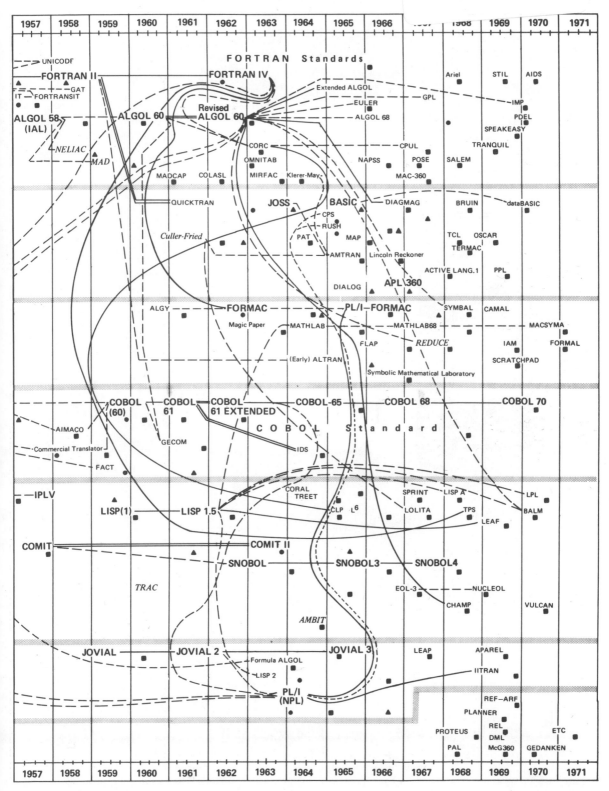

History
of Programming
Languages

From the ACM SIGPLAN History of Programming Languages
Conference, June 1–3, 1978

Jean E. Sammet, General and Program Committee Chairman
John A. N. Lee, Administrative Chairman

Editorial Board

This is a volume in the
ACM MONOGRAPH SERIES

Editor: THOMAS A. STANDISH, *University of California, Irvine*

A complete list of titles in this series appears at the end of this volume.

History
of Programming
Languages

Conference.

History of programming languages.

Edited by
RICHARD L. WEXELBLAT

Sperry Univac
Blue Bell, Pennsylvania

1981

ACADEMIC PRESS
A Subsidiary of Harcourt Brace Jovanovich, Publishers

New York   London   Toronto   Sydney   San Francisco

ACADEMIC PRESS, INC.
111 Fifth Avenue, New York, New York 10003

United Kingdom Edition published by
ACADEMIC PRESS, INC. (LONDON) LTD.
24/28 Oval Road, London NW1 7DX

Library of Congress Cataloging in Publication Data

History of programming languages.

(ACM monograph series)
Proceedings of the History of Programming
Languages Conference, Los Angeles, Calif., June
1–3, 1978.
Includes index.
1. Programming languages (Electronic computers)
––History––Congresses. I. Wexelblat, Richard L.
II. Title. III. Series: Association for Computing
Machinery. ACM monograph series.
QA76.7.H56 1978   001.64'24   80–24132
ISBN 0–12–745040–8

This book was prepared with the support of NSF Grant MCS 77-27208.
However, any opinions, findings, conclusions and/or recommendations
herein are those of the authors and do not necessarily reflect the views
of NSF.

PRINTED IN THE UNITED STATES OF AMERICA

81 82 83 84   9 8 7 6 5 4 3 2 1

Contents

v

Contents

V   COBOL Session/Chairman: *Michael Marcotty*
      /Speaker: *Jean E. Sammet*/Discussant: *Betty Holberton*

VI APT Session/Chairman: *John Goodenough*
      /Speaker: *Douglas T. Ross*

Contents

X JOSS Session/Chairman: *Thomas Cheatham*
/Speaker: *Charles L. Baker*

XI BASIC Session/Chairman: *Thomas Cheatham*
/Speaker: *Thomas E. Kurtz*

XII PL/I Session/Chairman: *Robert Rosin*
/Speaker: *George Radin*/Discussant: *Bruce Rosenblatt*

Contents

Appendixes

Editor's Introduction

These proceedings of the ACM SIGPLAN History of Programming Languages (HOPL) conference are a record, in the words of those who helped make the history, of a baker's dozen of the languages that set the tone of most of today's programming. It is difficult to describe the feeling that prevailed at the conference. There were no parallel sessions. Some attendees were graduate students, some pioneers, many were practitioners, and there seemed roughly an even division between industrial and academic affiliation. It was the first conference I attended where virtually everyone attended every session.

The Conference General Chairman's introduction (page xvii) provides a rationale for the languages chosen and what the speakers were asked to prepare. There was an official Conference Historian. (How can you have a "History of . . ." conference without a historian?) His introduction (page xxi) attempts to present the conference in the perspective of modern history-of-science scholarship.

The Keynote Address (page 7) was given by Grace Murray Hopper, Captain, USN, who was present at the birth of the industry and has remained an active participant. Her remarks indicate that a lot of what is considered novel and innovative today may well have first been done by her Remington-Rand Univac crew back in the 1950s.

The largest part of this volume is taken up with the languages themselves, in chapters each assembled in the following way:

The formal paper from the preprints (with some modifications by the authors).

A transcript of the formal conference presentation.

A transcript of the discussant's presentation. (There were discussants for APL, COBOL, FORTRAN, LISP, PL/I, and SIMULA only.)

A transcript of the question and answer session.

The full text of questions submitted in writing by the attendees (some with additional answers provided by the author).

Authors' biographies.

Summaries of the languages appear in Appendix A.

The order of the languages in this book is the order of the talks given at the conference. With the exception of JOSS, the formal papers were published as preprints in *ACM SIGPLAN Notices*, Vol. 13, No. 8 (August 1978). The papers are reprinted here with the permission of ACM and of the authors. In some cases, changes to the preprints have been made by the authors to correct typographical or factual errors. In a few cases, additional material was added.

Editor's Introduction

For ALGOL, two speakers were chosen initially to reflect the European and American points of view. An additional "short note" from another ALGOL pioneer has also been included.

The section on JOSS has a slightly different format since, due to a change in planned speaker, no paper for JOSS appeared in the preprints. To provide a broad historical outlook, the speaker was requested to make major revisions, expanding his talk into a formal paper.

No two speakers are alike and the transcripts of the talks reflect the differences. Some tended to repeat in the oral presentation the material in the formal preprint; others gave almost completely independent talks. In editing the transcripts, no attempt was made to remove redundancy. As far as possible, all that was said is included here. Editing has removed false starts and hesitations; punctuation has been added to try to clarify involved, run-on sentences. Interpolations are, for the most part, enclosed in brackets. Most sessions began and ended with administrative announcements which are omitted here.

Some of the talks were followed by formal presentations by discussants, and the transcripts of these are presented with the same type of editing as was used with the talks.

The question and answer sessions were handled at the conference by having written questions submitted to the session chairman during the talk. The chairman selected some of them to ask the speaker; the editing of the speakers' replies is similar to that indicated above.

The full text of all questions submitted is included and, in several cases, the authors have annotated this list, either keying the questions to the place in the transcript or the paper where it is answered or answering a question not covered at the conference.

Authors were asked to provide a brief biography highlighting their activities before the time period covered by the paper and their more recent work. For the most part, the biographies are the author's own words. In a few cases, the editor had to create a narrative biography from a terse *curriculum vitae*. If editorial license was carried too far in any case, my apologies. The pictures that accompany the biographies are candid photographs taken during the conference, and the subjects did not have a chance to select which pictures they preferred.

The after-dinner speeches at the conference banquet were devoted to humorous reminiscences and anecdotes about the languages and events during their development. The banquet anecdotes are not included in this volume because, although they are humorous to hear, the voice inflections make a big difference, and they are not necessarily amusing to read.

Audio and video tapes of the entire conference are available from ACM Headquarters: 1133 Avenue of the Americas, New York, New York 10036.

ACKNOWLEDGMENTS

Many people worked many hours to make the conference a success. The following is reprinted from the preprints:

It is . . . appropriate to acknowledge those who offered their time and energy.
Firstly, the chairmen who successfully surmounted a series of tough administrative problems:

Jean E. Sammet   General and Program Committee Chairman
JAN Lee   Administrative Chairman

Next the administrative committee chairmen who have done an excellent job of preparing for the conference:

Erwin Book	Local Arrangements
Billy Claybrook	Publicity
Susan Gerhart	Treasurer
Rorrie Ratkovich	Registrar

Next the "consulting historian" whose advice helped to put the plans for the conference in perspective and who also read and commented on most of the papers:

Henry Tropp

Then the members of the Program Committee who had the difficult task of deciding whom to invite . . . as well as making many decisions on the overall program organization:

Tom Cheatham	Michael Marcotty [replaced Ledgard in Feb. 1978]
John Goodenough	Robert F. Rosin
Henry Ledgard	Jean E. Sammet
JAN Lee	Henry Tropp
Barbara Liskov	

The Language Coordinators who worked to help the authors to get the papers done, done well, and done on time were:

ALGOL 60	David Gries, Tom Cheatham
APL	Philip S. Abrams, JAN Lee
APT	John Goodenough, Shizuo Hori
BASIC	Ted Lewis, Henry Ledgard
COBOL	Michael Marcotty, Henry Ledgard
FORTRAN	Bernard Galler, JAN Lee
GPSS	Julian Reitman, John Goodenough
JOSS	Charles Baker, Tom Cheatham
JOVIAL	Tom Cheatham, Christopher Shaw
LISP	Carl Hewitt, Barbara Liskov
PL/I	Robert F. Rosin, Michael Marcotty
SIMULA	Barbara Liskov, Richard Nance
SNOBOL	Michael Shapiro, Robert F. Rosin [end of reprinted material]

An oversight in the *SIGPLAN Notices* preprint volume—remedied here—is acknowledgment of those who prepared language summaries.

ALGOL 60	David Gries
BASIC	Ted G. Lewis
FORTRAN	Bernard A. Galler
GPSS	Julian Reitman
JOSS	Charles Baker
JOVIAL	Tom Cheatham
PL/I	Robert F. Rosin
SIMULA	W. R. Franta
SNOBOL	Michael Shapiro

APL, LISP, and APT summaries were prepared by the authors of the respective papers, and the COBOL summary was anonymous.

Editor's Introduction

Four students received NSF support to attend the conference:

John Favaro   Helen Gigley
Bruce Galler   Richard Miller

Although not directly related to these proceedings, I wish to acknowledge Bernard A. Galler's contributions as banquet master of ceremonies and in the closing session, both of which helped to establish and maintain the wonderfully supportive atmosphere. He titled the banquet presentations "The way we *really* were." And that was truly the feeling that prevailed.

The HOPL conference was notable not only for the subject matter, but also for the warm sense of shared interest in sharing experiences. The difficult task of converting this material and this feeling to a book was made easier by a diverse group of people.

David Beech, Roger Firestone, Fred Grampp, and C. T. Schlegel did preliminary editing of the transcripts. Three pioneers of the computer field helped in many areas, especially with clarification of early names and events: John Mauchly, Herman Lukoff, and Bill Schmitt. I would like to dedicate my effort in the preparation of this volume to John and Herman, both of whom died recently and both of whom provided so much help and support, even up to the last weeks of their lives.

Mrs. Elizabeth Emory, of Professional Transcription Services, Abington, Pennsylvania, did a magnificent job of transcribing the audio tapes—getting correct many proper names and much specialized jargon despite tape noise, unintelligibility, and a variety of European and American accents.

The authors were generally prompt in responding to my editorial requests, especially Geoff Gordon who had things to do twice due to carelessness in the editorial office.

A helpful editorial board (listed on page ii) was highlighted by the immense effort Jean Sammet put into both the conference and the proceedings and by JAN Lee who was also an infinitely patient advisor and intermediary. I also wish to acknowledge the support and assistance of the ACM Headquarters staff.

Robert M. McClure was "official" conference photographer and most of the photographs reproduced here are his. I also took some of the candid pictures. The video taping was done by a crew from California State University, Long Beach, directed by Dan Baker who is the Coordinator of Instructional Services.

Finally, my family not only tolerated the project, they helped. My son Alan typed most of the questions-submitted sections; my son David assisted with the index; and my wife Geraldine, a professional editor, taught me how to edit.

The National Science Foundation provided support for the conference and for the book preparation under grant MCS77-27208.

September 1980   RICHARD L. WEXELBLAT

xvi

Organization of the Conference

This conference was unusual in many ways and it seems appropriate to explain what its objectives were, what was and what was *not* intended, and to provide information about the way in which it was organized. There are four parts to this description: Basic Objectives and Rationale for Selection of Languages given here, and, in Appendix B, p. 721, the Major Elements of Organization and General Questions Asked of All Authors. This description is, with minor changes, taken directly from the preprints.

Basic Objectives

The History of Programming Languages Conference was intended to consider the technical factors which influenced the development of certain selected programming languages. It should be emphasized that this was not a conference on the entire history of programming languages nor entirely a conference on history. It was not even a conference on the entire history of the selected languages, but covered primarily their early developments. The emphasis was on the technical aspects of the language design and creation, and a number of significant steps were taken in advance of the conference to try to assure a high technical quality for the proceedings; these are discussed later in Appendix B entitled "Conference Organization." As a result of this conference, it was expected that people in the field of computer science would have a better understanding of the processes of language design as related to (a) the environment in which languages are developed and (b) the knowledge base available to the originators. It was also hoped that practitioners would have a better understanding of the reasons behind some of the quirks in the languages they are using. The people who attended the conference or who read this book can decide for themselves whether these objectives were achieved.

It is important to emphasize that by careful decision of the Programming Committee this meeting was *not* an occasion to confer honor or recognition on anyone, not even the invited speakers. Rather, it was a significant attempt to provide the appropriate written historical record for certain specific languages which met the criteria set forth by the Program Committee.

The Program Committee identified at least one major technical contributor to the origination of each language who agreed to participate in the conference by preparing a written paper and to be present at the conference in order both to present the paper and to participate in discussions. The speakers were chosen with careful consideration of the technical role played by each of them, and also considering their availability and probable willingness to undertake the large task of writing a high quality, historically significant paper. (Unfortunately, one of those people was not able to fulfil his commitment and another highly qualified speaker was chosen. This was unfortunately much too late for the preparation of a written paper for the preprints.) All the speakers did appear, and gave talks which, in many cases augmented the material in the written paper.

Several people have asked why a *conference* was held rather than simply having people prepare the papers and issue them in a book like this one. It was felt that a conference format and the audience discussion allowed after each presentation, would provide greater insight into the history of the events and decisions which formulated the languages in their early forms. Some of the speakers participated in the development of more than one language on the program; the expected "cross talk" which we hoped would occur among all attendees at a conference was deemed to be essential in bringing out the historical aspects of the early development. In several cases this hope was definitely fulfilled.

This conference was *not*—and was *not* intended to be—the *end* of any consideration of computing history, software history, language history in general, or even the history of the selected languages. On the contrary, it was intended to *initiate* the preservation of a historical record for the languages chosen, and to give impetus to others to continue adding to this record. If this conference or this book stimulate other conferences, or the preparation of other papers, or the preservation of historical records, then some of the objectives will have been achieved. Thus, these activities should be viewed as a first step rather than a final action in describing the history of programming languages.

Rationale for Selection of Languages

In developing the initial plan for this conference, which was done in May 1977, the Program Committee established both specific requirements and general criteria for the selection of languages. The specific requirements were that the languages (1) were created and in use by 1967; (2) remain in use in 1977; and (3) have had considerable influence on the field of computing. The cutoff date of 1967 was chosen to provide perspective from a distance of at least ten years. The general criteria for choosing the languages are the following (not necessarily in order of importance, nor with the requirement that each apply to each language): usage, influence on language design, overall impact on the environment, novelty (first of its kind), and uniqueness.

The above criteria were applied to develop the list of languages deemed appropriate for inclusion in this conference. The specific rationale for each language selected is as follows, where "today" refers to 1977, when the selection was made.

ALGOL 60: This language is an obvious landmark in the technical development of programming languages, both in terms of the concepts introduced and the first recognized use of formal notation for syntax. Most theoretical, and much practical, language and compiler work since 1960 has been based on ALGOL 60.

APL: This language has received widespread use in the past few years, increasing from a few highly specialized mathematical uses to many people using it for quite different applications, including those in business. Its unique character set, frequent emphasis on cryptic "one-liner" programs, and its effective initial implementation as an interactive system make it important. In addition, the uniqueness of its overall approach and philosophy makes it significant.

APT: This language has two major characteristics. The first is that it is in fact one of the earliest languages still in use today. Secondly, it is representative of a class of languages sometimes referred to as "special purpose" and sometimes referred to as "languages for specialized application areas." Since these have consistently represented about half of the total languages in use in the United States at one time, it is important to include APT as a representative of this class. It is not only a very early language still alive, but is also implemented on most computers. It has also been standardized by the American National Standards Institute.

BASIC: This language is widely used, and in many ways is the simplest of all the major languages in use today. It has wide educational use, and is a "first language" for many students. It has been implemented on most computers.

COBOL: This language is one of the most widely used, if not *the* most widely used language because of the predominance of the business data processing usage of computers. Its unique English-like style and emphasis on business data-processing applications make it important. It has been implemented on most computers.

FORTRAN: This is the oldest fairly general language in major use today. It is the first language to have become widely used. The importance of FORTRAN seems sufficiently obvious not to need further justification here.

GPSS: This is apparently the earliest of the simulation languages. Its unique block diagram style and its wide usage make it important. It introduced numerous simulation concepts in a unique distinct *language*. (The only other serious contender for inclusion in its place was SIMSCRIPT which appears to have come a little later. Although it was felt that the concepts and language style introduced by SIMSCRIPT were less significant than GPSS, actually both languages met the criteria. There seemed to be no need to include both and GPSS was chosen because it seemed to have a slight edge.)

JOSS: This was the first language designed specifically to be used in an interactive environment. It spawned many dialects and is still in use today.

JOVIAL: This language was an outgrowth of ALGOL 58 via JOVIAL's predecessor CLIP, which itself was an ALGOL 58 dialect. JOVIAL was the first language to attempt to include some significant numeric, logical, and data handling capabilities all in one language. It has been widely used by the Air Force, as well as by other groups, and it has been implemented on many computers.

LISP: The concepts in LISP are unlike those of any other language and that makes it significant in and of itself. In addition, it is widely used for most artificial intelligence and symbolic mathematical work.

PL/I: This was the first language to attempt to provide adequate facilities for scientific computations, business data processing, and systems programming all in one language. It was also the first of the really large languages.

SIMULA: In addition to its simulation capabilities added to ALGOL, this language introduced the concept of *class* on which much current theoretical work in data abstraction has been built. It has been implemented on many computers.

SNOBOL: This is a very widely used language for string manipulation. It is also implemented on most computers. (The only other possible contender for this class of language was COMIT, which is not in wide use today and does not meet the general criteria as well as SNOBOL.)

JEAN E. SAMMET

On Doing Contemporary History

The difficulties of doing research and writing on topics in contemporary history appear almost insurmountable: the faulty memory of participants, the vast volume of paper that must be perused for specific items, the desire to avoid hurting people's feelings during their lifetimes, the difficulty of objective assessments in a period that includes one's own lifetime experiences and what appear to be ever-changing political, social, environmental, and technological standards, etc., etc., etc. It is no surprise that the majority of historical scholars comfortably establish themselves in periods prior to 1900.

These difficulties grow even larger in any effort involving the history of the information sciences. Not only are most of the pioneers still alive and active, but the field is still evolving and changing, as are values and judgments regarding milestones and significant accomplishments. The field is so new and so volatile that events such as this Conference are themselves historic events in its development.

Yet, despite these difficulties, it is important to embark now on historical efforts of this nature. The development of the electronic computer and the subsequent evolution of programming languages is one of the major events not only of scientific, but of world history. It would be criminal for the contemporary community to avoid this effort just because of the impossibility of doing a final and definitive work. A start must be made now so that perhaps fifty or a hundred years hence those definitive works will be possible.

Clearly, one major thrust in historical efforts involves some form of oral history. The value of oral history as well as its dangers are fairly clear. Yet, oral history is a necessary source. On this topic, the late Ken May made the following comments in an address to the First International Research Conference on the History of Computing (Los Alamos, New Mexico, 10–15 June 1976):

> Computer people can . . . talk and write about what they have done and are doing—as you are at this conference. It isn't enough in any science to do things. It is necessary to communicate what has been done. . . . Not only communicate your scientific results but also talk about how they arose, who was involved, all those things that are often unrecorded. . . . People's memories are not precise. But that does not matter, because the essence of historical scholarship is to use memoirs and other primary sources with discretion. And so a person who has participated shouldn't worry about that bias that he has due to our participation. The historians will take care of that in due time by *comparing sources,* checking dates, and so on.

To add to Ken May's last comment above, in this Conference we made a serious attempt to have all authors check as much of their material as possible. John Backus' comments in his paper on the origin and timing of Laning and Zierler's work is an excellent example of this type of memory correction. Almost all of the authors began to unearth files and materials they had forgotten existed, and each had their memories questioned by individuals who reviewed their papers. I had the task of reviewing the various drafts of most of the papers in this collection. The contrast between the information in the first draft and the final version was significant as each of the authors was able to locate additional documentation. The effort on their parts was considerable, but the results were worth it. The quality of the papers and their enthusiastic reception at the Conference itself attest to that.

There is too much to do and the field is too complex for the burden of its history to be left to the professional historian. It is crucial that the participants themselves become historians as the speakers at this conference have done. In the traditional fields of the history of science it is not unusual to find the history of X emerging as an independent specialty, with a synergistic rivalry between historians of X who view themselves as historians first and X'ists second, and those who were trained primarily in X and entered the history of X by informal routes. That may well happen in the history of information science in the future; but for now, the energy and commitment of the latter group is needed with the full cooperation of the former.

As you read the papers in this volume you will see that, as high in quality as they are, they are not "definitive." Each will yield interesting future research needs. Each of them meets the basic criteria of this conference: they are excellent beginnings with full scale bibliographic and human resource possibilities. This volume is a challenge for continuing research and, in my opinion, a standard by which to measure it.

One last comment: I am often asked by individuals about what documents of historical significance they should preserve and what they should plan to do with them. These, and other related issues, are discussed in detail in a brochure produced by AFIPS (see reference list). However, a brief, general response is possible. Save your own material. Sure, you will want to throw some things away; but when in doubt, don't. However tempting, don't go on a wild burning spree. Second, think about giving your material to a depository, such as a university which has an archive. Don't leave it to your heirs, because heirs can do unpredictable things with your papers. Also, try to organize your material or identify segments of it, to help archivists sort it, file it, and catalog it.

REFERENCES

For readers interested in the vast technical literature on historiography,† the following items will provide a good beginning set of sources.

Kuhn, Thomas (1962). *The Structure of Scientific Revolutions.* Univ. of Chicago Press, Chicago, Illinois; 2nd rev. ed., 1970.
May, Kenneth O. (1973). *Bibliography and Research Manual of the History of Mathematics,* pp. 5–34. Univ. of Toronto Press, Toronto.
May, Kenneth O. (1975). Historiographic Vices. *Historia Mathematica* **2,** 185–187, 315–317.
May, Kenneth O. (1980). Historiography: A perspective for computer scientists. In *A History of Computing in the Twentieth Century* (N. Metropolis *et al.,* eds.), pp. 11–18. Academic Press, New York.

† Historiography: "The body of techniques, theories, and principles of historical research and presentation; methods of historical scholarship." *Random House Dictionary,* 1966.

Sarton, George (1957). *Study of the History of Mathematics and the Study of the History of Science,* Dover, New York (paperback).

AFIPS. *Preserving Computer Related Source Material.* Free copies of this brochure may be obtained by writing: AFIPS, 1850 North Lynn Street, Suite 800, Arlington, Virginia 22209.

HENRY TROPP

The Opening Session

Conference Chairman: Jean E. Sammet
Keynote Speaker: Grace Murray Hopper

CONFERENCE CHAIRMAN'S OPENING REMARKS

JEAN E. SAMMET: I'm happy to have this opportunity to open this Conference on the History of Programming Languages. It's something that I personally have been thinking about for almost seven years although the actual work on this has only been going on for the past one-and-a-half years. Most of you have not had the opportunity to look at the Preprints, and perhaps you haven't had too much time to even look at the program. For that reason I want to make sure that you understand something about what *is* intended, and frankly what is *not* intended be done in this conference. We view this as a start: perhaps the first of a number of conferences which will be held about various aspects of the computing field in general, software in particular, and even more specifically, programming languages. We hope that this conference and the Preprints and the final proceedings will stimulate many older people, many younger people, and many of those in the in-between category in the field to do work in history.

This conference, I repeat again, is certainly not the last set of words to be held on this subject. It's only a beginning. I want to emphasize also that it's *not* a conference on the entire history of programming languages, nor even on the entire history of the languages that we selected. As many of you have seen from some of the earlier publicity that we put out, we're trying to consider and report on the technical factors which influenced the development of languages which satisfied a number of criteria. First, they were created and in use by 1967; they remain in use in 1977, which is when we made the decisions; and they've had considerable influence on the field of computing. The criteria for choosing a language include the following factors, although not every factor applied to each language: we considered usage, influence on language design, overall impact on the environment, novelty, and uniqueness. Particularly because of the cut-off date of 1967, some languages which are in common use today are not included. We definitely wanted a perspective of 10 years before we started worrying about the early history of the language.

Furthermore, we made a very early decision, almost automatically, that this conference would be based on invited speakers for selected languages and not on contributed papers.

HISTORY OF PROGRAMMING LANGUAGES
Copyright © 1981 by the Association for Computing Machinery, Inc.
Permission for reproduction in any form must be obtained from Academic Press, Inc.
ISBN 0-12-745040-8

And I say this only so that you understand the background and not because other alternatives are better or worse, but simply—they're different.

Now, you'll find considerable variation when you hear the speakers and when you look at the papers in how far down in time they go on each language—whether in their oral presentation or in the paper. This depended to a considerable extent on the speaker. Our strong emphasis has been on the very early days of the technical development of the language, and some of the speakers became less involved as time went on and therefore could not speak with authority about later developments. Others are still heavily involved in the languages that they were concerned with initially, and so their timescale comes somewhat more up to date. That was, again, left up to the speakers.

Now, I want to say a little bit about how this conference was organized so that you understand a little bit about what the speakers had to go through to get here, and the speakers I think will understand what I mean, and when I get through, perhaps some of the rest of you will.

Certainly each speaker was an invited one in the true sense of the word. It was not a question of whether we were willing to accept their papers. They were invited, and we were going to accept them. On the other hand, we had certain methodologies that we tried to use. But before I even mention that, let me emphasize that the Program Committee selected *a* key person—not *the* key person—but *a* key person involved in the early technical development of the language. But the selections were based also not only on the involvement of the person, but potentially on the willingness and expectation that we had that the person would indeed write the paper, appear, and do the necessary work to get the papers written and the oral presentations made.

We did not feel that we could just ask a person to write a paper on the early days of language X, or even languages Y, Z, or PDQ. That was particularly true because, as I said, many of the speakers are not currently involved in the languages that they had a hand in the original design of. So we did two things: we created a concept called "Language Coordinator"—and this meant a person or persons who were going to assist the speaker in every way possible, with particular emphasis on reviewing drafts of the papers. The Program Committee, in order to maintain overall cognizance, had one person from the Program Committee as a Language Coordinator for each speaker. This is described somewhat more in the Preprints. Virtually all of the Language Coordinators that were not on the Program Committee, and of course, the Program Committee as well, I think, performed superbly. And it's because I think some of the Language Coordinators, some of whom were not even able to attend the Conference, are in some ways the unsung heroes of the quality—if we have quality—that I want to make sure they get the proper credit.

Now the second, and I think perhaps the most important step that we took in trying to help the authors write papers, was to develop a long set of questions, which we gave to all the speakers. We felt that the individuals writing the papers would have a little bit of trouble knowing what type of information to extract from the file, and perhaps also have some trouble in organizing it.

Incidentally, most of these papers are based very heavily on research of existing documents or hand notes, and not really just on memory. And if you look at the papers, you will find in most cases a very long bibliography which gives evidence of the documentation that was looked at in order to do this.

Now, in addition to the general questions that we gave to all speakers, we concocted sets of questions which were unique to each individual language, and gave them [to the appropriate speaker]. Now, these were meant to be guidance to the speakers. We did not expect, and certainly did not want a set of papers to be just a specific sort of "question/answer, question/answer." And as you'll see, they're not; and even given the basic set of questions which are in the Preprints, you'll find that everybody's personality manages to shine through in one way or another.

Now, when any conference starts, there's always a set of announcements that has to be made which are not necessarily of interest to the audience, but you're a captive audience and so you're going to have to listen anyhow.

Everybody should understand that we are preparing separate audio recordings, as well as a complete black-and-white videotape of all of the sessions, and of the banquet Friday night as well. Thus, if we have questions from the audience—and I'll get to that mechanism in a minute—but if we have any such person, then we must ask that the individual identify himself or herself. If you don't want to be so recorded, please don't go to the mike, because we're not going to delete anything later, and we will not be able to get back to the audience for clearance or anything like that. So, if you're worried about being recorded for posterity, please ask your questions off-line.

Now, while we have not worked out all of the details, we certainly intend—and it has been our plan from the very beginning—to make the audio recordings, and eventually the video, available to interested persons and groups for educational purposes. We envision classes, ACM chapters, and similar groups borrowing this material. For this reason, and because of the copyright laws, I want to make it very clear that nobody is allowed to make any recordings whatsoever of any part of this conference, nor to take any photographs. In addition to the video, we have two photographers that are making the official photographs for this. If any of you have any recorders with you, please put them away. The entire control of this for copyright protection purposes must remain with ACM. I give you my word, and that of all the others involved here, that it is our intention to make this material available as soon as we can, and in any way that seems practical. I cannot give you a time scale. It will be quite a while, but our intent from the very beginning has been to make this available.

Now, one of the problems, I think, from the point of view of the audience in attending a conference like this is—we're dealing with 13 languages, and you may be an expert in one, two, three—but I doubt that there's anybody who's an expert in all 13 of them. We want the speakers to be able to concentrate on the historical aspects and not have to provide tutorials on the languages themselves. For that reason, we have included in the Preprints for each language a one- or two-page summary of the language. And I urge you very strongly to look at the pages before the session. They will give you, I think, just enough of the flavor so that you will understand what the speaker is referring to from the technical side, without of course making you an expert on the basis of two minutes' perusal of two pages.

I referred a few minutes ago to the question mechanism. We're going to try something, and I quite frankly don't know whether or not it's going to work. Because of the size of the group, because we want to try and do things in a coherent fashion, we're going to try and deal with written questions and we will give priority to them. We have some question cards, and if there are any people now who think that they're likely to ask questions at the end of Captain Hopper's talk, which we will allow, if you will hold up your hands now, we have monitors who will be glad to give you some cards. If, during the session and as the talk is going on, a thought moves you and you want to hold up your hand, we will try and get a card to you. When you have a question written down, if you'd hold up your hand again, we'll try to get the monitors to pick them up, and I'm going to try and screen them in real time, and then read them from here. I frankly don't know whether this mechanism will work. We'll debug it this morning, and if it doesn't, we'll go back to the tried and true method of having people stand up at microphones. But, in any case, unlike some other keynote or opening talks, we have definitely allowed time for questions after Captain Hopper's talk.

As I think many of you know, we are planning to publish a book on this conference afterwards. It will contain the papers, the discussions, comments, questions, answers, other kinds of material. And there are also question boxes outside for you to put questions in that we will try and get answers to for inclusion with the proceedings. We also have what's been called a "Graffiti" board or sign up out there if you just want to write notes to which other people can comment.

Now, two more sets of sign-up sheets out there. The first and most important from the time point of view is this: you will note from the program that we have scheduled some "Birds of a Feather" sessions tonight, and we will make a determination on which are most suitable based on the space available, based on the number of people who have signed. For any of you who may not be familiar with this concept of "Birds of a Feather" sessions, all it means is a very informal gathering chaired by the person who suggested it in the first place. So there are sign-up sheets outside; if you would put your name as the session chairman, and the topic, and anybody who sees that and is interested please sign up, and we will indicate late in this afternoon's session which of those have been scheduled and where. In addition, as you will note from the program, there is a session *officially* scheduled for tonight by Henry Tropp concerned with "Doing Contemporary History," and that you do not need to sign up for. That's very official in any case.

One other sign-up mechanism, as you know—we are having a banquet tomorrow night which is going to have some tall tales or things of that kind, which will be the amusing part of this conference. We thought it might be interesting for those of you who wanted to sit with others who had language interests similar to yours to try and group by tables by language. So there are some sign-up sheets if you want to do that. If nobody wants to do that, we will simply keep the tables for free and open seating.

I'm sure you'll be glad to know I'm getting reasonably close to the end of my opening remarks. But there are, I think, a number of people and groups that ought to be thanked and I want to do that very specifically. First, I want to thank the National Science Foundation for providing the funding for the videotaping, much of the support for the audio taping, and transcription as well. They are also providing all kinds of support, and in particular they provided money to enable us to award four student scholarships. They're scholarships in name only because the people are working very hard, but these are four students who will be working as rapporteurs under the guidance of Professor Henry Tropp, and they will help contribute to the final record of the conference. The students are John Favaro from the University of California at Berkeley, Bruce Galler from the University of Michigan, Helen Gigley from the University of Massachusetts at Amherst, and Richard Miller from the University of Illinois.

And last, but very truly far from least, I want to acknowledge and thank two very different groups of people who helped make this conference possible. First, the speakers themselves who had to tear themselves away from their current activities, and I know in many cases that was extremely difficult. And they had to delve into dusty, and I do mean dusty, files and cartons. Secondly, the Program Committee and the administrative staff who helped organize the Conference. The Program Committee members are Tom Cheatham, John Goodenough, JAN Lee, Barbara Liskov, Mike Marcotty, Bob Rosin, Henry Tropp, myself, and for a while last year Henry Ledgard. The administrative aspects of this conference have been very ably handled under the overall, general supervision of JAN Lee with Erwin Book handling the local arrangements, Rorrie Ratkevich as the Registration Chairman, Sue Gerhart as the Treasurer, Dick Wexelblat, Proceedings Editor, Billy Claybrook, Publicity, and numerous people who helped them. In addition, for the historical record, I want to thank my secretary, Barbara Whitehill even though she's not here, who typed and sent out numerous papers pertaining to this conference.

I now want to give very special thanks to two people in particular. One is Henry, known as "Hank" Tropp, and the other is JAN Lee. Hank has served as the consulting historian, and we surely needed one, since none of us had any training in the history of science, and Hank does; and furthermore he got acquainted with an awful lot of the pioneers in this business in conducting the oral interviews for the AFIPS/Smithsonian Project a number of years ago. In my view, Hank has been of inestimable value to us in his specific service on the Program Committee, his reading and critique of all the papers, his overall advice on how to organize the conference to make it of maximum historical value, and his guidance to the four students who I suspect will get a better education from him in three days than they will from several courses that they could have otherwise taken.

And finally, I want to thank JAN Lee for his truly herculean efforts in handling all the administrative aspects of this conference, in addition to serving on the Program Committee. I think without his superb work we would have been in dire straits.

And now let me switch, thankfully I think from your point of view, to the introduction of our Opening Speaker.

INTRODUCTION OF
CAPTAIN GRACE MURRAY HOPPER

JEAN E. SAMMET: If there's anybody in the computer field in general, and the history of programming languages in particular, who needs no introduction, it is certainly Captain Grace Hopper. Nevertheless [laughter], because we are trying to create a historical record and some of this information may be a little bit more difficult to obtain 10, 20, 30, 50 years from now, I do want to provide somewhat of an introduction.

Dr. Grace Hopper graduated from Vassar College in 1928 and received a Ph. D. from Yale in 1934. She taught mathematics at Vassar from 1931 to 1943. In December 1943 she entered the United States Naval Reserve and attended U.S. Naval Reserve Midshipman School. (For some of you who were not born then, there was a war going on.) She graduated as a Lieutenant j.g. and was assigned to the Bureau of Ordnance Computation Project at Harvard. There she developed programs for the Mark I computer, the first automatically sequenced digital computer and forerunner of the modern electronic computer.

In 1946 she joined the Harvard faculty as a research fellow in engineering sciences and applied physics at the Computation Laboratory. There she worked on the Mark II and Mark III computers for the Navy. In 1949 she joined the Eckert–Mauchly Computer Corporation which was involved with the building of the first UNIVAC which was to be the first commercial large-scale electronic computer. While there, she supervised a department which, among its other achievements, created the first compiler, A-0, and its major follow-on, A-2, and one of the early mathematical languages which was originally called AT-3 and eventually renamed MATH-MATIC.

In early 1955 Dr. Hopper and her staff had preliminary specifications of a language which would be suitable for doing business data processing on computers and would also be easy to use. This was originally called B-0, and later named FLOW-MATIC. And as you will hear later, FLOW-MATIC was one of the major inputs to COBOL.

Now, lest anybody be confused by all the shifting back and forth between language names and two letters and words and so on, my recollection is that the systems being done in Remington-Rand Univac were originally named by the developers in letter–number style, and then some public relations people decided that was not too good, and so they renamed them with a whole new set of names.

Among Dr. Hopper's early significant publications and talks are "The Education of a Computer" presented at the ACM Annual Conference in 1952, and a talk entitled "Automatic Coding for Digital Computers" presented in Louisiana in 1955.

Dr. Hopper maintained close contact with the Naval Reserve throughout her industrial working career, and in 1967 was called to active duty in the Navy. She is currently [June 1978] a Captain with the title of Special Assistant to the Commanding Officer, Naval Data Automation Command.

I should tell you, and I intend to, Captain Hopper asked me to keep this introduction short which request I am obviously *not* honoring, but in moderate compliance with that I will not list her numerous honors and contributions to ACM, nor her numerous other papers and talks. But I do want to make a few personal comments which are pertinent to this.

In my view, Grace Hopper did more than any other single individual to sell the concepts of the higher level languages from both a technical and an administrative viewpoint. [Applause]

Furthermore, she did this when these comments and thoughts were often falling on deaf ears, and she had to battle her way through normal company funding authorization chains, and to convince the *users* that the systems she was developing would really help them. I believe, but can't guarantee, that she will tell you about some of these early days and the difficulties during her opening talk.

Now, it was clear to me and to the Program Committee that there is no person in the world more suitable to provide the opening talk on a conference of the history of programming languages. In many ways she embodies within her own person the entire history of programming languages right down to modern times, including her supervision of the development of the test validation routines for COBOL while she was in the Navy.

Now, when I talked to her about the introduction, she asked me to introduce her merely as "the third programmer on the first large-scale digital computer, Mark I," and not to say anything more because she wanted me to end with that. So in order to comply at least with that part of it, and with very deep personal admiration for the numerous contributions that Grace Hopper has made to this field, and as—in my view at least—the key person in the early history of programming languages, I want to introduce the third programmer on the first large-scale digital computer.

KEYNOTE ADDRESS

Grace Murray Hopper

Thank you very much. That gives me a nice opportunity to point out to the entire audience that the first large-scale digital computer in the United States was a *Navy* computer, operated by a *Navy* crew during World War II. There's a certain upstart service that tries to claim credit for computers nowadays, and they didn't even exist yet! [Applause]

Since this talk is being taped, I am forced therefore to remind you that nothing I say represents the plans and policies of the Department of the Navy or the Naval Service at large. Everything I say is purely the opinion of the speaker!

I'm appalled at you, in a way. You're all "Establishment." And I think I spent 20 years fighting the "Establishment." In the early years of programming languages, the most frequent phrase we heard was that the only way to program a computer was in octal. Of course a few years later a few people admitted that maybe you could use assembly language. But the entire establishment was firmly convinced that the only way to write an efficient program was in octal. They totally forgot what happened to me when I joined Eckert–Mauchly. They were building BINAC, a binary computer. We programmed it in octal. Thinking I was still a mathematician, I taught myself to add, subtract, and multiply, and even divide in octal. I was really good, until the end of the month, and then my checkbook didn't balance! [Laughter] It stayed out of balance for three months until I got hold of my brother who's a banker. After several evenings of work he informed me that at intervals I had subtracted in octal. And I faced the major problem of living in two different worlds. That may have been one of the things that sent me to get rid of octal as far as possible.

In putting material together, I go back to the days before there were programming languages, and I think I have to remind you of a few of the things that started all of this. I have here a copy of the manual for Mark I. I think most of you would be totally flabbergasted if you were faced with programming a computer, using a Mark I manual. All it gives you are the codes. From there on you're on your own to write a program. We were not programmers in those days. The word had not yet come over from England. We were "coders."

On the other hand, we did do some things to help us get programs written. And I managed to find another piece of paper which I find quite interesting because I find I have a relative subroutine in my hands which was written in 1944.

Mark I had built-in programs for sine, cosine, exponential, arctangent, ... On the other hand, because they were wired into the machine, they had to be completely general. Any problem that we solved, we found we did not need complete generality; we always knew something about what we were doing—that was what the problem was. And the answer was—we started writing subroutines, only we thought they were pieces of coding. And if I needed a sine subroutine, angle less than $\pi/4$, I'd whistle at Dick and say, "Can I have your sine subroutine?" and I'd copy it out of his notebook. We soon found that we needed just a generalized format of these if we were going to copy them, and I found a generalized subroutine for Mark I. With substitution of certain numbers, it can be copied into any given program. So as early as 1944 we started putting together things which would make it easier to write more accurate programs and get them written faster. I think we've forgotten to some extent how early that started.

The next thing that brought that to the fore was the building in England of the first computer over there and the book by Wheeler, Wilkes and Gill. They designed a set of subroutines before they built the machine. And they had a library of subroutines for that computer before it was implemented, and there was for the first time an available set of mathematical subroutines which were more or less standardized in the way you put data into them and the way you got data out of them, and made it possible to begin to write programs a *little* more rapidly. We didn't have ACM until 1947. Even then it didn't start publishing journals. There was very little communication throughout the industry unless you knew somebody. And in a way what I'm telling you comes from the basement of Croft Laboratory, and a very old factory building in North Philadelphia where we started work on UNIVAC I.

Those were precarious days. We used to say that if UNIVAC I didn't work, we were going to throw it out one side of the factory, which was a junk yard, and we were going to jump out the other side, which was a cemetary! There was little communication unless you knew someone; there were few places that we met: the University of Pennsylvania, Michigan, Harvard, MIT. Gradually we got to know each other a little bit, but there was very little communication . . . and very little publication, in the sense that you know it today. Therefore much of the interchange of information lay among the people you knew, and the places you went to.

The beginnings of ACM: we began to meet each other. There was a session at Harvard in 1948 which, I think, had the first session which began to cover something about the problems of programming. In fact there was a, . . . well, they had a whole long session on numerical methods and suggested problem solutions. There was also a shorter session, four papers—"Sequencing, Coding, and Problem Preparation." And I think that probably was one of the first sessions that was ever held on "What are we going to do about programming computers?"

The next group that stepped in to try to pull together the people in these fields and to get them to communicate with each other so that we could perhaps do a better job was the Navy. There was a series of three seminars held by the Navy on what was then called Coding, Automatic Programming, and various other names. ("Software" hadn't appeared yet.) And the first of those was held in 1951. I think most of us began to know each other at that time, and began to—even if we had no other way of communicating—would send to each other copies of what we were doing. And that was the beginning of the communications in this area.

This is a seminar on Data Handling and Automatic Computing, and it was held in March of 1951. There are some papers which verge on the question of programming, but as yet, nothing that even resembles a real assist to writing programs. I think the first two things to appear in this area that influenced me most were John Mauchly's "Short Order Code" and Betty Holberton's "Sort–Merge Generator."

John Mauchly's "Short Order Code" operated on a BINAC in 1949. It turned the BINAC into a floating decimal mathematical computer. He wrote words, and the first word might represent the X; there was a sign for equals, and sign for a, a sign for $+$ and a sign for b—because BINAC was a totally numerical computer. It had no alpha, so it was necessary to use two digits to indicate these various symbols. It was written in true algebraic format, but since there was no alpha, it didn't look very algebraic. But these pairs of digits did match the algebraic expressions. It was an interpretive system; the subroutines were stored in the memory and reference was made to the subroutines by the symbolic code which you put in.

I think this was the first thing that clued me to the fact that you could use some kind of a code other than the actual machine code. In other words, if you will, a "simulated computer" I guess we'd call it nowadays. To us it was a pseudo-code. It was not the original code of the computer, but it was a code which was implemented through a program. And I think Short Code was the first step in moving toward something which gave a programmer an actual power to write a program in a language which bore no resemblance whatsoever to the original machine code.

Short Code operated on BINAC in 1949. It was later transferred, reprogrammed, and used on UNIVAC by 1952. And it did constitute both a set of subroutines and a method for writing something in a pseudo-code. However, it was interpretive in that the program looked at each statement, jumped to the called-for subroutines, executed them, and went back and got the next statement. It did not write out an actual program.

I think the first step to tell us that we could actually use a computer to write programs was Betty Holberton's "Sort–Merge Generator." You fed it the specifications of the files you were operating on, and the Sort–Merge Generator produced the program to do the sorting and merging, including not only carrying out the operations, but also managing all of the input and output in the various tape units, and it contained, I think, what I would define as the first version of a virtual memory in that it made use of overlays automatically without being told to by the programmer. I think that meant a great deal to me. It meant that I could do these things automatically; that you could make a computer write a program.

Of course, at that time the Establishment promptly told us—at least they told me quite frequently—that a computer could not write a program; it was totally impossible; that all that computers could do was arithmetic, and that it couldn't write programs; that it had none of the imagination and dexterity of a human being. I kept trying to explain that we were wrapping up the human being's dexterity in the program that he wrote, the generator, and that of course we could make a computer do these things so long as they were completely defined. We did run up against that problem. I think I can remember sometime along in the middle of 1952 that I flatly made the alarming statement that I could make a computer do anything which I could completely define. I'm still of course involved in proving that because I'm not sure if anybody believes me yet.

But the Sort–Merge Generator gave rise to a whole family of other generators. I could wish that many of you today would go back and look at that Sort–Merge Generator. I think you might find the solution to some of today's problems. I think we've gotten far away from the concept of generator; with the mini- and microcomputers and the systems of computers, if we're going to dedicate them, we need more powerful generators. I'd love to have a good data handling generator, and I hope somebody's going to write one sometime during this year, to which I can feed specifications and receive as output the required program to do the job I have specified. I don't mean languages. I don't mean compilers. I mean generators for specific jobs.

The Navy sessions meant a great deal. The next one—the first one was 1951—the next one was 1954. I'll wait a minute for that. In the fall of 1951, October, I received an assignment to build a set of mathematical subroutines for UNIVAC I, to sufficiently standardize them so that everybody would be able to use them. As I went along in the process of standardizing the subroutines, I recognized something else was happening in the programming group. We were using subroutines. We were copying routines from one program into another. There were two things wrong with that technique: one was that the subroutines were all started at line 0 and went on sequentially from there. When you copied them into another program, you therefore had to add to all those addresses as you copied them into the new program—you had to add to all those addresses. And programmers are lousy adders!

The second thing that inhibited this was that programmers are lousy copyists! And it was amazing how many times a 4 would turn into a delta which was our space symbol, or into an A—and even Bs turned into 13s. All sorts of interesting things happened when programmers tried to copy subroutines. And there of course stood a gadget whose whole purpose was to copy things accurately and do addition. And it therefore seemed sensible, instead of having programmers copy the subroutines, to have the computer copy the subroutines. Out of that came the A-0 compiler.

Between October of 1951 and May of 1952 I wrote a compiler. Now, there was a curious thing about it: it wasn't what you'd call one today, and it wasn't what you'd call a "language" today. It was a series of specifications. For each subroutine you wrote some specs. The reason it got called a compiler was that each subroutine was given a "call word," because the subroutines were in a library, and when you pull stuff out of a library you compile things. It's as simple as that.

The program was a program which, given a call word, pulled a particular subroutine. Following the call word were the specifications of the arguments and results which were to be entered into the subroutine with no language whatsoever. The programs were butted, one bang against another. There was no attempt, really, at optimization. Because it was designed to let people write quickly the specs for a mathematical program, one time usually—one-time execution, and get an answer fast. And the main purpose was to get programs out fast, and get answers fast.

One of the reasons that we had to write programs faster, I think some people have forgotten. Mark I did three additions every single second, 23 digits to 23 digits. If you go back and look at the newspapers and magazines, you find she was the most fantastic thing man ever built. By the time we got to UNIVAC I, it was doing 3,000 additions every second, and it was chewing up programs awful fast. And the programmers had not accelerated in an equal degree! [Laughter] It was perfectly clear that we were going to have to produce programs faster.

There was also the fact that there were beginning to be more and more people who wanted to solve problems, but who were unwilling to learn octal code and manipulate bits. They wanted an easier way of getting answers out of the computer. So the primary purposes were not to develop a programming language, and we didn't give a hoot about commas and colons. We were after getting correct programs written faster, and getting answers for people faster. I am sorry that to some extent I feel the programming language community has somewhat lost track of those two purposes. We were trying to solve problems and get answers. And I think we should go back somewhat to that stage.

We were also endeavoring to provide a means that people could use, not that programmers or programming language designers could use. But rather, plain, ordinary people, who had problems they wanted to solve. Some were engineers; some were business people. And we tried to meet the needs of the various communities. I think we somewhat lost track of that too. I'm hoping that the development of the microcomputer will bring us back to reality and to recognizing that we have a large variety of people out there who want to solve problems, some of whom are symbol-oriented, some of whom are word-oriented, and that they are going to need different kinds of languages rather than trying to force them all into the pattern of the mathematical logician. A lot of them are not.

In any case, I started out to devise a means by which I could put these subroutines together to produce a program. Curiously, it did not occur to me that I should make two sweeps over it. I felt that it should be a single-pass compiler. In fact, the information defining a problem came in on one tape unit, and the program was written out on another one, because UNIVAC I only had 1000 words of storage and there wasn't room enough to keep a whole lot of junk in there while I was doing the compiling process.

I promptly ran up against the problem that in some cases, after making a test, I would jump back in the program for something I had previously processed and at other times I would jump forward in the program to a section of the program which had not been written and I did not know where it was. In other words, there were two types of jumps to be coped with: one which went back in the program; the other went forward in the program. Therefore, as the program was put together, a record was kept of where each subroutine was: they were numbered; the operations were numbered. And if I wanted to jump back to Operation 10, I could look at the record and find which line Operation 10 was at. But if I was at Operation 17, and I wanted to jump to Operation 28, I didn't yet know where it was.

And here comes in the curious fact that sometimes something totally extraneous to what you are doing will lead you to an answer. It so happened that when I was an undergraduate at college I played basketball under the old women's rules which divided the court into two halves, and there were six on a team; we had both a center and a side center, and I was the side center. Under the rules, you could dribble only once and you couldn't take a step while you had the ball in your hands. Therefore if you got the ball and you wanted to get down there under the basket, you used what we called a "forward pass." You looked for a member of your team, threw the ball over, ran like the dickens up ahead, and she threw the ball back to you. So it seemed to me that this was an appropriate way of solving the problem I was facing of the forward jumps! I tucked a little section down at the end of the memory which I called the "neutral corner." At the time I wanted to jump forward from the routine I was working on, I jumped to a spot in "neutral corner." I then set up a flag for Operation 28 which said, "I've got a message for you." This meant that each routine, as I processed it, had to look and see if it had a flag; if it did, it put a second jump from the neutral corner to the beginning of the routine, and it was possible to make a single-pass compiler and the concept did come from playing basketball! [Applause] I have a feeling that we would do well to train our computer people and specialists in many disciplines rather than in a single discipline because you never know what may prove useful. However, I'm afraid that that was the only compiler that was ever built that was a single-pass compiler.

Something rather interesting about it, though. At the time that it was written up, it was pointed out that there were some other things we might be able to do, and it was even suggested that it might—in line with the "anything which I can completely define"—it was pointed out that it might be possible even to build a differentiator.

With these concepts—incidentally, I have here the documentation of that A-0 compiler. It interests me today because of the failure of most of our people to document. In fact, I've probably never seen anything quite as completely documented as this is. In the first place, there's a write-up of the compiler and how it's going to work: the neutral corner, and all the rest of it. There is then a block chart of what it's going to do at a high level; a flow chart at a detailed level. The coding is here. Along with the coding, there are comments on it. The coding and the flow charts are keyed together with little circular things in the flow charts. And following that, there is a line-by-line description of exactly how the compiler works, in English, keyed both to the flow charts and to the coding. All this was done because I knew damn well nobody was ever going to believe it was going to work! And probably maybe that's one of the best reasons for documentation that ever existed—when you have to convince somebody that the darn thing will work.

It was running in May of 1952, and as Jean told you, the paper was given at the ACM meeting in Pittsburgh in May of 1952. A curious thing happened there. We did not put out proceedings in those days. I hauled 200 copies of the paper from Philadelphia to Pittsburgh on a Convair, and put them out at the back of the room so that people could pick them up as they wanted to, and I think I hauled 100 of 'em back again, which shows you the major interest that people expressed in trying to get some easier ways of writing programs.

To me the basic argument was that we were using subroutines which were checked out and known to work; we were putting them together with an automatic program which had been pretty well checked out too, and that only left the programmer the possibility of making major mistakes in logic.

In that same year of 1952, November of 1952, came Millie Coss's Editing Generator. One of the major problems in those early programs had been editing. You had to pull apart words and stick periods in, and put on dollar signs, and suppressed zeros, and much of it was done by hand coding. This seemed something which certainly—we knew exactly what was in the computer; we also knew exactly the format we wanted it to look like—that it would be possible to build a generator which would build an editing routine. Millie Coss went to work and in November of 1952 had operating a program which took in the format of the file, the format of the records, and the format of the output printed document, and produced the coding to get from one to the other. It also did a little bit of summing and things, and I think you could well call it the ancestor of most of the RPGs, and of those particular techniques.

Meantime, the long and cumbersome way of writing the input specifications to the A-0 compiler were becoming apparent, and it seemed much better to have a shorter way of writing that stuff. Now, I'll remind you that back in those days we were coding for computers. The concept of doing anything else had not occurred to us. Therefore, when we invented a new way of writing those programs, we used a code of course, and in fact, used a three-address code. Another thing drove us in this direction, and I think we often forget how much our surroundings influence our research decisions. All those things that we're aware of and yet are not aware of when we make decisions. And the fact was that we were living in an environment which consisted of a 12 alpha-decimal word, and it became perfectly obvious to us that the entire world operated in 12 alpha-decimal characters of which the first three defined an operation, the next three one input, the next three another input, and the last three the result. And it was clear that the world operated this way, and that the world lived in 12 alpha-decimal characters, and a three-address machine code.

That therefore was the code which was imposed on top of A-0. A translator was written, went on the front of A-0 which implemented a three-address machine code, and this became the A-2 compiler. I have here the original code for it and the write-up of the compiler. One interesting thing was that this combined the concepts of compiling and of generating, because when it came to compiling input and output routines, they became voluminous; there were so many of them, and just a few that did the arithmetic. And it was at this time that the I/O generators were written by Jim McGarvey, and the compiler actually contained generators which produced the input–output handling of the data.

Something else happened which curiously influenced and, if you will, slowed down the development of the languages from our point of view, in that that code proved to have some amazing virtues, and this is the reason I asked for a blackboard here. I'm going to try and show you what can happen to you when you become convinced that the whole world operates in a three-address code.

For instance, add x to y to give z. [ADD 00X 00Y 00Z]

Never mind there are some extra zeroes in there. Sometimes we needed those. Multiply z by t to give w. [MUL 00Z 00T 00W] Obviously, a beautiful way to write programs. This was $x + y = z$. This vas $zt = w$.

After that astounding remark that you could make a computer do anything which you could completely define, we felt impelled to do something about differentiation. We invented a new definition. We said if we put a number in front of a letter, it means the differential. 01X is dx. 15X obviously then is $d15$ of x. Perfectly permissible thing to do. All we did was leave the "d" out.

If a number follows—A12, A13, that just denotes an auxiliary storage location. And we found we could create a differentiator. What it did was pick up the first three letters, jump to a task routine; if it hit ADD it simply added ones, and it wrote down "ADD 01X 01Y 01Z" and it had nicely written "$dx + dy = dz$" which was totally correct.

When it got to multiply, it had to get a little cleverer. The task routine wrote down "MUL 00Z"—it added a 1 "01T"—moved to the next auxiliary storage location—"A14" "MUL 01Z, 00T, A15, ADD A14 and A15—you get 01W; and we'd written $z dt + t dz$ is equal to dw"—and the darned thing worked! And it was as silly a trick as that—to write the number in front of the letter.

MUL	00Z	01T	A14
MUL	01Z	00T	A15
ADD	A14	A15	01W

Of course as it kept on repeating the application of this, it got messier. It was finally given to Harry Kahrimanian, and in May of 1953, Harry put out his thesis at Temple University, "Analytical Differentiation by a Digital Computer." He had completed the work, extending from this original definition and using the A-2 compiler with its three-address code, had developed a differentiator.

Of course everybody promptly said that it couldn't possibly work because computers could only do arithmetic. They could not do calculus. That was very discouraging to Harry! [Laughter] Of course, but I always wanted to explore, to go a little bit further. We'd only added 1s here. We played with this on paper and on the computer, and we discovered we could get negative derivatives; we could also take d to the 1.08 derivative, and all sorts of interesting things like that. And nobody has yet told me what fractional derivatives are, so I hope somebody will explain that to me someday, but I can compute 'em under this definition! [Laughter] There are still some things to be explored from the ancient days.

With the A-2 compiler we began to try to get people to use these things. We found that we had to change from being research and development people and turn ourselves into salesmen, and get out and sell the idea of writing programs this way to customers. DuPont was the first to try A-2. It spread from there to the David Taylor Model Basin, I think, assisted by Betty Holberton and Nora Moser. To the Army Map Service. To the Bureau of the Census. And people began to try this game out. To NYU—it began to spread little bit by little bit to people who wanted to find a more rapid and easier way of writing programs.

The selling was an extremely difficult job because it had to involve not only selling the users, the customers, but also selling management, and persuading them that it was necessary for them to invest the time and money in building these program-assisting routines. And that was almost as difficult, if not more so, than selling to the users.

In July of 1953 John Mauchly prepared a paper on the influence of programming techniques on the design of computers, and it was published in the Proceedings of the IEEE. [IRE?] I think it was one of the first times that we tried to reach the entire community to say, "Look, we are going to be doing this kind of thing." And he mentions in the paper the need for assistance in designing computers. He brings up the Mark I and Mark II, brings up the fact that even when a standard subroutine program for full computer precision was to be used, it had to be copied with appropriate changes. He mentions the coding machine of Mark III. And the coding machine of Mark III was, of course, one of the things that led me to believe you could make programs somehow. The Wheeler, Wilkes, and Gill book. And then he goes on to the beginning of these generators. The Sort-Merge Generator. The Editing Generator. By then, Speedcoding had appeared with the IBM 701. The unwinding of programs and getting the computer to write out a complete program instead of having it all wound up in little knots.

The world began to look at the fact that maybe it was possible some way to provide assistance in developing programs. One of the other things I have here—which I will not go through for you except to mention what had to be done—this is a report written in December 1953, and it's a plea for a budget. All of that. The first two pages, about, are the plea for the budget. The rest of it is back-up documentation of what was happening in the world at that time.

I think it's interesting to find that the interpretive routines are mentioned. "Interpretive routines have been developed at many installations, notably Whirlwind, MIDAC, ILLIAC, SEAC, and IBM 701 Speedcoding." Interpretive routines were growing. It also gives the argument as to why we should be doing—it defines "interpreter" and "compiler"—and then it further gives the argument of why we should write programs instead of continuing to interpret at each step, because of course then the interpretive concept was the more popular one.

There were two papers that went out that year—September of 1953, Dick Ridgway's paper in Toronto, and bit by bit we were beginning to try and get the word out. July of 1953 was the first workshop sponsored by the Bureau of Census in Washington. By late 1953 we had the differentiator, the editing generator. By then A-2 had been successfully used at the Army Map Service, the Air Controller, Livermore, NYU, the Bureau of Ships, the David Taylor Model Basin. People were beginning to have some interest in the possibility of providing some assistance for writing programs. This even contains the letters—there were testimonial letters that were written saying, "Yeah, we used the compiler, and we find it useful, and it saved us some time." They're almost naïve to look at today, and yet they tell you a little bit about an atmosphere which was totally unwilling, or seemingly so, to accept a new development, because it was obvious that you always wrote your best programs in octal.

Probably the biggest step that year were two simultaneous developments. One was the beginning of FORTRAN. I have a copy here of a treasure which John Backus sent to me at the time: "Preliminary Report—Programming Research Group, Applied Science Division, International Business Machines Corporation, November 10, 1954. Specifications for the IBM Mathematical FORmula TRANslating System—FORTRAN" and the beginning of the true programming languages.

Simultaneous with that, at MIT, Laning and Zierler had written their algebraic translator. I've heard some people say that one led to the other. As far as I can tell, they were close to simultaneous, and neither one led to the other. In no case could it be possible that FORTRAN followed Laning and Zierler because this could not have been written between the time Laning and Zierler published and the time this was published.

It might interest you to look sometime at the original FORTRAN specs, though I suspect John will do his own job of educating you on that, but this was a tremendous step. This was the first of the *true* programming languages.

And yet I doubt if we could have gotten that far had we not had before that the generators, the compilers, the tools with which we would eventually implement the languages. I find today that many people are concentrating on the languages, and not doing very much about the tools with which to implement those languages. The art of building compilers, as far as I'm concerned, has been pretty badly stultified. There are excellent ways of building compilers for FORTRAN and ALGOL and Pascal and all the rest of the mathematical, logical programs, and then people try to use those methods to build a COBOL compiler, and it does not work. They are different, and the languages are different. And the distinction has not been made between the scientific engineering work, the mathematical work, and the data processing work. And the fact remains that in many ways they are different.

A little later, from Univac came AT-3. A-3 again was an extension of A-2, taking the 12-character, three address machine code, and extending it to a mathematical language. It's [AT-3] similar to FORTRAN in some cases; different in others. One of the things it did, which has never been done since, was to use exponents. At that time we prepared programs by typing on a typewriter onto a tape. Back in the early days of Mark I there was a gadget called a Unityper and you typed on tape. Of course, it disappeared and we had to reinvent that wheel some years later.

Since you could type directly on the tape, and since the Remington Rand typewriters had changeable type, we simply changed the type on the typewriter and decided that pulse codes mean what we say they mean. And we typed out stuff which looked like true mathematics: it had exponents and subscripts, and pulse codes meant what we said they mean. I don't think more than about 10 or 12 typewriters were modified like that, but we liked it a lot better being able to write our mathematics and have it look like mathematics directly, and have our exponents and subscripts explicitly typed out. That was true of MATH-MATIC which came out about that time.

Meantime, there was still the major difficulty of the data processors. Working with the people that I had worked with in data processing, I found that very few of them were symbol-oriented; very few of them were mathematically trained. They were business trained, and they were word-manipulaters rather than mathematics people. There was something else that was true of the data processing world: whereas in the mathematical–engineering world, we had a well-defined, well-known language; everybody knew exactly what—if you said "SIN" everybody knew it meant "sine"—they knew exactly what you meant, whether you were in Berlin or Tokyo, or anywhere in between. It was fully defined, already there. Everybody knew it. But there wasn't any such language for data processing. We took something over 500 data processing programs and sat down to write out what people were doing when they did data processing. We finally identified about 30 verbs which seemed to be the operators of data processing.

That December 1953 report proposed to management that mathematical programs should be written in mathematical notation, data processing programs should be written in English statements, and we would be delighted to supply the two corresponding compilers to translate to machine code. I was promptly told that I could not do that. And this time the reason was that computers couldn't understand English words. [Laughter] Well, I allowed as to how I never expected any computer anywhere to understand anything; that all I intended to do was to compare bit patterns. But it was not until January of 1955 that we were able to write a formal proposal for writing a data processing compiler. I keep it with me for a couple of reasons. One, to remind me that I always have to push into the future; and the other to remind me that any given moment in time there's always a line out here, and that line represents what your management will believe at that moment in time. [Laughter] And just you step over the line and you don't get the budget. I'd like to illustrate that:

This is the preliminary definition of a data processing compiler, dated 31 January, 1955. The language—the pseudo-code—is to be variable-length English words separated by spaces, sentences terminated by periods. One of the first things we ran into was nobody believed this. So we adopted an engineering technique. It's one that I wish more people would adopt. I'm surprised that we don't use it more often. When an engineer designs or builds something, he almost always builds either a pilot model or a bread board. He proves feasibility, he uncovers any difficulties he hasn't thought up theoretically, and he gets valid cost estimates. Best reasons in the world for building a pilot model.

We decided we'd build a pilot model of the compiler. And we started to work. Now, in the early compilers, there had been automatic segmentation and overlay. There had to be because of the size of UNIVAC I with only 1000 words of storage. Of course, we didn't call it by an interesting name. We just called it "using auxiliary storage." When it came to writing this data processing compiler, the first thing we found was that we were going to have to keep some lists. An operation list, a subroutine list, a jump list, and a storage list. Of course we quickly realized that management wouldn't know what a list was, and we changed that word to the word "file" and kept "files" so they'd understand all right.

The next thing that happened to us was that those got longer and longer and longer. And we only had 1000 words of storage. We had to do something, so we decided to use auxiliary storage. We tucked a small routine in the corner of the main memory, and if I didn't need a list for a while, I'd say, "Here's the Op File." It would grab it, put it on a tape unit, remember where it put it, and when I needed it again, I'd say, "Give me the Op File"—it's back in main memory, and I could work on it again. We did the same thing with the segments of the program in that model compiler. For instance, the heart of that compiler, the actual code generator, was called "DUZ". It was called DUZ because back in those days before we worried about phosphorus, DUZ did everything. [DUZ was a brand of soap with the slogan "DUZ does everything."] And if I didn't need DUZ for a while, I'd say, "Here's DUZ." It'd put it somewhere, and when I wanted it again, I'd say, "Give me DUZ"—it was back in the main memory, and I could work with it again.

Burroughs started using that technique about 20 years ago. I guess it was eight or nine years ago RCA reinvented it and called it "virtual storage." But it didn't really get to be respectable until IBM discovered it about five or six years ago. [Laughter and applause]

We got our little compiler running. It wouldn't take more than 20 statements. And on the back of this report, we put a nice little program in English. And we said, "Dear Kind Management: If you come down to the machine room, we'll be delighted to run this program for you." And it read: INPUT INVENTORY FILE A; PRICE FILE B; OUTPUT PRICED INVENTORY FILE C. COMPARE PRODUCT #A WITH PRODUCT #B. IF GREATER, GO TO OPERATION 10; IF EQUAL, GO TO OPERATION 5; OTHERWISE GO TO OPERATION 2. TRANSFER A TO D; WRITE ITEM D; JUMP TO OPERATION 8. It ended up: REWIND B; CLOSE OUT FILE C AND D; and STOP.

Nice little English program. But the more we looked at it, the smaller it looked. And we were asking for the biggest budget we had ever asked for. So we decided it would be a good idea if we did something more. We wrote a program. It went into the compiler and located all the English words and told us where they were, and we then replaced them. We said, "Dear Management: We'd also like to run this program for you. [Program spoken in French.] We'd like to run this French program for you." I don't know whether you recognized it, but the words are exactly the same and are in the same positions.

Well, if you do something once, it's an accident; if you do it twice it's a coincidence; but if you do it three times, you've uncovered a natural law! [Laughter] So—that's why they always tell you to "Try, try, try again." We changed the words again; the third program was an impressive one, of course. [Program in German language this time. With laughter] Beautiful words in this one! "We'd love to run this program for you."

Have you figured out what happened to that? That hit the fan!! It was absolutely obvious that a respectable American computer, built in Philadelphia, Pennsylvania, could not possibly understand French or German! And it took us four months to say no, no, no, no! We wouldn't think of programming it in anything but English.

What to us had been a simple—perfectly simple and obvious—substitution of bit patterns, to management we'd moved into the whole world of foreign languages, which was obviously impossible. That dangerous, dangerous point of something that's obvious, evident to the researcher, to the programmer—when it's faced by Management, is out of this world. It was nothing but a substitution of bit patterns, yet to management it was a move into all the foreign languages. The programs were identical, nothing but the bit patterns for the words changed. Incidentally, in building that compiler, we did something else—this is FLOW-MATIC. The A series was the mathematical compiler; the B series were to be the business compilers; it was those doggone sales people that wanted a fancier name and named them such things as MATH-MATIC and ARITH-MATIC and FLOW-MATIC. You can't do anything about the sales department, you just have to let 'em go ahead. But there was something we did in building this compiler that I find rather interesting, particularly since it survived so long. In order to quickly pick up the word—we didn't know anything about parsing algorithms at that point in time—and what happened was you picked up the verb, and then jumped to a subroutine which parsed that type of sentence. In order to do that quickly, and also to make it easy to manufacture that jump, the first and third letters of all the verbs in FLOW-MATIC were unique. That survived until last year in COBOL: that the first and third letters of all the verbs were unique. So, two things influenced FLOW-MATIC over and beyond mathematics and beyond programming languages. One was that we wanted to write the programs in anybody's language, which meant all the statements had to be imperative statements, because that was the only type of sentence in German that began with a verb. [Laughter] And the second was that we had to select the verbs, so that the first and third characters would be unique. One of our most difficult situations was of course display and divide, and that's why it had to be first and third characters. And there are certain of the other verbs which ran into that problem as well.

The data descriptions in that case weren't informal. We had forms, and you entered the data description in it. They were formalized. Frankly, I like the formalized things much better because I love filling in squares in answering questionnaires and things, and I always found it much easier to use a fixed format than I ever did to use an indefinite format, particularly because if you have a fixed format, you can always have the period be there; whereas if it's indefinite, then you have to remember to put the period on the end of the sentence, and that's one of my major difficulties.

To put that program—that compiler, on a 1000 word computer—perhaps I can appall you by what it meant. This is the chart of the tape operations. Did you ever see so many tapes spinning around? It took almost two hours sometimes to compile a program, because all the tape units were very busy spinning around at high speed, and yet that compiler was put on a 1000-word computer. Nowadays when people try to tell me that you can't put things on the minis or the micros, I have a tendency to pull some of these things out and say, "Of course you can! Let's not be ridiculous." 64K is a heckuva lot more memory than we had on 1000 words. A thousand 12-character words was only 12K, and all of FLOW-MATIC, and MATH-MATIC fitted in those memories. We can do a lot more with those micro-computers than we think we can. I think we've forgotten the size of the problems that those early computers tackled. UNIVAC I handled the whole premium file for Prudential Life. It did the entire payroll for U.S. Steel, including group incentive pay. It just did it slower, that's all. Now we have all the speed of the micros today.

When I look at the world today, what I see is a world in which I can have 300 UNIVAC I's all in one room, with all the power of those early computers. So, in a way, I'd ask you to look back at some of the tremendous things those early programmers did.

We finally convinced the Marketing Department that this thing could work. You might be interested later in looking at the first brochure that went out to try and sell to the general public the idea of writing data processing programs in English statements. It was a long, tortuous, and difficult job to get that concept accepted, because it was of course obvious that computers couldn't understand plain English, which made life very very difficult.

I also have, just in case anybody'd like to look at it, the list of the original verbs; the format with which they were defined, which incidentally, has survived through into today's COBOL compilers, COBOL manuals; and the specifications that started out the world in data processing of writing programs in plain English.

Now, of course, I still think we can go too far, and I would point out one thing about that language that implemented FLOW-MATIC: the fact that we could substitute those French and English words means that it was never anything but a code. It was not a language. Because the fact that we could take the words of those statements and substitute French words, German words, or anything else, meant that it was not a true language. It was actually a code.

I think sometimes we've lost track of the fact that we can make simpler languages if we stick to the format of a code of some kind and the exact definition provided by a code.

One other thing that came true from that particular language: by now the computers were going even a thousand times faster, and there was even greater demand for writing programs. Continuing on the subject of how the compilers were built, I think it was interesting that we used FLOW-MATIC to write our first COBOL—that it was possible to use it to write the first COBOL compiler. In between, something else had happened, and another unique compiler was produced, a compiler than ran on two computers.

The Air Materiel Command at Wright–Patterson wanted to write English language programs for their 1103. They had been writing English language programs on their UNIVAC. They wanted to write them on the 1103. A compiler was produced at Wright–Patterson, AIMACO, by the Air Materiel Command. First, you ran it on the UNIVAC I which translated the English into UNICODE, which was the assembly code of the 1103; it then picked the UNICODE off the UNIVAC I and walked it over and put it on the 1103, which produced the final program. And I think it's probably the only compiler I ever knew which worked halfway on one computer and halfway on a second computer, and it was done that way in order to build the compiler very very rapidly, and to make use of two existing pieces of software; the FLOW-MATIC on the UNIVAC I and the UNICODE already existing on the 1103. It's probably unique, and I don't think anything else was ever written in that particular way. But it might help us once in a while, when we need very badly to get a tool and to get it more rapidly than possible.

I was told to start talking to the days before 1956, the concentration was on meeting user needs, the concentration was not on the languages: it was on building the tools which later began to support the languages: the compilers, the generators, the supporting elements which now back up our definitions of languages. Languages came into use. People began to use 'em. There was another stage that had to occur. I think to some extent we had paid little attention to it in the early days. And that was that the implementers interpreted things differently. This particularly occurred in the case of COBOL. The Navy became very much interested in trying to make all the COBOL compilers give the same answers, even though they were on different computers. And it was that reason that I was called back and in the late 1960s at the Navy Department. A set of programs was built which would validate a COBOL compiler. They would compare the execution of the compiler against the standard, and monitor the behavior of the actions of the compiler. It was the first set of programs that was built to try to use software to check software.

I think this is an important element we've omitted. If we're going to have a language, it certainly should have the same answers on all the different computers. The set of COBOL validation routines was the first such set of routines to prove whether or not a compiler did in fact correctly implement the standards. I have the papers here that were published on the Federal COBOL Compiler Testing System. Recently they have also produced a set of routines for testing FORTRAN.

I think this is something we overlooked in our development of our languages. We overlooked the fact that we must see to it that those compilers properly implemented the language; that they did give common answers on different computers. A language isn't very useful if you get different answers on different computers. At least it isn't to an organization like the Navy which at any given moment has at least one of every kind of computer, and we *would* like to get the same answers from the same program on the different computers.

Another thing that's been happening as people have continued to develop the programming languages is that they persist in invalidating our older programs. I'd like to add something: put a burden on the programming language people. I'd like to insist that if they add something to a language, or change something in a language, they also provide us with the algorithm which will make the transfer in our programs so that we can automatically translate our programs, say, from COBOL 68 to COBOL 74. And if they don't do something like that pretty soon, I'm personally going to go around and shoot up the members of the language defining committees, because they are providing a large number of headaches. [Applause]

As I've gone through this, you may notice that in fact it was the Navy that ordered me to that first computer, the Navy that made it possible for us to develop COBOL, the Navy that made it possible for us to develop those test routines. I'm eternally grateful to an organization known as the United States Navy which ordered me to that first computer, and which throughout the 34 years since then, has given me the opportunities and the privileges of working in the computer industry, in the world of trying to make it easier for people to write programs. It's been a fascinating 34 years, and I'm forever grateful to the Navy for it, and for the privilege and responsibility of serving very proudly in the United States Navy.

Thank you. [Long applause]

TRANSCRIPT OF QUESTION AND ANSWER SESSION

SAMMET: We have questions for you.

CAPTAIN HOPPER: I can't answer questions sitting down.

SAMMET: I can't ask them standing up, so I'll sit down. There have been a number of questions that were turned in. I've tried to organize these in a little bit of coherence. The first one has been asked by a couple of people; JAN Lee for one, Richard Miller for another. If you were the third programmer on Mark I, who were the first two?

HOPPER: Richard Milton Block, now a consultant; he was on the engineering side; and Robert Campbell. I think he's now at MITRE. They were both Ensigns. I found out after I reported, they were brand new Ensigns—90-day wonders—they had heard that this gray-haired old college professor was coming, a j.g., and Dick Block paid Bob Campbell to take the desk next to me because he didn't want to have to. [Laughter] That's what comes of Ensigns! [More laughter]

SAMMET: I don't know whether it's Ensigns or Harvard—

HOPPER: They're both still in the industry!

SAMMET: A question from Aaron Finerman of SUNY at Stony Brook: Should not the Harvard group working on Mark I be given more credit for the development of programming and programming languages? There are few references to this group in the literature.

HOPPER: Yes, they should be. That was back in the days before there was much publication. The developments of the subroutines, the developments of first putting them together, the development of the coding machine above all, which was Aiken's concept; also it now turns out that Aiken was totally correct in saying that the programs and the data should be in separate memories, and we're just discovering that all over again in order to protect information. I think it's been very badly neglected. I could greatly wish that somebody might read those original manuals and find out what was done; find out the concepts. I think very few people seem to realize that Mark II was a multiprocessor. It could be operated as two independent computers: it could be operated as two computers which transferred information by a very interesting thing called a transfer register, which we could be interested in today; or it could be operated as one master computer and a slave computer; or all as one computer. The logic of that system has practically never been looked at because it was built in an awful rush out of relays, and—since by then we were using vacuum tubes and going on into electronics—very, very few people have ever bothered to look at the logic of that machine. And some of the people that are trying to build multiprocessors today would do well to read the Mark II manual. Some of the people that are building compilers and things today might well look at the Mark III coding machine. I think you're right. But that's prehistoric history, or something.

SAMMET: Two questions from Richard Miller: First question: Who brought Short Code from BINAC to UNIVAC?

HOPPER: Wait a minute—I'll tell you. If I can turn this pile upside down. They're out here on the West Coast now, I think, both of them. Robert Logan, and who was the other guy? I can't think of his name right now. You'll have to forgive me. Later I'll find out.

SAMMET: That can be looked up. Second question: Was there any consideration of codes other than three-address codes?

HOPPER: At this time? No. It was obvious that in mathematics you put two things in and got one out! And this wasn't constricted by the hardware, you see. It was a pseudo-machine. Of course I'd love to have one right now! One reason we didn't build three-address machines was along about then out came core storage and the whole aim became to shorten the word length so that it wouldn't cost too much to put the drivers on the core, and all of the manufacturers devoted their time and effort convincing us that we wanted single address, character-oriented machines. Now that we no longer have core storage, I hope we will break out of that restriction. It doesn't make sense anymore.

SAMMET: Okay. Next question from Saul Rosen at Purdue University. There were some interesting developments introduced in GP and GPX—namely FLEXIMATIC—on UNIVAC I. Would you comment on their significance?

HOPPER: They died! [Much laughter] So did BIOR—BIOR died too.

Transcript of Question and Answer Session

SAMMET: Do you care to say anymore? If you don't, I might!

HOPPER: Oh, you can say anything you want to. I've tried to concentrate on the things that had some existence and went forward. I didn't have time to cover everything. I'm sure there were some people who really wanted to know about BIOR.

SAMMET: Question from Bernie Galler of the University of Michigan. He says he recalls a remark that one of the early compilers took 47 passes on a program which contained only an END statement. Is that true, and why were so many passes needed?

HOPPER: No, it didn't take it for just one statement, but as you saw, that chart I held up did show the number of—of the ten tape units I think all of them were in action all the time on that first COBOL compiler. The reason was that Mark I [UNIVAC I] only had 1000 words of storage, and we had to make extended use of virtual storage. Some of them do the same thing today, only they cover it up by calling it virtual storage. Well, it's true! [Laughter]

SAMMET: Question from Bob Rosin at Bell Labs. It's rather long so let me read it verbatim: You express hope that microcomputers will allow people to rediscover some old and still-valid truths. We recently attended a microcomputer discussion in which the phrases "hand assembly" and "octal patch" were prominent. How can we enhance the probability that microcomputers will illuminate truths rather than allow people to ignore the hard-won and hard-learned discipline of programming?

HOPPER: I guess it's an education and marketing problem. I don't think we do nearly enough on spreading the word of what we're doing and what can be done. By and large, the people concerned with the large computers have totally ignored the so-called hobbyist community, though I would point out they are not a hobbyist community: they are small businessmen, doctors, lawyers, small towns, counties! They are a very worthwhile audience. But by and large I would say that the programming language community has ignored those people for years, and are still ignoring them. And we cannot be blamed if we haven't bothered to tell them that you can do something better than use binary. There are a few people—I've talked to a few, Bob Bemer and others—who are now making some effort to transfer what we have learned over the years and make it useful to the people with those computers. But so long as you are going to think that you've got to have a dinosaur to do anything, you are going to be out of tune with the world of the future. Does that answer it? We ain't done our job!

SAMMET: I agree with you. I think it's our fault. Last question—from Fritz Bauer of Munich, and I think while I know it will be covered to some extent by John Backus, I think he'd like your comments. He said that he thinks the work done, for example, by Rutishauser in the 1951–1952 time period should be mentioned in connection with the early historical development of the algebraic compilers.

HOPPER: When I started, I pointed out to you that I was talking from what I knew at that time in the basement of Croft Laboratory and in an old factory building. I had absolutely no idea of what Rutishauser, Zuse, or anyone else was doing. That word had not come over. The only other country that we knew of that was doing anything with the work was Wilkes in England. The other information had not come across. There was little communication, and I think no real communication with Germany until the time of ALGOL, until our first ALGOL group went over there to work with them. I think it's difficult for you in a seminar here to realize a time when there wasn't any ACM, there wasn't any IEEE Computer Society. There was no communication. There was no way to publish papers. And in fact, many of these documents that I have here are copied from Xerox— not even Xerox—they were Ozalid. They were mimeographed, and we mailed them to each other. My first copy of the FORTRAN was Ozalid. Not Xerox. It didn't exist. There *were* no meetings. There *were* no communications. How on earth could we know what other people were doing unless somehow or other, somewhere we managed to meet them? That's why those Navy seminars, the Harvard seminars, the MIT summer session computers, were so tremendously important. Michigan. Those were the places at which we met each other and were able to communicate with each other and find out what each other was doing. There wasn't any communication. That's one of the things we were up against. One of the things we hoped, in forming ACM, would meet that need. It's hard for me to explain to you that somebody in the basement of Croft, or that old factory building in Philadelphia, had very little communication with the outside world. And I didn't know what Rutishauser and Zuse were doing. I asked a while back if there was a copying machine—if any of you are interested, this was drawn in 1951; it's a cartoon which illustrates how a computer works, and maybe we could make a few copies of it if anybody's interested. It's rather fascinating. I found it when I was digging up this other stuff. Coffee??

SAMMET: It is now time for coffee.

FULL TEXT OF ALL QUESTIONS SUBMITTED

F. L. BAUER

I think, e.g., the work done by Rutishauser in 1951–1952 should be mentioned in connection with the historical development of algebraic compilers.

AARON FINERMAN

Should not the Harvard Mark I group at Harvard be given more credit for the development of programming and programming languages? There are few references to this group in the literature.

BERNARD GALLER

Captain Hopper— I recall a remark about one of your early compilers that it made 47 passes over a program that contained only an "END" statement. Is this true? Why were so many passes needed?

JAN LEE

Who were the first two programmers?

RICHARD MILLER

Who was involved in the UNIVAC-1103 compiler (FLOW-MATIC and UNICODE)?

If Grace was number 3 who was number 1 and number 2?

Who brought Short Code from BINAC to UNIVAC?

Was there any consideration of codes other than three-address code? Machine-dependent I assume!

SAUL ROSEN

There were some interesting developments introduced in GP and GPX (FLEXIMATIC) on UNIVAC I. Could you comment on their significance?

BOB ROSIN

You express hope that microcomputers will allow people to rediscover some old (and still-valid) truths. I recently attended a microcomputer discussion at which the phrases "hand assembly" and "octal patch" were prominent. How can we enhance the probability that microcomputers will illuminate truths rather than allow people to ignore the hard-won and hard-learned discipline of programming?

BRUCE WALKER

The best definition I ever heard of programming is, "Never forget that it is a waste of energy to do something twice, and if you know exactly what is to be done, you need not do it yourself at all." Unfortunately the reference is obscure (a science-fiction book "Skylark Three" by E. E. Smith, Ph. D., written in 1933).

FORTRAN Session

Chairman: JAN Lee
Speaker: John Backus
Discussant: George Ryckman

PAPER: THE HISTORY OF FORTRAN I, II, AND III

John Backus

IBM Corporation
Research Division

1. Early Background and Environment

1.1. Attitudes about Automatic Programming in the 1950s

Before 1954 almost all programming was done in machine language or assembly language. Programmers rightly regarded their work as a complex, creative art that required human inventiveness to produce an efficient program. Much of their effort was devoted to overcoming the difficulties created by the computers of that era: the lack of index registers, the lack of built-in floating point operations, restricted instruction sets (which might have AND but not OR, for example), and primitive input–output arrangements. Given the nature of computers, the services which "automatic programming" performed for the programmer were concerned with overcoming the machine's shortcomings. Thus the primary concern of some "automatic programming" systems was to allow the use of symbolic addresses and decimal numbers (e.g., the MIDAC Input Translation Program, Brown and Carr, 1954).

But most of the larger "automatic programming" systems [with the exception of Laning and Zierler's algebraic system (Laning and Zierler, 1954) and the A-2 compiler (Remington Rand, 1953; Moser, 1954)] simply provided a synthetic "computer" with an order code different from that of the real machine. This synthetic computer usually had floating point instructions and index registers and had improved input–output commands; it was therefore much easier to program than its real counterpart.

The A-2 compiler also came to be a synthetic computer sometime after early 1954. But in early 1954 its input had a much cruder form; instead of "pseudo-instructions" its input was then a complex sequence of "compiling instructions" that could take a variety of forms ranging from machine code itself to lengthy groups of words constituting rather clumsy calling sequences for the desired floating point subroutine, to "abbreviated form" instructions that were converted by a "Translator" into ordinary "compiling instructions" (Moser, 1954).

After May 1954 the A-2 compiler acquired a "pseudo-code" which was similar to the order codes for many floating point interpretative systems that were already in operation in 1953: e.g., the Los Alamos systems, DUAL and SHACO (Bouricius, 1953; Schlesinger, 1953), the MIT "Summer Session Computer" (Adams and Laning, 1954), a system for the ILLIAC designed by D. J. Wheeler (Muller, 1954), and the Speedcoding system for the IBM 701 (Backus, 1954a).

The Laning and Zierler system was quite a different story: it was the world's first operating algebraic compiler, a rather elegant but simple one. Knuth and Trabb (1977) assign this honor to Alick Glennie's AUTOCODE, but I, for one, am unable to recognize the sample AUTOCODE program they give as "algebraic", especially when it is compared to the corresponding Laning and Zierler program.

All of the early "automatic programming" systems were costly to use, since they slowed the machine down by a factor of five or ten. The most common reason for the slowdown was that these systems were spending most of their time in floating point subroutines. Simulated indexing and other "housekeeping" operations could be done with simple inefficient techniques, since, slow as they were, they took far less time than the floating point work.

Experience with slow "automatic programming" systems, plus their own experience with the problems of organizing loops and address modification, had convinced programmers that efficient programming was something that could not be automated. Another reason that "automatic programming" was not taken seriously by the computing community came from the energetic public relations efforts of some visionaries to spread the word that their "automatic programming" systems had almost human abilities to understand the language and needs of the user; whereas closer inspection of these same systems would often reveal a complex, exception-ridden performer of clerical tasks which was both difficult to use and inefficient. Whatever the reasons, it is difficult to convey to a reader in the late seventies the strength of the skepticism about "automatic programming" in general and about its ability to produce efficient programs in particular, as it existed in 1954.

[In the above discussion of attitudes about "automatic programming" in 1954 I have mentioned only those actual systems of which my colleagues and I were aware at the time. For a comprehensive treatment of early programming systems and languages I recommend the article by Knuth and Trabb (1977) and Sammet (1969).]

1.2. The Economics of Programming

Another factor which influenced the development of FORTRAN was the economics of programming in 1954. The cost of programmers associated with a computer center was usually at least as great as the cost of the computer itself. (This fact follows from the average salary-plus-overhead and number of programmers at each center and from the computer rental figures.) In addition, from one-quarter to one-half of the computer's time was spent in debugging. Thus programming and debugging accounted for as much as three-quarters of the cost of operating a computer; and obviously, as computers got cheaper, this situation would get worse.

This economic factor was one of the prime motivations which led me to propose the FORTRAN project in a letter to my boss, Cuthbert Hurd, in late 1953 (the exact date is not known but other facts suggest December 1953 as a likely date). I believe that the economic need for a system like FORTRAN was one reason why IBM and my successive bosses, Hurd, Charles DeCarlo, and John McPherson, provided for our constantly expanding needs over the next five years without ever asking us to project or justify those needs in a formal budget.

1.3. Programming Systems in 1954

It is difficult for a programmer of today to comprehend what "automatic programming" meant to programmers in 1954. To many it then meant simply providing mnemonic operation codes and symbolic addresses, to others it meant the simple process of obtaining subroutines from a library and inserting the addresses of operands into each subroutine. Most "automatic programming" systems were either assembly programs, or subroutine-fixing programs, or, most popularly, interpretive systems to provide floating point and indexing operations. My friends and I were aware of a number of assembly programs and interpretive systems, some of which have been mentioned above; besides these there were primarily two other systems of significance: the A-2 compiler (Remington-Rand, 1953; Moser, 1954) and the Laning and Zierler (1954) algebraic compiler at MIT. As noted above, the A-2 compiler was at that time largely a subroutine-fixer (its other principal task was to provide for "overlays"); but from the standpoint of its input "programs" it provided fewer conveniences than most of the then current interpretive systems mentioned earlier; it later adopted a "pseudo-code" as input which was similar to the input codes of these interpretive systems.

The Laning and Zierler system accepted as input an elegant but rather simple algebraic language. It permitted single-letter variables (identifiers) which could have a single constant or variable subscript. The repertoire of functions one could use were denoted by "F" with an integer superscript to indicate the "catalog number" of the desired function. Algebraic expressions were compiled into closed subroutines and placed on a magnetic drum for subsequent use. The system was originally designed for the Whirlwind computer when it had 1024 storage cells, with the result that it caused a slowdown in execution speed by a factor of about ten (Adams and Laning, 1954).

The effect of the Laning and Zierler system on the development of FORTRAN is a question which has been muddled by many misstatements on my part. For many years I believed that we had gotten the idea for using algebraic notation in FORTRAN from seeing a demonstration of the Laning and Zierler system at MIT. In preparing a paper (Backus, 1980) for the International Research Conference on the History of Computing at Los Alamos (June 10–15, 1976), I reviewed the matter with Irving Ziller and obtained a copy of a 1954 letter (Backus, 1954b) (which Dr. Laning kindly sent to me). As a result the facts of the matter have become clear. The letter in question is one I sent to Dr. Laning asking for a demonstration of his system. It makes clear that we had learned of his work at the Office of Naval Research Symposium on Automatic Programming for Digital Computers, May 13–14, 1954, and that the demonstration took place on June 2, 1954. The letter also makes clear that the FORTRAN project was well under way when the letter was sent (May 21,

John Backus

1954) and included Harlan Herrick, Robert A. Nelson, and Irving Ziller as well as myself. Furthermore, an article in the proceedings of that same ONR Symposium by Herrick and myself (Backus and Herrick, 1954) shows clearly that we were already considering input expressions like "$\Sigma\, a_{ij} \cdot b_{jk}$" and "$X + Y$". We went on to raise the question ". . . can a machine translate a sufficiently rich mathematical language into a sufficiently economical program at a sufficiently low cost to make the whole affair feasible?"

These and other remarks in our paper presented at the Symposium in May 1954 make it clear that we were already considering algebraic input considerably more sophisticated than that of Laning and Zierler's system when we first heard of their pioneering work. Thus, although Laning and Zierler had already produced the world's first algebraic compiler, our basic ideas for FORTRAN had been developed independently; thus it is difficult to know what, if any, new ideas we got from seeing the demonstration of their system.†

Our ONR Symposium article (Backus and Herrick, 1954) also makes clear that the FORTRAN group was already aware that it faced a new kind of problem in automatic programming. The viability of most compilers and interpreters prior to FORTRAN had rested on the fact that most source language operations were not machine operations. Thus even large inefficiencies in performing both looping/testing operations and computing addresses were masked by most operating time being spent in floating point subroutines. But the advent of the 704 with built in floating point and indexing radically altered the situation. The 704 presented a double challenge to those who wanted to simplify programming; first, it removed the raison d'être of earlier systems by providing in hardware the operations they existed to provide; second, it increased the problem of generating efficient programs by an order of magnitude by speeding up floating point operations by a factor of ten and thereby leaving inefficiencies nowhere to hide. In view of the widespread skepticism about the possibility of producing efficient programs with an automatic programming system and the fact that inefficiencies could no longer be hidden, we were convinced that the kind of system we had in mind would be widely used only if we could demonstrate that it would produce programs almost as efficient as hand coded ones and do so on virtually every job.

It was our belief that if FORTRAN, during its first months, were to translate any reasonable "scientific" source program into an object program only half as fast as its hand coded

† In response to suggestions of the Program Committee, let me try to deal explicitly with the question of what work might have influenced our early ideas for FORTRAN, although it is mostly a matter of listing work of which we were then unaware. I have already discussed the work of Laning and Zierler and the A-2 compiler. The work of Heinz Rutishauser (1952) is discussed later on. Like most of the world [except perhaps Rutishauser and Corrado Böhm—who was the first to describe a compiler in its own language (Böhm, 1954)] we were entirely unaware of the work of Konrad Zuse (1959, 1972). Zuse's "Plankalkül", which he completed in 1945, was, in some ways, a more elegant and advanced programming language than those that appeared 10 and 15 years later.

We were also unaware of the work of Mauchly et al. ("Short Code," 1950), Burks ("Intermediate PL," 1950), Böhm (1951), Glennie ("AUTOCODE," 1952) as discussed in Knuth and Trabb (1977). We were aware of but not influenced by the automatic programming efforts which simulated a synthetic computer (e.g., MIT "Summer Session Computer", SHACO, DUAL, SPEEDCODING, and the ILLIAC system), since their languages and systems were so different from those of FORTRAN. Nor were we influenced by algebraic systems which were designed after our "Preliminary Report" (1954) but which began operation before FORTRAN (e.g., BACAIC, Grems and Porter, 1956; IT, Perlis et al., 1957; MATH-MATIC, Ash et al., 1957). Although PACT I (Baker, 1956) was not an algebraic compiler, it deserves mention as a significant development designed after the FORTRAN language but in operation before FORTRAN, which also did not influence our work.

counterpart, then acceptance of our system would be in serious danger. This belief caused us to regard the design of the translator as the real challenge, not the simple task of designing the language. Our belief in the simplicity of language design was partly confirmed by the relative ease with which similar languages had been independently developed by Rutishauser (1952), Laning and Zierler (1954), and ourselves; whereas we were alone in seeking to produce really efficient object programs.

To this day I believe that our emphasis on object program efficiency rather than on language design was basically correct. I believe that had we failed to produce efficient programs, the widespread use of languages like FORTRAN would have been seriously delayed. In fact, I believe that we are in a similar, but unrecognized, situation today: in spite of all the fuss that has been made over myriad language details, current conventional languages are still very weak programming aids, and far more powerful languages would be in use today if anyone had found a way to make them run with adequate efficiency. In other words, the next revolution in programming will take place only when *both* of the following requirements have been met: (a) a new kind of programming language, far more powerful than those of today, has been developed; and (b) a technique has been found for executing its programs at not much greater cost than that of today's programs.

Because of our 1954 view that success in producing efficient programs was more important than the design of the FORTRAN language, I consider the history of the compiler construction and the work of its inventors an intergral part of the history of the FORTRAN language; therefore a later section deals with that subject.

2. The Early Stages of the FORTRAN Project

After Cuthbert Hurd approved my proposal to develop a practical automatic programming system for the 704 in December 1953 or January 1954, Irving Ziller was assigned to the project. We started work in one of the many small offices the project was to occupy in the vicinity of IBM headquarters at 590 Madison Avenue in New York; the first of these was in the Jay Thorpe Building on Fifth Avenue. By May 1954 we had been joined by Harlan Herrick and then by a new employee who had been hired to do technical typing, Robert A. Nelson (with Ziller, he soon began designing one of the most sophisticated sections of the compiler; he is now an IBM Fellow). By about May we had moved to the 19th floor of the annex of 590 Madison Avenue, next to the elevator machinery; the ground floor of this building housed the 701 installation on which customers tested their programs before the arrival of their own machines. It was here that most of the FORTRAN language was designed, mostly by Herrick, Ziller, and myself, except that most of the input–output language and facilities were designed by Roy Nutt, an employee of United Aircraft Corp. who was soon to become a member of the FORTRAN project.

After we had finished designing most of the language we heard about Rutishauser's proposals for a similar language (Ruthishauser, 1952). It was characteristic of the unscholarly attitude of most programmers then, and of ourselves in particular, that we did not bother to carefully review the sketchy translation of his proposals that we finally obtained, since from their symbolic content they did not appear to add anything new to our proposed language. Rutishauser's language had a FOR statement and one-dimensional arrays, but no IF, GOTO, nor I/O statements. Subscript variables could not be used as ordinary variables and operator precedence was ignored. His 1952 article described two compilers for this language (for more details, see Knuth and Trabb, 1977).

John Backus

As far as we were aware, we simply made up the language as we went along. We did not regard language design as a difficult problem, merely a simple prelude to the real problem: designing a compiler which could produce efficient programs. Of course one of our goals was to design a language which would make it possible for engineers and scientists to write programs themselves for the 704. We also wanted to eliminate a lot of the bookkeeping and detailed, repetitive planning which hand coding involved. Very early in our work we had in mind the notions of assignment statements, subscripted variables, and the DO statement (which I believe was proposed by Herrick). We felt that these provided a good basis for achieving our goals for the language, and whatever else was needed emerged as we tried to build a way of programming on these basic ideas.

We certainly had no idea that languages almost identical to the one we were working on would be used for more than one IBM computer, not to mention those of other manufacturers. (After all, there were very few computers around then.) But we did expect our system to have a big impact, in the sense that it would make programming for the 704 very much faster, cheaper, more reliable. We also expected that, if we were successful in meeting our goals, other groups and manufacturers would follow our example in reducing the cost of programming by providing similar systems with different but similar languages (Preliminary Report, 1954).

By the fall of 1954 we had become the "Programming Research Group" and I had become its "manager". By November of that year we had produced a paper: "Preliminary Report, Specifications for the IBM Mathematical FORmula TRANslating System, FORTRAN" (Preliminary Report, 1954) dated November 10. In its introduction we noted that "systems which have sought to reduce the job of coding and debugging problems have offered the choice of easy coding and slow execution or laborious coding and fast execution." On the basis more of faith than of knowledge, we suggested that programs "will be executed in about the same time that would be required had the problem been laboriously hand coded." In what turned out to be a true statement, we said that "FORTRAN may apply complex, lengthy techniques in coding a problem which the human coder would have neither the time nor inclination to derive or apply."

The language described in the "Preliminary Report" had variables of one or two characters in length, function names of three or more characters, recursively defined "expressions", subscripted variables with up to three subscripts, "arithmetic formulas" (which turn out to be assignment statements), and "DO-formulas". These latter formulas could specify both the first and last statements to be controlled, thus permitting a DO to control a distant sequence of statements, as well as specifying a third statement to which control would pass following the end of the iteration. If only one statement was specified, the "range" of the DO was the sequence of statements following the DO down to the specified statement.

Expressions in "arithmetic formulas" could be "mixed": involve both "fixed point" (integer) and "floating point" quantities. The arithmetic used (all integer or all floating point) to evaluate a mixed expression was determined by the type of the variable on the left of the "=" sign. "IF-formulas" employed an equality or inequality sign ("=" or ">" or ">=") between two (restricted) expressions, followed by two statement numbers, one for the "true" case, the other for the "false" case.

A "Relabel formula" was designed to make it easy to rotate, say, the indices of the rows of a matrix so that the same computation would apply, after relabeling, even though a new row had been read in and the next computation was now to take place on a different, rotated set of rows. Thus, for example, if b is a 4 by 4 matrix, after RELABEL $b(3,1)$, a reference to $b(1,j)$ has the same meaning as $b(3,j)$ before relabeling; $b(2,j)$ after $= b(4,j)$ before; $b(3,j)$ after $= b(1,j)$ before; and $b(4,j)$ after $= b(2,j)$ before relabeling.

The input–output statements provided included the basic notion of specifying the sequence in which data was to be read in or out, but did not include any "FORMAT" statements.

The Report also lists four kinds of "specification sentences": (1) "dimension sentences" for giving the dimensions of arrays; (2) "equivalence sentences" for assigning the same storage locations to variables; (3) "frequency sentences" for indicating estimated relative frequency of branch paths or loops to help the compiler optimize the object program; and (4) "relative constant sentences" to indicate subscript variables which are expected to change their values very infrequently.

Toward the end of the Report (pp. 26–27) there is a section "Future additions to the FORTRAN system". Its first item is: "a variety of new input–output formulas which would enable the programmer to specify various formats for cards, printing, input tapes, and output tapes". It is believed that this item is a result of our early consultations with Roy Nutt. This section goes on to list other proposed facilities to be added: complex and double precision arithematic, matrix arithmetic, sorting, solving simultaneous equations, differential equations, and linear programming problems. It also describes function definition capabilities similar to those which later appeared in FORTRAN II; facilities for numerical integration; a summation operator; and table lookup facilities.

The final section of the Report (pp. 28–29) discusses programming techniques to use to help the system produce efficient programs. It discusses how to use parentheses to help the system identify identical subexpressions within an expression and thereby eliminate their duplicate calculation. These parentheses had to be supplied only when a recurring subexpression occurred as part of a term [e.g., if $a*b$ occured in several places, it would be better to write the term $a*b*c$ as $(a*b)*c$ to avoid duplicate calculation]; otherwise the system would identify duplicates without any assistance. It also observes that the system would not produce optimal code for loops constructed without DO statements.

This final section of the Report also notes that "no special provisions have been included in the FORTRAN system for locating errors in formulas". It suggests checking a program "by independently recreating the specifications for a problem from its FORTRAN formulation [!]". It says nothing about the system catching syntactic errors, but notes that an error-finding program can be written after some experience with errors has been accumulated.

Unfortunately we were hopelessly optimistic in 1954 about the problems of debugging FORTRAN programs (thus we find on p. 2 of the Report: "Since FORTRAN should virtually eliminate coding and debugging . . . [!]") and hence syntactic error checking facilities in the first distribution of FORTRAN I were weak. Better facilities were added not long after distribution and fairly good syntactic checking was provided in FORTRAN II.

The FORTRAN language described in the *Programmer's Reference Manual* dated October 15, 1956 (IBM, 1956) differed in a few respects from that of the Preliminary Report, but, considering our ignorance in 1954 of the problems we would later encounter in producing the compiler, there were remarkably few deletions (the Relabel and Relative Constant statements), a few retreats, some fortunate, some not (simplification of DO statements, dropping inequalities from IF statements—for lack of a ">" symbol, and prohibiting most "mixed" expressions and subscripted subscripts), and the rectification of a few omissions (addition of FORMAT, CONTINUE, computed and assigned GOTO statements, increasing the length of variables to up to six characters, and general improvement of input–output statements).

Since our entire attitude about language design had always been a very casual one, the changes which we felt to be desirable during the course of writing the compiler were made equally casually. We never felt that any of them involved a real sacrifice in convenience or power (with the possible exception of the Relabel statement, whose purpose was to coordinate input–output with computations on arrays, but this was one facility which we felt would have been really difficult to implement). I believe the simplification of the original DO statement resulted from the realization that (a) it would be hard to describe precisely, (b) it was awkward to compile, and (c) it provided little power beyond that of the final version.

In our naïve unawareness of language design problems—of course we knew nothing of many issues which were later thought to be important, e.g., block structure, conditional expressions, type declarations—it seemed to us that once one had the notions of the assignment statement, the subscripted variable, and the DO statement in hand (and these were among our earliest ideas), then the remaining problems of language design were trivial: either their solution was thrust upon one by the need to provide some machine facility such as reading input, or by some programming task which could not be done with existing structures (e.g., skipping to the end of a DO loop without skipping the indexing instructions there: this gave rise to the CONTINUE statement).

One much-criticized design choice in FORTRAN concerns the use of spaces: blanks were ignored, even blanks in the middle of an identifier. Roy Nutt reminds me that that choice was partly in recognition of a problem widely known in SHARE, the 704 users' association. There was a common problem with keypunchers not recognizing or properly counting blanks in handwritten data, and this caused many errors. We also regarded ignoring blanks as a device to enable programmers to arrange their programs in a more readable form without altering their meaning or introducing complex rules for formatting statements.

Another debatable design choice was to rule out "mixed" mode expressions involving both integer and floating point quantities. Although our Preliminary Report had included such expressions, and rules for evaluating them, we felt that if code for type conversion were to be generated, the user should be aware of that, and the best way to insure that he was aware was to ask him to specify them. I believe we were also doubtful of the usefulness of the rules in our Report for evaluating mixed expressions. In any case, the most common sort of "mixtures" was allowed: integer exponents and function arguments were allowed in a floating point expression.

In late 1954 and early 1955, after completing the Preliminary Report, Harlan Herrick, Irving Ziller, and I gave perhaps five or six talks about our plans for FORTRAN to various groups of IBM customers who had ordered a 704 (the 704 had been announced about May 1954). At these talks we covered the material in the Report and discussed our plans for the compiler (which was to be completed within about six months [!]; this was to remain the interval-to-completion until it actually was completed over two years later, in April 1957). In addition to informing customers about our plans, another purpose of these talks was to assemble a list of their objections and further requirements. In this we were disappointed; our listeners were mostly skeptical; I believe they had heard too many glowing descriptions of what turned out to be clumsy systems to take us seriously. In those days one was accustomed to finding lots of peculiar but significant restrictions in a system when it finally arrived that had not been mentioned in its original description. Most of all, our claims that we would produce efficient object programs were disbelieved. Whatever the reasons, we received almost no suggestions or feedback; our listeners had done almost no thinking about the problems we faced and had almost no suggestions or criticisms. Thus we felt that our trips to Washington (D.C.), Albuquerque, Pittsburgh, Los Angeles, and one or two other places were not very helpful.

One trip to give our talk, probably in January 1955, had an excellent payoff. This talk, at United Aircraft Corp., resulted in an agreement between our group and Walter Ramshaw at United Aircraft that Roy Nutt would become a regular part of our effort (although remaining an employee of United Aircraft) to contribute his expertise on input–output and assembly routines. With a few breaks due to his involvement in writing various SHARE programs, he would thenceforth come to New York two or three times a week until early 1957.

It is difficult to assess the influence the early work of the FORTRAN group had on other projects. Certainly the discussion of Laning and Zierler's algebraic compiler at the ONR Symposium in May 1954 would have been more likely to persuade someone to undertake a similar line of effort than would the brief discussion of the merits of using "a fairly natural mathematical language" that appeared there in the paper by Herrick and myself (Backus and Herrick, 1954). But it was our impression that our discussions with various groups after that time, their access to our Preliminary Report, and their awareness of the extent and seriousness of our efforts, that these factors either gave the initial stimulus to some other projects or at least caused them to be more active than they might have been otherwise. It was our impression, for example, that the "IT" project [Perlis, Smith and Van Zoeren 1957] at Purdue and later at Carnegie–Mellon began shortly after the distribution of our Preliminary Report, as did the "MATH-MATIC" project (Ash *et al.*, 1957) at Sperry Rand.

It is not clear what influence, if any, our Los Angeles talk and earlier contacts with members of their group had on the PACT I effort (Baker, 1956), which I believe was already in its formative stages when we got to Los Angeles. It is clear, whatever influence the specifications for FORTRAN may have had on other projects in 1954–1956, that our plans were well advanced and quite firm by the end of 1954 and before we had contact or knowledge of those other projects. Our specifications were not affected by them in any significant way as far as I am aware, even though some were operating before FORTRAN was (since they were primarily interested in providing an input language rather than in optimization, their task was considerably simpler than ours).

3. The Construction of the Compiler

The FORTRAN compiler (or "translator" as we called it then) was begun in early 1955, although a lot of work on various schemes which would be used in it had been done in 1954; e.g., Herrick had done a lot of trial programming to test out our language and we had worked out the basic sort of machine programs which we wanted the compiler to generate for various source language phrases; Ziller and I had worked out a basic scheme for translating arithmetic expressions.

But the real work on the compiler got under way in our third location on the fifth floor of 15 East 56th Street. By the middle of February three separate efforts were underway. The first two of these concerned sections 1 and 2 of the compiler, and the third concerned the input, output, and assembly programs we were going to need (see below). We believed then that these efforts would produce most of the compiler.

(The entire project was carried on by a loose cooperation between autonomous, separate groups of one, two, or three people; each group was responsible for a "section" of the compiler; each group gradually developed and agreed upon its own input and output specifications with the groups for neighboring sections; each group invented and programmed the necessary techniques for doing its assigned job.)

Section 1 was to read the entire source program, compile what instructions it could, and file all the rest of the information from the source program in appropriate tables. Thus the compiler was "one pass" in the sense that it "saw" the source program only once. Herrick was responsible for creating most of the tables, Peter Sheridan (who had recently joined us) compiled all the arithmetic expressions, and Roy Nutt compiled and/or filed the I/O statements. Herrick, Sheridan, and Nutt got some help later on from R. J. Beeber and H. Stern, but they were the architects of section 1 and wrote most of its code. Sheridan devised and implemented a number of optimizing transformations on expressions (Sheridan, 1959) which sometimes radically altered them (of course without changing their meaning). Nutt transformed the I/O "lists of quantities" into nests of DO statements which were then treated by the regular mechanisms of the compiler. The rest of the I/O information he filed for later treatment in section 6, the assembler section. (For further details about how the various sections of the compiler worked, see Backus *et al.*, 1957.)

Using the information that was filed in section 1, section 2 faced a completely new kind of problem; it was required to analyze the entire structure of the program in order to generate optimal code from DO statements and references to subscripted variables. The simplest way to effect a reference to $A(I,J)$ is to evaluate an expression involving the address of $A(1,1)$, I, and $K \times J$, where K is the length of a column (when A is stored columnwise). But this calculation, with its multiplication, is much less efficient than the way most hand coded programs effect a reference to $A(I,J)$, namely, by adding an appropriate constant to the address of the preceding reference to the array A whenever I and J are changing linearly. To employ this far more efficient method section 2 had to determine when the surrounding program was changing I and J linearly.

Thus one problem was that of distinguishing between, on the one hand, references to an array element which the translator might treat by incrementing the address used for a previous reference, and those array references, on the other hand, which would require an address calculation starting from scratch with the current values of the subscripts.

It was decided that it was not practical to track down and identify linear changes in subscripts resulting from assignment statements. Thus the sole criterion for linear changes, and hence for efficient handling of array references, was to be that the subscripts involved were being controlled by DO statements. Despite this simplifying assumption, the number of cases that section 2 had to analyze in order to produce optimal or near-optimal code was very large. (The number of such cases increased exponentially with the number of subscripts; this was a prime factor in our decision to limit them to three; the fact that the 704 had only three index registers was not a factor.)

It is beyond the scope of this paper to go into the details of the analysis which section 2 carried out. It will suffice to say that it produced code of such efficiency that its output would startle the programmers who studied it. It moved code out of loops where that was possible; it took advantage of the differences between rowwise and columnwise scans; it took note of special cases to optimize even the exits from loops. The degree of optimization performed by section 2 in its treatment of indexing, array references, and loops was not equalled again until optimizing compilers began to appear in the middle and late 1960s.

The architecture and all the techniques employed in section 2 were invented by Robert A. Nelson and Irving Ziller. They planned and programmed the entire section. Originally it was their intention to produce the complete code for their area, including the choice of the index registers to be used (the 704 had three index registers). When they started looking at that problem it rapidly became clear that it was not going to be easy to treat it optimally. At that point I proposed that they should produce a program for a 704 with an unlimited number of index registers, and that later sections would analyze the frequency of execution of various parts of the program (by a Monte Carlo simulation of its execution) and then make index register assignments so as to minimize the transfers of items between the store and the index registers.

This proposal gave rise to two new sections of the compiler which we had not anticipated, sections 4 and 5 (section 3 was added still later to convert the output of sections 1 and 2 to the form required for sections 4, 5, and 6). In the fall of 1955 Lois Mitchell Haibt joined our group to plan and program section 4, which was to analyze the flow of a program produced by sections 1 and 2, divide it into "basic blocks" (which contained no branching), do a Monte Carlo (statistical) analysis of the expected frequency of execution of basic blocks—by simulating the behavior of the program and keeping counts of the use of each block—using information from DO statements and FREQUENCY statements, and collect information about index register usage. (for more details, see Backus *et al.,* 1957; Cocke and Schwartz, 1970, p. 511). Section 5 would then do the actual transformation of the program from one having an unlimited number of index registers to one having only three. Again, the section was entirely planned and programmed by Haibt.

Section 5 was planned and programmed by Sheldon Best, who was loaned to our group by agreement with his employer, Charles W. Adams, at the Digital Computer Laboratory at MIT; during his stay with us Best was a temporary IBM employee. Starting in the early fall of 1955, he designed what turned out to be, along with section 2, one of the most intricate and complex sections of the compiler, one which had perhaps more influence on the methods used in later compilers than any other part of the FORTRAN compiler. (For a discussion of his techniques, see Cocke and Schwartz, 1970, pp. 510–515.) It is impossible to describe his register allocation method here; it suffices to say that it was to become the basis for much subsequent work and produced code which was very difficult to improve.

Although I believe that no provably optimal register allocation algorithm is known for general programs with loops, etc., empirically Best's 1955–1956 procedure appeared to be optimal. For straight-line code Best's replacement policy was the same as that used in Belady's MIN algorithm, which Belady proved to be optimal (Belady, 1965). Although Best did not publish a formal proof, he had convincing arguments for the optimality of his policy in 1955.

Late in 1955 it was recognized that yet another section, section 3, was needed. This section merged the outputs of the preceding sections into a single uniform 704 program which could refer to any number of index registers. It was planned and programmed by Richard Goldberg, a mathematician who joined us in November 1955. Also, late in 1956, after Best had returned to MIT and during the debugging of the system, section 5 was taken over by Goldberg and David Sayre (see below), who diagrammed it carefully and took charge of its final debugging.

The final section of the compiler, section 6, assembled the final program into a relocatable binary program (it could also produce a symbolic program in SAP, the SHARE Assembly Program for the 704). It produced a storage map of the program and data that was a compact summary of the FORTRAN output. Of course it also obtained the necessary library programs for inclusion in the object program, including those required to interpret FORMAT statements and perform input–output operations. Taking advantage of the special features of the programs it assembled, this assembler was about ten times faster than SAP. It was designed and programmed by Roy Nutt, who also wrote all the I/O programs and the relocating binary loader for loading object programs.

By the summer of 1956 large parts of the system were working. Sections 1, 2, and 3 could produce workable code provided no more than three index registers were needed. A number of test programs were compiled and run at this time. Nutt took part of the system to United Aircraft (sections 1, 2, and 3 and the part of section 6 which produced SAP output). This part of the system was productive there from the summer of 1956 until the complete system was available in early 1957.

From late spring of 1956 to early 1957 the pace of debugging was intense; often we would rent rooms in the Langdon Hotel (which disappeared long ago) on 56th Street, sleep there a little during the day and then stay up all night to get as much use of the computer (in the headquarters annex on 57th Street) as possible.

It was an exciting period; when later on we began to get fragments of compiled programs out of the system, we were often astonished at the surprising transformations in the indexing operations and in the arrangement of the computation which the compiler made, changes which made the object program efficient but which we would not have thought to make as programmers ourselves (even though, of course, Nelson or Ziller could figure out how the indexing worked, Sheridan could explain how an expresssion had been optimized beyond recognition, and Goldberg or Sayre could tell us how section 5 had generated additional indexing operations). Transfers of control appeared which corresponded to no source statement, expressions were radically rearranged, and the same DO statement might produce no instructions in the object program in one context, and in another it would produce many instructions in different places in the program.

By the summer of 1956 what appeared to be the imminent completion of the project started us worrying (for perhaps the first time) about documentation. David Sayre, a crystallographer who had joined us in the spring (he had earlier consulted with Best on the design of section 5 and had later begun serving as second-in-command of what was now the "Programming Research Department") took up the task of writing the *Programmer's Reference Manual* (IBM, 1956). It appeared in a glossy cover, handsomely printed, with the date October 15, 1956. It stood for some time as a unique example of a manual for a programming language (perhaps it still does): it had wide margins, yet was only 51 pages long. Its description of the FORTRAN language, exclusive of input–output statements, was 21 pages; the I/O description occupied another 11 pages; the rest of it was examples and details about arithmetic, tables, etc. It gave an elegant recursive definition of expressions (as given by Sheridan), and concise, clear descriptions, with examples, of each statement type, of which there were 32, mostly machine dependent items like SENSE LIGHT, IF DIVIDE CHECK, PUNCH, READ DRUM, and so on. (For examples of its style see Figs. 1, 2, and 3.)

One feature of FORTRAN I is missing from the *Programmer's Reference Manual*, not from an oversight of Sayre's, but because it was added to the system after the manual was

Subscripts.

GENERAL FORM	EXAMPLES
Let v represent any fixed point variable and c (or c') any unsigned fixed point constant. Then a subscript is an expression of one of the forms: v	I
	3
	MU + 2
	MU − 2
c	5 * J
v + c or v − c	5 * J + 2
c * v	5 * J − 2
c * v + c' or c * v − c'	

The symbol * denotes multiplication. The variable v must not itself be subscripted.

Subscripted Variables.

GENERAL FORM	EXAMPLES
A fixed or floating point variable followed by parentheses enclosing 1, 2, or 3 subscripts separated by commas.	A(I)
	K(3)
	BETA(5 * J − 2, K + 2, L)

For each variable that appears in subscripted form the size of the array (i.e. the maximum values which its subscripts can attain) must be stated in a DIMENSION statement (see Chapter 6) preceding the first appearance of the variable.

The minimum value which a subscript may assume in the object program is +1.

Arrangement of Arrays in Storage.

A 2-dimensional array A will, in the object program, be stored sequentially in the order $A_{1,1}$, $A_{2,1}$, ..., $A_{m,1}$, $A_{1,2}$, $A_{2,2}$, ..., $A_{m,2}$, ..., $A_{m,n}$. Thus it is stored "columnwise", with the first of its subscripts varying most rapidly, and the last varying least rapidly. The same is true of 3-dimensional arrays. 1-dimensional arrays are of course simply stored sequentially. All arrays are stored backwards in storage; i.e. the above sequence is in the order of decreasing absolute location.

Fig. 1. Original FORTRAN Manual, p. 11. [Courtesy of International Business Machines Corporation.]

Any such routine will be compiled into the object program as a closed subroutine. In the section on Writing Subroutines for the Master Tape in Chapter 7 are given the specifications which any such routine must meet.

Expressions

An expression is any sequence of constants, variables (subscripted or not subscripted), and functions, separated by operation symbols, commas, and parentheses so as to form a meaningful mathematical expression.

However, one special restriction does exist. A FORTRAN expression may be either a fixed or a floating point expression, but it must not be a mixed expression. This does not mean that a floating point quantity can not appear in a fixed point expression, or vice versa, but rather that a quantity of one mode can appear in an expression of the other mode only in certain ways. Briefly, a floating point quantity can appear in a fixed point expression only as an argument of a function; a fixed point quantity can appear in a floating point expression only as an argument of a function, or as a subscript, or as an exponent.

Formal Rules for Forming Expressions. By repeated use of the following rules, all permissible expressions may be derived.

1. Any fixed point (floating point) constant, variable, or subscripted variable is an expression of the same mode. Thus 3 and I are fixed point expressions, and ALPHA and A(I,J,K) are floating point expressions.

2. If SOMEF is some function of n variables, and if E, F, ... , H are a set of n expressions of the correct modes for SOMEF, then SOMEF (E, F, ... , H) is an expression of the same mode as SOMEF.

3. If E is an expression, and if its first character is not $+$ or $-$, then $+$E and $-$E are expressions of the same mode as E. Thus $-$A is an expression, but $+$$-$A is not.

4. If E is an expression, then (E) is an expression of the same mode as E. Thus (A), ((A)), (((A))), etc. are expressions.

5. If E and F are expressions of the same mode, and if the first character of F is not $+$ or $-$, then

$$E + F$$
$$E - F$$
$$E * F$$
$$E / F$$

are expressions of the same mode. Thus A$-$$+$B and A/$+$B are not expressions. The characters $+$, $-$, $*$, and $/$ denote addition, subtraction, multiplication, and division.

Fig. 2. Original FORTRAN Manual, p. 14. [Courtesy of International Business Machines Corporation.]

STOP

GENERAL FORM	EXAMPLES
"STOP" or "STOP n" where n is an unsigned **octal** fixed point constant.	STOP STOP 77777

This statement causes the machine to HALT in such a way that pressing the START button has no effect. Therefore, in contrast to the PAUSE, it is used where a get-off-the-machine stop, rather than a temporary stop, is desired. The octal number n is displayed on the 704 console in the address field of the storage register. (If n is not stated it is taken to be 0.)

DO

GENERAL FORM	EXAMPLES
"DO n i $= m_1, m_2$" or "DO n i $= m_1, m_2, m_3$" where n is a statement number, i is a non-subscripted fixed point variable, and m_1, m_2, m_3 are each either an unsigned fixed point constant or a non-subscripted fixed point variable. If m_3 is not stated it is taken to be 1.	DO 30 I $= 1, 10$ DO 30 I $= 1, M, 3$

The DO statement is a command to "DO the statements which follow, to and including the statement with statement number n, repeatedly, the first time with i — m_1 and with i increased by m_3 for each succeeding time; after they have been done with i equal to the highest of this sequence of values which does not exceed m_2 let control reach the statement following the statement with statement number n".

The *range* of a DO is the set of statements which will be executed repeatedly; it is the sequence of consecutive statements immediately following the DO, to and including the statement numbered n.

The *index* of a DO is the fixed point variable i, which is controlled by the DO in such a way that its value begins at m_1 and is increased each time by m_3 until it is about to exceed m_2. Throughout the range it is available for computation, either as an ordinary fixed point variable or as the variable of a subscript. During the last execution of the range, the DO is said to be *satisfied*.

Suppose, for example, that control has reached statement 10 of the program

```
10    DO 11 I = 1, 10
11    A(I) == I*N(I)
12
```

Fig. 3. Original FORTRAN Manual, p. 20. [Courtesy of International Business Machines Corporation.]

written and before the system was distributed. This feature was the ability to define a function by a "function statement." These statements had to precede the rest of the program. They looked like assignment statements, with the defined function and dummy arguments on the left and an expression involving those arguments on the right. They are described in the addenda to the *Programmer's Reference Manual* (Addenda, 1957) which we sent on February 8, 1957 to John Greenstadt, who was in charge of IBM's facility for distributing information to SHARE. They are also described in all subsequent material on FORTRAN I.

The next documentation task we set ourselves was to write a paper describing the FORTRAN language and the translator program. The result was a paper entitled "The FORTRAN automatic coding system" (Backus *et al.*, 1957) which we presented at the Western Joint Computer Conference in Los Angeles in February 1957. I have mentioned all of the thirteen authors of that paper in the preceding narrative except one: Robert A. Hughes. He was employed by the Livermore Radiation Laboratory; by arrangement with Sidney Fernbach, he visited us for two or three months in the summer of 1956 to help us document the system. (The authors of that paper were: J. W. Backus, R. J. Beeber, S. Best, R. Goldberg, L. M. Haibt, H. L. Herrick, R. A. Hughes, R. A. Nelson, R. Nutt, D. Sayre, P. B. Sheridan, H. Stern, I. Ziller.)

At about the time of the Western Joint Computer Conference we spent some time in Los Angeles still frantically debugging the system. North American Aviation gave us time at night on their 704 to help us in our mad rush to distribute the system. Up to this point there had been relatively little interest from 704 installations (with the exception of Ramshaw's United Aircraft shop, Harry Cantrell's GE installation in Schenectady, and Sidney Fernbach's Livermore operation), but now that the full system was beginning to generate object programs, interest picked up in a number of places.

Sometime in early April 1957 we felt the system was sufficiently bug-free to distribute to all 704 installations. Sayre and Grace Mitchell (see below) started to punch out the binary decks of the system, each of about 2,000 cards, with the intention to make 30 or 40 decks for distribution. This process was so error-prone that they had to give up after spending an entire night in producing only one or two decks.

(Apparently one of those decks was sent, without any identification or directions, to the Westinghouse Bettis installation, where a puzzled group headed by Herbert S. Bright, suspecting that it might be the long-awaited FORTRAN deck, proceeded, entirely by guesswork, to get it to compile a test program—after a diagnostic printout noting that a comma was missing in a specific statement! This program then printed 28 pages of correct results —with a few FORMAT errors. The date: April 20, 1957. An amusing account of this incident by Bright is in *Computers and Automation* (Bright, 1971).)

After failing to produce binary decks, Sayre devised and programmed the simple editor and loader that made it possible to distribute and update the system from magnetic tapes; this arrangement served as the mechanism for creating new system tapes from a master tape and the binary correction cards which our group would generate in large numbers during the long field debugging and maintenance period which followed distribution

With the distribution of the system tapes went a *Preliminary Operator's Manual* (Operator's Manual, 1957) dated April 8, 1957. It describes how to use the tape editor and how to maintain the library of functions. Five pages of such general instructions are followed by 32 pages of error stops; many of these say "source program error, get off machine, correct formula in question and restart problem" and then, for example (stop 3624) "nonzero level reduction due to insufficient or redundant parentheses in arithmetic or IF-type formula". Shortly after the distribution of the system we distributed—one copy per installation—what was fondly known as the "Tome", the complete symbolic listing of the entire compiler plus other system and diagnostic information, an 11″ by 15″ volume about four or five inches thick.

The proprietors of the six sections were kept busy tracking down bugs elicited by our customers' use of FORTRAN until the late summer of 1957. Hal Stern served as the coordinator of the field debugging and maintenance effort; he received a stream of telegrams, mail and phone calls from all over the country and distributed the incoming problems to the appropriate members of our group to track down the errors and generate correction cards, which he then distributed to every installation.

In the spring of 1957 Grace E. Mitchell joined our group to write the *Programmer's Primer* (IBM, 1957) for FORTRAN. The Primer was divided into three sections; each described successively larger subsets of the language accompanied by many example programs. The first edition of the Primer was issued in the late fall or winter of 1957; a slightly revised edition appeared in March 1958. Mitchell planned and wrote the 64-page Primer with some consultation with the rest of the group; she later programmed most of the extensive changes in the system which resulted in FORTRAN II (see below).

The Primer had an important influence on the subsequent growth in the use of the system. I believe it was the only available simplified instruction manual (other than reference manuals) until the later appearance of books such as McCracken (1961), Organick (1963), and many others.

A report on FORTRAN usage in November 1958 (Backus, 1958) says that "a survey in April [1958] of twenty-six 704 installations indicates that over half of them use FORTRAN [I] for more than half of their problems. Many use it for 80% or more of their work . . . and almost all use it for some of their work." By the fall of 1958 there were some 60 installations with about 66 704s, and ". . . more than half the machine instructions for these machines are being produced by FORTRAN. SHARE recently designated FORTRAN as the second official medium for transmittal of programs [SAP was the first] . . ."

4. FORTRAN II

During the field debugging period some shortcomings of the system design, which we had been aware of earlier but had no time to deal with, were constantly coming to our attention. In the early fall of 1957 we started to plan ways of correcting these shortcomings; a document dated September 25, 1957 (Proposed Specifications, 1957) characterizes them as (a) a need for better diagnostics, clearer comments about the nature of source program errors, and (b) the need for subroutine definition capabilities. (Although one FORTRAN I diagnostic would pinpoint, in a printout, a missing comma in a particular statement, others could be very cryptic.) This document is titled "Proposed Specifications for FORTRAN II for the 704"; it sketches a more general diagnostic system and describes the new "subroutine definition" and END statements, plus some others which were not implemented. It describes how symbolic information is retained in the relocatable binary form of a subroutine so that the "binary symbolic subroutine [BSS] loader" can implement references to separately compiled subroutines. It describes new prologues for these subroutines and points out that mixtures of FORTRAN-coded and assembly-coded relocatable binary programs could be loaded and run together. It does not discuss the FUNC-TION statement that was also available in FORTRAN II. FORTRAN II was designed mostly by Nelson, Ziller, and myself. Mitchell programmed the majority of new code for FORTRAN II (with the most unusual feature that she delivered it ahead of schedule). She was aided in this by Bernyce Brady and LeRoy May. Sheridan planned and made the necessary changes in his part of section 1; Nutt did the same for section 6. FORTRAN II was distributed in the spring of 1958.

5. FORTRAN III

While FORTRAN II was being developed, Ziller was designing an even more advanced system that he called FORTRAN III. It allowed one to write intermixed symbolic instructions and FORTRAN statements. The symbolic (704) instructions could have FORTRAN variables (with or without subscripts) as "addresses". In addition to this machine dependent feature (which assured the demise of FORTRAN III along with that of the 704), it contained early versions of a number of improvements that were later to appear in FOR-TRAN IV. It had "Boolean" expressions, function and subroutine names could be passed as arguments, and it had facilities for handling alphanumeric data, including a new FOR-MAT code "A" similar to codes "I" and "E". This system was planned and programmed by Ziller with some help from Nelson and Nutt. Ziller maintained it and made it available to about 20 (mostly IBM) installations. It was never distributed generally. It was accompanied by a brief descriptive document (Additions to FORTRAN II, 1958). It became available on this limited scale in the winter of 1958–1959 and was in operation until the early 1960s, in part on the 709 using the compatibility feature (which made the 709 order code the same as that of the 704).

6. FORTRAN after 1958; Comments

By the end of 1958 or early 1959 the FORTRAN group (the Programming Research Department), while still helping with an occasional debugging problem with FORTRAN II, was primarily occupied with other research. Another IBM department had long since taken responsibility for the FORTRAN system and was revising it in the course of producing a translator for the 709 which used the same procedures as the 704 FORTRAN II translator. Since my friends and I no longer had responsibility for FORTRAN and were busy thinking about other things by the end of 1958, that seems like a good point to break off this account. There remain only a few comments to be made about the subsequent development of FORTRAN.

The most obvious defect in FORTRAN II for many of its users was the time spent in compiling. Even though the facilities of FORTRAN II permitted separate compilation of subroutines and hence eliminated the need to recompile an entire program at each step in debugging it, nevertheless compile times were long and, during debugging, the considerable time spent in optimizing was wasted. I repeatedly suggested to those who were in charge of FORTRAN that they should now develop a fast compiler and/or interpreter without any optimizing at all for use during debugging and for short-run jobs. Unfortunately the developers of FORTRAN IV thought they could have the best of both worlds in a single compiler, one which was both fast and produced optimized code. I was unsuccessful in convincing them that two compilers would have been far better than the compromise which became the original FORTRAN IV compiler. The latter was not nearly as fast as later compilers like WATFOR (Cress *et al.*, 1970) nor did it produce as good code as FORTRAN II. (For more discussion of later developments with FORTRAN, see Backus and Heising, 1964.)

My own opinion as to the effect of FORTRAN on later languages and the collective impact of such languages on programming generally is not a popular opinion. That viewpoint is the subject of a long paper (Backus, 1978). I now regard all conventional languages (e.g., the FORTRANs, the ALGOLs, their successors and derivatives) as increasingly complex elaborations of the style of programming dictated by the von Neumann computer. These "von Neumann languages" create enormous, unnecessary intellectual roadblocks in thinking about programs and in creating the higher level combining forms required in a really powerful programming methodology. Von Neumann languages constantly keep our noses pressed in the dirt of address computation and the separate computation of single words, whereas we should be focusing on the form and content of the overall result we are trying to produce. We have come to regard the DO, FOR, WHILE statements and the like as powerful tools, whereas they are in fact weak palliatives that are necessary to make the primitive von Neuman style of programming viable at all.

By splitting programming into a world of expressions on the one hand and a world of statements on the other, von Neumann languages prevent the effective use of higher level combining forms; the lack of the latter makes the definitional capabilities of von Neumann languages so weak that most of their important features cannot be defined—starting with a small, elegant framework—but must be built into the framework of the language at the outset. The gargantuan size of recent von Neumann languages is eloquent proof of their inability to define new constructs: for no one would build in so many complex features if they could be defined and would fit into the existing framework later on.

The world of expressions has some elegant and useful mathematical properties whereas the world of statements is a disorderly one, without useful mathematical properties. Structured programming can be viewed as a modest effort to introduce a small amount of order into the chaotic world of statements. The work of Hoare (1969), Dijkstra (1976), and others to axiomatize the properties of the statement world can be viewed as a valiant and effective effort to be precise about those properties, ungainly as they may be.

This is not the place for me to elaborate any further my views about von Neumann languages. My point is this: while it was perhaps natural and inevitable that languages like FORTRAN and its successors should have developed out of the concept of the von Neumann computer as they did, the fact that such languages have dominated our thinking for twenty years is unfortunate. It is unfortunate because their long-standing familiarity will make it hard for us to understand and adopt new programming styles which one day will offer far greater intellectual and computational power.

ACKNOWLEDGMENTS

My greatest debt in connection with this paper is to my old friends and colleagues whose creativity, hard work, and invention made FORTRAN possible. It is a pleasure to acknowledge my gratitude to them for their contributions to the project, for making our work together so long ago such a congenial and memorable experience, and, more recently, for providing me with a great amount of information and helpful material in preparing this paper and for their careful reviews of an earlier draft. For all this I thank all those who were associated with the FORTRAN project but who are too numerous to list here. In pariular I want to thank those who were the principal movers in making FORTRAN a reality: Sheldon Best, Richard Goldberg, Lois Haibt, Harlan Herrick, Grace Mitchell, Robert Nelson, Roy Nutt, David Sayre, Peter Sheridan, and Irving Ziller.

I also wish to thank Bernard Galler, JAN Lee, and Henry Tropp for their amiable, extensive and invaluable suggestions for improving the first draft of this paper. I am grateful, too, for all the work of the program committee in preparing helpful questions that suggested a number of topics in the paper.

REFERENCES

Most of the items listed below have dates in the 1950s; thus many that appeared in the open literature will be obtainable only in the largest and oldest collections. The items with an asterisk were either not published or were of such a nature as to make their availability even less likely than that of the other items.

Adams, Charles W., and Laning, J. H., Jr. (1954) May. The MIT systems of automatic coding: Comprehensive, Summer Session, and Algebraic. In *Proc. Symp. on Automatic Programming for Digital Computers*. Washington, D.C.: The Office of Naval Research.

Addenda to the FORTRAN Programmer's Reference Manual (1957) February 8. Transmitted to Dr. John Greenstadt, Special Programs Group, Applied Science Division, IBM, for distribution to SHARE members, by letter from John W. Backus, Programming Research Dept. IBM. 5 pp.

*Additions to FORTRAN II (1958). *Description of Source Language Additions to the FORTRAN II System.* New York: Programming Research, IBM Corp. (Distributed to users of FORTRAN III. 12 pp.)

*Ash, R., Broadwin, E., Della Valle, V., Katz, C., Greene, M., Jenny, A., and Yu, L. (1957). *Preliminary Manual for MATH-MATIC and ARITH-MATIC Systems (for Algebraic Translation and Compilation for UNIVAC I and II)*. Philadelphia, Pennsylvania: Remington Rand Univac.

Backus, J. W. (1954a). The IBM 701 Speedcoding system. *JACM* 1(1): 4–6.

*Backus, John (1954b). Letter to J. H. Laning, Jr.

Backus, J. W. (1958) November. Automatic programming: properties and performance of FORTRAN systems I and II. In *Proc. Symp. on the Mechanisation of Thought Processes*. Teddington, Middlesex, England: The National Physical Laboratory.

Backus, John (1978) August. Can programming be liberated from the von Neumann style? A functional style and its algebra of programs. *CACM* 21(8): 613–641.

Backus, John (1980). Programming in America in the nineteen fifties—some personal impressions. In *A History of Computing in the Twentieth Century (Proc. Internat. Conf. on the History of Computing, June 10– 15, 1976)* (N. Metropolis et al., eds.), pp. 125–135. Academic Press, New York.

Backus, J. W., and Heising, W. P. (1964) August. FORTRAN. *IEEE Transactions on Electronic Computers* EC-13(4): 382–385.

Backus, John W., and Herrick, Harlan (1954) May. IBM 701 Speedcoding and other automatic programming systems. In *Proc. Symp. on Automatic Programming for Digital Computers*. Washington, D.C.: The Office of Naval Research.

Backus, J. W., Beeber, R. J., Best, S., Goldberg, R., Haibt, L. M., Herrick, H. L., Nelson, R. A., Sayre, D., Sheridan, P. B., Stern, H., Ziller, I., Hughes, R. A., and Nutt, R. (1957) February. The FORTRAN automatic coding system. In *Proc. Western Joint Computer Conf., Los Angeles*.

Baker, Charles L. (1956) October. The PACT I coding system, for the IBM Type 701. *JACM* 3(4): 272–278.

Belady, L. A. (1965) June 15. *Measurements on Programs: One Level Store Simulation*. Yorktown Heights, New York: IBM Thomas J. Watson Research Center. Report RC 1420.

Böhm, Corrado (1954). Calculatrices digitales: Du déchiffrage de formules logico-mathématiques par la machine même dans la conception du programme. *Annali di Mathematica Pura ed Applicata* 37(4): 175–217.

Bouricius, Willard G. (1953) December. Operating experience with the Los Alamos 701. In *Proc. Eastern Joint Computer Conf., Washington, D.C.*, pp. 45–47.

Bright, Herbert S. (1971) November. FORTRAN comes to Westinghouse-Bettis, 1957. *Computers and Automation* 20(11): 17–18.

Brown, J. H., and Carr, John W., III (1954) May. Automatic programming and its development on MIDAC. In *Proc. Symp. on Automatic Programming for Digital Computers*. Washington, D.C.: The Office of Naval Research.

Cocke, John, and Schwartz, J. T. (1970) April. *Programming Languages and their Compilers* (Preliminary Notes, Second Revised Version, April 1970). New York: New York University, The Courant Institute of Mathematical Sciences.

Cress, Paul, Dirksen, Paul, and Graham, J. Wesley (1970). *FORTRAN IV with WATFOR and WATFIV.* Englewood Cliffs, New Jersey: Prentice-Hall.

Dijkstra, Edsger W. (1976). *A Discipline of Programming.* Englewood Cliffs, New Jersey: Prentice-Hall.

Grems, Mandalay, and Porter, R. E. (1956). A truly automatic programming system. In *Proc. Western Joint Computer Conf., San Francisco,* pp. 10–21.

Hoare, C. A. R. (1969) October. An axiomatic basis for computer programming. *CACM* 12(10): 576–580, 583.

*IBM (1956) October 15. *Programmer's Reference Manual, The FORTRAN Automatic Coding System for the IBM 704 EDPM.* New York: IBM Corp. [Applied Science Division and Programming Research Dept., Working Committee: J. W. Backus, R. J. Beeber, S. Best, R. Goldberg, H. L. Herrick, R. A. Hughes (Univ. of Calif. Radiation Lab., Livermore, Calif.), L. B. Mitchell, R. A. Nelson, R. Nutt (United Aircraft Corp., East Hartford, Conn.), D. Sayre, P. B. Sheridan, H. Stern, and I. Ziller.]

*IBM (1957). *Programmer's Primer for FORTRAN Automatic Coding System for the IBM 704.* New York: IBM Corp. Form No. 32-0306.

Knuth, Donald E., and Trabb Pardo, Luis (1977). Early development of programming languages. In *Encyclopedia of Computer Science and Technology.* Vol. 7, pp. 419–493. New York: Dekker.

*Laning, J. H., and Zierler, N. (1954) January. *A Program for Translation of Mathematical Equations for Whirlwind I.* Cambridge, Massachusetts: MIT Instrumentation Lab. Engineering Memorandum E-364.

McCracken, Daniel D. (1961). *A Guide to FORTRAN Programming.* New York: Wiley.

Moser, Nora B. (1954) May. Compiler method of automatic programming. In *Proc. Symp. on Automatic Programming for Digital Computers.* Washington, D.C.: The Office of Naval Research.

Muller, David E. (1954) May. Interpretive routines in the ILLIAC library. In *Proc. Symp. on Automatic Programming for Digital Computers.* Washington, D.C.: The Office of Naval Research.

*Operator's Manual (1957) April 8. *Preliminary Operator's Manual for the FORTRAN Automatic Coding System for the IBM 704 EDPM.* New York: IBM Corp. Programming Research Dept.

Organick, Elliot I. (1963). *A FORTRAN Primer.* Reading, Massachusetts: Addison-Wesley.

*Perlis, A. J., Smith, J. W., and Van Zoeren, H. R. (1957) March. *Internal Translator (IT): A Compiler for the 650.* Pittsburgh, Pennsylvania: Carnegie Institute of Tech.

*Preliminary Report (1954) November 10. *Specifications for the IBM Mathematical FORmula TRANslating System, FORTRAN.* New York: IBM Corp. (Report by Programming Research Group, Applied Science Division, IBM. Distributed to prospective 704 customers and other interested parties. 29 pp.)

*Proposed Specifications (1957) September 25. *Proposed Specifications for FORTRAN II for the 704.* (Unpublished memorandum, Programming Research Dept. IBM.)

*Remington-Rand, Inc. (1953) November 15. *The A-2 Compiler System Operations Manual.* Prepared by Richard K. Ridgway and Margaret H. Harper under the direction of Grace M. Hopper.

Rutishauser, Heinz (1952). Automatische Rechenplanfertigung bei programmgesteuerten Rechenmaschinen. In *Mitteilungen aus dem Inst. für angew. Math. an der E. T. H. Zürich.* No. 3. Basel: Birkhäuser.

Sammet, Jean E. (1969). *Programming Languages: History and Fundamentals.* Englewood Cliffs, New Jersey: Prentice-Hall.

*Schlesinger, S. I. (1953) July. *Dual Coding System.* Los Alamos, New Mexico: Los Alamos Scientific Lab. Los Alamos Report LA 1573.

Sheridan, Peter B. (1959) February. The arithmetic translator-compiler of the IBM FORTRAN automatic coding system. *CACM* 2(2): 9–21.

Zuse, K. (1959). Über den Plankalkül. *Elektron. Rechenanl.* 1: 68–71.

Zuse, K. (1972). Der Plankalkül. *Berichte der Gesellschaft für Mathematik und Datenverarbeitung.* 63, part 3. (Manuscript prepared in 1945.)

TRANSCRIPT OF PRESENTATION

JAN LEE: Our second session this morning, and the first session dealing explicitly with a language, is to be the paper by John Backus on the History of FORTRAN I, II, and III.

I had an interesting occurrence just before I left my office this week. I had a letter from Taiwan, believe it or not, saying, "In 1959 you wrote a program, and I have a customer

John Backus

who's very interested in this topic. Could you send me the source listing, etc., etc., of this?'' And believe it or not, I still do have the source listing. It turned out to be a language which, as Grace would have said earlier on, died, and I was looking back and saying, "Gee, 1959—why wasn't I programming in FORTRAN at that time? What was I doing?" And I realized of course that I was one of those people who were steadfastly resisting this movement into the algebraic field, and I guess I really didn't understand that you could do things with letters and alphabets and so on and so forth. So, amongst many many others, I was behind the times. And it keeps coming back to haunt me, which worries me.

This first speaker this morning is the man who was trying to educate the rest of us and say, "This is the way to go." John mentioned to me, when we were discussing how I should introduce him, that there was only one real thing to say—and I'll say that at the end, as we did with Grace. But I wanted to try and introduce him in two ways: one was —how would we have introduced him in 1955, if this were 23 years ago—what would we have said? At that point I guess we would say: Well, here's an IBM-er; he's a programmer, a very lazy programmer who feels that he wants to make everything much easier for everybody else; holds a Master's Degree in Mathematics from Columbia, and has currently moved from the Pure Science Division of IBM to the Applied Science Division of IBM, which as an engineer I feel means he saw the light about that time.

Since that time things have progressed 23 years, and so I say, "Okay, now where are we? How would I introduce him in 1978?" Well, he's an IBM Fellow, interested in programming languages, and is still a lazy programmer—John Backus.

JOHN BACKUS: Well, Grace Hopper is a hard act to follow, but that's my fate. Since I'm sure everyone has studied my paper very carefully already, I can skip parts of it, and that's fortunate because, of course, it would be impossible to cover everything in it.

I'd like to begin by getting some idea of the make-up of this audience. And to do that I'd like everyone who was involved in programming before 1960 to raise their hand. 1960 —Wow! Okay, let's try 1956. My gosh! 1954. Getting smaller. Okay—I'll stop there. Because that's the point where I'm going to begin—where Grace Hopper left off. I'd like to try to add something to what Grace Hopper has already said about what things were like in 1954, and the attitudes that prevailed then.

It's really difficult for a programmer today, who wasn't involved then, to realize how ignorant we were then, and how primitive the ideas and tools were that we felt were really advanced and sophisticated stuff. In late 1953 computers were pretty crazy things. They had very primitive instructions and extremely bizarre input–output facilities. Some were better than others. I think Grace had the benefit of rather good input–output facilities, but the rest of us didn't.

So, overcoming the difficulties of these computers and cramming programs and data into little tiny stores made programming really a black art. So each programmer had his own inscrutable tricks for making programs as fast and as complicated as possible. Some so-called automatic programming systems in 1953, would you believe, did the wonderful thing of providing decimal input or decimal input and output, and some did other wonderful things like providing symbolic addresses.

The most popular automatic programming systems, as Grace Hopper said, were interpretive systems. These just converted the peculiar host machine into a different synthetic machine which had floating point and improved I/O facilities and sometimes indexing. Could I have the first slide [Frame 1], please?

Name	Computer	Place developed
DUAL	IBM 701	Los Alamos
SHACO	IBM 701	Los Alamos
Summer Session	WHIRLWIND	M.I.T.
† David Wheeler's	ILLIAC	Univ. of Illinois
†SPEEDCODING	IBM 701	IBM New York

Frame 1. 1953 interpretive systems. These systems were all operating in 1953. Each provided a synthetic computer with floating point, indexing† and improved I/O.

Here are some 1953 interpretive systems that were running that I know of. Probably nothing is complete but I've done the best I can. So each one made its machine look like a different machine. It had an order code—you know, a machinelike order code, but it now could do floating point arithmetic, and things like that. So it made programming easier, but you were still really programming for a machine. So, in addition to these interpretive systems, as far as I know there were three compilers operating in 1953—there they are [in Frame 2]. I gather from what was said earlier, that the date for A-2 was earlier than that on the slide, but these dates are taken from an article by Knuth and Trabb and that was the date they gave, so I'm not responsible for that. We'll take a look at some sample programs for these systems in a minute. But let me just say that first of all, note that the AUTO-CODE system was a fixed point system. It didn't provide floating point, and it was really quite machine-dependent, as we'll point out a little more when we look at a program for it.

The A-2 language was not algebraic, but it did provide floating point operations. Its input language was not what we would call sophisticated nowadays. And in fact, its input language was somewhat more complicated and difficult to use than the machinelike languages of the interpretive systems.

Sometime in late 1954 or early 1955 the A-2 system acquired a pseudo-code that resembled the input languages of the interpretive systems that were listed on the previous slide.

The Laning and Zierler system was—I believe now everyone recognizes it to be—the world's first algebraic compiler. It was operating in May 1953, and possibly earlier. Some communications I've had from what used to be called the "Instrumentation Laboratory" indicated that it was perhaps earlier than that. Its input language was simple but elegant, and it compiled algebraic expressions into programs that were then interpreted by a floating point interpretive system.

(a) Alec Glennie's AUTOCODE, Manchester Mark I.
Not algebraic, very machine dependent, fixed point.
Early use: Sept. 1952

(b) Grace Hopper's A-2, UNIVAC.
Not algebraic, machine dependent, floating point.
Early use: late 1953 (A-0 & A-1 earlier)

(c) Laning & Zierler's system, WHIRLWIND.
Algebraic, machine independent, interpreter
executes compiled floating point instructions.
Early use: May 1953.

Frame 2. Compilers operating in 1953 (and earlier).

```
c@VA t@IC x@½C y@RC z@NC
INTEGERS +5 → c
     →t
   +t     TESTA Z
   −t
          ENTRY Z
SUBROUTINE 6 → z
   +tt → y → x
   +tx → y → x
+z+cx CLOSE WRITE 1
a@/½  b@MA  c@GA  d@OA  c@PA  f@HA  .@VE  x@ME
INTEGERS +20 → b  +10 → c  +400 → d  +999 → e  +1 → f
LOOP 10n
   n → x
+b − x → x
   x → q
SUBROUTINE 5 → aq
REPEAT n
  +c → i
LOOP 10n
  +an SUBROUTINE 1 → y
  +d − y TESTA Z
  +i SUBROUTINE 3
  +e SUBROUTINE 4
      CONTROL X
      ENTRY Z
  +i SUBROUTINE 3
  +y SUBROUTINE 4
      ENTRY X
  +i − f → i
REPEAT n
ENTRY A CONTROL A WRITE 2 START 2
```

Frame 3. An AUTOCODE program.

Now we can see some of the programs for these things. [Frame 3 shows an AUTOCODE program.] I'm sure you can't read that very well. It looks somewhat symbolic, but it really is more machine-dependent than it looks. Like "Test A" really refers to a particular machine register. "Close Right 1" means that that is the end of a subroutine, called "Subroutine 1," which is referred to later. I can't really explain these programs at all. I just wanted you to get a feel for what they looked like. This program is for a nonsense algorithm that Knuth and Trabb programmed for lots of early languages, to compare them, called the TPK Algorithm.

And here [in Frame 4] you can see the A-2 program that they coded for that same TPK Algorithm. The horizontal lines separate unit operations, and some of them you can see —the ones beginning "GM" are "generators" that Dr. Hopper mentioned; the single line operations are floating point instructions; and you see a couple of entries starting with OWNCO, and that is Machine Code that was necessary to use; the point I am trying to illustrate is that A-2 does not have a uniform input language. There's quite a variation in the formats of the unit operations; some take one line, some take 2, some take three, and some take four.

Now we can move on to [Frame 5] the TPK Algorithm for Laning and Zierler's system,

GMI000	000002	AA0040	038038	YT0036	038000	4RG000	000007
ITEM01	WS.000	AS0004	038040	GMM000	000001	5RG000	000006
SERV02	BLOCKA	OWNΔCO	DEΔ003	000194	200220	6RG000	000007
1RG000	000000	K00000	K00000	1RG000	011000	1CN000	000002
GMM000	000001	F00912	E001RG	GMM000	000001	2CN000	000014
000180	020216	000000	Q001CN	000222	200196	1RS000	000036
1RG000	001000	1RG000	008040	1RG000	012000	2RS000	000037
AM0034	034040	1CN000	000010	ALL012	F000Ti	OWNΔCO	DEΔ002
RNA040	010040	GMM000	000001	1RG000	013036	810000	820000
APN034	012038	000188	020238	2RG000	000037	900000	900000
AM0002	038038	1RG000	009000	3RG000	000006	1RG000	014000
						ЯØENDΔ	INFØ.Я

Frame 4. A-2 "TPK" ALGORITHM. [From Donald E. Knuth and Luis Trabb Pardo, The early development of programming languages. In *Encyclopedia of Computer Science and Technology*, Vol. 7, pp. 419–493. New York: Dekker, 1977.]

and we see that their language is algebraic. It has single subscripts which are denoted by the vertical bar, so that $v|j$ in the fourth line is V_j. Subroutines are indicated by the capital "F" with superscripts, and the superscripts are the "catalog number" of the subroutine, so you couldn't name subroutines except in that way. And it lacked a looping statement, a FOR statement, or what-have-you. But this language certainly is elegant by comparison with the earlier ones, and when you realize that it was running very early in 1953, if not earlier, you can get some idea of the accomplishment that it represented. And yet of course, as Grace Hopper said, the Establishment completely ignored this system for some peculiar reason.

In addition to the compilers that were actually operating in 1953, Heinz Rutishauser in Switzerland and Corrado Böhm in Italy had both published descriptions in 1952 of simple algebraic languages and their compilers. They really published the details of their compilers. And in fact, Böhm's compiler was actually written in its own language; the first example of such a thing.

And even earlier, Konrad Zuse in Germany had described in 1945 what was perhaps the most sophisticated programming language that was to emerge up to the mid 1960s. It was really a dilly. A very powerful language with data types and all kinds of things. He wrote many chess programs in that language at that early time.

For a discussion of these systems that I've shown, and other early systems—there are

$$
\begin{aligned}
& v|N = \langle \text{input} \rangle, && \text{CP 3,} \\
& i = 0, && z = 999, \\
1\ & j = i+1, && \text{PRINT } i,z. \\
& a|i = v|j, && \text{SP 4,} \\
& i = j, && 3\ \text{PRINT } i,y. \\
& e = i-10.5, && 4\ i = i-1 \\
& \text{CP 1,} && e = -0.5-i, \\
& i = 10, && \text{CP 2,} \\
2\ & y = F^1(F^{11}(a|i))+5(a|i)^3, && \text{STOP} \\
& e = y-400,
\end{aligned}
$$

Frame 5. Laning and Zierler "TPK" algorithm. [From Donald E. Knuth and Luis Trabb Pardo, The early development of programming languages. In *Encyclopedia of Computer Science and Technology*, Vol. 7, pp. 419–493. New York: Dekker, 1977.]

others—I recommend the article I mentioned by Knuth and Trabb in the *Encyclopedia of Computer Science and Technology.*

So I hope I've added a little something to what Grace Hopper said about the primitive state of affairs at the beginning of 1954. That was the point at which the story of FORTRAN begins.

About December 1953 I wrote a letter to my boss, Cuthbert Hurd, proposing that IBM should develop a practical automatic programming system for what was then the recently announced 704. He agreed, even without an argument. I don't know why Grace Hopper had so much trouble with her management! [Laughter] But we didn't have any at all. They kept backing us up for years and years without anything to show for it. But anyway, our plan was to produce a system that would output efficient object code. We felt that this was essential if the system was to be widely used for the big problems of the aerospace industry and that, of course, was the principal customer for the 704 at that time.

Most of the early systems we've seen, and many others, had hidden a lot of gross inefficiencies by virtue of the fact that most computing time was being spent in floating point subroutines. Because of that you could get away with a lot of clumsy treatment of looping and indexing, and references to arrays that escaped unnoticed because of all the time that was chewed up by floating point subroutines. But now we were confronted with the 704 which, for the first time, had built-in floating point and indexing, and we knew that this would make our goal of producing efficient object code very difficult because there was just nowhere to hide inefficiencies. You couldn't do clumsy calculations of subscript combinations and get away with it in that machine.

So by 1954, the FORTRAN group had become actually a group. It consisted of Irving Ziller—this is how he looks 24 years after the fact [Frame 6]; Harlan Herrick [Frame 7], and Bob Nelson [Frame 8]. Bob was actually hired to do technical typing for our group,

Frame 6. Irving Ziller.

Frame 7. Harlan Herrick.

but he and Irv Ziller were soon involved in planning and programming one of the most complex sections of the compiler. Nelson was later made an IBM Fellow, in fact, for his work on Virtual Memory, that we've heard mention of before! It's a rather broad term! And I was the fourth member of the group—so you can see me as I am. And I was its so-called "Manager." [See photo on p. 74.]

The early thinking of our group about the system that was to become FORTRAN is indicated by a paper that Herrick and I gave at the ONR symposium in May of 1954 which

Frame 8. Bob Nelson.

"[The programmer] would like to write $\Sigma a_{ij} \cdot b_{jk}$ instead
of the . . . instructions [for] this expression."
". . . a programmer might not be considered too unreasonable
if he were willing only to produce the formulas for the
numerical solution of his problem and perhaps a plan
showing how the data was to be moved from one storage
hierarchy to another and then demand that the machine
produce the results . . ."

Frame 9. From a May, 1954 article by Backus and Herrick. [From John W. Backus and Harlan Herrick, IBM 701 speedcoding and other automatic coding systems. In *Proc. Symp. on Automatic Programming for Digital Computers.* Washington D.C.: ONR, May 13–14, 1954.]

was organized by Grace Hopper. Her name seems to keep popping up in all these things. Here are some excerpts from that paper [Frame 9]. This shows that our plans for algebraic input were, in May of 1954, a bit more sophisticated than the Laning and Zierler language in that we had double subscripts and things like that. In fact I'd say that the goal suggested in the second paragraph about handling storage has yet to be satisfactorily achieved.

That brings up the questions of the influence of Laning's work on the FORTRAN language. A few years after FORTRAN was finished I was asked where we got the idea for algebraic input. Since I have a very poor memory, I recalled erroneously that we had begun work later than we actually had and that we had gotten the idea of algebraic input from seeing Laning and Zierler's system, and I went on believing this story for many years. But recently Dr. Laning was good enough to send me a copy of the letter I sent him in 1954 asking to see his system, and this letter—plus some recent discussions with Irv Ziller—made clear what really happened. The letter, in fact, makes clear that we first heard of Laning's work at the same ONR symposium at which those remarks appeared that I just showed you, and so we had already been thinking about algebraic input, and a fair number of other things. And so we can only conclude that we somehow had the idea for algebraic input independently of them, even though Laning and Zierler already had done their pioneering work and had their compiler running. As was common in those days news didn't get around very well.

So, before taking up the chronological account of the development of FORTRAN, I'd like to emphasize one other prevailing attitude in the period of 1954–1957, when we were working; and this was the firm belief that almost all programmers held—I guess JAN Lee was one of them—that no automatic programming system could produce code that was even comparable in efficiency to hand-coded programs. This belief came from their experience in coding for small, badly designed computers—that was truly a difficult task—and their experience with clumsy and slow automatic programming systems, of which there are quite a few. I was the author of one of them.

By the spring and summer of 1954, the design of the FORTRAN language was well underway. Most of the language was designed by Herrick, Ziller, and myself, but most of the input–output language was designed, mostly later on, by Roy Nutt, and we'll see a picture of him later on. Roy is one of the grand programmers of the profession. There's a myth—I don't know whether it's really true about him or not—that he sits down at the keypunch and programs. You'll have to ask him though whether that's true or not, . . . but he wrote an awful lot of programs for us.

There's very little I can say about how the language was designed. It never seemed like much of a problem to us, for some reason. Very early in our fooling around we had the

"Since FORTRAN should virtually eliminate coding and
debugging[!] . . ."
". . . an automatically coded problem . . . will be executed
in about the same time that would be required had [it]
been laboriously hand coded."
"Furthermore, after an hour course in FORTRAN notation,
the average programmer can fully understand . . . a procedure stated in FORTRAN language . . ."
". . . since each such [IBM] calculator should have a
system similar to FORTRAN . . ."

Frame 10. Excerpts from FORTRAN *Preliminary Report,* Nov. 1954.

notion of using algebraic expressions. It didn't seem to be very original. Subscripted variables didn't seem to be very original. And assignment statements. Shortly after that, Herrick, I believe it was, proposed the DO statement or "formula" as we used to call statements in those days. And the other features of the language just arose from the need to
make some machine function available. Many statements were machine-dependent
—things like IF DIVIDE CHECK or READ DRUM were popular items. And other statements arose from just writing test programs and finding we didn't have enough statements
to write the programs, so we'd make up one and add it to the language.

So we always regarded the real problem to be that of consistently producing object programs about as efficient as hand coded ones, because we figured that if we didn't do that,
no one would use the system.

By November of 1954 our group had produced a paper that really completely described
the FORTRAN language and, we'll see a few excerpts from that report [Frame 10]. As you
can see from the first quote, we were not exactly a group of pessimists, and the third quote
may have been more of a comment about the quality of programmers then than about the
ease of learning FORTRAN. And here [Frame 11] is part of the description of expressions
in that paper, just so you'll get some idea of style. I omitted the two longer ones, of course.
And here [Frame 12] are some of the many proposed additions to the system that are suggested at the end of the paper. There were quite a few of them. The description of the
proposed function definition facility is badly written, but it really does describe basically
what later appeared in FORTRAN II in 1958.

The last [item on Frame 12] is "summation." We had planned to put in a summation
operator that would take the index of summation, and the bounds, and the expression to
be summed.

So the language described in that 1954 preliminary report was very close to the actual
language that came out as FORTRAN. It had several features that were later dropped or
changed. For example, the DO formula, as it was called, could specify a distant sequence
of formulas to be iterated on. It didn't have to follow the DO statement. It could also spec-

    (i) Any constant or variable is an expression.
   (ii) If E is an expression not of the form $+F$ or $-F$, then
         $+E$ and $-E$ are expressions.
  (iv) If E is an expression, so is (E).
  (vi) If E and F are expressions, so is E $\times \times$ F. [sic]

Frame 11. Four lines (of six) from the "Formal description" of "expressions" from the *Preliminary Report,*
Nov. 1954.

John Backus

Begin Complex Arithmetic
Sort the vectors on tape N . . .
General Function: . . . the programmer [could] specify
the formula numbers of the formulas describing his
function and the arguments to be used in a given
instance. The value [would be obtained] having substituted the specified arguments for the original
arguments . . .
Summation

Frame 12. Excerpts from "Future additions to the FORTRAN system" from the *Preliminary Report,* Nov. 1954.

ify the statement that was to follow the last iteration separately. Expressions could be mixed mode, floating and fixed. And that got changed, I think, just because we didn't like the rules as to what happened with mixed mode expressions, so we decided, "Let's throw it out. It's easier." And it did leave in the principal uses of mixed modes—like even in FORTRAN I you could have an integer exponent and integer function arguments in a floating point expression. In IF formulas in this—Knuth calls it FORTRAN 0—you could use an inequality sign between two expressions and then give two formula numbers; one for the true case of the inequality, and one for the false case.

Then there was a RELABEL formula that's very hard to describe; it caused the subscripts of a particular array that you mention to be reinterpreted in a rotated fashion, and the purpose of that was to simplify calculations on arrays that were too large to fit in the store, so that the same stated calculation would work and you could read in the new row, wherever the current new row was supposed to go, and then rotate one place, and the whole calculation would still work. But it was too hard to describe, and much too hard to implement, so that got dropped.

FORMAT statements were lacking then, but they appeared as the first item in the section on future additions to the FORTRAN system, part of which I showed you. And apparently already at this time, we had been talking to Roy and that was probably his suggestion.

It's perhaps interesting to note that executable statements in FORTRAN 0 were called "formulas" but declarations such as EQUIVALENCE and DIMENSION statements were called "specification sentences."

The final section of this paper discusses FORTRAN programming techniques needed to produce optimum object programs. It discusses how the system identifies identical subexpressions and points out that DO loops would be treated optimally, whereas loops formed by IF's and GOTO's would not be.

In late 1954 and early 1955 Herrick, Ziller, and I gave five or six talks in various places about our plans for FORTRAN to groups of IBM customers who had ordered 704s. We described the language and our plans for producing optimized object programs. We estimated then that the compiler would be done in about six months, and this six-month interval was to remain the estimated time to completion for the next two years. And of course most of our listeners were extremely skeptical about all of our claims. Other groups had described in rosy terms their own automatic programming systems, and these had turned out to have a lot of restrictions and oddities in real life that had not been mentioned in the early descriptions. And in particular, many of those systems had been dreadfully slow.

So our claims were even more outlandish than those of others, and thus the skepticism

Frame 13. Roy Nutt.

they aroused was not really unreasonable. Our claims that we would produce efficient object code were especially disbelieved.

But one of these talks to customers had a very fortunate and crucial result. After our talk at United Aircraft, Walter Ramshaw, who was the head of that shop, agreed that Roy Nutt [Frame 13] would become a regular member of our group and contribute his expertise on input–output and assembly programs. As many of you know, Roy wrote the SHARE assembly program called SAP, and a lot of other utility programs for SHARE. All the time he worked with us he remained an employee of United Aircraft, and he used to travel from Hartford to New York two or three times a week from early 1955 up until early 1957.

There is no way to know what influence the FORTRAN preliminary report had on other groups. But some other groups produced algebraic compilers which were running before we distributed FORTRAN in April of 1957. They were able to do this in part because they had more modest goals. Mainly, they were not attempting to optimize their object programs. But we did have the impression that the fairly wide distribution of our preliminary report, plus the general awareness of many programming groups that we were involved in a fairly big effort and were pretty serious about it—that this provided a stimulus to some other groups that they might not have had otherwise.

In any event, the IT compiler at Purdue—it was later carried on at Carnegie Tech—the MATH-MATIC Compiler at Sperry Rand, and the BACAIC Compiler at Boeing were done at various points after late 1954. It's hard to be precise about when each of these began running, just as it's hard to be precise about when FORTRAN began running. For example, FORTRAN ran in various stages, and then the complete system ran for some unknown time before we distributed it. The only really definite date is when we distributed it.

In any case, whatever the order in which these systems began running, it's certainly clear that those three systems were running before we distributed FORTRAN.

John Backus

The most important of these compilers was the IT compiler for the IBM 650 that was done by Alan Perlis and his colleagues. It was begun in the fall of 1955 and since, like the others, it was less ambitious than FORTRAN, it was running about a year later. After FORTRAN and IT were both in operation for a while, Alan Perlis used to give some talks that really annoyed me. The idea of these talks was that he couldn't understand why those clods working on FORTRAN had taken 25 man-years to produce a compiler, since one of his graduate students had written an IT compiler in a single summer. He apparently didn't understand the problems of optimization in those days. I was annoyed only because I thought he did!

In any case, whatever the influence the FORTRAN preliminary report and our project had on the other projects that I mentioned, if it had any, it is clear that they didn't influence our design because we had our plans quite firm in November of 1954, before they had begun.

Work on the FORTRAN compiler got underway in January or February of 1955, and my paper for the conference goes into some detail about its construction, over, I might say, the objections of our chairman who doesn't think that's a proper subject for this conference. And it references other papers with further details. But now I would just like to sketch very briefly what each of the six sections of the compiler did and show you its principal architects if we haven't seen them already.

The main point to understand about the way the thing was put together was that each section was a separate and autonomous project in itself of one or two people. Each section really was an individual enterprise; each had its proprietor or proprietors and was designed, planned, and programmed by a very small group. That planning often involved the invention of a number of new techniques by the proprietors, and many of those techniques, of course, played an important role in future compilers. The proprietors of each section would consult with the neighboring sections and by doing so on and off for a long time, they gradually converged on specifications for their input from the preceding section, and the output they would give to the next section.

Section 1 read the entire source program. In that sense, the compiler was one-pass. It compiled instructions for the arithmetic expressions, and filed all the other information in tables for use by later sections.

Peter Sheridan [Frame 14] did the compilation and optimization of expressions in Section 1. His output rearranged the computation so that the recomputation of common subexpressions and unnecessary fetches and stores were avoided. That work as we'll discuss later often changed the way expressions were evaluated in a radical and surprising fashion. Roy Nutt handled the I/O statements in Section 1—the main thing that he had to do was replace the I/O "lists of quantities" that were involved by nests of DO formulas, which were then treated by the rest of the compiler in a regular fashion. Herrick did the table formation work in Section 1.

Section 2 optimized the treatment of DO formulas and references to arrays. To do so, it had to analyze the structure of the entire source program. There is not enough time to discuss the powerful and complex analysis of cases that it used to produce code. It yielded virtually optimal use of indexing and looping. Section 2 is the largest and one of the two most complex sections of the compiler. It was planned and programmed by Bob Nelson and Irving Ziller.

The degree of optimization they achieved was really not equalled again in subsequent compilers until the mid-60s when the work of Fran Allen and John Cocke began to be used

Frame 14. Peter Sheridan.

in fairly sophisticated optimizing compilers. They really did an incredible job, even taking out single instructions that you wouldn't believe could have been taken out of a program.

Originally Ziller and Nelson had planned to produce code which used only the three index registers for the 704, but as things progressed it began to appear that that was going to be extremely difficult to do in an optimal way. So at that point, I proposed that they should produce code for a mythical 704 that had an unlimited number of index registers, and that we would somehow produce later sections that would convert that program into one for a three-index-register machine.

This suggestion resulted in two new sections of the compiler, but before they could begin we had to have a Section 3 which consolidated all the information from Sections 1 and 2, and was a fairly involved program. This was programmed by Dick Goldberg [Frame 15].

Section 4 was programmed by Lois Haibt [Frame 16]. It made a statistical analysis of the frequency of execution of the different parts of the source program by simulating the execution of the source program. It also collected information about the usage of the fictitious and unlimited index registers.

The proprietor of Section 5 was Sheldon Best [Frame 17] who was loaned to us by Charles Adams at MIT. (Sheldon was really the same age as the rest of us, but that is the only picture we have that was taken when we were actually working on the project.) Section 5 did the actual transformation of a program with an unlimited number of index registers into one using only three. The index register allocation procedure that Sheldon devised for Section 5 was at least as optimal as any procedure developed during the next 15 years, and it probably is in fact optimal. Nobody has shown that it isn't. On the other hand, nobody has proved that it is—although his straight-line allocation procedure has

Frame 15. Dick Goldberg.

Frame 16. Lois Haibt.

Frame 17. Sheldon Best.

been proved to be optimal, and at the time, he had a fairly convincing argument that it was. His work was the basis of a lot of later work on the register allocation problem.

Finally, Roy Nutt wrote Section 6. This assembled the final program into relocatable binary. It also produced the storage map of the program and data, and obtained the library routines that were needed, including routines that interpreted the FORMAT statements in the program. Roy also wrote the FORMAT interpreter and all of the I/O program. The assembler took advantage of the special nature of its input and was about ten times faster than the standard SHARE assembler—SAP.

By the summer of 1956, large parts of the compiler were working; an algebraic subsystem was in productive use at United Aircraft from the summer of 1956 until the full system was distributed. From the late spring of 1956 until early 1957 the pace of debugging of the system was really intense. We would rent rooms at the Langdon Hotel across the street from where the computer was in New York, and we'd sleep there a little bit during the day and then stay up all night to get as much time on the machine as possible. We usually had it all to ourselves then. It was a really exciting period because by late summer and early fall we were beginning to get fragments of compiled programs out of the system, and we were often astonished at the code it produced. It often transformed the source code so radically that we would think it had made an error, and we'd study the program carefully, and finally realize it was correct. Many of the changes in the computation were surprising, even to the authors of the section responsible for them. But the changes really were effective in giving efficient programs, and they would, for example, make a major rearrangement of the program just to save a single instruction. For example, control transfers would appear in the program that corresponded to no control statement in the original program. And a given DO statement would sometimes produce no instructions if you put it in one context, and if you took the same identical DO statement and put it in a different context, it would produce a whole lot of instructions in a lot of different places in the object program.

So—in the summer of 1956 David Sayre [Frame 18], a crystallographer, rejoined our

Frame 18. David Sayre.

group. He had briefly consulted with Sheldon Best about Section 5 earlier. He began writing the FORTRAN programmer's reference manual. This manual stood for some time as a unique example of a clear, concise, and accurate description of a programming language, and it may still stand as such. It appeared in a glossy cover and handsomely printed in October of 1956, and there's a shot of the cover [Frame 19]. Here is the Table of Contents [Frame 20], and here's a sample program that appeared on Page 1 of Chapter 1 [Frame 21], to show you the flavor of things. Here is a description of arithmetic formulas [Frame 22]. You can see that it had very wide margins with headings out in the margin. Here is the description of DO formulas [Frame 23: see Fig. 3 in Paper]. It followed this general pattern of having a description of the general form of a statement and then some examples, and then text giving the details. And finally, there is a longer program that appeared toward the end of the manual [Frame 24], an example, showing various features.

The entire Reference Manual was only 51 pages long. That's some kind of record, I think, and as you noticed, the pages even had wide margins.

I'm afraid I haven't really done justice in this brief talk to the work my friends did on the

Frame 19. Cover of first FORTRAN Manual. [Courtesy of International Business Machines Corporation.]

TABLE OF CONTENTS

Frame 20. From the first FORTRAN Manual. [Courtesy of International Business Machines Corporation.]

Example of a Fortran Program

The following brief program will serve to illustrate the general appearance and some of the properties of a FORTRAN program. It is shown as coded on a standard FORTRAN coding sheet.

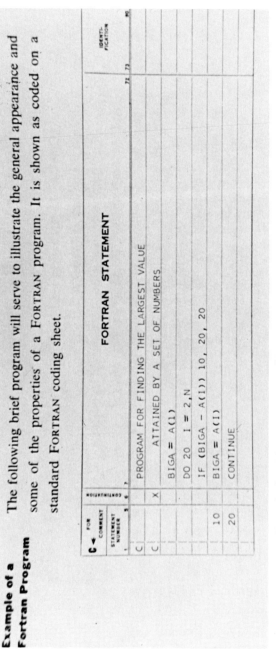

C ← COMMENT STATEMENT NUMBER	CONTINUATION	FORTRAN STATEMENT	IDENTIFICATION
C		PROGRAM FOR FINDING THE LARGEST VALUE	
C	X	ATTAINED BY A SET OF NUMBERS	
		BIGA = A(1)	
		DO 20 I = 2,N	
		IF (BIGA - A(I)) 10, 20, 20	
10		BIGA = A(I)	
20		CONTINUE	

Frame 21. From the first FORTRAN Manual. [Courtesy of International Business Machines Corporation.]

Optimisation of Arithmetic Expressions. The efficiency of the object program into which an arithmetic expression is translated may depend upon how the arithmetic expression is written. The section on Optimisation of Arithmetic Expressions in Chapter 7 mentions some of the considerations which affect object program efficiency.

GENERAL FORM	EXAMPLES
"a = b" where a is a variable (subscripted or not subscripted) and b is an expression.	A(I) = B(I) + SINF(C(I))

Frame 22. From the first FORTRAN Manual. [Courtesy of International Business Machines Corporation.]

John Backus

Given an N x N square matrix A, to find those off-diagonal elements which are symmetric and to write them on binary tape.

C ← FOR COMMENT / STATEMENT NUMBER	CONTINUATION	FORTRAN STATEMENT		72 73
		REWIND 3		
		DO 3 I = 1,N		
		DO 3 J = 1,N		
		IF(A(I,J)−A(J,I)) 3,20,3		
3		CONTINUE		
		END FILE 3		
		MORE PROGRAM		
20		IF(I−J) 21,3,21		
21		WRITE TAPE 3,I,J, A(I,J)		
		GO TO 3		

Frame 24. From the first FORTRAN Manual. [Courtesy of International Business Machines Corporation.]

project, but I hope that the paper does a better job of that. It's just that there's a lack of time to talk about what they did in sufficient detail.

About April of 1957, we felt the system was sufficiently free of bugs to distribute it. But before the system was finally distributed on magnetic tapes there was a vast confusion and a binary deck of the system was sent out to the Bettis installation at Westinghouse; this was just an unlabeled box of about 2000 binary cards with no instructions or data of any kind. It arrived there on a Friday afternoon, and Herb Bright and his colleagues at Westinghouse suspected that it just might be the FORTRAN system deck, so they proceeded to put blank tapes on every tape unit. They put cards in the card punch, and cleared the memory. They put this mystery deck in the card reader and pressed *start*. They observed some tapes moving, and after all the cards had been read, all the tapes rewound themselves and the machine stopped with the "ready" light on. They next put a small FORTRAN test program in the card reader and pressed "start" again. Again, some tapes were seen to move, plus others that hadn't moved the first time. And this time there was some action at the printer. It had printed a message saying that a comma was missing from a particular statement. The offending statement was corrected, and the source program placed in the card reader again, and "start" was pressed a third time.

After a few seconds of computing, the card punch produced a small deck of binary cards. Bright and his friends put the binary deck in the card reader and pressed the "start" button for the fourth time. Again, there were a few seconds of computing, and then the printer started up once more. This time it produced 28 pages of results. All the output from their test program was actually correct, with, of course, the exception of a few FORMAT errors. That took place on April 20, 1957, and it was probably the last time that Westinghouse Bettis was to have such a trouble-free run of FORTRAN for a long time.

Anyway, after the system was distributed, the proprietors of the six sections were kept very busy tracking down bugs. Hal Stern collected a stream of telegrams, letters, and phone calls from all over the country and distributed them to the appropriate people. He then collected the corrections and made up correction cards that he distributed back to all the installations.

In the meantime, Grace Mitchell had been working on a programmer's primer. It came out in the winter of 1957 and a slightly revised edition came out in March of 1958 [Frame 25]. By the fall of 1958, over half the instructions for some 66 704s were being produced by FORTRAN. SHARE, the 704 user's group, had made it their second official language (the first being SAP).

There is just enough time left, I hope to let me say a little about FORTRAN II. FORTRAN II was designed mostly by Nelson, Ziller, and myself. It provided some much needed subroutine definition facilities, and the ability to compile subroutines separately. It kept their symbolic names in the binary decks for each subroutine. These independent subroutine decks could be loaded by a linking loader that would put them together properly. It came out in the spring of 1958.

Frame 25. Cover of first FORTRAN Primer. [Courtesy of International Business Machines Corporation.]

George Ryckman

FORTRAN III was designed by Irv Ziller. It provided the ability to intermix FOR-TRAN statements and machine instructions with FORTRAN variables as addresses. It also introduced a number of features such as Boolean expressions and string handling facilities that later appeared in FORTRAN IV. In fact, most of the facilities of FORTRAN IV are to be found in FORTRAN III. It was mostly an internal IBM system and was first used in the winter of 1958–1959.

So, in closing, let me remark that there seems to be general agreement among the original FORTRAN group that it was one of the most enjoyable projects any of us ever worked on. We were graced by this wonderful independent status that Cuthbert Hurd and my subsequent bosses conferred on us, so that we were completely on our own. We knew we were going to provide a valuable tool, even if few others did, and we worked quite hard. But perhaps the best part was the uncertainty and excitement of waiting to see what kinds of object code all that work was finally going to produce. I only wish that programming today could be half as exciting and enjoyable as the FORTRAN project was.

Thank you.

TRANSCRIPT OF DISCUSSANT'S REMARKS

JAN LEE: Thank you, John. We invited John to prepare a paper on FORTRAN, and then we searched around to find somebody who might have some other thoughts, and I use that word "other" very carefully. We were somewhat concerned it might be "opposite" thoughts, "corroborating" thoughts, or any other. And we looked hard and long. You may notice that John said that one of the motivations for FORTRAN in those early days was this growing space industry. And so we looked to a down-to-earth space industry, and came up with General Motors, as a source of a Discussant. And then went to our friends at General Motors and said, "Okay—who was it out there who really bore the brunt of trying to get FORTRAN operational and knew what was going on?" and came up with George Ryckman. George has a Bachelor's Degree from the University of Virginia, and then went to the University of Michigan where he obtained a degree in Electrical Engineering. He's been at General Motors since 1952, starting off as a research engineer, supervisor of computer operations when FORTRAN was getting its feet on the ground, and now Assistant Department Head of the Computer Science Department at General Motors.

GEORGE RYCKMAN: Thank you, JAN. My remarks will deal primarily with the impact FORTRAN had on our organization, General Motors Research Laboratories, although I will have a few comments on the language design and its implementation. I'll begin with some pre-FORTRAN history, followed by our early experience with FORTRAN, some operational issues, and finally a comment on our more recent history.

In the three years prior to the first distribution of FORTRAN, we were preoccupied with programming and operating our first stored program machine, the IBM 701, and in preparing and installing its successor, the IBM 704. Still we took advantage of several opportunities to examine, critique and plan for FORTRAN at our installation. For example, my log book notes on March 17, 1955: "Received proposed additions to the FORTRAN: incorporated new symbols and formulas." And another entry on March 16, 1956: "FOR-TRAN code plates ordered for the keypunch machines."

We also suggested the IF SENSE LIGHT and IF SENSE SWITCH statements be added in order to monitor and control program execution at the computer console itself. From the first, FORTRAN seemed to offer inherent advantages over a myriad of langauges that we had up to that point, including Speedcoding, ACOM, which was a local three-address system we had, and a number of absolute, regional, and symbolic assembly languages.

From the standpoint of the engineer or scientist, the algebralike formula of FORTRAN appeared to have many specific advantages. The language was closer to his thought processes, required fewer pencil marks to program an algorithm, was easier to learn and retain, easier to read and change, and lent itself to more accuracy. All of these attributes netted out to two important predictions: first, the existing 15 to 20 full-time programmers would be more productive, but more importantly, through training classes and opening up the programming process to other groups, we could relieve the programming bottleneck. The big unknown, of course, at the time, was the other side of the equation; namely, the cost and computer time for translating and executing FORTRAN programs. And even though IBM was placing great emphasis on minimizing this cost, the answer had to wait until we had experience of our own.

The FORTRAN Translator arrived in April, as I remember—April of 1957, and by that time manuals had been distributed, some training had been conducted, and some programs had already been written. These programs included solutions for simultaneous algebraic and differential equations, an interpolation routine, and a program for graphing engineering results on a cathode-ray tube plotter. We very early learned that the Translator's diagnostics were not among its strong points. For example, the uninitiated could never understand why a missing parenthesis was cryptically known as a "nonzero level reduction." It was great sport in those days to scan the object program and either marvel at the Translator or question its sanity!

In spite of these problems, along with many translation errors, I can report that FORTRAN was a major success at GM Research. Between the internal and open shop programming groups, 40% of the 704 computer load was in FORTRAN by the end of 1957—a matter of eight months. A large fraction of this FORTRAN workload was converted from SAP but a more significant portion was worked generally by the other groups. Undoubtedly the rate of increase in computer workload at least tripled over what it would have been with the internal programming group using SAP. This estimate is based on some programmer productivity measurements that we made at the time.

Setting aside problem formulation and analysis time, studies showed that the programming and coding effort using FORTRAN was reduced by a factor between 5 and 10, compared to assembly language. Added to this, of course, was the fact that more people were trained to program the computer using FORTRAN.

Accompanying the reduction in programming effort was a decrease in the overall cost of the typical programming assignment. Taking into consideration the computer plus people costs of programming, compiling, recompiling and debugging, a cost reduction of $2\frac{1}{2}$ to 1 was achieved over a large set of programs.

In the real world, of course, these savings had less meaning simply because programs became larger, were more complex, and therefore the direct comparisons were no longer possible.

The greatest single design weakness of FORTRAN I was the lack of a full subroutine facility with load-time linking, because this generally limited the size of programs. In fact the mean free error time on the 704 was a major factor in running large programs; it just didn't hold out that long. The economics of compiling, testing, and recompiling were typically prohibitive with programs exceeding 300–400 statements. Later with the advent of FORTRAN II, the ability to break up a program into pieces substantially removed this restriction and the language became firmly established with virtually all application programming at GM Research.

At this point I'd like to address some of the operational issues of the earliest FORTRAN, the manner in which the compiler/translator ran on the 704. It did not come with an operating system, but rather took over the whole machine when it ran, so a programmer typically approached the machine, getting four tape units ready, a printer, a card reader, and a card punch. During translation, listings appeared on the printer and a binary object deck issued forth from the punch. The programmer transferred this binary deck from the punch to the reader, pushed "GO," and hoped. He finally retrieved the printed output and the card decks, and that completed a session. Rarely could all of this activity take place in less than 10 or 15 minutes per session, so machine time was scheduled in 15-minute blocks. All of this, I should say, was in marked contrast to our normal mode of operating a machine. Earlier in 1955, in a joint effort with North American, we had designed and implemented a so-called "multijob, tape-in, tape-out monitor system" for the 704. I guess today we'd call it an operating system. The resulting throughput advantages prompted us to initiate a similar system for FORTRAN, and in fact, we had already designed and all but checked out a new system for FORTRAN at the time it arrived. Within a month it was also running in an operating system. Incidentally, after suggesting SENSE LIGHT and SENSE SWITCH additions to FORTRAN, this nonstop automatic operation was rendered almost useless.

Fortunately the earlier monitor had done a good job of tuning our computer system because the translator was highly reliant and extremely brutal on tapes and drums. From an operational standpoint the only problem that plagued us for any extended period was the numerous program halts built into the translator. But the translator eventually learned that we would not put up with such laziness, and that if it had trouble with one source program, it should simply go on and get the next one.

In the intervening years, the FORTRAN load built up to virtually 100% of our computing. Only in the last ten years has it yielded grudgingly to PL/I; until today it still accounts for 50% of the load on three IBM 168 systems.

Our best, most efficient numerical analysis codes are still written in FORTRAN, as are some huge programs for structural and fluid flow analysis, just to name a few.

I've enjoyed delving into the archives for this discussion and also sharing it with you. I wish to thank the sponsors for the invitation to join you and the privilege of participating.

TRANSCRIPT OF QUESTION AND ANSWER SESSION

JAN LEE: Thank you, George. So, John, let me start off with the most general question. It is from Nancy Stern, and really it's not directly related to FORTRAN. "I notice that in the May 1954 article, the term 'programmer' was used. From your experience, when did the term 'programmer' begin and replace the word 'coder'?"

JOHN BACKUS: Well, the shortest answer I can give to that is—it's the same reason that janitors are now called "custodians." "Programmer" was considered a higher class enterprise than "coder," and things have a tendency to move in that direction.

LEE: Aaron Finerman, currently at SUNY, Stony Brook, says, "FORTRAN, as you noted, was greeted without enthusiasm by a skeptical if not hostile audience. To what then do you attribute its rapid acceptance? Was it the ease of programming, the efficient code it produced, or was it simply the thing to do? As a skeptical manager at the time, I have my own perspective but would like to have yours."

BACKUS: That's dangerous territory. I think there are a zillion different reasons why people took it up ultimately, but mainly it was economics. That's my belief—that it was the sort of a proposition you couldn't refuse unless you had problems of a special nature that FORTRAN didn't deal with very well.

LEE: Bob Bemer from H.I.S. asks: "How about a word on how long it took Sayre and Goldberg to pick up Best's section when he left your group?"

BACKUS: That was just something I would have liked to have mentioned in my talk but I didn't feel I had time. Sheldon Best wrote this enormously complex section 5, and then rather promptly left and went back to MIT before it was completely debugged. So David Sayre and Dick Goldberg, two good scholars, studied and studied and diagrammed the section and completed its debugging.

LEE: Was that a short episode, or a long one?

BACKUS: Well, it was no longer than the whole episode of debugging. That was quite long.

LEE: Tom Steel from AT&T asks: "Would you comment on the extent to which other works, specifically PACT, influenced FORTRAN development?"

BACKUS: Well, PACT was an ambitious project instituted by a number of aerospace companies in the Los Angeles area that performed a lot of services for the programmer, but —well, to make a short answer, I believe it had no influence because it began, you know, about the time we had frozen our design, if I'm not mistaken. At least, as far as we were aware then, that was the case.

LEE: Mr. Peterson from Bonneville asks: "Concerning FORTRANSIT, what connections existed between Perlis's IT and your FORTRAN?"

BACKUS: Well, IT was an algebraic translator for the 650, and there were lots and lots of 650s around in universities. And so a translator was written—Bob Bemer is the authority on this. I think he wrote it. A translator to translate FORTRAN programs into IT programs so that you could run them on 650s.

LEE: From Mike Shapiro of NCR: "Your paper tries to dispel the legend that three subscripts came from three index registers, and yet a later FORTRAN had a seven index register machine, and therefore had seven subscripts. What are your *current* thoughts on how many subscripts are needed?"

BACKUS: Well, I stick by my original story. The complexity of analysis that Bob Nelson and Irv Ziller had to do to optimally deal with indexing and looping rose exponentially as the number of subscripts went up. And that was, indeed, the reason we limited it to three. The fact that some later group decided to allow seven subscripts in a seven index register machine—that was out of my control. [Laughter]

LEE: Dr. Brebner from the University of Calgary asks: "With respect to FORTRAN, what do you consider was your best design decision, and what was your worst?"

BACKUS: Gosh! I just can't answer that right now. I'll try that one later.

LEE: Helen Gigley asks: "Why were the letters *I* through *N* chosen to designate integers?" [Laughter and applause]

BACKUS: Well, it just seemed for a while that people always used *I*, *J*, and *K* for subscripts, and we thought we'd be generous and add a few more.

LEE: Again from Helen Gigley: "Why was the decision to check at the bottom of a DO loop made?"—as opposed to the beginning, I presume.

BACKUS: For efficiency. You would have had an extra instruction, at least, if you'd done it otherwise.

LEE: Richard Miller asks—again, on the looping construct and the conditional construct: "Who wanted them originally, and was any support given by the hardware?"

BACKUS: No support was given by the hardware, to my knowledge, except that it provided the usual instructions that made it possible. And as far as who wanted it—we didn't know the answer to that. We just provided it, because it seemed like a convenient thing to do.

LEE: From David Dahm from Burroughs—and I think this goes back to Grace's talk. In her three-address system, pointing out that in Grace's system it was $x + y = z$, why did you decide to put the variable on the left of the equal sign as opposed to the right of the equal sign?

BACKUS: We thought it made programs more readable. If you put them on the right, the variable being assigned to would be a little hard to find, whereas, they're easy to find if they're on the left.

LEE: Juris Reinfelds from the University of Wollongong, Australia, asks: "Why and when was the decision made to interpret FORMATs, and does this not contradict your assumption of developing efficient execution code?"

BACKUS: I think Roy Nutt should answer that question.

ROY NUTT: That was strictly a matter of expediency. The original intent was to compile FORMAT statements, but we just couldn't get it done in time.

LEE: Roger Mills from TRW asks: "Was it your plan to have a subroutine facility from the very beginning, or did FORTRAN I show you it was a problem?"

BACKUS: Well, as the preliminary report indicated, we did intend to have it from the beginning, and in fact there were lots of things that never got into FORTRAN that were difficult to do—for example, summation never got in.

LEE: From Mike Shapiro again: "What comment do you have on the current trends in FORTRAN extensions?"

BACKUS: Well, I have some remarks on that in my paper. Not about FORTRAN extensions in particular, but about programming languages in general. I'm not in favor of any of them. I think conventional languages are for the birds. They're really low level languages. They're just extensions of the von Neumann computer, and they keep our noses pressed in the dirt of dealing with individual words and computing addresses, and doing all kinds of silly things like that, things that we've picked up from programming for computers; we've built them into programming languages; we've built them into FORTRAN; we've built them into PL/I; we've built them into almost every language. The only languages that broke free from that are LISP and APL, and in my opinion they haven't gone far enough.

LEE: John, thank you very much.

FULL TEXT OF ALL QUESTIONS SUBMITTED

BOB BEMER

How about a word on how long it took Sayre and Goldberg to pick up Best's section when he left?

M. A. BREBNER

With respect to FORTRAN, what do you consider was the best design decision, and what do you feel was the worst design decision?

DAVE DAHM

Why did you decide to put the variable being assigned on the left rather than the right of the "=" sign?
Where did the idea of the subscripted variable come from originally?

BILL DERBY

What language was used for your FORTRAN compiler, and how easily did it translate to the 704's successor?

KEN DICKEY

How were the bounds of your Monte Carlo simulation flow analysis (section 4 of compiler) arrived at (i.e., how did you bound your system)?

HAROLD ENGELSOHN

In the initial stages of planning, was there any conscious effort to allow for data processing as well as algebraic manipulation? If not, when were alphabetization capabilities, for example, added to FORTRAN?

Full Text of All Questions Submitted

AARON FINERMAN

FORTRAN, as you noted, was greeted without enthusiasm by a skeptical if not hostile audience. To what, then, do you attribute its rapid acceptance? Was it the ease of programming (compared to assembly language), efficient object code produced, or that it was simply the thing to do? As a (skeptical) manager at the time I have my perspective, but would like yours.

BERNIE GALLER

Bob Graham's early study (at Michigan) of the source code for FORTRAN showed that after the initial parse of a statement to determine its type, the original statement was passed to another module, and the analysis started over. Is this correct? Why wasn't information already at hand passed on to the next module?

HELEN GIGLEY

Why was the decision to check at the bottom of the DO loop made?
Why were the letters *I* through *N* designated for implicit integer variables?

JOEL GYLLENSKOG

Why was the decision made to remove blanks from the syntax? Why were key words rather than reserved words used?

RICHARD MILLER

What outside groups (i.e., outside of your design team) had influence in the design phase? Was it a pure IBM effort?
Comment: The optimality of DO loops as opposed to IF GOTO type loops has been seen since then in parallel processor software projects at Illinois. In particular in optimization phases.
The looping construct and the conditional construct—who wanted them, how much support was given by the hardware?

ROGER MILLS

Was it your plan to have a subroutine facility in the very beginning, or did FORTRAN I show the problem?

DIT MORSE

What do you remember about the interrelationship of the original language design and the hardware specifications of the 704?

N. D. PETERSON

For possible inclusion in the final post-meeting proceedings:

Future prospects of FORTRAN in terms of Structured Programming and adapting it to be better suited to structured programming.

Comments on extensions and FORTRAN-based package to handle expressions of the following kinds in source programs:

(1) Matrix algebra such as IBM's Scientific Subrouting Package.
(2) Differential equations such as MIMIC (Air Force).

Concerning FORTRANSIT: What connections existed, if any, between Perlis's IT and IBM's FORTRANSIT? Any other comments on the historical significance of FOR-TRANSIT?

JURIS REINFELDS

Why and when was the decision made to interpret FORMAT's? Does this not contradict the assumption of "efficient execution code"?

BOB ROSIN

One recalls the all too frequent FORTRAN diagnostic message which read something like: "Error in pass ONE PRIME". What was this pass, and who wrote it?

MIKE SHAPIRO

What comments do you have on current trends in FORTRAN extensions?

Your paper tries to dispel the legend that three subscripts comes from three index registers. Yet later FORTRAN for a seven index register machine had seven subscripts. What are your current thoughts on how many subscripts we need in "FORTRAN-like" languages?

T. B. STEEL JR.

Would you comment on the extent to which other work—specifically PACT—influenced the FORTRAN development?

NANCY STERN

I noticed that in your May, 1954, article, the term "programmer" was used. From your experience, when did the term "programmer" replace "coder"?

SELDON L. STEWART

Independently compilable subroutines versus local precedures:

(1) Given the value of independent compilability to programming libraries and complicated (systems) programs, why has this feature been so rarely included in higher level languages other than FORTRAN and its descendents?

(2) Was the assigned GOTO conceived of as a mechanism for implementing local procedures? If not, what was its origin?

BIOGRAPHY OF JOHN BACKUS

John Backus was employed by IBM as a programmer for the Selective Sequence Electronic Calculator (SSEC) in 1950, after receiving his Master's degree in mathematics from Columbia University. Later he headed the development of the Speedcoding interpretive system for the IBM 701. He also took part in the design of the IBM 704 and was the original advocate for its built-in floating point operations. From early 1954 until late 1958 he was manager of the programming research group (later department) in IBM during its development of FORTRAN.

While Backus was a member of the committees that designed ALGOL 58 and ALGOL 60, he joined IBM Research. In the course of efforts to define ALGOL 58 more precisely, he employed the syntax description technique known as BNF; this technique was improved and used by Naur to describe the syntax of ALGOL 60 in the ALGOL Report.

After his work on ALGOL, Backus spent a number of years working on the mathematics of families of sets. For the last eight years he has been developing a functional style of programming and its associated algebra of programs.

In 1963 Backus was appointed an IBM Fellow. He received the W. W. McDowell Award of the IEEE in 1967, the National Medal of Science of 1975, and the Turing Award of the ACM in 1977. He is a member of the National Academies of Science and of Engineering.

ALGOL Session

Chairman: Thomas Cheatham
Speakers: Alan J. Perlis
Peter Naur

PAPER: THE AMERICAN SIDE OF THE DEVELOPMENT OF ALGOL

Alan J. Perlis

Yale University
New Haven, Connecticut

1. Before ALGOL 58

History is contextual. The ALGOL† development was a product, perhaps a miraculous product, of its time. All developments proceed, almost implacably, from the primitive to the rococo, e.g., from ALGOL 58 through ALGOL 60 to ALGOL 68 with an appearance of a large number of offshoots (e.g., JOVIAL, MAD, NELIAC and Euler), extensions (FORMULA ALGOL and LCC), virile offspring (PASCAL), etc., occurring en route. The earliest developments appear clean, surprising us in the new views they reveal. One frets over why the vision that prompted the beginning weakened during the course of future developments. Perhaps it is inevitable that, as unexpected complexity is uncovered, smoothness, equal value if you will, in solutions cannot be maintained. Trivia cannot be identified easily, special cases overwhelm the search for general patterns, custom and habit move performance into the realm of objective concept, experience warps both intuition and reason, fear of instability burdens insight with caution. The elegance of ALGOL's offspring is a tribute to the grace and power of the original. ALGOL, a second-generation language, was more graceful than any of its predecessors, for example, FORTRAN, MATH-MATIC, and IT.

During 1956 and 1957, a programming revolution began. Programming aids, hitherto modest extensions of machine assembly language or interpreters executing the codes of

---

† "ALGOL" will refer to issues relating to the ALGOL 58—ALGOL 60 development. "ALGOL 58" and "ALGOL 60" will reference the explicit language they respectively identify.

suitable virtual machines, were being augmented to include free form, sentence oriented code formats. More of the "red-tape" issues of programming became the responsibility of these code processors. The programmer could devote more of his text to algorithmic issues and correspondingly less to machine related issues. More code writing could be done by the end user without totally reorganizing his use of time: His principal work did not need to cease when his programming began. This new style of programming appeared so fluid and machine-free that "language" or "algebraic language" replaced "code" in descriptions of the forms. Enough attention to machine details was given over to these language processors that their performance was blessed by the phrase "automatic programming." Examples of these languages were IT in 1956, MATH-MATIC in 1957, and FORTRAN in 1957. FORTRAN became the most widely used of these languages and shall be considered as representative of the class.

These languages exposed opportunities that most of the computing world had not anticipated and was not prepared to exploit. Many programmers believed that only machine assembly language could serve as a useful algorithmic base language. It was felt that there was a limited constituency of algorithms whose algebraic language descriptions were adequate to define the computation at hand.

It took strong support by IBM and concerned individuals within SHARE, to convert users of IBM 700 series computers to extensive use of FORTRAN. By the spring of 1958, a second version, FORTRAN II for the IBM 704, was released, and FORTRAN's acceptance steadily grew. Remington-Rand was exploiting the MATH-MATIC and UNICODE languages for its UNIVAC I and 1101-03 computers, respectively. Several universities were developing programming languages and processors for their computers. Carnegie Tech (now Carnegie–Mellon), Case, and Michigan spawned at least nine languages from IT (Evans and Perlis, 1959). An opening was thereby provided for universities that had not previously been involved in computer design to sponsor computer language research. These schools would later serve as nuclei for the development of computer science.

It almost seemed that each new computer, and even each programming group, was spawning its own algebraic language or cherished dialect of an existing one. Apart from local technical variations, these languages were much like others already present or under design. Since no theory of language design and no adequate measure of language suitability existed, why would any one language be permitted to predominate? Was it so unreasonable in those days to search for linguistic perfection? Since we haven't yet found perfection after 20 years of active search and trial, it probably was an unreasonable goal. However, if we remember that improvement in process, as much as product, is a goal of computing theory, the profusion of language developments was undoubtedly beneficial.

Profusion, to be beneficial, must lead to unification. The user's groups, e.g., SHARE, USE, and DUO, acting in the best interests of their memberships, pointed out the value of having a single programming language for communicating programs among users and, hence, to computers. That such a language could be defined was obvious. Indeed many such could be defined! Upon examination the many languages already designed and in use were more like each other than anything else, differing in matters of taste more than substance. Would such a "universal" language, once designed, achieve widespread acceptance and use? Or, to put it operationally, how could the computer world be made to achieve such a euphoric state? In periods of infancy, exuberance, energy, and simplistic visions dominate. In 1957 it seemed appropriate for ACM to support the petition of some user groups (USE, SHARE, and DUO, to be exact) for a study that would lead to a single (national) programming language that all could (would) use on their computers and in whose terms programs would be communicated between the users of all machines.

The petition, dated May 10, 1957, contained recommendations, one of which suggested that ACM appoint a committee to study, and recommend action for, the creation of a universal programming language. In 1957 computer users were already concerned about the difficulty of communicating programs, a difficulty caused by language and machine diversity and a lack of standards in almost every area relating to computer use. The petition did not specify whether this universal language be sought for at the machine or at the algebraic language level.

The ACM Council at the June 1957 national meeting of ACM supported the petition and requested that ACM president, John W. Carr III, appoint a committee to study the matter of creating a universal programming language. Carr quickly responded to the Council's request and appointed an ad hoc committee, composed of representatives of computer industry, users, universities, and the federal government, to issue the technical specifications of the proposed universal language. Membership in the committee included D. Arden (MIT), J. Backus (IBM), P. Desilets (Remington-Rand Univac), D. Evans (Bendix), R. Goodman (Westinghouse), S. Gorn (University of Pennsylvania), H. Huskey (University of California), C. Katz (Remington-Rand Univac), J. McCarthy (MIT), A. Orden (University of Chicago), A. Perlis (Carnegie Tech), R. Rich (Johns Hopkins), S. Rosen (Philco), W. Turanski (Remington-Rand Univac), and J. Wegstein (National Bureau of Standards).

The committee met three times. At the first meeting, in Washington, January 25, 1958, the committee agreed the language would be at the FORTRAN level, an "algebraic" language, since a universally acceptable computer instruction code was clearly out of the question. Looking at the situation today, one may ask why FORTRAN was not chosen, since it has now become more widely accepted than any other language. Today FORTRAN is the property of the computing world, but in 1957 it was an IBM creation and closely tied to use of IBM hardware. For these reasons, FORTRAN was unacceptable as a universal language.

At a second meeting at MIT in April, a subcommittee was formed to draft a language proposal for ultimate submission to ACM. The subcommittee included J. Backus, J. McCarthy, A. Perlis, and W. Turanski.

Even before the first meeting of the committee took place, a letter from GAMM (Gesellschaft für angewandte Mathematik und Mechanik) to Carr in October 1957 suggested that a unified language design effort between GAMM and ACM, rather than two distinct efforts, would better serve the computer field. A committee within GAMM had been working since 1955 on the design of a universal algorithmic language at the FORTRAN level.

The letter contained a number of important points:

1. None of the existing languages appears to overshadow the others sufficiently to warrant it being chosen as the universal language.

2. The situation would not be improved by the creation of still another nonideal language.

3. Each passing month will bring a large increase in the number of installations using existing languages, and thus increase the difficulty in arriving at a uniform formula language that will be widely used.

4. How can the logical structure of existing languages be adjusted to conform to a recommended common formula language?

2. The Zurich Meeting

It was proposed by GAMM that direct communication take place between the GAMM subcommittee for programming languages. F. L. Bauer of GAMM presented the GAMM proposal at a Philadelphia meeting of the ACM Committee on April 18, 1958. To accomplish unification of design, it was agreed that each committee would send four members to a meeting at Zurich, Switzerland, from May 27 to June 1, 1958. The Chairman of the ACM language committee (Perlis) and ACM President (Carr) chose four members to represent the ACM at Zurich. The four members chosen represented industry, university, and government. All were engaged in algebraic language design and compiler construction efforts.

The ETH (Eidgenossiche Technische Hochschule—The Swiss Federal Institute of Technology) in Zurich kindly extended its hospitality to provide a meeting place and support services for the meeting. The attendees at the meeting were F. L. Bauer, H. Bottenbruch, H. Rutishauser, and K. Samelson of GAMM, and J. Backus, C. Katz, A. J. Perlis, and, J. H. Wegstein of ACM. Professor Stiefel, a noted numerical analyst and the head of the applied mathematics group at ETH, opened the meeting with a few well-chosen welcoming words. He cautioned the group not to waste the precious days in a search for the perfect language and to heed Wittgenstein's observation that all too often "the best is the enemy of the good." He would have been relieved to know that the design of languages becomes so quickly proscribed by issues of taste, designer's myopia, the conflicts between generality and efficiency of performance, etc., that the search for the "best" is quickly diverted to a search for a few meaningful improvements.

As a background to this Zurich meeting, it is important to appreciate a distinction between the motivations and attitudes of the European and American groups. The former group had been engaged in a systematic effort to define a common language for a much longer period of time than the ACM group; a language that they hoped would become widely accepted and *used*. Europe was ripe and waiting for such a language. The existence in Europe of political partitions, a desire to avoid domination in Europe by IBM, and a general passion for orderliness made the future of a good language seem quite rosy. Except in England, assembly language was not in widespread use in Europe. It was believed that the algebraic language would confine machine language programming to a few important support programs on each computer. All other programming would be in the algebraic language.

All of the members of the American group were already deeply involved in *separate* language efforts. In the short time of one year, IT and FORTRAN, at least, had reached the inevitable refinement and expansion stages that (as we now know) accompany all language developments as a consequence of serious use. The experience of the Americans, as much as reason, prompted their various language designs and responses to language alternatives and possibilities. However, it was just the exposure to possibilities not yet thought of that made the American group optimistic about the value and the possible success of the proposed international language. Even if it were to be used widely only in Europe, that language, representing the best of what was known, could become a standard against which the old and new could be measured.

Developments, prompted both by reasoning about an abstraction and experience with languages being used, accounted for much of the excellence and balance in the language design that came to be known as IAL (the International Algebraic Language) achieved in a few days at the Zurich meeting. At one point during the meeting, the acronym ALGOL (Algorithmic language) was suggested as a name for the language under design. It was not adopted, perhaps because it did not emphasize the international (!) effort involved. Once publicized, discussed and debated, the "unspeakable" and pompous acronym, IAL, gave way in 1959 to the more verbal and source independent ALGOL. When a second version became an imminent possibility, the distinction between the earlier and later versions was captured in the names ALGOL 58 and ALGOL 60, respectively.

The eight who met, reasoned about, argued over, insisted on, and ultimately compromised over the issues during the eight-day period (the meeting was extended through June 3) behaved responsibly. No part of ALGOL 58 can be said to be the result of one man's intransigence. No part of the language is there only because all but one or two got so bored with tedious discussion about it that it was left in to avoid interminable bickering. (The perceptive cooperation that occurred at Zurich was to be repeated at the ALGOL 60 meeting in Paris about 18 months later under somewhat more difficult circumstances. A committee of thirteen is a different organism from a committee of eight. Five additional minds meant five additional voices that could not be permitted, on each issue, to give rise to five additional opinions.) No part of the Zurich language can be said to represent purely as a sop to the Americans who had traveled so far, or the Europeans who had worked so long. ALGOL 58 was truly the result of a joint effort.

Formal minutes of the daily activities of the conference were kept. Each evening the day's chairman and secretary had the minutes typed for the use at the next day's session. They represent the record of the stages through which the various language parts evolved to achieve their final form. No one chaired individual sessions. No chairman organized the flow of issues discussed; common sense and common purpose kept the meetings productive.

Several suggestions could not be taken up during the meeting period, either because of their peripheral importance or because no acceptably precise syntax and semantics for them could be found. Trees, lists, and recursion fall in these categories.

Several constructions were left in the language even though their presence would complicate translator construction. It would have been a linguistic restriction to have excised them, e.g., the placement of declarations arbitrarily within a program text.

Other constructions were included because experience had identified their utility. An example was multiple named, and multiple entry point procedures (e.g., a single procedure for sin, cos, and tan) and the copy statement that provided an analog to the open-subroutine and the macro, both of which had proved to be of significant value in assembly language programming.

Input and output parameters in procedure declarations were separately identified because it seemed natural to most of the group to look upon the procedure as a "mapping" from input (domain) to output (range). The parameter separation clarified this view. The use of empty subscript positions and empty procedure parameter positions permitted a more general procedure construction, e.g., a procedure for inner product could be defined that would handle both vectors and matrices. However, some natural generalizations were not possible because the only actual and formal correspondence permitted was matching indices of the empty parameter positions.

The separation between function and procedure, pioneered in FORTRAN, was maintained. It took the possibility of attachment of type to procedure and the choice of binding by name or value, introduced in ALGOL 60, to make the syntactic separation of function and procedure semantically unnecessary.

The proposal that there be three representations for the languages, reference, publication, and hardware, was a master stroke. It simultaneously freed designers, implementers, and users from pointless debates on issues over which none could expect to have much control. It made possible the appreciation of the ideas, the intent and the feel of the language, without the need of prior language alphabet projection onto local (usually limited) character sets.

As with so many clarifying concepts, the "three representation" proposal arose from a need for compromise. Joe Wegstein has reminded the author that, after two days of probing attitudes and suggestions, the meeting came to a complete deadlock with one European member pounding on the table and declaring: "No! I will never use a period for a decimal point." Naturally the Americans considered the use of comma as decimal point to be beneath ridicule. That evening Wegstein visited the opposing camps and proposed defining the three levels of language. The proposal was immediately adopted the following morning and progress resumed.

3. ALGOL 58

How are the merits (and shortcomings) of ALGOL 58 to be measured? As with every other member of a progressive sequence of artifacts, ALGOL 58 was better than its predecessors and weaker than its successors. ALGOL 58 was preceded by FORTRAN, IT and MATH-MATIC. The central ideas in these latter languages were captured in general and elegant constructions in ALGOL 58—types, compound statements, conditionals, loops, switches, and procedures. The major contribution of ALGOL 58 was the treatment of language issues in its design. Its major weaknesses were the tentative solutions of many of these same issues. ALGOL 58 was based on a model strongly derived from FORTRAN and its contemporaries. Consequently, it was oriented towards scalar arithmetic processing. The logic, arithmetic, and data organizations were close to those then being designed into real computers. Certain simple generalizations of computer instructions such as **switch,** for statement, if statements, and compound statement were included because their semantics and computer processing were straightforward consequences of single statement processing.

The major information transformer remained the assignment statement. Its data components were the, by now, accepted scalars, functions, and restricted procedure values. Side effects were not possible. Hence, problems arising from their presence were not discussed.

The simple data objects, integer, real, and Boolean, and their respective aggregate, the array, were classical. Character strings and bit vectors were mentioned in discussions, but were not admitted to the language in order to retain machine independence. The use of "type," as in "x is of type **real**," was analogous to that employed in logic. Both programming language design and logic dipped into the English language and came up with the same word for roughly the same purpose. But ALGOL 58 contained no constructive theory of data "type," and none was seriously discussed. It wasn't until 10 years later that such a constructive theory was discussed in the ALGOL framework (Galler and Perlis,

1967). The type of an identifier was set in a declaration whose lexicographic location was arbitrary, e.g., it could appear in the text contiguous to the earliest use of said identifier.

Control statements were recognized to be a class of constructions that called for the notion of compound statement. That notion, extended so nicely in ALGOL 60, is the main contribution of ALGOL 58 to programming languages. Though not in the IAL report, "clause" was used by Backus (Backus, 1960) to identify the control component attached to a compound statement in a control statement. That syntactic separation simplified the independent generalizations that came to be in ALGOL 60. Being a bracketing concept, the compound statement supported *nesting*. The notion of scope of control is present in ALGOL 58, but other important applications of scope, e.g., identifier scope, were missing. Why? Probably because the committee, balanced between a brief past and limited goals, did not design from a well-articulated set of language design criteria. Considering the limited time available to them and the apparently work-free ease with which linguistic concepts generalize, ALGOL 58 emerges as a testimonial to their sanity and good taste.

The unit of "operation" extension in ALGOL 58 is the procedure. Programs may contain procedures, but apparently procedures may not contain other procedures, though such nesting is desirable. How then may an ALGOL 58 program become a procedure within some still larger program? ALGOL 58 provides an answer by the simple expedient of requiring the process of "becoming" to be performed *outside of* ALGOL 58. The assembly process may take advantage of separate compilations to create new procedures from old programs. The ALGOL 58 report, in the section on procedure declarations, is quite explicit on what must take place, but not how, in this assembly process.

Nowhere was the language design more schizophrenic than in the handling of functions and procedures. The separation closely followed that of FORTRAN. Consider the four issues

    a. nature of the body

    b. parameter evaluation mechanism

    c. identifier collision

    d. place of use

and their treatment in functions and procedures

a.	expression	compound statement
b.	value of any actual parameter	text of any actual parameter
c.	nonparameter identifiers are global (free) to the definition	communication only through parameters
d.	an operand in an expression	a statement or an operand in an expression.

It should be pointed out that this schizoid behavior was not completely unintentional. The function was seen as serving a narrow but widely occurring purpose. Its syntactic and semantic complexity was intended to match the need of greatest usage—as an operand in an expression. The procedure served an arbitrarily "wide" purpose by representing arbitrary transformations, e.g., even those whose internal details were not represented in

Alan J. Perlis

ALGOL 58. As K. Samelson has pointed out to the author, the choice of "liberty through flexibility versus discipline through construction schemes," continually before the Zurich designers, also dominated the attentions of the Paris ALGOL 60 conferees, e.g., the control of side effects and the advantages of early binding.

This schizophrenia was resolved in ALGOL 60 by the introduction of blocks, typed procedures, call by value, and call by name. The linguistic distinction between function and procedure disappeared. The need for empty parameter positions in formal array, function and procedure parameters, was satisfied by call-by-name parameters. For example, the procedure,

real procedure $IP(z,y,n,j)$; **value** n;
  begin real a; $a := 0$;
    for $j := 1$ **step** 1 **until** n **do** $a := a + z \times y$;
    $IP := a$ **end**

when called as $IP(A[i], B[i], 70, i)$ computed the inner product of the vectors A and B, but when called as $IP(C[i,i], D[k,i], 70, i)$ computed the inner product of the diagonal of C and the kth row of D. This use of evaluation on the call side of an internal variable of a procedure is called Jensen's device, named after Jorn Jensen of the Danish Regnecentralen, who first noted this use of call by name *parameters*.

ALGOL 58 introduced into programming languages such terms as type, formal versus actual parameter, declaration, identifier, for statement, **switch,** compound statement, the **begin end** delimiters, three levels of language description, and the text substitution rule (call by name) for replacement of formal by actual parameter in procedure calls.

4. From Zurich to Paris

In the year following the publication of the Zurich report (Perlis and Samelson, 1958), a number of American comments about and recommendations for the improvement of the proposed language appeared in the *Communications of the ACM*. It seemed that while there was some American interest in implementing ALGOL 58, (e.g., within SHARE and IBM) more in the U.S.A. were interested in implementing a language derived from but not necessarily the same as ALGOL 58. In this category fall the efforts of the groups at the University of Michigan (MAD), Naval Electronics Laboratory (NELIAC), and System Development Corp. (JOVIAL). To these latter groups, ALGOL 58 was seen as a rich set of guidelines for a language rather than a standard to be adhered to. It suggested possibilities, yet neglected issues for which any real implementation must provide a solution, e.g., input-output. The Zurich group in its desire to avoid fixing on hardware dependent issues, left obvious gaps in the definition. Presumably individual implementations would fill these gaps so that the defined language would not be altered.

It should be remembered that the Zurich report was a draft. ALGOL 58 was not intended to be the language around which international conformity would immediately congeal. But it was a skeleton, internationally conceived, from which constructive improvements would lead to the sought after uniform language.

Unfortunately the skeleton was also convenient for the purposes of many who were mildly interested, at best, in the creation of the uniform language. Its incompleteness supported attitudes such as: no useful uniform language is logically possible; the language is at the wrong level; the need is for a uniform machine language. Yet, ALGOL 58's existence created a clamor within SHARE that IBM jettison FORTRAN in favor of ALGOL 58. One was reminded of a gold rush. Many in SHARE seemed in such a hurry to accept, implement, and proselytize, when what was needed was study, experimentation, and suggestions for improvement.

Shortly after the Zurich report was published, an IBM group in New York, led by R. Bemer and J. Green, began an experimental implementation of ALGOL 58 on the IBM 709. There was a reasonable amount of interest in this effort within the SHARE group. Indeed, SHARE had already formed an IAL committee at SHARE XI in September 1958. At a subsequent meeting in February 1959, the SHARE IAL committee recommended that ACM take steps to make ALGOL 58 a standard and that IBM implement an ALGOL 58 translator for their 700 series scientific computers. ACM chose to sidestep the recommendation. IBM described its translator progress at a subsequent SHARE IAL committee meeting in New York in May 1959. The SHARE IAL committee was never a major force in SHARE, and few SHARE members participated in its activities. The committee ultimately issued a report in the *Communications of the ACM* listing its proposal for improvement of the language (Bratman *et al.*, 1959).

SHARE and IBM enjoyed an uneasy partnership. While each was the captive of the other on certain issues, both agreed that their main order of business was the exploitation of IBM 700 series computers. How would ALGOL 58 affect their principal concern? Both chose not to treat ALGOL 58 as an inevitable standard whose acceptance in the United States would be hastened by their enthusiastic support. They were aware of the enormous resources it was taking to install FORTRAN as the central language component in increasingly complex traffic on their computers. Successive SHARE meetings revealed how the increasing dependence of SHARE and IBM on each other crystallized around FORTRAN. Since ALGOL 58 and FORTRAN were not obvious sublanguages of each other, full support of ALGOL 58 would only diminish the importance of FORTRAN. Neither IBM nor SHARE was interested in seeing that happen. Thus, ALGOL never had much of a chance to become the standard language on the large IBM scientific calculators (704, 709, 7090, 7094). By mid-year 1959, FORTRAN had won the day—and its acceptance, once achieved, was irreversible. The combination of adequate input–output, magnetic tape handling commands, reasonable object code optimization, a fit to the machine breed (IBM 704, 709, 7090, 7094), manufacturer language maintenance support, good system support software, and adequate language definition contributed to FORTRAN's acceptance.

The acceptance of FORTRAN within SHARE and the accompanying incredible growth in its use, in competition with a better linguistic vehicle, illustrated how factors other than language determine the choice of programming language of users. Programs are not abstractions. They are articles of commerce in a society of users and machines. The choice of programming language is but one parameter governing the vitality of the commerce. Perhaps it is just as well that IBM and its users accepted ALGOL 58 as a model for language development but did not settle upon it as a computing standard . . . too much would have to have been fixed too soon. The needs of the IBM community would have forced standardization prematurely.

ALGOL 58 was used as a basis for the development of the JOVIAL sequence of languages at SDC (Shaw, 1963), MAD language at the University of Michigan (Arden *et al.*, 1961), and the language NELIAC at the Naval Electronics Laboratory (Huskey *et al.*, 1963). These languages owed much to, but contained more than, their progenitor. Their existence and use enlarged everyone's field of view. For example, MAD's inclusion of definitions undoubtedly helped to round out ALGOL 68 almost a decade later. (The importance of the debate over the primacy of chicken versus egg is put in perspective by the existence of the poultry industry.)

Of great interest was the immediate use of ALGOL 58 as a language for expressing algorithms, or fragments of algorithms, in papers appearing in the *Communications* during 1959. Perhaps it was ALGOL 58's freedom from being tied to any one implementation, or hardware, or user's group, or vendor that made it seem the appropriate vehicle for expressing algorithms of general applicability. Papers touching on a diversity of topics, e.g., recursive list procedures (Carr, 1959), identifiers (Williams, 1959), symbol pairs (Bemer, 1959), card codes (Bright, 1959), and binary–decimal conversion (Taranto, 1959), used ALGOL 58 as the illustrative algorithmic notation. This role for ALGOL has continued to the present. No other programming language has been so widely used to convey algorithmic descriptions of general interest. Almost everyone in the United States who would be interested in ALGOL 58 was probably a member of ACM. Hence, the *Communications of the ACM* became the natural forum in which to publicize not only the usage of ALGOL 58, but recommendations for its revision.

The situation in Europe was quite different. The European Zurich contingent was affiliated with GAMM and certainly not respresentative of European computing groups. It was clear that the European circle of ALGOL 58 custodians had to be widened to include representatives of the major national computer societies of Europe. Invitations to attend a meeting in Mainz in November 1958, from the Zurich GAMM group, were accepted by computer specialists representing various computer organizations in France, England, Netherlands, Denmark, Sweden and West Germany. The ALGOL *Bulletin,* the European medium for disseminating ALGOL intensive matters, was established at a subsequent European conference in Copenhagen in February 1959, and the first of its issues appeared that March. P. Naur of the Danish Regnecentralen was its first editor.

At the first IFIP conference in Paris in June 1959, a resolution that both the *Communications* and the *ALGOL Bulletin* be the official media for discussions of proposals for ALGOL improvement and other ALGOL matters was adopted by those who were concerned about the development of ALGOL.

Throughout 1959 there appeared in the *Communications* American recommendations for improving ALGOL 58. Many were subsequently adopted at the January 1960 meeting that led to the definition of ALGOL 60. The American proposals were of somewhat different character from the European proposals that appeared in the *ALGOL Bulletin* during that same period. The Europeans were very concerned with the refinement of the procedure concept and linguistic control of identifier scopes. The Americans seemed more concerned with language flexibility, extension, and completion to include especially input–output.

The following proposals for changes in ALGOL 58 that appeared in the *Communications* during 1959 were considered at the Paris ALGOL 60 meeting:

1. Let Booleans be operands in arithmetic expressions, e.g., let *true* and *false* correspond to 1 and 0, respectively (Green, 1959a). The intent of this inoffensive suggestion was captured in ALGOL 60 through the conditional expression, but at a greater cost in notation. However, compressed notation was never an important goal of the ALGOL effort.

2. In switches, let the first component always be a NOP and compute the switch index MOD $(n + 1)$ if the switch has n components (Green, 1959a). The acceptable behavior of a switch when a subscript is out of range is at best a matter of taste, or, at worst, a matter of philosophy. What was finally adopted was: Subscript out of range is a NOP.

3. The for statement should be modified. Suggestions included were: Let the for statement be written as two assignments (initial and step) and one predicate (continuation condition). Thus **for** $v := 1(1)10$ becomes **for** $v := 1(v + 1)$ $(v < 10)$ which is not an improvement, but **for** $v := 1$ $(v + 1)(abs(x - y) > E)$ is more perspicuous than inventing a phony upper limit for v. If the assignments are omitted, **for** $abs(x - y) > E$ **do** is the **while do** form present in almost all languages derived from ALGOL 60. Refusal to cast the **for** clause as a general traversal scheme (initial value, next value, continuation condition) was probably a mistake—but the pressure to adhere to a form analogous to those in wide use in numerical analysis was probably the reason. Thus this proposal was not adopted at the Paris meeting, nor was the suggested parallel for statement, because of indecision over the appropriate semantics when the loops were of unequal duration. Booleans as **for** loop variable were also deemed unacceptable. However, the **for** list element was accepted and syntactic sugar was introduced, i.e., **step** and **until** (Green, 1959b).

4. The empty statement was proposed (Green, 1959b) and adopted.

5. Some modifications to the operation hierarchy were proposed:

a. Delete the exponential brackets and assign exponentiation, ↑, the highest precedence among dyadic operators (Kanner, 1959).

b. Let monadic operators bind more tightly than any dyadic operator e.g.,

$$2 \uparrow -7 \text{ means } 2 \uparrow (0-7) \text{ (Kanner, 1959)}.$$

c. Let all relational operators have the same precedence and lower than any arithmetic dyadic operator (Green, 1959b).

d. Let the dyadic logical operators have the precedence ∧ before ∨ before either or both of ≡ and ⊃. Let ¬ bind more tightly than any dyadic logical operator. All logical operators are of lower precedence than any relational operator (Green, 1959b).

The proposals a to d were adopted. Implied multiplication was not allowed, nor were relation sequences such as $y < x < w$ approved.

6. The conditional statement should be extended to include an **else** clause. This proposal was accepted as part of a redesign of the conditional statement.

7. Proposals were made to expand the types of variables that could appear in programs: string, lists, trees, matrices, and complex numbers were suggested. They were rejected at the Paris meeting. It was felt, rightly or wrongly, that these types would not fit harmoniously within the existing language units and insertion of additional units would be required. It was believed, I think rightly so, that the ALGOL language should not become a "weakly" connected set of linguistic constructions each useful for only a few of the variable types—creating what I call the "dumbbell" model of language.

8. Multiple assignment statements, e.g., $x := y := e$ were proposed (Green, 1959a) and adopted. However, an issue was thereby created that had not previously existed: In $A[i] := i := e$ what value of i is to be used in $A[i]$?

9. The conditional expression, as pioneered in LISP, was proposed (McCarthy, 1959) and adopted. Its inclusion made the language more uniform and suggested other unifor-

mizing extensions that would appear in future ALGOL derivates, e.g., name valued expressions.

10. Recursion was specifically proposed (McCarthy, 1959) even though it had not been explicitly forbidden in ALGOL 58. In any event, recursion became possible in obvious ways in ALGOL 60. Even though numerical analysis did not make much use of recursive procedures, inclusion of recursion made the language much more useful for important applications that would surface in the years immediately following ALGOL 60's birth.

11. Extensions were proposed for the do statement (Green, 1959b): Copy more than one statement sequence with the same substitutions and extend the scope of that for which substitutions could be made, e.g., include operator characters and even arbitrary strings as substituents. However, the do statement was dropped from ALGOL largely because no really pressing reasons could be summoned for keeping it.

12. Assignment of constants within declarations (Dijkstra *et al.*, 1959) was proposed. Often, identifiers serve the role of naming constants in a program, so the ability to assign in constant value at the point of identifier declaration seemed useful. However, the guarantee that these identifiers would not change their significance during a computation was not insured. Therefore, constant assignment seemed to be a special case of general assignment and not worthy of complicating the language.

13. Better control over the scope of, and aliases for, variables should be provided (Dijkstra *et al.*, 1959). A control somewhat like the FORTRAN COMMON or some other storage overlay scheme should be provided. A means for *local, global* differentiation between variables should be introduced. The effect of the FORTRAN EQUIVALENCE statement should be provided. While none of these specific proposals was adopted, the introduction of blocks provided much, though not all, of the facilities requested in these proposals. The simplicity and elegance of blocks had a great deal to do with the definition structure of procedures that finally emerged in ALGOL 60.

The American comments and proposals on identifier scopes and procedures were of far less consequence than the European proposals that led to blocks and inclusion of both call by value and name. The procedure proposal finally adopted in ALGOL 60 eliminated the need for a syntactic distinction between input and output parameters, as well as the need for specifying empty parameter positions in the formal and actual parameters.

During the entire period of ALGOL's development, one could point to significant differences between the European and American attitudes toward ALGOL. The European members of the committee felt deeply committed to the implementation and widespread use of the language as defined. They would make ALGOL a usable standard. It, and no other language, would be used for describing and communicating algorithms within the family of European computer groups. Even the Soviet block countries agreed to use ALGOL as a basis for their language developments.

Europe benefited from ALGOL. Not only could algorithms become communicable across national language barriers, but a language better than any extant had been defined. It was machine independent, both technically and politically. European-designed and -built computers were as suitable for hosting ALGOL processors as were, e.g., IBM computers. In particular, ALGOL 60 demanded enough new compiling techniques for processor constructions that European computer specialists would acquire superb proficiency in language processing techniques. And it wouldn't be busy work! A task of consequence had been set and none could do it any better than those who designed, studied, shaped, and used ALGOL.

The American group was more ambivalent toward ALGOL. All of its members recognized that ALGOL was an elegant synthesis, an important step forward in the crystallization of language ideas, and a great opportunity for the establishment of an international standard. However, most of the Americans at Zurich were involved in other language implementation efforts, e.g., the FORTRAN succession efforts at IBM, the UNICODE effort at Remington-Rand, and the IT-GAT-GATE developments at Carnegie Tech. They had already come to realize that language design was but the first step in a lengthy process leading to language acceptance and use. While the importance of software was not as universally appreciated then as it is now, IBM had certainly become aware of the commercial importance of FORTRAN and was considering other languages, such as Commercial Translator and COBOL, for their large data processing computer, the IBM 705. Already in 1959 in the United States there were almost two dozen groups engaged in programming language research and development, e.g., at Bendix, Burroughs, IBM, Remington-Rand and Philco (computer manufacturers); at Bell Labs, Boeing, Bureau of Standards, General Electric, Johns Hopkins Physics Lab, Los Alamos, Naval Electronics Lab, Naval Research Laboratory (research laboratories); at Carnegie Tech, Case Institute, Michigan, MIT, North Carolina, Purdue, and California (universities). For these groups, ALGOL did not necessarily fulfill the role of being the seed around which their actual programming efforts would crystallize. Instead, it was treated as a welcome abstraction, in whose terms many language and language processor issues could be treated in a machine independent way in the technical literature.

The Zurich language identified a linguistic form. During 1959, improvements, in this form were identified. These improvements, applied to ALGOL 58, led to ALGOL 60. But the simple graceful structure that was ALGOL 58 remained apparent within ALGOL 60. ALGOL 58 struck a nerve in the computer world. While it was not adequate of itself, it did foretell that what could be obtained by its careful modification would be superior to any language then known.

The Zurich language contained ambiguities, omissions, and some evidence of "linguistic schizophrenia" that aroused the interest of the European and American computer communities. These shortcomings suggested issues over which language designers have toiled ever since:

1. Lexical and dynamic scope of identifiers.
2. Lexical and dynamic control of binding. Indeed, the invention of linguistic techniques for asserting control of binding.
3. Defined types. Indeed, the prospect of programmer definable types.

During 1959 preparations were made in Europe and the United States for the next version of ALGOL. Some of these preparations have already been mentioned: Publication vehicles were set for the display of recommended changes to ALGOL 58 and the circle of contributing groups and individuals was widened. Sufficient progress in insight and interest was evident by early fall 1959 to warrant a second international meeting in Europe in early January 1960. The ACM Programming Language Committee met in Washington at the Bureau of Standards on November 5 and 6, 1959 to

1. resolve ambiguities in ALGOL 58;
2. draft a set of improvements and extensions based on items published in the *Communications* during 1959;
3. select the ACM representatives for the next European meeting.

Those present included Bemer (IBM), Evans (Bendix), Gorn (University of Pennsylvania), Rich (Johns Hopkins), Dobbs (SDC), Desilets (Remington-Rand), Goodman (Westinghouse), Levine (Philco), the Zurich Four (Backus, Katz, Perlis, and Wegstein), Green (IBM), McCarthy (MIT), and Turanski (Remington-Rand). The last seven named were chosen to attend the European meeting. They held a final preparatory meeting at MIT, November 30.

J. Wegstein proposed, and the ACM editorial board enthusiastically endorsed, on December 2, 1959, the establishment of a new department in the *Communications* for publishing algorithms in ALGOL. Other publications, e.g., *Numerische Mathematik* in Germany and BIT in Scandanavia, were to follow this same policy. Wegstein became the first editor. The alogrithms published in the *Communications* did much to enhance the popularity of ALGOL in the United States.

5. Paris and the ALGOL 60 Report

On December 19, 1959, Professor Bauer issued the letter of invitation to a meeting in Paris commencing January 11, 1960, and to be hosted by IBM World Trade Europe. William Turanski was killed in a tragic automobile accident a few days before the meeting began. The American contingent was reduced to six members. The Europeans attending the meeting were F. Bauer, H. Rutishauser, and K. Samelson, members of the Zurich conference, augmented by P. Naur (Denmark), A. van Wijngaarden (Netherlands), B. Vauquois (France), and M. Woodger (Great Britain). The participants were housed in the Hotel de Londres, where all meetings were held. Except for a daily excursion to an exterior cafeteria for lunch, the committee could be found each day hunched over global and local conference tables from post-breakfast to pre-bed. A few times a group sallied out to dinner in search of restaurant and bistro. After all, rumor had it, the meeting was being held in Paris! Even during these interludes conversation seldom strayed long from the task at hand.

The meetings were exhausting, interminable, and exhilarating. One became aggravated when one's good ideas were discarded along with the bad ones of others. Nevertheless, diligence persisted during the entire period. The chemistry of the 13 was excellent. On every point at issue there were opinions and solutions, with descriptive prose to support them that ranged from the technically clever to the breathtakingly simple. But there was rarely a complete cancellation. Progress was steady and the output, ALGOL 60, was more racehorse than camel.

This language proved to be an object of stunning beauty. It was sufficiently perfect and complete so that ensuing implementations were able to append necessities, such as input –output, in the style of ALGOL 60 but their addition propagated no significant changes in the body of the original language. Where ALGOL 58 was considered quite properly to be a draft, ALGOL 60 was appreciated, almost immediately, as a rounded work of art. It was a language from which almost every kind of computer specialist—numerical analyst, translator builder, computer designer, educator, and language theorist—could benefit.

While ALGOL 60 was no intellectual revolution, it was to become a universal tool with which to view, study, and proffer solutions to almost every kind of problem in computation. Rarely has a construction so useful and elegant emerged as the output of a committee of 13 meeting for about 8 days.

Eight reasons can be given for the success of the Paris meeting at which ALGOL 60 was defined. The committee had a good base from which to continue—ALGOL 58. Backus's IFIP paper (Backus, 1960) provided a notation in which the syntax of ALGOL 58, and its alternatives and derivatives, could be given precisely. A set of excellent proposals for consideration had accumulated during 1959. A draft organized in the style of the final report, containing the accumulated American and European proposals, was provided by Peter Naur to the committee when the meetings began. A permanent chairman, J. Wegstein, and secretary, M. Woodger, were in administrative control from the first meeting. All discussions of language issues were based on written subcommittee reports available to each member. Last, the committee was oriented scientifically and philosophically towards the definition of a useful, elegant, and artistic object.

The ALGOL 60 report (Naur *et al.*, 1960) was a fitting display for the language. Nicely organized, tantalizingly incomplete, slightly ambiguous, difficult to read, consistent in format, and brief, it was a perfect canvas for a language that possessed those same properties. Like the Bible, it was meant not merely to be read, but to be interpreted. It was no surprise that the precision with which the syntax of ALGOL 60 was defined was not attained for its semantics. Backus, in his IFIP paper, stated his intent to complement his formal syntactic description with a semantics one. Neither his nor any other adequate formal semantic definition technique was available to the ALGOL 60 designers. We now know that semantics is considerably more difficult to treat than syntax. Consequently, the semantics were given in English.

The authors wisely under-described the semantics, choosing an incomplete description, possibly leading to ambiguity, in preference to inconsistency. They can be forgiven for not being completely precise. To do so would have required agreement on a semantic model in which machine and implementation independence would have been preserved. At that time, no one knew how to define a semantic model with those properties. As a consequence, they underestimated the difficulties in getting efficient implementations of the **for** statement and evaluation of call-by-name parameters.

6. Post Paris

In the year following the publication of the ALGOL 60 report examples of ambiguity accumulated. Thus the report did not enable a reader to predict the unique value of an arithmetic expression when all of its operations and operands are specified (the issue of side effects). To some these were examples of intolerable language weakness; to others, just the opposite. ALGOL 60 was more subtle, more capable of rich interpretations, and more worthy of further scientific study than had been expected.

Many of the issues raised by ALGOL 60 have not been resolved to everyone's satisfaction to this day. Are global variables always harmful? What is the best replacement for call-by-name? Can semantics be independent of implementation? In some ways, ALGOL 60 raised as many problems as it solved. But, all along it has endured its imperfections and overshadowed its improvements.

Following the publication of the report in May 1960, ALGOL 60 entered the public domain. Its reception was not always friendly; often its weaknesses were overemphasized and its strengths were beyond the appreciation of those involved with it.

Some have said that, in the United States, ALGOL became a "political football." But it was only to those who measure progress by football results. SHARE, which enthusiastically endorsed the imperfect ALGOL 58, recoiled from the superior ALGOL 60. The on-again, romance between SHARE (and IBM) and ALGOL 60 titillated many, but was not really very important. The issues of ALGOL 60 input–output, standard subsets, and international maintenance were gradually solved in the early 1960s. But with it all, through its turbulent youth, ALGOL 60 maintained an excellent balance of trade—it exported far more to the computing world than it imported. To the ALGOL 58 terminology it added: block, call by value and call by name, typed procedures, declaration scope, dynamic arrays, **own** variables, side effects, global and local variables, primary, term, factor **step, until, while, if then else,** and bound pair. To translator technology was added the display, stack techniques, including static and dynamic level control, thunks, activation records, recursive descent parsers (Gries, 1971).

ALGOL 60 had sufficient linguistic structure to provide an incentive for the flowering of mathematical linguistics. Floyd (1962) showed that ALGOL 60, because of its declaration structure, was not context free though that fact had little effect on its parsers. It wasn't until ALGOL 68 that grammars formally exploiting declaration scope came into use (Koster *et al.,* 1969).

The Zurich language (and ALGOL 60 as well) was an invitation to implement a language processor. Later, it became an invitation to organize machines based on concepts that appeared in ALGOL—dynamic allocation of storage space for variables and data-typing (e.g., ICL, Burroughs, and Rice University efforts). Actually, some of these came from ALGOL and some from experience gained from processor implementation. ALGOL was not a partial description of an already implemented language. It opened up possibilities that were precluded for FORTRAN because of the latter's increasingly widespread use. Of course FORTRAN underwent improvements, but they were constrained by considerations arising from its heavy use: efficiency and improved control over the computer executing the object programs. FORTRAN was destined to evolve into an enormously vital computing tool, the international lingua franca of computation, the only language available on almost every computer, hence the only pragmatic medium for communicating application programs in which were accumulated the experiences of problem solvers. It was the ALGOL language that became the reference base for much of subsequent programming language development, both practical and theoretical. ALGOL's is the linguistic form most widely used in describing the new exotic alogrithms created in complexity theory. Improvements in our stock of available data processing algorithms, e.g., in sorting, graph analysis, and combinatorics, are given usually in ALGOL. Where important new linguistic inventions have occurred, they have been imbedded usually within an ALGOL framework, e.g., records, classes, definitions of types and their operations, dynamic syntax, and modules. New views of programming practice, such as structured programming and formal verification techniques, lean heavily on ALGOL-oriented programming. ALGOL has become so ingrained in our thinking about programming that we almost automatically base investigations in abstract programming on an ALGOL representation to isolate, define, and explicate our ideas. It comes as a shock to many that ALGOL is not the preferred representation for programs that investigate important programming questions, e.g., in interactive computation, in list string and array processing. Nonetheless, ALGOL deserves our affection and appreciation. It was a noble **begin** but never intended to be a satisfactory **end.**

ACKNOWLEDGMENTS

Though not cited directly in the paper, R. W. Bemer's fascinating "A Politico–Social History of Algol," *Annual Review in Automatic Programming* 5, pp. 151–238, Pergamon Press, 1969, was an invaluable source of information, about the human comedy surrounding ALGOL from conception through birth, and past toilet training.

Though their names have not figured prominently in the text, no history of ALGOL can fail to pay tribute to the special contributions of F. Bauer and the late H. Rutishauser. Rutishauser was the conscience and inspiration of both the Zurich and Paris committees. His vision of the nature and purpose of ALGOL never wavered, even when confronted with brilliant but erratic generalizations and annoying imperfections. Bauer, a man of iron will and scientific vision, guided the GAMM committee, arranged for the Zurich meeting and coaxed a wider circle of Europeans to participate in the ALGOL 60 effort. He, more than anyone else, made ALGOL a focus of attention for computer specialists in Europe.

REFERENCES

Arden, B. W., Galler, B. A., and Graham, R. M. (1961) Dec. MAD at Michigan. *Datamation* 7(12): 27–28.

Backus, John (1960). The Syntax and Semantics of the Proposed International Algebraic Language of the Zurich ACM-GAMM Conference. *Proc. International Conference Information Processing, UNESCO, Paris, 1959*, pp. 125–132.

Bemer, R. W. (1959) Apr. A Table of Symbol Pairs. *Comm. ACM* 2(4): 10–11.

Bratman, Harvey, *et al.* (1959) Oct. Recommendations of the SHARE Algol Committee. *Comm. ACM* 2(10): 25–26.

Bright, H. S. (1959) May. Card Code for IAL. *Comm. ACM* 2(5): 6–9.

Carr, John W. (1959) Feb. Recursive Subscripting Compilers and List-type Memories. *Comm. ACM* 2(2): 4–6.

Dijkstra, Edsgar W., *et al.* (1959) Algol subcommittee report—extensions. *CACM* 2(9): 24–26.

Evans, Arthur, Jr., and Perlis, Alan J. (1959) Sept. Letter to the Editor. *Comm. ACM* 2(9): 3–5.

Floyd, R. W. (1962). On the Nonexistence of a Phrase Structure Grammar for Algol 60. *Comm. ACM* 5(9): 48B.

Galler, B. A., and Perlis, A. J. (1967) Apr. A Proposal for Definitions in Algol. *Comm. ACM* 10(4): 204–219.

Green, Julien (1959a). Possible Modifications to the International Language. *Comm. ACM* 2(2): 6–8.

Green, Julien (1959b). Remarks on Algol and Symbol Manipulation. *Comm. ACM* 2(9): 24.

Gries, D. (1971). *Compiler Construction for Digital Computers.* Wiley, New York.

Huskey, H. K., Love, R., and Wirth, N. (1963) July. A Syntactic Description of BC NELIAC. *Comm. ACM* 6(7): 367–375.

Kanner, Herbert (1959) June. Letter to the Editor. *Comm. ACM* 2(6): 6–7.

Koster, C. H. A., Mailloux, B. J., Peck, J. E. L., and van Wijngaarden, A., eds. (1969). Report on the Algorithmic Language ALGOL 68. *Num. Math.* 14(2): 79–218.

McCarthy, John (1959) Aug. On Conditional Expressions and Recursive Functions (Letter). *Comm. ACM* 2(8): 2–3.

Naur, Peter, *et al.* (1960) May. Report on the Algorithmic Language Algol 60. *Comm. ACM* 3(5): 299–314. Also *Num. Math* 2: 106–136.

Perlis, A., and Samelson, K. (for the committee) (1958) Dec. Preliminary Report—International Algebraic Language. *Comm. ACM* 1(12): 8–22. Also (1959) Jan. Report on the Algorithmic Language Algol. *Num. Math.* 1: 41–60.

Shaw, C. J. (1963) Dec. A Specification of JOVIAL. *Comm. ACM* 6(12): 721–736.

Taranto, D., (1959) Binary conversion, with fixed decimal precision, of a decimal fraction. *CACM* 2(7): 27.

Williams, Franas A. (1959) June. Handling Identifiers as Internal Symbols in Language Processors. *Comm. ACM* 2(7): 27.

Peter Naur

PAPER: THE EUROPEAN SIDE OF THE LAST PHASE OF THE DEVELOPMENT OF ALGOL 60

Peter Naur

Copenhagen University
Copenhagen, Denmark

Introduction

In preparing this account of some of the developments leading to ALGOL 60, I have primarily sought to present such relevant information that is readily available to myself, but not otherwise accessible or well known. In addition I have tried to answer the specific questions formulated by the organizers of the Conference on the History of Programming Languages. The notes fall in three freely intermixed groups: those that relate to existing documents; those that reflect my own reasoning as a participant in the development, and those that try to answer the organizers' questions. Where the proper support has been lacking, I have left open holes in the presentation. Otherwise I have tried to be specific, giving names, dates, and reasons, as far as I have them available.

While this manner of presentation seems to me the best way to support more penetrating historical research into the period, it is also bound to give rise to controversy. First, it is openly one-sided, in the manner that any autobiography is. Further, by being specific, the presentation will offer sensitive points of attack to those who see the same development from a different angle and with different eyes. When these circumstances are combined with real events that involved differences of opinion and interest, strong reactions are bound to be provoked. This emerged clearly in the remarks from the reviewers of the draft of this paper.

In dealing with the reviewers' remarks I have decided to a large extent to leave my original formulation unchanged and to include the remarks in appendices to the paper. This seems to be the most consistent way to extend the scope of the account so as to include the views of others.

It should be made clear that my account is essentially incomplete in that the important European development that preceded the Zurich report is only briefly sketched in the quotation from H. Rutishauser's book given in Section 1.1 (cf. Appendix 5, Bauer's Point 1.1). My original plan was to include a detailed analysis of the documents from the time. However, when the original documents came into my hand, I had also seen the reactions of my colleagues to the first draft of my account. These latter made me realize that I would be the wrong person to report on the events happening before February 1959 when I joined the effort. Thus, although with regret, I decided to leave the account in its present incomplete state.

I wish to thank the language coordinator, David Gries, and the reviewers, F. L. Bauer, B. A. Galler, J. Sammet, and J. H. Wegstein, for their many useful notes on the draft. I am particularly grateful to Mike Woodger for his generous help in placing information and original documents at my disposal and for his encouragement. I also wish to thank P. Läuchli and K. Samelson for lending me original documents. The notes in Appendices 4, 5, 6, and 7, appear by permission from their authors.

My participation in the History of Programming Languages Conference is supported by Statens teknisk-videnskabelige forskningsråd, Copenhagen.

1. Background

1.1. The Roots and an Overview (Quotation from H. Rutishauser)

In the present account of the development of ALGOL 60, the center of attention will be the last phase in which the present writer took part. What went before that was highly significant, but since I cannot contribute to its description with anything that relates to my firsthand experience I shall cover the early phases with the aid of a quotation of a brief history of the complete development of the language, written by H. Rutishauser, one of the initiators of the language, who died in 1970. The quotation is taken from Rutishauser (1967) (cf. Appendix 5, Bauer's point 2.1). It has been edited to avoid footnotes and to give references to those original documents from the time that are known to me. Rutishauser writes:

§2. Historical Remarks on Algorithmic Languages

The very first attempt to devise an algorithmic language was undertaken in 1948 by K. Zuse (1948–1949). His notation was quite general, but the proposal never attained the consideration it deserved.

In 1951 the present author tried to show that in principle a general purpose computer could translate an algorithmic language into machine code. (Lecture at the GAMM (Gesellschaft für angewandte Mathematik und Mechanik) meeting, Freiburg i Br. March 28–31, 1951. Published in Rutishauser (1952)). However, the algorithmic language proposed in this paper was quite restricted; it allowed only evaluation of simple formulae and automatic loop control (it contained essentially the for-statement of ALGOL 60). Besides that, the translation method was intermixed with the idea of a *stretched program,* which at that time certainly had some merit as a timesaving device (see Rutishauser, 1953) but was not essential for the purpose to be achieved. For these and other reasons this paper did not receive much attention either.

In 1954 Corrado Boehm published a method to translate algebraic formulae into computer notation [Böhm (1954) officially presented at the ETH on July 10, 1952, as a thesis]. He considered neither subscripted variables nor loop control, but his method to break up formulae into machine instructions was at this state a noteworthy step towards the *pushdown methods* described by Samelson and Bauer (1959, 1960). Further early attempts to translate mathematical formulae into machine code were made in 1952 by A. E. Glennie (unpublished report) in England and in 1953 by A. A. Liapunov [cited in the introduction to Ershov (1959)] in Russia.

Thus by 1954 the idea of using the computer for assisting the programmer had been seriously considered in Europe, but apparently none of these early algorithmic languages was ever put to actual use.

The situation was quite different in the USA, where an assembly language epoch preceded the introduction of algorithmic languages. To some extent this may have diverted attention and energy from the latter, but on the other hand it helped to make automatic programming popular in the USA. Thus, when in 1954 Laning and Zierler (Adams and Laning, 1954) presented their algorithmic language—the first one ever actually used—and shortly thereafter the IBM FORTRAN System (IBM, 1954) was announced, the scientific world was prepared for this new concept.

Meanwhile at Darmstadt an international symposium on automatic computing was held in Oct., 1955 [the proceedings of this meeting are collected in Hoffmann and Walther (1956)], where, among other things, algorithmic languages and their translation into machine code were also discussed. Several speakers [mentioned in the proceedings: H. Rutishauser, A. Walther, and J. Heinhold] stressed the need for focusing attention on unification, that is, on *one universal, machine-*

independent algorithmic language to be used by all, rather than to devise several such languages in competition. This became the guiding idea of a working group called the *GAMM Subcommittee for Programming Languages,* which was set up after the Darmstadt meeting in order to design such a universal algorithmic language. [GAMM stands for Gesellschaft für angewandte Mathematik und Mechanik, i.e., Society for applied mathematics and mechanics. The proceedings of the Darmstadt meeting mention the formation of a GAMM committee for programming, chairman J. Heinhold, members H. Rutishauser and H. Unger].

This subcommittee had nearly completed its detailed work in the autumn of 1957, when its members, aware of the many algorithmic languages already in existence, concluded that, rather than present still another such language, they should make an effort towards worldwide unification. [cf. Appendix 5, Bauer's point 2.2]. Consequently, they suggested to Prof. J. W. Carr, then president of the ACM (Association for Computing Machinery), that a joint conference of representatives of the ACM and the GAMM be held in order to fix upon a common algorithmic language. This proposal received vivid interest by the ACM. Indeed, at a conference attended by representatives of the USE, SHARE, and DUO organisations and of the ACM, the conferees had likewise felt that a universal algorithmic language would be very desirable. As a result of this conference, the ACM formed a committee which also worked out a proposal for such a language.

§3. The ALGOL Conferences of 1958, 1960, 1962

At that point, direct contact between the GAMM subcommittee was established through F. L. Bauer in April, 1958, when he presented the GAMM proposal [presumably based on Bauer *et al.* (1958a)] at a Philadelphia meeting of the ACM group. A comparison of the proposals of the ACM and the GAMM indicated many common features. The ACM proposal was based on experience with several successful algorithmic languages. On the other hand, the GAMM subcommittee had worked for a much longer time at their proposal and had from the very beginning the universality of the language in mind.

3.1. ALGOL 58

Both the GAMM and ACM representatives felt that, because of the similarities of their proposals, there was an excellent opportunity for arriving at a unified language. They felt that a joint working session would be very profitable and accordingly arranged for a conference to be attended by four members of the ACM committee and four members of the GAMM subcommittee.

The meeting was held at Zurich, Switzerland, from May 27 until June 2, 1958, and was attended by F. L. Bauer, H. Bottenbruch, H. Rutishauser, and K. Samelson of the GAMM subcommittee, and by J. Backus, C. Katz, A. J. Perlis, and J. H. Wegstein of the ACM committee. (In addition to the members of the conference, the following persons participated in the preparatory work of the committees: GAMM: P. Graeff, P. Läuchli, M. Paul, F. Penzlin; ACM: D. Arden, J. McCarthy, R. Rich, R. Goodman, W. Turanski, S. Rosen, P. Desilets, S. Gorn, H. Huskey, A. Orden, D. C. Evans). It was agreed that the contents of the two proposals (Backus *et al.*, 1958; Bauer *et al.*, 1958b) should form the agenda of the meeting and the following objectives were agreed upon:

(a) The new language should be as close as possible to standard mathematical notation and be readable with little further explanation.

(b) It should be possible to use it for the description of numerical processes in publications.

(c) The new language should be readily translatable into machine code by the machine itself.

At this conference [unpublished proceedings: Zurich Conference (1958)] it was soon felt that the discrepancies between the notations used in publications on the one hand and the characters available on input/output mechanisms for computers on the other hand were a serious hindrance and might virtually prevent agreement upon a universal algorithmic language. It was therefore decided [cf. Appendix 4, Wegstein's point 1] to disregard printing usage and properties of input/output mechanisms and to focus attention upon an abstract representation (in the sense of a defining standard), called a *reference language,* from which appropriate *publication and hardware* languages might be derived later as isomorphic descendants of the reference language. (For the relation between reference, publication and hardware language, see Backus *et al.* (1959). It should be recognized that experience has shown that ALGOL programs may well be published in the reference language, and therefore extra publication languages are in fact unnecessary. On the other hand, hardware languages have proved necessary to such an extent that it was decided to standardize a few carefully selected hardware representation of the ALGOL symbols.) The notion was, therefore, that reference, publication and hardware languages should be three levels of one and the same language; the conference, however, would then discuss only the reference language. Accordingly, the algorithmic language ALGOL [on the origin of this name see Appendix 4, Wegstein's point 2 and Appendix 5, Bauer's point 2.2a], which was agreed upon at this conference and published in the ALGOL report (Backus *et al.,* 1959), is defined only on the reference level.

After publication of the ALGOL report (Backus *et al.,* 1959) much interest in the language ALGOL developed. At the initiative of P. Naur an ALGOL Bulletin (1959) was issued which served as a forum for discussing properties of the language and for propagating its use. The Communications of the ACM introduced an algorithm-section, in which numerical processes are described in terms of ALGOL. Elsewhere ALGOL was also used more and more for describing computing processes.

On the other hand it was soon found that certain definitions given in the ALGOL-58 report were either incomplete or even contradictory or otherwise unsatisfactory for the description of numerical processes. As a consequence many proposals were made to remove these defects (most of these proposals have been published in the *Communications of the ACM,* Vol. 2 (1959) and/or in the *ALGOL Bulletin,* No. 7).

3.2. ALGOL 60

In view of the constructive criticism that evolved and the proposals made, it was decided that another international ALGOL conference should take place. Accordingly, the GAMM subcommittee organized a preliminary meeting at Paris in Nov. of 1959, attended by about 50 participants from Western Europe, from which 7 delegates for the final ALGOL conference were selected. The ACM committee likewise selected 7 delegates at a preparatory meeting held in Washington D.C. at the same time. Both the European and the USA delegation made proposals for removing the inconsistencies from the ALGOL report and also for making changes in the language. These proposals took the criticisms as much as possible into consideration.

The conference, held at Paris, Jan. 11–16, 1960, was attended by J. W. Backus, F. L. Bauer, J. Green, C. Katz, J. McCarthy, P. Naur, A. J. Perlis, H. Rutishauser, K. Samelson, B. Vauquois, J. H. Wegstein, A. van Wijngaarden, M. Woodger (W. Turanski of the American delegation was fatally injured in an automobile accident just prior to the Paris conference). The proposals worked out prior to the conference again formed the agenda of the meeting, but in addition the conferees had at their disposal a completely new draft report prepared by P. Naur (ALGOL 60 document 5), which served as a basis for discussion during the conference.

From the beginning it was obvious that rather than just adding a few corrections to ALGOL 58, it was necessary to redesign the language from the bottom up. This was done, and accordingly ALGOL 60, as the language emerging from the Paris conference is officially called, was in many respects entirely different from ALGOL 58. It is defined on the reference level in the ALGOL-60 report (Backus *et al.,* 1960) edited by P. Naur. Since publication of the report, ALGOL 58 has become obsolete, but many of its features have been carried over into other algorithmic languages.

Here ends the quotation from Rutishauser.

In accordance with this description ALGOL 60 is the name of a notation for expressing computational processes, irrespective of any particular uses or computer implementations. This meaning of the name will be retained throughout the present account.

1.2. Centers and Individuals

ALGOL 60 was developed as an international, noncommercial, mainly informal, scientific activity of a unique kind, involving a number of computation centers or individuals associated with such centers. The central planning and control included mainly the organization of meetings and some publication. The necessary support was obtained locally and individually from the supporting computation centers or from research grant organizations. Most of the concepts of conventional projects, such as cost estimates and budget control, were never applied to the development activity as a whole. For this reason no meaningful estimate of the total cost can be made.

The organizational nature of the participating centers differed widely. Appendix 1, Table 1, gives the identity and a few notes about the European centers, including the names of the associated individuals. Appendix 1, Table 2, lists all individuals whose names appear somewhere in the available records, and their organization where known.

1.3. The Committees

Organizationally the development leading to ALGOL 60 had four phases:

1. 1955–1958 April: Preparatory work in several committees. In Europe: GAMM committee.
2. 1958 April–1959 January: The combined GAMM–ACM committee develops ALGOL 58, described in the Zurich report (Backus *et al.*, 1959).
3. 1959 February–1959 November: Open discussion of the Zurich report.
4. 1959 December–1960 March: The combined European–American ALGOL 60 committee develops ALGOL 60.

The work was started by some of the individuals who had originated the idea of it, notably H. Rutishauser, F. L. Bauer, and K. Samelson. This led to the formation of the GAMM subcommittee, having F. L. Bauer as chairman. This subcommittee made a deliberate effort to widen the circle of interest and support to suitable organizations in various European countries. This effort became effective from the later part of 1958. Thus a discussion of implementation problems taking place in Mainz, 1958 November 21, was attended by: B. Vauquois, Grenoble; P. J. Landin, London; W. Heise, Copenhagen; M. Woodger, Teddington; R. Basten, Stuttgart; K. Leipold, Munich; M. Poyen, Paris; W. Händler, Backnang; H. Rutishauser, Zurich; E. W. Dijkstra, Amsterdam; G. Ehrling, Stockholm; H. Bottenbruch, Darmstadt; K. Samelson, Mainz; F. L. Bauer, Mainz; Th. Fromme, Bad Hersfeld; M. Paul, Mainz. (Concerning ALGOL 58 implementation in Europe, see appendix 5, Bauer's point 2.2a.)

During the period of open discussion, 1959 February to November, any volunteer had the opportunity to contribute to the discussion channeled through the *ALGOL Bulletin*.

The selection of the European participants in the final ALGOL 60 committee was made in November 1959, during the open meeting taking place in Paris. The selection was proposed by the European participants at the Zurich meeting and endorsed by the full meeting. The idea behind the selection clearly was to make such additions to the earlier committee that would extend the geographical basis, as far as possible. The total number was limited to seven, by agreement with the ACM committee. Since H. Bottenbruch of the earlier committee wished to withdraw from the work the original members H. Rutishauser (Switzerland), F. L. Bauer (Germany), and K. Samelson (Germany), could be supplemented by the following four: P. Naur (Denmark), B. Vauquois (France), A. van Wijngaarden (Netherlands), and M. Woodger (Great Britain). This committee of seven met 1959 December 14–16 in Mainz and joined the ACM committee in the 1960 January 11–16 meeting in Paris. During these meetings there were no observers and the members acted essentially as equal individuals.

1.4. Contributors' Attitudes

The European participants in the work on ALGOL 60 shared, as the common idea, the belief in, and willingness to contribute to, a common programming language. Apart from that the attitudes differed widely from one participant to another. Some participants had worked on the principles of compiler construction, as described in the quotation from Rutishauser given in Section 1.1 above. (See also Appendix 5, Bauer's point 2.3.) There was hardly any clear distinction between language designers, implementors, and users; most participants in the work saw themselves potentially in all three roles, or at least in two of them. This also meant that the design of the language had regard to the problems of implementation. The concrete effects of this are difficult to identify, however. It is probably true to say that there was a general conviction that by limiting the number of mechanisms of the language and by adhering to a clear, systematic structure the problems of implementation would tend to stay within reasonable bounds.

1.5. Time Constraints

The final design of ALGOL 60 was scheduled during the 1959 June UNESCO conference in Paris. It was decided that proposals for the final language were to be collected until November 1959 and that a final design conference should be held in early 1960. The time limits thus imposed probably acted more as a spur than as a constraint on the design work. There is no reason to assume that a less tight schedule would have helped to remove the differences of the designers' opinions concerning the final language. Again, the reasons for the deliberate omissions from the final language, in particular details of input and output mechanisms (cf. Section 2.8 below), were probably only partly the tightness of schedule.

1.6. Discussion Techniques

In the present section on the manner in which the European discussions that led to ALGOL 60 were conducted, I shall give myself free rein in accounting for my motivations and feelings. This mode of presentation may give offense to my own modesty and the reader's sense of propriety. However, it appears to me necessary as a clue to several of the events in the development of ALGOL 60 with which I was mostly concerned. (See also Appendix 6, M. Woodger's note 1.)

As to the objective significance of the discussion techniques, it seems fairly clear that the strong emphasis on rapid exchanges of written formulations had a substantial influence on the development of the language itself. Besides, an account of the forms of discussion will make it clear how the later stages of the shaping of language ideas remains readily accessible from original documents.

Until the Mainz gathering November 1958 and the European ALGOL implementation conference 1959 February in Copenhagen, the European discussions had been concentrated in the closed GAMM committee. At the meeting in February 1959 the subject had been made open for discussion by the appearance of the Zurich report on ALGOL 58 in *Numerische Mathematik*. Much of the discussion at that meeting took the form of questions to the authors of the Zurich report from a wider audience, who had had the report available for a period of a month or two. During this meeting I developed an acute feeling of frustration because of the discussion form. I felt strongly that a verbal discussion was inadequate in settling the complicated questions, and in particular that the answers given to concrete queries were unsatisfactory because the time for their preparation was too short. In response to this feeling I developed the idea of a series of discussion letters, to be the medium for a more satisfactory form of discussion. This idea of an *ALGOL Bulletin,* to be circulated from Regnecentralen, was received positively, first by Niels Ivar Bech, the head of Regnecentralen where I was employed, and then by the group of implementors centered around F. L. Bauer and K. Samelson.

With this support I quickly formulated the rules of operation of the *ALGOL Bulletin,* which were stated in the first issue, of 1959 March 16. Among these rules, which run to two full pages, the most noteworthy are those that stress the clear division of contributions into separate parts, according to subject, each with an appropriate heading and separately numbered. I was much concerned with achieving a division of the debate into manageable units, so that lengthy repetitions of statements of a problem could mostly be replaced by brief reference to the "Zurich report" and to previous discussion.

The *ALGOL Bulletin* met with an active, positive response. A subcommittee on ALGOL at the UNESCO conference in Paris, members E. W. Dijkstra, W. Heise, A. J. Perlis, and K. Samelson, adopted the *ALGOL Bulletin* as the official collector in the eastern hemisphere of suggestions concerning the language (AB 4.1, 1959, June 15–20). Its contents during the period leading up to the period of meetings starting in November 1959 can be summarized as follows:

The ALGOL Bulletin

No.	Date of issue (1959)	Number of pages	Number of separate items of technical discussion
1	March 16	6	3
2	May 5	8	15
3	June 8	6	9
4	August 13	7	12
5	September 28	9	22
6	October 17	2	0
7	November 3	21	48

A major influence on the way ALGOL 60 was eventually described came from the paper given at the 1959 June UNESCO conference in Paris by John Backus (1959). To me personally this paper was in the first instance a disappointing surprise because of the lack of agreement between the language described in it and that of the Zurich report. This indicated that the common understanding among the members of the Zurich committee did not by far include everything that seemed clear enough in the Zurich report. As another disappointment, Backus's report did not contribute much to resolving the more subtle questions already raised by the Zurich report.

All this indicated to me the crying need for integrating the formulation of a precise and complete language description into the actual language development process. I was led to the conviction that the formulation of a clear and complete description was more important than any particular characteristic of the language.

Only in October 1959, during a second phase of studying Backus's Paris report, did I penetrate through his formal, syntactic description. This made me realize that his notation would be a highly valuable tool for the kind of description that I had in mind. However, this still left me with the problem of how to go about making the ALGOL committee actually use this notation and the precise prose formulations that would have to go along with it.

In this situation I seriously considered making an appeal to the members of the ALGOL committee concerning the style of the language description. However, before getting that far I concluded that the matter was too difficult to be solved just by an appeal and an explanation. The only hope was for me to produce samples of what was needed in a form that by its inherent quality would carry the day. In particular, I realized that it would be crucial to my plan that a substantial part of the new language description be written before the final meeting of the ALGOL committee in January 1960.

My situation was decisively improved when, during the November 1959 meeting in Paris, I was made a member of the ALGOL committee. In this way I took part in the meeting of the European part of the committee in Mainz in December 1959. This meeting was almost exclusively concerned with problems that led to the structure of blocks and procedures (cf. Section 2.10 below). The use of Backus's notation could only be mentioned in passing; my recommendation to that effect appears as one of 55 brief notes on revisions of the Zurich report as follows: "15) Change the syntactical description" (ALGOL 60 document 4A); Backus's notation was not used in the proposals from the meeting (ALGOL 60 document 2). (For another view of this see Appendix 5, Bauer's point 2.4.) The decisive action concerning the development of the new style of description was taken during the weeks following the Mainz meeting, when I worked out the results of this meeting according to the notions of language description that I had formed. In order to press the matter forward as much as possible, on January 2 I sent all other committee members a document of seven tightly typed pages, including samples of my proposed descriptions (ALGOL 60 document 3). This document contains the first appearance of my slightly revised form of Backus's notation (cf. Appendix 2; also Appendix 5, Bauer's point 2.6). The main result of this work was the 18-page draft report that I finished on January 9 and took along to the Paris meeting (ALGOL 60 document 5). This was structured in the manner known from the final report on ALGOL 60, and thus includes the partitioning into subsections giving syntax, examples, and semantics.

As was to be expected the meeting of the ALGOL committee in Paris, 1960 January 11–16, was dominated by intense and often heated discussions of the various characteristics of the language. Meetings of the full committee were chaired by Joe Wegstein, with Mike Woodger as secretary. Quite a number of questions were delegated to subcommittees, however. The results of the subcommittees were expressed in reports (ALGOL 60 documents 9, 11, 12, 15–18, 26, 27), while the minutes of the meetings were never made available to the members (see, however, Woodger, 1960).

As to the choice of notation and style of the description of the new language, my preparations were met with a response that was positive beyond my expectations. In fact, on the fourth day of the meeting the committee decided to take over my draft report (ALGOL 60 document 5) as the basis of the discussion of the new language, in preference to the Zurich report; moreover, I was invited to be the editor of the report of the meeting (for another view of this, see Appendix 5, Bauer's point 2.5). In order to support me in this capacity, I was given the option to decide on the most suitable mode of operation of the committee in discussing those parts of the language that were described in reasonably finished drafts. The procedure that I chose for this purpose was as follows. In a first phase the full meeting would read a suitable section of the documentation and have a brief discussion for clarification and insertion of corrections, but not for changes. In a second phase each member, working individually, would develop his proposals for changes in the form of written, concrete rewordings of the existing document. These proposals were collected by me, sorted and numbered according to subject, and typed in a copy for each member (ALGOL 60 document 31). In a third phase the full meeting would go through these proposals and would decide on each of them, usually by voting. This procedure was quite effective. Through the insistence on formulations in the form of wordings to the final report each member was urged to clarify his proposals to himself before proposing them to the full meeting, thus saving much time. A total of 80 proposals, many of them quite short, were formulated and decided upon, and this made the final editing of the bulk of the report of the meeting an easy matter. For myself as editor the procedure had the great advantage that in most matters I could proceed with confidence that the wishes of the committee were expressed clearly and positively.

1.7. Influence from Other Languages

It is probably true to say that the collective knowledge of the total group of participants in the development of ALGOL 60 included all there was to be known about programming languages at the time. However, the knowledge of each individual was mostly far more limited. My own experience stemmed primarily from my work with the EDSAC, Cambridge, England, in 1951 and 1953. This had given me a strong impression of the importance of closed subroutines, including the use of what in retrospect may be described as parameters called by name (Naur, 1977). Of later developments I had a reading acquaintance with R. A. Brooker's Autocode for the Manchester Mark I machine and with the first version of FORTRAN, but I had not tried to use them.

Undoubtedly, for the many participants who became active in the work after late 1958, the language ALGOL 58 as described in the Zurich report was the major influence, since this was the declared basis of the discussion.

1.8. Intended Purpose of ALGOL 60

The declared purpose of the development work on ALGOL has been stated in the quotation from Rutishauser given in Section 1.1. To this two remarks will be made.

First, the intended application area of the language is to some extent implicit in the historical situation. When talking about "standard mathematical notation" and "numerical processes," it is understood that the problem area is what later came to be known as "processes of numerical analysis" or even "scientific computing." The point is that at the time other application fields were only just emerging and not well understood. Scientific computing, on the other hand, could be based on an old tradition of computational methods derived as a part of mathematical analysis. The influence from this area on ALGOL 60 is clear partly from the fact that several of the most active contributors were also active in numerical analysis, and partly from the choice of subject of the sample programs given with the description of the language.

Second, the declared purpose of ALGOL includes potentials for contradictions of a fairly deep kind. These may be seen to lie at the root of at least some of the more persistent conflicts in the development of the language. The conflict arises between some view of what constitutes "standard mathematical notation" and some view of what is required of a language that is to be "readily translatable into machine code." An expression of this conflict is the difference between viewing a function as a closed transformation of a given input to yield a certain output and viewing it as a more or less open computational process that conceivably may have side effects. This conflict had a significant influence on the discussion leading to the procedure concept of ALGOL 60.

The users were often, but by no means exclusively, a direct concern in the design of the language. The declared objectives include that the language should be "readable with little further explanation." In the discussions of the details a recurrent theme is whether a feature or notation will enhance the readability.

2. Rationale of Content of Language

2.1. From Zurich Report to ALGOL 60: Topics and Treatment

The present account will be concerned almost exclusively with the development leading from the language described in the Zurich report (Backus *et al.*, 1959) to the language ALGOL 60 (Backus *et al.*, 1960). One reason for concentrating on this second phase in the development is that, at least in its European part, it includes the development of some of the most striking and original parts of the language, namely, block structure, with dynamic arrays and localization of the scope of entities, and procedures, with name-call of parameters and recursive activations. A further reason is that the development, which depends on many individual contributions, can be traced fairly accurately in the existing documentation. This means that the rationale behind the language can be displayed very concretely.

A subdivision of the description according to subject cannot be carried very far, because of the close interconnection between several of the most important issues. In the following sections several minor questions that can be treated separately are first discussed. This is followed in Section 2.10 by a discussion of the complex of questions related to the large-scale structure of programs.

The account will be based directly on the documents from the time, in particular the *ALGOL Bulletin* (1959). References to this series of documents will be given in the form "AB <section number>, <date>", where the date gives the time of writing.

2.2. Declaration of Named Constants

The discussion of declarations of named constants (or initializations) developed in a curious way. The SAAB group (AB 2.6, 2.7, 1959, Apr. 22) suggested that certain numbers,

Peter Naur

such as the mathematicians' π and e, should be made a fixed part of the language, and further that the language should give means for initialization of both simple and subscripted variables. The first of these proposals was rejected by a large majority after a brief discussion (AB 4.4, 1959, June).

Declarations of named constants were again recommended by E. W. Dijkstra, W. Heise, A. J. Perlis, and K. Samelson, forming a subcommittee at the UNESCO conference in Paris (AB 4.7, 1959, June 15–20). A question about the meaning of this proposal in case of an attempted assignment of a new value to the constant was posed by the group at Regnecentralen (AB 5.3.2, 1959, Sept. 10). This question was given two different answers by Rutishauser (AB 7.7, 1959, Oct. 21) and by the SAAB group (AB 7.48, 1959, Nov. 2). Otherwise the suggestion to have named constants met with approval. It also appears in the proposals from the American participants in the ALGOL 60 conference (ALGOL 60 document 6).

In spite of the general support of the idea the proposal to include it in the language was rejected on the last day of the meeting of the ALGOL 60 committee.

2.3 Arithmetic Expressions

The question of the meaning of an assignment of a real value to a variable declared integer was brought up by Naur (AB 4.15, 1959, July 1). In reply, Rutishauser stated that implicit rounding is performed (AB 5.10, 1959, Sept. 10). During the final ALGOL 60 conference the question of arithmetic expressions and assignments was discussed in a subcommittee, members: P. Naur, A. J. Perlis (ALGOL 60 document 16). The report of this subcommittee describes all combinations of arithmetic types and operators and identifies four alternatives for the assignment of a real value to an integer declared variable. In the absence of Rutishauser the meeting voted to leave this assignment undefined. Later the same day the issue was reopened by an appeal from Rutishauser: "Since I believe it is a grave error, I propose to accept possibility 2a [implicit rounding] of 2.5 in place of possibility 1 [undefined]." (ALGOL 60 document 31, item $\infty - 1$). This change of an earlier decision was then adopted by the full meeting.

2.4. Inclusion of Additional Types

A proposal to go beyond the basic types, Boolean, integer, and real, was made by Garwick (AB 4.16, 1959, Aug. 6). He suggested that the use of the Boolean operators with operands of type integer should be understood as manipulation of bit patterns. The suggestion was opposed by the Mailüfterl group (AB 5.11.1, 1959, Sept. 7) and by Rutishauser (AB 5.11.2, 1959, Sept. 10), whose objection was that with these operations the machine independence of ALGOL would be lost.

A more ambitious proposal for inclusion of additional types was made by A. van Wijngaarden and E. W. Dijkstra (AB 7.35, 1959, Oct.). They mentioned, "e.g., complex numbers, vectors, matrices, lists (sets) of quantities." The proposal is supported by a few, brief remarks about how the operators could be applicable "in the conventional meaning." The proposal does not seem to have stirred much attention during the discussions of the following months; the necessary understanding of user needs and implementation methods was lacking.

At the final ALGOL 60 conference J. Backus thought it was important to include string handling capabilities but "didn't try very hard to get together a good string proposal" (Backus, 1979). As a result string facilities were included in the final language only in the form of string constants used as parameters of procedure calls.

2.5. Simple Control Statements

A significant simplification in the area of simple execution control statements was achieved mostly through the medium of the *ALGOL Bulletin*. The start was made by Bring and Ehrling who suggested that the STOP of the Zurich report should be interpreted as a pause waiting for a restart signal, and that there was a need for DUMMY statement similar to FORTRAN's CONTINUE (AB 2.3 and 2.4., 1959, Apr.).

The new interpretation of the STOP statement met with some support but was opposed by Bauer and Samelson (AB 3.2.2, 1959, June 1), who suggested that the function of the proposed statement was fully covered by normal input functions.

As the next step in the discussion of STOP, Samelson suggested that STOP has essentially the same function as RETURN (AB 7.27, 1959, Oct.). Finally, during the ALGOL 60 conference Rutishauser suggested that RETURN is unnecessary (ALGOL 60 document 20; see also section 2.10 item 43 below). Thus both STOP and RETURN were found to be superfluous.

In response to the suggestion for a DUMMY statement Rutishauser, opposing the form of the original suggestion, suggested that the desired effect could be achieved by admitting the blank between two semicolons to act as a statement (AB 3.4, 1959, May 21). This suggestion was met with positive response from many sides.

2.6. The For Statement

The Zurich report described the controlling part of repetitive statements as " 'For' statements." M. Woodger, P. Landin, E. W. Dijkstra, and A. van Wijngaarden during the meeting in Copenhagen, 1959 February 27, suggested that these and similar parts of the language should belong to a separate category of the syntactic skeleton, quantifier statements. In the same vein K. Samelson suggested that the proper syntactic class of these parts is that of a clause (AB 7.26, 1959, Oct.).

The Zurich report permitted the repetitions of a for statement to be controlled either by a list of expressions or by a list of step-until elements. E. W. Dijkstra, W. Heise, A. J. Perlis, and K. Samelson, forming a subcommittee at the UNESCO conference in Paris, suggested that control by a list having an aribitrary mixture of the two kinds of elements should be permitted (AB 4.11, 1959, June 15–20).

J. Garwick and H. Rutishauser independently suggested that when the list defined by a step-until element is empty no executions of the controlled statement should take place (AB 7.14 and 7.15, 1959, Oct.).

In the Zurich report the three expressions of a step-until element were separated by parenthesis, with A **step** B **until** C being written $A(B)C$. This use of parentheses clearly may become confused with their use in function designators. A proposal to change the notation by using apostrophes instead of parentheses was made by the Siemens group (AB 7.29, 1959, Oct. 27). The final form of the for statement was based mostly on American proposals (ALGOL 60 documents 7, 25).

2.7. Conditional Statements

The Zurich report had an if statement and an alternative statement. A proposal to combine these and to admit also conditional expressions was made by K. Samelson (AB 7.25, 1959, Oct.). This agreed well with American proposals (ALGOL 60 document 6) and was adopted in the final language.

2.8. Machine-Dependent Auxiliary Information

The suggestion that programs might include auxiliary information that might serve certain machine-dependent purposes was made by E. W. Dijkstra, W. Heise, A. J. Perlis, and K. Samelson, forming a subcommittee during the UNESCO conference in Paris (AB 4.13, 1959, June 15–20). Proposals about how to understand this suggestion in more detail were made by the group at Regnecentralen (AB 5.8, 1959, Sept. 1, and 7.38, 1959, Oct. 15). Some of these proposals met with positive response but did not find their way to the final report on the language.

2.9. Input and Output

The Zurich report states that input and output operations will be taken care of by means of procedure declarations that are partly expressed in a different language than ALGOL itself. A suggestion for a manner in which input and output might be expressed in the language itself was made by E. W. Dijkstra, W. Heise, A. J. Perlis, and K. Samelson forming a subcommittee at the UNESCO conference in Paris (AB 4.6, 1959, June 15–20). This suggestion was clearly modeled on FORTRAN, and used format statements. This suggestion was incorporated in the draft report used as the basis for the ALGOL 60 conference (ALGOL 60 document 5). However, that conference decided to reject the proposal after hardly any discussion.

2.10. Blocks and Procedures

The present section, which accounts for the development of the intricate problems of blocks and procedures, is divided into 52 subsections, each corresponding to a separate contribution to the events.

1. The Zurich report (Backus *et al.*, 1959). For an understanding of the development during 1959 a fairly detailed knowledge of the relevant parts of the Zurich report is indispensable. In Appendix 3, full quotations from the Zurich report are given. These quotations are briefly and informally summarized below. The quotations and the summaries are similarly divided into sections numbered 1.1 to 1.7.

1.1. A *function* with parameters, e.g., $F(a,b,c)$, yields a single value, obtained through an application of the rules of a corresponding function or procedure declaration to the parameters. Certain functions have fixed meanings, e.g. abs, sign, entier, sqrt, and sin.

1.2. Any sequence of statements may be used to form a *compound statement,* e.g., **begin** A; B; C **end.**

1.3. A *procedure statement,* e.g., $P(a,b) =: (c,d)$, calls for the activation of a corresponding process, defined by a procedure declaration, using a and b as input parameters and c and d as output parameters. Very flexible parameter correspondences are permitted. As an example, an actual parameter of the form $A(p, \quad , \quad)$ may correspond with a formal parameter $F(\quad , \quad)$ since both have two empty positions. Certain procedures may be available without declaration and may perform input and output operations. During the activation of the procedure the formal parameters are replaced by the corresponding actual parameters, replacement being understood as symbol substitution. Return statements are replaced by suitable goto statements.

1.4. *Declarations* may be written anywhere and pertain to the entire program or procedure in which they occur. Their effect is independent of the state of execution of the program.

1.5. In *array declarations* the subscript bounds must be given as integer constants.

1.6. A *function declaration*, e.g, $G(u) := u + 3/h$, defines the rules for obtaining the values of the corresponding functions. The rule must be of the form of a single expression. This may contain the formal parameters and other variables, sometimes known as hidden parameters of the function.

1.7. A *procedure declaration* defines the actions activated by the corresponding procedure statements and functions by means of a series of statements. The heading of the declaration defines the forms of corresponding procedure statements and functions, each having certain inputs, outputs, and exits as parameters. One procedure declaration may define several different procedures and functions, having different names, entry points, and parameter lists. The procedure heading contains declarations concerning parameters. An array declaration concerning a parameter may contain expressions in its subscript bounds. All identifiers used within the statements of the procedure declaration have identity only within the procedure. The statements of the procedure declaration may be expressed in a language other than ALGOL.

Here end the summaries of the parts of the Zurich report.

The Zurich report is dated 1958 October 20 and became widely available in Europe around 1959 February 1. During the meeting in Copenhagen, 1959 February 26–28, requests for clarifications and proposals for modifications were discussed. No official proceedings of this meeting were produced, but the main points of the discussions are identified in a set of notes taken by M. Woodger (1959b). Apart from a question from A. van Wijngaarden concerning the possibility of jumping to a label inside a compound statement, thus avoiding entry through the **begin,** these notes indicate little that relates to the later discussions of blocks and procedures.

The following points 2 to 32 are abstracts of the contributions to the *ALGOL Bulletin* concerning procedures and what later became known as blocks, made before 1959 November 1.

2. A. Bring and G. Ehrling, AB 2.5.1–2.5.2.2, 1959 April. Discussion of array declarations, their possibly variable bounds [*dynamic arrays*], and procedures. Suggests that it is often unnecessary to give array declarations for input and output parameters in the procedure heading. Also that such array declarations may be used to produce a procedure working under more restrictive conditions. Further that declarations of internal arrays in a procedure have their natural place within the procedure itself. Discusses several ways of allocating storage for arrays of varying size within procedures. Suggests the need for a way to identify the open subscript positions of arrays given as actual parameters [*dummy variables*].

3. P. Naur and P. Mondrup, AB 2.5.3 1959 May 1. Refers to 1.5 and shows how the example discussed in 2 may be solved with the aid of arrays declared in the program, avoiding dynamic storage allocation.

AB 2 was distributed on 1959 May 5.

4. G. Ehrling, AB 3.5–3.6, 1959 May 10. Amplifies 2 by a discussion of ways to handle dynamic arrays. Suggests that the actual subscript bounds of an array given as parameter to a procedure may most conveniently be communicated as a hidden parameter. Suggests the need for indicating the maximum storage requirement of the internal arrays of a procedure by means of a special declaration.

5. P. Naur, AB 3.7, 1959 June 8. Discussion of the meaning of the distinction between input and output parameters of procedures. Asks about the effect of supplying the same variable as both input and output parameter in the same call, and suggests ways to avoid undesirable effects of doing so.

AB 3 was distributed on 1959 June 8.

6. E. W. Dijkstra, W. Heise, A. J. Perlis, and K. Samelson forming a subcommittee at the UNESCO conference in Paris, 1959 June 15–20, AB 4.9–4.10. Proposal that in the procedure heading a declaration of a particular form may be included, to indicate that the functions named in the declaration may be used within the procedure without being specified as procedure parameters [*require*]. The proposal is extended with a facility for renaming functions at the same time as they are declared to be accessible within a procedure, *equivalence*.

7. P. Naur, AB 4.14, 1959 July 1. Suggests that the identifier alone should suffice to identify an object. This would imply that differences in the empty parenthesis structures attached to identifiers would not suffice to differentiate objects.

AB 4 was distributed on 1959 August 13.

8. Regnecentralen, AB 5.6.2, 1959 Sept. 10. Describes an ambiguity in the meaning of the renaming mechanism of 6 in the case that the procedure referred to belongs to a set of several procedures defined by the same declaration.

9. Jan V. Garwick, AB 5.9.1, 1959 Aug. 21. Referring to 7, recommends that the same identifier could be used for several kinds of object.

10. H. Rutishauser, AB 5.9.3, 1959 Sept. 10. Referring to 7, stresses the power of the notation of empty subscript positions in referring to vectors extracted from an array. Stresses also the contribution of empty brackets to readability.

11. Regnecentralen, AB 5.9.4, 1959 Sept. 15. In response to 9 and 10, suggests a specific grouping of program objects as the basis for multiple uses of the same identifier.

12. Regnecentralen, AB 5.12, 1959 Sept. 5. Suggests that in array declarations in procedure headings (1.7) the bound expressions may contain only simple formal input variables, not arrays and functions. Reason: to remove unnecessary complications from translators, as illustrated by an example.

13. G. Ehrling, AB 5.13, 1959 Sept. 15. Suggests that procedure declarations may be nested indefinitely and that a procedure declared at a certain level of nesting should be accessible at all interior levels of nesting from that level unless the name of it is redefined. Thus any program may be made into a procedure by enclosing it between **begin** and **end** and adding a procedure heading. Library procedures will be referred to as if declared in a

level surrounding the main program. A special declaration is suggested to make it possible to get access to a library procedure even from a level where the name of it has been used for another function.

14. Regnecentralen, AB 5.15, 1959 Sept. 1. Question: why are switches not permitted as output parameters in procedure statements?

15. Regnecentralen, AB 5.16, 1959 Sept. 1. Proposal that labels and switches appearing as parameters in procedure headings and statements should be distinguished by being followed by colon.

16. Regnecentralen, AB 5.18, 1959 Sept. 26. Referring to 2 and 4, it is again stated that array declarations in procedure headings are superfluous. The question is asked why they were put there in the first place.

AB 5 was distributed on 1959 September 28.

17. H. Rutishauser, AB 7.4.1, 1959 Oct. 21. Referring to 12 it is claimed that the example given to support the suggestion cannot occur.

18. H. Rutishauser, AB 7.6, 1959 Oct. 21. Referring to the renaming proposal of 6 it is shown how the desired effect may be achieved with the aid of the procedure parameter mechanism.

19. H. Rutishauser, AB 7.10, 1959 Oct. 21. The proposal of 6 is reformulated as a "require" declaration that may be put in the procedure heading, for listing names of functions and procedures that are used, but not declared, within the procedure. Names of standard procedures are exempt.

20. Regnecentralen, AB 7.11, 1959 Nov. 1. Question: what should be the form of a procedure entered as input parameter to another procedure? Should a complete, empty bracket structure be included?

21. H. Rutishauser, AB 7.16, 1959 Oct. A discussion of the need for some sort of dynamic arrays, leading to a proposal for a fully dynamic array declaration, to be written just after the **begin** of the compound statement for which it is valid. Some suggestions are made about how the transition to this radical solution may be achieved by way of intermediate steps. The position of other declarations in the program structure is left as an open question.

22. H. Rutishauser, AB 7.17, 1959 Oct. 21. Answer to the query of 16: it is correct that array declarations in procedure headings are mostly superfluous. However, they serve to improve readability for humans.

23. K. Samelson, AB 7.22, 1959 Oct. Proposal: "A declaration is a prefix to a statement. It is valid for, and part of, the statement following it."

24. K. Samelson, AB 7.23, 1959 Oct. Proposal: "In all array declarations, subscript bounds may be arbitrary integer valued expressions."

25. Siemens, AB 7.39, 1959 Oct. 27. Discuss the need for means of structuring programs into blocks that do not need special mechanisms, such as procedure parameters, for communication with the surrounding program. No specific form is proposed.

26. A. van Wijngaarden and E. W. Dijkstra, AB 7.31, 1959 Oct. Proposal: "Declarations . . . pertain to that part of the text which follows the declaration and which may be ended by a contradictory declaration."

27. A. van Wijngaarden and E. W. Dijkstra, AB 7.33, 1959 Oct. " . . . We suggest that the level declaration **new** (I,I, . . .) has the effect that, the named entities have no relationship to identically named entities before in the following text, until the level decla-

ration **old** (I,I, . . .) which attributes to the entities named herein the meaning that they had before. These level declarations may be nested and form the only way to introduce a new meaning to a name . . . ."

28. A. van Wijngaarden and E. W. Dijkstra, AB 7.34, 1959 Oct. Suggest the introduction of the type declaration **dummy** for use with formal variables of function declarations and elsewhere.

29. H. Bottenbruch, AB 7.34, 1959 Oct. 26. Suggests that functions and procedures should be available inside procedure declarations without being communicated as parameters. Further that a procedure defined within another one should have direct access to the identifiers of that other procedure, thus making the "hidden parameters" of functions (cf. 1.6) also available for procedures.

30. H. Bottenbruch, AB 7.37, 1959 Oct. 26. Suggests that declarations should have a dynamic meaning, i.e., become valid when encountered during program execution.

31. Regnecentralen, AB 7.39, 1959 Oct. With reference to 13, the place of library procedures within the hierarchy of procedures is discussed. Several different possibilities are described. In conclusion it is recommended that library procedures are understood to be implicitly declared in a level surrounding the program and that they should be quoted in the heading of each interior level where they are used.

32. Regnecentralen, AB 7.40, 1959 Nov. 2. Referring to 21, the proposal for fully dynamic arrays is opposed on the basis of the claim that the handling of the limited storage capacity will remain with the programmer in any case.

AB 7 was distributed on 1959 November 3.

During the period following 1959 November 1 the discussions took place in meetings: 1959 November 12–14 in Paris, 49 participants; 1959 December 14–16 in Mainz, seven European representatives to the final ALGOL 60 conference; 1960 January 11–16 in Paris, the final ALGOL 60 conference. The following points summarize the reports of these meetings and some related contributions.

33. Subcommittee of Paris meeting 1959 Nov. 12–14, members P. V. Ellis, H. Bottenbruch, E. W. Dijkstra, P. Naur, K. Samelson, B. Vauquois, AB 8.1.2. Concerning dynamic arrays the subcommittee envisaged that these would only be allowed within procedures. It was recommended that all declarations will have to be written at the head of the program or of a procedure. Concerning the range within which a declaration should be valid, the subcommittee recognized the two extremes, by write up and by time succession, and in addition considered permitting dynamic declarations only when the two extremes are coincident. No unanimous recommendation could be given.

34. Subcommittee of Paris meeting 1959 Nov. 12–14, members E. W. Dijkstra, P. J. Landin, P. Naur, AB 8.1.2.2. Referring to 27, the notion of declarations **new** and **old** was recommended for serious consideration. Referring to 6 and 29 it was recommended that the notions of **require** and **equivalence** be extended to all kinds of entities, not only functions and procedures. Detailed proposals for a notation in the form of examples were given.

35. Subcommittee of Paris meeting 1959 Nov. 12–14, members H. Rutishauser, G. Ehrling, M. Woodger, M. Paul, AB 8.1.4. Recommends that procedures given as actual parameters may include n ($\geq k$) parameter positions of which k are empty, where the corresponding formal procedure has k empty parameter positions. Further that such parameters should be furnished with the appropriate bracket-comma-colon structure. It is noted

that this automatically prevents recursive activation through a parameter. Also that the empty parameter positions might be filled by suitably defined dummy variables.

36. Subcommittee of Paris meeting 1959 Nov. 12–14, members H. Bottenbruch, F. L. Bauer, W. L. van der Poel, J. Jensen, M. Woodger, AB 8.1.5. Dealing with the meaning of input and output parameters of procedures, cf. 5, the responsibility of avoiding unintended effects in special cases is generally left to the authors and users of procedures. As an exception, it is stated that a variable used purely as an input parameter will not be changed by the procedure statement.

37. European representatives to the ALGOL 60 conference, meeting in Mainz, 1959 December 14–16 (ALGOL 60 document 2).

37.1. Proposal: Any declaration is a prefix to a possibly compound statement and only valid for that statement. The declarations for a statement and any values of variables attached to them cease to be valid after exit from the statement. Identifiers that are thus declared to be local for a statement may be used independently outside that statement. Identifiers that are not declared to be local for a statement retain any significance that they have in the surrounding level. Labels and switches are local without needing a declaration.

37.2. Proposal: A procedure or function is formed from any statement by adding the heading giving the name, the list of formal input and output parameters, information concerning parameters, optionally the list of global identifiers, and optional information about global identifiers. The information concerning formal parameters and global identifiers is expressed in a notation that gives the complete structure of parameters and subscripts, to any level of nesting, with the aid of dummy identifiers. The dynamic entry to the procedure or function is the first statement following **begin.** At least one operational end must be indicated by a return statement. The value of a function must be assigned to the identifier naming the function.

37.3. Proposal: In a procedure call the actual parameters must have exactly the same nature as the corresponding formal parameters. Any expressions involved are to be evaluated when the procedure call is encountered.

As a personal comment, I believe that at the end of the meeting in Mainz the European representatives felt strongly that the proposal concerning declarations, 37.1, and the structure of procedures, 37.2, was a significant achievement. It managed to combine a variety of proposals into a scheme of great simplicity. There was also a clear feeling that the proposal would appear radical to the American representatives and would need the support of considerable persuasion in order to be accepted.

On the other hand, I felt that an important area had been neglected: the handling of procedure parameters. Neither discussion 36 nor proposal 37.3 contributed to an understanding of how the notions of input and output parameters on the one hand, and the replacement rule of the Zurich report, 1.3, on the other, should be reconciled.

These concerns, together with my feeling of an urgent need for a more precise and complete style of description, are the background of the following documents.

38. Memorandum to the international ALGOL committee from P. Naur, 1960 January 2 (ALGOL 60 document 3).

38.1. The reasoning behind the syntactical structure proposed by the European members.

38.2. The reasoning behind the following characteristics of the European proposal for procedures: only one procedure is defined in any one procedure declaration; partly empty parameter positions in procedure statements are disallowed; the necessity for empty bracket skeletons has been removed; a procedure heading will give complete information concerning the formal parameters; functions and procedures without parameters are possible; all functions are defined through declarations starting with the delimiter **function;** procedure declarations become similar in structure to other compound statements.

38.3. Draft formulation of the section on procedure statements for the final report on the language. The draft has syntactic rules expressed in my slightly modified form of Backus's notation (cf. Appendix 2; also Appendix 5, Bauer's point 2.6) appearing here for the first time, followed by examples and semantic rules. As the dominating part, the semantic rules include detailed explanations of the effects of parameter substitutions. The explanations are expressed in terms of cases, depending on the following descriptors: input or output parameter; kind of parameter (simple, array, function, procedure, label, switch); types of the formal and the actual parameter. A total of 15 different cases are described in terms of evaluations, replacements, and unique, internal variables. [In retrospect these rules may be described as an attempt to supply a complete definition of call by reference.]

39. Draft report on ALGOL 60 by P. Naur, 18 pages, 1960 January 9 (ALGOL 60 document 5). This describes the complete language according to both European and American proposals, as they were known at the time, with minor modifications, except for leaving open the description of if statement, for statement, alternative statement, do statement, and the semantics of procedure declarations. Throughout the description is based on subsections giving syntax, examples, and semantics. Following a proposal from A. Perlis, the international ALGOL 60 committee adopted the report as the basis for the discussions at the meeting in Paris, on 1960 January 14. This implied the adoption of the modified Backus notation for describing the syntax, a question that was never brought up for separate discussion.

During the ALGOL 60 meeting in Paris, 1960 January 11–16, the substance of the European proposals on program structure and the local significance of declarations was adopted with only one significant modification: the introduction of the notion of **own** variables proposed by J. Backus (ALGOL 60 documents 11, 31 item 163 by J. McCarthy). Procedures and their parameters caused more discussion, as clear from the documents summarized below.

40. Subcommittee of the ALGOL 60 meeting, members H. Rutishauser and F. L. Bauer, 1960 Jan. 13 (ALGOL 60 document 12). Proposal for reducing the number of parameter substitution cases given in 38.3. Not adopted.

41. Subcommittee of the ALGOL 60 meeting, members C. Katz, A. van Wijngaarden, M. Woodger, 1960 Jan. 14 (ALGOL 60 document 17). Proposal to abolish the distinction between input and output parameters. Replacement rules corresponding to call by reference are sketched. Adopted.

42. Subcommittee of the ALGOL 60 meeting, members J. Green, A. Perlis, K. Samelson, 1960 Jan. 14 (ALGOL 60 document 18). Proposal for procedure statement having input and output parameters, described in terms of a detailed replacement scheme. Not adopted.

43. H. Rutishauser, 1960 Jan. 14 (ALGOL 60 document 20). Proposal to abolish the return statement, thus making the function declaration of 1.6 unnecessary. Adopted.

44. H. Rutishauser, 1960 Jan. 14 (ALGOL 60 document 22). Proposal for "array functions", thus having expressions of the form $T[k](x)$. Not adopted.

45. Subcommittee of the ALGOL 60 meeting, membership not recorded, but believed to include A. Perlis and A. van Wijngaarden, 1960 Jan. 16 (ALGOL 60 documents 26, 27). Proposal for procedure statements and declarations. Functions are defined by procedure declarations that include assignment of a value to the procedure name. Both procedures and functions without parameters are admitted. No descriptions of the formal parameters are included in the heading. The treatment of each parameter in the call is controlled by a name part in the heading that lists those parameters whose names should be substituted. For all other parameters the value of the actual parameter is used as an initialization. No details of the meaning of name substitution is given. Adopted during the last hour of the meeting, at about 9 p.m.

When the meeting ended it remained my task to make a coherent report out of its agreements. Less than 12 hours after the adoption of 45 I became convinced that it introduced essential ambiguities into the language. This led to a quick exchange of letters among the representatives, as summarized below.

46. P. Naur to the members of the ALGOL 60 committee 1960 Jan. 17 (ALGOL 60 document 201). Claims that the scheme 45 introduces an ambiguity in a case like $A(f)$ where f is declared to be a procedure (functionlike) without parameters; seemingly it is not clear whether one value or the functional procedure will be supplied through the call. As a cure for this trouble it is proposed to reintroduce a distinction between declarations of procedures and functions and to disallow functions without parameters.

47. H. Rutishauser to the members of the ALGOL 60 committee, 1960 Jan. 20 (ALGOL 60 document 204). Points out that 45 also lacks all information about the types of formal parameters. Proposes to reintroduce a limited amount of description about the formal parameters into the procedure heading.

48. A. Perlis to the members of the ALGOL 60 committee, 1960 January 20 (ALGOL 60 document 205). Opposes the proposal of 46. Demonstrates that the ambiguity of 46 does not in fact exist, on the basis of a table showing the effect of call by name and value for 5 kinds of actual parameters: variable, label, array, expression, and procedure. Of particular interest is case 7: the actual parameter X is an expression, corresponding to the formal parameter U called as name:

Action induced by the call:
  a) The auxiliary procedure

procedure $\$n$; **begin** $\$n$: $\$n := X$ **end** $\$n$;

is defined. (See note 2.)
  b) Substitute the name $\$n$ for X in the call.
  c) same as case 9 [for which the actual parameter X is a procedure].
  Note 2. $\$n$ is an internal identifier. [. . .] It might be argued that case 7 not be defined. However, it is treated in such a simple way and the operational intent is so transparent that it seems silly to leave it undefined.

49. M. Woodger to the members of the ALGOL 60 committee, 1960 January 25 (ALGOL 60 document 208). Detailed description of the parameter treatment "as I understand it, based on my notes of 16th January." The rules distinguish between three forms of actual parameters: identifiers, subscripted variables, and other forms of expressions.

Identifiers are substituted, subscripted variables have their subscript expressions evaluated and the subscripted variables with constant subscripts so obtained are substituted, and other forms of expression are evaluated as an initialization of the formal variable. This scheme makes no use of a name list in the procedure heading.

To appreciate my situation as editor of the committee's report at this stage it should be clear that the full committee agreed on the urgency of the task. By now everyone was ready to see even his most cherished ideas abandoned if necessary in order to arrive at a publishable conclusion. It was quite clear that on the question of procedure parameters there was no agreement, and not even a common understanding. The last proposal adopted, 45, seemingly was understood in a coherent manner only by one member, Alan Perlis, as presented in 48. On the other hand, the only coherent alternative, 49, was virtually identical with proposals 38.3 and 40 that had been rejected, and moreover was inconsistent with the last proposal adopted, 45. When I saw that the clarification of 48 did in fact make my argument in 46 invalid, and moreover that the notion of 48 was clear and simple, I was pleased to go along with it. In addition, the proposal of 47 could be incorporated without difficulty. Thus the path was clear for the next documents. (For another view of these matters see Appendix 5, Bauer's point 2.7, the note on this in Appendix 6, Woodger's point 2, and the note in Appendix 8.2).

50. Report on the algorithmic language ALGOL 60, draft for the authors, edited by P. Naur, 1960 February 4 (ALGOL 60 document 213). This is essentially a carefully tidied-up collection of previous agreements. A few matters of detail have been filled in and changed. Thus a syntax for strings has been added; the delimiter **procedure** has been replaced by ⟨type⟩ **procedure** where appropriate; the listing of **name** in the procedure heading has been replaced by a listing of the complementary set, **value**. (See also Appendix 5, Bauer's point 2.8.)

51. P. Naur to the members of the ALGOL 60 committee, 1960 February 4 (ALGOL 60 document 212). Notes on the draft report, 50. Accounts briefly for the origin of the procedure concept, in particular how the proposal of 46 has been dropped. It continues: "In passing I would like to mention a fact which has been pointed out to me by Mr. Jensen: As a direct consequence of our new rules the partly empty arrays and procedures [cf. 1.3 and 35] are, in fact, automatically available. How this comes about in practice you will be able to see from the examples in sections 4.7.2 and 5.4.2 on the procedure Innerproduct."

52. The last substantial change of language concept was the admission of recursive procedure activations. This took place as follows. One of the proposals of the American representatives to the ALGOL 60 Conference was to add the delimiter **recursive** to the language, to be used in the context **recursive function** or **recursive procedure** at the start of declarations (ALGOL 60 document 6). This proposal was rejected by a narrow margin. Then on about 1960 February 10, while the draft 50 was being studied by the members of the committee, I had a telephone call from A. van Wijngaarden, speaking also for E. W. Dijkstra. They pointed to an important lack of definition in the draft report, namely, the meaning, if any, of an occurrence of a procedure identifier inside the body of the declaration other than in the left part of an assignment. They also made it clear that preventing recursive activations through rules of the description would be complicated because of the possibilities of indirect activations through other procedures and their parameters. They proposed to clarify the matter by adding a sentence to section 5.4.4: "Any other occurrence of the procedure identifier within the procedure body denotes activation of the pro-

cedure." I got charmed with the boldness and simplicity of this suggestion and decided to follow it in spite of the risk of subsequent trouble over the question (cf. Appendix 5, Bauer's point 2.8 and the oral presentation).

The reactions from the members of the ALGOL 60 committee arrived in a steady stream during the month of February 1960. Examples of the use of the language in realistic problems, to be included at the end of the report, were produced, procedure Euler by A. van Wijngaarden (ALGOL 60 document 214) and procedure RK by H. Rutishauser (ALGOL 60 document 221). The remarks and questions from H. Rutishauser led to several letters going back and forth between us (ALGOL 60 documents 217, 219–221), in which he continued to make new suggestions for improvement, while finally expressing his satisfaction with the result. Long lists of suggestions and corrections of detail were produced by most members of the committee. The tone of the letters was friendly and helpful but the attitude sceptical. With one exception: at the bottom of a five-page list of typed comments I found the following handwritten addition: "Otherwise we think you did a magnificent job and we'll go along with what you deem the best compromise of the various criticisms. A. J. Perlis (for A. Holt, J. McCarthy)" (ALGOL 60 document 215).

The suggestions from the members of the committee were incorporated in the final version of Report on the Algorithmic Language ALGOL 60, distributed to the approximately 100 addresses of the *ALGOL Bulletin* mailing list on 1960 March 2, and soon thereafter published in several journals (Backus *et al.*, 1960). This attracted much attention and gave rise to discussion and controversy. This, however, is beyond the present story.

3. A Posteriori Evaluation

3.1. Declared Objectives

Curiously, the ALGOL 60 Report (Backus *et al.*, 1960) includes no statement on the objective of the language. However, from its introduction it emerges clearly that it is to be regarded as the completion of the project described in the introduction to the Zurich report (Backus *et al.*, 1959). We are thus justified in taking over the objectives given in that document.

    I. The new language should be as close as possible to standard mathematical notation and be readable with little further explanation.
    II. It should be possible to use it for the description of computing processes in publications.
    III. The new language should be mechanically translatable into machine programs."

Taking these three points in order, it would, I feel, be impossible to claim that ALGOL 60 satisfies I. The part of the notation of ALGOL 60 that is similar to standard mathematical notation is confined to simple arithmetic and Boolean expressions. And even in this respect ALGOL 60 is deficient in so far as the notation is strictly linear and so does not admit the standard, two-dimensional form of mathematical expressions, a fact that has been pointed out by critics of the language all along.

While programming languages have been constructed that match standard mathematical notation of expressions to a much higher degree than does ALGOL 60, what seems to me of more interest is the question of how to handle the many other aspects of computational processes. Considering such aspects one may be led to the view that I cannot be satisfied and thus must be regarded as unreasonable. Such a view was expressed as early as January 1959 by M. Woodger (1959a):

> 3.3 A principal objective was to make the language as close as possible to standard mathematical notation and readable with little further explanation. In this I feel it has failed, and that indeed one cannot expect as much as this. Certainly the algebraic equations occurring as components of the expressions of the language are close to ordinary mathematical notation, but the logical structure of the processes intended, the control of the sequence of operations and of the use of storage requires a great deal of explanation and study before it is properly understood. There is of course no existing standard mathematical notation for this logical control.

To me this is a valid comment as far as objective I is concerned.

Point II of the declared objectives, on the other hand, was fully achieved. ALGOL 60 remains to this day a much used publication language. Within the application area for which it was designed, computation processes developed by numerical analysis, it has proved to be perfectly adequate, and it has even been found useful over a much wider field of problems.

Point III of the declared objectives likewise was fully achieved. The criticism that among the many ALGOL 60 compilers that have been made very few will handle the full ALGOL 60 language without exception to me carries little weight in this context. The parts of the language omitted in implementations have mostly been those that are of doubtful usefulness or are ambiguous in their meaning, or both. Their omission has had very slight influence on the overall usefulness of the language.

In my opinion those declared objectives of the language that were reasonable were achieved to a very high degree.

3.2. Implicit and Derived Objectives

In the present section we shall consider some motives in the work on ALGOL 60 that were not expressly included among the objectives, but that may have had a similar influence on the actual work.

A motive that was directly associated with the ACM ALGOL committee, as described in the introduction to the Zurich report (Backus *et al.*, 1959), was to establish "a single universal computer language". There was quite clearly a hope that ALGOL would become established instead of certain other languages, in particular FORTRAN. This hope was clearly disappointed, and one may ask why. A clarification of this question requires an account of the deliberations and decisions made within certain American organizations. This lies outside the scope of the present account. An analysis of the question has been published by Bemer (1969). Suffice it to say that in retrospect the attempt to establish ALGOL as a replacement for FORTRAN appears as a valiant effort that certainly deserved being tried, but that had only very slight chance of succeeding. Perhaps the simplest demonstration of the validity of this statement is the fact that PL/I, which also was charged with driving out FORTRAN, and had a much greater initial chance of success, likewise failed. For a further discussion of this aspect of programming languages, see Naur (1975).

Apart from the question of the success, in a political sense, of ALGOL 60 regarded as a "universal computer language", there is the question of the universality of the language in a technical sense. I believe it is true to say that although the attitudes of the participants on this question varied considerably there was a quite strong opinion that the scope of the language should remain limited to "computing processes." This we find expressed quite clearly by H. Rutishauser, in a response to a suggestion by Garwick that the language should include operations on bit patterns. Rutishauser writes (AB 5.11.2, 1959, Sept. 10):

> With the proposal [AB] 4.16 we would lose machine-independency of ALGOL, moreover it would mean a generalization of ALGOL towards a data-processing language. This however is—at least in my opinion—beyond the scope of the present ALGOL-group. Of course this does not mean that we cannot work on a universal data-processing language, but such activity should not interfere with our efforts to settle the definitions of ALGOL.

Thus the answer to the charge that ALGOL 60 failed to quality as a universal language is that it was not designed to be one.

Another set of implicit objectives may be said to have been derived from the basic idea of the whole development, that the language should be suitable to be used commonly, across divisions according to computer type, etc. From this idea it follows directly that the language must be described in a machine-independent way, and further that the description must meet the highest standards of clarity, unambiguity, and completeness.

As described already in Section 1.6 above, the problem of description was recognized as a separate issue during the language development. Moreover, the form of description chosen, based on subsections consisting of mutually supporting parts giving a formal syntax and semantical rules expressed concisely in prose, was subsequently recognized as a separate contribution of the language. In this context there has been a tendency to stress one-sidedly the use of a formal syntax language. It should be emphasized that the description of ALGOL 60 is based on three indispensable elements: (1) the formal syntax language; (2) the use in the syntax of full names for nonterminal symbols, providing immediate link between syntax and semantics; and (3) semantics expressed in concise, low-redundancy prose, consciously phrased to approach completeness while reducing inconsistency. In a posteriori evaluation of objectives one may ask to what extent this form of description meets the implied objective of a complete, unambiguous description. In comments concerning this question there has been a tendency to stress the fact that a number of deficiencies were found in the *Report on the ALGOL 60 Language* and that it was deemed necessary to publish the revised report (Backus *et al.*, 1962). Further, that even after this phase deficiencies in the description have been found. In evaluating these facts one may perhaps refer to the independent evidence of D. E. Knuth, who, in a very careful description of the known problems related to the description of the language states (Knuth, 1967): "The following list [of known trouble spots in ALGOL 60] is actually more remarkable for its shortness than its length. A complete critique which goes to the same level of detail would be almost out of the question for other languages comparable to ALGOL 60, since the list would probably be a full order of magnitude longer." Thus one may perhaps be allowed to claim that the objective of completeness and unambiguity in the description was achieved, as far as practically and humanly possible.

As an issue of some importance in the later influence from the language ALGOL 60, one may say that the implicit objective of simplicity and generality of concepts, closely related to clarity and completeness in the description of the language, to a significant extent entailed the need for innovation of language concepts as well. Thus one may regard the concepts of block structure and locality of quantities to be the result of a search for a simple and general solution for dynamic arrays and the need to give access to certain global quantities within procedures. A still more striking example of the influence from the form of description is the manner in which the procedure concept of the Zurich report was rejected in favor of the novel concept of the ALGOL 60 procedures. As described already in item 38.3 of Section 2.10 above, a detailed description of the procedures mechanism was produced in advance of the final meeting on ALGOL 60. As further described in item 40 of the same section, an attempt was made during the meeting to avoid the complexity of that description, without avail. This was a decisive incident in the change of outlook that led to the abolishing of the distinction between input and output parameters of procedures. It was brought about by an indirect attack on that concept, taking the form of a clear description of its meaning. The very length of that description, with the need for a number of subdivisions, became the evidence that the underlying concept was unacceptable.

3.3. Contributions of Language

ALGOL 60 contributed significantly to the field of programming language design in several ways that, although to some extent related, may be described in terms of five issues, as follows:

Contribution 1: A language suitable to be used as a computer programming language was defined independently of any implementation.

Contribution 2: A language suitable for the expression of algorithms in pure man to man communication was established.

Contribution 3: A new style of language description suitable for supporting contributions 1 and 2 was demonstrated.

Contribution 4: The language demonstrates what can be achieved if generality and economy of concept is pursued and combined with precision in description.

Contribution 5: The language included novel ideas, in particular in the areas of blocks and procedures.

Of these five contributions, items 1, 2, and 4 correspond rather directly to the objectives of the language. Item 5 was the concrete result of item 4.

Contribution 3 does not correspond to an objective stated in the Zurich report or the ALGOL 60 report. However, the importance of it was emphasized in the American proposal for the Zurich meeting (Backus *et al.*, 1958). This covers what I personally consider the best point of the language: the brevity, precision, and relative completeness of its description.

Each of the five contributions of the language has had an influence on the subsequent development. Tracing this in detail would be a major undertaking. Here only the barest outlines will be given. Thus as far as implementations of the language are concerned, suffice it to say that large numbers of implementations have been made, by many different implementors and for many different types of computers. The problems of implementation of the language have given rise to a substantial literature of its own.

Again, the use of the language in publications has been substantial. Several journals, including *Communications of the ACM, The Computer Journal,* and *BIT,* have published programs expressed in ALGOL 60 as a regular feature. It is probably true to say that for regular publication of general-purpose algorithms ALGOL 60 is the most used language.

As far as the influence from the style of description of ALGOL 60 on later developments is concerned, the most unexpected effect was the suggestion by Irons (1961) that the formal syntactic description of the language could be used to control the compiler for the language directly. This suggestion stimulated a large number of studies of the formal structure of computer languages and of compilation processes controlled directly by language descriptions. Although some of the claims made this approach appear to have been exaggerated, it has undoubtedly contributed substantially to the understanding and methodology of compiler construction.

In an outline of the influence from ALGOL 60 on later languages at least three different directions can be identified, corresponding to three different areas of main emphasis of the development. In the first direction of development the stress is on extensions of the language to cover further data structures and operations, while ALGOL 60 is retained as a subset of the new language. The outstanding example of this line of development is SIMULA (Dahl and Nygaard, 1966). In the second direction of development the stress is on the contributions 3 and 4 of ALGOL 60, leading to a higher degree of formalization and generalization of the language and its description. This is the direction taken in ALGOL 68 (van Wijngaarden *et al.*, 1969). In the third direction of development the size and style of description of ALGOL 60 are retained, but the mechanisms of the language are replaced by more recently developed concepts that to a still higher degree than ALGOL 60 itself combine simplicity and generality. An example of such a development is PASCAL (Wirth, 1971).

ALGOL 60 gave rise to many dialects. In fact, many of the implementations of the language include minor deviations from ALGOL 60 itself and thus are dialects. It is significant that the preliminary description, ALGOL 58 as described in the Zurich Report, inspired several dialects, such as MAD and JOVIAL, that deviate quite strongly from their origin and that early in their development became independent of it. By contrast, only a few of the close dialects of ALGOL 60 became significant as language developments. Thus one may claim that the striving for unification, that was part of the initial idea of the ALGOL development (cf. the introduction to the Zurich report), was to some extent successful.

Influence from ALGOL 60 on computer hardware design appears in a rather pure form in the Burroughs B5000 series of computers. In other computer designs a possible influence may be found in the provision of instructions for handling stacks and procedure calls, but in these cases the influence appears more as a general trend in which both other programming languages, such as LISP, and other application requirements have been active as influences.

3.4. Design Weaknesses

As described in Section 2.2, named constants were omitted from the language although it seemed fairly clear that they would be useful.

Other weak points of the design became the subject of much later discussion. One outstanding case is the concept of own with its lack of an initialization facility and its poor match with the procedure concept. Another case is the meaning of the for clause. This is related to questions of the side-effects and the order of evaluation of expressions. Several areas of difficulty are not just the result of oversights during the design of the language, but reflect differences of opinion of the design group. Thus the discussion of side effects of expressions and function calls reflects disagreement whether expressions should conform more to a mathematical transformation concept or more to an algorithmic processing concept.

The question of weaknesses of the language was taken up by many people soon after the publication of the ALGOL 60 Report, and an ALGOL Maintenance Committee was formed in the USA. The imminent risk of confusion arising from a high frequency of changes of the official specifications was soon realized by the authors, however, and it was decided to exercise severe constraints on changes. As a consequence, only one revision of the language was made, in 1962, touching only some obvious ambiguities while leaving the language virtually unchanged. The following five areas of difficulty were identified, but left for resolution at a later stage: (1) side effects of functions; (2) the call-by-name concept; (3) **own**: static or dynamic; (4) for statement: static or dynamic; and (5) conflict between specification and declaration. Such a resolution was never made within the frame of ALGOL 60.

A thorough discussion of the weaknesses of ALGOL 60 was eventually published by Knuth (1967).

3.5. Main Problems Related to ALGOL 60

Just as in the later phases of the language design, the main problems for the implementers were created by the blocks and procedures. However, as a result of a lively development effort soon after the publication of the language, these problems were understood and solved. In their solution they contributed substantially to a wider understanding of techniques of dynamic storage allocation.

For the users the biggest problems directly related to the language probably have been, partly the proper use of procedure parameters, partly the proper use of semicolon as a statement delimiter.

4. Implications for Current and Future Languages

As already sketched above, ALGOL 60 has had a substantial influence on later language developments, including SIMULA, ALGOL 68, and PASCAL. The reasons for this have been discussed in Section 3.3, "Contributions of Language."

Whether any further influence from the development of ALGOL 60 may still be expected is doubtful, since that development was very closely tied to its historical situation. However, if current and future language designers are looking for so far unattended aspects of the ALGOL 60 development that might again be found effective, the attention should be turned to the use of writing during the development process. Indeed, as described in Section 1.6, Discussion Techniques, the insistence on written contributions, both during the period of open debate and during the final design meeting, appears to me to have been of paramount importance for the intellectual quality of the language.

As for ALGOL 60 itself, it is still being used both for publications and for programming of computers to a substantial extent and will probably retain its influence in this manner for many years to come.

Appendix 1. Centers and Individuals

Cf. Section 1.2.

TABLE 1

European Centers Participating in the Development of ALGOL 60

The centers are ordered alphabetically by city name. Other identifications are included, with references to the city name. The list includes all European centers that appear in the mailing list of the ALGOL Bulletin until early 1960.

Amsterdam, Netherlands. Mathematisch Centrum (public service laboratory): Edsger W. Dijkstra, Aad van Wijngaarden, J. A. Zonneveld.

ASEA, see Västerås.

Backnang, Germany. Telefunken Gmbh (manufacturer). G. Beyer, W. Händler.

Bad Hersfeld, Germany. Zuse KG (manufacturer). Th. Fromme.

Bonn, Germany. Institut für Angewandte Mathematik, Universität Bonn. C. A. Petri.

Borehamwood, England. Elliott Brothers (London) Ltd. P. Shackleton.

Bull, Compagnie, see Paris 1.

Cambridge, England. The University Mathematical Laboratory. D. F. Hartley.

Chalmers Tekniska Högskola, see Göteborg.

Copenhagen, See København.

Darmstadt, Germany. Institut für Praktische Mathematik, Technische Hochschule. Hermann Bottenbruch, Heinz Schappert, Alwin Walther.

Didcot, England. Atomic Energy Research Establishment Harwell, Theoretical Physics Division. Ian C. Pyle.

Dresden, Germany. Funkwerk Dresden. G. Buchholz.

Eidgenössische Technische Hochschule, see Zürich.

Elliott Brothers Ltd., see Borehamwood.

English Electric, see London 1 and Kidsgrove.

Facit, see Stockholm 2.

Göteborg (Gothenburg), Sweden. Chalmers Tekniske Högskola (technical university). Ingmar Dahlstrand, H. Fuhrer.

Grenoble, France. Institut Fourier, Faculté des Sciences (university). Bernard Vauquois.

Hannover, Germany. Institut für Praktische Mathematik und Darstellende Geometrie, Technische Hochschule. Heinz Unger.

Harrow, England. Computer Development Ltd. J. H. Wensley.

Harwell, see Didcot.

Helsinki, Finland. Matematiikkakonekomitea. O. Varho.

Hersfeld, see Bad Hersfeld.

International Computers and Tabulators Ltd., see London 3.

Jena, Germany. Zeiss Werk (manufacturer). Dr. Kammerer.

Kidsgrove, England. English Electric Co. Ltd. F. Wetherfield.

Kjeller, Norway. Norwegian Defense Research Establishment. S. A. Övergaard.

København, Denmark. Regnecentralen (nonprofit computer development laboratory). Willy Heise, Jørn Jensen, Per Mondrup, Peter Naur.

Leidschendam, Netherlands. Dr. Neher Laboratorium. W. L. van der Poel.

Linköping, Sweden. Svenska Aeroplan Aktiebolaget (manufacturer). Börje Langefors, Sven Yngvell.

London 1, England. The English Electric Company Ltd., London Computing Service. Peter Landin.

London 2, England. Ferranti Ltd. George E. Felton, Stanley Gill.

London 3, England. International Computers and Tabulators Ltd. Peter V. Ellis.

London 4, England. University of London Computer Unit. A. R. Edmonds.

Lund, Sweden. Avdelningen för Numerisk Analys, Lunds Universitet. Carl-Erik Fröberg.

Mailüfterl Group, see Wien.

Mainz, Germany. Institut für Angewandte Mathematik, Johannes Gutenberg Universität. Friedrich L. Bauer, Manfred Paul, Klaus Samelson.

TABLE 1 (*Continued*)

Matematikmaskinnämnden, see Stockholm 1.
Mathematisch Centrum, see Amsterdam.
München 1, Germany. Max-Planck-Institut für Astrophysik. K. Hain.
München 2, Germany. Siemens und Halske AG. H. Gumin, Willy Heise, K. Leipold.
München 3, Germany. Technische Hochschule München. F. L. Bauer, P. Graeff, J. Heinhold, M. Paul, F.
    Penzlin, K. Samelson, Gerhard Seegmüller.
Munich, see München.
Napoli, Italy. Centro Di Calcolo Elettronico.
Norsk Regnesentral, see Oslo.
Oslo, Norway. Norsk Regnesentral. Ole-Johan Dahl, P. Gotaas.
Paris 1, France. Compagnie des Machines Bull. M. Bourgain, P. H. Dreyfus, Mme. Poyen.
Paris 2, France. College de France. M. Poyen.
Paris 3, France. Groupe Drouot. J. M. Barroux.
Paris 4, France. IBM France. Francois Genuys.
Regnecentralen, see København.
SAAB group, see Linköping.
Siemens, see München 2.
Standard Elektrik Lorenz AG, see Stuttgart.
Stockholm 1, Sweden. Matematikmaskinnämnden (public computer development laboratory). A. Bring, Stig
    Comét, Gunnar Ehrling.
Stockholm 2, Sweden. AB Åtvidabergs Industrier (Facit). A. Olsson, B. Westling.
Stuttgart-Zuffenhausen, Germany. Standard Elektrik Lorenz AG. R. Basten, W. Heydenreich.
Svenska Aeroplan Aktiebolaget (SAAB), see Linköping.
Teddington, England. National Physical Laboratory. Mike Woodger.
Telefunken Gmbh, see Backnang.
Tyresö, Sweden. Bo Nyman ABN AB. Bertile Owe.Uppsala, Sweden.
Uppsala Universitet, Klaus Appel.
Västerås, Sweden. ASEA (manufacturer). P. Gjerløv.
Vienna, see Wien.
Wien, Austria, Mailüfterl Group, Institut für Niederfrequenztechnik, Technische Hochschule. H. Zemanek.
Zürich, Switzerland. Institut für Angewandte Mathematik, Eidgenössische Technische Hochschule. P.
    Läuchli, Heinz Rutishauser, R. Schwarz.
Zuse KG, see Bad Hersfeld.

TABLE 2

European Individuals Participating in the Development of ALGOL 60

For persons attached to a center described in Table 1 the appropriate city identification is given. Other persons are indicated as "private." The list includes all persons who appear in the European part of the mailing list of the *ALGOL Bulletin* until early 1960. It is known to be incomplete as far as participants in meetings are concerned.

Appel, Klaus: Uppsala	Comét, Stig: Stockholm 1
Barroux, J. M.: Paris 3	Dahl, Ole-Johan: Oslo
Basten, R: Stuttgart	Dahlstrand, Ingmar: Göteborg
Bauer, F. L.: München 3, Mainz	Dijkstra, Edsger W.: Amsterdam
Beyer, G.: Backnang	Dreyfus, P. H.: Paris 1
Böhm, Corrado: Italy (private)	Edmonds, A. R.: London 4
Bottenbruch, H.: Darmstadt	Ehrling, Gunnar: Stockholm 1
Bourgain, M: Paris 1	Ellis, P. V.: London 3
Bring, A.: Stockholm 1	Felton, George E.: London 2
Brokate, K. G.: Böblingen, Germany	Fröberg, Carl-Erik: Lund
(private)	Fromme, Theodor: Bad Hersfeld
Buchholz, G.: Dresden	Fuhrer, H.: Göteborg

TABLE 2 *(Continued)*

Garwick, Jan V.: Haag, Holland (private)	Petri, C. A.: Bonn
Genuys, Francois: Paris 4	Poel, W. L. van der: Leidschendam
Gill, Stanley: London 2	Poyen, Mme J.: Paris 1
Gjerløv, P.: Västerås	Poyen, M.: Paris 2
Gotaas, P.: Oslo	Pyle, Ian C.: Didcot
Graeff, P.: München 3	Rutishauser, Heinz: Zürich
Gumin, H.: München 2	Samelson, Klaus: Mainz, München 3
Hain, K.: München 1	Schappert, Heinz: Darmstadt
Händler, W.: Backnang	Schwarz, R.: Zürich
Hartley, D. F.: Cambridge	Seegmüller, Gerhard: München 3
Heinhold, J.: München 3	Shackleton, P.: Borehamwood
Heise, Willy: København, from 1960:	Unger, Heinz: Hannover
München 2	Varho, O.: Helsinki
Heydenreich, W.: Stuttgart	Vauquois, Bernard: Grenoble
Jensen, Jørn: København	Ville, J. A.: Paris (private)
Kammerer, Dr.: Jena	Walther, Alwin, Darmstadt
Kudielka: Wien (private)	Wensley, J. H.: Harrow
Landin, Peter: London 1	Westling, B.: Stockholm 2
Langefors, Börje: Linköping	Wetherfield, F.: Kidsgrove
Läuchli, P.: Zürich	Wijngaarden, Aad van: Amsterdam
Leipold, K.: München 2	Woodger, Mike: Teddington
Mondrup, Per: København	Wynn, Peter: München (private)
Naur, Peter: København	Yngvell, Sven: Linköping
Olsson, A.: Stockholm 2	Zemanek, Heinz: Wien
Owe, Bertil: Tyresö	Zonneveld, J. A.: Amsterdam
Paul, Manfred: München 3, Mainz	Øvergaard, S. A.: Kjeller
Penzlin, F.: München 3	

Appendix 2. Backus' Syntax Notation and Its Modification

Cf. Section 1.6

The difference between the syntax notation introduced in Backus (1959) and that used in the ALGOL 60 report (Backus *et al.*, 1960) is demonstrated most simply by means of an example. Thus Backus (1959) has the following formula, which shows how a label may be attached to a statement:

<basic stmt> : ≡ <b stmt> $\overline{\text{or}}$

    <label> : <b stmt>

The corresponding rule in the ALGOL 60 report is as follows:

<basic statement> : : =

    <unlabeled basic statement> |

    <label> : <basic statement>

Thus the modified notation uses : := instead of : ≡ and | instead of $\overline{\text{or}}$. In addition, in the modified form the designations of the syntactic constituents, such as "basic statement," are chosen to be exactly the same as those used for the same items in describing the semantics, without abbreviation.

The significance of the modification has been discussed by Knuth (1964).

Peter Naur

Appendix 3. Quotations from the Zurich Report† Relevant to the Development of Blocks and Procedures

Cf. Section 2.10

1.1. From Part II, 3. Expressions

(iv)   Functions F represent single numbers (function values), which result through the application of given sets of rules to fixed sets of parameters.

Form: $F \sim I(P, P, \ldots, P)$

where I is an identifier, and $P, P, \ldots, P$ is the ordered list of actual parameters specifying the parameter values for which the function is to be evaluated. A syntactic definition of parameters is given in the sections on *function declarations* and *procedure declarations*. If the function is defined by a *function declaration,* the parameters employed in any use of the function are expressions compatible with the type of variables contained in the corresponding parameter positions in the function declaration heading (cf. *function declaration*). Admissible parameters for functions defined by *procedure declarations* are the same as admissible input parameters of procedures as listed in the section on *procedure statements.*

Identifiers designating functions, just as in the case of variables, may be chosen according to taste. However, certain identifiers should be reserved for the standard functions of analysis. This reserved list should contain

abs (E) for the modulus (absolute value) of the value of the expression E
sign (E) for the sign of the value of E
entier (E) for the largest integer not greater than the value of E
sqrt (E) for the square root of the value of E
sin (E) for the sine of the value of E

and so on according to common mathematical notation.

1.2. From Part II, 4. Statements Σ

(b)   Strings of one or more statements (see note below) may be combined into a single (compound) statement by enclosing them within the "statement parentheses" **begin** and **end.** Single statements are separated by the statement separator ";".

Form: $\Sigma \sim$ **begin** $\Sigma; \Sigma; \ldots ; \Sigma$ **end**

Note: *Declarations* which may be interspersed between statements have no operational (dynamic) meaning. Therefore, they have no significance in the definition of compound statements.

1.3. From Part II, 4. Statements Σ

(ix)   Procedure statements. A procedure serves to initiate (call for) the execution of a *procedure,* that is, a closed, selfcontained process with a fixed ordered set of input and

†Backus *et al.* (1959).

output parameters, permanently defined by a *procedure declaration*. (cf. *procedure declaration*).

Form: $\Sigma \sim I(P_i, P_i, \ldots, P_i) =: (P_0, P_0, \ldots, P_0)$

Here I is an identifier which is the name of some procedure, i.e., it appears in the heading of some procedure declaration (cf. *procedure declaration*), $P_i, P_i, \ldots, P_i$ is the ordered list of actual input parameters specifying the input quantities to be processed by the procedure.

The list of actual output parameters $P_0, P_0, \ldots, P_0$, specifies the variables to which the results of the procedure will be assigned, and alternate exits if any. The procedure declaration defining the procedure called contains in its heading a string of symbols identical in form to the procedure statement, and the formal parameters occupying input and output parameter positions there give complete information concerning the admissibility of parameters employed in any procedure call shown by the following replacement rules:

Formal parameters in procedure declaration	Admissible parameters in procedure statement
Input Parameters	
Single identifier (formal variable)	Any expression (compatible with the type of the formal variable)
Array, i.e., subscripted variable with $k(\geq 1)$ empty parameter positions	Array with $n(\geq k)$ parameter positions k of which are empty
Function with k empty parameter positions	Function with $n(\geq k)$ parameter positions k of which are empty
Procedure with k empty parameter positions	Procedure with k empty parameter positions
Parameter occurring in a procedure (added as a primitive to the language, see note below)	Every string of symbols S, which does not contain the symbol "," (comma)
Output parameters	
Single identifier (formal variable)	Simple or subscripted variable
Array (as above for input parameters)	Array (as above for input parameters)
(Formal) label	Label

Note: Within a program certain procedures may be called which are themselves not defined by procedure declarations in the program, e.g., input–output procedures. These procedures may require as parameters quantities *outside* the language, e.g., a string of characters providing input–output format information.

If a parameter is at the same time an input and output parameter, this parameter must obviously meet the requirements of both input and output parameters.

Within a program, a procedure statement causes execution of the procedure called by the statement. The execution, however, is effected as though all formal parameters listed in the procedure declaration heading were replaced, throughout the procedure, by the actual parameters listed, in the corresponding position, in the procedure statement.

This replacement may be considered to be a replacement of every occurence within the procedure of the symbols, or sets of symbols, listed as formal parameters, by the symbols,

Peter Naur

or sets of symbols, listed as actual parameters in the corresponding positions of the procedure statement, after enclosing in parentheses every expression not enclosed completely
in parentheses already.

Furthermore, any return statement is to be replaced by a goto statement referring, by its
label, to the statement following the procedure statement, which, if originally unlabeled, is
treated as having been assigned a (unique) label during the replacement process.

The values assignable to, or computable by, the actual input parameters must be compatible with type declarations concerning the corresponding formal parameters which appear in the procedure.

For actual output parameters, only type declarations duplicating given type declarations
for the corresponding formal parameters may be made.

Array declarations concerning actual parameters must duplicate, in corresponding subscript positions, array declarations referring to the corresponding formal parameters.

1.4. From Part II.

5. Declarations Δ

Declarations serve to state certain facts about entities referred to within the program.
They have no operational meaning and within a given program their order of appearance is
immaterial. They pertain to the entire program (or procedure) in which they occur, and
their effect is not alterable by the running history of the program.

1.5. From Part II, 5 Declarations Δ

(ii) *Array declarations* Δ. Array declarations give the dimensions of multidimensional
arrays of quantities.

Form: $\Delta \sim \textbf{array} \ (I, I, \ . \ . \ . \ I[l:l'],$
$I, I, \ . \ . \ . \ , I[l:l'], \ . \ . \ . \ )$

where **array** is the array declarator, the I are identifiers, and the l, and l' are lists of integers separated by commas.

1.6. From Part II, 5 Declarations Δ

(iv) *Function declarations* Δ. A function declaration declares a given expression to be a
function of certain of its variables. Thereby, the declaration gives (for certain simple functions) the computing rule for assigning values to the function (cf. *functions*) whenever this
function appears in an expression.

Form: $\Delta \sim I_N(I,I, \ . \ . \ . \ , I) := E$

where the I are identifiers and E is an expression which, among its constituents, may contain simple variables named by identifiers appearing in the parentheses.

The identifier I_N is the function name. The identifiers in parentheses designate the formal
parameters of the function.

Whenever the function $I_N(P, P, \ . \ . \ . \ , P)$ appears in an expression (a *function call*) the
value assigned to the function in actual computation is the computed value of the defining

expression *E*. For the evaluation, every variable *V* which is listed as a parameter *I* in the *function declaration,* is assigned the current value of the actual parameter *P* in the corresponding position of the parameter list of the function in the function call. The (formal) variables *V* and *E* which are listed as parameters in the declaration bear no relationship to variables possessing the same identifier, but appearing elsewhere in the program. All variables other than parameters appearing in *E* have values as currently assigned in the program.

Example: $I(Z) := Z + 3 \times y$
....
   $alpha := q + I(h + 9 \times mu)$

In the statement assigning a value to alpha the computation is:

   $alpha := q + ((h + 9 \times mu) + 3 \times y)$

1.7. From Part II, 5 Declarations Δ

(*vi*) *Procedure declarations* Δ. A procedure declaration declares a program to be a closed unit (a procedure) which may be regarded as a single compound operation (in the sense of a generalized function) depending on a certain fixed set of input parameters, yielding a fixed set of results designated by output parameters, and having a fixed set of possible exits defining possible successors.

Execution of the procedure operation is initiated by a *procedure statement* which furnishes values for the input parameters, assigns the results to certain variables as output parameters, and assigns labels to the exits.

Form: Δ ~ **procedure** $I(P_i) =: (P_0), I(P_i) =: (P_0), \ldots, I(P_i) =: (P_0)$ Δ; Δ; . . . ; Δ;
   begin Σ; Σ; . . . ; Δ; Δ; . . . ; Σ; Σ
   end

Here, the *I* are identifiers giving the names of different procedures contained in the procedure declaration. Each P_i represents an ordered list of formal input parameters, each P_0 a list of formal output parameters which include any exits required by the corresponding procedures.

Some of the strings " = : (P_0)" defining outputs and exits may be missing, in which case corresponding symbols "$I(P_i)$" define a procedure that may be called within expressions.

The Δ in front of the delimiter **begin** are declarations concerning only input and output parameters. The entire string of symbols from the declarator **procedure** (inclusive) up to the delimiter **begin** (exclusive) is the *procedure heading*. Among the statements enclosed by the parentheses **begin** and **end** there must be, for each identifier *I* listed in the heading as a procedure name, exactly one statement labeled with this identifier, which then serves as the entry to the procedure. For each "single output" procedure $I(P_i)$ listed in the heading, a value must be assigned within the procedure by an assignment statement "$I := E$", where *I* is the identifier naming that procedure.

To each procedure listed in the heading, at least one **return** statement must correspond within the procedure. Some of these **return** statements may however be identical for different procedures listed in the heading.

Since a procedure is a self-contained program (except for parameters), the defining rules

Peter Naur

for statements and declarations within procedures are those already given. A formal input parameter may be

(a) a single identifier I (formal variable)
(b) an array $I[, , \ldots ,]$ with $k(k = 1, 2, \ldots)$ empty parameter positions
(c) a function $F(, , \ldots ,)$ with $k(k = 1, 2, \ldots)$ empty parameter positions
(d) a procedure $P(, , \ldots ,)$ with $k(k = 1, 2, \ldots)$ empty parameter positions
(e) an identifier occurring in a procedure which is added as a primitive to the language.

A formal output parameter may be

(a) a single identifier (formal variable)
(b) an array with $k(k = 1, 2, \ldots)$ empty subscript positions.

A formal (exit) label may only be a label.

A label is an admissible formal exit label if, within the procedure, it appears in **goto** statements or **switch** declarations.

An array declaration contained in the heading of the procedure declaration, and referring to a formal parameter, may contain expressions in its lists defining subscript ranges. These expressions may contain

1. numbers
2. formal input variables, arrays, and functions.

All identifiers and all labels contained in the procedure have identity only within the procedure, and have no relationship to identical identifiers or labels outside the procedure, with the exception of the labels identical to the different procedure names contained in the heading.

A procedure declaration, once made, is permanent, and the only identifiable constituents of the declaration are the procedure declaration heading, and the entrance labels. All rules of operations and declarations contained within the procedure may be considered to be in a language different from the algorithmic language. For this reason, a procedure may even initially be composed of statements given in a language other than the algorithmic language, e.g., a machine language may be required for expressing input–output procedures.

A tagging system may be required to identify the language form in which procedures are expressed. The specific nature of such a system is not in the scope of this report.

Thus by using procedure declarations, new primitive elements may be added to the algorithmic language at will.

Appendix 4. Notes by J. H. Wegstein

1. To Section 1.1

A bit of the human side of this history would give it a little more life. For example, the 1958 meeting was held at the Eidgenossische Technische Hochschule and the emotional welcoming address by the director along with being surrounded by the walls of this famous institution were a real inspiration to the participants. However, after two full days of sparring the meeting came to a complete deadlock with one European member pounding on the table and declaring: "No!, I will never use a period for a decimal point." That evening

Wegstein visited the opposing camps and proposed defining the three levels of language. The proposal was immediately adopted the following morning and progress resumed.

2. To Section 1.1

The name ALGOL was not adopted in 1958 but emerged later and was applied retrospectively to the 1958 results. (At one point, Prof. Bauer [or Alan Perlis, cf. appendix 7,1] wanted to call it "agricola" pointing out that it would someday be as common as cola but he couldn't defend the prefix.)

Appendix 5. Notes by F. L. Bauer

1. General Remarks

1.1. To Introduction

The time between publication of the Zurich report and the Paris conference is viewed with the eye of a Copenhagen and possibly an Amsterdam observer. Much discussions went on between the four Zurich participants of the European side, quite naturally. This discussion was initially not at all and later only sporadically reflected in the *ALGOL Bulletin,* an undertaking set up by Peter Naur on his own. Although the four Zurich participants supported the *ALGOL Bulletin,* they could not publish there the technical details of the compiler design that was under way, and many observations and reflections did come directly from this experience.

The detailed, however very interesting, discussion of the development of even minor points of the language between Zurich and ALGOL 60 is justified if a similarly thorough treatment is given to the development from the GAMM proposal to the Zurich report. Otherwise, the presentation is an axiomatic approach, with the Zurich report (who does still remember its details?) as an axiom.

Hopefully, Alan Perlis will explain some of the deliberations that led to some of the interesting points of the Zurich Report. The development on the European side, however, is not in his scope.

1.2

Some of the "improvements" of the Paris conference over the Zurich report are doubtful. This can be seen from the fact that some of the U.S. ALGOL dialects, like NELIAC, based on ALGOL 58, turned out to be competitors to ALGOL 60. Some of the obscurities and ambiguities that made the Rome Revision necessary have been side effects of changes between Zurich and Paris. This should be pointed out by Peter Naur more clearly.

1.3

I recommend that the material that Samelson has made available to Peter Naur, in particular the two GAMM proposals from October 1957 and March 1958 (translation May 1958) and of the Zurich notes, be carefully studied and evaluated by Peter Naur and be given equal consideration as the ALGOL 60 development. [Note: "Formelgruppen" stands for "procedure."]

The "sectional character" of function definitions (p. 7) and the "section postulates" of

p. 10 are first steps towards the block structure. Unfortunately, these attempts were not fully appreciated by the American members of the Zurich conference. Other proposals were rejected on grounds of "experience with FORTRAN" (Backus); for example the notation $a + 3 \rightarrow s$ for an assignment, which expresses the natural flow of computation and supports optically optimization, was finally reverted.

2. Details

2.1. To Section 1.1

Rutishauser's Historical Remarks are from the introduction to his book, which is not just "his book on ALGOL 60," but is the Volume I, Part a, of a series planned under the title "Handbook for Automatic Computation." As Editors of this series in the famous Springer Grundlehren are listed F. L. Bauer, A. S. Householder, F. W. J. Olver, H. Rutishauser, K. Samelson, E. Stiefel. This project (so far, Vol. I, Part b, by Gries, Hill and Langmaack and Vol. II by Wilkinson and Reinsch have appeared, too) has a deep connection with the development of ALGOL, however. It was started in 1957 by the initiative of F. K. Schmidt, a mathematics professor in Heidelberg, who was consulting Springer. The handbook project called for the collection of experienced and tested (numerical) algorithms, thus making both a universal language for describing them and a compiler for operating them necessary. The handbook project was in particular an incentive for developing compilers in Munich, Zurich, and Oak Ridge (see below).

2.2. To Section 1.1, Rutishauser's § 2

The GAMM Subcommittee met at Lugano, October 16–22, 1957, to finalize the draft. At that meeting Bottenbruch and Bauer had just returned from a trip to the U.S., where they had been in contact with J. W. Carr, A. J. Perlis, and some others listed in Rutishauser's footnote. They reported that they had felt that an attempt of unification would be welcomed. Correspondingly, a letter was written to J. W. Carr, the President of the ACM, inviting cooperation. This led to the activity on the U.S. side that brought the establishment of the ACM Committee.

A similar invitation was at that time addressed to learned societies in other countries, but no reply was obtained.

2.2a. To Section 1.3

ALGOL 58 implementation started in Europe from a nucleus formed by the interested institutions in Zurich, Munich, and Darmstadt and, since April 1958, Mainz; a group which called itself ZMMD-Group. It was based on the work described in the German Patent Application "Verfahren zur automatischen Verarbeitung von kodierten Daten und Rechenmaschinen zur Ausübung des Verfahrens," Nr. B 44 122 IX 42m, submitted March 30, 1957.

By the way, the name ALGOL came up during one of the ZMMD-meetings in summer 1958, at an evening party. Somebody said "Algorithmic Language—ALGOL". Those among us who had studied astronomy did see the pun, and the name did stick on. In fact, the European side of the Zurich conference participants in 1958 had not liked the IAL (International Algebraic Language) favored by the American side; it went, however, into JOVIAL, etc.

2.3. To Section 1.4

At the November 1958 Mainz meeting of persons interested in ALGOL, the ALGOL 58 compiler programmed by M. Paul from Mainz was presented; it came into practical use for the Z22 in March 1959. In Zurich and Munich, similar progress was made.

2.4. To Section 1.6

It is amusing to see how Peter Naur looks at the use of the Backus notation from his personal point of view. Among Rutishauser, Samelson, and myself there was no question that we would like for the outcome of the Paris conference a form similar to the one Backus had used for its ICIP paper (some of us had been quite familiar with equivalent formulations in mathematical logic even before and did see the notational advantages.) Thus, there was no need to do more than mention the use of Backus's notation in passing. If Peter Naur had seen this a result of his "plan" to make an appeal to the members of the ALGOL Committee concerning the style of the language description, he was running into open doors.

2.5. To Section 1.6

Assuming that Peter Naur did not know this explains one of the strange incidents of the Paris ALGOL 60 conference. While Rutishauser, Samelson, and myself (and possibly others) had concentrated on preparing themselves for the conference by working through and sorting material of the European preparatory meetings, the last one being held in Mainz in December 1959, they were surprised by Peter Naur handing them out at the beginning of the Paris conference his 18-page draft report. Peter Naur had not been commissioned to do so; it was a fait accompli. It therefore sounds poetic if he has written that his draft Report was "chosen" as the basis of the discussion; the committee was simply forced to do so, after Peter Naur had gained this advantage. Likewise, he became automatically the editor; it was only a question of politeness to invite him. Since there was some concern that he would use this position to exert some influence of his own on the language (what has happened indeed, as he indicates himself), this development was not considered to be very healthy by some committee members. (I gave Peter Naur the warning, he would now be "the pope"—a role in which I would have preferred to see Rutishauser—but he seemingly did not appreciate the remark). On the other hand, this situation has certainly helped to get a draft of the report finished in spite of the very tight time schedule of the six day Paris Meeting.

2.6. To Section 1.6

In Section 1.6 and again in Section 2.10 item 38.3, Peter Naur speaks of "my slightly revised form of Backus's notation" and "my slightly modified form of Backus's notation." I think the minor notational difference is not worth mentioning. If some people speak of Backus–Naur form instead of the original Backus Normal Form, then they indicate that Peter Naur, as the editor of the ALGOL 60 report, brought this notation to a wide attention. Backus–ALGOL Form would be more appropriate anyhow.

2.7. To Section 2.10 item 49†

A particularly sad experience is described with the events after the conference‡ had ended. Samelson and others had unsuccessfully tried to have procedures as parameters

---

† See also Appendix 6, Woodger's point 2.   ‡ Paris, Jan. 11–16, 1960.

included in ALGOL 60 in a straightforward manner (This seemingly is not recorded by Peter Naur, showing the arbitrariness of working along the written notes only). Alan Perlis then with proposal 48 of Jan. 20 *admitted* that he understood the "call by name" to be a hidden introduction of procedure parameters (later to be known as Jensen's trick). The remark "seemingly was only understood in a coherent manner by one member" is therefore cynical and should be omitted. It was under great pressure that the conference had ended and a majority had voted down a minority in the controversial point 45. Straightforward introduction of procedure parameters (and of the lambda calculus), as it was advocated by the minority, would have outflanked some of the ambiguities that made the Rome revision necessary.

2.8. To Section 2.10 Items 50 and 52

Events described by Peter Naur in item 50 (replacing *name* listings by *value* listings!) and item 52 (the Amsterdam plot on introducing recursivity) show clearly that Peter Naur had absorbed the Holy Ghost after the Paris meeting. It should be mentioned, however, that there was not only scepticism among the committee members, but also resignation that there was nothing one could do when the editor did arbitrarily change the outcome of the conference: it was to be swallowed for the sake of loyalty. These feelings, however, seemingly have not been sensed by the editor. Otherwise, I think too, he did a magnificent job.

Appendix 6. Notes by M. Woodger

1. To Section 1.6†

I am very glad that you have described your technique for control over the discussions which led to the final report. This is a contribution still not recognized for what it was really worth, and possibly even unique—I know of no other comparable case.

2. To Appendix 5, Bauer's Point 2.7‡

I have puzzled long over Bauer's point 2.7 and over my notes made at the time. I have no idea what he refers to, and I believe that my notes taken at the time are fairly representative of what was discussed in open session, although I did not understand all the details of each argument. The copies enclosed cover the discussions on 15 and 16 January 1960. My marginal note to Perlis's proposal 1 of 4:45 P.M. on 15th January shows clearly that he was proposing to treat expressions given as parameters in just the manner of his letter of 20th January [cf. Section 2.10 item 40]. My note of proposal 2 by Samelson, and the voting on it (only Bauer supporting it) suggests that Bauer may be thinking of this one. My notes on the evening discussion of 15th January support this. But this is purely conjecture, and Fritz [Bauer] must be more specific if he is to be taken seriously.

† From letter to P. Naur, 1977 October 3.
‡ From letter to P. Naur, 1978 January 27.

Appendix 7. Comments by K. Samelson, 1978 December 1

For remarks on this see Appendix 8

1. To Section 1.1

The report starts with the background, viz. ALGOL 58, which Naur starts by quoting Rutishauser's book. To this and to the respective reviewers notes, two remarks should be added. The first is that initiative and drive in setting up contacts in particular to the ACM was primarily F. L. Bauer's, who thus might be called the initiator of ALGOL. Secondly, to the best of my recollection, Joe Wegstein, in his notes [Appendix 4,2], is in error ascribing the name proposal Agricola to Bauer (from whom it would have been in questionable taste). It was Alan Perlis who, in one of the lighter moments of the meeting, made the suggestion.

2. To Section 1.6

Next, some comments seem appropriate with regard to Section 1.6., headed "Discussion Techniques," essentially a presentation of Naur's own view of his part in preparing ALGOL 60, his way to editorship of the ALGOL 60 report and his part in the ALGOL 60 committee meeting in Paris, January 1960.

Well known facts are

that Naur was the initiator and editor of the *ALGOL Bulletin,*
that he was active in contributing there,
that he was an active participant in the preparatory conferences on the European side, viz. Copenhagen February 1959, Paris November 1959, Mainz December 1959,
that he surprised the entire ALGOL 60 committee with a draft compiling and consolidating the proposals made for the Paris meeting (*not* giving a new language design) which was accepted as a guide for the meeting, and
that on account of this work he was asked to be editor of the final report.

The narrative around these facts, however, to me seems to give more insight into certain facets of the author's personality, his energy and capacity for work on the one side, his style of cooperation on the other side, than into the history of ALGOL 60.

3. Concerning BNF

On the subject of BNF (which to me has always meant Backus Normal Form, since John Backus quite alone introduced it in his Paris '59 paper) for the ALGOL 60 report, I can only contradict him. As far as I, or even the entire GAMM group, is concerned no persuasion whatsoever was necessary to use it. Rather, BNF just needed to be presented by John to be accepted as a superior means of syntax description. When Naur [Section 1.6, tenth paragraph] says of the December '59 Mainz meeting "The use of Backus's notation could only be mentioned in passing . . . ," I would say this was so because it hardly needed mentioning, being so obvious, and there were much more problematical matters at hand.

Peter Naur

4. Concerning the ALGOL 60 Meeting in Paris

To the account of the way the ALGOL 60 meeting in Paris was conducted, I would add that the mode of operation to get the material for the report in shape proposed by Naur was effective as long as there was sufficient time for discussing the matters to be voted upon, and the will to cooperate could overcome material controversies, until, in the end, time was running out on us, and on the most controversial subject, procedures (cf. Section 2.10 item 40ff.). The foreseeable result was that the final votes, after insufficient deliberation, produced a procedure concept that even Naur, as editor, found inacceptable, whereupon he on his own made changes in the direction of previous concepts, repairing part (although far from all, in my opinion) of the damage, but threw in a few unnecessary changes, too.

5. Concerning the Central Controversy

This topic, procedure concepts, carries me right into the primary objection I have against the paper. There was considerable controversy in the development. Naur mentions it rather briefly in the next but last paragraph of 1.8, but in his discussion of the content of the language, Section 2, only treats the procedure case at length. Furthermore, in 1.8, he (to my mind and recollection) wrongly labels the opposing views. Thus he covers up rather than reports on the central controversy.

This conflict was not one between "standard mathematical notation" and language "readily translatable into machine code." These two, I found then as today, go very well together. The conflict really was between the wish for extreme "flexibility" and "power" of the language, giving freedom to the programmer to express his desires in as compressed (and puzzling) a way as he wished, and, at the other side, the wish to restrict syntax in order to secure transparency, in particular local readability, comprehensibility (today I would say verifiability), and translatability of programs.

That the liberalists (the "trickologists") were the stronger party shows up all over the ALGOL 60 report. Cases in point are: the dynamic for clause (allowing all kinds of manipulations with controlled variable, step, boundary values), functions (type procedures) with no restriction on side effects, procedure headings (disappearance of the separation of arguments, results and exits, of obligatory parameter specifications and specifications of parameter structure; preponderance of call-by-name concept), general designational expressions, even the introduction of blocks as distinct from statements (a major reason being that everybody agreed upon forbidding jumping into a block, but some people found it important to be able to jump into conditional statements, right over the if clause, which then required restrictions against jumping into for statements).

The restrictionists (the "safetishists") were essentially the GAMM group: Bauer, Rutishauser, Samelson (where I always have seen myself as the strictest one; others may see it differently), with occasional support by some other like Green or McCarthy. The hard core of the liberalists consisted of Naur, Perlis, and v. Wijngaarden, with most of the others tending to support them. The outcome was as sketched out above, with the largest, and most conspicuous object, procedures, in a particularly "flexible" (for trick programmers) and cumbersome (for translators and human readers) form partly due to the time pressure on the committee.

The wide divergence of opinions on this topic is illustrated by the last paragraph of section 3.2 of the paper. Here, the author presents the unification of procedure parameters as a decisive step forward, giving a clear description of meaning, where I always have seen a procrustean generalization "unifying" conceptually different classes of objects. This unification burdens the normal case with the problems arising from the exceptional case, where the normal case is the procedure with well-defined sets of input and output parameters, and the exceptional case is the procedure with parameters with parameter-dependent input–output characteristics (which in these days of structured programming no self-respecting programmer would touch). The closing paragraph of 3.5 (proper use of procedure parameters one of the biggest problems for users) seems to support this view.

I felt then, and today, that all these things were very much to the detriment of the language which was definitely not an exercise in language design but an attempt to create a universally acceptable (and, hopefully, accepted) programming language for numerical computations. Since safe (structured) programming has become the fashion in later years, many other people today may feel the same (if thinking of ALGOL 60 at all).

6. Concerning Recursive Procedures

There are some other points in Naur's account which I have to take up. The first is his remark on recursive procedures, (Section 2.10, item 52). The U.S. proposal was to introduce a particular delimiter **recursive** in order to tag recursive procedures, not the admissibility of recursive procedures proper which at the meeting was hardly questioned. The proposal was rejected because it was essentially useless. A delimiter as proposed would have made sense only in case recursive procedures were to receive special treatment by the translator (which alone would be concerned) but could not obviate a check for actual recursivity, and could only generate additional "errors" (of erroneous presence, or absence although needed), and it would probably be insufficient to mark recursivity via actual (for formal) procedure parameters. Saying nothing about recursivity automatically introduced it in full, and the meaning of procedure (or type procedure) identifiers in procedure bodies was always clear by syntactic position. Thus the "bold addition" "Any other occurrence of the procedure identifier within the procedure body denotes activation of the procedure" was superfluous. It only served to prohibit otherwise syntactically legal misuses of the procedure identifier, e.g., accumulating intermediate values computed iteratively under the final function identifier.

7. To Section 3.1

I have always been ignorant, and wondered very much about how the statement of objectives given in the Zurich report came to be left out of the ALGOL 60 report. Considering precision and thoroughness of both the editor and the report, simple oversight seems unlikely.

A possible reason is paragraph 1. "The new language should be as close as possible to standard mathematical notation, and be readable with little further explanation."

In Section 3.1. Naur takes a very "literal" view of this paragraph. Even there I think that he (and Woodger) judge far too severely disregarding the formulation "as close as possible" which takes into account both requirements presented by reading–writing devices (strict linearity of text) and by analyzing (parsing) techniques (reduction of context dependency).

However, in Section 1.8. Naur himself indicates that the term "mathematical notation" could be, and was, interpreted in a far wider sense than purely typographically by taking into account the intent, essentially the mathematical concept of a function as a mapping from domain to range, and e.g., an expression as expressing the mapping rule which absolutely excludes any kind of so-called side effects. This Naur himself contrasts with the concept of the more or less (I would say much more than less) open computational process that conceivably may have side effects which later was brought to "perfection" in ALGOL 68. This is again the basic conflict between linguistic discipline and unrestricted liberty mentioned above.

8. To Section 3.4

Section 3.4, Design Weaknesses, lists the five problem areas identified in the revision of 1962. Of these, four are connected with the procedure concept, which supports the view that the procedure concept was far from mature due—in part at least—to time restraints posed by the strict time schedule of the Paris meeting. Apart from this I feel that the most serious (and curious) lack in ALGOL 60 was that of a simple general repetitive clause of the **while** type. The ALGOL 60 **while** rather perversely couples a "controlled variable" to the **while** via the **for** making them into a kind of siamese twins whereas the **for** can be considered to be an important special case of the general **while.**

9. Concluding Remark

As a concluding remark I should add that I had grave doubts about the wisdom of the decision to treat the "history" of ALGOL 60 on a congress and in a publication since this could only raise old, long forgotten controversies. But since the decision was made, and the publication was presented, I felt compelled to add my admittedly personal (and, as such, possibly biased), view, attempting to balance the official report by the minority report I should have written—but abstained from doing so for unity's sake—in 1960.

Appendix 8. Remarks to Samelson's Comments in Appendix 7 by P. Naur

1. The Background of Samelson's Comments

For an understanding of some of my present remarks the sequence of events leading to Samelson's comments in Appendix 7 has to be clarified. Samelson first wrote his comments in response to my preliminary unpublished notes and report dating from 1977 August to October. These comments of Samelson's, which I shall refer to as version A, were dated 1977 December. He did not send them to me until 1978 February 14. At that time it was too late for me to take them into account in my report for the preprints of the History of Programming Languages Conference. However, in a letter to Samelson on 1978 February 21 I commented on them and in particular asked him to clarify the claims made by Bauer in Appendix 5, point 2.7, and the remarks to this made by Woodger in Appendix 6, point 2, and suggested that he bring his comments in accordance with the final version of my report. Samelson did not respond to this at the time. Meanwhile I made use of Samelson's version A in preparing my oral presentation at the conference in June (see transciption p. 147ff). The document brought along by Bauer to the conference (see the Question and Answer session) also is the unrevised version A. After two invitations from me, in letters of 1978 June 8 and October 5, Samelson finally produced version B of his comments, as given in Appendix 7, and sent them to me with a letter on 1978 December 11.

2. Concerning Bauer's Claim in Appendix 5, Point 2.7

On this background it is curious that Samelson's revised set of comments, Appendix 7, is silent on the question of Bauer's claim in Appendix 5, point 2.7, as was his version A. The matter is, however, clarified in the following remark by Samelson: "Fritz [Bauer] showed me the notes [Appendix 5], and as I had no clear recollection except that I knew I had at some time or other proposed a λ-like notation for function or procedure parameters, I thought that Fritz remembered better than I did, and let it pass. For your, and Mike [Woodger]'s remarks [Appendix 6, 2] I would now conclude, that Fritz mixed up times and events" (Samelson, 1978).

3. On Samelson's Comment on BNF

As concerns Samelson's remarks on the subject of BNF (Appendix 7, 3) I do not see the contradiction, cf. Section 2.10, item 39.

4. Concerning Samelson's Two Parties

Concerning Samelson's central section, Appendix 7, item 5, that presents the picture of two opposing parties, the "liberalists" and the "restrictionists," one of course must accept that Samelson views his own role and the events in the manner he describes. However, talking only about matters of which I have firsthand experience and evidence, Samelson misrepresents my motives and actions, and his picture is contradicted by the discussions as they emerge from the original documents. To a considerable extent it seems that Samelson's presentation is colored by events that took place after March 1960 and that thus lie beyond the period covered by my report.

The relevant questions have mostly been dealt with in my main report. Thus it should be clear that my own primary interest was in the area of clear, unambiguous language description, an interest that ought to accord well with what Samelson calls a "restrictionist" attitude, in particular in dealing with a language designed for wide use.

It may also be noted that many of the language points that Samelson claims were the result of the "liberalist" influence were already in ALGOL 58, established before two of the three "hard core liberalists" had joined the effort. This holds for the dynamic **for** clause, designational expressions, and procedure parameters called by name. In fact, the presence of procedure parameters called by name in ALGOL 58 was due to Samelson himself, who in referring to the first draft of the ALGOL 58 report says: " . . . where I (to my later deep regret) filled a gap left open by the Zurich conference inserting the strict text replacement rule for procedure parameters (pre–"call by name")" (Samelson, 1977). Up to the time of the ALGOL 60 report no opposition to these features of ALGOL 58 was voiced by the "restrictionists."

Further, the outstanding new dynamic feature of ALGOL 60, the dynamic array declaration, after having been advocated by Ehrling (Section 2.10, items 2 and 4), was strongly supported by Rutishauser, claimed to be a "restrictionist" (see Section 2.10, item 21), while it was initially opposed by me, claimed to be a "liberalist" (Section 2.10, item 32).

On the question of procedures, I, far from proposing new radical ideas, spent much effort in trying to save a procedure concept that retained the "restrictionist" separation of input and output parameters (ALGOL 60 documents 5, 10, and 14). In the final round my main influence was that I followed Rutishauser's "restrictionist" suggestion for parameter specifications (Section 2.10, item 47), while also insisting that the proposal already adopted by the full committee should be understood and described clearly. How these actions can be reconciled with a membership of Samelson's "hard core liberalists" I fail to comprehend.

Altogether Samelson's claim that many of the problematic features of ALGOL 60 were due to the influence of a "stronger party of liberalists" has no support in the recorded facts. Concerning several of the features, for example, the undesirable dynamic possibilities of the **for** statement, there was simply no discussion. If in the period leading up to ALGOL 60 the members of the "restrictionist party," Bauer, Rutishauser, and Samelson, had specific proposals for avoiding these possibilities, they failed to communicate them to the ALGOL community.

More generally I feel that any attempt to describe the discussions leading to ALGOL 60 in terms of parties having clearly identifiable views and goals will be misleading. Neither the problems, nor people's views, were that simple. The description of conflicting views in Section 1.8 is not meant to imply that a corresponding grouping of the ALGOL 60 authors into parties existed.

5. On the Admission of Recursive Procedures

My answer to Samelson's remarks on the admission of recursive activations in ALGOL 60 (Appendix 7, 6) is given in my oral presentation, the transcript of which appears below.

6. The Omission of Objectives

The answer to Samelson's question (Appendix 7, 7) about the omission of the statement of objectives in the ALGOL 60 report is simple. The introduction to the report was drafted by the chairman of the meeting, Wegstein (ALGOL 60 document 28), and adopted by the full meeting with a few corrections. In the draft ALGOL 60 report this introduction was taken over unchanged. The omission of the statement of objectives was an oversight, committed by the full committee of which Samelson himself was a member, first during the meeting in Paris, and again during the weeks of scrutiny of the draft. It is quite unnecessary to look for sinister actions by "hard core liberal party members" behind this omission.

7. On the Conflicts of the Present Discussion

Finally, in response to Samelson's final remarks (Appendix 7,9), it appears from the above discussion that to Samelson the old facts are as forgotten as the old controversies. Most of the conflict of the present discussion would disappear if Samelson would consider the facts as they are recorded in the original documents, instead of blaming the imperfections of ALGOL 60, to which he has contributed equally with the rest of the authors, on a "liberalist party" existing only in his own imagination.

REFERENCES

AB, see *ALGOL Bulletin.*

Adams, C. W., and Laning, Jr., J. H. (1954). The MIT systems of automatic coding. In *Proceedings of a Symposium on Automatic Programming for Digital Computers*, pp. 40–68. Washington, D.C.

ALGOL 60 documents (1959–1960). Unpublished technical memoranda prepared in connection with the ALGOL 60 conference in Paris, 1960, Jan. 11–16. During the conference the available documents were numbered 1 to 30. Here the numbers 31 and 201 to 221 have been used for further related documents.

2: European representatives to the ALGOL 60 conference (1959) Dec. 14–16. Meeting of the European representatives to the ALGOL conference. Mainz. 4 pp.

3: Naur, P. (1960) Jan. 2. Material related to the coming international ALGOL conference in Paris. Copenhagen. 1 + 7 pp.

4A: European ALGOL committee (1959) Dec. 19. Aide-memoir on revisions of the Zürich report. Mainz. 2 pp.

5: Naur, P. (1960) Jan. 9. ALGOL 60—draft report. Regnecentralen, Copenhagen. 18 pp.

6: American representatives to the ALGOL 60 conference (1960) Jan. Proposals for the conference. 12 pp.

7: Turanski, Wm. (1960) Jan. 11. Report on ACM proposal for for-clauses. 2 pp.

8: Katz, C. (1960) Jan. 11. Report on switch declaration and do statement for ACM. 1 page.

9: Perlis, A. (1960) Jan. 12. A proposal on the global-equivalence controversy. 2 pp.

10: Naur, P. (1960) Jan. 11. Procedure declaration (supplement to document 5). 3 pp.

11: Backus, J., Green, J., Samelson, K., and van Wijngaarden, A. (1960) Jan. 13. Report of the committee on local, etc. . . . . 1 page.

12: Bauer, F. L., and Rutishauser, H. (1960) Jan. 13. Semantics of procedure statements. 2 pp.

13: Vauquois, B. (1960) Jan. 13. Proposal about subscripted variables. 1 page.

14: Naur, P. (1960) Jan. 13. Summary of parameter replacement rules of document 5. 1 page.

15: Naur, P., and Perlis, A. Meaning of types and assignments. 1 page.

16: Naur, P., and Perlis, A. (1960) Jan. 13. Types of expressions—assignments. 3 pp.

17: Katz, C., van Wijngaarden, A., and Woodger, M. (1960) Jan. 14. Report of the committee on procedure declarations and procedure calls with only one list of parameters. 1 page.

18: Green, J., Perlis A., and Samelson, K. (1960) Jan. 14. Procedure statements. 3 pp.

19: Naur, P. (1960) Jan. 14. Addition to document 5—conditional statements. 2 pp.

20: Rutishauser, H. (1960) Jan. 14. Remark concerning function declaration. 1 page.

21: McCarthy, J. (1960) Jan. 14. Namechange. 1 page.

22: Rutishauser, H. (1960) Jan. 14. Array-functions. 1 page.

23: Naur, P. (1960) Jan. 15. Compound statements and blocks (correction to document 5). 1 page.

24: McCarthy, J. Scopes of identifiers. 1 page.

25: For statement. 2 pages.

26: Procedure statements (1960) Jan. 16. 2 pp.

27: Procedure declarations (1960) Jan. 16. 2 pp.

28: Wegstein, J. H. Report on the algorithmic language ALGOL 60 (draft for the introduction). 3 pp.

29: Wegstein, J. H. At the end of the introduction add. 1 page.

30: Samelson, K., and Woodger, M. Syntax of expressions and statements. 2 pp.

31: ALGOL 60 committee (1960) Jan. 13–16. First and second list of suggested changes in document 5. Each item is authored by a member of the committee. The items are numbered 101 to 175, followed by 173–175 (used again) and $\infty - 1$. 33pp.

201: Naur, P. (1960) Jan. 17. To the members of the ALGOL 60 committee. Paris. 2 pp.

202: van Wijngaarden, A. (1960) Jan. 19. Letter to P. Naur. Amsterdam. 1 page.

203: McCarthy, J. (1960) Jan. 20. Letter to P. Naur. Cambridge, Massachusetts. 1 page.

204: Rutishauser, H. (1960) Jan. 20. Letter to the members of the ALGOL 60 committee. Zurich. 2 pp.

205: Perlis, A. (1960) Jan. 20. Letter to the members of the ALGOL 60 committee. Pittsburgh, Pennsylvania. 1 page.

206: Wegstein, J. H. (1960) Jan. 21. Letter to P. Naur. Washington, D.C. 1 page.
207: Bauer, F. L., and Samelson, K. (1960) Jan. 22. Letter to P. Naur. Mainz. 1 page.
208: Woodger, M. (1960) Jan. 25. Letter to the members of the ALGOL 60 committee. Teddington. 3 + 5 pp.
209: Katz, C. (1960) Jan. 25. Letter to P. Naur. 2 pp.
210: Rutishauser, H. (1960) Jan. 25. Letter to the members of the ALGOL 60 committee. Zurich. 1 page.
211: Green, J., and Backus, J. (1960) Jan. 26. Telegram to P. Naur. White Plains, New York. 1 page.
212: Naur, P. (1960) Febr. 4. Letter to the members of the ALGOL 60 committee. Copenhagen-Valby. 1 page.
213: Backus, J., *et al.* (1960) Febr. 4. Report on the algorithmic language ALGOL 60 (draft). Copenhagen-Valby. 26 pp.
214: van Wijngaarden, A. (1960) Febr. 4. Letter to the members of the ALGOL 60 committee. Amsterdam. 4 pp.
215: Perlis, A. J. (for Holt, A., and McCarthy, J.) (1960) Febr. Comments on the report draft. Pittsburgh, Pennsylvania. 5 pp.
216: Bauer, F. L., and Samelson, K. (1960) Febr. 12. Letter to P. Naur. Mainz. 2 pp.
217: Rutishauser, H. (1960) Febr. 14. Letter to P. Naur. Zurich. 5 pp.
218: Woodger, M. (1960) Febr. 16. Letter to P. Naur. Teddington. 2 pp.
219: Rutishauser, H. (1960) Febr. 17. Letter to P. Naur. Zurich. 2 pp.
220: Naur, P. (1960) Febr. 18. Letter to H. Rutishauser. Copenhagen-Valby. 1 page.
221: Rutishauser, H. (1960) Febr. 26. Letter to P. Naur. Zurich. 4 pp.

ALGOL Bulletin (1959). Mimeographed discussion letters (P. Naur, ed.). No. (AB) 1, 1959 March 16, 6 pp.; No. 2, 1959 May 5, 8 pp.; No. 3, 1959 June 8, 6 pp.; No. 4, 1959 Aug. 13, 7 pp.; No. 5, 1959 Sept. 28, 9 pp.; No. 6, 1959 Oct. 17, 2 pp.; No. 7, 1959 Nov. 3, 21 pp.; No. 8, 1959 Dec. 12, 15 pp. Regnecentralen, Copenhagen.

Backus, J. (1959). The syntax and semantics of the proposed international algebraic language of the Zurich ACM-GAMM conference. *Proc. International Conf. on Information Processing,* pp. 125–132, UNESCO.

Backus, J. (1979). Jan. 16. Letter to P. Naur. 3 pp.

Backus, J. W., Desilets, P. H., Evans, D. D., Goodman, R., Huskey, H., Katz, C., McCarthy, J., Orden, A., Perlis, A. J., Rich, R., Rosen, S., Turanski, W., Wegstein, J. (1958). Proposal for a programming language. Unpublished memorandum. 20 pp.

Backus, J. W., Bauer, F. L., Bottenbruch, H., Katz, C., Perlis, A. J. (ed.), Rutishauser, H., Samelson, K. (ed.), Wegstein, J. H. (1959). Report on the algorithmic language ALGOL. *Num. Math.* **1:** 41–60. Also (1958). Preliminary report—international algebraic language. *Comm. ACM* **1**(12): 8–22.

Backus, J. W., Bauer, F. L., Green, J., Katz, C., McCarthy, J., Naur, P. (ed.), Perlis, A. J., Rutishauser, H., Samelson, K., Vauquois, B., Wegstein, J. H., van Wijngaarden, A., and Woodger, M. (1960). Report on the algorithmic language ALGOL 60. *Num. Math.* **2:** 106–136. Also *Comm. ACM* **3**(5): 299–314.

Backus, J. W., *et al.* (1962). Revised report on the algorithmic language ALGOL 60. *Num. Math.* **4:** 420–453. Also *Comm. ACM* **6**(1): 1–17. Also *Computer J.* **5:** 349–367.

Bauer, F. L., Bottenbruch, H., Graeff, P., Läuchli, P., Paul, M., Penzlin, F., Rutishauser, H., and Samelson, K. (1958a). Formelübersetzungsprojekt Zürich-München-Darmstadt—Projektstufe 1: Festlegung der Formelsprache—Interner Bericht No. 2c. Unpublished memorandum. 21 + 23 pp.

Bauer, F. L., Bottenbruch, H., Rutishauser, H., Samelson, K., under cooperation of Graeff, P., Läuchli, P., and Paul, M.(1958b). Proposal for a universal language for the description of computing processes. Unpublished memorandum, Zurich. 1 + 21 pp.

Bemer, R. W. (1969). A politico-social history of ALGOL. In *Annual review in automatic programming.* (M. Halpern and C. Shaw, eds.), Vol. 5, pp. 151–237. Oxford: Pergamon.

Böhm, C. (1954). Calculatrices digitales du dechiffrage de formules logico-mathematiques par la machine même. Thesis ETH Zurich.

Dahl, O., and Nygaard, K. (1966). SIMULA—an ALGOL-based simulation language. *Comm. ACM* **9**(9): 671–82.

Ershov, A. P. (1959). *Programming programme for the BESM computer* (translated from Russian by M. Nadler). Oxford: Pergamon.

Hoffmann, W., and Walther, A. (1956). *Elektronische Rechenmaschinen und Informationsverarbeitung.* Nachrichtentechnische Fachberichte, Bd. 4. Braunschweig: Vieweg.

IBM (1954). *Specifications for the IBM mathematical formula translating system FORTRAN.* Preliminary report. Applied Science Division, Internat. Business Machines Corp., New York.

Irons, E. T. (1961). A syntax directed compiler for ALGOL 60. *Comm. ACM* **4**(1): 51–55.

Knuth, D. E. (1964). Backus Normal Form vs. Backus Naur Form. *Comm. ACM* **7**(12): 735–736.

Knuth, D. E. (1967). The remaining trouble spots in ALGOL 60. *Comm. ACM* **10**(10): 611–618.

Naur, P. (1975). Programming languages, natural languages, and mathematics. *Comm. ACM* **18**(12): 676–683.

Naur, P. (1977). A vector-handling subroutine using call by name written for EDSAC in 1951. Unpublished.

Rutishauser, H. (1952). Automatische Rechenplanfertigung bei programmgesteuerten Rechenmaschinen. Mitt. No. 3 aus dem Inst. für angewandte Math. der ETH. 45 pp. Basel: Birkhaeuser.

Rutishauser, H. (1953). Bemerkungen zum programmgesteuerten Rechnen. Vorträge über Rechenanlagen. pp. 34–37. Max-Planck-Institut für Physik, Göttingen.

Rutishauser, H. (1967). *Description of ALGOL 60.* Handbook for Automatic Computation, Vol. I, part a. Berlin and New York: Springer-Verlag.

Samelson, K. (1977). Nov. 21. Letter to P. Naur. 1 page.

Samelson, K. (1978). Dec. 11. Letter to P. Naur. 2 pp.

Samelson, K., and Bauer, F. L. (1959). Sequentielle Formelübersetzung. *Elektronische Rechenanlagen* **1**: 176–182.

Samelson, K., and Bauer, F. L. (1960). Sequential formula translation. *Comm. ACM* **3**(2): 76–83.

van Wijngaarden, A. (ed.), Koster, C. H. A., Mailloux, B. J., and Peck, J. E. L. (1969). Report on the algorithmic language ALGOL 68. *Num. Math.* **14**(2): 79–218.

Wirth, N. (1971). The programming language PASCAL. *Acta informatica* **1**: 35–63.

Woodger, M. (1959a). Report on a visit to Germany and Switzerland in November 1958. Unpublished memorandum. Teddington, National Physical Laboratory. 5 pp.

Woodger, M. (1959b). Copenhagen ALGOL conference. Unpublished, handwritten notes 6 pp.

Woodger, M. (1960) Jan. 10–16. ALGOL 60 conference in Paris. Unpublished, handwritten notes. 17 pp.

Zurich conference on "universal language" (1958) May 27–30. Unpublished summaries of the agreements of the conference. Zurich. 20 pp.

Zuse, K. (1948–1949). Über den allgemeinen Plankalkül als Mittel zur Formulierung schematisch-kombinativer Aufgaben. *Arch. Math.* **1**: 441–449.

TRANSCRIPTS OF PRESENTATIONS

THOMAS CHEATHAM: We're now to talk about that great compromise, ALGOL. We have two representatives: Alan Perlis, who, when ALGOL was born, was one of the American representatives; and Peter Naur, who was one of the European representatives. And we have proposed that what we shall do is have these gentlemen talk for a half hour apiece, and we will then field all the questions in the half hour remaining at the end, rather than have them after each speaker.

By the time of ALGOL, Alan was head of the Computer Science Department at Carnegie Institute of Technology, which of course has since been renamed. He received his Ph.D. in Applied Mathematics from MIT, and then got into computing very very quickly, working at BRL, Purdue, and Carnegie, with a strong interest in programming languages. We heard about the IT system this morning. John Backus remarked on that, one of the earlier programming languages on the 650. And there were other systems as well.

At the present time, Al is Professor of Computer Science at Yale University, where he continues his interest in programming languages, and is perhaps the most noteworthy APL freak on the East Coast.

ALAN J. PERLIS: ALGOL came into existence in several stages. Its first stage might very aptly be called the FORTRAN stage, because it owes a great deal to FORTRAN and, to a lesser degree, the other languages that were in existence prior to the first ALGOL meeting in Zurich in 1958. The various theological periods of ALGOL's history can be classified as indicated on Frame 1: there was Pre-ALGOL 58, the primitive period; Zurich where ALGOL 58 was forged, no pun intended; ALGOL 58, the language itself which emerged from that first meeting; the period from Zurich to Paris when the world attempted to come to grips with ALGOL; ALGOL 60 and its Testament which emerged from the meeting in Paris in 1960, and I call it a "testament" because as those of us know who used it to explain ALGOL 60, we very often, said that the "ALGOL report is like the Bible; it's meant to be interpreted and not read or understood."

After Paris there was the period called the "Post-Paris Blues" when the world came to grips with a language which was a little bit more complicated and deeper than they had anticipated, which required more of them in understanding its nature and what its translators would have to be able to do than people were prepared to accept. Consequently, ALGOL 60, for the best of reasons as well as the poorest of reasons, created a large amount of controversy and some ill will, largely in the United States more than in Europe. Finally we come to the current state which has been going on now for more than fifteen years. ALGOL is now so pervasive it's part of our atmosphere. Whenever any programmatic question comes up involving languages, it is immediately cast into ALGOL terms to determine how it is affected by ALGOL and how ALGOL affects it. Does it represent an improvement? Does it represent a new point of view?

The real success of ALGOL, I think, is in that last statement I made—that ALGOL has become an indigenous part of the computing environment, even to those who don't use ALGOL, who would never be caught dead using it, etc.

Those are the various stages in which ALGOL has existed. In more detail, we should recall that John W. Carr, president of the ACM in 1957, was very much interested in programming languages, seeing their use and understanding flourish, and fortunately for all of us, Fritz Bauer from Europe, a member of the GAMM group, contacted Carr and suggested that the GAMM group that had been working on programming language definition could join profitably with the ACM group working on programming languages, and together they might produce a better language than either would produce separately.

At that time, largely because of the success of FORTRAN, people were becoming very much aware of the potentials of so-called algebraic language programming. Alongside every computer then being conceived of there was such a language. There was a dire prospect, which has since been verified, that every computer would have its own language. And it was obvious also that these languages would be very little different from each other; differing only in matters of taste rather than any deep new startling insight into com-

Pre-ALGOL 58

Zurich

ALGOL 58

Zurich to Paris

ALGOL 60 and its Testament

Post-Paris Blues

ALGOL as Atmosphere

Frame 1. ALGOL's theological periods.

puting. Consequently, it seemed highly appropriate that ACM, through its committee, and GAMM, through its group, attempt to derive a standard language. At that time the word "Universal" was applied to it, meaning, I suspect, Germany and the East Coast of the United States! The West Coast was still deep into assembly language programming at that time. (That's a joke.)

The GAMM group had been working since 1955. Its membership, at least that part of the group that came to Zurich, Fritz Bauer and Samelson from Munich, Professor Rutishauser from Zurich, and Dr. Bottenbruch from Darmstadt, had been laboring long and hard over the definition of a programming language, largely one that would be useful to numerical analysts. When one examines their report submitted to the conference in Zurich, one senses the strong influence of numerical analysis.

The American group was much more concerned with translation issues, largely because all represented on the American committee were deeply involved in translator-building efforts. They were concerned with the problems of mapping language into machine code. Very few were numerical analysts. There was an interesting difference, both in background and perspective, between the European and the American groups which met in Zurich.

The Americans had already become aware in two short years of the inevitable consequence of building or defining a language, and that is, it will not stay fixed. Having defined it once, there would be a version 2, 3, 4, etc. Indeed, the IT language, mentioned by John Backus this morning, spawned at least nine dialects within a period of about three years.

The American view of the promise of ALGOL contained the hope that some new view of a programming language would emerge that none of us—using the word collectively— had thought of. For the Europeans, the issue was much more serious and pragmatic. It was necessary for the Europeans that a language be created that the numerical analyst could use, that would run on their computers and enable them to avoid, at least for a small period of time, being inundated by IBM.

So the two groups collided in Zurich with two different points of view about what should be attained. And yet, when one looks at the proposals that came from ACM and from GAMM, one is struck by their similarity. The differences are not major. Each of them dealt with what we've now come to call the "standard parts" of a "high level language" as indicated in Frame 2. Both were preoccupied with scalar processing. The assignment statement was the main transformer of information. Conditionals, loops, procedures, and jumps were there, and they were there because both groups had their feet very firmly implanted, as John [Backus] mentioned this morning, in the von Neumann machine. For

Scalar data & arrays

Assignments

Conditionals

Loops

Procedures

Jumps

Frame 2. The standard parts.

Alan J. Perlis

each of the constructions present, both groups had pretty good ideas how they could be mapped into machine code. Many ideas, as a matter of fact.

So both proposals had these constructions as their basis, and they differed only in rather small details, some of which have turned out to be more important than others. For example, the Americans, following the FORTRAN approach, had the variable being assigned to on the left. The Europeans had it on the right. The Americans used an equals sign for the assignment, thus hiding the fact that there is a direction to the assignment; the Europeans used a directed arrow pointing to the right. When ALGOL 58 came out, neither equals nor directed arrow was used, but a colon–equal and it pointed to the left. Indeed, throughout the meeting in Zurich that took place within one week, there was a very sanguine attitude voiced by all eight, *compromise at all costs*. Indeed, Professor Stiefel, as I mentioned in my paper, made a short opening address to the participants in which he said: "The best is the enemy of the good." By which he meant of course, "Don't seek for the perfect language. Otherwise you'll kill the week." He would have been relieved to know that neither the eight who were there, or any group since then, has found the perfect language.

Frame 3 shows an example—as a matter of fact, this is the **procedure** that was in the ALGOL 58 report, showing the constructs, most of which are now obvious to us all. This is a **procedure;** hence there is an identifier in the procedure, which has its same name indicating the commencing point, the starting point of the procedure. ALGOL 58, by the way, allowed a particular lexical procedure body to have within it many separate subprocedures which could link with each other in arbitrary ways. That very fine idea went out the window in ALGOL 60. At the end is the **return** indicating the termination of the procedure. The **return** also went out in ALGOL 60—the return from the procedure being replaced by falling out the bottom. Notice, the declaration **integer** k in there occurs at the end of a procedure. ALGOL 58 allowed one to put declarations anywhere. In ALGOL 60 they migrated to the beginning of blocks, a most natural place for them.

In the middle there is an **if** statement. Following the **if** statement is one of ALGOL 58's major contributions to programming: the compound statement. It's interesting in looking back at both the ACM and the GAMM proposals that both had the idea of the compound statement but neither described it as it appeared in ALGOL 58 and later served as the skeleton for the block idea in ALGOL 60.

Indeed, the compound statement idea in the American proposal showed up largely in

```
procedure Simps(F(), a, b, delta, v);
begin Simps: Ibar := V*(b − a); n := 1
             h := (b − a)/2
             J := h*(F(a) + F(b))
    J1:      S := 0
             for k := 1(1)n
             S := S + F(a + (2*k − 1)*h)
             I := J + 4*h*S
             if (delta < abs(I − Ibar))
             begin Ibar :=I; J := (I + J)/4
             n := 2*n; h := h/2
             goto J1 end
             Simps := I/3
return; integer (k, n)
end
```

Frame 3. ALGOL 58.

the need to identify a set of contiguous statements which could be copied from one part of the program into another—the open subroutine idea. It was absolutely essential that some lexical scope be identified. What the ACM group did was identify it by a pair of labels; a left label and a right label, rather than a pair of brackets such as **"begin," "end".**

The European proposal had **section**s which are disturbingly like what we later have come to call, in modern programming terms, "modules." **Section**s had the property that they're either imbedded in one another or disjoint. But again, the purpose of **section**s was to identify a scope within if statements, for statements, and copies which were in both languages.

In the ALGOL 58 discussions initially, the if clause—the word "clause" first appearing, by the way, in John Backus's 1959 IFIP paper in which his syntactic language was first made public. The if clause was first considered in ALGOL 58 as the left parenthesis for the compound statement; later it was replaced by the **begin** so that both **if** and **for**—the iteration statement—would use the same pair of brackets, left and right.

An interesting story about this particular procedure—I find it very amusing: The meeting was in June '58, and in September '58 I had the good fortune to go to the Soviet Union along with three other Americans to tell the Soviets about all the wonderful things we were doing in computing. I took along this procedure where the word *delta* was replaced by the Greek letter δ, and I think I had an α in it also in place of one of the other letters. And I showed it to Ershov in Moscow, and I said, "This is an example of a language developed at Zurich, ALGOL 58." Ershov said, "Oh, we'll run it in our computer." And I said, "You can put this text on your computer directly?" "Of course." So he disappeared through a door into an adjoining room, came back, and he said, "In a short while, we'll go and watch it run on the machine." I said, "What's behind the door?" So—we went through the door and behind the door there was a roomful of coders sitting at desks, and some of them were translating this program into three decimal character sequences, α being mapped into the integer 001, δ into the interger 002, etc., coding = into another character, and then that whole string of decimals laid out, and then sent into the machine where it was ultimately translated and run. The Russians by very simple means had solved the character input problem that had vexed so many of us for so long. Don't ever underestimate the Soviets' ability to solve problems.

ALGOL 58 was originally called the "International Algebraic Language," a very pretentious name, but sometime or other during the meeting—I don't recall just when—it was decided that it really should be called ALGOL; someone—it wasn't me—suggested that ALGOL would be a much better name, although the report, in order to ensure a more substantial following, called it the International Algebraic Language.

The ALGOL 58 language showed some of the schizophrenia which had been in both of the ACM and the GAMM proposals: Functions and procedures should be treated differently in the four areas mentioned in Frame 4, the nature of the body, the parameter evaluation mechanism, identifier collision, and place of use. Functions could only be used in expressions; procedures were statements. Functions delivered a value. Their parameters were called by value; procedures by text substitution. Nonparameters are global in functions; communication with the procedures is only through parameters. A function is only an operand. A procedure is a statement or an operand. One of the major virtues of ALGOL 60 was removing this schizophrenia, and providing only one mechanism called the "procedure."

Following the ALGOL 58 report, in the United States through the mechanism of the

(a) Nature of the body
(b) Parameter evaluation mechanism
(c) Identifier collision
(d) Place of use

Function	Procedure
(a) expression	statement
(b) value	text substitution
(c) nonparameters are global	communication only through parameters
(d) as operand	as statement or operand

Frame 4. Function–procedure schizophrenia.

Communications of the ACM and in Europe through the *ALGOL Bulletin,* proposals were made for alterations in ALGOL 58. I've listed in Frame 5 eight classes of proposals that were made during the course of the year 1959 within the United States. Interestingly enough, the American proposals were of a different nature from the European proposals. The American proposals were largely concerned with extensions to the language, the lack of input–output bothered people, extension of types—adding more types of variables; and sprucing up the syntax.

In Europe, on the other hand, the major concern was with the issues of the procedure and, in a sense, the scope of identifiers. Looking back, it seems quite clear that though the language has a much nicer shape because of the American proposals, the substantive changes came from the European modifications proposed during 1959—those that led to the definition of call-by-name parameters and blocks.

It's interesting to follow, as indicated in Peter Naur's splendid paper [and in Frame 6] the tortuous, step-by-step process by which blocks finally came into being. That concept, now so well understood by all students almost immediately, began with a set of declarations and ended in an understanding of how long a variable exists in such a block environment and was arrived at over the year 1959 in painfully slow steps, by people that are as bright as or brighter than anyone here. It only shows that what we know how to do is simple, and what we don't know how to do is complicated, and so it will always be.

Men of the stature of Dijkstra, Naur, Samelson, Rutishauser, labored long and hard through the year of 1959 to come up with something that we now take so much for granted, and is such an obviously desirable programmatic concept. But it wasn't in those days.

If we look at some of the exports from the ALGOL effort—both 58 and 60—into the

1. Arithmetic
   Boolean   Precedence

   $\uparrow \times / + - [<, >, =, \neq, \geq, \leq\} \wedge \vee \{\equiv \supset\}$ (dyadic)

2. **for** statement
   for $V := 1(1)(V*G \geq E)$

3. Multiple assignments
4. Recursion
5. Constant assignment
6. Scope of variable definition
7. Generalization of **do** statement
8. Dummy statement

Frame 5. Proposals for change (American).

1. Need for dynamic arrays.
2. Procedure declarations be nested

$\therefore$ Programs $\rightarrow$ procedures within the language.

3. Place dynamic array declaration just after **begin** of compound statement over which it is valid.
4. A declaration is a prefix to, and valid for, the statement.
5. Must be able to structure program into blocks between which communication occurs without use of parameters.
6. *new* $(l_1, \ldots, l) \ldots old (l'_1, \ldots, l')$ with lexical scope
7. Dynamic arrays *only* within procedures.
8. Finally (Mainz meeting Dec. 1959) blocks as given in the ALGOL 60 report.

Frame 6. Passage to blocks and procedures.

programming world, we find on this list, [illustrated in Frame 7] a partial one, of its contributions: BNF—not that ALGOL provided BNF, but a need to describe ALGOL provided in a sense a need for BNF and Backus gave it to us. An interesting aside—I must get back at Backus for what he said this morning—if one reads Backus's paper in the IFIP proceedings of 1959, one finds there an innocent sentence which says: "I hope to follow the syntactic description of language by a semantic description in a paper to follow in a short while." We're still waiting, all of us—not only from him of course, but from anyone, to give us an adequate semantic language for describing the intent of programming languages.

But clauses, blocks, types—types for example. Where did that come from? Did it come from a prolonged contact with logicians? No at all! Types, in a sense, came into programming because we needed a word to indicate types, and we used it the same way logicians did; they don't own it.

The procedure, function unification—call by value, call by name. Never has anything been more maligned than call by name, but it is still with us.

Side effects—to some people side effects were terrible, an indication of language destruction. Anarchy. To others, side effects were wonderful. And the ALGOL 60 group divided itself neatly into two parts: the conservatives and the radicals. The conservatives who felt that side effects are bad for one's health and one's moral life; and the others who feel that side effects give one a chance to play and probe.

Own variables—own variables came into ALGOL 60 largely at the request of John Backus, and they are very desirable. We never really found out how to define them and

BNF
clauses
blocks
types
procedure–function unification
call by value, call by name
side effects
own variables
   and
compiler technology
mathematical linguistics
linguistic growth
formal semantics

Frame 7. ALGOL 60.

Alan J. Perlis

implement them. That doesn't mean that they're wrong, just that we're not smart enough to learn how to control them.

Finally—compiler technology. It's hard to imagine any language that has had more effect on the technology of translator construction than ALGOL 60. It was ALGOL 60 that really pointed a finger at, focused on the absolute necessity of learning how to define, control and manipulate stacks. ALGOL 60 would have been impossible to adequately process in a reasonable way without the concept of stacks. Though we had stacks before, only in ALGOL 60 did stacks come to take a central place in the design of processors.

Mathematical linguistics—thought it's not fair to say that mathematical linguistics got its start from ALGOL 60, it is fair to say that ALGOL 60 provided a fertile soil in which the techniques of mathematical linguistics could be developed.

Linguistic growth—unlike FORTRAN, which was designed for a specific machine, and for which the issues were coding efficiency and properly so, ALGOL was designed for arbitrary, unknown machines. Consequently, the design of ALGOL focussed on linguistic structure. They were the first languages, both ALGOL 58 and ALGOL 60, in which linguistic issues forged to the front.

And finally, formal semantics—because of the ambiguities and annoyances in ALGOL 60, the difficulties in providing efficient translation, not recognized by the 13 people who created it, a need for formal semantics became evident.

Finally, in Frame 8 is a list—a partial one, to be sure—of programming languages, many of which I'm sure you are familiar with, by name if not by value, which owe a tremendous amount to ALGOL 58 and ALGOL 60. Some of these languages are the grafting of ALGOL onto, for example, a list-oriented language as in M-LISP. Some of them are the grafting of ALGOL onto tree processing as in FORMULA ALGOL. SIMULA, for example, is a language with many important new ideas that was grafted on top of ALGOL. Many people have tended to be confused over what it is that is SIMULA and what it is that is ALGOL. In many people's minds, SIMULA as a language is totally tied to ALGOL, so strong and pervasive has been the influence of ALGOL.

ALPHA, a language developed by the Soviets, is an extension of ALGOL 60, allowing for better input notation. APLGOL—if you want to have structured programming in APL, what do you do? You bathe it in ALGOL!! Thus misinterpreting and misunderstanding exactly what structure means in programming by arguing for example that only if one has a nest of **whiles,** proper indenting, no **go to**s, etc., can one be or have programs that contain structure. So pervasive has ALGOL's influence been that it's also cast shadows on the programming field, some of which it's going to take a long time to dispel.

EULER	ALPHA
ALGOLW	MLISP
PASCAL	APLGOL
LCC	MESA
Formula Algol	BLISS
SIMULA	C
PL/I	EUCLID
ALGOL 68	ECL

Frame 8. ALGOL 60 and its offspring. "ALGOL is a gene in every language and plays a significant role in its development."

And finally, as I would like to say, ALGOL is a gene in every language, and plays a significant role in its development, not often to the benefit, but always—always ALGOL has played a role in every programming language, give or take a few, that has developed since it came out. It has completely colored our thought. It is the mother's milk of us all. Thank you.

CHEATHAM: As we announced at the beginning, we're going to go right ahead with Peter's talk, and then have the questions for both at the end.

At the time we're talking about—the invention of the ALGOLs, Peter was at Regnecentralen in Copenhagen. He had come there recently to work on the DASK Computer. Peter's degree was in astronomy, a field which he practiced for some years before getting into the ALGOLs. Indeed, in his notes, he points out that one of the things he did with computers in astronomy was to compute the orbit for a comet whose preliminary computations had been done by Herb Grosch in 1945. [Correction: this was precomputer work, done by hand, published in 1945, using work by Grosch done a few years earlier, P. N.]

During the ALGOLs, Peter was editor of the *ALGOL Bulletin,* which was one of the most marvelous communication devices I've ever run across, a way of getting information about ALGOL spread around to a large community very quickly. And he ended up as the editor of the ALGOL report.

At present point in time, Peter is a professor of datalogy at the University of Copenhagen, where he retains an interest in programming methodology and software engineering.

PETER NAUR: The origin of ALGOL in Europe [Frame 1] can be traced right back to the origin of computers in Europe, to the pioneering work of Zuse. Actually the very first source of ideas of algorithmic languages in Europe was the work on the so-called Plankalkül published by Zuse in 1948. The line ahead to ALGOL can be traced clearly from the next similar activities by Rutishauser in Switzerland in 1951 and similar work by Böhm, also in Switzerland.

The idea of a common language can also be traced this way [Frame 2]. That was made first, as far as I can trace, at the meeting in Darmstadt in 1955 by Rutishauser and immediately seconded by Walther and Heinhold. They were from Germany.

This led to the formation of the committee of GAMM, which is the German Society of Applied Mechanics and Mathematics [Frame 3]. This set up a working committee to work on a common language to avoid the great multiplicity of languages. You see the eight members who worked on this committee on this slide. And they worked for several years and had a proposal almost finished when they decided to contact the Americans, and this then led to the collaboration of the ACM committee and the GAMM committee at the Zurich meeting in 1958. This meeting had four European members and four American members. Their names we see here in Frame 4.

This meeting was very successful. We already heard from Al Perlis about much of what

European origins of algorithmic languages:

1948 Zuse, Germany
1951 Rutishauser, Switzerland
1952 Böhm, Italy, working in Switzerland

Frame 1

First suggestion for a common algorithmic language

1955 October Darmstadt Symposium

Rutishauser, Switzerland
Walther, Germany
Heinhold, Germany

Frame 2

Subcommittee of GAMM
Gesellschaft für angewandte Mathematik und
  Mechanik

Bauer	Paul
Bottenbruch	Penzlin
Graeff	Rutishauser
Läuchli	Samelson

1957 October Contact to ACM

Frame 3

1958 May 27—June 2
Zurich meeting of ACM–GAMM committee

Europeans: Americans:

Bauer	Backus
Bottenbruch	Katz
Rutishauser	Perlis
Samelson	Wegstein

Frame 4

it did. And the group turned out their report which was dated 1958 October 20 [Frame 5]. This is the report—sometimes called the IAL Report, or the ALGOL 58 report, or the Zurich report. It's all the same thing.

This in Europe led to vigorous activity. There were a number of meetings. I have a slide here showing the main points [Frame 6]: a meeting in November, 1958, in Mainz, where the idea was spread to several other countries beyond the original central European countries of Switzerland and Germany. There was a meeting in February 1959 in Copenhagen. This became the start of the *ALGOL Bulletin,* an informal communication letter which I myself set up because I felt that we needed such a thing. There was a meeting in June of 1959 in Paris where the final plan for the revised language was made. There were meetings in November of 1959 in Paris and December 1959 in Mainz.

The final Paris conference on ALGOL 60 was in 1960 January [Frame 7], with the seven European members and the six Americans. There should have been seven, but one American member, Turanski, was killed [in an accident] just before the meeting and could not take part in the final meeting although he contributed to the preparations.

By some good fortune we have some pictures of this final meeting which might amuse you. Well here is, except for the photographer who was John McCarthy, the whole set of people [Frame 8]. You see there is a hand showing; this was the one and only unanimous vote of the meeting. And the issue of this vote was: "Do you agree to have your picture taken?" Apart from that, there was absolutely no unanimous agreement at that meeting, I can assure you.

I have other pictures. Here [Frame 9] we have Joe Wegstein and Bernard Vauquois. Joe Wegstein was the chairman of the meeting. This [Frame 10] is Mike Woodger who was the secretary. Now we come thick and fast [Frame 11], you can see the names: van Wijngaarden, Rutishauser, and Bauer; here [Frame 12] we have Charlie Katz and myself. Here [Frame 13] we have Fritz Bauer, Wijngaarden, myself, and Klaus Samelson. Here [Frame 14] we have Wijngaarden and Perlis, and Julian Green. This [Frame 15] is John Backus and Fritz Bauer in intense discussion at the blackboard. Here [Frame 16] we have Klaus Samelson, myself, and Julien Green. I'm afraid this is not any better, we don't have really good pictures of Julien Green. This [Frame 17] is a nice one of Perlis and Wijngaarden in

1958 October 20
Report on the Algorithmic Language ALGOL
  (edited by A. J. Perlis and K. Samelson)
Zurich report
ALGOL = IAL = International Algebraic Lan-
  guage = ALGOL 58

Frame 5

1958	November, Mainz
1959	February, Copenhagen, start of ALGOL Bulletin (edited by Naur)
1959	June, Paris, UNESCO
1959	November, Paris
1959	December, Mainz

Frame 6

1960 January 11–16
Paris conference on ALGOL 60

Europeans:	Americans:
Bauer	Backus
Naur	Green
Rutishauser	Katz
Samelson	McCarthy
Vauquois	Perlis
van Wijngaarden	Wegstein
Woodger	

Frame 7

close collaboration. And then finally [Frame 18]—well, you see, John McCarthy took the pictures. This one is not actually taken at the meeting, but I could add it just to make a complete set of people.

Well, we worked of course hard for that time, and finally we made our report which was then published on March 1 of the same year, the ALGOL 60 Report [Frame 19]. This then became the subject of a lot of discussion, and it was revised once. The revised report came out in 1962.

I could tell you a lot about all this. I had to concentrate on the last phase of this whole development because I only came into this myself at the beginning of 1959, which was fairly late as you can realize. Also, I could tell you a lot of things in detail, but I have to concentrate on a few things. Actually just two main questions. One is a question of procedure parameters, and one the question of recursive procedures. What I would like to try is to illustrate partly some of the technical questions, partly some of the modes of discussion which were applied in settling the language; also some problems of the history writer, and

Frame 8. Paris conference on ALGOL 60. Seated clockwise from left: Julien Green, Klaus Samelson, Charlie Katz, Peter Naur, Mike Woodger, Joe Wegstein, Bernard Vauquois, Aad v. Wijngaarden, Alan Perlis, Heinz Rutishauser, Fritz Bauer, and John Backus.

Frame 9. Joe Wegstein (left) and Bernard Vauquois.

into all this there will be the question of the interplay of actual language concepts and the description of them.

So now I will go ahead with the first issue, the question of procedure parameters, which is one limited part of the whole language development question, but one which I think illustrates some of these points rather nicely.

I will show you first an example of a procedure in ALGOL 60 [Frame 20]. This is the first part of it, this is the heading, to show you—well, you've already seen from Al Perlis's example—the flavor of it. I just point out a few important points here. First of all, this is a procedure heading; it can only define one procedure which is here called *"Transtrace"*—this is something which transposes a matrix and also finds the trace of it, a very trivial thing. You see that the parameters appearing in the heading, they're just simple identifiers. We have something called a **value** part here, which is not in the older language, and also in the specifications down here, the **array** B and **real** p, Tr, we have just identifiers.

The next slide [Frame 21] shows the procedure body of this, which is not really anything of great interest to you, I'm sure. I just remind you that in this language we have this block structure and we have the declarations at the top attached to the **begin,** making this procedure body a block.

Now I want to show you a similar construction in the older language, in the ALGOL 58, and doing so I am somewhat at a disadvantage because ALGOL 58 was a sketch. I mean, it was a magnificent thing, but many details in this language are blurred, and if you try to really express yourself in it, you may get into trouble. And I am not quite sure that what I write is proper ALGOL 58. I wouldn't be able to tell for sure. But in any case, this brings out some of the problems.

Frame 10. Mike Woodger.

This is again, the procedure heading [Frame 22]. And one interesting thing is, here we can have several procedures introduced or declared by one declaration. We have two names, *Transtrace* and *Trace,* two different things introduced or declared by the same total construction.

Then another interesting thing is these empty brackets which you see in the form *B*[,]. They were a means for indicating a subvector of a matrix, or submatrix of a matrix. That was of course a rather interesting feature of this language.

We also see a division of the parameter part in two. There is something first coming and then there is an equal colon (=:) turning to the right, which divides the list of parameters into two things, one which is input parameters, and then the output parameters.

And as a final point here, the description of parameters further down shows a complete declaration-like construction, **array** (*B*[1,1:*p*,*p*]), not like in the final language, just a single identifier. This is particularly problematic in case that your parameter is a procedure. It's really quite blurred what is intended to be placed in this language in such a case.

The next slide [Frame 23] then shows just the first part of this procedure body with an entry for one of the two actual actions; the next [Frame 24] is the end of it, the second entry with a *"Trace,"* and we have a **return,** and we have a declaration, **integer** (*i,j*), which can be put anywhere, which is characteristic of this language.

We should also mention that this procedure concept of the old language introduced for every procedure body a completely closed universe of names. There was no communica-

Frame 11. From left: Aad Wijngaarden, Heinz Rutishauser, and Fritz Bauer.

Frame 12. Charlie Katz (left) and Peter Naur.

Frame 13. From left: Fritz Bauer, Aad van Wijngaarden, Peter Naur, and Klaus Samelson.

Frame 14. Aad van Wijngaarden (left), Alan Perlis, Julien Green.

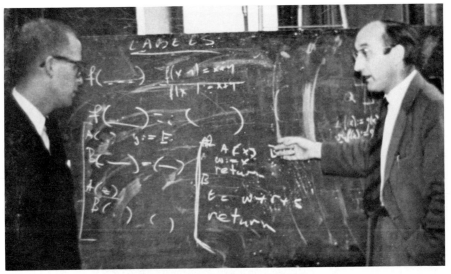

Frame 15. John Backus (left) and Fritz Bauer.

tion to the outer world except through parameters. In this way of course, recursive activations were ruled out by the language itself.

Now, the issue that I really want to discuss in a little bit more detail is the question of parameter rules. The language ALGOL 58 had talked really about two different rules for what to do in the case of a call of a procedure [Frame 25]. On the one hand, we have this division of parameters into input and output parameters, and that implies something about

Frame 16. Klaus Samelson (left), Peter Naur, and Julien Green.

Frame 17. Alan Perlis (left) and Aad van Wijngaarden.

Frame 18. John McCarthy.

Peter Naur

1960 March 1, Report on the Algorithmic Language
ALGOL 60 (edited by P. Naur)

1962, Revised Report on the Algorithmic Language
ALGOL 60

Frame 19

how they're handled at the call. On the other hand, the ALGOL 58 report very clearly has a paragraph talking about replacement; that is, that at call time, the formal parameter is supposed to be replaced, literally, as a substitution of text, by the actual parameter.

Now having such two rules really makes for some trouble, at least in sort of unusual cases. And I'll show you an example of how this can be problematic. I show another little procedure [Frame 25] "*Modifitrace*" which at the same time modifies a given matrix and finds a trace of it. You are supposed here to supply as input a matrix B, and I also have to mention B as an output parameter because it is modified in the process. Then, supposedly this M will be a modifier of, I think, the diagonal elements, and the trace will have to be formed in the output parameter T. This is a perfectly trivial little thing to do, of course. The only trouble arises when you call it in a somewhat strange way, as we will see in this further slide here [Frame 26]. The inside of it is really trivial. I form the trace by summing the diagonal elements and I modify the diagonal by this constant M. That's all there is to it. But the case here [last line of Frame 26] is that I have replaced M in the input by the same S as I had replaced the T by—you see, there is again an S here. Of course, one might say, "Why do you do this?" And that is the answer *some* people would give to this sort of argument. In any case, this seemed to me at the time to be at least worth considering, this sort of thing: What is the meaning of these two parameter substitution rules? What is the meaning, on the one hand, of the input–output distinction? And, on the other hand, in relation to the substitution rule, how are we to understand this?

This was discussed at length during 1959 [Frame 27]. I believe I myself was the first to raise this problem in June 1959 in the *ALGOL Bulletin,* where then it could be commented on by anyone interested. Nothing much came out until the meeting in Paris in 1959. That was not the final meeting, you will remember. This was an open meeting with something like 50 participants from Europe. And here this problem was taken up in a subcommittee with members as you see here on Frame 27. And they submitted a somewhat strange response to the question. It says something like: "a procedure is to be written in such a way that it achieves its intended purpose, which may be expressed by a comment in the procedure heading." They also said: "one cannot expect a procedure to be foolproof," and "one cannot expect that the maker of a procedure has foreseen every conceivable use to which it may be put." It was a sort of general philosophical argument, or warning, to gen-

Example of ALGOL 60 procedure:

procedure
    Transtrace (B, p, Tr);
value p;
array B;
real p, Tr;
comment Transposes matrix B and finds its trace,
    Tr;

Frame 20

```
begin integer i,j; real w;
Tr := 0;
for i := 1 step 1 until p do
    begin Tr := Tr + B[i,i];
    for j := 1 step 1 until i−1 do
        begin w := B[i,j]; B[i,j] :=
        B[j,i]; B[j,i] := w
        end
    end
end Transtrace;
```

Frame 21

Example of procedure according to the Zurich
report (ALGOL 58)

procedure
   Transtrace $(B[\, , \,], \text{p})$
    $= : (Tr, B[\, , \,])$,
   Trace $(B[,], p) = : (Tr)$;
   array $(B[1,1:p,p])$;
   integer (p);

Frame 22

eral users, but it really did not at all try to clarify what is the semantics of the procedure call. What is the semantics of parameter correspondences?

This was to me quite unsatisfactory, so before the final meeting—I don't know whether I intended it as a provocation—at any rate, I felt that something had to be done, so I tried to describe the procedure of the Zurich report as carefully as I could. And that became really an unpleasant document of several pages of rules, subcases—something like 15 or 16 of them altogether, depending on the nature of the actual and the formal parameters and so on. It was some attempt to make sure that this was not forgotten, that this was not ignored, that we would know how to make compilers for this language.

Then we were at the final meeting and the question of course will somehow be taken up, and immediately people look at these things. They decide, some of them, that this proposal of mine is unacceptable which, in a way, it was; and they try then in various ways to do better. There was a subcommittee of two members [Frame 28] trying to reduce the number of cases. This was not received very well by the full committee; it was not adopted. So presumably it was somehow not adequate.

Then new subcommittees were set up, one other subcommittee with three members [Frame 29]. Actually it took the step to suggest that the trouble is that we have this distinction between input and output parameters, and that to me was quite a sensible thing. A similar other subcommittee made another proposal where they retained this distinction and that was not adopted. So in this way we may say that this idea of input–output parameters was killed, indirectly perhaps, by describing it carefully; it showed that it was just too complicated to survive.

But this did not completely finish off the whole concept. Something else had to be done, and finally the meeting had a subcommittee [Frame 30], which, on the very last evening of the meeting when everybody was really exhausted, came along with a proposal which is essentially what we have now, very briefly described, and that was adopted: this business of having a name part, and then otherwise calling by value.

This seemed to be all right, until I woke up the next morning and decided it wasn't. I

```
begin
Transtrace:
for i := 1(1)p;
  begin for j := 1(1)p;
    begin w := B[i,j];
    B[i,j] := B[j,i];
    B[j,i] := w
    end
  end;
```

Frame 23

```
Trace:
Tr := 0;
for i := 1(1)p;
  Tr := Tr + B[i,i];
return;
integer (i,j)
end
```

Frame 24

Algol 58 parameter rules:

(1) Input and output parameter
(2) Replacement (call by name)

Example:

procedure *Modifitrace*
$(B[,], p, M) = : (B[,], T);$
array $(B[1,1:p,p]);$
integer $(p);$

Frame 25

begin $T := 0;$ **for** $i := 1(1)p;$
  begin $T := T + B[i,i];$
    $B[i,i] := B[i,i] + M$
  end; return; integer (i)
end

Problematic: formal param.:
$(B[,], p, M) =: (B[,], T)$
Parameters in call:
$(A[,], 5, S) =: (A[,], S)$

Frame 26

could not understand it, and I was supposed to report on it, you see. So I sent out a letter to every member that something had to be done [Frame 31]. And this then led to a rapid exchange of letters among the members on the meaning of this procedure concept. This was clarified very adequately by Perlis, and actually later careful studies of notes taken by Mike Woodger, the secretary, show that what he clarified was perfectly what had been proposed during the meeting, but I would say quite clearly, not fully understood by the committee. The whole thing took place under the great pressure of time and other issues to be discussed, of course.

Well, this is the way this concept came in. We can discuss a little bit of the consequences of it [Frame 32]. There are certain desirable consequences of the parameters called by name, that is, desirable flexibility. And that included the power of empty parameter and subscript positions. This was a surprise, I believe, to most of us, that the empty parameter positions of the old language which had been kicked out really came in in a new way. This is what is now called the Jensen Device. And for that reason I thought there would be general agreement that call by name was a good concept.

I'll just give you an example of this Jensen Device, as it appears in the ALGOL 60 report. This is a terribly long slide [Frame 33]. It's really the last line which is interesting, because this shows you how we can express the inner product of two vectors, one which is B, another one which is subvector taken out of three-dimensional array, and we have this P which is really the pointer, a parameter that controls which positions will be actually worked on in the inner product.

Now, the side effects of functions—the undesirable effects of this became a major point of controversy later. And I can point now to a difficulty of history writing in this area. Many of us who took part in that discussion, in the subsequent discussion would develop rather strong views, and it's very difficult nowadays to forget this feeling that came in later, in trying to describe what happened actually in the first place. It's very difficult to avoid such an influence on our discussion.

Well, this was the first issue, and the major issue, in my discussion. I have now another

European discussion of procedure parameters:

1959 June: Problem raised (Naur)
1959 Nov.: Leave problem to the programmer
    (Bauer, Bottenbruch, Jensen, van der Poel,
    Woodger)
1960 Jan.: Proposal for parameter handling (Naur)

Frame 27

Procedure parameters during ALGOL 60 conference, 1960 January

Proposal for reducing the number of parameter treatment cases (Bauer, Rutishauser). Not adopted.

Frame 28

Proposal to abolish the distinction between input and output parameters (Katz, van Wijngaarden, Woodger). Adopted.

Proposal for a scheme for retaining input and output parameters (Green, Perlis, Samelson). Not adopted.

Frame 29

similar issue which I can discuss with you, to illustrate how things took place, and that is the question of recursive procedures.

Recursive procedures were becoming known just barely at the time, and mostly through McCarthy's work on LISP, which was presented at various meetings. Also there was the indication that recursive processes would be useful in compilers, in certain quarters.

The actual idea of having recursiveness in ALGOL 60 was made by the Americans; there was an American proposal which I quote here [Frame 34], and it was a very brief suggestion that we should have a delimiter **recursive** to tack onto a declaration, and it just said that if a functional procedure uses itself then this should be the form of the declaration: nothing more—no attempt to draw the consequences of scope rules or parameters, things like that. That was completely left out.

This was taken up during the meeting at a certain stage, long before other issues of procedures had been clarified. And there was a vote taken on this particular proposal. Frame 35 shows what I have in my notes—a vote on forbidding recursive functions, and the vote was for forbidding—6; and against—5.

In the final language description, this whole issue was then ignored. The final description of ALGOL 60 as it was drafted did not in any way mention recursiveness or otherwise, and it so happened that the procedure concept which was then defined made recursiveness almost the obvious thing, because you have access from inside the procedure body to anything outside, so why should you not have access to your own identifier, and in this way, to the possibility of recursive call?

This was not really recognized—I didn't recognize it when I drafted the report. And then the authors had this draft in their hands during February 1960, and the only place where they became aware of this was in Amsterdam where Dijkstra and van Wijngaarden were discussing this draft. And they decided that it would be a good thing to clarify the issue. This is what van Wijngaarden tells me now. So, they called me on the telephone [Frame 36] and suggested that I add just one sentence to the report: "Any other occurrence of the procedure identifier (that is, than on the left-hand side of an assignment) within the procedure body denotes activation of the procedure." And this would then make it official that this was not illegal and obviously this would be a recursive activation.

Now, this is the way this recursiveness came in, and it was quite clear, I think, in the telephone call that the alternative would of course be to say clearly that this could not be done; that this was not permissible. And it was quite clear that this would be very difficult

Proposal for procedure parameter treatment based on a name part in the procedure declaration heading (Perlis, van Wijngaarden + ?). Adopted during the last hour of the conference.

Frame 30

1960 January 17–25

Exchange of letters among the committee members, concerning the meaning of the last proposal adopted.

Frame 31

Peter Naur

Consequences of parameters called by name:

Desirable:

Flexibility, including the power of empty parameter and subscript positions (Jensen's device)

Undesirable:

Side effects of functions and parameters

Frame 32

Example in ALGOL 60 report:

procedure *Innerproduct*
(a,b) Order:(k,p) Result:(y);
value k; **integer** k,p;
real y,a,b;
begin real s; $s := 0$;
for $p := 1$ **step** 1 **until** k **do**
    $s := s+a \times b$; $y := s$
end *Innerproduct*:
Call: $(A[t,P,u],B[P],10,P,Y)$

Frame 33

to do effectively. It is not an easy thing to make sure that you stop recursiveness in the description of ALGOL 60.

Now again, the question of history in this area: how the authors understood all this is really not clear. And my conclusion at the present time is that there was no common understanding on this issue. In the written paper there is an appendix [Appendix 5, item 2.8] with notes by Bauer, and he uses the words "the Amsterdam plot on introducing recursivity" in referring to this telephone call. I have asked the other authors on their view of this issue. Samelson [Appendix 7, item 6] says, very differently, that saying nothing about recursivity automatically introduced it in full, and this is fairly closely what van Wijngaarden [1978 May 10] also would say. I talked to him on the telephone the other day. McCarthy [1978 March 28] has written to me about this when I asked him, and he writes back quite a lot, and says also that "it was a surprise to me when the report was interpreted as admitting them. Therefore I think Bauer is correct in what I take to be his contention: that the decision of the Paris meeting was reversed in the writing of the report."

Yet another view is sentences by Al Perlis [1978 March 27] in a letter I had a short time ago. Perlis says that "we really did not understand the implications of recursion, or its value, at the ALGOL 60 meeting in Paris. McCarthy did, but the rest of us didn't." And the question—"did the vote on the American proposal turn down recursion, or the explicit labeling of recursive procedures?" This is an obvious question. I mean, what did this vote really mean, you see. Well, that is not clear at all: it's not clear to me, personally, and it's quite clear that some members would say "Having this **recursive** delimiter sitting there doesn't help anybody, because the thing that makes it recursive is recursive activation, and not putting this delimiter there"—see? So it could be that some of the people who turned down this proposal did it because it was a bad proposal for other reasons, and not because they were against recursion. It's not clear!

Well, that is really the end of my presentation, I would say. In these questions there was

Recursive procedures—American proposal to the
    ALGOL 60 conference:

"If a function or a procedure uses itself, then the
    form of the declaration shall be:

recursive function
    $I(I,I \ldots , I) := E$
    or [. . .]"

Frame 34

ALGOL 60 committee meeting vote on the
    American proposal:

Forbidding recursive functions:

For   6
Against   5

Frame 35

1960 February 10 (approx.)
Van Wijngaarden (plus Dijkstra)

Any other occurrence of the procedure identifier
within the procedure body denotes activation
of the procedure.

Frame 36

just no clear understanding among the authors; that this is part of how this language was constructed, and it couldn't be otherwise.

Generally I would like to conclude that I hope I've given you the impression that this language was constructed in a true collaboration of many people over quite a considerable time. And of course there were differences in opinion and interest, and thus the final result is a compromise, and it is quite possible to find weak points in it. I would then finally say that to me personally this whole effort was quite gratifying. I think the result of this language on the world at large was perhaps even more significant than one could really have good reason to expect from the way the whole thing took place.

Thank you.

TRANSCRIPT OF QUESTION AND ANSWER SESSION*

1. ALGOL versus FORTRAN

THOMAS CHEATHAM: The first question comes in three or four versions, versions by Mike Marcotty from General Motors, Daniel Solomon from McGill, and the one I'll read by Aaron Finerman from Stony Brook—his was to Perlis, but I think either one of you could field this: He says: "You once described FORTRAN as the language of the streets, graffiti upon the bathroom walls. You also indicate, and correctly so, that ALGOL's contributed much to the language and compiler development. Why then is FORTRAN so widely used in the real world, almost to the exclusion of all other languages except COBOL, while ALGOL is noted only for its contributions?" [Long pause while Naur and Perlis stare at each other.]

ALAN PERLIS: I think the answer is very simple. The use of the language is not determined solely, or even largely, by its linguistic perfection. Programming is an activity—it's part of a commerce. The exchange of programs, the writing of programs, the use of programs, the running of them, the maintenance, their debugging, all of that has a place in the use of a programming language. FORTRAN—I never said was graffiti on the bathrooms of the world. What I did say was that FORTRAN is the lingua franca of the computing world. It is the language of the streets in the best sense of the word, not in the prostitutional sense of the word. And it has survived and will survive because it has turned out to be a remarkably useful part of a very vital commerce. And those people, in a sense, who think of programming as merely dealing with algorithms, and all their problems being concerned with algorithmic questions, ought to look at the stability of FORTRAN as a counterexample to that view.

---

* Headings provided by P. Naur. [Members of the ALGOL 60 Committee (and others) in the audience participated in the discussion from floor microphones.]

Transcript of Question and Answer Session

CHEATHAM [to Naur]: Would you like to comment further?

PETER NAUR: No, no.

2. The Meaning of the Acronym BNF

CHEATHAM: The next question is from Bernie Galler of the University of Michigan, and he asks: "BNF is sometimes pronounced Backus–Naur–Form and sometimes Backus–Normal–Form. What was the original intention?"

NAUR: I don't know where BNF came from in the first place. [It was not used during the ALGOL 60 conference in Paris in January 1960.] I don't know—surely BNF originally meant Backus–Normal–Form. I don't know who suggested it. Perhaps Ingerman. [This is denied by Peter Z. Ingerman (1978).] I don't know.

CHEATHAM: It was a suggestion that Peter Ingerman proposed then?

NAUR: . . . Then the suggestion to change that I think was made by Don Knuth in a letter to the *Communications of the ACM,* and the justification—well, he has the justification there. I think I made reference to it [Knuth (1964) in references to Naur's paper], so there you'll find whatever justification was originally made. That's all I would like to say.

3. The Influence of Formal Linguistics

CHEATHAM: Another question that's somewhat related, from John Favaro, U.C. Berkeley—"Did the ideas of the formal linguists like Chomsky have a genuine effect on the actual development or didn't they receive much attention until people were worrying about the actual problems of compiling?"

NAUR: That question I think definitely should be put to John Backus. I would myself be quite curious to hear what John says about his background when he made this suggestion for the notation. He around?

JOHN BACKUS: As to where the idea came from—it came from a class that I took from Martin Davis. He was giving it at Atlanta State, talking about the work of Emil Post and the idea of a production. It was only in trying to describe ALGOL 58 that I realized that there was trouble about syntax description. It was obvious that Post's productions were just the thing, and I hastily adapted them to that use. And I'd just like to add that the main thing was simply the recognition that syntax needed careful description that really brought it about. It was Peter Naur's recognition of exactly the same fact independently—I just happen to have written this funny little paper that he happened to read—that caused him to use it. But I would say it was a parallel discovery, namely, that syntax had to be accurately described; that was the real thing. One last thing I'd like to add is that Peter Naur's conduct of the *ALGOL Bulletin* and his incredible preparation for that Paris meeting in which ALGOL was all written down already in his notebook—he changed it a little bit in accordance with the wishes of the committee, but it was that stuff that really made ALGOL the language that it is, and it wouldn't have even come about, I don't think, had he not done that.

4. The Influence of Committee Sizes

CHEATHAM: The next question is from Richard Miller. "What effects resulted from the increase in the size of the 1960 committee from the smaller 1958 committee?"

NAUR [to Perlis]: Well, that you must say because you were on both.

PERLIS: I think it had primarily a very beneficial effect in that it enlarged the points of view available for discussion. In particular, the addition of someone like John McCarthy with his background in list processing and recursion, adding to the European committee Peter Naur, Mike Woodger with his interest in logic—all of this just improved the sets of views available—it enlarged the points of view of the committee. So I would say that it was by and large an enormously useful thing to have had the committee enlarged. It was also politically essential. If the original group of eight had been the sole purveyors of ALGOL 60, it probably would not have achieved the widespread acceptance in Europe as quickly as it did, and that was essential for ALGOL, because it sure didn't receive much success in the United States.

5. Input–Output in ALGOL

CHEATHAM: The next question is from Paul Abrahams from New York University. "Why was I/O omitted from ALGOL 60?"

NAUR: In a way, it wasn't, of course. It was there all the time. The suggestion in the old language and in the new language—it said you could have procedures doing things which were not defined within the language itself. Then of course I would admit, certainly, that politically it was very unfortunate that we did it this way—that we ignored any details. That I think was mainly a question of expediency. We realized, I think, if we tried to do anything much in this area, we would get stuck. I believe this was the reason why the committee decided, without much discussion, to drop any such discussion on this question. Actually, my draft had a few sections suggesting a few things on input–output, and they were just wiped away. I think the overwhelming feeling of the committee was that that would be the only feasible way to go ahead.

6. ALGOL as a Standard Language for Numerical Computation

CHEATHAM: Next question is from John McCarthy, Stanford: "Didn't the ALGOL committee violate its charter to produce a standard language for numerical computation?"

NAUR: Well, some people may say so. I think it's a matter of taste, probably. As a matter of fact, ALGOL 60 is an extremely useful language for numerical algorithms. It's being used to this day extensively, so I don't think it's true that it's not useful for that purpose. I suppose the suggestion may be that in some ways it went too far in other directions which are not needed in a numerical analysis, and in that way somehow spreading its ideas—I don't know whether that is John's suggestion. That point can certainly be made.

CHEATHAM: I wonder if McCarthy, who is in the audience, or Bauer, who is in the audience, would like to make a comment?

MᴄCᴀʀᴛʜʏ: When I was invited to be on the committee, I didn't think that it was going to be the way it turned out to be, which, to put things sort of bluntly, is an academic log-rolling kind of thing where it would be a sort of thing like, "We'll get my good idea in, in exchange for getting your good idea in." I think the fact that the language was not implementable as a whole was a fault of the committee going beyond its charter. Now, of course it's true that my own interests were not in the numerical area, and I made some contribution to the debacle—not much. But it does seem to me that we simply didn't do what we had promised our sponsors we'd do. We got too interested in getting things into it.

Pᴇʀʟɪs: I think there's another answer to that, John, and that is, when you sit down to define an object of the complexity of a language such as ALGOL 60, there is an internal dynamics to the definition that runs roughshod over all of one's good intentions. So that when one looks at what actually happened, I think, in ALGOL 60, one event led to another and one definition's shortcoming led to expansion of some other definition. It would have been extremely difficult, I think, to have adequately defined the purview of the committee so that we would never have constructed anything that would take us outside that bound. We had no such well-defined limitation before us. The question John has raised really has no answer because I don't know that we did go outside the boundaries of numerical analysis because we don't know what they are.

7. ALGOL and the Commerce of Computing

Kʀɪsᴛᴇɴ Nʏɢᴀᴀʀᴅ: I want to return to another earlier question we're relating to the success of languages. We are having here a conference on the history of programming languages, but whereas we have been asked to give our papers, it is bound to be only one part of the story, and I think Perlis mentioned a very important point. Programming languages are a very important part of a very important commerce, and if you are going to have the real full story, then you must also have the story of the commercial reactions and interests in the various languages. When we designed SIMULA, we felt quite strongly the resistance against ALGOL from IBM. And we felt that it was said that ALGOL was a "long-haired" language; it was such-and-such; it was a distinction between commercial and scientific, etc., etc., which was in line with certain commercial interests. So I think we are going to cover an important part of the story at this conference, but another very important part, I feel, is only briefly going to be touched upon.

Pᴇʀʟɪs: I think that my use of the word "commerce" has been, at least in that case, misinterpreted. My use of the word "commerce" was not meant to imply that it was IBM's self-interest which determined that FORTRAN would grow and that ALGOL would wither in the United States. It certainly was the case that IBM, being the dominant computer peddler in the United States, determined to a great extent—that the language FORTRAN would flourish, but IBM has peddled other languages which haven't flourished. FORTRAN flourished because it fitted well into the needs of the customers, and that defined the commerce. SHARE is the commerce. The publication of books on FORTRAN is the commerce. The fact that every computer manufacturer feels that if he makes a machine, FORTRAN must be on it is part of the commerce. In Europe, ALGOL is part of a commerce that is not supported by any single manufacturer, but there is an atmosphere in Europe of participation in ALGOL, dissemination of ALGOL, education in ALGOL, which makes it a commercial activity. That's what I mean by "commerce"—the interplay and communication of programs and ideas about them. That's what makes commerce, and that's what makes languages survive.

8. Samelson's Set of Comments

CHEATHAM: We have a comment from Professor Bauer that he has brought—the comment is concerned with some information—a proposal of Samelson's that he has dug up and brought with him and is contributing to the whole ALGOL story. I wonder if Professor Bauer would like to make a comment.

BAUER: Can't you read it?

CHEATHAM: Yes, but I wondered if you had any further comments to make on the proceeding. I will read it. It says: "In his Appendix 6, Peter Naur quotes Mike Woodger, asking for specific details about my remark 2.7 in Appendix 5. Woodger is right that I referred to Samelson's Proposal 2. Fortunately, I could persuade Samelson to give permission to include his six-page review in the proceedings of this conference. It is herewith submitted. It contains clarifications to the above-mentioned controversy as well as other pertinent remarks." [Cf. Naur's paper, Appendices 7 and 8.]

BAUER: Yes. I think there's little I can add to it. Samelson's six pages are here. They contain quite some pertinent opinion in particular to the main issue of the procedure semantics, and it would be too much to go into the details, so I can only say whoever is interested should read this additional material in case it is published in the minutes.

9. What Makes a Language Survive

HOPPER: When I think about the dissemination and use of a language, I might remind you of the example of COBOL which most of the manufacturers attempted to kill, which was largely sponsored and developed by its own users. And I think it's the users of a language who see to it whether it grows and develops and is used or not. Certainly COBOL is a good example of that. Besides which, the Establishment didn't like it either.

10. Attention to Implementation During the Design of ALGOL

CHEATHAM: We have another technical question: "Was thought ever given as to how the language and especially the dynamic storage allocation would be implemented at the Zurich meeting?" This is from Richard Miller.

PERLIS: There was no discussion at Zurich. ALGOL 58 did not necessarily require dynamic storage allocation. ALGOL 60 did, with the introduction of the block feature. So let's assume that the question was meant to deal with ALGOL 60.

NAUR: Well, my memory is not very exact on exactly how much implementation was discussed during these meetings. My general impression, which may be contradicted by better memories, is that very little was discussed, so that the ideas of the dynamic storage allocation needed for blocks and procedures—well, for procedures, I think it was obvious that it was not—there was no time; the procedure concept did not exist until the last minute of the conference. The block structure of course had been prepared by European discussions about a month before the final meeting, but again, I don't remember clearly that too much attention was paid. But it could well be that the general idea of having a stack for your variables was around. I can't contradict it, and I can't confirm it. Maybe somebody else would reply to this.

11. The Attitudes of IBM and SHARE to ALGOL

BACKUS: I'd like to return to the issue of the earlier question of commerce of programming languages. I don't often stand up to defend IBM's action. I'm sure IBM has blocked lots of progress in its time. But in the question of blocking ALGOL, I'd like to just point out one thing that I don't think has been mentioned—that after ALGOL 58 was designed, that I was supposed to be SHARE's representative to that meeting, and I came back and reported to SHARE that they should adopt ALGOL 58. And SHARE did adopt it, enthusiastically supported it, had a committee—and in all of this, IBM was perfectly willing and almost eager to support ALGOL. And it was only because SHARE finally decided that it didn't want ALGOL—that ALGOL was changing too much; I mean, it was what John McCarthy said; we didn't fulfill our obligations of a certain kind to make a practical, realizable language; we didn't have input–output and other things; that caused SHARE to drop ALGOL. Therefore IBM didn't see that it could expend the rather enormous expense it would have taken to support something that its major customers didn't want.

12. More on Attention to Implementation

BAUER: To the previous question on implementation. In the committee meeting, in the plenary meeting, there was not time to discuss implementation. In subgroups, frequently there were hints among the groups that they knew quite well how they would have to implement it. So I found that Julien Green knew quite a lot of things he had to do if he had to implement certain things. It was clear from some of his side remarks. For the European group, Samelson, Rutishauser, and I—we had a clear plan for such a compiler, including block structure, including storage allocation even for the recursive situations. This has not been made clear so far. Rutishauser had such a scheme already in 1957, in a mental way described. He had drafted as a rule how a programmer should set up procedures, as he called them, "that can have other procedures through the back door." His back door, of course, was open to any procedure. It was exactly what Alan Perlis said—be open to any recursive use, too. However, we knew—at least Samelson, Rutishauser, and I—we knew exactly what we had to pay at that moment for including this in full generality, and it has been stated before that we had been on the pragmatic side. Our attitude was that we wanted rather to have something that could be used rather than something that was flying in the sky. There is continual disagreement about this. I know this. And Perlis was on the other side. I could quote from Samelson [in Naur's paper, Appendix 7, item 5], and I think I do now. He groups the members into two groups. He calls the ones the "liberalists trickologists" and the others as "restrictionists, safetishists–conservatives." And he says the restrictionists were essentially the GAMM group–Bauer, Rutishauser, Samelson; and I quote from Samelson: "where I always have seen myself as the strictest one; others may see it differently. With occasional support from others like Green or McCarthy. The hard core of the liberalists consisted of Naur, Perlis, and van Wijngaarden with most of the others tending to support them."

McCarthy: Two points. My first point is that my recollection of the meeting was that discussions of implementability as a criticism of any proposal was explicitly out of order in the ALGOL 60 Paris meeting. It was stated that everyone was a gentleman and no one would propose something that he didn't know how to implement, but there was no guarantee that the combination of proposals was implementable, and it wasn't. The second point is that I really thought that one of the goals of ALGOL was to knock off FOR-TRAN. I believe that many people at the time considered that a goal, and I considered it a quite practical goal, because I in particular didn't like the control structure of FORTRAN, and I thought that it was easily possible to do much better than that. Now, later on there certainly were some explicit statements that the ALGOL committee was a vehicle for group research, or something like that. These were approving statements, and so I think it was a mistake. And I think this mistake applies not merely to ALGOL, but it is the danger in every committee-produced language that there is a kind of academic log-rolling going on. It was true, I think, in PL/I, and it will be true probably in the Defense Department's shiny new language [Ada], and I think that the only way to avoid it is to require full implementations before final adoption of the language, and that's a very expensive thing to do, but it just has to be done.

Cheatham: If Joe Wegstein is here and would like to comment . . . . Do you have a comment, Joe?

Wegstein: I have no comment.

13. More on the Influence from Commerce

Nygaard: I was, to some extent, misunderstood. I didn't say that the private computer manufacturer decides the whole history. I just said that it played an important part in the development. And what I described as the feeling in Norway is true. It may have been different in other countries, but we felt it.

FULL TEXT OF ALL QUESTIONS SUBMITTED†

1. Michael Marcotty

To what do you attribute the antagonism to ALGOL in the United States?

Answer: Section 1, 7, 9, 11, 13.

2. Daniel Salomon

Why do you think ALGOL never became more popular than FORTRAN?

Answer: Section 1, 7, 9, 11, 13.

† Peter Naur has been kind enough to annotate the full set of questions and to provide answers to several that were not asked at the session. The section numbers refer to the subheadings that Professor Naur placed in the transcription of the Question and Answer Session. Ed.

3. AARON FINERMAN

You once described FORTRAN as the language of the streets, graffiti upon the bathroom walls. You also indicate, and correctly so, that ALGOL had contributed much to the language and compiler development. Why then is FORTRAN so widely used in the real world, almost to the exclusion of all other languages except COBOL, while ALGOL is noted only for its contributions?

Answer: Section 1, 7, 9, 11, 13.

4. BERNIE GALLER

"BNF" is sometimes pronounced "Backus Naur Form" and sometimes "Backus Normal Form." What was the original intention?

Answer: Section 2.

5. JOHN FAVARO

Did the ideas of the formal linguists like Chomsky have a genuine effect on the actual development, or did they not receive much attention until people were worrying about the problems of compiling ALGOL?

Answer: Section 3.

6. RICHARD MILLER

What effects resulted from the increase in size of the 60 committee from the 58 committee?

Answer: Section 4.

7. PAUL ABRAHAMS

Why was I/O omitted from ALGOL 60?

Answer: Section 5.

8. JOHN MCCARTHY

Didn't the ALGOL committee violate its charter to produce a standard language for numerical work?

Answer: Section 6.

9. FRITZ BAUER

In his Appendix 6, P. Naur quotes M. Woodger asking for specific details about my remark 2.7 in Appendix 5. Woodger is right that I referred to Samelson's proposal 2. Fortunately I could persuade K. Samelson to give permission to include his six-page review in the proceedings of this conference. It is herewith submitted, it contains clarifications to the above-mentioned controversy as well as other most pertinent remarks.

Answer: Samelson's comments are included as Appendix 7 to Naur's report and commented on in Appendix 8.

10. RICHARD MILLER

Was thought ever given as to how the language, and especially the dynamic storage allocation, would be implemented at the Zurich meeting.

Answer: Section 10, 12.

11. RICHARD MILLER

Implementation was clearly brought up between Zurich and Paris. Could you comment on the effects of this discussion.

Answer by Naur: In the European discussions conducted via the *ALGOL Bulletin,* implementation questions as such were not prominent. However, it runs like an undercurrent through the discussion of language features that implementation was continually kept in mind, often resulting in hints to the implementor or in remarks on efficiency. Also the demand for clear language definitions was a result of implementors' requirements. This undoubtedly contributed strongly to keeping the language small, simple, and clear. And in fact, a few months after the publication of the ALGOL 60 report the first European implementation was in operation in Amsterdam, soon to be followed by many others.

12. RICHARD MILLER

$$\textbf{procedure } Simps \ (F(\ ), \ a, \ b, \ delta, \ v);$$
$$\uparrow$$
$$?$$

Could you explain (possibly again!) the parenthesis set and the parameter problem more generally.

Answer by Naur: In a procedure heading in ALGOL 58 a formal parameter could be, for example, $G(\ ,\ ,\ )$, which would indicate that the corresponding actual parameter should be a procedure call having, in this example, three open parameter positions, for example $H(a,\ ,b,\ ,\ )$, or $K(\ ,\ ,c,\ )$. A similar mechanism was available for subscripted variables as parameters. Further examples are given in my talk in Frames 22, 25, and 26. The feature is described formally in Appendix 3 of my report.

13. RICHARD MILLER

Who thought up the scope rules (as expressed in the block structure) and when? What was available in ALGOL 58 compared to 60?

Answer by Naur: The matter is treated fully in Section 2.10 of my report.

14. DIT MORSE

When/how did **own** appear?

Answer: see answer to 15 below.

15. CARY COUTANT

Why were own variables implemented without including a mechanism for initializing them, thus destroying their advantage (partially) by requiring a global boolean at least?

Answer by Naur: The concept of **own** was a very late idea, not adequately prepared and poorly executed, cf. my report Sections 2.10, remark before item 40, and 3.4.

16. JURIS REINFELDS

Comment: The concept of context dependent procedure declarations is probably the largest single cause of the lack of wide acceptance of ALGOL.

This mechanism prevents independent compilation of single procedures; complicates the comprehension of procedures and does not give the programmer any additional power over non-nested procedure definitions.

Question: Why was this mechanism included in ALGOL?

Answer by Naur: Whether a separate part of a program, such as a procedure declaration, can be compiled independently depends entirely on the capabilities of the linkage editor. The claim that independent compilation of ALGOL 60 procedures is impossible is therefore an expression of unwillingness to provide a linkage editor having the appropriate capability but invalid as an argument against ALGOL 60. The arguments leading to the blocks and procedures of ALGOL 60 have been given in my report, Section 2.10.

17. RICHARD MILLER

What might have been the effect of BNF on 58 or even FORTRAN had it been available?

18. RICHARD MILLER

What about the approach: an international committee, versus a team or committee of industry people, versus a team within a single company.

19. ALLEN BRADY

ACM enforced a requirement until 1965 or so that all submitted algorithms be written in ALGOL. Under George Forsythe's tenure submitted algorithms then had to be verified ahead of time (there was a B 5000 at Stanford). At that time (during the Forsythe era) pressure was mounting to accept algorithms written in FORTRAN and ACM succumbed. Would it not be fair to say that initially a strong effort was made on the American side to promote ALGOL?

REFERENCES TO PRESENTATIONS AND QUESTIONS AND ANSWERS

Ingerman, P. Z. (1978) Sept. 20. Letter to R. L. Wexelblat.
McCarthy, J. (1978) March 28. Letter to P. Naur
Perlis, A. (1978) March 27. Letter to P. Naur.
Wijngaarden, A. van (1960) Feb. 10 approx. Telephone call to P. Naur.
Wijngaarden, A. van (1978) May 10. Telephone call to P. Naur. Summary of contents in letter of 1978 June 8 from P. Naur to A. van Wijngaarden.

BIOGRAPHY OF ALAN J. PERLIS

After receiving the Ph.D. in mathematics from MIT in 1950, I was employed as a research mathematician in the computing laboratory of the Ballistic Research Lab at Aberdeen Proving Grounds until January 1952. I returned to MIT to work at Project Whirlwind at MIT, developing programs for Whirlwind. In September 1952, I accepted an assistant professorship in mathematics at Purdue. My major responsibility was to guide the development of a university computing facility. An IBM CPC, installed in October 1952, was replaced by a Datatron 205 in the spring of 1954. In 1955, a group of us at Purdue began the development of a compiler for the language IT (Internal Translator) that we had defined. A version was operating at Purdue in 1957. In September 1956, I accepted the position of director of the newly formed computing center and associate professor of mathematics at Carnegie Tech, my alma mater. A version of IT was running on the center's IBM 650 in November 1956 and within a year was in wide use on 650's at a number of university computing centers. Research in programming languages dominated my professional life from then on, and I was honored to become the chairman of the ACM Programming Languages Committee in 1957 and a delegate to the conference in Zurich in 1958 at which ALGOL 58 was defined. In 1958, I became the first editor of a new publication, the *Communications of the ACM*.

After ALGOL 60, in 1962, I was elected president of the ACM. I was chairman of the math department at Carnegie from 1960 to 1964 and co-chairman of an interdisciplinary doctoral program in systems and communications sciences that led to the establishment of a large ARPA supported program in computer science that, in turn, prompted the establishment in 1965 of a graduate department of computer science. I became the first chairman of that department and gave up my directorship of the computation center. During the 1960s I was a member of both the NIH and NSF advisory computer committees and a member of the NAS Computer Science & Engineering Board.

In 1966, I gave the first ACM Turing lecture. I have received three honorary doctorates in science from Davis and Elkins, Waterloo, and Purdue. In 1971, I accepted the Eugene Higgins Chair in Computer Science at Yale. In 1977, I was elected to the National Academy of Engineering.

BIOGRAPHY OF PETER NAUR

Born in Frederiksberg near Copenhagen, 1928. From the age of 12 I got deeply interested in astronomy and soon began to be active in computations of the orbits of comets and minor planets. My experience goes back to computing with the aid of logarithms and includes a long period of work with desk calculators. My work in this area began to be published in 1943. A major project in this line was an orbit for a comet, based on a preliminary calculation done by Grosch, published in 1945. I started at the Copenhagen University in 1947, finished my degree in 1949. 1950–1951 I spent in Cambridge, England, where I used the EDSAC to compute the motion of planets and comets. This was a decisive exposure to computers and their programming. I remained mostly an astronomer until 1959, but still retained important ties with computing, in the USA in 1952–1953, again in Cambridge in 1953, and as a consultant to the building of the first Danish computer DASK at Regnecentralen, Copenhagen, from 1955. My final switch to computing as a full-time activity happened early in 1959, when I joined Regnecentralen. I was immediately assigned to the group that was preparing to exploit the new language, ALGOL. Regnecentralen was host to a European ALGOL implementation conference in February 1959, which led to the circulation of the *ALGOL Bulletin,* a discussion letter, from Regnecentralen. As editor of the *ALGOL Bulletin* I was drawn into the international discussions of the language, and was selected to be member of the European language design group in November 1959. In this capacity I was the editor of the ALGOL 60 report, produced as the result of the ALGOL 60 meeting in Paris in January 1960. Thus when ALGOL 60 was produced I was a computer-oriented astronomer, recently switched fully to computing.

The design of ALGOL 60 was followed immediately by my participation at Regnecentralen in the development of compilers, for ALGOL 60, in several versions, for several computers, during the years 1960 to 1967, and for COBOL during 1963–1965. From these projects my interest gradually turned to the central methods and techniques employed within them, and to the fundamental concepts of computer methods and to software engineering. Since 1969 I am professor of datalogy (computer science) at Copenhagen University. My later interests have been mainly in the area of programming methodology.

LISP Session

Chairman: Barbara Liskov
Speaker: John McCarthy
Discussant: Paul Abrahams

PAPER: HISTORY OF LISP

John McCarthy

1. Introduction

This paper concentrates on the development of the basic ideas and distinguishes two periods—Summer 1956 through Summer 1958, when most of the key ideas were developed (some of which were implemented in the FORTRAN-based FLPL), and Fall 1958 through 1962, when the programming language was implemented and applied to problems of artificial intelligence. After 1962, the development of LISP became multistranded, and different ideas were pursued in different places.

Except where I give credit to someone else for an idea or decision, I should be regarded as tentatively claiming credit for it or else regarding it as a consequence of previous decisions. However, I have made mistakes about such matters in the past, and I have received very little response to requests for comments on drafts of this paper. It is particularly easy to take as obvious a feature that cost someone else considerable thought long ago. As the writing of this paper approaches its conclusion, I have become aware of additional sources of information and additional areas of uncertainty.

As a programming language, LISP is characterized by the following ideas: computing with symbolic expressions rather than numbers, representation of symbolic expressions and other information by list structure in the memory of a computer, representation of information in external media mostly by multilevel lists and sometimes by S-expressions, a small set of selector and constructor operations expressed as functions, composition of functions as a tool for forming more complex functions, the use of conditional expressions for getting branching into function definitions, the recursive use of conditional expressions as a sufficient tool for building computable functions, the use of λ-expressions for naming functions, the representation of LISP programs as LISP data, the conditional expression interpretation of Boolean connectives, the LISP function *eval* that serves both as a formal definition of the language and as an interpreter, and garbage collection as a means of handling the erasure problem. LISP statements are also used as a command language when LISP is used in a time-sharing environment.

Some of these ideas were taken from other languages, but most were new. Toward the end of the initial period, it became clear that this combination of ideas made an elegant mathematical system as well as a practical programming language. Then mathematical neatness became a goal and led to pruning some features from the core of the language. This was partly motivated by esthetic reasons and partly by the belief that it would be easier to devise techniques for proving programs correct if the semantics were compact and without exceptions. The results of Cartwright (1976) and Cartwright and McCarthy (1978), which show that LISP programs can be interpreted as sentences and schemata of first-order logic, provide new confirmation of the original intuition that logical neatness would pay off.

2. LISP Prehistory—Summer 1956 through Summer 1958

My desire for an algebraic list-processing language for artificial intelligence work on the IBM 704 computer arose in the summer of 1956 during the Dartmouth Summer Research Project on Artificial Intelligence, which was the first organized study of AI. During this meeting, Newell, Shaw, and Simon described IPL 2, a list-processing language for RAND Corporation's JOHNNIAC computer, in which they implemented their Logic Theorist program. There was little temptation to copy IPL, because its form was based on a JOHNNIAC loader that happened to be available to them, and because the FORTRAN idea of writing programs algebraically was attractive. It was immediately apparent that arbitrary subexpressions of symbolic expressions could be obtained by composing the functions that extract immediate subexpressions, and this seemed reason enough to go to an algebraic language.

There were two motivations for developing a language for the IBM 704. First, IBM was generously establishing a New England Computation Center at MIT, which Dartmouth would use. Second, IBM was undertaking to develop a program for proving theorems in plane geometry (based on an idea of Marvin Minsky's), and I was to serve as a consultant to that project. At the time, IBM looked like a good bet to pursue artificial intelligence research vigorously, and further projects were expected. It was not then clear whether IBM's FORTRAN project would lead to a language within which list processing could conveniently be carried out or whether a new language would be required. However, many considerations were independent of how that might turn out.

Apart from consulting on the geometry program, my own research in artificial intelligence was proceeding along the lines that led to the Advice Taker proposal in 1958 (McCarthy, 1958). This involved representing information about the world by sentences in a suitable formal language and a reasoning program that would decide what to do by making logical inferences. Representing sentences by list structure seemed appropriate—it still is—and a list-processing language also seemed appropriate for programming the operations involved in deduction—and still is.

This internal representation of symbolic information gives up the familiar infix notations in favor of a notation that simplifies the task of programming the substantive computations, e.g., logical deduction or algebraic simplification, differentiation or integration. If customary notations are to be used externally, translation programs must be written. Thus most LISP programs use a prefix notation for algebraic expressions, because they usually must determine the main connective before deciding what to do next. In this LISP differs from almost every other symbolic computation system. COMIT, FORMAC, and Formula Algol programs all express the computations as operations on some approximation to the customary printed forms of symbolic expressions. SNOBOL operates on character strings but is neutral on how character strings are used to represent symbolic information. This feature probably accounts for LISP's success in competition with these languages, especially when large programs have to be written. The advantage is like that of binary computers over decimal—but larger. (In the late 1950s, neat output and convenient input notation was not generally considered important. Programs to do the kind of input and output customary today wouldn't even fit in the memories available at that time. Moreover, keypunches and printers with adequate character sets didn't exist.)

The first problem was how to do list structure in the IBM 704. This computer has a 36-bit word, and two 15-bit parts, called the address and decrement, were distinguished by special instructions for moving their contents to and from the 15-bit index registers. The address of the machine was 15 bits, so it was clear that list structure should use 15-bit pointers. Therefore, it was natural to consider the word as divided into four parts, the address part, the decrement part, the prefix part, and the tag part. The last two were three bits each and separated from each other by the decrement so that they could not be easily combined into a single six-bit part.

At this point there was some indecision about what the basic operators should be, because the operation of extracting a part of the word by masking was considered separately from the operation of taking the contents of a word in memory as a function of its address. At the time, it seemed dubious to regard the latter operation as a function, since its value depended on the contents of memory at the time the operation was performed, so it didn't act like a proper mathematical function. However, the advantages of treating it grammatically as a function so that it could be composed were also apparent.

Therefore, the initially proposed set of functions included *cwr,* standing for "Contents of the Word in Register number" and four functions that extracted the parts of the word and shifted them to a standard position at the right of the word. An additional function of three arguments that would also extract an arbitrary bit sequence was also proposed.

It was soon noticed that extraction of a subexpression involved composing the extraction of the address part with *cwr* and that continuing along the list involved composing the extraction of the decrement part with *cwr.* Therefore, the compounds *car,* standing for "Contents of the Address part of Register number," and its analogs *cdr, cpr,* and *ctr* were defined. The motivation for implementing *car* and *cdr* separately was strengthened by the vulgar fact that the IBM 704 had instructions (connected with indexing) that made these operations easy to implement. A construct operation for taking a word off the free storage list and stuffing it with given contents was also obviously required. At some point a *cons* (a, d, p, t) was defined, but it was regarded as a subroutine and not as a function with a value. This work was done at Dartmouth, but not on a computer, since the New England Computation Center was not expected to receive its IBM 704 for another year.

In connection with IBM's plane geometry project, Nathaniel Rochester and Herbert Gelernter (on the advice of McCarthy) decided to implement a list-processing language within FORTRAN, because this seemed to be the easiest way to get started, and, in those days, writing a compiler for a new language was believed to take many man-years. This work was undertaken by Herbert Gelernter and Carl Gerberich at IBM and led to FLPL, standing for FORTRAN List Processing Language. Gelernter and Gerberich noticed that *cons* should be a function, not just a subroutine, and that its value should be the location of the word that had been taken from the free storage list. This permitted new expressions to be constructed out of subsubexpressions by composing occurrences of *cons*.

While expressions could be handled easily in FLPL, and it was used successfully for the Geometry program, it had neither conditional expressions nor recursion, and erasing list structure was handled explicitly by the program.

I invented conditional expressions in connection with a set of chess legal move routines I wrote in FORTRAN for the IBM 704 at MIT during 1957–1958. This program did not use list processing. The IF statement provided in FORTRAN I and FORTRAN II was very awkward to use, and it was natural to invent a function XIF(M,N1,N2) whose value was $N1$ or $N2$ according to whether the expression M was zero or not. The function shortened many programs and made them easier to understand, but it had to be used sparingly, because all three arguments had to be evaluated before XIF was entered, since XIF was called as an ordinary FORTRAN function though written in machine language. This led to the invention of the true conditional expression which evaluates only one of $N1$ and $N2$ according to whether M is true or false and to a desire for a programming language that would allow its use.

A paper defining conditional expressions and proposing their use in ALGOL was sent to the *Communications of the ACM* but was arbitrarily demoted to a letter to the editor, because it was very short.

I spent the summer of 1958 at the IBM Information Research Department at the invitation of Nathaniel Rochester and chose differentiating algebraic expressions as a sample problem. It led to the following innovations beyond FLPL:

(a) Writing recursive function definitions using conditional expressions. The idea of differentiation is obviously recursive, and conditional expressions allowed combining the cases into a single formula.

(b) The *maplist* function that forms a list of applications of a functional argument to the elements of a list. This was obviously wanted for differentiating sums of arbitrarily many terms, and with a slight modification, it could be applied to differentiating products. (The original form was what is now called *mapcar*).

(c) To use functions as arguments, one needs a notation for functions, and it seemed natural to use the λ-notation of Church (1941). I didn't understand the rest of his book, so I wasn't tempted to try to implement his more general mechanism for defining functions. Church used higher order functionals instead of using conditional expressions. Conditional expressions are much more readily implemented on computers.

(d) The recursive definition of differentiation made no provision for erasure of abandoned list structure. No solution was apparent at the time, but the idea of complicating the elegant definition of differentiation with explicit erasure was unattractive. Needless to say, the point of the exercise was not the differentiation program itself, several of which had already been written, but rather clarification of the operations involved in symbolic computation.

In fact, the differentiation program was not implemented that summer, because FLPL allows neither conditional expressions nor recursive use of subroutines. At this point a new language was necessary, since it was very difficult both technically and politically to tinker with FORTRAN, and neither conditional expressions nor recursion could be implemented with machine language FORTRAN functions—not even with "functions" that modify the code that calls them. Moreover, the IBM group seemed satisfied with FLPL as it was and did not want to make the vaguely stated but obviously drastic changes required to allow conditional expressions and recursive definition. As I recall, they argued that these were unnecessary.

3. The Implementation of LISP

In the Fall of 1958, I became Assistant Professor of Communication Sciences (in the EE Department) at MIT, and Marvin Minsky (then an assistant professor in the Mathematics Department) and I started the MIT Artificial Intelligence Project. The project was supported by the MIT Research Laboratory of Electronics, which had a contract from the armed services that permitted great freedom to the Director, Professor Jerome Wiesner, in initiating new projects that seemed to him of scientific interest. No written proposal was ever made. When Wiesner asked Minsky and me what we needed for the project, we asked for a room, two programmers, a secretary, and a keypunch, and he asked us to also undertake the supervision of some of the six mathematics graduate students that RLE had undertaken to support.

The implementation of LISP began in Fall 1958. The original idea was to produce a compiler, but this was considered a major undertaking, and we needed some experimenting in order to get good conventions for subroutine linking, stack handling and erasure. Therefore, we started by hand-compiling various functions into assembly language and writing subroutines to provide a LISP "environment." These included programs to read and print list structure. I can't now remember whether the decision to use parenthesized list notation as the external form of LISP data was made then or whether it had already been used in discussing the paper differentiation program.

The programs to be hand-compiled were written in an informal notation called M-expressions intended to resemble FORTRAN as much as possible. Besides FORTRAN-like assignment statements and **gotos,** the language allowed conditional expressions and the basic functions of LISP. Allowing recursive function definitions required no new notation from the function definitions allowed in FORTRAN I—only the removal of the restriction —as I recall, unstated in the FORTRAN manual—forbidding recursive definitions. The M-notation also used brackets instead of parentheses to enclose the arguments in order to reserve parentheses for list-structure constants. It was intended to compile from some approximation to the M-notation, but the M-notation was never fully defined, because representing LISP functions by LISP lists became the dominant programming language when the interpreter later became available. A machine readable M-notation would have required redefinition, because the pencil-and-paper M-notation used characters unavailable on the IBM 026 keypunch.

The READ and PRINT programs induced a de facto standard external notation for symbolic information, e.g., representing $x + 3y + z$ by (PLUS X(TIMES 3 Y)Z) and $(\forall x)(P(x) \lor Q(x,y))$ by (ALL (X) (OR (P X) (Q X Y))). Any other notation necessarily requires special programming, because standard mathematical notations treat different operators in syntactically different ways. This notation later came to be called "Cambridge Polish," because it resembled the prefix notation of Lukasiewicz, and because we noticed that Quine had also used a parenthesized prefix notation.

John McCarthy

The erasure problem also had to be considered, and it was clearly unesthetic to use explicit erasure as did IPL. There were two alternatives. The first was to erase the old contents of a program variable whenever it was updated. Since the *car* and *cdr* operations were not to copy structure, merging list structure would occur, and erasure would require a system of reference counts. Since there were only six bits left in a word, and these were in separated parts of the word, reference counts seemed infeasible without a drastic change in the way list structures were represented. (A list handling scheme using reference counts was later used by Collins (1960) on a 48-bit CDC computer).

The second alternative is *garbage collection,* in which storage is abandoned until the free storage list is exhausted, the storage accessible from program variables and the stack is marked, and the unmarked storage is made into a new free storage list. Once we decided on garbage collection, its actual implementation could be postponed, because only toy examples were being done.

At that time it was also decided to use SAVE and UNSAVE routines that use a single contiguous public stack array to save the values of variables and subroutine return addresses in the implementation of recursive subroutines. IPL built stacks as list structure and their use had to be explicitly programmed. Another decision was to give up the prefix and tag parts of the word, to abandon *cwr,* and to make *cons* a function of two arguments. This left us with only a single type—the 15-bit address—so that the language didn't require declarations.

These simplifications made LISP into a way of describing computable functions much neater than the Turing machines or the general recursive definitions used in recursive function theory. The fact that Turing machines constitute an awkward programming language doesn't much bother recursive function theorists, because they almost never have any reason to write particular recursive definitions, since the theory concerns recursive functions in general. They often have reason to prove that recursive functions with specific properties exist, but this can be done by an informal argument without having to write them down explicitly. In the early days of computing, some people developed programming languages based on Turing machines; perhaps it seemed more scientific. Anyway, I decided to write a paper describing LISP both as a programming language and as a formalism for doing recursive function theory. The paper was *Recursive functions of symbolic expressions and their computation by machine, part 1* (McCarthy, 1960). Part II was never written but was intended to contain applications to computing with algebraic expressions. The paper had no influence on recursive function theorists, because it didn't address the questions that interested them.

One mathematical consideration that influenced LISP was to express programs as applicative expressions built up from variables and constants using functions. I considered it important to make these expressions obey the usual mathematical laws allowing replacement of expressions by expressions giving the same value. The motive was to allow proofs of properties of programs using ordinary mathematical methods. This is only possible to the extent that side effects can be avoided. Unfortunately, side effects are often a great convenience when computational efficiency is important, and "functions" with side effects are present in LISP. However, the so-called pure LISP is free of side effects, and Cartwright (1976) and Cartwright and McCarthy (1978) show how to represent pure LISP programs by sentences and schemata in first-order logic and prove their properties. This is an additional vindication of the striving for mathematical neatness, because it is now easier to prove that pure LISP programs meet their specifications than it is for any other programming language in extensive use. (Fans of other programming languages are challenged to write a program to concatenate lists and prove that the operation is associative.)

Another way to show that LISP was neater than Turing machines was to write a universal LISP function and show that it is briefer and more comprehensible than the description of a universal Turing machine. This was the LISP function $eval[e,a]$, which computes the value of a LISP expression e, the second argument a being a list of assignments of values to variables. (a is needed to make the recursion work.) Writing $eval$ required inventing a notation representing LISP functions as LISP data, and such a notation was devised for the purposes of the paper with no thought that it would be used to express LISP programs in practice. Logical completeness required that the notation used to express functions used as functional arguments be extended to provide for recursive functions, and the LABEL notation was invented by Nathaniel Rochester for that purpose. D. M. R. Park pointed out that LABEL was logically unnecessary since the result could be achieved using only LAMBDA—by a construction analogous to Church's Y-operator, albeit in a more complicated way.

S. R. Russell noticed that $eval$ could serve as an interpreter for LISP, promptly hand coded it, and we now had a programming language with an interpreter.

The unexpected appearance of an interpreter tended to freeze the form of the language, and some of the decisions made rather lightheartedly for the "Recursive functions ..." paper later proved unfortunate. These included the *cond* notation for conditional expressions, which leads to an unnecessary depth of parentheses, and the use of the number zero to denote the empty list NIL and the truth value **false**. Besides encouraging pornographic programming, giving a special interpretation to the address 0 has caused difficulties in all subsequent implementations.

Another reason for the initial acceptance of awkwardnesses in the internal form of LISP is that we still expected to switch to writing programs as M-expressions. The project of defining M-expressions precisely and compiling them or at least translating them into S-expressions was neither finalized nor explicitly abandoned. It just receded into the indefinite future, and a new generation of programmers appeared who preferred internal notation to any FORTRAN-like or ALGOL-like notation that could be devised.

4. From LISP I to LISP 1.5

(a) Property lists. The idea of providing each atom with a list of properties was present in the first assembly language implementation. It was also one of the theoretical ideas of the Advice Taker, although the Advice Taker (McCarthy, 1960a) would have required a property list for any expression about which information was known that did not follow from its structure. The READ and PRINT programs required that the print names of atoms be accessible, and as soon as function definition became possible, it was necessary to indicate whether a function was a SUBR in machine code or was an EXPR represented by list structure. Several functions dealing with property lists were also made available for application programs which made heavy use of them.

(b) Insertion of elements in lists and their deletion. One of the original advertised virtues of list processing for AI work was the ability to insert and delete elements of lists. Unfortunately, this facility coexists uneasily with shared list structure. Moreover, operations that insert and delete don't have a neat representation as functions. LISP has them in the form of the *rplaca* and *rplacd* pseudo-functions, but programs that use them cannot be conveniently represented in logic, because, regarded as functions, they don't permit replacement of equals by equals.

(c) Numbers. Many computations require both numbers and symbolic expressions. Numbers were originally implemented in LISP I as lists of atoms, and this proved too slow for all but the simplest computations. A reasonably efficient implementation of numbers as atoms in S-expressions was made in LISP 1.5, but in all the early LISPs, numerical computations were still 10 to 100 times slower than in FORTRAN. Efficient numerical computation requires some form of typing in the source language and a distinction between numbers treated by themselves and as elements of S-expressions. Some recent versions of LISP allow distinguishing types, but at the time, this seemed incompatible with other features.

(d) Free variables. In all innocence, James R. Slagle programmed the following LISP function definition and complained when it didn't work right.

$$testr[x, p, f, u] \leftarrow \textbf{if } p[x] \textbf{ then } f[x] \textbf{ else if } atom[x] \textbf{ then } u[\,] \textbf{ else}$$

$$testr[cdr[x], p, f, \lambda:testr[car[x], p, f, u]].$$

The object of the function is to find a subexpression of x satisfying $p[x]$ and return $f[x]$. If the search is unsuccessful, then the continuation function $u[\,]$ of no arguments is to be computed and its value returned. The difficulty was that when an inner recursion occurred, the value of x in $car[x]$ wanted was the outer value, but the inner value was actually used. In modern terminology, lexical scoping was wanted, and dynamic scoping was obtained.

I must confess that I regarded this difficulty as just a bug and expressed confidence that Steve Russell would soon fix it. He did fix it, but by inventing the so-called FUNARG device that took the lexical environment along with the functional argument. Similar difficulties later showed up in ALGOL 60, and Russell's turned out to be one of the more comprehensive solutions to the problem. While it worked well in the interpreter, comprehensiveness and speed seem to be opposed in compiled code, and this led to a succession of compromises. Unfortunately, time did not permit writing an appendix giving the history of the problem, and the interested reader is referred to Moses (1970) as a place to start. (David Park tells me that Patrick Fischer also had a hand in developing the FUNARG device.)

(e) The "program feature." Besides composition of functions and conditional expressions, LISP also allows sequential programs written with assignment statements and **gotos**. Compared to the mathematically elegant recursive function definition features, the "program feature" looks like a hasty afterthought. This is not quite correct; the idea of having sequential programs in LISP antedates that of having recursive function definition. However, the notation LISP uses for PROGs was definitely an afterthought and is far from optimal.

(f) Once the *eval* interpreter was programmed, it became available to the programmer, and it was especially easy to use because it interprets LISP programs expressed as LISP data. In particular, *eval* made possible FEXPRS and FSUBRS, which are "functions" that are not given their actual arguments but are given the expressions that evaluate to the arguments and must call *eval* themselves when they want the expressions evaluated. The main application of this facility is to functions that don't always evaluate all of their arguments; they evaluate some of them first, and then decide which others to evaluate. This facility resembles ALGOL's *call by name* but is more flexible, because *eval* is explicitly available. A first-order logic treatment of "extensional" FEXPRs and FSUBRs now seems possible.

(g) Since LISP works with lists, it was also convenient to provide for functions with variable numbers of arguments by supplying them with a list of arguments rather than the separate arguments.

Unfortunately, none of the above features has been given a comprehensive and clear mathematical semantics in connection with LISP or any other programming language. The best attempt in connection with LISP is Michael Gordon's (1973), but it is too complicated.

(h) The first attempt at a compiler was made by Robert Brayton, but was unsuccessful. The first successful LISP compiler was programmed by Timothy Hart and Michael Levin. It was written in LISP and was claimed to be the first compiler written in the language to be compiled.

Many people participated in the initial development of LISP, and I haven't been able to remember all their contributions and must settle, at this writing, for a list of names. I can remember Paul Abrahams, Robert Brayton, Daniel Edwards, Patrick Fischer, Phyllis Fox, Saul Goldberg, Timothy Hart, Louis Hodes, Michael Levin, David Luckham, Klim Maling, Marvin Minsky, David Park, Nathaniel Rochester of IBM, and Steve Russell.

Besides work on the LISP system, many applications were programmed, and this experience affected the system itself. The main applications that I can remember are a program by Rochester and Goldberg on symbolic computation of impedances and other functions associated with electrical networks, J. R. Slagle's thesis work on symbolic integration directed by Minsky, and Paul Abrahams's thesis on proof checking.

5. Beyond LISP 1.5

As a programming language, LISP had many limitations. Some of the most evident in the early 1960s were ultraslow numerical computation, inability to represent objects by blocks of registers and garbage collect the blocks, and lack of a good system for input–output of symbolic expressions in conventional notations. All these problems and others were to be fixed in LISP 2. In the meantime, we had to settle for LISP 1.5, developed at MIT, which corrected only the most glaring deficiencies.

The LISP 2 project was a collaboration of Systems Development Corporation and Information International Inc., and was initially planned for the Q32 computer, which was built by IBM for military purposes and which had a 48-bit word and 18-bit addresses, i.e., it was better than the IBM 7090 for an ambitious project. Unfortunately, the Q32 at SDC was never equipped with more than 48K words of this memory. When it became clear that the Q32 had too little memory, it was decided to develop the language for the IBM 360/67 and the Digital Equipment PDP-6; SDC was acquiring the former, while III and MIT and Stanford preferred the latter. The project proved more expensive than expected, the collaboration proved more difficult than expected, and so LISP 2 was dropped. From a 1970s point of view, this was regrettable, because much more money has since been spent to develop LISPs with fewer features. However, it was not then known that the dominant machine for AI research would be the PDP-10, a successor of the PDP-6. A part of the AI community, e.g., BBN and SRI, made what proved to be an architectural digression in doing AI work on the SDS 940 computer.

The existence of an interpreter and the absence of declarations make it particularly natural to use LISP in a time-sharing environment. It is convenient to define functions, test them, and re-edit them without ever leaving the LISP interpreter. A demonstration of LISP in a prototype time-sharing environment on the IBM 704 was made in 1960 (or 1961). (See Appendix.) L. Peter Deutsch implemented the first interactive LISP on the PDP-1 computer in 1963, but the PDP-1 had too small a memory for serious symbolic computation.

The most important implementations of LISP proved to be those for the PDP-6 computer and its successor the PDP-10, made by the Digital Equipment Corporation of Maynard, Massachusetts. In fact, the half word instructions and the stack instructions of these machines were developed with LISP's requirements in mind. The early development of LISP at MIT for this line of machines and its subsequent development of INTERLISP (née BBN LISP) and MACLISP also contributed to making these machines the machines of choice for artificial intelligence research. The IBM 704 LISP was extended to the IBM 7090 and later led to LISPs for the IBM 360 and 370.

The earliest publications on LISP were in the Quarterly Progress Reports of the MIT Research Laboratory of Electronics. McCarthy (1960b) was the first journal publication. The *LISP Programmer's Manual* by Phyllis Fox (1960) was published by the Research Laboratory of Electronics and the *LISP 1.5 Programmer's Manual* by McCarthy *et al.* (1962c) was published by MIT Press. After the publication of McCarthy and Levin (1962), many LISP implementations were made for numerous computers. However, in contrast to the situation with most widely used programming languages, no organization has ever attempted to propagate LISP, and there has never been an attempt at agreeing on a standardization, although recently A. C. Hearn has developed a "standard LISP" (Marti *et al.*, 1978) that runs on a number of computers in order to support the REDUCE system for computation with algebraic expressions.

6. Conclusions

LISP is now the second oldest programming language in present widespread use (after FORTRAN and not counting APT, which isn't used for programming *per se*). It owes its longevity to two facts. First, its core occupies some kind of local optimum in the space of programming languages given that static friction discourages purely notational changes. Recursive use of conditional expressions, representation of symbolic information externally by lists and internally by list structure, and representation of programs in the same way will probably have a very long life.

Second, LISP still has operational features unmatched by other languages that make it a convenient vehicle for higher level systems, for symbolic computation and for artificial intelligence. These include its run-time system that gives good access to the features of the host machine and its operating system, its list structure internal language that makes it a good target for compiling from yet higher level languages, its compatibility with systems that produce binary or assembly level programs, and the availability of its interpreter as a command language for driving other programs. (One can even conjecture that LISP owes its survival specifically to the fact that its programs are lists, which everyone, including me, has regarded as a disadvantage. Proposed replacements for LISP, e.g. POP-2 (Burstall *et al.*, 1968, 1971), abandoned this feature in favor of an ALGOL-like syntax, leaving no target language for higher level systems.)

LISP will become obsolete when someone makes a more comprehensive language that dominates LISP practically and also gives a clear mathematical semantics to a more comprehensive set of features.

Appendix. Humorous Anecdote

The first on-line demonstration of LISP was also the first of a precursor of time sharing that we called "time stealing." The audience comprised the participants in one of MIT's Industrial Liaison Symposia on whom it was important to make a good impression. A Flexowriter had been connected to the IBM 704 and the operating system modified so that it collected characters from the Flexowriter in a buffer when their presence was signalled by an interrupt. Whenever a carriage return occurred, the line was given to LISP for processing. The demonstration depended on the fact that the memory of the computer had just been increased from 8192 words to 32768 words, so that batches could be collected that presumed only a small memory.

The demonstration was also one of the first to use closed circuit TV in order to spare the spectators the museum feet consequent on crowding around a terminal waiting for something to happen. Thus they were on the fourth floor, and I was in the first-floor computer room exercising LISP and speaking into a microphone. The problem chosen was to determine whether a first-order differential equation of the form $M\ dx + N\ dy$ was exact by testing whether $\partial M/\partial y = \partial N/\partial x$, which also involved some primitive algebraic simplification.

Everything was going well, if slowly, when suddenly the Flexowriter began to type (at ten characters per second):

"THE GARBAGE COLLECTOR HAS BEEN CALLED. SOME INTERESTING STATISTICS ARE AS FOLLOWS:"

and on and on and on. The garbage collector was quite new at the time; we were rather proud of it and curious about it, and our normal output was on a line printer, so it printed a full page every time it was called, giving how many words were marked and how many were collected and the size of list space, etc. During a previous rehearsal, the garbage collector hadn't been called, but we had not refreshed the LISP core image, so we ran out of free storage during the demonstration.

Nothing had ever been said about a garbage collector, and I could only imagine the reaction of the audience. We were already behind time on a tight schedule, it was clear that typing out the garbage collector message would take all the remaining time allocated to the demonstration, and both the lecturer and the audience were incapacitated by laughter. I think some of them thought we were victims of a practical joker.

REFERENCES

Abrahams, Paul W. (1963). *Machine Verification of Mathematical Proof.* Ph.D. Thesis in Mathematics, MIT, Cambridge, Massachusetts.

Abrahams, Paul W. (1967). *LISP 2 Specifications.* Systems Development Corporation Technical Report TM-3417/200/00, Santa Monica, California.

Abrahams, Paul W., Barnett, J., *et al.* (1966). The LISP 2 programming language and system. *Proceedings of the Fall Joint Computer Conference,* pp. 661–676.

Allen, John (1978). *Anatomy of LISP.* McGraw Hill, New York.

John McCarthy

Berkeley, Edmund C., and Bobrow, Daniel, eds. (1964). *The Programming Language LISP, Its Operation and Applications.* Information International Incorporated, Cambridge, Massachusetts (out of print).

Burstall, R. M., Collins, J. S., and Popplestone, R. J. (1968). *The POP-2 Papers.* Edinburgh Univ. Press, Edinburgh.

Burstall, R. M., Collins, J. S., and Popplestone, R. J. (1971). *Programming in POP-2.* Edinburgh Univ. Press, Edinburgh.

Cartwright, Robert (1976). *A Practical Formal Semantic Definition and Verification System for Typed LISP.* Stanford Artificial Intelligence Laboratory Technical Report AIM-296, Stanford, California.

Cartwright, Robert, and McCarthy, John (1978). *Representation of Recursive Programs in First Order Logic* (to be published).

Church, Alonzo (1941). *Calculi of Lambda Conversion.* Princeton Univ. Press, Princeton, New Jersey.

Collins, G. E. (1960). A method for overlapping and erasure of lists. *Communications of the ACM* 3: 655–657.

Fox, Phyllis (1960). *LISP 1 Programmers Manual.* Internal Paper, MIT, Cambridge, Massachusetts.

Gelernter, H., Hansen, J. R., and Gerberich, C. L. (1960). A FORTRAN-compiled list processing language. *Journal of the ACM* 7(2): 87–101.

Gordon, Michael (1973). *Models of Pure LISP.* Experimental Programming Reports, No. 31, University of Edinburgh, Edinburgh.

Hearn, Anthony (1967). *REDUCE, A User-oriented Interactive System for Algebraic Simplification.* Stanford Artificial Intelligence Laboratory Technical Report AIM-57, Stanford, California.

Hewitt, Carl (1971). *Description and Theoretical Analysis (Using Schemata) of PLANNER: A Language for Proving Theorems and Manipulating Models in a Robot.* Ph.D. Thesis, MIT, Cambridge, Massachusetts.

McCarthy, John (1959), Letter to the Editor. *CACM* 2(8).

McCarthy, John (1960a). Programs with common sense. *Proceedings of the Symposium on the Mechanization of Thought Processes.* National Physiology Lab., Teddington, England.

McCarthy, John (1960b), Recursive functions of symbolic expressions and their computation by machine, part I. *CACM* 3(4): 184–195.

McCarthy, John (1963a). A basis for a mathematical theory of computation. In *Computer Programming and Formal Systems,* (P. Braffort and D. Hirschberg, eds.), pp. 33–70. North-Holland Pub. Amsterdam.

McCarthy, John (1963b). Towards a mathematical science of computation. *Proceedings of IFIP Congress, Munich, 1962.* pp. 21–28. North-Holland Publ., Amsterdam.

McCarthy, John, and Talcott, Carolyn (1979). *LISP: Programming and Proving* (to be published). Versions of most chapters are available at the Stanford Artificial Intelligence Laboratory.

McCarthy, J., Minsky, M., *et al.* (1959a). Quarterly Progress Report No. 52, Research Lab. of Electronics, MIT, Cambridge, Massachusetts.

McCarthy, J., Minsky, M., *et al.* (1959b). Quarterly Progress Report No. 55, Research Lab. of Electronics, MIT, Cambridge, Massachusetts.

McCarthy, J., Minsky, M., *et al.* (1960). Quarterly Progress Report No. 56, Research Lab. of Electronics, MIT, Cambridge, Massachusetts.

McCarthy, J., Minsky, M., *et al.* (1962a). Quarterly Progress Report No. 63, Research Lab. of Electronics, MIT, Cambridge, Massachusetts.

McCarthy, J., Minsky, M., *et al.* (1962b). Quarterly Progress Report No. 64, Research Lab. of Electronics, MIT, Cambridge, Massachusetts.

McCarthy, John, with Abrahams, P. W., Edwards, D., Hart, T., and Levin, M. (1962c). *LISP 1.5 Programmer's Manual.* MIT Press, Cambridge, Massachusetts.

McCarthy, J., Minsky, M., *et al.* (1963a). Quarterly Progress Report No. 68, Research Lab. of Electronics, MIT, Cambridge, Massachusetts.

McCarthy, J., Minsky, M., *et al.* (1963b). Quarterly Progress Report No. 69, Research Lab. of Electronics, MIT, Cambridge, Massachusetts.

McCarthy, J., Minsky, M., *et al.* (1965). Quarterly Progress Report No. 76, Research Lab. of Electronics, MIT, Cambridge, Massachusetts.

McCarthy, J., Minsky, M., *et al.* (1966). Quarterly Progress Report No. 80, Research Lab. of Electronics, MIT, Cambridge, Massachusetts.

Marti, J. B., Hearn, A. C., Griss, M. L., and Griss, C. (1978). *Standard LISP Report.* University of Utah Symbolic Computation Group Report No. 60, Provo, Utah.

Mathlab Group (1977). *MACSYMA Reference Manual.* Laboratory for Computer Science, MIT Version 9, Cambridge, Massachusetts.

Mitchell, R. W. (1964). *LISP 2 Specifications Proposal*. Stanford Artificial Intelligence Laboratory Memo No. 21, Stanford, California.

Moon, David A. (1974). *MACLISP Reference Manual*, Project MAC Technical Report, MIT, Cambridge, Massachusetts.

Moses, Joel (1970). *The function of FUNCTION in LISP or Why the FUNARG Problem Should Be Called the Environment Problem*. MIT Artificial Intelligence Memo 199, Cambridge, Massachusetts.

Newell, A., and Shaw, J. C. (1957). Programming the logic theory machine. *Proceedings of the 1957 Western Joint Computer Conference*. IRE. pp. 230–240.

Rulifson, J., *et al.* (1968). QA4—A language for writing problem-solving programs. *Proceeding IFIP 1968 Congress*, TA-2, pp. 111–115.

Sussman, G. Winograd, T., and Charniak, E. (1970). *Microplanner Reference Manual*. AI Memo 203, AIL MIT, Cambridge, Massachusetts.

Teitelman, Warren (1975). *INTERLISP: Interlisp Reference Manual*. Xerox PARC Technical Report, Palo Alto, California.

Weisman, Clark (1967). *LISP 1.5 Primer*. Dickenson Press, Belmont, California.

Many reports and memoranda of the MIT and Stanford Artificial Intelligence Laboratories have dealt with various aspects of LISP and higher level systems built on LISP.

TRANSCRIPT OF PRESENTATION

BARBARA LISKOV: Welcome to the session on LISP.

John McCarthy is going to talk about LISP. At the time of the development of LISP, he was an Assistant Professor in Communications Science at MIT. Previously he had received his Ph.D. from Princeton in Mathematics in 1951, and then had worked as Assistant Professor of Mathematics at Dartmouth. His interests at the time were in AI, time sharing, and theory of computation—especially program verification. Today, John McCarthy is Professor of Computer Science at Stanford University, and I believe that his interests are still the same.

JOHN McCARTHY: Well, what I have today I think will be maybe curious rather than instructive. Now that you know about this history business, you could entitle it something like "The Opinions of the Late John McCarthy." I found writing it a great strain, and I look forward to the Conference on History of Programming Languages that will be held 20 years from now when none of the people who were involved in the particular languages will be allowed to give papers, and when one of us, so to speak, dodders up to the microphone and says something, people will listen politely and continue on with what they were discussing previously.

First, there was this questionnaire [see "Questions sent to Authors" in Appendix B—ed.], and the questionnaire had various questions on the administrative history of the project which can be summed up in "Whoever said you could do that?" And so I would like to answer these questions with regard to LISP: No one ever said we could do it. As far as that part of LISP after September of 1958 where people actually began code things, the way it took place is that Marvin Minsky and I asked Jerry Weisner, who was the head of the Research Laboratory of Electronics, if we could have an Artificial Intelligence project. [Jerome B. Weisner is now President of MIT.] And he said, "Yes, what do you need?" And we said, "We need two programmers, a secretary, and a keypunch." And he said, "Well, how about taking also six graduate students?" And we said, "Oh, yes—graduate students, too." The Research Laboratory of Electronics had agreed to support six graduate students of mathematics, and they didn't know quite what to do with them, so they

John McCarthy

ended up graduate students on the artificial intelligence project. We did artificial intelligence, and it seemed reasonable to do the LISP language at that time, so we did it.

I should say that was when the country still had some basic trust in the judgment of scientists as to what science was likely to be useful, so Weisner had this large grant or contract with the Armed Services jointly, and so there never was any proposal that said, "This is what we would like to do. Please let us do it." So that's a little different from the way things are now, and it had certain advantages. Maybe now there are too many people wanting to do things. I don't know.

What I would like to do is mainly base this talk on the different features of LISP and how they got that way. Because LISP forms a kind of neat whole, one might think that it was planned that way, but it really wasn't. It sort of grew and then, one might say, snapped into some kind of local maximum, or maybe a local minimum, in the space of programming languages.

I'd like to have the first slide [Frame 1]. What we have here is a LISP program in three different notations. The top one is the notation that I like to use for publication these days. As you see, it's the shortest. It's a function for computing a new list whose elements are alternate elements of the original list. So here's an example of the results of ALT, and let me read this definition. "If the list is null, or if *cdr* of the list is null (and *cdr* of the list is the list with the first element deleted), then you just take the list back." So a list of 0 or 1 element is changed into itself. Otherwise, you take the first element of the list, the *cdr* of the list, and put it on the front of a list formed by taking the function ALT applied to *cddr* of the list, which is the list which is gotten by deleting the first two elements. So that's a simple example of a recursive definition of this kind of thing.

This is the internal form of ALT as you would feed it to MACLISP, which is one of the current popular variants of LISP. This is approximately a 1958 form of publication notation. Now, I should say that this is a publication notation in that there never was a compiler that would read this notation. In the first place, when LISP got started there weren't any brackets on the keypunch, and we needed to distinguish brackets from parentheses, and there was a sort of lot of dithering about how to translate from the notation that one would really like to something that could be really keypunched. While various things were done, none of them became very popular, and instead, this kind of notation became popular with some minor variants at the beginning about the first part of it, which I won't go into. But this part from the *cond* on is the form that it took early in 1959.

Now, LISP is characterized by a fair number of features, and I want to describe where they came from. The first one is computing with symbolic expressions rather than numbers. That came about because there was a goal to do artificial intelligence research, and the idea that facts about the world had to be represented as sentences in some kind of a

alt x ← **if n** *x* ∨ **n d** *x* **then** *x* **else a** *x* . *alt* **dd** *x*

```
(DEFUN ALT (X) (COND
        ((OR (NULL X) (NULL (CDR X))) X)
        (T (CONS (CAR X) (ALT (CDDR X))))
))
```

alt[x] = [null[x] ∨ null[cdr[x]] → x; T → cons[car[x]; alt[cddr[x]]]]

alt (A B C D E) = (A C E)

Frame 1

formalism. Also there was a desire to do purely algebraic computations like differentiation and integration.

The next is representation of symbolic expressions and other information by list structure in the memory of the computer. I should have a slide on list structure, but I don't. I will have to assume that you know what it looks like.

This idea came from Newell, Simon, and Shaw, and was represented in their various languages called IPL (1 through N). And they talked about some variant of this, I guess it must have been the first one, at the Dartmouth Summer Research Conference on Artificial Intelligence in 1956, and they described its various virtues; that is, the representation of information by lists, which meant that the size of the information was variable; the ability to add and delete elements in the middle, which in fact LISP rarely uses; and the idea of recursive subroutines with a programmed stack. The language IPL itself was a machine language. If you think about the average of those languages that John Backus showed this morning, it sort of looked like one of those. So while it had list operations as elementary, it didn't have any way of combining them algebraically.

Representation of information in external media, mostly by multilevel lists and sometimes by S-expressions, came along naturally, later.

Selector and constructor operations expressed as functions and composition of functions as a tool for forming more complex functions; well, this idea in some sense—the idea of using an algebraic language came from FORTRAN. FORTRAN didn't exist at the time. This was 1956. So there was the FORTRAN Project. Then the question came as to what were the appropriate operations for operating on list structure. And the kind of list structure that was meant was something whereby a computer word was divided into two halves. One half was, so to speak, the data half, and the second half was the pointer half that pointed to the next word. That is, that gave the address of the next word in the list structure, and so forth. And when you wanted to extend lists, then you got new words from a free storage list, and somehow things got back on the free storage list when you didn't need them anymore, usually by erasure.

The data item of a list could itself be a pointer to a list, and therefore a list as a whole was represented by the location of its lead element. This really was the Newell–Simon–Shaw idea, and the idea of using this algebraically was apparent once one considered trying to get something that had the notational advantage of FORTRAN.

What the operations were gave some trouble. The most obvious thing was extracting parts of a word, and so that was used. And then it became clear that what you wanted to do was think of a register and memory as a function of its location; so there was a function called "*cwr*"—Contents of Word in Register number so-and-so. So if you had a 15-bit quantity, that is, representing an address, as we were thinking about it for FORTRAN, then *CWR* of that would be the 36-bit quantity which was the contents of the word in that. And then you could take it apart with these extracters, and it sort of gradually developed that, well, what you were really interested in were not these operations separately, but certain compositions of them. So one had *contents of the address part of register number . . . ,* and writing it out or saying it out in that long way—"contents of the address part of register number . . ."—is somewhat reminiscent of the mental agony that was involved in thinking that that was the thing that you really wanted. So it has this sort of monument which still exists in the *car*. And then this ancient computer, the IBM 704, which was, in fact, at the time an aspiration rather than a fact (for Dartmouth, that is) had this other part of the word called the decrement part. So *cdr* came along there.

John McCarthy

This much provided a basis for discussing doing list processing in FORTRAN, and one of the results of the Dartmouth Summer Research Conference on Artificial Intelligence was that Nat Rochester at IBM, who had been one of the participants, decided to do some work on AI, and he hired Herbert Gelernter, and they took a problem of Minsky's. Minsky's idea was that if you were going to do theorem proving the way humans did, then you ought to use examples, and in particular, you should not try to prove things that were false in examples. And the easiest domain in which to do this was elementary plane geometry, where you would use a diagram of some kind.

Well, in any case, this involved symbolic computation where suitable list structures would represent geometric figures, and also would represent assertions about these geometric figures, like "the two sides were equal," or something like that. So some kind of list processing was in order, and it was decided to do this in FORTRAN, and so there was this FORTRAN List Processing Language. On that project I served as a consultant. But after a while they began to get good ideas that I'd never even heard of. I would say the major one which is reflected in LISP is the fact that the constructor operation, which was clearly necessary, that takes two 15-bit quantities, puts them in a word so that you can make more list structure—that that should be a function whose value is the location of the new word and that list structure, or the structure representing algebraic expressions and so forth could best be done by composing such functions. That was Gelernter's idea.

I still had a somewhat purist view of the distinction between functions and operations, and I was being rather stubborn about it, that that was a kind of subroutine that didn't return a value, and I showed that it should return a value. So at that point one had *car, cdr,* and *cons.* So we have composition of functions as a tool for forming more complex functions. And of course that's mathematics. Mathematics has always done that, but as far as computing is concerned, LISP owes that to FORTRAN.

The next thing which is an innovation is the use of conditional expressions for getting branching into function definitions. So we want to use conditional expressions, from something which is in ALGOL—**if** *p* **then** *a* **else** *b*—so the value of it depends on the test. And that came up through an inconvenience in FORTRAN. I was writing a chess program in FORTRAN, and I kept having these things that were conveniently done by conditional expressions: **if** *p* **then** *a* **else** *b.* But what you had to do in FORTRAN was use this FORTRAN IF statement, which was particularly inconvenient because it was difficult to write and difficult to read, because you could never remember if you said IF an expression less than 0, then it goes this way, equals 0, it's that way, and greater then 0. . . . One was always getting it wrong. So there was a great incentive to try to get away from that.

And so I invented this FORTRAN IF function, IF of three arguments—IF (P,A,B)—but it had the blemish that in order to work you had to compute P, A, and B before you got started. And in the examples that were used in the chess program, this was merely a minor inefficiency, one of a large number of inefficiencies in the chess program, so it wasn't overly worrisome, but it certainly gave an aspiration to have a conditional expression that would be computed in the sense that if P was true, it would compute A, and would not compute B at all, and so forth.

The recursive use of conditional expressions is a sufficient tool for building computable functions. That in a way is kind of a key idea of LISP. It was not in FLPL. There was a certain opposition to recursion among the FLPL people. I didn't quite understand why except that FORTRAN didn't do it, and it would be very difficult to. We even considered *mapcar*[*u*, *f*] ← **if n** *u* **then** NIL **else** *f*[**a** *u*] . *mapcar*[**d** *u*, *f*]

maplist[*u*, *f*] ← **if n** *u* **then** NIL **else** *f*[*u*] . *maplist*[**d** *u*, *f*]

diff[*exp*, *var*] ← **if a** *t* *exp* **then**[**if** *exp* = *var* **then** 1 **else** 0]
      else if a exp = PLUS **then**
          PLUS . *mapcar*[**d** *exp*, λ*x*.*diff*[*x*,*var*]]
      else if a *exp* = TIMES **then**
          PLUS, *maplist*[**d** *exp*, λ*x*. TIMES.*maplist*[**d** *exp*,
λ*y*.**if** *x* = *y* **then** *diff*[**a** *y*, *var*] **else a** *y*]]

diff[(TIMES X (PLUS X Y 3)),X] = (PLUS (TIMES 1 (PLUS X Y 3))
(TIMES X (PLUS 1 0 0)))

Frame 2

a project to make FORTRAN do it by means of a kind of trick, a function that would modify the FORTRAN program that called it. But that was in fact never implemented.

The remaining features of this arose in connection with an example [Frame 2]. This example in itself drove a number of the features of LISP, and that was to try to write a function that would differentiate an algebraic expression. The example here down below is that we have the expression which is really x times $(x + y + 3)$, which is to be differentiated with respect to x. And the answer is given down here with no simplification. Notice that we have an inner product there, that TIMES 1(PLUS X Y 3) which of course—since we have a product one of whose factors is 1 should be simplified, and then we have a sum, one of whose terms is 1 and the other two are 0 which we simplify away, and so forth. But of course, simplification is in fact a much harder problem than differentiation.

So we wanted to write that. And I've written it in kind of the modern blackboard notation, or publication notation that's going to be in my book, and so we wanted to differentiate an expression with respect to a variable. So if the expression is atomic, then it's either a variable itself or it's a number. In either case, unless it's the same as the variable with respect to which we are differentiating, the partial derivative had better be 0; otherwise the derivative is 1. So that gets us out there, and that looked very good, if you compare that with writing a program of some kind, and it seemed that it was at least reasonably close to the informal definition of differentiation.

The next thing is: What if it's a sum? Its being a sum is represented by the first element of the list being +, so the test is fine. And if you differentiate a sum, then as everybody who's taken calculus knows, the derivative of a sum is the sum of the derivatives. So obviously it's going to start out being + here. But then came a little problem: how do you talk about the sum of the derivatives, and in programming it, there were clearly two kinds of programs that could be written.

One is where you have a sum of a fixed number of terms, like just two, where you regard a sum as a binary operation. And then you could write down the formula easy enough. But the other was where you have a sum of an indefinite number of terms, and you'd really like to make that work too. To make that work, what you want to be able to talk about is doing the same operation on all the elements of a list. You want to be able to get a new list whose elements are obtained from the old list by just taking each element and doing a certain operation to it.

In order to describe that, one has to have a notation for functions. So one could write this function called *mapcar*. This says, "Apply the function *f* to all the elements of the list." If the list is null then you're going to get a NIL here. Otherwise you are going to apply the function to the first element of the list and put that onto a front of a list which is obtained by doing the same operation again to the rest of the list. So that's *mapcar*. It wasn't called *mapcar* then. It was called *maplist*, but *maplist* is something different, which I will describe in just a moment.

That was fine for that recursive definition of applying a function to everything on the list. No new ideas were required. But then, how do you write these functions?

And so, the way in which to do that was to borrow from Church's Lambda Calculus, to borrow the lambda notation. Now, having borrowed this notation, one of the myths concerning LISP that people think up or invent for themselves becomes apparent, and that is that LISP is somehow a realization of the lambda calculus, or that was the intention. The truth is that I didn't understand the lambda calculus, really. In particular, I didn't understand that you really could do conditional expressions in recursion in some sense in the pure lambda calculus. So, it wasn't an attempt to make the lambda calculus practical, although if someone had started out with that intention, he might have ended up with something like LISP.

Then we might go to the very next term where we want to differentiate a product. And a further complication immediately arises. It's clear that the derivative of a product is a sum of terms, each term of which is a product, and each factor of the inner products corresponds to one term of the original product that you're differentiating. But the thing is either differentiated or not, and it's differentiated or not according to whether the index of the factor is the same as the index of the summand in which it's going to appear. Well, I've said that correctly, but probably too rapidly. But I won't say it again!

So, anyway, it turned out that you needed for this purpose to be comparing not the elements of the lists themselves, but the sublists, which effectively compares their indices.

Well, in any case, while I was spending a summer at IBM, the summer of 1958, I spent a fair amount of time writing that definition. I don't say it took me all summer to write it, but one might say pretty much. I forget whether I did anything else, but I didn't get any further on this project than just that. And so, in the fall of 1958, when the Artificial Intelligence Project started at MIT, LISP existed to this extent, in that we had the idea of this kind of a language.

The there are some other ideas that are in LISP. One of them is the representation of LISP programs as LISP data, and the fact that that could be done was always clear, but the idea that this had some high priority came about in a fairly peculiar way. The original way in which we started to implement LISP is that we had the intention of producing a compiler. But the FORTRAN people were expressing their shock of having spent 30 man-years on FORTRAN, which seemed like a lot at that time, and it didn't seem like these graduate students would hold still long enough that we could get 30 man-years of work out of them. So that seemed fairly formidable, and anyway, we wanted to do it right. So what was going on in the fall of 1958 was a lot of hand-coding of LISP functions into the assembly language for the IBM 704, and adopting a number of conventions. For example, one of the conventions that was adopted different from IPL was to use a linear stack rather than use a LISP-type list as a stack. So there were saving and unsaving routines for handling variables, and input and output was written.

Then I decided to write a paper about this which was to be entitled "Recursive Functions of Symbolic Expressions and Their Computation by Machine, Part I." Now, there was to have been a Part II, and Part II was to contain some applications to algebraic computation because I felt that we should really justify this by doing some integration and differentiation and algebraic simplification and so forth. Well, other people did that, and the Part II never appeared.

But one of the contentions made in Part I was that this style of recursive functions was a neater way of doing basic computability theory than Turing machines. In order to illustrate that contention, what was done was to write a function that played the role of the universal Turing machine; that is, a universal Turing machine in Turing machine theory is a machine that, when it is given the description of another machine on its tape, and also given space to represent blank tape, then it will carry out that computation that the other machine would have done. In LISP, it is the function *eval,* one version of which is given in the LISP Micromanual that is included in the paper [referring to the language summary —ed.], but that function which was intended for kind of theoretical purposes, almost for rhetorical theoretical purposes, required deciding on a representation of LISP functions as LISP data which is approximately the one given there in the second expression. And I must say, that one was done without a great deal of thought, and in particular the *cond* is deeper in parentheses than is necessary.

Now, when Steve Russell saw that one, he said, "Why don't I program it, and we'll have an interpreter for LISP?" And he did, and we did. That was a little bit surprising, somehow, that an interpreter suddenly appeared.

There are a couple of other things, garbage collection as a means of handling the erasure problem, and also the fact that LISP is a reasonably good command language in a time-sharing environment.

I just want to finish off with one remark, and that is the question "How come LISP has survived this long?" because most of the languages that were created in that period are long since dead. People who have tried to make better languages than LISP to do the same thing have in some sense succeeded, but I've figured out why it survived so long, and that is that one of the things that everybody, including me, thought was a vice of LISP was, in fact, a virtue. So, therefore, some of the attempts to improve it went in the wrong direction. And the thing that was a virtue when everybody thought it was a vice was all these parentheses, that is, the fact that the primary way of programming in LISP is as LISP data, and this has made LISP very good for big systems in which programs produce more program and things of this kind.

Well, I've used up my time without getting really beyond April 1959. It has actually had some additional history in the last 19 years that I don't have time to go into.

TRANSCRIPT OF DISCUSSANT'S REMARKS

BARBARA LISKOV: Our discussant on LISP is Paul Abrahams, who is one of those six graduate students that McCarthy had to take on in order to get his project going. He was a graduate student at MIT during the early development of LISP and worked on the original LISP system. His doctoral dissertation, "Machine Verification of Mathematical Proof," was one of the early applications of LISP. Today, Paul Abrahams is an Associate Professor of Computer Science at the Courant Institute of Mathematical Sciences. His interests are in compiler design, programming methodology, and programming languages. In the subsequent period he's worked on several other implementations of LISP, but he says in recent years he's had a change of faith and has been heavily involved in the standardization and implementation of PL/I.

PAUL ABRAHAMS: I started my career in LISP as a very enthusiastic and very interested graduate student at MIT. In the time since then I may have achieved an undeserved prominence in connection with LISP, since my name happens to start with AB and comes ahead of all the others in alphabetical lists.

One thing I hope to do in this talk is to provide a slightly different perspective on some of the early ideas. You should realize, when you consider LISP in comparison with most of the other languages with the notable exception of APL, that LISP was really the work of one mind. The rest of us mostly added things. We implemented it, we added trimmings, but basically LISP was John McCarthy's invention, in the same sense, for example, that APL was Ken Iverson's invention. This makes it harder to really determine all that went on because if you look at the early history of ALGOL or FORTRAN or PL/I, there were lots of project memos flying back and forth, and so there's a lot more written documentation to go on. Unfortunately, we don't have quite so much in the case of LISP.

When I was researching this talk, I figured that the natural source to go to was Artificial Intelligence Memo Number 1. In fact, there did exist such a thing, even though it didn't have that title. I would say that for anybody who really wanted to trace back how LISP got started, that is the thing to look at. Its title is "An Algebraic Language for the Manipulation of Symbolic Expressions," and it is dated September 16, 1958. If you read that memo, you get really a very interesting picture of the flavor of LISP as it started out: LISP was a language to solve problems rather than an object of beauty. There were these two main threads of thought that led to it: IPL (the Newell, Shaw, and Simon list processing language) and FLPL. If you look at IPL in comparison with LISP as it started out, there are quite a number of similarities.

LISP originally was a very clever synthesis designed to get certain jobs done. The notion of list structure appeared in IPL, and in fact, IPL had field extracters that bore some resemblance to those one finds in LISP. For example, IPL had four field extractors. There was a symbol field which was like the *car* portion in LISP and a link field which was like the *cdr* in LISP. There were two others, *P* and *Q*, whose role was very mysterious and I never did find out quite what those did. The first LISP functions had more field extractors, and then it was discovered that they could be dispensed with.

I should mention in that connection, people often wonder about the origin of *car* and *cdr*. There are two levels to the story of how they originated. The first level is that the IBM 704 had an address field and a decrement field, and the address field stored one part of the LISP word and the decrement field the other. But the second part of the story is that they seem to be backwards. Namely, if you look at a picture of LISP's structure, you discover that *car*, which is the right part of the word, is on the left; but *cdr*, which is the left part of the word, is on the right. Now, that turned out to be a peculiarity of SAP, the IBM assembly language that was being used. In SAP you wrote "address,,decrement." So in fact, *car* and *cdr* didn't even mirror the machine, they mirrored the assembly language.

Getting back to some of the resemblances between IPL and early LISP, one notion that one finds in IPL is the notion of attribute value lists. These were the precursors of the property lists that are so very useful in LISP. Another thing that one finds in IPL is the notion that programs can be looked on as data, and in fact you can create them, you can build them. And if you look at how you construct data structures in IPL, and how you write an IPL program, they look much the same. The idea of interpretation had a great deal of importance in IPL, and so did recursion and the notion of using a public pushdown stack.

So LISP started out with the thought of "Let's see what we can do in building something that is an effective means of carrying out certain kinds of computations." In this early period, list processing was not the thing that we now take for granted. You now think of it as almost like addition; it's just something you use. But at that time it had a capital "L" and a capital "P." The very name of LISP stands for *List Processing*, and that was the original conception of the language.

There were a lot of things that were really quite novel and had no counterpart in either IPL or FLPL; for example, as John pointed out, the use of conditional expressions. In the ALGOL talk, it never really came out directly that conditional expressions were one of John's major contributions to the ALGOL effort. There's a certain incestuous quality to the history of these early languages.

In the early versions of LISP, you had to do erasure explicitly. In fact, there was a built-in function called *eralis* which stood for *erase list*. List erasure was replaced later by a much more elegant idea: Garbage Collection. It doesn't sound elegant, but in fact it is, and it's an idea that has been taken over in many other languages and many other contexts since then.

One of the early objectives of LISP was being able to do algebraic manipulation; the differentiation program was a classic example. Building the Advice Taker was another objective, and a third objective was just being able to have something you could use effectively in artificial intelligence.

And then, two years later came John's paper, "Recursive Functions of Symbolic Expressions." That changed the whole ball game, and it changed how people perceived LISP. Now all of a sudden, LISP was not merely a language you used to do things. It was now something you looked at: an object of beauty. It was something to be studied as an object in and of itself.

And ever since that day there has been a continual tension between those who love LISP for its purity and those who want to use it to do various kinds of computing. Certainly a lot of computing has been done with LISP. But that wasn't true at the very beginning. It used to be said that the main purpose of LISP was to produce more LISP, and the first outside application that I knew of, that I can remember anyway, was an algebraic system developed by Anthony Hearn. But there were also a number of applications in the LISP community: for example, my own work on the Proof Checker, which was one of the earlier large LISP programs. What made a program large in those days was much smaller than what makes a program large nowadays.

I'd like to mention some of the effects of this tension between the pure view of LISP and the view of LISP as a language that you actually program in. In the original version we had these functions *car* and *cdr*. There was also something else that John mentions in his paper which was really an accident of implementation; the falsity function F and NIL were the same. They were both represented as zero, because that was convenient. It also turned out that the equality predicate EQ was defined in a very peculiar way so that it was true if one of the elements was atomic; otherwise it was undefined. One or both were atomic. That too was just a peculiarity that arose from the way things were implemented.

Later on, when people were interested in writing programs, for example, John devised the program feature which let you write things that looked much more like sequential programs, and again, there was a very fancy justification of this in terms of a state vector. You could prove that the program feature could be reduced to something that could be expressed in pure LISP, but that was beside the point. The program feature was really a convenience.

Then there were other dirty things that got introduced. For example, *rplaca* and *rplacd* —the things that let you modify list structure. That is something that the purists have always been very unhappy about who have looked at LISP, but at the same time, programmers have tended to use a great deal.

There was one area that I got involved in which was the development of some input–output features. For example, in the original LISP, it was only possible to read in list structure. But often you wanted to read in arbitrary character strings, and so I provided a set of facilities for doing that. The compiler introduced a whole other set of practical considerations. The way, for example, one looked at variable bindings became very different when you were dealing with compiled programs versus interpreted programs. With interpreted programs you had an A-list; with compiled programs you had special variables to deal with.

We were under a lot of pressure in those days because it was not very easy to use the machine. For example, on the IBM 704, typically, we had 48-hour turnaround time. That's something that has only been duplicated, to my knowledge, at the NYU computing center at the end of the semester. One of the standard tricks that we had for cadging a little extra computer time was to sign up for so-called "programmer-present time" which you were allowed to have exactly five minutes of, and we always managed to squeeze out one extra minute. We didn't really have any need to be present; it was just a way to get a scheduled shot on the machine.

There were a number of early applications of LISP which really gave people more of a feeling of what they could do with it: A lot of work in algebra, my work with the Proof Checker. One of the earlier large programs was Jim Slagle's program for doing integration. According to the reports, it took 15 minutes to do one integral.

So there was a very active group of people using LISP in those days. Since then, LISP has become in effect a standard language in a very important application area, namely, artificial intelligence. So I feel that the value of LISP lies even more in its use in that application area than in its beauty as an object for the beholder.

JOHN MCCARTHY: Let's see—before taking these questions, let me make a couple of comments on Paul's thing: the idea of the *rplaca* and *rplacd,* which are pseudo-functions in LISP—that is, they do return a value but they mainly have a side effect which makes changes in the middle of list structure. That there should be some such thing was in from the very beginning. Maybe its implementation was somewhat delayed, or at least its implementation in the interpreter was a little bit delayed. The idea that there should be a program feature was in some sense in before the idea that there should be recursive functions. So it's not a case of pure features which were found to be inadequate in practice and then were supplemented. It's that some of the features which were put in for practical purposes turned out to make a neat unit, that is, the so-called pure LISP unit; and the other features somehow, well, remained theoretically anomalous and we still don't have a quite adequate theory of them. Well, actually, Michael Gordon has an adequate theory of it, but it's too complicated for almost anybody else.

TRANSCRIPT OF QUESTION AND ANSWER SESSION

BARBARA LISKOV: Okay—I have a question here from Aaron Finerman from Stony Brook, and he says, "Do you believe that LISP has made any long-lasting contributions to the more 'normal' programming languages, e.g., FORTRAN and ALGOL, COBOL, etc.?"

JOHN MCCARTHY: Well, yes, sure. The easiest example is conditional expressions, which I think will be around for a long time. The definition of a function by recursion of the kind which I gave in my two slides I think is something that eventually will be in those languages to supplement their existing features. I think this is, so to speak, part of the mathematics of computing, and indeed, from a theoretical point of view, one of the major approaches; the whole fixed point theory is based on this kind of recursive definition. So, I think those features are here to say.

LISKOV: I have a couple of questions on garbage collection. One is from Bruce Walker of Logicon, and he asks, "Was the Garbage Collector original, or did it exist in any earlier list processing languages?" And a related question is from Richard Miller, who says, "What could be considered the real reason for going to garbage collection instead of reference counting? How long did it take to solve the erasure problem?"

MCCARTHY: I'm pretty sure that as far as a list-processing language is considered, garbage collection is original with LISP. I wouldn't be sure that garbage collection was not used in particular programs. In fact, I would almost guess that you could find examples quite a lot earlier than LISP. What was the next question there?

LISKOV: It was about garbage collection instead of reference counting. Sort of the history of the mechanism.

MCCARTHY: When I decided that we really couldn't stand erase, that is, that it was going to make everything absolutely ugly to have to explicitly erase lists once you've got nice definitions like that differentiation example, then both garbage collection and reference counting immediately presented themselves as ways of doing it. And in the case of the 704, garbage collection was clearly superior because there were six bits left in the word after you had the address and decrement fields, and it did seem like a sublist might easily have more than 64 references to it. So, it would have meant a complete rewrite in order to do it by reference counting. So that seemed very difficult, whereas garbage collecting was rather easy to represent.

Now, George Collins, who was making a list-processing system for the CDC 1604, which had a 48-bit word, and also 15-bit addresses, and therefore had a lot more bits left over in the word, made the reverse decision. He casually referred to the "elegant but inefficient" method of garbage collection, and I gave him an argument on that, which would be roughly speaking that at the time when LISP gets inefficient, the reference counting thing doesn't work at all. So . . . both were considered.

LISKOV: Here's another question from Richard Miller: "You wrote an interpreter before a compiler, as you pointed out in your talk. Did the *eval* function as written in LISP have any effect on LISP continuing as a primarily interpreted language?"

MCCARTHY: I think so. In some sense, there wasn't any other way to do it. That is, once the idea became clear that the *eval* function, the universal function could serve as an interpreter, then there was no kind of alternate way of doing things that anyone ever seriously considered.

LISKOV: I have a comment here that you might like to respond to. This is from Paul Berry of I.P. Sharp Associates. He says, "IPL 1 to N and LISP had an effect that may not be obvious to people in computing because it rarely led directly to executable programs. Namely, they inspired among psychologists a number of models of human information processing, that is, metaphors rather than programs, which have continued to be influential in that rather amorphous field."

McCARTHY: Well, I'll comment on that. It doesn't seem to me that IPL and LISP itself had these effects. It's the programs that people wrote in IPL and LISP which they explicitly attempted to model these phenomena. Maybe that's what he meant.

FULL TEXT OF ALL QUESTIONS SUBMITTED

PAUL BERRY

IPL1–N and LISP had an effect that may not be obvious to people in computing because it rarely led directly to executable programs. Namely, they inspired among psychologists a number of models of human information processing (metaphors rather than programs) which have continued to be influential in that rather amorphous field.

AARON FINERMAN

Do you believe that LISP has made any long-lasting contributions to the more "normal" (e.g., FORTRAN, ALGOL, COBOL) programming languages?

RICHARD MILLER

What could be considered the real reason for going to garbage collection instead of reference counting? How long did it take to solve the "erasure" problem?

Will M-expressions ever return? Note page 220 1st column 3rd paragraph of the preprints.

You wrote an interpreter before a compiler. Did the *eval* function as written in LISP (and given in the preprints) have any effect on LISP continuing as a primarily interpreted language?

When did the desire for compactness and mathematical influence really begin to affect LISP. You noted that some things were added and later pruned out of the language. Can you give examples of this? Did anyone really attempt to do program proving in a serious way?

Beyond the comments about *car* and *cdr,* how much effect did the machine architecture have on the language? Did the fact that you were only trying to get on one and not that you actually had one affect the early design of the language?

BRUCE WALKER

Was the garbage collector original or did it exist in any earlier list processing language?

Dᴀᴠɪᴅ S. Wɪsᴇ

In the preprint you describe how FUNARG solved the problem of a free (or nonlocal) binding changing before its intended use. Was the adoption of dynamic scoping, which gave rise to this problem (rather than ALGOL-like static scoping), a conscious choice?

BIOGRAPHY OF JOHN McCARTHY

John McCarthy holds a B.S. in Mathematics from Caltech (1948) and a PhD. in Mathematics from Princeton (1951). At Princeton he was first a Proctor Fellow and later Higgins Research Instructor in Mathematics. He has also been on the faculty of Dartmouth and M.I.T. and is now Professor of Computer Science and Director of the Artificial Intelligence Lab at Stanford.

He participated in the development of ALGOL 58 and ALGOL 60 and created the LISP programming system while at MIT, where, with Marvin Minsky, he organized and directed the Artificial Intelligence Project.

ACM's Turing Award was given to him in 1971.

V

COBOL Session

Chairman: Michael Marcotty
Speaker: Jean E. Sammet
Discussant: Betty Holberton

PAPER: THE EARLY HISTORY OF COBOL

Jean E. Sammet

IBM Corporation
Federal Systems Division

1. Introduction

Before starting this historical description of COBOL, it is essential to point out several factors relating to my involvement with this particular paper.

First, during the entire time that I had any involvement with COBOL, I was working for Sylvania Electric Products in Needham, Massachusetts. At that time, Sylvania was producing large scale computers for the army, and was contemplating going into the more general purpose computer business. Thus, it is clear that I was not an employee or representative of IBM at the time of the activities I am describing. My views as expressed herein are purely my own and do not represent those of either Sylvania or IBM, then or now.

Second, this paper naturally presents only one person's view of the activities that went on. Because this was a committee, other members obviously may have different views; it is hoped that such views can be brought forth at a different time. I certainly do not claim to speak for the committee, although I hope that many of the participants would concur with most of my statements. The people listed in the Acknowledgments, which includes several of the committee members, have reviewed drafts of this paper, and I have taken their suggestions into consideration. However, quite naturally the entire responsibility for any comments and opinions, or accidental misstatement of facts, in this paper is mine.

Third, let me indicate my role in the COBOL effort. I was appointed as chairman of two of the major subcommittees, which operated at different points in time. I also served on the six-person subgroup that developed the detailed specifications. As the chairman of the statement language subcommittee, I wrote reports after each of our subcommittee meetings and much of the material in this paper is based on those reports written *at that time*.

HISTORY OF PROGRAMMING LANGUAGES

Jean E. Sammet

This paper was prepared by using all the items in the bibliography as well as my hand notes from many of the committee and subcommittee meetings. This final paper differs from the preprint version somewhat, but primarily from an editorial rather than a substantive viewpoint, except for Section 2.1.1. Major additions were made there as a result of receiving information which I did not have when the preprint version was prepared.

2. Background

2.1. Origins and Creation of the COBOL Committee

Many people are aware—because of histories published in the COBOL standard (ANSI, 1968) and elsewhere—of the origins of COBOL. Unfortunately, some of the common beliefs about the origin of COBOL, or the common perceptions of the people and activities involved, are not necessarily accurate. This section attempts to show how the committee was started and under what auspices.

2.1.1. Pre Department of Defense Activity

On April 8, 1959, there was a meeting of computer people, including representatives from academia, users, and manufacturers, held at the University of Pennsylvania Computing Center. Present at the meeting were I. Edward Block, Ben Cheydleur, Saul Gorn, Grace Hopper, Robert Rossheim, and Albert E. Smith. The purpose of the meeting was to

1. Define the objectives for a first formal meeting on common business languages.
2. Prepare an agenda for this first formal meeting.
3. Decide who should participate in this first formal meeting.

(Block, 1959). Block's report indicated that the "meeting was the result of a request by Mary K. Hawes (ElectroData Division, Burroughs Corporation) to plan a formal meeting involving both users and manufacturers where plans could be prepared to develop the specifications for a common business language for automatic digital computers."

In the light of later timing developments, it is worth noting that Block's report on the meeting said, "To achieve the ultimate, the development of the language could take up to ten years, but it was a general feeling that this ultimate would be too costly and that a timetable of perhaps two years for completion of an approximation to this ultimate is all that could be tolerated."

They decided to ask the Department of Defense, through Charles Phillips, to sponsor the first formal meeting, and they recommended a specific list of invitees consisting of 7 people from 7 computer manufacturers, and 14 people from user organizations.

A meeting was scheduled for May in the Pentagon. In a talk at the ACM annual conference on Sept. 1, 1959, Phillips commented on the reaction of the Department of Defense to this undertaking by saying (Phillips, 1959b):

> The Department of Defense was pleased to undertake this project; in fact, we were embarrassed that the idea for such a common language had not had its origin by that time in Defense since we would benefit so greatly from the success of such a project, and at the same time one of the Air Force commands was in the process of developing one of the business languages: AIMACO.

2.1.2. May 1959 Pentagon Meeting

A meeting was held at the Pentagon on May 28–29, 1959. It was chaired by Mr. Charles A. Phillips, then Director of the Data Systems Research Staff, Office of the Assistant Secretary of Defense (Comptroller). About 40 people attended the meeting, including 15 people from about 7 government organizations, 11 users and consultants (including one, but only one, person from a university), and 15 representatives of manufacturers. The manufacturers represented were Burroughs, GE, Honeywell, IBM, NCR, Philco, RCA, Remington-Rand Univac, Sylvania Electric Products, and ICT. I was present at the meeting as the senior of two Sylvania representatives. Because the actual list of attendees at that meeting is of historical importance and the information is almost inaccessible, it is included as an Appendix to this paper.

There was considerable discussion about the potential need or desirability for a common business language (CBL). The needs expressed then are still relevant now, e.g., time and cost of reprogramming, inflexibility of programs on a single machine, desirability of interchange among machines.

Perhaps the most important outcome of that meeting, aside from the actual decision that something should be done, was a listing of the desired characteristics of the proposed CBL (Phillips, 1959a, p. 2):

  a. Majority of group favored maximum use of simple English language; even though some participants suggested there might be advantage from using mathematical symbolism.

  b. A minority suggested that we steer away from problem-oriented language because English language is not a panacea as it cannot be manipulated as algebraic expressions can.

  c. The need is for a programming language that is *easier to use,* even if somewhat less powerful.

  d. We need to broaden the base of those who can state problems to computers.

  e. The CBL should not be biased by present compiler problems.

The other major output of the meeting is one that is the least clearly known or understood, namely the creation of *three* committees. Again, I quote from Phillips (1959a, p. 3):

  a. It was agreed that three groups will be set up with short, medium and long-range objectives, and the Executive Committee will coordinate the efforts of these groups.

  b. The short-range committee is to do a fact-finding study of what's wrong and right with existing business compilers (such as FLOWMATIC, AIMACO, COMTRAN, etc.) and the experience of users thereof. This short-range group is due to complete its work in three months, i.e., by September 1, 1959.

  c. A similar conference will be convened to receive and discuss this report. (Notice will be given to those on the mailing list when this conference is scheduled.)

  d. The group also agreed to the need for intermediate and long-range committees (to be later designated). The long-range committee would probably take several years to complete its task of coming up with a proposed optimum CBL.

Figure 1 is an extract from Phillips (1959a) showing the composition of the Short-Range and Intermediate-Range Committees as of the time that Phillips wrote this summary of the meeting.

The importance of the notion of Short and Intermediate-Range Committees (the Long-Range Committee never really did get established) is absolutely crucial to an understanding of the development of COBOL. Note that the mission of the Short-Range Committee

Jean E. Sammet

Short-Range Committee

Chairman
Joseph Wegstein   National Bureau of Standards

Members
Colonel Alfred Asch   USAF, Hq., Air Materiel Command, Dayton, Ohio
William Carter   Datamatic Division, Minneapolis-Honeywell, Newton Highlands, Massachusetts
Ben F. Cheydleur   Manager, Advanced Programming Department, RCA Electronic Data Processing Div., Camden, N.J.
Mrs. Mary K. Hawes   Burroughs Corporation, ElectroData Div., Pasadena, California
Mrs. Frances E. Holberton   Chief Programming Research Branch, Applied Mathematics Laboratory, David Taylor Model Basin, Washington, D.C.
Miss Jean E. Sammet   Sylvania Electric Products, Needham, Massachusetts
William Selden   Data Systems Division, IBM Corporation, White Plains, New York
E. F. Somers   Sperry Rand, Philadelphia, Pa.

Intermediate-Range Committee

Chairman
A. Eugene Smith   Navy Department, Bureau of Ships

Members (as so far designated; additional members and advisors to be added later)
Lester Calkins   U.S. Steel Corporation
Gregory M. Dillon   DuPont Company
Roy Goldfinger   IBM Corporation
Jack Jones   Air Materiel Command, Dayton, Ohio
William P. Keating   National Cash Register Company
Colonel Gerald Lerner   USA—Signal Corps ADPS School, Ft. Monmouth, New Jersey
Robert Rossheim   Sperry Rand UNIVAC Division

Fig. 1. [Source: Phillips (1959a). (Typeset for ease of reading.)]

(see Fig. 2) was to *explore* and "to recommend a short-range composite approach (good for at least the next year or two)." This wording is clearly ambiguous, and at the time, there was some discussion as to whether or not we were to try and create a language. It was by no means clear *then* that we were to do anything *except* try and *combine* the three known languages of the time. These were FLOW-MATIC (Remington-Rand Univac, 1958), which had been developed under the leadership of Grace Hopper, and which was actually in use by customers at the time; AIMACO (Air Materiel Command, 1959), devel-

I - Fact-Finding and Short-Range Language Committee (Task Group No. 1)

    A. Mission-To report by September 1, 1959, the results of its study of the strengths and weaknesses of existing automatic compilers (especially AIMACO, FLOWMATIC and COMTRAN); and to recommend a short-range composite approach (good for at least the next year or two) to a common business language for programming digital computers. This group will explore a "problem-oriented but machine-independent language." This is defined as: "A language which will permit the description of the problem in such precise terms as to convey the management needs and objectives while providing a regimented and firm basis for exploration of these objectives in a language which would not be geared to a specific data processing system, but to which each data processing system might be applied to provide for the accomplishment of the objective in the most practical manner."

Fig. 2. [Source: Phillips (1959a). (Typeset for ease of reading.)]

oped by the Air Force under the overall leadership of Col. Alfred Asch, with much work and supervision being done by Jack Jones, a civilian, and with some help from Grace Hopper's group; and COMTRAN (IBM, 1959), soon renamed Commercial Translator and existing at that time as only a manual produced by IBM; no implementation had even been started. The COMTRAN specifications had been produced by a group whose manager was Bob Bemer and whose technical leader was Roy Goldfinger.

The psychological and philosophical effect of this May 1959 meeting profoundly affected what was to happen over the next 3–6 month period. I believe the Short-Range Committee definitely understood that it was to create only an *interim* language. There was such a short time scale for reporting that the Short-Range Committee could do nothing very significant and creative. In addition to the three languages already cited, RCA said it was starting to develop its own business data-processing language, and so was Sylvania. The hope of the Short-Range Committee was to try and "nip these in the bud" so that all manufacturers would be using the same common language, rather than having each develop its own. It was definitely felt that the Intermediate-Range Committee would have the time and resources to develop a really good and long lasting business data processing language. I am certainly convinced in my own mind that had the Short-Range Committee realized at the outset that the language it created (i.e., COBOL) was going to be in use for such a long period of time, it would have gone about the task quite differently and produced a rather different result. But I believe that most of us viewed our work as a stopgap measure—a very important stopgap indeed, but not something intended for longevity.

2.1.3. CODASYL Executive Committee

Although not directly involved with the technical creation of COBOL, the CODASYL Executive Committee must be mentioned here to provide perspective on its role in supervising the COBOL development. As part of the May 28–29 meeting, it was felt (Cunningham, 1959) "that a Steering Committee be formed to charter [sic] a course of action for the orderly progression toward a 'common or basic business language.'" This Steering Committee met on June 4, 1959, and decided (Cunningham, 1959) that the work and organization of the entire activity would be called "Committee [sic] on Data Systems Languages" (CODASYL) and that an Executive Group was needed to coordinate the work of the various subcommittees, and selected the following members of the executive committee:

Chairman: Charles A. Phillips (Office of the Secretary of Defense)
Vice-Chairman: Joseph F. Cunningham (Air Force Department)
E. J. Albertson (U. S. Steel Corporation)
Gregory Dillon (Dupont Company)
Mel Grosz (Esso Standard Oil Company)
Chairman, Task Group #1 (= Short-Range Committee): Joseph H. Wegstein (National Bureau of Standards)
Chairman, Task Group #2 (= Intermediate-Range Committee): A. E. Smith (Department of the Navy)
Chairman, Task Group #3 (= Long-Range Committee): not specified
Advisors to the Executive Committee: Grace M. Hopper (Sperry Rand Company)
Robert W. Bemer (IBM Corporation)

Jean E. Sammet

While it is true that the CODASYL Executive Committee was essentially self-appointed, it is equally true in my judgment that that group, under the leadership of Charles Phillips, did a great deal to shepherd COBOL through the political thickets of the competing manufacturers.

2.2 Short-Range Committee Activities (June–December, 1959)

2.2.1. First Meeting (June 23–24, 1959)

The first meeting of the Short-Range Committee was held at the National Bureau of Standards, June 23–24, 1959, with Joe Wegstein as chairman. (Part of those two days was spent in subcommittee meetings.)

Before the June meeting, we at Sylvania had made a comparative study of the verbs in FLOW-MATIC 1 and 2, Commercial Translator, and AIMACO, and that tabular comparison appears in the minutes of the committee meeting (Asch, 1959); it showed there was great similarity among the languages. Mary Hawes (Burroughs) had sent the committee a memo describing her ideas on requirements for data descriptions.

Much of the following material is either a direct or an indirect quote from the minutes of that meeting, prepared by Colonel Alfred Asch (1959). The committee decided to use the terms "data-description" and "procedural statements." Subcommittees were set up to deal with each of those; Mary Hawes (Burroughs) was appointed chairman of the former, and Jean Sammet (Sylvania) was appointed chairman of the latter (subsequently referred to as the Statement Language Task Group). Two other subcommittees were set up—one to deal with an application survey, and the other to obtain usage and experience information. A survey of nine user organizations was actually conducted by the Air Materiel Command: a first version of this is included in the minutes of this meeting (Asch, 1959).

An important decision of the committee was to agree (Asch, 1959) "that the following language systems and programming aids would be reviewed by the committee: AIMACO, Comtran [sic], Flowmatic [sic], Autocoder III, SURGE, Fortran, RCA 501 Assembler, Report Generator (GE Hanford), APG-1 (Dupont)." (Since this is a direct quote, the names of the languages are given here as shown in the original document cited, although the name Comtran was later changed to Commercial Translator, and FLOW-MATIC is the proper form for that language name.) It is beyond the scope of this paper to give a comprehensive (or even a superficial) description of each of these and its influence on COBOL. However, in practice, the languages that were considered most significant as input were AIMACO, FLOW-MATIC, and COMTRAN (shortly thereafter renamed Commercial Translator.) As already noted, the first two were in actual use but the latter was only a set of specifications; its implementation had not started.

Although IAL (later renamed ALGOL 58) was not on that list, the committee members were aware of it. However, I don't recall how much any of us actually knew about it (beside Wegstein who had been *on* the IAL committee); I don't believe IAL had any influence on our deliberations, except for the character set which is discussed in Section 2.4.4.

See Section 2.4 for a further discussion of the technical inputs to COBOL.

Even in this early first meeting, there was considerable technical discussion. For example, Mary Hawes presented her ideas on data description and some of that also appears in the minutes; we discussed the AIMACO file design and there was, of course, discussion of the differences in the verbs from the different languages.

2.2.2. Subsequent Meetings: July–August, 1959

The Task Group on Statement Language met July 8–9, July 22–24, August 6–7. Technical considerations are discussed in Section 3.1. While much technical work was going on, the politics were not buried. Because this was probably the first attempt by competitive computer manufacturers to work together toward a common goal, the marketing considerations of all groups were extremely relevant. Thus, much of the time at a July 22 meeting of the Statement Language Task Group was spent getting statements of commitment from the various manufacturers. All said in essence that they would implement this language "but"—and then each manufacturer had some constraint to go along with the "but."

One of the problems with having two separate task groups to deal with the statement language and data descriptions was that each had to make assumptions about what the other was doing. This need was perhaps felt more by the Statement Language Task Group than by the other group. Thus, at the July 22 meeting, there was considerable concern expressed by our task group that no meeting on data design had even been held, while we were into the third meeting on the statement language. At this July 22 meeting, a preliminary set of verbs was actually developed and it was also agreed that a very simple language would be specified by September 1 with a definition of a more complex version after September 1. (Note that this split of time was forced because of the requirement to make a report to the CODASYL Executive Committee by September 4.) One of the decisions was that the four arithmetic verbs, ADD, SUBTRACT, MULTIPLY, and DIVIDE would be included, but that the use of formula notation would be deferred for the more complex version after September 1. There was a very strong minority dissent to that decision (from those who wanted the formulas included in even this very early version).

By the August 6 meeting, there was a brief indication of some of the preliminary work done on the data designs. (Section 3.1.2. discusses the approach taken for the data description.)

The Short-Range Committee met August 17–19 with much of the time spent in subcommittees. By the end of August 17, the Statement Language Task Group had a complete set of verbs and the various notes (currently called semantics) which would apply to each one. As one looks at this material, it is clearly primitive by today's standards. However, considering the short length of elapsed calendar time and the need for strangers from competing manufacturers to work together, it does seem rather impressive. My favorable prejudices in this matter are obvious and other more objective people can certainly reach a different conclusion!

On August 18 the Short-Range Committee voted unanimously in favor of the three parts of a program—procedure, data description, and environment; the latter at that time was thought to consist of (1) a select function which would indicate features involving hardware units, hardware names, buffers, etc., and (2) a configuration statement which would indicate the machine on which the program was to be (a) compiled and (b) executed. The task of specifying those features was assigned to the Statement Language Task Group. Thus, the idea of allowing cross-compilation was considered at a very early stage, although never achieved in a major way, and the configuration statement was merely for documentation.

During the August 17–19 meeting, there was a great deal of discussion about the validity, usefulness, etc., of what the committee had done so far. Some people felt that it showed much too much the result of a design by a committee and embodied too many compromises. Others felt that it was indeed better than the three main existing languages which had been considered—AIMACO, Commercial Translator, and FLOW-MATIC. Some people felt the new language had gone too far, i.e., was too complex (e.g., subscripts) whereas others felt that it was still too simple (e.g., lack of formulas). Considerable discussion centered around the idea that each manufacturer might implement only a subset; this concept was discarded because of the recognition of what that would do to portability (although that word was never used). Interestingly enough, there was considerable debate about whether or not subscripts should be included. Some felt that was much too complicated a feature for the data-processing users. It should be emphasized again that much of this debate took place within the framework of the requirement for us to make a report to the CODASYL Executive Committee by early in September. Information had come from the Intermediate-Range Committee (Short-Range Committee, 1959a, p. 16) that it had decided their approach would be to start from an overall systems approach and they would *not* have as part of its function the maintenance and extension of a short-range language. It was pointed out in the general discussion that this Short-Range Committee was not asked to come up with a specific language but was only asked to examine others. That argument and similar ones were forcefully presented by the IBM representatives. Joe Wegstein, as the chairman, indicated that he felt that this committee should do what it thought best and come to as much of an agreement as possible for its September 4 report. One transcript of part of this meeting (Short-Range Committee, 1959a) has him saying in part, "I also want to point out . . . in the Constitutional Convention, if they had not taken this attitude, we would not have a constitution."

Actual specific votes by the committee were taken on individual verbs and many other issues; only one vote per organization was allowed. However, many "straw votes" were taken long before formal voting to allow someone to see what the general sentiment was on a particular issue.

After much debate at the next meeting, held August 27–28, a report was turned in to the CODASYL Executive Committee (Short-Range Committee, 1959b). In essence, it said

2. CONCLUSIONS

The following report is hereby presented to the Executive Committee. The PDQ Committee considers this to be a framework upon which an effective Common Business Language can be built. It feels that the work is complete enough for presentation to the Executive Committee. However, the report to date contains rough spots and requires some additions. Therefore, it is recommended that the PDQ Committee be authorized to complete and polish the system by December 1, 1959. At that time, the completed system can be presented to the Executive Committee with the recommendation that the system be turned over to the manufacturers and users for implementation and application.

It is requested that a directive for the following be issued immediately:

1. Continued existence of the PDQ Committee in order to complete the system by December 1, 1959.
2. Continued existence of the PDQ Committee beyond that date in order to monitor the implementation.

It is felt that there has been a constructive exchange of views and ideas within the PDQ Committee. It is further felt that a Common Business Language is desirable, practical, and within sight.

Fig. 3. [Source: Short-Range Committee (1959b, Sept. 4). (Typeset for ease of reading.)]

we have a good start but more work is needed and we asked permission to continue the existence of the PDQ (a pseudonym for Short-Range) committee in order to complete the language by December 1, 1959. The exact wording of the conclusion of this report is shown in Fig. 3. The outline of the statement language portion of the report is shown as Fig. 4. Numerous verb formats were included in great detail with an indication of whether or not the Short-Range Committee had accepted them (with the vote recorded) or whether they were still unsettled in some fashion. This report also contained the description of verb formats, known in today's terminology as a metalanguage, and this is discussed in more detail in Section 3.2.

It is absolutely essential to recognize that—as best I can recall and after careful scrutiny of all my detailed notes—by this point in time there had been *no indication* by any of the Honeywell representatives of the technical content of the work being done under their contract to the newly formed Computer Sciences Corporation. This matter became an enormous bone of contention over the next few months. (See Section 2.2.4.)

One of the interesting side issues was the relatively late involvement (or attempted in-

APPENDIX A—STATEMENT LANGUAGE OUTLINE

		Pages
I. GENERAL PRINCIPLES OF STATEMENT LANGUAGE		(A1–A6)

I. GENERAL PRINCIPLES OF STATEMENT LANGUAGE — (A1–A6)
  1. CHARACTER SET
  2. WORDS
    2.1 Nouns
      2.1.1. Data Names
      2.1.2. Statement Names
      2.1.3. Suffixes
      2.1.4. Subscripts
    2.2 Literals
    2.3 Actions
    2.4 Specials
      2.4.1 Connectives
      2.4.2 Noise Words
      2.4.3 Comments
      2.4.4 Separators
  3. STATEMENTS
    3.1 Rules of Formation
    3.2 Statement Names
    3.3 Statement Sequencing and Correcting
      3.3.1 Format of Sequence Numbers
      3.3.2 Corrections
II. VERB LIST — (A-7)
III. VERB FORMATS
  Notation for Verb Writeups — (A-8)
  Verb Writeups — (A-9–A-40)

Accept	Divide	Overlay	Close (Revision #1)
Add	Edit	Perform	Open (Revision #1)
Alter	Enter	Read	Read (Revision #1)
Begin	Fill	Replace	Write (Revision #1)
Close	Go	Stop	
Copy	If	Subtract	
Define	Multiply	Write	
Display	Open		

Fig. 4. [Source: Short-Range Committee (1959b, Sept. 4). (Typeset for ease of reading.)]

ASSOCIATION FOR COMPUTING MACHINERY
2 East 63rd Street
New York 21, New York

September 1, 1959

Dr. Charles Phillips
Department of Defense
Washington, 25, D.C.

Dear Dr. Phillips:

A topic of discussion at the most recent meeting of
the Council of the Association was the Department of Defense
Data Processing Language Committee and its activities

The Council directed me to invite you and your
Committee to consider using the Association for Computing
Machinery for furthering your objectives by:

1) Contributing reports to the ACM publications,

2) Contributing papers to the ACM meetings and,

3) Placing recommendations before the Council for action.

In particular, I would like to call your attention to
the ACM Committee on Computer Languages under the chairmanship
of Professor Alan J. Perlis of Carnegie Tech. You might contact
Professor Perlis directly about specific avenues of cooperation.

The Association, in summary, wishes to commend you and
your Committee for its most important work, and extends its
facilities to aid on this project in which so much interest exists.

Sincerely yours,

signed

Jack Moshman

Secretary

Fig. 5. [Source: Phillips (1959, Sept. 4). (Typeset for ease of reading.)]

tervention and support) of ACM. Figure 5 shows a letter from the ACM secretary offering ACM support. To the best of my knowledge, there was no response from CODASYL which had any effect.

2.2.3. September 4 Report to CODASYL Executive Committee

On September 4, 1959, the CODASYL Executive Committee met to hear the report from the Short-Range Committee. After introductions from Joe Wegstein, the main presentations were made by Mary Hawes, chairman of the task group on data descriptions, and Jean Sammet, chairman of the task group on procedural statements. From the minutes of that meeting (Phillips, 1959, Sept. 4, p. 3), "The recommendation for continuation of the Short-Range Committee to complete the system by December 1, 1959, was approved. The indefinite continuation beyond that date to monitor the implementation of the language was also approved."

2.2.4. Relationship of FACT to COBOL

Eventually a significant bone of contention arose from trying to evaluate how much effect—if any—the Honeywell-800 Business Compiler (later renamed FACT) (Honeywell, 1959) had on COBOL. As was stated earlier, the three main inputs to COBOL in terms of influencing the work were FLOW-MATIC, AIMACO, and Commercial Translator; the first and last of these had the most significant influence because AIMACO was really a minor modification of FLOW-MATIC. Although work on FACT, which at that time was called the Honeywell-800 Business Compiler, was going on during the summer of 1959, the Short-Range Committee was not given any written information on this, and to the best of my recollection, was not even told any of the technical details of the work going on. We finally did receive manuals; I still have mine and the "Received date stamp" on it is October 12, 1959. Now obviously if I did not receive a manual until then, and *if* the Honeywell representatives on the committee did not say anything about the technical content, I claim that it cannot have had much influence up until then.

Early in October, FACT manuals were made available to the entire Intermediate-Range Committee, which immediately became very enthusiastic about FACT. Specifically, in October it passed a motion whose exact wording I do *not* have, but the essence of which was that FACT was a much better language than the specifications produced by the Short-Range Committee so far, and hence should be adopted as the basis of the first common business language (Sammet, 1959c). As can be imagined, this had the effect of a major bombing on the Short-Range Committee, which was very unhappy about the Intermediate-Range Committee recommendation and certainly did not agree with it. Since the Intermediate-Range Committee had only the September 4 Short-Range Committee specifications, and since in my view (and theirs) FACT was really a good and an advanced language, any technical comparison would clearly be on the side of FACT. However, the difficulties of dealing with machine independence, and the interaction of competing manufacturers certainly made the creation of a *common* business language orders of magnitude more difficult. It is interesting to speculate what COBOL might have looked like had the FACT language specifications been available in June 1959 when the other three major inputs were!

In fairness to the historical record I wish to include a bit of information which I don't believe I knew then and which was just sent to me in a letter from Dick Clippinger (1977). He was the Honeywell representative to the Intermediate-Range Committee and informs me that *he* did *not* make the proposal to adopt FACT as the Short-Range Committee output and left the meeting when it was made and did not vote on it.

(Timing overtook the Intermediate-Range Committee resolution on FACT; by the time the CODASYL Executive Committee got around to considering it formally, they had already accepted the final Short-Range Committee report for publication and the question died (Phillips, 1960, Feb. 12).)

What becomes considerably more subjective is how much influence the Honeywell language had *after* we had received the manuals. For myself, I can only say that it had minimal influence. To the best of my recollection, I was certainly much too busy to study it in any detail, and while I believe that I glanced at it, I can honestly state that I recall it had little or no influence on *my* thinking with regard to COBOL. It is certainly true that some of the elements in even the early version of FACT were more advanced than those in COBOL. Indeed, it would be surprising if this were not true, since the FACT language designers had the same inputs that the COBOL committee had, but had the double advantage of designing for only a single machine (the Honeywell 800), and without the constraints of a group of competing manufacturers.

A further discussion of the FACT situation as it relates to attribution in the published versions of COBOL appears in Section 2.3.2.

The basic difficulty of the entire situation (as I saw it then and recall it now) was the difference between the alleged importance and contributions of FACT to COBOL as seen by Honeywell, and the opposite opinions on this held by the rest of us. In other words, Honeywell thought FACT had made a significant contribution and the rest of the Short-Range Committee did not.

Some of the Honeywell view is included in Clippinger (1961), particularly pp. 255–256.

2.2.5. Producing the December 1959 Version of COBOL

Meetings of the Short-Range Committee were held September 17–18, October 5–9, and October 19–21. Improvements and further language developments, all based on the September 4 report, were considered. According to my hand notes, it was at the September 17 meeting that six specific names for the language were suggested, but *not* agreed to. They were the following:

BUSY	Business System
BUSYL	Business System Language
INFOSYL	Information System Language
DATASYL	Data System Language
COSYL	Common Systems Language
COCOSYL	Common Computer Systems Language

The next day, the name COBOL was finally agreed to as an acronym for *CO*mmon *Bus*iness *O*riented *L*anguage. Unfortunately, my notes do not show who made that suggestion.

During and between these meetings in September and October, various methods were used to expedite the work, but we continued to get bogged down by the size of the committee trying to work. Finally, on the third day of the October 19–21 meeting, a suggestion—I believe from Gertrude Tierney (IBM)—was made that a six-person group should be appointed to try and develop the specifications. This had been considered by several of us because we felt that the committee itself was too large and too unwieldy to actually get the work done. After much discussion about what could and should be done, including a discussion of the Intermediate-Range Committee resolution with regard to the Honeywell language (see Section 2.2.4), Tierney's suggestion was accepted. Joe Wegstein appointed a six-person committee, consisting of Gert Tierney and Bill Selden (IBM), Howard Bromberg and Norman Discount (RCA), and Vernon Reeves and Jean Sammet (Sylvania). To the best of my recollection, the six of us had felt that we could get the job done and semi-volunteered. We did indeed work for two solid weeks in New York City, including some literally round-the-clock sessions, and on November 7, 1959, produced a final specification (Bromberg *et al.*, 1959) which was sent to the Short-Range Committee for its consideration. At the Short-Range Committee meeting, November 16–20, two types of discussions took place—technical and administrative/political. The latter pertained to the way in which the final report should be described and presented, and when. The former obviously dealt with the technical language specifications themselves. By and large, the work of the six person group was generally accepted although the Short-Range Committee did consider the details carefully. However, a few items of some significance were changed which, at least in my view, turned out to be serious mistakes. Prime among these had to do with changes on the conditionals and the DEFINE. (See Section 3.1.1.) According to my hand notes, after days of discussion, the 16 voting attendees at the meeting accepted the technical content and voted to establish an editing committee consisting of the six people who had put together the November 7 draft (Bromberg *et al.*, 1959) and with myself as chairman. This committee was to do editing only and was morally bound not to make any changes; if we felt changes were necessary, we were instructed to attempt to get a consensus by phone. This phoning to authorize technical changes was actually done successfully in a few cases where the editing process uncovered some glaring errors in the language specifications (e.g., need for restriction on the maximum size of numbers in arithmetic operations, handling the literal delimiter). Finally, after another two weeks of round-the-clock work (this time in Boston), a document entitled "COBOL—Specifications for a *CO*mmon *B*usiness *O*riented *L*anguage," dated December 1959, was finished, (Short-Range Committee, 1959c). (Although they were not officially members of the editing committee, I believe that Dan Goldstein, Betty Holberton, and Nora Taylor were present during most of the work in Boston and contributed to the editing.) The title page of this report contained the following statement:

> This report was prepared by the Short-Range Committee of the Committee on Data Systems Languages. This report is a technical reference manual detailing the specifications of COBOL. It is not intended to be a training or teaching manual, and assumes a fair knowledge of data processing on the part of the reader.

As is to be expected, even the exact way in which this was to be transmitted to the CODASYL Executive Committee had some political problems. In particular, the Minneapolis–Honeywell representative originally *declined* to sign the committee transmittal letter to Phillips (Wegstein, 1959) with the explanation (Gaudette, 1959a),

> because there are major deficiencies which reduce its effectiveness as a common language. These deficiencies are: (1) the lack of a powerful output processor; (2) the inability to process card input files directly; (3) the absence of built-in sort routines; and (4) the weakness for handling records of a highly variable nature.

This November 30 letter of Gaudette was never actually sent, and eventually he wrote another one (Gaudette, 1959b) which I believe was formally submitted and which said in part,

> We join in the decision of the Short-Range Task Group . . . and . . . request the privilege of filing this letter . . . to more fully express our views . . . the following additional attributes would serve to make it a more powerful and effective common language: (1) a powerful output processor; (2) the ability to process card input files directly; (3) built-in sort routines; and (4) the ability to handle records of a highly variable nature.

As best as I can recall, the general response by the rest of the committee to all these comments was that we felt some of the proposed features (e.g., card input) were inappropriate whereas others (e.g., built-in sort routines) we agreed were desirable; however, we did not have time to develop specifications for even those facilities we did approve.

2.2.6. Manpower Estimates

There is no good way to estimate the manpower to bring COBOL even this far purely from a language development viewpoint and impossible to say anything about the implementation efforts. However, based purely on what my notes and records say about when meetings were held and who was there, I estimate the Short-Range Committee effort to produce the input to the Government Printing Office in the spring of 1960 was between two and four man-years, of which about 90% was expended before January 1960. The lower number certainly does *not* include work done by the Short-Range Committee members (or others in their organizations) *between* meetings. The higher number includes some of that, but certainly *not all* of it. Neither number includes any work on implementation.

2.3. COBOL in 1960

2.3.1. Production of COBOL 60

I have gone into considerable detail to describe the first six months of the COBOL work and to record my view of some of the circumstances and pressures surrounding the initial development. While significant changes were made in the development of COBOL 61 (primarily to improve some of the technical deficiencies that arose from the rapid time scale in which we worked) the fundamental concepts and structure and layout of COBOL were indeed established in that six-month period of June–December 1959. (See Section 2.3.3 for discussion of COBOL 61.)

The CODASYL Executive Committee met January 7–8, 1960, and accepted the report (Phillips, 1960, Jan. 7–8) "for publication and recommended its adoption for usage by the entire data processing community after required typographical and other minor corrections had been made." The Executive Committee "established an ad hoc Editorial Board and designated Joseph Wegstein as Chairman. . . . Due to Mr. Wegstein's expected absence from the country for a short period, initial editorial work will be done by Mrs. Frances E. Holberton of the David Taylor Model Basin, the other member of the Editorial Board." In actuality, all the editing was done by Holberton, according to correspondence from both of them to me as part of the review of this paper (Holberton, 1978; Wegstein, 1977).

There was also a discussion at this meeting regarding the publication mechanism, and the Executive Committee decided to arrange (if possible) for the Government Printing Office to produce the COBOL report; that was subsequently done. The editing work was primarily concerned with cleanup of some minor items that had been slightly mishandled by our December editing group in our haste to get the thing finished; however, Holberton had to contact the Short-Range Committee members to get concurrence on some of the changes and corrections she deemed necessary.

The CODASYL Executive Committee also spent a considerable amount of time on the maintenance problem and essentially accepted the Short-Range Committee recommendations, albeit with some modifications. The essence of the plan was that there would be two groups, one composed of users and another composed of the manufacturers. Concurrence of both would be needed for changes or clarifications to be approved.

The Short-Range Committee was dissolved. Perhaps the most important decision that was made was to agree (Phillips, 1960, Jan. 7–8)

> that Basic COBOL as recommended in the Short Range Committee's report would be accepted as the minimum that would be required from all computer manufacturers; i.e., no computer manufacturer could correctly claim his computer accepts COBOL unless he provides a compiler that will deal with every element included in Basic COBOL, as defined.

(The actual language specifications contained much more than the subset of elements which were designated as Basic COBOL.)

On February 12, 1960, the CODASYL Executive Committee met and made certain decisions that were quite crucial from both a practical and an historical viewpoint. They said (Phillips, 1960, Feb. 12), "This first publication of COBOL should be identified as 'preliminary specifications' for a programming language and that a statement should be included to caution prospective users that there is no guarantee, expressed or implied, that programs written with COBOL will run on any processor." Different wording was used in the actual GPO report, but it did contain a legal disclaimer that there was no responsibility by the committee. Secondly, the list of people who had participated in the work of the Short-Range Committee at one time or another which had been *included* in the December 1959 Short-Range Committee report was to be *eliminated* from the final GPO report. This list of names did not appear again in any place until the publication of the COBOL standard in 1968 (ANSI, 1968). This list is shown in Fig. 6. Thirdly, they decided (Phillips, 1960, Feb. 12), "There is no intent to characterize the report as a 'military document.' It will be published by the Government Printing Office as a government report." (Nevertheless, because apparently government regulations require the name of the requesting department to appear on the cover, the COBOL 60 GPO report clearly includes the words "Department of Defense" on the cover in large letters.)

2.3.2. Attribution of Inputs

One of the most interesting items from a political point of view was not discussed at all. It pertains to the printed attribution of languages which were used as input to the design of COBOL. The 1960 GPO manual (Department of Defense, 1960, p. I-2) stated: "Ideas and information were drawn from many sources; in particular, from the FLOW-MATIC System . . . the Commercial Translator System . . . and the AIMACO System . . . ." Then the citations for (only) the specific Remington-Rand and IBM manuals were shown: (Remington-Rand Univac, 1958; IBM, 1959). The acknowledgment for the 1961 version of COBOL (Department of Defense, 1961, p. I-5) revised that wording to delete AIMACO entirely and said "The authors and copyright holders of the copyrighted material used herein: FLOW-MATIC . . . Commercial Translator . . . FACT . . . have specifically authorized the use of this material, ..." Thus, FACT was shown as input to COBOL for the 1961 version but not for the 1960 version, although in my own personal view it had no more effect on COBOL 61 than on COBOL 60. To the best of my recollection, the decision to include FACT in this acknowledgment was made unilaterally by Charles Phillips, although conceivably he may have consulted someone before doing so; I do not believe the committee had the chance to decide on this. As partial proof of this, I note that the COBOL 1961 specifications produced by a Special Task Group of the CODASYL Executive Committee and accepted May 5, 1961, definitely did *not* include FACT in

Jean E. Sammet

2. ATTRIBUTION

The following people have participated in the work of the SHORT-RANGE COMMITTEE at one time or another.

Col. Alfred Asch	Air Materiel Command USAF
Robert S. Barton	Burroughs
Howard Bromberg	Radio Corporation of America
William Carter	Minneapolis-Honeywell, and later IBM
Ben F. Cheydleur	Radio Corporation of America
Miss Deborah Davidson	Sylvania Electric Products, Inc. and later CEIR
Norman Discount	Radio Corporation of America
William Finley	Sperry Rand
Charles Gaudette	Minneapolis-Honeywell
Roy Goldfinger	International Business Machines
Dan Goldstein	Sperry Rand
Mrs. Mary K. Hawes	Burroughs, and later Radio Corporation of America
Duane Hedges	Air Materiel Command
Mrs. Frances E. Holberton	David Taylor Model Basin USN
Miss Sue Knapp	Minneapolis–Honeywell
Karl Kozarsky	Radio Corporation of America
Roy Nutt	Computer Science [sic] Corporation
William Logan	Burroughs
Rex McWilliams	Radio Corporation of America
Vernon Reeves	Sylvania Electric Products, Inc.
Gerald Rosenkrantz	Radio Corporation of America
Miss Jean E. Sammet	Sylvania Electric Products, Inc.
William Selden	International Business Machines
Edward F. Somers	Sperry Rand
Mrs. Nora Taylor	David Taylor Model Basin USN
Miss Gertrude Tierney	International Business Machines
Capt. Erwin Vernon	Air Materiel Command
J. H. Wegstein, Chairman	Bureau of Standards

Fig. 6. [Source: Short-Range Committee (1959c, Dec.). (Typeset for ease of reading.)]

the acknowledgments (see CODASYL Special Task Group, 1961, p. I-7). It also did *not* include AIMACO, which by that time was almost dead and also was not copyrighted. Future versions of COBOL have included the acknowledgment of copyrighted material from FLOW-MATIC, Commercial Translator, and FACT, but have not mentioned AIMACO.

2.3.3. Production of COBOL 61

The Short-Range Committee proposed (Wegstein, 1960) a maintenance mechanism which involved two committees—a Manufacturers Committee with one voting member from each company interested in implementing COBOL, and a Users Committee with individuals from user groups. These groups were to handle both clarifications and proposals for language changes by a very complicated method which essentially required agreement by both groups. (The Short-Range Committee proposal was eventually adopted with some modifications.)

A severe conceptual problem arose during 1960. An informal document of my own (Sammet, 1960b) which I believe was never sent to anybody, said in part:

> Much less has been accomplished in the preceding 9 months than in the 6 months required to issue the original Short-Range Committee report. . . . There are only three people on the current Manufacturers Group who were on the original committee and still representing the same com-

pany. . . . Both as individuals and companies, they seem to feel that it is partially their job to rewrite the language. . . . Changes are being made just because people have "bright ideas" without regard to the fact that this is supposedly a language already developed and fixed. . . . IBM, Minneapolis–Honeywell, and General Electric all have differing languages. They naturally are interested only in forcing COBOL into some mold relative to their own language. . . .

At a meeting held August 25–26, 1960, the Manufacturers Group passed a resolution saying essentially that COBOL should be updated at most once per year. On September 2, 1960, the Users Group of the COBOL Maintenance Committee passed a resolution saying, in part that "Resolution of . . . ambiguities will be the first order of business for the COBOL Committee." In September–October, 1960, the CODASYL Executive Committee agreed to establish a "Special COBOL Task Group" whose objective was "to make an intensive and complete review of the COBOL report, as published in April 1960 . . . all supplements . . . all proposals pending . . . or submitted . . . during its special session . . . . This action is to be started September 26, 1960, and shall be completed . . . not later than November 15, 1960." (Source for this paragraph is Phillips, 1960b.)

At the same time, the Executive Committee decided to eliminate the terms "Basic COBOL," "Extended COBOL," and "Levels of Implementation" where such terms had been used previously, but had caused confusion. They said that beginning with COBOL 1961, there should be a "Required COBOL" and "Elective COBOL," with the former being a subset of the latter, and the latter containing primarily elements which were very machine oriented.

As part of the ground rules for establishing the special task group, the CODASYL Executive Committee (Phillips, 1960b) stated that "only those members representing manufacturers who have made firm written commitments to develop COBOL compilers . . . shall vote." This concept was objected to by R. F. Clippinger of Minneapolis–Honeywell with the statement shown in Fig. 7. Phillips (1960b) said,

> The Honeywell statement lists several ways in which it is contended that COBOL is still inferior to FACT. It is interesting to note that these are the same points contained in a letter from the Honeywell representative on the Short Range Task Force dated November 30, 1959. Although Honeywell held membership in the group that developed the initial specifications of COBOL and has been a member of the Manufacturers Group of the Maintenance Committee . . . no proposals were submitted to any of these groups by Honeywell to rectify these deficiencies. The Maintenance Committee will be gratified to note that Honeywell now intends to present such proposals.

This special task group was chaired by Jack Jones (Air Materiel Command) and Greg Dillon (Dupont); according to Jones (1977) the two of them were to protect the user interests since no other users were on the committee. The committee first met in September 1960 and completed the work in February 1961, although the Executive Committee had said it was to be done by November 15, 1960. (In those days all of us had yet to learn how long it takes to define and/or clarify a language!) Again based on comments from Jones (1977), we met every other week for a full week during most of that period.

COBOL 61 kept the basic structure but made a number of changes which created incompatibilities with COBOL 60. For the remainder of 1961 and throughout most of 1962, the Maintenance Committee was concerned primarily with extensions, and that is where most of the CODASYL COBOL work has concentrated since then.

STATEMENT BY R. F. CLIPPINGER TO BE INSERTED IN THE MINUTES OF COBOL COMMITTEE

Minneapolis Honeywell believes that a strong, common business language is to the advantage of the USER and also to the advantage of the manufacturer with the most effective equipment. Therefore Honeywell is in favor of a strong, common business language.

Honeywell has and will continue to contribute to the creation and definition of COBOL.

COBOL, as currently defined, is still notably weak and inferior to FACT in the following ways: (1) It possesses no effective way of creating a file from information on paper tape or cards. (2) It possesses no SORT verb. (3) It defines no collation sequence. (4) It lacks the automatic housekeeping for convenient handling of records containing an indefinite number of subgroups at one or more levels. (5) It possesses no report writing generator.

Honeywell will present proposals to rectify these weaknesses.

Honeywell draws attention of the USERS to two major acts of arbitrary and unjust-ified discrimination by the Executive Committee of CODASYL against Honeywell.

1. When the Development Committee, one of two major committees of the CODASYL Conference proposed almost unanimously that FACT (Honeywell Business Compiles) [sic] be made the basis of COBOL, the Executive Committee did not even meet to consider this proposal.
2. The Executive Committee has arbitrarily decided that General Electric, Sperry Rand, National Cash Register, Sylvania, Radio Corporation of America and International Business Machines may vote and Burroughs, Control Data Corporation and Minneapolis Honeywell may not vote on the definition of required elements of COBOL-61.

Whether or not the Executive Committee has the power to penalize three out of eight manufacturers, each of whom is contributing on a voluntary basis to the creation of COBOL is debatable. The wisdom of the decision is less debatable.

CODASYL is a voluntary effort. It draws its strength from the desires of the USERS to have a useful product. When voting rules are arbitrarily manipulated to achieve unspecified purposes, CODASYL loses much of that strength.

In conclusion Honeywell supports COBOL, is devoted to the goal of making it strong and will implement it when it is strong enough.

Fig. 7. [Source: Phillips (1960b, Oct. 6). (Typeset for ease of reading.)]

2.3.4. The First COBOL Compilers

One of the interesting events of 1960 with regard to COBOL was the action and reaction of several of the manufacturers. RCA and Remington-Rand Univac were involved in a "race" to produce the first COBOL compiler. IBM was having internal qualms about what to do about COBOL; this latter problem is described in Bemer (1971) and certainly kept IBM out of any COBOL race.

Perhaps the most significant event, though, took place December 6 and 7, 1960 (Phillips, 1960, Dec. 6; Bromberg, 1961). Essentially the same COBOL program was run on both the RCA and Remington-Rand Univac computers with changes only the Environment Division and perhaps one or two trivial changes elsewhere. The significance of this lay in the demonstration that compatibility could really be achieved. Manuals were available in 1960 —see RCA (1960a) and Remington-Rand Univac (1960). The attitudes of these companies and their internal activities are very interesting but are better described by people who are in a firsthand position to do so, rather than by me. (See, e.g., the article by Bromberg, 1961.)

2.4. Technical Contributions of the Known Languages

It is beyond the scope of this paper to do even a superficial study of all of the work which precedes COBOL. However, it is worth noting the preliminary definition of a data-processing compiler by Grace Hopper (1955) which contains the following two crucial sentences as part of the description of the compilation process: "in the case of a *verb,* the catalog entry will lead to a generator or subroutine and its satellite routines in a volume of the library. In the case of a *noun,* the catalog entry will lead to a standard item design and its satellite routines in a volume of the library." In my opinion, these sentences are crucial, since they point the way to a data description that is separate from the executable code.

A number of source documents for the predecessors to COBOL are listed in Sammet (1969, p. 377–378). Only the most important ones relative to COBOL are included in this paper.

2.4.1. Specific Contributions of FLOW-MATIC and Commercial Translator

A complete analysis of all the contributions made by FLOW-MATIC and Commercial Translator would require more time and space than is feasible within this paper, and is indeed worthy of a separate study. Some of their contributions have been mentioned already, but in this section I will attempt to summarize the major contributions of each language. (In all cases, unless another source is indicated, these evaluations are purely mine.)

The early versions of FLOW-MATIC were called B-∅ (Remington-Rand Univac, 1956). FLOW-MATIC's major contributions were:

(1) It worked! It was in practical use in or shortly after 1957 by several organizations, including Dupont, Metropolitan Life Insurance Company, U.S. Steel, Westinghouse, U.S. Navy's David Taylor Model Basin, Wright–Patterson Air Force Base, and Ontario Hydro of Canada, according to Hopper (1977).

(2) It used full data-names instead of short symbolic names (as in FORTRAN). Although FLOW-MATIC was limited to 12 character names because the UNIVAC word was only 12 characters, the principle of writing SOCIAL-SECUR rather than something like SOSEC was established.

(3) It used full English words for commands, e.g., ADD, COMPARE. The combination of this with the data-names made the program fairly readable in English.

(4) It used less than full machine words for each data item. Note that FORTRAN assumes each number is in a single machine word. In a data processing problem where some fields only required a single character (e.g., to distinguish between MALE and FEMALE) while others might require 15 characters (e.g., a long part number), it would not make sense to define a file which required a separate machine word for each field. This required a fairly complex data description relative to FORTRAN and similar languages. (See next point.)

(5) It separated data descriptions and instructions. This is so well known and understood now it is hard to image what a conceptual breakthrough it was in the mid-1950s.

In considering Commercial Translator's contributions to the early development of COBOL, it must be remembered that at that time only the language specifications existed, i.e., there had been no implementation and therefore no users. Preliminary specifications had been developed as early as March 1958. However, the more formal manual (IBM, 1959) seems to have appeared just around the time of the May 1959 Pentagon meeting. In addition to this timing situation, it must be remembered that Commercial Translator was able to build on FLOW-MATIC. These comments are not made to downgrade the importance of Commercial Translator, but merely to put into perspective the contributions made by the "second of anything" rather than the first.

The major contributions of Commercial Translator were the five given by Bill Selden (IBM) as reported in Sammet (1959, July 13) and the sixth added by me; the parenthetical remarks were *not* in that report, but are current comments of mine:

(1) Formula expressions. (These were not allowed in FLOW-MATIC, and as will be discussed later, the decision to include or exclude them from COBOL became a major bone of contention.)

(2) Conditional variables. (This facility allowed the user to write IF SENIOR rather than IF CLASS EQUALS SENIOR.)

(3) Many levels in data design. (FLOW-MATIC only allowed one level of field.)

(4) IF . . . THEN clausing.

(5) Suffixing. (This provided a mechanism for using the same field names in different files by appending the name of the file.)

(6) (Although *not cited* by Selden, the PICTURE clause was taken over almost directly into COBOL.)

2.4.2. Contributions of FACT

Sections 2.2.4, 2.3.2, and 2.3.3 have shown my view of some of the difficulties with FACT and its role in the early development of COBOL. As stated earlier, I don't feel it had any effect on COBOL 60 nor on COBOL 61. It certainly made a contribution to versions later than COBOL 61, primarily because of the addition of the concepts of a SORT verb, and the concept of a Report Writer. There may have been other, but less obvious, contributions made to some of the later versions of COBOL but time did not permit a study of this.

2.4.3. Interaction of the Four Languages

Because the three manufacturers with "independent" languages were also attempting to produce COBOL, they naturally wanted to bring their own languages as close to COBOL as possible, and conversely. Thus, it seems fair to say that COBOL, Commercial Translator, and FACT had some intertwining effect on each other. This point is made more definitively by both Clippinger (1961) and Bemer (1971). Since FLOW-MATIC II never really existed as a separate set of language specifications as best I can determine, it played no significant role in this interaction.

2.4.4. Relevance of Algebraic Languages

Although the data-processing languages previously cited were the main inputs to COBOL, the committee was certainly aware of, and reasonably knowledgeable about, both FORTRAN and IAL (later called ALGOL 58). In fact, it is the latter which provided a significant influence on the choice of the COBOL character set, because we were appalled at the impracticality of the concept of characters which simply did not exist—in other words, the reference language of IAL. Even by 1959, it was clear that every implementation of IAL or any of its dialects had to make a transliteration of some kind into a hardware language, which in our view destroyed the usefulness of the reference language. Therefore, we were adamant that we would deal only with existing entry hardware equipment, which at that time was primarily limited to a keypunch. However, we did not entirely have blinders on and recognized that the equivalent of typewriter characters could be used (particularly with paper tape). Therefore in certain cases, (e.g., the relational characters) we provided both symbols and English words as well.

2.5. Documentation

Documentation was handled fairly informally, in the sense that there were no requirements in the early development for what could or should be documented. In particular, there was no record kept of the reasons behind certain decisions, except insofar as individuals might have these in their hand notes. At the September 17, 1959, meeting there was a considerable discussion as to what the first public description should have as its objective. Even at that time there was a considerable discussion of the difference between the language manual issued in the name of CODASYL and the individual manuals that would be issued by each manufacturer. The following items indicate early manuals that were produced from various manufacturers, and some of the earliest published papers or texts of technical talks given (Anonymous, 1960a,b; Clippinger, 1961; DeJong, 1960; Lanzarotta, 1961; RCA, 1960a,b; Remington-Rand Univac, 1960; Sammet, 1960a,c, 1961a,c; Willey *et al.*, 1961). The entire May 1962 issue of the *Communications of the ACM* contains articles on COBOL 61.

2.6. Intended Purpose and Users

Although from the very beginning COBOL was concerned with "business data processing," there was never any real definition of that phrase. It was certainly intended (and expected) that the language could be used by novice programmers and read by the management. We felt the readability by management could and would be achieved because of the intended use of English, which was a fundamental conclusion from the May 1959 Pentagon meeting. Surprisingly, although we wanted the language to be easy to use, particularly for nonprofessional programmers, we did not really give much thought to ensuring that the language would be easy to learn; most of our concentration was on making it "easy to read" although we never provided any criteria or tests for readability.

COBOL was intended for use only in the United States, even though experience from Grace Hopper's group had shown that the transliteration into another natural language at this level was trivial. I believe that subsequently other countries (e.g., Germany, Japan, Netherlands, and Sweden - but not France) have used COBOL with English key words but their own data names. What this does to *their* readability is left to the imagination! [This information was confirmed and/or supplied by Grace Hopper (1977).]

The biggest dispute with regard to the users came in the committee conflict about the perceptions of what business data processing people could and should do in such a higher level language. At that time, the primary experience was with the users of Remington-Rand FLOW-MATIC. We had the not too surprising problem that those representatives tended to pontificate and issue pronouncements based on their experience, while the rest of us were somewhat unwilling to accept the gospel as issued that way. Certainly the biggest and worst example of this came in the dispute over the way of providing arithmetic capability. In essence, those committee people who felt they knew the business-type users said that those users could not (and should not) be forced to use formulas, and hence it was necessary and appropriate to supply the four arithmetic verbs: ADD, SUBTRACT, MULTIPLY, and DIVIDE. Conversely, those people on the committee (including myself) who had mathematical training said that we had no objections to providing those verbs but that we could *not* tolerate a situation in which somebody who *understood* what a formula was nevertheless was prevented from writing one! This dispute raged for many months, directly and indirectly, as best as I can recall, and it was the type of argument for which there simply was no compromise except the one that we ended up with—include both facilities, i.e., the four arithmetic verbs on one hand and permitting formulas on the other, albeit with the formula to be triggered by the verb COMPUTE.

COBOL was designed from its inception to be used on large computers (by 1959 standards although by 1978 standards they would be considered minicomputers), intended for business data processing use. In particular, machines for which COBOL was certainly being considered were the UNIVAC I and II, the IBM 705 and 709, the Honeywell 800, RCA 501, Sylvania MOBIDIC, Burroughs B-5000. The desire for "business data processing" computers intuitively would seem to exclude binary machines since at that time they were not considered suitable for business data processing even though AIMACO itself was being designed for the binary Sperry Rand 1105. However, since Sylvania's machine was binary and I was heavily involved with the committee, I could not allow language restrictions on using binary computers; simultaneously, the IBM people had at least one binary machine (the 709) on which they were contemplating implementing COBOL. As indicated earlier, when Remington-Rand changed its mind and put out a binary machine as UNIVAC III, they changed their mind in midstream on the importance of making COBOL usable on a binary machine.

In the middle of 1959, there was no thought of interactive capabilities and not even any serious consideration of requiring COBOL compilers to be imbedded into an operating system; while some of the latter existed, they were few and far between, and COBOL was certainly not going to be designed for usage in that environment. This in fact caused bitter discussions on the committee, because the input–output facilities were provided in different ways by computer manufacturers in their other software. Thus different manufacturers had differing types of I/O Executives and tape handling and tape labeling conventions which they did not want to have overridden by COBOL requirements, or which might be considered to be in conflict with COBOL.

2.7. Comments on Personal and Company Interrelationships

The following comments represent some highly subjective and purely personal judgments on some of the people and interrelationships, albeit without including any names. First, the members of the Short-Range Committee were generally strangers to each other (except, of course, those from the same company). Secondly, it was quite clear that the disputes between people from the same organization were often as great (and sometimes greater) than between people from different organizations, and this applied to virtually all the organizations involved, whether manufacturers or users. In my opinion, this was natural because I have always felt that most issues in language design are matters of personal taste rather than either science or economics. Thus, those organizations which had two representatives seldom had an "organization position"—not even the manufacturers! Some of the group considered themselves purely as language designers, whereas others also had the responsibility for the implementation. The former group naturally could afford to be much more cavalier about the features that would be difficult to implement. As time went on, representatives from RCA and Remington-Rand Univac became increasingly reluctant to make changes in the language specification because of work they had done so far with regard to the implementation. I felt their position was quite reasonable, even though many of us tried to overrule them.

As best I can recall my view at that time, I felt there was a strong anti-IBM bias in this committee from me and some (but certainly not all) of the others. Since I was not working for IBM at the time, I can freely (although *not* with pride) admit that in some cases suggestions or decisions were made on the basis of doing something differently than IBM did it. For example, we felt that the verb used for loop control should *not* be called DO because that was being used in FORTRAN. (I should hasten to point out that the greatly different specifications for the PERFORM was another reason for not using the same word, and the reason for having different specifications is that we felt the FORTRAN DO was not technically adequate for COBOL.)

One of the difficulties with IBM from the committee's viewpoint was their oscillation on what position they were taking with regard to COBOL (see Bemer, 1971). Some of the IBM people who were not on the committee delighted in saying that the language did not really exist; their rationale seemed primarily to be that it was not defined in BNF!

Another of the factors involving people was the significant change in the committee personnel in 1960. New people wanted to redo the work of the Short-Range Committee—sometimes with good technical justification, but often because they just "preferred" it that way. (Further elaboration of this problem is given in Sammet (1961b).)

Finally, in my own personal opinion the whole situation with Minneapolis–Honeywell (as described in Sections 2.2.4, 2.3.2, 2.3.3, and 2.4.2) engendered a great deal of bitterness on both sides at that time. However, it would be inaccurate to leave an impression that such bitterness continued "forever." While obviously no specific date can be given to its disappearance, it is certainly true that Honeywell did implement COBOL, did send representatives to meetings, and eventually dropped FACT entirely. It is unlikely that many people outside the COBOL committees of 1959–1961 even know there ever was any bitterness.

Considering all of the people and organizational problems which existed, in hindsight it seems almost miraculous that we achieved anything!

3. Rationale for Content of Language

3.1. Language Design Principles

The primary issue on language design faced at the June 1959 meeting was the division of the language—and the work—into statement language and data description. From this it became natural to divide the program itself into separately marked divisions—Procedure and Data. The need for the Environment Division came later in the deliberations. (See Section 3.3.)

By today's standards of some of the important elements of language design, a vast amount of time was spent arguing about syntactic issues—what punctuation should be used and where, what should be done about reserved words which had to differ from division to division, etc. The prime motivation behind this emphasis was the desire for readability and naturalness. There were numerous irregularities in syntax—primarily because so many cases were determined on an individual basis. It is interesting to see the list of items that were considered of major controversy in the development of the language as of August 17. (See Fig. 8.)

There was great emphasis on simplicity, but simplicity in this context really meant the

POINTS OF GREATEST CONTROVERSY
WITHIN THE
STATEMENT LANGUAGE TASK GROUP

Prepared by Jean Sammet
August 17, 1959

An attempt has been made to list the most controversial points in the material agreed upon to date. This list may not be conclusive but it covers at least the material handled in the first four meetings. The order of the points is random and therefore not significant.

An attempt has also been made to summarize the major arguments for and against the decision although, naturally, much of the detail has been omitted.

It will be noted that in very many cases—most notably points 1, 9, and 10—the basic argument was that it was powerful and flexible and many people would like to have it. The opposing argument generally was based on the fact that the situation is a very complicated one and had a very limited use. There does not appear to be any real answer to the statement made by the proponents of additional power that people need not use it if they do not want it, and that local installation rules may use only a subset of the language if desired.

1. THE USE OF "IF–THEN" AND/OR BOOLEAN EXPRESSIONS WILL NOT BE ALLOWED AT THIS TIME.

    For: Many situations require the power and flexibility of this type of formalism.

    Against: This is too complicated for normal data processing and is only needed in specialized cases.

2. A SENTENCE IS TO BE HANDLED BY A PERIOD FOLLOWED BY AT LEAST ONE SPACE.

    For: The normal ending marker of the sentence is indeed a period. However, a period is not sufficient because of its use in a literal. (Note: If the literal is marked, then this does not matter since it can always be clearly distinguished.

    Against: In a hard copy coming from paper tape, it is impossible to tell whether or not there is a space if there is a carriage return. The normal procedure is indeed to have a carriage return, and therefore, it will be impossible to determine whether or not the format is correct.

    Comment: Words must end with a space; therefore, if a period is preceded by a space, it is all right except in the case of something like .3. However, in this case, the problem is solved if we say that an end of sentence is specified by a period surrounded by spaces.

Fig. 8. [*Source:* Sammet (1959a, Aug. 17, 18). (Typeset for ease of reading.)]

3. KEY WORDS AND/OR PUNCTUATION WILL BE USED TO DEFINE PARAMETERS.

For: This is far easier to implement. It is also safer in reading in the sense that you know which words really matter, since the format is fixed.

Against: This often requires unnatural expressions.

4. SYMBOLIC NAMES WILL BE USED TO IDENTIFY STATEMENTS.

For: This is very nmemonic [sic] and has all the advantages of normal symbol code. When the original flow chart is prepared, it is easier to work with symbolic names.

Against: Sequence numbers are required to allow reordering and causes essentially a double set of names. Once the program has been written, it may be harder to refer to the flow chart by symbolic names.

Comment: The judicious use of symbolic names allows convenient use of flow charts.

5. SEQUENCE NUMBERS MAY NOT BE ADDRESSED.

For: The compiler and possibly the program will be much more complicated if it is possible to write "Go to" sequence numbers"." [sic]

Against: It is sometimes very convenient to be able to use the sequence number rather than a symbolic name.

6. DATA AND STATEMENT NAMES WILL HAVE THE SAME FORM.

For: This is nmemonic [sic] and avoids the necessity of a double set of rules.

Against: These are conceptually quite different and should be made to look different. There is great possibility of confusion.

7. THE SAME NAME MAY NOT BE REPEATED WITHIN A FILE.

For: This is by far the simpler situation.

Against: A tremendous amount of flexibility is lost because the same reasons which make it desirable to allow the same name in several files also apply to duplication of names within files.

8. THE "DEFINE VERB" SHOULD HAVE A LIBRARY OPTION WHICH AUTOMATICALLY INSERTS THE NEW SUBROUTINE INTO THE COMPILER LIBRARY.

For: If a problem is moved from one installation to another, it is only necessary to append the statements to the basic problem in order to have it run.

Against: This reduces the readability and "commonness of the language".

9. THE USE OF SYMBOLIC EXPRESSIONS FOR ARITHMETIC OPERATIONS IS NOT ALLOWD [sic] IN THIS TIME.

For: This is too complicated for normal data processing use, and is unneeded in general.

Against: Many problems could make great use of this and those who do not wish to bother need not use the symbolism.

10. SUBSCRIPTS ARE ALLOWED.

For: Many problems require this type of handling and elimination would penalize the machines which have index registers.

Against: This is too complicated for normal data processing uses.

Fig. 8. (*Continued*)

11. THE WORD "IF" WILL BE USED INSTEAD OF THE WORD "COMPARE".

For: This is a more natural way of expressing the action, and lends itself easily to future extensions.

Against: "If" is not an imperative command as are all of the other verbs. The extension to Boolean functions should not be made in the future.

12. PRESENT FORMAT OF INPUT–OUTPUT VERBS

For: The mere naming of a file should not automatically open it. The opening of a file should not automatically provide the first unit record. File information is often read into an area other than the normal file area and similarly is often written from different areas.

Against: The first "Read" of a file should suffice to start all the mechanism needed to obtain the first unit record.

13. THE FOUR ARITHMETIC VERBS SHOULD HAVE AS FEW KEY WORDS AS POSSIBLE.

For: This eliminates a large amount of writing.

Against: Additional Key words provide for an easier and safer scan.

14. THE "PERFORM" VERB DOES ALLOW HANDLING OF BOTH OPEN AND CLOSE [sic] SUBROUTINES.

For: This permits the programmer to make use of "accidentally useful" chunks of coding without rewriting.

Against: It is necessary to establish two sets of stringent rules for the two types of subroutines for there is great possibility of error.

15. THE REQUIREMENT OF THE WORDS "FROM, BY, TO," IN THE "PERFORM" VERB IS ESSENTIAL.

For: If one of the six possible sequences is required, this may not be natural to all people. If the sequence does not happen to be the one now commonly used in Fortram, [sic] this inconveniences a large body of users.

Against: The requirement for the key words is inconsistent with the general policy of having as few as possible.

ADDITIONAL POINTS OF CONTROVERSY
Based on August 17, 1959 Meeting of
STATEMENT LANGUAGE TASK GROUP
Prepared by Jean Sammet
August 18, 1959

For earlier controversial points, see first report on this subject.

16. KEY WORDS WILL BE CONSIDERED IN CONTEXT AND CAN BE USED ANYWHERE AS LONG AS THE MEANING IS CLEAR.

For: Present scanning techniques indicate that this is no problem, and it improves the readability.

Against: The scan is harder and it is undesirable to depend on context for the meaning.

17. THE USE OF POSITIONS IS ALLOWED ON THE RECEIVING END OF THE MOVE VERB.

For: This allows a good amount of individual handling of characters.

Against: All kinds of problems present themselves in attempting to specify the result of a Move when the receiving area does not have the same format as the source area.

Fig. 8. (*Continued*)

18. SEQUENCE NUMBERS ARE REQUIRED ON EVERY SENTENCE

For: The use of preprinted forms makes this very easy. The difference in collating sequence makes it very difficult to determine a rule of succession for every possible alphanumeric configuration, and this is what is needed if every sentence does not contain a sequence number.

Against: It is inconvenient and unnecessary to require sequence numbers for every sentence. It is possible to establish a rule of succession and allow implied sequence numbers until the next stated one.

19. FORMAT OF CORRECTION VERBS SHOULD BE ESTABLISHED BY EACH COMPILER WRITER.

For: This depends so heavily on the collating sequence and the media format that it is very difficult to do in general. It is not inherently part of the statement language.

Against: This is as much a part of a "common language" as any action verb.

20. THE EXACT FORMAT OF THE MEDIA IS NOT A FUNCTION OF THIS COMMITTEE

For: This is something to be specified by each compiler writer and is not part of the language.

Against: In order to permit the goal of moving a program from one computer to another it is necessary that the format for each media [sic] be completely established.

21. THE "LEADING" OPTION IN THE "MOVE" VERB IS ELIMINATED

For: This is a special case which can be handled in other ways.

Against: This is so common an occurrence it should be allowed in the language.

22. THERE SHOULD BE AN OPTION IN THE OVERLAY "VERB" FOR "OVERLAY FROM STATEMENT-NAME"

For: This is similar to present FLOWMATIC.

Against: This is unsafe and therefore undesirable.

Fig. 8. (*Continued*)

inclusion or exclusion of specific features, such as IF–THEN, Boolean expressions, and subscripts. Simplicity certainly was not defined in terms of any of the concepts that are used for that term in the environment of the late 1970s (e.g., few special cases, single notation for the same concept, consistency).

3.1.1. Statement Language (= Procedure Division)

At the first meeting of the Statement Language Task Group, we posed a list of problems to be considered. A copy of the original listing, which was included in the chairman's report on the meeting, is shown as Fig. 9. It will be noted that there are several of my hand notes on there which came from later discussions. In the light of today's language considerations, it should be noted that a great many of the questions that are asked there are still relevant today for many aspects of new language design. Note particularly question 9, "How can the language be designed to include particularities of each machine and still remain universal?" This is, of course, still an unsolved problem!

At this same meeting it was decided (Sammet, 1959, June 29) that "the criteria to be used in making the decisions are the following, in decreasing order of importance:

PROBLEMS TO BE CONSIDERED BY TASK GROUP ON

STATEMENT LANGUAGE

7-6-59 What time scale for implementation do we want? i.e. should we start now with ultimate or take simpler case + expand.

[My answer: Complic. should be specified but subset available for rapid implementation .

1. Clausing

    a) How many individual sentences can be combined together?

    b) Can a sentence contain more than one call word? If so, how many, and what are the restrictions?

    c) Is extraneous wording -- for example, commentary or misspellings or different connectives -- allowed?

    d) How many operands per verb will be allowed? (See also 4b.)

2. Punctuation *+ Notation*

    What is the significance or lack of significance to different symbols and spaces?

    Forms of punc:
    # ; ( ) /
    ; :

3. Data References

    a) Are prefixes and/or suffixes allowed? If so, in what form?

    b) How are the data references in the statement language connected to the data descriptions?

    Literals

4. Philosophy of Verb Structure

    a) Should there be many options for each verb, or should there be a longer list of verbs with little or no variation allowed?

    b) How many operands per verb should be allowed? (See also 1d.)

    c) What type of complexity and compounding should be allowed?

5. Open-endedness

    a) How are clausing and compounding related to allowance of new verbs?

    b) What means should be provided for the addition of new verbs or phrases? Is the use of a "Define" the best way to do this?

Fig. 9

6. Types of Processing Allowed

    a) What types of processing beyond very basic "data processing"

       should be allowed? Suggestions include

             Algebraic or Operations Research manipulation

             Logical

             Compiler Writing (i.e. Bootstrapping the compiler) *incl corrs*

    b) If items beyond normal data processing are to be allowed, when

       should the language for these be formulated?

7. Symbols or English

    Should the words "add, multiply, subtract, and divide" be used,

    or should the symbols " + X -/" be used? *Equal =*

8. Input-Output and Intramemory Transfer

    What is the best way to handle movement of data?

9. Configuration Problems

    How can the language be designed to include peculiarities of each

    machine and still remain universal?

7-6-59 10. *Sentence naming + correcting*
        ✓ Op nos ¢/or symbolic names
        Correction pseudops?

✓11. Indexing
  12. Allowable chars + rules for combining
  13. Media layout

Fig. 9 (*Continued*)

Jean E. Sammet

(1) Naturalness.
(2) Ease of transcription to required media.
(3) Effectiveness of problem structure.
(4) Ease of implementation.''

Among some of the key technical decisions that were taken at the second meeting of the Task Group on Statement Language were the following: (1) there will be few verbs with many options rather than a large number of individual verbs; (2) the sentence "AND GO TO" will be allowed after any applicable sentence. (That was considered normal and harmless then; today, of course, that is considered a heresy. The ability to put GO TO at the end of every sentence was dropped although the GO TO was, of course, kept as a separate verb.) (3) the first word of every sentence will be the verb; this later required some circumlocution in dealing with "IF" which by no stretch of the English language can be considered a verb but which nevertheless had to be treated as one. It also forced the inclusion of the word "COMPUTE" preceding a formula. (In retrospect, I believe this decision was made almost automatically because of the FLOW-MATIC influence. Grace Hopper (1977) told me that the reason for starting every statement in FLOW-MATIC with a verb was to facilitate translation into other natural languages; apparently all the natural languages she was considering started imperative sentences with a verb.) (4) new verbs may be added by use of a DEFINE operation that effectively causes the named set of statements to be executed whenever the new verb is used. (This appears to be one of the earliest suggestions for the use of a macro in a higher level langauge and also provided in a style which is compatible with the overall language style.)

With regard to the actual verbs to be included, we were heavily influenced by the list in FLOW-MATIC which certainly seemed to provide most of the necessary functional capability. More of the arguments came over specific syntax and the complete functional capability of each verb. As one illustration, it is incredible to remember how much time was spent arguing over the rules for moving a data item from one field to another. A large number of issues crops up in something like that, e.g., should decimal points of the sending and receiving fields be automatically aligned, what rules for truncation or fill in (at either side) are needed if the two fields are unequal size, and what type of conversion from one internal format to the other should be done automatically.

More powerful verbs such as SORT were excluded from the early discussions simply for lack of time. After all, the first issues to be settled were such weighty ones as to whether or not a sentence would end with a period, and where spaces would and would not be allowed, and other rules of punctuation. In almost all cases, decisions were made using the criteria of ease of reading.

Functions were not included in the language because they were felt to be unneeded. At that time, the classical definition of function meant a mathematical function such as sine or cosine or even absolute value. It was felt that these had no use in business data-processing applications.

There was much debate over the loop control and subroutine capability. We wanted the numerous and powerful variations that eventually went into the PERFORM verb. However, there was considerable debate about the need and/or desirability of open versus closed subroutines, with the "open subroutine" contingent eventually emerging triumphant; the feeling for and against open subroutines was almost evenly divided.

It was a subject of great debate as to whether the first occurrence of a READ or a

WRITE verb for a file should automatically open it. The decision finally was no and a separate OPEN verb was put into the language and required for use before the first READ or WRITE of a file. There was also considerable debate about what the OPEN, CLOSE, READ, WRITE verbs would do because some manufacturers feared that the COBOL specifications would interfere with their standard I/O facilities.

While it was recognized that a library facility was needed, it was not considered of major importance relative to other features and because of lack of time the INCLUDE verb was deemed satisfactory, although it was quite weak.

The driving force behind considerations of all the "statements" was the concept of readability. For example, the character set was chosen to be something that was physically available on most data-entry machines (and thus emphasized the keypunch). This had an enormous influence on the syntax of the language because it was felt that we could *not* use the technique of a reference language that was in ALGOL 58.

The concept of noise words (i.e., words which were not required syntactically but allowable in certain places to enhance readability) was influenced by the desire for readability. There was, of course, considerable debate even over this simple concept. For example, given the initial premise did that mean "one could put any word in place of a specific noise word" or "could a particular noise word be used anywhere the user wanted"; many other similar questions were posed. Our decision was that a particular word could be used where shown to enhance readability, but the only choice the user had was to include it or exclude it where specified. Thus, one had the format

```
READ file-name RECORD INTO data-name;
AT END any imperative statement.
```

In that format, the words RECORD and AT are noise words not needed in any way for the logic of processing the statement. We did not entirely envision at that time the enormous headache to come from having to write out in great gory detail the data names and verbs. On the other hand, some of us, particularly including myself, pushed very hard for a DEFINE verb which would allow substitutions. Thus, we wanted a DEFINE which would allow one to write DEFINE SSN = SOCIAL-SECURITY-NUMBER. The intent was that the compiler would accept the SSN which was easier for the user to write and put out on the listing SOCIAL-SECURITY-NUMBER, which would then be used in future listings. The arguments for and against this are quite obvious; the arguments in favor have to do with ease of writing, whereas the arguments against have to do with the fact that this clearly diminishes the readability of the original version of the program that COBOL was supposed to be serving. This capability was *not* included in COBOL 60, but it is ironic to note that a number of software houses have over the past number of years produced programs which they sell which allow the user to do exactly this.

It is interesting to note that the DEFINE (in its two different conceptual forms—one dealing simply with name substitution and the other providing a major macro capability) were in and out of various drafts of COBOL during the period June–December, 1959. The DEFINE for name substitution was *not* included in the December 1959 language, whereas the macro DEFINE *was* included. The latter remained in the language until (at least) 1965; it was removed sometime between COBOL 65 (Department of Defense, 1965) and COBOL 68 (CODASYL, 1969) on the grounds that nobody had implemented it! Incidentally, the COBOL 65 manual just cited is the last one printed by the U.S. Government

Jean E. Sammet

Printing Office. Since then the COBOL Journals of Development (which are different from the standard) have been printed by the Canadian government.

Another feature that was in an early draft of the language but taken out was an overlay facility. It was eventually taken out before the December 1959 version on the grounds that it was simply too diffficult for the programmers for whom COBOL was aimed.

One of the problems that exists in COBOL is the very large list of reserved words, i.e., words which the user cannot use for a data name or a paragraph name because they are key words in the verb formats. They were included to help the implementer. We tried very hard to make it easier for the user by keeping the same set of reserved words in all three divisions; this proved to be absolutely impossible to do if we were to still maintain the readability.

There was some thought given to the desirability of having COBOL able to be used to write its own compiler. For that reason, a few things were put in to help, most notably the EXAMINE verb.

It was recognized that COBOL would not contain all the facilities needed, and that people might have to "escape" to another language, either assembly language or another high level language—hence the ENTER verb.

Among the heaviest points of controversy were the power of the conditional sentence itself, and the Boolean conditions which could be expressed. Actually, the COBOL conditional sentence form which was adopted turned out to be more powerful than the ALGOL 60 **if then else** construction (although few people seem to recognize or acknowledge this). Abbreviated conditions were allowed as an elegant feature contributing to both ease of writing and readability. Thus, instead of having to write

$$X = 2 \text{ OR } X = Y \text{ OR } X = Z$$

the user could write

$$X = 2, \, Y \text{ OR } Z$$

The use of "implied subjects" or "implied objects" was allowed, thus permitting the user to write

```
IF X = Y MOVE A TO B;
IF GREATER ADD A TO Z;
OTHERWISE MOVE C TO D.
```

instead of

```
IF X = Y MOVE A TO B;
IF X IS GREATER THAN Y etc.
```

However, the development of the conditional procedure structure and the conditionals themselves was done on a very ad hoc basis; we decided on rules that seemed to produce "natural" constructions to both write and read.

A number of issues about arithmetic arose. As indicated earlier in Section 2.6, the business people purportedly did not like the formulas and hence we had the COMPUTE verb on one hand and the ADD, SUBTRACT, MULTIPLY, and DIVIDE verbs on the other. Note that it was necessary to use the word COMPUTE preceding the formula because of the general format which required every sentence to start with a verb!

Floating point was considered unnecessary in business data-processing operations and therefore was omitted although some manufacturers later included it in their own versions. We actually did consider including the facility whereby the user could define the precision which he wished used in carrying out the arithmetic calculation. (This concept thus foreshadowed the PL/I inclusion by approximately five years.) However, it was not included in COBOL because it was felt to be too difficult to implement. Nevertheless, we felt that there had to be some way to maintain compatibility among various computers as far as precision was concerned. We therefore established 18 decimal digits as the maximum to be used for any field, and then went on to require that intermediate results had to be carried out to one more place on the right and one more place on the left than the maximum field size. Eighteen was chosen for the simple reason that it was *dis*advantageous to every computer thought to be a potential candidate for having a COBOL compiler. Thus no manufacturer would have a built-in advantage in efficiency.

One of the minor, albeit interesting things with regard to syntax has to do with the DIVIDE verb. Certainly I think most people feel it is easier or more natural to say DIVIDE A BY B, instead of saying DIVIDE B INTO A. However, after much debate we chose the latter in order to maintain the consistency of having the receiving field as the last stated variable for the four arithmetic verbs.

Considerable thought was given to the flow of control. We did not go as far as the infinitely nested block structure of ALGOL 60. However, we did introduce a hierarchy of: simple statements, compound statements, sentences, paragraphs, sections. Only the last two could be given names. Because of the powerful (and complex) conditional control statements that were provided, the flow of control often depended heavily on whether the user wrote a semicolon or a period. For example, consider

```
IF A = B THEN MOVE X TO Y;
          OTHERWISE ADD D TO E;
                    MULTIPLY F BY G.
     MOVE H TO J.
```

If A = B, control transfers to the sentence "MOVE H TO J" after executing "MOVE X TO Y" because of the semicolon after "ADD D TO E." If there were a period after the "E," then control would transfer to "MULTIPLY F BY G."

3.1.2. Data Description

One of the major arguments in the data description area had to do with free form versus a columnar approach. The latter was being used in Commercial Translator, but many people felt that the free form was more natural. Thus, one of the many compromises made in the Data Division was to allow both the PICTURE Clause, as well as the long stream of words used to define the data. This was done primarily because Commercial Translator had developed the PICTURE Clause and several people (including several not from IBM) were very anxious to have it used because it was a lot easier to write whereas others felt that the readability of the numerous words in the Data Description was more desirable.

One of the most fundamental decisions in describing data was to decide that we would describe data as a continuous stream of information from the point at which the data started. This is in contrast with simply describing each field or subfield as it appears by defining its starting position in a word; in particular this led to the FILLER clause which was to be used to take up space when there was no data. The reason for doing it this way was because we felt it would provide more machine independence. It was taken for granted that every data item must be described in the Data Division; there were no defaults defined.

One of the significant contributions of COBOL over any of the languages then considered as primary inputs was a ''recursive'' data description. In this context, ''recursive'' means that the same method can be used to describe data at all levels in the hierarchy (although some aspects apply only to the lowest level of data in the hierarchy). Furthermore, the hierarchy of data could occur to any desired depth. Thus, Commercial Translator, which had developed a good data description, nevertheless allowed only a few levels of field or subfield. COBOL made the jump to allowing any level number up to 49, which was an arbitrary number chosen because it was felt to be large enough for any practical application. The numbers 77 and 88 were chosen as arbitrary (and purportedly easily remembered) numbers to identify the special concepts of noncontiguous constants and noncontiguous working storage (77) and condition names (88).

One of the biggest problems, and perhaps one of the biggest failures, of COBOL was trying to come to grips with the difference between trying to describe data internally and externally. Obviously, we could not have the Data Division describe the data as it was represented internally because there was so much difference from one computer to another. (For example, consider the internal representation of negative numbers.) On the other hand, trying to describe the data as it appeared externally was possible, but then led to difficulties in getting efficient translations into internal formats and consistent results in execution. We ended up with some strange looking things, plus something that I believe was felt to be satisfactory at the time; namely, a clause in the Data Description called USAGE. The purpose of that was to allow the user to indicate how he wanted the data used and to allow the compiler to determine the best way to store it internally. The most common ''usages'' were felt to be computational and display, with the implementor allowed to provide several instances of each. This feature was not in COBOL 60 but was one of the significant features added in COBOL 61. For example, if the usage of a field was to be for calculations, then the storage would be quite different than if it were simply to be used for output. Furthermore, the compiler could do some optimization of storage and/or execution time by deciding whether to store the data in one format and convert before ''using it,'' or store it initially in the needed form.

3.1.3. Names

Much debate centered around what rules to use for naming variables. The Data Description task group recommended that there be a maximum of 30 characters allowed for names, and that there be a difference between the description for a file and for data. The maximum of 30 characters per name was chosen because on one hand it seemed to allow people enough characters to write out the names of variables as they chose (e.g., SO-CIAL-SECURITY-NUMBER) and on the other hand was not tied to the individual characteristics of any particular computer!

One of the rather hotly disputed points with regard to data names was whether or not at least one alphabetic character needed to be included. The argument in favor was fairly obvious, namely, that it made the implementation easier because data names could be more easily separated from numbers. The argument in favor of allowing purely numeric data names was that part-numbers and other such things were often purely numeric, and it was felt desirable to allow these to be used as data names in the program (e.g., to allow inventory programs to use part numbers as variables). The decision made was to help the implementor by requiring a letter in the data name—but we did not go all the way to ease the implementation because we did not require the letter to be the first character.

One of the items in the data descriptions which took a considerable amount of time to settle was the concept of "qualification." This came about because we recognized the desirability of using the same data name in more than one file (e.g., ADDRESS). However, if the Procedure Division simply referred to the data name ADDRESS, it would be unclear which particular one was meant, and so we had to devise a method of distinguishing among potential duplicates. By expanding the concept of suffix in Commercial Translator, we derived the general concept of "qualification" which simply means "provide enough upper level names in the hierarchy in which this data name appears to make it unique."

A major difficulty, both conceptual and syntactic, was the mixing of subscripts and qualification. Obviously both had to be allowed simultaneously, but the rules became somewhat mind-boggling; after a while it became clear that qualification had to occur first to get into the correct field, record or file of the variable, and then the subscripting was needed to pick out the particular instance.

3.2. Language Definition

The whole matter of the actual technique for defining COBOL is in my mind one of the most significant and interesting aspects of the early development. First, it must be recognized that the very famous paper by John Backus (1959) presenting his metalanguage did not appear until the UNESCO 1st International Conference on Information Processing in June 1959, and I am not sure how many of us saw or heard about it even then. I am not sure that the word "metalanguage" had occurred to very many of us on the Short-Range Committee; however, those of us working on the Statement Language task group clearly had to find a way to describe the verbs that we were working on and we did exactly that. We developed something which we called a "notation," as early as August 13, 1959, although some details were changed over the next month. Unfortunately, because on one hand we *called* this a notation, and on the other because it was a metalanguage quite different from that proposed by Backus in his paper, it became very fashionable and quite common to say (at least orally if not in writing) in 1959–1961 that COBOL had no formal definition. I think anyone who looks will indeed recognize that the *syntax* of COBOL was (and still is) defined in just as formal a way as ALGOL 60; the obvious difference in report size is due to the far greater power and complexity of COBOL.

I would venture to guess that more languages are defined today using some variation of the COBOL metalanguage than are actually defined using (even a variation of) BNF. BNF has, of course, become a generic term and I have been amused to see in some cases that the metalanguage used was that of COBOL but it was referred to as BNF. In reality, each serves a somewhat different purpose and there are certain language elements which are easy to define in one and hard in the other, and conversely. I did write a paper (Sammet, 1961c) which does describe the COBOL Procedure Division using BNF. I think it is fair to say that the COBOL syntactic philosophy (e.g., few verbs with many options per verb) simply could not have been carried through, if we had used BNF from the beginning. BNF lends itself well to certain types of language design but not to languages like COBOL which are structured to have many, many syntactic options.

Jean E. Sammet

3.3. Portability (= Machine Independence)

Obviously, from the very beginning, portability was a major, if not *the* major, objective (although the phrase "machine independence" was used at that time). It was recognized that many aspects of the language (e.g., those related to physical file units or switches) were dependent on a particular machine and eventually we got to the point of relegating those to the Environment Division. However, there was considerable discussion about how much machine independence could be achieved and at what price. In the ideal world, we felt that one should be able to take a deck of cards from one machine and move it to any other and change merely the Environment Division. However, we also recognized that in the real world that wasn't likely to happen. The amount of machine independence, of course, depends somewhat on the way the user writes the program. After a while it became clear that one could fairly easily write a Procedure Division that was machine independent but that it was much harder to do this with the Data Division and still maintain efficiency for a particular machine. Thus, if one laid out a file for a machine that had 36 bits, this was not necessarily the optimal way of laying out a file for one that had 24 bits, even though the words and phrases used to describe the data would be the same, and the same description could physically apply to both.

Many of the technical discussions centered around the controversy between (a) the general agreement of wanting machine independence, and (b) the desire of each manufacturer to make sure that the language could be used to its utmost effectiveness with its machine(s). There were two main examples of this controversy. At that time the largest RCA machine was the 501, and it, along with the IBM 705, was the only variable word-length machine for which COBOL was being contemplated. Therefore, several features in the Data Division were included to try to allow their users to write efficient data descriptions for a variable word-length machine (e.g., SYNCHRONIZED was optional but did not really solve the problem). Another point of controversy arose over the relevance of binary machines. Sylvania's MOBIDIC was binary and although IBM also had a binary computer (namely, the 709), their main data-processing machine was a 705 which was character oriented. One of the more amusing things that happened was a constant dispute between the Remington-Rand people and the Sylvania people on this subject of binary. The former argued that no data-processing user would choose to use a pure binary machine because it was not appropriate for data processing. Since Sylvania was making such a machine for use by the Army, with data processing to be included among its other uses, Sylvania naturally did not accept that argument and felt that while certainly the users should *not have to learn binary,* nevertheless the data description had to take binary into consideration. Up to that point it was just a normal argument; the amusing thing occurred when, sometime during the deliberations of the Short-Range Committee, Remington-Rand announced the availability of the UNIVAC III, a binary machine. All of a sudden, the Remington-Rand representatives changed their opinion and indeed recognized that one had to be able to use this language on a binary machine.

Another debate on the problem of machine independence arose when we were considering the concept of allowing a file to be read backward. If a computer has a basic machine command to read a tape in reverse, then obviously this is easy to implement. Some people argued that it should be in the language because it was a useful facility and those manufacturers whose computer did not have a READ REVERSE machine command could nevertheless execute this by backing up the tape two records and reading forward one. This potential READ REVERSE command was finally thrown out on the grounds that although it could be logically implemented by everybody, the penalty in efficiency was too great on machines without the machine command.

One of the very mistaken notions *outside* the Short-Range Committee was that the Environment Division was supposed to make the programs machine independent. On the contrary, the Environment Division was intended to be that portion of the program which contained *all* the machine-*dependent* features, e.g., allocation of tapes, hardware switches, and specific computer configurations. Some people have questioned why this division was included at all, since it clearly—and by definition—had to be rewritten when the program was moved from one computer to another (even if nothing else had to be touched). The answer is quite simple—we wanted the information which was needed for each program to be presented in a uniform way. This was meant to ease training problems, improve readability, and provide documentation.

3.4. Machine and Compiler Environment

We assumed little or no operating systems, but we did assume a large computer of that vintage (see Section 2.6), which is equivalent to some of today's minicomputers. We made some concessions to smaller machines, by originally defining a subset of COBOL 60 called Basic COBOL. The Environment Division was established to both require and allow any user to specify machine-related information in a consistent way. Obviously, there was no question of that information being the same in going from one machine to the other. Both COBOL 60 and 61 contained in the Environment Division the clauses Source Computer and Object Computer. Even at that time, we hoped to have cases of cross compilation.

Even though we did not assume very much in the way of an operating system, we did recognize the need for some interaction with I/O and similar capabilities which might be provided by the computer manufacturer. Thus, the verb USE and the phrase ON SIZE ERROR, as well as clauses in the File Description relating to tape labels, all were meant to interact somehow with the environment.

Considerable attention was paid to implementation with perhaps more emphasis on ease of compiling than on efficiency of object code. For example, there was a lot of controversy about the use of symbolic names versus sequence numbers for statements, on the grounds that the sequence numbers would allow easy reordering although on the other hand it would be harder to parse if one could write "GO TO sequence number"; we decided to allow the pure numeric procedure indentifiers.

By today's standards, of course, most of the items which were felt to be difficult to compile are trivial, but they were not that easy in those days. For example, one of the reasons that COBOL has a maximum of three subscripts is because I pushed very hard for three subscripts on the grounds that (a) more than three were probably not needed in a realistic data-processing environment and (b) the people in my office responsible for implementing the compiler had what they considered to be an excellent algorithm for handling three subscripts but it did not work beyond three. By the time they found out how to generalize the algorithm, COBOL had been set with three subscripts.

Unfortunately, very little was done about including debugging facilities. There was considerable discussion about how to prevent errors, but naturally there was very little agreement on how best to do that. This is still an area of research in 1979.

3.5. New versus Modification of Language Concepts

In my view, we were not consciously trying to introduce new language concepts, but rather we were trying to combine the best features and ideas from the languages which were considered the major inputs. Nevertheless we did break much new ground, and did introduce some new concepts; these are discussed in Section 4.2.

3.6. Influence of Nontechnical Factors

Based on my experience, I personally think that COBOL was influenced in its technical design by nontechnical factors more than any other language that I am aware of. These factors include (a) the time pressure, plus (b) the obvious need to obtain compatibility across machines, and (c) the simultaneous constraints imposed by different manufacturers with different equipment and differing schedules for the production of their first compiler. All of these factors made a situation that I suspect would not be tolerated today as an environment for language design.

4. A Posteriori Evaluation

4.1. Meeting of Objectives

I am admittedly prejudiced, but I think the language met most of its original objectives. It has achieved a significant amount of compatibility, and I think programs can be made easy to read. The places where I think it failed to meet the objectives are discussed in Section 4.3. The users apparently seem to think that the language met its objectives, but that may be hard to demonstrate, since they really have not had much choice! COBOL had become a de facto standard even before it became an official one. This was due—at least in part—to the pressure from the Department of Defense which essentially insisted that computer manufacturers provide COBOL compilers.

I think there is no question that the machine independence—or at least as much as could be achieved from COBOL—played a major role in user acceptance. Much of this independence minimizes training and conversion costs. I have no idea how many programs have been moved from one computer to a fundamentally different machine without changing anything but the Environment Division.

I honestly don't know whether some of the things we did helped or hindered the objectives (e.g., noise words which increase readability but also increase complexity for both users and implementors).

I believe the computer science part of the computer community thinks COBOL is a dismal failure. I think that many computer scientists fail to realize the difficulty of producing a language for business data processing such that the language is effective and usable across a wide range of computing equipment. Furthermore, many computer scientists object to the use of English from a stylistic point of view.

4.2. Contributions of Language

In my view, the largest contribution made by COBOL was to be good enough to become what appears to be the most widely used language in the late 1970s, although of course there is no accurate way to measure usage. Nevertheless, intuitively, it appears to be true that a very large number of business data-processing applications are written using COBOL, and I believe that the majority of computers are used for business data-processing applications. There were additional contributions made; for example, it showed that a group of competing manufacturers could work together to produce something useful to the entire field. The goals of machine independence have been met moderately well. (See the previous section.)

It seems fair to say that the separate Data Division—wherein one data description can be used for many *programs*—gave impetus to the concepts of Data Base Management Systems where one data description can be used for many *applications*.

The item that I consider one of the largest contributions of COBOL was certainly not one of its objectives, and often is not appreciated. I refer specifically to the metalanguage which was developed, which has become at least as widely used as BNF and may conceivably be even more widely used. As I stated earlier in Section 3.2, this point is often overlooked by computer scientists. Finally, I think that the other major contribution of COBOL was to really put into practical usage and show how to develop in a practical environment some of the fledgling ideas for business data-processing languages that originally appeared in FLOW-MATIC.

Another contribution made by COBOL was to demonstrate that "language maintenance" could be accomplished in an orderly fashion, and by a committee. As described in earlier sections, from almost the beginning of the Short-Range Committee's deliberations, the need for maintenance (in the sense of clarification and enhancement) was recognized to be important. I think this has prevented the spawning of any major dialects, although many manufacturers have added to their own COBOL compilers some special features that they felt were valuable to their customers. The fact that the language maintenance really worked which made it easier to develop a language standard (except for the subsetting problem) than was true for FORTRAN where there were a large number of dialects from the very beginning. (Although it is beyond the time scale that I am trying to cover in this paper, I also note that the development of the official standards under ANSI auspices (ANSI, 1968, 1974) was done with the cooperation of the COBOL language developers. CODASYL and its COBOL committee (which has sometimes functioned with different names) have always been considered the *authority* on making changes or clarifications to the language.)

It seems to me that COBOL has not had the impact on language design that it deserves; I say this because I think that the difficulties of trying to develop data descriptions which apply across many machines is a significant technical contribution. Unfortunately, the leaders of the computer science community have taken a very negative view of COBOL from its very inception and therefore have not looked carefully enough to see what good ideas are in there which could be further enlarged, expanded or generalized.

COBOL 60 introduced many specific language concepts or features which were either completely new or significant improvements over the state of the art in 1959; a partial list, written in no particular order follows:

(1) A truly readable language which also provides good program documentation.
(2) A data description which really is machine independent (if one ignores efficiency considerations).
(3) Recursive data definitions, allowing for any reasonable number of levels of subfields.

(4) A powerful conditional (i.e., IF THEN ELSE) structure.

(5) Abbreviations for writing conditionals.

(6) Noise words for ease of readability.

(7) Specifications for a high-level language macro (DEFINE), although it was never implemented and was subsequently removed from the language.

(8) Clear separation (at least in concept) of procedural statements which are to be executed and the description of data, from those features which are definitely machine or operating system dependent.

(9) Useful metalanguage.

(10) Semiautomatic segmentation.

(11) A machine independent language based on realistic hardware facilities.

In summary then, I feel COBOL's major contributions were:

(1) It was good enough to remain in very wide use for over 20 years.

(2) The concept of a data description which could be used to describe data for many differing computers, and which was clearly separated from executable statements. These facilities in turn paved the way for concepts of Data Base Management Systems.

(3) A specific metalanguage which has been widely used.

(4) The handling of language maintenance in an orderly way.

(5) Specific language concepts and features (listed just above).

4.3. Mistakes or Desirable Changes

In my view, the largest mistakes were in the area of the alignment of the Data Division and the Environment Division, and the omission of the collating sequence specification. Let me deal with the latter first.

During the deliberations which led to COBOL 61, several of us tried very hard to include in the Environment Division the requirement for the user to specify the collating sequence under which he was writing the program. (The need for this has since become obvious and it was put into the 1974 ANSI standard.) Others on the committee objected at that time because of the obvious inefficiencies that would occur if a compiler had to automatically provide the conversion from the collating sequence specified by the user, to the one which was inherent to the object machine.

Considering the distribution of features between the Data and Environment Divisions, there are some things that we put into the former which really belong in the latter, e.g., some of the file description. Certainly the failure of COBOL to include full block structuring after we went as far as four levels of a procedural hierarchy (statement, sentence, paragraph, section) is a deficiency. The omission of parameter passing for subroutines was a significant weakness.

In spite of the favorable words included earlier about the orderliness of the language maintenance, I must point out that frequent language changes (which I personally deem inappropriate) have been made simply because the personal viewpoints of individuals involved in the COBOL language maintenance (and the people themselves) have changed. I am not referring to changes made because of advances in languages, compilers, applications, and equipment (e.g., random access devices, teleprocessing); I am referring simply to matters of personal taste wherein the change of an individual can change the language because a new person simply prefers something different (e.g., identification of comments). I think certain changes have been made which are not justifiable in terms of advances in the language (e.g., punctuation rules, comments). Some of the changes made to COBOL since its inception were the addition of features which we initially felt were desirable but did not have enough time to include; the best examples of these were the Report Writer and the Sort verb, both of which were put into COBOL 61 Extended (Department of Defense, 1962).

The total number of changes suggested to COBOL is so large and they are so lengthy that there is simply no way to indicate their type or quantity, even in just the early days, let alone since then. It *is* worth noting that according to Jones (1977) a large number of the suggestions for changes have come from Europe and Japan.

4.4. Problems

I think the biggest problems were the needs to satisfy machine independence on one hand, and provide a powerful language on the other. In my opinion this is still an unsolved problem.

5. Implications for Current and Future Languages

I personally do not see much language development in 1979 which is, or admits to being, significantly influenced by COBOL. I think the main reason for this (as I have indicated several times already) is that most computer scientists are simply not interested in COBOL. (This is in spite of the fact that most languages which have meaningful data and record handling capabilities took those basic concepts from COBOL.) Since it is the computer scientists and their students who do most of the new language development, it is not surprising that COBOL has not had much effect. This is really sad, because the technical contributions they could make, and the related education of students are thus lost. On the other hand—and somewhat fortunately—COBOL has essentially the control structures needed for structured programming which is one of today's important language concepts.

The main lesson that I think should be learned from the early COBOL development is a nontechnical one—namely, that experience with real users and real compilers is desperately needed before "freezing" a set of language specifications. Had we known from the beginning that COBOL would have such a long life, I think many of us would have refused to operate under the time scale that was handed to us. On the other hand the "early freezing" prevented the establishment of dialects, as occurred with FORTRAN; that made the development of the COBOL standard much easier. Another lesson that I think should be learned for languages which are meant to have wide practical usage (as distinguished from theoretical and experimental usage) is that the users must be more involved from the beginning.

I think that the long-range future of COBOL is clearly set, and for very similar reasons to those of FORTRAN— namely, the enormous investment in programs and training that already exists. I find it impossible to envision a situation in which most of the data-processing users are weaned away from COBOL to another language, regardless of how much better the other language might be.

Jean E. Sammet

Appendix. List of Attendees at Pentagon Meeting, May 28–29, 1959*

NAME	ORGANIZATION
Government Representatives	
Asch, Col. Alfred	USAF, Hq. Air Matl. Comd.
Campaigne, Howard	NSA
Coulter, Cdr. P. H.	OASD (Comp)
Cunningham, Joseph F.	Hq. USAF
Gammon, W. Howard	OASD (Comp)
Gregg, Col. C. R.	Hq. USAF
Griffin, L. L.	Navy Management Office
Holberton, Frances E.	David Taylor Model Basin
Hyman, Paul J.	OASD (S&L)
Knitter, Lt. H. Robert	USASROL Ft. Monmouth, N.J.
Phillips, Charles A.	OASD (Comp)
Smith, A. E.	Navy BuShips
Stock, W. S.	OASD (Comp)
Tweed, N. B.†	Armed Forces Sup. Support Ctr.
Wegstein, J. H.	National Bureau of Standards
Users and Consultants	
Albertson, E. J.†	U.S. Steel Corp.
Bright, Herb†	Westinghouse-Bettis
Canning, Richard G.†	Canning, Sisson & Associates
Conway, Ben†	Price Waterhouse and Co.
Dillon, Gregory M.†	DuPont
Dowkont, A. J.	Rand Corp.
Goren [sic], Saul†	Univ. of Penn.
Jones, Fletcher	Computer Sciences Corp.
Kaufman, Felix†	Lybrand Ross Bros. & Montgomery
Kinzler, Henry†	Metropoliton Life Ins. Co.
Perry, George†	Traveler's Life Ins. Co.
Manufacturers	
Ashforth, H. N.	Int'l. Computers & Tabulators, Ltd.
Barton, Robert S.	Burroughs Electrodata
Bemer, R. W.	I.B.M.
Carter William C.	Honeywell-Datamatic Div.
Cheydleur, B. F.	R.C.A.
Hawes, Mary K.	Burrough's [sic] Electrodata
Hopper, Grace M.	Remington-Rand Univac
Keating, William P.	National Cash Register
Konig, Rudolf J.	General Electric Co.
Kozarsky, Karl	R.C.A.
Lavine, Louis	Philco
Pearlman, Robert	Sylvania Electric
Rosen, Saul	Philco
Rossheim, Robert	Remington Rand Univac
Sammet, Jean E.	Sylvania Electric

* *Source:* Phillips (1959a).
† Attended May 29, 1959, only.

ACKNOWLEDGMENTS

Several drafts of the preprint version of this paper were read by Henry Ledgard, Michael Marcotty, and Henry Tropp; all of them made numerous suggestions for improving wording and substance, and I am most grateful to them. In addition, the following people who had either direct or tangential involvement with COBOL in the time period discussed in this paper were sent a draft: R. W. Bemer, H. Bromberg, R. Clippinger, N. Discount, D. Goldstein, B. Gordon, B. Holberton, G. M. Hopper, J. L. Jones, C. Phillips, J. Wegstein. Constructive comments were received from most of them, but in some cases they are in disagreement with my views or interpretations or my memory. That is not surprising, and I am grateful to all of those who took the trouble to make suggestions for improving the paper. In addition to the above, Aaron Finerman made many editorial suggestions on the final preprint version to improve its form to that printed here.

REFERENCES

ACM (1962) May. *Communications of the ACM.* **5**(5). (Contains 13 papers on COBOL.)

Air Materiel Command (1958) August 25. *AIMACO Compiler, The AIMACO Compiling System Manual.* AF-WP-0-SEP 58 750. (Although not shown on the manual, this presumably was issued by AMC at Wright-Patterson Air Force Base, Ohio.) (This is for the UNIVAC 1105.)

Air Materiel Command (1959) June 30. *The Air Materiel Command Compiler For Electronic Data-Processing Equipment (AIMACO).* Wright-Patterson Air Force Base, Ohio: Headquarters, Air Materiel Command, AMC Manual No. 171-2. (This is for the UNIVAC 1105.)

Anonymous (1960a). March. Editorial—The High Cost of Computer Babble. *Management and Business Automation.*

Anonymous (1960b). March. COBOL—Common Language for Computers. *Management and Business Automation.* pp. 22–24, 37–39.

ANSI (formerly USAS) (1968) August 23. *USA Standard COBOL.* New York: American National Standards Institute; Sponsor: Business Equipment Manufacturers Association. USAS X3.23-1968.

ANSI (1974) May 10. *American National Standard Programming Language COBOL.* New York: American National Standards Institute; Secretariat: Computer and Business Equipment Manufacturers Association. ANSI X3.23-1974. (Revision of X3.23-1968.)

Asch, Alfred (1959) July 29. *Minutes of Committee Meeting on Data Systems Languages held at Bureau of Standards, June 23–24.*

Backus, John W. (1959). The Syntax and Semantics of the Proposed International Algebraic Language of the Zurich ACM–GAMM Conference. In *Proceedings 1st International Conference on Information Processing, UNESCO, Paris,* pp. 125–132. Oldenbourg, Munich and Butterworth, London.

Bemer, Robert W. (1960) March. Comment on COBOL. *Management and Business Automation.* p. 22.

Bemer, Robert W. (1971). A View of the History of COBOL. *Honeywell Computer Journal.* **5**(3): 130–135.

Block, I. E. (1959). *Report on Meeting held at University of Pennsylvania Computing Center, April 9, 1959.*

Bromberg, Howard (1961) February. COBOL and Compatibility. *Datamation.* **7**(2): 30–34.

Bromberg, Howard, *et al.* (1959) November 7. COBOL. (Specifications submitted by 6-person working group to Short-Range Committee.)

Clippinger, Richard F. (1961). FACT—A Business Compiler: Description and Comparison with COBOL and Commercial Translator. In *Annual Review of Automatic Programming* (Richard Goodman, ed.), Vol. 2, pp. 231–292. New York: Pergamon.

Clippinger, Richard F. (1977) December 20. Letter to Jean Sammet. (Written as part of a review of a draft of this paper.)

COBOL Manuals—See Department of Defense (all entries) and CODASYL (1969) March.

CODASYL (1960) September 23. *Updating and "Freezing" COBOL Specifications.* (Fairly formal and important document but with no specific identification as to writer or issuer. Obviously prepared in connection with, or by, CODASYL Executive Committee.)

CODASYL Special Task Group (1961) May 5. *COBOL—1961, Revised Specifications for a Common Business Oriented Language.* (Material submitted to CODASYL Executive Committee to be published as COBOL-61.)

CODASYL (1969) March. *CODASYL COBOL Journal of Development 1968.* Ottawa, Canada: Dept. of Defence Production. 110-GP-1.

CODASYL—See also Department of Defense (all entries), Short-Range Committee (all entries), Phillips, Charles (all entries), and Cunningham, Joseph (1959).

Cunningham, Joseph F. (1959) June 4. *The Problem of Specification of a Common Business Language for Automatic Digital Computers.* (Report on CODASYL Steering Committee meeting held June 4, 1959.)

d'Agapeyeff, A., Baecker, H. D., and Gibbens, B. J. (1963). Progress in Some Commercial Source Languages. In *Annual Review in Automatic Programming* (Richard Goodman, ed.), Vol. 3, pp. 277–298. New York: Pergamon.

DeJong, John H. (1960) October. COBOL, Computer Language of the Future. *Data Processing.* pp. 9–12.

Department of Defense (1960) April. *COBOL, Initial Specifications for a Common Business Oriented Language.* Washington, D.C.: U.S. Gov. Print. Off. #1960 0—552133.

Department of Defense (1961). *COBOL—1961, Revised Specifications for a Common Business Oriented Language.* Washington, D.C.: U.S. Gov. Print. Off. #1961 0—598941.

Department of Defense (1962). *COBOL—1961 EXTENDED, Extended Specifications for a Common Business Oriented Language.* Washington, D.C.: U.S. Gov. Print. Off. #1962 0—668996.

Department of Defense (1965). *COBOL—Edition 1965.* Washington, D.C.: U.S. Gov. Print. Off. #1965 0—795-689.

Gaudette, Charles H. (1959a). Draft Letter to Charles Phillips, Chairman CODASYL Committee. [Gaudette was Minneapolis-Honeywell representative on the Short-Range Committee.]

Gaudette, Charles H. (1959b). Letter to Joseph Wegstein, Chairman Short-Range Task Group [sic]. [Gaudette was Minneapolis-Honeywell representative on the Short-Range Committee.]

Holberton, Betty (1978) January 10. Letter to Jean Sammet. [Written as part of review of a draft of this paper.]

Honeywell (1959). *The Honeywell-800 Business Compiler, A Preliminary Description.* Newton Highlands, Massachusetts: Minneapolis-Honeywell Regulator Company, DATAmatic Division.

Hopper, Grace M. (1955). January 31. *Preliminary Definitions, Data Processing Compiler.* [Informal working paper with text description and flow charts and a sample program in English, French, and German.]

Hopper, Grace M. (1977). December 27. [Information in hand notes by Jean Sammet of telephone conversation between Hopper and Sammet.]

Humby, E. (1963). Rapidwrite. In *Annual Review in Automatic Programming* (Richard Goodman, ed.), Vol. 3, pp. 299–309. New York: Pergamon.

IBM (1959). *General Information Manual, IBM Commercial Translator.* New York: IBM Corp. F28-8013.

Jones, John L. (1977) December. [Hand notes on a draft of this paper.]

Lanzarotta, Santo A. (1961) March. The Editor's Readout. *Datamation.* 7(3): 21.

Phillips, Charles A. (1959a). *Summary of Discussions at Conference on Automatic Programming of ADPS for Business-Type Applications, The Pentagon, May 28–29, 1959.* [Issued by Phillips several months after May meeting.]

Phillips, C. A. (1959–1961) *Minutes, Meeting of the Executive Committee of the Conference on Data Systems Languages.* [Note—Some are identified as "Committee" rather than "Conference."] 1959 July 7; 1959 September 4; 1959 November 25; 1960 January 7–8; 1960 February 12; 1960 April 7; 1960 June 1; 1960 December 6; 1961 February 15; 1961 May 5; 1961 July 18.

Phillips, Charles A. (1959b). *Report from Committee on Data Systems Languages.* (Oral presentation to Association for Computing Machinery, Boston, Massachusetts, September 1, 1959.)

Phillips, Charles A. (1960a) October. A Common Language to Program Computers for Business Problems, Second Report. *Computers and Automation.* (Based on talk given to Association for Computing Machinery, Milwaukee, Wisconsin, August 1960.)

Phillips, Charles A. (1960b) October 6. *Memo to Members of the COBOL Special Task Force with Subject: Resolution of Manufacturers Group and Statement of R. F. Clippinger.*

RCA (1960a) May. *RCA 501 COBOL Narrator, Preliminary User's Manual.* Cherry Hill, New Jersey: Radio Corporation of America, Electronic Data Processing Division. P 501-03.031.

RCA (1960b) Dec. *RCA 501 COBOL Narrator, Programmer's Reference Manual.* Cherry Hill, New Jersy: Radio Corporation of America, Electronic Data Processing Division. P 501-03.032.

Remington-Rand Univac (1956) August 15. *The B-0 Compiler Working Manual.* [This was clearly developed by Remington-Rand Univac, but no identification appears on the document. Only the words "Automatic Programming Development" appear on the title page, and it was then marked Company Confidential.]

Remington-Rand Univac (1958). *FLOW-MATIC Programming System.* Philadelphia, Pennsylvania: Remington Rand Univac, Management Services and Operations Research Dept. U 1518.

Remington-Rand Univac (1960) September. *B-2, FLOW-MATIC Programming (Preliminary User's Reference*

Manual to Accompany COBOL Manual, April, 1960) Second Edition. Philadelphia, Pennsylvania: Sperry Rand Corporation, Remington-Rand Univac Division, Research Automatic Programming.

Sammet, Jean E. *Report No. N for Task Group on Statement Language* (shown with N, date of meeting, and date of report). 1. June 24, 1959, June 29, 1959; 2. July 8–9, 1959, July 13, 1959; 3. July 22–24, 1959, July 27, 1959; 4. August 6–7, 1959, August 13, 1959; 5. August 17, 1959, August 17, 1959 (written same day); 6. August 19, 1959, August 19, 1959 (written same day).

Sammet, Jean E. (1959a) August 17, 18. *Points of Greatest Controversy within the Statement Language Task Group* and *Additional Points of Controversy*.

Sammet, Jean E. (1959b) August 26. *Report Number 7—Statement Language Principles and Verbs*.

Sammet, Jean E. (1959c) October 16. *Special Meeting of the Intermediate Range Committee of CODASYL*. (Memo to Short-Range Committee.)

Sammet, Jean E. (1959d). Hand notes for all meetings.

Sammet, Jean E. (1960a) August. *Technical Description of COBOL*. (Paper presented orally at ACM Annual Conference, Milwaukee, Wisconsin.)

Sammet, Jean E. (1960b) September 7. Informal document.

Sammet, Jean E. (1960c) September 16. (See SHARE 1960.)

Sammet, Jean E. (1961a). A Detailed Description of COBOL. In *Annual Review in Automatic Programming* (Richard Goodman, ed.), Vol. 2, pp. 197–230. New York: Pergamon.

Sammet, Jean E. (1961b) March. The Sylvania View—More Comments on COBOL. *Datamation*. 7(3): 33–34.

Sammet, Jean E. (1961c) September. A Definition of the COBOL-61 Procedure Division Using ALGOL 60 Metalinguistics. Summary in *Preprints of 16th National Meeting of the ACM*. pp. 5B-1 (1)–(4).

Sammet, Jean E. (1969). *PROGRAMMING LANGUAGES: History and Fundamentals*. Englewood Cliffs, New Jersey: Prentice-Hall.

SHARE (1960) September 16. Panel on COBOL (J. Sammet) and Commercial Translator (R. Talmadge) chaired by K. Wright. SHARE XV, Session 11.

Short-Range Committee (1959a) August 18–20. Draft Transcription of August 18–20 Meeting. [This is a raw transcript which has had a little editing.]

Short-Range Committee (1959b) September 4. *A Report to the Executive Committee of the Committee on Data Systems Languages by the Fact Finding and Short Range Language Committee*. [Contains very early, very preliminary specifications including "notation" = "metalanguage."]

Short-Range Committee (1959c) December. *COBOL, Specifications for a Common Business Oriented Language*. [Technical reference manual submitted to CODASYL Executive Committee; eventually published as COBOL-60 after some editing and a few changes; see Department of Defense 1960.]

Sperry Rand (see Remington-Rand Univac).

Talmadge, Richard (1960) September 16. (See SHARE, 1960.)

USAS (See ANSI, 1968).

Wegstein, Joseph H. (1959) November 20. [Letter to Charles Phillips transmitting final report of Short-Range Committee, which is item identified as Short-Range Committee (1959c) December.]

Wegstein, Joseph H. (1960) February 2. Memo to CODASYL Executive Committee on Subject: "Proposed Details for COBOL Maintenance."

Wegstein, Joseph H. (1977) December 28. Letter to Jean Sammet [Written as part of review of a draft of this paper.]

Willey, E. L., *et al.* (1961). A Critical Discussion of COBOL. In *Annual Review in Automatic Programming* (Richard Goodman, ed.), Vol. 2, pp. 293–304. New York: Pergamon.

TRANSCRIPT OF PRESENTATION

MICHAEL MARCOTTY: This morning our subject is COBOL, and our main speaker is Jean Sammet. At the time of the start of the COBOL effort, Jean was Section Head for the MOBIDIC programming at Sylvania Electric Products. Between 1956 and 1957 she taught one of the earliest programming courses given for academic credit. In the second semester she used an early FORTRAN manual, playing the standard trick of staying about one chapter ahead of the students, because this was the only information that was available.

Jean E. Sammet

KEY DATES IN EARLY COBOL HISTORY
1959 (Slide 1)

"The Early History of COBOL"

1959–1961

how and why

it all started

Frame 1

KEY DATES IN EARLY COBOL HISTORY
1959 (Slide 1)

May 28–29	Pentagon Meeting
June 23–24	1st Meeting of Short Range Committee
June–Aug.	Meetings of Short Range Com. and its Task Groups
Sept. 4	Preliminary Short Range Com. Report to Executive Com.

Frame 2

Nevertheless, they produced some programs and ran them—"He who reads may run." Now Jean is Programming Language Technology Manager for IBM's Federal Systems Division, and is going to talk to us about the early history of COBOL.

JEAN SAMMET: Thank you. I certainly intend to talk to you this morning about the early history of COBOL. I want to emphasize that at the time that this activity took place I was working for Sylvania Electric Products—not for IBM. And what I'm about to say represents my own personal views and perspective of this activity and not the official view of either Sylvania or IBM.

I'm going to start by showing you a number of slides which simply give you some key dates, in order to put into perspective the overall activity [Frame 1]. And I'm going to cover a span from around May, 1959, until around June, 1961. And I simply want to give you a focus for the time and the activity, and then I will come back and talk in more detail.

[Frame 2 shows that] the first of the activities was the very famous meeting in the Pentagon on May 28 and 29 of 1959. I'll have a lot more to say about that in a little while. The Short-Range Committee met for the first time in June. There were more meetings in July and August, and in September there was a preliminary Short-Range [Committee] report for the Executive Committee, and I'll define what all those terms mean as I go along.

[Frame 3 shows that] in September to October there were meetings of the Short-Range Committee. Then in a two-week period a six-person group developed some specifications. In November the Short-Range Committee modified and approved the specs. There were a final set of specs produced by an editing group in December.

[Frame 4 shows that] in January 1960 the CODASYL Executive Committee accepted

KEY DATES IN EARLY COBOL HISTORY
1959 (Slide 2)

Sept.–Oct.	Meetings of Short Range Com.
Oct.–Nov. (2 weeks)	6 person group develop specs.
Nov. 16–20	Short Range Committee modify & approve specs.
Dec.	Final specs produced by editing group

Frame 3

KEY DATES IN EARLY COBOL HISTORY
1960 (Slide 3)

Jan. 7–8	CODASYL Executive Com. accepts Short Range Com. report
Spring	Final editing done
June	COBOL 60 specs issued as DOD report

Frame 4

KEY DATES IN EARLY COBOL HISTORY (Slide 4)		COBOL PROGRAM CONSISTS OF 4 DIVISIONS	
Spring–Summer 1960	Maintenance activity	Identification	—Provide user identification information
Sept. 1960–Feb. 1961	Special Task Group develops COBOL 61	Environment	—Provide machine-dependent information
June 1961	COBOL 61 specs issued as DOD report	Data	—Define files and records
		Procedure	—Specify executable actions
Frame 5		**Frame 6**	

the report. There was final editing done in the spring, and in June, COBOL 60 specifications were issued as a DOD report.

[Frame 5 shows that] in the spring and summer of 1960 there was maintenance activity. Later in that year there was a special task group to work on COBOL 61, and in June of 1961, the specs were issued.

Now, just to give you some focus on what a COBOL program consists of—because I'll have quite a bit to say about these different parts—a COBOL program consists of four divisions [Frame 6]: an Identification Division, an Environment Division, a Data, and a Procedure Division. The last two are the most important, but there are some conceptual interests in even the Environment Division.

Now, since I know some of you have never seen COBOL before, some of you have deliberately never seen COBOL before!—I want to show you just for your edification what a COBOL program looks like. Frame 7 is a small sample of an actual COBOL Environment Division. Frame 8 is a small sample of the File Section of the Data Division. This is just part of the Data Division. Frame 9 is an example of the Record Description. And you'll notice—and I'll say a lot more about this later—you'll notice a difference between words of that kind and something more cryptic and symbolic. And finally [Frame 10] the Procedure Division.

Now—I want to go back to this Pentagon meeting on May 28 and 29, 1959, because that's when it all started. [As can be seen in Frame 11,] there were present 7 government representatives, 11 users and consultants, and representatives from 10 computer manufacturers. The invitations were issued by the Department of Defense, and in particular, by Mr. Charles Phillips. The key results of that particular meeting were to form three committees, and eventually the CODASYL Executive Committee. It's crucial to understand the overall spirit of the Pentagon meeting, [as summarized in Frame 12]. First of all, there were many manufacturers that were starting to develop business data-processing

SMALL SAMPLE OF ACTUAL COBOL ENVIRONMENT DIVISION:

```
ENVIRONMENT DIVISION.
CONFIGURATION SECTION.
OBJECT-COMPUTER. IBM 705.
INPUT-OUTPUT SECTION.
FILE-CONTROL. SELECT INPUT-FILE-1
     ASSIGN TO TAPE 5.
     SELECT FILE-2 ASSIGN TAPE 6.
```

Frame 7

SMALL SAMPLE OF ACTUAL COBOL DATA DIVISION—FILE SECTION:

```
DATA DIVISION
FILE SECTION
FD INPUT-FILE-1; RECORDING MODE IS F;
BLOCK CONTAINS 5 RECORDS;
LABEL RECORDS ARE STANDARD;
DATA RECORD IS INPUT-RECORD.
```

Frame 8

SMALL SAMPLE OF ACTUAL
COBOL DATA DIVISION—RECORD DESCRIPTION

```
01 INPUT-RECORD.
   02 NAME       CLASS IS ALPHABETIC;
                 SIZE IS 40.
   02 ID-NUMBER  PICTURE 9 (10).
   02 ADDRESS    CLASS IS ALPHANUMERIC;
                 SIZE IS 47.
      03 STREET  PICTURE 9 (40).
      03 STATE   PICTURE A (2).
      03 ZIPCODE PICTURE 9 (5).
```

Frame 9

SMALL SAMPLE OF ACTUAL
COBOL PROCEDURE DIVISION:

```
OPEN INPUT EMPLOYEE-FILE,
     OUTPUT FILE-1, FILE 2.
SELECTION SECTION.
PARAGRAPH-1. READ EMPLOYEE-FILE
     AT END. GO TO YOU-KNOW-WHERE.
IF FIELD-A EQUALS FIELD-B PERFORM
     COMP ELSE MOVE FIELD-A TO
     FIELD-B.
```

Frame 10

languages and compilers. There was an intuitive desire to prevent proliferation; there was a belief that something *could* be done, and that something *should* be done. And perhaps most importantly of all, it was taken for granted that this would be an English-like, business-oriented language. I don't recall much debate about that; it was simply assumed that was the way it was going to be.

The Short-Range Committee was formed [as Frame 13 shows] with membership from six computer manufacturers, three government representatives, and the chairman, Joseph Wegstein of the National Bureau of Standards. There were four subcommittees formed: two major, which were the Statement Language and Data Description Subcommittees; these are the groups which eventually produced the drafts of what became known as the Procedure Division and the Data Division. And then there were some subcommittees that I considered minor in terms of their effect: the Applications Survey, and the User-Experience Survey.

The organizations represented on the Short-Range Committee [Frame 14] were these six computer manufacturers, and I've used their current names [Burroughs, Honeywell, IBM, RCA, Sylvania, Univac] because I'm not sure what they were officially called then, and three government users: NBS as the Chairman, the Air Force, and the David Taylor Model Basin. One of those people was Betty Holberton, who's the discussant for this.

Now, the Short-Range Committee mission, [shown in Frame 15] as of that May meeting, was to report by September 1, the results of a study of the existing compilers, AIMACO, FLOW-MATIC, and COMTRAN—you heard about two of these [FLOW-MATIC and AIMACO] from Grace Hopper yesterday. COMTRAN I'll say a little bit more about later.

MAJOR ASPECTS OF PENTAGON MEETING
May 28–29, 1959

Organizations present: 7 government
                        11 user/consultants
                        10 computer mftrs.

Invitations issued by Dept. of Defense
   (Charles Phillips)

Key results: Form 3 committees and
              eventually CODASYL
              Executive Committee

Frame 11

OVERALL SPIRIT OF PENTAGON MEETING

- Many manufacturers starting to develop business data processing languages and compilers

- Desire to prevent proliferation

- Belief that something could be done

- Belief that something should be done

- Taken for granted—
   English-like business oriented language

Frame 12

SHORT RANGE COMMITTEE ORGANIZATION

- Membership: 6 computer manufacturers
  3 government representatives
  Chairman (Joseph Wegstein, NBS)

- 4 Subcommittees (2 major, 2 minor)
  —Major: Statement Language
  Data description
  —Minor: Application survey
  User experience survey

Frame 13

ORGANIZATIONS REPRESENTED ON SHORT RANGE COMMITTEE

Computer Manufacturers (current names)

Burroughs   IBM   Sylvania
Honeywell   RCA   UNIVAC

Government Users

National Bureau of Standards (Chairman)
Air Materiel Command (Air Force)
David Taylor Model Basin (Navy)

Frame 14

The next point is perhaps the most important point that I'm going to make the entire time, so if you don't remember anything else that I say, please remember that *we were to recommend a short range composite approach good for at least the next year or two.* And that, in my view at least, colored the entire way in which we went about this. Had our objective been stated differently, had our directives been different, we might have approached this differently. Whether it would have been better or worse, I don't know—but different, certainly. We were to explore a problem-oriented but machine-independent language.

Now we need to know what COBOL was intended to do and what it was not. [See Frame 16.] It was intended for business data processing, but we never really defined what that meant. We felt the program could be written by novice programmers, but it was to be able to be read by managers due to the English nature of it. And there was a definite emphasis on the ease of reading, not on the ease of writing. Those of you who have written COBOL programs well understand that!

Some more points about the intended purpose and the users [are in Frame 17]. There were a number of disputes on the user capability about formulas, Booleans, and subscripts. I'll say a little bit more about that later. The large computers as of 1959, and the ones that were considered to be those on which COBOL was to be able to be run, were the ones that are listed in Frame 17, and as a minor purpose we felt COBOL should be able to write its own compiler.

Very specifically *not* intended or considered as purposes [Frame 18], interactive capability in 1959 (except a few far-thinking people had considered that). Not intended to be imbedded in an operating system because there really weren't very many, if any, but there were some tie-in facilities provided. We did not intend a good library system.

A key point in the development of any language is to see what influenced it [Frame 19].

SHORT RANGE COMMITTEE MISSION
AS OF May 28–29, 1959

- Report by Sept. 1, 1959 results of study
  of existing compilers
  (AIMACO, FLOWMATIC, COMTRAN)

- Recommend short-range composite approach
  good for at least next year or two

- Explore problem-oriented but
  machine-independent language

Frame 15

INTENDED PURPOSE AND USERS

(Slide 1)

- Business data processing
  [but this was never really defined]

- Program could be
  a) written by novice programmers
  b) read by managers (due to English)

- Emphasis on ease of reading,
  <u>not</u> on ease of writing

Frame 16

INTENDED PURPOSE AND USERS

(Slide 2)

- Disputes on user capability re
  formulas, Booleans, subscripts

- Use of large computers (as of 1959)
UNIVAC I, II	IBM 705, 709
Honeywell 800	RCA 501
Sylvania MOBIDIC	Burroughs B 5000

- Minor purpose—self compilation

Frame 17

The major influences were the two languages—FLOW-MATIC from Remington-Rand Univac done under Grace Hopper's direction—Commercial Translator being done in IBM by a group under the general technical leadership of Roy Goldfinger, who was working for Bob Bemer at the time.

The ALGOL 58 character set had an influence; namely, we felt it was very poor and so we were not going to follow it. In particular, we were very disturbed by the very characteristic that the ALGOL people were very happy about, namely, that they could use any old characters they wanted. We felt that we needed to have a character set that could really be used on existing keypunch machines.

BNF had no influence because it was too late. You will recall yesterday that there were several references made to this famous paper of John Backus's which was presented in June in 1959 at the UNESCO meeting, and again, I'll have a little bit more to say about that later, but in any case it really had no influence on COBOL. Little or no influence, the Honeywell Business Compiler, which later became called FACT and again, that became known to us too late.

The language design principles [Frame 20], first of all, were to separate the executable statements and the description of data. This was the difference between the Procedure and the Data Divisions, and this was the concept that had been so clearly put forth in FLOW-MATIC. We were to put machine-dependent information into the Environment Division, and the reason for that was consistency. A number of people have said, "Why did you have an Environment Division when it's clear that has to be rewritten when you move a program from one machine to another? And so why bother at all?" We felt that all programs ought to be written the same way even if the actual text had to change when you moved from one machine to another.

Now, the criteria [Frame 21] that we used for the statement language, at least as of June 29 (which was really the first meeting of that subcommittee)—we wanted naturalness. We wanted ease of transcription to the required media; that meant that it had to be a really

INFLUENCES ON COBOL

**NOT INTENDED OR
CONSIDERED AS PURPOSES**

- Interactive

- Imbedded in operating system
  (but some tie-in facilities provided)

- Good library system

Frame 18

Major:	FLOW-MATIC (Rem.-Rand Univac)	
	Commercial Translator (IBM)	
	ALGOL 58 character set	[poor]
None:	BNF	[too late]
Little or none:	Honeywell Business Compiler (FACT)	[too late]

Frame 19

LANGUAGE DESIGN PRINCIPLES
                                                    (Slide 1)

- Separate executable statements and
  description of data
  (PROCEDURE, DATA Divisions)

- Put machine dependent information
  into ENVIRONMENT Division
  (for consistency)

Frame 20

LANGUAGE DESIGN PRINCIPLES
                                                    (Slide 2)

Criteria for statement language
  (as of June 29, 1959)

- Naturalness

- Ease of transcription to required media

- Effectiveness of problem structure

- Ease of implementation

Frame 21

usable, keypunch character set and not 128 characters that nobody had. We wanted effectiveness of problem structure, and naturally we gave lip service to ease of implementation. Everybody always says that.

Now, in the COBOL 60 development, the first of the major elements was a September 4 report [Frame 22]. Remember, the committee had just started to meet in June; we had a few meetings over the summer, and we produced a report which was pretty crude. We then received permission from the CODASYL Executive Committee to finish by December 1. They were very gracious to us! And the reason for this crude report in September was that our original charter was to report by September. But if you will recall [Frame 15], the mission was to develop a composite approach. The mission did not say "develop a language." But nevertheless, we did.

[Frame 23 shows that] the December, 1959 report had full specifications, was accepted by the CODASYL Executive Committee; it had final editing done by Betty Holberton and was the first one issued by the Government Printing Office in April 1960.

[For] COBOL 61 development [Frame 24], we had manufacturers and users with separate groups, each required to approve clarifications and enhancements. It was a special task group in September 1960 to February, 1961 to produce specifications. I believe we were told to produce them by December [1960], but you know, language designers don't produce things on time anymore than programmers do. There were to be some changes to COBOL 60 and this was issued by the Government Printing Office in June of 1961. And at least from a time point of view, that's as far as I'm going to go.

Now, one of the more exciting activities occurred in December of 1960 with the first compilers [Frame 25]. RCA and Remington-Rand were able to run the same program on the RCA 501 and the UNIVAC I—or maybe it was UNIVAC II, I don't remember. But with very few changes besides the Environment Division. And at that time, in the trade press there was a great deal of publicity about competition between them.

**MAJOR ELEMENTS OF COBOL 60
DEVELOPMENT**   (Slide 1)

Sept. 4, 1959 REPORT

- Crude specifications

- Permission received from CODASYL
  Executive Committee to finish by
  December 1, 1959

Frame 22

**MAJOR ELEMENTS OF COBOL 60
DEVELOPMENT**   (Slide 2)

December 1959 REPORT

- Full specifications

- Accepted by CODASYL Executive Com.

- Final editing done by Betty Holberton

- Issued by GPO April 1960

Frame 23

Jean E. Sammet

COBOL 61 DEVELOPMENT

- Manufacturers and Users— separate groups, each to approve clarifications and enhancements

- Special Task Group (Sept. 1960–Feb. 1961) to produce specifications

- Some changes to COBOL 60

- Issued by GPO June 1961

Frame 24

FIRST COMPILERS

December 6–7, 1960

RCA and Remington Rand run same program with very few changes besides Environment Division

Frame 25

Now, let me consider [Frame 26] some of the problems that were considered by the Statement Language Task Group at its earliest meeting. There was the whole matter of clausing—how we combine sentences, and whether we should or should not have extraneous words. There was a philosophy of verb structure in which we debated at length between many options per verb, or many verbs with no options. And those of you who are familiar with COBOL understand that, or at least are aware of the fact that we opted for the many options per verb.

In terms of the data references, we considered prefixes and suffixes, and we had to worry about how the data references and information got connected to the statements which were to be acting on them.

The next set of problems [Frame 27] involved open endedness. We were very open-minded about worrying about open endedness, and we were concerned with getting new words and new phrases. We were very concerned about the scope of the processing; whether this should or shouldn't allow algebraic and operations research, or logical processing or compiler writing. And then we were concerned with punctuation, forever and eternally concerned with punctuation! The number of hours that were spent worrying about commas, semicolons, and periods is a number that is too high to contemplate.

Another set of very important problems [Frame 28] had to do with the debate between symbols versus English, and it really went to the heart of who the intended users were. In essence, the people who were supporting, if you will, the business data-processing community who allegedly had no knowledge of algebra or mathematics or anything like that, felt that we had to have words of the kind ADD, SUBTRACT, MULTIPLY, and DIVIDE, and that such people were not capable of comprehending or writing, or didn't want to use symbols of the kind that most people learn in high school.

PROBLEMS TO BE CONSIDERED BY STATEMENT LANGUAGE TASK GROUP AS OF June 29, 1959 (Slide 1)

Clausing	—Combining sentences
	Extraneous words

Philosophy of verb structure
          —Many options per verb
  or   Many verbs with no options

Data References—Prefixes/suffixes
          Connection of statements to
            descriptions

Frame 26

PROBLEMS TO BE CONSIDERED BY STATEMENT LANGUAGE TASK GROUP AS OF June 29, 1959 (Slide 2)

Open endedness —New verbs
          New phrases

Types of processing
          —Algebraic/operations research
          Logical
          Compiler writing

Punctuation

Frame 27

**PROBLEMS TO BE CONSIDERED BY
STATEMENT LANGUAGE TASK GROUP
AS OF June 29, 1959** (Slide 3)

Symbols vs. English

<u>ADD, SUBTRACT, MULTIPLY, DIVIDE</u>
vs.
<u>+ X − /</u>

Input–Output
Configuration problems—machine
  independence versus efficiency

Frame 28

**EARLY KEY DECISIONS OF
STATEMENT LANGUAGE TASK GROUP
AND THEIR FINAL STATUS**

- Few verbs with many options   (Kept)
- ''AND GO TO'' allowed after
  each sentence   (Dropped)
- First word of each sentence
  must be the verb   (Kept)
- New verbs added
  via DEFINE   (Kept till 1965)

Frame 29

Some of us—I think most of us that had had mathematical training were of course in favor of the symbols. We were indeed sympathetic to the fact that there were individuals who wanted to be able to write the thing that way, but we did say that if anybody could cope with this complexity we felt they ought to be allowed to.

We were very concerned with input–output, naturally. And from a very early stage, with the configuration problem and worrying about machine independence versus efficiency.

The early key decisions and what happened to them were the following [in Frame 29]. We had few verbs with many options; we talked about having the phrase AND GO TO allowed after each sentence, and maybe in advance of what we were afraid we would be accused of, we dropped that. We did of course keep a GO TO in the language; that wasn't such a heresy then as it is now.

A key point having to do with the implementation—the first word of each sentence must be the verb—we kept. And new verbs being added by a DEFINE macro was kept until 1965 when it was dropped from the language on the grounds that nobody had implemented it. Then the software houses came along and they implemented it for a cost.

I want to emphasize [in Frame 30] some of the major points of controversy as of August [1959] at least. Should we allow IF . . . THEN and Boolean expressions? The main contenders, if you will, were the "COMPARE" philosophy that was in FLOW-MATIC versus the IF . . . THEN philosophy that was in COMTRAN. Should the sentence be ended by a period and a blank? Should the symbolic names rather than numbers be used for statement identification?

We then went on [Frame 31] with such esoteric [sarcasm intended] ideas as whether or not data and statement names should have the same form; whether you could repeat the

**SOME EARLY POINTS OF CONTROVERSY
AS OF August 17, 1959** (Slide 1)

Should

- IF—THEN and Boolean expressions be allowed?
- sentence be ended by PERIOD BLANK?
- symbolic names (rather than numbers) be used for statement identification?

Frame 30

**SOME EARLY POINTS OF CONTROVERSY
AS OF August 17, 1959** (Slide 2)

Should

- data and statement names have same form?
- same data name be repeated in the file?
- there be a DEFINE verb?

Frame 31

Jean E. Sammet

SOME EARLY POINTS OF CONTROVERSY
AS OF August, 17, 1959 (Slide 3)

Should

- formulas be allowed or not?

- subscripts be allowed or not?

- PERFORM verb handle both open and closed
  subroutines?

- key words be allowed anywhere?

- sequence numbers be required on every
  statement?

Frame 32

same data name in the file, or whether if you wanted to talk about ADDRESS, you had to talk about ADDRESS 1 and ADDRESS 2 and so on; and whether there should be a DE-FINE verb.

Some more points of controversy [Frame 32]: the formulas of course, whether subscripts should be allowed. Some people argued that was too complex for the data-processing users for whom this was intended. Should the PERFORM verb which was to do the loop control allow open and closed subroutines, or just one or the other, or both? Could key words be allowed anywhere, and were sequence numbers to be required on every statement? Remember, those were in the days of punch cards, and people were worried about decks dropping.

Now, some key decisions that were made relating to some of these questions [are in Frame 33]. The form of conditionals—and I'll say a little bit more about that later—did allow quite a bit of flexibility in the sense of having combined AND and OR. We had a very flexible conditional statement. In fact, it is in my view the most flexible of any language that exists to date. We allowed extensibility, at least at that time, by the DEFINE verb to add both abbreviations and new verbs. Now, some of the other decisions that we made [Frame 34]—we had the issue about the formula with the symbols, versus the four words, and that is an issue on which there was simply no compromise. There are people who say, "It must be this way," and some other people who say, "It must be that way." And we did what any self-respecting group would do, which was to allow both.

KEY DECISIONS/ISSUES ABOUT
STATEMENT LANGUAGE (Slide 1)

- Form of conditionals, e.g.,

  DOG AND CAT OR PIG

- Form of conditional statements

- Extensibility via DEFINE verb
  for abbreviations
  for new verbs

Frame 33

KEY DECISIONS/ISSUES ABOUT
STATEMENT LANGUAGE (Slide 2)

- Formulas (with symbols) versus

  ADD, SUBTRACT, MULTIPLY, DIVIDE

- Open versus closed subroutines

- Implied subjects and objects, e.g.,

  IF A EQUALS B ... ELSE
  IF GREATER ...

- Grouping of executable statements

- Importance of punctuation

Frame 34

CONDITIONALS AND IMPLIED SUBJECTS, OBJECTS ARE POWERFUL, FLEXIBLE

```
X = 2, Y OR Z
```

instead of

```
X = 2 OR X = Y OR X = Z
- - - - - - - - - - - - - - - - -
IF X = Y MOVE A TO B;
IF GREATER ADD A TO B;
OTHERWISE MOVE C TO D.
```

Frame 35

MAIN CRITERION FOR ALL STATEMENTS WAS READABILITY— THUS

- Physically available character set
- Allowance of Noise Words
- Sufficiently long data names

Frame 36

One of the other issues was the open versus the closed subroutines. Then we had a whole discussion about implied subjects and objects. And the next slide will show you something more about that. The grouping of executable statements: remember, we did not then have the information from ALGOL 60 since this was now 1959, and we did not have the significant contributions from there. And what we could glean from the ALGOL 58 report somehow didn't appeal to us. And so we were concerned about the grouping of executable statements, but we did not go the whole way. Again, another key issue was the importance of punctuation.

Now, in my view, the conditionals and implied subjects and objects are very powerful and flexible. For example, [Frame 35 shows] you can write "X = 2, Y OR Z" instead of the normal way of writing "X = 2 OR X = Y OR X = Z." That simply saves you a lot of writing on the one hand and is quite natural on the other.

One could also say, "IF X = Y MOVE A TO B," which is not very significant, but now notice that you're allowed to say, "IF X IS GREATER ADD A TO B." In all other languages, you must repeat both of these. You would have to say, "IF X IS GREATER THAN Y, ADD A TO B." But here we were allowed to say "IF GREATER" — meaning the comparison that was here, and then of course there was the OTHERWISE. And that [implied subjects and objects] turned out to be a great boon in terms of ease of writing. It's not so hard to write "IF X = Y," but if you have data names of the form SOCIAL-SECU-RITY and other things like that, and you have to repeat that two or three times, it's a bit much from a writing point of view.

Now the main criterion for all the statements was readability. Thus [Frame 36] we insisted on a physically available character set; we allowed noise words, which simply means words which were not syntactically required, but could be put in for readability, and [we allowed] sufficiently long data names.

Now, let me talk about the data description [Frame 37]. One of the key issues was whether it should be free form, rather than columns or on preprinted forms. The FLOW-MATIC example had been preprinted forms, the COMTRAN (then renamed Commercial Translator) was somewhat more free form, and we ended up with completely free form. A very important point is the next one: that the data is a continuous stream from the starting point of storage. The alternative is to say that for each item of data you indicate where, in some kind of a memory map, or where in some external paper, it is actually starting. But we chose to say the data would be continuous from wherever it started, and if there was space that was not being used, then there was something or other called FILLER which in essence meant that one did not care about what was in there.

Jean E. Sammet

<table>
<tr><td>KEY DECISIONS/ISSUES ABOUT
DATA DESCRIPTION   (Slide 1)</td><td>KEY DECISIONS/ISSUES ABOUT
DATA DESCRIPTION   (Slide 2)</td></tr>
</table>

<table>
<tr>
<td>

- Free form (rather than columns or preprinted form)

- Data is continuous stream from starting point of storage

- Recursive Data descriptions

- External versus internal data
  [never solved satisfactorily]

</td>
<td>

- Size of names—30 characters
  (because independent of any existing machine word size)

- Qualification (to allow duplicate names)

- Machine <u>independent</u> Data Description versus <u>efficient</u> Data Description

- Use of binary machine

</td>
</tr>
<tr><td style="text-align:center">Frame 37</td><td style="text-align:center">Frame 38</td></tr>
</table>

The recursive data descriptions—and there's apparently some confusion in that—what I mean is that we could use the same data description for each level of data, whether it be a field or a group of fields, or a group of group of fields.

And of course the major issue had to do with the external versus internal data which we never did solve satisfactorily. That is to say, obviously if we were going to describe data as it was to be represented internally, we were never going to get machine independence because these machines were completely different. On the other hand, describing it externally presents a whole lot of technical problems which at least in my view have not been solved satisfactorily yet.

Now [Frame 38], some of the key decisions and issues about the data description: the size of names was chosen to be 30 characters because this was inconvenient for every computer that existed then. If we had chosen any other number—[for example] if we had chosen 12, that would have favored Univac; if we had chosen 6 that might have favored IBM; the RCA people had a variable word-length computer, and so we didn't know what number would help them. But anyhow, 30 was sort of unpleasant for everybody and so we used that.

We allowed a concept called "qualification" which allowed you to use the word AD-DRESS or SOCIAL-SECURITY-NUMBER or something, to use that same data name in many files and fields, and then you tacked some other stuff on to show which one you really meant.

We opted, as best we could, for a machine-independent data description, versus an efficient data description, but that whole issue pervaded the discussion and to some extent still does. And a very key issue was the use of binary machines. Now, I was from Sylvania which at that time had thoughts about going into the computer field, and their computer was binary, so I was very anxious that there be provisions in the data description to allow data to be represented in a binary machine. I certainly did not expect individuals and users to handle this on a binary machine *per se* in terms of bits, but I certainly did expect that we would have the facilities in there. And I can't resist telling the story, and a very true one, that one of the representatives from Remington-Rand was opposing this very very bitterly, and he kept saying, "Users will never buy binary machines for data processing, and there-fore we don't need to have this kind of capability," and so forth and so on. This went on for several months, and at one meeting he came in and sort of said to me and one of the other people who was concerned with binary machines, and allowed as to how maybe we weren't so wrong after all. And we wondered what caused this change of heart, until shortly thereafter we saw the announcement of UNIVAC III from Remington-Rand which

LANGUAGE DEFINITION ISSUES

(Slide 1)

**DELIBERATE EXCLUSIONS
FROM LANGUAGE**

- Floating point

- Functions

- Strong library facilities

- Term "metalanguage" probably unknown to committee

- BNF <u>not</u> known to most members

- COBOL definition severely criticized because it was not BNF!

- Separate notation (= metalanguage) defined

Frame 39   **Frame 40**

happened to be a binary machine. And since they clearly wanted to have COBOL on that machine, you know, that caused somewhat of a change of heart.

Now, there were some things deliberately excluded from the language [Frame 39]. Floating point—there was felt to be no need for that. Functions—the reason that was excluded was because in those days one thought conceptually about functions in terms of mathematical function—trig functions, exponential, and so on—and clearly that was not needed in a business data-processing language, and so we didn't think we needed functions at all. And we excluded strong library facilities. And I'll have some comments later about where I think we made good and bad decisions.

Now, my favorite point with regard to COBOL has to do with the language definition issue [Frame 40] which may surprise you because you don't think this necessarily has much to do with COBOL per se. But first of all, the term "metalanguage" was probably unknown to the committee. We didn't know as much then as we think we know now, and I'm not sure whether any of us had ever even heard that word. Certainly, BNF as a concept was not known to us. Again, remember, John's paper was only being presented in June; we were meeting in June, and I don't think any of us even saw the paper thereafter. [This refers to Backus (1959). See the references in the formal paper—ed.] When COBOL was defined it was severely criticized because the definition was not BNF. A number of people went around saying COBOL simply had not been defined because its definition was not a BNF definition. But we did define a separate notation, and probably the biggest mistake we made out of sheer naïveté was to call it a "notation" and not a "metalanguage." I think had we called it a "metalanguage," certain aspects of the history of computer science might be rather different!

The reason I say that is that this notation which was used is the one that is frequently used today and is referred to as BNF. The notation that we developed [Frame 41] was some braces in which you could list vertically a number of elements meaning "Choose one from", square brackets to mean "optional." You did or didn't have to have that particular thing there. Underlining would mean "required" and three dots mean "repeat." Now, those of you who have looked at language definitions will note that there seem to be three kinds of metalanguages used. A few people use pure BNF; somewhat more people use an augmented form of BNF, but which is inherently still BNF. Some people use this [i.e., the COBOL] pure notation, and most people use a mixture of both. But I think the mixture tends to have predominantly more of the COBOL metalanguage than the BNF, and I say this not in any disparagement of the BNF metalanguage which I think is one of the greatest contributions that has been made to the whole computer field. But I point out

Jean E. Sammet

LANGUAGE DEFINITION ISSUES

(Slide 2)

- Notation (= metalanguage) developed:
{	}	choice
[	]	optional
underlining		required
· · ·		repeat

Frame 41.

**CONTRIBUTIONS OF COBOL—
VIEWED FROM TODAY** (Slide 1)

- Manufacturers successful joint effort

- Separate data description
  (leading to DBMS)

- Machine independent data description

- Metalanguage

- Orderly language maintenance and enhancement

Frame 42

that because we called this a "notation" and because most of the people concerned with computer science were interested in ALGOL and therefore familiar with BNF—somehow we just lost a battle we didn't even know we were supposed to be fighting!

Now, let me talk about the contributions of COBOL viewed from today, [Frame 42]. First of all, the manufacturers had a successful joint effort. I think this was the first time that computer manufacturers had gotten together to try and create a language in a fairly competitive environment. It was certainly not the first time that groups had gotten together. The PACT example which was referred to yesterday had been done on the West Coast primarily by a lot of the aerospace and related R & D outfits. But those, while they were competitive, they were presumably competitive about what planes they were going to build and not about what computers they were going to sell. There certainly were manufacturers' representatives on the ALGOL 58 committee, but somehow that had an entirely different flavor and so the issue of competition was not that important.

But here you had six computer manufacturers with varying degrees of involvement in the computer field, all working together, bound and determined to try and produce a successful language.

There was a separate data description. Now, that was the breakthrough that came from FLOW-MATIC. In my view, it leads to the current work in DBMS. Some people may feel that's a farfetched claim, and maybe it is, but I think that the original concept of separating the data description from the actions that you want to perform on it, and making that a very clear delineation was a very significant concept, originally proposed in FLOW-MATIC, somewhat extended in COBOL, and as I say, has led very much to the DBMS work today.

The machine-independent data description—and again, there I think we made a contribution not as large perhaps as we could have or should have, but the data description is machine independent if you are willing to sacrifice efficiency. And that's a fairly important point. If you start out saying, "I want a data description that is as efficient as possible for this particular machine," then when you come to run it on the other one, surely it will be inefficient on another machine, and perhaps it may not work unless you've been careful in writing it in the first place. Conversely, if you make a sincere attempt to make the thing independent in the first place, then you should be able to succeed to a very large degree in getting over onto another machine. The metalanguage I think is a significant contribution of COBOL, again, because it turns out in real life that most people, or many people at least who really do not have any intellectual or other kind of axe to grind, will in fact use the COBOL metalanguage or a minor variation thereof rather than BNF. And it turns out to have some interesting implication on the languages that you can define. There are some language features that are very easy and very nice to define in BNF that you cannot do in the COBOL metalanguage. Conversely, there are some things that are very easy and very nice to do in the COBOL metalanguage that you just can't do in any practical way with regard to the BNF. And probably the best illustration of that has to do with choice. If you want to have a choice of, let's say, two or three elements, followed by a choice of another two or three elements, in the COBOL metalanguage you can represent that simply by two contiguous braces, and you list vertically the elements from which you make the choice. In BNF, essentially you have to list all of the combinations.

Now, the great disadvantage to that choice mechanism in COBOL of course is that it is vertical and, you know, the world moves horizontally—at least on paper—and so some expediencies have been developed to get around that by listing things horizontally, and so on.

The next point is the contribution that I think was made by COBOL, orderly language maintenance and enhancement. And again, I think that's a terribly important point. You heard Al Perlis yesterday talk about FORTRAN in an environment; that is to say, a language is only part of an environment. And certainly the creation of the language specifications is just the tip of the iceberg. There need to be, certainly, clarifications, normally enhancements, and up until that point in time, there really had not been very much thought given to that. The ALGOL 58 people, as far as I recall, put forth this activity, the ALGOL 58 report, but without at that time committing themselves to any maintenance and enhancement; whereas by 1959 the COBOL committee knew it had to do this, and therefore when we turned in the [December 1959] report to the CODASYL Executive Committee, part of our proposals had to do with language maintenance and enhancement.

Now, some more of the contributions of COBOL viewed from today [Frame 43]: we had a very powerful conditional statement, as I say, I think it is the most powerful of any language today, but I'm not 100% certain of that. We had semiautomatic segmentation. That is to say that the user is allowed to indicate some priorities and say that this particular section of code should be grouped together because it was going to be executed together, whereas some other group was to be executed together, and so on; and the compiler was supposed to do the right thing, and create the stuff efficiently, and by and large those early compilers did. A first attempt, crude though it was, at paging.

Realistic use of hardware—again, I contrast this with ALGOL 58, which was the only other model that we had, and we stayed with the hardware we had and not the character set that didn't exist.

A readable language—clearly a readable one. And I think it was the first high-level language macro facility in the pure sense of the word, with a DEFINE which allowed you to

---

**CONTRIBUTIONS OF COBOL—
VIEWED FROM TODAY** (Slide 2)

- Powerful conditionals
- Powerful conditional statements
- Semi-automatic segmentation
- Realistic use of hardware
- Readable language
- 1st High Level language macro facility

Frame 43

**MISTAKES AND/OR DESIRED CHANGES
(BASED ON COBOL 60 AND WITH
RESPECT TO THAT TIME FRAME)**

- No collating sequence
- Some features in Data Division belonged in Environment Division
- No parameters for subroutines
- Inadequate library facilities

Frame 44

---

define a new verb in terms of existing ones, and the compiler was supposed to do the right thing. As I say, unfortunately it never got implemented and it was eventually removed from the language. But nevertheless it was there.

Now, some of the mistakes and desired changes [Frame 44] based on COBOL 60, and with respect to that time frame—now, I emphasize very strongly, with respect to that time frame; I think it is quite fair to criticize the COBOL committee for things they should have done at *that* time given the state of the art. I think it's less fair to criticize any person or any group for not having a good enough crystal ball to see what was going to happen two or three or ten years in the future. And that first mistake that I think we made, that finally has been rectified, is the lack of collating sequence. Now, what we wanted, some of us, and I guess I'm proud to say I was one of the ones that wanted to put the collating sequence in—but I can tell you what the problem was. What some of us said was: if this is truly to be machine independent, we need to include in the Environment Division or somewhere a specification. We had to include the statement about the collating sequence that was intended for that particular program, on that particular machine, because if you write something that says IF ALPHA IS LESS THAN NUMERIC, that may test positive, that is to say YES on one machine and NO on the other, depending on what the internal structure and collating sequence of the machine is. Now, clearly, from an intellectual point of view, this can be handled by the compiler; you just make sure that the compiler makes all the tests based on the collating sequence that the programmer is using, and not on the one that the machine is using. And so the concept was very simple, very clear, [and] I think should have been put in, but the counterargument was that the inefficiency that would be caused would be so great that everybody would run and holler and therefore it wouldn't be used, and therefore why bother??

The next mistake that we made was that some features in the Data Division belonged in the Environment Division. We couldn't really judge that as well as we should, but there are some things about the files which we put into the Data Division meaning that we thought they could be made machine independent, and in reality they cannot.

No parameters for subroutines—no decent parameter mechanism for subroutines was probably the biggest mistake that we made, and I certainly think we should have known better. I can't find any excuse for not doing that.

Inadequate library facilities, again, was a mistake we made. I think we should have included that. We should have been smart enough to see that that was going to be important. I'm not sure whether at that time we had the example of the JOVIAL COMPOOL that you'll hear more about. I don't think we did. We should have been smart enough to think

**IMPLICATIONS FOR CURRENT/FUTURE
LANGUAGE DEVELOPMENT**

- Experience with real users and compilers
  needed before freezing specs

- Computer scientists should learn and
  teach COBOL

- Will probably continue to be very heavily
  used

- Has kept up with changes in equipment

Frame 45

of that kind of problem ourselves. We certainly did include some library facilities; I don't mean to, if you will, to knock ourselves completely. We did include some, because we knew, for example, that there were going to be libraries of these data descriptions. The basic concept was that we wanted to allow an installation or a project group to write one Data Description which would be easily available in a library, and then as many Procedure Divisions as they needed for each of their different applications.

Now, let me talk about the implications for current and future language development [in Frame 45]. The first and most obvious—but it was not entirely obvious then—is that experience with real users and compilers is needed before freezing the specs. Now, those of you who have had any experience in the standards activity know the problem, but for those of you who don't, there is always a problem in standardizing on whether you're too early or too late. If you're too late, then everybody has gone off from some common base in 29 different directions and you have technical, administrative, management, and political problems in trying to bring all the stuff back together again. But at least everybody knows by then, through experience, because of trying different things, what's good and what's bad. But you have that problem of bringing everything together.

Conversely, if you do it very early, you don't have everybody going off left, right, and sideways, but you have, in essence, a standard based on things that maybe weren't as clearly thought through and explored as they should be. And this is certainly an important lesson that needs to be considered with regard to the development of DoD-1, the proposed Department of Defense language, and I think they're quite well aware of this.

The other aspect of this is that COBOL became a de facto standard, and the reason it became a de facto standard is very simple. Charlie Phillips, who had been the honcho and the person who convened this Pentagon meeting, who chaired the CODASYL Executive Committee, issued a letter to computer manufacturers after we got this, which said in essence that if they wanted to sell computers to the Department of Defense, they were going to have to have a COBOL compiler, unless they could prove they were doing scientific computations. Now I hesitate to use the word "edict" for that, but it's a mighty powerful club to a computer manufacturer who, at that time, felt quite rightly that the Department of Defense was a very large and a very major customer. And I point that out here because we have the following anomaly: COBOL was established pretty much as a de facto standard, not in the ANSI sense, but in the real working sense, because of the activity and the pressure from the Department of Defense. And it was standardized, again not in the ANSI sense, but in the practical sense, before all of us really knew what we were doing. And some changes of course have had to be made to COBOL since then; on the other hand, I think the basic structure has proven to be sound. In my view, many of the changes that have been made since then have been matters of personal taste and not based on really new concepts or changing equipment. COBOL has kept up with changing equipment.

Now, the second implication for current and future language development is that in my view the computer scientists should learn and teach COBOL. (I'm waiting for the groan. The size of the groan is directly proportional to the number of computer scientists in the audience—sometimes, anyhow.) What has happened over the past 20 years is that the computer science faculty, and some of my best friends are there, have chosen to ignore COBOL for two reasons: on the one hand, they consider it beneath them, undignified, not elegant, not conceptually important, and so on. That's in essence what they say. My view, which they *don't* say, is that it's too hard! It is! It's significantly more difficult because you're dealing with complex data structures. And in my view there are a number of lessons to be learned from looking at COBOL, and I don't care whether you look at the present form or the early form. But I think for myself that it's a shame that a number of students will graduate with at least Bachelor Degrees in COBOL Science—I'm sorry—Bachelor Degrees in [Laughter and Applause!!] will graduate with Bachelor Degrees in Computer Science without having had any more than perhaps a minimum exposure to COBOL which has a number of very interesting concepts.

Anyhow—so much for that amount of proselytizing which will, I'm sure, have no more effect now than it has when I've said this in other places! COBOL will continue to be very heavily used. I think that's important. I think it's important because it means that attempts which are made somehow to kill COBOL just are not going to work. And I'm not saying necessarily that COBOL should continue to be very heavily used. I do think it should. But, that's quite different from saying that I believe that it *will* continue to be very heavily used.

Now, it's extremely difficult to determine what usage of a language means. In a different environment, and with different talks, and some of you may even have heard this—I have a whole slide that talks about the impossibility of measuring the usage of a language. You don't know whether you're talking about the number of programmers or the number of programs or the amount of computer time, and on and on. Nevertheless, without having any way to measure this, intuitively it seems to be apparent that—I hope I have enough cop-out words there—it seems to be true that COBOL is the most widely used programming language. The reason being that there are a large number of data-processing computers—that is to say, computers used for data processing, a large number of small ones, and there in the business environment that is at least one of the two major natural languages. (In this context, ''natural'' refers to choice rather than to the English-like nature of COBOL. The other major choice is RPG, which I do not personally consider a high level language although many other people do.)

One point I should make in this context, and it has to do with the standardization and the experience. A number of you have seen language rosters that I have put out for a number of years—and seen tabulations—and consistently in the data-processing area, the business data-processing area, there have only been three or four languages, whereas in the numerical scientific there tend to range anywhere from 10 to 20, or maybe even as high as 30 in all kinds of other areas. And the reason for that is very simple. The initial standardization by COBOL, the initial pressure on the manufacturers to support it whether they wanted to or not, are all very important.

Finally, COBOL has kept up with changes in equipment. There are a number of changes in COBOL 74 that were not in COBOL 60 or any of the versions up until then. And so I think the COBOL maintenance activity has done a very good job of keeping up with the changes in equipment. And that's something that needs to be kept in mind for future language development.

TRANSCRIPT OF DISCUSSANT'S REMARKS

MICHAEL MARCOTTY: Thank you very much, Jean. Now, before we go to the questions, I'm going to introduce a Discussant, Betty Holberton, who has been for a long time in this business. Between 1945 and 1947 she was a mathematician, one of the original six programmers developing trajectories for the first electronic computer, ENIAC, at the Aberdeen Proving Ground. Then between 1947 and 1950 she joined the Eckert–Mauchly Corporation as a Logic Design Engineer, one of a team of six on logic design for the first commercially available electronic computer, UNIVAC I. Later, with Remington-Rand, she developed techniques for sorting and merging of data on electronic computers and, as Grace Hopper mentioned yesterday, pioneered in the field of automatic computer programming. This effort resulted in the first sort-generator produced in the computer industry. Between 1953 and 1956 she was at the David Taylor Model Basin, in the Applied Math Lab there, and she was a member of the DoD Sponsored COBOL Development Committee. She's going to give us some discussion on her views of what went on. Betty.

BETTY HOLBERTON: I'm going to try to give you a little of the flavor of the times, as I see it. By 1951 engineers had well accepted the computer, but the business world was still very skeptical about it, because they had such questions as, "How do I know the data is on the magnetic tape?" And "What is the legal implication of data on a magnetic tape?" which I had no answer for. However, I tried to assist in the first problem by recording a section of tape at 20 pulses per inch on the UNITYPER, followed by a section of 200 bpi by the computer, sprinkling iron filings on that, and lifting it off with Scotch tape, and sandwiching it in between another piece, and with a pulse code chart, a magnifying glass, and the Scotch tape, I was prepared for any emergency. I still have that Scotch tape.

The field had overoptimism. Even Mauchly, in describing a data-processing task and how it would be done, would give an estimate of the speed or the amount of programming effort, and I would do a mental calculation, and would normally have to multiply it by at least a factor of 2 because he had forgotten about the housekeeping problems in control, or the debugging and documentation.

The signs of the time were exaggeration. The exaggeration of the success of use of computers. It was often hard to determine when a paper was given at a conference whether what was being described had actually been implemented, or was it still in the mind of the spokesman. But one thing that I did attempt to get from every conference was, what was the latest estimate of the cost of one bit of fast storage, and what was the estimate of the speed of the circuit? Because this was very important, what direction we were going to go in the future of automatic programming? Unless we could solve an economic problem there, we were going to be living with memories of 1000 words which was very difficult to handle.

I attended that first meeting that Jean spoke about at the Pentagon, where the decision was made to have English as the language; where also it was decided that the manager could read this program. Now, my image of a manager was the senior member of a tab shop who had moved over to take this new installation, and was in charge of a group of programmers that he could not even communicate with. And in my mind, I saw no way he was going to read this program. But near the end of the meeting, which had approximately 40 people there, Charlie Phillips who conducted the meeting, asked each one of us to give some statement on what we thought the future would be in this project. And he started to the left of me and went around clockwise, and it began with exaggerated claims, and very unrealistic hopes, and I began to wonder what I would say. My thoughts turned back to David Taylor Model Basin where we had attempted to get programmers to use Grace Hopper's A-0 and B-0 and FORTRAN, and when one person would try it, the word would get around: the compiler was too slow; it had bugs; the object code was too slow. And we had to start an open shop and train engineers from other laboratories before we got any takers. The professional programmer was afraid of job security.

Then as the remarks of the meeting reached a crescendo, one gentleman opposite me said he had a severe problem with a lack of program documentation, and if this language could improve the picture—this picture, he was for it. And anything else it did he considered a fringe benefit. Well, I certainly thought it could do that. I don't recall what anybody else said, or even what I said, but I was going to try to tackle that problem.

To expect the Short-Range Committee to develop a language and write the report in three months was gross optimism on the part of the Executive Committee. To ask the manufacturers to implement the language and the users to write programs in the language that would survive for only two years to me was unthinkable. So, I asked Grace Hopper if she could send me a cost estimate of implementing a compiler. So on August 8, 1959, she supplied me with this information, which I still have today, in which she stated, in 1959 dollars, it would have cost approximately $945,000 and $45\frac{1}{2}$ man-years of effort. In no way was this language going to be an interim solution. This language was going to be "it" as far as I was concerned.

As I viewed the problem, if the Committee worked full time on the solution, did not get sidetracked and change its approach, and then whatever time would be needed to get the job done I felt would be given by the Executive Committee. By early December, before the final report of the Short-Range Committee was issued, I was informed that I would be charged with the final editing of the publication. I do not believe that I was aware that the report was going to be circulated for review outside of the Committee, which it was, because I did not receive a copy of this letter until January 15 with a request for comments to be received by the 29th. However, in early January I had noticed some substantive issues that had to be resolved before publication; otherwise the manufacturers would have problems implementing the language. The Short-Range Committee had been dissolved, and the Technical Committee, which was the manufacturers, had begun work. However, with Wegstein's and Phillips's permission, two meetings lasting seven days were held with the Short-Range Committee to resolve these problems. By April there had been a complaint about the editing procedure. And I'd like to read from this letter, dated April 19, addressed to me. It says: "Today Charles Phillips is conducting a joint meeting between the old Short-Range Committee and the editorial group which was supposed to have edited the COBOL Manual and released it for publication with a representative from the Maintenance Committee participating as an observer. This meeting is brought about as a result of the opinion of members of the Short-Range Committee that the editorializing of the COBOL Manual had made changes which, while generally acceptable to the Technical Committee, had not been intended initially by the Short-Range Committee and they felt that it was proper procedure to warrant a discussion of these changes before publication."

So on the 19th, a meeting was held (of the Short-Range Committee) and I have a copy of the minutes in which very few little things—but one thing was very interesting. This is Nora Moser's minutes of the 19th in Phillips's office, and this was related to the PERFORM verb. It says, "There are two minor changes." And in the first one, she says, "Hurrah." In the second one, she says, "6 a and b, notes removed." And then in quotes, "They weren't mine anyway." She had rewritten the PERFORM verb.

The documentation was completed, ready for publication on the 29th of April in 1960, but GPO had never gotten around to scheduling the printing of it until June 24.

In closing I'd like to say what I feel are the reasons why the initial COBOL effort was successful, which goes along somewhat with what Jean has said. But one of the things that I felt helped it along was that the language did not require any program definition, or any data files to be restyled: only how you wrote the program. And this was very important to the acceptance of a new language without additional change. The joint effort of the implementors and the users was significant. And Phillips's letter which Jean mentioned, asking each implementor to make a statement on August 12 of 1960 was also significant. And DoD's requirement on implementation—and I'll be stronger than Jean, I'd say that was a pressure. But in the end I'd like to say that Grace Hopper's continued effort to inform management was very important because, in my opinion, the option of using compilers, left to the user, might easily have made it go down the drain because they resist change.

TRANSCRIPT OF QUESTION AND ANSWER SESSION

MICHAEL MARCOTTY: First, I have a series of questions on the readability of COBOL. I'm going to try and lump them together, and I think start with a question from Dan McCracken which says, "Program readability was a commendable design goal and ahead of its time, but how did it come about that the main emphasis was on readability by managers, instead of readability by programmers? Was there any evidence at that time that managers wanted to read programs?"

JEAN SAMMET: Well, with regard to the first part of the question, I think it was taken for granted that if the managers could read it, so could the programmers. While there was no concrete evidence that the managers wanted to be able to read this, I think the assumption was that programming was becoming more important, it was going to require more supervision and more management, and to the extent that such supervision could be exercised directly by the manager reading the code, that this would be a good thing. Now, there was no concrete evidence. I think it was sort of an intuitive feeling, and we've come full circle, 20 years later, into a concept called "Chief Programmer" and "Walk-Throughs" and all kinds of other things which have very similar connotations.

MARCOTTY: Roger Mills from TRW: "Did the COBOL Committee seriously believe that users could not handle grade-school operations of add, subtract, multiply, and divide?"

SAMMET: Some members of the COBOL Committee felt that way. I was not one of them.

BETTY HOLBERTON: Neither was I.

SAMMET: Quite seriously, there was a strong sentiment, particularly from the Remington-Rand people, that the users did not want to use formulas, did not want to use algebraic symbols in the normal course of writing an arithmetic expression.

MARCOTTY: Question from Brian Webb: "How and why did the statement indentation and numbering schemes come into being?"

SAMMET: To the best of my recollection, it was felt that we needed to produce a consistent output; that is to say, we wanted literally to be able to move a deck of cards (after all, that's all we had then)—to move a deck of cards from one machine to another. Now, clearly, if you didn't know what you were going to find in column 7 or 22 or something of that kind, you'd be in some difficulty. So between the desire for readability on the one hand, which had to do with indentation, and the importance of this machine interchangeability which would enforce consistency, we came up with those particular rules about what was to be where.

MARCOTTY: Question from Bob Rosin, Bell Labs: "Do you now have second thoughts about the conservative position with regard to character sets? Specifically, don't you now believe that we would all be using 128 characters in compiler interaction if CODASYL had required this in 1959?"

SAMMET: No!

HOLBERTON: No way!

SAMMET: No, I have not changed my mind. I still think we were right. And I say that, having previously said there were some things I think we did that were wrong—I still think we were right on a realistic character set. I think that if we had chosen 128, we would have simply had the same incompatability problem that exists with regard to ALGOL and the problem of mapping onto—you know, first 48 characters, and then even now 64. The world is based on a 64 character typewriter.

MARCOTTY: This is another one from Roger Mills: "If the goal was to write in English, why did DEFINE provide for abbreviations?"

SAMMET: There was quite a debate about that. The DEFINE was in and out, in and out, in the early six-month period, and the DEFINE as originally proposed had two components to it; one which was to abbreviate words, the other which had to do with providing new verbs by way of macros. The one having to do with abbreviation of words was an attempt to straddle the fence between the readability and the writability. It was clear that you had to allow people to write out SOCIAL-SECURITY-NUMBER to get readability, and it was equally clear that to require them to do that all of the time was going to lead to hand-cramps and all kinds of other things of that kind. And so, the attempt was made by some of us to include a DEFINE in which the individual could, at the very beginning of his program, write DEFINE SSN = SOCIAL-SECURITY-NUMBER, and all the appropriate things would be done by the compiler, and all the listings would show SOCIAL-SECURITY-NUMBER. And the counterargument is exactly the one that Roger seems to imply, that the doing of that would cause lack of readability because of the cryptic nature of the abbreviations, and so on. And hence, that aspect of it was voted out of the December 1959 report. It never got in there, although it had been in varying versions, whereas the macro facility did. I think it's too bad, and as I say, when the software houses started coming out with these packages for a fee, I kept thinking it was a shame that this had not been kept in COBOL where it would have been in for free, or at least as basically part of the compiler.

MARCOTTY: Now some questions on the make-up of the Committee. Richard Miller: "For the invitations to the initial Pentagon meeting, how was the invitation list made up; in particular, was academic representation considered?"

SAMMET: There were academic people there. I don't know—you'd have to ask Charles Phillips. I have the list of people who were invited and so on. The list of organizations, I believe, is in the paper. How the list was concocted, I don't know. I think all the computer manufacturers were invited, and presumably any users and consultants and so on that were believed to have knowledge, competence, interest, and so forth, in this; then within each individual organization they, of course, made the decision on who was to go.

HOLBERTON: Jean, there was an original list which was fairly short that came out about three weeks before the invitations, and the word must have gotten around because a number of people asked to attend this, so it then grew from about 15 to 46; something like that.

SAMMET: Grace Hopper is, I think, hopefully going to shed some light on this.

GRACE HOPPER: Part of that original list was based on the people who were already using FLOW-MATIC and who had already experimented in looking at COMTRAN and FACT. So it was the people who were already concerned, and had shown concern in use of compilers and such a language in data processing. But that was, I think, part of the original list, and then it spread when they told people, and some other people asked to be invited.

SAMMET: Very good.

MARCOTTY: Question from Stan Whitlock: "Where and when did CODASYL come from, and how was it tied to COBOL?"

SAMMET: I'm sorry—I meant to bring that out in the formal presentation, and I just forgot. At this Pentagon meeting, there was a group of people that set up a Steering Committee which then created an Executive Committee, which called itself CODASYL. And in different documents, CODASYL stands for *Conference* On Data Systems Languages or *Committee* On Data Systems Languages. Some of the official reports from them are labeled one way, and some are labeled the other. CODASYL as an organization never existed. It was a mailing list of 300 or 400 people for a while. There was a CODASYL Executive Committee which was in essence self-appointed, and I do not mean that in any disparaging way because they did a great deal of very useful technical work—that is to say, the CODASYL Executive Committee themselves, and they had two technical advisors, both of whom are in the audience—Grace Hopper and Bob Bemer. Grace at the time with Remington-Rand; Bob Bemer with IBM at the time. And they [i.e., the Executive Committee] are the ones that appointed and supervised and everything else. But it was a self-appointed group, if you will, and there never was any meeting under the auspices of CODASYL until a ten-year anniversary meeting which was in 1969. The CODASYL Executive Committee was supervising the Short-Range Committee which it had created, and the Intermediate-Range Committee which was one of the ones that was coming out of the [May 1959] Pentagon meeting. Perhaps I can take this opportunity to forestall what I believe was a question asked about what happened to those other committees. There was an Intermediate-Range Committee formed, and there was allegedly to be a Long-Range Committee formed. The Long-Range Committee never got formed. All that got formed was a group to plan it. And they never planned it, and so it never formed. The Intermediate-Range Committee got formed, but had a fair amount of trouble getting going because they were supposed to follow on to what the Short-Range Committee was doing: they were supposed to do it right. That is to say, the Short-Range Committee was to do something that was going to last for a year or two, and the Intermediate-Range Committee was then supposed to do something that was really going to last. But somehow it didn't quite work out that way. Now, there were some things done under the auspices of the Intermediate-

Range Committee. It was very good work that was done under their auspices, but that's getting us a bit far afield.

MARCOTTY: Question from Bruce Galler: "The ALGOL Committee was made up of mostly academic people, while the COBOL Committee was made up mostly of government and business people. How did the operation of these committees differ in these respects?" Maybe Joe Wegstein, if he's in the audience, who was on both these committees, might like to comment on this?

JOE WEGSTEIN: Well, the COBOL Committee had these people from their various manufacturers who had a lot of vested interest, and were very intense about that sort of thing in connection with everything being done. Whereas, the ALGOL Committee had a bunch of senior professors of Europe and an oddball collection from the U.S., and—all very temperamental and very intense about mathematical aspects of programming. So there was quite a difference. I don't know if that satisfies the question or not, but that was about the difference, I'd say.

MARCOTTY: Thank you. A question from Aaron Finerman: "COBOL has long had features that other languages are now starting to incorporate. Although it is somewhat verbose, it compensates by carrying a built-in documentation within the program, yet it continues to be viewed with great disdain, as is data processing in general, by many computing scientists. It is rarely taught in prestigious computer science departments, where it is still regarded as an abomination. Have you any comments?"

SAMMET: To some extent I addressed some of that during the talk, but I'm glad for an opportunity to comment further on that because I must admit, it's not a planted question. I didn't know he was going to ask it, but it is a subject on which I must say I do have very strong feelings. I think that to a very large extent there has been a snob reaction from the very beginning of COBOL. The computer scientists of the early 1960s, the late 1959, were to a large extent the ALGOL people, and those people concerned with ALGOL. Clearly, COBOL which was designed for practical usage was certainly not considered very elegant, and in fact I think intellectually was perhaps not very elegant. It was just useful. And usefulness and elegance are not necessarily the same thing. I think on the one hand, as I say, the snob appeal, that this was not being done by the academic people who were the influential ones in the computer science field, the disdain for business data-processing as being something of intellectual importance, even though I should think by now it should be more obvious even to those people than they seem to realize—the importance of the intellectual concerns with business data processing, data base management systems problems, the entire organizational problem, and so on. And I think there's a second reason, and I'm sure this will step on a great many toes. I think simply the data-processing activity is much harder. It really is hard to worry about files and machine independence and how you lay out files efficiently and still keep the machine independent, how you worry about conversion programs and so on. And it's always been a very great source of sadness to me that so many people who clearly have the intellectual capability to deal with these kinds of problems on an abstract basis, have not chosen to do so, either in their research or in their computer science department teaching. I think COBOL ought to be taught because there are concepts in there which are important and which are useful, and business-data processing has a large significant, intellectual component. But most of the senior key computer science faculty people don't agree.

MARCOTTY: In fact, I think you said that COBOL was hard to teach and Roger Mills . . .

SAMMET: I didn't say that!

MARCOTTY: Oh. Roger Mills asks: "If COBOL is so hard to teach, how could it be easy to learn?" [Based on misinterpretation of comment at bottom of p. 259? Ed.]

SAMMET: I never said it was hard to teach. I don't know—I have not taught COBOL directly per se, so I can't tell you of my own knowledge whether or not it's hard to teach. We did intend it to be easy to learn. I'm not sure we achieved that.

MARCOTTY: From Bruce Galler: "In the preprint article on COBOL it is stated twice that COBOL has far greater power and complexity than ALGOL 60. Could you be more explicit about this?"

SAMMET: Yes—given another two hours or so. Let me try and do that succinctly. First and foremost is the concept of the whole data structures. The moment you're dealing with ALGOL 60 you are dealing with only two data types, fixed and floating point essentially, real and rational, whatever words are being used. In COBOL you have the entire complexity of data and files, and that just in and of itself is literally, in my view, an order of magnitude more difficult than dealing just with the algebraic part of the activity. That's wherein the complexity comes. The power is because you do have the capability of dealing with all of this data material and you do, as I say, have fairly powerful conditional statements and conditional expressions and things of that kind which, I believe, are more powerful than, certainly, those in ALGOL 60.

MARCOTTY: Question from Saul Rosen: "Considering the performance of the early COBOL compilers with multihour compilations on the RCA 501 for example, do you think COBOL would have survived without the pressure applied by the Department of Defense in requiring COBOL on all machines?"

SAMMET: No.

HOLBERTON: I don't either.

SAMMET: But I think it would not have survived even if the compilations *had* been fast! There's no question in my mind that the pressure from the Department of Defense is to a very significant degree what made COBOL succeed because the manufacturers, particularly over a period of time—IBM, Honeywell, and Remington-Rand, which had other languages in varying stages of development, completion, and what-have-you—eventually, for more or less economic reasons, had to drop their own language in support of COBOL because they *had* to support COBOL in order to get that business, and it became on the one hand economically unfeasible to support it, but I think there was also some pressure from the users other than the Department of Defense which said that they really want a single language. Maybe COBOL isn't a good one or isn't the best one, and so on, but at least it's *a* language that everybody's got and we're going to use that rather than a language which they might consider better, but which wasn't going to be available on the machines.

MARCOTTY: Questions from Alan Ambler and Richard Miller can be summed up as: "What is the history of the PICTURE concept?"

SAMMET: Oh, that's clear. That came from Commercial Translator. That was in the Commercial Translator preliminary specifications [see bibliography, IBM, 1959] that we got after the Pentagon meeting, and was taken over almost hook, line, and sinker into COBOL. There was a debate, again similar to the debate on formulas versus the statements ADD, SUBTRACT, MULTIPLY, and DIVIDE—there was a similar debate on whether or not one should have the PICTURE clause which is very symbolic and cryptic, and just has letters and numbers to tell you what the data description is, as contrasted with a whole set of words like SIZE and CLAUSE and DATA TYPE and so on. And we did the same thing there that we did with the other controversy. Namely, we included both.

HOLBERTON: And I was for the PICTURE clause. Hook, line, and sinker.

MARCOTTY: From Paul Abrahams: "What thought was given to comments in COBOL? Why aren't they allowed in the Data Division?"

SAMMET: We didn't think they were needed in the Data Division.

HOLBERTON: That was a mistake. That was really a mistake.

MARCOTTY: Question from Mike Shapiro: "In your paper you note that the 18-digit precision limit was chosen to put every candidate computer at a disadvantage. However, 18 digits fit nicely in 64 bits—binary or compressed decimal. Was this ignored because it was presumed only binary coded decimal or other decimal would be used? Or were there other reasons for the magic number 18?"

SAMMET: With regard to the 64 bits—at the time the machines we were considering as potential candidates for COBOL to be used on, I don't think any of them had 64 bits.

HOLBERTON: I think that 18 thing came in from the National Debt at that time! [Laughter and Applause]

SAMMET: I don't recall that! That may indeed be correct; I don't recall it! But the 18 bits [digits] were chosen because we wanted something that was going to be large enough in terms of size of numbers that could be represented, but indeed again, to be equally inconvenient to everybody—and I don't think we had any 64-bit computers around at that time that we were consciously thinking of. The fact that it's turned out to be convenient for them later is their good luck or skill or something.

HOLBERTON: Or preplanning.

SAMMET: Yes.

MARCOTTY: Question from Nancy Stern: "You mentioned several languages which influenced the development of COBOL. Did FORTRAN, despite its scientific nature, have any influence at all on the design of COBOL?"

SAMMET: From my point of view that's a bit hard to answer. We were of course as familiar as one could be with FORTRAN—you know, a whole couple of years after its issuance on the scene, and so we knew what was there. And we knew what kinds of things could and couldn't be done, but to the best of my recollection, and Betty can also comment, to the best of my recollection, we didn't look at FORTRAN very much because there wasn't anything in FORTRAN that wasn't in FLOW-MATIC or Commercial Translator, and those were the models that we clearly had to follow as input. Betty?

HOLBERTON: Jean, in going over my files (which were a couple of file drawers) for this meeting, I came across a comparison that I had written down in which one whole column was FORTRAN. So that I know I was looking at what was in each one of these languages, so that very often a choice could have been one or the other, in the statement area. But as far as the data description area, none of them fitted across machine lines. But it was considered.

MARCOTTY: Question from Dan McCracken: "To my mind, COBOL's main innovation was the separation of the Data Description from the imperative statements. Whose idea was this?"

SAMMET: Well, it's clear: that came from FLOW-MATIC.

MARCOTTY: Question from Peter Wegner: "What lessons can be learned from the development of COBOL that are relevant to the development of DoD-1?"

SAMMET: I think the main lesson is the nontechnical lesson. It has to do with the maintenance and the surrounding mechanisms for controlling the language, for controlling its compilers, for making sure that everybody is doing the same thing when what you want is compatability. That's one thing. The second thing has to do with a point that I had, I guess, on the last slide [Frame 45] which says that some real testing by users for writing programs is needed before freezing [the work from] either of the two organizations that are now selected to produce the potential candidate languages. And I would sincerely hope that a lot of sample programs would be written in both of those candidate languages long before any decision is made on which of them to pick. And presumably the mechanics of the contracts and so on, and the DoD selection process will allow that. But I think those are the two main things: that some real experience has to be gained by writing at least some sample programs, and that also the environment, the maintenance—the whole maintenance facility has to be looked at and handled very carefully so that one doesn't go off on cloud 9—and this has been done very well in the COBOL area, and I think that needs to be done in DoD.

HOLBERTON: I was wondering also about phasing into the construction of these compilers on the basis of certain modules and things like that to start with, so before you go the whole hog, that you can determine whether this is going to be a workable tool. Which actually was done in COBOL by the technical committee, to phase the various aspects of the language into the implementation.

SAMMET: Yes. The COBOL Committee early on had all kinds of subsets and things of that kind which we tried to promulgate and kept changing.

MARCOTTY: Although we have still some more questions, we don't have more time. I'd like to thank Jean and Betty for a very enlightening hour and a half on COBOL.

FULL TEXT OF ALL QUESTIONS SUBMITTED*

STAN WHITLOCK

Where and when did CODASYL come from and how was it tied to COBOL?

Answer: See Section 2.1.3 and the Discussion transcript.

NANCY STERN

(1) Besides those already mentioned, who served on the Short-Range Committee?
(2) Also—the original May 28 meeting included 11 user/consultants in addition to government and computer manufacturers. Yet the Short-Range Committee included computer manufacturers and government reps only. Why no users on this committee?

Answer: (1) Original and/or eventual participation in the Short-Range Committee is shown in Figs. 1 and 6. However, less than half the people listed in either figure played a significant role. Some of the people listed just attended part of one meeting, and some of the original members listed for the Short-Range Committee did not really participate in any major way. For example, one changed companies and was not involved any further.
(2) I believe the government people were considered to be users. Also, I believe (although I am not sure) that it was thought that language design could and should be done primarily by the computer manufacturers who would have to implement the language, and they were supposed to look out for the interests of their users.

BRUCE GALLER

The ALGOL committee was made up of mostly academic people while the COBOL committee was made up mostly of government and business people. How did the operation of these committees differ in these respects? Maybe Joe Wegstein, who was on both committees, could comment on this.

Answer: See discussion transcript.

BERNIE GALLER

I have heard it said that the main initiative (or motivation) for calling the first meeting at the Pentagon was to help the smaller manufacturers head off IBM's expected dominance in the commercial language field. Can you comment on this?

Answer: As best I am able to determine, the motivation was that stated in Section 2.1.1 and 2.1.2. (Section 2.1.1 has been significantly changed from the preprint due to my having obtained further information.)

BRUCE WALKER

What happened to the medium-range and long-range committees?

Answer: The CODASYL Long-Range Committee was never created. I believe the In-

---

*·Jean Sammet has annotated the full set of questions and provided answers to several that were not asked at the session. Section headings and figures refer to the paper on pp. 199–243.

termediate-Range Committee became involved in Decision Tables and produced some work there. Also, I believe that it was transformed into, or spawned, two other groups— the Language Structure Group and the Systems Committee. The former produced the Information Algebra and the Systems group issued a number of excellent documents on data bases.

JACK VALE

COMTRAN was an early attempt to do commercial work (done partly by Tom Kasparian of IBM). Did COMTRAN influence COBOL design? How?

Answer: See Section 2.4.1 re design influence, and Section 2.1.1 re the project leadership of Goldfinger and Bemer.

DICK UTMAN

Sammet said she would comment further on the influence of the FACT language and she didn't. Would she?

Answer: See Sections 2.2.4, 2.4.2, and 2.4.3.

NANCY STERN

You mentioned several languages which influenced the development of COBOL. Did FORTRAN—despite its scientific nature—have any influence at all on the design of COBOL?

Answer: See the discussion transcript.

DAN McCRACKEN

Program readability was a commendable design goal, and ahead of its time. But how did it come about that the main emphasis was on readability by *managers,* instead of readability by programmers? Was there any evidence at the time that managers *wanted to read programs?*

Answer: See discussion transcript.

STEPHEN LANGDON

Did the participants in the original COBOL development sincerely believe that the use of an English-like language would enable nonprogrammers (e.g., managers) to understand programs, or did they hope that this claim would assist in the spread of computer use (which they all had an interest in)?

Answer: Yes. We sincerely believed managers would be able to understand the programs and that more people would find them easier to write.

JON J. SCHILD

Do you think anything will ever be done about COBOL's tendency to excessive verbosity?

Answer: It was a design objective to provide good readability, and an English-like language. This naturally leads to verbosity but I think the fundamental ideas were sound and I personally see no reason to change this concept.

ALLEN AMBLER

What is the history of the PICTURE concept?

Answer: It was introduced in the first *Commercial Translator* Manual (IBM, 1959).

BERNIE GALLER

I believe FORTRAN II was already available, with separately compiled subroutines. Why did COBOL require all procedures to be contained in the program? (This is not the same as inadequate library facilities.)

Answer: I don't remember.

ROGER MILLS

If the goal was to write in English, why did DEFINE provide for abbreviations?

Answer: See discussion transcript.

RICHARD MILLER

Why was DEFINE removed?

Answer: See Section 3.1.1, and also the discussion transcript answer to Roger Mills' question. I really think it was too far ahead of its time for most people to appreciate it.

PAUL ABRAHAMS

What thought was given to comments in COBOL? Why aren't they allowed in the Data Division!

Answer: The early COBOL had a NOTE verb which was specifically to allow comments in the PROCEDURE Division. I believe (but am not positive) that we considered allowing comments in the DATA Division and decided they were not needed. (See also the discussion transcript.)

MIKE SHAPIRO

In your paper you note that the 18-digit precision limit was chosen to put every candidate computer at a disadvantage. However, 18 digits fit nicely in 64 bits, binary or compressed decimal (3 digits = 10 bits). Was this ignored because it was presumed only binary coded decimal (pure or excess 3) or other decimal would be used? Were there other reasons how the "magic number" 18 derived?

Answer: See discussion transcript.

BOB ROSIN

Do you now have second thoughts about the conservative position with regard to character sets? Specifically, don't you now believe that we would all be using 128 characters in computer interaction if the CODASYL had required this in 1959? (Opinion—NOT to have adopted a large character set in fact forced us all to suffer for years.)

Answer: See discussion transcript. In addition, let me point out that for years no two identical ALGOL programs could necessarily be identified as being the same once they were transliterated into a machine-readable form. The major compatibility and readability objective of COBOL would have been severely damaged. In 1959 we were not smart enough to foresee the use of typewriters as a major input form! I feel very strongly about this issue, because the choice of character set affects the syntax very strongly, as is obvious from such dissimilar languages as COBOL, PL/I, and APL. In the latter case, see Iverson's oral presentation in which he comments on the effect on the design of APL from deciding to use a typewriter ball.

Roger Mills

Did the COBOL committee seriously believe that the users could not handle grade school operators of $+$, $-$, $\times$, $/$?

Answer: See discussion transcript.

Bryan Webb

How and why did the statement indentation (and numbering) scheme(s) come into being?

Answer: See the discussion transcript. We really wanted to make sure that a deck of cards for one compiler could be read and translated by another compiler, and for this a standard format was essential! Procedure names could be either alphanumeric, or pure numeric. I believe the latter was allowed to permit user sequencing if he chose.

Dan McCracken

In my mind, COBOL's main innovation was the separation of the data description from the procedure statements. Whose idea was this?

Answer: The basic idea came from FLOW-MATIC. See also the quote from Grace Hopper in Section 2.4, which could be interpreted as the genesis of this concept.

David Zook

Who originated the separate Data Division in FLOW-MATIC? Why was it done?

Answer: See the answer to Dan McCracken's question.

Richard Miller

(1) For the invitations to the initial Pentagon meeting, how was the invitations list made up? In particular was academic representation considered?

(2) Why did you not consider a library system?

(3) Do you feel that the Environment Division ideas to provide machine independence really work?

Answer: (1) See the discussion transcript and also Section 2.1.1 of the paper which has been significantly modified on this point from the preprint version.

(2) COBOL 60 did have primitive capabilities for a library system, but the details were left to the implementor. (See also the transcript of the talk.) In other words, we considered it but at too primitive a level.

(3) The Environment Division was *not* to provide machine independence. On the contrary, it was defined as requiring change from one computer to another. See the last paragraph of Section 3.3.

R. MORGAN MORRISON

(1) Why did the language design group decide to allow or require the writing of the contents of a loop to be written "OUT OF LINE" from the PERFORM verb that controlled the loop execution?

(2) When was the COMPUTE verb introduced into the language and was this verb a consequence of the early FORTRAN development?

(3) Can you account for the continuing growth of COBOL as an applications language?

Answer: (1) I believe we wanted to allow the flexibility of permitting the user to write code which could be used either in a loop (i.e., under control of the PERFORM) or else just executed a single time in a normal flow of control situation.

(2) See Sections 2.6 and 3.1.1

(3) The implementation by virtually all manufacturers (under early pressure from the Department of Defense) made it easily available, and competitive languages disappeared. The continued existence of CODASYL to provide needed language extensions, and the creation of the ANSI standards provided the necessary language stability with controlled improvements. By now the investment in training and programs is enormous, and COBOL is a useful language for its intended application area.

RICHARD MILLER

(1) Were those early specifications implementable?

(2) What effects do you feel that COBOL has had on language design?

(3) Who (and when) developed the PICTURE concept?

Answer: (1) Yes—see Section 2.3.4, which discusses the the early RCA and Remington-Rand Univac compilers.

(2) Most languages which have introduced the concept of data records (e.g., PL/I) have adopted the COBOL concepts, although in the computer science community they seldom give COBOL the credit. The metalanguage (as discussed in Section 3.2) has been used for defining some languages, although unfortunately computer scientists refer to it as BNF even though it is distinctly and substantively different.

(3) The PICTURE clause was introduced in the first Commercial Translator manual (IBM, 1959).

BRUCE GALLER

In the preprints article on COBOL it is stated twice "COBOL has far greater power and complexity than ALGOL 60." Could you be more explicit about this, please?

Answer: See discussion transcript.

BILL JONES

Why has COBOL continued to resist including a completely general statement compounding facility (like **begin end** in ALGOL)?

Answer: I don't know. You might also ask why other languges have continued to resist including some of the good ideas of COBOL.

N. D. PETERSON

Do you have any speculations as to the practicality of adding floating point and mathematical functions to a later version of COBOL.

Answer: Floating point (and I believe mathematical functions) has been added by one or more manufacturers to their implementations.

SAUL ROSEN

Considering the performance of the early COBOL compilers—with multihour compilations on the 501 for example—do you think that COBOL would have survived without the pressure applied by the Department of Defense in requiring COBOL on all machines?

Answer: See discussion transcript.

BERNIE GALLER

Why did the work of the Short-Range Committee last beyond "a year or two?"

Answer: Because the initial investments in compilers and training and in improving the language was so large no group seemed to want to try to provide a replacement.

JURIS REINFELDS

Would you agree that Business BASIC will replace COBOL as the most *widely* used data-processing language?

Answer: NO! I am not personally familiar with the details of Business BASIC, but I don't think COBOL will be replaced by *anything* as the most widely used data-processing language for the same reasons that FORTRAN cannot get replaced even by significantly new and better languages, or by simpler ones such as BASIC. There is too heavy an investment in programs and training for users to want to switch from COBOL.

HELEN GIGLEY

One of the stated objectives of COBOL was to be to "broaden the base of those who can state problems to computers." Do you feel this objective has been realized or has COBOL become another linguistic encoding of the same statement of problems that other languages offer?

Answer: Prior to PL/I, no other language (except the forerunners, or languages parallel in time, to COBOL) gave the user the capability of dealing with large data files with complex data structures. So I don't really believe that there are *other significant* languages which offer a "statement of problems" of the business data-processing type. Admittedly, as the problems themselves become more complex, the people who are going to state the solutions to those problems must also become more skilled and knowledgeable about their application, *and* about the programming language, *and* about the entire computer environment. Writing even something as relatively well understood as a payroll program is not something that can be done by "just anyone," regardless of the languages available.

ROGER MILLS

If COBOL is so hard to teach, how could it be easy to learn?

Answer: See discussion transcript.

KEN DICKEY

There are many myths about Grace Hopper's early connections with COBOL. Do you wish to clarify this relationship here?

Answer: Grace Hopper was one of the two technical advisors to the CODASYL Executive Committee (see Section 2.1.3). Several of the people who worked in the group she headed at Remington-Rand Univac were on the COBOL committee. The influence of FLOW-MATIC, which had been developed by her group, was major, since it was the only business data-processing high-level language in use prior to the start of COBOL. I believe it is fair to say that the influence of her work and her thoughts was high, but she did not have any direct participation on the Short-Range Committee itself.

PETER WEGNER

What lessons can be learned from the development of COBOL that are relevant to the development of DoD-1?

Answer: See discussion transcript.

AARON FINERMAN

COBOL has long had features that other languages are now starting to incorporate. Although it is somewhat verbose, it compensates by carrying a built in documentation with the program. Yet it continues to be viewed with great disdain, as is data processing in general, by many computing scientists. It is rarely taught in "prestigious" computer science departments, where it is still regarded as an abomination. Have you any comment?

Answer: See discussion transcript.

MIKE SHAPIRO

Why do you think academicians chose to ignore COBOL rather than accept it as a challenge?

Answer: Many have a snobbish attitude and feel it is beneath their dignity. See further comments on this point in discussion transcript answer to Aaron Finerman.

BIOGRAPHY OF JEAN E. SAMMET

From 1955 to 1958, Miss Sammet was the first group leader for programmers in the engineering organization of the Sperry Gyroscope company on Long Island.

She taught what were probably among the earliest computer courses given for academic credit. In 1956–1957, she organized and taught graduate courses entitled "Digital Computer Programming" and "Advanced Digital Computer Programming" in the Graduate Applied Mathematics Department at Adelphi College on Long Island. (By today's standards, those were very elementary courses in basic programming and coding, using UNIVAC and the 704.) During the second year she taught those courses (1957–1958) she used FORTRAN which had just been released.

In 1958, she joined Sylvania Electric Products in Needham, Massachusetts, as Section Head for MOBIDIC Programming. The primary task of the section was the preparation of the basic programming package for MOBIDIC (a large-scale computer of that time frame) under a contract to the Signal Corps as part of the Army FIELDATA program. She held that position at the time the COBOL effort started, and supervised the initial specification and design of the COBOL compiler on MOBIDIC.

Miss Sammet joined IBM in 1961 and has had several positions, including that of Programming Language Technology Manager. In 1979 she became Software Technology Manager in the Federal Systems Division.

Miss Sammet was President of the Association for Computing Machinery (1974–1976). She was elected to the National Academy of Engineering in 1977 and received an honorary Sc. D. from Mount Holyoke College in 1978.

VI

APT Session

Chairman: John Goodenough
Speaker: Douglas T. Ross

PAPER: ORIGINS OF THE APT LANGUAGE FOR AUTOMATICALLY PROGRAMMED TOOLS

Douglas T. Ross

SofTech, Inc.

1. Introduction

From The New Yorker:

> Cambridge, Mass., Feb. 25—
> The Air Force announced today that it has a machine that can receive instructions in English, figure out how to make whatever is wanted, and teach other machines how to make it.
> An Air Force general said it will enable the United States to "build a war machine that nobody would want to tackle."
> Today it made an ashtray.
> —*San Francisco Chronicle*
> . . . *In a sulk, probably.*

This quote from *The New Yorker* magazine of March 28, 1959, resulted from a newspaper article, from a wire service story, covering a press conference held at the Massachusetts Institute of Technology, February 25, 1959. (Souvenir aluminum ashtrays, milled in three dimensions by the first APT System, were indeed included in the press kit!) The press conference, jointly sponsored by the Aircraft Industries Association (AIA, now the Aerospace Industries Association), the Massachusetts Institute of Technology (MIT), and the Air Materiel Command (AMC) of the United States Air Force was attended by over 60 members of the technical and popular press and resulted in extensive coverage throughout the world for the next few months. The widespread attention which this event received was not misplaced, for it represented the true inauguration of the era of computer-aided manufacturing which still is in the process of vigorous evolution today, some two decades later.

Douglas T. Ross

The February 1959 press conference (MIT, 1959a) formally marked the completion of the opening phase of APT System development and roughly the midpoint of my own active involvement in the creation and determination of the basic structure of APT. APT stands for "Automatically Programmed Tools," and the APT language, in more elaborate form, is now an international standard for the programming of numerically controlled machine tools.

Although I have been almost overwhelmed by the amount of work involved, I am both honored and pleased with this opportunity to present a personal summary of those hectic and historic times. When first invited to prepare this paper, I envisioned a simple set of reminiscences which would be fun and easy to do. But when confronted with the almost 70 shelf feet of archival working papers, reports, and records which I have retained over the years, (two large file cabinets worth of which concern APT), I realized I was faced with a major undertaking. I have tried to minimize my personal opinion as much as possible by referring back to the original source documents which exist in such profusion. I hope I have done this in a way that is both entertaining and instructive.

I hope that I will not be accused of immodesty for writing this paper in the first person, but quite frankly I am not an impartial historical scholar and know of no other way than to provide this personalized account. I hope to share with you some of the excitement of discovery that comes from the detective work needed to place specific undated bits and pieces into what must have been the actual sequence—long since forgotton—as supported by evidence in the source material itself. I have been surprised many times by the evidence that discoveries and observations were made years earlier than I would have guessed or remembered, and I think these provide a useful and enlightening commentary on the historic roots of many concepts of computer science and language design which today are recognized as of central importance. I will try to point these out when they occur in the story.

1.1. An APT Theme for This Paper

There are many stories that could be written about APT. By its very nature and timing, APT simply had to be an exciting, dynamic, driving, multithreaded, and multifaceted brew of historic firsts—and it was. This means that any story of APT must be complex, for the historic truth of what happened from 1956 to 1960 was indeed complex. Conceptual, technical, technological, organizational, and political problems, each of which could form the basis for a historical paper, all were intertwined and all were influential on each other. Therefore, in order to treat the subject of APT *language* development as a separable component in a way that will provide some useful perspective from the present day, looking back in time, I have tried to select a theme which will allow us to see some pattern relevant to this one aspect, without doing violence to the validity of the historical record. I will try to state that theme briefly here and to refer back to it with fair regularity as my story unfolds, but I am sure that my effort will only be partially successful. So many nonlanguage topics must be treated in order to characterize the subjects and issues that are of thematic importance that I am sure that the theme itself will occasionally be swamped, shortly to resurface like an intrepid white-water canoeist.

My theme itself is a discovery, not an invention, and is a direct result of my many weeks of struggle through the mass of material available to me. Although 20 years had completely blanked it from my memory, I found that at the very beginning of the APT effort I had an extremely clear and "modern" view of both the nature and substance that the language should have well before any real substantive progress had been made. This surprised me. I was not, however, surprised at the many high and low points, that showed clearly in my reconstruction of the activities of building the initial APT system itself. Those parts I did recall, in flavor at least (although again many of the actual timings surprised me and intrigued me in my reconstruction efforts). But when I finally got to examining the first complete APT language presented in the Phase I *APT Part Programmer's Manual,* of early 1959 (Ross, 1959), I was struck by the observation that although the funny punctuation made the language somewhat stilted, nonetheless an amazing number of the original high-flown objectives for the language had in fact been achieved. Out of the white-water hurly-burly of those two years of hectic project activity had emerged a reasonably user-oriented, English-like language. Again, the canoeist is a valid analogy.

My attempt to understand this phenomenon—how with no valid precedents to go on and with the most chaotic possible working environment (with essentially no time for research, but only breakneck development) this desired end result came about—supplied my theme. When I asked myself *why* did the APT language turn out to be "English-like" and well-suited to the needs of its part-programmer users in spite of the fact that there was no theoretical basis for language design or implementation or management of large, dispersed, team programming efforts, I could see only one pattern which emerged from the historic record which I had reconstructed. That pattern, or theme, seems to have four primary premises. These premises, combined with the factual observation that our efforts were indeed successful, yield a conclusion which seems to explain the reason for that success. The four premises are:

1. The entire field of automatic programming for numerical control was brand new. Therefore, with respect to language design, *the semantics of the language had to come first* and the syntax of the language had to derive from the thinking or viewpoint engendered by technical ability to have a "systematized solution" to the general problem area.

2. For many pressing reasons, the project and the work to be done had to be broken into many pieces to be worked on by many people at different locations. This implied that even though there were no guidelines to go by, *some form of viable modularity had to be imposed on every aspect of the solution.* The system had to have a structure mirroring the structure of the systematized solution.

3. Lacking today's compiler-building technology, *both the syntactic (translation) and semantic (execution) processes had to be cohesive modular units within the system structure.*

4. In order to satisfy the requirements for the system and language as a whole, *both the syntactic and semantic aspects of both the language and the system had to be open-ended,* so that both the subject matter and the linguistic treatment of it could be extended as the underlying manufacturing technology evolved. In particular, the system had to be independent of geometric surface types, and had to be able to support any combination of machine tool and control system.

These four premises, which I will cite when they occur in the record and which were religiously observed from the beginning, combined with the fact that we were indeed able to get the job done, seemed to (and this is the theme) *supply the equivalent of a theoretical framework* matching almost feature for feature the current high-technology, theoretically founded approach to building advanced man–machine computer application systems. In other words, even though we stumbled frequently along the way, and at times created rather awkward and juvenile versions of what we now accept as required, nonetheless we did manage to get all of the essential pieces done in essentially the right way, in essentially the right places so that even today some twenty years later, the structure of both the language and the system are essentially the same and have been found to have stood the test of time well. In effect *we were forced by the nature of our problem and the necessity of our approach to it to anticipate much of the well-structured methodology* that from today's vantage point seems essential and almost inevitable. As we will see, however, the first time through, that inevitability was not quite so obvious!

1.2 An Overview

Before commencing on the story itself, I will present a brief overview of the rough chronology of times, places, people, and events to provide a bit of orientation. Much as different periods of development can be observed, after the fact, in the evolution of style in painters and artists, the beginnings of APT also break naturally into a number of overlapping but nonetheless distinctive *periods* during which the focus of attention highlighted first one and then another and then another aspect of the overall subject.

The *first major period* covers roughly September 1956 to January 1957, during which I and my green staff at MIT came up with the first overall formulation of the APT System concept and documented it in the *first Interim Report of the project* (Ross and Pople, 1956). We laid out a system structure distinguished by three styles of three-dimensional programming (by points, by space curves, and by regions) and a system structuring technique based upon the simulation of a *specialized APT computer* on a general-purpose computer. My coverage of this first period here is preceded by historical background with respect to numerical control and the MIT Milling Machine Project, as well as of my Computer Applications Group. Since some of the system and language design objectives which formed the starting point for my theme come from background working papers generated during the preparation of the Interim Report, a couple of side excursions set the tone of my thinking as the project actually got underway.

To me a very interesting pair of discoveries which I never would have guessed if I had not found the evidence in my papers, is the fact that my concepts of *plex* programming via "reversed index registers" (and the modern equivalents of beads, records, controlled storage classes, and abstract data types) as well as the essential difference between "input" and "control" of my 1970s formulation of plex ideas in the form of *Structured Analysis* both were recognized as important and documented by me way back then in the fall of 1956. These are among the events that form the source for that first Interim Report formulation of APT.

The *second period* concerns our initial activities in conjunction with the Aircraft Industries Association—a trade association of all of the major companies involved in any way with aircraft manufacturing. We first made contact with them early in 1957 and the second period stems from their interest in having MIT put on a *Special Course covering all aspects of numerical control*. Their interest stemmed from the fact that a major Air Force "buy" of $30 million (yes! 1957 dollars!) worth of numerically controlled machine tools was scheduled to start, with installations in many of their plants beginning in the summer of 1957. The companies had to figure out how to put them into productive use. Although there was as yet no APT language, I present here my lecture about language design for numerical control from that course, for it also forms a cornerstone in my thinking about APT language before it actually existed.

Our APT research progress showed the greatest promise for meeting the needs of the aircraft industry in time to be of use, so that the *third period* covers the AIA decision to form the APT Joint Effort. This began with a *kickoff meeting at MIT the week of May 20, 1957,* which launched the world's first major cooperative programming venture, combining government, university, and industry, with the Air Force sponsoring MIT leadership of a 14-company team effort.

Still there was no APT language. The *fourth period* which I consider took place primarily on two days of a weekend (May 25, 26, 1957), followed by spot efforts over the next two weeks as I generated the *first memorandum defining the initial APT language* (Ross, 1957c), intended merely as a starting point and designed primarily to permit the simplest possible translation approach. The memo is brief and historically interesting so I present it here in its entirety.

The *fifth period* concerns most the *structuring of the APT System and the stages of evolution* of how to treat the input translation, instruction preprocessing, and definition preprocessing portions of that system which in modern terms constitute the lexical analysis and parsing of APT language expressions. Although I don't go into detail here, I try to indicate a bit of the struggle that led to modular program structuring which from there on served the same role as the modern high-technology approach to compiler construction. I also cover progress in the computational aspects of the geometric semantics of the language which led to the first paring down of expectations to a Field Trial system appropriate for testing.

The *sixth period* concerns the *construction of the Field Trial APT language,* with side excursions into the preparation of the first two major papers describing APT, one presented at the Third Annual Contour Machining Conference (Ross, 1957d), and the other at an ACM session of the American Association for the Advancement of Science (AAAS) (Ross, 1957f). Extracts from these papers once again provide a concise expression of the kind of thinking that lay behind the day-to-day work.

The Field Trial distribution marked the end of MIT's official coordination of the APT Joint Effort, which from then on passed into the hands of a succession of leaders from industry. The transition was not easy, however, and difficulties continued to plague the project so that the *seventh period* centers around a *"Post-Coordinator's Report"* in the fall of 1958 (Ross, 1958f) which draws together many of the syntactic and semantic problem areas and supplies solutions which completed the specifications for the Phase I APT system—the first really complete APT system and language, which is the ending point for this historic analysis.

The *eighth period* covers the actual *Part Programmer's Manual of the Phase I APT language,* citing how its features evolved from the initial and Field Trial formulations, through the evolutionary stages cited in the papers, into the first complete formulation. I also point out how the concomitant evolution of the syntactic and semantic processing, as covered in the Project Report and Coordinator Report descriptions, made possible the various language features, and cite how they match with many of the original high-blown objectives of the first Interim Report and the Special Numerical Control Course of the spring of 1957.

The *ninth period* covers the public presentation of these almost-working results in the *February 25, 1959 Press Conference at MIT,* and I also briefly outline some of the syntactic and semantic language features which purposely were left out of Phase I but which later came into subsequent phases of APT evolution, in several cases anticipating powerful language features (such as macros and phrase substitution) found in today's high level languages.

APT has undergone continuous evolution and extension from the beginning up to the present day and therefore I make no effort to extrapolate or to provide a tutorial summary of modern-day numerical control programming, computer graphics, and computer-aided design—all of which are part of the same evolutionary development. But I hope that my efforts to present an organized analysis of these early developments will be found to support the theme which I discovered threaded through the historic record—that because we were forced to be modular and open-ended, in a very difficult and brand new appplication area, the fact that we succeeded ensured that the resulting system and language were "modern" by today's standards, even though done some twenty years ago.

1.3 Generality in Specialty

The fact that APT was the first and most widely used of the special purpose application-oriented languages counts for something. But more importantly, it seems that APT is particularly apt as a subject for study in the history of programming languages. Being a language for a specialized area—automatic programming of numerically controlled machine tools—might appear to make it *in*appropriate, because it would appear to lack generality. But it turns out that, because the application area was brand new and never before had been attacked in any way at all, the study of the origins of the APT language necessarily involves much greater attention to semantics than is the case with respect to more general-purpose languages which obtained most of their background ready-made from the fields of mathematics and logic. There is no way to separate the origins of the APT language from the origins of numerical control itself, and of the community of users of numerical control. More so than for any other historic language, APT requires a complete consideration of every aspect of relevance to language design.

This perhaps surprising generality of interest in a specialized language is further bolstered by the fact that, because it involved so many firsts, including the first introduction of the use of computers in large segments of the manufacturing industry, we were forced at the time to be very explicit about our thoughts, objectives, and motivations in designing the APT language and APT system, in terms addressed directly to the intended users. Thus, among my many source documents are specific writings concerned with the very subject of the motivations behind the design of the APT language. It is not necessary to speculate at all about what was in my mind twenty years ago, for we can find it expressed directly on paper, written at that time. To me, this has been one of the most interesting discovery aspects, for it shows that we were very much aware of what we were doing and that we expressed ourselves in surprisingly "modern" terms. I will present verbatim extracts at appropriate points in my story and let the modern reader be the judge.

1.4 Source Material

As to my source material itself, it is held together and (meta-)commented on in an ongoing, continuing fashion by an extensive series of "daily resumes" (Ross, 1956b–1963), which were a form of professional diary which I kept with surprisingly complete regularity from

October 30, 1956, through May 20, 1959,
December 15, 1959, through March 10, 1960,
December 4, 1961, through October 2, 1962,
February 1, 1963, through November 29, 1963,

finishing with a few bits and pieces in connection with the IFIP Congress in 1965. Every day or so, and often periodically during the day, I would merely grab my dictating machine and say whom I had met with about what, or what I had read that had interested me, what trips I had taken, etc., and, in general, what I was thinking about. I started this practice initially shortly after the beginning of the APT Project at MIT when it became apparent to me that I could not keep all my activities straight without some help. I decided that the time of my secretary in transcribing these daily resume notes would be well invested in allowing me to know what was going on. This blow-by-blow description—all 833 pages of it—is, of course, invaluable reference material for historic reconstruction.

In addition to the resumes, my files contain the expected correspondence and reports, extensive technical memoranda series, trip reports, notes, and meeting handouts, as well as many clumps of actual original working papers and working drafts which led to published material, sample computer runs, and the like. At the time, the MIT Servomechanisms Laboratory supplied us with pads of unlined yellow paper (yellow since it was nonreproducible by the Ozalid process and much of our work was classified). In my group we attempted to retain working papers for continual back-checking, and we said, "Find it fast in the Yellow Pages." Only a few of them have survived, but those that have are interesting indeed.

To provide concise reference to these materials in my files (which ultimately will reside in the MIT Archives) I have used the following condensed notation: [R56123] means "resumes 1956 December 3"; [C570123] means "correspondence 1957 January 23"; [N57223, p4] means "page 4 of working paper notes 1957 February 23," etc., and [p3] means "page 3 of the most recently cited reference," etc.

2. Background

Because of the importance of the pragmatic and semantic components of APT language design, it is appropriate to begin with a brief overview history of the events before, during, and after the time period (from the fall of 1956 through the spring of 1959) actually covered by the story of this paper. I will interweave a bit of my own history and that of my Computer Applications Group at MIT with that of numerical control itself in order to lay the proper foundation for the personalized account which follows.

I came to MIT in the fall of 1951 as a Teaching Assistant in the Mathematics Department, following my completion of an Honors Degree in Mathematics at Oberlin College in June. I started in the Servomechanisms Laboratory (now the Electronic Systems Laboratory) with a summer job in June 1952 and stayed with the lab until departing to form SofTech in July 1969. As is evidenced most accessibly by the excellent article (Pease, 1952) in the September 1952 issue of *Scientific American,* 1952 also was the year of completion of the first phase of the introduction of numerical control to the world, with the operation of the MIT numerically controlled milling machine at Servo Lab (MIT, 1952).

As is described more completely elsewhere (Ward, 1968), the development of numerical control, proper, began with a proposal by John T. Parsons of the Parsons Corporation,

Douglas T. Ross

Traverse City, Michigan to the United States Air Force that punched tape and servomechanism control be applied to a milling machine to produce automatically the templates required in the production of helicopter rotor blades. Parsons received a contract from the Air Force in July 1949, and subcontracted the control work to the Servomechanisms Laboratory in 1949. In February 1951 the Air Force contract was switched directly to Servo Lab which was to receive continuing sponsorship for numerical control hardware, software, and adaptive control, followed by computer-aided design, computer graphics hardware and software, and software engineering and software technology, for almost 20 years.

My entry to Servo Lab was in 1952 in the field of airborne fire control system evaluation and power density spectra analyses. (I later completed a Masters Thesis on Improved Computational Techniques for Fourier Transformation (1954) as well as all course requirements for the Ph.D. in pure mathematics by taking courses throughout this period as a part-time student. I never completed the doctorate program, since qualifying examinations would have covered material in pure mathematics that I had not studied for years and there was, of course, no computer science doctorate program at that time.) The MIT Digital Computer Laboratory with its Whirlwind I computer (Everett, 1951) had recently spun off from Servo Lab and I taught myself to program it in the summer of 1952, completing my fall teaching schedule while also taking a full course load and being a full-time staff member at Servo Lab.

From the fall of 1952 and for the next seven years I was heavily involved in the application of a new form of air mass ballistic tables to the evaluation of airborne fire-control systems, especially for the B-58 bomber. A series of projects eventually involved the installation of manual intervention and Charactron display tube equipment on the ERA 1103 Computer (precursor to the UNIVAC 1100 series of computers) at Eglin Air Force Base in Florida. This work, which preceded and heavily overlapped with the early APT developments, had a very strong influence on my approach to the numerical control programming and calculation problem. The problems were of similar complexity and involved the same style of "systematized solution" using three-dimensional vector calculations, intermixing a heavy use of logical decisions with simple approximating calculations in a complex network modeling the reality of the situation (Ross and McAvinn, 1958). This also was the source of the foundations of my plex philosophy and approach to general problem modeling and solution.

In the four years from the summer of 1952 to the summer of 1956, I was involved in a broad range of small and large projects. I and my small group of programmers had developed a Mistake Diagnosis Routine for interpretive checking of arbitrary programs, and various program debugging and preparation aids. We commissioned programmers of the Digital Computer Laboratory to prepare a symbolic assembly system for preparing ERA 1103 computer programs on Whirlwind, as well as a "director tape" program for Whirlwind, which probably was the first JCL-driven operating system. We were the first to use the then-classified manual intervention and multiple scope equipment (developed for the Air Defense System) for general interactive man–machine problem solving. I wrote the first two-dimensional freehand, graphic input program (1954) starting computer graphics, and we installed the first interactive on-line typewriter keyboard (1955). All of these features including automatic logging and playback of manual actions were included in the Servo Lab Utility Routine Program (SLURP) System (Ross, 1958b), including a system called "Group Control" (MIT, 1959b, Vol. VII) for automatic paging between core memory and drum storage to allow large programs to operate in limited memory.

Many of these activities were simultaneously underway in the summer of 1956, including a multiorganization "Pre-B-58 Project" (MIT, 1958b) for the evaluation of the tail turret of the B-58 airplane, with programmers under my direction in St. Louis, Eglin, and MIT shuttling back and forth developing both hardware and software for Whirlwind and the ERA 1103. A number of the important concepts behind this work were summarized in my first professional paper on Gestalt programming, presented that spring at the 1956 Western Joint Computer Conference in California (Ross, 1956a). I set aside an example of push-button control of (pre-Sputnik) satellite launching, and instead illustrated that paper with an example of control of an automatic factory—appropriately enough for APT.

2.1 The MIT Milling Machine Project

While these many activities were forming the background of myself and my programming group, the MIT Numerical Control Project was also progressing full steam on several other parallel paths from 1952 to 1956. Through numerous contacts with machine tool builders and aircraft companies, large numbers of test parts were produced on the milling machine and were studied for economic impact. Many parts were programmed entirely by hand, but throughout this period John Runyon developed a comprehensive subroutine library on Whirlwind (Runyon, 1953) for performing many of the necessary calculations and automatically producing the coded instructions for the punched paper machine tool control tape. Many parts were produced by a combination of manual and subroutine means. Improvements also were made to the hardware of the control system and machine tool director during this period, along with documented economic studies and much educational documentation and promotional material.

In 1953 the primary sponsorship support for the engineering-based milling machine project switched from the Air Force to the Giddings and Lewis Machine Tool Co. which sponsored the development of a new production tool director on a commercial basis. During this period, the Air Force–sponsored economic studies were completed (Gregory and Atwater, 1956) and the Air Force–sponsored engineering project commissioned the development, by Arnold Siegel of the Digital Computer Laboratory, of the first automatic programming language and system for higher-level language preparation of machine tool control tapes. Arnie did a wonderfully elegant prototype demonstration system for two-dimensional parts consisting of straight lines and circles called for respectively by symbolic names beginning with *S* or *C* and with mnemonic punctuation for indicating near and far intersection points and controlling the tool motion on the right or left side of the specified curve, see Figure 4 (later). The resulting MIT report and *Control Engineering* article (Siegel, 1956a, b) stimulated a great deal of interest.

Based upon this success and that of the Runyon subroutine library, the engineering project submitted a proposal to the Air Force that numerical control work be continued at MIT with a concentration on automatic programming rather than further engineering. Then in 1955 the entire engineering project staff (except for Alfred Susskind, who remained at MIT for teaching and research) left the Laboratory to form Concord Controls, Inc., with Giddings and Lewis backing, to manufacture the Numericord director system on a commercial basis (MIT, 1956).

Douglas T. Ross

2.2 The Computer Applications Group

The Air Force accepted the Servo Lab proposal. Beginning in June of 1956 the laboratory was under contract to inaugurate a new program in numerical control, this time emphasizing automatic programming for three-dimensional parts to be produced by three- and five-axis machine tool director systems. Naturally enough, this work was assigned to my group. In recognition of the many projects which we already were serving in addition to the milling machine project, we were commissioned as the Computer Applications Group at that time. Since I was understaffed for the work already underway, an entire new recruiting effort was immediately instituted. John Ward, then Executive Officer of the Laboratory was acting Project Engineer, but technical responsibility fell to me.

Late in the summer we hired our first programmer trainee, Jerome Wenker, but actual work on the project was forced to wait until the arrival in September of three new Research Assistants with engineering backgrounds. They were Samuel M. Matsa, Harry E. Pople, Jr., and George Zames. Thus the revitalized milling machine project got underway in September 1956, three months late, with everybody including myself completely inexperienced in numerical control and, except for me, also inexperienced in either programming or language design. Furthermore, the contract called for quarterly Interim Engineering Reports, the first of which was to report on our progress from the start of the contract through September 30! Hardly an auspicious beginning for so ambitious an undertaking, especially since the Pre-B-58 Project was beginning to encounter the first of a long series of great technical difficulties, so that that project forms the bulk of my daily resumes for many months to come. We were all bright, eager, and hardworking, however, and set to work immediately with enlightened if somewhat naive vigor.

3. Period 1: Initial APT Formulation (September 1956 through January 1957)

3.1 Changes from the Siegel System

My date stamp on my own copy of Arnie Siegel's MIT report reads "September 28, 1956." Arnie was a good friend, and I'm sure I met several times with him to go over his programs and gather his thoughts on how we ought to proceed. His system was based upon a simple character-driven Input Translation Program like those used elsewhere in the symbolic assemblers that had been written at the Computer Lab. The translator then selected from a library of closed subroutines which analytically computed the required intersections of straight lines and circles and employed the same calculations as Runyon's cutter center offset routines and punched-tape code generation (recorded on magnetic tape for offline punching). His system also produced meaningful error diagnostics and was elegant and easy to use.

I saw immediately that although the input and output portions of the Siegel system could be extended, the language and calculating methods would have to be completely different, for in order to handle arbitrary three-dimensional shapes the calculation of curves and endpoints by closed-form solutions would be impossible. Furthermore, the "automatic programming language" (it was still several months before the term "part programming language" was introduced in APT, probably by Boeing) would have to be considerably more elaborate than that used in Arnie's little prototype. I was familiar with parametric methods, having completed a course in differential geometry as part of my mathematics training, but planes, spheres, cones, cylinders, and quadric surfaces were the primary building-block shapes which had occurred in the parts that had been programmed thus far. Airfoil sections and smooth faired surfaces described by arbitrary meshes of points in space were also handled by special Whirlwind routines (Bromfield, 1956). Therefore, the more natural approach seemed to be to describe the three-dimensional motion of a cutter through space by means of a space curve resulting from the intersection between two three-dimensional surfaces.

From the extensive use of vector methods in the fire control system evaluation work, and from the natural match between a rectilinear coordinate system for calculation and the rectilinear control directions of the machine tool, it was quite natural to base all considerations on a three-dimensional vector approach. As I recall, Arnie was mildly disappointed to find that such major surgery would be required on the framework of his prototype system, but he agreed that, especially since the closed-form mathematical solutions were impossible, the changes were necessary. Unfortunately, except for these few startup contacts, Arnie had no involvement with our project except for helping with the course the following spring (Section 4), and the Kick-Off Meeting (Section 5.3).

In any case, the earliest written record about APT that I find in my files is a letter [C561010] from me to Joseph Albert, then an engineer in the Manufacturing Research Department of Lockheed Aircraft Corporation, Marietta, Georgia, in reply to his October 4 letter to the Lab Director, Professor J. F. Reintjes, inquiring about our use of Whirlwind for preparing tapes for our milling machine. After referring him to the relevant reports (including Arnie's, but suggesting that Runyon's report "would be of the most immediate interest to you") I then describe our new method "which is now in its infancy [and] is restricted to the case of planes and spheres, although a direct extension to include cones, cylinders, surfaces of revolution, and quadratic [sic, not the correct "quadric"] surfaces is planned. A report describing this work is scheduled for publication."—So we were well underway.

3.2 Project Start-Up

The yellow-page draft Interim Report material appears to start with some notes spoken into the dictaphone [N569?] in the process of a kickoff meeting of some sort, probably in late September 1956. The notes mention starting off with only planes and spheres, using them to both define curves and program with regions, and also include the ideas of directed distance and normal vectors "to get somebody's surface in" [p1]:

> We will put in only as much vocabulary into the language as we presently need to motivate the study and make it workable for ourselves. The making of this thing into a really useful system, since we have limited manpower, we would like to have assistance from other people in establishing a vocabulary for the language, in other words, which particular surfaces are to be used or how surfaces are to be specified in particular. . . . Now here is a problem—How do you work out a way of talking about a part in terms of regions?—What are the necessary things are not self-explanatory and that's where we will be working [p2]. . . .
>
> First of all we want to establish that the problem is one of language. Then, what kind of language? Well, we want our language to be just between the man and his problem, independent of

the particular machine tool that is going to be used but, . . . we do have to compromise some-what on this ideal language. In other words, our language will be influenced by the particular tool and by the particular computers to some extent, but our goal is to have it as nearly independent of these quantities as possible . . . [p3].

Certainly not written or dictated English, but it is a record of our early thinking and of the beginning of the APT language. This establishes premise number 4 of my theme (Section 1.1).

3.3 System Structure and Semantics

Evidently starting from this initial group meeting, sometime in September or October, I prepared four pages, single spaced, of typewritten outline with corrections in ink [N5610?] starting out:

I. Introduction

We now give breakdown of problem into major areas as reference for all future reports and work . . .

The contents verify that from the beginning I had the view that the (as yet unnamed) APT system would be modeled on the structure of a computer, with an *input translation program* preparing pseudo instructions to be interpreted by a *control element program* which in turn would select the modes of behavior of an *arithmetic element program* producing a sequence of cut vectors to be output in the language of a chosen machine tool and machine tool director system. The arithmetic element program (or ARELEM, as it is now known) calculates cut vectors just as an ordinary computer calculates numbers as answers. These yellow-page outline notes are of historic interest because they document the evolution of terminology to that still in use in APT today. The section [p1] entitled "II. *Progress*" reads as follows:

Have chosen to work on PD [part description] of simulated computer first because all other parts hinge on its form.
Method of Part Description: At Computer Level: by point moving in some pattern over the sur-face of the part, i.e., view as point cutter. Viewed as point moving in steps by sequence of straight line *cut vectors,* but need not imply that actual cutter will use linear interpolation. This view merely gives discrete points on the surface and space between points may be treated in many ways depending on particular director used. Point by point calculation is required for digital treat-ment of problem. The sequence of cut vectors are [sic] made to approximate an *elementary seg-ment* of a *determined curve,* defined as follows:
The point cutter is to move on some *determining surface* but staying [p2] in the *driving plane.*
The intersection of the driving plane and the determining surface is the determined curve. The elementary segment of the determined curve is determined by the intersection of the determined curve with the *check surface,* the end point being called an *intersection point.*
Thus an elementary segment is defined by a DP, a DS and two CS's., as the section of the deter-mined curve between the two intersection points.

After a few more lines about the simulated computer, we find [p2]

Operation Code—the operations which the simulated computer can do. For present, simplified case

    DS =
    DP =
    CS =
    GO!
    Tolerance =
    END

A very interesting point is that this paper has black ink pen corrections which include changing the first two instructions to "PS =" and "DS =" and these corrections are carried through the rest of the pages. This shows that the current APT system and APT language terminology of *part surface, drive surface,* and *check surface,* see Fig. 1, resulted in this fashion as an improvement over the original idea sometime on or before November 2, 1956 (for which my resume says, "The introductory part of the milling machine report now seems to be in fairly good shape. Progress on the body of the report is up to the equations for part surface = sphere" [R56112], so that the term "part surface" was established by then).

The remainder of the outline [N5610?] contains no further language features except for a discussion of

> ways to automatically determine which direction to take when there exists two possibilities. . . . Decided to use just $K1 \cdot K2 > 0$ to define "forward" and have "go forward!" plus "go reverse!" modes of "GO!." [If the dot product is zero] then forward = right if think of standing on K1 with head in direction of N1 and look in direction of K1. This is easy to remember and can be used to treat arbitrarily complex parts. [p3, 4]

The meaning of forward, right, and left being based upon orientation with respect to the surface normal still is true of APT language, but later underwent several versions of implementation after this initial definition, as we will see. In any case, the outline pages show that although the problem was averred to be one primarily of language, it is clear that we approached the problem from the *semantics* of that language, not its syntax, from the beginning. This establishes premise number 1, of my theme (Section 1.1).

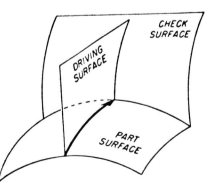

Fig. 1. Space curve determined by surfaces.

3.4 Generalized ARELEM

The heart of APT semantics is the Arithmetic Element program, ARELEM. We did not stay very long with the very simple plane-and-sphere case. The November 9 resume states

Jerry Wenker started thinking about a general design for part description. It involves an iterative technique for using normals to surfaces as well as programs for directed distance to surfaces to handle arbitrary situations. I talked with him about this and we developed several improvements on the technique and I pointed out that it was very similar to what we were now doing in the [Pre-B-58] evaluation program . . . [R56119].

This is an important date for it marks the beginning of ARELEM developments that were not to receive really satisfactory resolution until our Second-Order MIT ARELEM was finally developed in 1961—well after the end of the story I tell here. But by November 19, I "wrote section on the new elementary calculation for milling machine report" [R561119], so by this date we knew the complete structure of the intended new system.

3.5 Glimmerings of Plex

Two weeks later "most of the day was spent in milling machine conference considering primarily the use of index registers. The results are summarized in Milling Machine Conference Number 1" [R561129, 30]. When I first saw that in the resume, I made the side note "I don't know whether those notes are still available. I wonder if even this early I had the idea of 'reverse index registers' or Plex programming (Ross, 1961). If so, it predates my even hearing of McCarthy's LISP system (in 1959)" (Ross, 1977b). This note was written in October 1977 before discovering that I did indeed still have the yellow-page minutes of that conference with my crew, from which the following extract is pertinent (Ross, 1956c):

It is desirable to be able to program by areas instead of by curves as we now do. This we feel may be accomplished by allowing an arbitrary number of *surface registers,* i.e., the locations for part surfaces, check surfaces, and driving surfaces. The motion over the surface of a part, whether by zig-zag or by spiral motion, will be called facing. The use of many surface registers allows a facing to have an arbitrary boundary [p1] and contain an arbitrary number of intermediate part surfaces. In order to have compact representations of complicated facing motions, we need to have indexing capabilities.

Indexing may be done on many levels and in many ways. The quantities which may be indexed are program addresses, data addresses, or data. When an instruction is tagged for indexing it is tagged whether the index is to be modified or not modified before the indexing operation, and modification always applies a check against an associated criterion. The instruction is also tagged whether the check with the criterion should cycle, terminate, or start. If cycled, then the index is reset and the instruction remains active. If terminate, the index is not reset and that instruction is ignored until the index is reset by some other means. If start, the instruction is not executed until the criterion is reached.

All indexable quantities (which are all quantities) have stored with them an increment in their appropriate units. . . . [p2]

The notes go on to describe the grouping of surface data together for such accessing so it does seem that what later was to become the "*n*-component element" and "bead" programming with pointers of AED (Ross *et al.*, 1970), "records" (Wirth and Hoare, 1966) and "abstract data types" in other languages (Liskov *et al.*, 1978), and even the "controlled storage classes'' of PL/I (ANSI, 1976) were recognized by us as useful in 1956. In fact, the incorporation of the logical control information in a complete cross reference network for problem solution (which is further born out by the subsequent four sides of yellow-page working papers [N56121, 2] which I generated on December 1 and 2, 1956, over the weekend, leading to a "new method of language and driving surface derivation" [R56123]) is still my understanding of how the "guarded commands" of Dijkstra (1975) should be thought of and used. Thus twenty years is both a long time and a short time in the history of programming.

3.6 Language Intentions

While these semantic-oriented ARELEM developments were going on, work on the Interim Report continued. In a November 7, 8 visit, our Air Force contract monitor, Bill Webster, requested that the Interim Report "should be as up to date as possible and not terminate at the September 30 date. This will entail an appreciable amount of additional writing" [R56119]. I have a yellow-page handwritten pencil draft [N561215, 16] written over the weekend on December 15 and 16, 1956 addressed specially to the "point of view of language being the most important item and the system reflects the structure of the language" [R561214+17]. The draft itself was never used, but for our purposes here, of understanding the state of mind with regard to language design at that time, a few exerpts are illuminating.

> The objective is to instruct the machine tool to perform some specific operation, so that sentences similar to the imperative sentence form of English are required. . . . Declarative statements are also necessary. Examples of declarative sentences used to program a numerically controlled machine tool might then be of the form:
>
> > "Sphere No. 1 has center at (1, 2, 3) and radius 4"
> > "Airfoil No. 5 is given by equation . . . "
> > "Surface No. 16 is a third order fairing of surface 4 into surface 7 with boundaries . . . "
>
> An imperative sentence might have the form:
>
> > "Cut the region of Sphere No. 1 bounded by planes 1, 2, and 3 by a clockwise spiral cut to a tolerance of 0.005 inch."
>
> These sample sentences, although written here in full English text for clarity, are indeed representative of the type of language toward which the present study is aimed" [N561215, 16, p2].

The draft continues to discuss the vocabulary and "*syntactical rules* for combining words to express and communicate ideas. In general terms, the syntactical rules determine the *structure* of the language, while the vocabulary determines the *substance* of the language [p3]. . . . All of the elements of syntactical structure and each word in the vocabulary of the language must be matched by an appropriate computer program. Therefore the structure and substance of the language influence directly the system of computer programs" [p4]. This establishes premise number 3 of my theme (Section 1.1).

3.7. The Name "APT" and Glimmerings of Structured Analysis

The last portion of this December 15, 16 draft shows that it was at this time that I first came up with the acronym "APT." The pages I have end with *"The APT System Concept",* as follows:

Douglas T. Ross

The preceding sections have introduced the basic approach to the problem of programming of machine tools, from an abstract and ideal point of view. It was mentioned above that the ideal language must be modified in practice to suit the particular machine to a computer, as well as to suit the human and his problem. A very instructive and helpful visualization of these influences may be gained by considering the practical problem from a system point of view. The general structure of an *A*utomatic system for the *P*rogramming of machine *T*ools (abbreviated APT system) is shown in Fig. 1. The "variable parameters" for APT system design are shown as vertical inputs to the principal system components—the human and the computer [N561215, 16, pp5, 6].

Thus was the APT system christened, although in the final December 27 [R561227] rewriting of the report I say " . . . called APT systems (an abbreviation of *A*utomatically *P*rogrammed *T*ool systems)" (Ross and Pople, 1956, p. 4) which holds to this day.

I actually do not have the original "Fig. 1," but instead have the new figure (shown here as Fig. 2) which was used in the final Interim Report [p5] and elsewhere. I do, however, have a yellow typed page, with carbon [R5612?], which talks about the original Fig. 1 and which I clearly wrote in the intervening ten days. It is of interest in its own right because it shows that the "variable parameters" of the original Fig. 1 (which was closely related to

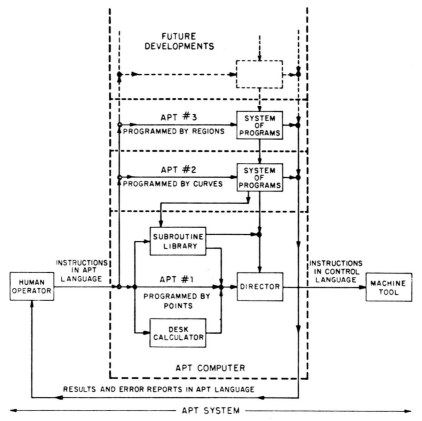

Fig. 2. The APT system concept.

Fig. 2) were in fact the all-important "control" of my latest creation—Structured Analysis (circa 1973) (Ross, 1977a).

> The characteristics of any particular APT system will depend upon the vertical "inputs" shown —the experience, design practice, and APT system capabilities which influence the human, and the various programs which control the computer. Conversely the development of a particular system with certain prescribed characteristics is centered in the study or design of these "inputs." Thus, the overall task can be broken into convenient sections by considering each of these "inputs" as a separate problem. The solution of any of these problems will of course be influenced by the interdependence imposed by the overall system [R5612?].

This establishes premise number 2 of my theme (Section 1.1), so all four premises were, as I said, observed from the beginning.

The historically interesting fact is that I clearly understood that there was a profound difference between "inputs" (without quotes) and " 'inputs' " (with quotes), including their vertical placement, and that they led to hierarchic modular design. The December 14 resume says, "Spent all day hashing over the Milling Machine Report trying a number of new introductory sections. A number of good ideas were brought up but were too difficult to whip into shape, such things as a hierarchy of programmable systems, etc." [R561214]. This was immediately preceding my preparation of the above-mentioned handwritten draft [N561215, 16], that weekend.

Although I have stated in my writings about Structured Analysis that it had its roots in my early plex thinking, I have attributed the four-sided box notation (with its *input, control, output,* and *mechanism* meanings for the four sides) to the "cell-modeling" notation of Shizuo Hori (Hori, 1972) [who headed the APT Long Range Program follow-on to our early work for many years (Dobe, 1969)]. Although I am sure that neither Shiz nor I were aware of it, it might be that he was influenced by my Fig. 2 and the way I talked about APT, for I did indeed talk with him during his own early developments of his ideas. But in any case it is clear why in the 1970s I found the four-sided box notation so attractive and so natural as an expressive medium for my own plex notions when I came to formalize them as Structured Analysis. I have always claimed that all of my work merely tries to solve the same philosophical problem in working form—the problem of *plex* (Ross, 1961, 1975)—which really started to form in my mind in the early nineteen fifties and was quite important in my thinking during this formative APT period.

So by the end of December 1956, the name, nature of language, method of semantic calculation and the general system structure of APT was available. In the report we even said

> The above sequence [of APT systems programmed by points, curves, and regions] has not been terminated since there is not necessarily an end to the growth potential of the APT computer. Conceivably it can grow until all design and analysis for machined parts is included in the automatic programming system, and the APT computer is programmed simply by describing the function which a machined part is to perform (Ross and Pople, 1956, p. 4).

—a clear call for what later became computer-aided design (Ross, 1960; Coons and Mann, 1960). APT I, programmed by points, never existed, but at MIT we did proceed to make both APT II, programmed by space curves, and APT III, programmed by surface regions, on the Whirlwind I computer (Ward, 1960), see Fig. 2.

Douglas T. Ross

4. Period 2: Special N/C Course for The AIA (December 1956 through April 1957)

The publication of the first Interim Report marks the end of the first, primarily background, phase of APT language development. The next phase, our first contact with the Subcommittee for Numerical Control (SNC) of the AIA, overlapped and coincided, for the Interim Report came back from the printer while Don Clements and I were in Dallas meeting with the AIA, January 21–25, 1957 [R570121-25, p3]. (On December 6, Don Clements had been appointed Project Engineer [R56126]. He had been working on other projects in the laboratory previously.) On November 7 and 8, Bill Webster, the Air Force Contact Monitor, and his boss Colonel Dick visited with us and Bill suggested that we contact Bernard Gaiennie of Northrop, Los Angeles, Chairman of the Subcommittee for Numerical Control of the Aircraft Industries Association, and also that we should get in touch with Kenneth Wood of Boeing, Seattle, to ask him about a report on Boeing preparations for numerical control [R56117, 8]. Numerous phone calls, letters, and meetings at MIT document not only our going to the Dallas meeting, but also AIA's request that MIT present a Special Course on Numerical Control [R56124].

During the Dallas AIA meeting, my resume says, "Frank Reintjes [Servo Lab Director] called Vic Benetar of Lockheed there in Dallas and informed them that we were now considering giving a one week course at the end of March during vacation. Frank feels that he should pick up the ball as far as organizing the course and that with a one week thing we should be able to handle it all right" [R570121-25, p2]. There follow some other items concerning the content of the course and how it would be funded, but these are only of interest to historians of numerical control as such. The course itself did indeed take place with fancy printed brochure, tuition of $275.00, etc., from Monday, March 25, to Wednesday, April 3, 1957 (MIT, 1957b, R57218).

For the purpose of APT history proper, one interesting component of the course is the series of lectures presented by myself and Arnie Siegel in the middle four days of the course. We covered the computer programming process, using as examples a mouse solving a maze to emphasize logical programming, and finding the intersection of a circle and a parabola to illustrate systematized solution iterative calculation methods [also used in my 1958 AAAS paper, described later]. Programming principles were covered from computer architecture and binary number systems through actual programs coded in IBM 704 assembly language. Arnie described his automatic programming system and I presented APT, including curve and region programming.

The most important item for APT language background, however, was the lecture which I presented, on Friday, March 29, on *"Design of Special Language for Machine Tool Programming"* (Ross, 1957a), which I reproduce here in its entirety from the handout notes from the course (MIT, 1957c). Not only are most of the principles still valid today, but it shows very precisely the nature and trend of my thinking just prior to the first creation of APT language proper. In the oral lecture, itself, I illustrated the principles in geometric terms by means of a number of styrofoam models which I had made up in our shop from $6.86 worth (I still have the March 6, 1957 purchase requisition) of styrofoam balls, dowels, and blocks, as used in Christmas store decoration [N5736]. These geometric shape description principles, describing objects as joins and intersections of simpler objects, have only come into practical use in the mid-1970s through the work of Braid and Voelker (Braid, 1975; Voelcker and Requicha, 1977).

As we will see, I was forced to make many compromises with these design principles when APT language design actually got underway. But I feel that even today the points made in this brief lecture still are valid for user-oriented application language design. In any case, the special course was a success in completing the technical background for APT language development, so now it is time to take up the story of the physical environment in which that development took place.

Design of Special Language for Machine-Tool Programming†

Douglas T. Ross

A. Need for Human Convenience

1. Previous lecture has shown that computers can be used to perform most of the repetitious tasks of programming machine tools, and that, using automatic assembly techniques, detailed computer coding is not necessary.

It still is necessary, however, for the human to consider masses of detail, in order to express his wishes in a form which the Subroutine Library can handle. The way he thinks about the problem is governed by the Subroutine Library.

For complicated parts the amount of detailed information required of the human can be very great. This situation is dangerous because humans cannot handle quantities of detailed work reliably.

2. It is necessary to find a more natural, less detailed way for the human to express himself.

B. Language Design

1. In order to have a truly convenient way for humans to program machine tools to make parts, we must first determine what are the important properties of parts in general.

The Δx, Δy, Δz and feedrate information required by a numerically controlled machine tool are certainly a complete set of properties for arbitrary parts, but, as we have seen, these properties are far from convenient for humans.

We must find properties which are much more general, more similar to the way humans think.

This is not an easy task, however, because the properties still must be very explicit so that the computer will be able to fill in all of the necessary details which are implied.

2. Once the properties have been found, then we can assign English-like words to them so that they are easy for people to remember and use.

There must also be very explicit rules for combining these words to make meaningful statements about parts.

These rules should also be similar to the rules of English grammar so that it is easy and natural for the human to express himself.

3. The effect of choosing properties, assigning words to them, and establishing rules for combining these words, is that a special-purpose language with very explicit meanings and capabilities has been designed for "talking" to the computer about parts to be machined. It is important, for human convenience, to allow for redundancy in this language, so that the human can express himself in whatever way is natural at the moment.

C. Suggestions for Language Design

1. At the present time, language design is an art. No scientific procedures are known and each problem area requires its own special treatment.

† Friday, March 29, afternoon session.

Douglas T. Ross

A number of helpful steps can be outlined, however, which appear to be applicable to most problem areas.

2. The kind of statements which are to be made about a problem area are generally of two kinds:

Declarative or descriptive statements ("say"-type statements) which establish definitions and basic relationships among the things which are to be discussed.

Instruction statements ("do"-type statements) which use the relationships and definitions, and tell what action is to be carried out.

The distinction between "say"-type statements and "do"-type statements is helpful in deciding what kinds of words and rules are needed in the language.

3. It is not necessary (indeed impossible) to consider all possible statements which will be made in the language, since we can consider only the *kinds* of things we wish to say and do.

At this stage we need to know only a few representative *things* to say things about, and *things* to do.

Examples of "say" statements

The _____ is on the _____.
The _____ is the same size as the _____.
A _____ with a _____ will be called a _____.

Examples of "do" statements

_____ the _____ to _____.
_____ing followed by _____ing will be called _____ing.
If you have _____ed, _____ the _____.

4. It is also possible to establish a wide variety of *modifiers* for the language, knowing only a few representative *things* to be modified.

Well-chosen modifiers can be very important to the language since they allow complicated ideas to be expressed by simple statements. They allow variations of meaning without drastically changing the form of the statements.

Things which we *say* things about can be modified according to size, quantity, relationship to other things, etc. "Say"-things may also be modified by other "say"-things.

Example: There are _____ _____s on the _____ of the _____.

Things which we say to *do* can be modified according to how quickly, how carefully, and in what mode or version they are to be done, etc.

Example: _____ _____ly to the _____ and then _____ _____ _____ly.

5. With the kinds of "say"-and "do"-statements determined and modifiers established, the main features of the language are set.

The next step is to "flesh out" the skeleton of the language with the necessary *thing* vocabulary.

Usually there will be many more "say"-things than there are "do"-things, since problem areas are usually quite restricted in scope.

D. Results of Language Design

1. The primary purpose of a language is to provide a means for a human to express himself in a given problem area.

If the language design process has been successful, the vocabulary and rules for modifying and making statements will be easy to learn and natural to use.

2. The language also serves another very important function which is not as easily recognized. It helps the human to organize his thinking about the problem area.

Since the important features of the problem area are represented by the various parts of the language, thoughts about a particular problem are automatically directed and channeled to the essentials of the problem by attempts to make statements in the language.

3. A language will usually be in a constant state of growth and revision.

As more and more particular problems are encountered, additions to the "say" *thing* vocabulary will frequently be necessary to introduce new objects, etc., into the language.

If it is found that an expression in the language occurs very frequently, the expression itself can be given a name to be added to the vocabulary.

Occasionally new *modifiers* will also be required for a particular problem. These new modifiers can be used with many of the old words in the vocabulary so that a whole new class of expressions are made possible.

Finally, the whole problem area will tend to expand with usage so that additions of "do"-things to the vocabulary, and even revision of the rules for making statements may be made.

E. Practical Aspects of Language Design

1. Although ideally language design should be influenced only by the problem area and the characteristics of humans, since the language is to be used to accomplish some task involving a computer and other machines as well, a number of other factors necessarily influence the design.

A universal factor throughout the design process is the economics involved. The advantage to be derived from a given aspect of the language must be balanced against the difficulties in incorporating that aspect into a complete and working system.

2. A written form of the language must be designed which is not too cryptic to be easily remembered and used by the human, but which is relatively easy for a computer program to translate.

The written language should also lend itself readily to transcription from hand-written copy to the input medium of the computer.

The language should be sufficiently readable and understandable that untrained personnel can process the statements reliably.

3. Translation programs must be written to recognize the meaning of statements in the language and initiate appropriate computer behavior.

Since the language is likely to be in a continual state of flux and improvement, it should be relatively easy to make the corresponding changes in the translation programs.

F. Computer-to-Human Languages

1. Whenever a language must be designed (as above) for humans to make statements to computers it is also necessary, to a greater or lesser extent, for the computer to make statements back to the human.

2. It is always necessary for the computer to inform the human of any errors which the human has made, and which the computer can detect.

These statements should be made in the same language the human uses, so that they can be easily understood.

3. Often it is desirable for the computer to report back to the human, its progress in solving the problem.

These statements may be made either in the form of written statements or pictures.

In the case of machine tool programming the computer might draw a picture on an output oscilloscope of the part being made, and give written statements about crucial points of intersection, etc., to greater precision than could be drawn.

This information allows the human to check that he has instructed the computer properly.

4. Most of the points made above about language design apply equally well to computer-to-human languages.

Douglas T. Ross

G. Computer-to-Machine Languages

1. Computer-to-machine languages are influenced by a different set of conditions than languages which involve humans.

2. The primary condition is to match input and output media so that additional transcription and processing is not required.

Because of the large investment in equipment there are a great many practial problems involved, and several groups are now working on suitable standards.

3. It is permissible to have limited flexibility in computer-to-machine languages, since the required flexibility can be achieved by computer programming.

4. As a backlog of experience is built up it may prove best to make specially designed computers for machine-tool problems.

At the present time, however, not enough is known about the field so that programming of general purpose computers is probably better than attempting special hardware design.

5. Period 3: The APT Joint Effort (January 1957 through May 1957)

5.1. Initial Meetings

As I have already stated, the original suggestion that we get in touch with the Subcommittee for Numerical Control (SNC) of the Aircraft Industries Association (AIA) came during a November 7, 1956, visit of Bill Webster, our Air Force sponsor, to MIT. I first made contact with the SNC Chairman, "Barney" Gaiennie on December 4th [R56123+4], and by the 18th had received an invitation to the January 21 and 22 meeting in Dallas Texas [R561218, 19]. In my reply of December 26, I suggested that "20 to 30 minutes toward the end of the meeting [be allotted to] a short oral presentation of our goals" [C561226].

Don Clements and I both attended the Dallas meeting, and although I seem not to have received the official AIA minutes, my resume [R570121-25] on returning states, "I gave them a brief description of what we were trying to do, and everybody seemed to be quite excited about the prospects, although I tried to make it clear that these things were probably a little bit in the future." A subgroup under Jerry Jacob of Sperry Rand was responsible for "the computer end of things, and a meeting is planned . . . at the end of February at which Lockheed, Boeing, North American, and Chance Vought will be represented. I will plan to attend this meeting and we will try to make definite assignments for working areas at that time." In the discussion, 14 companies planned to use IBM 704 computers, and my single yellow page of notes from the meeting [N570121] has a box drawn around the phrase, "Package APT #2 with language!"—evidently my first decision to speed up our work to help out the industry. There also was considerable discussion of the desire for a special course, as we have already considered.

The Computer Programmer's Meeting actually took place March 1st in Los Angeles, immediately following the Western Joint Computer Conference. The AIA minutes (AIA, 1957a) state "Mr. Ross explained that these charts indicate a proposed program to handle the general case of automatic machine tool control programming. He invited companies interested in this effort to send experienced programmers to MIT and offered to provide guidance aimed at coding this program in an acceptable form for a particular general purpose computer. [I had first broached this idea to some Lockheed visitors at MIT on February 7 [R5727]]. While the offer was gratefully acknowledged, it was determined that most aircraft plants are presently utilizing their computing staff manpower to the fullest extent on current problems. Most companies indicated that they will closely follow the work done at M. I. T. and several may ultimately accept M. I. T.'s offer'' [p3]. So the seed was sown, but the time was not yet ripe.

My own resume notes of March 4 reporting on the meeting lend a bit more color.

> I described to them the work we have done here at MIT including region programming, and as discussion developed I proposed our generalized programming by curves system and passed around several copies of the diagram that Jerry [Wenker] had made. I finally was able to show them the distinction between a subroutine library approach to this problem and the system approach which we follow. And they all were quite happy about the system approach but could not get over the idea that it was more difficult than a subroutine library. I battled with them quite strenuously on this point urging them to pool their programmers and at least do a programming by curves system for 704s. Boeing is mostly completed with their subroutine library, however, so they are quite firmly entrenched in this way of doing things, and the feeling of the group seems in general to be that they were somehow afraid of the system approach in spite of my statements that I expected Jerry to have the system all programmed in a month on Whirlwind [for planes and spheres—which still was very optimistic]. The net results [sic] was that several subgroups were formed, one of which will be a planning group to consider the overall problem of input translation –output translation and calculations. MIT is a member of this group along with 4 of the aircraft companies. . . . Am hoping for another go around in this group to convince them that the system approach is really no more difficult than the subroutine library approach and much cleaner [R5734].

5.2 The Fateful Decision

There are almost eight weeks between the March 1 Los Angeles Programmer's Meeting and the April 23, 24 Los Angeles Programmer's Meeting, followed immediately by the April 25, 26 SNC Meeting. These are significant meetings, for on April 26, the SNC gave official approval to the idea of having MIT lead the construction of the first APT system based upon our research, beginning with a kickoff meeting the week of May 20, 1957 at MIT. In the eight weeks leading up to these meetings were (1) the preparation for and presentation of the ten calendar day Special Course at MIT, (2) the preparation for and execution of two debugging trips to Florida on the Pre-B-58 fire control system evaluation project of five days and ten days respectively, (3) continual work with the programmers on the Editor Generator and Logging features of SLURP, (4) work on the APT II and APT III Whirlwind programs, and (5) the start of writing of the third Interim Report. Personnel problems were acute. On February 25, George Zames left the project to transfer to the Research Lab of Electronics at MIT, on April 15 Harry Pople left for six months of Air Force duty, and on February 25 we learned that Sam Matsa would leave the project in June, at the end of the semester (he actually left in November) [R571127]. Therefore, during this period I had extensive meetings with both Mathematics and Electrical Engineering Departments attempting to line up replacement research assistants as quickly as possible [R57225-57418].

I have no resume notes for the April Los Angeles meetings, but I do have five pages of penciled notes on lined yellow paper taken at those meetings [N57423-26], as well as the handouts. I don't seem to have a copy of the official AIA minutes of the SNC meeting for reference, but my recollection is quite clear regarding an anecdote which in any case is the most interesting aspect of the meeting, in my mind. On the afternoon of April 25 the Tru-Trace Corporation gave a demonstration of their new numerical control system to the sub-committee and invited us to a dinner at a local restaurant following the demonstration. By way of hospitality they arranged an open bar at the restaurant until the private dining room to which we had been assigned could be made ready. Unfortunately, some local group such as Rotary or Toastmaster was already occupying the room and it was not until late in the evening that our dinner was ready. In addition to the several hours of open bar (always with the continuing understanding that our room would shortly be available so "you better get your last drink while you can") the restaurant management included copious wine with the meal to compensate for the delay.

As I recall it, the first thing on the agenda the following morning was the vote to approve the launching of the APT Joint Effort! I have often wondered whether the result might have been different had the TruTrace open bar been of normal spigot rather than firehose proportions. We will never know for indeed the SNC vote was favorable and APT was officially launched. (Later in a May 10 letter to attendees at the TruTrace demonstration [C57514], Mr. George Fry, President of TruTrace, states, "I want to personally apologize to you for the unexpected delay encountered before dinner, and we hope that it did not cause you any severe problem in maintaining your schedules.") (!) It didn't. Our schedule problems were to come later!

The minutes of the Programmer's Meeting (which I do have) (AIA, 1957b) summarize the main structure that I proposed for the APT simulated computer and then contained the following:

2. Information made available and views expressed:

(a) The various individual computer programming approaches of North American Aviation Co., Lockheed (Marietta), and Boeing, were examined and compared. The M. I. T. programming concept was reviewed and it was the concensus of opinion that this approach is more efficient in the long view due to its capability to expand and take into consideration future more sophisticated time saving programming procedures. However, many points of similarity and/or compatibility were discovered among all the approaches.

(b) Much of the work in programming already accomplished by individual plants is applicable, with modification, to a new superior common approach. . . .

(e) With early and effective work by each assignee, it should be possible to complete the project by October 1957.

(f) M. I. T. was considered to be in the best position to coordinate the efforts of all plants in this joint programming effort. Such coordination would include any necessary instruction in the system concepts, determination of information on progress and results, assistance with technical problems insuring common philosophies and compatibilities, maintaining surveillance over individual progress, and coordinating the final results for distribution. . . . [p3]

An attachment to the minutes "First group of common manuscript and computer language terms defined by the Numerical Control Data Processing Group during the meeting held on 23–24 April at AIA Los Angeles" lists meanings for 10 basic words still found in the APT language. My second page of notes from the meeting shows that clockwise (CW) and counterclockwise (CCW) circle definitions of motion (as in Siegel's system) also were discussed, but were not included in the list. My notes also show that 56 man-months were estimated for the October 1957 target date for the first system, excluding project coordination by MIT and parallel efforts for the IBM 650 computer. Ultimately AFML did partially sponsor IBM to develop a pared-down version APT, called ADAPT, for the 650 (IBM, 1963).

Upon returning to MIT from the meetings, I was greeted by a letter from J. B. (Bill) Rankin of Convair, Forth Worth stating, "Since we returned from the course at M. I. T., Numerical Control activity has intensified at Convair, Ft. Worth, to such an extent that I had to miss the AIA meeting in Los Angeles. The purpose of this letter is to tell you that we have generated an acute interest in your APT program. However, we do not want to be the only participant . . . " [C57429], to which I replied post haste that they had been assigned to work on the "Preprocessing portion of the A. I. A. APT II system, with counsel from MIT" and that I thought the October date was "realistic" although "It will not be easy to coordinate the efforts of so many different organizations, but with the fine spirit shown by all concerned I think we should be able to succeed quite nicely" [C57429]. Programmers are perennially optimistic.

5.3. The Kickoff Meeting

My May 1, 1957, memorandum *"Preparations for Joint Programming of AIA APT II System"* invitation to the Kickoff Meeting described the nature of the system, mentioned that the project would operate under "a semi-democratic procedure", and laid out an agenda for the May 20 through May 24 meeting, covering both technical topics as well as details of how the project itself would be organized (Ross, 1975b). At the meeting itself, I explained that "semi-democratic" meant that we would have full democratic discussions as long as I felt progress was being made adequately and we were on track, but when I didn't think so, I would invoke my semi-democratic authority and we would do things my way—we had a job to do. I don't think I abused this authority but I did indeed invoke it at various times even during the Kickoff Meeting itself [R57520-24, p2]. Throughout its long history, the APT Project had a strong sense of mission and a high esprit de corps. The people involved were eager, talented, and very good to work with.

My own files actually contain very little information on the Kickoff Meeting itself. I have only one page of resume summarizing the meeting and some notes titled "Working Group Translation Meeting, Thursday AM Session May 23, 1952" which is a very rough transcript (evidently) of a Dictabelt copy of a tape recording made during the session [N57523]. My resume states

> We had a good turnout for the joint programming effort for the A. I. A. APT II. One difficulty, however, was I was plagued and beseiged by intestinal and digestive difficulties for the whole week but Don [Clements] and Arnie Siegel and Dale Smith of North American did very nicely in running both parts of the meeting when I was incapacitated. We made excellent progress in defining all of the various tasks in [sic] barring any difficulties within individual plants about getting men and money assigned to this work. Had a tape recorder at the meetings and we got most all of the important parts of the discussion on tape. It turned out the translation program actually could be made quite straight forward by stealing the symbolic section out of the SHARE assembly program and making the language entirely a function of punctuation. Convair, San Diego feels they can handle the job in its present form. M. I. T. will handle preprocessing for the control element, since that involves making up the pseudo instructions for control element which we must design anyhow. The other portions of the system appear to be in good hands and will be handled adequately. We established a system of semi-monthly reports to M. I. T. and to coordinating sponsors of the various tasks and M. I. T. will issue monthly reports to the entire group and the

A. I. A. as well. The first one is to be due for the Denver meeting. During the meeting we revised the radius of curvature calculation for the APT II system to correspond to that of APT III and also decided that a more sophisticated check service calculation is required. I have just developed a check surface calculation . . . '' And regarding the language itself: "Since we also left the Translation Program completely independent of spelling of words etc. we can throw the problem of machine tool programming language back into the laps of Benetar and Carlberg. I should do so in a letter describing the structure of the translation program" [R57520-24].

Since this paper concerns the history of the APT Language rather than of APT itself, I will not go into the structuring of the project or how the system and work was organized except when they influenced the syntax or semantics of the language. (Each company assigned six-character symbols beginning with their unique company letter, for interfaces, and each programmer specified his required inputs etc. [R574(sic)29, p3]). Starting with June 14, 1957, a series of "2D APT II" memoranda summarized both technical and project coordination matters in a series ending with my "Post Coordinators Report re Phase I System" on July 25, 1958.

6. Period 4: The Origins of APT Language
(May 24, 1957 to June 14, 1957)

I did the basic design of the APT language literally over one weekend—not by design, but out of necessity. How that came about is as follows.

6.1. Prior Language Suggestions

I had, of course, the influence of Siegel's language, and our Special Course preparation discussions. But also, at the March 1 Programmer's Meeting, Boeing handed out a slightly updated description of their "Numerical Control Library Routines" (Boeing, 1957b) (also presented in the Dallas Meeting) and also a one page "Part Programming Language Numerical Control Program-Tentative" (February 27, 1957) (Boeing, 1957a). Several of the APT words such as SETPT (set point), TRACO (Transform coordinates), ONKUL, OFKUL (coolant on and off), as well as XLARG, XSMAL (large and small X coordinates for multiple intersections) seem to have come from this list, for I do not remember these five-letter spellings being bandied about at MIT earlier. Also in preparation for the April 23–24 Programmer Meeting, I received a March 27 letter with attachments A through F from Ed Carlberg of Boeing (Carlberg, 1957) stating "It should be our goal to present to the SNC on April 25 a united Steering Committee opinion and/or recommendation in the field of data processing compatibility, with the further goal of obtaining industry concurrence at the next Study Group meeting in May." Attachment A is a ten-page paper on "Numerical Control Compatibility" in which Ed stresses compatibility with a minimum of standardization. He outlines 13 steps going from the engineering drawing to the machine tool and finds that the "manuscripts [will] allow the greatest flexibility and will be the easiest item to exchange of any of the possible points" [p5]. He goes on:

> Standardizing on the definitions is of much greater importance than on the actual word itself. If one plant calls it a "curve" and another a "circle," this means only minor re-programming or manual revisions to the manuscript in order to trade manuscripts. But if the *definition* is not standard, then a complete new manuscript starting from the part drawing is required. The number of words in a language will vary from plant to plant. . . . Certainly all the SNC can do at this point

is to establish a minimum language . . . [p6]. The other possible compatibility points (except the subroutine library) [have] unnecessary restrictions in the data processing without compensating benefits . . . [p7]. Thus there would seem to be no point in pursuing the study of compatibility points beyond the manuscripts [p8].

He then goes on to emphasize also the need for subroutine "entry–exit (or front end)" compatibility so that "plants can interchange these detail subroutines, with only main control modifications required" [p9]. Interestingly enough, he finished, "Of the two, the trading of parts is much more important from a long range, national defense standpoint. This compatibility should receive the bulk of our attention" [p10]. To this date, however, part program portability is just as difficult and rare as computer program portability. But as this shows, initially the industry did not desire the constraint of a standard language but wanted to achieve compatibility while retaining freedom to choose the words.

Attachments B and C provided definitions for the list of words referenced previously in the March 1 Programmer's Meeting, showing that the Boeing language was fixed-column card format, invoking program selection from the subroutine library approach. Items D and E then apply this to the preparation of a "manuscript" for the AIA Test Piece, an aluminum part with curves and pocketing which had earlier been established by the SNC. Attachment F presented Boeing subroutine standards for the IBM 704.

Among the assignments made at the Los Angeles meetings in April had been one to Vic Benetar of Lockheed, Georgia to propose the "standard manuscript language." On May 15, I received his initial recommendations for use in the meeting (Benetar, 1957). The list of 10 words had now grown to 17 including some which may have come from the Boeing list mentioned earlier. Vic also recommended 7 forms of circle definition, 10 forms of lines, 8 forms of points, and a general curve given by a list of points. The list of words is more closely related to Siegel's language than APT, however, for LINE and CIRCC were recommended for moving along a line or counterclockwise around a circle, and as in Siegel's system all the symbolic names for circles began with C, lines began with S, and points began with P. Although I am sure this proposal must have been discussed somewhat, I cannot recall being influenced by it in my initial design of the APT language. I remember feeling that since Benetar's suggestions carried none of the flavor of our three-dimensional, more generalized work, I would have to suggest the basic language form myself if things were to match up right in the long run. Although I said in my Friday, May 24 resume "we can throw the problem of machine tool programming language back in the laps of Benetar and Carlberg. I should do so in a letter describing the structure of the translation program" [R57524], over the weekend I instead wrote my own language, on May 25 and 26, 1957.

6.2. The First Language Memo

Memorandum 2D APT II-2, dated June 14, 1957, is the first APT language definition. The memo is titled *"A Proposed APT Language for the 2D APT II"* by Douglas T. Ross, [signifying a two-dimensional, curve programming, APT system language] (Ross, 1957e). My resumes indicate that it actually was primarily written over the weekend of May 25 and 26 (as I have described many times from memory over the intervening years). The resume for May 27 says

Started working out a language for the AIA APT II to suggest to Benetar on the basis of the results of our [kickoff] meeting. I have decided that we probably should have multiple words in the major word portion of the instructions and these sections will be separated by commas. In this way all of the instructions modifying the main instruction will appear on the same card. If not stated, they will remain the same as before. This can easily be programmed by having indicators set whenever a word occurs and each program will check with these indicators when appropriate. I have also decided not to store inside–outside information with surfaces for this system, since it is easier to merely say where the tool should go. In our final system we should have both possibilities. In a place where questions arise such as planes where it is not really sure which is the inside or the outside in the canonical form [this] can be handled again in terms of the normal. I suppose it could be handled, however, by saying whether you go through the surface or just up to the surface when you reach it. I will summarize these considerations in a letter and send it to Vic and suggest that the completion of the language be a function of the subcommittee and he with the help of Carlberg might consider themselves a project group for this task [R57527].

I never followed through with the letter, since I did the memo instead. The reference to going "through the surface or just up to the surface" later became GO PAST and GO TO (along with GO ON) to control the check surface calculation.

Because of its historical importance, the six-page initial language definition memorandum is included here in its entirety. The general types of APT language statements still apply today, with the use of modifier words separated from parameters by a slash and the incorporation of useful default cases, (which we always have preferred to call "normal" cases!)

MASSACHUSETTS INSTITUTE OF TECHNOLOGY
Servomechanisms Laboratory
Cambridge 39, Massachusetts

Memorandum 2D APT II-2

SUBJECT: A Proposed Basic Language For The 2D APT II

FROM: Douglas T. Ross

DATE: June 14, 1957

The following pages present the format and vocabulary of a proposed language for the 2D APT II System. The format is defined by the types of statements which can be made in the language. Notice that the character *space* is completely ignored and that use is made of space in the vocabulary to provide easy readability. Since card format is to be variable field, the double dollar sign indicates the termination of a statement, and a complete statement need not appear on a single card. The form of instructions have been chosen for generality and for ease in converting into the coded form required for the initial control element program. Notice that the type of curve which is to be followed is derived from the definitions of the symbols used. The modifiers DNT CT and TERM permit symbolic positioning of a tool and establish meanings of later modifiers. For the initial system at least it will not be possible to use NEAR and FAR in definitions since the preprocessing programs will not have any means for determining the current output position so that the words NEAR and FAR would have no meaning. Note that it is possible to include a number which specifies feedrate in any statement immediately preceding the double dollar sign. In order to simplify the examination of the number of parameters for automatic selection of preprocessing routines it may be desirable to precede feedrate by an additional "/" so that feedrate is uniquely shown. To assist in the interpretation of the language an example is given on the last page. The programming for the example would read in English as follows:

"Execute the following instructions at a feedrate of 80 inches per minute. From point P, don't record cutter coordinates, but go to point Q. With the tool on the left, don't record cutter coordinates, but go left on A to the near intersection of A and B. Then go left on B to C, go right on C to D, go left on D to E''. (Notice that the near intersection has been used in all cases because if no specification of NEAR or FAR is given, NEAR is assumed by definition). ''Cross curve E and go along F to the far intersection of G. Then go clockwise on G to the near intersection of G and H, and counterclockwise on H to the (NEAR) intersection of H and I. Considering the tool to be on the right, terminate as though you were to go left on I, then stop. This is the end of the program''.

LANGUAGE FORMAT

A. TYPES OF STATEMENTS

Definition

Symbol = Modifier, . . . , Modifier, <u>Name</u> Parameter, . . . , Parameter $$

    = , , , , / , , , , $$

Non-Definition

Symbol) Modifier, . . . , Modifier, <u>Instruction</u> / Parameter, . . . ,

Parameter $$) , , , , / , , , , $$

Parameter Definition

Symbol) Modifier, . . . , Modifier, <u>Parameter Name</u> = Parameter, . . . ,

Parameter $$) , , , , = , , , , $$

Special Words

Symbol) Modifier, . . . , Modifier, <u>Word</u> $$

) , , , , $$

Synonyms

Symbol = Parameter or Symbol $$

    = $$

B. INSTRUCTIONS

Terminated by '','' or ''/''

<u>FROM</u>   S
Defines current cutter location S. S must be a *point*

<u>GO TO</u>   S
Move cutter center to S. S must be a *point*

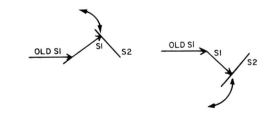

<u>GO LFT</u>   S1, S2
<u>GO RGT</u>   S1, S2

Douglas T. Ross

Go left or Right on curve S1 until S2 is reached.
(These instructions are usually used to go from one curve to the next. If only one symbol is given, it is interpreted as the new S2, and S1 is taken to be the previous S2.)

GO FWD   C̶R̶O̶S̶S̶   S1, S2
GO BAK   B̶A̶C̶K̶   S1, S2

[in original]

Cross onto S1 and go forward until S2 is reached. Back up onto S1 and go in reverse direction until S2 is reached. (These instructions are used when curves are tangent or intersect at small angles. Two symbols are always required.)

GO CLW   S1, S2
GO CCW   S1, S2

Go clockwise or counterclockwise on S1 until S2 is reached. (These instructions are treated as the appropriate one of the previous four instructions.) If only one symbol is given it is interpreted as the new S2, and S1 is taken to be the previous S2 *if* GO LFT or GO RGT are appropriate; an alarm is given if CROSS or BACK are appropriate.)

PS IS   S1
DS IS   S1
CS IS   S1

Part, driving, or check surface is S1

C. MODIFIERS

Terminated by "," or "/"

TL RGT
TL LFT

Cutter (tool) to right or left of curve when looking in direction of movement. These words also modify all following instructions.

DNT CT

Don't cut for this instruction *only*. (This modifier is used to prevent storage of cutter coordinates, etc., for the instruction which it modifies. The instruction, therefore, has the sole function of establishing cutter position and direction for later left, right, etc., instructions.)

TERM

Terminate the sequence of cutter motions as though this instruction were to be executed next. Applies only to this instruction. (This modifier is the converse to DNT CT since it defines the end position of the cutter. If only one symbol is used in the instruction being modified the modifier TERM causes it to be interpreted as S1 *not* as S2 as in the usual case.)

NEAR
FAR

Go on S1 until the near or far intersection of S1 and S2 is reached, with respect to the specified direction of motion. "NEAR" will give the first intersection, "FAR" will give the second intersection, "FAR, FAR" will give the third intersection, etc. (If no specification of NEAR or FAR is given, NEAR is assumed. "NEAR, FAR" or "NEAR, NEAR" will give a translation alarm, but will be treated as NEAR alone.)

D. DEFINITION NAMES

Terminated by "," or "/"

CIRCL	Circle
ELIPS	Ellipse
PARAB	Parabola
HYPRB	Hyperbola
LINE	Line
POINT	Point
CURVE	Curve
INT OF	Intersection of
TAN TO	Tangent to
SPHER	Sphere
PLANE	Plane
QDRC	Quadric
SURFC	Surface
ZFNXY	$Z = F(X, Y)$
YFNX	$Y = F(X)$
CONE	Right circular cone
CYLNR	Right circular cylinder
CTR OF	Center of

Note: Each of these names has an associated canonical form, but preprocessing allows data to be given in other forms in many cases.

E. DEFINITION MODIFIERS

Terminated by "," or "/"

1
2
⋮

Integers tell which of several preprocessing programs to use with the name being modified. Not needed if data format distinguishes cases.

LARG X	(or Y or Z)
SMAL X	(or Y or Z)
POS X	(or Y or Z)
NEG X	(or Y or Z)

These modifiers are used with INT OF or TAN TO to tell which of multiple intersections or tangents to use. As many may be used as necessary.

F. PARAMETER NAMES

Terminated by "="

<u>TOL</u>   N

Maximum allowable deviation from the defined curve = N

<u>TL DIA</u>   N
<u>TL RAD</u>   N

Diameter or radius of cutter. (For ball, or face or end mill)

<u>CR RAD</u>   N

Corner radius of cutter

<u>TL 1</u>   (or 2 or . . .) N1, N2,
N1, N2, . . . are the parameters for a tool of type 1 (or 2 or . . .)

<u>FED RT</u>   N
Feedrate = N inches per minute.

G. SPECIAL WORDS

Terminated by "$$"

<u>DNT CT</u>

Don't cut any of the following instructions.

<u>CUT</u>

Cut all of the following instructions. (Used only to over-ride a previous DNT CT Special Word).

<u>TL RGT</u>
<u>TL LFT</u>
<u>NEAR</u>
<u>FAR</u>

Same as Modifiers, but apply to all following instructions (NEAR assumed if not specified)

<u>STOP</u>

Planned machine stop where all programmed motions are stopped, including the tape transport.

<u>END</u>

End of program or tape.

OTHER WORDS which depend on auxillary functions of the particular machine tool being used.

H. EXAMPLE

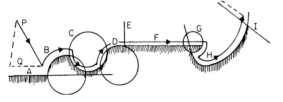

```
        FED RT = +80. $$              NOTE: ANY INSTRUCTION
             FROM / P $$              HERE CAN HAVE FEEDRATE
      DNT CT, GO TO / Q $$            GIVEN BEFORE "$$"
TL LFT, DNT CT, GO LFT, NEAR / A, B $$  IF ONLY ONE SYMBOL IS
          GO LFT / B, C $$            USED IT IS THE DESTINATION
          GO RGT / C, D $$            CURVE (EXCEPT FOR "TERM")
          GO LFT / D, E $$            I. E. COULD HAVE
      FAR, CROSS / F, G, $$           "-----------------------------------------------
    NEAR, GO CLW / G, H $$            GO LFT / B, C $$
          GO CCW / H, I $$            GO RGT / D $$
TL RGT, TERM, GO LFT / I $$           -----------------------------------------------"
             STOP $$                  INSTEAD OF
             END $$                   "-----------------------------------------------
                                      GO LFT / B, C $$
                                      GO RGT / C, D $$
                                      -----------------------------------------------"
```

So it literally is true that I designed the APT language over a weekend and that its principal syntactic features were determined by the requirement that its translation be controlled entirely by the statement format punctuation. The basic simplicity of the core of the language has made it easy for part programmers to learn. As we will see, later difficulties with the calculating portions of ARELEM, as well as the more sophisticated requirements of elaborate geometric definitions and transformations, enriched the language considerably (and made certain portions more of a challenge to use correctly) but the basic sense of the language has stood the test of time well.

7. Period 5: Evolution of the System (May 1957 through May 1958)

7.1 Project Organization

The Language Memo was written immediately following the Kickoff Meeting as the project was just getting underway. The first MIT Coordinator's Report was issued by Clements June 21, 1957 (Clements, 1957), and reports progress in some areas, and not in others. There is neither time nor space to go into details here, but Fig. 3, the Press Conference version of a diagram extracted from the first paper on APT (Ross, 1957d) (written between September 13 and 27, and presented October 24, 1957, at the Third Annual Contour Machining Conference in Los Angeles) shows both the system structure and the company assignments, originally and in February 1959. The key elements to note concerning the language aspects are that Input Translation (INTRAN), Definition Preprocessing (DEFPRE), and Instruction Preprocessing (INSPRE) constitute the translator proper. They served to compile interpretive code for CONTROL and ARELEM, in which resided the real semantics of the language. ARELEM turned out a cutter location tape (CLTAPE) format to a changeable Postprocessing and Output program. Machine-tool-dependent vocabulary was passed directly through, in sequence, for handling by the chosen postprocessor. A library of Unit Normal and Directed Distance subroutines, with one canonical form for the data of each surface type, and the Diagnostic system completed the system architecture still followed pretty much today. These company assignments realized the modularity cited in premises 2 and 3 of my theme (Section 1.1).

Douglas T. Ross

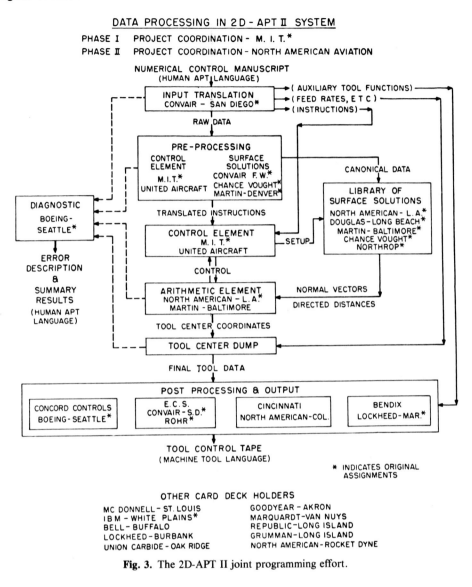

Fig. 3. The 2D-APT II joint programming effort.

7.2 Systematized Solutions

The basic idea that a systematized solution provides the semantic framework for a specialized application language, thereby permitting an integrated, cohesive approach still seems not to be widely recognized even in the 1970s, although it is in many ways the essence of any strong argumentation based on abstract data types. Twenty years ago the concept really was difficult for people to grasp, even with our simulated computer analogy.

The question of systematized solution was considered of such importance that the majority of Chapter 1 in Interim Report Number Three, covering the period from January 1 to

March 31, 1957 (MIT, 1957a), is devoted to illustrating the principle by generalizing a program to find the intersection of a parabola with a circle (from the Special Course) to a program to find the intersection between two arbitrary plane curves.

> Just as the example of the previous section solved for the intersection of any two curves providing the defining functions were known, the two systems to be described [for APT II and APT III] move a cutter along a space curve or over an entire region, providing the analogous defining quantities are available. . . . As [is] described more fully in the last chapter of this report, it is planned to attempt the same type of systematized solution to the problem of translation of languages, so that the translation portions of the APT computer can have the same generality and flexibility as the calculating portions of the computer. The resulting systematized approach to the problems of APT system design will, it is hoped, result in a basic structure and an accompanying methodology which will allow APT systems to continue to grow and change to meet the varying needs of their users [p13].

In fact, the last chapter of that report concludes with

> At the present time, it seems possible that the two research efforts outlined above—determining the principles of language design and language translation—may provide sufficient cross fertilization to make it possible to devise a special metalanguage which can be used to describe special-purpose languages of the type under consideration. If this is indeed possible, then it may prove feasible and desirable to devise a program to write translation programs based upon a description in the metalanguage, of the rules and vocabulary of the subject language. Such a program would represent an important advance in APT system design, since the individual programmer could add to the language of the system at will [p52].

According to my resume that was probably written May 15, 1957, a good four years before I developed my Algorithmic Theory of Language (Ross, 1962), and seven years before the initial version of my AED JR system (Ross, 1964) which actually did what was suggested here. The prospect was very real to me at the time, however, and I suspect that it was this initial connection between systematized solution and metalanguage which caused me to emphasize in the Algorithmic Theory of Language that language design was primarily semantic rather than syntactic. This also was the reason why when we finally did develop the AED language we did not go beyond AED-0 (Ross et al., 1970), and instead extended the language by "integrated packages" of functions (corresponding to the abstract data types of today) so that the language was extended semantically without syntactic extensions. This enabled AED to possess in the middle 1960s, features that other high-level languages only achieved many years later.

As we will see, even though the tremendous turmoil of practicalities of APT system development caused many of these rich concepts to be set aside initially, some of them did come to the surface and had an effect later in the Definition Preprocessing and Macro features, which were my last contributions to APT language development in 1960, predating similar features in other high level languages.

7.3. Evolution of the Translator

As I have mentioned, the starting idea for the Input Translator (including the funny punctuation) came out of the May 23, 1957, session of the Kickoff Meeting. "The translation program actually could be made quite straight forward by stealing the symbolic section out of the Share assembly program and making the language entirely a function of punctuation. Convair, San Diego feels they can handle the job in its present form"

Douglas T. Ross

[R57520-24]. But by June 10, Convair dropped out of the project (Kinney, 1957), and not until a month later were they cajoled to return. Finally, Charlie Swift did visit with me at MIT for the whole day of August 14 [R57814] at which time we worked out the basic translation scheme involving a data table filled from card reading, a syllable table for words, a symbol table, and communication to the preprocessing programs—all controlled by the statement punctuation.

Things were progressing very erratically in the widely dispersed project, so by August 30 I joined Don Clements in preparing the Coordinator's Reports. The "new style" (i.e., no-holds-barred commentary on any and all aspects of the project) Coordinator's Report (Ross and Clements, 1957) begins to show further evolution of the language ideas. The discussion of the input translation process shows that it was what would today be called a "lexical scanner."

The fact that the APT language at this point in time had only four statement types which were determined entirely by their punctuation had a profound influence on the evolution of the language at this early stage. The September 27 Coordinator's Report discusses various modifications to the input translation process to allow transient modifiers to both precede and follow words which they modify, and in the next Coordinator's Report, October 22, I made what became the final design evolution for this early stage of INTRAN by suggesting that a table for modifiers similar to that for parameters should be used so that the sequence of words would be passed along intact to INSPRE and DEFPRE. This, in effect made the input translation program into a proper lexical scanner which merely recognized, translated into internal form, and type-classified the words in the sequence they were encountered in the input string. This greatly simplified the scheme and I said, "This rather major change [may make Convair] feel that their task is becoming too simple and that their talent is not being made use of" (Ross and Clements, 1957, Oct. 22). Interestingly enough, on October 31 (after the above simplifications) I received a copy of an October 24 letter from Charlie Swift to Ed Carlberg (Swift, 1957) saying that it was useless for the Convair programmers to attempt to continue their task until the language was more pinned down. Therefore, the suggestion when it was received, was well received.

The final change to the translator structure which formed the framework for further language design developments also was recommended in the October 22 Coordinator's Report. This consisted of the specification that INSPRE should be allowed to call DEFPRE as a subroutine. The Instruction Preprocessor handled all words to the left of the slash (/) while the Definition Preprocessor was invoked only whenever there was an equal sign (=) in column seven. By allowing INSPRE to call DEFPRE, the language was considerably enriched and made much closer to my original desires for the language because the programmer now could write, for example, "TL LFT, GO RGT, LINE/P1, P2 $$," i.e., geometric definitions did not have to be given separate symbolic names but could be nested in the motion instruction itself.

The final clincher to the translation scheme is contained in the following letter of November 27 (Ross, 1957e) to B. J. McWhorter of Convair which I quote in its entirety to give a first hand feel for both the methods we were using and the flavor of the informal communication which, in those days, took the place of "formal specifications":

> We just received your progress report of October 20 and although I have not given it very careful perusal, there are a couple of things I thought I would bring to your attention and see if you can get them into the deck that you will send us by December 1. The change is slight and comes about because of the fact that we plan to handle surface definitions as instructions in Phase I, and also

since your progress report does not seem to have quite as much flexibility as you said you needed when you were here. The change is, therefore, that the modifiers on page 7 of your report, XLRG, etc., should go to the right of the major punctuation, /, as well as the TAN TO etc., modifiers on page 8. In other words, all of your important modifiers will appear in the translated parameter table. I would suggest that the coded form for TAN TO etc., be changed to read (1, 0, 2) etc., when coded in SAP. Or if you do not need to distinguish the two classes of modifiers, then just number those on page 8 from 9 through 14. These coded forms will then all appear in the symbol table and not in the syllable table which is reserved for words to the left of the major punctuation. Your example, then, would be changed to read as follows:

LIN 1 = LINE, 3/ LARGE Y, TAN TO,
CIR 1, SMALL Y, TAN TO,
CIR 2 $$

I should also point out to you that the geometric type of the figure which appears in the decrement of symbol table entries as you give them on page 7 will only use the right hand 6 bits of the decrement. You should mask out these 6 bits since we may very soon have junk in the left hand half of the decrement. If you can describe any of the special cases for which you want additional information in the decrement in a rough way, please let us know since we are at present planning to assign these additional positions on the basis of control element requirements.

One further thing, is that type 1 modifiers, i.e., numbers, still may appear in the translated modifier table as modifiers to the principal word, in case you need this information for selecting among preprocessing routines. If control is passed to your program by the instruction preprocessor, then we would prefer to have the numerical modifier follow the principal word, i.e., LINE, 3 instead of 3, LINE in your example. Since we will have recognized the word LINE as calling for your preprocessor, we can still pass that along to you as the principal word in which case the 3 will be the last entry in the translated modifier table.

I hope this letter is not too hastily written and that you can make sense out of it. The new language memo is almost completed and so far I plan to put in only canonical forms for surface definitions but if you have any additional suggestions to pass along at this time please do so immediately. We are looking forward to getting a deck of cards from you soon for Phase I. Hope you had a happy Thanksgiving.

With these changes, the evolutionary pathway for the language enrichment was established. From this point on, the interactions of the semantics of the language, in terms of our ability to carry out the geometric computations, could be reflected directly in a simple choice of a new syntactic word and the corresponding control element action. Even though there was no formal metalanguage definition, the (now) well-understood relationship between the Input Translation lexical scanner, INSPRE, and DEFPRE, and the Control Element program and ARELEM provided, in an informal way, the mechanism for a fairly clean enrichment of the language (taking the place of a formal language theory). The next stages of evolution had to do with the semantic vocabulary areas—a process that, due to the complexity of both the subject matter and the project organization, was to continue for another three years.

7.4. The ARELEM Problem

My primary contention in this paper is that it is orders of magnitude more difficult to create truly new, deep, application-oriented languages such as APT. In order to be successful, they must be based upon a world view that both matches the thought processes of

Douglas T. Ross

the intended end users and also is amenable to efficient, reliable, and comprehensive computations. Only if the coverage of the world view is complete, comprehensive, and reliable can the user himself think completely, comprehensively, and reliably in terms of the language. This is why throughout the actual historical development of APT as well as throughout this paper, I have repeatedly returned to the theme of the "systematized solution," for it embodies this *abstraction of the essence of the entire problem area in generic form* so that each specific problem that is posed in the language in fact has a workable solution. In the case of APT, this required the establishment of a methodology for solving the dynamic three-dimensional geometric problem of approximating arbitrarily closely, the sculpturing of arbitrary dimensional parts composed of arbitrary surfaces by means of broken-line motions of rotating tools, described by arbitrary surfaces of revolution, with five degrees of freedom—three of position and two of tilt.

To appreciate the intellectual difficulty of the task you must realize that the "mind's eye view" of ARELEM is completely different from that of a person considering the problem. A person can appreciate the fact that the task is difficult if he is told that the problem is to consider an arbitrary-shaped tool (a surface of revolution) which can be steered through space, and his problem is to do that steering in such a way as to cut an arbitrary-shaped part out of a chunk of material. Both the speed and direction of approach, as well as the actual point of contact, must be very precise so that there is no chatter or gouging, etc. Clearly the problem is nontrivial.

With the concept of arbitrary shapes somehow floating and moving in space in a precise and coordinated fashion firmly in mind, now consider the problem once again from the "mind's eye view" of the actual ARELEM computation. In this case, there is no direct concept of shapes, surfaces, and smoothness of surfaces and motions. Instead, there are only sets of three-dimensional coordinates making sharp angular constructions of vectors, vectors, and more vectors. Everything is extremely discrete, jumpy, and disjointed. There is only a staggeringly complex construction of points and straight lines connecting those points. Even such a simple concept as curvature (a small segment of a circular arc in some oriented plane, with a point in the center of that arc) is not directly known but must be approximated by an appropriate construction which includes

(1) the selection of the orientation of the plane specifying the direction in which curvature is to be measured,
(2) the selection of some appropriate base point from which two directions can somehow be selected,
(3) from which two applications of the directed distance subroutine for the surface can be invoked to provide,
(4) two points exactly on the surface in question,
(5) at which the unit surface normal vectors can exactly be calculated,
(6) from which suitable projections into the plane can be made to allow,
(7) the construction of two circle radii and the chord between them so that,
(8) the curvature can be estimated.

(And throughout the process, remember that the directions for the directed distances must yield points *on* the curve of intersection between the plane and the unknown surface, if the whole approximation process itself is to have any validity.) So it takes all that merely to approximate a single curvature in a single direction. From this horrible description of the simplest of all ARELEM operations you can perhaps appreciate the difference between the human and ARELEM viewpoints. Points and vectors between points (relations between points)—that is all ARELEM has to go on. That is all that unit normals and directed distances supply. There are no analytic functions known to ARELEM, for whatever their form, they would limit its generality and applicability at its most basic level. The APT world is primitive indeed.

This paper is about language design, and this brief belaboring of the computational difficulties is included only to pin down the fact that ultimately every aspect of the APT language must be reduced to these same, very primitive terms. Furthermore, when, because of the mathematical vector constructions within ARELEM, multiple cases must be selected from, words with meanings suitable to the mind of the part programmer must be included within the language so that he can supply the appropriate constraint to the degrees of freedom of the vector computation. Several APT words arose from this source.

7.5. Evolution of ARELEM

It should not be surprising that the solution to this problem required several years, and that the viewpoint and terminology of the APT language went through an evolutionary development during this period, corresponding to the successes and numerous failures of ARELEM calculations.

Throughout the early period from 1957 to 1959, the primary difficulties driving this evolution hinged on the gradual weaning from the holdovers of the methods that were successful in the much simpler two-dimensional case in which tool center offsets are applied separately after the approximation to the desired curve has been established. In the case of two dimensions, even for arbitrary curves, tool center offset requires merely the expansion of the curve in the direction of the surface normal the fixed amount of a tool radius. To be sure, such addition of a normal direction thickness to a convex curve can lead to cusps and other difficulties, but except for the detection of these anomalies (and the corresponding problem that, of course, an inside curve can have no sharper radius than the tool radius) the problem is quite tractable. Therefore, a completely workable, comprehensive, and reliable two-dimensional system can be created with this underlying viewpoint of a zero-radius "point cutter" followed by a separate "tool center offset" computation.

Even though the initial AIA joint effort APT system was to be "2D APT II" this always was recognized as a mere waystop, and from the beginning ARELEM was to be three-dimensional (Ross, 1957b). The difficulty was that we did not realize at that time that the concept of a separate tool center offset for three dimensions is essentially unworkable. Furthermore, the urge to creativity, coupled with the fact that we had only incomplete documentation on our Whirlwind APT II programs (MIT, 1957a, R57122, 3) then being debugged, caused O. Dale Smith, of North American Aviation (NAA), to make the first IBM 704 ARELEM with a new and different set of equations (Smith and Corley, 1958). This both introduced new problems and made it impossible to exchange results between the two efforts—both of which suffered from the deadly "point cutter with cutter center offset" syndrome! Thus there was a long period of "improvements" in the basic ARE-

Douglas T. Ross

LEM computation in which case after case of anomalous behavior was corrected for by the application of special treatments (R580114, AIA, 1959). Interestingly enough, most of the linguistic aspects of these problems were of a general enough nature to last. Even when I finally devised the successful MIT ARELEM (with the assistance of Clarence Feldmann from late 1959 through 1961, see Section 12), both the situations and viewpoints for the proper application of the words FROM, INDIR, MAXDP, and TNCKPT remained valid. Quite probably most current users of the language are unaware that those terms entered the thought framework of APT at such an early and rudimentary stage.

7.6. Evolution of Semantics

My voluminous records would permit almost a blow by blow account of the evolution of the meanings of almost every APT language word and construct. But suffice it to say that with much travail, and many Coordinator's Report exhortations, progress was laboriously made on all fronts during the summer and fall of 1957 (Ross and Clements, 1957). At the October 3 and 4 meeting of the AIA Subcommittee for Numerical Control I requested that the cooperating companies "take a relatively simple part that they plan to produce by numerically controlled machines and try to program it by using the language which was supplied in the 2D APT-II Memorandum 2, and to send the result to MIT by November 1. This would show up any inadequacies in the current language proposal and enable MIT to provide a more usable language" (AIA, 1957c, p. 4). Also at that meeting it was decided that since the October date could not be met, the new target would be a January 1, 1958 distribution of a system, if the companies sent their program decks to MIT by December 1. As it turned out, this date, too, could not be met, for the last deck reached MIT February 3, 1958 [R5823], and the February 4 Coordinator's Report states "It is hoped that a working system can be performing before the next SNC Meeting on February 20." The March 13 Coordinator's Report says

At the (SNC) meeting it was reported that a successful part program had been run using the 2D-APT II program and that the debugging operation was still in progress. . . . On this note, SNC arranged [that] a "field trial" distribution of the program was to be made in the early part of March as a sort of shakedown before a formal distribution of the program. . . . The target date for the distribution of the more finished version of Phase I was selected as the first of May. During the interval between the March distribution and the May distribution, MIT agreed to produce an edited and comprehensive version of the documentation and to furnish a corrected card deck to the APT Project Coordinating Group [headed by O. D. Smith of North American] for distribution to the industry. There will be included in the May distribution, three items: A part programmer's manual, a computer programmer's manual and descriptive brochure. This will complete MIT's formal participation in the joint effort. After May, the MIT project will revert to a consultant status and concentrate on further research efforts for AMC [Air Materiel Command] (Ross and Clements, 1957).

Thus was the Field Trial first version of APT defined. We now move back again in time to pick up the language definition thread that led to the corresponding Field Trial Part Programmer's Manual.

8. Period 6: The Field Trial APT Language (November 1957 through April 1958)

8.1. Two Papers on APT

To set the background, on August 15, 1957, I had received an invitation from George Fry, President of TruTrace (who had given the demonstration prior to the AIA decision to start APT), to present a paper at the Third Annual Contour Machining Conference to be held at Los Angeles October 23 through 25. Since this would be the first chance to describe APT and the AIA Joint Effort in a public forum, I accepted [C57819]. The paper was actually written sometime between September 13 and 27, disrupted by various activities including a week long debugging trip to Eglin A. F. B. [R57913-927]. Figure 3 from that paper (Ross, 1957d) has already been presented. Figures 4 and 5, also from that paper, show Siegel language and APT language versions of a sample part program. At the time, this was the most complete part programming example I had written since the original June 14 Language Memo (Ross, 1957c). Compare the placement of the modifiers with the sample line in the letter to McWhorter (Section 7.3). (Notice that the October 22 Coordinator's Report with the improved translation scheme was completed just before I departed for this Los Angeles paper presentation.)

Upon my return from Los Angeles, the November 8 resume says, "We have got some sample parts programmed in APT language from some of the companies, some very good and some really sad" [R57118, p2]. So I also had those examples with their high incidence of tangent check surfaces as stimulation. According to the resume of November 12 through 18,

> Harry Pople has returned from his stint in the Air Force. . . . I also described to him briefly the use of the Scope Input Program as a possible flexible input language for APT programming. He seemed quite taken with the idea. We will save this for a little bit in the future, however, and only try to do a very *pilot* model to begin with. . . . I will start working on the draft of the language memo today [R571112-18].

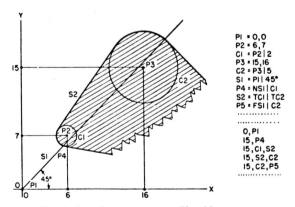

Fig. 4. Sample part program, Siegel language.

Douglas T. Ross

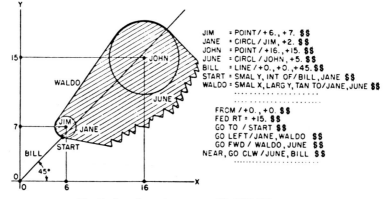

Fig. 5. Sample part program, 2D-APT-II language.

As I mentioned earlier (Section 2), I had written the first computer graphics input program in 1954, and here I was suggesting its use for part programming, even though it was to come only many years later.

The November draft of the APT language memo (which I have) [N5711?] never was completed because it was interrupted by the activities of other projects, but in particular, another paperwriting stint. On October 7 I received an invitation to present a paper on APT at the ACM-sponsored session at the annual meeting of the American Association for the Advancement of Science in Indianapolis in late December [C57107]. On October 9 I was further informed that "the paper you are to present . . . has been selected by the Association's Public Information Committee as one which should be reported widely to the general public. For your own protection I trust that you will cooperate with us . . ." and requesting 100 copies of a nontechnical abstract of the paper by December 15 [C57109].

I started thinking about the paper December 2, sent the abstracts in on December 12, and "most of the time before Christmas was spent in writing the AAAS paper and taking a week's vacation from December 23 on. The paper finally came out quite well and was well received at the meeting" [R57123-58019]. It made the front page of the Indianapolis Star as I got on the airplane Sunday morning, December 29, and upstaged Crawford Greenawalt 15 column inches to two in the next day's Wall Street Journal, etc. [R57123-58019]. But the paper was later rejected for publication in the *Communications of the ACM*. "While very interesting [it] is too highly expository for publication. . . . The *Communications* would, however, be interested in publishing a description of the programming language and a small example of its use. The philosophy of program construction, while interesting, parallels that in any other development of a specialized programming language. What would really be worth while would be a discussion of the steps by which a language for your particular class of problems has been developed" (Perlis, 1958). I certainly did not agree with this putdown and was still in the throes of language design and therefore I made no further efforts with ACM. Perhaps this paper 20 years later will fill the bill. Throughout my career editors and reviewers have reacted poorly to the same work that others (often years later) give me awards or accolades for.

The emphasis in the AAAS paper (Ross, 1957f, 1958a) was on the "systematized solution [which] greatly clarifies the obscure problems which arise in spatial geometry, language design, language translation, and system organization. It is not improbable that continued work along these lines can lead to a design machine which will assist in the design process itself and then automatically produce a part to meet the specified conditions" [p16]. Although the language aspect is only mentioned in the AAAS paper, I illustrated for the first time, the idea of "ignorable words" with the sample statement "GO RGT, WITH, TL FT, ON, CIRCLE/CENTER, PNT 3A, RADIUS, +5.025 $$" [p26]. I also discuss some of the ground rules for "applying the principles of systematized solution to the problem of language translation" [p28]. My yellow-page handwritten notes for the paper are of interest to me because they say, "Man is programmed by the language we design for him to use, since only way he can get the system to perform is to express his wishes in the specified language form" [N5712?, p7], which is the earliest trace I have of my stock statement that a language designer bears a heavy burden of responsibility because he provides the major part of the solution of any problem that ever will be solved with his language because he programs (constrains) the thought processes of the human who will use the language to solve a problem.

In any case, these were the sources of background leading up to the April 1958 Field Trial Part Programmers Manual for APT. The original June 1957 language memo, the clarification of semantic content brought out by refinements of input translation, instruction and definition preprocessing, and control and ARELEM interaction, along with the sample part programs of the Contour Machining Conference paper, test programs from the companies, philosophically based first draft attempt at a field trial language memo, and finally the AAAS paper all taken together constituted the background source for the first true APT Part Programmer's Manual embodying the definition of a complete APT language.

8.2. The Field Trial Language

Whereas the June 14, 1957 2D APT II-2 Language Memo (Ross, 1957c) consisted of six pages, the April 29, 1958 *2D-APT II Part Programmer's Manual* (*Field Trial Version*) (Ross, 1958e) was 50 pages long. The flavor of the language at that stage is concisely conveyed by the now-famous "MIT Teardrop" sample part, see Fig. 6 (a combination of Figs. 1, 2, 3 from the Manual). Page 21 also, however, illustrates the more complex nesting of a geometric definition in a complex motion instruction, with post-processor control, by

TL LFT, ON KUL, FAR, 2, GO FWD,
ELIPS/+4.5, +5., . . . $$

But page 36 points out that in this more complex form, "feedrate may *not* be added before the $$," whereas it could be in the simpler forms. (Several other restrictions evidence various growing pains in the coordination between the program modules, in this case, between INSPRE, DEFPRE, and CONTROL. Once INSPRE passed control to DEFPRE, it could not send feedrate to CONTROL, as it usually did, and DEFPRE would only return control, not the value of feedrate it could have found!)

Examination of Fig. 6 also shows that at this point the flat plane of the two-dimensional part was considered the Drive Surface (DS), whereas later this was made the Part Surface (PS). The example is missing a crucial comma in line 17, but neatly side-steps the startup problem covered in detail on pages 28 and 29 of the manual, where a sequence of three DNT CT, GO TO instructions demonstrates how "Illegal Use of Vertical Motion" can be

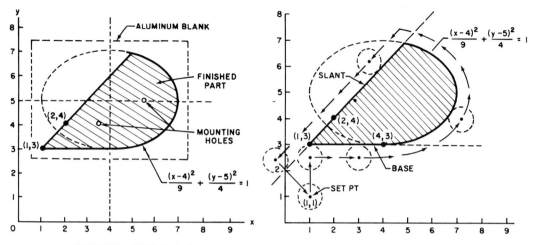

GIVE DATA FOR SAMPLE PART

SYMBOLS AND TOOL PATH

Line Number	Portion of APT Program	APT Statements	Type of Statement
1		DS = PLANE/+0.,+0.,+1.,+3. $$	Definition
2		SET PT = POINT/+1.,+1.,+3. $$	"
3	GEOMETRIC	Y AXIS = LINE/+0.,+0.,+3.+0.,+1.,+.3. $$	"
4	DEFINITIONS	BASE = LINE/+1.,+3.,+3.,+4.,+3.,+3. $$	"
5		CONIC = ELIPS/+4.,+5.,+3.,+.33333, +0.,+0.,+0.,+.5,+0. $$	"
6		SLANT = LINE/+1.,+3.,+3.,+2.,+4.,+3. $$	"
7	PARAMETER	TL DIA/+1.0 $$	Instruction
8	DEFINITIONS	TOLER/+.005 $$	"
9		FEDRT/+80. $$	"
10	TOOL	HEAD 1 $$	Special
11	CONTROL	MODE 1 $$	"
12	INSTRUCTIONS	ON SPN $$	"
13		ON KUL $$	"
14		DS IS / DS $$	Instruction
15	STARTING	FROM/SET PT $$	"
16	INSTRUCTIONS	GO TO/+0.,+1.,+3. $$	"
17		TL ON GO RGT/Y AXIS, BASE $$	"
18	CUTTING	TL RGT, GO RGT/BASE $$	"
19	INSTRUCTIONS	GO FWD/CONIC $$	"
20		GO LFT/SLANT, BASE $$	"
21	CUT FINISH	TERM, GO LFT/BASE $$	"
22	INSTRUCTIONS	GO TO/SET PT $$	"
23	PROGRAM	OF KUL $$	Special
24	FINISH	OF SPN $$	"
25	INSTRUCTIONS	END $$	"
26		FINI $$	"

Fig. 6. "MIT Tear Drop" sample part.

avoided by a slanting dodge seen by ARELEM, but resulting in a simple vertical plunge by the machine tool. Since sense of direction came from comparison of the most recent motion with the direction of the tool axis, a plunge was impossible for ARELEM!

9. Period 7: The Postcoordinator Report (July 1958)

It was a lot of work putting together the first APT Field Trial System. Clarence Feldmann, who was to work closely with me for the next 20 years, had joined the project as a Research Assistant, June 28, 1957 [R57628] and had been responsible for MIT's INSPRE and CONTROL modules, as he rapidly learned the ropes. He, Harry Pople, Jerry Wenker, and Bob Johnson, loaned to the project by IBM, were the prime movers, although a week's visit to MIT by Dale Smith in February [R58210-17] also helped greatly with ARELEM integration, at the start.

The April 15, 1958, Coordinator's Report (Ross and Clements, 1958) says "Accompanying this memorandum are the rest of the computer program writeups for the field trial of the 2D-APT II Phase 1 system. . . . The IBM Service Bureau, shipped the field trial card decks [some 8000 cards to 16 companies] via Railway Express on April 10, 1958." Finally, the May 1 Coordinator's Report says that "The programmer's memo of instructions for the field trial version of the 2D-APT II Phase 1 system was mailed on April 30. On May 6, 1958 another mailing will occur which will contain a deck of cards for the sample part program described in detail in the report, instructions for running this test part through the system and up-to-date deck corrections. It is hoped that this manual and this test part will allow the recipient companies to start actual field trial tests for the system on their own." From that point on, the official debugging of the APT System was intended to take place in industry with coordination by Dale Smith of North American.

Although ostensibly MIT was to concentrate on the documentation, following the distribution of the APT Field Trial decks, we also continued with full-scale development and debugging runs on APT II and APT III on Whirlwind, along with intensive debugging of the 704 APT system. United Aircraft had joined the AIA Joint Effort, and by March 4, Dale Smith suggested that they take over the Instruction Preprocessor and Control Element responsibility from MIT (Clements, 1958). By this time also Sam Matsa, now at IBM, had obtained a go-ahead to develop an APT III region programming system for the IBM 704 [R58312-17], and United Aircraft was going to collaborate with IBM on this effort, which shortly was christened AUTOPROMT (for automatic programming of machine tools). It was decided that IBM would concentrate on the region programming aspects, while United Aircraft concerned itself with the incorporation of 2D APT II for the curve programming necessary for initial passes and treatment of region boundaries.

After various interchanges, a fruitful meeting between MIT and United Aircraft programmers took place at MIT on July 2, 1958. Ken Kaynor and Richard Leavitt met with myself and Clarence Feldmann, and a number of syntactic and semantic language issues were finally settled (Kaynor, 1958).

There was a meeting of the Numerical Control Panel (the new name of the SNC) in Seattle July 16 through 18 at which both Dale and I made presentations on the status of the Field Trial distribution and rework. A polling of the companies represented showed that great difficulties were being encountered, but that most were still counting on APT being successful and switching to it once it was (AIA, 1958). I also met with the people at Boeing "going over the greatest parts of the Phase I system which is now defined as that system which MIT will now write up. Discussion was concerned primarily with post processing and the translation and preprocessing'' [R58714-21].

Upon returning to MIT, on Tuesday, July 22, I ''had a long go around with Harry and Clare concerning the shortcomings of the APT II system and the APT documentation. . . . After much hashing around, we finally decided that we would issue a postcoordinators report describing all the changes that are necessary to make the field trial version into a Phase I system . . . and at the same time request changes in the SHARE write-ups'' [R58722].

On July 24, ''Don and I called Dale Smith and although he seemed somewhat taken aback at first, after we explained what we meant by a postcoordinators report he seemed to think it was a good idea'' [R58724]. The report itself was issued July 25 (Ross, 1958f) and, in effect, it constituted the specifications for the program changes necessary to allow me to actually get down to work completing the Part Programmer's Manual.

The remaining portions of the crystalization of APT language ideas took place in my writing, correspondence, and discussion over the next few months. By November 14 ''Drafting and typing are well underway'' [R581113 + 14], but it was not actually received back from the printers for mailing until mid-February 1959 [R59210-18]!

10. Period 8: The First Real APT Language (August 1958 through November 1958)

10.1. The Phase I Part Programmer's Manual

For all the ups and downs in deciding how to handle the syntactic and semantic processing, this first really complete version of the APT language (Ross, 1959) ended up with a number of very interesting features which not only strongly influenced the subsequent development of APT, but were strongly influential on my thinking in the design of the phrase substitution and object-oriented-language features of AED. They do come quite close ''except for the funny punctuation'' to the objective of having APT be an ''English-like'' language. The Press Conference handout example, Fig. 7, illustrates this best.

By the time the instruction preprocessor was allowed to handle all translation and call on the definition preprocessor when necessary, and when the same words, such as TO, ON, PAST, were allowed to appear either as modifiers in the major section or as parameters in the minor section, very English-like idea flow was made possible, especially if ignorable words were used, too.

The manual states [p1–7]:

There are four types of APT statements containing one, two, or three principle [sic] sections, separated by distinguishing punctuation characters. These are:

Definition statement

Symbol = major section/minor section

Instruction statement

Major section/minor section

Synonym statement

Symbol = minor section

Special statement

Major section

Each word exhibits a certain modifying power with respect to the overall meaning of the entire part program . . . called Modal (M), One-shot (O), Transient (T), and variable One-shot or Modal (O-M).

Figure 8 [p1–11] lists the entire present vocabulary of the APT system and shows whether each word is to be placed in the major or minor section of an APT statement. . . . The words are arranged into *classes* with appropriate headings such as "motion instructions" and "parameter names," and within some of the classes, words are further grouped into *sets* by means of brackets. Only one word from any set (or if there is no bracket, only one word from the entire class) may appear in any single APT statement, unless a class contains several *bracketed* sets, in which case one word from each set may appear. There are of course many exclusions from this general rule, e.g., if one word is chosen at random from each of the classes and sets, then a meaningless statement will result. Once the meaning [sic] of the individual words are understood, however, if the words are selected such that they make good English sense, then the resulting APT statement will be acceptable.

A word which has *modal* meaning need be written only once in the part program, after which its meaning applies to all succeeding statements until another word from the same set is given. . . .

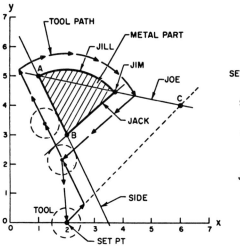

```
A    =  POINT / 1, 5
B    =  POINT / 2, 3
C    =  POINT / 6, 4
        TL DIA / +1.0, INCH
        FEDRAT / 30, IPM
SET PT = FROM, POINT / 2, 0
        IN DIR, POINT / C
SIDE  =  GO TO, LINE / THRU, A, AND, B
        WITH, TL LFT, GO LFT, ALONG / SIDE
JILL  =  GO RGT, ALONG, CIRCLE / WITH, CTR AT, B, THRU, A
JOE   =  LINE / THRU, A, AND, C
JIM   =  POINT / X LARGE, INT OF, JOE, WITH, JILL
JACK  =  LINE / THRU, JIM, AND, B
        GO RGT, ALONG / JACK, UNTIL, TOOL, PAST, SIDE
        GO TO / SET PT
        STOP, END, FINI
```

Care To Match Wits With A Giant Brain?
Marvelous new APT System, using large computers and automatic machine tools lets you cut out complex metal parts just by writing down the instructions. Read the "APT language" part program above, comparing with the picture, and see how brainy these brains are getting to be. Abbreviations are TL = tool,

DIA = diameter, FEDRAT = feedrate, IN DIR = in direction of, LFT = left, RGT = right, CTR AT = center at, INT OF = intersection of. MIT scientists working for Air Force developed new Automatically Programmed Tool (APT) system with cooperation of Aircraft Industries Association companies.

Fig. 7. Sample part program.

Symbol	=	Major Section Words (Separated by Commas)			/	Minor Section Words (Separated by Commas)
Symbols (Examples)		Motion Instructions	Modifiers	Geometric Names		Definition Modifiers
A1		FROM O	TL LFT M	POINT O		TO O
2S32		IN DIR O	TL RGT M	LINE O		ON O
SET PT		GO TO O	TL ON M	CIRCLE O		PAST O
Y AXIS		GO ON O	CUT O-M	ELLIPS O		TAN O
LINE 5		GO PAST O	DNT CUT O-M	HYPERB O		CTR AT O
JOHN		GO TAN O	NEAR O-M	PARAB O		AT ANGL O
		GO DELTA O	FAR O-M	PLANE O		RADIUS O
Special Words		GO RGT O	2 T	SPHERE O		INT OF T
REMARK		GO LFT O	3 T	CONE O		TAN TO T
		GO FWD O	4 T	CYLNDR O		X LARGE T
		GO BAC L O		ELL CON O		X SMALL T
		GO BAC R O	Director Words	ELL CYL O		Y LARGE T
		GO UP O	(Concord Control)	PAR CYL O		Y SMALL T
		GO DOWN O	MODE 1 M	HYP CYL O		Z LARGE T
			MODE 2 M	TAB CYL O		Z SMALL T
		Special Instructions	MODE 4 M	ELLPSE O		RIGHT T
		Z SURF M	P STOP O	ELL PAR O		LEFT T
		TN CK PT M	STOP O	HYP PAR O		LARGE T
		LOOK TN M	HEAD 1 M	HYPLD 1 O		SMALL T
		LOOK DS M	HEAD 2 M	HYPLD 2 O		
		LOOK PS M	HEAD 3 M	QADRIC O		Numbers (Examples)
		2D CALC M	OF KUL M	VECTOR O		+123.4
		3D CALC M	ON KUL M			-0.01234
		PS IS M	END O	Parameter Names		+123
		FINI O	LOKX M	TOLER M		-123
			ULOKX M	FEDRAT M		123
		Ignorables		MAX DP M		
		WITH AND		TL RAD M		Pre-Defined Symbols
		ALONG		TL DIA M		
		INCH		COR RAD M		
		DEG		COR DIA M		
		IPM		BAL RAD M		
		THRU		BAL DIA M		
		UNTIL		GNRL TL M		
		JOINT				
		TOOL				

Fig. 8. Complete initial vocabulary for the APT II system.

One-shot words apply only to the statement in which they occur and do not modify the meaning of words in other APT statements. . . . *One-shot-or-Modal* words have either one-shot or modal meaning depending upon what kind of statement they are used in. If they are used in a special statement they have modal meaning whereas if they are used in a definition or instruction statement (i.e., a statement punctuated with a /) their meaning is one-shot. Once a one-shot meaning has been executed, the meaning will revert to the modal setting. . . . *Transient* words modify only the word immediately preceding or the word immediately following their occurrence. Thus the combination FAR, 3, means the third far intersection; whereas the combination X SMALL, INT OF, means the intersection with the smallest X coordinate. When transient modifiers are bracketed into sets in Figure 8, it means that two words from the same set may not be used to modify the same single word, even though several set uses may appear in a single statement [pp1–10, 12, 13].

It is, of course, essential to know the meaning of each individual word as well. For example, FROM applies only to a point in space and tells ARELEM the location of the tool following a manual set up procedure by the machine operator. Thus, FROM/LINE would be meaningless and unacceptable. Similarly, INDIR, meaning ''in the direction of,'' works only with points or vectors, not the other geometric quantities.

The first glimmerings of the need for INDIR show in my daily resume for February 25, 1958 [R58225], but the word itself is first referenced in the resume for April 2 and 3 [5842,-3], even though it was excluded from the Field Trial language (Ross, 1958e). Along with GO TO, ON, PAST, TAN a surface, INDIR finally solved the start up problem (although ARELEM could not do GO TAN, and probably should not have been asked to). Similarly, allowing TO, ON, PAST, and TAN to be parameters on the right of the slash in a motion instruction, gave complete control over termination of cutting conditions, thereby eliminating the word TERM from the language. To eliminate an illegal jog motion when backing up from a tangent check surface condition, GO BAC became GO BACR or GO BACL to convey the part programmer's intention so that an alarm could be generated in the illegal cases.

Z SURF, which for a long time was restricted to being equivalent to Z PLANE [R58827-29], specified a surface on which all implicitly defined points should lie. I recognized the need for it as early as August 30, 1957 (Ross and Clements, 1957), but it never was properly specified, so that the initial preprocessing package (C58324, McWhorter, 1958) set the Z coordinate of every point defined equal to zero—hardly three dimensional.

I invented the "tangent check point," TN CK PT, solution to the tangent check surface problem July 22, 1958 [R58722]. If the step size were selected small enough (limited by MAXDP [R58417-55]) the tangent check surface calculation would be guaranteed to see the check surface if it looked from the current tool position to the tangent check point rather than looking in the surface normal direction. Thus, for example, a single check point interior to a convex part would insure that all surfaces of that part could properly be found. The three LOOK instructions tell whether to use that or the drive surface or part surface normal for tangent check surface calculations. These arose when it was found that the old unreliable surface normal method was in fact preferable for certain classes of parts in which tangent check points would need to be changed repeatedly and yet the normal vector method would work satisfactorily. Hence the part programmer was given this control.

2D CALC and 3D CALC were intended to switch ARELEM calculations from three to two dimensions and back (Ross and Clements, 1957, Aug. 30). This capability wasn't actually implemented until considerably later.

An interesting phenomenon is that PS IS is all that remains in the 2D APT II system in this initial official language. DS IS and CS IS were later reinstated, but at this point in time, the addition of TO, ON, PAST, and TAN as definition modifiers allowed them to be completely replaced for two-dimensional work, in addition to doing away with word TERM, as has previously been described (Kaynor, 1958). Literally the last word in APT, decided on at the July 2 MIT/UAC meeting, is the word FINI which indicates the very end of each part program so that the APT processing programs can reset to their original condition (Kaynor, 1958).

Each geometric name has a corresponding collection of "preprocessing formats" which prescribe the wording and punctuation of the minor section of a statement (Ross, 1959, Ch. 7). By means of the = sign, a symbolic name can be given by the geometric quantity thus properly defined. By means of synonym statements, symbols may also be assigned for numbers or other symbols. Symbolic numbers may be used wherever numbers are called for and many of the definition formats call for the use of symbolic geometric quantities. If no geometric name is given with FROM, INDIR, GO TO, or GO ON, then point is assumed. Similarly, GO DELTA (the incremental GO TO) has vector as normal case. *Ignorables* can be written any place to make the reading more English-like, but are completely ignored by the system.

Under parameter names, TOLER was a single mathematical tolerance specification to match the existing ARELEM, even though the need for separately specifiable inside and outside tolerance had been recognized at MIT since at least January 1957 when the "se-

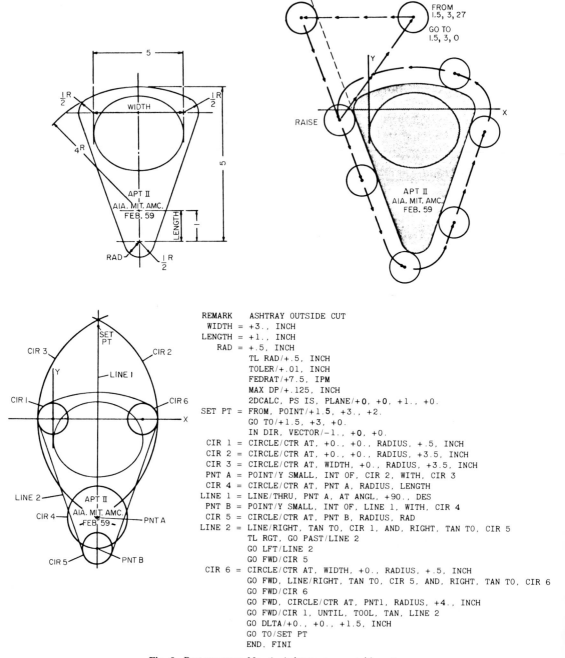

```
REMARK     ASHTRAY OUTSIDE CUT
  WIDTH = +3., INCH
 LENGTH = +1., INCH
    RAD = +.5, INCH
           TL RAD/+.5, INCH
           TOLER/+.01, INCH
           FEDRAT/+7.5, IPM
           MAX DP/+.125, INCH
           2DCALC, PS IS, PLANE/+0, +0, +1., +0.
 SET PT = FROM, POINT/+1.5, +3., +2.
           GO TO/+1.5, +3, +0.
           IN DIR, VECTOR/-1., +0, +0.
  CIR 1 = CIRCLE/CTR AT, +0., +0., RADIUS, +.5, INCH
  CIR 2 = CIRCLE/CTR AT, +0., +0., RADIUS, +3.5, INCH
  CIR 3 = CIRCLE/CTR AT, WIDTH, +0., RADIUS, +3.5, INCH
  PNT A = POINT/Y SMALL, INT OF, CIR 2, WITH, CIR 3
  CIR 4 = CIRCLE/CTR AT, PNT A, RADIUS, LENGTH
 LINE 1 = LINE/THRU, PNT A, AT ANGL, +90., DES
  PNT B = POINT/Y SMALL, INT OF, LINE 1, WITH, CIR 4
  CIR 5 = CIRCLE/CTR AT, PNT B, RADIUS, RAD
 LINE 2 = LINE/RIGHT, TAN TO, CIR 1, AND, RIGHT, TAN TO, CIR 5
           TL RGT, GO PAST/LINE 2
           GO LFT/LINE 2
           GO FWD/CIR 5
  CIR 6 = CIRCLE/CTR AT, WIDTH, +0., RADIUS, +.5, INCH
           GO FWD, LINE/RIGHT, TAN TO, CIR 5, AND, RIGHT, TAN TO, CIR 6
           GO FWD/CIR 6
           GO FWD, CIRCLE/CTR AT, PNT1, RADIUS, +4., INCH
           GO FWD/CIR 1, UNTIL, TOOL, TAN, LINE 2
           GO DLTA/+0., +0., +1.5, INCH
           GO TO/SET PT
           END. FINI
```

Fig. 9. Part program No. 1. Ashtray cam outside cut.

cant cut" of maximum length allowed by a complete tolerance band was used in APT III [R57017, 8].

Figure 9 shows (the Press Conference ashtray version of) the Geometric Definitions, Tool Path, and Part Program for the first sample part completely worked out in the manual. (The center portion was a three-dimensional "saddle surface" hyperboloid of one sheet, pocketed by decreasing indexed elliptic cylinders, with a slanting gouge for a cigarette at each upper corner.) The example is interesting because it showed the use of the geometric definitions to perform ruler-and-compass constructions to define the complete geometry given very sketchy input requirements. The same outside shape and two other insides of this part were also worked out in the manual. The second outside part program illustrated how the flexibility of the language would allow the part programmer to program a path directly. He could simply start out from the beginning and define quantities as he went along by adding symbols to earlier statements and using those in constructing definitions for later statements, rather than doing all the definitions beforehand as in the first example.

10.2. Phase II Extensions

I don't think there ever was a completely functional APT system corresponding to this first Part Programmer's Manual. Once the Seattle Meeting decided that Phase I would be defined to be "the system that MIT was documenting" I very carefully kept out of the Part Programmer's Manual any ideas that might smack of a possible Phase II [R58725-29]. In fact, it is probably true that it was not until well after the San Diego Project effort in 1961, in which the truly definitive APT system was generated by programmers from many companies working together in the same place for an extended period of time, did APT ever have a set of documentation that adequately matched the system then in use. The whole project was so difficult and drawn out, however, the lack of current documentation seemed like a normal state of affairs to APT participants.

A few historic highlights are worth citing even though they don't show in the first APT Part Programmer's Manual because they showed up much later in subsequent development or have not been pinned down as to time, in my previous discussion here.

(1) The use of symbolic names for geometric quantities minimizing numerical parameters so that entire families of part shapes can be accommodated by the automatic programming system, comes from my discussions January 29 through 31, 1957, with Arnie Siegel in preparation for the Numerical Control Course at MIT.

(2) The various check surface types, including their use as decision surfaces, was seen February 11, 1957 in Whirlwind APT II discussions.

(3) February 12, 1957, again in discussions with Siegel regarding the course, is the first place that the terms "preprocessing" and "postprocessing" for those major sections of the APT system structure make an appearance.

(4) April 29, 1957 I first proposed the *tabulated cylinder* (which like an aurora borealis passes parallel lines through an arbitrary chain of points in space) as the general way to handle arbitrary two-dimensional curves in a way that properly fits into the three-dimensional case.

(5) On August 15, 1957, NAA raised questions on using filleted end mill cutters to cut pocketing with sloping bottoms as in the AIA Test Part No. 1. They suggest the idea of a "limit surface to control the extent to which any of the other surfaces, part surface, driv-

ing surface, check surface apply'' (Ross and Clements, 1957, Aug. 30, p. 11). We actually did incorporate such limit surface capabilities in our MIT ARELEM in 1960, but I believe that this is still a current topic to be accomplished in the current CAM-I Advanced NC Project even today.

(6) The ''CL tape'' cutter location tape standard of APT came out of talks I had at North American with Dale Smith in early October 1957 and was selected by me at Carlberg's urging by ''semi democratic authority'' in preference to a less-flexible scheme then being proposed by Boeing, on December 3, 1957. (It was later refined somewhat.)

(7) The first test run of CONTROL and ARELEM together took place sometime in January 14 through 16, 1958 on the IBM 704 at MIT.

(8) On March 14, 1958, in his first Coordinator's Report (Smith, 1958), Dale Smith presented a proposal for automatic pocketing based upon indexing of drive surfaces. We also had considered indexing in our APT work at MIT, and this type of operation did get incorporated in APT in the APT Macro facility about 1961 (AIA, 1961).

(9) Under ''Loops and subroutines in the part program'' Dale also recognized that there is more to indexing, but evidently he was not aware of our suggestion [R57211] that check surfaces be used as actual *decision surfaces* for part program logic control. I had included labeled instruction statements in my original June 14, 1957 Language Memo (Ross, 1957c) for this purpose.

(10) We first talked about iterating a general tool shape into the valley formed by multiple check surfaces on April 7, 1958.

(11) While writing the Post Coordinator's Report July 25, 1958, I saw (with Pople) that using the terms N, E, S, W would be preferable to the RGT, LFT, FWD, BAC, especially to go with later coordinate transformations, but it never got into APT.

(12) On October 17 through 20, 1958, I say, ''Talking a little bit more long range with Clare, I pointed out that we could use the connectives AND and OR really with no need for parentheses since we would want to follow any such statement by suitable IF clauses which would automatically determine the meaning. This is somewhat different than FORTRAN since we can, in our case, make the system figure out what we mean by what we say in later statements. In strictly mathematical problems this is not possible. . . . The problem of macrocoding such as is required in tool shape and director specifications [also mentioned in the March 14 Dale Smith report], as well as the inclusion of FORTRAN and SAP language in APT programs also should be included in Phase II. The writing of a general normal vector and directed distance program would facilitate the inclusion of arbitrarily defined surfaces.''

These not only presage the phrase substitution of AED, but were in fact included in my later recommendations to the APT project which became viable features in subsequent versions. It may be of interest to APT aficionados to know that their consideration was documented this far back in time.

10.3. Macros and Phrase Substitution

One of the most interesting aspects of the extensions of APT beyond the initial Phase I language was the way in which several of the more powerful language and translation features that would later become important also in general-purpose programming languages arose in a completely natural fashion much earlier in APT. I believe that the reason this happened is that because of its subject matter (and perhaps any truly application-oriented language would share this property) APT had to be, from the beginning, what I now call an *"object-oriented language."* (Ross, 1975); in other words, a language in which the viewpoint and terminology reflected in the vocabulary, syntax, semantics, and even the pragmatics of the language are concerned directly with describing and manipulating specific real objects of the area of discourse. The attitude of the user and of the designer of the language is concerned directly with the subject matter and not with how that subject matter may be represented in a computer. This means that the language is concerned exclusively with objects, and with properties of or operations on those objects. [This means that the types, in the sense of today's abstract data types (Liskov *et al.,* 1978; Shaw *et al.,* 1977; etc.), are concerned with descriptors and operators of the type.] There is no place in either the thinking or the language for "pointers" or "references," which are strictly representational matters.

In the case of APT, two important features came up early and naturally—macros and nested definitions (i.e., phrase substitution). The first ideas for macros in APT (which I have previously cited) have to do with making repetitive patterns of holes, (DRILL), or in carrying out the reliable control of feedrate in the drilling-like start-up of a pocketing operation, (PLUNGE). These were considered macro instructions and called "macroinstructions" (Smith, 1958, No. 1, p. 10) because they involved repetitive patterns of the more elementary GO types of APT instructions. It was then but a short step to see that the same process applied to both rough and finish cuts in part programming, from which the application of the macro pattern generation concept applied equally well in the motion-instruction domain in general. This in turn brought out the idea that the same concern for safe control of feedrate during a plunge operation should be applied to the same concerns for general part programming, and the idea of packaging stylized patterns of general part-programming-standards macros was a natural consequence.

All of this took place well before the development of the SAP macro facility in 1960 by McIlroy of Bell Labs (McIlroy, 1960). (My resume of February 10 through 29 [sic!], 1960, says, "Got a writeup of the new SAP MACRO system just this morning. It appears that these facilities will suit very well our flow diagramming and coding conventions and will make the generation of the compiler or whatever system I ultimately end up with much easier and more powerful. The boys from Bell Labs did a very good piece of work here" [R60210-29]. In fact, our early APT macro thoughts included conditional macros, for that is how "loop-logic" was to be exploited for rough and finish cuts. This was, in fact, the purpose of the "symbol = . . . " beginning of the statement types in my original June 14 1957, Language Memo (Ross, 1957c), although it was dropped for a time and did not come back until Dale Smith's Coordinator's Report #4 of August 20, 1958 (Smith, 1958, No. 4) lists "symbolic statement identification" along with "completely variable field card format." But it is not until his "Prognostications" of Report #7, dated January 13, 1959 (Smith, 1959), that we find among other things "Addition of logical part program jump instructions" and "Addition of macro instructions" as separate headings. I believe it was sometime after that that I finally was able to start getting people to see that from the beginning I had intended that these all be one set of thinking.

The matter of nested definitions or phrase substitution, in which any phrase of a given type can be substituted wherever any other phrase of the same type can occur, may go back as far as my original discussions with Arnie Siegel, especially in the context of the preparation for the Numerical Control Course we gave for AIA at MIT [R57212], but I can't really vouch for that. The earliest APT language, like Siegel's language, only allowed symbols to be given to geometric quantities and then those symbols were written in instructions or other definitions—but not the definitions themselves. I do know, however, that once we had seen that DEFPRE could be called from INSPRE [R58930-107] (and I spoke of it at the time as "nesting definitions in instructions") the idea of nesting definitions within *definitions* was a natural step. The problem was that the definition preprocessor control was not up to that task at the time. (It was a simple dispatcher, not a compiler.) Therefore it is not until the September 1959 Coordinator's Report of Len Austin (who followed Dale Smith as Coordinator) that we find nested definitions as an assigned APT Phase II item (Austin, 1959). I had been pressing for its inclusion ever since writing the portion of the Phase I Part Programmer's Manual in which instruction statements were converted into definition statements after the fact by writing "symbol = . . . " at the beginning of an already-written statement in the "path-oriented" second program of the rocker arm cam sample part (see Section 10.2).

The important thing to notice about these macro and nested definition language features is that they both became full-blown in concept and purpose, if not in practice, at least by early 1959 and certainly were brewing in 1957. My recollection is that they came from the needs of the application area, rather than from any influences of general-purpose programming thinking (although I can't fully vouch for that). In any case they were very influential on my own formulation of plex and my Algorithmic Theory of Language which, as I have already cited, also had its roots in the same period. [Another interesting aside is that my resume shows that on April 16 through 18, 1959, a symbolic manipulation conference was held at MIT (no formal auspices) at which "I talked for a short time on multimode control as applied to list searches (Ross, 1958d), group control and proposed a modified list structure which seems more appropriate to our design machine application" [R59416-511] which was my first public discussion of my "n-component element" plex ideas (although I did not at that time have the word "plex"). This predates by almost exactly one year the May 20–21, 1960, Philadelphia ACM conference on Symbol Manipulation at which my note published in CACM March 1961 (Ross, 1961) was presented. As I have cited here, the start of this thinking was "Milling Machine Conference Number One" in 1956 (Ross, 1956c). Since most people seem to associate 1961 (the CACM late publication date) with the start of my plex thinking, I thought it would be interesting to point out these earlier dates.]

11. Period 9: The Press Conference (November 1958 through February 1959)

The official launching of APT on the world was, of course, the Press Conference of February 25, 1959 (MIT, 1959a), with which I opened this paper. According to my resumes, over a year went into its preparation [R580131], triggered by the significant press coverage of my AAAS paper reverberating through the month of January 1958. Nothing actually happened, of course, for a long time as the Field Trial effort struggled past the projected May 1st date. On June 9, 1958, I received an invitation to present a paper at the ASME annual meeting in New York City December 1 through 5, 1958, in a special program sponsored by the Aviation and Machine Design Divisions [C5869]. I accepted and proposed the title "A Progress Report on the 2D APT II Joint Effort for Automatic Programming of Numerically Controlled Machine Tools" [C58630]. On August 13, I started writing, and by August 29 I was putting the finishing touches on the ASME paper [R58827-29]. A figure in that paper (Ross, 1958g) shows the state of my thinking at that point in time with regard to the Fig. 8 language chart of the final Part Programmer's Manual. At that point in time, "miscellaneous" words was a catchall category. I had not yet decided to treat INDIR as a motion instruction because it set the sense of direction for all the rest. ZSURF was ZPLANE at that point, and direct setting of the drive and check surfaces was included. A few spellings are also different, but the language itself was almost complete when this paper was submitted on August 29, 1958.

By mid November George Wood of the MIT public relations department took over [R581113 + 14]. His primary suggestion was that we try to arrange some sort of demonstration along with the release. By January 9 we had decided to make souvenir ashtrays from the part programming example and have sense switch control of scope plots, etc. [R581229-59019]. The Press Conference itself took place February 25, 1959.

> We had a little over 60 press people present, split almost equally between popular and technical press. The impact of the conference was, I think, beyond anyone's expectations. We evidently made the front page several places and received some radio and TV coverage as well. . . . Lowell Thomas also made a pun on APT, saying that with APT almost anything was apt to happen. . . . One of General Irvine's statements was taken out of context so that the press releases said that he said that APT would make possible a war machine that the Russians wouldn't dare to tackle. Whereas actually what he had said was more of this kind of development could lead to such a situation. We haven't yet begun to get the technical press and magazine coverage which should be more factual than the newspaper coverage. . . . The amount of notoriety that has reflected on me personally is quite unnerving but I seem to be surviving well enough and I hope my professional colleagues will take most of the noise with a grain of salt [R59219-34].

It was, however, a first class job all around with a much higher than usual communication of valid technical information into the public consciousness. It was, I think, more than mere hoopla, for the added credibility of this widespread attention helped to see the APT Project through the many ups and downs in the later months and years. (The resume for January 29–February 5, 1959 says "We are going to call this the APT Project rather than the Joint Effort.")

12. Period 10: The MIT ARELEM Epilogue (July 1959 through July 1962)

Although APT was used for production parts from mid-1959 on, in various places, the performance of ARELEM was extremely erratic and unreliable. To wrap up the story and provide a tie to my later development of plex, my Algorithmic Theory of Language (the application of plex to the subject of language), and AED, I will cite briefly the subsequent history.

As we were finishing up the Phase I documentation, in the summer of 1959, the AIA APT Project asked us to look into the ARELEM problem at MIT. Even though we were switching our Air Force sponsorship from APT to the subject of computer-aided design and computer graphics, we carried along an APT collaboration task until July of 1962. During that period, with Clarence G. Feldmann (and part of the time with John F. Walsh) I worked out a completely new approach which became known as the "MIT ARELEM," which still forms the basis for the APT system used widely today (MIT, 1961). We did two complete versions of this ARELEM analysis, the First-Order Analysis being based primarily upon linear approximations, the Second-Order Analysis directly taking into account the curvature approximations to yield much more efficient results. Both analyses gave "guaranteed cut vectors" in the sense that using the actual points of tangency to the surfaces involved, the "deepest point of gouge" was determined with respect to independent inside and outside tolerance bands at both ends of the straight-line cut vector, as well as in the middle of the cut. We also, in our MIT version, had a scheme called "parabolization" which is a generalized scheme for drastically speeding up and guaranteeing the convergence of iterative vector computations. Both versions of the program also incorporated adaptive "learning" to generate excellent starting conditions for the cut vector iterations. The scheme for efficiently selecting the appropriate tool segment for use with a given center of curvature of a surface is interesting because it corresponds almost exactly to the guarded commands of Dijkstra (1975), including several very efficient algorithms for evaluation of "simultaneous Boolean expressions" with a minimum number of steps (MIT, 1961, pp. 61–66).

Although we had all of these versions of the MIT ARELEM working at MIT at various times, it was a lengthy process and went through several stages of interaction with the on-going AIA APT Project. The very first incomplete version was made mostly workable by programmers from Chance-Vought and was used in AIA APT for a short time even though we were continuing with the developments further at MIT. Feldmann spent many months and many trips working directly with the San Diego APT Project, first helping them to program the First-Order Analysis in FORTRAN, and later incorporating portions of the Second-Order Analysis as well. To our knowledge the AIA APT never did incorporate the complete MIT Second-Order Analysis with parabolization, and the work had dragged out to such an extent and we were so deeply into the beginnings of AED by 1962, that we never did complete the documentation of the final analyses beyond the quite complete descriptions that appeared in our MIT project Interim Reports. By that time, however, the APT Long Range Program was beginning at Armour Research Foundation (now IITRI) (Dobe, 1969) so that the APT Project managed to get along without our further intensive assistance.

The programming and testing of the MIT ARELEM from 1959 through 1961 was the place where we first worked out the ideas and approaches to n-component element plex programming using "reverse index registers." Each tool segment and each surface had many parameters which were kept together in a block of contiguous storage with different components accessed by an appropriate setting of an index register which pointed to the head of the block and the offset with respect to the index picked up the component. We also used the same method to embed transfer instructions in the n-component elements so that an indexed transfer jump through the element would act as a switch in a program. In this way merely by changing the index register pointer from one tool segment to another or one surface to another, the entire collection of programs constituting ARELEM would radically change both its data and its flow-of-control behavior. Although now commonplace in advanced programming languages, this was a radical innovation in 1959. It was, however, very natural in the context of our ARELEM analysis and the nature of the problem we were solving.

One thing that has always disappointed me is that this entire massive effort had so little direct impact on the other developments in programming language and computer science developments. For the most part the (by now) several hundred computer programming people who have worked on the system have been from industry, not academia. Paper writing, except addressed to the "in group," has been almost nonexistent. The continual evolution of more sophisticated features in systems which were in daily productive use meant that almost never was a complete, elegant package available for concise description and documentation. Finally, the system and problem area itself is so complex and elaborate that it is difficult to isolate a single topic in meaningful fashion for presentation to those not familiar with the complete APT and numerical control culture. For the most part, APT was viewed with respect, but from a distance, by members of the computer science community, even though many of the significant developments of the 1970s first were tried out in the 1960s in APT.

In any case, I hope that this historical look into the beginnings of APT has helped to redress the balance, somewhat. I believe the hypothesis of my theme—that although old, the original APT was "modern," because otherwise it could not have been done—is supported by the facts from which I found it emerging. The one solid conclusion I have reached is that it is much easier to make history than to write about it. I now have added to my APT files endless notes and cross references that may, someday, be useful to real historians. All I can really say is that an awful lot of people did an awful lot of good work in those days. I'm glad I was part of it all.

REFERENCES

AIA (1957a) March 26. *Report of the Meeting of the AMEC/SNC Study Group for Manuscript Codes, Computer Programming and Computer Sub-Routines Held on 1 March 1957 in Los Angles, California.* Los Angeles, California: Aircraft Industries Association Memo AMEC-57-34.

AIA (1957b) April. *Report Concerning the Meeting of the AIA/AMEC-SNC Control Data Processing Group Held at AIA, Los Angeles, California on 23–24 April 1957.* Los Angeles, California: Aircraft Industries Association (draft copy; no doc. number).

AIA (1957c) October 18. *Report of the AMEC/Subcommittee for Numerical Control held at AIA, Los Angeles, California, on 3–4 October 1957.* Los Angeles, California: Aircraft Industries Association Memo AMEC-57-87.

AIA (1958) August 20. *Report of AMEC/Numerical Control Panel Meeting held in Seattle on July 16–18, 1958.* Los Angeles, California: Aircraft Industries Association Memo AMEC-58-44.

AIA (1959) October 9. *Meeting Report, Proceedings of Computer Programmers Meeting, August 24–26 (Project 358-12.3).* Los Angeles, California: Aerospace Industries Association Memo MEC-59-69. (Section VIII, p. 12, starts MIT ARELEM work.)

AIA (1961). *APT Documentation (6 Vols.).* Washington, D.C.: Aerospace Industries Association. (Results of the APT III Central Project at San Diego, California.)

ANSI (1976). *American National Standard Programming Language PL/1.* New York: American National Standards Institute, Doc. No. ANSI X3.53-1976.

Austin, L. (1959) September. *Summary of September 1959 Monthly APT Progress Reports.* St. Louis, Missouri: McDonnell Aircraft Corporation (no number).

Benetar, V. (1957) May 10. *Subject: Standard Manuscript Language,* Marietta, Georgia: Lockheed Aircraft Corp. Memo to AIA AMEC/Subcommittee for Numerical Control (no number).

Boeing (1957a) February 27. *Part Programming Language, Numerical Control Program—Tentative.* Seattle, Washington: Boeing Airplane Co. Numerical Control Mathematical Programming Memo, 1 p.

Boeing (1957b) February 28. *Numerical Control Library Routines A. M. C. Skin Mills—Preliminary Outline.* Seattle, Washington: Boeing Airplane Co. Memo, 16 pp.

Braid, I. C. (1975) April. The Synthesis of Solids Bounded By Many Faces. *Communications of the ACM* **18**(4): 209–216.

Bromfield, G. (1956) January 12, *Numerical Control for Machining Warped Surfaces,* Cambridge, Massachusetts: MIT Servo Lab Rep. No. 6873-ER-14.

Carlberg, E. F. (1957) March 27. Letter to D. T. Ross with Attachments A–F.

Clements, D. F. (1957) June 21. *Coordinator's Report for Period May 20–June 20.* Cambridge, Massachusetts: MIT Servo Lab Memo 2D APT II-6.

Clements, D. F. (1958) March 4. Letter to O. D. Smith.

Coons, S. A., and Mann, R. W. (1960) October. *Computer-Aided Design Related to the Engineering Design Process.* Cambridge, Massachusetts: MIT Servo Lab Rep. No. 8436-TM-5, 13 pp. DDC No. AD252061.

Dijkstra, E. W. (1975). Guarded Commands, Nondeterminacy and Formal Derivation of Programs. *Communications of the ACM* **18**(8): 453–457.

Dobe, J. W. (1969) April. The APT Long Range Program: Progress to Date; Plans for the Future. Glen View, Illinois: *Numerical Control Society Sixth Annual Meeting and Technical Conference Proceedings.*

Everett, R. R. (1951). The Whirlwind I Computer. *Proceedings of the 1951 EJCC.* New York: AFIPS, p. 70.

Gregory, R. H., and Atwater, T. V., Jr. (1956) March 1. *Economic Studies of Work Performed on a Numerically Controlled Milling Machine.* Cambridge, Massachusetts: MIT Servo Lab Rep. No. 6873-ER-18. See also *Journal of Engineering* **8**(6): 337–352 (1957).

Hori, S. (1972) July. The Structure of Functions and its Application to CAM Planning. *NC Scene* Glen View, Illinois: Numerical Control Society. July: 2–5.

IBM (1963) January. *ADAPT, A System for the Automatic Programming of Numerically Controlled Machine Tools on Small Computers.* San Jose, California: Final Tech. Eng. Rep. (Air Force Contract AF33(600)-43365).

Kaynor, K. (1958) July 8. Memo to R. Nutt. *Subject: Conclusions reached at MIT on July 2, 1958.*

Kinney, G. E. (1957) June 10. Letter to G. W. Jacob. Copy received by D. T. Ross 1957, June 18.

Liskov, B., Snyder, A., Atkinson, R., and Schaffert, C. (1978) August. Abstraction Mechanisms in CLU. *Communications of the ACM* **20**(8): 564–576.

McIlroy, M. D. (1960) April. Macro Instruction Extensions of Compiler Languages. *Communications of the ACM* **3**(4): 214–220.

McWhorter, B. J. (1958) April 10. Letter to D. T. Ross, with enclosures. Contains excellent description of INTRAN-DEFPRE processing method.

MIT Servo Lab. (1952) July 30. *Final Report on Construction and Initial Operation of a Numerically Controlled Milling Machine.* Cambridge, Massachusetts, Rep. No. 6873-FR-1. Reprinted in Appendix B of Ward (1960).

MIT Servo Lab. (1956) March 15. *Design, Development and Evaluation of a Numerically Controlled Milling Machine.* Final Report. Cambridge, Massachusetts, Rep. No. 6873-FR-2. Reprinted in Appendix A of Ward (1960).

MIT Servo Lab. (1957a) January 1 through March 31. *Automatic Programming for Numerically Controlled Machine Tools.* Cambridge, Massachusetts, Rep. No. 6873-IR-3.

MIT Servo Lab. (1957b) February 18. *Programming for Numerically Controlled Machine Tools.* Cambridge, Massachusetts. (Special course brochure printed by MIT Summer Session Office.)

MIT Servo Lab. (1957c) March 23–April 3. *Course Outline and Workbook for the Special Course on Programming for Numerically Controlled Machine Tools.* Cambridge, Massachusetts (no report number).

MIT Servo Lab. (1958a) January 1–June 30. *Automatic Programming of Numerically Controlled Machine Tools.* Cambridge, Massachusetts, Rep. No. 6873-IR-6 and 7, ASTIA No. AD-156060.

MIT Servo Lab. (1958b) April. *Research in Defense Techniques for Airborne Weapons, 1957 Annual Report* (Vol. 2). Cambridge, Massachusetts: Servo Lab Rep. No. 7668-R-5(2).

MIT Servo Lab. (1959a) February 25. *APT Press Conference.* Cambridge, Massachusetts, Appendix C of Ward (1960).

MIT Servo Lab. (1959b). *APT System Documentation.* Ross, D. T. (1959) June. Vol. I, *General Description of the APT System,* 85 pp. Ross, D. T. (1959) May. Vol. II, *APT Part Programmer's Manual,* 130 pp. Ross, D. T. Vol. III, *APT Calculation Methods* (not published). MIT and AIA participating company staffs (1959) May. Vol. IV, *A Description of the APT Computer Programs,* 162 pp. Feldmann, C. G. (1959a) May. Vol. V, *Operator's and Troubleshooter's Manual,* 27 pp. Feldmann, C. G. (1959b) May. Vol. VI, *Modification and Change Procedures,* 54 pp. McAvinn, D. (1959) December. Vol. VII, *Group Control for Automatic Manipulation of Computer Programs which Exceed Core Memory,* 59 pp.

MIT Servo Lab. (1961) January. *Investigations in Computer-Aided Design* (December 1, 1959 to May 30, 1960). Cambridge, Massachusetts, Interim Eng. Rep. No. 8436-IR-1.

Pease, W. (1952) September. An Automatic Machine Tool. *Scientific American* **187**(3): 101–115.

Perlis, A. J. (1958) March 27. Letter to D. T. Ross rejecting Ross (1957f) for publication in CACM.

Ross, D. T. (1956a) February 7–9. Gestalt Programming: A New Concept in Automatic Programming. *Proceedings of the 1967 WJCC.* New York: AFIPS, pp. 5–9.

Ross, D. T. (1956b) through 1963. *Daily Resumes* (unpublished). Lexington, Massachusetts (to be placed in MIT Archives), 833 pp.

Ross, D. T. (1956c) November 30. *Machine Tool Programming Conference No. 1* (unpublished memo draft), Cambridge, Massachusetts.

Ross, D. T. (1957a) March 29. *Design of Special Language for Machine-Tool Programming.* Cambridge, Massachusetts, published in MIT (1957c), pp. 3/29.5–9. (Reproduced here in Section 4, in full.)

Ross, D. T. (1957b) May 1. *Preparations for Joint Programming of AIA APT II System.* Cambridge, Massachusetts: MIT Servo Lab. Rep. No. 6873-TM-2. (Distributed to AIA/AMEC/Subcommittee for Numerical Control.)

Ross, D. T. (1957c) June 14. *A Proposed Basic Language for the 2D APT II.* Cambridge, Massachusetts: MIT Servo Lab. Memo 2D APT II-2, 6 pp. (Reproduced here in Section 6, in full.)

Ross, D. T. (1957d) October 23–25. *Some Recent Developments in Automatic Programming of Numerically Controlled Machine Tools.* Presented at Third Annual Contour Machining Conference (no Proceedings). Published in Ross (1958a).

Ross, D. T. (1957e) November 27. Letter to B. J. McWhorter.

Ross, D. T. (1957f) December 28. *Development of a Research Effort in the Automatic Programming of Numerically Controlled Machine Tools.* Presented at Association for Computing Machinery Session of the Indianapolis meeting of the American Association for the Advancement of Science (no Proceedings). Published in Ross (1958a).

Ross, D. T. (1958a) January 7. *Papers on Automatic Programming for Numerically Controlled Machine Tools.* Cambridge, Massachusetts: MIT Servo Lab. Rep. No. 6873-TM-3.

Ross, D. T. (1958b) April. *The SLURP System for Experimental Programming.* Section III-E in MIT (1958b).

Ross, D. T. (1958c) April. *A Philosophy of Problem Solving.* Section III-D in MIT (1958b).

Ross, D. T. (1958d) April. *A Multi-Mode Control Element.* Section III-C in MIT (1958b).

Ross, D. T. (1958e) April 29. *2D-APT II Post Programmer's Manual (Field Trial Version).* Cambridge, Massachusetts: MIT Servo Lab. Memo 2D APT II-16.

Ross, D. T. (1958f) July 25. *Post Coordinators Report re Phase I System.* Cambridge, Massachusetts: Servo Lab. Memo 2D APT II-19.

Ross, D. T. (1958g) November 30. *A Progress Report on the 2D-APT-II Joint Effort for Automatic Programming of Numerically Controlled Machine Tools.* New York: ASME Paper No. 58-A-236 at ASME Annual Meeting. Published in condensed form, two parts, *Mechanical Engineering* **81**(5): 59–60, 70 (1959) May. Also published as Chapter II in MIT (1958a).

Ross, D. T. (1959) May. *APT Part Programmer's Manual.* See Vol. II of MIT (1959b).

Ross, D. T. (1960) September. *Computer-Aided Design: A Statement of Objectives.* Cambridge, Massachusetts: MIT Servo Lab. Rep. No. 8436-TM-4, DDC No. AD252060, 22 pp.

Ross, D. T. (1961) March. A Generalized Technique for Symbol Manipulation and Numerical Calculation. *Communications of the ACM* **4**(3): 147–150.

Ross, D. T. (1962) November. *An Algorithmic Theory of Language.* Cambridge, Massachusetts: MIT Servo Lab. Rep. No. ESL-TM-156, DDC No. AD296998, 68 pp.

Ross, D. T. (1964) September. *AEDJR: An Experimental Language Processor.* Cambridge, Massachusetts: MIT Servo Lab. Rept. No. ESL-TM-211, DDC No. 453881, 53 pp.

Ross, D. T. (1975) December. *Plex 1: Sameness and the Need for Rigor* and *Plex 2: Sameness and Type,* with "are: pres. pl. of BE" (1976 April). Waltham, Massachusetts: SofTech, Rep. Nos. 9031-1.1, 2.0, and 10. Abstracted in Ross (1976).

Ross, D. T. (1976) March. Toward Foundations for the Understanding of Type. *SIGPLAN Notices* 1:**8**(2), Part II, *Proceedings of Conference on Data: Abstraction, Definition and Structure,* pp. 63–65. Abstracted from Ross (1975).

Ross, D. T. (1977a) January. Structured Analysis (SA): A Language for Communicating Ideas. *IEEE Transactions on Software Engineering* **3**(1): 16–34.

Ross, D. T. (1977b) October. *Comments on APT Items in D. T. Ross Daily Resumes* (unpublished). Lexington, Massachusetts.

Ross, D. T., and Clements, D. F. (1957 and 1958). *Coordinator's Report(s),* Cambridge, Massachusetts: MIT Servo Lab. Memos: 2D APT II-9 for Period August 1–August 30; 2D APT II-10 for Period September 1–September 27; 2D APT II-11 for Period September 28–October 21; 2D APT II-12 for Period October 22–February 4, 1958; 2D APT II-13 for Period February 5–March 13; 2D APT II-14 for Period March 14–April 4; 2D APT II-15 for Period April 5–April 15; 2D APT II-17 for Period April 15–May 1.

Douglas T. Ross

Ross, D. T., and McAvinn, D. (1958) December. *Data Reduction for Pre-B-58 Tests of the XMD-7 Fire-Control System*. Vol. 3. *Evaluation of Fire-Control System Accuracy*. Cambridge, Massachusetts: MIT Servo Lab. Rep. No. 7886-R-3, ASTIA AD 207 353.

Ross, D. T., and Pople, H. E., Jr. (1956) June 26–December 31. *Automatic Programming of Numerically Controlled Machine Tools*. Cambridge, Massachusetts: MIT Servo Lab. Rep. Nos. 6873-IR 1 and 6873-IR-2.

Ross, D. T., Rodriguez, J. E., and Feldman, C. G., eds. (1970) January. *AED-0 Programmer's Guide*. Cambridge, Massachusetts: MIT Servo Lab Rep. No. ESL-R-406 (published by SofTech, Waltham, Massachusetts).

Runyon, J. H. (1953) December 1. *Whirlwind I Routines for Computations for the MIT Numerically Controlled Milling Machine,* Cambridge, Massachusetts: MIT Servo Lab. Rep. No. 6873-ER-8.

Shaw, M., Wulf, W. A., and London, R. L. (1977) March. Abstraction and Verification in ALPHARD: Defining and Specifying Iteration and Generators. *Communications of the ACM* **20**(8): 553–564.

Siegel, A. (1956a) March 1. *Information Processing Routine for Numerical Control*. Cambridge, Massachusetts: MIT Servo Lab. Rep. No. 6873-ER-16.

Siegel, A. (1956b) October. Automatic Programming of Numerically Controlled Machine Tools. *Control Engineering* **3**(10): 65–70.

Smith, O. D. (1958 and 1959). *AIA Coordinator's Report*(s). Los Angeles, California: Aircraft Industries Association memos: 1. AMEC-58-17; 1958 April 4; for Period through 1958 March 14. 2. AMEC-58-45; 1958 August 25; for Period through 1958 August 7. 3. AMEC-58-47; 1958 August 27; Definition Preprocessing Memo. 4. AMEC-58-47; 1958 August 27; for Period through 1958 August 20. 5. AMEC-58-55; 1958 October 8; for Period through 1958 September 9. 6. AMEC-58-62; 1958 October 30; for Period through 1958 October 22. 7. AMEC-59-5; 1959 January 20; for Period through 1959 January 13. 8. AMEC-59-11; 1959 February 24; Work Assignments 1959 February 18.

Smith, O. D., and Corley, C. F. (1958) February 10. *APT-II Arithmetic Program*. Los Angeles, California: North American Aviation. SHARE-type writeup submission to 2D APT II Field Trial.

Swift, C. J. (1957) October 24. Letter to E. F. Carlberg.

Voelcker, H. B., and Requicha, A. A. G. (1977) December. Geometric Modeling of Mechanical Parts and Processes. *IEEE Computer* **10**(2): 48–57.

Ward, J. E. (1960) January 15. *Automatic Programming of Numerically Controlled Machine Tools*. Final Report. Cambridge, Massachusetts: MIT Servo Lab. Rep. No. 6873-FR-3.

Ward, J. E. (1968). Numerical Control of Machine Tools. New York: *McGraw Hill Yearbook of Science and Technology,* pp. 58–65.

Wirth, N., and Hoare, C. A. R. (1966) June. A Contribution to the Development of ALGOL. *Communications of the ACM* **9**(6): 413–431.

TRANSCRIPT OF PRESENTATION

JOHN GOODENOUGH: The first paper in this session tells about the origins of APT, a language for use with numerically controlled machine tools. The paper is by Doug Ross, and Doug Ross began his career in computing in 1952, as an MIT graduate student in pure mathematics. Although a mathematician, from 1952 to 1956 he was a member of the MIT staff and was programming numerical and support software for the Whirlwind computer. In 1956 he was appointed head of the Computer Applications Group at the Electronic Systems Laboratory at MIT, and at that time his work on APT began. Twenty-two years later, Doug is chairman of the board of SofTech, a company he founded in 1969. Among his current technical interests and activities is an Air Force–sponsored effort on integrated computer-aided manufacturing, an effort that is like APT in that it is focused on improving manufacturing through the use of computers. Interestingly enough, this effort is sponsored by the Air Force Materiel Laboratory, the same group that supported the initial development of APT. Doug.

Frame 1

DOUGLAS ROSS: Archivists measure archival material in shelf feet. [Frame 1] Well, I happen to have 70 shelf feet of material gathered over the years, of which about five or six major file drawers have to do with APT [Frame 2], and this was really an oppressive thing when it came to writing this paper, because I felt that I had to go back into all that to get to the original material wherever possible.

Frame 2

Anyhow, in there I found this copy of the cover of a *New Yorker* magazine from 1959 [Frame 3]—some of you may go back that far and remember having seen it—but inside was this story [Frame 4]. "Cambridge, Mass., February 25: The Air Force announced today that it has a machine that can receive instructions in English and figure out how to make whatever is wanted and teach other machines how to make it. An Air Force General said it will enable the United States to build a war machine that nobody will want to tackle. Today it made an ashtray." And of course, the *New Yorker* has to go on and say, "In a sulk, probably."

Well, there really was such an ashtray. In fact, I have one here [Frame 6]. And this is my story of the origins of APT. The particular press conference [Feb. 25, 1959, Frame 6] that that wire service story came from in the *San Francisco Chronicle* took place at MIT, was sponsored jointly by the Aircraft Industries Association, now renamed the Aerospace Industries Association, MIT, and the Air Force Materiel Laboratory. And here was the kit that we handed out, and there is the ashtray. It had a hyperbolic paraboloid three-dimensional surface in there. But of course, APT was really built to do much more than make ashtrays [Frame 7]. This is the engine mount from an F-100 fighter aircraft. It actually was not produced with APT but instead was one of the earliest test parts done by a combination of hand programming and using subroutines on the Whirlwind computer, those subroutines being developed by John Runyan.

The machine tool itself was first described in 1952 [Frame 8], in the same summer that I joined the laboratory. I didn't have anything to do with the machine tool itself, but here it is [Frame 9], and over here is the paper tape reader, and then these banks of electronics control the three axes of the machine tool. This slides back and forth; this goes in and out; and this goes up and down to move a tool, as you can see, around a part in space and whittle out whatever shape you wanted. The electronics themselves were built out of existing telephone relay equipment and so forth, and here you see the three banks of equipment for the three axes [Frame 10].

The encoded instructions on the punch tape were very detailed, using a Hamming checking code and all that sort of thing, and so the idea of APT was to create a high-level language that would accept the description of a part just in terms of its dimensions and relationships among them, and then control the path of a tool going around the outside. And so you see [Frame 11], from $1\frac{1}{2}$, 3, and 2—some point up in the air—go to $1\frac{1}{2}$, 3, and 0—that's a plunging motion of 2 inches, down to the level of the work pieces, at which time the various go forward instructions would take it around the part.

Here's an example of the language itself [Frame 12]. This is the one for the outside of the ashtray, and you can see that the language has symbolic names for the dimensions. In fact, in the demonstration program, we allowed arbitrary choice of these parameters so that you could see how entire families of similar parts could be made because after specifying such things as the tool radius, the tolerance that's to be used, and the feed rate in inches per minute, and the max *dp*, the maximum step size of the calculations, and those things, then came a whole string of instructions having to do with geometric relationships. And in fact, over here you can see the ruler-and-compass type of constructions that you could do with the language itself to construct all of the necessary geometric data which then the GO instruction would cause the tool to cut out. We'll see more examples as we go along.

Frame 3. Cover of *The New Yorker,* March 28, 1959 (not reproduced here for copyright reasons).

CAMBRIDGE, MASS., Feb. 25—The Air Force announced today that it has a machine that can receive instructions in English, figure out how to make whatever is wanted, and teach other machines how to make it.

An Air Force general said it will enable the United States to "build a war machine that nobody would want to tackle."

Today it made an ashtray.—*San Francisco Chronicle.*

In a sulk, probably.

Frame 4. Anecdote from *The New Yorker*.

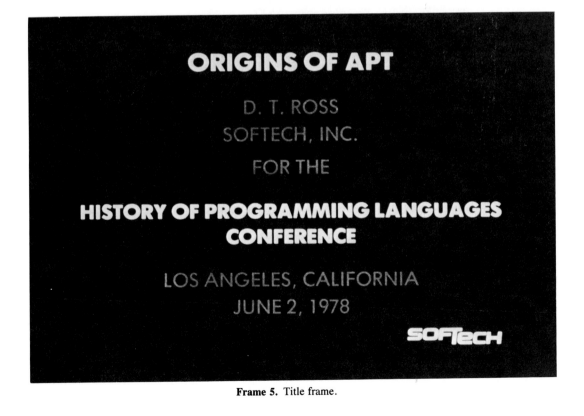

ORIGINS OF APT

D. T. ROSS
SOFTECH, INC.

FOR THE

HISTORY OF PROGRAMMING LANGUAGES CONFERENCE

LOS ANGELES, CALIFORNIA
JUNE 2, 1978

SOFTech

Frame 5. Title frame.

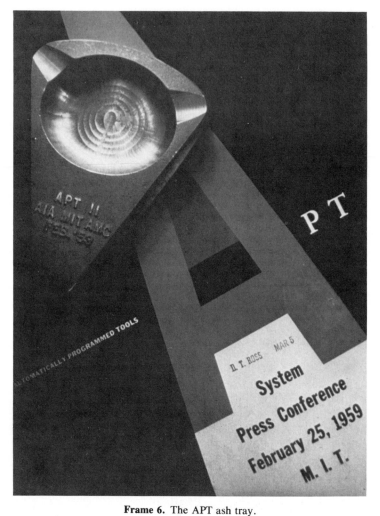

Frame 6. The APT ash tray.

But the important thing is that the language was very complete—was, from the beginning, by its nature—it had to be a fully typed language, and we'll see that that had quite a few impacts on the development of APT itself.

Now, the Electronic Systems Laboratory was originally called the Servomechanisms Laboratory, and this [Frame 13] was a big 8 × 12 or 16 foot chart that used to be out at our front door, that showed the whole series of development that had the same sponsorship for 20 years from the Air Force Materials Lab, starting with the machine tool, then APT, which stands for Automatically Programmed Tool, and then we went on into the Computer-Aided Design Project, in which we developed both the hardware and software of computer graphics, developed our AED system which, incidentally, is one of the more powerful of the ALGOL extensions. AED stood for Algol Extended for Design. It still is being used. It was the first language with types and complex data structures and that sort

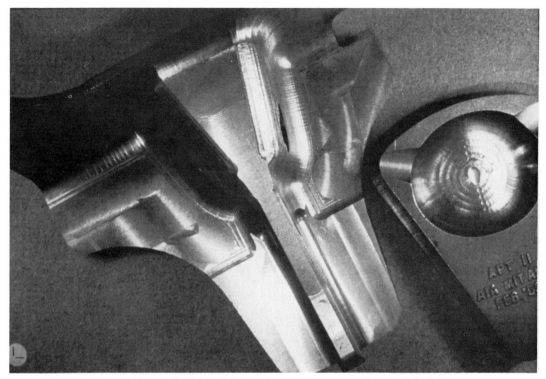

Frame 7. F-100 Engine mount and ash tray.

of thing. But all of this work, including the software engineering and software technology, sprung out from the same series of developments. And as John indicated, is still going on today.

The time span of APT was almost abrupt [Frame 14]. It started in June 1956. The previous engineering project had left the Laboratory in a body to form a private company, Concord Controls, to produce numerically controlled machine tool directors on a commercial basis, but they left behind a proposal to the Air Force that automatic programming should be further investigated. The contract actually started in June, but I had a whole string of other projects going and had no staff at all or anybody who knew anything about any of this, including myself, by the way, until September when the students arrived. And at that time, had Sam Matsa and George Zames along with Jerry Wenker who was very green, brand new, mathematical background, but we had to train him to be a programmer; that's what we started with in September.

Now, in January 1957 we were put in touch with the subcommittee for numerical control of the Aircraft Industries Association by Bill Webster, our contract sponsor, and we thought that they would be able to tell us what we should be doing in our research. At that point we finished up our first interim report, had APT all defined, in terms of its structure —as you'll see—and so forth. But we really didn't know what we were doing too much. So we thought the subcommittee would be able to tell us, because they'd been working on

Douglas T. Ross

Frame 8. Cover of *Scientific American,* September 1952, special issue on Automatic Control. [Reprinted by permission. Copyright © 1952 by Scientific American, Inc. All rights reserved.]

this, and the Air Force was purchasing $30 million—and in those days that was really a lot of money—worth of machine tools that were supposed to be put into practice by the aircraft companies in 1957. Some of these machine tools were for such things as wing skins that are 12 ft wide and 60 ft long, whittling out great upper panels for the B 52 wing panels; that sort of thing. We used to say, ''Look out below. Here come all these expensive tools that are supposed to be put to practice.''

Well, it turned out actually that the brief report on the progress that we'd made in our research turned out to be very interesting to that group because they were sort of floundering around as to what to do. So they asked us to give a special course on numerical

Frame 9. Photographs of machine tool from September 1952 *Scientific American*. [Photo by Bernard Hoffman.]

Frame 10. Photographs of relay panels from September 1952 *Scientific American*. [Photo by Bernard Hoffman.]

control, which we did, from soup to nuts, including talking about what a computer is, and binary and everything else. And then as a result of a series of meetings with the subcommittee, they decided to form the APT Joint Effort. We had a kickoff meeting at MIT in the week of May 20 to 24, and actually started out, I believe it was—we started with 14 companies all ganging together with MIT as the leader; eventually it built up to 19 companies, I believe, that were active. Some 25 or so got copies of the deck. And at one point I added up the number of warm bodies that were involved in this first round and came up with the magic number of 55 programmers that were involved in making this first system.

So the first language for APT, actually, I created by default in two days on one weekend when one of the assigned companies was unable to get on with its job defining a language. And then we had this period of the evolution of the APT System with programs being collected. We hoped we'd be finished in October. We actually collected the programs in December to February. Put them all together and finally shipped the first field trial version out the door on April 10. Then came a period when we turned over the coordination to the AIA itself, and Dale Smith of North American was the next coordinator. We jumped back in with a post-coordinator report to be of some further help. Finally we came out with the Phase 1 language which is the one that was announced at the press conference.

Then the system proceeded and had still more difficulties. It's a very very complicated problem to do all this three-dimensional calculation that had never been done before. And so we jumped back in even though we'd switched now to the computer-aided design project and were incidentally working with such things as playing around with LISP and coming up with the basic ideas of my algorithmic theory of language and *plex* and everything else that led to AED and structured analysis and the things we're doing today. But we did, for this period from roughly July of 1959 through June of 1962, work on finally getting the semantics of the language, the calculating programs to where they would fly over the long pull. And my proudest point about APT is that it's only just recently that there have been any major changes to either the language, which still is very much the same—it's a standard—but also, more importantly, to the structure of the system.

Now, remember, this was in 1956, the fall of 1956 that we were doing this. This whole structure was, you see, laid out and known before we actually started the project going [Frame 15]. We decided that we had to approach this problem as a simulated von Neumann type of computer. So we had an input translation stage which—I go through it in the paper—the stages of evolution that made this result in an actual, proper, lexical processor. The parsing of the language was done in what we called preprocessing, which was of two forms; both instruction preprocessing, and definition preprocessing; definition preprocessing making heavy use of this Library of Surface Solutions for all the different kinds of geometric objects. Then there was a control element which interpreted the code that was compiled by the preprocessing, which was the proper parsing functions. Then this very complex program—the arithmetic element program, which in effect, instead of adding and subtracting numbers, moved tools around in space with respect to surfaces, and then the output was a tool center dump, because from the beginning the system had to have separate postprocessing and output. It was machine-tool-independent, as well as computer-independent intended from the very beginning, and by virtue of this separation, there are

Frame 11. See Fig. 9 (top) in Paper, p. 328.

Frame 12. See Fig. 9 (bottom) in Paper, p. 328.

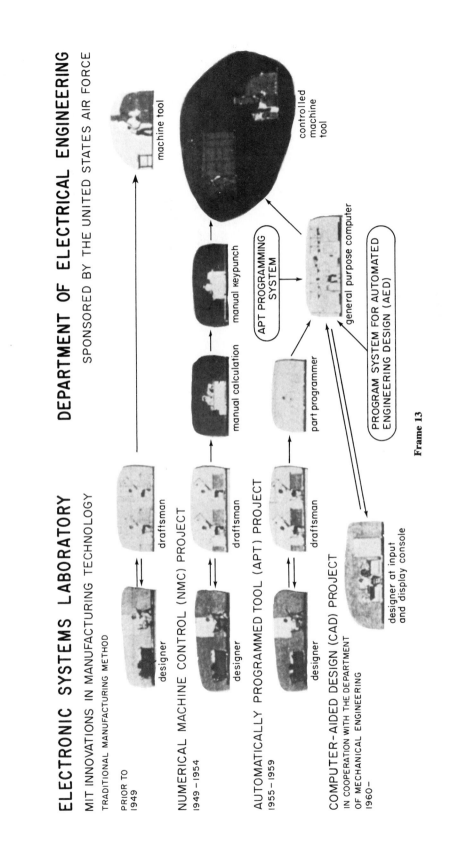

ELECTRONIC SYSTEMS LABORATORY

MIT INNOVATIONS IN MANUFACTURING TECHNOLOGY

TRADITIONAL MANUFACTURING METHOD

PRIOR TO
1949

designer

draftsman

machine tool

NUMERICAL MACHINE CONTROL (NMC) PROJECT

1949 – 1954

designer

draftsman

manual calculation

manual keypunch

AUTOMATICALLY PROGRAMMED TOOL (APT) PROJECT

1955 – 1959

designer

draftsman

part programmer

APT PROGRAMMING SYSTEM

COMPUTER-AIDED DESIGN (CAD) PROJECT

IN COOPERATION WITH THE DEPARTMENT
OF MECHANICAL ENGINEERING

1960 –

designer at input
and display console

DEPARTMENT OF ELECTRICAL ENGINEERING

SPONSORED BY THE UNITED STATES AIR FORCE

controlled
machine
tool

general purpose computer

PROGRAM SYSTEM FOR AUTOMATED
ENGINEERING DESIGN (AED)

Frame 13

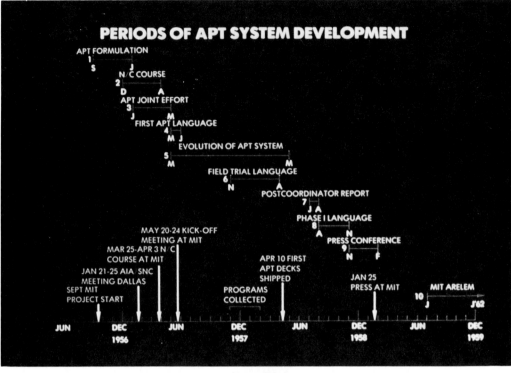

Frame 14

now, I believe, several hundred postprocessors, and it got to be the same way that nobody could sell a machine tool unless they had an APT postprocessor. And of course we had diagnostics as well.

Also, this chart will show some of the names of the people—and the companies that were involved in this rather large project.

APT itself—this [Frame 16] is a picture from the first interim report that came out in the fall of 1956—we defined APT I to be point-by-point motion of a tool, which is similar to running a drill press, or making discrete motions in space. And so we sort of considered that to be what had gone on in the past. And then we had APT II which was a language in which you thought of programming in terms of three-dimensional space curves, and APT III was to be something that was programmed in entire regions, where you'd whittle out entire surfaces at one time. Now, we actually had research programs going in January for all three of these areas, just starting, of course, in 1957.

Now, when I was trying to write this paper, I was struggling with this blur of information that I had in all my records, and out of it came a very interesting theme which I then used to structure the final talk, and the paper [Frame 17]. And that is that because of three basic things—for example, the semantics of the language had to come first in the design of this language. We had absolutely no prior history in this field. Arnie Siegel had done (as

Frame 15. See Fig. 3 in Paper, p. 312.

Frame 16. See Fig. 2 in Paper, p. 294.

THEME 1

SEMANTICS HAD TO COME FIRST

NO PRIOR HISTORY

SYNTAX REFLECTED VIEW

Frame 17

you will see, I'll give an example of it) a little prototype language for two dimensions with straight lines and circles, but that was the only thing that had ever been done in this area. So that the meaning of three-dimensional geometry and tool motion and so forth had to come first, and then the syntax had to reflect that because that was the only way we had to understand the problem.

The second part of the theme is that the system had to be modular [Frame 18]. Again, it was done in 14 different sites all over the country. I had originally proposed that the companies send people to MIT to work with us, but that was one of these economic crunches and they were even counting pencils at the time, so that I had to design the thing to be done all over the country by different portions of the development team on this very tight schedule, and from the beginning we had to have machine tool independence. This forced the system to be modular. We couldn't have done it otherwise.

The third part of the theme is that similar modularity had to apply to both the syntax and the semantics of the language and furthermore they had to be open ended [Frame 19]. We knew that we did not have the option of even considering making a one-time short-term thing. This was just the beginning step of what was intended to be a long-term evolution.

So the result of these conditions of the project was that we were forced to anticipate [Frame 20] almost all of the modern well-structured methodology, and I believe (this took me by surprise. I'd forgotten when most of these things happened) . . . I was amazed to find that we were doing things three years earlier than I remembered, and had been talking about for years with people when I actually got to looking through my records. So I think that this makes APT an interesting language to study because in a way, it's more pure than any of the other languages in that the very semantics, the very meaning of the language itself was unknown.

Now, here's the way that APT functions [Frame 21]. You see, in order to handle three dimensional curves, they are generated actually by intersecting surfaces. So we have a *part surface* and a *driving surface* which intersects along a curve. That's what the tool is supposed to move along. Actually it moves in the valley between them. And it keeps going until it bumps into a *check surface*—checking tangency conditions, either to the surface, on the surface, or past the surface. Then you can go either right or go left, along the next intersection, you see, and that combination will make the path of the tool through space.

Now here's Arnie Siegel's prototype language [Frame 22]. *P* stood for point, *C* for circle, and *S* for straight line. And down here, 15 inches per minute—go along these sequences of curves to whittle out the part. The same sample part, done now in the earliest

THEME 2

HAD TO BE MODULAR SYSTEM

DISPERSED DEVELOPMENT TEAM

MACHINE TOOL INDEPENDENCE

Frame 18

THEME 3

SYNTAX (TRANSLATION) AND
SEMANTICS (EXECUTION)
HAD TO BE MODULAR
AND OPEN-ENDED

Frame 19

of the APT languages [Frame 23], was much more mnemonic, you see, with names and talking about conditions of being tangent to, or *small x* and *large y* to pick out multiple intersections, and again, quite readable. One of the main intentions of the language was that it be, again, very English-like because the part programmers, as we came to call them as distinct from computer programmers, were not of academic background.

This is the course that we gave at MIT [in 1958, Frame 24], and from the notes for that and working papers, I found this bit of—here's the purchase requisition [Frame 25] for going out and purchasing a bunch of Styrofoam rods and balls and blocks like they use for Christmas decorations, so that I could make a bunch of models which I actually waved around. They're long since gone, but this was my effort to show people what it was to do language design in this area. And in fact, I find it intriguing that this form of description of objects in terms of algebra of unions and joins of objects, which was not the way that APT language is built, has just recently in the last few years come into its own and I find people saying, "Aha! You missed it in APT. Why didn't you do it this way?" And so I love to point out that, yes, I thought of it the same way too, but it just didn't fit the circumstances at the time.

Here's some of my actual handwritten notes from the lecture on language design which I do commend to you, even if you read nothing else in my paper [Frame 26]. This is in there verbatim, and it is from the spring of 1957 and is about actually designing language when we had no basis for having done that before, and here for example I'm giving examples of SAY statements. The *blank* is on the *blank*. The *blank* is the same size as the *blank* [Frame 27]. Where you can fill in these various forms. A *blank* with a *blank* will be called a *blank*. And here are examples of DO statements, which had to do with the motions. And here are some more examples of similar things—this is the actual lecture notes from that course. And again, it appears in the paper.

Here's [Frame 28] the memo, May 1, that called for the kick-off meeting at MIT, and it shows that we were going to be the coordinator, and a "semidemocratic procedure will be used to establish all rules," and so forth. Now, "semidemocratic" turns out to be very useful. What that meant was that we would have full and open democracy in debate and so forth, as long as I thought things were on track, and going all right. And as soon as I didn't: boom! We'd do it my way! And it worked very effectively. In fact, I evidently used it during that first week, even though my resumes say that I was afflicted with all sorts of intestinal troubles during the week—but one of the attendees sent me a Special Delivery two-page letter almost in tears saying, he hoped we were still friends and so forth. So evi-

THEME 4

THESE FORCED APT TO ANTICIPATE
MOST MODERN WELL-STRUCTURED
METHODOLOGY.

Frame 20

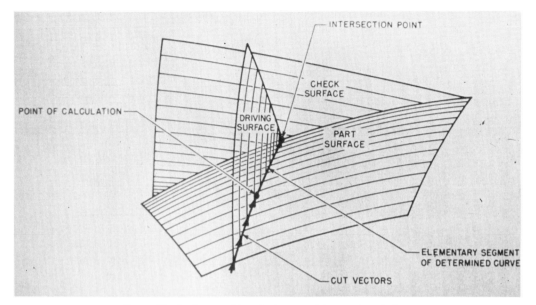

Frame 21. Surfaces and terminology used in part description.

dently I came down very hard at some point during the meeting. But it was quite essential in order to get things done that we have one set of mind and leadership making the thing happen.

Now, this is a page from a copy of what I used to (this is what made writing my paper so difficult too) I kept what I called "Daily Resumes" [Frame 29] where I just took my dictating machine and would say who I met with about what. Because I had about four or five other projects going simultaneously, some of them in much hotter water than APT, at the same time, and also involving multiple programmers at multiple sites working on evaluation of fire control systems for the B-58 airplane and that sort of thing. So I had to keep my sanity. The only way I could keep track of what was going on was to do this daily technical diary. This is from that two-day weekend when I first did APT [Frame 30]. Notice, it has a typo; it was 1957—May 27, 1957, not 1956. But it does pin down the results. Right after the meeting, you see, I decided on the basic structure of the language; that it would have left and right sides [Frame 31].

Here's an example from the first year. APT, like COBOL, has geometric definitions and parameters definitions in different sections of the program [Frame 32]. Then control instructions [Frame 33] starting instructions, and finally END FINI allowed you to run multiple programs at one time.

Here's the actual final language that was distributed. This was the entire syntax of the language in this one chart [Frame 34]. This is our form of metalanguage, and with just a few rules to describe the entire thing. Of course there were many more things for the forms of definition of the geometric quantities.

Frame 22. See Fig. 4 in Paper, p. 319.

Frame 23. See Fig. 5 in Paper, p. 320.

Douglas T. Ross

Frame 24. Attendees at 1959 MIT course. [Blank spot present in original.]

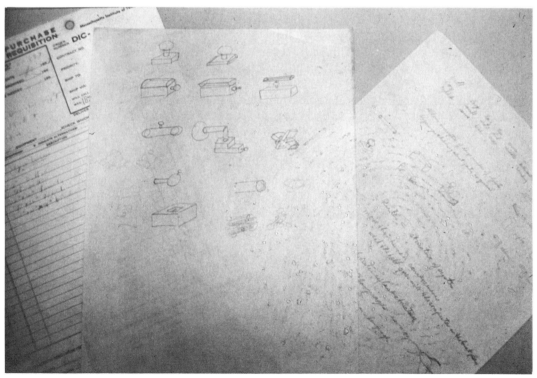

Frame 25. Relating to the styrofoam models.

Frame 26. Notes from language design lecture.

3/28.7

4. It is also possible to establish a wide variety of modifiers for the language, knowing only a few representative things to be modified.

Well-chosen modifiers can be very important to the language since they allow complicated ideas to be expressed by simple statements. They allow variations of meaning without drastically changing the form of the statements.

Things which we say things about can be modified according to size, quantity, relationship to other things, etc. "Say" - things may also be modified by other "say" - things.

Example: There are _____ _____ s on the _____ of the _____.

Things which we say to do can be modified according to how quickly, how carefully, and in what mode or version they are to be done, etc.

Example: _____ _____ ly to the _____ and then _____ _____ _____ ly.

5. With the kinds of "say" - and "do" - statements determined and modifiers established, the main features of the language are set.

The next step is to "flesh out" the skeleton of the language with the necessary thing vocabulary.

Usually there will be many more "say" - things than there are "do"-things, since problem areas are usually quite restricted in scope.

Frame 27. Syntactic models.

D. T. ROSS   MAY 6 1957

MASSACHUSETTS INSTITUTE OF TECHNOLOGY
Servomechanisms Laboratory
Cambridge 39, Massachusetts

D.S.R. Project 6873

MEMORANDUM

TO: AIA/AMEC/Subcommittee For Numerical Control

FROM: Douglas T. Ross

SUBJECT: Preparations for Joint Programming of AIA APT II System

DATE: May 1, 1957

-   - - - - - - - - -

Introduction

At its April 25th and 26th meeting in Los Angeles, the AIA/AMEC/
Subcommittee for Numerical Control approved the proposal of the Numerical
Control Data Processing Group for a joint effort to produce a system of
computer programs for automatic programming of two-dimensional parts. The
system of programs will be patterned after the work of Boeing, Lockheed,
Georgia, North American, and MIT, and will be called the AIA APT II system.
The problem has been broken into many parts and each participating plant
will be responsible for programming a part of the system. The Servomechanisms
Laboratory, MIT, has been chosen as project coordinator, and a meeting of all
programming personnel who are to execute the actual work has been scheduled
for May 20 through May 24 at MIT. This memorandum outlines the proposed
agenda for the MIT meeting, and describes briefly the current ideas on the
AIA APT II system as outlined at the Subcommittee Meeting.

Since MIT is acting merely as coordinator and representative of
the Data Processing Group and the Subcommittee in this work, a semi-
democratic procedure will be used in establishing all rules, regulations,
procedures, and deadlines. By combining the ideas and suggestions of those
in attendance, it should be possible to arrive at a smoothly functioning
and efficient organization. It is hoped that an optimistic progress report
can be made to the Subcommittee at its next meeting.

Topics To Be Discussed at MIT

Most of the people attending the meeting, although experienced
programmers, will not be familiar with the many problems which arise in
designing automatic programming systems for numerically controlled machine
tools. Therefore, the first item of business will be a series of presentations
describing the proposed AIA APT II system, and all of its components, including
the language, thoroughly and in great detail. The material will be gone

Frame 28. Announcement of kickoff meeting.

Monday Resume

May 27, 1956   121

went over Chapter I with Don again so that he could give it to
Merener. He is also going to work on Chapter II and I said that
III was ready as far as I was concerned if the figure numbers were
corrected. Worked out an approved check surface calculation. Jerry and
will include this in the appendix preceding the present appendices
APT II and APT III.

Wrote a letter to Dr. Wall sending him the line of sight
questions and telling him that Dave McAvinn would write him further.

Started working out a language for the A.I.A. APT II to suggest
star on the basis of the results of our meeting. I have decided that
probably should have multiple words in the major word portion of the
instructions and these sections will be separated by commas. In this way
all of the instructions modifying the main instruction will appear on the
one card. If not stated, they will remain the same as before. This can
easily be programmed by having indicators set whenever a word occurs and
each program will check with these indicators when appropriate. I have
also decided not to store inside outside information with surfaces for
this system, since it is easier to reach say where the tool should go. In
a final system we should have both possibilities. In a place where
questions arise   such as planes where it is not really sure which
is the inside or the outside in the canonical form. This, of course, can
handled again in terms of the normal. I suppose it could be handled,
however, by saying whether you go through the surface or just up to the
surface when you reach it. I will summarize these considerations in a
letter and send it to Wie and suggest that the completion of the language
a function of the subcommittee and he with the help of Carlberg,

Frame 29. A daily resume.

MASSACHUSETTS INSTITUTE OF TECHNOLOGY
Servomechanisms Laboratory
Cambridge 39, Massachusetts

Memorandum 2D APT II-2

SUBJECT: A Proposed Basic Language For The 2D APT II

FROM: Douglas T. Ross

DATE: June 14, 1957

- -

The following pages present the format and vocabulary of a proposed language for the 2D APT II System. The format is defined by the types of statements which can be made in the language. Notice that the character space is completely ignored and that use is made of space in the vocabulary to provide easy readability. Since card format is to be variable field, the double dollar sign indicates the termination of a statement, and a complete statement need not appear on a single card. The form of instructions have been chosen for generality and for ease in converting into the coded form required for the initial control element program. Notice that the type of curve which is to be followed is derived from the definitions of the symbols used. The modifiers DNT CT and TERM permit symbolic positioning of a tool and establish meanings of later modifiers. For the initial system at least it will not be possible to use NEAR and FAR in definitions since the preprocessing programs will not have any means for determining the

Frame 30. Resume of first APT language design.

Frame 31. APT example.

Frame 32. See top of right side of Fig. 6 in Paper, p. 322.

Frame 33. See middle of right side of Fig. 6 in Paper, p. 322.

Frame 34. See Fig. 8 in Paper, p. 326.

Frame 35. See Fig. 7 in Paper, p. 325.

Frame 36. Press packet.

Frame 37. From the press packet.

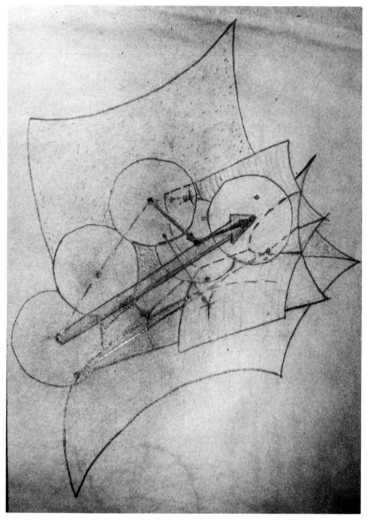

Frame 38. Tool motion.

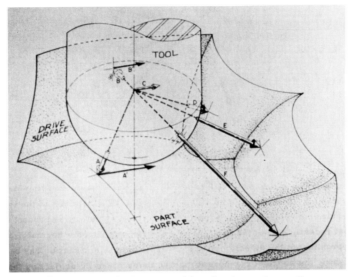

Frame 39. Typical cutter position showing surface pulls.

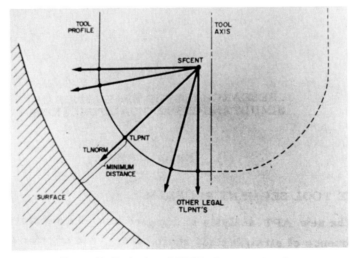

Frame 40. Projection of SFCENT onto tool profile.

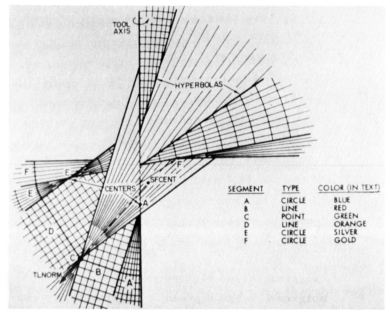

Frame 41. Complete "colored" regions for sample tool.

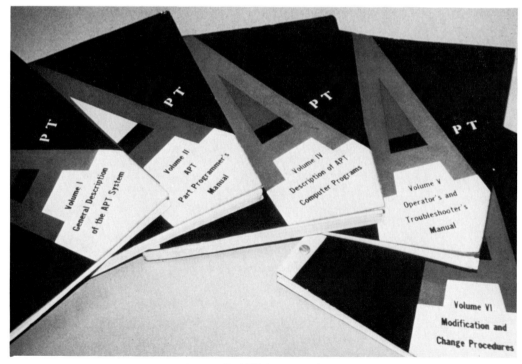

Frame 42. APT documentation.

Frame 43. APT documentation.

Frame 44. Mickey's nephew.

Frame 45. Souveniers of APT TV program.

Frame 46. APT memorabilia.

This [Frame 35] just shows how, again, with ignorable words you get very English-like: go right along the circle with a center . . . and so forth, made it so that it was very easy for people to use the language [Frame 36]. And there's how we all looked at the time [Frame 37]. This was Bill Webster who was the sponsor, and yours truly at an earlier age. [Carl Perry is also in this slide—Ed]

These are just some things about the arithmetic element calculations [Frames 38 and 39] that merely led to all sorts of further complexities including, as I point out in there, (this is essentially the guarded command of Dijkstra), for selecting tool segments [Frames 40 and 41]. And these are the documents—again, the general description for our programmers' manual, description for the computer programmers, how to run the system, and how to change it [Frame 42].

And here [Frame 43] was the later documentation that came out of the subsequent system. They brought all the programmers into one place at San Diego to do the system that actually got into production use, and here's [Frame 44] the one I wanted to get to, because we were having this conference here. This was my daughter's Mickey Mouse guitar, well beat up because it was well loved, and if you look down here, here's one of [Mickey's] nephews who was the sample for this test of how fast could I write a complex part program. And sure enough, it worked, and here was this computer display when we were doing a public television program on it [Frame 45].

So this [Frame 46] is the slide I wanted to finish with. APT is about all these things which are equally important. I think the cheerful little Mickey Mouse there says just as much about the language as all the rest. It was a really great time to be doing things and quite a different language in many respects—it had a preprocessor, full macro definition in fact, that it was defined in 1958, actually got into the language in 1959, and in 1960 and 1961, and also led to all the things about typed language and so forth. They all had their roots back here and were not just talked about but done. Thanks.†

TRANSCRIPT OF QUESTION AND ANSWER SESSION

JOHN GOODENOUGH: We have a question from Dave Thompson "What's the relationship of ADAPT to APT? I know a version of ADAPT that runs on the XDS 940 for example."

DOUGLAS ROSS: Right. ADAPT was the outgrowth, remember, I said this thing was intended to be machine-independent, computer-independent as well as machine-tool-independent, and from the beginning the main effort of the AIA group was on the [IBM] 704 because the surveys showed that that's what most people had. But there also was an effort right from the beginning to do things for smaller machines. And there was a [IBM] 650 effort, which later was funded again by the Air Force with IBM where they did develop this smaller version of APT for smaller machines. Also the APT III Region Programming that I mentioned—we had a very complete system working at MIT and Sam Matsa left the

---

† Note: The material on pages 339–365 was edited from the transcribed tape recording of the oral presentation at the conference. The author would have preferred to have had a different version of the talk printed here. Copies of that version are available from Mr. Ross (SofTech, 460 Totten Pond Road, Waltham, Massachusetts 02154).

Douglas T. Ross

project in 1958 to go work for IBM to start off the 650 small machine version, but instead convinced them to do a region programming which became known as AUTOPROMT and was another one of the strong languages in that day.

GOODENOUGH: A question from Richard Miller: "What kind of computer hardware was available at the time?"

ROSS: As I say it was primarily—people had 1103s. We were using an [ERA, later UNIVAC] 1103 on the pre-B-58 fire control system tests that we were doing down in Florida, and some of the companies had those. But for the most part it was 650s or the 704. Incidentally, I also wanted to mention that, with respect to this question of compiling on one machine and running on another, remember, one of the talks yesterday it was said that the UNIVAC was used to prepare programs for the 1103; we happened to do the same thing, preparing programs on Whirlwind and flying the tapes down to Florida, to run on the 1103 also down there at the same time.

GOODENOUGH: A last question: "What kind of numerical control machinery was available?" This is also asked by Richard Miller.

ROSS: There was quite a wide range even at that time, ranging from small milling machines, up to these great huge things with multiple axes, also. We also were supposed to be able to handle five degrees of freedom on the tool: x, y, z, and two angles of rotation. But the actual language for five-dimensional control came quite a bit later, even though we had that work to do our research systems at MIT, including limit surfaces where a tool comes over and runs across the sharp angle between two surfaces that intersect, all that sort of thing. And so the machine tools just kept proliferating, and as I say, there are now hundreds of them. Still very little in the way of machine portability. In the language itself, the things about turning coolant on and off and things controlling feed rate, passed through to the postprocessor, and so they still remain machine-dependent. It's even harder to get portability in machine tool programming than it is in computer programming, evidently.

GOODENOUGH: Thank you very much.

FULL TEXT OF ALL QUESTIONS SUBMITTED

RICHARD MILLER

You mentioned a Hamming code was used. Who was responsible for its introduction? Did your hardware specifically have this capacity?
What kind of computer hardware was available? And also what kind of Numerical Control machinery was available?

DAVE THOMPSON

What is the relationship of ADAPT to APT? I know of a version of ADAPT on an XDS 940 at the National Bureau of Standards in Boulder, Colorado.

BIOGRAPHY OF DOUGLAS T. ROSS

Douglas T. Ross received the degree of A. B. cum laude in Mathematics from Oberlin College in 1951, and the S. M. degree without course specification from MIT in 1954. He completed the course requirements for the degree of Ph.D. in Mathematics at MIT in 1956.

He has held many positions at MIT, including Head of the Computer Applications Group at the Electronics Systems Laboratory, Lecturer in the Electrical Engineering Department, and Project Engineer for the MIT Computer-Aided Design Project. His activities included:

directing development of integrated system of program development, integration, and testing tools for production of large-scale military programs;

creating and directing development of APT System for automatic programming of numerically controlled machine tools, now an international standard;

leading MIT Computer-Aided Design Project including research and development in language theory, language design, generalized compiler construction, computer graphics hardware and software, and design applications.

In 1969, SofTech was founded. Mr. Ross was President from 1969 to 1975 and is now Chairman of the Board of Directors.

He was an organizer and participant in the NATO Software Engineering Conferences in Germany (1968) and Italy (1969).

Mr. Ross received the Joseph Marie Jacquard Award from the Numerical Control Society in 1975. The paper "Theoretical Foundations for the Computer-Aided Design System" co-authored with J. E. Rodriguez, now Senior Vice President of SofTech, received the Prize Paper Award at the AFIPS Spring Joint Computer Conference in 1963. The paper "AED Approach to Generalized Computer-Aided Design" shared the Prize Paper Award at the 20th Anniversary National Meeting of the Association for Computing Machinery in August 1967. In 1980 he received the Distinguished Service Award from the Society for Manufacturing Engineers.

JOVIAL Session

Chairman: John Goodenough
Speaker: Jules I. Schwartz

PAPER: THE DEVELOPMENT OF JOVIAL

Jules I. Schwartz

Computer Sciences Corp.

1. The Background

1.1. The Environmental and Personnel Setting

The time was late 1958. Computers that those who were involved with the first JOVIAL project had been using included the JOHNNIAC (built at RAND Corporation), the IBM AN/FSQ-7 (for SAGE), 701, and 704. A few had worked with board wired calculators. Some had never programmed. For those using IBM, the 709 was the current machine. There were various other manufacturers at the time, some of whom do not exist today as computer manufacturers.

The vacuum tube was still in vogue. Very large memories, either high-speed direct access or peripheral storage, didn't exist, except for magnetic tape and drums on some computers.

The first large-scale system which was built and maintained by thousands of people was in the process of being installed after a considerable amount of effort, expense, and technological innovation. Called SAGE, it was a large real-time system (very large by 1958 standards). It had, among other things, an interesting and very valuable (even by today's standards) utility system for assisting in development. This included the Communication Pool. The Comm Pool's purpose was to permit the sharing of System Data among many programs by providing a centralized data description. Programming for SAGE had been done in machine language, as was almost all programming up to that time.

FORTRAN existed and had been in use for a few years, but use of higher level languages wasn't nearly as common as the use of such languages today. Certainly the majority of people involved in compiler efforts at that time, and in particular the initial JOVIAL language development and compiler effort, had almost no experience with such activities.

HISTORY OF PROGRAMMING LANGUAGES

369

I had had experience with the language and compiler called PACT (Project for Automatic Coding Techniques) which was developed and described in 1954–1955 (Melahn *et al.*, 1956). But actually this experience, largely because of the nature of that language and the computer the first version ran on (the IBM 701), was not particularly valuable for the development of languages in the ALGOL class.

One of the significant things that got the JOVIAL language and compiler work started was an article on Expression Analysis that appeared in the 1958 *Communications of the ACM* (Wolpe, 1958). The fact that this was actually quite a revelation to us at that time seems interesting now. Since that day, of course, there have been many developments in the parsing of mathematical and logical expressions. However, that article was the first exposure many of us had to the subject. Some of us who had just finished work on some other projects (including SAGE) began experimentation with the processing of complex expressions to produce an intermediate language utilizing the techniques described. There was no compiler language at the time in our plans, but the idea of being able to understand and parse complex expressions in itself was of sufficient interest to motivate our efforts.

Another article which was to have great influence on our future development was also published in the *Communications of the ACM* in 1958. This was the description of what was then called the International Algebraic Language (IAL, later called ALGOL), which had been defined by what became (and for the most part had been) an esteemed group of computer people (Perlis and Samelson, 1958).

1.2. The Economic and Situation Stimulus

JOVIAL really got its beginning because of the launching by the Air Force of another large system. This one followed SAGE and it was called the SACCS System. SACCS was to be developed from scratch. This meant new computers, a new system, new programming techniques, and a new operating (executive) system. All of these had to be developed before the operational program could be developed. The main computer was the IBM AN/FSQ-31. Other communications computers (built by ITT) were also utilized.

1.3. The Technical Base for JOVIAL

The two major influences on the language of JOVIAL were, first, the International Algebraic Language, which served as the language architectural base, and SAGE, which contributed to the knowledge of many of the problems and ideas needed to solve the large programming system problem. IAL was chosen as the base language for several reasons. One was that at the time it appeared as if it would become the commonly accepted standard for languages. Secondly, it seemed like a better technical basis for a new language than FORTRAN, which was the only other possibility. SAGE influenced such matters as data handling, Communication Pool, and the need for a variety of types of variables (items or elements). These things were deemed essential to the programming of SACCS and served as the basis for the first definition of JOVIAL.

1.4. Organizational and People Beginnings

The first actual contribution to the language effort that eventually led to JOVIAL was the small study which took place at SDC in California in the latter part of 1958. As stated before, it started with experimentation with the analysis of logical and mathematical expressions. And, although the intent was not, at the time, to start developing a language, that was not completely out of the realm of possibility. (But it should be remembered that up until then language development was not a wide-spread phenomenon. Within a year or two, it would become as wide-spread as certain viruses.) Key members of this study were Erwin Book, Harvey Bratman, and myself. During the latter months of 1958, I was transferred to New Jersey to work on the SACCS project. This transfer came shortly after the publication of the description of IAL in the *Communications of the ACM* that was referenced above. Based on the experience with SAGE and the reading of the IAL description, I recommended to the SACCS development managers, prior to my transfer, the use of a higher level language to program the system. To my and a number of other people's surprise, this recommendation was accepted.

Actually the final recommendation was made in New Jersey, where the SACCS program was to be developed. This written recommendation was done with a paper typed on about seven or eight onion-skin pages around December 1958. The title of it was "OVIAL —Our Version of the International Algebraic Language". It was a brief description of some of the language concepts which could be implemented in order to develop the SACCS program. This paper was accepted as the beginning of the project, and the first work was begun. (I realized some years later that I had not kept that paper. There were not many copies, and it was never a formally issued document. At the time it seemed like a relatively small item and not likely to be continued much in the future, at least outside of the particular SACCS development environment. So the paper didn't seem very important to me. Now it would be of great interest to me for several reasons. One is its historical interest to me and perhaps some others. Secondly, I am quite curious what my first ideas were at that time for the language I called OVIAL.)

The project that was formed to develop this language and compilers for it was called the CUSS (Compiler and Utility System for SACCS) project. It was part of the SACCS Division of System Development Corporation which at the time was serving as a subcontractor to IEC. IEC was part of the ITT complex, formed specifically to develop the SACCS system.

During this period of the organization and beginning of the JOVIAL effort in New Jersey, the other members of the team who did some of the initial language investigation also started a project to develop a language. Eventually this language was called CLIP (Compiler Language for Information Processing) (Bratman, 1959; Englund and Clark, 1961). These two activities, the one in New Jersey and the one in California, were rather independent efforts, the one in California being somewhat research oriented, while the one in New Jersey on JOVIAL was operationally oriented—and in fact with a fairly difficult schedule (which wasn't met).

The people on the CUSS project were primarily implementors. With the exception of my own experience with the language PACT in 1954 and 1955, nobody else on the project had any experience with compilers or languages. Some had had experience in the development of the SAGE system. For some members of the project, this was their first programming experience. The list of people who served at least sometime on the CUSS project (and their current, or last known affiliation, where known) follows:

Jules Schwartz	(Manager)
Moe Spierer	(Manager 709 JOVIAL)(CSC)
Hank Howell	(Manager Q-31 JOVIAL)(SDC)

Jules I. Schwartz

Paul McIsaac	(Data Vantage)
John Rafferty	(IBM)
Patricia Weaver	(Unaffiliated)
Emmanuel Hayes	(Century Data Systems)
Lynn Shirley	(Consultant)
Jack Friedland	(Consultant)
Donna Neeb	(CSC)
Richard Brewer	(TELOS)
Stan Cohn	(Unknown)
Mike Denlinger	(Unknown)
John Bockhorst	(Northrop)
Phil Bartram	(Unknown)
Frank Palmer	(SDC)
Ed Foote	(IBM)
John Dolan	(Unknown)
Patricia Metz	(Unknown)

Some of the members of the CLIP Project, in addition to Book and Bratman mentioned previously, were:

Howard Manelowitz
Don Englund
Harold Isbitz
Ellen Clark
Ellis Myer

1.5. History of the Name

Since it has been stated that this paper on JOVIAL will serve as some sort of permanent record of the language, this seems like the right place to describe the origin of the name. For many people this seems to be the most important and best known part of the language. I have over the years met many people who know the name (and that Jules is part of it) but know nothing about the language. There is a discussion of this in Sammet's book on languages (Sammet, 1969), but the following expands somewhat on that.

As stated above, the name OVIAL was the one originally recommended, which meant Our Version of the International Algebraic Language. In the late 1950s, society wasn't quite as free thinking as it is today. The name OVIAL seemed to have a connotation relative to the birth process that did not seem acceptable to some people. So, during a meeting, held approximately January 1959, at which a number of technical issues were discussed—a meeting attended by members of the staff of the SACCS Division Management, the CUSS project, and IEC personnel—the subject of an acceptable name for the language was initiated. Someone in the group, and it's not known by me who it was, suggested the name JOVIAL. This seemed like the easiest transition from OVIAL. The question then was the meaning of the "J." Since I was standing in front of the room conducting the meeting at the time, somebody—perhaps somebody other than the one who suggested JOVIAL—suggested it be called Jules' Own Version of the International Algebraic Language. This suggestion was met with laughter by the assembled group. The meeting ended shortly afterward without actually finalizing the discussion of the name.

I left town for a trip soon after. Upon my return I found that the IEC people had put in the performance contract an obligation for SDC to develop the language called "JOVIAL (Jules' Own Version of the International Algebraic Language) and compilers for this language for the IBM 709 and AN/FSQ-31." The AN/FSQ-31 computer wasn't due to be installed for quite some time, but the 709 was available and was to be used by user personnel for a variety of kinds of work. (I didn't remember who the IEC people were, but was told in 1976 by Joe Ceran, now of CSC, who was then one of the IEC personnel at the meeting.) Thus, along with the dates for various deliveries, the name JOVIAL, which included my first name, became the official term.

1.6. Objectives

Both compilers were to be delivered to the Strategic Air Command in Omaha and to be used for a variety of functions. The AN/FSQ-31 Compiler was intended for the programming of the SACCS System, the 709 for a variety of other ongoing SAC functions as well as the early development of the Q-31 Development System prior to the availability of the Q-31. The JOVIAL language was to be the same for both the 709 and Q-31. The compilers were to be programmed in JOVIAL.

1.7. Schedules and Allocated Manpower

I have not been able to find the original contract statements containing the actual schedules that were required. Whatever they were, it is quite certain that they didn't get met. As I recall, the first version of the compiler for the language was scheduled something like six months after the beginning of the effort on the IBM 709. Since the AN/FSQ-31 wasn't due to be installed for quite some time afterwards, that had a much later scheduled delivery. The number of people on the project soon after it got started was around nine and it grew to a maximum of about 15 people as the CUSS project continued. The actual first users of JOVIAL, aside from the compiler developers themselves, were to use the first processor, which was an interpreter, not a compiler, for a very simple subset of the language, which was available in about 12 months (around January 1960).

People within the SACCS development effort began to use the language for very simple things (e.g., short subroutines for conversion, calculations, expression analysis). There were somewhere around eight man-years' effort before the language began to be used. About 25 man-years of effort were expended before very heavy use of the 709 Compiler took place. The first programs to make use of the compilers (outside of the compiler builders) were the utility and executive systems that were to be used for the further development of the SACCS system. The compiler development itself utilized the early compilers. Once the earliest subset of the language was available in a machine-coded compiler, the compiler was immediately reprogrammed in that language. From then on, all versions were programmed in some version of JOVIAL.

Jules I. Schwartz

1.8. Planning and Procedures

Today there are a variety of concepts for orderly development, including structured programming, structured design, top-down development, continuously evolving specifications, and in general rigorous planning and disciplined effort. These ideas were unknown to the original JOVIAL development. The language design actually proceeded largely in parallel with the implementation of the compilers. There were some basic concepts (e.g., IAL, SAGE data definitions) and enough definition to get started with the development, but a firm baseline never existed, and changes were made almost daily. The early documents were limited and essentially working papers, subject to considerable change. No reasonably complete "final" documents were published until the end of the major work.

The main "management technique" used was frequent interaction among all personnel, including the project leaders, where changes, techniques, and progress were discussed on an individual and group basis. Although not to be recommended as the major way to run a project, it seemed to work for this project (where most personnel, although rather inexperienced, were quite capable and hard-working). No detailed plans or schedules or systematic growth from design through testing were ever written or followed. The only real test case was the compiler itself.

The first official document on JOVIAL was published in April 1959 (Schwartz, 1959a) and the second in May 1959 (Schwartz, 1959b). These described a number of the concepts and details of the language. Additional documents came out on the state of the language over the next six months.

Since one of the major emphases of this language was to be the development of the compiler in the language itself, many of the ideas for the language came from those who were actually in the process of developing parts of the compiler. Changes were suggested by those people as they programmed.

Many of the important parts of the language were developed in an incredibly short time. A good example of this is the Data Definition Capability, which was the original heart of JOVIAL. It was not well defined when we embarked on the development effort. It had to be developed as the compiler development proceeded. When it was determined that we couldn't postpone the data definition any longer, it was developed in about 30 minutes. One other person (H. Howell) and I examined each possible type and structure and developed the syntax for them immediately (Howell, 1960). Those who know the original JO-VIAL will readily agree that that part of the language could have been developed in only 30 minutes. Many of the syntactic improvements over the years have been in that area, although the capability provided has always been well received. Other language features (such as the CLOSE Routine and Item Switch—discussed below) were decided on and added in minutes. Rarely did language features require more than a day to determine both need and structure. STRING Items (discussed below) were one exception, mainly because of objections by the compiler producers.

1.9. Documentation and Early Versions

As stated previously, the first document describing the language was published in April 1959 (Schwartz, 1959a). It was superseded by another in May (Schwartz, 1959b). The next two language documents appeared in September (Bockhorst and Reynolds, 1959;

Schwartz, 1959c). In early 1960 work began in California on JOVIAL itself in addition to CLIP, so documents began to appear in the spring of 1960 (Shaw, 1960a) on the language JOVIAL and some plans for JOVIAL on computers other than those being developed in New Jersey. However, those versions of JOVIAL were not identical to the East Coast version.

The early use of the interpreter (for language version J0) occurred in January of 1960, about a year after the system was started. The first compiler for the language version called J−1 (J minus one) was available for the compiler developers in the fall of 1959. That compiler was used to program the next version of the language—called J1—which was available in the winter of 1960. This was used to produce the J2 version. The J2 version was delivered in March of 1961 (Schwartz and Howell, 1961). It ran on the IBM 7090, which had replaced the 709 by that time.

The AN/FSQ-31 version of J2 was delivered some months later. Usage of the 709 version really began back with the J1 version of the compiler for the development of utility systems. In Omaha, at SAC Headquarters, it began with the delivery of the 709 J2 version in March of 1961.

What eventually became a standard was the J3 version of JOVIAL. That was originally described by Chris Shaw (Shaw, 1960b, 1964). This version was developed in California. Chris Shaw was responsible for most of the early formal descriptions of JOVIAL.

The first formal presentation on JOVIAL was given at the International Symposium on Symbolic Languages in March of 1962 (Schwartz, 1962).

2. Rationale of the Content of the Language

2.1. Language Objectives

The actual major objective of the original JOVIAL was a language for programming large systems, although it has typically been referred to as a Command and Control Language. These were systems which required the contributions of many people. Also, they would not be constrained to utilize limited sections or instructions of the computer, nor to work with strictly computational problems. These properties certainly seem to serve the Command and Control problem, but serve equally well the programming of a compiler or operating system.

A natural result of this basic objective was the requirement for flexibility. The language had to be able to handle a variety of situations. The necessity for people to use machine language often would not be considered satisfactory, even in those cases in which machine language had always been assumed necessary in the past.

Another language objective was a reasonable level of machine independence. The fact that two compilers for two totally different computers was the original contractual objective of the language helped to achieve this latter objective (Wilkerson, 1961).

2.2. Things Which Were Pretty Much Ignored in the Language

One thing which was given little attention until the first versions of the compiler began to be used to compile themselves was compiler speed. Capabilities were added to the language independent of their effects on compilation speed. This was not true of some other languages being developed at that time, one of which was NELIAC, which has similar overall objectives but tended to emphasize compilation speed to a much greater extent.

Another thing which was ignored was language elegance. An example of this was given previously in the discussion of how the Data Description part of the language was developed. Almost everyone on the project had no foundation in language design, including the managers. Consequently, although the example of IAL existed for a relatively formal description of a language, the formality of JOVIAL tended to be ignored. This could not have been completely bad, I think. It certainly had its weak points, but in fact JOVIAL actually turned out to be very natural for people to use. Many language features were developed as actual needs were recognized, leading to useful, if inelegant, results. The Data Definition area easily fits here. It contained quite a bit of flexibility and power, along with reasonable programming transparency, but syntactically was a string of hard-to-memorize characters required in specific sequence. Long string constants were defined in a very awkward way (e.g., 18H (THIS IS AN EXAMPLE)), requiring considerable counting and recounting for changing. The use of the symbols "($" and "$)" for liberally used brackets was a bad choice. Imprecision in semantic definitions did not help in making all versions totally compatible, even when there were attempts at compatibility.

Another thing which was ignored was standardization with other efforts. Even other efforts within SDC at that time were ignored—partially because of the need for (if not the achievement of) meeting of schedules on the SACCS effort. It was also partially because of the physical distance between the JOVIAL efforts (for much of the time period of the Project, the coast-to-coast trip was by propeller-driven aircraft) and the not unusual tendency for people to ignore other people's work. And the initial inspiration of IAL didn't lead to continued following of it. No further attention was paid to IAL (or ALGOL, as it was eventually called) after the initial design.

2.3. Things Excluded in the Language or Given Little Attention

One of the major initial exclusions of the language was input–output. This can be attributed to SAGE. In the SAGE system no program except the central control program did any input–output. Consequently, it was felt that the great majority of programs would not require input–output for the SACCS System. JOVIAL thus did not include it initially. Eventually, subroutines were written and called Through Procedures (Bockhorst, 1961). One of the original omissions (and still omitted) is interrupt handling or any other obviously real-time instruction or capability. Instead, JOVIAL gave access to parts of the machine through various operations and modifiers. These included access to parts of words in arbitrary groupings of bits or bytes, which allowed one to inspect interrupt or message registers, therefore obviating the absolute need for more direct commands in this area. In the initial versions of the language no real debugging facilities were added. But the Communications Pool provided capability for supporting systems to give considerable debugging capability at both the individual program and system level. Also, no data allocation statements were put into the initial version of the language.

One thing which was allowed in the language but somewhat ignored in the compiler were multidimensional arrays. The language provided for them, but the efficiency of handling anything more than a single subscripted variable was not stressed in the compiler.

(However, single-subscripting was handled quite well.) This resulted in relatively little interest in JOVIAL for programming multidimensional matrix problems. It was felt, in justification of the latter, that the use of multidimensional arrays for the kinds of systems for which JOVIAL was to be used would be minimal.

2.4. Major Language Features

The basis of JOVIAL taken from IAL included such things as compound statements. The use and syntax of compound statements was the same as defined in IAL. The major operators were generally the same, including a switch which was similar to the IAL switch. The statement structure, labelling, and ending were the same. Procedure calls, at least initially, were similar to IAL's, and the general loop structure and FOR statements were similar.

The biggest departure (and the original one) from IAL was in the Data Definition area. Where IAL provided primarily for floating point arrays and some integer values, the JO-VIAL language included at the lowest data description level entities which were called "items" (based on the SAGE term) which had a variety of types. The types included floating point, fixed point (where the scaling was specified to be a part of the item), Hollerith and Standard Transmission Code character strings (in the initial version, these were limited to reside within one computer word), and status valued items. These latter represented with symbolic values finite states such as GOOD, FAIR, and POOR, or ON and OFF, or any predefined set of values. In the JOVIAL program these are referred to by the symbolic names (e.g., IF WEATHER = V(CLOUDY)), although internally they are assigned integer values by the compiler.

Items were assigned to the next higher level of hierarchy, which was an "entry" in JO-VIAL. Each entry contained all of the elements or the items that were necessary to describe particular objects (such as Aircraft and Persons). All entries for an object were contained in a "table", the top level of the hierarchy.

Tables could take on several forms. These were serial, parallel, and variable.

In the serial table, all words containing an entry were contiguous. As an example, a serial table containing the items A, B, C, D, E, and F in a three-word entry would appear as follows:

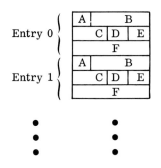

A parallel table containing the same items could appear as in the following:

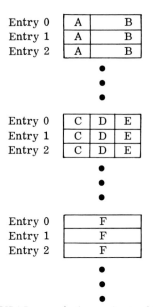

Indexing in both cases with JOVIAL was independent of the entry size or parallel/serial format. For example, the sequence:

```
FOR I = 0, 1, 10$
D1($I$) = 5$
```

would set D1 in the first 11 entries to the value 5 for either of the above (and would work in the serial case if fewer or more words were in an entry).

It was also possible to utilize a variable format which might have a different structure for each entry, as follows:

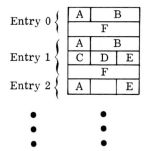

In the variable case, there would normally be some item in each entry (say A1 in this example) which would provide assistance in stepping from one entry to the next. This was not done automatically by the compiler. A sequence of the following kind would be possible:

```
          FOR I = 0$
BEGIN X1.   IF A1($I$) = 3$ D1($I$) = 5$
          I = I + A1($I$) $
          IF A1($I$) = 0$ STOP $
          GOTO X1$
END
```

This sequence would set all existing D1s to 5 until the end of the table, where only three word entries contained D1, and the end was signaled by an A1 equal to 0.

Another data type was added to the language—much to my chagrin because of its awkwardness—during its early implementation. This was called STRING and it provided for a rather complex combination of character string elements in a variety of formats within an entry. This went beyond the original concept of items and character string items. (This was one of the only "committee type" additions to the early language.)

These data types and data structures provided for a comprehensive capability for access to almost any configuration of logical or arithmetic values. Items could be either full or part words. (No item could be more than one word. This was changed in later versions of the language.) Also, access to parts of items (discussed below) was provided. The point of this was not only the definition of data structures. It was to provide it in such a way that the programmer would not need to know where the item was placed within a word, which word in an entry it was in, and in most cases the size of the items and other facts about it. In some cases, the type itself did not have to be known.

Thus, the JOVIAL program could remain largely unaffected by changes in the data description. That was a crucial part of the language. Also, in some ways this capability was used to show that in fact JOVIAL would produce more efficient code for programming systems than the machine language as used for SAGE. The following type of example was used as an illustration.

In SAGE, "pseudo-instructions" (macros) were used in machine language when referring to Communication Pool items. The purpose was to prevent any assumptions about the size or position of items by programmers while producing reasonably good code for specific situations. (Programs had to be reassembled when the Communication Pool changed.) Four such pseudo instructions were:

ETR Perform an AND to the Accumulator with a mask the size and position of the item.

POS Shift the accumulator so that the least significant bit of the item is in the least significant bit of the accumulator.

RES Shift the accumulator left so that the least significant bit of the accumulator moves to the least significant bit position of the item.

DEP Deposit into the word containing the item from the proper bit positions of the accumulator.

At least one instruction was generated for each pseudo-instruction.
Thus, to add two items and store in a third, the following sequence had to be used.

```
CLA ITEM1    Move ITEM1 to accumulator
ETR ITEM1
POS ITEM1
STO TEMP     Save ITEM1
CLA ITEM2    Move ITEM2 to accoumulator
ETR ITEM2
POS ITEM2
ADD TEMP     Add the two items
RES ITEM3
DEP ITEM3
```

This sequence generated a minimum of 10 instructions (on the SAGE computer). In JO-VIAL, the same operation would appear in the following statement:

$$\text{ITEM3 = ITEM1 + ITEM2\$}$$

Depending on the definitions of the items, this statement could generate as few as three instructions because of the capability of the compiler to analyze the entire statement.

The Communication Pool is essentially the Data Definition for all items and tables to be used by the subprograms of the system. In some versions of JOVIAL compilers the Communication Pool is syntactically identical to the Data Definition section within a program. In other versions, however, the Communication Pool actually has a different format from the Data Definitions and has more information than the JOVIAL programs themselves permit. Such things as allocation information can be put into the Communication Pool for both programs and data. The Communication Pool is used for more than compiling programs. It can also be used for such things as simulating data for testing. It allows for the entry of the item name and its value without the programmer having to specify where to place the value or its internal form. The Communication Pool also can serve as a tool for data reduction after tests are run. This is because the Data Reduction Program can examine the information as it exists after a run and use the Communication Pool definition to translate it to a readable form for the user or the tester (Tjomsland, 1960).

Another significant feature of the JOVIAL language from its earliest version was the provision for access to bits and bytes of items. Modifiers for this provided access to a variable number of bits or bytes of the item, starting from any position within the item. The expressions are BIT (i,j\$)(*item*) and BYTE(i,j\$)(*item*), where i is the starting bit or byte and j the number of them. These provide a good deal of power. However, the efficiency of this form when i and j are both variable is at best adequate, but normally much worse. The simpler expression where only one of a constant number of bits or bytes was referenced can produce more efficient code.

Access to entries of tables also was given in JOVIAL. Thus, one can move whole entries other than on an item-by-item basis. A modifier was provided which provided access to the count of entries in a table for use or modification. For example, the statement NENT(TABLE) = NENT(TABLE) + 1\$ increments the count of entries in TABLE.

Some other rather unique forms were added to the early JOVIAL to resolve certain problems. One was the CLOSE Statement. This provided for a closed subroutine with no entrance or exit parameters, but it maintained and could use the value of a subscript when it was within its domain of definition. The LOC modifier was added. This modifier, which stands for "(absolute) core location," provided the capability of getting to the location of a part of memory. The expression LOC(TABLE or ITEM) enabled one to reference relocatable information. Today, pointers can be used for this without some of the awkwardness and inadequacy available only with LOC. Another kind of flexibility which was provided (and which created problems for compiler writers) was the fact that the step factor in the FOR statement (FOR I = A, B, C; with B being the increment or the decrement for I) was allowed to be a variable. It could be either negative or positive, and in fact during the loop was allowed to change sign. Of course, that was not the normal case, but the need for providing for it in the compiler was one of those things which created some of the early compiler problems in achieving efficiency and speed.

NENT, BIT, BYTE, LOC, ENT, MANT, and other terms are examples of functional modifiers which were added during the early development of JOVIAL. These were utilized to satisfy a number of the problems which required language solutions. They can normally be used in "right" or "left side" expressions. For example, the statement

```
BIT($I$) (ITEM) = 1$
```

causes the Ith bit of ITEM to be set to 1. (When the number of bits or bytes is 1, it doesn't have to be specified.)

Although the purpose of the language was to provide for machine oriented programming without the use of machine language, the originators were realistic enough to know that there would be a requirement for the use of machine language, at least occasionally. Particularly in the early versions, at a minimum, access to input and output required some machine language operations.

Access to machine language is easy in JOVIAL. The operator DIRECT signals the beginning and the operator JOVIAL the end of machine language. Within the machine language, it was expected that users would need access to JOVIAL (and Comm Pool) defined items and tables. Thus, an operator was defined to give access to these from within the machine language part of the program. This operator was called ASSIGN and it permitted one to place an item in the accumulator or the accumulator to an item. The compiler automatically took care of the shifting of the item as it would in normal JOVIAL statements. (The scaling of the accumulator was specified by the programmer in the ASSIGN statement.) Actually, the ASSIGN combined the functions available in the pseudo-instructions of SAGE shown above. Another capability of interest was called the Item Switch. A Numeric switch is provided as in IAL for a series of branches based on normally continuous integer values of an item. But this was not sufficient for things like status items which were, first of all, symbolically named where users could not assume values for the names. Also, the Item Switch could be used for other item types such as character strings, which can have quite random values.

2.5. Language Design Methodology

The primary technical driving forces for JOVIAL are quite clear. Given that the basic structure would be that of IAL, the major question was what would have helped in the programming of SAGE, since it was assumed that the programming of SACCS would have a similar set of problems. These included the use of a large number of people, different types of data, more logic operations than calculation, and the need for item packaging to save space and access certain machine registers. For example on the SAGE computer there was no floating point arithmetic. Everything was fixed point. So, although the SACCS computer had floating point, it was assumed that fixed point arithmetic would be useful for it as well. Other major influences were those things found necessary to program the compiler itself. That was the source of most of the early modifications to the language. Other ideas came from early users who were beginning to use the language. They discussed and wrote about problems that they had found in using the language.

It would be quite an extreme exaggeration to say that a strict methodology or control system was used in developing the JOVIAL language. As stated earlier, much of the development came from innovation when needs were recognized. Most problems were resolved by adding to or modifying the language. Many problem resolutions had as a goal the obviation of the need to resort to machine language. This mode of working led to some extremely fast decisions, some awkward syntax, some difficulties for the compilers, but a quite practical and usuable language.

The basic approach was essentially as described before. The base language was chosen, and it was initially implemented in a variety of processors. Compiler work was begun with a minimal form of the language. Data Definitions were added for the total range of data that was to be needed both for the compiler and for the application systems. As time went on, modifiers and other forms were added as need arose. The language continued to evolve for some years thereafter, both within the original effort and in California and other places as the language was used elsewhere.

3. A Posteriori Evaluation

It is always difficult to provide an accurate objective account of a product's success or failure (even when one's name isn't directly involved). This is true for many reasons, including the fact that nothing is ever absolutely good or bad. But the following attempts to present a reasonable assessment of JOVIAL's effect on the world.

3.1. Meeting of Objectives

In general, it seems that JOVIAL met its goals. There have been a large number of systems of many types produced using JOVIAL. Most of these have been for areas which up until the time when JOVIAL was developed were not thought programmable in other than machine language.

For the first decade of use there were really never very many serious complaints about the language capability (after the first year or two of development). The difficulties and complaints tended to be largely the result of early implementations. The early compilers were, to put it mildly, not very reliable. They were extremely slow. The first compiler on the 709 took eight hours to compile itself. In those days the probability that one could compile for eight straight hours and get a properly punched binary deck for output was less than 0.5. Of course this slowness was also recognized when compiling other sizeable programs. This, combined with the fact that the compiler might produce erroneous results, could dampen even the most ardent enthusiasm. But even with these kinds of problems, there was little drive on the part of early users to disassociate themselves from the use of the language. Rather strong statements were used to point out compiler problems, but once many of the early difficulties were overcome with the compiler the language was considered quite satisfactory.

Another interesting fact was pointed out by someone responsible for teaching early users how to use the language (Rizzo, 1962). The initial capability didn't provide much tutorial assistance, so that learning of the language was not easy and the documentation, although it improved with time, wasn't the best for beginners. But those who were responsible for training and criticized this lack of good teaching aids also pointed out that once people got over the hurdle of learning JOVIAL there were very few questions and very few problems in using what they learned. Most people found the language relatively easy to retain and use for everyday work.

The fact that the SAC organization under Colonel William Shirey in Omaha (the first non-SDC users) continued to use the language on a fairly heavy basis, despite some early tough going, was critical in keeping the JOVIAL language alive. This led to an eventual spread of use in the Air Force. It is also true that its use spread without support from any major manufacturer. Almost all the JOVIAL compilers that were produced until the mid–late 1960s were done under contract to a government agency for a specific system. Manufacturers were evolving COBOL and FORTRAN at that time. Of course a number of other languages were also in development in the period from 1960 to 1965, such as MAD, NEL-IAC, ALGOL 60, SNOBOL, JOSS, and hundreds of others. But JOVIAL maintained its progress during that period.

The objective of moving JOVIAL–coded programs and the compilers from computer to computer was partially met. The initial effort in New Jersey provided compilers for two computers for the same language almost simultaneously. When one moved a program from a computer with six characters in a word to another which had eight-character words, the fact that the early compilers didn't provide for character string items of more than one word in length certainly made the portability imperfect. Similar results occurred because of the restrictions on scaled fixed point items. However, considering the type of programming which was permitted (much more variable than possible with FORTRAN), portability was reasonable. I'm not sure that it had too much effect on the ultimate success or failure of the language. Most users tended to program for a machine and stay with it on that machine. It is true that very few JOVIAL compilers handled the same version of the language. After the J2 effort, most others produced different subsets of J3.

The objectives for JOVIAL that were set originally were not changed. The flexibility and power of the language continued to be objectives throughout and were reasonably well satisfied. In fact, as people developed the language further there were actually some restrictions put in that did not exist in the early version. These included restriction to equal types for formal and entrance parameters of procedures. Restrictions on the step factor of the FOR Statement were implemented in some later versions.

3.2. Contributions of the Language

It is hard to say what contribution to programming technology in general or to other languages JOVIAL actually made.

There are a number of languages which contain some of the capabilities or characteristics of JOVIAL. Most often they are in a different format and except for certain situations it's not possible to directly relate that language to JOVIAL itself. A good example of this is PL/I. JOVIAL knowledgeable reviewers of PL/I when it was first developed pointed out that many of the characteristics of JOVIAL had been adopted in PL/I. However, there's no official acknowledgement of the use of JOVIAL as one of the bases for PL/I to my knowledge.

Nevertheless JOVIAL had things to offer and, whether directly or indirectly, should have contributed something to the technology. It was one of the first system programming languages and helped show that languages were capable of serving that purpose. It was one of the early, if not the earliest, compilers coded completely in its own language. It provided for data structures, types, and operations that permitted programming outside the realm of the strictly computational. It was even possible to use it for commercial programming. Although certain problems occurred in the early versions with rounding and report formatting, JOVIAL was used for the programming of a wide variety of systems. It provided for access to subparts of elements and words, which in early computers with small memories was very important, and is still valuable today for a variety of things. It was a language really aimed at flexibility and nonconstraint on the program. These were all contributions and valuable factors for the people who used it. They have helped maintain the language's use for a lengthy period, although the initial intent of the language was actually intended for only one specific set of users and a single system.

There have been quite a few versions of JOVIAL. I don't know them all and within each version there were variations with different implementations, so that there is unlikely to be a comprehensive list of all the capabilities that actually were in each version. A list of the names for different varieties or versions of JOVIAL includes: J0 (Olson *et al.*, 1960), J−1, J1, J2 (Schwartz and Howell, 1961), J3 (Shaw, 1961, 1964), and J3B (Department of the Air Force, 1967). This was the original Air Force standard version, J3 being the version developed in California in parallel with the development of J2 in New Jersey for the SACCS contract. Other versions included J4, J5, and J5.2, the latter two being outgrowths of a version called Basic JOVIAL (Perstein, 1968), which was actually an attempt to provide a working version with a fast compiler. (For example, it didn't include fixed point arithmetic). This was developed because of the criticism of the slowness of the compiler. Basic JOVIAL was itself derived from an experimental version called JX2 (developed in 1961), which rivaled other compilers in speed but did not have enough language. When timesharing came in the early 1960s, another interpretive version of a subset of JOVIAL was produced. It had language capability similar to JOSS (if not the elegance) in that it provided for arithmetic, formatting, simple terminal input–output, and other capabilities useful for interactive users. That was a version of JOVIAL which had quite different objectives than the original system programming language. This version was called TINT and was described in a paper at the 1965 IFIP Conference (Schwartz, 1965).

Although the preceding references to the various versions of JOVIAL may appear rather mind-boggling, it is actually probably an understatement. With the exception of some Air Force sponsored versions of J3, little control was exercised over the language. So, for reasons of implementation pressure, computer idiosyncrasies, particular needs or lack of needs, and individual choice, one will note differences within "versions" as well as among different ones. New versions were sometimes labeled after compilers were developed. However, the major aspects generally were implemented, and there was "near-compatibility" in most versions.

JOVIAL has served as a direct contributor to at least several languages. One language which is in use today in Europe is CORAL (Woodward and Wetherall, 1970). Many of the initial concepts for CORAL were taken from the JOVIAL of the early 1960s. A language which has been used by Computer Sciences Corporation for much of its systems programming work is called SYMPL. It consists of elements of JOVIAL and FORTRAN and some other properties developed at CSC. SPL, a Space Programming Language which was developed by the Air Force Space Command some years ago, was based to a large extent on the experience with JOVIAL. Others, such as CMS II used by the Navy and perhaps PL/I as stated before, have had either a direct or some indirect relationship with JOVIAL.

In the early 1970s a group was formed by the Air Staff under Leo Berger to produce a new standard version of JOVIAL. They developed a specification for a language called J73 (Department of Defense, date unknown). There have been several implementations of it, and it is being used on a variety of computers at the present time. This is the first version which, by design, is not upward-compatible with other versions. Some version of JO-

VIAL, or several versions of JOVIAL in some cases, have existed on just about every major manufacturer's computers and some less well-known computers over the years. A minimum of ten companies have produced JOVIAL compilers.

JOVIAL was adopted in the mid-1960s as a standard language (Department of the Air Force, 1967) for the Air Force and that's where most of its use has been. It also was for a short period of time adopted by one part of the Navy (NAVCOSSAT). This adaptation of JOVIAL for the Navy was done on the basis of a comparative study comparing JOVIAL, a number of other languages, and machine language. However, there were a number of criticisms of the particular study, and the future of JOVIAL in the Navy became somewhat tenuous. (An interesting sidelight to that particular study was the fact that the first time it was run the machine language version of the program was assumed to be the base with which to compare other languages' efficiency and size. But the machine language program actually came out worse in these respects than some of the higher level languages involved. This caused the people responsible for the study to rerun it. Machine language fared better the second time.)

In 1961, members of the RAND Corporation conducted a study to compare JOVIAL with FORTRAN to see if JOVIAL or any language really merited being used as a Command and Control language at the time. The actual test consisted of seven problems, five of which utilized multidimensional arrays within several statements. The basis of the test was to see how well these would be compiled. FORTRAN won handsomely on all of the array problems with respect to generated code.

JOVIAL compared favorably on the nonmatrix problems. JOVIAL was much worse in compilation time, which didn't help its cause. In any case, based on that experiment, which seemed inadequate for the choosing of a Command and Control language, the people doing the study recommended that no language be adopted for Command and Control use at that time. The main thing proven by some of this is that we haven't mastered the art of comparative studies. The conclusion may have been right, but it always seemed to me that if so, it was in spite of the method used to reach it (Haverty and Patrick, 1963).

JOVIAL has been used by a variety of services and some other organizations, including the FAA, the Air Force (of course), the Navy (for some things and a variety of research and system projects).

Since the earliest versions of JOVIAL, the most significant changes that have been added are in the area of input–output. There are now a number of input–output commands in the language. Dynamic control of data allocation has been entered through data structure definitions, and pointers have been added in J73. Some syntax improvements have been provided in the language, particularly in the data definition area and in some of the modifiers. Some types have been purified to a certain extent. Originally, arrays and tables were separate. For example, when one defined an array he couldn't include items, and arrays couldn't be part of tables. That has been changed. There are a number of other changes which have taken place. Many of the key ones, of course, are being implemented in J73.

3.3 Mistakes and Omissions

The first major omission which constrained the use of JOVIAL considerably was its lack of input–output. This of course was actually a planned omission from the beginning. But its use for systems other than large systems where it is assumed that just one or several routines would service all input–output is of course diminished by this lack of input–output for individual programs. The lack of formatting and the ability to output or input by format or other convenient means (which is still an official omission from the language) has kept the language at arms length for many applications. Actually formatting has been implemented in at least a few versions. One which included formatting was the interpretive version called TINT (Schwartz, 1965). That was essential for it to operate as an interactive user oriented language. JOVIAL syntax awkwardness in certain areas probably didn't affect its use from the point of view of those who started using the language but helped keep certain communities uninterested in the language. The early implementation problems, particularly the speed and size of the initial compilers, which were 50,000 or more instructions, helped keep down any overwhelming use that might have occurred otherwise. To a great extent these implementation problems were due to the fact that features which made compiling difficult were sometimes added with reckless abandon. And, of course, the lack of efficiency in certain areas—particularly multidimensional arrays—restricted its application by programs which required them. It is unlikely that much interest would have been generated in JOVIAL for programming outside of its major areas of current use even if it had been much improved in these areas. Other languages such as FORTRAN and COBOL are accepted for programming these problems.

3.4. Problems and Trade-Offs

The hurry-up mode in the early versions created incompatibilities among different versions, particularly those separated geographically and those developed by different groups. And, of course, this detracted from portability among versions. The overall emphasis was for flexibility and generality of the language, which in turn led to a variety of implementation problems. This caused reliability, speed, and code generation difficulties. But the trade-off was made. There is a question whether in the long run it was a bad trade-off. The flexibility and the generality were probably worth some initial difficulties. Time for implementation was always a problem in this development. The language was defined rapidly, and the compilers were written quickly. There wasn't a lot of planning by the individuals and the managers concerned, but I think to some extent that this hurrying was as much a question of personalities as pressure. The people who were involved liked to do things in a hurry, were not very academically or research oriented, and they liked to see things run (typical system programmers). So I sometimes wonder if there hadn't been imposed deadlines (which in many cases of course were missed anyway) whether the people would have done a significantly more studious effort. (I'm certain that the tendency to "produce" rather than "study" is true for me, who was responsible through J2.)

4. Implications for Current and Future Language

Certainly, whether or not directly a stimulus, the work that went on in the early JOVIAL is now represented in a variety of ways. System programming languages are quite common. Complex data definition capability in a variety of languages certainly is not unusual today. Much of the system programming language work today is based to a large extent on PL/I, but it is also based on other languages as well. This concept within JOVIAL did prove feasible and valuable.

The original JOVIAL work was not a committee effort. There were relatively few people who actually helped design the language. Most of the people involved hadn't done this kind of work before and were basically implementors, or programmers. The fact that it wasn't a committee effort in many ways created the positive characteristics of the language as well as some of its negative ones. The language did maintain its original objectives, and its major characteristics remained fairly consistent throughout its early development. Perhaps the influence of others who had some better or more experience in this area could have been valuable, but it is also quite possible that with a variety of other contributors, it would have lost some of its flavor. For initial efforts on language design, an individual driving effort is probably a good idea.

I'm not certain what the future of JOVIAL is. The Department of Defense is trying to standardize once and for all on a language. This is one of those efforts which is going to take a long time to resolve. Meanwhile JOVIAL itself is being implemented and used for a number of projects. It has of course much more competition now in the areas for which it was intended. Also, competition from entrenched languages like COBOL and FORTRAN for things outside of what are typically JOVIAL applications, or considered to be JOVIAL applications, is much too intense to assume that it'll ever go beyond that. It's probably more likely that it will continue to have about the same percentage of use in the world as it has had until now. Hopefully, it will have influenced the Department of Defense standard language [Ada] which is eventually chosen to some degree.

REFERENCES

Bockhorst, J. (1961). *JOVIAL I/O (7090)*. Paramus, New Jersey: System Development Corporation SDC Rep. FN-L0-34-3, S1.

Bockhorst, J., and Reynolds, J. (1959). *Introduction to "JOVIAL" Coding*. Lodi, New Jersey: System Development Corporation SDC Rep. FN-L0-139.

Bratman, H. (1959). *Project CLIP*. Santa Monica, California: System Development Corporation SDC Rep. SP-106.

Department of Defense (date unknown). *Military Standard, JOVIAL* (J73/I), MIL-STD-1589.

Department of the Air Force (1967). *Standard Computer Language for Air Force Command and Control Systems*. Washington, D.C.: Air Force Manual AFM 100-24.

Englund, D., and Clark, E. (1961) January. CLIP Translator. *Communications of the ACM* **4**(1): 19–22.

Haverty, J. P., and Patrick, R. L. (1963). *Programming Languages and Standardization in Command and Control*. Santa Monica, California: Rand Corporation Memo RM-3447-PR and DDC Doc. AD-296 046.

Howell, H. L. (1960). *JOVIAL—Variable Definition For the 709 Translator*. Paramus, New Jersey: System Development Corporation SDC Rep. FN-L0-34-2-52.

Kennedy, P. R. (1962). *A Simplified Approach to JOVIAL*. Santa Monica, California: System Development Corporation SDC Rep. TM-555/063/00.

Melahn, W. S., *et al.* (1956) October. PACT I (A series of 7 papers). *Journal of the Association for Computing Machinery* **3**(4): 266–313.

Olson, W. J., Petersen, K. E., and Schwartz, J. I. (1960). *JOVIAL and its Interpreter, a Higher Level Programming Language and an Interpretive Technique for Checkout*. Paramus, New Jersey: System Development Corporation SDC Paper SP-165.

Perlis, A. J., and Samelson, K. (1958) December. Preliminary Report—International Algebraic Language. *Communications of the ACM* **1**(12): 8–22.

Perstein, M. H. (1968). *Grammar and Lexicon for Basic JOVIAL*. Santa Monica, California: System Development Corporation SDC Rep. TM-555/05/01A.

Rizzo, M. (1962). *Critique of the JOVIAL User's Manual, FN-L0-34-3*. Paramus, New Jersey: System Development Corporation SDC (internal use only) Rep. N-L0-2109/000/00.

Sammet, J. (1969). *Programming Languages: History and Fundamentals*. Englewood Cliffs, New Jersey: Prentice-Hall.

Jules I. Schwartz

Schwartz, J. I. (1959a). *Preliminary Report on JOVIAL*. Lodi, New Jersey: System Development Corporation SDC Rep. FN-L0-34.

Schwartz, J. I. (1959b). *JOVIAL—Report #2*. Lodi, New Jersey: System Development Corporation SDC Rep. FN-L0-34-1.

Schwartz, J. I. (1959c). *JOVIAL—Primer #1*. Lodi, New Jersey: System Development Corporation SDC Rep. FN-L0-154.

Schwartz, J. I. (1960a). *JOVIAL—A Description of the Language*. Paramus, New Jersey: System Development Corporation SDC Rep. FN-L0-34-2.

Schwartz, J. I. (1960b). *JOVIAL—Clarifications and Corrections for FN-L0-34-2*. Paramus, New Jersey: System Development Corporation SDC Rep. FN-L0-34-2-51.

Schwartz, J. I. (1962). JOVIAL: A General Algorithmic Language. In *Proceedings of the Symposium on Symbolic Languages in Data Processing*, pp. 481–493. New York: Gordon & Breach.

Schwartz, J. I. (1965). Programming Languages For On-Line Computing. In *Proceedings of the IFIP Congress*, Vol. 2, pp. 546–547. Washington, D.C.: Spartan Books.

Schwartz, J. I., and Howell, H. L. (1961). *The JOVIAL (J-2) Language for the 7090 Computer*. Santa Monica, California: System Development Corporation SDC Rep. FN-6223/100/00.

Shaw, C. J. (1960a). *The Compleat JOVIAL Grammar*. Santa Monica, California: System Development Corporation SDC Rep. FN-4178.

Shaw, C. J. (1960b). *The JOVIAL Lexicon: A Brief Semantic Description*. Santa Monica, California: System Development Corporation SDC Rep. FN-4178, 51.

Shaw, C. J. (1960c). *Computers, Programming Languages and JOVIAL*. Santa Monica, California: System Development Corporation SDC Rep. TM-555, Part 1.

Shaw, C. J. (1961). *The JOVIAL Manual, Part 3, The JOVIAL Primer*. Santa Monica, California: System Development Corporation SDC Rep. TM-555/003/00.

Shaw, C. J. (1964). *Part 2, The JOVIAL Grammar and Lexicon*. Santa Monica, California: System Development Corporation SDC Rep. TM-555/002/02.

Tjomsland, I. A. (1960). *The 709 JOVIAL Compool*. Paramus, New Jersey: System Development Corporation SDC Rep. FN-3836.

Wilkerson, M. (1961). *JOVIAL User's Manual*. Subtitled *JOVIAL Language Specifications for 7090 and MC Compilers*. Paramus, New Jersey: System Development Corporation SDC Rep. FN-L0-34-3.

Wolpe, H. (1958) March. Algorithm for Analyzing Logical Statements to Produce Truth Function Table. *Communications of the ACM* **1**(3): 4–13.

Woodward, P. M., and Wetherall, P. R. (1970). *The Official Definition of CORAL 66*. London: HM Stationery Office.

TRANSCRIPT OF PRESENTATION

JOHN GOODENOUGH: The next paper is by Jules Schwartz on the JOVIAL language. Mr. Schwartz began his career in computing at Columbia University in 1953 when he was a graduate student in Mathematical Statistics. He joined the RAND Corporation in 1954 where he worked with early systems such as the JOHNNIAC Computer, some IBM 701 scientific routines, and the development of a higher level language, PACT, for the IBM 701. In 1956 and 1957 he was part of the SAGE (Semi-Automatic Ground Environment) development effort at Lincoln Laboratory. When System Development Corporation was spun off from RAND, Jules Schwartz went with SDC. He began his work on JOVIAL at the System Development Corporation in 1958.

Currently Jules is at Computer Sciences Corporation , where he is responsible for a staff which consults, manages, audits, and plans projects both in the commercial and in the government sectors. He has also continued some work in language design, most recently a few years ago for a Data Base Management system called DML (Data Management Language) for use on CSC's Infonet System.

JULES SCHWARTZ: Thank you. If I appear sleepy today there's a good reason. Yesterday, during Al Perlis's discussion, I learned for the first time that when the first ALGOL specifications were published, the committee already knew that the name was to be changed to ALGOL. But they published the specifications using the name IAL (International Algegraic Language). So I've been plagued all night with the specter of the ALGOL committee having decided to call the original specs ALGOL. In that case, what would be the name of the language we're discussing today? JOVALGOL just doesn't work.

Well, as we already know—and of course, you know today if you didn't know yesterday—when the development of JOVIAL began, the world of computing was quite different than it is today. Computers were vacuum tube based; most were quite small, even relative to today's small computers. Utility routines such as one-card load programs, and small memory dump routines, were used as individual programs rather than part of major systems controlled by a job control language. Assembly language programming was used in most environments.

My own experience with things like languages and compilers was limited to several things. One was work on the PACT [Project for Automatic Coding Techniques] language that was described in the 1956 ACM Conference, which, although called an automatic programming language, was not syntactically anything like ALGOL or FORTRAN. I, with several other people, namely, Irwin Book of SDC and Harvey Bratman also of the System Development Corporation, had experimented with the expansion of algebraic and logical expressions, based on an article in an ACM *Communications* of 1958 by H. Wolpe of IBM. Other than that, and reading the IAL (International Algebraic Language) specifications, my language experience was nil.

By the time JOVIAL began, one large Command and Control System had been developed, and was in the process of its initial installation. The development of it had started in 1954. It was called SAGE, and it was a system built to track and intercept hostile aircraft. It had a significant influence on JOVIAL.

The actual design of JOVIAL began in 1958. Its purpose was to program another large Air Force Command and Control System called SACCS, with the actual designation 465-L. JOVIAL has been called a command and control language because of its use for systems like 465-L. However, I prefer to call it a system programming language. A demonstration of its capabilities can best be described, I think, by listing the objectives of the language when it was developed, and presenting brief examples of how JOVIAL satisfied these.

The major objective of JOVIAL was to permit people to program complete systems in a higher level language. This capability was provided through various facilities, the first one being a comprehensive data definition and referencing capability.

[Frame 1] gives an example of part of the data definition capability. Now, incidentally, through all these examples, you'll see dollar signs liberally sprinkled. This should not

ITEM XYZW	F	$	Floating Point
ITEM RMN	I	7 S $	Integer
ITEM XTUVW	A	14 U 6 $	Fixed Point
ITEM ABC1	H	5 $	Hollerith
ITEM VIX	S	V(CLOUDY)	
		V(RAIN) V(FAIR)$	Status

Frame 1. Items—examples of definitions.

Jules I. Schwartz

```
    TABLE     RQW2   V    150   M$        Variable-length, serial,
                                          medium-packed
    BEGIN     ITEM...$
              ITEM...$
              .
              .
              .
    END
```

Frame 2. Tables.

be construed as an indicator of wealth, greed, or success on my part. When the language was first implemented, there was, as we all know now, a shortage of characters available on keypunches. In this case we decided to use the dollar sign to help form the character set. One major place they are used is as end of statement symbols, as can be seen. The other is as part of left and right brackets, to help form the left and right subscript brackets, which will appear later.

Now, [Frame 1] illustrates the definition of items. Items are the lowest level of named objects in the language. These are five examples of item definitions as they originally existed in the JOVIAL language. Each one illustrates a different type of item. Item XYZW is defined as a floating point item, by the character F. The second item, RMN, is an integer item. It has seven bits and it's signed; the S means it's signed. The next item is a fixed point arithmetic item. It can be used for numerical calculations with fixed point arithmetic. It has 14 bits and the 6 means there are 6 bits to the right of the point; the U means there is no sign; it's always positive. The next item, ABC1, is a Hollerith or character string item. It has five characters. The last item is a status item. It provides for name values of an item without committing the programmer to know or to specify in code the actual numeric values for the values. Internally, however, the item is assigned a numerical value for each of the statuses represented. The statuses, in this case, are CLOUDY, RAIN, and FAIR.

[Frame 2] represents some of the kinds of structures that were made available with JOVIAL. (Actually the next five slides) The major structure is called the table. The first example here is table RQW2. Table RQW2 has a variable length designated by V, meaning that it can have a varying number of entries, where an entry is a set of items. This particular table has a maximum of 150 entries. This can be seen in the header. And it is to be "medium packed"—M stands for "medium packed," meaning that the compiler will allocate the individual items of the table to fit into machine-oriented parts of the computer

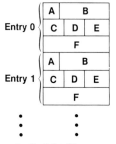

Frame 3. Serial table—example.

```
TABLE    RMT3     R    75 3 P$              Fixed-length, Parallel,
                                            Hand-packed
BEGIN    ITEM XY  I    15 U 2 4 D $         Word 2, BIT 4, Dense
         .
         .
         .
```

Frame 4. Parallel table.

word which are easily accessible. In the early days of JOVIAL these would most likely have been the address field, the operation field, and a few others. Today most machine-oriented fields probably could be bytes or characters.

Following the table header, the definition of an entry is included between the BEGIN and END. That's where the items are listed.

Table RQW2 is defined as a serial table. Actually it's defined as a serial table by using the default which in this case implies "serial." An example of a serial table is [in Frame 3]. A serial table groups all items of an entry into a contiguous set of words. Entry 0 is the first entry; Entry 1 is the second, and all items within that table are in contiguous words.

Table RMT3, whose definition is [in Frame 4] is defined by the P as a parallel table. The parallel format is illustrated [in Frame 5]. The parallel table is structured so that moving between entries on the same item, such as from A of entry 0 to A of entry 1, is in increments of 1, and between words within an entry, such as from item A of entry 0 to item C of Entry 0, is done by incrementing by the number of entries. That's the parallel structure.

Getting back to table RMT3 [in Frame 6], it's defined as fixed length by the R (for rigid table). This means that it has a fixed number of entries. 75 is the number of entries. In this case, the number 3, which follows the 75 in the header, means that there are going to be three words per entry, and the fact that this is stated in the table definition means that the programmer himself will assign item positions within each entry. Again, the definition of the entries or the items within the entries follows the table header. The difference between these and the other item definitions discussed before is that the programmer will provide information such as word 2 of the entry, bit 4 of the word for the starting position, and D for "dense"—dense as opposed to medium packed which we saw before. Dense means

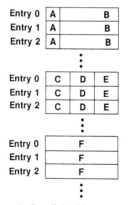

Frame 5. Parallel table—example.

TABLE	RMT3	R	75 3 P$	Fixed-length, Parallel, Hand-packed
BEGIN	ITEM XY	I	15 U 2 4 D $	Word 2, BIT 4, Dense

.
.
.

Frame 6. Parallel table.

it's not going to be accessible by referencing a machine field such as the address or operation codes. In other words, the dense item is tightly packed within a word.

Also in JOVIAL one can define arrays. Arrays of any number of dimensions were possible in the original versions of JOVIAL.

After structures and items, the next major capability which provided for generalized programming was direct access to bits and bytes, or characters, within items in JOVIAL. The next slide [Frame 7] shows examples of that use. The first example says: set bit 3 of IT3 (the item IT3) equal to 1. The second example as it would be stated in JOVIAL would set the two bytes, starting with the Ith byte of Item HXY to the two bytes of Item PRQ starting with the Jth byte.

The last example says to set the J bits of the Xth occurrence of item MNP, starting with the Ith bit to the J bits starting in bit K of the Yth occurrence of item RQL. In other words, you're setting a variable number of bits to a variable number of bits from one item to another where both items are indexed.

A second major objective of the language was freedom from machine specifics. Although the programming of very general and system oriented functions was permitted, one of the ways this was done was through a set of modifiers. Some of the modifiers are shown [in Frame 8]. With NENT one can access or modify the number of entries in a table. MANT gives access to the mantissa of a floating point number, CHAR, the characteristic, SIGN, the sign of an item, ENT, the whole entry of a table, and LOC, the absolute location of a table. An example of the syntax and use of a modifier is shown at the bottom of the slide.

In the first example at the bottom, the number of entries of table TABX is incremented by 2. It's set to the number of entries of the same table plus 2. And in the second example, the sign of item1 is set to 1. (Actual statements in JOVIAL would have had dollar signs at the end.)

The third objective of JOVIAL was an attempt to make the program independent of the data definition. That is, although the data definition could change, the program itself should remain unchanged. One example of this is the ability to mix data types in a variety of ways, within arithmetic expressions, on assignment statements, and elsewhere.

Another example of freedom from the data definition shows in the kinds of switches JOVIAL allows. First of all, it allows the subscript or numeric switch, where the switch point was simply based on the value of the subscript and the switch call, such as the first example on the next slide [Frame 9], where one branches to ABLE subscripted by I. In this

```
BIT($3$) (IT3) = 1$
BYTE($I, 2$) (HXY) = BYTE($J, 2$) (PRQ)$
BIT($I, J$) (MNP($X$)) = BIT($K, J$) (RQL($Y$))$
```
Frame 7. Bit and byte—examples of use.

NENT   Number of Entries
MANT   Mantissa
CHAR   Characteristic
SIGN   Sign
ENT   Entry
LOC   Location

Use Example

```
NENT(TABX) = NENT(TABX) + 2
SIGN(ITEM1) = 1
```

Frame 8. Modifiers—examples.

case, the branch would be the "Ith" label on the switch declaration. Another kind of switch initiated in JOVIAL was called the item switch. In this switch, the value of the switch point is contained in an item and may not necessarily be chosen from a set of sequential integers known by the programmer. In this case, the switch labeled BAKER is based on the value of the item RPQM which is a status item, the values you see to the right: CLOUDY, RAINY, and FAIR. This call will go to R1, R2, or R3 depending on whether the value of RPQM is CLOUDY, RAINY, or FAIR. And of course, in this case the item could have had more values than just CLOUDY, RAINY, or FAIR—all of which are unknown to the programmer.

Another example of independence from data structure in programs is on the next slide [Frame 10]. This particular program, without going into detail, cycles through a table setting values of DX based on the values of AB. It does it whether the table is serial or parallel, and independent of the number of words in an entry. So that if the structures involved change from serial to parallel, or parallel to serial, or the number of words changes in an entry, the program doesn't have to change.

In addition to these capabilities, JOVIAL does provide rather easy access to machine language, although the object has always been to avoid its use as much as possible. Another objective of the language, and probably one of the first languages with this objective, was that the compiler should be written in its own language. JOVIAL compilers were always programmed in JOVIAL.

Some of the basic ideas for the language came from the programming of SAGE. It was the first large real time system, utilizing about 1000 or more people for development and installation. SAGE provided ideas for the kinds of facilities that would be needed in a language to program large systems. One of the key ideas of SAGE was in the area of data definition. SAGE was programmed in machine language but used the concept of a central data dictionary. This concept was implemented with the Communication Pool, or Comm Pool, which was the central data definition used to assemble programs. The SAGE Com-

Subscript (Numeric) Switch

```
SWITCH ABLE = (S1, S2, S3...Sn) $        Declaration
GOTO ABLE($I$)$                          Call
```

Item Switch

```
SWITCH BAKER(RPQM) = (V(CLOUDY) = R1, V(RAINY)
                     = R2, V(FAIR) = R3)$ Declaration
GOTO BAKER($I$)$                          Call
```

Frame 9. Switches—examples.

```
FOR I = ALL(AB)$
BEGIN
  IF AB($I$) = 3$
  DX($I$) = 5$
END
```

Frame 10. Accessing tables independent of structure.

munication Pool also provided definitions of items of the various types that were eventually defined in JOVIAL. The Comm Pool capability was applied to JOVIAL, permitting the data definition to exist outside of programs.

SAGE provided a scheme for accessing data through pseudo-instructions to permit constant programs even when changes were made in the central data definition.

[Frame 11] gives an example of how that was done in SAGE. Again, I'm not going to go into detail, but there were operators in the machine language programs, such as ETR for Extract, Position with POS, and Restore and Deposit. These were pseudo-instructions in SAGE. Using these, the programmer did not have to know the actual positions of items within words, but could manipulate them anyway, such as in this example of an addition of two items.

One of the problems with this technique as used in SAGE was that to add these two items together—ITEM1 + ITEM2—which is shown on the bottom of the example, took a minimum of 10 instructions, one for each pseudo-instruction. One of the arguments used for the development of JOVIAL was the fact that one could have the same data transparency, plus the generation of more efficient machine code with JOVIAL than was possible with machine language, because the compiler could take advantage of the particular situations of ITEM1, ITEM2, and ITEM3 to do the same operation, and actually turn out better code.

So SAGE was one of the major contributors to JOVIAL.

The other very strong contributor to JOVIAL, and actually the basis for the architecture and the name of the original language, was the definition of IAL, later called ALGOL. This definition appeared in 1958 in the *Communications of the ACM*. The basic structure of JOVIAL, and of course many other languages, was taken from IAL. A number of

```
SAGE:
  CLA ITEM1    Move ITEM1 to accumulator
  ETR ITEM1    Mask ITEM1
  POS ITEM1    Position ITEM1 to the least significant position
  STO TEMP     Save ITEM1
  CLA ITEM2    Move ITEM2 to accumulator
  ETR ITEM2    Mask ITEM2
  POS ITEM2    Move ITEM2 to the least significant position
  ADD TEMP     Add the two items
  RES ITEM3    Move to position of ITEM3
  DEP ITEM3    Store in ITEM3
JOVIAL:
  ITEM3 = ITEM1 + ITEM2$
```

Frame 11. Accessing items in SAGE—adding two items.

changes were initially made to IAL for JOVIAL, particularly in the data definition area, but as time went on, no attempts were made to incorporate concepts from succeeding versions of ALGOL, not at least in the first few years.

Another of the very important subjects of JOVIAL was schedules. This was not always a happy subject in the days when JOVIAL was being developed. The original contractual commitments were for several compilers to be produced by System Development Corporation in parallel, one on the IBM 709, and the other on the AN/FSQ-31 Computer. The IBM 709 version, according to the contract, was to be delivered within six months, the Q-31 some months later. The work began at the end of 1958. The actual first formal delivery of the JOVIAL 709 compiler was made to SAC (Strategic Air Command) in Omaha in early 1961. A little calculation will show that it missed the original schedule by a fair amount.

However, a variety of intermediate versions of JOVIAL processors was produced prior to the formal delivery and used for a number of in-house activities, one of which was programming the compilers.

Another interesting aspect of this development in retrospect was the management practices used at the time. Today there are probably more people that have worked with compilers in the world than there were total programmers in the world at the time of the JOVIAL development. The only person with previous experience on the original JOVIAL project was myself, and at best my experience was very distant and limited. The project that developed both the 709 and the Q-31 compilers varied in size from around 6 to 15 people over its life. For some of these people—and a fair number of them—this was their first programming job. They were hired to do this and trained. Management practices were, to put it favorably, informal. To put it bluntly, almost nonexistent. One of the major problems with management was that the language was evolving as the compilers were being implemented. Major language features were developed in literally minutes! With minor exceptions, there were no committees involved. One couldn't define things in minutes with committees. The fact that there were no committees involved in the original version of JOVIAL, was, I believe, good for the development. Most of the early features were added by me, or one of several others working on the project (most of the time with my concurrence).

Frequently, language features were determined as needs were recognized by compiler writers who were programming in JOVIAL. Features were also put in or changed as early users began to use it, in-house users, generally.

No complete language description existed at the beginning of compiler building. Informal documents were written which served as an adequate baseline, but frequently compiler code was produced based only on spoken communication. Updates of previous documents were eventually produced, after things were implemented in most cases. The first comprehensive attempt for a stable language description was produced at the time of the first compiler delivery, which was about $2\frac{1}{2}$ years after the project started.

Other formal JOVIAL language descriptions were written in the following years. They were written mostly by people associated with another version of JOVIAL being produced by SDC on the West Coast. You have to understand—the version I was talking about up to now was produced on the East Coast, for 465-L. The West Coast efforts initially produced compilers for computers other than the ones that were being used on the East Coast. An example of these computers were the Philco 2000, the AN/FSQ-7, which was the original SAGE computer, and the CDC 1604, among others. However, these efforts generally were also for versions of JOVIAL other than the versions being produced on the East Coast.

The West Coast team grew from the early experimentation with expression analysis which was worked on by Bratman (SDC), Book (SDC), and myself. When I left for the 465-L effort in 1958, that nucleus expanded and continued research into languages and compilers. A language called CLIP evolved from this effort, in parallel with early JOVIAL work on the East Coast. However, as time progressed, more effort was devoted to JO-VIAL on the West Coast and the work on CLIP eventually stopped.

But the West Coast group continued with expansion, refinement, and formalizing of JO-VIAL, and in fact, are responsible for the version that eventually became the Air Force Standard. Most of the formally published literature on JOVIAL was written by Chris Shaw on the West Coast. He's now at Xerox.

As the years continued, many other companies became JOVIAL compiler producers. Examples are PRC, CSC, Abacus, SofTech, and a number of others. Computer manufacturers were not a major factor in producing or preserving the language initially, although versions of JOVIAL have existed for almost all major and not-so-major computers that have been in existence since those days.

With all these companies and computers, and with the exception of the eventual Air Force published standard, very little control over the language existed, and a great number of variations were eventually produced.

These are some of the versions [Frame 12]. These are each a version of JOVIAL, J0, J−1, J1, J2, . . . it goes on. If this isn't sufficiently mind-boggling in its size, it should be realized that it isn't a complete list. And for each of these variations, different subsets of that variation were produced within compilers. In summary, although someone familiar with a particular version of JOVIAL would probably recognize other variations as being part of the JOVIAL family, he would also find that he'd better study the specific version very carefully before producing any code.

JOVIAL did prove to be quite general and useful for a sizeable number of tasks, but several areas of concern stand out quite distinctly in my mind. First, the original compilers were slow—very slow. One of the things which was not a concern when language features were being designed was the effect of a feature on the compiler. This was coupled with the language's emphasis on generality and the use of fairly slow computers by today's standards. Also there was the rather small level of experience of the staff, although most of the people were quite good, and quite hard-working. Also, the compiler was programmed in

J0 J-1 J1 J2	The Original East Coast Set
J3 J3B	The West Coast Versions—The Eventual AF Standard
BASIC JOVIAL JX-2 J5 J5.2	Relatively Fast Compilers
J73 J73I	Current AF Developed Versions

Frame 12. Some versions of JOVIAL.

its own language. All these things contributed to long periods of compilation. At first it took eight elapsed hours to compile the compiler on the 709, and that's with nothing else running on the computer. Also, for a variety of reasons, some of which are probably obvious, the initial compilers were not very reliable. This, together with the lack of speed, not infrequently led to long periods of waiting for wrong or nonexistent results. This caused considerable tension on the part of early users! It also created a fair degree of strain for those of us who had their names associated with the language!

Even with these and other problems, however, the language continued to grow in use, and there was no significant attempt to avoid its use among most of the early users. It did prove to be quite general, although not elegant syntactically nor particularly easy to learn; it was easy to use, and once learned, easy to retain. It has been used for a wide variety of programs, many of which were other than Command and Control Systems. It has been compared against other languages in contests of various kinds, and has usually come out fairly well. It was probably the first language with a large compiler totally programmed in itself, and it was also the very first, (or near to it) System Programming Language. It was one of the first high-level languages used for total programming of a large Command and Control System.

JOVIAL, in a variety of flavors, continues to exist today and to be used for numerous applications. The newest versions have resulted from an Air Force–sponsored design committee's efforts begun in the early 1970s. These are the J73 versions which appeared on the last slide. Several other languages have used JOVIAL as part of their original design basis. Some languages, such as PL/I, now have quite similar kinds of objectives and capabilities, although it's not clear that their design was based directly or indirectly on JOVIAL itself.

The Department of Defense is in the process of trying to find a standard language, and a few versions of JOVIAL have been part of the several languages examined for this standard. If JOVIAL is not chosen, its use will probably decrease over the next decade. But considering that JOVIAL originally had very short-range objectives, narrow support, the rather over-ambitious nature of the original efforts, and a variety of other early problems, it has survived and been used in a larger number of situations than one might have expected. It has been and will most likely continue to be used for some time. This provides great satisfaction to its early developers, who thought of it in very short-range terms back in 1958.

Thank you.

TRANSCRIPT OF QUESTION AND ANSWER SESSION

JOHN GOODENOUGH: One of the questioners, John Favaro, asks (I'm going to rephrase a bit): One of the arguments you said that was in favor of developing JOVIAL was the fact that you could develop more efficient programs using it, although it seems with most other languages, people are always concerned that if you're developing a system implementation language, it'll be less efficient than using assembly language. Was there really a lot of opposition to that argument at the time?

JULES SCHWARTZ: Yes, of course there's always opposition, particularly in some areas. For example, JOVIAL did allow an unlimited number of dimensions for arrays, but little use was made of this feature. It was very inefficient once one got beyond a single subscript. But in the area I was talking about, which provided the ability for programs to refer to tightly packed or otherwise structured items without having to worry about where they were in the word, JOVIAL did provide the ability for the compiler to produce better code for a particular setup than the programmer himself. In that area, and some others (including single dimension arrays), it did quite well.

GOODENOUGH: A couple of people have asked, "What communication did you have with people implementing other ALGOL 58 dialects, such as MAD and NELIAC?"

SCHWARTZ: Almost none with MAD. NELIAC—there was communication after one of the contests. It was an experiment to compare the two to see which language the Navy would use. NELIAC was the Navy base language, originally. JOVIAL wasn't. And in at least one version of the contest, JOVIAL was chosen by the Navy. That created a lot of communication! But JOVIAL didn't stay as the Navy language. [As far as ALGOL, eventually there was communication, but it didn't have continued influence on the early JOVIAL.]

GOODENOUGH: You mentioned that the term "byte" is used in JOVIAL. Where did the term come from?

SCHWARTZ: As I recall, the AN/FSQ-31, a totally different computer than the 709, was byte oriented. I don't recall for sure, but I'm reasonably certain the description of that computer included the word "byte", and we used it.

FRED BROOKS: May I speak to that? Werner Buchholz coined the word as part of the definition of STRETCH, and the AN/FSQ-31 picked it up from STRETCH, but Werner is very definitely the author of that word.

SCHWARTZ: That's right. Thank you.

GOODENOUGH: A question from Richard Miller: "Could you comment further on the fact that JOVIAL was always used to compile itself? Who was primarily responsible for this decision?"

SCHWARTZ: Oh, I think those of us who were on that original project out here on the West Coast—Erwin Book and Harvey Bratman, and others. The idea always was, for some reason, to compile the language in itself. It seemed quite logical at the time.

ERWIN BOOK: We also were kind of influenced by UNCOL [Universal Compiler Language] at the time and we thought to make a technology whereby we had one generator for all computers translating into an intermediate language. Then one could have different translators producing code for each different computer that we wanted—and that's the way the JOVIAL compilers are all built. The front end is reproduced very easily, and you just write a translator and that intermediate language is kind of half an UNCOL, but very limited.

GOODENOUGH: How much influence did FORTRAN have?

SCHWARTZ: FORTRAN really had, I would say, almost none on JOVIAL. It was really just getting started in those days. I think we had one fellow on the project who had used it.

The rest of us had read specs, but anything we did had really come from the IAL specs, plus our own invention.

GOODENOUGH: How many problems resulted from the many variations of declarations and the large number of descriptors in the language?

SCHWARTZ: I happened to read in preparing this material, much of the old documentation. (I got this from Chris Shaw, whom I mentioned as the guy who wrote much of the early documentation. He also collected every piece of paper that was written, informally or otherwise, and he donated it to me.) One of the documents was by people responsible for teaching and seeing that other people used the language. One of their remarks was that it was kind of difficult to teach the language, but they also said that they noticed—and these people were totally unbiased—that once people learned JOVIAL, they didn't have many problems. They remembered it, and they never had to go back to the documents. So, it seems that initial learning was the worst problem.

GOODENOUGH: The language uses items as its term of declaring an individual variable, which is different from the way FORTRAN or IAL uses REAL and INTEGER as its declaration mechanism. How did you come to make that particular choice?

SCHWARTZ: That was really based largely on the way the SAGE definitions were done (although SAGE had a machine language orientation). We added some things, but it was based on SAGE, which used the name "item" in Comm Pools and tables.

GOODENOUGH: Do you have any further comments on the name of the language, beyond what's in [pp 369–388] and in Jean Sammet's book?

SCHWARTZ: No, but I think if it had been called anything else, somebody else would probably have been chosen to be up here today. No, the preprint does give, I think, the fairly complete story on how the name came about.

GOODENOUGH: Thank you very much.

FULL TEXT OF ALL QUESTIONS SUBMITTED†

CHUCK BAKER

In JOVIAL data descriptions, some data attributes are bound at compile time (item type, length, etc.). Others are bound at execution time (table length). How was the choice of when to bind made? Would you change these choices now?

KEN DICKEY

Implicit in the design of the language is a high level of programming awareness (assembly language, data mixing, etc.). To what measure is this due to desire for flexibility, and what measure to time constraints?

---

† Jules Schwartz has annotated the full set of questions and provided answers to several that were not asked at the session.

Answer: Largely to flexibility and the fear of getting stuck without it.

JOHN FAVARO

What experiences convinced you that system programming should be done in a high level language? How much opposition was there at the time?

Answer: If not much opposition, certainly skepticism existed. It seemed desirable enough that it was worth the attempt, and some efficiency improvement was possible if one tried to achieve flexibility.

BERNIE GALLER

Was the term "byte" used in JOVIAL? Where did it come from?

Answer: See discussion transcript.

FORREST HOWARD

What was the bootstrap procedure to get JOVIAL to the point where it compiled itself?

Answer: The first compiler $(J-1)$ was written in machine language.

RICHARD MILLER

Could you comment further on the fact that JOVIAL was always used to compile itself? Who was primarily responsible for this?

Answer: See discussion transcript.

RICHARD MILLER

Do you have any further comments on the name beyond what is in the preprints and Jean Sammet's book?

Answer: See discussion transcript.

RICHARD MILLER

Why items and not specific types as in the REAL, INTEGER, etc., of FORTRAN or IAL?
What influence did FORTRAN have?
How many problems resulted from the many variations of declarations and the large number of descriptions?

Answer: See discussion transcript.

BOB ROSIN

To what extent did ALGOL 58 influence the design of JOVIAL? Did you communicate with people implementing ALGOL 58 dialects—e.g., MAD, NELIAC?

Answer: See discussion transcript.

BIOGRAPHY OF JULES I. SCHWARTZ

While attending Graduate School at Columbia University, Jules Schwartz became acquainted with some early computing devices at T. J. Watson Center in New York. He joined RAND Corporation in 1954 where he worked on the JOHNNIAC Computer, primarily in the development of utilities and on the IBM 701, where major work was on the PACT Compiler (one of the early high-level language efforts). He joined the SAGE System development at Lincoln Laboratory in late 1955, where his major contribution was to the Lincoln Utility System. After SDC was split off from RAND, he became involved with various system efforts, which eventually led to language work and the development of JOVIAL.

After JOVIAL, beginning in the early 1960s, he became responsible for a wide variety of projects, including early time-sharing systems, Data Base Management, continued language efforts, and other activities. By the end of the 1960s, he was the Director of Technology at SDC.

In 1970, he joined CSC, where his primary responsibilities have been consulting, managing, auditing, and working on a variety of commercial and Government Systems. In the process, he has been responsible for design of several general- and special-purpose languages.

VIII

GPSS Session

Chairman: Barbara Liskov
Speaker: Geoffrey Gordon

PAPER: THE DEVELOPMENT OF THE GENERAL PURPOSE SIMULATION SYSTEM (GPSS)

Geoffrey Gordon

IBM Corporation
Data Processing Division

1. Background

The General Purpose Simulation System (GPSS) is a programming system designed for the simulation of discrete systems. These are systems that can be modeled as a series of state changes that occur instantaneously, usually over a period of time. Complexities in their analysis arise because there are many elements in the system, and there is competition for limited system resources. The simulation technique uses numerical computation methods to follow the system elements through their changes of state, and predicts properties of the system from measurements on the model.

GPSS came into existence rapidly, with virtually no planning, and surprisingly little effort. It came rapidly because it filled an urgent need that left little time for exploring alternatives. The lack of planning came from a happy coincidence of a solution meeting its problem at the right time. The economy of effort was based on a background of experience in the type of application for which the language was designed, both on the part of the designer and the early users.

1.1. Analog Experience

Regarding my own background, I began simulating, with analog computers, in the early 1950s when working on guided missile studies at the Research Laboratories of the General Electric Company in England. Analog simulation is, of course, a different technique from digital simulation. However, no one who has worked with analog simulation can fail to have been impressed by the way an analog computer gets its user involved with the problem being solved. Putting together the elements of an analog computer to study a system feels almost like building the system itself, and it is extremely gratifying to get results that can be immediately related to elements of the system. There seem to be no intermediaries, no complicated procedures to follow, and no experts to interpret results.

In developing GPSS there was no conscious effort to base the design on analog computers, but I feel sure the block diagram notation and the emphasis on making the simulation directly accessible to system analysts rather than through programmers, that are characteristics of GPSS, were unconsciously influenced by the analog computer experience.

1.2. Early Digital Experience

I began simulating with digital computers, also at an early date; starting in 1954, with a machine called MOSAIC, built in England at the Telecommunications Research Establishment: a machine that seems to have slipped through the cracks of computer history. When I came to the USA in 1955, I continued similar work at the Electronics Division of the Westinghouse Corporation, using an IBM 650 machine.

None of these early simulation efforts could be described as a language development. They used essentially continuous simulation techniques to solve the equations of motion of missiles, and they were all written either in machine or assembly language. However, they gave me experience in modeling and the general programming techniques of generating, gathering, and reporting simulation statistics.

At the end of 1956 I joined the Bell Telephone Laboratories, Murray Hill, New Jersey, initially to work on a project aimed at designing a digital computer for Bell System's revenue accounting needs. The work included writing what would now be called an emulation program for the proposed machine, but otherwise did not involve simulation.

When that project was terminated, however, I began writing simulation programs for some message switching systems that were under development. This work began to demonstrate some general concepts. It became apparent that the individual items of equipment, whether they were switching devices, communication channels, or message storage units could be represented as simple server units, with their own service discipline and capacity. The system models were essentially networks of such units. The system design problems usually involved balancing the use of fast, costly devices, like markers, that served telephone calls or messages one at a time, against relatively slow multiple-access devices like cross-bar switches. The contrast between the two device types was emphasized by referring to them as being time-shared and space-shared.

Correspondingly, the models used single-server and multiple-server entities as basic elements: elements that were to become the facilities and storages of GPSS.

Again this work did not result in any form of simulation language. However, subroutines for representing the elements of switching systems and for generating and gathering statistics were developed. Those, of course, were the days of punched cards. I soon got to the stage of assembling models from small, carefully saved decks of cards, with a few cards being added or repunched. It was apparent that a lot could be made from a few, fully tested, and well understood routines, and I am sure this predisposed me to interpretive programming.

1.3. The Sequence Diagram Simulator

Experience with these simulation studies led to my being asked, in 1959, to work on a project in the Systems Research Department. The project, led by John P. Runyon, was to develop a tool for studying advanced switching system designs. Switching systems were being described by sequence diagrams; that is, by directed graphs whose nodes correspond to operations performed in the system and whose directed paths of connected nodes represent possible sequences of events. Professor D. L. Dietmeyer of the University of Wisconsin Electrical Engineering Department, who was an employee of the Laboratories for the summer of 1959, was asked by John Runyon to write a simulator based on the sequence diagram model. He wrote the first version of the program, and I took over this work when he was about to return to the university at the beginning of the fall term.

I succeeded in getting the program running toward the end of 1959 and left the project in early 1960. About that time, Mr. B. A. Tague joined the Systems Research Department, and he subsequently made substantial improvements to the program.

The program assumed that the action at a sequence diagram node could take time and involve the use of up to three items of equipment which were described as being either single or multiple servers. A series of marks, representing telephone calls, moved through the nodes. The departure of a mark from a node could be by way of three possible paths with the choice being made either randomly or conditionally upon the availability of the equipment defined at the destination nodes.

A paper describing the first version of this Sequence Diagram Simulator was presented at a meeting of the IEEE (Dietmeyer *et al.*, 1960). A version of the program was also run at the University of Wisconsin.

In describing the results of the previous year's work, what had begun as a program to simulate switching systems was described as being for traffic-handling systems. To demonstrate the more general nature of the program this implied, the example chosen to illustrate its application was the movement of people through a supermarket.

The program proved to be simple to use, and it met its goal of "estimating such quantities as delays, queue lengths and occupancies at an early stage of design when only a rough description of a system is available" (Dietmeyer *et al.*, 1960). More detailed systems, however, needed somewhat contrived sequence diagrams or required modification of the program, and I did subsequently apply the program to some switching system studies at Bell Laboratories by making such modifications.

A conclusion drawn when discussing what was described as the problem of "simplicity versus flexibility" was that the problem "can be to some extent resolved by retaining the basic structure of the program . . . , which is of itself adequate for use by non-programmers for a large class of problems, and acknowledging that other problems will require program modification" (Dietmeyer *et al.*, 1960).

1.4. The Gordon Simulator

In June 1960 I joined the Advanced Systems Development Division (ASDD) of IBM, initially at White Plains, New York, but eventually Yorktown Heights, New York. (The division has since been disbanded.) The division had been established toward the end of

Geoffrey Gordon

1959, essentially as an applied research facility, to investigate the design and application of systems based on new technologies.

The division was heavily engaged in the design of teleprocessing systems. These involve entering transactions from remote terminals into a central computer. Application programs for processing the transactions have to be located and, possibly, read into a computer. Usually, records stored off-line need to be referenced and updated, and a reply has to be sent to the terminal that submitted the transaction. The terminals share a communication network under the control of switching units. Problems are raised by the need to share computer resources between messages and data records, and the need to construct an economical communication network by sharing lines between several terminals.

There were concerns with the design of individual system elements, with the response time of the system, and with predicting the effect of the system on the organization that would use it.

GPSS came to be used extensively in the study of many teleprocessing systems developed within ASDD. Among the systems studies at that time that used GPSS and were later to be publicized were a stock exchange system (Smith, 1962), urban traffic control (Blum, 1964), a steel mill (Boyd *et al.*, 1964), organization of a computer center (Smith, 1962), a voice answer-back telephone interrupt system (Velasco, 1964), and an airline reservation system (Perry and Plugge, 1961). Another IBM group that was to make a great deal of use of GPSS was the Data Services Group, stationed in Houston, Texas, in support of the Real Time Computer Complex for the National Aeronautics and Space Agency (Stanley and Hertel, 1968).

The people engaged in these studies formed a mixed group. Many were system designers, with operations research or electrical engineering experience, from the product development laboratories of IBM. Others were industry specialists from the marketing division with knowledge of particular application areas. There were also people brought into IBM for their work experience in the application areas, most of whom had little or no experience of computers.

I joined a Mathematics and Programming Department under the leadership of Dr. D. V. Newton. The role of the department was to assist in solving design problems by applying mathematical techniques, and supplying algorithms for performing application functions. Within the department were several mathematicians attempting to describe some of the more critical factors, such as channel interference and communication line polling, by queuing models which could show the effect of traffic load on response time, and compare the effects of different priorities and polling disciplines. However, the simplifications needed to produce solvable models made it difficult to judge how valid the results would be.

The potential value of simulation in giving more realistic models had been recognized, and one person (Mr. H. Mechanic) had begun to look at the possibility of developing a mathematical notation suitable for describing a system simulation. Ultimately, the intention was to write a compiler to implement the language. I, naturally, considered the Sequence Diagram Simulator, but quickly found that the level of detail needed to simulate the type of system and equipment being considered in ASDD would require a great deal of reprogramming. The problem of "simplicity versus flexibility" that had arisen with the Sequence Diagram Simulator had to be resolved at a different level if simulation was to be used effectively on the many ASDD projects. I suggested developing a system description language based on the Sequence Diagram Simulator approach, and it was agreed that I look into the possibilities.

The development work on which I now began fell within the scope of the department's role, so no special project or budget was established: the work was regarded as a research project. Periodic reviews would be made, and, no doubt, had no significant progress been made by the end of the year, the project would have been terminated in the course of planning the next year's efforts. As it happened, significant progress was soon made and it was the mathematical language project that was dropped later in 1960.

I was not aware of the work on the SIMSCRIPT language, another general purpose discrete simulation language. Judging by publication dates, this must have begun about that time or soon after (Markowitz *et al.*, 1963).

I began writing a program implementing a block diagram language, choosing a relatively simple table-oriented, interpretive structure that would make changes easy. It was written using the SAP assembly language on the IBM 704 system. All subsequent IBM versions of GPSS, up to and including GPSS V, were also written in the assembly language of whatever machine for which they were designed.

While, in general, block diagrams cannot be considered a fundamentally different concept from a sequence diagram, the particular properties being sought were that there should be a number of fixed block types, and that each should embody only one particular function.

I was the only programmer, but, from the beginning, I planned to work closely with other members of the division involved in system designs. They were very helpful in explaining the detailed logic of the equipment and procedures, and helping to define block types. In particular, Mr. R. A. Merikallio, who was responsible for many models, was very active in assessing the developing program and feeding back suggestions for improvements.

In addition to finding that many types of system could be described, it transpired that the block diagram language provided an excellent means of communication. When I talked with a system analyst we could quickly agree on a block diagram to describe the main elements of a system. By progressively refining the block diagram, the details of the system description could be expanded.

If I had to pick an event that established this point, it was when I went to the west coast laboratory of ASDD, then located at San Jose, to help in a problem with random access disks operating on a channel. I arrived one morning, knowing nothing about the details of the problem, and left that evening with a working simulation model that had already produced significant output. The project engineer (Mr. Don Fisher) continued to use the model to produce further results. This was not the first problem solved with the program, but it was the first to demonstrate the potential for the quick solution of problems: the others had progressed through a series of stops and starts as program changes were made and bugs were removed. It was also typical of the way the program was being used at that time. I would produce a block diagram, working with someone familiar with the system to be simulated, and that person would learn enough about the program to run it and make changes and extensions.

The existence of the program by then had become well known within IBM, and it was being used on problems brought to ASDD from other divisions. In addition, copies of the program at various levels of completion, and with various assortments of bugs appeared around IBM. While I knew the development of the language was far from finished, I decided to document what had been produced to satisfy the demand that was growing for the program. The result was a cleaned-up program with a user's manual, produced as an internal ASDD technical memorandum. This was an IBM confidential document dated October 25, 1960 (Gordon, 1960).

The program had never really been given a name, but, by default, it came to be known as the Gordon Simulator.

1.5. The First GPSS

Experience with the Gordon Simulator had uncovered some anomalies. Minor changes in the block diagram that logically made no difference could cause significant differences. Some examples are: adding or removing blocks that do not represent system actions, like blocks gathering statistics; changing the order of blocks when the sequence of the actions they represent is irrelevant; or moving the calculation of a time from one block to another.

The basic cause was the manner of handling simultaneous events. The apparently minor change could alter the order in which simultaneous events were processed and, sometimes, like the proverbial tiny pebble that moved, cause a complete change in the subsequent course of events. The result was not really an error, since, in the circumstances, the new sequence of events could just as easily have occurred as the first—but it looked like an error. The diagnosis of the trouble had been made early in the use of the program, but, with the pressure of work, the trouble had gone untreated. A lot of thought was now put into redesigning the simulation algorithm to remove the anomalies. The technical details are explained in Section 3.5.

At the beginning of 1961, a complete rewrite of the program was begun in order to implement the new algorithm that was developed, as well as to incorporate some new block types. A project was established with budget to cover three people. I was joined by two programmers, Messrs. R. Barbieri and R. Efron, and the program continued through the summer of 1961.

The program was initially IBM confidential, but, as its use within IBM spread, it was apparent that many other people could use it. The program was brought to the attention of the Cross Industry Marketing Group of IBM, then managed by Mr. Steve Furth, who had among their responsibilities the promotion of application programs of potential use to diverse industrial users. They considered the program to be of general interest, and agreed to sponsor the program as an IBM product.

The confidential classification of the program was removed early in 1961 so that copies of the then existing program could be given to people outside IBM, on the understanding that it was not supported by IBM. (It was an IBM type III program, for which there is no commitment to correct errors.)

It took a few more months to stabilize the program and produce proper documentation. When this was done, a press release was made on September 27, 1961, announcing the program as an IBM type II program (that is, with a commitment to correct errors.) A user's manual, dated October 6, 1961 was issued, and the program was made available for use on the IBM 704, 709, and 7090 systems (Gordon, 1961a).

Again the program had not been given a title, and in the haste of preparing for its release it was just called a General Purpose Simulator, or GPS. I shortly realized that this acronym was used by Professors Newell and Simon for a program called General Problem

Solver, being used in connection with their work on artificial intelligence. I quickly changed the name to a "General Purpose Systems Simulator," or GPSS. Later, with the GPSS III release, the name was changed slightly to the "General Purpose Simulation System."

Not only in name but also in substance, I consider that program to be the first that can properly be called the General Purpose Simulation System, although it had only 25 block types. More block types were to be added to later versions, and a major change in the internal structure of the program was to be introduced in the next version of the program, but this 1961 program contained the essential elements of GPSS. In particular, it had the simulation algorithm that was to remain a feature of all following IBM versions of GPSS, at least through GPSS V.

A paper describing the program was presented at the Eastern Joint Computer Conference, held in Washington, D.C., in December 1961 (Gordon, 1961b). Another paper describing that first version of the GPSS program was published (Gordon, 1962a). Later, the flowcharts of that same version of the program were released (Gordon, 1962b).

1.6. Later IBM Developments

Development work continued in ASDD after the release of the first program, and a second version, GPSS II, was released in 1963 (IBM Corp., 1963). Most of the coding for that program was done by Mr. R. Efron, and we published a joint paper describing the program (Efron and Gordon, 1964).

The number of blocks had expanded to 33, and there was an important change in the program structure. While the first program had been table-oriented, GPSS II used list processing techniques, in a manner described later, in Section 3.5. The simulation algorithm remained unchanged (although the BUFFER option was added) but the execution was made more efficient. The system numerical attributes (described later, in Section 2.4) were also introduced with this version.

The first GPSS program had required the user to assign all block numbers absolutely, but GPSS II had an assembly program which included a macro generator. The coding for this assembler was done by Mr. G. H. Bean.

In 1963, responsibility for further development of GPSS was transferred to the Data Processing Division of IBM, to a department called Systems Marketing Techniques Development (SMTD), managed by Mr. R. M. King.

A reorganization of the GPSS program, by Mr. E. Olson, led to a version that ran much faster than GPSS II, both in execution and assembly. As a result, it earned the name of ZIP/ZAP, but it was not released. Further work by Messrs. J. Bult and R. Gould, however, led to a version that was released as GPSS III (IBM Corp., 1965a; Herscovitch and Schneider, 1965). It was made available for the IBM Systems 7090/94 (IBM Corp., 1965b) and 7040/44 (IBM Corp., 1965c).

There were several major changes reflecting the users' reaction to the program, including one of the input format. The fixed form of input statements used in the earlier versions of the program was changed to free format. This meant that GPSS III was not compatible with GPSS II. Subsequent versions, however, remained compatible.

The documentation of the program was also considerably improved by a manual prepared by R. A. Merikallio that included full details of how the program was internally organized. There were some changes in block types, the main improvement being the introduction of the concept of chains. These allow a user to implement queuing disciplines other than the FIFO discipline that had been implicit in earlier versions.

Soon after release of the GPSS III program, IBM announced the System 360. A GPSS/360 version of the language was released in March 1967 (IBM Corp., 1967a; Gould, 1969). It was available for running under OS/360 (IBM Corp., 1967b) and DOS/360 (IBM Corp., 1967c). This version introduced the concept of groups, which allow transactions, not necessarily otherwise connected together, to be recognized as being members of a common set, irrespective of where they reside in the block diagram. It is possible to carry out various search and processing functions on members of the group.

The SMTD group were continually simulating computer systems. By using the macro capability associated with the assembly program of GPSS it was possible to define models of standard computer system elements, and, in effect, create a problem-oriented language for describing computer systems. Based on this experience, the group developed from the GPSS program another simulation program called CSS, the "Computer Simulation System," which was considerably more efficient than GPSS for that type of application, both in terms of storage and execution time. The design of this program was the work of Mr. R. M. Tomashulo. The first version, which was an internal IBM program, was programmed by J. Bult. A second version, which was made public, was the work of Messrs. H. Herscovitch and R. Ramsay (IBM Corp., 1970c).

In 1970, GPSS V was released by IBM (IBM Corp. 1970a,b). By that time responsibility for the program had been transferred to the Scientific Industry Development group in Chicago. The programming was done by J. Bult and R. Gould.

Two important extensions introduced by GPSS V were the ability to place part of the model on external storage, where it could be accessed dynamically, and allowing parameters and savevalues to have fullword, halfword, byte size, and floating-point formats. The user could also reallocate the storage space assigned to the different program entities. As discussed in Section 1.8, some of these ideas had been introduced in non-IBM versions of the program.

1.7. The Generalized Monitor System

An interesting extension of GPSS II was carried out in ASDD during 1963. It had occurred to me that there was a strong similarity between tasks performed by the GPSS simulation algorithm and the tasks performed by a control program. In simulating a control program, the simulation is maintaining records of the system resources being simulated that essentially duplicate the records kept by the control program. Also, the simulation algorithm, like a control program, must be organized to respond to stochastic events, even though the "randomness" is internally generated rather than being the result of an interrupt from an external source.

I proposed an experiment in which the GPSS program was modified in such a way that it would drive a real-time data processing application. The system built for this experiment was called the Generalized Monitor System. The design and programming was done by Messrs. G. H. Bean, J. J. Davis, H. A. Mulkiewicz, and C. J. VanTassel (Bean et al., 1963).

A PROCESS block was designed to transfer control from the simulation algorithm to an operational program. There could, in principle, be any number of such blocks. Those that were occupied by transactions represented programs that were currently being multipro-grammed. A limit on that number was placed by using a conventional GPSS storage to limit the number of transactions simultaneously in the block diagram. A modified form of GPSS storage represented actual system storage by taking account of addresses.

Normal GPSS operations would determine when conditions were correct for the execu-tion of an operational program to begin, just as would be done in a simulation of the system. Entry into a PROCESS block would then start execution of the program. An operational program issuing an I/O command did so through a macro that would suspend the transac-tion representing the execution of that program, by making it a delayed transaction. Modi-fications to delayed transactions saved machine register values. A channel trap in re-sponse to the I/O request reactivated the transaction, but control returned to the simulation algorithm to select, by priority, which transaction would next gain control of the CPU.

At that time, I had reporting to me a group concerned with an information retrieval ap-plication called SDI (Selective Dissemination of Information). Abstracts of documents which had keywords could be searched to retrieve documents meeting logical combina-tions of keywords. Part of the database for that application was used in the experiment. The selected database was put on several tapes attached to two channels. Requests, in the form of any one of eight specific logical formats, between up to four keywords, could be entered from a card reader or a tape.

The experiment was run on an IBM 7090 at the Thomas J. Watson Research Center, Yorktown Heights, New York. It was a remarkably successful experiment, demonstrating that the GPSS algorithm could act as a real-time control program. The results raised vi-sions of being able to design real-time systems by simulation and use the simulation model description as a basis for generating a working system. Unfortunately, IBM was about to reap the hurricane associated with producing OS/360, and ASDD was about to go into a major reorganization forced by the loss of programmers in the hurricane. Somehow, the thrust of this experiment was also lost.

1.8. Other GPSS Programs

Following release of the initial GPSS program several other computer manufacturers and simulation users made other versions of GPSS available. No standards have been es-tablished for the language, so that most of these alternative versions, while generally based on one of the IBM releases of the language, have not remained compatible with the IBM versions or among themselves.

Among the other computer manufacturers that have produced versions of GPSS are UNIVAC (Gorchow, 1968), CDC (Goldman, 1968), Honeywell (Batchelor, 1968), RCA (Bannan, 1968), and DEC (Digital Equipment Corp., date unknown).

One of the earliest users of GPSS, outside IBM, was the Norden Division of United Technologies Corporation. A group under the leadership of Mr. Julian Reitman began using the program early in 1962.

The group was concerned with the simulation of large military defense systems, and needed to run GPSS for large scale models. They were, therefore, among the first users to become concerned with problems of excessive amounts of storage space and running time in GPSS models. As a result, they developed an interactive version of GPSS, called

GPSS/360-Norden (Walde *et al.,* 1968). It first used an IBM 2250, but later a Tektronix 4012 graphic display terminal. The terminal was used to create input and interrogate output, and also to interrupt the program, and either modify or abort long simulation runs.

Because the models involved large amounts of input data, the program was also modified so that, not only could matrices of data be entered from the graphic terminal, but the data could be stored on a disk file and made dynamically available to a model, or be passed from model to model.

The relative ease of learning GPSS made it attractive for teaching simulation, in particular, to people without a technical background. Professor T. J. Schriber of the Graduate School of Business, University of Michigan, was among the first to develop a course, used both within graduate courses and for a summer school, that has been taught for many years (Schriber, 1974).

Among his co-workers, Mr. J. Henriksen became particularly interested in simulation languages to the point where he has developed a version of the GPSS/360 language that runs several times faster than the original IBM version (Henriksen, 1975). He has also produced a version which has interactive capabilities (Henriksen, 1977). An interactive version of GPSS, based APL, has also been produced (IBM Corp., 1976a,b). The design and programming of this version was done by Mr. M. Wolin of IBM.

2. Rationale and Content of the Language

2.1. Block Diagram

The GPSS user has to describe the system being simulated as a block diagram, using specific block types. The first program had 25 block types. Later versions increased the number until the GPSS V version had 49. Each block type can be used any number of times, subject to an upper limit on the total number of blocks that can be used.

Moving through the system being simulated are temporary entities, such as messages, data records, and people. These entities are represented in GPSS by transactions that, conceptually, move through the block diagram. Transactions are created by a block type called GENERATE, and they are removed by TERMINATE blocks. System action times are represented by having a transaction stay in an ADVANCE block. Other block types are concerned with allowing a transaction to take over or relinquish control of a facility or space in a storage.

If a transaction is unable to move; for example, by not being able to take control of a facility, or not finding sufficient space in a storage, it is said to be blocked. The program automatically recognizes when the blocking condition has been removed and continues the progress of the transaction at that time.

Alternatively, when a potential blocking condition occurs, another course of action can be taken, by using a TRANSFER block, which has several ways of selecting between different paths for the transaction.

2.2. Block Types

The blocks described so far give the basic traffic-handling capability that was present in the Sequence Diagram Simulator. Other block types introduce concepts that expand the ability to describe systems. Finding these block types was essentially a matter of trial and error. Analyzing aspects of a system design would suggest extensions, and the environment in which the development was being conducted gave ample opportunity to test the results.

In retrospect, there were two surprising results: the relatively small number of block types that were needed, and the range of system types that could be described. As was pointed out in the conclusions of the paper that described the first GPSS program (Gordon, 1961b), "Experience has shown that the rather limited language . . . has not been a significant restriction on the users; instead, it has tended to clarify the description of system concepts."

In quieter moments, there was speculation on whether there is a finite set of block types fundamental to the description of all discrete systems, or, more realistically, to systems with given, nontrivial properties. No serious attempt was made to find such a set, or even to restrict the number of block types for the sake of parsimony, but it was interesting to review the reports of modeling problems that came from the harried users, and see how often they could be resolved with the then existing set of block types.

With regard to the range of system types that could be covered, the development work had not been started with the express purpose of defining a general purpose language. However, from the beginning GPSS was being used for many types of system, ranging from precisely engineered systems to less-well-defined systems like office procedures and production processes. The only point at which a greater generality was consciously sacrificed, because it was not needed for the type of systems being developed in ASDD, was in the elementary way of specifying mathematical functions and calculations.

Other simulation languages that were to be developed gave more freedom of expression. Yet, a survey of six discrete simulation languages, including GPSS, prepared in connection with a workshop on simulation languages (Teichroew and Lubin, 1966), concluded that "there is as yet no conclusive evidence that one simulation language is best for a variety of problems. In fact the evidence so far seems to indicate to the contrary: a number of problems have been programmed with approximately equal ease in several languages."

2.3. Parameters

Temporary entities, represented by transactions, need to have attributes; for example, transactions representing work-pieces may need to carry a machining time, or transactions representing job lots may need to carry the number of items in the lot. For these purposes, transactions carry data words, called parameters. Initially, there could only be one parameter to a transaction, in the form of a 35-bit integer; the second version of the program expanded the number to eight; GPSS/360 allowed 100, with the option of being either fullword or halfword size; and GPSS V added floating-point and byte size parameters, with up to 256 of each type.

2.4. System Numerical Attributes

The decisions in a system depend upon more than the availability of resources, represented by facilities and storages. The user is, therefore, given access to a number of system variables that reflect the current state of the system. As a group, they are called System Numerical Attributes, or SNAs. Typical examples are the current content of a storage, the length of a queue, or the current clock time. They are denoted by standard symbols. Their values are calculated at the time they are requested, and they are made available globally, except that parameter values are included in the set of SNAs, and they are only available locally; that is, a reference to a parameter value is for the value associated with the transaction invoking the reference.

Mathematical combinations of SNAs are allowed, using the operations of addition, subtraction, multiplication, division, and modulo division. The result of the calculation is called a variable, and variables are included in the set of SNAs. Variables can also be defined using logical operators.

2.5. Statistics Gathering

Certain statistics on the use of facilities and storages are collected automatically. In addition, some block types are included for the express purpose of gathering statistics, rather than representing system actions. Some gather statistics about queues that build up in the system. Others sample and tabulate values of any SNA. In particular, the time taken for transactions to move from one part of the system to another can be tabulated.

In all cases, the statistics gathering is automatic: the user indicates what statistics are to be collected, and does not have to provide the computational algorithms. This not only saves the user from programming, but also avoids pitfalls in defining the calculations, which have several subtle points in the correct handling of end conditions and accuracy.

The statistics that are gathered, both automatically and by user request, are printed at the end of a run in a fixed format. Again, the user is not required to do any programming, or provide specifications.

Beginning with GPSS/360, it was possible to replace or supplement the standard output report with an edited version. Unwanted parts of the standard output can be omitted, and data that have been saved can be printed, along with explanatory text. It is also possible to print tabulated data graphically.

2.6. Testing System Conditions

Transaction flow can depend upon more than just the ability to take control of a facility or enter a storage. Logic switches were introduced as two-state devices to represent any condition the user cares to define. One block type controls the setting of a logic switch, and another, the GATE block, can test the status of a switch. The GATE block can also test the status of any facility or storage, wherever it might be in the block diagram, thereby giving a ''look-ahead'' capability. A GATE block not finding the specified condition can either hold up the transaction until the condition does exist, or it can divert the transaction to some other course of action. Groups of GATE blocks can be tested to check for simultaneous conditions.

A TEST block behaves like a GATE block, but it makes a comparison between any two SNAs. Since the SNAs include variables, which are combinations of simple SNAs, an extensive range of conditions can be checked by a TEST block.

2.7. Indirect Addressing

At first, a parameter could only be used as an input to a function, or to provide the amount by which a storage content or a table interval is incremented. It was quickly realized that the greatest use of a parameter was for providing an indirect addressing capability. By allowing the parameter to supply some value, such as an entity number, one block could process several types of transactions. For example, in the simulation of a computer, the logic for processing different message types could be the same, but it might involve channels or terminals that depend upon the particular type. Blocks were arranged to accept parameter values as the argument for most fields.

Some other SNAs were found to be useful for indirect addressing. It was finally arranged that all SNAs could be used to supply the argument of almost any block field, giving an extensive indirect addressing capability, although the intelligent use of many of the SNAs in most of the fields stretched the imagination.

2.8. Interruption

A storage of one unit capacity appears to be logically equivalent to a facility. A conceptual difference, however, is that, while only the transaction that has taken over a facility can release it, there is no necessary connection between the transactions occupying space in a storage and those giving it up. Some examples where this property of a storage might be useful were conceived, but their significance was probably overrated.

However, there was a practical reason for maintaining the distinction between a facility and a storage of unit capacity. To ensure that only the transaction that seized a facility can release it, a record has to be kept of which transaction has control of the facility. This is a tolerable amount of recordkeeping but, in the case of a storage, which can have a very large capacity, it is impractical to keep records of all individual transactions using space in a storage.

An advantage of having a record of the ownership of a facility is that it is then possible to simulate the interruption of the facility. The GPSS program includes the concept of priority, by which a transaction of higher priority can precede a lower priority transaction when attempting to enter a block. Priority, by itself, does not allow one transaction to interrupt another. One block type, however, allows a transaction of one priority to interrupt a lower priority transaction in its use of a facility. The interrupted transaction can be given back the use of the facility at the end of the interruption, or it can be removed from contention altogether. Similar options can be exercised for the transactions that happen to be waiting for the facility at the time of interruption.

2.9. Transaction Sets

As has been briefly mentioned, list structuring was incorporated in the program from the second version, but, at that time, the user was unaware of the structure. GPSS III, however, exploited the structure by allowing the user to construct chains. One block type places transactions on a chain, and another block type allows other transactions to remove them. The ordering on the chain can be according to the value of a parameter, thereby allowing more complex queuing disciplines than the simple FIFO discipline inherent in the basic GPSS simulation algorithm. The unlinking can depend upon SNAs both for controlling the condition for a transaction to be removed and the number of transactions removed. Again, since variables are SNAs, some very complex relationships can be used in making decisions.

The concept of groups, introduced with GPSS/360, forms sets of transactions that are free to move independently through the block diagram: even to leave the system. Transactions can be entered in the group, examined for particular values of their parameters or priority, removed according to those values, or have parameter values changed.

2.10. Synchronization

An important requirement is to be able to represent coincident events. In GPSS terms, this means being able to synchronize the movement of transactions in the block diagram. One block type creates copies of an original transaction. The program is able to keep track of the copies (by linking them in a circular chain.) A MATCH block type, working in pairs, can arrange that two copies must have arrived, one at each of the blocks, before they can both proceed further. Two other block types can collect a given number of copies at the block before; in one case, letting them all proceed; or, in the other case, destroying all but one and letting that one proceed. These block types, therefore, give the ability to marshal or assemble transactions.

3. Program Organization

3.1. Clock Time

The technique of simulating discrete systems consists of following the changes of system state over a period of time. Consequently, the program must contain a number representing current clock time. A change of state is called an event, and, as far as the model is concerned, the change occurs instantaneously. Between changes, the system remains quiescent. In most discrete systems for which simulation would be considered, the intervals between state changes are randomly distributed.

One method of organizing clock changes is to advance the clock to the next (potential) event time. The clock then moves in uneven steps over quiescent periods. An alternative is to advance the clock in small, discrete (and usually uniform) steps, checking whether an event is due to occur at the new time. The method of advancing to the next most imminent event time was chosen for GPSS, and there seems little doubt that this is the best choice for a general purpose discrete simulation program because uniform steps will, much more often than not, find no change to be made.

A less obvious choice is the nature of the time unit. It was decided to express time in integral units so that the clock time is a fixed-point number. The usual virtues in using floating-point numbers; allowing a large dynamic range, and permitting fine graduations, seemed to have little value for the type of simulation being considered. Another factor in the choice of an integral clock was the fear that round-off errors associated with floating-point calculations might result in two events that should be simultaneous occurring at slightly different times, or that some minor change in the manner of specifying the calculation might cause a change of order in two events. As will be discussed in Section 3.5, there was a great deal of concern with ensuring that simulation runs were strictly repeatable.

The use of an integral clock was to have an unexpected advantage. One of the difficulties encountered by newcomers to simulation is understanding the degree of abstraction to use when creating a model. The choice of a time scale, is one of the factors involved: too fine a scale relative to the major event time spans, will result in excessive computing. A user who chooses to define a time unit of, say, milliseconds and then tries to include activities operating on a time scale of, say, minutes is made acutely aware of the extreme range of event times when translating all times to a common unit. Floating-point calculations will absorb and mask the wide range.

However, the choice of an integral time scale was to cause some embarrassment. Comparing GPSS output results for simple queuing systems with known mathematical results often shows significant differences. The discrepancies arise because truncating times to integral values distorts results by restricting the number of possible output values (Scher, 1977). The distortions produced by an integral clock are not significant in a system simulation, when the time unit has been properly established, but the anomalous results obtained comparing results to theory are disturbing.

3.2. System Data

Data are introduced into the program in the form of functions or savevalues. Functions describe a relationship between two variables. Savevalues are words of numeric data, organized individually or in two-dimensional matrices. User-defined calculations of the data are carried out by the use of variable statements. Dynamic system data, computed automatically, are available as SNAs. Initially all data values were integral, but later, floating-point values were allowed. (However, floating-point operations were always used in the evaluation of functions.) No alphabetic data are accepted, other than symbolic names of entities which appear in output reports.

It is also possible to introduce transactions that have already been created, with preset data, and placed in external storage. These could have been written by a separate program, or, more commonly, they are created in a previous GPSS run. Whichever way they are created, the transactions are read into the block diagram at a simulated time that is specified at the time of creation.

It was decided not to compute functions from their mathematical form. Two considerations were involved. It was expected that the users would be system designers working with experimentally derived data, or plain estimates of functions, so that there was no need for high accuracy. Second, the major use for functions was thought to be for generating random numbers with nonuniform distributions. The probability integral transform method was seen as being the best method of generation. This involves evaluating the inverse of the (cumulative) distribution. Since only the (negative) exponential distribution, and certain very elementary functional forms, give closed mathematical formulae for this operation, some form of approximation would be needed anyway.

Consequently, functions are represented as tables of numbers connecting inputs to outputs, with the option of representing continuous functions by linear interpolation between the defined points, or leaving the function in discrete form, when the value of the output remains constant between the defined points.

3.3. Data Structure

The distinction between transactions as temporary entities which move through the system, and facilities and storages as permanent entities is important when selecting data structures. The permanent entities can be described in tables of fixed size and formats, as is done in GPSS. For earlier versions of the program, table sizes were fixed or they could be set to values elected by the user at initial program load. The GPSS V version allows the user to reallocate the sizes on each individual execution. Some modeling entities, such as the functions, tables, and variables, can vary in the amount of data to be recorded. A fixed-size table is then used to hold basic information, and extra space is taken from a common pool. Prior to GPSS V, transaction records were fixed in size (for a given run). In GPSS V, changes due to selecting the number of parameters also result in linking extra space from a common pool.

The main concerns with organizing transaction data, however, are the facts that the number of active transactions fluctuates, and transactions are created and destroyed in an unpredictable order. List-processing techniques proved to be an excellent method of organizing these records, as will be described in Section 3.5.

3.4. Interpretive Mode

Although the prime purpose of defining a block diagram type of input was to clarify system concepts, it was apparent that a block type could be represented by a subroutine with each specific instance of a block type that occurred in a particular model supplying input data. Interpretive execution was chosen as a simple means of implementation which also has the advantage of allowing simple execution error reports.

A compiler is generally considered to provide faster execution. However, early problems solved with GPSS were not very large. The actual running time compared with the time and effort spent in constructing a model seemed unimportant. It was thought that most applications of the program would be similarly balanced; that is, a relatively large expenditure of time and effort constructing the model, and a relatively small amount spent on the actual running of the model. The large models that were later to be programmed in GPSS, and that were to be used for extended periods of time were not foreseen. As a result, a major dissatisfaction with GPSS has been its slow running speed.

3.5. Simulation Algorithm

The simulation algorithm is concerned with maintaining the records of events and executing them in the correct sequence. The main elements of the algorithm used in GPSS will be described in this section. A complete description is given elsewhere, (Gordon, 1975). The topics not covered here are the handling of transactions that are interrupted, waiting for a matching condition, or are placed on a user chain. Each of these conditions results in a transaction being temporarily removed from the sets of transactions discussed here, and handled separately in a manner that does not affect the main algorithm.

The program proceeds by moving transactions from block to block in the correct chronological order and with regard to their relative priorities. A transaction may move into a block that requires no action time, either because it has been defined as zero, or it may be calculated to be zero. In that case, the transaction is allowed to continue immediately. Once a transaction begins to move, it moves until it enters a block with a nonzero time, leaves the system, or becomes involved in one of the special conditions, described above, that are not being discussed here.

Transactions due to move at some known time ahead of the clock represent future events. Those that are blocked, waiting for some change of system state, are called, in GPSS, current events. (The name "ready events" would have been better.) The records of future and current events are kept separate. It is not necessarily true that dividing the transactions into these two sets is more efficient, and no tests were made on the subject. It was assumed that most simulations would have a significant number of blocked events and it would be more efficient to segregate the records of the blocked events.

When all events that can be executed at the current clock time are completed the time of the next most imminent future event is used to update the clock. The conditions for moving the transaction involved in that event, and any future event transactions due to move at the same time must be tested. However, to move them without reference to the delayed transactions could violate the priority rules, because the movement of a future event transaction, which has its own priority, can cause the unblocking of a current event transaction of higher priority. The records of the future events that have become due are, therefore, merged with the current event records before attempting to move any transactions. By itself, this does not solve the problem of resolving priorities properly, but it places the entire problem in the context of how to process the current events.

To simply scan the current events sequentially from beginning to end runs the risk of having one transaction move and, in so doing, unblock a transaction that is of higher priority, or is of the same priority but appears earlier in the current events list. The transaction becoming unblocked will then have been passed in the scan. To continue the scan might allow a lower priority transaction that is waiting for the same change of condition to proceed ahead of the higher priority transaction. Even if there is no other lower priority transaction waiting for the same change, the program might be unaware of the unblocking until the next scan, and so cause the movement of an unblocked transaction to occur later than it should.

It might be argued that, in the actual system, the probability of exact simultaneity is zero, when time is considered infinitely divisible, in which case, the order of simultaneous events, at least of the same priority, is not very important. However, the Gordon Simulator had not used the algorithm described here, and a number of anomalies arose. As a result, a great deal of attention was paid to this matter of handling ''simultaneous'' events for two reasons. It is important to be able to trace the exact sequence of events when trying to debug a model. It is also to be expected that a repetition of a run will produce exactly the same results. Of course, using a different sequence of random numbers is not a true repetition, and will produce a different result within statistical limits.

It may be philosophically unimportant how simultaneous events of the same priority are handled, but in practice, it has a very disturbing effect on users who have not thought about this problem to find that they do not get an exact repetition when they expect one. While it might be thought unusual for the circumstances to arise or be noticed, it happens that people learning simulation tend to practice with simple models that deliberately, or through their simplicity, do in fact produce these circumstances. Their faith in the accuracy of a program is considerably shaken by apparent anomalies.

The solution that was developed for GPSS depends upon the highly structured nature of GPSS. The blocking of a transaction depends upon the status of the facilities, storages, and logic switches associated with the model. As a result, it is usually possible to associate the blocked transaction with the condition for which it is waiting. A flag in the transaction record can then be set to stop the program from attempting to move the transaction until the flag is reset. Correspondingly, when the state of a GPSS entity changes, it is possible to turn off the flags of the transaction waiting for the new state.

The scanning of the current events in GPSS is restarted whenever it has been determined that a movement of a transaction has changed the state of a GPSS entity, and, in so doing, has reset the flag of a blocked transaction. The scan is not usually restarted until processing of the transaction that caused the change has been completed. (The BUFFER option allows the user to force an immediate rescan.)

Both the future and current event records are organized as chains. A transaction record can be on one chain or the other. Future events are organized chronologically, and in priority order for coincident events. Current events are organized by priority. On both chains, coincident transactions of the same priority are kept in order of arrival. Secondary chains, called delay chains, are formed for each possible blocking condition of each facility, storage or logic switch that exists in the model. The delayed transactions remain on the current events chain, but they are also chained to the appropriate delay chain. When any GPSS entity changes state the program uses the delay chains to locate transactions that become unblocked.

There are times when more than one entity change can release a blocked transaction. For example, the TRANSFER block, choosing conditionally between two paths, can be blocked on both paths. Whichever path become available first should be taken. It is feasible to put the blocked transaction on two delay chains. However, the TEST block can be more complicated. It also has two exits, but the conditions to be met at either exit could involve variable statements that may involve many GPSS entities. To check the effect of all possible changes automatically would require a virtually unlimited ability to place a single blocked transaction on many delay chains simultaneously. This is technically feasible, but it was decided not to complicate the program beyond the level of allowing a transaction to be on more than one delay chain at a time. In the more complex conditions, the blocked transaction is not put on any delay chain. Instead, it is left on the current events chain with its flag unset so that the status of the transaction is retested on each scan, at a cost of extra execution time.

The algorithm that has been described ensures that when any blocked transaction is released by a system change, the program automatically recommences its progress through the block diagram. Although the algorithm has been described in list-processing terms, the first GPSS program, which did not use that programming technique, nevertheless implemented the same algorithm.

3.6. Random Numbers

In all IBM versions of GPSS a multiplicative congruence method of generating random numbers has been used. The early programs used a single random number stream, although the seed could be reset to get a different sequence. The 360 version introduced a generator that produces eight random number streams. The method is described in (IBM Corp., 1970a) and (Gordon, 1975). Tests of this generator, which has been given a generally satisfactory rating, have been published (Felder, 1968). Some of the results of those tests have also been reproduced elsewhere (Reitman, 1971).

3.7. Associated Coding

The first GPSS program had not allowed a user to associate non-GPSS coding with the program. GPSS II, however, introduced a HELP block which allowed a user to transfer to a program that had been written in assembly language and assembled. To make effective use of the HELP block, the user had to understand the internal structure of GPSS and know the names of specific locations.

The HELP block had existed in the first version but its existence was not made public. I had put it there to help in debugging the GPSS code. The debugging of a simulation language program is not easy because errors can occur at several levels. There can be a bug in the basic code, a logical fault in the simulation algorithm, an error in the simulation input, or some erratic behavior in the model. In the early 1960s, as well, it was never wise to rule out the possibility of a machine error. A designer needed help and that was precisely what the HELP block was for: it was used as a probe to dump selected data dynamically when all other debugging efforts failed.

I was reluctantly persuaded to include the HELP block in the GPSS II release. It was argued that the HELP block would allow a user to recode parts of a large model that had become cumbersome or slow. My reluctance was really an aversion to writing the documentation that was needed to use the block properly. I argued that a project using large models would have the talent to understand the structure of GPSS from the published flowcharts, with some guidance. The block was included but with poor documentation: a mistake that was to cost me many hours on the telephone.

Later versions of GPSS gave better documentation as well as expanding the block function by allowing the HELP block coding to be done in FORTRAN or PL/I. The block, however, still caused trouble because many newcomers to GPSS would not at first see the full powers of GPSS and regarded the HELP block as their salvation.

4. A Posteriori Evaluation

4.1. User Considerations

My early experience in using the program convinced me that, if it were properly organized and documented, engineers and analysts would be able to use the program themselves, even if they were not trained in programming. As far as possible, using the program was to be like using a special purpose machine, avoiding programming terminology and practices. This potential elimination of an intermediary in the form of a programmer who has to interpret the system designer's ideas was considered a highly desirable characteristic.

Nowadays, this attitude may seem unnecessarily cautious. However, at the time the program was being developed, programming tended to be avoided, or approached very reluctantly by engineers and analysts. That attitude became less prevalent. Moreover, as the field of simulation expanded, more people with programming backgrounds became involved. As a result, to many users, particularly those on large projects, the language was to become somewhat restrictive. The emphasis placed on simplicity of use, however, was a major factor in the rapid acceptance of the program.

4.2. Documentation

In keeping with the desire to avoid the appearance of programming, the program documentation at first excluded any mention of the way the program worked internally. The purpose was to avoid giving the user any suggestion that it was necessary to understand programming in the sense of following either computer coding or program logic charts.

This undoubtedly was too severe. As the use of the program expanded to more complex models, particularly computer control program models, it became important to understand, in some detail, exactly how the simulation algorithm worked. This detail was added to the documentation by Mr. Merikallio.

4.3. Block Structure

The block diagram language enhanced the illusion that the user was not programming, but describing a system. It also proved to be a great asset in teaching the program, and encouraged what would now be described as top-down programming, by permitting the system description to be steadily expanded from a general to a more specific block diagram.

Block diagrams were also an asset in improving understanding between the various people who needed to know about the system. Even people who do not have experience in GPSS programming but do know what the system does, or should do, are usually able to follow how the system has been represented, when shown the block diagram with a commentary by the person who constructed it. Misunderstandings about the precise logic of a system design are undoubtedly reduced. In fact, in the ASDD environment in which the program first developed, there were times when a block diagram describing the logic of a system design was being used as a document of transmittal between groups engaged in the development of the system.

4.4. Error Checking

As another aid to the user, the program has many built-in error stops. In view of the highly structured nature of the modeling principles used, it is possible to foresee most execution errors, such as attempting to release equipment that is not in use, and describe them directly in terms of the model rather that in terms of the program execution fault that is caused. The error dump that is given, also describes the status of the system in terms of the model, rather than just being a write-out of memory contents.

It was, perhaps, over-optimistically thought that all execution errors could be foreseen and that, assuming no machine errors, users would never need to consult a memory dump. Initially there were 43 error stops. The list grew until the GPSS V version of the language was to have over 700 error stops, many associated with entities and concepts not in the earlier programs. It cannot be claimed that all possible errors were eventually covered by this finite set of error messages, but it soon became very unusual for the program to stop at any but these prediagnosed errors. This was another factor in the gaining confidence in the use of the program.

4.5. Process Interaction

An important aspect of GPSS that helps to simplify its use is the fact that the simulation algorithm automatically restarts the progress of a blocked transaction when the blocking condition has been removed. If a user commits a transaction to a set of connected events scheduled over a period of time and represented by a string of blocks (i.e., what can be called a process) the individual events are eventually carried out without the user having to check continually the conditions for further advancing.

In discussions of simulation programming techniques, this approach has come to be called process interaction (cf. Kiviat, 1969; Fishman, 1973; Franta, 1977; Gordon, 1978). Without this technique, there is a potential for introducing errors by overlooking the consequences of a system change in releasing blocked events, particularly since the unblocking can be the result of an interacting series of unforeseen circumstances.

On the other hand, a function missing in the GPSS simulation algorithm is the ability to cancel a committed event. This was really an oversight, since the mechanism for performing the function exists. When the function is needed, a transaction can be made to take control of a facility, so that, if an event associated with the transaction is to be cancelled, the facility can be preempted and the transaction displaced.

4.6. Simultaneous Events

The somewhat lengthy, and no doubt tedious, description of the simulation algorithm given in Section 3.5, may reflect an excessively pedantic concern with the problem of resolving simultaneous events correctly. In most system simulations, it is sufficient that the order of executing events that occur "simultaneously" be the matter of chance that the description implies (but not the order of releasing delayed events.) Adopting this compromise would give a simpler algorithm that reduces the number of scan restarts.

The original concern with how users might react to minor anomalies is probably no longer necessary. Nevertheless, it seems imprudent that there should be an "uncertainty principle" in connection with the execution of a simulation. There is currently a good deal of research on the topic of simulation algorithms which will, presumably, lead to more satisfactory solutions (Vaucher and Duval, 1975; Wyman, 1975).

4.7. Storage Requirements

A frequent criticism of GPSS has been the relatively large amount of memory space needed for running the program. There are two aspects to the problem. The need to build a model from a fixed set of block types sometimes leads to a more clumsy representation of a system than could be given with a less restrictive language. This, however, is not a major cause of excessive space. The more important factor is the interpretive mode of operation. Each block or entity is represented, not by in-line code, but with a few entries of coded data in tables that are submitted to a single copy of the block type routine. In earlier GPSS programs these tables were fixed in size, which resulted in space being assigned but unused. The GPSS V program, however, allows the user to reallocate the sizes to save space overall. The ability in GPSS V to select byte and halfword size parameters and save-values, and also to pick the number of parameters, helps to save space.

Another factor contributing to excessive space is the fact that subroutines that are not wanted in a particular run are nevertheless loaded (e.g., for block types not used in that run.) The major phases of the program, loading, assembly, execution, and report writing are implemented by modules of coding that overlay each other. In addition, a user of the HELP block has the option of choosing whether the block routine shall be resident or not. More selection could, perhaps, be offered by omitting block subroutines that are not needed, or giving an option of making them dynamically available from external storage.

Geoffrey Gordon

Better use of programming methodology could, undoubtedly, provide more available space to satisfy the large GPSS model user. However, there seems to be a "Parkinson's" law of simulation saying that models will eventually expand to fill all available space.

4.8. Timing

By far the biggest criticism of GPSS is its slow execution time, relative to other simulation languages. As the number of simulation languages increased, comparisons of execution times were made and GPSS usually finished last.

In the defense of GPSS it had been argued that comparisons based on execution times are unfair, since there are advantages for GPSS that are not reflected in such comparisons. The ease of using GPSS helps make the total time spent developing a model and getting results less than for some other languages.

The over-cautious simulation algorithm is one cause of slow execution. The main fault lies, however, with the interpretive mode of operation. A repetitive programming overhead is involved in each move of a transaction into a block. It is necessary to find which block type is being entered and prime the corresponding subroutine with the values for the particular instance about to be executed. However, the ability to interpret which block is causing an error is invaluable.

On the other hand, interpretive programming has been the most obvious and simplest means of implementing the block diagram approach used by GPSS. This approach to system descriptions has had advantages that have been discussed in earlier sections. It has provided a disciplined system description language, that has smoothed the way for many simulation users; made possible a very effective error-reporting system; and, perhaps most significant of all, allowed a simulation algorithm that relieves the user of many routine scheduling tasks.

Will the next GPSS be interpretive?—Probably not. Most likely it will have an interpretive appearance with a set of predefined block types, but with the ability to redefine the block types and intersperse some other established programming language. Almost surely, it will be executed by a compiler, leading to the irony of a compiler simulating an interpreter.

REFERENCES

Bannan, V. J. (1968) July 26. Technical note in *IEEE Trans. on System Sci. and Cybernetics.* SCC-4(4): 447.

Batchelor, R. E. (1968) July 10. Technical note in *IEEE Trans. on System Sci. and Cybernetics.* SCC-4(4): 446–447.

Bean, G. H., J. J. Davis, H. A. Mulkiewicz, and C. J. VanTassel (1963) June 28. Techn. Rep. 17-115. *An experiment to evaluate a generalized monitor (GMX) for real-time systems.* Yorktown Heights, New York: IBM Corp. ASDD.

Blum, A. M. (1964). A general purpose digital simulator and examples of its use and application: part III-digital simulation of urban traffic. *IBM Systems J.* 3(1): 41–50.

Boyd, D. F., H. S. Krasnow, and A. C. R. Petit (1964). A general purpose digital simulator and examples of its application: part IV—simulation of an integrated steel mill. *IBM Systems J.* 3(1): 51–56.

Dietmeyer, D. L., G. Gordon, J. P. Runyon, and B. A. Tague (1960). Conference paper CP 60-1090. An interpretive simulation program for estimating occupancy and delay in traffic-handling systems which are incompletely detailed. *IEEE Pacific general meeting,* San Diego, California.

Digital Equipment Corp. (date unknown). *GPSS-10 for the PDP-10 data processing system.*

Efron, R., and G. Gordon (1964). A general purpose digital simulator and examples of its application: part I— description of the simulator. *IBM Systems J.* 3(1): 21–34.

Felder, H. (1968). The GPSS/360 random number generator. In *Digest of second conference on the application of simulation*. New York: Assoc. for Computing Machinery.

Fishman, George (1973). *Concepts and methods in discrete event digital simulation*. New York: Wiley.

Franta, W. R. (1977). *A process view of simulation*. New York: Am. Elsevier.

Goldman, David (1968) July 16. Technical note in *IEEE Trans. on System Sci. and Cybernetics*. SCC-**4**(4): 446.

Gorchow, Neil (1968) June 21. Technical note in *IEEE Trans. on System Sci. and Cybernetics*. SSC-**4**(4): 446.

Gordon, Geoffrey (1960) October 25. *A general purpose systems simulator* (unpublished manual). White Plains, New York: IBM Corp. ASDD Commercial Dept.

Gordon, Geoffrey (1961a) October 6. *Preliminary manual for GPS—A general purpose systems simulator*. Tech. Memo 17-048. White Plains, New York: IBM Corp. ASDD.

Gordon, Geoffrey (1961b). A general purpose systems simulation program. In *Proc. EJCC, Washington, D.C.,* pp. 87–104. New York: Macmillan.

Gordon, Geoffrey (1962a). A general purpose systems simulator. *IBM Systems J.* **1**(1): 18–32.

Gordon, Geoffrey (1962b) July 7. Tech. Memo 17-096. *Flow charts and programming description of the general purpose systems simulator (IBM 7090, 709, & 704 versions)*. Yorktown Heights, New York: IBM Corp. ASDD.

Gordon, Geoffrey (1975). *The application of GPSS V to discrete system simulation*. Englewood Cliffs, New Jersey: Prentice-Hall.

Gordon, Geoffrey (1978). *System simulation*, 2nd ed. Englewood Cliffs, New Jersey: Prentice-Hall.

Gould, R. L. (1969). GPSS/360-an improved general purpose simulator. *IBM Systems J.* **8**(1): 16–27.

Henriksen, James O. (1975). Building a better GPSS: a 3.1 performance enhancement. In *Proc. 1975 Winter Simulation Conf.,* pp. 465–469. Montvale, New Jersey: AFIPS Press.

Henriksen, James O. (1977). An interpretive debugging facility for GPSS. In *Proc. 1977 Winter Simulation Conf.,* p. 331–338. Elmont, New York: WSC/SIGSIM.

Herscovitch, H., and T. Schneider (1965). GPSS III—An extended general purpose simulator. *IBM Systems J.* **4**(3): 174–183.

IBM Corp. (1963). *General purpose systems simulator II*. White Plains, New York: IBM Corp. Form B20-6346.

IBM Corp. (1965a). *General purpose systems simulator III: User's manual*. White Plains, New York: IBM Corp. Form H20-0163.

IBM Corp. (1965b). Program No. 7090-CS-15X.

IBM Corp. (1965c). Program No. 7040-CS-14X.

IBM Corp. (1967a). *General purpose simulation system/360: User's manual*. White Plains, New York: IBM Corp. Form H20-0326.

IBM Corp. (1967b). Program No. 360A-CS-17X.

IBM Corp. (1967c). Program No. 360A-CS-19X.

IBM Corp. (1970a). *General purpose simulation system V: User's manual*. White Plains, New York: IBM Corp. Form SH20-0851.

IBM Corp. (1970b). GPSS V, Program Nos. 5734-XS2 (OS) and 5736-XS3 (DOS).

IBM Corp. (1970c). *Computer System Simulator: Program description and operations manual*. White Plains, New York: IBM Corp. Form SH20-0875.

IBM Corp. (1976a). *APL GPSS for APLSV* (Program No. 5796-PJF) and for *VS APL* (Program No. 5796-PJG).

IBM Corp. (1976b). *APL GPSS: Program description and operations manual*. White Plains, New York: IBM Corp. Form SH20-1942.

Kiviat, P. J. (1969). *Digital computer simulation: computer programming languages*. Tech. Memo RM-5883. Santa Monica, California: Rand Corp.

Markowitz, Harry M., Bernard Hausner, and Herbert W. Karr (1963). *SIMSCRIPT—A Simulation Programming Language*. Englewood Cliffs, New Jersey: Prentice-Hall.

Perry, M. N., and W. R. Plugge (1961) May. American Airlines' SABRE electronic reservation system. *Proc. AFIPS Conf. WJCC*, 19: 593–601.

Reitman, Julian (1971). *Computer simulation applications: discrete-event simulation for the synthesis and analysis of complex systems*. New York: Wiley.

Scher, Julian M. (1977). On the precision of probabilistic process generators in GPSS. *Proc. 1977 Winter Simulation Conf.,* pp. 341–347. Elmont, New York: WSC/SIGSIM.

Schriber, T. J. (1974). *Simulation using GPSS*. New York: Wiley. (Originally published in preliminary form by Ulrich's Bookstore, Ann Arbor, Michigan, 1972.)

Smith, E. C., Jr. (1962). Simulation in systems engineering. *IBM Systems J.* **1**(1): 33–50.

Geoffrey Gordon

Stanley, W. T., and H. F. Hertel (1968). Statistics gathering and simulation for the Apollo real-time operating system. *IBM Systems J.* **7**(2): 85–106.

Teichroew, Daniel, and J. F. Lubin (1966). Computer simulation—discussion of the technique and comparison of languages. *Commun. ACM.* **9**(10): 723–741.

Vaucher, J. G., and Pierre Duval (1975). A comparison of simulation event list algorithms. *Commun. ACM.* **18**(4): 223–230. See also corrigendum **18**(8): 462.

Velasco, C. R. (1964). A general purpose digital simulator and examples of its application: part II—simulation of a telephone intercept system. *IBM Systems J.* **3**(1): 35–40.

Walde, William A., David Eig, and Sherman R. Hunter (1968). GPSS/360-Norden, an improved system analysis tool. *IEEE Trans. on System Sci. and Cybernetics.* SSC-**4**(4): 442–445.

Wyman, F. Paul (1975). Improved event-scanning mechanism for discrete event simulation. *Commun. ACM.* **18**(6): 350–353.

TRANSCRIPT OF PRESENTATION

BARBARA LISKOV: The first language that we're going to talk about is GPSS, and our speaker is Geoffrey Gordon. GPSS was developed within the Advanced Systems Development Division of IBM. This was a division that was formed principally to investigate the design and application of information processing systems using telecommunications, both for the design of the systems themselves, and for understanding the impact of the systems on the organizations that were to use them.

Geoffrey Gordon had just joined this division when the work on GPSS started, and by the end of the GPSS development he was the manager of simulation development within that division.

Today Geoff is still at IBM. His title is Consultant Systems Engineer, working out of New York City, and he's concerned mostly with computer applications in the public utilities industry, particularly with applications in the Bell Telephone System.

GEOFFREY GORDON: Thank you, Barbara. If you're wondering what the difference is between an IBM Fellow and an IBM Consultant—IBM Fellows lecture in short sleeves and Consultants have to wear suits. [Laughter—John Backus, who is an IBM Fellow, previously lectured in a short-sleeved shirt.]

Well we are getting a little more specific in the use of languages, and simulation is a specific area for which there has been a lot of language development. GPSS is even more specific in being applied to discrete systems. These are systems which are characterized by state changes. There are complexities in analyzing them from a couple of causes; usually there are many elements in the system, and there's usually competition for limited resources in the system. In fact, the computer itself is a very good example of a discrete system, as it jumps from task to task and manages input–output operations.

Simulation is essentially a numerical computation technique. Given some numerical representation of a system, which shows the current state, the technique is to follow the state changes and extract information from the model, much as you would like to experiment on a real system. So, simulation is an excellent application of computers. In fact, for most large-scale discrete system simulations, it's essential to use a digital computer.

I appreciate that many, if not most, of you won't be too familiar with this area, or with GPSS in particular, so I'd like to start with a couple of minutes giving a very simple little example of a GPSS program.

The example I pick is the flow of traffic through a network of streets [Frame 1]. For

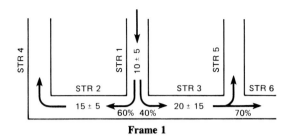

Frame 1

simplicity, let's leave them as one-way streets. Imagine traffic coming in at this street. When it gets to the bottom, some (of the traffic) turns left and some turns right. It moves along some other streets. If it goes this way (i.e., turns right), it has to turn up (at the end of the street). If the traffic goes this way (i.e., turns left), it has another choice of splitting at the corner here.

What the GPSS user has to do is to draw a block diagram to represent the system, using some very specific block types.

[Frame 2] is the block diagram representing the network of streets. I've deliberately drawn it to correspond physically to the same layout [as Frame 1.] That, of course, isn't necessary.

In this example there are four specific block types. Up here is a GENERATE block which creates transactions. These transactions each represent a vehicle. Here are AD-VANCE blocks representing streets, and associated with each block is some time, which is representative of the transit time. In this case, it's chosen from a uniform distribution.

These blocks are TRANSFER blocks which make the traffic choose between paths, and a figure here (within the block) decides how much (traffic) goes one way and how much goes the other way. This one is an unconditional TRANSFER. This block, and this block, and this block are TERMINATE blocks which simply destroy the transactions when you have no further interest in them.

Having drawn that block diagram, each block has to be transferred into a (GPSS) statement [Frame 3], and the upper half of this slide is the GPSS program corresponding to that

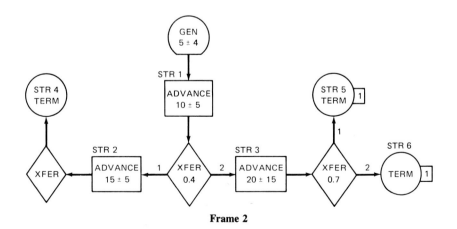

Frame 2

Geoffrey Gordon

```
        * TRAFFIC SYSTEM MODEL
        *
1               GENERATE   5,4              CREATE CARS
2       STR1    ADVANCE    10,5             MOVE DOWN STREET 1
3               TRANSFER   .4,STR2,STR3     40% TURN LEFT
4       STR2    ADVANCE    15,5             MOVE ALONG STREET 2
5               TRANSFER   ,STR4            GO TO STREET 4
        *
6       STR3    ADVANCE    20,15            MOVE ALONG STREET 3
7               TRANSFER   .7,STR7,STR6     70% GO INTO STREET 6
8       STR7    TERMINATE  1
9       STR6    TERMINATE  1
        *
10      STR4    TERMINATE
        *

                START      1000             RUN FOR 1000 TERMINATIONS
        RELATIVE CLOCK     12623      ABSOLUTE CLOCK   12623
        BLOCK COUNTS
        BLOCK CURRENT       TOTAL
            1       0        2514
            2       2        2514
            3       0        2512
            4       1        1512
            5       0        1511
            6       0        1000
            7       0        1000
            8       0         320
            9       0         680
           10       0        1511
```

Frame 3. GPSS coding and output example.

simple (traffic) model. Each block is (described by) one line. There's the name of the block here; here are some parameters controlling the times (for ADVANCE blocks) or percentages of turning either way (for TRANSFER blocks.) There are some symbolic names (listed) down here. Each statement can carry remarks and you can intersperse comments.

The bottom half here (of the slide) is the output for this particular model when it has run 1000 vehicles. In this simple example, all that comes out is the time—the simulated clock time—at which the simulation finished, and some block counts. These numbers (in the right column) are the numbers of times each of those blocks was entered, plus here (in the left column) the number of transactions sitting in the block at the time the simulation finished.

This report is produced automatically. That's one of the features of GPSS. You can, in fact, edit it (the report). That is, you can wipe out some information you don't want; put in comments; and it's possible to do some of (the report) in graphical form. But, by and large, the output of GPSS is an automatic report, so the user does not have to do any programming for that.

The system could have certain resources [Frame 4]. This block diagram, for example, illustrates the use of a facility, which is one (kind) of resource available to the system. The facility has the property that it can only be used by one transaction at a time. This model, for example, might represent a machine tool. Here's a GENERATE block which is creat-

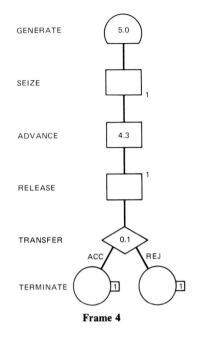

GENERATE

SEIZE

ADVANCE

RELEASE

TRANSFER

TERMINATE

Frame 4

ing transactions, in this case representing work-pieces. This SEIZE block allows a trans-action to take over the facility, and this block here—RELEASE—makes it give up the facility. In the meantime, here's an ADVANCE block which represents the length of time for which that transaction has control of that facility. There are other ways of representing types of resources.

Now, no invention stands entirely on its own, so I'd like to discuss some of the factors which I feel led up to the development of GPSS [Frame 5]. The topics I would like to cover are some work I did on analog computers; some work on switching systems generally; in particular, a simulator called the Sequence Diagram Simulator, work that I did while I was at Bell Labs; the so-called Gordon Simulator; and GPSS itself.

First of all, to talk about analog computing. Now, I'm aware that I may just be rational-izing after the fact here, but I began simulating with analog computers when I was working in England—working for the GEC company [the British General Electric Company] on missile systems. Analog simulation is an entirely different technique from digital simula-tion. However, anyone who has ever used an analog computer will be very much aware of how much they get you involved with the system you're working with. What you do on an

ANALOG COMPUTERS
SWITCHING SYSTEM SIMULATION
SEQUENCE DIAGRAM SIMULATOR
GORDON SIMULATOR
GPSS
Frame 5. Chronological developments.

analog computer is you draw a block diagram of the computer. You can build up sub-models representing components of the system, and, when you put these together, you wire them together very much as though you were building a system. It's like a one-to-one correspondence between the computer and the actual system. I feel myself that this block diagram approach was really what influenced me strongly—subconsciously—when it came to looking at discrete systems.

I actually began using digital computers for some simulation work of the same nature; namely, simulating missile systems in flight. I began using a computer in England called MOSAIC.

Just as an aside, I put a comment in the paper saying that this seemed to be a computer that fell through the cracks of computer history: the reason being, since I have worked on that machine, I've never found anybody who has even heard of it. So, I thought I'd test out Henry Tropp, our resident historian, by telling him I put this comment in and I said it ought to be a nice spot for a scholarly footnote. I'm glad to say that he knew all about MOSAIC, so I think this is a good omen for the quality of the history we're going to get from Henry. [See note on p. 436. Ed.]

I thought of this machine when Grace Hopper was talking about three address machines and octal programming. This particular machine had an 81-bit word, which is a 27-octal word, and it had four addresses. This was a case where, if you could actually *write* five instructions a day, you felt you had achieved something. [Laughter]

I came to the USA in 1955 to work with Westinghouse, and, for a while I continued the same sort of work, simulating missiles on digital computers, mostly on an [IBM] 650.

I was very interested in John Backus's story about that box of 1000 unlabeled cards arriving at Westinghouse in, I think he said, April of 1957, because my first contact with FORTRAN was a class given at the Westinghouse Research Center, which couldn't have been later than May, perhaps June, of 1957, about a month or two after that box of cards arrived. I think that's a remarkable reflection on the courage of people in those days.

That early work on digital computers really was of the nature of what we would now call "digital–analog" work. It didn't lead to any languages; and there wasn't any point in my trying to write a language because that had, in fact, already been done by Gordon Selfridge who had come out early in 1957 with a digital–analog simulator, written for a 650 machine.

I joined Bell Labs in 1957, and after working on the design of their own computer, which they dropped, I got to working on simulating switching systems. Again, I didn't really get into language development. Those were the days of punched cards, and what I found was that I quickly got to the point of making up models out of decks of subroutines and punched cards by just putting the cards together, or changing one or two, and I think that is what influenced me towards interpretive programming. I soon came to realize that when you had a well-debugged subroutine, it was worth hanging on to it.

I eventually got to work on a project with a man named John Runyon in the Switching Research Department, to work on a Sequence Diagram Simulator. They were working on advanced switching systems designs, and describing the switching systems by sequence diagrams. John Runyon started a project to try to come up with a method of simulating the systems directly from the sequence diagram description. That was a program that I got running late 1959 or early 1960, and we published a paper describing that Sequence Diagram Simulator in August of 1960.

By that time I had left (Bell Labs) and joined IBM, joining the Advanced Systems Development Division. It's a division that no longer exists. It was created largely to look into the design and application of what IBM called Teleprocessing systems, which is the amalgamation of telecommunications and data processing. Now, these are quite complex systems, and it was clear that simulation could be a major aid in designing these systems. However, at the time, simulating discrete systems, particularly when they were stochastic in nature, was quite difficult. It required quite a major, skilled programming effort.

I was in a department under Dr. [D. V.] Newton called Maths and Applications. Its function was generally to help the systems analysts design systems. At that time, they were mostly trying to apply queuing theory to look at such matters as polling disciplines and channel interference.

I suggested trying to work on a simulation language, based on the experience I'd had with the Sequence Diagram Simulator. I had the feeling that we could develop a language which would make it possible for the system analysts to build their own models with little or no help from skilled programmers. Now, you have to realize the atmosphere of those days. A lot of engineers and analysts still regarded programming as a black art. They really didn't want to touch it. So, if you could put into their hands a tool that they could use easily, they would use simulation. But, otherwise, their tendency would be to say ''That's a programmer's job; let him do it.''

I began working (on GPSS) very soon after I joined IBM, which was June of 1960. I mentioned to Doug Ross, who was talking about APT this morning, the way I got the work done. Doug mentioned he had one of his graduate students, Sam Matsa, join IBM, and he was writing a large piece of the complex of APT programs. Sam was on so tight a schedule that he rented the whole night shift of the Service Bureau's machine in New York City. So the way I used to work was to sit around while he was working, and I'd slip in when he wasn't using the machine; working through the nights. That's how I got the work done —but I didn't tell Doug, I never paid for that time!

I had a working program in the fall of 1960, and I began working very closely with the systems analysts in the Division. What I found was that a block diagram was not only an effective language for describing systems, but it was also a very effective means of communication. I could sit down with a systems analyst, and in a very short while come up with a block diagram of the main structure of a system. He, quite quickly, could understand the blocks well enough to progress, filling out the block diagram with more and more detail as he explained the internal parts of the system.

So there was a great deal of interaction. I had many people using the program while I was writing and debugging it, and I got a lot of feedback on what was good and what was bad, as well as a lot of suggestions from the users as to how the program might be improved.

The program got to be known quite well around IBM, and copies of the program in various stages of completion, with lots of bugs, popped up. So I sat down and decided to write a cleaned-up version. I put that out with a user's manual dated October 25, 1960. We never actually bothered to name the program, and, by default, it came to be known as the Gordon Simulator.

Now there were a number of anomalies using that program. For example, putting a block in, say, for measuring statistics which had nothing to do with the system's logic. Sometimes you'd find a minor change like that—or maybe reversing the order of two blocks, where the order wasn't relevant to the system's logic—could cause a totally different output.

When I looked into it, the cause was the fact that simultaneous events were being

GPSS	BARBIERI, EFRON, & GORDON		1961
GPSS II	EFRON & GORDON		1963
ZIP/ZAP	OLSEN	(INTERNAL)	1965
GPSS III	BULT & GOULD		1965
GPSS/360	BULT & GOULD		1967
GPSS V	BULT & GOULD		1970

Frame 6. IBM developments.

treated differently. They'd be done in a slightly different order. Now simultaneous events might be just coincidental events, but more often than not, it was a case of several transactions becoming unblocked simultaneously as a result of one system change. If the program were to take the unblocked transactions in one order, you'd get one result: taken in another order, you'd get another result. Now that isn't really surprising. Whichever way it went is an equally likely outcome of the system, but to users, it looked like an error. It really shakes their confidence to apparently repeat a run and find a totally different result. So, I began looking very carefully at how to work out the algorithm to avoid these sorts of anomalies, and, in early 1961, I designed a new algorithm, and started rewriting the program. The program actually got announced, or released—it had been a confidential program up to that point—early in 1961, and then, later that year, the new program I wrote was announced as what IBM called a type II program, what we now call a Program Product. That was on September 27, 1961.

There had been steady development all along, but I feel myself that it's that program, that was publicly released in 1961, which was really the first GPSS because of the algorithm it had.

Here, quickly, is the sequence of developments within IBM[Frame 6]. That program was released in September 1961—I worked on that with two other programmers, Bob Barbieri and Dick Efron. Efron and I went on then to produce a second version of that program which was released in 1963. At that point, responsibility for further development went to another part of IBM, and I was no longer responsible. A man named Bob Olson organized a program a good deal faster—hence it got the name ZIP/ZAP—but that wasn't a released program; it was used internally. Instead John Bult and Bob Gould came along. They produced a third version of the program that came out in 1965. When the (IBM System) 360 was announced, they went on to produce a 360 version, and later they were to produce the current version, which is GPSS V.

Other computer manufacturers have come out with GPSS programs [Frame 7]. There

BURROUGHS	(GPSS V)
CDC	GPSSV/3600
DEC	GPSS-10 (GPSS/360)
HONEYWELL	GPSS-6000 (GPSS V)
RCA	SPECTRA 70 FLOW (GPSS/360)
UNIVAC	GPSS II—VERSION E
J. O. HENRICKSEN	GPSS-H (GPSS V)
M. WOLIN	APL GPSS (GPSS V)

Frame 7. Other versions.

BLOCK DIAGRAM LANGUAGE

AUTOMATIC DETECTION OF UNBLOCKING

SIMULTANEOUS EVENT HANDLING

ERROR REPORTING

Frame 8. GPSS characteristics.

have been no standards for GPSS, and most of these programs are not completely consistent. Other manufacturers who have turned out versions are Burroughs, CDC, DEC, Honeywell, RCA, and Univac. A couple of individuals have also turned out programs. (J. O.) Henricksen had turned out a program called GPSS-H, which is based on GPSS V. In the paper I've wrongly attributed that program to 360. More recently, there is an APL version of GPSS (written by M. Wolin.)

We could discuss many aspects of GPSS, but I'd like to address these four topics (shown on Frame 8): the block diagram language—just say something about the way GPSS detects the unblocking of transactions—I want to say some more about the simultaneous event handling—and a quick word about error reporting.

One important aspect of GPSS which was unique at the time, and I think probably still is, is that it detects when a blocked transaction becomes unblocked [Frame 9], and automatically goes on to continue the motion. Having committed a transaction to a process, the user does not have to worry about it getting blocked halfway done; the GPSS system will take care of that.

The way this is done depends upon the rather highly structured nature of GPSS; the fact that the resources (of the simulated system) are represented specifically by facilities and storages. For each facility in the system, for example, there can be six states of that facility which could cause a transaction to be blocked. For example, a transaction might want

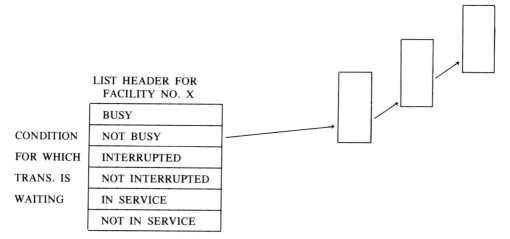

Frame 9. Detection of unblocking.

Geoffrey Gordon

CHAIN FUTURE EVENTS CHRONOLOGICALLY
CHAIN CURRENT (BLOCKED) EVENTS BY PRIORITY
FLAG BLOCKED EVENTS AS INACTIVE
MERGE NEW EVENTS WITH CURRENT EVENTS
SCAN CURRENT EVENTS LOOKING FOR ACTIVE EVENTS
MOVE THAT TRANSACTION AS FAR AS POSSIBLE
USE DELAY CHAINS TO MAKE UNBLOCKED EVENTS ACTIVE
RESTART SCAN IF ANY SUCH CHANGE OCCURS

Frame 10. Main scanning algorithm.

to get access to a facility, or it might want the facility to be busy. Whatever the condition, a chain is set up to link together all the transactions waiting for that particular facility to be in that particular condition. These are called delay chains. When that facility changes state, the system is able to use those delay chains to locate the particular transactions that were waiting for that state, so the system becomes aware of the fact that it has unblocked some transactions.

In addition to being on the delay chains, transactions are also on one of two other chains. One chain is a chain of all future events, which are events that will occur ahead of the current clock time. The other chain is known as the current events chain, which are events that are currently blocked—they are unable to move.

The essence of the simulation algorithm, which I will not describe in detail [Frame 10 shows a flowchart of the algorithm], is that as the clock advances transactions are moved from the future events chain as their time becomes due, and they're merged with the current events chain. The current events chain is then scanned, and whenever a transaction moves, if the movement of that transaction changes the status of a facility or storage, the delay chains let the system find out "Did a transaction become unblocked?"

If a transaction did become unblocked, the scan starts again. The point being that as you scan down a chain, the released transaction might be of a higher priority than the one you're just working on. So, if the scan continues, it will miss the higher priority transaction. By going back, it makes sure that the transactions are always handled in priority order, and in first-come, first served order. It gets rid of the anomalies I mentioned earlier on, at a cost of rather an excessive amount of scanning.

I finished the paper by mentioning a few areas in which I feel that there could be considerable improvement in GPSS. [Frame 11 was not shown.] That question of the slow time due to constant rescanning is certainly one of the areas in which a great deal more work can be done.

Thank you.

MORE LANGUAGE FLEXIBILITY
IMPROVED UNBLOCKING DETECTION
REEVALUATION OF SIMULTANEOUS EVENT HANDLING
MORE EFFICIENT SIMULATION ALGORITHM
COMPILER MODE EXECUTION
MORE EFFICIENT USE OF STORAGE

Frame 11. Needed improvements.

TRANSCRIPT OF QUESTION AND ANSWER SESSION

BARBARA LISKOV: First I have a question from Jim Mitchell. He says, "Would you characterize the differences between event-driven and time-driven simulation?"

GEOFFREY GORDON: Well, GPSS is event-driven. The difference is a question of what mechanism you use for advancing clock time. The two alternatives are to move the clock to the time of the next most imminent event, which is the procedure used in GPSS and in most discrete system simulations, or to move the clock forward a small—usually uniform—increment of time, and having moved it forward, then look around to see if there are any events due to occur at that time. Generally, the event-driven method will be more efficient in discrete simulation. It's not difficult, however, to dream up cases where the other method is more efficient. It's a system engineering type of decision. It depends upon the particular model and particular circumstances. By and large, event-driven is more efficient in discrete simulation.

LISKOV: Here's a question from Richard Miller: "How much of the System 360 did you know about at the time of the release of GPSS? Did the fact that 360 was coming have any effect on GPSS?"

GORDON: No. I knew very little about 360 at the time that the program was released, and it had very little effect on the design. One of the troubles with writing languages and getting them popular is that you tend to set them in concrete. Once they've been released, there's a lot of resistance to changing them. So when the 360 came out, the program had to run exactly like the previous program, maintaining consistency. All the programs, with the exception of the first, were always kept compatible. The new program was kept so that the old program's models would run on it.

LISKOV: Okay—I have one last question here that I'd like to ask, except that I can't read one word of it. It's from Dick Nance. He says . . .

GORDON: Let me try: "The early versions of GPSS 2 and 3 had a multiplicative random number generator as you state, but GPSS V utilizes a . . . "

LISKOV: What's the word? Dick Nance, would you like to tell us that word?

RICHARD NANCE: Table shuffling of the multiplier.

GORDON: I don't know who did that. I've been unable to find out who exactly suggested that idea. The question is related to the fact that the early programs had a relatively simple but effective multiplicative congruence number generator—a single one. GPSS V has eight (generators) in which the seeds are randomly swapped. It turns out that testing has been done on that generator, and they say it's quite good, but I have no evidence for showing that the swapping improves the efficiency.

LISKOV: Okay. Thank you very much.

[The author has provided answers for two further questions submitted at the session. Ed]

NANCE: You close your paper with the comment on a compiled implementation "simulating" an interpreter—the predominant implementation of GPSS to this point. Why not two distinct implementations—The interpreter to be used in model development, testing, and debugging, and the compilier to be used in analysis mode.

GORDON: That comment was only a speculation made in a final section discussing possible further developments. It recognized the fact that a major criticism of GPSS has been its slow execution time. Running in an interpretive mode is, of course, a major cause of the slow rate of execution. My comment was to the point that a compiler implementation would probably be essential to get a suitably fast program but, since I feel the interpretive mode plays an important part in simplifying the use of the language by assisting in debugging, I would like to see that property preserved. An implementation that could switch modes would be an excellent solution.

I have pointed out in the paper that the algorithm for scanning events can waste time because it will frequently cause a rescan when it is not needed. However, the algorithm greatly assists debugging by ensuring that runs can be made reproducible. When the debugging phase is over, the scanning algorithm could be reorganized. That alone may be enough of a mode change to speed up execution.

ALLEN BRADY: Considering the criteria for choosing representative languages, why was SIMSCRIPT excluded?

GORDON: I was, of course, not in any way involved in the selection of languages for presentation at this conference, as, I am sure, is true of any other authors of papers that have been presented. I do not feel, therefore, that I can answer that question. [This question is addressed in the Conference Chairman's introduction. Ed.]

[The MOSAIC reference mentioned on p. 430 is: A. W. M. Coombs, MOSAIC—The Ministry of Supply Automatic Computer. In *Automatic Digital Computers*, pp. 38–42. London: HMSO, 1954.]

FULL TEXT OF ALL QUESTIONS SUBMITTED

ALLEN BRADY

Considering the criteria for choosing representative languages, why was SIMSCRIPT excluded?

RICHARD MILLER

How much of the System 360 did you know about at the time of the release of GPSS? Did the fact that the 360 was coming have any effects on GPSS?

You mentioned that you had experience with simulation before getting into GPSS. Who else (if anyone) affected the kinds of things that GPSS could do (the statistical techniques)?

JIM MITCHELL

Would you characterize the differences between event-driven and time-driven simulation?

RICHARD NANCE

The early versions of GPSS (II and III) had a multiplicative random number generator as you state. But GPSS utilizes a shuffling of the multipliers. Who suggested this approach and for what reasons?

You close your paper with the comment on a compiled implementation "simulating" an interpreter, the predominant implementation of GPSS to this point. Why not two distinct implementations—the *interpreter* to be used in model development, testing, and debugging, and the *compiler* to be used in the analysis mode?

BIOGRAPHY OF GEOFFREY GORDON

When the GPSS language first appeared, Geoffrey Gordon was Manager of Simulation Development in the Advanced Systems Development Division of IBM, soon after joining the corporation from Bell Telephone Laboratories. The division had been formed principally to investigate the design and application of information processing systems using telecommunications. Simulation was an essential tool for studying these complex systems, both for the design of the systems themselves and for understanding the impact of the systems on the organizations that were to use them.

At that time, however, the application of simulation to such complex, discrete systems involved a considerable amount of skilled programming effort. The GPSS program made a profound difference by giving systems analysts a means of constructing and running simulation programs quickly and easily. It has been described in Jean Sammet's history of programming languages as "the first language that made simulation a practical tool. . . ."

GPSS has since gone on to become a very widely used discrete simulation language, and Geoffrey Gordon has gone on to become well known, not only as the originator of GPSS but also as the author of two widely used textbooks on the topic of System Simulation, as well as contributions to encyclopedia and handbooks on Computer Science and Operations Research.

Today, Geoffrey Gordon is still with IBM, as a Consulting Systems Engineer, working out of New York City. He is concerned mostly with computer applications in the public utilities industries, particularly with applications in the Bell Telephone System.

SIMULA Session

Chairman: Barbara Liskov
Speaker: Kristen Nygaard
Discussant: Ole-Johan Dahl

PAPER: THE DEVELOPMENT OF THE SIMULA LANGUAGES

Kristen Nygaard

Norwegian Computing Center and University of Oslo

Ole-Johan Dahl

University of Oslo

Preface

The organizers of this conference have told us that we should write at least 25 pages of manuscript, but that we may produce as many pages more as we wanted. Perhaps they did not envisage the possible consequences, but we have taken their words at face value.

This paper has implied a vast amount of work and archeological activities. We are grateful to SIGPLAN for defining a task to which resources had to be allocated by our institutions and which forced us to write down an account of our work from 1961 to 1971. While we are writing this preface, those years are very much alive to us. We realize that we lived through this period in a state of semimadness, a combination of very hard work, frustration, and euphoria.

The observations which have impressed us most are:

that the results of the SIMULA effort were completely dependent upon the joint beliefs, work, ideas and advice of a very large group of people, and

that at many stages the whole effort continued just because of lucky circumstances.

Have we told the truth about SIMULA's history? Yes, to our best knowledge, we have. But—have we told the whole truth? No, we have not.

SIMULA's history is intertwined with that of the Norwegian Computing Center. And

HISTORY OF PROGRAMMING LANGUAGES
Copyright © 1981 by the Association for Computing Machinery, Inc.
Permission for reproduction in any form must be obtained from Academic Press, Inc.
ISBN 0-12-745040-8

the emergence of NCC in the 1960s is an important part of the history of informatics in Norway. It is too early to tell that history, but our professional society is now starting at least to collect all the stories remembered. In this paper we are deliberately vague when we want to avoid accusations against persons and institutions, and yet indicate problematic situations.

In our time travel during the last few months, many of those involved have put their memories at our disposal. We want to express our gratitude. In the actual writing we have been assisted by Birger Møller Pedersen and Paul Wynn of the NCC, and the typing has been very competently done by Lise Tschudi assisted by Eileen Schreiner.

1. Background

The development of the SIMULA I and SIMULA 67 languages was carried out at the Norwegian Computing Center (NCC). The early background for the development is, however, our work at the Norwegian Defence Research Establishment (NDRE) in the 1950s.

KN started his conscript service at the NDRE in 1948 as assistant to Jan V. Garwick — the father of computer science in Norway. Their first main task was to carry out resonance absorption calculations related to the construction of Norway's first nuclear reactor. After extensive work had been invested in a traditional numerical approach, Monte Carlo simulation methods (by "hand") were successfully introduced instead in 1949–1950. KN headed the "computing office" until mid 1952, and then became a full time operational research worker.

OJD joined the NDRE in 1952, also as a soldier doing his conscript service. Garwick and his assistants had, since 1949, followed the development of electronic computers. A BULL punched-card calculator had, in 1951–1953, been extended at the NDRE into a card-programmed electromechanical computer. In 1954 it was decided that NDRE should acquire a Ferranti MERCURY computer, then at the design and construction stage, and in the following years the NDRE milieu developed basic software which was fairly advanced for its time.

In the late 1950s, the NDRE milieu started work in language design, in which Garwick and OJD were particularly active.

From 1956 on the operational research (OR) activities expanded rapidly. In the large scale OR jobs, simulation once more turned out to be the only feasible tool for analysis of sufficiently realistic models. Also, it became evident that no useful and consistent set of concepts existed in terms of which the structure and interaction in these complex systems could be understood and described. Since the task of writing simulation programs for the MERCURY computer became important, the lack of tools for this task was a serious obstacle.

In May 1960 KN left the NDRE to build up the NCC as a research institute in computer science, operational research and related fields. Many of the civilian tasks turned out to present the same kind of methodological problems: the necessity of using simulation, the need of concepts and a language for system description, lack of tools for generating simulation programs. This experience was the direct stimulus for the ideas which in 1961 initiated the SIMULA development.

NCC is a semigovernmental research institute, established in 1958, working within informatics, operational research, numerical analysis, and applied statistics. The task of the institute basically is to assist in disseminating new methods and tools in these fields to the user environment in Norway. In fulfilling this task, NCC is supposed to take on practical jobs and to develop new knowledge through pure and applied research.

NCC is supervised by the Royal Norwegian Council for Scientific and Industrial Research. The institute is funded by research contracts with customers and contributions from the Research Council. Today (1978) approximately 60% of NCC's income stems from customers, 40% from the Research Council. Of this 40%, 75% is grants to the institute's activities in general, and 25% (10% of the total) earmarked contributions to specified research projects. The staff amounts to 76, of which 55 are research workers. The customers of NCC come from private commerce and industry, public agencies, other research institutions, and (since 1971) trade unions. NCC has played an important part in the Norwegian and later Scandinavian development of workers' influence on planning, control and data processing systems.

2. SIMULA I

2.1. Early History

The ideas for a language which could serve the dual purpose of system description and simulation programming originated at the NCC in the spring of 1961. The first written reference to SIMULA is found in a letter dated January 5, 1962, from KN to the French operational research specialist Charles Salzmann (Nygaard, 1962a):

> The status of the Simulation Language (Monte Carlo Compiler) is that I have rather clear ideas on how to describe queueing systems, and have developed concepts which I feel allow a reasonably easy description of large classes of situations. I believe that these results have some interest even isolated from the compiler, since the presently used ways of describing such systems are not very satisfactory.
>
> I hope that later developments, for which I have a number of ideas, will include e.g. stochastic inventory situations amongst the situations which may be described by the language.
>
> The work on the compiler could not start before the language was fairly well developed, but this stage seems now to have been reached. The expert programmer who is interested in this part of the job will meet me tomorrow. He has been rather optimistic during our previous meetings.

The naïve optimism evidenced by this quotation was perhaps an asset. Had we at that time known the magnitude of the efforts ahead, we had at least had a more difficult task in getting the necessary resources for the project.

The "expert programmer" was of course OJD, who had been contacted by KN in December 1961 when the first set of apparently powerful ideas had appeared. Then it became evident that the "SIMULA project" could only be carried out successfully if it combined:

experience in operational research, particularly related to large, complex systems of many different kinds, with

experience and knowledge in computer programming language design and implementation.

OJD immediately got interested and participated in a long series of discussions with KN during the spring of 1962. In May we felt that we had a language proposal which we could present to other people. At that time OJD had become involved to such an extent that he decided to leave NDRE for NCC. He started his work at the NCC in March 1963, after having finished his current project at NDRE (implementing a homemade ALGOL-like programming language).

In May 1962 Univac launched a big campaign for their new computers, the famous UNIVAC 1107 and the (now forgotten) UNIVAC III. KN was invited to join the "Univac Executive Tour" to the US, and accepted with the intention of reversing the sales mission by selling SIMULA to Univac. To the surprise of all involved, both parties succeeded: The NCC got a UNIVAC 1107 in August 1963. Univac and NCC entered a software contract, and NCC had completed the SIMULA I compiler in January, 1965. The politics surrounding these events was complex, often tough, and gave some of those involved wounds which were difficult to heal.

There was no initial enthusiasm for SIMULA in NCC's environment, and we were told that:

1. There would be no use for such a language as SIMULA.
2. There would be use, but it had been done before.
3. Our ideas were not good enough, and we lacked in general the competence needed to embark upon such a project, which for these reasons never would be completed.
4. Work of this nature should be done in countries with large resources, and not in small and unimportant countries like Norway.

We had, however, the support of the board of NCC, and SIMULA was linked to the acquisition of NCC's UNIVAC 1107 computer.

2.2. The Main Development Stages

The SIMULA I language went through four main stages:

1. The summer of 1961–the autumn of 1962: The initial ideas based upon a mathematically formulated "discrete event network" concept and a programming language reasoning which had no specific implementation situation in mind. The main references are a working document (Nygaard, 1962b, in Norwegian) and the SIMULA presentation at the IFIP World Congress in Munich, August 1962 (Nygaard, 1963a).

2. The autumn of 1962–September 1963: Development of the early approach, increased flexibility introduced by the possibilities of ALGOL 60, at the same time restricted by the assumption of SIMULA being implemented by a preprocessor to ALGOL 60 combined with a "procedure package". The main references are Nygaard (1963d) and Dahl and Nygaard (1963), the latter being the language definition of the SIMULA I software agreement between Univac and NCC (Agreement, 1963).

3. September 1963–March 1964: Decision to implement SIMULA I through a modification and extension of Univac's ALGOL 60 compiler, based upon a new storage management scheme developed by OJD. The introduction in February 1964 of the "process" concept, utilizing the new possibilities available. The main reference is Dahl and Nygaard (1964a).

4. March 1964–December 1964: The implementation of the SIMULA I compiler. Minor language modifications and extensions based upon implementation experience and programming test cases. The main reference to the resulting SIMULA I language is Dahl and Nygaard (1965).

In this section we will describe the SIMULA I of stage 2 and its transition into the SIMULA I of stage 3. The reasoning which motivated this transition and thus the final SIMULA I language will be presented in Section 2.3.

Using the July 1963 paper (Nygaard, 1963d) as a platform, we find that the basic concepts of SIMULA at that time were:

1. A *system,* consisting of a finite and fixed number of *active* components named *stations,* and a finite, but possibly variable number of *passive* components named *customers.*

2. A station consisting of two parts: a *queue part* and a *service part.* Actions associated with the service part, named the station's *operating rule,* were described by a sequence of ALGOL (or ALGOL-like) statements.

3. A customer with no operating rule, but possibly a finite number of variables, named *characteristics.*

4. A real, continuous variable called *time* and a function *position,* defined for all customers and all values of time.

5. The possible sequence of positions for a given customer implied that a customer was generated by a service part of a station, transferred to the queue part of another (or the same) station, then to the service part of that station etc., until it disappeared by not being transferred to another queue part by the service part of some station.

Since this structure may be regarded as a *network,* and since the events (actions) of the stations' service parts were regarded as instantaneous and occurring at *discrete points of time,* this class of systems was named *discrete event networks.*

It should be noted that at this stage:

1. Each *individual* station had to be described by a declaration:

station ⟨identifier⟩; ⟨statement⟩

the ⟨statement⟩ being single, compound, or a block.

2. Customers were declared *collectively* by

customer ⟨customer list⟩

where the ⟨customer list⟩ elements had the format

⟨identifier⟩ (⟨list of characteristics⟩) [⟨integer expression⟩]

the ⟨integer expression⟩ indicating the upper limit to the number of this type of customer being present.

3. A system was declared by

system ⟨identifier⟩ := ⟨station list⟩

where the elements of the ⟨station list⟩ were identifiers of stations.

The best way to give the reader a feeling for the language at this stage is to present some fragments of an example—an "airport departure" model.

system Airport Departure := arrivals, counter,
fee collector, control, lobby;
customer passenger (fee paid) [500]; **Boolean** fee paid;

⋮

```
station counter;
    begin accept (passenger) select:
            (first) if none: (exit);
    hold (normal (2, 0.2));
    route (passenger) to:
    (if fee paid then control else fee collector)
    end;
station fee collector, etc.
```

The language elements "accept-select-if none," "hold," and "route-to" describe the nodes of the network and the interconnections. The syntax is that of ALGOL procedure calls, but according to Dahl and Nygaard (1963) "these are not procedures in the strict ALGOL sense. . . . Various details must be added behind the scenes by a preprocessor." For instance, the "hold" statement represented a time delay in the operation of the station, which implied that control would have to leave the station and return to it at a later time. Each new life cycle of a station would be started automatically at the appropriate times.

At the next stage, March 1964 (Dahl and Nygaard, 1964a), the simple network idea had been replaced by the more powerful concept of models consisting of interacting processes operating in "quasi-parallel" (see Section 2.3.2). The processes were declared collectively by **activity** declarations. At this stage the preprocessor idea had been abandoned, the language would be implemented by extending the ALGOL compiler and changing parts of the run time system (Dahl, 1963, 1964).

Process queues were now represented by explicitly declared ordered "sets." They were manipulated by "wait" and "include" statements and a special **extract–select** construct which also made quantities declared local to the selected process, the "attributes," accessible from the outside. Thereby processes were also data carriers, like the "customer" objects one year earlier.

```
SIMULA begin comment airport departure;
set q counter, q fee, q control, lobby (passenger);
    counter office (clerk); . . .
activity passenger; Boolean fee paid;
    begin fee paid := random (0, 1) < 0.5; . . . ;
        wait (q counter) end;

activity clerk;
begin
counter: extract passenger
    select first (q counter) do
    begin hold (normal (2, 0.3));
            if fee paid then
                begin include (passenger) into: (q control);
                    incite (control office) end
```

```
              else
              begin include (passenger) into: (q fee);
                     incite (fee office) end;

          end
          if none wait (counter office);
          goto counter
      end
   :
   end of SIMULA;
```

Curiously enough the wait-incite operator pair makes our set concept of 1964 act as a waiting mechanism not unlike the concept of condition variables introduced by Hoare for process synchronization in monitors (Hoare, 1974). (Hoare never saw our paper.) Our operator pair is analogous to Hoare's wait-signal.

At this stage all the major features of SIMULA I were present. Some important details were adjusted, however, along with the language implementation. In order to increase flexibility, sets were allowed to contain processes of different kinds, and process pointers were introduced as explicit language elements. Consequently the mechanism for accessing the attributes of a process had to be remodelled.

```
      inspect ⟨process reference⟩
          when passenger do . . .
          when staff do . . .
          otherwise . . .
```

The **incite** operator was replaced by the more generally applicable construct

```
      activate ⟨process reference⟩
```

The SIMULA I compiler was finished at the end of 1964, and the language definition user's manual appeared in May the following year (Dahl and Nygaard, 1965).

2.3. The Development Process

2.3.1. System Description

From the very outset SIMULA was regarded as a *system description language,* as evidenced by the title of the IFIP 1962 Munich paper, "SIMULA—an extension of ALGOL to the description of discrete event networks" (Nygaard, 1963a). The design objectives were stated in Nygaard (1963d, pp. 2–3).

1. The language should be built around a general mathematical structure with few basic concepts. This structure should furnish the operations research worker with a standardized approach in his description so that he can easily define and describe the various components of the system in terms of these concepts.

2. It should be unifying, pointing out similarities and differences between various kinds of network systems.

3. It should be directing, and force the operations research worker to consider all aspects of the network.

4. It should be general and allow the description of very wide classes of network systems and

other systems which may be analyzed by simulation, and should for this purpose contain a general algebraic and dynamic language, as for example ALGOL and FORTRAN.

5. It should be easy to read and to print, and should be suitable for communication between scientists studying networks.

6. It should be problem-oriented and not computer-oriented, even if this implies an appreciable increase in the amount of work which has to be done by the computer.

Two years later, in May 1965, the design objectives were restated in the SIMULA I Manual (Dahl and Nygaard, 1965, pp. 4–5):

1. Since simulation is the method of analysis most commonly to be used for the systems in which we are interested, SIMULA is a dynamic language:

It is designed to describe sequences of actions, not permanent relationships. The range of variation in decision rules and interactions between components of systems is so wide that it is necessary to let the language contain a general algorithmic language. An important reason why ALGOL has been chosen is that its block structure is similar to what was needed in SIMULA.

2. SIMULA should be built around a few basic concepts, selected to provide the research worker with a standardized approach to a very wide class of problems and to make it easy to identify the various components of the system.

3. Attempts have been made to make the language unifying—pointing out similarities and differences between systems, and directing—forcing the research worker to consider all relevant aspects of the systems. Efforts have also been made to make SIMULA descriptions easy to read and print and hence a useful tool for communication.

4. Taking the above objectives into account, SIMULA descriptions (supplemented by the necessary input, output and data analysis statements) should without any rewriting be able to produce simulation programs for electronic computers through compilers.

Comparing the two versions of the design objectives, it is seen that the three main differences are:

1. In 1963 SIMULA was related to "discrete event *network* systems." In 1965 the term "network" had disappeared.

2. In 1963 it was stated that SIMULA "should be built around a *general mathematical structure* with few basic concepts."

Also it was said in Nygaard (1963d) that "our present idea is that the first SIMULA compiler should be ALGOL-based, and ALGOL is used here. A later version may be FORTRAN-based, using the same basic concepts." In 1965 SIMULA's nature as a *"dynamic language"* (i.e. algorithmic language) and its relationship to the block structured programming language ALGOL was strongly emphasized.

3. In 1963 it was said that SIMULA "should be problem-oriented and not computer-oriented, even if this implies an appreciable increase in the amount of work which has to be done by the computer." In 1965 SIMULA's problem orientation was still stressed, but its computer orientation was also underlined.

Let us examine the reasons for each of these modifications of the design objectives.

When we started the development of SIMULA, we felt that we had a rather wide range of system examples available to test our ideas against. The situation was, however, that all these systems could be conceived as consisting of components of two distinct kinds: permanently present *active* components, and a variable number of transient *passive* components moving between and being acted upon by the active ones. Such a system could in a natural way be regarded as a network.

First we observed that, e.g., the airport departure system could be considered from a "dual" point of view: It could be described by active passengers, grabbing and holding the passive counter clerks, fee collectors, etc. Then we realized that it was also possible to adopt an "in-between" or "balanced" point of view: describing the passengers (customers) as active in moving from station to station, passive in their interaction with the service parts of stations. These observations seemed to apply to a large number of situations. Finally, in our search for still wider classes of systems to be used to test our concepts, we found important examples of systems which we felt could not naturally be regarded as "networks" in the sense we had used the term (e.g., the "epidemic system" described in Dahl and Nygaard, 1966.) The result of this development was the abandonment of the "network" concept and the introduction of processes as the basic, unifying concept.

The second modification of the design objectives was related to the first. We no longer regarded a system as described by a "general mathematical structure" and instead understood it as a variable collection of interacting processes—each process being present in the program execution, the simulation, as an ALGOL stack.

From then on the program execution, existing as a dynamic system within the computer's store, became prominent in our discussions. Graphical representations of simplified (but structurally identical) versions of the program executions were used as *models* of the systems described by the language. More and more our reasoning on language properties was related to desirable features of these model systems. (The textbook *SIMULA BEGIN* is a later example of the systematic pedagogical use of such graphical models (Birtwistle *et al.*, 1973).)

It turned out that this approach was essential in the teaching of SIMULA I, and it was an important mode of thinking when SIMULA 67 was developed and later taught. Instead of deriving language constructs from discussions of the described systems combined with implementation considerations, we developed model system properties suitable for portraying discrete event systems, considered the implementation possibilities, and then settled the language constructs. An obvious consequence was that we abandoned the idea of a FORTRAN-based version of SIMULA I (see Section 2.5). ALGOL's stack structure had, in its generalized form, become an essential feature of SIMULA I and a main reason for its success.

Finally, let us consider the modification of the 1963 design objective, that SIMULA "should be problem-oriented and not computer-oriented, even if this implies an appreciable increase in the amount of work which has to be done by the computer." This design objective caused much discussion and disagreement between us. But, as the language gradually developed, we felt that the expected conflict between problem orientation and computer orientation diminished and to some extent disappeared. Instead we often discovered that, with the language approach chosen, good system description capabilities seemed to result in a more simple and logical implementation. Another reason for the modification was that we realized that the success of SIMULA would, regardless of our insistence on the importance of problem orientation, to a large extent depend upon its compile and run time efficiency as a programming language.

2.3.2. Storage Allocation

The initial plan was that the simulation facility should be implemented as a procedure package and a simple preprocessor on top of ALGOL 60. One idea that looked promising at the time came from the observation that ALGOL, by its recursive block mechanism, did cater for multiple occurrences of user defined data structures rather like the "customers'' that would go from one "station" to the next in our simulation models. Also the station descriptions had block format. It turned out, however, that the block structure of ALGOL was not very helpful, in fact the preprocessor would have to fight against it by breaking up the blocks, making local variables nonlocal, etc. There was no hope of integrating special purpose operations like "hold (time interval)" completely into the language, since it implied a kind of "parallel" processing foreign to ALGOL and conflicting with ALGOL's strict dynamic stack regime of procedure calls and storage allocation.

During the spring of 1963 we became more and more convinced that the project was on a wrong track, and started toying with the idea of making nontrivial changes to ALGOL by breaking with the stack regime. Since that would have grave consequences for the storage management of the ALGOL run time system, we had to dig from that end.

During the summer and autumn of 1963 a storage allocation package was designed, based on a two-dimensional free area list (Dahl, 1963). The inner lists contained areas of the same size, which we felt would be numerous in typical steady state situations; the outer list contained the inner ones ordered according to area size. Each area had a "used" bit in its first and last words to facilitate the recombination of neighbouring free areas. Thus the system had stack allocation as a special case, and could at the same time utilize the entire noncontiguous store of our computer.

With this solution to the storage allocation problem the search space for useful dynamic structures was drastically increased, and in February 1964 the SIMULA process concept was born, ranging from pure data structures to quasi-parallel ALGOL programs. Quasi-parallel execution of processes implied that control would switch from one process to another as the result of special sequencing statements such as "hold." Each temporarily inactive process had a "reactivation point" (represented by a system variable local to the process) which identified the program point where control should resume operations next time it entered the process. With the new storage allocation package quasi-parallel sequencing statements could be allowed at arbitrary program points, e.g., inside procedures called by the processes, since their data stacks could grow and shrink independently (Dahl, 1964). Furthermore processes could be created and destroyed in arbitrary order.

2.3.3. Security and Consistency

During the summer of 1963 Bernard Hausner, then working at RAND Corporation, Santa Monica, U.S., was employed by the NCC (see section 2.5). Hausner was one of the fathers of SIMSCRIPT (Markowitz et al., 1963), and through him we got to know the SIMSCRIPT language and its implementation rather well. This was our first encounter with the pointer concept in a high-level language. To some extent, however, our reaction to SIMSCRIPT can best be described as that of a "cultural clash." It helped to make an important design goal conscious and explicit.

Our language had to provide programming "security" to the same extent as ALGOL 60 itself: Any erroneous program must either be rejected by the compiler (preferably), or by run time checks (if unavoidable), or its behavior must be understandable *by reasoning based entirely on the language semantics,* independent of its implementation.

A main aspect of security was to achieve compiler controlled data access. As far as processes only interacting through nonlocal data were concerned, the problem was solved merely by applying the usual ALGOL access rules, with user convenience and computer efficiency thrown into the bargain (no subscripts needed to distinguish "my" local variables from those of other processes of the same kind). However, there was a need to obtain access to the contents of an object from outside the object. In a model containing "customers" and "clerks" the active agent would need access to its own data as well as those of the partner during "service."

The **inspect . . . when . . . when . . . otherwise** construct did provide the required compiler control, at the expense of run time tests to determine the type of the inspected object. However, the testing was turned into a potentially constructive language mechanism, rather than unproductive run time checking. Compiler control required that outside access be limited to the outermost block level of a process. This had the advantage that a process could prevent outside interference by hiding local data in inner blocks.

Another aspect of security had to do with de-allocation of storage. For reasons of implementation simplicity and efficiency one would like de-allocation to be explicit, say through a "destroy" statement, or self-destruction by control going through process **end.** However, the only way this could be combined with security would have been a process referencing regime essentially ensuring one pointer at a time to any process. Unable to find such a scheme providing sufficient programming flexibility we implemented a reference count scheme, an idea borrowed from Weizenbaum (1962), and also added a "last resort" garbage collector.

Automatic data retention was felt to be a fairly dangerous approach, in the sense that bad programs might easily lead to the flooding of memory by useless data, the resulting error message not giving many clues as to which pointers were responsible. To reduce that danger we insisted that procedures and ordinary subblocks should be self-destructive on exit, as they are in ALGOL 60. Combining these two different de-allocation strategies led to two possibilities of conflict with respect to data accessing security.

1. A process could outlive its dynamic parent, i.e., the block instance containing the generating expression which gave rise to the process. As a result the process might access nonexisting data through its formal parameters. The remedy chosen was to forbid all kinds of call by name parameters to processes (including procedures, labels, and switches), only excepting arrays which had to be allocated as separate objects anyway. The restriction was sometimes painful, but it did conform with the notion that a process breaks loose (becomes "detached") from its parent upon generation and starts a life of its own.

2. A process could outlive its textually enclosing block instance (by being pointed to by data nonlocal to the latter), thereby accessing nonexisting nonlocals. A remedy was to require that all processes be declared (by **activity** declarations) local to a special block, identified by the prefix **SIMULA.**

SIMULA begin . . . end

Furthermore the SIMULA block must be the outermost one or must be embedded in an *ordinary* ALGOL program. This latter requirement was enforced by the following compiler stratagem: the special SIMULA vocabulary was part of the compiler dictionary only inside a SIMULA block, with the single exception of the word **SIMULA;** the latter was removed from the dictionary inside a SIMULA block. (It would still be possible to have dynamically nested instances of a SIMULA block, by embedding it in a recursive procedure. But to our knowledge nobody has ever found a use for this construct, or even checked that the compiler could handle it properly).

Kristen Nygaard and Ole-Johan Dahl

The SIMULA block would correspond to the simulation model as such. It was not unnatural to require that processes, running in quasi-parallel, should also be declared "in parallel" and as direct components of the model.

A final aspect of security concerned the ALGOL rule that the value of a variable is undefined upon declaration. With reference variables in the language (see below) it was very clear that "undefined values" would have to be treated explicitly and cautiously by the implementation. The best way we could find of combining reasonable efficiency with full programming security was to revise ALGOL on this point and assign neutral initial values to all variables. Fortunately this revision could not change the behavior of any correct ALGOL program.

2.3.4. Process Referencing

The concept of "process sets" was planned to be a prominent feature of the language, together with associated scanning mechanisms and with "selector expressions" as the only means of process identification. In this respect we were influenced by the design of SIMSCRIPT; certainly the term "set" was borrowed from that language, in SIMULA I meaning "ordered set of processes." It was questions of efficiency and algorithmic generality that made us abandon that approach and settle for "process pointer" as a basic data type.

As the language and its implementation took form, efficiency issues came more into the foreground. Not only should the language implementation be efficient, but the language itself must be such that users were *invited to make efficient programs*. In particular all built-in mechanisms ought to have execution times independent of model size.

One of our standard examples was a queue of high- and low-priority customers. Rather than having any easy-to-use selector expression that would search the queue for a priority customer, it would be better to maintain separate queues for the two kinds of customers. Thereby customer selection would become independent of queue size.

Still, some kind of built-in list mechanism was required for queueing and similar purposes, so an abstract ordered set concept was included as a second new data type, implemented as two-way circular lists. It seemed attractive at the time to emphasize the "abstract" nature of the set concept and enable processes to be members of arbitrarily many sets at the same time. This could be achieved by using auxiliary "element" objects to represent a process in different sets. At the same time all process references were made indirect through element objects by providing only "element pointers" in the language. Thereby "successor" and "predecessor" functions could be implemented without implicit searching.

No special scan/select mechanisms were included, except the natural extension of the ALGOL **for** statement to control pointer variables. Unfortunately the ALGOL **while** construct insists on advancing the controlled variable before testing it, which meant that the "set head" had to come out into the open and make our sets look less abstract than we had intended.

```
set S; element X; . . .
X := head(S);
for X := suc(X) while exist(X) do
    inspect X when . . . do . . .
```

Admittedly the inspect construction was a clumsy and fairly inefficient device for taking brief looks at objects in passing. However, we rationalized by referring to the "invitation-to-efficiency" principle: the clumsier the better, searching is abominable anyway.

In retrospect the introduction of "multimembership" sets was a mistake. First the "sets" were really process sequences allowing multiple process occurrences, whereas simple process chains would have been more appropriate for most purposes. Second, natural abstract set primitives like $P \in S$ and $S := S - \{P\}$ for given process P and set S were not efficient operations for the chosen set representation. So, contrary to good principles, functions like "member (P, S)," searching S for an element representing P, found their way into the language as built-in procedures. Third, there was an ever-present overhead in process referencing caused by the fact that all process pointers were directed through separately allocated "element" objects.

2.3.5. Process Scheduling

If (avoidable) searching in space is bad, then searching for the correct point in time is even worse. The May 1963 language specifications (Dahl and Nygaard, 1963) contain a statement

PAUSE (⟨Boolean expression⟩)

to that effect (awaiting the truth of the Boolean expression). The idea was quietly buried, and we made do with *passivate, activate, hold,* and *cancel* statements as described in Dahl and Nygaard (1964a). There was *direct* activation for immediately invoking the next active phase of a process, comparable to a procedure call and activation with *time delay* (including *hold*) not unlike the CAUSE–AT mechanism of SIMSCRIPT.

A simple way to implement model time scheduling is to maintain a list of scheduled processes sorted by time attributes. The list (we called it the "sequencing set," SQS) was made to look like a generalized ALGOL activation stack by an invariant stating that the currently operating process is at the end of the SQS. (And its time attribute is the current model time). Admittedly scheduling with a time delay is then not an $O(1)$ operation, and to improve efficiency, the SQS was represented by a kind of binary tree (left heavy, postordered). The tree preserved the order of elements with equal time values and had $O(1)$ algorithms for removal and for LIFO and FIFO insertion. Worst-case insertion was $O(n)$, but according to experiments (Myhrhaug, 1965), the "average" behavior was much better.

Recently the insertion algorithm was analyzed with respect to exponentially distributed time delays (Jonassen and Dahl, 1975), and the average performance in that case was found to be $O((\ln n)^2)$.

The decision, made early 1964, not to include any mechanism for "interrogative sequencing" (Dahl, 1968b), was a fairly natural one at the time. It was based on considerations of efficiency and ease of implementation, and on the growing conviction that the language must give the user full sequencing control in order to be a sufficiently general purpose modeling tool.

As a result of discussion with colleagues, especially those from the CSL group (Buxton and Laski, 1962), it became clear that the case for interrogative sequencing was stronger than we had originally realized (see, e.g., Blunden, 1968), compared to the "imperative" sequencing of SIMULA (and SIMSCRIPT). The dilemma may be explained as a choice between a statement

$$\textbf{await} (\langle \text{Boolean expression} \rangle)$$

in process **P**, and a **passivate** statement in P together with matching occurrences of **activate** P in other processes. Advantages of the former are:

1. It is obviously easier to use, and more self-documenting.

2. It leads to better program decomposition in terms of processes; process P is made more self-contained.

3. Properly implemented it protects the user from making the error of forgetting necessary occurrences of **activate** P. This kind of programming error is especially nasty since the observable consequences are negative: events that should have happened in the model do not take place.

Yet, we feel that our design decision was the right one, for the following reasons:

1. The notion of waiting until a given condition becomes true is not well defined within the framework of quasi-parallel processes, since only one process may run at a time. Thus, any realization can only approximate the idea, which means that sequencing decisions that ought to be in the hands of the user, will have to be arbitrarily made by the implementation. A ''good'' implementation is likely to be so complicated that the exact model behavior is hard to predict from the program text in complex cases.

2. There is no a priori upper limit to the cost of executing an **await** statement. The cost is likely to increase with the size of the model (as is true for searching in space too).

From 1 and 2 we draw the conclusion that interrogative sequencing should not be among the language primitives. Whether it should be added as an auxiliary mechanism on top of the language is perhaps a question of time, money, programming skill, and taste. Fortunately one has learned to achieve program decomposition (cf. point 2 above) by isolating sequencing strategies as separately verifiable *class*-like program components, representing such concepts as abstract resource schedulers, communication channels, or even interrogative schemes. (Compare the monitor concept of Hoare (1974) for parallel programming.)

Our attitude and feelings towards interrogative sequencing has been conditioned by experience and perhaps cultural factors. Two incidents from the year 1965 are worth recounting. At the IFIP Congress 65 in New York, May 24–29, 1965 (Nygaard and Dahl, 1965), we were able to show results from our first real-life simulation model (of a paper mill lumbering yard). For the first time we could exchange information on typical simulation execution speeds and found that SIMULA I's performance was very much better than what a number of people in that audience were accustomed to.

Some of the first SIMULA programs written outside our center were part of Univac's acceptance tests for our compiler. One of the programs, a model of the job flow through an operating system, appeared to go into a tight loop. After running it for 15 minutes while nothing happened we were convinced that another bug had been discovered in the run time system. It turned out that the program was built around a loop of the form

```
wait: if nothing has happened then
      begin hold (one drum cycle);
      goto wait end
```

According to the program, the computer was switched on at 8 A.M., and the data provided the first job arrival at 9 A.M. Since the drum cycle was 34 milliseconds, approximately

100,000 events had to be executed before anything happened. After some simple repro-gramming a whole day's work was simulated in a few minutes of computer time, which goes to show that the "invitation-to-efficiency" may well be turned down by language users.

2.4. Relation to Other Languages

SIMSCRIPT was the only simulation language that we were closely acquainted with during the design phase of SIMULA. From the preceding sections it will be evident that it had a considerable impact through its list processing and time scheduling mechanisms. It also contained a set of random drawing and other utility routines, which served as a model for our procedure library. Information on GPSS (Gordon, 1962) was available to us through IBM Norway, but the GPSS system looked more like a generalized simulation model than a programming language. Consequently we did not study it very closely. Only later did it occur to us that the "transactions" of GPSS could in fact be looked upon as processes in quasi-parallel. Tocher's work on GPS (e.g., Tocher, 1963), gave us a greater awareness of some of the practical considerations and difficulties of large scale simulation. However, his system design appeared to be too specialized. SOL (Knuth and McNeley, 1964a, b) came to our attention too late (July 1964) to have an effect on our design, but we were impressed with its beauty and realized that others before us had had the idea of quasi-parallel processes in an ALGOL-like setting.

At the time when we offered our SIMULA introduction paper (Dahl and Nygaard, 1966) to the ACM, October 1965, Don Knuth was serving as the programming language editor. He wrote us a very generous letter, typical for him, which added to our pride and became the starting point of a long and lasting friendship. Other good friendships resulted from contacts and discussions with the CSL designers John N. Buxton and John Laski.

By far the most important language ancestor of SIMULA I is of course ALGOL 60 it-self. Through its orthogonal design, concept economy, strictness of definition, and degree of compile time error control it set a standard of quality that we could only hope to ap-proach, but which was well worth striving for. The concept central to us was the dynamic block structure. In retrospect the two main lessons were:

1. The distinction between a piece of program text and an execution, or "dynamic in-stance" of it.

2. The fact that data and operations belong together, and that most useful program con-structs contain both.

In ALGOL, blocks (including procedures) are seen externally as generalized operations. By introducing mechanisms for quasi-parallel sequencing, essentially the same construct could play the role of processes in parallel, and through mechanisms for naming block in-stances and accessing their contents they could function as generalized data objects. The essential benefits of combining data and operations in a single construct were already there to be explored.

One result of this exploration was the discovery that "procedure attributes" might be useful. The following example of a class of "abstract" car objects is quoted from the Lan-guage Definition document (Dahl and Nygaard, 1965), Section 5.3:

```
        activity car;
        begin real V, X₀, T₀;
              real procedure X; X := X₀ + V * (time − T₀);
              procedure update (Vnew); real Vnew;
              begin X₀ := X; T₀ := time; V := Vnew end;
              ⋮
        end;
```

The attributes X, V and update were used by a police survey process to enforce a speed limit on a given road section. (It is perhaps a pity that the representation variables X_0 and T_0 could not be hidden away in a subblock.) Another discovery was the fact that SIMULA had become a powerful list processing language. A second example in the same document defines a process for scanning the leaves of a tree, advancing to the next leaf with each activation.

It should be mentioned that D. Ross, through his AED project (Ross and Rodriguez, 1963), independently and unknown to us had developed an ALGOL-like language also exploiting the idea of adding operators to data structures.

One factor which contributed to the comparative success of the SIMULA I project was the fact that we had a good ALGOL compiler to start with. It had been developed at Case Institute of Technology in Cleveland by J. Speroni, W. Lynch, N. Hubacker, and others. They had extended the ALGOL language by a rather nice I/O system, including an elaborate generalized parameter list mechanism. The compiler was finished and installed in Oslo late spring 1964 (which was in the nick of time for our project schedule). Our implementation effort amounted to about one man-year's work on the run time system, including built-in procedures, and one man-month for extending the compiler.

2.5. The Software Agreement between Univac and NCC

In the second half of May 1962, Univac arranged the "Univac Executive Tour." A Douglas DC-8 was filled with prospective customers who were shown Univac's new computers and production facilities. KN was invited to participate by Stig Walstam, Director of Univac Scandinavia. KN came into contact with James W. Nickitas, then Assistant to Luther Harr, director of Univac Europe. Nickitas was told about SIMULA and also about another NCC software project: a linear programming package based upon a new algorithm developed by Sverre Spurkland at NCC. Nickitas immediately arranged a meeting at a hotel in New York for himself, KN, and three important people within Univac's software activities: Alvin M. Paster (Manager, Systems Research), his boss Robert W. Bemer (Director, Systems Programming), and Bemer's boss, William R. Lonergan. In the setting of the Executive Tour, a certain measure of polite interest was of course to be expected. But Paster, Bemer, and Lonergan turned out to be really interested, both in SIMULA and the LP package. (They knew that NCC recently had contracted a Danish GIER computer and would not buy Univac equipment.) Bemer at once invited KN to present SIMULA at the session which he was to chair at the IFIP 62 Congress in Munich. When the Executive Tour arrived at St. Paul, KN was very impressed by the brand-new UNIVAC 1107, and this both pleased Nickitas immensely (he was deeply in love with that computer himself) and also gave him another idea which he started to work on.

On May 29 the Executive Tour had arrived in Washington, D.C. After a dinner at the

Mayflower, Nickitas, who is of Greek descent, invited KN to a Greek nightclub. While they were listening to bouzouki music, watching a beautiful belly dancer, Nickitas presented the following informal proposal: Univac needed in the near future a good UNIVAC 1107 demonstration site in Europe. If NCC would be willing to provide Univac with SIMULA and the LP package, Univac would be willing to sell the 1107 at a substantial discount. When KN returned and told this story, most people raised serious doubts as to the state of his mind. In the end of June, however, Luther Harr, Nickitas and Walstam turned up in Oslo and presented the offer officially at a meeting with the NCC board. During the meeting, it became clear that Luther Harr either was in a very generous mood, or he had not read his lesson sufficiently well and did not realize that SIMULA and the LP were to be a part of the payment for the 1107. KN then asked him if Univac was definite in their decision to offer NCC a software contract for these items, and this was confirmed. Nickitas was foaming, but could do nothing. Afterwards, Nickitas took the incident with grace and became a very close friend of us as well as NCC. But Univac was from then on not too happy when money was discussed in relation to SIMULA.

After a summer of intensive computer evaluation studies the GIER contract was cancelled and UNIVAC 1107 purchased by the NCC. Alvin M. Paster became Univac's man in the subsequent software contract negotiations. Univac's letter of intent was dated October 12, 1962, and it also contained Univac's first contract proposal (Paster, 1962). The contract work was delayed because of the long communication lines (the contract was with Univac headquarters, New York) and because NCC had internal troubles associated with the very rapid expansion necessary to take over a large scale computer.

Another factor also complicated the picture: Univac decided to support an alternative basic software package for the 1107 ("Package B" as opposed to the original "Package A"). KN was sent to the US in November 1962, as a representative for the European 1107 users to make an evaluation of the situation, which was critical also for SIMULA: what would the quality be of the proposed new Package B ALGOL 60 compiler, to be developed at Case Institute of Technology in Cleveland? (The Package A ALGOL 60, later to be dropped, was contracted from General Kinetics Inc.).

KN returned as a convinced Package B supporter, and had established very useful contacts with Joseph Speroni and others participating in the Case ALGOL 60 project. In Los Angeles he had lectured on SIMULA at the RAND Corporation and got Bernie Hausner interested. Hausner was the chief implementor in the SIMSCRIPT team (Markowitz et al., 1963). He was promptly offered a job at the NCC, which he later accepted, and arrived on July 1, 1963.

At a meeting at NCC on May 2, 1963, Univac to our surprise confronted us with a proposal for an extension of the contract: we should also implement a SIMSCRIPT compiler. The reason was that Univac had met a US market demand for SIMSCRIPT. They did not lose interest in SIMULA, but used Hausner's presence at NCC to force us into SIMSCRIPT as well, as an "initial step" towards implementing SIMULA. (It was believed, also by us, that we could use important parts of a SIMSCRIPT compiler as a platform for SIMULA.) Another awesome new person now also entered the scene: Mr. C. A. Christopher, Univac's Director of Procurement. We never met him, but his presence was very much felt as the representative of the world of law, money and vast administrative hierarchies. Our first encounter with this new world was the first page of his contract text proposal, where we read:

WITNESSETH:

WHEREAS, Univac desires to have a program developed and implemented which will solve Linear Programming Problems, a Simscript Compiler developed and implemented, and a SIMULA Compiler developed and implemented, all for a UNIVAC 1107 Computer System, and

WHEREAS, NCC is willing and able to design, develop, implement, check out and document such aforementioned programs for the stated purposes on the terms and conditions hereinafter set forth.

NOW, THEREFORE, in consideration of the premises and of the mutual convenants herein contained, the parties hereto agree as follows.

The contract text was worked out and agreed upon. It specified Robert L. Hengen as the Technical Supervisor and C. A. Christopher as the General Contract Administrator for Univac, KN serving in both these functions for NCC. Hengen was, however, substituted by Alvin M. Paster. Paster gradually got other responsibilities and Hengen returned in February, 1964. The contract was dated June 1, 1963, signed June 1 by the NCC and July 3 by Univac (Agreement, 1963).

The SIMULA part of this contract clearly describes (in Article III B) the SIMULA compiler as a preprocessor to the ALGOL compiler. It also has our language specifications of May 18, 1963 (Dahl and Nygaard, 1963) as an appendix, defining the SIMULA language. It states that variations in the language have to be approved by Univac. The payment was $35,000, according to a payment schedule which assumed that the SIMSCRIPT part of the contract should be completed first. It is also implicitly assumed that the SIMULA compiler should be ready for acceptance tests by July 3, 1964 (366 days after the contract was signed). The contract gave NCC 60 days maintenance responsibility after it had been accepted by Univac, and it described the details of the acceptance procedure.

The SIMSCRIPT compiler was to be completed very quickly, in five months, for the sum of $25,000. Already in August–September 1963 it became clear that it would not be sensible to transform the SIMSCRIPT IBM 7090 compiler into an 1107 compiler. NCC immediately told this to Paster during a visit at NCC late September, and Univac agreed to terminate this section of the contract. During this visit Univac got our proposal of making a SIMULA compiler with a new storage management scheme, and not only a preprocessor and procedure package in ALGOL. Communication between Univac and NCC was problematic, and for various reasons our work was delayed. In February 1964 the terms of the contract were modified (Christopher, 1964). SIMSCRIPT was officially terminated. The delivery date was changed to January 1, 1965. The payment schedule was revised: $33,000 had already been paid ($8000 for SIMSCRIPT), $20,000 was to be paid by March 31, 1964, and $30,000 was to be paid upon Univac's acceptance of the SIMULA and LP products. (The main reference to the history of the contract work is Nygaard (1965a).)

In February 1964 the SIMULA language could be reconsidered with the freedom made available by the new storage management scheme developed in the autumn by OJD. The process concept was developed and reported in March (Dahl and Nygaard, 1964a). From then on only minor language revisions were made.

A major problem encountered was the late arrival of the Case ALGOL 60 compiler (May–June 1964) and the lack of suitable documentation, particularly relating to its interface with the EXEC II operating system. Two American visitors during the summer of 1964 provided useful assistance in this situation: Ken Walter from Purdue and Nicholas Hubacker from Case. At the NCC Bjørn Myhrhaug and Sigurd Kubosch were members of the SIMULA team. The work during the summer and autumn went on with much effort and little drama. Progress reports were forwarded to Univac as before, but we only got a reaction once (through a Telex) when we urgently requested an acknowledgment of the arrival of our reports. Our impression was that the personnel with knowledge of the contracts left Univac and did not inform those who took over their responsibilities. (We got, however, the scheduled March 1964 payment of $20,000).

When the SIMULA I compiler was ready, on the date specified by the revised contract, January 1965, Univac was notified, but we got no reaction. During our visit to the US in May 1965, in connection with the IFIP 65 World Congress, we had a meeting with Ira A. Clark (Technical Coordinator for Systems Programming, Univac, St. Paul) and W. J. Raymond (Systems Programming Manager, Univac International Operations, New York).

Clark's attitude toward SIMULA was initially very negative, and for good reasons. It turned out that he, who had got the responsibility for handling the contract, had never seen our letter. Later on it was discovered, we were told, in an abandoned desk at the Univac New York headquarters.

Clark later on was very helpful as our contact during the acceptance tests which followed. Univac forwarded their test problems to be run in Oslo on October 27, 1965. On January 10, 1966, a Telex informed us that Univac was accepting SIMULA I, and a letter from Ira A. Clark (dated January 27, 1965) said

> We have examined the results of test cases submitted as acceptance runs for the SIMULA compiler. In every case, the compiler performed successfully and useful results were obtained. The personnel in the Center were very helpful in doing everything necessary to analyze our test cases, insure the accuracy of our work, successfully compile these SIMULA tests, and provide helpful comments and listing annotation of output.

SIMULA I was for some time Univac Category III Software. This implied that Univac distributed the compiler, but NCC had the maintenance responsibility. When NCC had completed a comprehensive technical documentation, SIMULA I was (in May 1967) made Category I software. (NCC had a maintenance agreement with Univac until Univac adapted the SIMULA I compiler to its EXEC-8 operating system).

In spite of our efforts, Univac had lost interest in our LP package, and a last letter from C. A. Christopher (1965, Dec. 15) stated: "To date we have made payments to you of $53,000. I realize that time and effort were put into the other projects but with negative results. We feel that the total paid NCC to date represents full and adequate reimbursement for the SIMULA Compiler."

2.6. The Response to SIMULA I

At the NCC the use of SIMULA I for simulation programming started immediately and spread rapidly. In 1965 three SIMULA I courses were given at NCC. The use of SIMULA I up to December 1965 is reported in Nygaard (1965b). A later version of this report covers the period up to June 1968 (Hegna et al., 1968).

A visit to Stockholm in February 1965 triggered off an important development. We were lecturing three days at the Royal Swedish Institute of Technology and were pleased to note the first day that two representatives from the big Swedish company ASEA seemed to be very interested. The second day we were disappointed to find that the ASEA people did not turn up. The third day they returned however, Niels Lindecrantz of ASEA bringing an offer: ASEA would consider using SIMULA for a number of jobs if we were willing to do a test job free of charge. We were requested to program and run a large and complex job shop simulation in less than four weeks, with a simulation execution efficiency which was at least four times higher than that job on the FACIT computers. We accepted, succeeded and got the other jobs. (A simplified version of this program is one of the main examples used in Dahl (1968b).)

In addition to the money from Univac, NCC got a number of other benefits. Our Operational Research Department could take on jobs which otherwise would have been impossible to accept. Customers got important problems solved. The first SIMULA-based application package, for simulation of logic circuits, was implemented (Stevenson, 1967). The NCC developed international connections, and we got into direct contact with many of the other research workers developing programming languages, particularly simulation languages, at the time. We had at an early stage ideas for using SIMULA I as a tool in real-time programming, but these plans never materialized (Nygaard, 1963e, in Norwegian).

Burroughs was the first of the other computer manufacturers to take an interest in SIMULA I, for two reasons:

the advocacy of Don Knuth and John L. McNeley, the fathers of SOL,
the general ALGOL orientation within the company.

In 1968 SIMULA I was made available to Burroughs B5500 users. The language was modified and extended, the reasons being discussed in a letter from John S. Murphy of Burroughs, Pasadena (Murphy, 1968).

Another early interest in SIMULA I developed in the Soviet Union, reported in Nygaard (1968b). The main center of activity was the Central Economical Mathematical Institute of the Russian Academy of Sciences in Moscow (CEMI). The CEMI Computer Science department was headed by E. I. Yakovlev. KN was invited to the Soviet Union twice in the summer of 1966, and gave one-week courses in Moscow, Leningrad, Novosibirsk, and some lectures in Kiev. A number of reciprocal visits resulted and a cooperative agreement was in effect for some time. OJD and Myhrhaug lectured on SIMULA I and SIMULA 67 implementation in Moscow, and a team in Yakovlev's department later implemented SIMULA I on a URAL 16 computer. The project leader was K. S. Kusmin. Implementation on the BESM 6 computer was discussed but never carried out. The SIMULA I manual (Dahl and Nygaard, 1965) was translated into Russian.

During the first years of SIMULA's life, the NCC had to do most of the teaching of the language. We soon discovered that this was not a trivial task. As a result we developed the pedagogical approach in which the process concept was the first one introduced, then the reference ("element") concept and informal versions of the statements followed. Procedures and formalized versions of the statements were introduced later. Graphical models were used extensively (see Section 2.3.1).

Those familiar with FORTRAN very often had difficulties in unlearning that language. Those familiar with ALGOL were better off, but still found it problematic to substitute ALGOL's single-stack picture of the world with SIMULA's multistack picture. Quite often the newcomers to programming seemed to absorb SIMULA faster than the oldtimers.

When SIMULA I was put to practical work it turned out that to a large extent it was used as a system description language. A common attitude among its simulation users seemed to be: Sometimes actual simulation runs on the computer provided useful information. The writing of the SIMULA program was almost always useful, since the development of this program (regarded as a system description) resulted in a better understanding of the system. Semiformalized SIMULA programs, with the input, output, and data analysis statements omitted, proved to be useful in discussing the systems' properties with people unacquainted with programming.

SIMULA was intended to be a system description and simulation programming language. Some users discovered that SIMULA I also provided powerful new facilities when used for other purposes than simulation. After the first introduction phase we became more and more interested in this use of SIMULA I, and we soon discovered a number of shortcomings within the language. The resulting discussions on the possible improvements to SIMULA I in 1965–1966 initiated the development of SIMULA 67.

3. SIMULA 67

3.1. From SIMULA I to SIMULA 67

During 1965 and the beginning of 1966, most of our time went to using and introducing SIMULA I as a simulation language. Tracing facilities were designed and implemented (Dahl *et al.*, 1966), but were never used very much (at the NCC). When the first large jobs had been successfully completed and a number of users had learned the language, we became more and more interested in the possibilities of SIMULA I as a general purpose programming language. A first reference to a "new, improved SIMULA" occurs in a letter dated September, 1965 (Nickitas, 1965). We explored SIMULA I's list structuring and coroutine capabilities, the use of procedure attributes etc. Gradually we realized that a number of shortcomings existed in the language.

1. The element/set concepts were too clumsy as basic, general purpose mechanisms for list processing. Even for simulation modeling our experience showed that simple process pointers might be better, combined with an inherent set membership capability of processes, restricted to one set at a time.

2. The inspect mechanism for remote attribute accessing turned out to be very cumbersome in some situations. (Try to compute X.A+Y.A using inspect statements.) Then Hoare's record class proposal appeared (Hoare, 1965, 1966, 1968), which showed how full security could be obtained in constructs like X.A by compile time reference qualification, and how reasonable flexibility of run time referencing could be obtained by the idea of record subclasses.

3. We were beginning to realize that SIMULA I's simulation facilities were too heavy a burden to carry for a general purpose programming language. Certainly the multistack structure was a big advantage, but quasi-parallel sequencing had many applications independent of the concept of simulated time.

4. We had seen many useful applications of the process concept to represent collections of variables and procedures, which functioned as natural units of programming although they had no "own actions." It occurred to us that the variables of such an object could play the role intended for the not very successful **own** variables of ALGOL 60, since they survived individual procedure activations. In our experience, however, such data would often be associated with a group of procedures rather than just one. The difficulties inherent in the **own** variable concept were related to generation and initialization. However,

SIMULA objects were generated by explicit mechanisms, and initializing actions could be naturally assigned as "own actions" of the object.

5. When writing simulation programs we had observed that processes often shared a number of common properties, both in data attributes and actions, but were structurally different in other respects so that they had to be described by separate declarations. Such partial similarity fairly often applied to processes in *different simulation models,* indicating that programming effort could be saved by somehow preprogramming the common properties. Parametrization could not provide enough flexibility, especially since parameters called by name, including procedure parameters, had been banned for processes (for good reasons, see Section 2.3.3). However, the idea of subclasses, somehow extended to apply to processes, might prove useful.

6. We were itching to revise the SIMULA implementation. The Univac ALGOL compiler, although efficient for most ALGOL programs, was terribly wasteful of storage space whenever the number of process activation records was large, as it would be in most simulation models. This made memory space our most serious bottleneck for large scale simulation. Jan V. Garwick, back from work in the US, had shown us a nice compacting garbage collector (now well known, said to have been designed for the implementation of a language called LISP 2). Some experimentation indicated that it was more efficient than our combined reference count/garbage collecting scheme. Furthermore it could take advantage of active deallocation at exit from procedures and blocks, simply by moving the free pointer back whenever the deletion occurred at the end of the used memory. Thus, ALGOL programs could be run with hardly any overhead at all, and most SIMULA programs would benefit too.

Our discussions during the spring and summer of 1965 had been rather academic: what should be revised *if* a revision was to be made. In the autumn of 1965 the Technical University of Norway in Trondheim contacted NCC and expressed its interest in implementing a new ALGOL 60 compiler on the UNIVAC 1100 series. The possibilities of basing a SIMULA compiler upon an ALGOL 60 compiler designed with SIMULA in mind seemed attractive. From February 1966 the term "SIMULA II" started to appear in our correspondence.

We started at that time a cooperation with a team headed by Knut Skog and Kristen Rekdal at the Technical University. NCC's part of that work faded out from December 1966 onwards, when the SIMULA 67 ideas were developed. The compiler was completed by the Technical University and marketed under the name "NU ALGOL."

This was the background for our language discussions during the autumn of 1966. All six points listed above were motivating us, but in retrospect it appears that points 2 and 5—attribute accessing and common properties of processes—were the most important ones. That is, important in the sense that our work to resolve these problems resulted in the class/subclass concepts which structured the rest of the new language. The subclass idea of Hoare (1968) was a natural starting point, but there were two difficulties:

1. We needed subclasses of processes with own actions and local data stacks, not only of pure data records.

2. We also needed to group together common process properties in such a way that they could be applied *later,* in a variety of different situations not necessarily known in advance.

Much time was spent during the autumn of 1966 in trying to adapt Hoare's record class construct to meet our requirements, without success. The solution came suddenly, with the idea of "prefixing," in December 1966. We were thinking in terms of a toll booth on a bridge, with a queue of cars which were either trucks or buses. (This example reappears in Dahl and Nygaard, 1968.) A "stripped" list structure, consisting of a "set head" and a variable number of "links," had been written down, when we saw that both our problems could be solved by a mechanism for "gluing" each of the various processes (trucks, buses) on to a "link" to make each link-process pair *one block instance.* Such a language feature would not be difficult to implement. Now each of the processes in the example would be a block instance consisting of two *layers: A prefix layer* containing a "successor" and "predecessor," and other properties associated with two-way list membership, and a *main part* containing the attributes of either a truck or a bus. In order to obtain compiler simplicity and, at the same time, security in attribute referencing, it was necessary that the two-layer property of these processes be known at compile time and that the prefix and main part be permanently glued together into one block instance.

The syntax for this new language feature was easy to find. The "links" could be declared separately, without any information about the other process classes which used link instances as a prefix layer. Since the processes of these other process classes were at the same time both "links" and something more, it was natural to indicate this by textually prefixing their declarations with the process class identifier of this common property, namely, "link." These process classes would then be "subclasses" of "link."

It was evident that when prefixing was introduced, it could be extended to multiple prefixing, establishing hierarchies of process classes. (In the example, "car" would be a subclass of "link," "truck" and "bus" subclasses of "car.") It was also evident that this "concatenation" of a sequence of prefixes with a main part could be applied to the action parts of processes as well. Usually a new idea was subjected to rather violent attacks in order to test its strength. The prefix idea was the only exception. We immediately realized that we now had the necessary foundation for a completely new language approach, and in the days which followed the discovery we decided that:

1. We would design a new general programming language, in terms of which an improved SIMULA I could be expressed.
2. The basic concept should be *classes* of *objects.*
3. The prefix feature, and thus the subclass concept, should be a part of the language.
4. Direct, qualified references should be introduced.

The development of the first SIMULA 67 proposal, based upon these decisions, is described in the next two sections.

3.2. The Lysebu Paper

The IFIP Technical Committee 2 (on programming languages) had decided in the autumn of 1965 that an IFIP Working Conference on simulation languages be held in Oslo in the spring of 1967. The decision was the result of a proposal made by the Norwegian representative to TC2, at the time, OJD. At New Year 1967 preparation had been under way for more than a year, and the time and place of the conference had been fixed for May 22–26 at Lysebu, a resort in the hills outside Oslo. We naturally hoped to be able to complete the design of our new language in time for the Lysebu conference. According to the conference schedule, preprints of all papers were to be distributed to the participants at the end of March. Consequently we were in a hurry, but fortunately the most difficult work had already been done, and the initial version of the paper (Dahl and Nygaard, 1967a) was ready in time. We had a fairly clear idea of how to unify the old processlike objects and the new concept of self-initializing data/procedure objects (Section 3.1, point 4), and at the same time remove the special purpose "model time" concept from the former. Since the term "process" could not apply to the unified concept, we introduced the more neutral word "object" as a technical term.

An object would start its life like an instance of a function procedure, invoked by the evaluation of a generating expression. During this phase the object might initialize its own local variables. Then, on passage through the **end** of the object or as the result of a new basic operation "detach," control would return to the generating expression delivering a reference to the object as the function value. In the former case the object was "terminated" with no further own actions, in the latter case it had become a "detached object" capable of functioning as a "coroutine." The basic coroutine call **resume** (⟨object reference⟩) would make control leave the active object, leaving behind a reactivation point at the end of the resume statement, and enter the reference object at its reactivation point. (The Lysebu paper mentions a third primitive operation "**goto** (⟨process reference⟩)" terminating the active object, but on this point revisions were made later.)

A declaration giving rise to a class of objects might well have been called an *object class* (in analogy with Hoare's *record class*). In choosing the shorter term **class** we felt that we had a good terminology which distinguished clearly between the declared quantity (the class) and its dynamic offspring (the objects). Our good intentions have not quite worked out, however. Many users tend to use the term *class,* or perhaps *class instance,* to denote an object, no doubt because *object* does not occur as a reserved word of the language. (As an afterthought, around 1978, we might have insisted that all class declarations must be prefixed, and defined a primitive outermost prefix *object* containing detach and resume as local procedures. (See also Wang and Dahl, 1971.))

The idea of class prefixing and concatenation was the most important step towards our goal. It had become possible to define classes primarily intended to be *used as prefixes.* Our idea was that some of the special purpose concepts of SIMULA I could be expressed by such "prefix classes" available to the programmer as plug-in units.

It was easy to describe "circular list processing" (like "sets" in SIMULA I) by means of a little class hierarchy for list elements (**class** link) and list heads (**class** list, later called "head"), with a common prefix part containing forward and backward pointers. Now any class prefixed by "link" would give rise to objects that could go in and out of circular lists, using procedures like "into" or "out" declared within its prefix part together with the list pointers. The lists themselves would be represented as "list" objects, possibly augmented by user defined attributes.

In order to explain the process concept as a prefix class it became necessary to extend the concatenation mechanism slightly. The original rule was that the operation rule of a concatenated class consisted of the operation rule of the prefix class followed by that of the main part. For a process object it was necessary to have predefined actions both at the beginning and at the end of its operation rule. So the prefix class had to be given a "split body" whose operation rule consisted of initial actions and final actions textually separated by a special symbol **inner.**

Now the task was simple. The prefix class was named "process," which meant that the term **activity** of SIMULA I would be represented by the much more descriptive term "process **class.**" The Lysebu paper shows a class "process" containing a **real** variable "evtime" representing model time, and a **ref** (process) variable "nextev" used to describe the SQS as a one-way list of process objects. (In an actual implementation we intended to use the logically equivalent binary tree technique, mentioned in Section 3.2.5). Obviously the sequencing primitives of SIMULA I could be represented by procedures manipulating the SQS, keeping it sorted with respect to evtime values, and passing control by resume operations. The "final actions" of a process were needed to remove the now dying object from the SQS and pass control to its successor on the SQS. Now only two problems remained: where to store the SQS pointer, and how to represent the "main program" of a simulation model.

We had independently, while exploring the linguistic consequence of the prefix notation, considered block prefixes as a natural extension. The reason for this was the fact that an ordinary in-line block could be viewed as the body of a very specialized anonymous class. We were quite pleased to discover that this very idea had been used before, through the ad hoc notation

SIMULA begin · · · end

of SIMULA I for making available the non-ALGOL simulation facilities.

Now everything fell into place. We only had to collect the various bits and pieces like prefix classes, procedures, and nonlocal variables (the SQS pointer) into one big class, appropriately named SIMULA and intended to be used for block prefixing. Its "initial actions" were used to initialize the SQS, containing a specialized process object impersonating the main program, whereupon control would proceed as it should: to execute the first active phase of the latter.

One ad hoc rule was needed to make the whole thing run: "an instance of a prefixed block is a detached object by definition." Thereby the main program could function as a coroutine in quasi-parallel with its local process objects. (It was later discovered that this effect could have been achieved in a somewhat more natural way (Wang and Dahl, 1971).)

It goes without saying that the class/subclass constructs had not been fully explored as general purpose programming tools at the time of the first version of the Lysebu paper (March 1967). However, the possibility of using class declarations to define "language dialects oriented towards special problem areas" is pointed out, and so is the importance of "making user defined classes generally available."

The generalization to hierarchies of "language dialects" was fairly obvious. In June 1967 the "SIMULA class" had been renamed and reorganized as a two level hierarchy,

class SIMSET, and
SIMSET **class** SIMULATION,

reflecting the fact that circular list handling could be useful for other purposes than simulation modelling. (We never quite got rid of the term "set" from SIMULA I.) This kind of hierarchy points towards a technique of level-by-level bottom-up program design not unlike that of Dijkstra in constructing his THE operating system (Dijkstra, 1968).

No mention of the class concept as an abstraction mechanism is made in the Lysebu paper. It took several years of slowly growing understanding (see, e.g., Dahl, 1970; Dahl and Hoare, 1972), until the fundamental difference between the internal ("concrete") view of an object and an external ("abstract") one finally was made clear by Hoare (1972).

It is worth noticing that the Lysebu paper, as distributed prior to the conference, does not mention the concept of virtual attributes. In fact, a preliminary version of that mechanism was developed in April–May and is described in a paper dated May (Dahl and Nygaard, 1967b), also available at Lysebu. The concept was discussed at the conference, and a short section on virtuals has been added to the paper as it appears in the conference proceedings (Buxton, 1968). (This conference report is still today quite refreshing reading.)

We had seen that the class/subclass facility made it possible to define generalized object classes, which could be specialized by defining subclasses containing additional declared *properties*. However, the concatenation mechanism was not quite flexible enough for adding details to the *operation rules*. Something like procedure parameters still seemed to be needed for classes.

As discussed in Section 2.3.3 the ALGOL-like call-by-name parameters were out of the question for reasons of security and storage allocation strategy: the actual parameter could be lost during the lifetime of an object. The problem then was to find a name-parameter-like mechanism that would guarantee a safe place for the actual parameter. After much trial and error we hit on the virtual quantity concept where the actual would have to be declared *in the object itself,* but at a deeper subclass level than that of the virtual specification. Now generalized objects could be defined whose behavior pattern could be left partly unspecified in a prefix class body. Different subclasses could contain different actual procedure declarations.

The implementation efficiency of virtual quantities was good, since no change of environment was needed to access a virtual from within the object. Unfortunately we chose to model the virtual specifications after the parameter specifications of ALGOL, which meant that the parameters of a virtual procedure had to be run time checked.

It has later been shown that virtual quantities make it possible to directly use class hierarchies for top-down programming, but in a fairly clumsy way. Consequently this way of using classes has not received much attention.

3.3. The Common Base Conference

As reported in Section 3.5 a SIMULA 67 Common Base Conference (CBC) was arranged June 5–9, 1967, at the NCC, two weeks after the Lysebu conference.

The following papers were submitted to the CBC:

1. The Lysebu paper (Dahl and Nygaard, 1967a, Mar.),
2. "SIMULA 67 Common Base Proposal" (Dahl and Nygaard 1967b, May), and
3. "Proposals for Consideration by the SIMULA 67 Common Base Conference" (Dahl and Nygaard, 1967c, June).

The most controversial subject discussed at the CBC was what we called "in-line" declarations. We had realized that the indirect naming of objects through reference variables often represented wasteful overhead for the programmer as well as the program execution (not to speak of the garbage collecting effort). It would be useful to have a direct naming mechanism, in fact treating objects as ("in-line") compound *variables*. The Common Base Proposal, Section 8.3 reads:

8.3 In-line declarations

8.3.1 Syntax

⟨in-line object⟩ ::= ⟨identifier⟩ ⟨actual parameter part⟩

⟨in-line declaration⟩ ::= ⟨class id⟩ ⟨in-line object⟩|

⟨in-line declaration⟩, ⟨in-line object⟩

8.3.2 Semantics

A class identifier, underlined, may be used as a declarator. The identifier of a declared ⟨in-line object⟩ is a qualified ref variable, initialized to refer to a generated object of the stated class, and with the given actual parameters.

Assignment to the variable is not allowed. (Procedure declarations local to the class may be used to simulate en-bloc assignment of attributes.)

The implementor has the option to represent the declared variable by the associated object itself, rather than by the associated ref value.

(The important problem of reference variables elsewhere in the system pointing to an in-line object was not mentioned. To allow that would have grave consequences for the garbage collector.)

The proposals of (2) were, however, to be replaced by a set of much more ambitious proposals, (3), intended to unify the concepts of "class" and "type." These ideas were to some extent inspired by discussions at the Lysebu conference, and in particular the papers of Garwick (1968) and McNeley (1968). (Actually the paper presented to the CBC was an iteration of (3) produced during two hectic days and nights prior to the CBC. This paper has been lost.) Essentially the proposals were as follows:

1. Let C be a class identifier. Then

$$\mathbf{def}(C) \ V \ \langle\text{actual parameter part}\rangle$$

is a declaration which defines a variable named V of "type" C.V is an (in-line) object of class C initialized according to its operation rule and the actual parameter part. Thus, the above declaration is comparable to

$$\mathbf{ref}(C) \ X; \text{ followed by } X := \mathbf{new} \ C \ \langle\text{actual parameter part}\rangle$$

except that the latter generates an "off-line" object. The types C and ref(C) are distinct and an operation like X := V is therefore illegal. An ad hoc restriction on the class body (that it must contain no occurrence of the reference expression "this C") ensures that no reference values pointing to an in-line object can ever occur. Given a reference value X of type ref (C) to an object, then "X." is an expression of type C denoting that object. (Since it is mentally difficult to distinguish correctly between a reference to, or "name on," a thing and the thing itself, we felt there should be a notational difference forcing the programmer to precise thinking.)

2. Each basic type is a predefined class with local data and procedures defined outside the high level language. There is a one-to-one correspondence between operator symbols and a certain preselected set of identifiers (such as "becomes," "plus," greater," etc.). Thus a declaration line "integer a" means

$$\mathbf{def}(\text{integer})a;$$

where "integer" is a predefined class. And a statement like "a := b∗c+d" means

$$a.becomes(b.times(c).plus\,(d))$$

where the closing parentheses are positioned according to operator priority, and the identifiers refer to procedures local to the class "integer." A consequence of this transformation rule was that operations such as :=, =, +, etc., would be available for a user defined type if and only if the class body contained procedures with the corresponding names.

3. Whenever a formal parameter is specified to be of type C, a corresponding actual parameter must belong to C or to a subtype (subclass) of C. This proposal opened up for a lot of interesting possibilities such as introducing side effects to assignment operations on variables belonging to subtypes of the basic ones (McNeley, 1968), without changing their meaning as operands in basic type expressions. It also made it possible to unify the concepts of function procedure and prefixed class; an instance of the procedure would be an object whose prefix part played the role of the function value.

No doubt the above proposals were prematurely presented. Although the final proposal document has been lost, we are sure that we had not managed to work through all the consequences for the language and its implementation during the two short weeks available between the Lysebu conference and the CBC.

Anyway, we made a valiant attempt to get our new proposals accepted by the CBC, but failed. The parties who had committed themselves to implementing the new language felt they were too complicated and cautiously rejected them, (NCC, 1967). We were in no position to overrule these parties. It was crucial for the continuation of the whole SIMULA 67 effort to get at least one major manufacturer (in this case Control Data, see Section 3.5) to commit itself to implementations. Unfortunately the simpler proposal of (2) was swept aside too.

The concept of virtual quantities was thoroughly discussed by the CBC. The discussion led to an interesting and nontrivial improvement of our own proposal. By a slight change of the binding rule for actuals it became possible to *redefine* previously bound virtuals. An actual declaration provided at a deep subclass level of an object would have precedence (throughout the whole object) over definitions at more shallow levels. This meant added flexibility in designing application languages. "Default" actuals for virtual procedures, provided at an application language level, now were replaceable in user defined subclasses. For instance, default error printouts might be replaced by corrective actions applicable in user defined situations.

One beauty of the principle of required qualification of references lies in the fact that it solves completely, at least for disjoint classes, one of the problems of language consistency discussed in Section 2.3.3. No object can lose its textual environment by active deletion of block/procedure instances, because any reference to an object must occur within the textual scope of the object class declaration and is therefore embedded in that environment.

However, in order to utilize the full capabilities of class concatenation it was deemed necessary to allow prefix sequences to cross block levels. In particular, predefined classes declared nonlocally to a user program, must be available for prefixing within the program. But then consistency is lost, since an object belonging to a local subclass may lose part of its textual environment if pointed to by a nonlocal reference. In order to prevent this phenomenon we had to devise an ad hoc rule restricting reference assignments (and class pre-fixing), the so called "Rule R" (see, e.g., Dahl and Nygaard, 1967d), Section 4.1.2:

> A reference assignment is legal only if the left hand quantity is declared within the scope of the class qualifying the right hand side and all its subclasses, scopes defined after effecting all concat-enations implied by class and block prefixes.

(It must be admitted that the wording of this rule is more compact than understandable). The rule would (as far as we know!) restore full security and consistency, even if unquali-fied references were allowed. However, it was very unnatural, too implicit, and therefore very difficult to grasp, to observe, and to enforce. A simpler rule of "same block level," called "Rule S," was apparently too restrictive:

> All classes of a prefix sequence must belong to the same block head (which may be that of a concatenated class or a prefixed block). Qualification is required for all references.

These matters were discussed by the CBC, but no recommendation was given, except to forbid unqualified references. Soon afterwards it occurred to us, however, that the es-sential capabilities of the prefixing mechanism could be salvaged and full security retained by applying the Rule S to class prefixes, but not to block prefixes. Sufficient flexibility could now be obtained by embedding predefined classes in a textually enclosing class C, say, (also predefined). Now these classes could be made available for class prefixing in any desired block head by prefixing that block by the class C. Since that technique would be the standard way of implementing application languages in any case, we were fairly happy. Still, there are situations in which Rule S is a nuisance.

Our various proposals to the CBC contained nothing about string handling and input–output. The CBC unanimously stressed the importance of having such facilities included as well defined parts of a "Common Base Language." Consequently a working group was established consisting of members of the implementation teams and persons from the NCC. One hoped that the class/subclass concept might lead to fruitful constructs. The proposals of the group should be submitted for approval to the "SIMULA 67 Standards Group" (see Section 3.5), which was also established by the CBC. Of the remaining re-corded decisions of the CBC (NCC, 1967) one notes a recommendation on the syntax of "external class" declarations (for the inclusion of separately compiled classes). Every-thing considered, the CBC played a very constructive role during the birth of SIMULA 67. Among other things it helped the first implementation efforts to get off the ground by re-jecting our premature proposals. However, if the CBC had been delayed a couple of months, SIMULA 67 might well have contained a general type concept. As an immediate follow-up of the CBC we produced a document called "The SIMULA 67 Common Base Definition," dated June 1967 (Dahl and Nygaard, 1967d), which, except for the missing string and I/O facilities, gives a surprisingly accurate description of the language as it exists today. In the preface are listed those whom we felt at that time had given us useful advice: C. A. R. Hoare, Jan V. Garwick, Per Martin Kjeldaas, Don Knuth, John Buxton, John Laski, Pat Blunden, and Christopher Strachey.

The Rule S, which later was made part of the Common Base, is mentioned as an "op-tional restriction." The introduction of the document refers to plans for a "full SIMULA 67 language," as opposed to the Common Base, which would contain a unification of the type and class concepts. But this dream was never to be realized.

3.4. The SIMULA 67 Common Base.

According to the CBC the SIMULA 67 Common Base (SCB) had been frozen in June, except for string handling and I/O facilities. The responsibility for the latter was assigned to a working group reporting to the SIMULA Standards Group (SSG). In actual fact a few adjustments were made to the SCB during the autumn of 1967, along with the development of the new facilities. But all decisions and proposals were made in contact with the implementation teams headed by P. M. Kjeldaas in Oslo and J. Newey in Paris (see Section 3.5).

At NCC Bjørn Myhrhaug was given responsibility for the development of the string and I/O proposals. Myhrhaug had for a long time been most useful as a partner in the implementation work and as a "sounding board" in our language discussions. Now he became a member of the design team and thus a co-author of SIMULA 67.

In October Myhrhaug had his first string handling proposals ready (Myhrhaug, 1967b). There were three alternatives, two of which introduced in-line strings of compile time defined lengths as a new primitive type. We rejected both of them for two reasons: insufficient flexibility, and the fact that they were based on concepts unrelated to those of the SCB.

The third proposal was based on classes and a new basic type *character*. There were two classes, "string descriptor" and "string," the latter containing a character array, the former identifying a substring of a string object and a "scan pointer" for sequential character access, together with various operators declared as procedures. We felt that these constructs would provide good flexibility and could be implemented with reasonable execution efficiency, also on computers without direct character accessing capability. The price was a certain amount of overhead in run time data structure, and a syntactic overhead which was unacceptable. The latter could, however, be alleviated by defining "string descriptor" as an "in-line object type" using operator notation for operations like "becomes" and "equal." True enough, this new construct could not be defined within the SCB, but it was consistent with our (still evolving) plans for a "complete" SIMULA 67 with classlike types. The new type was later called *text* in order to avoid confusion with ALGOL's string concept.

The input–output facilities were in some ways easier to design. The proposals converged on a hierarchy of classes corresponding to different kinds of files. (However, some details in the "printfile" class kept worrying the SSG for several years.)

The first meeting of the SIMULA 67 Standards Group was held in Oslo, February 10, 1968. The last of a series of proposals by Myhrhaug (1968) was presented at the meeting, together with recommendations by the Working Group. The proposals were approved (SIMULA Standards Group, 1968), and the NCC was instructed to "provide a new SIMULA 67 Common Base Definition paper within 6 weeks." The NCC actually worked twice as long to produce it. The first complete and authoritative Common Base Definition is dated May 1968 (Dahl *et al.*, 1968a).

It so happened that the first batch of the new SCB documents came out of the printing mill the day before the ten-year anniversary conference for ALGOL in Zurich. Myhrhaug arrived late for the conference with 45 kg overweight baggage and reported difficulties in passing the customs control. The inspector had become very suspicious when, on opening one of the books, his eyes fell upon the following example (Dahl *et al.*, 1968a, pp. 22–27):

class hashing; **virtual: procedure** hash; . . .

One adjustment to the old SCB, approved by the February meeting of the SSG, deserves to be mentioned, since it is related to basic ways of thinking of objects, values and references. We had discussed during the summer of 1967 whether references were so different from other kinds of operands that they needed a special set of operator symbols. The answer had been a tentative "yes, perhaps," but the possible gain in clarity had not seemed important enough to warrant the expense. Faced with our new text type the old question appeared in a new light. A text could either be thought of as a string descriptor ("text reference") or as a character sequence ("text value"), and we needed some notation for distinguishing between them. The operators ":−," "==," and "=/=" were chosen for reference assignment and reference equality/inequality, respectively. It was then natural to apply these operator symbols to object references as well. A similar distinction was made between parameter transmission "by reference" and "by value." This had only syntactic consequences for the old SCB, since an object transmitted by reference is the same as an object reference transmitted by value.

At the beginning of 1968 we regarded the Common Base as a statue with one leg missing. Our plan was to "complete" the language and provide an experimental in-house Univac implementation by extending the Common Base compiler now in progress on our UNIVAC 1107 (Nygaard, 1967). We were now thinking in terms of class declarations giving rise to in-line references to off-line objects, and analogous "type" declarations giving rise to in-line objects. (*text* could be seen as a type prefixed by a class, whose objects were references with additional descriptive information.) Some of our views at the time are expressed in a letter from OJD to Tony Hoare (Dahl, 1968a).

We had had some correspondence with Hoare during the preceding autumn, and through him we had seen some of his correspondence with Niklaus Wirth. This contact had been very stimulating and refreshing. We invited Hoare and Wirth to a three day meeting, February 4–6, to discuss types and classes (Nygaard, 1968a). We also wanted to consult them on our string handling and I/O proposals, about to be submitted for approval by the SSG. They kindly accepted our invitation, and we had a series of discussions which were very useful to us, since they clarified our own thoughts considerably. It turned out that their views and ours differed so much (Wirth, 1968) that we could not follow their advice in specific matters (which implies that neither of the two is responsible for any shortcomings of SIMULA 67's text and I/O facilities).

One concrete result of the meeting was that the **while** statement of PASCAL was included in the Oslo compilers and later proposed as a "recommended extension" of the SCB. It is now a part of the SCB.

The Common Base paper consumed most of our time during the spring. From the summer of 1968 on there were no resources for a continuation of work on the "complete SIMULA 67." OJD moved to the University of Oslo, KN had to concentrate on "SIMULA politics," and the implementors had enough problems to cope with within the Common Base.

3.5. The Fight for the SIMULA 67 Compilers.

Fairy tales end with the heroine getting her prince, and everybody (except the witch) living happily ever after. As language designers we often feel that people believe that one has "succeeded" and that a language "exists" as soon as it is defined, and that the subsequent implementation is a mere triviality, even if time consuming. The implementors very often are only briefly mentioned in a preface to some report.

In fact it is when the language is reasonably well described and thus the implementation task defined, that the main, tedious, and frustrating part of the struggle for a language's existence really starts. The actual writing of compilers is one aspect of this struggle. To obtain the resources necessary for this work is another aspect, to establish an organizational framework for distribution, maintenance, language standardization and development, is a third aspect. Finally, a fourth one is to make the language known and used.

We believe that these aspects of the histories of the various programming languages are usually quite dramatic and very often without a happy ending. We also suspect that this is the case even when large, powerful organizations are involved.

In the case of SIMULA 67 very scarce resources were at hand. The NCC is a small institute in a small country, without a worldwide organizational network to support its activities. We are not presenting the true history of SIMULA 67 unless we tell this second part of the story, at the same time mentioning a few of those who contributed to SIMULA 67's survival.

SIMULA I was originally only considered as a system description and simulation language, not as a general programming language. SIMULA I was implemented for UNIVAC 1100 series computers, later on also for Burroughs B5500 and URAL 16.

Our ambitions for SIMULA 67 were much higher: we wanted SIMULA 67 to become an "existing" general programming language, "existing" in the sense that it was available on most of the major computer systems, being used over a long period of time by a substantial number of people throughout the world and having a significant impact upon the development of future programming languages. We felt, of course, that SIMULA 67 was worth fighting for. What were our resources?

In 1968 NCC entered a difficult reorganization period. (The NCC is described in Section 1). From 1963 on NCC had been operating a UNIVAC 1107 and acted also as a computer service bureau. Now the 1107 was sold, and NCC was itself to become a user of other organizations' computers. A number of employees associated with our function as supplier of computing power left the institute. Even if NCC now was supposed to focus upon research and development work, large new long-range projects were not particularly popular in this turbulent period.

As mentioned earlier, the SIMULA I ideas were not received with enthusiasm in NCC's environment. The reception of SIMULA I in the professional world had made it difficult to maintain that the language was a poor one and its designers incompetent. This time it was stated (without any knowledge of the new language) that

1. Obviously SIMULA 67 was a wonderful language, but
2. Programming languages would have an average life time of about five years. Consequently, SIMULA 67 should not be implemented by NCC unless we could be certain of covering the total expenses by sales income over a five year period.

We were convinced that the language situation would be different in the coming decade from what it had been in the previous one. Neither users nor computer manufacturers would be willing to accept a stream of new languages. Also, in the research world it would be demanded that what had been achieved in the sixties should now be consolidated and evaluated through practical use of the most advanced high-level languages which had been developed.

We felt that in the next decade a large number of languages would cease to "exist," and that only about a dozen would survive: COBOL and FORTRAN because of conservatism and the colossal investment in programs written in these languages, PL/I because of IBM support, and then, at a lower scale of usage, some ten other languages. We wanted SIMULA 67 to be in that group.

SIMULA I had been developed during NCC's expansion years in the early 1960s, within KN's research department, established in 1963 and named the "Department for Special Projects." This department consisted in 1967 of six persons, the total staff of NCC being about 120 persons at that time.

Even if KN had a decisive influence on the work in the department, it was not possible to allocate more than at most four persons to SIMULA 67 implementations, and not possible to get additional resources from other departments unless such implementations were set up as projects intended to be profitable from a strictly economic point of view.

Another argument against SIMULA 67 implementation projects was a valid one, but greatly exaggerated: A modern, commercial compiler would require investment on a much greater scale than the SIMULA I compiler, and we were told that IBM was using about five hundred man-years on their PL/I effort. We realized that our objectives for SIMULA 67 would require much larger resources than SIMULA I, but could not accept that this should rule out SIMULA 67. (We often quoted the story about the two businessmen debating whether to locate an important software project in the US or in Europe, the question being settled by the remark: "We have to locate the project in Europe, since in the US it is not possible to put together a sufficiently small team.")

To sum up: our resources in manpower and money were very modest, and we had to provide economic arguments for the implementations of SIMULA 67. We had other resources, however: the reputation of SIMULA I, and the fact that SIMULA was linked to ALGOL 60. Simulation was becoming more and more important, and in Europe people started asking for SIMULA when computer purchase contracts were negotiated.

We had defined our objective as making SIMULA 67 a member of the small group of programming languages which in ten year's time would still "exist" in the sense defined earlier. Obviously, we had very great odds against us, and we had to plan very carefully. Some aspects of our strategy and tactics will be described below.

In practice, the language could be regarded as "existing" only if implementations of a high standard were available on the most important computers. In our environment that implied giving top priority to implementations on Control Data, IBM and Univac computers.

By "high standard" we understood:

1. Compilation and run time execution speeds comparable with the most efficient ALGOL 60 compilers.

2. Availability of comprehensive and well written documentation and educational material.

3. The existence and effective operation of distribution and maintenance organizations for the compilers.

We also felt, based upon the fate of ALGOL 60, that the implementations should be compatible as far as possible, and continue to be so. This implied:

1. String handling and input/output facilities should be defined as a part of the SIMULA 67 language.

2. The establishment of an organization which had the exclusive power to state what was "legal SIMULA 67" and adopt changes to that SIMULA 67. This organization had to be set up to provide conservatism, but also such that its members had genuine common interests in the spreading and development of the language.

Compatibility considerations also were important in other respects. Should SIMULA 67 contain ALGOL 60 as a subset? We disagreed with some basic design features of ALGOL 68, and compatibility with that language was ruled out. We also doubted that ALGOL 68 would be accepted by a large proportion of the ALGOL 60 user community and we felt that we could improve certain features of ALGOL 60 in SIMULA 67. On the other hand, ALGOL 60 is a beautiful language and the advantages of staying compatible were indeed very great. We decided that the possibility of running ALGOL 60 programs on SIMULA 67 compilers and of "growing" from ALGOL 60 to SIMULA 67 would attract many ALGOL 60 users. We needed their support, even with the limited size of the ALGOL community, and made only small modifications in the ALGOL 60 part of SIMULA 67.

A minor, but not unimportant point was the name of our new language. SIMULA is an abbreviation of "simulation language," and very obviously so. The new language was a general, high-level programming language and a system description language. In the short run the language would benefit from a name presenting it as an improved version of the simulation language SIMULA. In the long run the SIMULA name possibly might slow down the language's acceptance as a general purpose language. We decided that we were forced to give priority to the short term advantages and named the language SIMULA 67. Today the language suffers from the predicted long range effects.

In the spring of 1967, we did the basic groundwork in the design of the SIMULA 67 run-time system features. At the same time Control Data decided that they wanted SIMULA implemented both on their 3000 and 6000 series of computers because of customer demands. Among the customers were the Kjeller Computer Installation [KCIN, serving the Norwegian Defence Research Establishment (NDRE)] and the University of Oslo.

Negotiations between NCC and Control Data (acting through Control Data Norway) were started on March 1, 1967, and a contract was signed on May 23, 1967 (Agreement, 1967). According to this contract and discussions with Control Data:

1. Control Data intended to implement SIMULA 67. The 6000 series compiler would be implemented by Control Data, Europe. The 3000 series compiler would be implemented by KCIN.

2. At the insistence of Svein A. Øvergaard, director of KCIN, a firm "SIMULA 67 Common Base" language definition should specify what was to be implemented. A SIMULA Common Base Conference should meet "within the first ten days of June 1967."

3. A new organization named the "SIMULA 67 Standards Group" (SSG) was to be established. Eligible for membership of the SSG would be organizations which were responsible for development and/or maintenance of SIMULA 67 compilers. NCC would be an ex officio member and have the right to veto decisions in the SSG. Control Data should apply for membership. (The statutes of SSG are found in Statutes, 1967.)

4. NCC would provide SIMULA 67 implementation guidance to Control Data.

This was the initial platform for the SIMULA 67 implementation efforts. In June the University of Oslo, through its Computer Department headed by Per Ofstad, joined the project. The 3000 series work was carried out in a cooperation between KCIN ("upper" 3000 series) and the University ("lower" 3000 series).

In order to make the initial and basic definition of SIMULA 67, named the "SIMULA 67 Common Base Language", and to set up the SSG, the "SIMULA 67 Common Base Conference" convened at the NCC in the period June 5–9. Present at the conference were representatives from Control Data, KCIN, people from the University of Oslo, and some individual computer scientists invited by the NCC. The conference succeeded in making the necessary basic decisions, deferred certain decisions for further study, and established the SSG, with Control Data and NCC as the initial members, KN being the first chairman. (Today the SSG has ten member organizations representing active implementations). Some of the decisions at the conference were rather important and have been discussed earlier in this paper.

The *real* freezing of SIMULA 67 happened during the autumn of 1967. *Formally* the freezing was achieved by decisions made at the SSG meeting in Oslo on February 10, 1968 (see Section 3.4).

We also planned from the outset that an "Association of SIMULA Users" (ASU) should be the framework for contact between the end users of SIMULA and for channelling their demands and complaints to the SSG and its members (having compiler maintenance responsibility). The ASU was established five years later, in September 1972, with Robin Hills being Chairman the first two years. ASU has since then had annual conferences and a series of workshops on a wide range of issues. (The first conference was in Oslo, the second in Monte Carlo). The present active membership is approximately 500.

The last element of the organizational strategy was the SIMULA Newsletter. After a few abortive attempts (NCC, 1968b) the Newsletter has been published regularly by the NCC since May 1972 and is now distributed to approximately 1000 subscribers. The reasons for the delays in setting up the ASU and the Newsletter were simple: we had to economize carefully with our scarce manpower resources and we did not get SIMULA users in any quantity until 1971.

In the beginning of 1968 the SIMULA 67 Common Base Language was quite well defined and the initial stage of the organizational plan in operation. Later on that year OJD became the first Professor of Informatics at the University of Oslo. He participated in the Control Data 3000 series implementations, but was mainly absorbed by the task of building up informatics at the University of Oslo. Also, in the beginning of 1968, the "battle for the compilers" started and lasted till the summer of 1969 when it was finally decided that NCC should implement and market SIMULA 67 on the IBM 360/370 computers and complete and market SIMULA 67 for the UNIVAC 1100 series computers.

The Control Data projects started in 1967 and were carried out in Paris under the direction of Jacques Newey (6000 series). In Norway the two 3000 series implementations were run as a joint KCIN/University project under the direction of Per Martin Kjeldaas of KCIN. There was some contact between the Oslo and Paris teams. In Oslo the work on the lower 3000 series compiler was pushed ahead, since the test facilities were better at the University. Both compilers were, however, ready in the spring of 1969 and turned out to satisfy the "high standard" criteria for efficiency stated earlier.

The Norwegian teams had some financial support from Control Data Europe. In return Control Data Europe obtained the right to use and distribute the 3000 series compilers.

The University and KCIN had maintenance contracts for their respective compilers. The 3000 series team directed by Kjeldaas consisted of Dag Belsnes, Ole Johnny Dahle, Øivind Hjartøy, Øystein Hope, Ole Jarl Kvammen, Hans Christian Lind, Åmund Lunde, Terje Noodt, Tore Pettersen, and Arne Wang.

At the NCC the situation was more complex. When the class/subclass concepts were invented, SIMULA 67 emerged and the "SIMULA II" ideas were dropped. Our work in the Department for Special Projects in 1967 and early 1968 was, in addition to the language definition, mainly directed towards the development of the basic design of SIMULA 67 compilers. We were always running implementation studies in parallel with the language design. A concept was not incorporated in the language until we had a sensible way of implementing it. One of the few exceptions was the "type proposal" (Section 3.3). A result of this work was the "SIMULA 67 Implementation Guide" (Dahl and Myhrhaug, 1969). This report contained the results of a quite substantial investment and was regarded as a commercial secret until it was released in 1971. The report was sold as a part of NCC's consultancy contracts with SIMULA 67 implementors. [See KN's letter to Hoare, then working at Elliott–Automation Computers Limited, dated November 3, 1967, for conditions offered (Nygaard, 1967).]

Bjørn Myhrhaug, Sigurd Kubosch, Dag Belsnes, and OJD were active in these design studies. Gradually Sigurd Kubosch (originally from Germany) became more and more involved with the UNIVAC 1100 series compiler, later on joined by Ron Kerr (from Scotland), and they did the main bulk of work on that implementation.

Kubosch and Kerr worked mostly alone and without the major support which the IBM compiler project later received. Their task was made even more difficult because NCC changed from using UNIVAC 1107 (with EXEC II) to UNIVAC 1108 (with EXEC 8) in the middle of the project. A first, rather restricted version was ready in the summer of 1969, being released to Univac, St. Paul, for evaluation purposes and to the Technical University in Trondheim. The compiler was gradually extended and improved. When it was clear that we had a marketable product, and that we had to market it ourselves, we were able to allocate Kubosch and Kerr to write comprehensive documentation. There had been no resources for that earlier. The first commercial delivery of the UNIVAC 1100 series SIMULA System took place in March 1971 to the University of Karlsruhe, West Germany.

In the spring of 1968 it was made clear to us that NCC could only support the production of Univac and IBM SIMULA 67 compilers if we could establish a financial arrangement which secured NCC the same payoff on these products as on our strictly commercial projects. Preferably, NCC should not run any economic risk.

The financial pressure was brought to bear upon SIMULA 67 at a time when NCC, as mentioned earlier, had large reorganizational problems. From a narrow SIMULA 67 point of view this was a lucky circumstance, since the insistent pressure was never followed up by administrative decisions. Time passed by and in the summer of 1969 the work on the Univac compiler and the support for the IBM compiler had developed to a stage beyond "the point of no return."

In the autumn of 1968 Harald Omdal was employed by NCC to assist KN in finding suitable financial arrangements for the two compiler projects. Omdal, former director of the Joint Computing Center of the four largest Norwegian commercial banks, was working as a private consultant. After initial work by Omdal on designing alternatives, he and KN visited in the spring of 1969 a number of large Scandinavian companies to obtain their financial partnership in the production of an IBM 360/370 compiler. We got a pleasant reception, interest in later use of SIMULA 67, and some, but not many positive responses. We were not too surprised. Why should these companies pay in advance for something they could get without risk later? The whole idea of this type of project support had to be abandoned.

We also contacted IBM in Norway and Sweden. Both IBM and we were rather careful in these discussions. IBM wanted to support advanced national programming research in Scandinavia. To accept SIMULA 67 as an IBM-supported language would, however, be a major decision with far-reaching economic implications. Such a decision could only be made at IBM headquarters in the U.S. On our side, we were afraid of giving IBM control over the 360/370 compiler because of the risk of the language and its compiler being put on the shelf.

The results of these contacts were in the end positive and very important. IBM agreed to support the project by granting NCC a very substantial amount of computer time for developing and testing the compiler (40 hours on a 360/75 in Stockholm and 200 hours on a 360/40 in Oslo).

The event which finally triggered off the IBM compiler project occurred in the summer of 1969: the Swedish Agency for Administrative Development (Statskontoret) decided, with the support of the Swedish Defence Research Establishment, to participate in the project through two highly qualified programmers. Jacob Palme played an important role in this decision. The IBM 360/370 SIMULA 67 compiler project was headed by Bjørn Myhrhaug, and the team consisted of Lars Enderin and Stefan Arnborg (from the Swedish Defence Research Establishment), and the NCC employees Francis Stevenson, Paul Wynn, Graham Birtwistle (all from the United Kingdom) and Karel Babcicky (from Czechoslovakia). When Myhrhaug got a leave of absence, Babcicky was project leader for a period. Myhrhaug also was coordinator for both the Univac and IBM projects, being succeeded by Birtwistle. The first public release of the IBM compiler took place in May 1972 (to the governmental data center in Stockholm).

Univac had mixed reactions towards SIMULA 67. From a commercial point of view SIMULA I was a useful but not very important part of their software library. They felt no market demand for an improved language and, in particular, no reason to share SIMULA with other manufacturers From a professional point of view, however, many within Univac were actively interested in getting SIMULA 67. A long series of discussions and contract negotiations with various Univac agencies followed, but a contract was never signed.

We think it can be safely said that the UNIVAC 1100 series and the IBM 360/370 series compilers both satisfy the criteria for "high standard" described earlier. It is interesting to observe that they were developed in two completely different ways. The two-man UNIVAC 1100 series compiler team worked their way with little support, using a long time, and were asked to provide comprehensive documentation at a late stage. The seven man IBM 360/370 series compiler team worked in a well supported and carefully planned project, documenting as they went along. The end result was that both compilers proved efficient and successful and both consumed approximately 15 man-years. Our initial estimate had been 8–10 man-years, assuming no suitable ALGOL 60 compiler available (Nygaard, 1967). We underestimated to some extent the design and programming work and to a great extent the documentation effort.

At the NCC a team of four persons, headed by Karel Babcicky, is now constantly employed in handling our SIMULA activities. For many years Eileen Schreiner has been our "SIMULA secretary" keeping all threads together and serving on the board of the ASU.

We have mentioned that the attitude toward SIMULA I and SIMULA 67 was rather negative in certain parts of NCC's environment. In other parts of that environment, among professional people, the attitude has been mainly positive. Within the NCC itself, SIMULA has had wholehearted and generous support. The period in which (in our opinion) too shortsighted economic considerations threatened the development was quite brief, atypical and had its reasons. Anyhow, an institute organized as the NCC is forced to take economics into account, and the compiler projects represented in the years 1968 – 1971 a significant economic burden for the institute.

Has SIMULA 67 then been an economic success or a failure for the NCC? That is a difficult question to answer, since it is not easy to measure the economic side effects of the SIMULA efforts. The experience gained has been the platform for later, straightforwardly profitable jobs, e.g., other language projects. SIMULA itself has made it possible to do jobs within operational research and data processing which otherwise would have been much more costly or beyond our capabilities. The international acceptance of SIMULA 67 has contributed to the Institute's reputation. In direct money terms, SIMULA 67 has not produced a profit. On the other hand, distributed over the eleven years since 1967, serious losses have not been incurred.

Today it is generally accepted that SIMULA has been a worthwhile effort, both for NCC and its environment. We have since then, in 1973–1975, developed a new type of language—a pure system description language—called DELTA (Holbæk-Hanssen et al., 1975), starting from the SIMULA platform. From DELTA we are now deriving a new systems programming language, called BETA (Kristensen et al., 1977) in cooperation with research workers from the Universities in Århus and Ålborg in Denmark. Whereas DELTA cannot be compiled, BETA of course can. Will the NCC embark upon the implementation of BETA, having had the SIMULA experience? This remains to be seen.

4. Concluding Remarks

The organizers of this conference have suggested that we should discuss our own languages' "implications for current and future languages." We find this difficult because of our personal involvement and think that other research workers are better judges on this subject. However, we are in the lucky situation that we may refer to Peter Wegner's recent article, "Programming Languages—The first 25 years" (Wegner, 1976), which contains many comments on SIMULA 67. Instead, we would like to conclude our paper with some reflections on our experiences from the process of developing a programming language.

In the spring of 1967 a new employee at the NCC in a very shocked voice told the switchboard operator: "Two men are fighting violently in front of the blackboard in the upstairs corridor. What shall we do?" The operator came out of her office, listened for a few seconds and then said: "Relax, it's only Dahl and Nygaard discussing SIMULA". The story is true. The SIMULA 67 language was the outcome of ten months of an almost continuous sequence of battles and cooperation in front of that blackboard—interrupted by intervals when we worked in our neighboring offices (communicating by shouting through the wall if necessary) or at home. (The people arranging this conference asked us to provide material relating to the development of our respective languages. We felt that the best thing we could have done was to bring along that blackboard. But we did not know for certain whether we would be flying a wide-body aircraft.)

In some research teams a new idea is treated with loving care: "How interesting!," "Beautiful!." This was not the case in the SIMULA development. When one of us announced that he had a new idea, the other would brighten up and do his best to kill it off. Assuming that the person who got the idea is willing to fight, this is a far better mode of work than the mode of mutual admiration. We think it was useful for us, and we succeeded in discarding a very large number of proposals. The class/subclass concept was perhaps the only one which was immediately accepted, whereas the virtual concept perhaps was the one which went through the longest sequence of initial rejections before it finally was given a definition acceptable to both of us.

When we started working together, we had quite different backgrounds. KN had quit programming in 1954, at a time when an essential aspect of the art was to program an algorithm with the minimum number of machine code instructions. His reasoning was always related to suitable language mechanisms for the description of systems in the real, physical world. OJD had been working on typical programming tasks and programming language design and implementation, with little experience from the problem area of operational research. In the initial stages of our cooperation we had communication problems. Gradually the area of common knowledge and understanding increased. We believe that our differences turned out to be a useful resource in our work, since each of us developed his own "role" in the team. In this way we were more likely to create ideas together which none of us would have created alone. We have later on both been working in close-knit teams with other people and we have found that we have had to develop other roles in these teams, the resource situation not being the same.

Sometimes we are asked questions like: "Who invented the virtual mechanism?" or "Who got the prefix idea?" Even if an answer could be given it would only tell who brought an idea forward the last of a long sequence of steps, and thus be of little interest. We tried once (when OJD was applying for his current position at the University of Oslo) to sort out at least certain rough areas of "ownership" in our relations to SIMULA I and SIMULA 67. When we found that each of us owned one half of the "reactivation point," we discontinued the effort.

We have been criticized for "dropping" SIMULA 67 after it had been developed. It is said that other people, e.g., Tony Hoare, Jean Ichbiah, Don Knuth, Jacob Palme, have done the real job of promoting the language. This is partially true, and we are grateful for their interest. One reason for the increased use of SIMULA 67 in recent years, especially within the United States, is undoubtedly the very successful DEC 10 implementation produced by a Swedish team in 1973–1974. Arnborg and Enderin, who also took part in the IBM implementation, were key members of that group. Ingrid Wennerström was another important member. Jacob Palme again played a decisive role in initiating the work. OJD's work on structured programming has been based on a SIMULA 67 platform, and has contributed to making SIMULA 67 known in the scientific community. Graham Birtwistle took the main burden in writing a comprehensive SIMULA 67 textbook (Birtwistle *et al.*, 1973). NCC and its staff has invested a substantial effort in promoting SIMULA 67 in many other ways: courses in many countries, publication of the SIMULA Newsletter, contacts with users in general. It was SIMULA 67's simulation capability which made it possible to get support for the implementation of the first set of compilers and to sell these compilers to customers. If we had used our very scarce resources for writing papers and as traveling lecturers, SIMULA 67 might have been a paper language today, not a living one with an active user community.

REFERENCES

The letter P, D, or C following each reference should be understood as follows: P—publication, D—document, C—correspondence.

Agreement (1963) June 1. *Agreement made 1st day of June by and between Sperry Rand Corporation (Univac) and the Royal Norwegian Council for scientific and industrial research (by NCC).* (D).

Agreement (1967). *Agreement on implementation of the SIMULA 67 language between Control Data A/S Norway and the Norwegian Computing Center, Oslo May 23, 1967.* NCC Doc. (D).

Agreement (1969) September. *Draft outline for a SIMULA 67 agreement between UNIVAC and the Norwegian Computing Center.* (D).

Birtwistle, G. M., Dahl, O.-J., Myhrhaug, B., and Nygaard, K. (1973). *SIMULA BEGIN.* Studentlitteratur, Lund, Sweden and Auerbach Publ., Philadelphia, Pennsylvania. (P).

Blunden, G. P. (1968). Implicit Interaction in Process Models. In Buxton, J. N., ed, *Simulation Programming Languages,* pp. 283–287. Amsterdam: North-Holland Publ. (P).

Buxton, J. N., ed. (1968). *Simulation Programming Languages.* Proceedings of the IFIP Working Conference on Simulation Programming Languages, Oslo, 1967. Amsterdam: North-Holland Publ. (P).

Buxton, J. N., and Laski, J. G. (1962). Control and Simulation Language. *Computer Journal* 5(5). (P).

Christopher, C. A. (1964) February 28. Letter to Leif K. Olaussen, Director NCC. (C).

Christopher, C. A. (1965) December 15. Letter to Leif Olaussen, Director, NCC. (C).

Clark, I. A. (1966) January 27. Letter to Leif Olaussen, Director, NCC. (C).

Clark, I. A. (1967) January 24. Letter to Kristen Nygaard, NCC. (C).

Dahl, O.-J. (1963) November. *The SIMULA Storage Allocation Scheme.* NCC Doc. 162. (D).

Dahl, O.-J. (1964) February/March. *The SIMULA Data Structures.* NCC Doc. (D).

Dahl, O.-J. (1968a) January 24. Letter to C. A. R. Hoare, Elliott-Automation Computers, Herts., England. (C).

Dahl, O.-J. (1968b). Discrete Event Simulation Languages. In Genuys, F., ed., *Programming Languages,* pp. 349–395. New York: Academic Press. (P).

Dahl, O.-J. (1970). Decomposition and Classification in Programming Languages. In *Linguaggi nella Società e nella Tecnica.* Milan: Edizioni di Comunita. (P).

Dahl, O.-J., and Hoare, C. A. R. (1972). Hierarchical Program Structures. In Dahl, O.-J., Dijkstra, E. W., and Hoare, C. A. R., *Structured Programming,* pp. 175–220. New York: Academic Press. (P).

Dahl, O.-J., and Myhrhaug, B. (1969) June. *SIMULA 67 Implementation Guide.* NCC Publ. No. S-9. (D).

Dahl, O.-J., and Nygaard, K. (1963) May. *Preliminary presentation of the SIMULA Language (as of May 18th 1963) and some examples of network descriptions.* NCC Doc. (D).

Dahl, O.-J., and Nygaard, K. (1964a) March. *The SIMULA Language. Specifications 17 March 1964.* NCC Doc. (D).

Dahl, O.-J., and Nygaard, K. (1964b) July. *The SIMULA Project.* Tech. Prog. Rep. 1, July 1964. NCC Doc. (D).

Dahl, O.-J., and Nygaard, K. (1965) May. *SIMULA—A language for programming and description of discrete event systems. Introduction and user's manual.* NCC Publ. No. 11. (D).

Dahl, O.-J., and Nygaard, K. (1966) September. SIMULA—an ALGOL-based Simulation Language. *CACM* 9(9): 671–678. (P).

Dahl, O.-J., and Nygaard, K. (1967a) March. *Class and subclass declarations.* NCC document. (As presented at the IFIP Working Conference on Simulation Programming Languages, Oslo May 1967.) (D).

Dahl, O.-J., and Nygaard, K. (1967b) May. *SIMULA 67 Common Base Proposal.* NCC Doc. (D).

Dahl, O.-J., and Nygaard, K. (1967c) June. *Proposals for consideration by the SIMULA 67 Common Base Conference, June 1967.* (D). [See author's comment on pp. 465–466. Ed.]

Dahl, O.-J., and Nygaard, K. (1967d) June. *SIMULA 67 Common Base Definition.* NCC Doc. (D).

Dahl, O.-J., and Nygaard, K. (1968). Class and subclass declarations. In Buxton, J. N., ed., *Simulation Programming Languages,* pp. 158–171. Amsterdam: North-Holland Publ. (P).

Dahl, O.-J., Myhrhaug, B., and Nygaard, K. (1966). *SIMULA. Simula Tracing System.* NCC Doc. (D).

Dahl, O.-J., Myhrhaug, B., and Nygaard, K. (1968a) May. *The SIMULA 67 Common Base Language*. NCC Publ. S-2. (D).

Dahl, O.-J., Myhrhaug, B., and Nygaard, K. (1968b) October. *Some uses of the External Class Concept in SIMULA 67.* (Presented by P. M. Kjeldaas at the NATO sponsored conference on Software Engineering, Garmisch, Germany, 7th–11th October 1968); referred in the conference report *Software Engineering, 1968*, Naur, P., and Randell, B., eds., p. 157. NCC Doc. (D).

Dahl, O.-J., Myhrhaug, B., and Nygaard, K. (1970) October. *Common Base Language*. NCC Publ. No. S-22. (Revised edition of S-2.) (P).

Dijkstra, E. W. (1968) May. The Structure of THE Multiprogramming System. *CACM* 11(5). (P).

Garwick, J. V. (1968). Do we need all these languages? In Buxton, J. N., ed., *Simulation Programming Languages*, pp. 143–154. Amsterdam: North-Holland Publ. (P).

Gorchow, N. (1966) January 10. Telegram to Leif Olaussen, NCC. (C).

Gordon, G. (1962) September. A General Purpose Systems Simulator. *IBM Systems Journal* 1. (P).

Hegna, H., Lund, O. J., and Nygaard, K. (1968) June. *User's experience with the SIMULA language*. NCC Doc. (D).

Hoare, C. A. R. (1965) November. Record Handling. In *ALGOL Bulletin* No. 21. (P).

Hoare, C. A. R. (1966) May. Further Thoughts on Record Handling. In *ALGOL Bulletin* No. 23. (P).

Hoare, C. A. R. (1968). Record Handling. In Genuys, F., ed., *Programming Languages*, pp. 291–347. New York: Academic Press. (P).

Hoare, C. A. R. (1972). Proof of Correctness of Data Representations. *Acta Informatica* 1:271–281. (P).

Hoare, C. A. R. (1974) October. Monitors: an operating system structuring concept. *CACM* 17(10): 548–557. (P).

Holbæk-Hanssen, E., Håndlykken, P., and Nygaard, K. (1975) September. *System Description and the DELTA Language*. DELTA Project Rep. No. 4, NCC Publ. No. 523. Oslo: Norwegian Computing Center. (P).

Ichbiah, J. D., and Morse, S. P. (1969) December. *General Concepts of the SIMULA 67 Programming Language*. DR. SA. 69. 132 ND. Compagnie Internationale pour l'Informatique. (P).

Jonassen, A., and Dahl, O.-J. (1975). Analysis of an Algorithm for Priority Queue Administration. *BIT* 15(4): 409–422. (P).

Knuth, D. E., and McNeley, J. L. (1964a) August. SOL—A Symbolic Language for General Purpose Simulation. *IEEE Transactions on Electronic Computers* ED-13(4): 401–408. (P).

Knuth, D. E., and McNeley, J. L. (1964b) August. A Formal Definition of SOL. *IEEE Transactions on Electronic Computers* ED-13(4): 409–414. (P)

Kristensen, B. B., Madsen, O. L., and Nygaard, K. (1977) September. *BETA Language Development*. Survey Rep. 1. November 1976. (Revised version, September 1977.) RECAU-76-77, DAIMI PB-65, NCC Publ. No. 559. (P).

Markowitz, H. M., Hausner, B., and Karr, H. W. (1963). *SIMSCRIPT, A Simulation Programming Language*. Englewood Cliffs, New Jersey: Prentice-Hall. (P).

McNeley, J. L. (1968). Compound Declarations. In Buxton, J. N., ed., *Simulation Program Languages*, pp. 292–303. Amsterdam: North-Holland Publ. (P).

Murphy, J. S. (1968) July 10. Letter to Kristen Nygaard, NCC. (C).

Myhrhaug, B. (1965). *Sequencing Set Efficiency*. Working Paper. (D).

Myhrhaug, B. (1967a) April 25. Letter to I. A. Clark, Systems Programming, Univac, Minnesota. (C).

Myhrhaug, B. (1967b) October. *A note on string handling facilities in SIMULA 67 Common Base*. NCC Publ. No. D24. (D).

Myhrhaug, B. (1968) January. *Proposal for string and input/output definition in SIMULA 67 Common Base. Preliminary presentation*. NCC Publ. No. 212. (D).

Naur, P., *et al.* (1960) May. ALGOL 60 Report. *CACM* 3(5). (P).

Naur, P., *et al.* (1963) January. Revised ALGOL Report. *CACM* 6(1): 1–17. (P).

NCC (1967) June. *Recommendations from the SIMULA 67 Common Base Conference, NCC, June 1967*. (D).

NCC (1968a). *1107/1108 SIMULA 67 Project*. Internal Information No. 1, July 22. (D).

NCC (1968b) July 26. *SIMULA Newsletter* No. 1. (D).

Nickitas, J. W. (1965) September 13. Letter to Kristen Nygaard, NCC. (C).

Nygaard, K. (1962a) January 5. Letter to Charles Salzmann, CFRO, Paris. (C).

Nygaard, K. (1962b) September 24. *Diskret-begivenhets nettverk* (Discrete event networks). Note, in Norwegian. (D).

Nygaard, K. (1963a). SIMULA, An Extension of ALGOL to the Description of Discrete Event Networks. In *Proceedings of the IFIP Congress, 62*, pp. 520–522. Amsterdam: North-Holland Publ. (P).

Nygaard, K. (1963b) April 17. Letter to C. A. Christopher, Director of Procurement, Univac (C).

Nygaard, K. (1963c) May 18. Letter to A. M. Paster, Manager Systems Research, Univac, New York. (C).

Nygaard, K. (1963d). A Status Report on SIMULA—A Language for the Description of Discrete-event Networks. In *Proceedings of the Third International Conference on Operational Research,* pp. 825–831. London: English Universities Press. (P).

Nygaard, K. (1963e) September 19. *Opparbeidelse av kompetanse innenfor Real-time Systemer* (Building up competence on real-time systems). Note, in Norwegian. (D).

Nygaard, K. (1965a) August 15. *The Software Contract between UNIVAC and the Norwegian Computing Center.* NCC Doc. (D).

Nygaard, K. (1965b). *Report on the use of SIMULA up to December 1965.* NCC Doc. (D).

Nygaard, K. (1966) February 17. Letter to S. M. Haffter, Univac Sperry Rand Corporation, Lausanne. (C).

Nygaard, K. (1967) November 3. Letter to C. A. R. Hoare, Elliott-Automation Computers, Herts., England. (C).

Nygaard, K. (1968a) January 29. Letter to Niklaus Wirth, Rechenzentrum der Universität, Zürich. (C).

Nygaard, K. (1968b) April 2. *En redegjørelse for samarbeidet mellom Det russiske vitenskapsakademi og Norsk Regnesentral om bruk av programmeringsspråket SIMULA i Sovjet* (An account of the cooperation between the Russian Academy of Science and the Norwegian Computing Center on the use in the Soviet Union of the programming language SIMULA). Note, in Norwegian. (D).

Nygaard, K. (1968c) September. *Oversikt over NR's SIMULA-engasjement* (Survey of NCC's commitment to SIMULA). Note, in Norwegian. (D).

Nygaard, K. (1968d) September. *Markedsføring av SIMULA 67* (Marketing of SIMULA 67). Note, in Norwegian. (D).

Nygaard, K. (1969) September 26. Letter to Peter Weil, Manager, Contracts and Pricing, Univac, England. (C).

Nygaard, K., and Dahl, O.-J. (1965). SIMULA—A Language for Describing Discrete Event Systems. In *Proceedings of the IFIP Congress, 65,* Vol. 2, pp. 554–555. Washington, D.C.: Spartan Books; New York: Macmillan. (P).

Palme, J. (1968). A comparison between SIMULA and FORTRAN. *BIT* **8**:203–209. (P).

Paster, A. M. (1962) October 12. Letter to Kristen Nygaard, NCC. (C).

Reitan, B. (1969) September 4. Letter to Kristen Nygaard, NCC. (C).

Roach, (1963) July 3. Telegram to Kristen Nygaard, NCC. (C).

Ross, D. T., and Rodriguez, J. E. (1963). Theoretical Foundations for the Computer-aided Design System. In *Proceedings of the SJCC,* p. 305. (P).

SIMULA Standards Group (1968). *Report from the meeting of the SIMULA Standards Group, held in Oslo, Norway, February 10, 1968.* (D).

Statutes (1967) May 23. *Statutes for the SIMULA Standards Group.* NCC Doc. (D).

Stevenson, F. (1967) November. *LOGIC, A computer program for simulation of digital logic networks.* NCC Doc. (D).

Tocher, K. D. (1963). *The Art of Simulation.* London: English Universities Press. (P).

Wang, A., and Dahl, O.-J. (1971). Coroutine Sequencing in a Block Structured Environment. *BIT* **11**: 425–449. (P).

Wegner, P. (1976) December. Programming Languages—The first 25 years. *IEEE Transactions on Computers* C-**25**(12): 1207–1225. (P).

Weizenbaum, J. (1962) March. Knotted List Structures. *CACM* **5**(3): 161–165. (P).

Wirth, N. (1968) February 14. Letter to Kristen Nygaard, NCC. (C).

TRANSCRIPT OF PRESENTATION

BARBARA LISKOV: Our speaker on SIMULA will be Kristen Nygaard. At the time that SIMULA was developed, Kristen Nygaard was the Director of Research at the Norwegian Computer Center, and apart from his work on SIMULA he was also responsible for building up the NCC, as it's called, as a research institute. He had been working in computing since 1948, and in Operations Research since 1952. Today, Kristen Nygaard, continues as Director of Research at NCC, but directs only his own projects. He also holds the rank of Professor at the University of Oslo, and his current research interests include programming languages and the social aspects of computing.

KRISTEN NYGAARD: During the writing of the paper for this conference, the authors had an abundance of letters from Jean Sammet and the language coordinators, but little communication between themselves. As it turns out, we have each chosen our own style. Those of you who have read our paper will know that it at least partially is in the form of an "action thriller." We are not certain whether it is fun to read or not, but it was on the point of becoming funnier. Two slides illustrate this.

Frame 1 shows a typical passage from the paper—from the "Greek nightclub episode." Observe the words "watching a beautiful belly dancer."

Quotation from the Greek
night club episode
(final version):

"While they were listening to bouzouki music, watching a beautiful belly dancer, Nickitas presented the following informal proposal,....."

Frame 1

Now observe the next to final version of the manuscript, (corrected at the last minute) in which we are not content with passive observation [Frame 2].

Also, our very competent typist felt that the sex angle was not sufficiently well handled. Her feeling materialized in terms of a very resolute insistence on writing SINSCRIPT instead of SIMSCRIPT (a prominent language which to our regret is not presented at this conference).

When one looks at one's own work at a distance, one is able to sort out the essentials and talk briefly. Having had the rather large job of writing our paper, we are in trouble because the SIMULA development once more has become very close. To sum up seven years of rather hard work in 25 minutes has become a difficult task; therefore, you must excuse me for using a manuscript. I will *close* my lecture with acknowledgments of some persons and one important activity outside of our own effort.

I will *start* by stating that SIMULA was, and is, a collective effort by many persons. SIMULA exists as a living language with an active user community, and the reason is a series of good implementations by some exceptionally competent teams. I admired the way in which John Backus brought his team members into the picture, and I wish that I

Quotation from the Greek
night club episode
(original version):

"While they were listening to bouzouki music, washing a beautiful belly dancer, Nikitas presented the following informal proposal,....."

Frame 2

Kristen Nygaard

had been able to do the same thing. I want to mention one name, however, that of Bjørn Myhrhaug, who designed SIMULA's string-handling and input–output; Ole-Johan Dahl and I very much would have liked to see him here.

SIMULA did not start as a programming language, and during all of its development stages reasoning outside traditional programming played an important part in its design. The first ideas came from operational research. My own work in that field told me that we needed a set of concepts and an associated language in terms of which one could understand and describe the complexity of the systems one had to deal with. It was also evident that simulation had to be the main tool for analysis. Consequently, from the very start in 1961, SIMULA was labeled both a system description language and a simulation programming language.

I was working within operations research, and had at the time lost contact with programming after leaving that field in 1954. I realized that I was not competent to design such a language alone, and since I knew Ole-Johan from my time at the Norwegian Defense Research Establishment, I tried to get him interested. I succeeded, and from then on, and through all the important development stages of SIMULA we worked together. It is impossible, even just between us, to find out who was responsible for which language concept. This may sound like a beautiful pastoral scene of peaceful cooperation. It was not. And the following story is true:

In the spring of 1967 a new employee at the Norwegian Computing Center came running into the telephone exchange and, very shocked, told the operator: "Two men are fighting in front of the blackboard on the first floor corridor!" The operator went out of her cubicle, listened for a few seconds, and said, "Relax—it's only Ole-Johan and Kristen discussing SIMULA!"

When we started, Ole-Johan knew much about programming and next to nothing about systems thinking. I knew something about systems and next to nothing about programming. Today Ole-Johan knows much about systems thinking.

SIMULA started from a mathematically oriented concept of a network consisting of passive customers flowing through a network of active stations. However, we realized that the processing and decision rules to be described and simulated made it necessary that the language, quoting from a very early document, "had to include a general algorithmic language such as ALGOL or FORTRAN." John Backus said in his speech yesterday that language design was a relatively easy part of the task. I understood him that way. That was not the case with the two SIMULA languages. It was a long and tedious process of working and reworking our concepts before we gradually arrived at the SIMULA of today.

At this point I want to mention another important aspect of our method of working. We always discussed how to implement as we went along, and never accepted anything unless we knew it could be implemented efficiently.

Our network concept dissolved for two reasons: we discovered that we could regard the networks as consisting of active customers and passive stations equally well as the opposite, what we labeled a "dual view." We then realized that an in-between approach in many situations was very useful, and also discovered many situations which couldn't be described well by the network concept.

At this stage, the influence of ALGOL 60 became more and more prominent. It had at earlier stages been both an inspiration and an obstacle. We found the stack to be the obvious way of organizing a system component's action sequence. We believed, and it is specifically stated in our SIMULA contract with Univac, that we should implement SIMULA through a preprocessor to ALGOL 60.

In the spring of 1963 we were almost suffocated by the single-stack structure of ALGOL. Then Ole-Johan developed a new storage management scheme in the summer and autumn of 1963. The preprocessor idea was dropped, and we got a new freedom of choice. In February 1964 the process concept was created, which is SIMULA 67's class and object concept (but integrated at that time in simulation facilities, and without a subclass feature).

Frame 3 sums up some essential facts about SIMULA I. When we moved on to SIMULA 67 we had realized that SIMULA also was a powerful general programming language. Sometimes it is remarked that SIMULA's usefulness as a tool for implementing data types was a welcome lucky coincidence. I do not agree because many of the uses to which SIMULA has been put are the logical and necessary consequences of the system approach married to the ALGOL block concept.

It is true, however, that we did not grasp all of the implications of SIMULA at the time of creating its concepts. The transition from SIMULA I to SIMULA 67 is described in our paper, and I only want to summarize this by the next slide [Frame 4]. When we developed SIMULA we were not concerned with most of the questions which were essential to the ALGOL 60 fathers. We more or less took the algorithmic capabilities of ALGOL 60 for granted. Alan Perlis said to me yesterday that we should have developed SIMULA as the common superstructure for both ALGOL, FORTRAN, and possibly other languages. That was also our initial idea. But as our insight in what we regarded as a proper systems approach increased, this became more and more impossible. The ALGOL block concept which, with its integration of data, patterns for actions (procedure declarations) and actions became the cornerstone of our thinking.

At this stage, I want to illustrate what I mean by "system thinking." Our main reference frame was a set of examples of systems in the world around us: job shops, airports, epidemics, harbors, etc. For this reason, the dynamic systems created by the program execution was first and foremost a model of the system described by the program. This reasoning was carried over to our understanding of more traditional parts of programming as well. Let us examine this approach in a little more detail.

In Frame 5 a sketch of an ALGOL program is showed on the left and a simplified model of the corresponding program execution on the right. What is physically generated is organized as a stack. Systems which may be usefully thought of as such stacks, are described conveniently by ALGOL. Frame 6 states this with other words.

Moving on to SIMULA, each component, now called an "object" in our model system (the program execution) is itself a stack. And therefore what is SIMULA? Here we have a

SIMULA I

developed:
   June 1961–March 1964

design objectives:
   system description
   simulation programming

basic feature:
   the process concept

Frame 3

SIMULA 67

developed:
    December 1966–January 1968

design objectives:
    system description
    high level programming
    application languages
    (e.g. simulation)

basic features:
    the object/class concept
    prefixing and subclasses
    the virtual concept

Frame 4

number of stacks with the static enclosures, and SIMULA is the world regarded as a nested collection of interacting stacks [Frame 7]. When we examine what was new in SIMULA 67, two main and interrelated features were prefixing and virtual procedures. The prefixing with block concatenation made it possible for us to use Tony Hoare's ideas of reference qualification, and still keep the flexibility we wanted. It also provided the possibility of building up hierarchies of concepts [Frame 8]. As you know, using prefixing by Class *A*, an object of Class *B* contains an *A*, and its prefix and main parts are glued together as one integrated block instance.

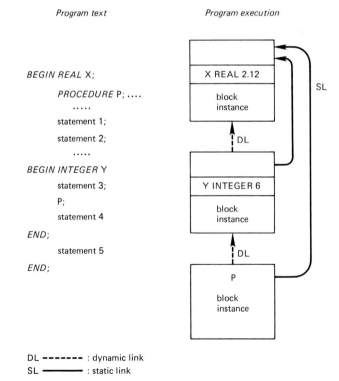

Program text   *Program execution*

BEGIN REAL X;
    PROCEDURE P; ....
        .....
    statement 1;
    statement 2;
        .....
BEGIN INTEGER Y
    statement 3;
    P;
    statement 4
END;
    statement 5
END;

X REAL 2.12 / block instance

SL

DL

Y INTEGER 6 / block instance

DL

P / block instance

DL ------- : dynamic link
SL ——— : static link

Frame 5

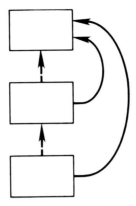

Frame 6. ALGOL 60—the world regarded as a stack of block instances.

One thing which should be mentioned in passing is that we tried by a last minute desperate effort to get a type concept into SIMULA 67 (in terms of in-line types). We did not succeed for reasons which are explained in our paper.

My last visit to the U.S. was in 1970. At that time the class concept only had a certain curiosity and entertainment value. I except people like Don Knuth, John McNeley, Bob Bemer, Al Paster, and some others. Today it's interesting and pleasant to observe that the situation is different. But—and there is a "but"—I still think that many people who refer to SIMULA only grasp parts of it. In fact, those who understand SIMULA best are not the people in programming research, but rather SIMULA's simulation users. The computer scientists like SIMULA as a vehicle for implementing data types. But many of them have never discovered the use and implication of the class/subclass feature. If they have, most have not exploited the virtual concept. And only very few, including Tony Hoare and Per Brinch Hansen, have realized what I feel is the most important property of SIMULA, that it is a multistack language. The computer-based systems we now have to

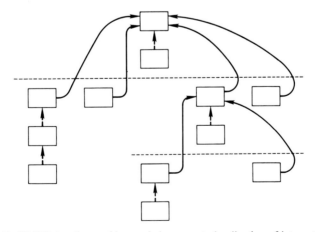

Frame 7. SIMULA—the world regarded as a nested collection of interacting stacks.

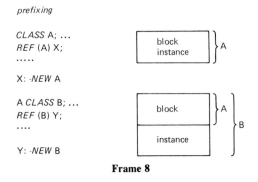

prefixing

CLASS A; ...
REF (A) X;
.....

X: -NEW A

A CLASS B; ...
REF (B) Y;
....

Y: -NEW B

Frame 8

implement are networks of human beings, production equipment and computing equipment. For these systems I'm convinced that SIMULA's multistack framework is useful.

When I planned this presentation, I expected to use much of my time in discussing SIMULA politics. As I wrote along, my mind changed, as you have observed. Politics was, however, an essential part of the SIMULA venture, and it is described in detail in our paper. I will conclude my speech by pointing out what I feel were the most essential political elements of that venture.

When SIMULA 67 was developed, the Norwegian Computing Center employed approximately 120 persons. Of these 120, three persons could be assigned to language development. Backus told us that he got the resources he wanted. Grace Hopper's situation was more like ours. [Refer to the FORTRAN and Keynote presentations. Ed.] In 1962 we were told that (1) there would be no use for SIMULA; (2) there would be use, but it had been done before; (3) we would not succeed; (4) we should not make such efforts in a small and unimportant country like Norway.

In 1967 we were told that SIMULA was wonderful, but the lifetime of a programming language was only three to five years, and we have to earn back our expenses during that time period.

We had very small resources, and we had to fight for them. We wanted SIMULA to be an "existing" language, and our definition of that term is given on Frame 9.

These were our ambitions. To achieve these objectives, we needed the compilers to be of "high standard," a term which is defined on Frame 10.

The period from the spring of 1968 until the summer of 1970 was a crucial phase in SIMULA 67's life. The Control Data implementations were on the way, but SIMULA would not exist unless we got it onto IBM and Univac, and this was something which we

"Existing" language:

— available on most of the
   major computer systems

— being used over a long
   period of time by a
   substantial number of
   people throughout the world

— having a significant impact
   upon the development of
   future programming languages.

Frame 9

Condition for "existence"—
"high standard":

— Compilation and run time
  execution speeds comparable
  with best ALGOL 60 compilers.

— Availability of comprehensive
  and well written documentation
  and educational material.

— The existence and effective
  operation of distribution and
  maintenance organizations
  for the compilers.

Frame 10

had to do at the Computing Center. And we were in a difficult situation at that time, described in the paper.

In the summer of 1970 the NCC compilers had passed their "point of no return"; it was more costly to drop them than to complete them. Still, our resources were limited, as shown on Frame 11.

For this reason it was essential for SIMULA's success that we already in 1967 had designed an organizational strategy which was carried out during the subseqent five years [Frame 12].

The Norwegian Computing Center was at all stages, except a brief interval, very loyal to the SIMULA effort. And when you are shown loyalty, you also feel loyalty in return. Captain Grace Hopper concluded her opening address by expressing her gratitude and dedication to the organization she had served. I feel the same towards the Norwegian Computing Center and our comrades there. I could stop here, but I have to thank some of those outside the Norwegian Computing Center who were essential to the success of SIMULA. What I'll present to you is my own "short list" of names. Ole-Johan's may be slightly different, so I'll give it to you as my list.

First of all—and underlined—is Jan V. Garwick, the father of computer science in Norway. He was Ole-Johan's and my own first boss, and we are in great professional debt to him. Then follows a series of people at that time associated with Univac. Without Univac's immediate interest at an early stage, SIMULA would at least have been seriously delayed.

Stig Walstam brought us in contact with key Univac people in May 1962, as, e.g., Bob Bemer who listened for twenty minutes and then interrupted me by stating "Why don't you go to Munich [the IFIP World Conference in Munich] and discuss it?" And he was interested in discussing negotiations with Univac. But then Jim Nickitas, the man who got the whole thing started within Univac, the man who had faith in us at the Computing Cen-

Norwegian Computing Center:
120 persons

IBM SIMULA team:
7 persons (peak)

Univac SIMULA team:
2 persons

Frame 11. Resources.

Ole-Johan Dahl

Strategy:

— getting SIMULA 67 implemented
   on IBM, Univac and Control Data
   computers
— SIMULA Common Base Conference
   (June 1967) and
   SIMULA Common Base Language
— SIMULA Standards Group (SSG)
— Association of SIMULA Users (ASU)
— SIMULA Newsletter

Frame 12

ter, and was material in the Computing Center getting the 1107 computer. Al Paster, our main contact during our work with the concept. Bernie Hausner, staying with us for a while, and telling us about SIMSCRIPT. We learned from it; we copied it to a slight extent, and we learned what we wanted to be different. Joe Speroni behind our ALGOL compiler for our SIMULA I; Don Knuth, John McNeley—who very generously supported us. Eugen I. Yakovlev and Kirill S. Kusmin in the Soviet, at the Zentralniya Ekonomika Mathematicheskiya Institut in Moscow. Then Tony Hoare who is the single person whose ideas have meant most to us. Jean Ichbiah has done a big job in telling other people about SIMULA. Robin Hills, the first chairman of the Association of SIMULA Users. Jacob Palme . . . (I understand from the Johnny Carson show you have a big research project going on here in the states: trying to develop a T-shirt without anything printed on it! Henry Tropp has asked us to give references. I'm loyal to that. But it has not been developed in Sweden, and Jacob Palme is a person who has SIMULA 67 on his T-shirt.) But he has done very very much more. There are many others, and I'll use my leeway by ending up and saying—above all—well, it is at the bottom, but it is in fact, on top—ALGOL 60. Our gratitude first and foremost goes to ALGOL 60, and to all of the elegance and clearness which this language has, and which we have tried to carry over in SIMULA. Thank you.

TRANSCRIPT OF DISCUSSANT'S REMARKS

BARBARA LISKOV: As I'm sure you're all aware, SIMULA was in fact a two-man project. The other member of this team was Ole-Johan Dahl, and he's going to be a discussant for SIMULA today. At the time that the ideas for SIMULA came up, he was working for the Norwegian Defense Research Establishment for Jan Garwick. As a matter of fact, he was working on an implementation of an ALGOL-like high-level language that was going to be implemented—if I have this correctly—on a machine with 1000 words, and a drum of 16K words. Anyway, in 1962, Ole-Johan Dahl moved to the Norwegian Computing Center and started working full-time on SIMULA. Today he's Professor of Informatics at the University of Oslo and his primary research interest is in program specification and verification.

OLE-JOHAN DAHL: I would like to use another few minutes in talking about ALGOL and its surprisingly many kinds of applications, especially of course the block concept of

ALGOL, which turned out to be able to model all we felt that we needed for simulation models—that was the first SIMULA language. It also could be extended to the more general purpose class concept of SIMULA 67.

I have listed five different kinds of uses of blocklike constructs in SIMULA 67, all under the disguise of what we call a *class* or *class body*. I know that SIMULA has been criticized for perhaps having put too many things into that single basket of class. Maybe that is correct; I'm not sure myself. But it was certainly great fun during the development of the language to see how the block concept could be remodeled in all these ways.

So, the first and simplest instance of class is of course the pure data structures that you have in languages such as Pascal, ALGOL 68 and others; recordlike things, which you get out of an ALGOL block simply by deleting the block tail, keeping the declarations of variables and arrays.

The next example can be called "generalized data objects." You get them by including not only variable declarations in your class body block head, but also procedure declarations. The discovery was made in 1964–1965 that these so-called "procedure attributes" could be useful. And people like Tony Hoare have since shown us that what is really lying there is the concept of an abstract data object, with the procedures as abstract operators. The only thing we needed to do to ALGOL in order to make blocks look like data objects, was simply to devise a naming mechanism for block instances. And a mechanism of looking into blocks from the outside.

Next on my list is the process concept. It merely required us to include some very simple mechanisms for coroutinelike sequencing in addition to ALGOL's procedure activation mechanism. Having that, we had all the power of ALGOL programs going in quasiparallel.

Then, the fourth on the list is the class prefixes. Now this was, as Kristen mentioned, a less trivial addition. The idea of prefixing one class by another one, and thereby composing a composite object consisting of two layers. But this enabled us to use the class mechanism for a kind of abstraction, collecting common properties of different kinds of objects into a single class, and making it available for use at later times as a kind of plug-in unit, where a given class could be extended into more concrete classes at later times by adding more properties.

And finally, the prefix mechanism could be used for ordinary in-line blocks too. This turned out to be a very interesting application, rather like collecting together sets of interrelated concepts into a larger class, and then using that larger class as a prefix to a block. The class would function as a kind of predefined context that would enable the programmer to program in a certain style directed toward a certain application area. Simulation, of course, was one of the ideas that we thought of, and we included a standard class in the language for that particular purpose.

There are two more points on my list of mechanisms that we proposed for inclusion in the language at the Common Base Conference which was held in June or late May of 1967. To use these class objects as generalized variables so that the concept of a class could be used rather like a generalized type concept, like integer and real. And finally we also saw the possibility of unifying the class and procedure concepts.

Now, as I said, it was great fun to see how easily the block concept could be remodeled and used for all these purposes. It is quite possible, however, that it would have been wiser to introduce a few more specialized concepts, for instance, a "context" concept for the contextlike classes. As a matter of fact, one of our disappointments with the usage of

SIMULA during the past years is the relatively little usage of the context-building capability of the language. Maybe this is also due to the fact that it is not at all an easy task to make good contexts. Thank you.

TRANSCRIPT OF QUESTION AND ANSWER SESSION

BARBARA LISKOV: There have been a number of questions, and I'll start with this one from Richard Miller: "Do you think the fact you were in a small group and country working on a project that many other groups were also working on helped push you on to the high quality work that you wanted?"

KRISTEN NYGAARD: Yes. I think that we benefitted from the fact that we had very complete control in a small group of what we were doing. I believe in team development of such a project. I'm skeptical of committee projects in designing languages. ALGOL 60 succeeded. They had a number of very brilliant people. They succeeded also because they had an apparently innocent but in fact very cunning secretary with devious manners, Peter Naur, to help the whole thing succeed. I address this comment also to the television cameras, which (we are told) records for history.

LISKOV: I have a question from Richard Nance at Virginia Tech: "Using the Kiviat–Lackner classification of simulation languages, both SIMULA and GPSS are described as process interaction languages. GPSS is narrowly focused on the interaction of temporary objects with permanent objects. Did SIMULA evolve from the same view, and how well can SIMULA treat interaction among permanent objects?"

OLE-JOHAN DAHL: I think it is fair to say, looking back now, that the conceptual origins are much more similar than we thought they were at the time. Our starting point was also the concept of a network through which things were flowing, and as I have understood, that is also the basic view of GPSS. About the distinction between temporary and permanent objects, I really can't see any great distinction between them. To me, a permanent object is an object that gets created at the start of an execution and lasts the whole time.

LISKOV: Here's another question from Richard Miller: "Could you comment further on the possible use of parallelism in SIMULA programs? When was this idea thought of?"

NYGAARD: I guess that you are talking about real physical parallelism as opposed to quasi-parallelism. Quasi-parallelism, to portray parallelism, was of course essential from the very outset. It occurred to us that this could be carried over to true parallelism, and in fact, there exists a note, in Norwegian, from 1963, about developing SIMULA into a real-time language. When we discovered it, among much dust, I reread it with quite some nervousness. But it turned out that the ideas there were not too bad, but of course we didn't at that time at all really understand all the problems related to physical parallelism. I think that we *could* incorporate such features in SIMULA, but I don't think it *will* be done. There are versions of SIMULA now with extended operating systems for running programs in parallel, but not in the nature of, say, concurrent Pascal.

LISKOV: Thank you very much.

FULL TEXT OF ALL QUESTIONS SUBMITTED

Ulf Beyschlag

SIMULA turned out to be a successful, nearly profitable programming language project. This without the strong backing of a manufacturer or a widespread academic community. What problems did you face and how do you see the chances for further projects with these characteristics?

Per Brinch Hansen

Many computer scientists now refer to SIMULA as the origin of the idea of abstract data types, that is, as a program module that makes a clear distinction between externally available abstract operations and internal implementation details of these abstract concepts. Was this viewpoint evident to you and Dahl from the beginning or was it a happy (unexpected) consequence of the SIMULA 67 class concept?

Richard Miller

The class concept of SIMULA has become the prototype of the data abstraction techniques now coming into vogue in languages such as CLU and ALPHARD. Was this usage of the class apparent during the design? When did it become apparent?

(For Professor Dahl in particular, but. . . .) Could you describe your attempts (and eventual success) in developing the multiple stack concept for SIMULA. In particular, what options were available to you at the time and how were they used or eliminated?

Do you think the fact that you were in a small group and country working on projects that many groups were also working on helped push you on to the high quality work that you wanted?

Richard Nance

Using Kiviat–Lackner classification of simulation languages, both SIMULA and GPSS are described as process interaction languages. GPSS is narrowly focused on the interaction of temporary objects with permanent objects. Did SIMULA evolve from the same view? How well can SIMULA treat interaction among permanent objects?

BIOGRAPHY OF KRISTEN NYGAARD

Kristen Nygaard was born in 1926 in Oslo, Norway. He worked with the Norwegian Defense Research Establishment from 1948 to 1960 in computing and programming (1948–1954) and operational research (1952–1960). His master's thesis (1956) on abstract probability theory was entitled "Theoretical Aspects of Monte Carlo Methods." From 1957 to 1960 he was head of the operational research groups in the Norwegian defense. He was Cofounder and first chairman of the Norwegian Operational Research Society (1959–1964). Starting in 1960 he was employed by the Norwegian Computing Center, becoming its director of Research in 1962. Among his activities have been: building up the NCC as a research institute (in the 1960s), operational research, SIMULA I, and SIMULA 67.

After working on SIMULA 67 he did research for Norwegian trade unions on planning, control, and data processing, all evaluated in light of the objectives of organized labor (1971–1973). Other research and development work included: the social impact of computer technology, the general system description language DELTA (1973–1975); and the programming language BETA (1976–1980). He was Professor in Aarhus, Denmark (1975–1976) and in Oslo (from 1977 on). His work in Aarhus and Oslo included research and education on system development and the social impact of computer technology. He is a member of the Research Committee of the Norwegian Federation of Trade Unions. He has cooperated with unions in a number of countries.

BIOGRAPHY OF OLE-JOHAN DAHL

Ole-Johan Dahl was born in 1931 in Mandal, Norway. He worked with the Norwegian Defense Research Establishment from 1952 to 1963 with computing and programming under Jan V. Garwick. From 1956 onwards his main activity was software development. His master's thesis ("Numerical mathematics," 1957, University of Oslo) addressed the representation and manipulation of multidimensional arrays on a two-level store computer. His main contribution at the NDRE was a high level programming language, MAC, used locally during the early 1960s (first specification dated 1957, the implemented version modified as the result of ALGOL impact). In 1963 he joined the Norwegian Computing Center for full-time work on SIMULA, and in 1968 he became professor of computer science, then a new discipline at the University of Oslo. His main research during recent years has been in the areas of program architecture, specification tools, and verification techniques.

From 1964 to 1976 he was the Norwegian delegate to IFIP Technical Committee 2 (Programming Languages), and from 1970 to 1977 a member of IFIP Working Group 2.2 (Language Definition). He has been a member of IFIP Working Group. 2.3 (Programming Methodology) since its founding in Oslo in 1969.

JOSS Session

Chairman: Thomas Cheatham
Speaker: Charles L. Baker

PAPER: JOSS—JOHNNIAC OPEN-SHOP SYSTEM†

Charles L. Baker

Ocean Data Systems, Inc.,

JOSS,‡ the JOHNNIAC Open Shop System, was conceived in early November 1960 at the RAND Corporation in Santa Monica, California. RAND had always been a pioneer in computing, with a long history of innovative research in both hardware and software, and continuing this tradition was certainly a strong motivation for the JOSS Project. But without doubt, the single most important factor was the continuing presence of JOHNNIAC itself.

1. The JOHNNIAC—the Beginning of JOSS

The RAND JOHNNIAC was basically a computer of the Princeton class, following the original logical design of the group at the Institute for Advanced Study, under the direction of mathematician John von Neumann. Other IAS machines included the ORACLE at Oak Ridge, the MANIAC at Los Alamos, and the ILLIAC at Illinois.

As early as 1958 the debate had begun. I quote from the "JOHNNIAC Manifesto" written in March of that year (unattributed authorship): "The present JOHNNIAC is far removed, by evolution, from the original design. Much of its circuitry is now transistorized; its memory consists of magnetic cores; it has one of the fastest printers of any machine.

---

† Note: The format of the JOSS section of this book is different from the format of the other language sections. Due to circumstances beyond the conference program committee's control, there was no paper on JOSS in the preprints and indeed, at one point we feared there would be no talk on JOSS at the conference. Fortunately, Chuck Baker came to the rescue at the last minute, giving a talk that was well presented and well received.

The Editorial Board for these proceedings decided to ask him to revise his remarks into a formal paper, feeling that the additional information gained thereby would serve the historical record more than just an edited transcript. The paper presented here is, then, a history of JOSS based on, but going beyond, the oral presentation at the conference. The Question and Answer Session has also been revised and answers expanded beyond the original. The transcript of the oral presentation is omitted as it is too similar to the paper. Ed.

‡ JOSS is the trademark and service mark of the RAND Corporation for its computer program and services using that program.

Charles L. Baker

Despite these significant improvements, JOHNNIAC is still a long way from being a modern, or even a complete, computer. Unfortunately, the design art has progressed faster than our machine.'' It was recommended that a decision as to what to do with JOHN-NIAC be reached ''no later than April 15.''

Now, nearly three years later, in the late fall of 1960, the question was still being debated, and a series of meetings held on November 8 and 9 led directly to JOSS. Present at the creation, so to speak, were Paul Armer, Head of RAND's Computer Sciences Department; Willis Ware, Associate Department Head; and RAND researchers Keith Uncapher, Tom Ellis, and J. C. (Cliff) Shaw, the true ''father'' of JOSS. Cliff's notes from that two-day session record that he proposed ''a possible full-time use of JOHNNIAC to service the 'Open Shop' via remote hard-copy stations. The point is that here is a real-life challenge and an opportunity to tangle with such communications and monitoring problems on a small scale.''

This was not a spur-of-the-moment suggestion on Cliff's part. Much thinking had gone into the various possibilities and problems of such a project, and with his customary thoroughness, Cliff had collected these into a handwritten set of notes titled ''Possible use of JOHNNIAC in a Open-Shop system using personal communication stations.'' Sample quotations from this document, dated November 7, indicate the directions which JOSS would eventually take:

> Accommodate 12 users simultaneously. . . .
> User can communicate inputs, inserts, deletes, and changes. . . .
> Activating the routine, stopping, interrupting, restarting, dumping, tracing (with a question mark) and other meta-processes. . . .
> Floating point decimal arithmetic, and only such arithmetic. . . [Here Cliff notes that with double-precision, a test case with only a 10 (or 8) bank desk calculator becomes difficult!]
> A linear form for algebraic statement. . . .
> Variables: single character from upper or lower case Roman. . . .
> Vectors and Matrices. . . [Again, with a question mark.]
> System transforms input from external form to internal list structure form on command, and then interprets this internal form at execution time. . . .
> Express equations to evaluate so that sequence control is separate from the equations. . . .
> Evaluate expressions in control statements themselves. . . .
> Any expression will simply be evaluated and the value used. . . .
> Simple I/O processes as well as more elegant ones, which can produce final reports on vellum copy. . . . [This, before the age of the ubiquitous office copier.]

Interspersed throughout Cliff's notes are extensive discussions of how such facilities might be implemented on JOHNNIAC, along with rough estimates of the expected performance of the resulting system.

Although there is no formal record of any final decisions reached at the November meetings—quite in character for discussions about JOHNNIAC at RAND—apparently the go-ahead was given to proceed with JOSS. Nearly two and a half years of hardware and software development followed, and numerous major design decisions and changes took place as a feasible system evolved. During this period, the hardware effort was under the direction of Tom Ellis and Mal Davis, while Cliff produced nearly all of the software himself, with the assistance of Leola Cutler and Mary Lind.

What were the facilities provided by JOHNNIAC? Figure 1 outlines the basic characteristics of the machine: 4K of 40-bit core supplemented by a 12K moving-head drum, two

JOHNNIAC CHARACTERISTICS	JOHNNIAC FEATURES

WORD LENGTH: 40 BITS

INSTRUCTION LENGTH: 20 BITS

CORE MEMORY: 4096 WORDS

DRUM MEMORY: 12288 WORDS

ARITHMETIC REGISTERS: 2

ADD TIME: 50 μsec.

Fig. 1

NO FLOATING POINT ARITHMETIC

NO INDEXING OR INDIRECT ADDRESSING

NO ERROR CHECKING OR MEMORY PROTECT

NO INTERRUPTS OR CHANNELS

NO COMPARE OR ZERO TEST

NO SUBROUTINE LINKAGE

Fig. 2

arithmetic registers, an add time of 50 microseconds, and from a programmer's point of view, a dreadful two-instruction-per-word format.

And JOHNNIAC provided other programming "conveniences" as well [Fig. 2]: no floating-point arithmetic, no indexing or indirect addressing, no error checking or memory project, no I/O interrupts or channels, no compare or zero test instructions, and no subroutine linkage. There was system software to match: a primitive linking loader providing a minimum of relocation ability and essentially no symbolic capability of any kind.

Nevertheless, JOHNNIAC was physically quite large. In this picture of Cliff at the console [Fig. 3], the sole peripheral facilities—a line printer and a collator for card input—can be seen, while in the background is the "main frame" of the machine. Not visible is a large basement full of power supply equipment, including literally hundreds of variacs for slowly powering up and powering down the machine, and a room containing the large, garbage-can-sized magnetic drum.

In view of the limited I/O facilities, it is not surprising that major hardware additions were required to support the remote typewriter terminals. This gear, known as the Multiple Typewriter Communications System (MTCS), was built to service up to 12 remote stations and to multiplex their communications on a line-at-a-time basis with JOHNNIAC.

For the remote terminals themselves, the IBM Model 868 electric typewriter was chosen [Fig. 4]. A rather large electronics package (by today's standards) was required at each station, along with an array of lights, switches and buttons in a separate control box alongside the typewriter.

Great care was taken in the choice of a character set for the typewriters [Fig. 5]. Wherever possible, the conventional graphics were retained in their usual position, and

Fig. 3

Fig. 4

these, *as well as the nonprinting graphics,* were communicated to JOSS and became part of the JOSS language.

Certain characters were assigned special meaning; a number of these do not appear on the standard typewriter keyboard [Fig. 6]. These include a large centered dot, used to denote multiplication; a five-pointed elevated asterisk to denote exponentiation; the absolute value bar; and the paired relational symbols. Special meaning was assigned to the number or pound sign, which is used as a strikeout symbol (backspace does not erase), and to the dollar sign and the underscore.

Proprietary control of the JOSS typewriter is provided by the console electronics and the MTCS: either JOSS has control for output purposes, or the user has control, for typing into JOSS. This is indicated by a RED/GREEN light pair on the control box [Fig. 7]. When JOSS turns control over to the user, the light changes from red to green, the keyboard unlocks, the ribbon color changes to green, and an audible signal is given. Control is returned to JOSS by either a carriage return or page; the light turns to red, the ribbon changes to black, and the keyboard is locked.

JOSS TYPEWRITER GRAPHICS

CONVENTIONAL

- LETTERS: abc...xyzABC...XYZ
- PUNCTUATION: . , ; : ' " ? ( ) [ ]
- DIGITS: 1 2 3 . . . 9 0
- NON-PRINTING:
  SPACE, BACKSPACE, TAB, SHIFT,
  CARR.RTN., PAGE

Fig. 5

SPECIAL

- OPERATOR: $+ - \cdot / * |$
- RELATION: $< \leq = \neq \geq >$
- OTHER: $ # _

Fig. 6

JOSS CONSOLE RED/GREEN STATES

CONTROL	• JOSS HAS CONTROL
	• USER HAS CONTROL
KEYBOARD	• LOCKED
	• UNLOCKED
RIBBON	• JOSS TYPES IN BLACK
	• USER TYPES IN GREEN

Fig. 7

```
JOSS at your service.
Initials please: RAND
Project number: 3407
Department: CSD
```

Fig. 8

To sign on to JOSS, the user turns on the console power at the control box [Fig. 8]; JOSS responds with "JOSS at your service. Initials please:" and turns control over to the user. A carriage return after each response elicits the next prompt from JOSS. [In program figures italics indicate user inputs; roman indicates JOSS outputs. Ed.]

When the sign-on is completed, JOSS ejects to the top of a new sheet of paper [Fig. 9], records the date and time, types a centered page number, spaces down to allow a one-inch margin, and turns control over to the user. This paging feature can be initiated at any time by the user, and automatically occurs at the botton of each page of output. It is part of the JOSS language.

2. The JOSS Language

Only a few examples are necessary to provide a nearly complete overview of the JOSS language [Fig. 10]. The user may type in a direct command as in Type 2 + 2., followed by a return, and JOSS responds with a restatement of the expression and its evaluation. *Any* JOSS command may be modified by the addition of a conditional clause, as shown and will be carried out only if the indicated relationship holds.

JOSS requires a letter-perfect input, including capitalization, spacing, and a final period on each command; if this is not the case, JOSS responds as it does to all meaningless inputs: with a single universal error message, "Eh?" All rumors aside, it is indeed only a coincidence that it takes JOSS precisely as long to type "Eh?" as it takes the user to say "Oh bleep!" It is, however, a great timesaver.

The verb Set is used to indicate the assignment of a value to a variable [Fig. 11]; JOSS commands can deal with these in the usual way in linearized expressions. The verb Type can have as its object, a list of expressions; each of these is evaluated and the response typed on a separate line. In this example, note the use of the dot for multiplication and the raised asterisk for raising to a power.

The use of square brackets and paired absolute value bars, along with parentheses,

JOSS OUTPUT PAGE HEADING

```
11:31 4/15/66 RAND 3407

8½" x 11" PAPER
1" MARGINS
```

Fig. 9

```
Type 2+2.

        2+2 =           4
Type "ok" if 500<3*6≤1000.

ok

Type 2+2

Eh?
```

Fig. 10

Charles L. Baker

```
Set x=3.

Type x.
                    x =        3

Type x+2, x-2, x·2, x/2, x*2.
                x+2 =        5

                x-2 =        1

                x·2 =        6

                x/2 =        1.5

                x*2 =        9
```
Fig. 11

```
Type [(|x-5|·3+4)·2-15]·3+10.
[(|x-5|·3+4)·2-15]·3+10 = 25

x=7

Type ([x-7|·3+4)·2 *

Type ⌈(|x-5|·3+4)·2-15⌉·3+10.
[(|x-5|·3+4)·2-15]·3+10 = 25
```
Fig. 12

greatly increases the readability and typability of extended expressions [Fig. 12]. Still, mistakes in typing can occur; if the user wishes, he may backspace and strike over or strike out any previously typed characters (this editing being performed by MTCS), or in extremis use the asterisk to tell JOSS to ignore the line in error. The asterisk may also be used at the beginning of a line to indicate a comment.

Linearization of the standard functions is provided in the usual way, using parentheses or brackets to enclose the argument(s) [Fig. 13]. Additional spacing on output can be requested by using the underscore to denote a null element in a list of expressions. When JOSS cannot carry out the requested evaluation, an appropriate error message is returned.

The usual transcendental functions are provided [Fig. 14], and yield nine-decimal-digit accuracy throughout their ranges; special care is taken to hit "magic values" on the nose. Note that JOSS switches over to scientific representation of numbers when required.

A particularly useful set of functions is provided in JOSS to allow number dissection [Fig. 15]: they include the integer part, fractional part, digit part, and exponent part. (These latter two are shorter and more mnemonic than mantissa and characteristic, which few of us can keep straight.) An added bonus of these functions is that they allow a fair degree of symbolic manipulation within the JOSS language at no extra cost in complexity. Originally included somewhat as an afterthought, they have been heavily exploited by JOSS users and contribute a great deal to the construction of concise programs.

The care with which JOSS carries out decimal arithmetic is illustrated by the next example [Fig. 16]. Ten to the eighth power minus 0.05 yields ten to the eighth as the result. However, if the 0.05 is increased by one in the ninth significant digit, the resulting answer is as shown, which is the correct value obtained when 99,999,999.9499999999, the exact result, is rounded to nine significant digits. This accuracy—true decimal result rounded

```
Type sqrt(3), _, sqrt(4).
          sqrt(3) =        1.73205081


          sqrt(4) =        2.
Type sqrt(-1).
I have a negative argument for sqrt
```
Fig. 13

```
Type sin(.5), cos(.5).

        sin(.5) =            .479425539
        cos(.5) =            .877582562
Type exp(0), exp(1), exp(20).

        exp(0) =            1
        exp(1) =            2.71828183
        exp(20) =           4.85165195·10*8
```

Fig. 14

to nine significant digits, is provided for addition, subtraction, multiplication, division, and square root.

Indirect commands, that is, commands which are to be stored by JOSS for later interpretation and execution are indicated by preceding the command with a numeric step label [Fig. 17]. This label, which can have any positive value less than ten to the ninth, more than carries its weight as a linguistic device. In addition to distinguishing direct and indirect commands, it serves as the instruction to JOSS actually to store the step; it uniquely identifies and sequences stored steps; it indicates whether the step being stored is an addition, insertion, or replacement; it serves to group individual steps into collections which are termed parts; and finally, it can be denoted by an algebraic expression. In this example, part one consists of two steps: the first computing the hypotenuse of a triangle with sides a and b, and the second typing the sides of the triangle as formal output by means of a user-supplied form. Forms, like steps, are identified by (integer) numeric values, and are entered on two lines to allow the full line width for the resulting output. Within the body of a form, underscores denote fields for the values of the variables; all other information is output literally.

A third indirectly stored step instructs JOSS to execute the commands in part 1 (here, steps 1.1 and 1.2) repeatedly, varying the value of the variable b from 1, in steps of 1, to the value of a. The for clause, which may be appended to any Do command, direct or indirect, can be extended to include multiple ranges of any increment, and may also be composed of a list of values, or a list of ranges, or indeed any combination which will fit on a single line.

To initiate the execution of the stored program, the direct Do command, specifying iteration values for b, is given [Fig. 18].

The resulting output from JOSS consists of six lines of output, formatted according to

```
y= -1.23456·10*2
Type y, ip(y), fp(y), dp(y), xp(y).

            y =         -123.456
        ip(y) =         -123
        fp(y) =            -.456
        dp(y) =         -1.23456
        xp(y) =            2
```

Fig. 15

```
Type 10*8-.0500000000.
10*8-.0500000000 =        1·10*8
Type 10*8-.0500000001.
10*8-.0500000001 =        9.99999999·10*7
Type sqrt(.5).
     sqrt(.5) =           .707106781
Type [sqrt(.5)]*2.
[sqrt(.5)]*2 =            .5
```
Fig. 16

the specified form. It is relatively easy to modify the JOSS program that generates this output so that only Pythagorean triples are typed: append the conditional clause "if the fractional part of C equals zero" to the Type command, and extend the range of iteration of the variable a. Further niceties, such as separate pages for output, column headings, etc., can be added and tested interactively, and indeed, this is the usual way in which the JOSS user proceeds.

One of the distinguishing characteristics of the JOSS language is the richness of the results that can be obtained with a relatively modest repetoire of commands [Fig. 19]. There are actually only 13 verbs, which are grouped according to their usage. Of these 13, seven are simple imperatives (Form, Go, Cancel, Line, Page, Done, and Stop), and only six verbs refer to the objects of discourse of the language (Delete, Type, Set, Do, Demand, and To).

These objects of discourse are themselves few in number [Fig. 20]: steps, parts, forms, and values, the latter category consisting either of variables (simple, singly or doubly indexed) or of algebraic expressions. Type and Delete may refer to any of these, while Set and Demand are applicable to variables only, and Do and To may refer either to steps or to parts.

3. Philosophy of JOSS

Over the years, it became apparent that there was an underlying philosophy which guided the direction in which JOSS and its immediate successors at RAND evolved [Fig. 21]. At first, these were unstated, or at least not written down, but after working with JOSS for even a short length of time, one could say, with some degree of assurity, that a certain proposed feature, or behavior, either was or was not "JOSS-like." Even-

```
Delete all.                        Do part 2 for a = 1(1)3.
1.1 Set c = sqrt(a*2 + b*2).       a = 1   b = 1   c = 1.414
1.2 Type a, b, c in form 1.        a = 2   b = 1   c = 2.236
Form 1:                            a = 2   b = 2   c = 2.828
a =__   b =__   c =__.___          a = 3   b = 1   c = 3.162
2.1 Do part 1 for b = 1(1)a.       a = 3   b = 2   c = 3.606
Do part 2 for a = 1(1)3.           a = 3   b = 3   c = 4.243
```
| **Fig. 17** | **Fig. 18** |

JOSS Verbs   JOSS OBJECTS OF DISCOURSE

Direct	Both	Indirect		
•Form	•Type	•Demand	step n.nn	all steps
•Delete	•Set	•To	part n	all parts
•Go	•Do	•Done	form n	all forms
•Cancel	•Line	•Stop	a, b, ..., y, z	all values
	•Page		A, B, ..., Y, Z	
			all	

Fig. 19

Fig. 20

tually, in 1967, some of these were collected in a RAND paper, "JOSS: Rubrics." I quote Webster's: "Rubric: A heading of a statute in a code of law, originally printed in red; hence, any brief, authoritative rule or direction." Or, for JOSS, a guiding principle of design and implementation.

A few rubrics are evident from the examples just presented. JOSS commands are limited to one line. They take the form of an imperative English sentence. They begin with a verb. They may be modified by a conditional clause. They conform to the conventional rules of spacing, capitalization, punctuation, and spelling.

JOSS is a complete, self-contained system, acting as a single active agent [Fig. 22]. That is, the JOSS user is always communicating with a single set of software that always recognizes the same message in the same way, and there are no modes or internal states of which the user must be aware. Similarly, a message to JOSS is never "passed off" to another processing system to determine its nature and content.

JOSS machine hardware and software are completely "sealed off," in that their nature cannot be detected by the user [Fig. 23]. JOSS is independent of its implementation, and, at least in theory, can be programmed for any computer with the requisite facility for handling typewriter terminals. At the same time, the ability to "seal off" JOSS has itself been "sealed off," so that the user must always deal directly with JOSS, and not with a higher level system constructed in the JOSS language.

JOSS provides exact input and output for all elements of the language, and maintains a complete isomorphism between its internal and external states [Fig. 24]. This isomorphism is particularly useful with regard to symbolic manipulation using numbers for symbols—in that if the user can determine that the fourth digit of a number is, say, 5, then JOSS number dissection functions can likewise determine this fact. Any user can do an exact simulation of JOSS (with due allowance for some uncertainty in the last digit of transcendental functions) using pencil and paper and a good set of tables. This feature is of high utility when tracking down "bugs" in JOSS programs.

JOSS commands are quantized [Fig. 25]. That is, JOSS never presents itself to the

JOSS

RUBRICS

GUIDING PRINCIPLES OF
DESIGN AND IMPLEMENTATION

Fig. 21

JOSS IS A
COMPLETE
SELF-CONTAINED
SYSTEM, ACTING AS A
SINGLE ACTIVE AGENT

Fig. 22

Charles L. Baker

JOSS MACHINE HARDWARE AND
SOFTWARE ARE COMPLETELY
"SEALED OFF"
AND THE ABILITY TO
"SEAL OFF" JOSS
HAS ITSELF BEEN
"SEALED OFF"

Fig. 23

JOSS PROVIDES
EXACT INPUT AND OUTPUT
FOR ALL ELEMENTS OF THE
LANGUAGE, MAINTAINING COMPLETE
ISOMORPHISM
OF INTERNAL AND EXTERNAL STATES

Fig. 24

user in a state where it has only partially interpreted and executed a step. Either a step "runs" to its conclusion, or the effect is that the step has caused no changes at all. (A Type command may not finish—the user can interrupt JOSS if output "runs away"—but since this command causes no changes in the state of JOSS, the effect is essentially the same.) Interpretation is distinct from execution, and serves to verify that execution will proceed without difficulty. For example, a Do command is interpreted only once, and may be deleted during execution without ill effects. (This behavior is the basis of many of the intriguing "JOSS puzzles" concocted by RAND's Oliver Gross, which usually took the form of "what was the deleted step?") Both of these rubrics contribute greatly to the ease of using JOSS and of debugging JOSS programs.

The JOSS language is constructed so that the general case applies whenever possible [Fig. 26]. This leads to simple rules with no exceptions. The most notable of these is the universal rubric "wherever a number can appear in a command, an arbitrarily complex expression denoting a number can also appear." This is especially powerful when referring to steps, parts, and forms, but applies equally well to the value of an index of a vector or matrix and to the values which are part of the for clause of a Do command.

Equally important to the user, these rules can generally be discovered by simple testing at a JOSS console. Whenever in doubt, the procedure is to try it and see what happens. Since JOSS provides a complete hard-copy record of each user session, it is possible to reconstruct any situation from the typed protocol (in green and black, eliminating ambiguity as to who said what to whom), and in a desperate situation, the user can seek out an "expert" for further consultation.

Perhaps the most important characteristic of a computer language such as JOSS is the behavior of the system in response to the commands of the language. Usually, most of the designers' time is spent in figuring just what should occur as the result of "well-formed" statements, with consequent emphasis on speed, efficiency and the like. Inasmuch as JOSS is intended for the casual user, however, "not-so-well-formed" statements are often the rule rather than the exception, and a great deal of emphasis has been placed on informative and relevant error messages to the user [Fig. 27]. JOSS never tries to second-guess the user, and does insist on letter-perfect input. In general, JOSS error messages say, "Don't do that." rather than, "You shouldn't have done that; please start over from

JOSS COMMANDS ARE
QUANTIZED
FURTHER,
INTERPRETATION IS
DISTINCT FROM
EXECUTION

Fig. 25

JOSS LANGUAGE IS CONSTRUCTED
SO THAT THE
GENERAL CASE APPLIES
LEADING TO
SIMPLE RULES
WITHOUT EXCEPTION

Fig. 26

```
                              JOSS ERROR RESPONSES

                          Stop.
JOSS ERROR REPORTS:       Don't give this command directly.
   "DON'T DO THAT."       Do part A.
    RATHER THAN           I can't find part 3.
   "YOU SHOULDN'T         Type 2*2, 4*4*4, 6*6*6*6.
  HAVE DONE THAT."        I have an overflow.
                          Type 123456789.012/3.
                          Please limit numbers to 9 digits.
        Fig. 27                          Fig. 28
```

the beginning." This is possible largely because of the distinction JOSS makes between interpretation and execution.

In response to a direct Stop, JOSS responds with a rule [Fig. 28]. When an object is denoted by an expression, JOSS evaluates the expression when reporting an error. When requested to type a list of values, JOSS makes sure that all values are within proper range before carrying out the execution of any part of the command. When presented with unallowable inputs, JOSS again reports with a rule.

JOSS exhibits similar behavior while carrying out indirect commands as well [Fig. 29]. In this example, the Do command is first interpreted, and since it is acceptable, it will run to conclusion if at all possible. The first step to be done, however, cannot be executed, and JOSS informs the user not only of the error, but of the step where the error was found. The user can supply the missing value, and Go directs JOSS to carry on from the point of interruption (Cancel would tell JOSS to forget about it.) and the do now runs to completion.

It is perhaps instructive to present one or two examples of non-JOSS-like behavior [Fig. 30]. JOSS would never indicate that a variable was undefined, and then report the value of that variable. Nor would JOSS report two different values (one internal and one external) to the user. This contradictory state of affairs inevitably occurs somewhere in

```
       JOSS ERROR RESPONSES


  1.1 Type x/y.
  Go.                                NON-JOSS BEHAVIOR
  I have nothing to do.
  Do step 1.1 for x = 1,2.       Error at step 5.1:  x = ???
  Error at step 1.1:  y = ???    Type x.
  y = 4
  Go.                                     x =           0
             x/y =      .25       Type y if y ≠ 1.
             x/y =      .5                 y =           1
            Fig. 29                        Fig. 30
```

JOSS CHRONOLOGY		
NOV. 7–9, 1960	FIRST PROPOSAL FOR JOSS	
MAY 11, 1962	FIRST EXTERNAL PAPER ON JOSS	
APR. 16, 1963	FIRST DEBUGGING RUNS	
MAY 29, 1963	JOSS 99 OPERATIONAL	
MAR. 21, 1964	FILMING OF JOSS MOVIE	
JAN. 8, 1965	JOSS 666 OPERATIONAL	
FEB. 11, 1966	LAST DAY OF JOSS SERVICE	

Fig. 31

JOSS DERIVATIVES		
JOSS	JOHNNIAC	RAND
JOSS-II	PDP-6	RAND
AID	PDP-6/10	DEC
TELCOMP	PDP-1/7	BBN/MGH
SON of JOSS	PDP-7	MGH
ISIS	IBM-1410	UCI
CAL	SDS-940	UCB, ETC.
PI L/L	IBM-360/50	PITT/UCI/CMU

Fig. 32

the implementation, and in the case of JOSS, a great deal of effort was expended, both on the detection of such anomalies and on their elimination.

Once, when asked what the important features of JOSS were, Cliff Shaw replied, "It's the little things that count. Hundreds of 'em!"

4. Chronology—JOSS Derivatives

In speaking or writing about JOSS, it is almost impossible to avoid the use of the present tense: "JOSS is. . . ," "JOSS will. . . ," "JOSS can. . . ," etc., and yet, as evidenced by this conference, JOSS is really a part of history [Fig. 31]. The chronology of JOSS proper is rather brief, with a few well defined dates marking the important events. It is perhaps unusual that these events can be pinpointed exactly. November 9, 1960, is the exact starting date; February 11, 1966, was the last date of JOSS service; Cliff's young son, David, was the last user. (JOHNNIAC was formally decommissioned one week later, and now resides in the Los Angeles County Museum.) Of that slightly more than five-year period, JOSS was operational for nearly three years, but the full capabilities of "JOSS 666" were available only during the final 13 months of that period.

During this active lifetime, JOSS was demonstrated to literally hundreds of visitors to RAND, including many who would be responsible for designing and implementing the new wave of interactive time-sharing systems. To further disseminate information about JOSS, a 20-minute, color, sound film was made, depicting a "typical" user session; this film was widely circulated to industrial, academic, and government groups throughout the world. Although perhaps unable to fully appreciate the countless details which underlie its almost deceptive simplicity, almost everyone in the business had at least heard about JOSS by the end of JOHNNIAC's useful lifetime.

Many subsequently developed interactive systems can be termed "JOSS Derivatives" in the sense that they were direct outgrowths, on different hardware, of JOHNNIAC

CITRAN	IBM-360/50	CAL TECH
FILECOMP	GE 4	MEDINET
ESI	PDP-5/8	ADR
MATH	IBM-360/50	IBM
JEAN	ICT-1900	ICT
FOCAL	PDP-5/8	DEC
AMTRAN	IBM-1620/B5500	NASA
MUMPS	PDP-9	MGH
ABLE	IBM-360/50	ICC

Fig. 33

JOSS-INFLUENCED		
HYTRAN	EAI-8000	EAI
INTERP	B-5000	BURROUGHS
TINT	IBM-Q32	SDC
BASIC	GE-265,635	DARTMOUTH
RUSH	IBM-360/50	ABC
CPS	IBM-360/50	IBM
MINIJOSS	MERCURY	RAE

Fig. 34

JOSS [Fig. 32]. Replacing JOSS at RAND was JOSS II, which uses Selectric typewriter terminals and the DEC PDP-6 to service 30 consoles, many remote from RAND at selected Air Force installations. JOSS II provides extended facilities in the JOSS language, notably formulas and conditional expressions along with long-term storage for JOSS programs. Other systems were adapted to meet the individual needs of their respective organizations.

Another direct implementation of JOSS was provided by IBM's MATH/360 which is a direct transcription of JOSS II for the IBM 360/50 [Fig. 33]. Several variants of this implementation appeared at overseas IBM laboratories; JOSS was translated into French, German, and perhaps several other languages. The final direct extension of JOSS was implemented in 1970–1971 at International Computing Company, Bethesda, Maryland. This extension is called ABLE and includes facilities for text manipulation, report generation, and extensive dynamic data base file creation and maintenance facilities, along with a direct interface to batch processing programs. JOSS II, MATH/360 and its variants, and ABLE all adhere closely to the JOSS rubrics.

Another category of systems can be best termed JOSS-influenced [Fig. 34], in that although the systems were designed and implemented with different goals, and hence with different emphasis on matters such as speed and efficiency, and were often aimed at a different category of user than JOSS, at least some resemblance between the languages can be discerned. Some of these designers had direct, and often extensive contact with JOSS, while others had only a short demonstration of an early version of the system. Regardless of the extent of influence, however, JOSS did provide an early "existence theorem" that powerful interactive systems could be built and programmed with modest resources, and in this role, if in no other, JOSS was a significant milestone in the history of programming languages.

REFERENCES

Baker, C. L. (1966) July. *JOSS: Introduction to a Helpful Assistant*. Rand Corporation RM-5058-PR.

Baker, C. L. (1967) February. *JOSS: Console Design*. Rand Corporation RM-5218-PR.

Baker, C. L. (1967) March. *JOSS: Rubrics*. Rand Corporation P-3560.

Bryan, G. E. (1966) November. *JOSS: Introduction to the System Implementation*. Rand Corporation P-3486.

Bryan, G. E. (1967) August. *JOSS: 20,000 Hours at the Console—A Statistical Summary*. Rand Corporation RM-5359-PR.

Bryan, G. E. (1967) August. *JOSS: Assembly Listing of Supervisor*. Rand Corporation RM-5437-PR.

Bryan, G. E. (1967) January. *JOSS: User Scheduling and Resource Allocation*. Rand Corporation RM-5216-PR.

Bryan, G. E. (1967) June. *JOSS: Accounting and Performance Measurement*. Rand Corporation RM-5217-PR.

Bryan, G. E., and Paxson, E. W. (1967) August. *The JOSS Notebook*. Rand Corporation RM-5367-PR.

Bryan, G. E., and Smith, J. W. (1967) August. *JOSS Language*. Rand Corporation RM-5377-PR.

Gimble, E. P. (1967) May. *JOSS: Problem Solving for Engineers*. Rand Corporation RM-5322-PR.

Greenwald, I. D. (1966) September. *JOSS: Arithmetic and Function Evaluation Routines*. Rand Corporation RM-5028-PR.

Greenwald, I. D. (1966) September. *JOSS: Console Service Routines (The Distributor)*. Rand Corporation RM-5044-PR.

Greenwald, I. D. (1967) February. *JOSS: Disc File System*. Rand Corporation RM-5257-PR.

Marks, S. L. (1971) August. *The JOSS Newsletter, November 1967–June 1971*. Rand Corporation P-3940/7.

Marks, S. L., and Armerding, G. W. (1967) August. *The JOSS Primer*. Rand Corporation RM-5220-PR.

Shaw, J. C. (1964) August. *JOSS: A Designer's View of an Experimental On-Line Computing System*. Rand Corporation P-2922.

Shaw, J. C. (1965) April. *JOSS: Examples of the Use of an Experimental On-Line Computing Service.* Rand
Corporation P-3131.
Shaw, J. C. (1965) May. *JOSS: Conversations with the JOHNNIAC Open-Shop System.* Rand Corporation P-
3146.
Shaw, J. C. (1965) May. *JOSS: Experience with an Experimental Computing Service for Users at Remote Type-
writer Consoles.* Rand Corporation P-3149.
Smith, J. W. (1967) August. *JOSS: Central Processing Routines.* Rand Corporation RM-5270-PR.

FULL TEXT OF ALL QUESTIONS SUBMITTED†

THOMAS CHEATHAM

If JOSS is so great, why isn't it in use everywhere?

Answer: In a sense it is, as almost every interactive language has at least some features introduced by JOSS. As to JOSS itself, we made several mistakes in the way the system was publicized, although even in the light of the later developments we would probably have to repeat these mistakes. The first mistake was in retaining the name JOSS for the post-JOHNNIAC implementation of the language, regardless of the additions that were made. The linguistic power of these systems is many times that of the original JOHN-NIAC JOSS; nevertheless, people always judge JOSS by the system as it was first implemented: by the early papers that were presented by Cliff Shaw, by the first demonstrations in 1963, and by the film that was circulated beginning in 1964.

The name had to be retained, however, to get the Air Force to give RAND the money to continue JOSS post-JOHNNIAC, because so many RAND and Air Force types liked JOSS so well. We were really stuck with the name if we were to continue. (We could imagine the Air Force saying, ''We gave you money to build JOSS and you built JL/1.'') Internally, we used JOSS II to designate this follow-on system, but in all formal publications JOSS was used, regardless of the versions.

However, the Air Force didn't give us very much money, and so we had constraints on the manufacturer we chose to be the follow-on hardware supplier. The Digital Equipment Corp. was in a race with IBM, and won. DEC gave us almost no publicity, and it is unlikely that this would have been the case with IBM. If we had gone with IBM we would maybe have had enough money for a 360/40. Later on, the implementation of MATH/360 showed that even on a 360/50 JOSS was about three times slower than on the PDP-6, so that this mistake, too, would have had to be repeated.

A third reason was that there wasn't much documentation for the JOSS user, but that's because JOSS is a secret vice, best practiced in private. That is, one could go off in a room alone and do JOSS. This same virtue is what makes the pocket calculator so attractive: you make your dumb mistakes in, say, learning Polish notation for a Hewlett–Packard calculator by yourself, all alone, and nobody knows. The same is true for JOSS, and as a result, little attention was given to preparing material for potential users—or implementers elsewhere. A number of excellent papers were published a number of years later, but these, unfortunately, had little impact on the computing community.

Anyone interested in programming language design should read the classic paper by J.

† With answers by C. L. Baker.

W. Smith, *JOSS: Central Processing Routines,* which was published in 1967. He talks about iterative expressions, designatory expressions, formulas—the whole repertory of facilities available for non-procedural processing in the advanced version of JOSS.

AARON FINERMANN

Do you believe that JOSS had much effect on Project MAC and later interactive systems?

Answer: It's hard to say what the immediate effects were beyond the fact that JOSS was a truly remarkable accomplishment on the JOHNNIAC, and that it wasn't hard to extrapolate to what could be done with a modern machine. Beginning in 1963, RAND was literally inundated with people who came to see JOSS—and JOSS was like the proverbial elephant visited by the blindmen. Each came and experienced it, and went away with his own impression. Clearly, everyone had his view—it was deceptively simple. You looked at JOSS and you knew instantly what it would do, if you knew anything at all about computer systems. You went home and said, "Why didn't I think of that?" Perspecuity is one of the outstanding traits of JOSS, but it's hard to say what people took away after seeing JOSS.

RICHARD MILLER

Was there an independent run-time system for JOSS, or was access to the machine just access to JOSS?

Answer: Access to JOSS was access to JOSS alone. In the PDP-6 version, the entire RAND building was wired with JOSS outlets, and you could roll the mobile JOSS Terminal around with ease [Fig. 35]. Everyone had a plug in his own office, and he went out, found a terminal not being used, brought it back, and plugged it in. There was no business about passwords, log-in account numbers, fees, or anything like that. You had to know that your initials were 1 to 4 letters, and that a project number had 1 to 4 digits. We didn't verify either of these.

PAUL ARMER

Would you comment on the relationship between the JOSS II terminal and the 2741?

Answer: At the time JOHNNIAC JOSS was implemented, there were, of course, no remote terminals, and only the IBM model B typewriter was available for use when RAND engineers designed and built the JOSS console. Several years later, RAND was successful in interfacing an IBM Selectric typewriter to this console on an experimental basis. This was probably the first use of the Selectric typewriter in a remote terminal; we liked its operation so well that we decided to specify the Selectric for JOSS II terminals. The 2741 was IBM's response to this requirement. The 2741 did not, however, provide the paging control that we felt we had to have [Fig. 36]. The proposal from DEC, however, did include this feature, and they built the JOSS II terminals to satisfy our requirements in nearly every respect. What was never provided by the 2741 (nor, to my knowledge in any terminal other than those built for RAND by DEC) was the feature of proprietary control, so that it is completely unambiguous as to who is saying what to whom when: who has

Fig. 35

Fig. 36

control; red or green; locked or unlocked; two-color ribbon control; etc. using *simultaneous* two-way communication protocol.

RICHARD MILLER

How did JOHNNIAC affect the restrictions made on the language?

Answer: Mostly by its extremely limited facilities. A better question might be, "How did the lifting of the restrictions imposed by JOHNNIAC affect the language?" The answer to this can be seen by comparing the language described in Bryan and Paxson (1967) and Bryan and Smith (1967) with the original JOSS.

HELEN GIGLEY

What features of JOSS do you feel have contributed to its continued usage?

Answer: Not only is JOSS easy to learn (most every language designer puts forth that claim), but more to the point is the fact that, like bicycle riding or ice skating, once learned, it's almost impossible to forget. Even after a lapse of weeks, months, or years, the wobbliness doesn't last long, and it all comes back with a little practice.

RICHARD MILLER

The Form appears to be just the COBOL picture in a somewhat restricted form. Did this or the FORTRAN FORMAT affect this?

Answer: Details of COBOL did not penetrate as far west as RAND until JOSS design was well under way. The FORTRAN FORMAT is largely nonpictorial and was useful as a model only insofar as it provided a checklist of features which might be provided by JOSS. The true antecedent or progenitor of the JOSS Form was in fact the "Electric Accounting Machine Layout Form," which was used by those oldtimers such as Cliff Shaw who did computing in the early days on tabulating equipment, and served as a sort of programming form for guiding the wiring of machine control panels. It's a very old idea, and still useful.

RICHARD MILLER

Were outside users (outside of RAND) afraid to implement JOSS because of JOHNNIAC?

Answer: Because JOHNNIAC was a one-of-a-kind machine, available only at RAND, there was no way that actual experience in using JOSS could be evaluated by another organization before the decision to implement it was made, and there was a natural reluctance to implement without such an evaluation. Too, any organizations (at that time) with sufficient resources to undertake a major implementation such as JOSS probably had ideas of their own as to how the new technology of time sharing (where all such systems were grouped indiscriminately) could best be put to use. IBM did implement JOSS II for the 360 from RAND-supplied PDP-6 listings and documentation, and it is this version of JOSS II that is in current use at RAND.

BIOGRAPHY OF CHARLES L. BAKER

Charles L. Baker has been active in the field of computer science for more than 25 years. During this period he has directed and participated in systems analysis, design, and computer programming projects in the application areas of aircraft and aerospace engineering, oceanography, meteorology, military command and control, antisubmarine warfare, economic modeling and forecasting, and business-data processing. In addition, he has participated in all phases of computer software specification and development for both batch and on-line, interactive systems, including operating systems, compilers, assemblers, and data management components.

Currently he is a Senior Technical Director at Ocean Data Systems, Inc., where his responsibilities include design and development of multiuser interactive color graphics systems.

He holds a B.S. in Physics from MIT (1951) and has had graduate studies in Aerospace Engineering and Numerical Analysis at UCLA (1952–1954).

In 1955, while working for Douglas Aircraft, he was a delegate to the Project for the Advancement of Coding Techniques (PACT). He worked on the CPC I and CPC II calculators and installed the Douglas IBM 701 system.

From 1956 to 1967 he worked for the RAND Corporation. Among his activities were: project leader for the JOSS II on-line computer service; coordinating the research to determine the nature and extent of computer problem-solving support required. Technical activities included design and specification of the JOSS II remote typewriter console, interfaced to the computer through a unique private-wire installation which distributes "JOSS computer-power" automatically to any of 300 individual wall outlets in the RAND complex. As part of responsibility for operational evaluation of JOSS as implemented on RAND's JOHNNIAC computer, supervised production of, wrote script for, and appeared as narrator in a film, *JOSS.*

During period 1956 through 1961, he programmed the Information Processing Language Five (IPL-V) system for the IBM 704, 709, 7090, and 7044 series of machines, specified many features of the final, complete system, and participated in the preparation of the IPL-V Users' Manual.

As first acting secretary of SHARE, he organized the SHARE Operating System working group which produced the first large-scale operating system, SOS for the IBM 709. He submitted the initial proposal for the Modify and Load concept which was adopted as the basis for the SHARE Assembler, Compiler, and Translator, features of which are incorporated into all current computer operating systems.

XI

BASIC Session

Chairman: Thomas Cheatham
Speaker: Thomas E. Kurtz

PAPER: BASIC

Thomas E. Kurtz

Darthmouth College

1. Background

1.1. Dartmouth College

Dartmouth College is a small university dating from 1769, and dedicated "for the education and instruction of Youth of the Indian Tribes in this Land in reading, writing and all parts of learning . . . and also of English Youth and any others" (Wheelock, 1769). The undergraduate student body (now nearly 4000) outnumbers all graduate students by more than 5 to 1, and majors predominantly in the Social Sciences and the Humanities (over 75%).

In 1940 a milestone event, not well remembered until recently (Loveday, 1977), took place at Dartmouth. Dr. George Stibitz of the Bell Telephone Laboratories demonstrated publicly for the first time, at the annual meeting of the American Mathematical Society, the remote use of a computer over a communications line. The computer was a relay calculator designed to carry out arithmetic on complex numbers. The terminal was a Model 26 Teletype.

Another milestone event occurred in the summer of 1956 when John McCarthy organized at Dartmouth a summer research project on "artificial intelligence" (the first known use of this phrase). The computer scientists attending decided a new language was needed; thus was born LISP. [See the paper by McCarthy, pp. 173–185 in this volume. Ed.]

1.2. Dartmouth Comes to Computing

After several brief encounters, Dartmouth's liaison with computing became permanent and continuing in 1956 through the New England Regional Computer Center at MIT,

HISTORY OF PROGRAMMING LANGUAGES

515

Thomas E. Kurtz

sporting a new IBM 704 and heavily subsidized by IBM. The earliest use of this machine was without the aid of either an operating system or a higher level language. John Kemeny and I learned the Share Assembly Language (SAP), how to read memory dumps, and the joys of two-week turnaround (my schedule of train trips to Boston). Before the IBM 704 was installed at MIT, we used a similar machine through the courtesy of General Electric at Lynn, Massachusetts.

Disturbed by the intricacy of programming in assembly language and despairing of ever teaching it to our students and colleagues, John Kemeny devised DARSIMCO (DARtmouth SIMplified COde). In it, the common arithmetic operations were expressed as templates of two or three SAP instructions. Thus, to perform A + B = C, one wrote as a single template:

```
LDA A
FAD B
STO C
```

Similar templates were devised for subtraction, multiplication, division, and simple looping. This was, then, Dartmouth's first crack at a simple computer language. Little used, since FORTRAN became available the following year, DARSIMCO reflected Dartmouth's continuing concern for simplifying the computing process and bringing computing to a wider audience (Dartmouth, 1956).

FORTRAN appeared on the MIT machine in 1957. Its acceptance was tempered by its alleged inefficiency in comparison with assembly language. This allegation had little effect on us, and we quickly dropped both SAP and its dialect DARSIMCO. One incident in particular comes to mind. I had a project to calculate certain statistical percentage points over an array of third and fourth moment values. Indoctrinated by the maxim that FORTRAN was inefficient, and that one could and should save valuable machine cycles by coding directly in assembly language, I did just that. After several months of trying, reading memory dumps, and trying again, I admitted failure. I had consumed about one hour of valuable 704 time, and untold hours of my less valuable time. I then programmed the same computation in FORTRAN, inefficiently, I am sure. The answers appeared. About five minutes of computer time were used. This lesson—that programming in higher level languages could save computer time as well as person time—impressed me deeply.

1.3. Computing Comes to Dartmouth

An LGP-30 small computer arrived at Dartmouth in June of 1959. This computer had a memory of 4K 30-bit words on a drum that rotated 30 times a second, and had 16 simple instructions. Several undergraduates were persuaded that summer to explore what could be done with the new toy. One student, without any prior background in computing, prepared a simple higher level language and language processor he called DART (Hargraves, 1959). Obviously influenced by FORTRAN, but wishing to avoid scanning general arithmetic expressions, he required parentheses around all binary operators and their operands. Hardly earth-shaking, but one conclusion was inescapable: a good undergraduate student could achieve what at that time was a professional-level accomplishment, namely, the design and writing of a compiler. This observation was not overlooked.

At the same time E. T. Irons, then a graduate student at Princeton, spent the summer in Hanover while working on a syntax-directed compiler (Irons, 1961). Our attention was thus drawn to the International Algebraic Language known also as ALGOL 58. A group of four students (Stephen Garland, Robert Hargraves, Anthony Knapp, and Jorge Llacer) and I began to design and construct an ALGOL 58 compiler for the LGP-30. A paper (Samelson and Bauer, 1960) discussing what is now known as bottom-up parsing, provided the efficient scanning algorithm needed for a slow and small computer. Shortly, ALGOL 60 appeared (Naur, 1960), and our effort shifted to it.

Since the limited size of the LGP-30 precluded a full implementation of ALGOL 60, certain of its features (arrays called by value, own arrays, strings, variable array bounds, and recursion) were omitted; but we did include parameters called by name, using "thunks" (Ingerman, 1961; Irons and Feurzeig, 1961), and integer labels. We dubbed our work ALGOL 30, since it was for the LGP-30 (Kurtz, 1962a, Feb., 1962b, Mar.). From this project emerged a small group of undergraduate students who were well equipped to perform further work in the development of computer languages. For instance, one student (Garland) discovered that compound statements and blocks could be included in the Samelson and Bauer scanning algorithm. This simple fact was not published until some years later. (I have been unable to identify the source I clearly remember; the closest is Gries, 1968.)

The ALGOL 30 system suffered one defect that hindered its wide use as a student-oriented language: it was a two-pass system. The intermediate code was similar to relocatable binary, but had to be punched onto paper tape. Compilations could be "batched," but the delays between presenting the source code tape and the final execution were too great to allow widespread student use. It was clear that a "load-and-go" system was needed. Thus was born SCALP, a Self Contained ALgol Processor (Kurtz, 1962c, Oct.).

The design of SCALP (by undergraduates Garland and Knapp, and myself) was limited by having only one-third of the available 4K word memory for the compiler, another third for the run-time support routines (including software floating point routines), and the final third for the compiled user code. Several drastic decisions were made, the most severe of which was to limit the *for-loop* construct to only the *while* element, since one could obtain the *step-until* element as a special case.

Two other details of SCALP are worth mentioning. The student's program was compiled almost as fast as the source code paper tape could be read in. Furthermore, once in execution, a program could be traced and patched using the symbols of the source code. These two features allowed five or six student jobs to be completed in 15 minutes. Thus, quick turnaround and the ability to deal only with the source language were confirmed as essential for a student-oriented system. Hundreds of students over the next several years learned and used SCALP until it was replaced by BASIC (Kurtz, 1963a, Jan.).

Another experiment in language design occurred around 1962. The language was called DOPE—Dartmouth Oversimplified Programming Experiment (Kemeny, 1962). Kemeny was assisted by student Sidney Marshall. Intended to offer a smooth transition from flowcharting to computer programming on the LGP-30, it expressed typical flowchart operations as two or three operand commands. For example, the assignment C = A + B appeared as

        7 + A B C

and Z = SIN(X) as

        10 SIN X Z

Thomas E. Kurtz

Only one arithmetic operation per line was allowed. Variables could be single letters or letter–digit combinations, a harbinger of BASIC. The letters E through H were reserved for vectors, each allowing components numbered 1 through 16. In addition to the four main arithmetic operations $(+, -, \cdot, /)$, the commands included four functions (SQR, EXP, LOG, SIN), a jump (T), and a three-way branch (C)—shades of FORTRAN! Loops began with Z and ended with E, and allowed only unit step sizes. Input–output commands included an input (J), input and print a label (A), print a number (P), and print a new line (N).

Though not a success in itself, DOPE presaged BASIC. DOPE provided default vectors, default printing formats, and general input formats. Line numbers doubled as jump targets. Uppercase letters and lowercase letters could be used interchangeably.

While no one of these language projects (DARSIMCO, DART, ALGOL 30, SCALP, DOPE) was an unqualified success in its own right, they all were influenced by our goal to simplify the user interface. They taught us something about language design. And they confirmed that programming talent was available as we prepared for our next computing venture.

2. Rationale for BASIC

2.1. Goals of the Project

Dartmouth students are interested mainly in subjects outside the sciences—only about 25% major in science or engineering. While science students will learn computing naturally and well, the nonscience group produces most of the decision makers of business and government. We wondered, "How can sensible decisions about computing and its use be made by persons essentially ignorant of it?" This question begged the conclusion that non-science students should be taught computing. The hard question was thus not "whether" but "how." It seemed to us inescapable that to learn about computing one must deal with it directly; that is, one must actually write programs. Merely lecturing about computing would not work. But having large numbers of nonscience students learn to write programs in assembly language, or even FORTRAN or ALGOL, was clearly out of the question. The majority would balk at the seemingly pointless detail. What could we do?

The approaches common at the time seemed inadequate for our purpose. Typical access to computing, requiring punched cards and involving both programming and administrative hurdles, might be acceptable to technically minded students, but certainly not to others. Typical introductory courses that were really baby courses in numerical methods would not be elected by the majority of the students in whom we were interested. Furthermore, Dartmouth's English, foreign language, and distributive (humanities, sciences, social sciences) requirements weighed heavily against introducing whole new courses about computing.

We gradually settled on a fourfold approach. First, we would have to devise a computer system that would be friendly, easy to learn and use, and not require students to go out of their way. While we felt that our students would not accept punched cards, we did feel they would accept time sharing, a technique that had been demonstrated previously at MIT and elsewhere (Corbato *et al.*, 1962; McCarthy *et al.*, 1963). (Around 1960 or 1961, after a visit to the PDP-1 time shared computer at MIT, I can clearly recall John McCarthy saying, "Why don't you guys do time sharing?" Shortly afterward I said to Kemeny, "I think we ought to do time sharing." Kemeny responded, "OK." And that was that!) Computing could thus be brought to the comfort of work areas readily available to students. The newly developed ASCII code and inexpensive communications and terminals (Teletype models 33 and 35) came along in the nick of time. And we concluded, bravely perhaps, that we could design and construct a time-sharing system that would be friendly and easy to use. We had absolutely no doubt about the easy-to-use part. As to the design and construction, we were willing to believe that our undergraduate students could tackle literally any programming job we gave them. (For many years, this proved true. Only when the systems jobs required continuous attention for more than several terms did this approach falter. Still, Dartmouth students over the years accomplished far more than anyone might have been willing either to predict in advance, or to believe by hindsight.)

The second part of the project was to develop a new language—again, one that was easy to learn and use. While Kemeny instantly realized (in the spring of 1963) the need for designing a new language, I preferred to believe that, although existing languages such as FORTRAN and ALGOL were not suitable, reasonable subsets of these languages could be devised. This belief proved wrong. For example, the compound statement is a central concept in ALGOL; one cannot construct a nontrivial *for-statement* without it. But the idea of a compound statement posed pedagogical problems; it would have to be defined and explained. I had even toyed with the notion (Kurtz, 1963b, May) that

> **for** i := 1 **step** 1 **until** n **do**
> **begin** a := b **end** next i;

which is legal ALGOL, could be written

> **for** i := 1 **step** 1 **until** n **do**
> a := b **next** i;

With FORTRAN, a subset wouldn't make sense if it violated the IJKLMN convention. But how many nonscience students could appreciate the distinction betwen integer and non-integer variables. Other problems included remembering the punctuation in the DO and IF statements, and the order of the three statement numbers in the IF statement. Very early, then, I agreed with Kemeny that a new language was needed to meet our requirements.

The third component of the project concerned the student's initial introduction to computing. For reasons given earlier, a whole course was not practical. On the other hand, the principal motivation for a student to learn computing would come from applications in which the student might have a direct interest. Accordingly, we made plans to introduce computing as an *adjunct* to two courses: second-term calculus, and finite mathematics. The applications of computing came from the topics of the course. Over the years about 85% of all Dartmouth students have taken at least one of these courses (Kemeny and Kurtz, 1968).

The fourth and final element was the decision to operate the computer with open access. Dartmouth has a large open-stack library, and it was natural for us to carry over this philosophy into our computing operation. Achieving open access was aided by the virtual absence, in those days, of government-supported research at Dartmouth. We were thus freed from the major constraint found at other large institutions—the apparent requirement to charge students and faculty for computer services lest income from government grants be jeopardized.

The ideas neatly summarized above did not arise overnight, but actually evolved gradually over the years since 1956, and depended in crucial ways on the nature of Dartmouth as a small liberal arts university. Although Kemeny and I, and our student programmers, did most of the work, we were backed at all times by President John S. Dickey, Dean of the Faculty Leonard M. Rieser, and Dean of the Thayer School of Engineering Myron Tribus. In fact, Tribus writes (letter, 1977 November 7):

> I remember quite vividly an afternoon conversation with John Kemeny in which we agreed that certain requirements would be met even if it meant indefinitely postponing the computer.
>
> a. Students would have free access.
> b. There would be complete privacy. No one would know what the students were doing.
> c. The system should be easy to learn. The computer should contain its own instructions.
> d. The system would be designed to save the time of the user even if it appeared that the computer was being "wasted."
> e. Turnaround time should be sufficiently rapid that students could use the system for homework.
> f. The system would be pleasant and friendly.

In early 1964, with the assistance of two grants from the NSF and educational discounts from General Electric, Dartmouth acquired a GE-225 computer (replaced in the summer of 1964 by a GE-235) combined with a Datanet-30 and a disk that could be accessed from either machine (Kemeny and Kurtz, 1968). Kemeny had begun work during the summer of 1963 on a compiler for a draft version of BASIC; GE provided access to GE-225 machines in the area. Design and coding for the operating system began in the fall of 1963, with the main responsibility falling to students Michael Busch and John McGeachie. The pace quickened in February of 1964 when the equipment arrived on the campus. The first BASIC program under time sharing was run on May 1, 1964, around 4 A.M. Three terminals in May became eleven by June, and twenty in the fall.

The design of BASIC and of the operating system went hand-in-hand. Extant notes, memoranda, and recollections are concerned more with the design and development of the operating system than with BASIC itself. On the other hand, the project had a single set of goals, and these goals applied as much to the design of BASIC as to the design of the time-sharing system. For example, Memo No. 1 (Kurtz, 1963c, Nov.) reads:

> The Time Sharing System should be externally simple and easy to use for the casual programmer . . . .

A little later, the same document states:

> . . . flexible, including compiling in standard languages. However, no attempt will be made at making the use of the Time Sharing equipment be compatible with standard use of a computer.

(Presumably, "standard" meant "batch.") This latter quote sets the record straight: the Dartmouth system was always a multilingual system, even in its conception. And finally, on p. 2 of that memo:

> In all cases where there is a choice between simplicity and efficiency, simplicity is chosen.

Need I say more.

2.2. BASIC and Time Sharing

In addition to reflecting a common set of goals, the language BASIC and the time-sharing system in which it resides were, and still are, inextricably meshed. It is impossible for us to talk about one without the other. For example, each statement in BASIC begins with a line number, primarily to aid editing. To cooperate, the operating system monitor assumed that all inputted lines of text that started with a digit were part of a program. In addition, all programs were *automatically* sorted by line number prior to their being listed or run. Additions, deletions, and changes to programs could thus be made without overtly involving an editor. On the other hand, all inputted lines of text that started with a nondigit were assumed to be monitor commands. The discrimination between program lines and commands occurred at the earliest possible juncture in the operating system, rather than deeply within some editor, thus encouraging efficiency and rapid response. (A user wishing to create or change a text file lacking line numbers needed to overtly invoke an editor.)

A second example is the choice of monitor commands, such as HELLO, NEW, OLD, SAVE, LIST, RUN, and GOODBYE. Short common English words as system commands encouraged computer use by nonexperts. The true impact of this choice is almost beyond comprehension to a computer specialist, who is quite at home with "logon," "catalog," "execute," and "logoff," or their single letter abbreviations that are so common. Persons who use BASIC but don't understand the distinction between a language processor and an operating system monitor are incredulous when they learn that NEW, OLD, and RUN are not part and parcel of BASIC. The moral is obvious: simple and understandable command languages, like simple programming languages, are essential if nonexperts are to use the computer.

A final example is that the user deals directly only with his BASIC program. He need not even know that such things as "object code" exist. The user could compile (by typing RUN), receive error messages, edit by typing line-numbered lines, and recompile, all within seconds. Execution would automatically occur if there were no errors. This approach obviously required that compilation be fast, which in turn meant that it had to be single-pass. BASIC was always, and still is, a language simple enough to permit single pass compilation. Forward GO TO references and functions defined near the end of a program could be handled with linked lists and a "clean up" pass to fill in the missing transfers.

We make the point later that BASIC originally was not a true interactive language, since the INPUT statement that allowed data to be entered from the terminal during execution was not added until later. But BASIC lives, and has always lived, in interactive time sharing environments. While conceptually possible, a "batch" version of BASIC that used punched cards would be unthinkable.

2.3. Other Influences on BASIC

The relation of BASIC to FORTRAN and ALGOL is apparent. From FORTRAN comes the order of the three loop-controlling values—initial, final, step—thus permitting the step size to be omitted if it is unity. From ALGOL come the words FOR and STEP, and the more natural testing for loop completion *before* executing the body of the loop. These and other similarities are not surprising, since we knew both languages, and we did not hesitate to borrow ideas.

Thomas E. Kurtz

We also knew about the interactive language JOSS, but we preferred to stay nearer the main stream of "standard" languages. Several JOSS conventions—decimal points in line numbers, and periods after statements—did not appeal to us. Kemeny and I also had conversations with Richard Conway and others from Cornell about CORC, their "friendly" student-oriented language designed for card input (Conway and Maxwell, 1963). Like BASIC, CORC required the word LET for an assignment statement and made no syntactic distinction between integers and "real" numbers. Unlike BASIC, CORC simplified data input by fixing the format, provided an approximate equality, included a simple block structure, and required declaration of all variables. Interestingly, the educational goals stated in the article are similar to Dartmouth's, except that CORC was intended primarily for engineering students while BASIC was directed to liberal arts students.

BASIC was also influenced by the earlier DARSIMCO, which was really an approach to assembly language programming. For example, a BASIC program consists of a number of "instructions." Each instruction consists of three parts: the "instruction number," the "operation," and the "operand." This similarity is exhibited in the first BASIC program to appear in published form (Kemeny and Kurtz, 1964a, p. 4):

Instr. no.	Operation	Operand
10	LET	X = (7+8)/3
20	PRINT	X
30	END	

2.4. Compiling versus Interpreting

While its implementation is not strictly part of a language, it is important to realize that Dartmouth BASIC was *always* intended to be compiled. A strong argument favoring an interpretive environment concerns "direct" versus "indirect" mode; that is, a user can enter a statement for direct execution, or change the program, *after* execution of the program has begun. This feature was never considered important for BASIC. We were concerned lest interpretative execution times would be prohibitive for any but the smallest programs. Instead, BASIC was intended to be a simple compiler-based language designed for use with terminals rather than cards, and for quick turnaround rather than batch-type delays.

The bias toward interpretive language processing in interactive environments was probably also influenced by the slowness of many compilers, which employed multiple passes. (One horror story claims that a certain FORTRAN compiler required 45 seconds to compile a program consisting *only* of the END statement; this was because the termination routine was located at the end of a long subroutine tape.) We estimated that a BASIC "compile" would require no more time than a "linking load". Load-and-go compiling placed a limit on program size, since the entire object code was assumed to be present in memory; this limitation proved more theoretical than real. As BASIC grew, program sizes were allowed to grow without conceding the single-pass ideal.

Another argument advanced in favor of interpreting involved instant syntactical error analysis. This approach went too far, in our view, and posed too great a load on the computer. In addition, it required users to compose programs in a restricted manner, giving them error messages before they had a chance to make obvious corrections on their own. BASIC at Dartmouth *never* checked for errors line-by-line. Instead, our strategy separated program construction from compiling. If there were errors, reasonable error messages in English, limited to five in number per compilation, were produced only after the user requested a run. For small programs, this response occurred within five or ten seconds.

Despite the fact that both the Dartmouth and the General Electric implementations use compilers, BASIC is widely believed to be an interpretive language. Perhaps the reason is that most minicomputer implementations of BASIC use interpreters, for good reasons only loosely related to BASIC itself. Furthermore, minicomputers became quite widely available, and were the principal agents in the spread of BASIC. For instance, all of these minicomputers used interpreters for BASIC: the HP 2000, the DEC PDP/8, the DEC PDP/11, the DG NOVA, the WANG, and even the early DEC PDP/10. But BASIC itself, particularly at Dartmouth, possesses few properties that would a priori incline it toward being interpretive. In fact, its closest relative in many ways is FORTRAN, which was never thought to be interpretive.

3. Descriptions of BASIC

This section details the features of the sequence of BASICs developed at Dartmouth. The early versions were the most influential, but later versions are included to illustrate how the language has grown without sacrificing the original goals. What we omit, with deep regret, is the study of the many versions of BASIC developed elsewhere. Features have been catalogued for the more commonly available versions (Isaacs, 1973), and the diversity seems greater than the unity. All of these versions should however receive credit for helping to make computing more accessible to more people, which is the unifying theme that underlies BASIC.

3.1. BASIC, the First Edition

The first version of BASIC (Kemeny and Kurtz, 1974a) is similar to the proposed American National standard Minimal BASIC (ANSI, 1978). It included the statements or "instructions": LET, PRINT, END, FOR, NEXT, GOTO, IF THEN, DEF, READ, DATA, DIM, GOSUB, RETURN, and REM. A variable name consisted of a single letter or a single letter followed by single digit. (This restriction did not seem severe to us for two reasons: first, composing programs is quicker if shorter names are used; second, being mathematicians, we were accustomed to short variable names. As I recall, two arguments for short variable names were: we were concerned about symbol table lookup time, and we wanted space independence so that, for instance, FOR I = 1 TO NSTEP2 would be recognized as FOR I = 1 TO N STEP 2.) Subscripted variables were named by single letters and could have one or two dimensions.

Expressions, which were called "formulas," were governed by the usual rules. The exponentiation operator was the up-arrow $\uparrow$, a symbol then available on a Teletype. This symbol was selected " . . . since on a teletype typewriter it is impossible to print superscripts, . . ." (Kemeny and Kurtz, 1964a, p. 5). The exponentiation operation $A \uparrow B$ took the absolute value of A, no doubt in order to calculate it by EXP(B*LOG(ABS(A))). The manual explained that to compute $X \uparrow 3$ when X could be negative, one should use X*X*X. Through an error in the treatment of unary minus signs (Kemeny, personal communication, 1978 Feb. 7), $-X \uparrow 2$ was incorrectly interpreted as $(-X) \uparrow 2$. This was corrected in the third edition of BASIC.

Ten intrinsic functions were provided: SIN, COS, TAN, ATN, EXP, LOG, SQR, ABS, RND, and INT. The first four had the usual definitions and used radian measure. The next two used base e, not base 10. SQR provided the square root of the absolute value. ABS was of course the absolute value function. RND provided a "random" number between 0 and 1, but was quaint in one way: no doubt we were merely being lazy when we required that RND have a dummy argument. Although in later versions we quickly removed this unfortunate syntax, the damage had been done, and our bad choice later resurfaced in several ugly forms. The first version of INT truncated toward zero. That is, ". . . INT(3.45) = 3, INT(-34.567) = -34, . . " (Kemeny and Kurtz, 1964a, p. 31). INT was changed in the third edition of BASIC to conform to the "floor" function, in order to allow rounding by using INT(X + .5) for both positive and negative values of X. The GE-225 word size (20 bits) seduced us into making a third unfortunate decision—all function names had to have three letters, 20 bits being enough for three six-bit characters.

Regarding variable types, we felt that a distinction between "fixed" and "floating" was less justified in 1964 than earlier. The ratio of the execution times between floating and fixed calculations was diminishing. Furthermore, to our potential audience the distinction between an integer number and a non-integer number would seem esoteric. A number is a number is a number. Since all numeric variables were of type "number," there was no need either for explicit typing, as in ALGOL, or implicit typing, as with the FORTRAN IJKLMN convention.

We now consider the individual "instructions." The assignment statement required (and still requires) the word LET. We felt the assignment idea to be particularly tricky, and the word LET helped. LET X = X + 1 is easier for novices to understand than is X = X + 1. Furthermore, we felt it important that *all* BASIC statements begin with an English word. The "instruction" END was required to be the last statement in a program.

The PRINT statement allowed expressions, used the comma as a separator, and allowed quoted material. The comma was "a signal to move to the next print zone (or to a new line if we are in the fifth zone)" (Kemeny and Kurtz, 1964a, p. 25). The comma could be omitted when the quoted material was combined with a simple variable or expression, as in PRINT "FIRST NO. =" A, "SECOND NO. =" B (Kemeny and Kurtz, 1964a, p. 25); later versions of BASIC required either a comma or a semicolon between the quoted material and the expression.

A cornerstone of BASIC is that numbers are automatically printed in a fixed format, thus freeing the user from having to learn about formatting. The format used depended on the number. If the number happened to be an integer, it was printed that way, without a decimal point. If the number was not an integer, but could be represented in a fixed decimal format with the decimal point adjacent to one of the six significant figures, it was so printed. Otherwise, an exponential format was used, with six significant digits and a power of ten. Six significant digits, which was within the accuracy of our hardware, was felt to be adequate for most applications.

The FOR and NEXT statements were designed to be more general than the FORTRAN DO and CONTINUE, but without allowing recalculation of the stepsize or final value, as permitted in ALGOL. The running variable is of course available to the programmer. We allowed noninteger values in the loop statement. This decision caused us fewer serious problems than it might have, for the reason that arithmetic was done in binary floating point, and the results truncated rather than rounded. Thus, for instance, the value 0.1 was internally slightly less; consequently, a typical FOR statement FOR X = 1 TO 10 STEP .1 worked as the unsuspecting programmer expected; namely, it provided 101 values of X = 1, 1.1, . . . , 9.9, 10. But since negative numbers on the GE-225 were represented as two's complements, −0.1 truncated became slightly larger in absolute value, and the construction FOR X = 10 TO 1 STEP − .1, fortunately less common, would *not* provide values of X = 10, 9.9, . . . , 1.1, 1.

The GOTO statement requires some explanation. We had already decided that BASIC programs would have line numbers. Why not, then, have the GOTO statement use the already existing line numbers? For those who program mentally, forward-pointing GOTOs required picking line numbers for later portions of the program. But this nuisance seemed preferable to defining a new syntactical entity called ''label'', and explaining this to students. Whatever the strengths or weaknesses of this decision, it was made, it is simple, and it *is* BASIC.

The IF-THEN statement allowed a relational expression using any one of the six relational operators: =, <, >, >=, <=, <>. The relational expression did not have to be enclosed in parentheses, as it did in FORTRAN. The two-way branching was pedagogically simpler than the three-way IF statement in FORTRAN.

The first version of BASIC allowed two methods for aiding program organization: the DEF defined function and the subroutine. DEF could be used to define up to 26 additional functions, with three-letter names ranging from FNA to FNZ. These had to have exactly one argument, and were restricted to a single line. They would appear anywhere in the program.

Subroutines were provided by a subroutine jump, GOSUB, which used a stack for the return address, and a RETURN statement to effect the return. In violation of present theories about program structure, a subroutine could have multiple entry points, and multiple exit points, but could not pass arguments. Some of us have learned how to use GOSUB with discipline, but BASIC itself remains laissez faire on this issue.

READ and DATA operated in an obvious manner. The interesting point is that READ was the *only* input statement in the first version of BASIC. Thus, not only was the first version of BASIC not interpretive, it wasn't even interactive!

The REM statement was included. We of course knew that FORTRAN had its C statements and ALGOL its comments, but the reason is not recorded for choosing the statement name REM or REMARK in BASIC.

The DIM statement for specifying array bounds was optional. In the absence of a DIM statement for an array, BASIC provided default subscript ranges of 1–10 in each dimension. The terms *vector* and *matrix* were used here. In later editions of the manual, we used the less mathematical *list* and *table*.

The conventions for creating and editing programs using line numbers were defined in this manual. One could SAVE programs, RUN (compile and go), and LIST them, but not much more. It was suggested that debugging could be aided by inserting extra PRINT statements. To start a new program, one had to type HELLO and reenter the user number, which was the student's regular ID number. Running time was computed to the nearest second, so that the trailing message "TIME: 0 SECS." was common, and the manual warned the user to "not be shocked" by it (Kemeny and Kurtz, 1964a, p. 17). The user was admonished that "since the space on the disks is limited, users are asked not to

Thomas E. Kurtz

save a program unless they really expect to use it again'' (Kemeny and Kurtz, 1964a, p. 18).

The mathematical flavor of what was done is reflected in the examples appearing in the first manual: average of 100 logarithms, quadratic equation solver, maximum value of a function, Simpson's Rule, product of two matrices, binomial probabilities. The program that found the maximum value of a function took ''1 MINS. 11 SECS.'' on the GE-225 (Kemeny and Kurtz, 1964a, p. 37). (A penciled notation states that the same problem in FORTRAN on a 1620 model II required 4 minutes 55 seconds.) In the manual we promised that with the forthcoming GE-235, the problem should take less than 10 seconds. Just for fun, that same problem required 1.181 seconds in 1977 (in Dartmouth BASIC on a HIS 66/40 computer). Finally, the manual promises that ''a second language, MATRIX, will be designed specially for matrix work'' (Kemeny and Kurtz, 1964a, p. 39).

3.2. BASIC, the Second Edition

Starting with the third edition of BASIC, each new edition of the manual signaled a significantly different version of BASIC. Since 1966 we have therefore identified the versions of BASIC by the edition number of the manual. On the other hand, the first and second editions of the manual each referred to the original version of BASIC, with only minor changes. The manuals themselves differ in that the first edition was organized as a reference manual while the second edition was organized as a primer, reflecting BASIC's principal clientele.

One other historical fact: although neither the first edition nor the second edition was actually signed, my memory records that John Kemeny wrote the first edition while I wrote the second edition.

The manual for the second edition (Kemeny and Kurtz, 1964b, Oct.) bears a date only five months after that of the birth of BASIC. In that brief time, the semicolon was added as an allowable print separator. Its purpose was to ''pack'' numeric output by using only the actual spaces needed, up to the nearest multiple of three spaces. (This unfortunate glitch, rectified in later versions, can be traced in non-Dartmouth implementations.)

The other important addition was that the zero subscript, as in A(0) or B(0,0), was now allowed. Polynomial coefficients could now be represented naturally as, for instance, C(0), . . . , C(N).

A slightly different version of BASIC called CARDBASIC was also described in the second edition. It was designed for card input and printer output, and operated in background, which shared time slices with the foreground users. CARDBASIC contained the first version of the MAT statements, which had been promised in the first edition. These statements appeared in regular BASIC in the third edition, and are therefore described in the next section. There were of course other features, such as allowing longer programs and more data. CARDBASIC differed in one other important way: it did not allow the zero subscript. CARDBASIC lived a short life, since one of our goals was to eliminate dependence on punched cards.

I make one last observation about the second edition. Long before the current surge of interest in structure and style in programming, the following sentences appeared (p. 48):

> There are some matters that do not affect the correct running of programs, but pertain to style
> and neatness. For instance, as between two or more similar ways to prepare a part of a program,

one should select the one that is most easily understood unless there is an important reason not to do so.

And, after some hints about data organization, the following appeared (p. 49):

No doubt the user will be able to devise other ways to make a program neat and readable. But again, the important consideration in style is to program in a way that makes it more understandable and useful to both oneself and others in the future.

These sentences give little hint as to what the user was supposed to do in order to achieve good style, but at least the thought was there. Since then several stylistic ideas have been tried, and there is now a book about structure and style using elementary BASIC (Nevison, 1978).

3.3. BASIC, the Third Edition

There were only two major changes to Dartmouth BASIC in the 15 months since the second edition. By 1966 we knew our efforts would shortly be directed to a GE-635 computer, and we therefore felt that further development of BASIC for the GE-265 was pointless. The manual (Kemeny and Kurtz, 1966) records a few minor changes. A SGN (signum) function was added, and it was noted that repeated exponentiation was left-associative. A RESTORE statement was added to reset the internal pointer to the data block, which was constructed from the totality of the DATA statements. The precedence of the unary minus sign was finally corrected (p. 40) so that $-X \uparrow 2$ would be interpreted as $-(X \uparrow 2)$.

The first major addition was that of the INPUT statement, which accepted data from the terminal during execution. BASIC was at last an interactive language!

The second major addition was the collection of MAT statements, originally tested in CARDBASIC (see the previous section). These allowed operations on arrays of one and two dimensions. When it mattered, a vector—an array of one dimension—was treated as a column vector. The following operations were described:

```
MAT READ A, B, C
MAT PRINT A, B; C
MAT C = A + B
MAT C = A - B
MAT C = A * B
MAT C = INV(A)
MAT C = TRN(A)
MAT C + (scalar expression)*A
MAT C = ZER
MAT C = CON
MAT C = IDN
```

In MAT PRINT, the semicolon caused packed printing while the comma caused printing in zones. The * stood for matrix multiplication, not element-by-element multiplication. INV and TRN produced an inverse and transpose, respectively. ZER and CON produced arrays of zeros and ones, respectively, while IDN produced an identity matrix. The statement MAT READ A(M,N) caused the array A to be redimensioned before the reading took place. Redimensioning was also allowed with the ZER, CON, and IDN functions. MAT A + B*A and MAT A = B were specifically disallowed. It was stated (p. 47) that the former would "result in *nonsense*" and that the latter could be achieved by the statement MAT A = (1)*B.

The MAT statements in CARDBASIC (Kemeny and Kurtz, 1964b, Oct.) had dealt with arrays whose subscripts started with 1. In the third edition (Kemeny and Kurtz, 1966), subscripts started with 0, and the MAT statements were changed accordingly. Thus, for example, CON(3,4) was a four-by-five array of ones. This also meant that the upper left hand corner of a matrix was the element subscripted (0,0). Needless to say, we were not completely happy with our choices.

On a happier note, here was the first appearance in BASIC of indentation to suggest the scope of a loop (p. 19).

3.4. BASIC, the Fourth Edition

By 1965–1966, system use had grown to about thirty simultaneous Teletype model 33 and 35 terminals, a number of which were off campus in secondary schools and colleges. Plans were afoot to replace the hardware with a GE-635 and move to a new building. Although the third edition continued in use into the fall of 1967, a new experimental version of BASIC appeared on the GE-635 in the spring of 1967. It was described in the Supplement to the BASIC Manual, Third Edition (Kemeny and Kurtz, 1967).

The software for the new hardware was developed jointly by General Electric and Dartmouth; GE wrote the operating system while Dartmouth wrote the compilers and editors. Both General Electric and Dartmouth contributed to the design of this version of BASIC. For instance, GE made suggestions concerning strings and files, presumably to improve compatibility with their Mark I BASIC (phone conversation, Neal Weidenhofer, 1978 February 15).

The Supplement notes that the previously required dummy argument for the RND function was omitted, and a new statement, RANDOMIZE, was added to "randomize" the starting point of the random number sequence. Defined functions were now allowed to have no arguments. The ON-GOTO statement was added as a multiple-way branch. In order to "increase the similarity between the ON and IF-THEN" all variations—IF-THEN, IF-GOTO, ON-THEN, and ON-GOTO—were permitted. The argument of the ON-GOTO was truncated and, if out of range, caused a program halt.

The semicolon PRINT separator now produced contiguous printing. A TAB function was added, with the column positions numbered from 0 to 74. Multiple assignments in a single LET statement were allowed, as were assignments to subscripted variables having subscripted variables as subscripts. For the first time, BASIC initialized all variables to zero.

Two major additions appeared. The first provided string variables and arrays of strings (one-dimensional only) together with all relational operators, thus allowing the sorting of alphabetical information. The DATA statement was expanded to allow unquoted string constants as data. String data and numeric data were retained in two separate pools, regardless of how they might be intermixed in the source program. A statement RESTORE$ was provided to reset the pointer to the string data. (RESTORE* reset the numeric data pointer, while RESTORE reset both; this feature persisted until the sixth edition of

BASIC in 1971.) One serious error was made, with the good intention of making things easier for the casual programmer—trailing spaces were ignored in string comparisons. Thus "YES" and "YES ƀ" were treated as equal. (This feature persists into Dartmouth's current BASIC, but will almost certainly disappear in the next version.)

The other major change was in the MAT package. There were a few minor additions, such as allowing MAT A = B, and various options for MAT PRINT. But the important change was that MAT now ignored the zeroth row and column. A programmer could now expect to find the "corner" element of a matrix in position (1,1). This compromise has worked well over the years, despite theoretical and esthetic arguments against it. One statement, MAT INPUT V, where V is one-dimensional array variable, was added to permit arbitrary amounts of input, separated by commas. Though not strictly speaking a MAT operation, this capability was urgently needed. A zero-argument function NUM was added to provide the actual number of data entered.

The manual for the fourth edition finally appeared (Dartmouth, 1968). Since most of the new features had been described in the Supplement to the Third Edition (Kemeny and Kurtz, 1967), only a few additional features now made their appearance.

Multiple-line defined functions were allowed, though they still accepted only numeric arguments and produced only numeric values. The CHANGE statement was added to change a string to a numeric vector consisting of the ASCII codes for each character of the string, and vice versa. The zeroth element of the vector contained the number of characters. This capability proved extraordinarily useful, since any conceivable string operation could be carried out by equivalent operations on numbers.

3.5. BASIC, the Fifth Edition

This, the first version of BASIC to exist with the DTSS operating system, was described initially in two supplements to the fourth edition of BASIC (Dartmouth 1969 February, April). The fifth edition manual appeared in late 1970 (Dartmouth, 1970).

Important changes appeared in this version of BASIC. The most significant was the addition of files. DTSS was designed around a random access file system. The catalog entry for each file included a number of "device addresses" so that a file could be distributed over several devices. The address of any particular point in the file could be calculated easily from these device addresses. We were thus able to allow both sequential files, which we called "terminal format" files, and random access files. The latter could contain either numeric or string data, but not both. A FILES statement associated filenames with file reference numbers, which were really the ordinal numbers of the filenames in the FILES statement. (This stringent early binding requirement was relaxed with the FILE statement, described shortly, and was eliminated in the sixth edition of BASIC.) For random access files, the file type was indicated explicitly in the file name. Numeric file names required a "%" following the filename proper, while string files require a "$xx", where xx was a constant integer that gave the maximum string length.

The FILE statement was introduced to allow changing the file name associated with a particular file reference number. This more natural file opening mechanism became more commonly used, even though the FILES statement remained; the user merely specified unnamed scratch files in the FILES statement and specified his real files in several FILE statements.

Thomas E. Kurtz

In order to help casual programmers distinguish between sequential and random-access files, separate statements were provided. The PRINT and INPUT statements applied to sequential files. IF END was used to determine the end-of-file condition. Both input and printing operations could take place on the same file.

For random-access files, the principle statements were READ and WRITE. The location of the file pointer was given by a LOC function, and the file length by LOF. The RESET statement for this type of file could set the pointer to any location in the file. The end of the file was detected by a statement such as:

```
IF LOC(#1) >= LOF(#1) THEN <process end of file>.
```

Two program segmentation features were added in this version. The simplest was CHAIN, which allowed a program to initiate the execution of another program. CHAIN permitted almost any system structure, although it was inefficient at times. It could, for instance, allow a program to create a whole new program, and then transfer to it. At this stage, only simple chaining was allowed, though later versions allowed file passing.

The other segmentation feature was called subprograms, although it was really a variant of overlaying. The variable names of the several segments were common, as if in a giant COMMON, but the line numbers were independent. These so-called subprograms were referred to by reference number, and obviously had to be compiled with the main program. There were a number of petty restrictions with this feature, and by hindsight it is easy to conclude that this was a bad idea. It did serve, however, to allow construction of moderately large systems using BASIC. The most notable was the first version of IMPRESS, a system for analyzing social science survey data (Dartmouth, 1972).

These two segmentation features were similar to features designed by GE for its Mark I BASIC on the GE-265 computer. It is not known whether Dartmouth devised them independently or copied them from GE.

This version contained corrections of previous minor flaws, such as now leaving the for variable untouched if the for loop was to be executed zero times. Two-dimensional string arrays were added. The individual characters of a string could be obtained only through the CHANGE statement. Defined functions could now have string arguments and values. Several new functions were added: CLK$, DAT$, LEN, USR$, STR$, VAL, ASC, and TIM. They provided, respectively, the wall clock time, the date, the length of a string, the current user number, the printed form of a number but without leading or trailing spaces, the numeric value of a string presumed to represent a number, the ASCII number of a character, and the elapsed running time of a job. In-line comments appeared for the first time, using the apostrophe as a separator.

The CHANGE statement was amplified to allow specifying the bit size of the characters. Thus, CHANGE A TO A$ BIT 4 allowed the string A$ to contain decimal digits, each requiring only four bits, thereby obtaining greater packing densities for data. (This feature was added to accommodate Project IMPRESS.)

User defined functions were allowed to be recursive, but were implemented so inefficiently that they were (arbitrarily) prohibited from being recursive in the subsequent version of BASIC.

In the MAT package, MAT A = A*B was still not allowed.

3.6. BASIC, the Sixth Edition

In the fall of 1969, even prior to the appearance of the manual for the fifth edition of BASIC, we began designing the sixth edition. In addition to Kemeny and myself, the group included three former students who had returned to Dartmouth as faculty: Stephen Garland, John McGeachie, and Robert Hargraves. It is probably the best-designed and most stable software system Dartmouth has ever written. Previous versions had been hastily designed, introducing many flaws to be corrected in subsequent versions, which appeared often. This time we designed thoughtfully and slowly. Ideas were carefully discussed. Specifications were written down in advance. Undergraduate programmers Kenneth Longmuir and Stephen Reiss began their work only after the design was essentially complete. The compiler and runtime support routines were extensively tested, and were operated as an experimental version for over three months during the summer of 1971. The manual was prepared in advance and published *prior* to the official installation of the new version (Mather and Waite, 1971). A formal specification was prepared; it appeared two years later (Garland, 1973). This new version went into regular operation on September 21, 1971. There were almost no problems, conversions having taken place during the summer. This stands in our mind as a rare and shining example of how a major system change should take place.

Though not part of the ancient history of BASIC, the design of the sixth edition at Dartmouth is discussed here for several reasons. First, it really is the culmination of the original BASIC project, having grown from the rapidly changing earlier versions. Second, it appeared first in 1971, which was seven years from the initial version, and which was about seven years ago. Third, it has been used since 1971 without significant change, a rarity among university-built software.

Major changes were made to subprograms, files, the string package, and output format control. (Minor changes were also made, but these will not be discussed here.)

The most significant change was the scrapping of the previous subprogramming feature, and its replacement by subprograms that connect to the calling program only through the calling sequence. The statements used are CALL, SUB, and SUBEND. Parameters are specified by reference. There is no syntactical distinction between input and output parameters. Unlike early FORTRAN, parameters and arguments are matched at each CALL for correct type and number. Unlike ALGOL, parameters cannot be specified "by name," nor can there be global variables. Since the subprograms exist independently of the calling program, they can be separately compiled and collected into libraries. They can also overlay one another, thus allowing BASIC to be used for constructing large systems. Indeed, the management information system (FIND) used at Dartmouth is written almost entirely in BASIC (McGeachie and Kreider, 1974).

The second major change was to files. The FILES statement was dropped completely. The FILE statement provides execution-time binding of file names to file reference numbers. The requirement for file typing by trailing character was removed, since BASIC can almost always tell what the user wants. The ambiguous case occurs in writing to an empty random-access string file; here, the MARGIN statement specifies the maximum string length for such a file. Two new functions were added to permit file type checking by the programmer. In the previous version, a nonexistent file name appearing in a FILE statement would cause termination. In this version, no error can occur on a FILE statement. A program can then use special functions to determine if the file actually exists, and what operations are permitted on it. Naturally, if an inconsistent operation is attempted, termination still occurs.

That we should expand string manipulation in BASIC was clear. Less clear was what substring notation should be used. We therefore chose to use string functions, since they could be changed more easily than new syntax. The SEG$ function provides a substring, while the "&" causes string concatenation. The POS function can locate a given string expression in a string. Together, these functions allow all string operations. For example, assignment into the interior of a string can be done by constructing the desired string with SEG$ and &.

A form of "image" formatting was added. It is employed by including in the PRINT statement a string expression which specifies the image (rather than the statement number of an "image" statement).

A final note: MAT A = A*B is now legal.

4. Dartmouth and General Electric

The history of Dartmouth time sharing and the BASIC language is intertwined with the early history of the General Electric time-sharing business. It is therefore appropriate here to outline key events in the relationship. This will not be a complete history, nor will it extend credit to all that are due it.

Our first technical contact with General Electric occurred in the summer of 1962. Anthony Knapp (a student) and I visited GE in Phoenix and examined the GE-225, the Datanet-930 (a predecessor to the Datanet-30), and the dual access disk controller. On returning to Dartmouth, Knapp sketched, in two weeks, an outline of a time-sharing system using that equipment. A descriptive document entitled MESS (Knapp and Kurtz, 1962) was mailed to everyone we had met, no doubt in the hope that GE would immediately want to give us a computer on which to carry out our ideas. MESS elicited no response.

Our own plans nevertheless gathered steam, and in April of 1963 Dartmouth sent to General Electric a letter of intent to purchase a system. During the summer of 1963, John Kemeny developed a compiler for a draft version of BASIC, using GE-225 computers in the New England area. Our own hardware arrived in February of 1964, with assists from GE educational discounts and two NSF grants made in January 1964.

During the spring and summer, persons from the Engineering Department at General Electric in Phoenix followed our progress. They provided both moral and material assistance—a FORTRAN compiler and additional magnetic tape drives, for example. In the fall, Dartmouth demonstrated at the Fall Joint Computer Conference in San Francisco, with General Electric providing the costs of the display. In December of 1964 and January of 1965 a copy of the Dartmouth system, including BASIC and ALGOL, was installed in the Engineering Department in Phoenix.

Shortly thereafter, operation of that machine was transferred to GE's already-established service bureau business. Since the hardware was a marriage of the GE-235 and the Datanet-30, the new system was named the GE-265. Additional copies were put into operation as their service bureau business grew.

In 1965 we attempted to obtain support from GE for our continuing software work. Louis Rader, then a Vice President of General Electric, responded in September of 1965 by offering to place an entire GE-635 system in the Kiewit Computation Center then under construction. The terms included joint use of the machine for three years, and a joint project to develop an operating system for that machine. GE was to retain title to the machine for the period of the agreement, which started on October 1, 1966.

While Dartmouth ceased in 1965 enhancing its third edition version of BASIC (see Section 3.3), GE added important features to its version for the Mark I service. These features included strings and files (phone conversation, Derek Hedges, 1978 February). They also designed a CHAIN statement, borrowed from an early version of FORTRAN, and a CALL statement, which was similar to the CALL feature found later in the fifth edition of Dartmouth BASIC (see Section 3.5).

Software teams from both sides formed in the spring of 1966. The Dartmouth team included Kemeny, Kenneth Lochner, and myself, together with students Sidney Marshall, David Magill, Sarr Blumsen, Ronald Martin, Steven Hobbs, and Richard Lacey. A GE-635 computer at RADC, Griffiss AFB, Rome, New York, was used in the summer and fall to develop and operate MOLDS, a multiple user on-line debugging system designed by Marshall.

A GE-635 was installed at Dartmouth in late 1966 and early 1967. Using MOLDS, GE personnel developed a Phase I operating system for this machine. Dartmouth developed the fourth edition of BASIC to specifications prepared jointly with GE, and provided communications software. This work continued through 1967 until Phase I became operational in September of 1967, allowing Dartmouth to sell its GE-265. Both Dartmouth people and GE customers shared the new machine under the terms of the joint agreement.

In April of 1967, having completed its part of the Phase I development, Dartmouth began designing its own "ideal" operating system, which was called Phase II. Joining the group at this time were former students Stephen Garland and Robert Hargraves. Marshall continued but with the new title Chief Designer. The project group, which included many other persons, met weekly to resolve problems; Kemeny served as chairman and final arbiter.

General Electric established additional sites in the fall of 1968, and transferred its commercial customers to them. Dartmouth continued to use Phase I until late March 1969, when Phase II replaced it. The name Phase II was changed to DTSS shortly thereafter.

The fourth edition of Dartmouth BASIC (see Section 3.4) was the original version on the GE Phase I operating system, which shortly became the Mark II service. GE continued to modify and use that version of BASIC, whereas Dartmouth replaced it in 1969 with its own fifth edition of BASIC.

After 1967 there was little exchange of software with GE, though both sides made numerous good faith efforts to exploit the association and achieve mutual benefits. The title to the GE-635 passed to Dartmouth in September of 1969. An additional three year agreement was then executed, but little occurred under its terms other than the gift from General Electric to Dartmouth of several additional major pieces of GE-635 hardware. All contractual association with GE ceased on September 30, 1972.

While working together from 1966 to 1968 posed problems for both sides, there is no question that each benefited enormously from the association. Dartmouth obtained a large machine far beyond its own means at that time. General Electric started in time sharing initially by adopting the original Dartmouth system (Mark I on the GE-265), and later shifted to a larger system (Mark II on the GE-635) through close association with Dartmouth.

Thomas E. Kurtz

5. Evaluation

5.1. A Priori Evaluation

Our goal was to provide our user community with friendly access to the computer. The design of BASIC was merely a tool to achieve this goal. We therefore felt completely free to redesign and modify BASIC as various features were found lacking. We have always remained loyal to our overall goals, while at the same time we allowed the language to grow to meet the increasingly sophisticated tastes. We did not design a language and then attempt to mold the user community to its use.

Little a priori evaluation of BASIC exists. A memorandum (Kemeny and Kurtz, 1963) prepared for internal use discussed time sharing, simple user interfaces, and open access computing, but failed to mention BASIC, and made only a passing reference to the need for a "simple language." Although two proposals were submitted to the NSF in 1963 and funded in 1964, neither dealt primarily with BASIC. One was a facilities proposal based on research, the other dealt with course content improvement. Understandably, there were doubts about our ability to develop a time sharing system using undergraduate students as programmers. Nonetheless, the two grants were made.

5.2. A Posteriori Evaluation

BASIC and the associated system commands spread rapidly. The original version, for the GE-265, was replicated in perhaps fifty sites, and for several years served General Electric as its Mark I time sharing system. Other users of the GE-265 included Call-A-Computer and several educational institutions.

The Dartmouth approach served as the model for two of the most widely used small time sharing systems ever developed: the HP 2000, and the DEC PDP/11-RSTS. Almost all small systems now offer BASIC, either exclusively or with other languages. Although one of COBOL or FORTRAN is probably the most widespread language in terms of number of lines of code ever written, it is my opinion that more people in the world know or have seen BASIC than any other computer language. I can only wildly guess that perhaps five million school children have learned BASIC on some minicomputer.

In 1973 when consideration was being given to the possible standardization of BASIC, we discovered that the number of commercial time-sharing service bureaus that offered BASIC was greater than the number offering any other language (SPARC, 1973). Some criticized that it was too late to standardize BASIC. Perhaps, but committee X3J2 has been one of the largest and most enthusiastic of the language standards committees. The standard for Minimal BASIC (ANSI, 1978) is in the final stages (as of 1978 February). Close cooperation with ECMA/TC21 (the European counterpart of X3J2) has ensured that the European and American standards are technically equivalent. Work continues on enhancements to Minimal BASIC.

Developing a standard for BASIC has suffered from the multiplicity of different versions. The major differences have been catalogued (Isaacs, 1973), and Isaacs admonishes the user to stick to elementary BASIC for transportability. Indeed, the standards committee X3J2 was charged to develop a standard for Minimal BASIC first, partly because it might fail if it tried to do more.

BASIC is truly a product of grass roots efforts. Hobbyists can and do write their own compilers, adding their own innovations. Rather than being a single language with dialects, BASIC is really a class of languages, all with a common core. Variations and features abound. From Dartmouth's point of view, some languages called BASIC really shouldn't be, since they violate one or more of our original criteria, although they may have borrowed other features. For instance, our dogma prohibits the optional LET, several statements on one line, and a single statement continued over several lines.

In some ways, the effort to standardize BASIC has suffered from the same malady that plagued the early FORTRAN standards efforts: the multiplicity of variations that had to be reconciled. If anything, the task is more difficult since BASIC grew unchecked for nine years (from 1964 to 1973) before the effort began. In contrast, APL was designed by a single person and copied almost exactly, so that it became its own standard. COBOL was designed as a standard language to begin with. ALGOL was also designed before it was used, so that the ALGOL 60 Report serves as its standard.

What would we change if we were to start over? We now know that spaces should be used to improve clarity, and to indicate scope through indentation. We also now know that the selection of variable names is far too limited. Requiring spaces around keywords, as ANS Minimal BASIC does, and multicharacter variable names go hand in hand. This change is high on our wish list.

We also now know the limitation of the primitive GOTO and IF THEN statements in BASIC. A version called SBASIC (Garland, 1976) dispenses with GOTO, IF THEN, GOSUB, and ON GOTO, all of which target to line numbers, and replaces them with the DO and LOOP for loops, the IF, THEN, ELSE, and CONTINUE for decision mechanisms, the PERFORM, DEFINE, and DEFEND for subroutines, and the SELECT CASE for multiple-way branches. While the particular constructs selected are not ideal in all cases, SBASIC has been taught in several elementary courses with very good results. My own opinion is that GOTO has an attractive simplicity for novices, but that it should be discarded at an early stage in favor of structured constructs.

Finally, to paraphrase, one graph is worth a thousand numbers. About 10% of all BASIC programs at Dartmouth produce graphical output. This being the case, graphical statements have been added to the language by means of a preprocessor. The statements include PLOTTER < device > , VIEWPORT, WINDOW, CLEAR, BORDER, AXIS, PLOT, and others. Also included are picture definitions similar to subprograms, simple ways of applying transformations such as translation and rotation, and three-dimensional perspectives (Garland, 1976; Arms, 1977; Hardy, 1978).

6. Implications

BASIC has become the most widely known computer language. Why? Simply because there are more people in the world than there are programmers. If ordinary persons are to use a computer, there must be simple computer languages for them. BASIC caters to this need by removing unnecessary technical distinctions (such as integer versus real), and by providing defaults (declarations, dimensioning, output formats) where the user probably doesn't care. BASIC also shows that simple line-oriented languages allow compact and fast compilers and interpreters, and that error messages can be made understandable.

Thomas E. Kurtz

ACKNOWLEDGMENTS

I would like to thank the numerous persons who read early drafts of this paper, suggested changes, and filled lapses in my own faulty memory. John Kemeny especially recalled important facts and ideas. More than that, our close collaboration of 22 years has made it difficult to separate our respective contributions to the overall effort.

I would also like to thank Henry Ledgard and Ted Lewis, the reviewers, for their many helpful suggestions. My special thanks go to Stephen Garland, who kept better files than I concerning the early days, and to Kent Morton, who corrected numerous stylistic flaws. As is customary, the author accepts final responsibility for all remaining errors, factual and otherwise.

Finally, the author expresses his deep appreciation to Jean Sammet for organizing the History of Programming Languages Conference, thereby goading the author into writing about a subject that has appeared only rarely in the technical literature.

REFERENCES

ANSI (1978). *American national standard programming language: minimal BASIC,* X3.60—1978. New York: American National Standard Institute.

Arms, W. Y. (1977). *Graphics with SBASIC* (unpublished memo). Hanover, New Hampshire: Kiewit Computation Center.

Conway, R. W., and Maxwell, W. L. (1963). CORC—the Cornell computing language. *CACM* **6**(6): 317–321.

Corbato, F. J., Merwin-Daggett, M., and Daley, R. C. (1962). An experimental time sharing system. In *AFIPS Conference Proceedings,* Vol. 21. Palo Alto, California: National Press.

Dartmouth (1956). *DARSIMCO.* Hanover, New Hampshire: Dartmouth College.

Dartmouth (1968). *BASIC,* 4th ed. Hanover, New Hampshire: Dartmouth Publ.

Dartmouth (1969a) February. *BASIC,* 4th ed. (supplement, version I). Hanover, New Hampshire: Kiewit Computation Center.

Dartmouth (1969b) April. *BASIC,* 4th ed. (supplement, version II). Hanover, New Hampshire: Kiewit Computation Center.

Dartmouth (1970) September. *BASIC,* 5th ed. Hanover, New Hampshire: Kiewit Computation Center.

Dartmouth (1972) July. *The IMPRESS manual.* Hanover, New Hampshire: Project IMPRESS.

Garland, S. J. (1973). *Dartmouth BASIC, a specification.* Hanover, New Hampshire: Kiewit Computation Center TM028.

Garland, S. J. (1976). *Structured programming, graphics, and SBASIC.* Hanover, New Hampshire: Kiewit Computation Center SP028.

Gries, D. (1968) January. Use of transition matrices in compiling. *CACM* **11**(1): 26–34.

Hardy, S. (1978) February. *Graphics in BASIC and structured BASIC.* Hanover, New Hampshire: Kiewit Computation Center TM110.

Hargraves, R. F. (1959) October. *DART I.* Hanover, New Hampshire: Dartmouth Computation Center.

Ingerman, P. Z. (1961) January. Thunks. *CACM* **4**(1): 55–58.

Irons, E. T. (1961) January. A syntax directed compiler for ALGOL 60. *CACM* **4**(1): 51–55.

Irons, E. T., and Feurzeig, W. (1961) January. Comments on the implementation of recursive procedures and blocks in ALGOL 60. *CACM* **4**(1): 65–69.

Isaacs, G. L. (1973). *Interdialect translatability of the BASIC programming language.* Iowa City, Iowa: American College Testing Program. ACT Tech. Bull. No. 11.

Kemeny, J. G. (1962) May. *Dartmouth oversimplified programming experiment.* Hanover, New Hampshire: Dartmouth Computation Center.

Kemeny, J. G., and Kurtz, T. E. (1963). *A proposal for a college computation center.* Hanover, New Hampshire: Dartmouth College.

Kemeny, J. G., and Kurtz, T. E. (1964a) June. *BASIC instruction manual.* Hanover, New Hampshire: Dartmouth College.

Kemeny, J. G., and Kurtz, T. E. (1964b) October. *BASIC,* 2nd ed. Hanover, New Hampshire: Dartmouth College Computation Center.

Kemeny, J. G., and Kurtz, T. E. (1966). *BASIC,* 3rd ed. Hanover, New Hampshire: Dartmouth College.

Kemeny, J. G., and Kurtz, T. E. (1967). *BASIC,* 3rd ed. (supplement). Hanover, New Hampshire: Dartmouth College.

Kemeny, J. G., and Kurtz, T. E. (1968). Dartmouth time sharing. *Science* **162**: 223–228.

Knapp, A. W., and Kurtz, T. E. (1962). *MESS, a master executive supervisory system.* Hanover, New Hampshire: Dartmouth College.

Kurtz, T. E. (1962a) February. *ALGOL for the LGP-30, a comparison.* Hanover, New Hampshire: Dartmouth Computation Center.

Kurtz, T. E. (1962b) March. *ALGOL-30 system operating instructions.* Hanover, New Hampshire: Dartmouth College Computation Center. Procedure Manual CCM-5.

Kurtz, T. E. (1962c) October. *A Manual for SCALP, a self-contained Algol processor.* Hanover, New Hampshire: Computation Center.

Kurtz, T. E. (1963a) January. *Programming for a Digital Computer.* Hanover, New Hampshire: Dartmouth College.

Kurtz, T. E. (1963b) May. *Languages* (unpublished memo). Hanover, New Hampshire: Dartmouth College.

Kurtz, T. E. (1963c) November. *Background for the time sharing system.* Hanover, New Hampshire: Dartmouth Computation Center Time Sharing Project Memo No. 1.

Loveday, E. (1977) September. George Stibitz and the Bell Labs Relay Computer. *Datamation* pp. 80–85.

Mather, D. G., and Waite, S. V. F., eds. (1971). *BASIC,* 6th ed. Hanover, New Hampshire: University Press of New England.

McCarthy, J., *et al.* (1963). A time sharing debugging system for a small computer. In *AFIPS Conference Proceedings,* Vol. 23, pp. 51–57. Washington, D.C.: Spartan Books.

McGeachie, J. S., and Kreider, D. L. (1974). Project FIND—an integrated information and modeling system for management. In *AFIPS Conference Proceedings,* Vol. 43, pp. 529–535. Montvale, New Jersey: AFIPS Press.

Naur, P., ed. (1960). Report on the algorithmic language ALGOL 60. *CACM* 3(5): 299–314.

Nevison, J. M. (1978). *The little book of BASIC style.* Reading, Massachusetts: Addison-Wesley.

Samelson, K., and Bauer, F. L. (1960) February. Sequential formula translation. *CACM* 3(2): 76–83.

SPARC (1973). *Proposal for an American National Standard project under committee X3, the BASIC programming language.* Washington, D.C.: CBEMA.

Wheelock, E. (1769). *The Dartmouth College Charter.* Portsmouth, New Hampshire: King George III.

TRANSCRIPT OF PRESENTATION

THOMAS CHEATHAM: For the rest of the session, we'll turn our attention to the BASIC language. Professor Tom Kurtz is going to talk about that. In 1964 Tom was an Associate Professor of Mathematics, teaching mainly Statistics at Dartmouth College, and at the same time, the Director of the Dartmouth College Computing Center. Initially they had an LGP 30, [but] in the Spring of 1964 they got their first Dartmouth time-sharing system, and then on to BASIC. At the present point in time, Tom is a Professor of Mathematics, teaching about half-and-half in Statistics and Computer Science, having, I guess wisely, given up the Computing Center.

THOMAS E. KURTZ: This is the last talk of the day. I would like to believe that the plan was to save the best for last. I'm not sure about that, but I do have one firm principle myself and that is not to cut into the cocktail hour, so I'm in complete accord with the firmness of the management to hold the talks on schedule.

In a way, this is like a reunion for me, because I got my start in computing in [the summer of] 1951 at the National Bureau of Standards Institute for Numerical Analysis, which was located on the UCLA campus. As a matter of fact, there was one other person who was also a student in that program that summer; that was Ken Iverson. And I think it's kind of interesting that out of six summer students who were involved that year, and who happened to be students of a man named Forman Acton, two of them went on to invent or coinvent computer languages.

Thomas E. Kurtz

I have a disclaimer. The views expressed are my own and do not necessarily represent those of ANSI Committee X3J2, of which committee I have the dubious honor to be chairman; nor of Dartmouth College and its well-known president, John Kemeny.

Now, as a matter of fact, from the very beginning, ever since I went to Dartmouth in 1956, John Kemeny and I have collaborated on a number of computing projects. Many of these are mentioned in the paper [pp. 529–551]. We worked together in the development of BASIC and the Dartmouth Time-Sharing System. Very early on, as either a form of a mutual admiration society, or possibly an attempt to be able to point the blame at the other fellow in case one got into difficulty, we followed the lead of Sir Edmund Hillary and Tenzing Norgay in that neither has to this day informed the rest of the world exactly who was the first to step on the top of Mt. Everest.

About that time—this is by way, incidentally, an introduction for John Kemeny, who, I suppose, if asked, would say he couldn't attend today because he's busy being president. About that time, I remember looking at a payroll disbursement form which showed him listed as $\frac{1}{12}$th on the systems programming project. That was in 1967. I don't remember what the other $\frac{11}{12}$ths were, but they involved a number of things including teaching, fundraising, and what-not. He's a man for all seasons. Actually, he immigrated to this country in 1939, and, as I mentioned, he was a systems programmer for a while during the early days of the BASIC Dartmouth Time-Sharing project, and all of this led me, in 1971, after he had become President of the College, to introduce him with the phraseology: "So you see, in a democracy even a systems programmer can become President!"

Dartmouth is a liberal arts college. Most of the students are not science students, although a good many of them do take mathematics. And we could clearly see at that time—Kemeny and myself (when I say "we" it's always Kemeny and myself)—we could clearly see at that time that there would be a problem of the two societies: those who knew about computing, that is, the professionals—the black bag people; and the "other" people in the society: the managers, the politicans, the lawyers, and, if you want, leaders. What could we do about solving the problem, or at least mitigating the problems of these two societies? We felt that many of the approaches then being used to educate about computing were not acceptable for a variety of reasons. Lecturing about computing doesn't make any sense, any more than lecturing on how to drive a car makes sense. You just can't get the idea across.

So we decided that students had to write computer programs. We had both written computer programs in assembly language so we knew quite clearly that that was not going to be accepted. Perhaps it would be accepted by engineering students and other science students, but it wouldn't be accepted by English majors, history majors, Greek majors, and so on, who are in a vast majority at Dartmouth. So that was clearly out.

With respect to that, I remember an experience that I had in 1957 when I was programming certain statistical percentage points and attempting to use machine language because, as it's been brought out in earlier talks, FORTRAN, which had just arrived on the scene at MIT, was too inefficient and one should use machine language. Well, I used machine language and I even have the records at home, although I don't have the programs. I burned up—I think that's the only fair way to say it—I burned up over an hour of IBM 704 time trying to get my program to work and it never did. Poring over octal dumps, and all the rest of the stuff, I never did get it to work. I'm not a very good programmer.

I then reprogrammed it in FORTRAN, because I had been taught FORTRAN by the MIT people, and it was a very inefficient coding job that I did. But I got the thing to work and the total amount of computer time that I used was five minutes. So that made a very deep impression on me. For klutzes like me, one had to use higher level languages.

Well, we considered FORTRAN and ALGOL at Dartmouth, but only briefly because they are still too complex if you're going to try to teach them to nonscience people. We were also discouraged by the mode of operation of the computers then in existence—namely, using punch cards as a method of supplying information. We felt that punch cards would be a turn-off—you know, fold, spindle, mutilate, and so on. Too many people would be prejudiced against them anyhow. We also didn't like the idea that folks would have to ask for permission to use the computer. I think [Charles] Baker's comment about JOSS—completely open shop—was completely in accord with what we felt our approach to computing should be.

So, a new approach was needed. I remember about in 1960 or 1961 I was chatting with John McCarthy, who had left Dartmouth in 1958 and gone to MIT, and I remember his words very clearly because they made a deep impression on me. He said, "You guys ought to do time sharing." So that was one of the components. Namely, we decided very early on that we should do time sharing rather than something else like punch cards or whatever.

We also decided that a new language was needed. Now this decision did not arise over-night or instantly—but, going through a series of trials and errors with FORTRAN and ALGOL, I tried to construct subsets of FORTRAN and ALGOL that would, I thought, be acceptable. But it's perfectly clear that ALGOL wouldn't be ALGOL without the compound statement, so that that was out. And there were so many details that characterized FORTRAN as FORTRAN; if you tried to get rid of those then it really wouldn't be FORTRAN anymore.

So in any case, the decision was reached early on an agreement—unspoken agreement—that a new language was needed. Thus was born BASIC, and of course that's the purpose of this conference—that particular part of the approach.

We also decided that we needed a new approach to teaching. We wanted an approach which would be almost self-instructional. As a matter of fact, the preliminary lectures that we put together a few years later—the first time we did it we gave four hours of lectures, and the next time we did it, we gave three hours of lecture, and then the next time we did it we gave two hours of lecture, and now they're condensed to a couple of video tapes that run a total of less than one hour if you sit through both of them.

And finally we decided, again in keeping with the JOSS philosophy, that the computing would be open access to the students, so they wouldn't have to get prior permission, but could just use their student ID number. This is an ID card. [Speaker held up an ID card.] I don't know what it's used for. Oh, yes I do. It's used for taking out library books. But the same number that appears on the card is also the person's user number. And user numbers are validated before the students even show up on campus, so the instant they arrive on campus they can go to the computing machine and work it.

Now, even though this is a conference on computer languages and not operating systems, the development of BASIC went hand-in-hand with the development of the Dartmouth Time-Sharing System. As a matter of fact, most of the early memoranda, the proposals to the National Science Foundation, and other things of that sort, referred to the Time-Sharing System, and not to the language BASIC. There's hardly any early documentation of the details of the development of the language BASIC or why it was developed, and most of what I'm telling you is what I've been able to piece together in retrospect.

However, a common set of principles applied to all aspects of the work, and I guess they can be quite simply summarized by a sentence in a memorandum which is called "Time-Sharing Project Memorandum No. 1" [Frame 1].

"The time-sharing system should be externally simple and easy to use for the casual programmer." On the next page of the memorandum [Frame 2] we also see the same idea a little further developed. "The basic idea so far generated for the time-sharing executive routine reflects one important principle: in all cases where there is a choice between simplicity and efficiency, simplicity is chosen."

Now, I was surprised when I dug out this memorandum to find these words because I hadn't realized that we'd been so clear in our objectives even before the machine had arrived on campus and even before we had begun to cut any code. I signed that memorandum, although I'm sure the views expressed in that memorandum were discussed by Kemeny and several other people from the math department as well as a bunch of student programmers who were working with us at the time.

I asked myself—as the conference has been going on I asked myself, "What's unique about BASIC?" We know the uniqueness of what FORTRAN did for the world, and we know what ALGOL did for the world, and so on. It seems clear that in BASIC there are no new syntactic or semantic ideas that haven't been thought of before. I finally came to the conclusion that if there is any uniqueness in BASIC, it's simply that it is the only language on the program during these three days [of the conference] that is completely a synthesis of other languages. I hope it's not a compromise by committee.

So let's look at some of the details. I'm not going to ask you to take a tutorial in the BASIC language. If you want to do that, you can. On the other hand, I think I'm assuming that most of you do know a little bit about BASIC because it is quite ever-present and sometimes it's hard to avoid. Even if you *wish* to avoid it, sometimes it's hard to avoid.

One characteristic of BASIC is similar to several other languages that have been discussed at this conference: an English word starts each statement. Instead of the SET of JOSS, BASIC chose the LET statement. That completes the set of statements because the assignment statement is the only one that's left over. All of the other statements in most of the other programming languages begin with an English verb. I think (shades of COBOL as well) that every statement should begin with an imperative English verb. Another characteristic of BASIC is one line, one statement. And furthermore, since it was designed to live in a time-sharing environment with line numbers on programs, the line numbers double as the statement labels. There was early criticism made of that, but that is BASIC, that was BASIC, and that's just the way it is. It hasn't been so bad, as a matter of fact.

Another characteristic of BASIC is its lack of declarations. Even in those cases where some form of declaration was needed we allowed a default dimension for arrays if you didn't want more than ten elements in the array. We also decided that there would not be a distinction between real and integer, which is a characteristic of FORTRAN, and that typ-

This memo will contain a brief discussion of the status of the Time Sharing System, and will serve to record some of the thoughts and ideas that have been generated to date.

1. Broad Specifications

   A. The Time Sharing system should be externally simple and easy to use for the casual programmer. This requirement is more important in light of the student training that will be done using this system.

Frame 1. Time-sharing project memorandum No. 1, Nov. 6, 1963, from page 1.

III.   Some Thoughts on the Time Sharing Program

The basic ideas so far generated for the Time Sharing Executive routine reflect one important principle: In all cases where there is a choice between simplicity and efficiency, simplicity is chosen. Every effort will be made to design a system convenient for the user.

Frame 2. Time-sharing project memorandum No. 1, from page 2.

ing would be explicit by variable name form. This principle became more important a few years later when string types were added to the language.

[Frame 3] illustrates one problem that I found using FORTRAN as a teaching language. With the implicit integer typing of variables beginning with I, J, K, L, M, or N, one needed to do something as shown in text line 140 in order to properly develop the mean of a number by dividing the sum by the number of items. And the same program in BASIC is shown down below.

I think one other comment that can be made about this is that in many respects, BASIC is closer to FORTRAN than to any other language. It's very easy to hand translate a simple program in FORTRAN to BASIC and vice versa.

A couple more features to point out: we decided that input—all input—would be free-format and all output would be fixed format. Again, influenced by the intricacies—nay, the complexities—of the FORTRAN FORMAT statement—I never could get it right.

This is a real BASIC program [Frame 4]. It's a very simple one, obviously. I hope you can read it the same way you could read a COBOL program, even though you aren't managers, perhaps. [Frame 5] is the output, and the purpose of this program is simply to point out that there are several different output formats that are automatically picked by the printing routine, depending on how the number happens to come out. If it happens to be an integer, it prints it as an integer, as in the middle example there. If it happens to be a noninteger decimal in a certain range, then it's printed as the first case. Otherwise, it's printed in the familiar exponential format down below.

A couple of other features. The FOR/NEXT looping statement is a lot like the ALGOL statement. It uses the ALGOL verb and like ALGOL, in contrast with the FORTRAN

```
LIST

HOPL-VAR   26 MAY 78   10:21

100 *Program fragment in FORTRAN
110
120       DO 17 I = 1, N
130    17 S = S + X(I)
140       XN = N
150       XMEAN = S/XN
160
170
180 'Same program fragment in BASIC
190
200 FOR I = 1 TO N
210     LET S = S + X(I)
220 NEXT I
230 LET M = S/N
240
250
READY
```
Frame 3

```
LIST

HOPL-INP   26 MAY 78   10:34

100 'Illustrates free form input
110 'and fixed form output.
120
130   PRINT "Type numerator, denominator";
140   INPUT N, D
150   LET Q = N/D
160   PRINT "Quotient =", Q
170   PRINT
180   GO TO 130
190
200   END
READY
```
Frame 4

```
RUN

HOPL-IMP   26 MAY 78   10:35

Type numerator, denominator? 5, 3
Quotient =      1.66667

Type numerator, denominator? 120, -20
Quotient =      -6

Type numerator, denominator? 3, 129
Quotient =      2.32558 E-2

Type numerator, denominator? STOP
Program halted

STOP
0.180 CRU    0.200 CPU
READY
```

Frame 5

DO, it makes the test before entry into the loop; but like FORTRAN and in contrast to ALGOL, the STEP element is optional and is the third element in the three element sequence specifying the range of the looping statement. You can leave it off if you mean the STEP size to be unity. So there's a mixing of the two languages there.

The IF–THEN statement is more like the ALGOL variety; that is, it's a two-way branch, and I remember at the time not liking the three-way branch that was part of FORTRAN. I remember yesterday, John McCarthy made a statement that he couldn't remember which way it was going to go. I was planning to make the same statement. I could never remember which way it was supposed to go, or whether there was a comma there or not after the conditional part of the clause. So in BASIC then, we tend to use English words instead of punctuation because English words are easier to remember. It's easier for somebody to remember an English word sequence for an instruction than to remember the punctuation, whether it's a comma or semicolon or whatever.

Error messages—I was very happy to see in Charles Baker's talk the attention paid to error messages in the JOSS language. But even so, most error messages in the implementation of languages that were around in those days were pretty cryptic. I can remember, of course, poring over octal dumps and code numbered errors, "error #240". You'd have to go to the computer center library and get the magic code book and look up error #240 and figure out—this is a "general system error!" This happens even today, I'm sorry to say.

[Frame 6] is a page-and-a-half from the newsletter of the MIT Information Processing Services Center, and it has to do with the decoding of a certain type of error condition that may arise from the running of a FORTRAN program. Let me just paraphrase. I'll show you the program blown up in a minute so you can see what what the actual error is.

There's a lot of stuff printed out in octal, hexadecimal, rather. "The system completion code is a clue to what happened—both 0C4 and 0C5 result from an invalid address which may have been generated by an improper subscript . . .," and so on. And the way you find this out is to take the last six digits of the program status word, and you can, let's see, subtract from that the address in register 15, in hexadecimal; this number corresponds to the location shown in the statement label map. There you get the mapping back to the fact that this is really statement number 5, and you look at the source code and see statement number 5, and the only thing that could possibly be wrong is that the subscript is out of bounds.

WHAT HAPPENED?

Adapted with permission from System Network Computer Center Newsletter (Louisiana State University).

This article features FORTRAN error number 240. User completion code 240 from a FORTRAN program indicates that the routine that intercepts most system completion code interruptions in a FORTRAN program has received control. In other words, an abnormal termination has occurred.

This situation can be recognized by the presence of 3 diagnostics:

      (1) IEW199I ERROR - USER PROGRAM HAS ABNORMALLY TERMINATED

      (2) a COMPLETION CODE - SYSTEM=000 USER=0240 in the JCL listing.

      (3) IHO240I message in the output listing.

The following simple program caused an addressing exception (system completion code 0C5 or 0C4) which resulted in a FORTRAN 240 error.

```
0001            DIMENSION ARRAY (10)
0002            SUM=0.
0003            DO 10 I=1,100
0004            ARRAY(I) = I
0005            SUM = SUM + ARRAY(I)
0006     10     CONTINUE
0007            STOP
0008            END
```

It was compiled with the MAP option, as follows:

      // EXEC FORCGO,PARM.C='MAP'

producing the following statement-label map which shows locations (hexadecimal displacements from the beginning of the routine to the beginning of the instructions for each statement), compiler-generated statement numbers, and programmer-assigned statement labels (if any).

```
                    STATEMENT LABEL MAP
       LOCATION         STA NUM         LABEL
       00012C              2
       000134              3
       000140              4
       000160              5
       00016C              6              10
       000184              7
```

Execution of the above program produced the following messages:

    IHO9001 EXECUTION TERMINATING DUE TO ERROR COUNT FOR ERROR NUMBER 240

    IHN2401 STAE - ABEND CODE IS: SYSTEM 0C5, USER 0000. IO - NONE
      SCB = 07F458. PSW IS FF95000DA2070488.

    TRACEBACK ROUTINE CALLED FROM ISN REG. 14 REG. 15 REG. 0 REG. 1

        MAIN   00004648 01070328 FD000008 0007F7F8

    ENTRY POINT= 01070328

    SUMMARY OF ERRORS FOR THIS JOB   ERROR NUMBER   NUMBER ERRORS

                            240   1

What happened and where?

The system completion code is a clue to what happened. Both 0C4 and 0C5 result from an invalid address which may be generated by an improper subscript.

```
The last six digits of the PSW (Program Status Word) contain the address of the  next  in-
struction  to  be  executed.  This is the instruction that would have been executed if the
abnormal termination has not occurred.  We can calculate the address of the FORTRAN state-
ment corresponding to this instruction.  Subtract the address in register 15 from the  ad-
dress in the PSW.  (Remember they are hexadecimal.)

                              70488
                             -70328
                                160

This number corresponds to the hexadecimal location shown in the Statement Label Map.  Lo-
cation 160 is the beginning of the instructions for statement number 5.  This is  not  the
statement  that caused the abnormal termination.  It is the statement that would have been
executed next if the abnormal termination had not occurred.  Statement number 4 is the one
that caused the interruption.  We can therefore conclude that subscript  I  of  ARRAY  was
probably much larger than 10, the DIMENSIONed size of ARRAY.

This example is rather trivial, but the procedures shown can be used to  track  down  most
240  errors  in FORTRAN programs.  If more information is required, the LIST option may be
used in addition to MAP.  LIST provides a list of actual instructions in  pseudo-assembler
code with hexadecimal displacements.

FORTRAN error-tracing is discussed in more detail in ARCS  memo  PP-16,  and  hexadecimal
arithmetic  in  ARCS  memo  PP-11.   Both are available from the Publications Office, Room
39-484.
```

Frame 6 (*Continued*)

Now, as I say, I don't mean this to be critical, but I do wish to make a point! And the point is that FORTRAN is not supposed to calculate subscript-bound correctness, because that leads to inefficiencies in the program; I'll grant that point. On the other hand, the termination routine as part of this system could just as easily have done the hexadecimal arithmetic and the looking up in the statement label map, and tell the programmer that it was statement number 5 that was the cause of the error.

Just to contrast this, let me move to the same program that's written in BASIC and, of course, BASIC requires subscript-bound checking on each and every reference to a subscript, which undoubtedly slows the execution of the program down, but it also means that the user gets quite a clear idea of a subscript out of bounds when he does that [Frame 7]. As you can see, the array is dimensioned to contain 10 elements, and the loop tries to push it to 100, and so we get into trouble.

And just to make the point that this is not so much a language as it is an implementation problem, [Frame 8] is the offending FORTRAN program of [Frame 6] slightly changed, with a little indentation and so on, but it's otherwise the identical program. It is run on a different implementation of FORTRAN, and you see this particular implementation does calculate the subscript and determine that it's out of bounds.

We made some mistakes in BASIC. I would like to publicly confess to them now. We had a lot of fun with it, as a matter of fact. Like many languages it was designed on the fly. Version 1—oh, gee! That's wrong. We need this. Out comes Version 2. Oh gee! We need something else. Out comes Version 3, and finally the manual for Version 1 appears! One of the mistakes we made early is that we made the wrong decision on the unary minus signs, so that if you tried to calculate $EXP(-X \uparrow 2)$—and those of you who are statisticians know that this is the normal curve—it would come out the wrong way.

Another important point is that in the early version of BASIC, the zero subscript was not allowed; subscripting was one to whatever you said in the dimension statement. In

```
LIST

HOPL-BAS  26 MAY 78  10:19

100 'Array bound error program
110 'in BASIC
120
130 DIM A(10)
140 LET S = 0
150 FOR I = 1 TO 100
160    LET A(I) = I
170    LET S = S + A(I)
180 NEXT I
190 END
READY

RUN

HOPL-BAS  26 MAY 78  10:19

Subscript out of bounds at 160

STOP
0.117 CRU   0.111 CPU
READY
```

Frame 7

an early revision the zero subscript was added, to allow somebody to represent polynomial coefficients using simple array notation in BASIC, and there's always a zero-num-
bered coefficient. And to this day that has caused problems. In X3J2 that's the one issue
that we could not resolve in our development of the Minimal BASIC standard. Every time
we took a vote on the subject—and we took many many votes—it came out to be a 14-to-
14 tie. And there we had to resort to a committee compromise, and the two-humped camel
that has resulted is what is known as the OPTION BASE statement.

Another mistake that we made because we were lazy, is that we had added a packed
output, using a semicolon in the print list, so that the numbers would be packed fairly
close together on the page if you wanted to save paper or save typing time. The only trouble is that we made this the nearest multiple of three characters instead of the actual pack-

```
LIST

HOPL-FOR  26 MAY 78  10:20

100 *Array bound error program
110 *in FORTRAN
120
130      DIMENSION ARRAY(10)
140      SUM = 0.
150      DO 10 I=1,100
160         ARRAY(I) = I
170         SUM = SUM + ARRAY(I)
180   10   CONTINUE
190      STOP
200      END
READY

RUN

HOPL-FOR  26 MAY 78  10:20


Subscript error at 160.

STOP
0.137 CRU   0.160 CPU
READY
```

Frame 8

ing, because we had a machine that could contain three characters in one word—it was a 20-bit machine, and you can get three characters in one word, and we were just simply lazy. And I can report that that particular error—I guess one should call that a feature, actually— has migrated into several other versions of BASIC, some of which I'm told still exist to this day.

I'd like to conclude with a couple of thoughts. I think BASIC as a language represents the idea that life can be simple for the casual user, even though it does create some messy problems for the implementer, or appears to be inelegant for the language designer. There are some syntactic production rules in BASIC that are kind of ugly because we were trying to make things easy for the casual user.

The second point is that BASIC is only part of the total system. Another point is that one of the advantages of a language like BASIC is that a casual user such as the Chairman of the Math Department—and this is true—can remember how to write a program in BASIC with six month intervals between such program writing, without consulting the manual.

Finally, I think it's fair to say that more persons in the world know how to write simple programs in BASIC than in any other language. It is true that most of them are probably still unable to vote or buy a drink. And if FORTRAN is the lingua franca, then certainly it must be true that BASIC is the lingua playpen.

TRANSCRIPT OF QUESTION AND ANSWER SESSION

THOMAS CHEATHAM: The first question kind of responds to that last point. Richard Miller asks, "Did you ever think that BASIC would become as widespread outside of Dartmouth as it has?"

THOMAS E. KURTZ: No.

CHEATHAM: Any explanation as to why it has?

KURTZ: Well, we did a little missionary work. With the aid of some NSF grants, we got some terminals in some high schools and colleges around New England, and I think the word leaked out, and when it came time for Hewlett–Packard and Digital Equipment to develop systems for schools, they zeroed in finally on an implementation of the Dartmouth system, and I think that's what did it. I don't know for sure. It was not the GE connection, in my opinion.

CHEATHAM: Ken Dickey from Humboldt State asks, "In view of the scientific users you did have at Dartmouth, why such limited precision? Was this machine-dependent, did the users have an option for extended precision, and so forth?"

KURTZ: At Dartmouth all floating point was done in double-word floating point. It wasn't called double precision, but it was 40-bit precision. So that in that version of hardware, things were okay. And then when we got new hardware, that was the standard 36-bit precision so there was no major problem there either. In our BASIC at Dartmouth we have steadfastly refused to add double precision as a data type, although there is a black market version of BASIC floating around on campus which does everything in double precision, including, I believe, the looping arithmetic!

CHEATHAM: John Stier from SUNY Stony Brook asks, "Why did you not include JOSS-type immediate statements which would have provided a desk calculator facility for the really casual user?"

KURTZ: That's actually a long discussion. I've been thinking about that quite a bit, trying to present from the point of view of the debate why I believe that the method that we chose is the reasonable method. There are a number of reasons; all worked together. One is that we felt that we wanted an implementation of the language that would allow one to run large programs. So this suggested to us at least that it not be interpreted, but be compiled. And we didn't have any problem with compiling the language because we had very fast compilers from the very beginning. Not really one pass because we had to handle the forward GOTO, and we used linked lists for filling in those later on. But it's essentially a one-pass compiler, compile and go; so we didn't face the inefficiencies of the compile phase. Another reason was that the hardware configuration that we had was a two-machine configuration, and it would have been very difficult to handle a lot of interaction between the user and the actual running program. The command scanning and the master-minding of the whole time-sharing system was in one machine; the actual computation, the compiling, and the consequent execution was in a separate machine. It would have been very very difficult to build a system around these two machines that would have imitated the JOSS environment.

CHEATHAM: Mike Marcotty from GM Research asks, "If clarity was more important than efficiency, then why was the programmer not allowed to choose more mnemonic names for his variables?"

KURTZ: I believe there are several reasons for that. Of course I'd been brought up on multicharacter variable names of ALGOL, but John Kemeny had been brought up on single-character variable names in several other language projects that he'd been identified with. Furthermore, both of us were mathematicians and we were quite used to the idea of single-letter variable names. Still furthermore, for various reasons that we now believe to be bad, we decided that the implementation should be blank insensitive, and it's kind of hard to tell which are variable names and which are keywords; that means that if you allow multicharacter variable names, then you have the problem of disallowing those that happen to look like function names, or happen to look like key words. And so you have the key word problem. And a fourth reason was that John Kemeny didn't know how to construct a symbol table!

CHEATHAM: Next question is from Jim Dehnert at UC Berkeley: "Given the intent of BASIC to provide a beginners' or teaching language, how do you view its widespread use as a production programming language for professionals?"

KURTZ: Well, it's not widely used as a production programming language. It really depends on the implementation, if I understand the question. At Dartmouth, the implementation is quite rich. It contains, for example, independently compilable subprograms, which can be used for automatic overlaying; it contains full access to the file system, and so on. So it really depends on the implementation. One of the problems with the language is that it isn't really *a* language. It's a group of languages, some of which are very small, and some of which are very big, and they're all over the map. And so it really depends on the implementation.

CHEATHAM: Aaron Finerman from SUNY Stony Brook notes that "Recent emphasis in programming languages has been on such things as data structures, control structures, modularity, and so on. And of course that contrasts with the idea of BASIC. The question is, if you had it all to do over again, would BASIC be as basic?"

KURTZ: Well, I don't know because this comes under the category of hypothetical considerations, and I'm not exactly sure. I can tell you what we are now thinking of in terms of the next evolutionary step for BASIC at our own institution, and that is to do such things as: add multicharacter variable names; drop blank insensitivity because we think blanks should be used to improve readability; add certain structural elements—the DO loop, the expanded IF–THEN–ELSE construction, case statements, primitive plotting statements, and a few other things of that sort. We've already experimented with some of these, and are planning others, so that this is the direction we're going. On the other hand, we're not trying to make it the all-purpose language for all people. For example, we won't have the string handling capability that SNOBOL provides; and we won't have the business-data processing capability that COBOL provides, and so on. We'll stop short of that. And so on—we won't have the matrix capability that APL provides, etc.

GEORGE RYCKMAN: Would you state for the record when the Dartmouth Time-Sharing System was first used? [Question from the floor]

KURTZ: The Dartmouth Time-Sharing System was first used at Dartmouth on May 1, 1964, at 4 A.M. in the morning!

CHEATHAM: Eastern Daylight Time? Are there any other questions or comments? Thank you.

FULL TEXT OF ALL QUESTIONS SUBMITTED

JIM DEHNERT: Given the intent of BASIC to provide a beginners' or teaching language, how do you view its widespread use for production by professionals?

KEN DICKEY: In view of the "scientific" users you did have, why such limited precision (was this machine dependent; was there a user option to extend precision)?

AARON FINERMAN: Recent emphasis in programming languages has been on such characteristics as data structures, control structures, modularity and readability—in an attempt to make programs more reliable, BASIC deemphasizes these characteristics in favor of simplicity of use. Can you comment on these conflicts between reliability and simplicity? If you had it to do all over again, would you make BASIC as basic?

MICHAEL MARCOTTY: If clarity was more important than efficiency, why was the programmer not allowed to chose more mnemonic names for variables?

RICHARD MILLER: Would it have been possible to separate the BASIC language from the run-time commands? Even now, many BASIC subsystems include the commands RUN, etc., and the response READY that appear in early versions of the Dartmouth system.

Did you ever think that BASIC would become as widespread outside of Dartmouth as it has?

Do you feel that the large number of dialects of BASIC is detrimental to the language?

JOHN STIER: Why did you not include JOSS-type immediate statements, which would have provided a desk-calculator facility to the *really* casual user?

BIOGRAPHY OF THOMAS E. KURTZ

Dr. Kurtz received his Ph.D. in statistics from Princeton in 1956, his first contact with computing having occurred in 1951 at the Summer Session of the Institute for Numerical Analysis at UCLA. He joined the Mathematics Department of Dartmouth College in 1956 as an instructor. Besides teaching statistics and numerical analysis, he served as the Dartmouth contact to the New England Regional Computer Center, which was supported in part by IBM at MIT. In 1959 Dartmouth obtained an LGP-30 computer, and Kurtz became the first director of the Dartmouth Computation Center.

Around 1962, Dr. Kurtz and Dr. John G. Kemeny (then Chairman of the Mathematics Department) began jointly to supervise the design and development of a time-sharing system for university use. This effort culminated in the first Dartmouth Time-Sharing System and the computer language BASIC in the late spring of 1964.

Subsequently, Kurtz served as Director of the Kiewit Computation Center from 1966 to 1975, and as Director of the Office of Academic Computing from 1975 to 1978. In 1978 he returned to full-time teaching as Professor of Mathematics, concentrating on statistics and computer science.

Outside of Dartmouth, Kurtz served as Council Chairman and Trustee of EDUCOM, as Trustee and Chairman of NERComP, and on the so-called Pierce Panel of the President's Scientific Advisory Committee. He also served on the steering committees for two NSF-supported activities: the CONDUIT project (which distributes program sets for instructional use), and the CCUC conferences on instructional computing. He has served as well as Principal Investigator of half a dozen NSF- or ARPA-supported projects dealing with computing and the instructional use thereof. In addition, he continues to serve as Chairman of committee X3J2, which is developing a standard for the BASIC computer language.

PL/I Session

Chairman: Robert Rosin
Speaker: George Radin
Discussant: Bruce Rosenblatt

PAPER: THE EARLY HISTORY AND CHARACTERISTICS OF PL/I

George Radin

IBM Corporation
Research Division

1. Introduction

Source material for a written history of PL/I has been preserved and is available in dozens of cartons, each packed with memos, evaluations, language control logs, etc. A remembered history of PL/I is retrievable by listening to as many people, each of whom was deeply involved in one aspect of its progress. This paper is an attempt to gather together and evaluate what I and some associates could read and recall in a few months. There is enough material left for several dissertations.

The exercise is important, I think, not only because of the importance of PL/I, but because of the breadth of its subject matter. Since PL/I took as its scope of applicability virtually all of programming, the dialogues about its various parts encompass a minor history of computer science in the middle 1960s. There are debates among numerical analysts about arithmetic, among language experts about syntax, name scope, block structure, etc., among systems programmers about multi-tasking, exception handling, I/O, and more.

I must acknowledge my debt particularly to Jim Cox for help in the search through the archives, but also to Marc Auslander, David Beech, Pat Goldberg, Marty Hopkins, Brian Marks, Doug McIlroy, John McKeehan, Erich Neuhold, John Nicholls, Bruce Rosenblatt, for help and criticism of early drafts, and to Warner King, Elliot Nohr, and Nat Rochester for making the material available. Finally, because Mike Marcotty and Bob Rosin (the PL/I language cordinators for this conference) were unhappy with the early drafts and provided specific suggestions, the following paper is much improved.

HISTORY OF PROGRAMMING LANGUAGES
Copyright © 1981 by the Association for Computing Machinery, Inc.
Permission for reproduction in any form must be obtained from Academic Press, Inc.
ISBN 0-12-745040-8

2. Background

In the early 1960s computer applications, programmers, and equipment were much more clearly divided among scientific, commercial, and special-purpose lines than they are today. There were computers designed primarily for scientific applications, such as the IBM 7090 and the IBM 1620, scientific operating systems for these computers, a scientific programming language (FORTRAN), and a user's group for installations whose primary applications were scientific (SHARE). Similarly there were computers oriented toward commercial applications, such as the IBM 7080 and the IBM 1401, system facilities for these, a commercial language (COBOL), and a users' group installations involved primarily in commercial applications (GUIDE). Finally, there was a bagful of special purpose computers such as the IBM 7750 and Harvest and special languages such as JOVIAL.

Moreover, there were accepted characteristics which distinguished these categories. Scientific users needed floating-point arithmetic, arrays, subroutines, fast computation, fast compilation, and batch job scheduling. Commercial users needed decimal arithmetic, string-handling instructions, fast and asynchronous I/O, compilation which produced efficient object code, and excellent sort programs. Special-purpose users needed capabilities like variable length bit string arithmetic, macro libraries (such as COMPOOL in JOVIAL), pattern matching operators, list handlers, and very fast response for real time.

The trouble was that this elegant separation was no longer a realistic characterization of installations and projections were that matters were going to get worse. Applications and users refused to stay properly compartmentalized.

The stereotype of a scientific programmer who is willing to wait two hours for a blinking computer finally to display the answer on its console lights was giving way to the professional who wanted a camera-ready report in a beautifully readable format. The files that scientists were processing were as voluminous as those in many commercial installations. They too needed sorts and I/O managers.

Commercial users were doing linear regressions and factor analyses on market data. They needed floating point and arrays.

Installation managers objected to buying two sets of hardware, maintaining two operating sytems, and educating two sets of application programmers who could not talk to each other or share programs.

Becoming increasingly aware of this situation, IBM reached the conclusion that it could best serve its customers' (and hence its own) interests by developing a single product line and a single family of operating systems which satisfied the requirements of all three user types. Thus System/360 and OS/360 development was begun.

It was for this same reason that IBM and SHARE formed the Advanced Language Development Committee of the SHARE FORTRAN project in October of 1963. This group was charged with specifying a programming language which would meet the needs of all three of these user types as well as those of systems programmers.

Bob Evans, IBM Vice-President, recalls that David J. Farber, now Professor of Electrical Engineering at the University of Delaware, was the principal catalyst in his decision to organize this group with qualified user professionals combined with IBM programmers. A meeting was held in October, 1963, at the Motel-on-the Mountain in Suffern, N.Y., attended by IBM and SHARE management. At this meeting the SHARE committee members were already named and present. They were:

Hans Berg, from Lockheed, Burbank, who had direct experience in training programmers and in the problems of running a computing installation,

Jim Cox, of Union Carbide, who had experience not only in FORTRAN and assembly language programming, but also in using IBM's existing business language, Commercial Translator, and

Bruce Rosenblatt, of Standard Oil of California (the chairman of the committee) who, in addition to experience in programming and installation management, best understood SHARE's expectations for the committee.

The IBM committee members were:

C. W. Medlock, a FORTRAN compiler expert who had developed loop optimization algorithms,

Bernice Weitzenhoffer, who had wide experience in both FORTRAN and COBOL programming, and

myself (the IBM project leader) whose background lay primarily in scientific programming and programming language theory (pursued in university and consultant environments).

Tom Martin of Westinghouse Corp. (manager of the Systems Division of SHARE) and Paul Rogoway of Hughes Dynamics, Inc. (chairman of the SHARE FORTRAN project within the Systems Division) were not official members but attended almost all meetings and participated in the decision-making process. Similarly, Larry Brown and Ray Larner, IBM FORTRAN compiler developers, were virtually full-time committee participants.

The committee met generally every other week for three or four days (long weekends, in fact), mostly in New York and Los Angeles. The non-IBM members retained the demanding responsibilities of their full-time jobs during this period. Language definition was, for them, mostly a moonlighting activity. IBM management, being more directly a beneficiary of the activity, allowed their employees compensatory time off, but this was often an official gesture rather than a practical occurrence. The meetings were held in hotel suites, in New York primarily, but also in California. At times the most vocal opponents of the activity were not FORTRAN advocates but neglected wives (and husbands).

Procedures at the meetings were largely informal. Since the non-IBM committee members had signed a confidential disclosure agreement with IBM, we attempted, at the first several meetings, to learn about IBM's New Product Line (which became S/360) and, particularly, its operating system (later called OS/360) and language processors. Minutes were not officially taken. When an area was to be defined, one or more small subgroups were formed to develop specific proposals. These were then presented to the committee as a whole, preferably preceded by a written description mailed Special Delivery before the meeting.

The major constraint which confronted the committee throughout the development process was a series of very early, but seemingly rigid, deadlines. In order to be included in the first release of IBM's New Product Line, we were first informed that the language definition would have to be complete (and frozen) by December 1963. In December we were given until the first week in January 1964, and finally allowed to slip into late February. Thus, not only was the total time for language definition very short, but even this period was punctuated by "deadlines" which gave a sense of crisis to the activity. (An interesting example of the subjectivity of history can be found in my vivid recollections of these deadlines compared to Bruce Rosenblatt's remark in a recent letter to me [19]: "I was not conscious, as a non-IBMer of any missed deadlines; though I felt earlier commitments were requested, I thought we (the committee) had successfully avoided these when the subject came up.")

In spite of this pressure, PL/I did not make the first release of OS/360. It has been suggested that this late introduction was primarily what accounted for COBOL's early success over PL/I. While this can never be proven, it is clear that much of the long and demanding work in PL/I language development would have been made much easier had the designing committee been given six months or a year at the beginning to lay down a carefully defined language base.

Since the background of the group was so strongly FORTRAN-oriented, and the committee reported to the SHARE FORTRAN project, starting the language development with FORTRAN as a base seemed as obvious choice. (In fact, for the first several meetings, the language was referred to as FORTRAN VI.) Bruce Rosenblatt recalls that FORTRAN compatibility was part of the original charge to the committee. As part of its New Product Line software development IBM had supported proposals for such a new language. But even in these proposals, strict upward compatibility with FORTRAN was soon abandoned.

In a detailed FORTRAN VI language definition written by Larry Brown and Ray Larner [20] the introduction stated:

> FORTRAN VI is not intended to be compatible with any known FORTRAN IV. It includes the functional capabilities of FORTRAN IV as well as those capabilities normally associated with "commercial" and "algorithmic" languages. In order to embrace these capabilities in a usable and practical language, it has been found virtually impossible, and certainly undesirable, to retain FORTRAN IV as a compatible subset.

Nat Rochester, in "A FORTRAN VI Proposal" [21] wrote:

> Compatibility with FORTRAN IV would preclude having a simple elegant streamlined language because FORTRAN IV itself is heavily burdened with curious restrictions and complexities that have accumulated during the long history of additions that maintained an approximate compatibility with earlier versions.

Finally, a report of a meeting held in Los Angeles on February 11, 1963 [22], where IBM language experts and programming management discussed the future of FORTRAN, began:

> The purpose of the meeting was to decide whether there should be a FORTRAN V or whether we should move directly to FORTRAN VI. F5 was defined as a compatible extension of F4 to provide field and character handling capability, making it suitable for "information processing" as distinct from purely scientific or business applications. F6 was defined as a new language, incompatible with existing FORTRAN's, with a simplified syntax designed in part for ease of compiling, suitable for scientific "information processing" and business applications, and open-ended with regard to real-time, control and other applications.

After several weeks of investigation the SHARE–IBM committee unanimously agreed to abandon the direction of compatible extensions to FORTRAN IV and start the language definition from scratch. In a recent letter to me, Doug McIlroy credits (or blames) me with being responsible for this decision. I certainly was responsible for persuading the technical and management community in IBM to accept it. In too many meetings with IBM I was faced with strong objections from FORTRAN language experts to the introduction of yet another language. In addition to the reasons given by Brown and Larner, the arguments I recall which argued for incompatibility are:

The syntax of FORTRAN does not lend itself to free-form representation on display terminals. In particular, statement labels were recognized by their column position on a card (or card-image file).

Declarations in FORTRAN are organized by type rather than by identifier. For instance, all 10 by 10 arrays can be declared together and all floating-point variables can be declared together. This generally results in the attributes of a single variable being scattered across several statements. The committee wanted to be able to isolate the description of a variable, perhaps even keeping it in some compile-time library.

Storing arrays by column (as in FORTRAN) rather than by row is awkward even for scientific users but is quite unnatural to commercial application programmers, who think in terms of tables rather than matrices. It is mostly possible to keep this mapping unknown to the programmer, but there are uses of overlays and I/O which expose it.

In fact, the FORTRAN programmer's capability to take advantage of data mapping by unconstrained overlaying in COMMON was not a practice the committee wanted to perpetuate.

In addition to these specific arguments, two more basic points were made in these debates. First, it was demonstrated that after ALGOL block structure was added (a recognized requirement which, however, did not get defined in time to be included in the first language report) together with all the extensions required for commercial and systems applications, the result would be a langauge so different from FORTRAN that the benefits to IBM of staying compatible (e.g. compiler development cost) hardly seemed worthwhile. Second, the application programmers who would benefit from FORTRAN compatibility did not include the large and important group of commercial programmers. They would have to learn a new language in any case, and therefore it was unfair to them to compromise this language in order to benefit scientific programmers.

In retrospect, I believe the decision was correct. Its major drawback was that, by taking FORTRAN as a base, we could have gone, in any orderly way, from a well-defined language to an enhanced well-defined language. We could have spent our time designing the new features instead of redesigning existing features. By starting over, we were not required to live with many technical compromises, but the task was made much more difficult.

My recollections of the language debates are that at every stage of its evolving definition, the language was constrained by compiler and object code performance objectives when running under OS/360 (in its changing forms). Thus, for instance, the definitions of I/O features and multitask execution could not conflict sharply with those functions as provided by the operating system. Facilities for separate compilation were matched to those supported by the link editor. Thus, while the definers always tried to focus on requried functions rather than specifically on OS/360 facilities, so that the language would remain "system-independent," it was constrained to be a system-independent language which would execute efficiently on a S/360.

Bruce Rosenblatt, in comments on an early draft of this paper [19], reveals the different perspective which the non-IBM committee members had on this issue: "Your comments on our attempt to achieve compatibility with OS surprised me. I had no idea what OS was and felt frustrated in trying to find out at the time. Maybe in the later development process this held true, but certainly not in our original deliberations.''

Once the decision was made to become incompatible with FORTRAN, a name other than FORTRAN VI was needed. A language designed for such a wide application set needed a general name. APL was already taken. MPPL (for Multi-Purpose Programming Language) was considered. NPL (for New Programming Language) seemed a good choce, since it would tie the language, within IBM, to the New Product Line. This name remained until, in 1965, its prior use by the National Physical Laboratory in England required a change to PL/I. Again this new name linked the language, within IBM, with S/360 and OS/360. (PL/360 would have made this link too strong since we were determined to be system-independent.)

The first document describing the language, (SHARE, 1964, March) [1] was presented to SHARE at its March meeting in San Francisco. (Appendix A contains several examples developed for the SHARE meeting showing programs written in this ''new'' programming language compared to the ''old'' FORTRAN IV.) The reaction was anything but indifferent. It was widely praised for its breadth, its innovations, and its attention to programmers of varying sophistication. It was criticized for its formlessness, complexity, and redundancy. One SHARE member later compared it to a 100-blade Swiss knife; another wondered why the kitchen sink had been omitted from the language. At the end of the meeting, however, the language was endorsed by SHARE, and IBM decided to develop several processors for S/360. Shortly after the SHARE meeting a more complete version of this document, entitled ''Specifications for the New Programming Language, April, 1964'' was distributed [2].

Since the language was to appeal to commercial programmers, the GUIDE users' group appointed Bob Sheppard of Proctor and Gamble as a member of the committee. At this same time SHARE added Doug McIlroy of Bell Telephone Laboratories to the committee because of his strong background in numerical analysis, and systems programming.

In June 1964 the committee produced a second version, ''Report II of the SHARE Advanced Language Development Committee'' [3]. Some of the major differences between this document and the April specification were:

The explicit verb SET for assignment statements was removed. The language reverted to the FORTRAN (A = B) syntax, i.e., A = B rather than SET A = B.

Binary numeric data types were introduced. The April document defined only decimal.

The April document defined a data type called ADDRESS, which could take as values statement labels, procedure names or files. The June document separated these into three separate data types.

The DO group was introduced. The April document had specified the FORTRAN-like syntax in which the label of the last statement in the group is explicitly named in the DO statement.

The semicolon terminator was introduced.

The storage classes TEMP and HELD, corresponding to ALGOL's distinctions, were introduced.

The ''RETURN TO label variable'' form was added.

The level of acceptance of this language by SHARE and by IBM can be seen in a statement attached to this June document, signed jointly by Thomas W. Martin, Manager

SHARE Systems Division, and Carl H. Reynolds, Manager of Programming Systems, Data Systems Division, IBM Corporation:

> The attached report represents the efforts of the joint IBM/SHARE Committee to identify the functions and features needed in an extended language and to propose a particular embodiment thereof. Because of its belief that the committee's results are a significant step forward, it is the intention of the IBM Corporation to use this report as the basis of specification for the New Programming Langauge.

At about this same time IBM decided that the major part of NPL compiler development would be done in its laboratory in Hursley, England. Although product planning and language control remained officially in the U.S. for at least the initial period, NPL (and then PL/I) was primarily a Hursley responsibility (Responsibility for the language and its compilers has recently moved to the IBM Laboratory in Santa Teresa, California.)

In November 1964 the Hursley laboratory produced a document much more detailed than the reports of the Advanced Language Development Committee [4]. It ran to 200 pages and represented the definition of the language from which the implementors would develop their compilers. Then in December 1964 this document was published for external distribution as "NPL Technical Report, IBM World Trade Laboratories (Great Britain) Ltd" [5]. Some significant language changes between this document and the June report were:

A 60-character set replaced the original 48-character set. Special characters (such as | for "OR") were added primarily for NPL operations and delimiters.

"BEGIN . . . END" blocks were introduced, supported by the members of the IBM laboratory in Vienna, Austria. They argued, in a paper called "Block Concept for NPL" [9], for the elimination of ALLOCATE and the inclusion of blocks. Paul Rogoway (who had now joined IBM) and I objected because we wanted the function of dynamic storage allocation at other than block entry. We prevailed and both functions were included.

%INCLUDE was removed, but many new compile-time facilities were added. (%INCLUDE was brought back into PL/I in the language supported by the first available compiler, called the F-compiler.)

STATIC, AUTOMATIC, and CONTROLLED storage classes replaced TEMP and HELD.

"IF . . . THEN . . . ELSE" was introduced. The June specification did not have the THEN delimiter.

When compared to the relatively small changes undergone by FORTRAN or ALGOL 60 in their first years, the language described in this document is remarkably unlike the PL/I described in later documents such as GC 33-0009-4 [6] which defines the language supported by the present IBM Checkout and Optimizer compilers for PL/I. Further language evolution has resulted in a 1976 PL/I American National Standard [7], and an ECMA Standard [8]. An ISO Standard is near approval at this writing.

The period between April and November 1964 was marked by a staggering amount of language definition, debate, presentation and early compiler implementation. It is impossible in this short paper to describe this activity properly. Let me briefly mention three major parts of the discussion.

George Radin

Literally as soon as the March report was typed, Kurt Bandat, Viktor Kudielka, Peter Lucas, and Kurt Walk of the IBM Vienna Laboratory began an intensive critique of the language. As early as April 3 they produced a 52-page "Review of the Report of the SHARE Advanced Language Development Committee" [10]. This review disclosed syntactic errors, ambiguities, problems generally, and made recommendations, many of which were accepted.

Also as soon as the March document was available, the Programming Language Evaluation department was formed in IBM, at the Time/Life building in New York City, under Paul Comba. This was a group of nine highly experienced programmers with extensive background in high-level languages. They selected 22 representative programs from various application areas which had already been written in existing languages (6 FORTRAN, 5 COBOL, 5 ALGOL, 6 JOVIAL). They reprogrammed all 22 in NPL and compared this language to the originals with respect to criteria such as ease of programming, size of programs, readability. On July 20, 1964, they produced a 185-page report describing their conclusions: "A Comparative Evaluation of the New Programming Language" [11]. As an aid to their own learning the group developed a formal syntax of NPL, which was also published in this report. The following is a direct quote from the overall conclusions of this report:

Overall Conclusions

The goals set by the developers of NPL have been stated in terms of improvements and extensions over the current FORTRAN. Because of this, and because FORTRAN is the most widely used programming language, our overall evaluation gives the greatest weight to the comparison of NPL with FORTRAN. The following remarks refer to Section 1.1 of the April 15 Specifications.

1. Extensions to include additional applications

NPL has undoubtedly succeeded in this stated goal. The programs exhibited in Part 2 of this report are a partial proof of this. The range of these extensions is indeed extremely wide. (Because of these extensions, it is likely that NPL will not need any provision for the inclusion of assembly language subroutines.) Whether the character string operations of NPL will prove adequate for writing programming systems remains doubtful. We have not evaluated this aspect.

2. Clarity, and removal of arbitrary restrictions.

NPL has succeeded outstandingly when compared with FORTRAN and with the other languages except ALGOL (Iverson's programming language, while not considered here, is much more general than NPL; however there are serious problems involved in implementing Iverson's language in its totality). NPL is a little more prolix than FORTRAN. In a few cases it requires constructs that are less convenient than FORTRAN and look unnatural to FORTRAN users, but these cases are relatively minor. Some of them may be removed by redefining NPL on a 60 character set.

As to the claim that NPL is easier to teach and easier to use, we believe it will prove to be valid *PROVIDED:*

(a) subsets of NPL are defined;
(b) an authoritative formal definition of the syntax of NPL is given;
(c) teaching aids to explain the more complicated parts of NPL (e.g., the valid combinations of attributes and their default interpretations) are developed.

3. Bringing the language in line with current practice of machine use

The adequacy of NPL with respect to I/O control, trap supervision, monitored operations and multi-programming is not evaluated in this report, since the I/O facilities were inadequately defined when this study was undertaken and there are, in general, no facilities in the other languages corresponding to trap supervision, monitored operations and multiprogramming. It is clear nevertheless that the inclusion of some of the facilities in NPL is a most important advance. . . .

The comparison of NPL with COBOL for commercial programming shows that NPL has most of the facilities of COBOL and some very useful additional ones. NPL is usually more flexible, simpler, and less verbose. Of the COBOL facilities that are lacking in NPL, many are minor or specialized; only a few are substantial. NPL should not be presented as a language that can fully replace COBOL, but it is likely that a large number of commercial shops will find it superior and eventually will want to convert to it.

The comparison of NPL with ALGOL shows that NPL has gone a long way toward incorporating many ALGOL concepts, and has a much richer repertoire of extended arithmetic operations than ALGOL does. The structure of NPL statements and programs is not as simple as that of ALGOL; in part this could be remedied by redefining NPL on 60 characters, in part it is a consequence of the additional facilities offered by NPL. We believe that a large number of ALGOL users whose interests extend beyond the formulation of algorithms for numerical analysis will find that the additional facilities of NPL more than compensate for its comparative lack of elegance. As a publication language, NPL cannot compete with ALGOL unless a publication version of NPL is developed.

The comparison of NPL and JOVIAL shows that NPL has all the essential capabilities of JOVIAL with the exception of status variables and arrays of string variables, and less convenient switching capabilities. NPL should prove strongly competitive with regard to JOVIAL.

In conclusion NPL is a very strong and powerful language. It can be further strengthened by:

a definition of NPL on a 60 character set.
the definition of subsets and the development of teaching aids,
a formal definition of the syntax,
a publication version of NPL.

As soon as the language and compiler responsibility was moved to Hursley, England, intensive work began in that laboratory to solidify the language and build compilers. Ray Larner, Larry Brown, and Tom Peters moved to England to participate in this effort. Hursley management (John Fairclough, the lab director, George Bosworth, manager of programming, John Nash, manager of the F-compiler, and I. M. (Nobby) Clarke, manager of the Library) were determined to stabilize the language at a level at which an efficient compiler could be built on schedule. In fact, from 1965 until today, the success of PL/I is due almost entirely to the Hursley programmers who made it well defined and usable, who built the compilers for it, and who participated in the standards activities (John Nicholls, David Beech, Brian Marks, Roger Rowe, Tony Burbridge among many others).

Questions were being raised about whether it was possible to build an efficient compiler for such a large and complex language. In October 1964 a committee was formed to investigate the compiler activity, analyze the language, and generally predict the characteristics of NPL compilers. This committee was chaired by Mike Roberts and had participants from the original NPL committee (Jim Cox, who had since joined IBM, and myself), managers of compiler groups (Jack Laffan, John Nash, Bob Sibley) and a member of the original FORTRAN compiler group (Dick Goldberg).

In November 1964 [23] the committee reported. Its conclusions are summarized in the following quote from its report:

The mission of the committee was to determine whether NPL as defined by Hursley V (the November document) would necessarily result in slow compilers or inefficient object code. A brief summary statement is that there is no single feature in the language (as distinct from currently planned implementations) that will cause major and unavoidable inefficiencies in object code. The sum total of all the features has a strong effect on compile speed. Object code inefficiencies, where found, can be mitigated by the suitable restriction of, or interpretation of, features in the language of by considerable effort at compile time. There will be a continuing need for such restriction and interpretation especially until a compiler is implemented.

The standard for comparison chosen was ASA FORTRAN IV. Every subsequent reference to FORTRAN means ASA FORTRAN IV. The general consensus is that a compiler for NPL will require about four times as much coding as a FORTRAN compiler. It is also generally agreed that those NPL programs which are essentially FORTRAN programs written in NPL will take twice as long to compile as would the same programs written in FORTRAN and compiled with a FORTRAN compiler programmed to the same design criteria. (The agreed figures for the NPL-COBOL comparison are twice as much for coding and a factor of 1.5 for compile time.) It is the expectation of the committee that the compile time per statement for programs using the full facilities of NPL will be at most 20 percent greater than the compile time per statement for those NPL programs which are essentially FORTRAN programs written in NPL.

A good summary of the reaction of the ALGOL community to NPL is found in a report from Paul Rogoway to Nat Rochester, his manager, describing a meeting in Hursley on July 24, 1964, where NPL was described to "European University Computing Leaders." I quote:

The NPL presentation was not particularly well organized but most of the significant features of the language were presented. In general the audience was overwhelmed by the language—some members by its power, most by its apparent largeness. The experience reemphasized the crying need for a tutorial presentation of a subset of the language geared to the computing interests and needs of the scientific or FORTRAN–ALGOL audience. There was nearly unanimous feeling that the language would appear to be a fine one, but more definite judgement was reserved, pending further study of the June 15 document (copies of which were distributed to the attendees Tuesday afternoon).

Most of the attendees are ALGOL users and generally agreed that the language is a superset of ALGOL. Serious concern was raised over any instance (such as the WHILE clause) where the same language has a different meaning in NPL from ALGOL. Also, many persons suggested that the point of departure for the new language development should have been ALGOL rather than FORTRAN.

The most significant observations came from three individuals representing interestingly enough three distinct interest groups. A FORTRAN user involved in application programming asked for certain additional function in the language such as an ON clause for overflow of storage; the director of a university computing center expressed concern about compilation speed and subsetting and/or teachability of the language; and an ALGOL father requested an escape character and a single form of the FOR statement.

There was general agreement that the NPL Task Force, and the ALGOL Committee are attacking the same problem from two opposite directions. SHARE from a pragmatic direction, the ALGOL persons from a theoretical one. It was further agreed that cooperation between the two groups is desirable and that much could be gained by attempting to describe equivalent features in an identical manner.

In the fall of 1964 a Language Control Board was established in the New York Programming Center. In 1966, this Board was moved to Hursley. As its attempts to clarify and improve the language proceeded, it became clear that none of the 1964 language documents were adequate as a base from which to work. Ray Larner and John Nicholls (joined by David Beech, Roger Rowe, and, later, David Allen) took the first steps toward developing a formal semantic definition of PL/I (called Universal Language Definition II). This was followed by a formal definition developed in the Vienna Laboratory by a group managed by Kurt Walk ("Abstract syntax and interpretation of PL/I (ULD Version III)") [14]. Later, this was superseded again by the ECMA/ANSI definition referred to earlier. Thus, while it began as a language informally specified with many ambiguities and omissions, PL/I has evolved into one of the most precisely defined languages in use.

Since 1964, many languages both within and outside IBM have been developed as variants on PL/I. The most important of these was EPL, a language development in early 1965 by Bob Morris and Doug McIlroy of Bell Laboratories for use by the MULTICS project. MULTICS [16], a joint Bell Labs, G.E., MIT system project, was looking for a suitable systems programming language at the time NPL was being defined. The only other serious contender was MAD, a language based on ALGOL 58 developed at the University of Michigan, which lacked recursion and adequate data structures, and did not interface well with the interrupt mechanism of MULTICS.

NPL had all the necessary features and was already designed. Thus EPL was developed as a subset of NPL. (It lacked complex data types, aggregate expressions, and all I/O.) In about a year the EPL compiler was operational. Almost all of MULTICS was written in this language, accounting for much of the productivity and maintainability of the system.

Today, among IBM program products, there are more PL/I compiler licenses sold to IBM S/370 customers than FORTRAN licenses. PL/I is still second to COBOL among IBM customers for commercial applications. PL/I and a variant for systems programming have been used successfully to program several large operating systems and compilers (notably MULTICS, OS/VS Release 2 Version 2, the PL/I Checkout compiler). Several pedagogical subsets have been defined and used in introductory programming books [15]. Thus to a large degree, the goals of the original designers have been realized. It is being widely used for scientific, commercial, and systems programming.

3. Design Criteria

It will be helpful, in evaluating PL/I, to review the explicit design criteria of its originators, as well as to see what they did not aim for. There are six such objectives, developed by the Advanced Language Committee members and reported in the January, 1965 *Communications of the ACM* in a paper by Paul Rogoway and myself [13]. They are quoted below:

Freedom of expression: If a particular combination of symbols has reasonably sensible meaning, that meaning is made official. Invalidity is a last resort. This will help to insure realistic compatibility between different NPL compilers.

Full access to machine and operating system facilities: the NPL programmer will rarely if ever need to resort to assembly language coding. No facility was discarded because it belonged more properly to assembly or control card languages.

Modularity: NPL has been designed so that many of its features can be ignored by the programmer without fear of penalty in either compile time or object time efficiency. Thus, manuals can be constructed of subsets of the language for different applications and different levels of complexity. These do not even have to mention the unused facilties. To accomplish this end, every attribute of a variable, every option, every specification was given a default interpretation, and this was chosen to be the one most likely to be required by the programmer who doesn't know that the alternatives exist.

Relative machine independence: Although NPL allows the programmer to take full advantage of the powerful facilities of System/360 and Operating System/360, it is essentially a machine-independent language. The specific parameters of the language such as size of numbers, kinds of input/output devices, etc. are independent of the characteristics of any particular machine.

Cater to the novice: Although the general specification is there for power, beauty, growth, etc., the frequently used special case is specifiable redundantly in an explicit way. As an extreme example, it is possible to invoke in a consistent way any of the sixteen Boolean functions on two logical variables by calling for $BFb_1b_2b_3b_4(arg_1, arg_2)$. The $b_i(i = 1, \ldots, 4)$ are independently either zero or one. The operators specifying union and intersection are, however, still explicitly allowed as: $arg_1 \mid arg_2$, arg_1 & arg_2. This approach allows the compiler to maximize efficiency for the commonly-used case, and again, permits the novice to learn only the notation which is most natural to him.

NPL is a programming, not an algorithmic language: Programming languages are most often written on coding sheets, punched at key punches or terminals, and listed on printers. While the specification of a publication language is considered essential, the first and most important goal of syntax design has been to make the listings as readable, and to make the writing and punching as error-free, as possible. A free-field format has been chosen to help the terminal programmer.

This is an unusual set of objectives when viewed after fifteen years, not so much for what it includes, which is generally reasonable, as for what it omits. Nowhere do we find many of the goals in favor today:

e.g., a solid theoretical basis,
   extensibility from a simple base language,
   interactive facilities,
   producing well-structured programs,
   ability to prove correctness.

(Bruce Rosenblatt recalls that extensibility was discussed by the committee, and that the decision to avoid reserved key words was a result of this objective.)

It was still of overriding importance, as it was with FORTRAN, that object code be efficient. Convenience was the key word rather than simplicity. This was a language defined more in the spirit of English than of Mathematics. (There were irregular verbs and idioms.) Success was measured primarily by the ease of specifying large classes of programs in the language. If the right primitives were available, the language succeeded; if tedious procedures had to be written to provide the required functions, the language failed.

4. Rationale and Evaluation of Contents of NPL-PL/I

This section discusses some of the more interesting characteristics of the December 1964 language and evaluates them in the light of our experience.

Program Structure

The lexical rules in NPL (which remained largely unchanged as PL/I developed) have proven to be easy to learn and quite natural (especially as compared to COBOL and FORTRAN). They removed all mention of column numbers, allowed blanks and comments freely wherever separators were allowed, and thus were naturally adaptable to different media.

The use of semicolons as statement terminators instead of as separators (as in ALGOL) is an interesting small example of the fundamental differences between the two languages. The ALGOL decision provides a more regular basis for extending the language. The PL/I decision is more readable when listed on a printer with only the standard upper case font. Some studies [17] have suggested that this PL/I usage is easier to learn and less prone to errors but, like all human factors studies, this is quite subjective.

The NPL designers decided also to develop a syntax which did not require that keywords be reserved. This decision was made in order to allow language extensions without invalidating old programs.

An interesting example of the subjectivity of language syntax is the debate over the assignment statement. Since all other statements in NPL began with a verb, it would have simplified the syntax (and thus the parse phase of compilation) to have specified assignment as:

$$SET \text{ variable} = \text{expression};$$

which was, in fact, the syntax in the March report.

Going to a distinct assignment operator as in ALGOL:

$$\text{variable} := \text{expression};$$

would also have been reasonable. The committee, being uncertain about the correct decision, informally polled the general SHARE body. The results were completely inconclusive. Each choice had its strong adherents and its equally persuasive detractors. As a result the committee decided to revert to the FORTRAN syntax since it was the most widely understood. The impact of this decision on the compiler was very small. The major problem has been the human confusion caused by using the same symbol for the boolean equality operator and the assignment operator, as in:

$$A = B = C;$$

Facilities for defining aggregates of statements had been provided by subroutines in FORTRAN, and by blocks in ALGOL. The NPL design approach here again reveals its concern with performance over simplicity. The functions provided by this level of structure were separated and a different syntactic form defined for each so that their separate usage could easily be recognized for customized implementation.

To delimit a group of statements simply for control (as in IF THEN clauses or DO WHILE iterations) the syntax DO; . . . END; was defined. This required no more runtime overhead than a branch.

To delimit a group of statements in order to define scope of variables, and to allow storage sharing among blocks of disjoint scope, the ALGOL-like BEGIN; . . . END; block was used. This defined a dynamic as well as static state and so a prologue was required in order to establish this state on entry to the block.

Finally to delimit a group of statements which can act either as a subroutine (i.e., the object of a CALL) or as a function that is invoked within an expression, the syntax PROCEDURE; . . . END; was used.

George Radin

Control Flow

The NPL designers attempted to be very ambitious in the definition of dynamic structure and flow, an attempt that still accounts for much of PL/I's strength and usability, but that introduced some complexity and optimization problems. For separate reasons the following facilities were provided, some of which, even individually, were quite unusual in a high level language:

creation of asynchronous executing tasks,
ON conditions specifying blocks to be invoked when specific conditions occurred,
recursive procedures with static, as well as automatic, storage,
variables whose values are labels (for computed GO TO as well as abnormal returns from procedures).

It was not so much the problems associated with each of these facilities that caused trouble as their interactions. In this area it would seem that the language had not achieved its goal of modularity. However, several PL/I procedure attributes and compiler options were added to allow the programmer explicitly to declare that some particular language feature would not be used (such as recursion or tasking). The fact that such assertions could cause the compiler to produce efficient code without requiring large compiler modifications argues that some sets of these features were indeed defined to be reasonably independent.

An example of this interaction was the definition of label variables. Consider what had to be contained in the value of a label variable. This value had to include the level of recursion and the name of the task as well as the name of the block in the procedure in which the label occurred. Restrictions had to be defined to preclude label variables from containing values which no longer were active.

Thus, in NPL, label variables could not be static or controlled. On assignment, the persistence of the variable on the left was constrained to be no greater than that on the right. For example,

```
P: PROCEDURE (A);
        DECLARE A LABEL,
                B LABEL;
   L:B=L;
     A=B;
   END;
```

would result in the value L persisting in A after return from P.
    In

                    GO TO label variable;

the variable's value was constrained to be in the same block activation as the GO TO statement so that GO TO could not be used for RETURN. But this could not in general be assured at compile time and so code had to be generated to check for it at run time. (This is an example of a facility carefully defined so that a sophisticated optimizing compiler could find the cases where efficient object code could be safely generated. Often, however, in real compilers developed by programmers under schedule, compile speed and space constraints, this sophisticated analysis is not achieved.)

Similarly, because

RETURN TO label variable;

was allowed freely in NPL, such a return could collapse any number of blocks and procedures and commence at any label in the returned-to procedure. Thus every procedure invocation which passed a label variable to another procedure had to expect this abnormal control flow and suitably materialize its state (that is, ensure that all variables modified in registers were copied back into storage, and all subsequent references got fresh copies from storage). (Eventually, as PL/I developed, the constraints on GO TO were dropped as was the RETURN TO form, since it had become redundant.)

The NPL document said nothing to preclude passing a label variable across tasks. But it did not define what happened if its value were used in a RETURN TO statement. In general, tasking was one of the more inadequately designed features of NPL. This facility was greatly improved as PL/I evolved but still has quite limited use. A tasking proposal considerably different from that in PL/I was proposed for the ANS PL/I standard. This too was finally rejected primarily because of difficulties in achieving an adequate definition.

In retrospect it is hard to understand how asynchronous processing capability could have been defined in NPL without locking, queueing, event posting, waiting, or any method by which to program synchronization. No explicit definition of atomicity or synchronization was given which would restrict a compiler's ability to move code freely. Thus in general it was difficult to allow tasks to cooperate at all.

Programming languages before NPL (and most languages still) had few general facilities to define actions which were to be taken when conditions such as reading an end of file, overflow, bad data, new line, occurred. Often the conditions could not even be sensed in the language, and assembly language patches were required. Even where the condition could be sensed and explicit "IF THEN ELSE" clauses inserted wherever it could occur, the resulting program was quite awkward.

The NPL designers were determined that entire real applications should be programmable in the language and these programs be properly reliable and safe. Thus they introduced 23 types of conditions and the executable statement:

ON condition action;

This facility provided a powerful control structure for coping with these infrequent occurrences. It resulted, however, in a complex total control flow when coupled with the other aspects of dynamic flow in NPL. For instance, inheritance and stacking of actions were defined across procedure and block invocations. When a condition occurred, the block specifying the action was to be executed (almost) in the state which pertained when the ON statement was executed. This required the ability to suspend one state temporarily and reinstate another. Thus some information necessary to handle the exception might be inaccessible in the ON unit since it was accessible only in the context of the exception itself.

ON conditions, as a general mechanism to take action when unusual or infrequent situations occur, are always more difficult to define and sometimes more difficult to use than would be desired. It is hard, however, in retrospect, to point to the subsequent invention of a simpler or more usable facility. The conclusion that, therefore, the facility should not be in a programming language at all simply was inconsistent with the NPL objectives.

George Radin

Storage Management

STATIC storage in NPL was directly modeled after FORTRAN storage management. STATIC INTERNAL corresponds to FORTRAN local storage and STATIC EXTERNAL to FORTRAN named COMMON. Since NPL supported recursion, AUTOMATIC storage had to be introduced. Allowing recursion at the *procedure* level does not require dynamic stacking at *block* entry. But AUTOMATIC variables local to blocks were defined so that binding of extents could be deferred as late as block entry time. This did require dynamic stack management and has caused considerable run-time complexity. It was included primarily because the NPL designers in 1963–1964 were quite concerned with storage efficiency, because late binding offered a function that was considered to be useful in some future interactive environment, and because the designers again reasoned that an intelligent compiler could recognize the cases where extents could be bound earlier.

CONTROLLED storage, like ON conditions, was introduced to provide, at the NPL language level, functions hitherto available only to assembly language programs invoking operating system services. The NPL definition, however, provided more extensive function than that offered by most operating systems.

Generations of CONTROLLED variables were allowed so that programmers could implement dynamic storage allocation with arbitrary numbers of separate allocations. Extents could change between generations; only the number of dimensions and the data type (and structuring) had to be constant. (This last facilty has resulted in controlled storage being significantly less efficient than STATIC or AUTOMATIC. But, since there is no facility in PL/I to create new names at runtime or to grow an existing allocation, its removal would result in a real functional restriction in the language.)

While both CONTROLLED storage and multitasking are each useful functions, their interaction illustrates the problems which combinations of such functions can introduce into a language. Consider the definition of CONTROLLED storage in a multitask program as it appears in the November 1964 NPL document [4].

> An attached task has almost the same access to the attaching task's data as it would have if it were executed synchronously; that is, when it is attached, all allocations of CONTROLLED data known to the attaching task are passed to the attached task. However, subsequent allocatons in the attached task are known only within the attached task and its subsequent descendants; subsequent allocations in the attaching task are known only within the attaching task and its subsequent descendants. Thus the stack of allocations for a CONTROLLED variable splits into separate stacks, with a common part preceding task initiation and separate parts after task initiation. A task may only free storage which it allocated. All storage allocated within a task is destroyed when that task is completed.

This definition is also illustrative of one of the most serious and pervasive problems with the NPL document [4] a problem which resulted primarily from the scope of the definition and the pressures of its schedule. It is a short paragraph attempting to define a very complex, powerful facility and thus leaving unanswered many detailed points. For example, can the creating task free the shared generation? If so, it can now access the previous generation; can the created tasks also now access this generation? (It should be noted that even this document represented a major improvement in level of definition over the much shorter, more ambiguous document developed by the Advanced Language Development Committee [3].)

Another innovation in the NPL storage model was the concept of auxiliary storage. In all programming languages, and in most systems without virtual memory, data which cannot fit within available main memory must be explicitly written to auxiliary storage using I/O facilities. This means that files must be defined, opened, and written. The mapping of data aggregates to records must be defined by the programmer.

In NPL the statements SAVE and RESTORE were defined to permit moving the current values of a variable to auxiliary storage, and subsequently retrieving them, without requiring that the user cope with the complexities of I/O. The function was provided in great generality and required extensive run-time support. Stacks of generations of SAVEs were allowed, as was retrieval by key. (These stacks were similar to those of controlled variables. One would expect a similar approach to tasking, but in fact tasking was not mentioned in the section on SAVE and RESTORE.) The complexity of implementation, and a general feeling that virtual memory would eventually provide a better solution to the same problem led to the eventual removal of SAVE and RESTORE from NPL.

It is surprising, in retrospect, to recall that one of the most powerful aspects of PL/I, widely used for systems programming, was not in the original NPL definition at all. Namely, all notions of pointers, areas, offsets and based variables are completely missing. Moreover, none of the criticisms about the various versions of the language noted this omission. (Similarly, the notion of a reference is missing from ALGOL 60.)

This part of the language was introduced when one PL/I compiler group attempted to program their compiler in PL/I, and when General Motors stated their need for pointers in their graphics applications. An early description of these facilities in PL/I was a paper by Bud Lawson, produced in October 1965, entitled "A Guide to PL/I List Processing" [12]. After discussing the problem in general, Bud introduces the notion of a based variable (but without that explicit attribute) and a pointer:

> This facility to operate upon pointers and list data elements is provided by extending the CONTROLLED storage class to include pointer variable. For example, consider the following declaration.

DECLARE ALPHA FLOAT CONTROLLED (P);

> This declares ALPHA to be a floating point variable, and that the pointer P will be used to identify the location of ALPHA when ALPHA is referenced. P is assumed contextually to have the attribute POINTER due to its position in the CONTROLLED attribute. This new form of controlled variable will be referred to as a *based variable*. It does not imply stacking of allocations of data. Instead, it provides a descriptive device for describing the structure of data that exists in any storage class (STATIC, AUTOMATIC or CONTROLLED).

It has been argued that the UNSPEC built-in function (which returns the underlying bit representation of its argument) and the ADDR built-in function (which returns the address of the first byte of its argument) coupled with free pointers containing real memory addresses, exposed too much of the underlying storage structure. Certainly much sophisticated optimization has been made more difficult because of these features. On the other hand they made feasible the programming of many procedures which would otherwise have been written in assembly language.

George Radin

Data Types

Nowhere is the "swiss knife" aspect of NPL more apparent than in its unparalleled variety of data types. Even though the language still lacked entry variables, areas, offsets, pointers, and events, the interactions of its many data types accounted for much of its apparent complexity.

Except for label and file variables, data were of two types: arithmetic or string. Strings were character or bit and could be of fixed or varying length. Facilities for substring selection, concatenation, searching, etc. were provided.

The question of whether a language should treat strings as one-dimensional arrays is still debated today. The Bell Labs "C" language [18], for instance, supports only a single-character scalar data type which must be declared in an array to represent a string. An insight into the level of discussion in 1964 can be gained from this quote from a memo to Fred Brooks, from me, dated July 24, 1964 [25]. Fred, manager of OS/360 at the time, had asked the question at an earlier meeting.

> The type string is, as you have remarked, unnecessary. We could have introduced instead a type character and a type bit (or logical), each being of constant length 1. We could then use the mechanism of a vector of characters or bits to accomplish the string facility. This has two interesting consequences:
>
> a. People (and there really are some) who have not had any previous exposure to the concepts of vectors, arrays, dimensions, etc., are going to run very quickly back to COBOL unless we publish a manual for them which cleverly disguises these notions in more familiar terms. Even some people who do know about vectors will find it hard not to think of JOE as a scalar. But more important if JOE is really (J,O,E), SAM is really (S,A,M) and DANIEL is really (D,A,N,I,E,L), note that (JOE,SAM,DANIEL) is not an array. I think confusion, rather than clarity, will result.
> b. Suppose we adopt the proposed approach. A character string is then just a vector. The concatenation of two character strings is just the concatenation of two vectors. We don't have this facility yet, but it's obviously necessary, so we'll introduce it. Analogously, we will have to introduce, for vectors, an infix notation to reference a substring, an index function to search the vector for a given pattern, a variable length facility since fixed length strings are intolerable. Now, having provided all this for arrays of dimensionality one, we will certainly feel compelled to generalize the facilities to higher dimensionality. Of course, here the notations became a bit more complicated since A concat B is ambiguous for arrays unless one states the dimension to be concatenated. You see that what you are asking turns out not to be the treatment of strings as arrays, but quite the contrary. I'm not knocking the proposal, but the way. We suggested it several times at our SHARE committee meetings and were greeted by great reluctance among the implementors (and we really couldn't blame them).

Another debatable question was whether bit strings should be treated like character strings or like variable-length binary integers. NPL chose the former direction, which results in left justification and, hence, unnatural conversions between bit and binary. This can result in undesirable effects when the bit strings are meant to represent numbers.

In the April 1964 paper from the Vienna Lab which reviewed NPL [10], a proposal was made to reverse this decision, that is, to treat bit strings as numbers:

> Operations on bit strings are [in this proposed change, ed.] defined as bit-by-bit operations (with the exception of CONCAT), beginning at the *right* side of the strings. If the strings are of different lengths, the shorter string is extended on the *left* side with zeros to the length of the longer string, for all operations. The bits are numbered from right to left.

Remark

This rule has the advantage that the numeric value assigned to a string . . . is preserved by the extension. . . .

Remark

The inconsistency of the rules for bit-and-character strings seems to be unavoidable, since it is due to a fundamental difficulty (writing numbers beginning with the most significant digit).

Arithmetic data could be "numeric fields" or in "coded form." (A numeric field was defined as a character string whose PICTURE attribute enables a unique numeric value to be determined. Thus arithmetic data could be stored with explicit decimal points, dollar signs, leading blanks, etc.) Arithmetic data could be decimal or binary, fixed or floating point, real or complex. The "precision" could be specified by declaring the total number of digits and the number of digits to the right of the decimal (or binary) point.

Arrays were allowed to have arbitrary dimensionality and arbitrary lower and upper bounds for each dimension. Cross sections of arrays were specifiable by inserting asterisks in those dimensions which were to vary (e.g., A(I,*) referred to a vector, which was the *i*th row of A). Structures of arbitrary depth were defined with name qualification to ensure uniqueness of references.

The decimal and numeric field facilities and structures were largely taken from COBOL, the fixed binary, floating point, and arrays from FORTRAN. What is remarkable is that, with very few exceptions, the attributes were orthogonal. (For instance, any radix was allowed with any mode and any encoding or precision; arrays of structures and structures with array elements were permitted.) The language and compiler complexity that this freedom ultimately caused was not fully anticipated by the NPL designers. This is illustrated by the fact that while, already in the NPL document of 1964 [5], great detail is given to the specification of the PICTURE attribute, conversion is covered entirely in a little over one page. The later PL/I document required 17 double-column pages, with many tables, to define all the permissible conversions.

Many combinations are seldom used (e.g., fixed decimal components of complex numbers). Others have, in fact, not been widely used even though one can create examples in which they are appropriate (e.g., fixed binary data which are not integers). The developers of NPL, and PL/I later, always intended that numeric data attributes describe the ranges of values and the precise meaning of operations on data, and not imply an internal representation. (Honeywell PL/I, for instance, represents FIXED DECIMAL as binary numbers with power of ten scaling; thus DECIMAL and BINARY integers are represented identically.) What has happened, in spite of this intent, is that those data types which correspond closely to S/360 machine-supported operands are used almost entirely (e.g., fixed binary integers of precisions 15 and 31). Using data types which are much different from these and using conversions with loss of information (e.g., float to fixed) often results in unexpected program behavior.

It is always difficult to define arithmetic and assignment for programming languages or for machines. Numerical analysts disagree among themselves; there are conflicting goals which cannot all be satisfied. For instance, a subject of continuing debate in NPL, and later in PL/I, was whether the result of an operation should be uniquely defined by the attributes of its operands (which simplifies language definition and compilation), or whether the result should be influenced by its eventual use (which often leads to more useful and expected answers). Taking the former approach (as in FORTRAN), 3/2 + .5 might yield 1 + .5 = 1.5, while 3/2 + 1/2 might yield 1 + 0 = 1. Taking the latter approach might always yield 2, but is difficult to define in general and would make finding common subexpressions for optimization difficult until the text had been translated to a lower level. PL/I rules yield the expected 2 in these cases but surprise the programmer who tries 3/2 + 9 when OVERFLOW is disabled.

The basic principle which PL/I follows is to preserve precision when the hardware allows it, and to use overflow otherwise. This principle, and the specific PL/I precision rules, were debated at great length during the standard definition process. Every alternative proposal was found to have its own set of problems and so, in the end, the PL/I rules were preserved.

But the debate continues, centered largely around fixed point division. I quote from a recent letter to me from Doug McIlroy recalling the NPL debate [24]:

> One case in point that I remember especially is the rules for arithmetic: We all had hoped to make definitions that would yield generally agreeable answers for most plausible expressions and work well with constants, which should have indicated value without forcing type. One old shibboleth stuck with us all the way through: Commercial users were expected to balk unless division of fixed point numbers yielded fixed point results. Rules that made sense, gave all the bits you were entitled to, and catered for fixed point divide, eluded us, despite any number of tries at different bottom up or top down ways to arrive at coercions. To this day I believe that had we cut the Gordian knot of fixed point divide, there would have followed a more plausible and less demanding rule. (If you declare your integers to be full single precision numbers, the minute you add two of them you get double precision arithmetic.)

Many programming language definers take the easy way out. They simply do not define the results of computation and assignment in any detail. This results in languages which are proudly "machine independent" but programs which are not. Machine architects contain the problem generally by not allowing mixed attribute facilities at all. Where they do, as in the Move Character Long instruction in S/370, the specification is as complex as it is in PL/I.

One of the more controversial PL/I decisions concerned the order of computation and assignment for array expressions. In APL, monadic and dyadic operations on arrays are performed right to left, one operator at a time. Thus

$$A \leftarrow A + A[1]$$

means the same as

$$TEMP \leftarrow A[1]$$
$$A \leftarrow A + TEMP$$

In PL/I, however

```
A = A + A(1);
```

meant the same as

```
DO I = 1 TO N;
  A(I) = A(I) + A(1);
END;
```

Thus the new value of A(1) is added to A(2) . . . A(N).

There are good arguments for either decision. The PL/I approach can produce more efficient code and does not require temporaries. There are cases also where storage hierarchies are accessed much more efficiently. The APL approach seems more natural to programmers. (The ANSI standard PL/I has, in fact, changed to the APL approach.) What is most interesting historically, however, is that the problem does not seem to have been recognized in the NPL document. Not until the PL/I (F) document was there an example inserted to call attention to the difference.

I/O Facilities

ALGOL chose to leave I/O as a facility for each system to provide as it wished. Thus, while algorithms specified in ALGOL will run on different systems, programs may not. FORTRAN invented the concept of a format list and a data list, thus allowing entire programs to run, provided the files which they accessed were compatible and the control statements properly modified. COBOL introduced more extensive facilities for the processing of records and preparing of reports than any other language before or since.

The NPL designers were determined that both FORTRAN and COBOL programmers should not find their product lacking in the functions they were accustomed to, and that the external data management facilities which they were told would be available to OS/360 assembly language programmers would be invokable in NPL. Thus more than 10% of the NPL definition dealt with I/O. It had more extensive format-list capability than FORTRAN and, while not as rich as COBOL functions generally, it reflected what little was then known of the OS/360-to-be features such as the TITLE option (for DD names), the SORT statement (designed to invoke the SORT utility), and the TASK option on READ and WRITE (for asynchronous I/O). It is interesting to observe that ANSI made very little change to PL/I in the name of operating system independence (although asynchronous I/O has been removed). Hence either the NPL designers succeeded in their goal of generalizing these OS/360 facilities or the OS system facilities have been widely adopted in the industry.

Compile-Time Facilities

NPL compile-time facilities were developed with conventional macro assemblers in mind. The functions, with the exception of macro procedures, were all standard. The syntax was constrained to allow one-pass processing. Surprisingly, although equivalence to JOVIAL motivated much of NPL's fixed binary data definition, %INCLUDE, PL/I's equivalent of COMPOOL, was removed from the language in the December 1964 document.

Implicit and Default Attributes

Perhaps because of the FORTRAN background of its designers, NPL (and PL/I) did not require that all attributes be explicitly declared. If identifiers were not declared at all, implicit or contextual data types were assigned consistent with their use in the program (e.g., GO TO L; implied that L was a label variable). If the rules for implicit declaration established the variable as numeric, NPL adapted the FORTRAN convention of assigning fixed binary type to identifiers whose names began with the letters I through N, float otherwise. (This rule has been removed in the PL/I standard.) NPL, however, responding to an outstanding request for extension to FORTRAN, added an IMPLICIT statement, by which any set of attributes could be implied for variables whose names began with specific letters.

But the real complexity (and confusion) entered the language with default, rather than implied attributes. NPL did not require that all attributes be explicitly declared for all variables. The missing attributes were given default values depending on the ones which were explicitly presented. (E.g., explicitly declaring a variable to be BINARY gave it a default scale of FLOAT; explicitly declaring FLOAT gave it a default radix of DECIMAL; the default lower bound of an array dimension was 1.) Given all the different kinds of attributes in PL/I, defining natural and consistent defaults for any sensible subset became a sizable task.

Today the computer science community generally does not approve of all this defaulting, nor of implicit conversions. If the program is not explicitly correct, we generally argue that it should not compile. But how much, one may ask, is this change in objectives due to the fast, cheap turn-around offered by contemporary systems? Would we be as willing to be forced to resubmit if each submission meant a day's delay?

5. Implications for Current and Future Languages

NPL was a language defined too quickly. Its virtues resulted primarily from the combined intuitions (and programming experience) of its definers. (They convened "knowing" what they wanted in the language.) Its faults were largely ambiguity and incompleteness.

In retrospect it appears that these definers correctly assessed the unique strengths of the languages from which they drew inspiration. They took from FORTRAN the notions of separately compiled subroutines sharing common data and the DO loop. From COBOL they introduced data structures, I/O, and report generating facilities. From ALGOL they took block structure and recursion. A major contribution of NPL was not only its original facilities but the combining of these borrowed characteristics into a consistent single language.

If one reads the 1964 NPL documents and compares them with PL/I today, it becomes clear that the Hursely language definers did much more than simply clarify and extend. They took an impressive first effort (NPL) and, spending many years in the process, fashioned a well-defined, usable programming language.

In the first years (1964–1966), these clarifications were motivated largely by the need to know precisely what to compile, to make compilation tractable, and to make object code reasonably efficient. They were eventually motivated also by users' comments, particularly from SHARE and GUIDE, but, in the years between the NPL document and the release and wide use of the PL/I(F) compiler in 1966, little real programming experience existed to demonstrate language change requirements.

Like almost all of its contemporary languages, PL/I suffered from being defined at a single level. If it was felt that a facility was useful and could be compiled reasonably it was added to the language. In a subsequent wave of language definition ALGOL 68, SIMULA, PASCAL, and PL/I compile-time facilities turned (in very different ways) to extension facilities as a means of adding data types and operators.

The strongest characteristic of PL/I is its breadth and detail. It is really feasible to write entire application (and even system) programs in the language without resorting to assembly language. It may be that programming in the 1980s will be divided between applications programmers, who will want to communicate in many different, very high-level, special-purpose languages, and highly skilled systems programmers, who will provide the processors, libraries, and services for the former. Even more important than its wide use in scientific and commercial application programming is the role PL/I (and its derivatives) may play as a language for these systems programmers.

Appendix A

(NEW = Language Described in Share Report of April, 1964; OLD = FORTRAN IV)

```
                NEW                                          NEW

                PROCEDURE PROBLEM1                           PROCEDURE PROBLEM2
                GET (A, B, C, D) ' E(14, 5) '                DECLARE PEOPLE (20), FIXED,
RDACD.          GET (X) 'E(14, 5) '                            =20*0 / SALARY (20), =20*0
                ON EOF RETURN                                  / AGE, FIXED,
                IF ( X EQ D ) ( SET FOFX = 0 GO TO                     PICTURE(ZZZ) / INCOME, FLOAT
                    PTALINE )                    RDACD.       GET(AGE, INCOME) 'F(3), E(10,2)'
                IF ( X LT D ) SET FOFX = X*(A*X + B)          IF ( AGE NE-1 ) ( SET I = AGE /5 + 1
                    + C                                              SET PEOPLE (I) = PEOPLE (I) + 1
                        ELSE SET FOFX = X*(-A*X + B)                 SET SALARY (I) = SALARY (I)
                            - C                                        + INCOME
PTALINE.        PUT (X, FOFX) ' E(14,5) '                            GO TO RDACD )
                GO TO RDACD                                  DO LOOP I = (1,20)
                END                                          IF ( PEOPLE(I) NE 0 ) SET SALARY (I)
                                                                = SALARY (I)/PEOPLE(I)
                                                            SET AGE = 5*I - 5
                                             LOOP.          PUT(AGE, SALARY(I), PEOPLE(I))
                                                                'F(3), E(10,2), F(7)'
                                                            RETURN
                                                            END
```

```
        OLD                                          OLD

C       PROBLEM 1                            C       PROBLEM 2
        READ (5,1) A, B, C, D                        INTEGER AGE
6       READ (5,1) X                                 REAL INCOME
        IF ( X - D) 2,3,4                            DIMENSION PEOPLE(20), SALARY(20)
2       FOFX = X*(A*X + B) + C                       DATA(PEOPLE(I), SALARY(I),I=1,20)/40*0.0/
        GO TO 5                              1       READ (5,3) AGE, INCOME
3       FOFX = 0.0                                   IF ( AGE + 1 ) 8,4,2
        GO TO 5                              2       I = AGE/5 + 1
4       FOFX = X*(-A*X + B) - C                      PEOPLE(I) = PEOPLE (I) + 1.0
5       WRITE (6,1) X, FOFX                          SALARY(I) = SALARY(I) + INCOME)
        GO TO 6                                      GO TO 1
1       FORMAT ( 4F14,5 )                   4       DO 7 I = 1,20
        END                                          IF ( PEOPLE(I) ) 8,6,5
                                            5       SALARY(I) = SALARY(I)/PEOPLE(I)
                                            6       AGE = 5*I - 5
                                            7       WRITE (6,3) AGE, SALARY(I), PEOPLE(I)
                                            8       STOP
                                            3       FORMAT ( 13, F10.2, F7.0 )
                                                    END
```

George Radin

```
                NEW                                              NEW

              PROCEDURE PROBLEM3                              PROCEDURE PROBLEM4
              DECLARE FIXED PRIME / FACTOR                    DECLARE FLOAT I/L
              DO LOOP2 PRIME = (3,1000,2)          RDACD.  GET(R, F, L)'E(14,5)'
              DO LOOP1 FACTOR = (2,SQRT(PRIME))            ON EOF RETURN
LOOP1.IF  ( MOD(FACTOR,PRIME) EQ 0 ) GO TO LOOP2           SET R = R**2
              PUT(PRIME) 'F(4)'                             SET F = 6.2832*F
LOOP2.        CONTINUE                                      SET FACTOR = F*L
              RETURN                                        GET(CO, CF) 'E(14,5)'
              END                                           PUT(R, F, L) 'E(14,5)'
                                                            DO LOOP E = (1.0,3.0,0.5)
                                                            PUT (E)'E(14,5)'
                                                            DO LOOP C = (CO,CF,1.0E-8)
                                                            SET I = E / SQRT( R +
                                                                (FACTOR-1/(F*C))**2 )
                                                  LOOP.   PUT(C, I) 'E(14,5)'
                                                            GO TO RDACD
                                                            END


                OLD                                              OLD

C     PROBLEM 3                                   C     PROBLEM 4
        INTEGER PRIME, FACTOR                            REAL I, L
        PRIME = 3                                 7  READ (5,1) R, F, L
3     A = PRIME                                          R = R**2
        A = SQRT(A)                                       F = 6.2832*F
        J = A                                             FACTOR = F*L
        DO 1 FACTOR = 2,J                                READ (5,2) CO, CF
        IF ( MOD(FACTOR,PRIME) ) 1,2,1                   WRITE (6,1) R, F, L
1     CONTINUE                                            E = 1.0
        WRITE (6,5) PRIME                        9  WRITE (6,1) E
5     FORMAT ( 120)                                       C=CO
2     PRIME = PRIME + 2                           5  I = E / SQRT( R + (FACTOR-1/(F*C))**2 )
        IF ( PRIME - 1000 ) 3,7,7                        WRITE (6,2) C, I
7     STOP                                                C = C + 1.0E-8
        END                                               IF ( C - CF ) 5,5,6
                                                  6  E = E + 0.5
                                                          IF ( E - 3.0 ) 9,9,7
                                                  1  FORMAT (3F14.5 )
                                                  2  FORMAT (2E14.5 )
                                                          END
```

REFERENCES

1. SHARE, *Report of the SHARE Advanced Language Development Committee,* March 1, 1964.
2. SHARE, *Specifications for the New Programming Language,* April, 1964.
3. SHARE, *Report II of the SHARE Advanced Language Development Committee,* June 25, 1964.
4. IBM, *The New Programming Language,* IBM UK Laboratories, November 30, 1964.
5. IBM, *NPL Technical Report,* IBM World Trade Laboratories (Great Britain), December 1964.
6. IBM, *OS PL/I Checkout and Optimizing Compilers: Language Reference Manual,* GC33-0009-4, IBM Corporation, October 1976.
7. American National Standards Institute, *American National Standard Programming Language PL/I,* ANSI X3.53, New York, 1976.
8. European Computer Manufacturers Association, *Standard for PL/I,* Standard ECMA-50, Geneva, 1976.
9. Bandat, K., Bekic, H., and Lucas, P., *Block Concept for NPL,* IBM Laboratory, Vienna, July 1964.
10. Bandat, K., Kudielka, V., Lucas, P., and Walk, K., *Review of the Report of the SHARE Advanced Language Development Committee,* IBM Laboratory, Vienna, April 1964.
11. Comba, P., *A Comparative Evaluation of the New Programming Language,* IBM, New York, July 1964.
12. Lawson, H. W., Jr., *A Guide to PL/I List Processing,* SDD-PL/I, IBM, New York, October 1965. See also Lawson, H. W., Jr., PL/I List Processing. *CACM,* **10**(6): 358–367 (1967) June.

13. Radin, G., and Rogoway, H. P., NPL: Highlights of a New Programming Language. *Communications of the ACM,* **8**(1): 9–17 (1965) Jan.
14. Walk, K., Alber, K., Fleck, M., Goldmann, H., Lauer, P., Moser, E., Oliva, P., Stigleitner, H., and Zeisel, G., *Abstract Syntax and Interpretation of PL/I* (ULD Version III), Tech. Rep. TR 25:098, IBM, Vienna, April 1969.
15. Conway, R. W., and Gries, D., *A Primer on Structured Programming Using PL/I, PL/C, and PL/CT,* Winthrop Publ., Cambridge, Massachusetts, 1976.
16. Corbato, F. J., and Vyssotsky, V. A., Introduction and Overview of the Multics System. *Proc. AFIPS FJCC,* Vol. 27, pp. 185–196. Spartan Books, Washington, D.C., 1965.
17. Gannon, John D., and Horning, James, The Impact of Language Design on the Production of Reliable Software. Presented at the *International Conference on Reliable Software, 1975;* published in *Technical Report CSRG-45,* University of Toronto, Toronto, Ontario, December 1974.
18. Kernighan, B. W., and Ritchie, D. M., *The C Programming Language.* Prentice-Hall, Englewood Cliffs, New Jersey, 1978.
19. Rosenblatt, Bruce A., Letter to George Radin, December 1977.
20. Larner, Raymond A., and Brown, Lawrence C., *FORTRAN VI Language Notebook,* IBM memo, February 1964.
21. Rochester, N., *A FORTRAN VI Proposal,* IBM memo, 1963.
22. IBM report, February 1963.
23. IBM memo, November 1964.
24. McIlroy, M.D., Letter to George Radin, December 1977.
25. Radin, George, IBM memo to Dr. F. P. Brooks, July 24, 1964.

TRANSCRIPT OF PRESENTATION

ROBERT ROSIN: The speaker on PL/I is George Radin. He earned his Bachelor's Degree in English Literature at Brooklyn College in 1951, Master's in English Literature in 1952 at Columbia, and in 1961, a Master's in Mathematics at New York University. In 1963, at the time PL/I activity really took shape, he had already joined IBM in February of that year. He was in the New York Programming Center, and was working on advanced technology for compilers. More recently he's had many activities inside of IBM and currently is Senior Manager in the Computer Sciences Department at the Thomas J. Watson Laboratory in Yorktown Heights. George Radin.

GEORGE RADIN: When I discovered that we were scheduled to talk about PL/I at 8:30 on Saturday morning, I called Jean Sammet and I asked her, "How come us?". She assured me that it required a language of the wide popularity and audience appeal of PL/I to guarantee a full crowd at this outrageous hour, and I believe that *that* was the reason that we were chosen [Laughter] [Frame 1].

   [Frame 2] acknowledges my debt to many helpers and readers and rememberers and critics. The order is random, except for Jim Cox [now of IBM], who spent many days helping me find the material, read it, and filter it. And material exists in great volume for a history of PL/I. It exists in the files of many people who never throw anything away; it exists in large numbers of cartons, each packed with memos and evaluations and language

THE EARLY HISTORY AND CHARACTERISTICS
OF PL/I

GEORGE RADIN

Frame 1

George Radin

CONTRIBUTORS TO PAPER:
JIM COX
MARC AUSLANDER
DAVID BEECH
PAT GOLDBERG
MARTY HOPKINS
BRIAN MARKS
DOUG MCILROY
JOHN MCKEEHAN
ERICH NEUHOLD
JOHN NICHOLLS
BRUCE ROSENBLATT
WARNER KING
ELLIOT NOHR
NAT ROCHESTER
BOB ROSIN
MIKE MARCOTTY
Frame 2

control logs, and other things. It exists also in the memories of many people, each of whom was involved in some aspect of PL/I design.

The paper that you have [on pp. 551–575] is an attempt to do what we could in several months to gather together some of the more interesting aspects of that language design. I believe that material is left for several dissertations, and I believe also that the exercise is an important one, not just because PL/I is an important language, but because of the breadth of its subject matter.

PL/I took as its scope virtually all of programming, and so the dialogs about its various parts really encompass a minor history of computer science in the early and middle 1960s. If you read through the archives of PL/I, you find innumerable debates among numerical analysts about arithmetic (some of those debates were continued at 8 o'clock this morning right here, in fact), among language experts about syntax and name-scope and block structure, among systems programmers about multitasking, exception handling, I/O, and other things. Because of the very objective of PL/I (primarily to be able to program an entire application in it), there is nothing that has been deliberately omitted from its subject matter scope. And for that reason, it provides a very interesting study in the beliefs and some of the mistaken dogmas of that period.

I've been asked to start with a brief and—this morning, I've been asked to make it very brief—overview of some of the essential technical characteristics of PL/I.

PL/I deals with programs [Frame 3]. Programs are collections of external procedures, and an external procedure is composed of internal procedures and blocks and statements, and internal procedures and blocks are of course also composed of internal procedures, blocks, and statements, quite conventionally. The structure resembles ALGOL and in some respects resembles FORTRAN, and resembles most conventional languages.

Statements in PL/I are terminated by semicolons, not separated by semicolons as they are in ALGOL, and that's another separate discussion as many of you know. Variables may be declared in DECLARE statements. PL/I supports a staggeringly wide variety of data types [Frame 4]. Numeric variables can be binary or decimal, fixed or floating point, real or complex, with specifiable precision. Character and bit strings can be of fixed or varying lengths. Pointer variables whose values are instances of variables, file variables,

STRUCTURE

— PROGRAM IS A COLLECTION OF PROCEDURES
    (INTERNAL OR EXTERNAL)

— PROCEDURES MAY BE BLOCK-STRUCTURED
    BEGIN...END
    DO......END

— STATEMENTS TERMINATED BY SEMI-COLONS
    P: PROCEDURE (A);
        DECLARE A CHAR (*),
                B FIXED BINARY (31,0),
                C ENTRY;
        B = A+2;
        CALL C;
        END;

Frame 3. Brief overview of PL/I.

entry variables, label variables, etc. And what is most important—and characterizes PL/I —is that any mixture, almost, of variable types is allowable in expressions, with implied conversion. If you look at PL/I documentation, you will find that much of the complexity and the size is due to the necessity of defining the result of all such operations on variables of mixed type.

Another characteristic which accounts for the size and complexity of the definition is that variables need not be explicitly declared at all. This use results in implicit typing; that is, typing by the contextual appearance of a variable in a program. And even when a variable is declared, all of its attributes do not have to be declared. And the missing attributes are deduced from those present.

For instance, [in ANS PL/I] if you declare X to be binary and nothing else, then it is given the default attributes "fixed" and "real." Again, there are many pages in the documentation of PL/I which define for every subset of explicit declarations what the defaults are. Among the objectives of PL/I was the desire to allow specific application subsetting; that is, to define these defaults in such a way that if you don't know what is being defaulted

DATA TYPES

— WIDE VARIETY
    NUMERIC
    CHARACTER/BIT STRINGS
    POINTER
    FILE
    ENTRY/LABEL

—MIXED TYPE EXPRESSIONS

—IMPLICIT AND DEFAULT DECLARATIONS

—STORAGE CLASSES
    STATIC
    AUTOMATIC
    BASED
    CONTROLLED

Frame 4

George Radin

because it is not in your subset, you get what you expect. Now, that didn't always happen, but that was the goal.

PL/I also supports a large variety of storage classes. There is static, which corresponds roughly to ALGOL **own** or to FORTRAN COMMON. There is automatic, which is simply temporary stack data available during a single activation of a procedure. There are based variables which are simply templates superimposed on other variables or on storage to provide an interpretation of the bits. And there's a controlled storage class which allows the explicit allocation and freeing of generations of a variable.

And then there are many other features [Frame 5] which I will not dwell on. There are extensive I/O facilities, many of which were borrowed from FORTRAN and from COBOL. There is a notion in PL/I of tasking—that is, of processes which can execute asynchronously and which can synchronize on events. There are variables whose values are events. There are compile-time facilities—that is, a notion of a preprocess which produces as its output a PL/I procedure and takes as its input, in its most general sense, simply a character string. And there is the ability to specify actions which are to be taken when certain conditions occur, such as end of file or overflow.

So much for an overview of some of the essential characteristics of PL/I which give it much of its flavor.

Now, in the late 1950s and early 1960s, computer installations, applications, and people —at least in the IBM view of the world, and in the view of IBM customers, which is really all I can speak of with any real understanding or knowledge—the world was divided very much like Gaul was in Caesar's time; namely, into three distinct parts—much more so than today—into scientific, commercial, and special purpose application lines.

For instance, there were computers for scientific applications such as the IBM 7090 and the 1620 [Frame 6]. There were scientific operating systems for these computers. There was FORTRAN which was a scientific language. And there was even SHARE which was a user's group primarily devoted to installations whose prime applications were, in fact, scientific.

Similarly, there were computers for commercial applications such as the 7080 and the 1401. There were systems facilities for these. There was, of course, a commercial language: COBOL. And there was a user's group for installations whose prime applications were commercial, that is, GUIDE.

And finally there was a bagful of computers for special applications such as the IBM 7750 and Harvest, and there were special languages such as JOVIAL.

And moreover, it was a truism in the field that these special people, special groups, required special kinds of systems characteristics. Scientific users, we all knew, needed floating-point arithmetic and arrays and subroutines, fast computation and fast compilation, and batch job scheduling. We all knew that commercial users need decimal arithmetic and string handling, fast and asynchronous I/O, compilation which produced efficient object

OTHER FEATURES

— EXTENSIVE I/O

— MULTITASK/EVENTS

— COMPILE-TIME FACILITIES

— ON-CONDITIONS

Frame 5

IN EARLY SIXTIES,

SCIENTIFIC	COMMERCIAL	SPECIAL-PURPOSE
7090	7080	7750
FORTRAN	COBOL	JOVIAL
SHARE	GUIDE	

THIS SEPARATION WAS NO LONGER WORKING.

Frame 6

code regardless of how long the compiler took, and excellent sort programs. And then we knew of special purpose users who needed capabilities like variable length bit string arithmetic such as you saw yesterday in JOVIAL, macro libraries (such as COMPOOL in JOVIAL), pattern matching operations, list handlers, and very fast response for real time.

The problem was that by the early 1960s this elegant separation of applications was coming apart and projections were that matters were going to get worse. Applications and users refused to stay properly compartmentalized. The stereotype of a scientific programmer who was willing to wait for two hours for a blinking computer finally to display the answer on its console lights was giving way to the professional who wanted a camera-ready report in a beautifully readable format. Scientific users wanted report generation facilities. The files that scientists were processing were as voluminous as those in many commercial installations. And so they, too, wanted sorts and I/O management routines. Commercial users began doing linear regressions and factor analyses and all sorts of statistics on market data. And so they, too, wanted floating-point arithmetic and array, handling facilities.

And installation managers, by and large, objected to buying two sets of hardware, maintaining two operating systems, and educating two sets of application programmers who could not talk to each other and could not share programs.

And so, as this situation became increasingly obvious, IBM reached the conclusion, as you all know, that it could serve its customers', and therefore its own, best interests by developing a single product line and a single family of operating systems which satisfied the requirements, they hoped, of all three of these user groups. And that's how System/360 and OS/360 development was begun.

It was this same reason, this desire to unify what was essentially a very strictly compartmentalized environment which motivated IBM and SHARE, the scientific users group of IBM customers, to form the Advanced Language Development Project of the SHARE FORTRAN Project in October of 1963 [Frame 7]. And this group was charged with specifying a programming language that would meet the needs of all three of these user types as well as those of systems programmers.

Now the point that I intend to make increasingly in this talk is that it's the last objective, namely, to satisfy the needs of systems programmers, which has evolved into being the most important objective, a fact I believe that was dimly conceived at the time that the committee was first formed, and in fact, in its first few years.

And so a meeting was held in October of 1963 at the Motel-on-the-Mountain in Suffern, New York, attended by IBM and by SHARE management. At this meeting, the SHARE committee members were already named and present. They were Hans Berg, from Lockheed, Burbank, Jim Cox, who was then with Union Carbide, and Bruce Rosenblatt, of Standard Oil of California, who was the chairman of the committee.

The IBM committee members were C. W. Medlock and Bernice Weitzenhoffer, both of

George Radin

Advanced Language Development Committee
of the SHARE FORTRAN Project
Formed October, 1963

Members:
Hans Berg
Jim Cox
Bruce Rosenblatt (Chairman)

C. W. Medlock
Bernice Weitzenhoffer
George Radin
Tom Martin
Paul Rogoway
Larry Brown
Ray Larner

Doug McIlroy
Bob Sheppard

Frame 7

whom had had extensive experience in compiler development, and myself, who was fresh into IBM, less than a year out of some private consulting and university computing primarily, and who had begun an unsuccessfully completed dissertation on programming language theory.

Tom Martin of Westinghouse, who was manager of the Systems Division of SHARE, and Paul Rogoway, of Hughes Dynamics, who was chairman of the SHARE FORTRAN Project within this Systems Division, were not official members of the committee, but attended almost all the meetings and participated in the decision making process. And similarly, Larry Brown and Ray Larner, who were FORTRAN compiler people from IBM, also were virtually full-time members of the committee.

The committee met generally every other week for about three or four days on weekends, and the meetings were all held in hotel suites, mostly in New York City, sometimes in California, in Los Angeles. At that time there was a great deal of controversy—unlike later when it became noncontroversial entirely—particularly among FORTRAN people, about the existence of such a language development effort. But I would argue that many times the most vociferous opponents of the committee were the wives and husbands of the committee members, since the activity dominated virtually all the weekend time through that autumn and winter.

The non-IBM committee members signed a nondisclosure agreement with IBM, and therefore we were able to peruse IBM's plans with respect to the new product line and its operating system. And so we attempted to be briefed upon the architecture of that system and the characteristics of the operating system, which was later called OS/360, and its language processors. There was remarkably little learned which was reflected in the language, I would say, because subsequent to that, OS/360 underwent major revisions. And so that activity, while it was motivated to prevent inclusion into the language of any characteristics which would be impossible or extremely difficult to implement well on that system, resulted in very little specific language in PL/I.

The procedures at the meetings were very informal. We did not take minutes officially. When an area was to be defined, we broke up into subgroups and each subgroup developed a specific concrete proposal for that aspect of the language. These were then presented to the committee during the intervening week or two weeks, preferably by special-delivery letters, and then at the next meeting we discussed the proposals and arrived at all decisions, I believe, by consensus.

The rather predominant attendance at this committee of people whose backgrounds were primarily devoted to optimizing compilers lends a great deal of flavor to the language. There was always the motivation of "Can we produce good code?" John Backus talks about the importance of producing good code from FORTRAN. But even by the time of PL/I design, the importance of producing good code was absolutely not taking second place to any other characteristic of the language.

Now, the major constraint that confronted the committee throughout its development process was a series of very early (missed, but at the time seemingly rigid) deadlines. We were told, for instance, that in order to be included in the first release of IBM's new product line, we would have to complete and freeze the language specifications by December of 1963. Now, since we started in October of 1963 and worked every other weekend, that didn't give us very much time. In December we were told that in fact we had another month, and so we were given until January of 1964, and then finally we were allowed to slip until late February. It's a characteristic of that design process, not only that the total elapsed time for definition was short, but that, in fact, it itself was broken up into a series of steps at each of which we felt, or were told, that we needed to produce the entire language specification. And so there was a sense of crisis to the activity all through its development. That was not all bad; but many of its effects were unfortunate, I think.

Now, the background, as you can see, was that almost all the group was strongly FORTRAN-oriented. The committee reported to the SHARE FORTRAN Project and so, starting the language development with FORTRAN as a base seemed at first to be an obvious choice. And in fact, for the first several meetings the language was referred to as FORTRAN VI. But after several weeks of investigation, the committee unanimously agreed to abandon the direction of compatible extensions to FORTRAN IV and to start the language definition from scratch.

In the paper I quote some independent evaluations and reasons at some length for going in that direction, but by and large the arguments that I recall, which made us decide to go incompatible [Frame 8], were:

First, we felt that the syntax of FORTRAN was not free-form enough to allow it to be presented on display terminals. In particular, we did not want to live with statement labels being recognized by column positions on cards or on card image files.

Secondly, declarations in FORTRAN, as you know, are organized by type rather than by identifier. For instance, you can declare all 10 by 10 arrays together, and all floating-point variables together; and this results, generally, in the attributes declared for a single variable being scattered throughout statements in the program. We wanted, however, to be able to isolate the attributes of a single variable, so that we could keep that in a library,

NOT COMPATIBLE WITH FORTRAN:

WANTED: — FREE-FORM SYNTAX
         — DECLARATIONS GROUPED BY IDENTIFIER
         — ARRAYS STORED BY ROW
         — CONSTRAINTS ON OVERLAYING
         — MANY NEW FACILITIES
         — EQUAL FOCUS ON COMMERCIAL PROGRAMMING

Frame 8

or keep it along with the data itself; and therefore we preferred the COBOL-like sorting in which the major sort was the identifier and the minor sort was the attribute, which was incompatible with FORTRAN.

Thirdly, the well-known decision of FORTRAN to store arrays by column rather than by row is awkward even for scientific programmers and is quite unnatural to commercial application programmers who think in terms of tables rather than matrices. Now, it's true that it's mostly possible to keep this mapping unknown to the programmer. But there are uses of overlays and of I/O which expose the mapping. In fact, FORTRAN's capability that it gives to programmers to take advantage of data mapping by unconstrained overlaying in COMMON was a practice that we did not want to perpetuate.

Now, these are specific arguments. In addition, there were two really more basic points that were continually made in the debates.

First, we felt that after we put in all the things that we really thought we needed in the language—most importantly ALGOL block structure, and the extensions that we needed to support commercial applications—the result would be a language which was already so different from FORTRAN that the benefits to anybody of it being a formally compatible extension would be minimal.

And secondly, we felt that most of the programmers who would be programming in this language would come not from the scientific community, but from commercial applications and special-purpose applications, and compatibility with FORTRAN for them would be no advantage at all; and therefore it was poor justification to make any compromises based upon catering to the learning requirements of scientific programmers who might, in fact, be the group most capable of learning a new language.

Now, in retrospect—and I've been thinking about this for a while, since I started writing this paper—I think the decision was correct, although it had some disadvantages. Its major drawback was that if we had gone with compatible extensions to FORTRAN, we could have gone in an orderly way from a well-defined language to an enhanced well-defined language. We could have spent our time designing the new features instead of redesigning existing features. By starting over, we were not required to live with many technical compromises, but the task was made much more difficult.

Once the decision was made to become incompatible with FORTRAN, we needed a name other than FORTRAN VI. Now, a language designed for such a wide application set needed a general purpose name, and APL was already taken. We considered MPPL for Multi-Purpose Programming Language. And then we decided on NPL, for New Programming Language. At the time, within IBM, the 360 Series was called the New Product Line [Frame 9]. And so we felt that, at least within IBM, this choice would tie the language to the new product line, and in fact this name, NPL, remained the name for the language until in 1965, its prior use by the National Physical Laboratory in England required a change. At that time we changed to PL/I, again because the "slash" would somehow link the language, within IBM at least, to System/360 and OS/360.

The first document which described the language was called the "Report of the SHARE Advanced Language Development Committee," and was presented to a SHARE meeting in March of 1964 at the Jack Tar Hotel in San Francisco. That was a traumatic week. There were, I believe, more strong opinions voiced on either side during that week than at any meeting that I have attended, certainly before, and I think since, on any subject.

The language was widely praised by many people for its breadth, its innovations, and its attention to programmers of varying sophistication. It was widely criticized for its form-

ORIGINAL NAME: NPL
(CHANGED TO PL/I IN 1965)

NPL DOCUMENTS:

— REPORT OF THE SHARE ADVANCED LANGUAGE DEVELOPMENT
   COMMITTEE, MARCH 1, 1964
— SPECIFICATIONS FOR THE NEW PROGRAMMING LANGUAGE,
   APRIL, 1964
— REPORT II OF THE SHARE ADVANCED LANGUAGE DEVELOPMENT
   COMMITTEE, JUNE 25, 1964
— NPL TECHNICAL REPORT, IBM WORLD TRADE LABORATORIES,
   (GREAT BRITAIN) LTD., DECEMBER, 1964

Frame 9

lessness, its complexity, and its redundancy. One SHARE member later compared it to a 100-blade Swiss knife. Another wondered why the kitchen sink had been omitted. At the end of the meeting, however, the language was endorsed by the SHARE body and IBM decided to develop several large processors for System/360. And shortly after this meeting, [in April,] a more complete document entitled "Specifications for the New Programming Language" was distributed.

In June of 1964 the committee produced a second version which was called Report II of the SHARE Advanced Language Development Committee. There is an interesting quote in the back of that document which is signed by both Carl Reynolds, who was the Manager of Programming Systems in the Data Systems Division of IBM, and Tom Martin, who was the manager of the SHARE Systems Division. I think it gives us a reasonable feeling for what the status, as perceived by both SHARE and IBM, of the language was at that time. I quote:

> The attached report represents the efforts of the joint IBM/SHARE committee to identify the functions and features needed in an extended language and to propose a particular embodiment thereof. Because of its belief that the committee's results are a significant step forward, it is the intention of the IBM Corporation to use this report as the basis of specification for the New Programming Language.

In November of 1964 the IBM Laboratory in Hursley, England, produced a document which was much more detailed than the reports of the Advanced Language Development Committee. It ran to about 200 pages, and it represented the definition of the language from which the implementers would develop their compilers. Then in December of 1964 this document was published for external distribution as the NPL Technical Report by IBM World Trade.

When you compare the changes that PL/I has undergone in its first years of development with the changes that FORTRAN underwent and ALGOL did, it's remarkable how different these early documents were to, for instance, the PL/I language definition described in GC-33-0009, which is the language implemented by the IBM Checkout and Optimizing compilers for PL/I. Many significant language changes happened in those years, and, I might say, mostly developed by and controlled by IBM Hursley, in England.

Further language evolution has resulted in a 1976 PL/I ANSI Standard and an ECMA Standard.

I'd like to spend a little time describing the period from April to November of 1964; that is, from the time the first SHARE document was produced and IBM UK at Hursley was

George Radin

identified as the focus of PL/I compiler development, to the time that the second document, namely, the one produced by Hursley, was published. It was a period which marked the most fervent language development activity and debate, within IBM, within SHARE, and within GUIDE at that time, that I have ever recalled. Bernie [Galler] was talking about a period of constant highs.† If there was ever a period of constant highs in the PL/I development process, it was between April and November of 1964. In fact, as soon as the March document was available, IBM formed a Programming Language Evaluation Department in the Time/Life Building in New York under Paul Comba [Frame 10]. And the first thing that that group did was to select 22 representative programs from various application areas which had already been written in existing languages: six from FORTRAN, five from COBOL, five from ALGOL, and six from JOVIAL. They reprogrammed all 22 in NPL, and then they compared this new language to the originals with respect to such criteria as ease of programming, size of programs, readability, etc. In July of 1964 they produced a 185-page report which described their conclusions, which is called "A Comparative Evaluation of the New Programming Language."

Now, all evaluations of languages are subjective and suspect. And all can be debated. I'm not quoting from this one to give you a definitive comparison of the languages, but to give you a feeling of how the language was viewed with respect to these others at that time within that community. I will just quote briefly from representative conclusions with respect to various languages.

For instance, when they compared NPL with COBOL for commercial programming, they found that NPL "had most of the facilities of COBOL and some very useful additional ones." "NPL," they wrote, "is usually more flexible, simpler, and less verbose." Of the COBOL facilities that are lacking in NPL, many are minor and specialized; only a few are substantial. NPL "should not be represented as a language that can fully replace COBOL, but it is likely that a large number of commercial shops will find it superior and eventually will want to convert to it." And in fact, a large number of commercial shops have, although by no means all.

Comparing NPL with ALGOL, they wrote, "NPL has gone a long way toward incorporating many ALGOL concepts and had a much richer repertoire of extended arithmetic operations than ALGOL does. The structure of NPL statements and programs is not as simple as that of ALGOL; in part this could be remedied by redefining NPL on 60 characters"—which, as you know, was later done. "We believe that a large number of ALGOL users whose interests extend beyond the formulation of algorithms for numerical analysis will find that the additional facilities of NPL more than compensate for its comparative lack of elegance. As a publication language, NPL cannot compete with ALGOL unless a publication version of NPL is developed."

†[At the conference banquet.]

Finally, in comparing NPL with JOVIAL, they wrote, "NPL shows that it has all of the essential capabilities of JOVIAL with the exception of status variables and arrays of string variables, and has less convenient switching capabilities. NPL should prove strongly competitive with regard to JOVIAL."

And so the evaluation and, in fact, the spirit, at least within the SHARE and IBM community that I was acquainted with, was quite bullish at that time about the language.

As soon as the language and the compiler responsibility was moved to Hursley, intensive work began in that laboratory to solidify the language and to build compilers. And as compilers were being specified, questions began to be raised about whether it was possible indeed to build an efficient compiler for such a large and complex language.

In October of 1964 a committee was formed. You may notice that the IBM and SHARE approach to addressing problems is that committees are formed. That is one way to attack problems and it has its well-known disadvantages. But it has some advantages as well. And so a committee was formed to investigate the compiler activity, to analyze the language, and generally to predict the characteristics of NPL compilers. In November the committee reported, and I'll quote briefly from a summary of its conclusions:

> A brief summary statement is that there is no single feature in the language . . . that will cause major and unavoidable inefficiencies in object code. The sum total of all features [, however,] has a strong effect on compile speed. Object code inefficiencies, where found, can be mitigated by the suitable restriction of . . . features in the language or by considerable effort at compile time.

I quote that because it's an important characteristic of PL/I strategy, one which sometimes worked but did not always work. Namely, the idea was: if you can put something in, and it doesn't hurt you either in compile time or in object code efficiency, or in learning, then that's a great thing to do: some people benefit, and nobody gets hurt. Where that can work, the language becomes quite useful. But often that doesn't work, because, in fact, even though theoretically one can optimize, one can discover at compile time that certain facilities are not being used, or are being used in a constrained way, and so can optimize the special case. Schedules and resource constraints of the compiler development often don't let you take advantage of that theoretical possibility. And so the result is that while the language permits such optimization in the face of complexity, the compilers do not provide it.

I think that a good summary of the reaction of the ALGOL community to NPL can be found in a report which describes a meeting that took place in Hursley on June 24, 1964, where NPL was described to what, in the report, are called "European University Computer Leaders" [Frame 11]. Let me quote from that report, which describes this meeting and what everyone said and the results.

— IBM NPL COMPILER EVALUATION
— ALGOL LEADERS MEETING
— FORMAL DEFINITION EFFORTS
    "ABSTRACT SYNTAX AND INTERPRETATION OF PL/I"
    (ULD VERSION III) APRIL 1969
— EPL ACTIVITY
    BOB MORRIS
    DOUG MCILROY

Frame 11

In general the audience was overwhelmed by the language—some members by its power, most by its apparent largeness. The experience reemphasized the crying need for a tutorial presentation of a subset of the language geared to the computing interests and needs of the scientific, or FOR-TRAN–ALGOL audience.

(Eventually Paul Rogoway did produce such a Scientific Programmers' Guide for PL/I. But that was always an intent in the language definition. There was going to be a book which was PL/I for Scientific Programmers and it wouldn't have PICTURES. And there was going to be a book for Commercial Programmers and it wouldn't have array expressions or whatever. So it was to be an underlying unified base from which various people would see the subset and the flavor that in fact they wanted.) [Continuing from the European University Computer Leaders report . . .] "there was nearly unanimous feeling that the language would appear to be a fine one, but more definite judgement was reserved pending further study of the June 15 document."

"Most of the attendees," the report goes on, "are ALGOL users and generally agreed that the language is a superset of ALGOL." I find that a surprising quote.

"The most significant observations came from three individuals representing interestingly enough three distinct interest groups. A FORTRAN user involved in application programming asked for certain additional function in the language such as an ON clause for overflow of storage . . ." Notice, by the way, this typical dialogue: "What about this language?" "Well, it's awfully big and awfully complex." "Okay. What shall we do about it?" "Well, you should add the following. . . ." It really did happen all the time.

The director of a university computing center expressed concern about compilation speed and subsetting and/or the teachability of the language; and an ALGOL father requested an escape character and a single form of the FOR statement.

There was general agreement, that the NPL task force and the ALGOL committee are attacking the same problem from two opposite directions; SHARE from a pragmatic direction, the ALGOL persons from a theoretical one. It was further agreed that cooperation between the two groups is desirable, and that much could be gained by attempting to describe equivalent features in an identical manner.

(I don't believe that that recommendation was pursued.)

In the fall of 1964 a Language Control Board was established first in the New York Programming Center, and then in 1966 was moved to Hursley. This Language Control Board was a very important aspect of PL/I development. If you had a question concerning what you thought was ambiguous in the language specification, you brought it up and it was officially logged by the Control Board, and at the meeting an official interpretation was defined. The language began to be defined as questions were raised, and as points were brought out. If you had a proposal for a language change or a language enhancement, of course that also came into the report. Or, if you even had a proposal for rewording something to make it clearer. There were literally hundreds of such language points, and a large on-going activity to clarify the language and to really make it as well-defined and unambiguous as possible.

But given this rather informal description, even augmented to 200 pages by the Hursley group, it became clear that none of these documents was really adequate as a base from which to work. And so Ray Larner and John Nicholls [of the Hursley Lab] at that time took the first steps towards developing a formal semantic definition of PL/I, which was

PL/I Documents

- OS PL/I CHECKOUT AND OPTIMIZING COMPILERS: LANGUAGE
  REFERENCE MANUAL, GC33-0009-4, IBM CORPORATION,
  OCTOBER, 1976
- AMERICAN NATIONAL STANDARDS INSTITUTE, "AMERICAN
  NATIONAL STANDARD PROGRAMMING LANGUAGE PL/I,"
  NEW YORK, N.Y. ANSI X3.53, 1976

Frame 12

called the Universal Language Definition II.† And this was followed by a formal semantic definition developed in the Vienna Laboratory which was called Abstract Syntax and Interpretation of PL/I, ULD Version III, and produced in April of 1969.

Later, this was superseded by a formal definition which comprises the ECMA/ANSI language specification. And thus, interestingly, while PL/I began as a 30- or 40-page informal document, produced in some haste by the SHARE/IBM committee, containing many ambiguities, many alarming omissions of things which in retrospect should have been clearly defined—and I can describe some examples of those if you like—it evolved finally into what I assert is probably the most well-defined programming language in use today because of all this activity in formal semantic definition [Frame 12].

Since 1964 many languages have been developed, both inside and outside IBM as variants of PL/I. One of the most important of these was EPL [Early (implementation of) PL/I], which is a language developed in early 1965 by Bob Morris and Doug McIlroy of Bell Labs for use by the MULTICS Project. MULTICS, which was a joint Bell Labs, G.E., MIT systems project, was looking for a suitable systems programming language at the time that NPL was being defined. NPL, for some reasons which are defined in the paper, seemed to have all the necessary features of a systems programming language, and it was already designed. And therefore EPL was developed as a subset of NPL. And in about a year, the EPL compiler was operational. As many of you know, almost all of MULTICS was written in this language and, according to the implementers, accounts for much of the productivity and maintainability of that system.

Today, among IBM program products, there are more PL/I compiler licenses sold to IBM customers than there are FORTRAN licenses. There are not as many as there are COBOL licenses sold to commercial customers, but there are many.

PL/I and variants which are aimed primarily at systems programming, have been successfully used to program several large operating systems, and several compilers. There have been pedagogical subsets defined and used in introductory programming books. Therefore I would argue that, to a large degree, the goals of the original designers have been realized. It is being widely used for scientific, commercial, and systems programming.

Now, I thought it would be interesting to spend a little bit of time reviewing the explicit design criteria that the originators said they had when developing the language [Frame 13]. And, what is even more interesting, to understand what they did not say their design criteria were. There are six such objectives which were developed by the committee and

---

† I believe the Hursley definition was just called the Universal Language Definition. ULD II was the first version from the Vienna Lab and ULD III was the second Vienna version. Ed.

George Radin

DESIGN CRITERIA
- FREEDOM OF EXPRESSION
- FULL ACCESS TO MACHINE AND OPERATING SYSTEM
  FACILITIES
- MODULARITY
- RELATIVE MACHINE INDEPENDENCE
- CATER TO THE NOVICE
- NPL IS A PROGRAMMING, NOT AN ALGORITHMIC LANGUAGE

Frame 13

were reported in an ACM paper by Paul Rogoway and myself, in 1965 [Ref. 13 in Paper]. Let me talk to them.

The first is summarized—these are mostly quotes, but I'll paraphrase—as freedom of expression. And by that we meant that if a particular combination of symbols has a reasonably sensible meaning, then we will make that meaning official. We said invalidity is the last resort. We did not want a language for which there were many compilers and for which the compilers themselves chose to define permissive diagnostics; that is, to be more intelligent than the language allowed, but in different incompatible ways. And therefore, if there was any sensible interpretation of a combination of programming characteristics, then we said, "that's the official one," rather than trying to allow the many unofficial ones de facto to spring up.

The second objective is full access to machine and operating system facilities. That means that it was an important objective that you could write an application totally in PL/I—or NPL, at the time—without resorting to assembly language coding. And so we never omitted a function from the language because it really belonged to assembly language, or it really was an operating system facility, or it really belonged on a job control card. There was nothing that we felt the programmer wanted to say to the system which we excluded from the language.

The third [objective], which I discussed before, is modularity. Namely, this paper went on to say, "NPL has been designed so that many of its features can be ignored by the programmer without fear of penalty, in either compile time or object time efficiency." I went into that earlier.

A fourth objective is relative machine independence, which meant that although we were careful not to introduce into the language characteristics which would preclude efficient implementation on the System/360, in fact we attempted to parameterize precision and lengths in such a way that the language itself would be applicable to many different machines and, in fact, it was.

Now, I won't go through the others, but I will say that this is an unusual set of objectives when you look at it after 15 years, not so much for what it includes, which is generally reasonable and laudable, but for what it omits. Nowhere do we find goals like having a solid theoretical basis, being extensible from some simple base, being amenable to interactive use, producing well-structured programs, or ability to prove correctness, or any of the criteria that one would expect to find in languages being designed today. In fact, it harkens much more closely back to FORTRAN. Code efficiency was of overriding importance; convenience was the key word, rather than simplicity. This was a language which was defined more in the spirit of English than of mathematics. There were many irregular verbs and many idioms, and we measured success by the criterion of "If you have some-

Summary

- NPL was defined too quickly
- Correctly chose what to take from FORTRAN, COBOL, ALGOL
  - Combined these into a unified language
  - Defined at a single level

It is feasible to write entire applications in PL/I

It has become a widely used systems programming language

Frame 14

thing to say, can you say it naturally and easily in the primitives of the language?'' rather than ''Can you say it minimally in the few primitives of the language?''

Finally, let me summarize what I think are the overriding characteristics of PL/I [Frame 14]. In some sense, NPL was a language defined too quickly. Its virtues resulted primarily from the combined intuitions and programming experience of its definers. When they convened, they knew what they wanted in the language. Its faults were largely ambiguity and incompleteness.

Now, in retrospect, I believe that the definers of the language correctly assessed and took over the unique strengths of the languages from which they drew inspiration. They took from FORTRAN the notions of separately compiled subroutines, sharing common data, and the DO loop. From COBOL they introduced data structures, I/O, and report generating facilities. From ALGOL they took block structure, and we thought we took recursion, until a couple of days ago.

A major contribution of NPL was not only its original facilities but the combining of these borrowed characteristics into what I would assert is a consistent single language.

The strongest characteristic of PL/I is its breadth and detail. It really is feasible to write entire application programs and in fact to write entire operating systems, in PL/I virtually without resorting to assembly language at all.

Now, what about the future? Well, let me make a guess. I think that PL/I, like ALGOL and FORTRAN and COBOL, was designed for a kind of programmer who, while perhaps not a vanishing breed, is possibly a nongrowing breed, and that in fact, in the 1980s we will see more programmers who wish to program in languages which are higher level than those four, languages which are more specialized toward their idioms and their specific applications, and fewer languages which are just at that middle level, like the ones that I specified. And therefore what will be really required will be tools, among which are languages, for developing the processors, run-time libraries, and operating systems for these myriad new languages. Rather than replacing FORTRAN or COBOL, which is an objective that I think (while certainly having failed) is even becoming of little interest, replacing assembly language as a facility for writing such systems programs may in fact be an important role that PL/I will play in the future.

Thank you.

TRANSCRIPT OF DISCUSSANT'S REMARKS

Robert Rosin: I said, in introducing George, that there were in fact two people for whom it's a distinct privilege and pleasure to be the session chairman. Bruce Rosenblatt received his Bachelor's Degree at the University of California, Berkeley, in Mathematical

Bruce Rosenblatt

Statistics in 1951, and thereafter joined the Standard Oil Corporation. In 1963, at the time of the formation of the IBM/SHARE 3 by 3 Committee, he was Manager of the Computer Systems group in Standard Oil, and in fact was also past-Chairman of the FORTRAN committee of SHARE. Today he's still with the Standard Oil Corporation, Consultant in Computer Systems, focusing primarily on hardware and software systems, their acquisition and utilization.

BRUCE ROSENBLATT: I can't help telling you a story today that Carl [C. J.] Reynolds [then at IBM] told at a meeting I recently attended—and it best expresses my feeling about the whole conference that we've had here. Carl's story went something like this:

There was a young man who lived in the Midwest in a very small town, and very early in his life he encountered a flood, and his activity during the next few years was to repeat his feelings about the flood and what had gone on during this time. He continued to do this and tell this story over and over again, until everybody in town essentially avoided him, and he wasn't able to find anyone who would listen to his story anymore. Finally, the man died and went to heaven. When he got to St. Peter, St. Peter said, "You have one wish that we will grant you." He said, "I'd like to be able to tell my story just one more time. I want to talk about the Great Flood and have an audience that would appreciate my story." St. Peter said, "Fine. We'll certainly grant that wish. If you report back here at 8:30 tomorrow—you can have the palatial auditorium, and we'll have it filled with people." So he dutifully reported back at 8:30 the next morning, and St. Peter said, "The audience is here. It's yours for as long as you want them. Just remember one thing. Noah's in the audience!"

That's sort of how I feel today with all of the people who have been on the podium before me.

George has described the environment that existed in the 1963–1964 time frame pretty well. I'd like to add just a couple of comments. By this time, the users—at least the users in the industrial community where I was working and therefor most familiar with—had come to rely almost exclusively on the vendors for supplying basic software needs. The compilers and the operating systems which we used on our computers, we looked to the vendors to supply. That isn't to say that we didn't do a lot of modification, but basically we looked to the vendors to supply these.

The SHARE FORTRAN committee—and I guess all SHARE FORTRAN committees since then—had developed a long list of enhancements which we felt should be placed in the language to avoid having to resort to assembly language code for those activities which we wanted to carry on which couldn't be done in FORTRAN, and, secondarily, to try and encompass the great and burgeoning amount of data processing—commercial data processing [as opposed to scientific processing] which we saw in our various installations.

We, as I guess again all SHARE FORTRAN committees have felt since then, felt we were having very little effect on IBM in either getting them to listen or adopt any of these enhancements that we wanted to see put in the system. And so we were extremely pleased when IBM came to SHARE and suggested the formation of the 3 × 3 committee of three IBMers, and three SHARE people.

Our first activity when the committee was formed was, as George indicated, to survey the current state of the art, because most of us who at least came from the commercial side of the house didn't have a background in building and designing languages. And I guess one of the things that was a major disappointment, concern, and surprise to me was that

IBM either wasn't willing or didn't have an awful lot of research in language activities which they would share with us. And we found further that the FORTRAN language which, granted, was in very very preliminary design phases so far as being designed for the 360, had surprisingly few enhancements planned. It's our belief that the industrial community certainly broadened and added to the functions which were in 360 FORTRAN or in the PL/I language which we finally defined as part of our activities.

I guess the point that I'm most interested in making here is that the industry has done nothing but grow since that time, and more and more we look to the vendors as the suppliers of the programming languages or the programming systems which we use today. This means that in many cases we find people working for the vendors who have had no experience in user shops. And we think it most necessary that they do work and have user participation in the development of their systems to really have successful systems.

George didn't mention in his talk this morning, but he does in his paper, the fact that we didn't have as one of our objectives the development of an interactive programming language. In actual fact, it wasn't a written objective, but we certainly spent an awful lot of time during the course of our deliberations trying to figure out how to make an interactive language. As a matter of fact, one of the points George made was that we didn't want to have a position-sensitive language was certainly the result of our thoughts of trying to get a language which would be interactive. Jim Cox, as a matter of fact, remembers that the reason we introduced the semicolon and the SET statement which was our version of the assignment statement originally, was to make the language more easily usable on an interactive basis.

My own thoughts on this hark back to a point George made about the OS/360 operating system. Here again, we were very unsuccessful in making contact with the group within IBM who were developing the operating system. The reason we felt this was important was that at the time there was a group of us within the PL/I committee who very strongly felt that we should try to develop a language which incorporated not only the normal [programming] specification that one sees in a language, but also the job control information so that one wouldn't have to hop back and forth between language and an operating system. In order to do this we felt it very important that we have some idea of what might be incorporated in the operating system. Due to our failure to make the contact with the operating system people, probably due to our naïveté, and certainly due to the time constraint, we finally had to abandon this activity.

One of the points—certainly one of the ambitions of the PL/I design, as George has mentioned and certainly as is pretty obvious to everybody—is that we would produce a language which would encompass both the business and the scientific user community as it was at that time. It was particularly important to note that while there was a COBOL, most of the commercial programming (at least in most of the industrial shops I was aware of) was still being done in assembly language; so there was a very large uncommitted group which, if we were able to design the system right, we felt we could get to use PL/I, and consequently achieve a single programming language for all of our shops.

I think none of us realized, or even contemplated the possibility, that a compiler wouldn't be available at the time of the first shipment of OS/360, and consequently none of us really thought out what this meant. I know in our own shop it meant that if we were to do on the 360 what we had intended to do, we either had to program in assembly language, or adopt COBOL. And so very reluctantly, we adopted the COBOL language. As a result of this a lot of programmers and programming shops with no previous experience with higher-level languages learned how to program in COBOL. This introduced an awful lot of COBOL programs, which otherwise wouldn't have existed.

So, the result of this, later, as time went on was to create a further impedance to the problem of translation or movement of this group of people and the programs they had built into a new language.

The second thing that I think we failed to understand was the problem of doing the conversion from FORTRAN and what later proved to be this COBOL community that had developed. I think possibly we were all somewhat naive about the conversion as a result of our experience in going from FORTRAN II to FORTRAN IV which I think most of us on the committee had participated in. This conversion had gone very well, partially because we had written conversion aids. But I think we all failed to understand the large number of people and the large number of programs that these people had written, that had been put together since the time the FORTRAN II to FORTRAN IV conversion was made. And so I think that one of the things that we did—in our naïveté at the time—was to underestimate the conversion problems and this certainly led to, I think, some major reasons that maybe some people have not moved to the PL/I language.

The other problem that I think we should have addressed, and George talked about it several times during the course of his statement, was subsetting the PL/I language. It was, as we indicated, our intent to develop subsets for the scientific, commercial, and other special-interest groups. We full well expected to do this activity as part of our on-going work. However, as all of you are probably aware, very little, if any, has ever really been done in this area. As a result, those people who want to learn, or who learn PL/I must learn the language in its entirety, which, as you're all aware, is a rather large chore. In particular, I think that we would have served ourselves and the computer industry by having built those subsets; in particular I think it would have enabled PL/I to have been taught more readily in the colleges and universities particularly in those areas where one is not really interested in teaching programming methodology.

Finally, I guess I must admit that one thing has become clearer to me as time has gone on, and I think to the rest of the programming community, and that's that programming languages per se are not the end-all of programmer productivity. I think it's fair to say that those people who have and who are successfully using FORTRAN, ALGOL, and other higher-level languages for their work and find these satisfactory would gain very little productivity by moving to PL/I. The primary attraction offered by PL/I is its great breadth and the capability of writing a program or a number of programs requiring different disciplines in a single all-encompassing language.

TRANSCRIPT OF QUESTION AND ANSWER SESSION

GEORGE RADIN: I've gotten a preview of some of these questions while Bruce was talking, and I'm going to need help—so, all you friends, feel free.

ROSIN: Let me start out with a friendly one. Dan McCracken lists the language on his card as "PL/X." He says, "Please settle a bet. Did you guys intend it to be PL/I (Roman I), or PL/1 (Arabic 1)?"

RADIN: Well, the only thing I can say about that is that the first draft of my paper had it all as PL/1 (Arabic), and—what is it today, by the way? [Laughter] I don't remember. Who does?

ROSIN: It's my understanding that IBM copyrighted several PL/Ns—I wonder what those Ns were expressed in. Anyone know? We don't have any authorities.

TOM STEEL: Just a brief comment on this subject. Officially, as far as the American National Standards Institute is concerned, it is a Roman I. There was a formal vote taken on the subject and Roman won!

ROSIN: And Roman won by 52% I'll wager. It'll be interesting to see whether IBM chooses to follow the standard. [Laughter] The second question is, I think, the briefest statement of several that were somewhat related, and is from Steve Franklin "Was there any consideration given to making NPL a compatible extension of ALGOL 60?"

RADIN: Well, the SHARE/IBM committee as you've seen was heavily FORTRAN oriented and had some COBOL experience. It had really no direct involvement with ALGOL. Many of us knew about ALGOL, but I believe none of us had programmed in ALGOL and we did not, to my knowledge, give any serious consideration to moving to an ALGOL base once we had decided we would not work from a FORTRAN base. The people in the Vienna Laboratory in IBM, however, were quite anxious that we would do that, in fact. There are reports and memos, and there was a good deal of debate from that community, which is to be expected from a European community, to do that. But of course they were not successful.

ROSIN: Tom Steel had a comment. Let me read you what he wrote; I think it's relevant. He said, "Regarding your comment on the interaction with the ALGOL community, it is the case that efforts at cooperation were pursued. The authorization for the original ANSI effort explicitly called for this as a result of a compromise negotiated at a meeting held during a coffee break at an ANSI X3 meeting in Phoenix. The workers on both sides ignored management." Continuing with questions on outside influence, let me read one from Bob Bemer: "Many languages at the time of PL/I's origin allowed spelled-out or abbreviated operators. The examples on page 240 (I assume that's 240 of the Preprints; is that right, Bob? [referring to Appendix A on pages 573–574 of this volume]) show 'NE' for Not Equals, 'EQ' for Equals. What are the historical reasons for *not* and *or* demanding unique printing characters with damaging effect to the ASCII code? Was PL/I expected to be batch only and not used with terminals?

RADIN: Jim—could you comment on that? Jim Cox who was a member of the committee.

JIM COX: We originally tried to design the graphics that were on the 029 or the—I've forgotten the numbers now, but the keypunch that was in wide use—that did not have "less than" or "greater than" or any of those things. And then as System/360 developed within IBM we developed the EBCDIC code and the character set that went along with it, and so we switched over some time during the compiler development to adopt those characters.

PETER NAUR: On the question of the approach from the PL/I design group, I think it should be recorded that I was personally approached by representatives of IBM, by Fred Brooks in particular, during the spring and summer of 1964 it must have been. I got in my hand some of the specifications, and had a chance to comment on them. After a month or two, I think, we peacefully agreed that I would not be a suitable man on his project. The whole thing at that stage was to me so un-ALGOL-like, by the sheer size, the sheer lack of conceptual economy, that I could really not do anything to it. But there was a positive approach by Fred Brooks. I thought that might be of interest.

ROSIN: Thank you. The next question, in a similar vein is from Richard Miller. The question is related to one of your early slides. "Was JOVIAL actually considered a special purpose language by IBM?"

RADIN: Well, that's words—special purpose, or general purpose. JOVIAL, and the applications that JOVIAL supported, were in fact considered in the language design process of NPL, and in particular, fixed binary numbers and fixed binary arithmetic and the specified binary point came directly from JOVIAL, and if I recall, the application which it was to have supported was one of long input tapes which came from analog to digital conversions which had sequences of bits with an implied binary point. And the second JOVIAL characteristic which we explicitly put into the language was that we took JOVIAL COMPOOL, or the spirit of JOVIAL COMPOOL, and introduced the INCLUDE facility into NPL. So that JOVIAL's characteristics certainly were understood and included.

ROSIN: And you did consider JOVIAL to be particularly a special purpose language at that time?

RADIN: As I said—that's a word. Yes, I guess so.

ROSIN: Let me follow on with this, as long as we're in the context of nits in the language. Paul Abrahams asks: "Were there any reasons for left-justifying bit strings on assignment other than symmetry with behavior of character strings?"

RADIN: I guess I discussed that in the paper, and it's hard for me to do so, because I think that was an error. The reasons were precisely that we felt that strings were strings and that we should have symmetrical facilities and symmetrical rules for character strings and for bit strings. It has been my experience that in fact bit strings almost always represent numbers, and therefore the truncation rules ought to be amenable to treating them as numbers, and that the PL/I decision in that case was really wrong. I'm sorry we made it.

ROSIN: Let me follow on with another question from Paul Abrahams: "Could you explain the decision not to include varying strings without a maximum length?"

RADIN: Yes. There are many things in the language which, in this flavor, make it unlike languages like SNOBOL, for instance, and LISP. The language does not require a sophisticated, underlying storage management mechanism which does dynamic space reclamation and garbage collection. Rightly or wrongly, the language was defined in a FORTRAN OS Region spirit in which in fact the job was given a certain amount of memory and could exercise in that memory. And therefore we were very suspicious of underlying mechanisms which allowed this kind of unlimited growth. In character strings, in the ability of arrays to grow, of areas to grow, in the ability of creating new names and therefore new storage of things in a dynamic and unanticipated way—in that sense, the language is quite statically defined.

ROSIN: At the risk of offending some people who have submitted some rather good philosophical and more general questions, and we may run out of time to present them, I'd like to address one more nit that I know has influenced negatively thousands of programmers. Daniel Salomon and John Schild ask similar questions. Let me phrase it in Schild's context: "If PL/I was meant to be compatible with OS/360, why does it use the OS endfile symbol /* as a comment indicator?"

RADIN: Did we know about JCL at that time?

BRUCE ROSENBLATT: No, I think we really didn't have any knowledge—as I indicated during my talk—of OS and the JCL that OS was using. So, it was a happenstance situation.

RADIN: Two good ideas—arrived at independently! [Applause]

ROSIN: R. Morrison presents a challenge: "Please comment on IBM's heavy-handed introduction of PL/I to the computing community. Do you think that in retrospect, PL/I has been able to gain wider acceptance in spite of IBM's early association with the language, or do you think that PL/I has declined in utilization when compared with more recent programming languages such as ALGOL 68 or PASCAL because of IBM's association with PL/I?"

RADIN: You understand that's awfully hard to answer. But let me try in some spirit. First of all, these are all my personal views. I think that the use of PL/I to a large extent was enhanced by IBM support. I refuse to add the adjective. But in another respect, I think that the late 1950s and the early 1960s were in many respects a time of very ambitious desires for unification. I was reminded by Fred Brooks yesterday of that. There was a desire for unified field theories in physics and universal languages and universal systems. And the 1970s see quarks and leptons of various flavors and colors, and minicomputers— and so the 360 has not become a universal standard, nor has PL/I become a universal standard. And I believe it would be wrong to attribute to IBM, rightly or wrongly, I mean for good or bad, the power to move the currents of that kind of social climate that strongly. I simply believe that this is a period of diversity and less so of desires to find unifying, minimal constructs, and for that reason, and perhaps for other reasons, PL/I is not the unifying universal construct either.

ROSIN: I have two questions from Bernie Galler that are almost identical—if I don't raise one of them, I probably won't be able to leave the platform. The second one is: "Mark Elson told me, just before his death, that the compile-time facility was the best that could be done once it was realized that a built-in definition facility to expand the language would have been valuable. Can you comment on this?"

RADIN: Jim, can you?

COX: Yes. One of the things we learned about PL/I after the definition phase, once we started trying to implement it, was that it was a big job, and we ended up consuming the entire programming resource of the Hursley laboratory, just to try and get the compiler under control for the language as it was defined and understood at that point. Now, we always wanted to work on extension facilities, and we were very fortunate to find a group of very talented people in the IBM Boston Programming Center. Pat Goldberg was one of those. And I think primarily because the Atlantic Ocean was in the middle, we defined the compile-time facilities to be a macropreprocessor. You know, strictly a preprocessor that took character string text and put out PL/I programs that would then go into the compiler. And so we very heavily compromised some of the grand ideas of language extensibility that came along after the original definition, but before the compiler was shipped, in order to have something that would be in the nature of extensibility.

ROSIN: Helen Gigley asks for George to prepare a doctoral dissertation. She says, "Good code and/or optimization have been mentioned as criteria for several language implementations. Would you please define them?"

RADIN: Well, I've been working in optimizing compilers lately, in research, within the context of variants of PL/I, in fact, and we've been trying to produce code such that when good systems programmers examine it they are pleasantly surprised and often pleasantly shocked. And I can assert that given PL/I with some very few constraints, it is indeed technically possible to produce such code, which competes very well with very good systems programmers. That's sort of my criterion.

ROSIN: Dick Wexelblat says that he has an amusing—according to Wexelblat's criteria, it's not clear what that means—but Dick Wexelblat has a comment to make.

WEXELBLAT: A lot of people were interested in PL/I in the old days and would prefer to forget it. [Donald] Knuth may be among them. Tony Hoare was the chairman of the European PL/I standards committee, and at a meeting in Vienna, we were discussing whether we could define a subset in the "spirit" of PL/I, and Tony Hoare said, "No, it's impossible. The spirit of PL/I is to be a *big* language!"

FULL TEXT OF ALL QUESTIONS SUBMITTED

PAUL ABRAHAMS

How much consideration was given to pointers and offsets in the original design? Were they introduced as a quick fix, or after much contemplation? Were typed pointers even considered? Was the relationship between BASED and CONTROLLED examined.

Were non-IBM machines considered when BINARY/DECIMAL was designed? If so, which ones?

Were there any known applications of scaled fixed binary when NPL was designed? Who used it in practice?

Were the ⌐< and ⌐> operators included just because they are in COBOL?

How were PL/I PICTURES derived from COBOL pictures?

Explain the decision not to include varying strings without a maximum length.

Were there any reasons for left-justifying bit strings on assignment other than symmetry with the behavior of character strings?

BOB BEMER

Many languages (at the time of PL/I origin) allowed spelled-out or abbreviated operators. The examples on page [573] show "NE" for "not equals," "EQ" for "equals." What are the historical reasons for "Not" and "Or" demanding unique printing characters, with damaging effect to the ASCII code? Was PL/I expected to be batch only, and not used with terminals?

ERWIN BOOK

In the light of current language design theory, what additions or deletions would you make to PL/I today?

NEIL CUADRA

What is the history of the cell concept in PL/I?

STEVE FRANKLIN

Was any consideration given to making NPL a compatible extension of ALGOL 60?

BERNIE GALLER

The late Mark Elson told me just before his death that the compile-time facility was the best that could be done once it was realized that a built-in definition facility to expand the language would have been valuable. Can you comment on this?

I believe you told me once (1964) that there was a rigid policy that: "Designers must not specify anything into PL/I that would imply any particular implementation method—for machine independence reasons." This ruled out a built-in definition facility, for example. Was this a good policy? What was its impact?

HELEN GIGLEY

"Good code" and/or optimizations have been mentioned as criteria for several language implementations. Would you please define them?

J. F. GIMPEL

What do you feel to be those PL/I deficiencies that most inhibited its widespread use?

·DAN MCCRACKEN

Please settle a bet: Did you guys intend it to be PL/I or PL/1?

RICHARD MILLER

We would like to know whether the ALGOL–PL/I cooperation noted in the preprints and the talk was ever pursued. George commented that he didn't know, does anyone else?

Was JOVIAL actually considered as a *special-purpose* language by IBM during the decision phase of the language (deciding when to do it and *if* to do it)?

Could you comment on the effects that the different labs of IBM (Hursley, Vienna, Watson, etc.) had on PL/I. Do you think this separation of function was beneficial?

ROGER MILLS

What ever happened to the idea that a programmer could specify what type of programmer he/she was, hence the prologue could be cut since FORTRAN programmers doing algorithms may not understand or want asynchronous tasking, controlled or automatic storage, etc.?

R. Morgan Morrison

Please comment upon IBM's "heavy handed" introduction of PL/I to the computing community.

Do you think that, in retrospect, PL/I has been able to gain wider acceptance in spite of IBM's early association with the language or do you think that PL/I has declined in utilization, when compared to more recent programming languages such as ALGOL 68, C, or PASCAL, because of IBM's association with PL/I?

Daniel Salomon

How did it happen that the symbols /* were chosen as a delimiter by both PL/I and OS/360 JCL?

Jon Schild

If PL/I was meant to be compatible with 360 OS, why does it use the OS end-of-file symbol (/*) as a comment indicator?

T. B. Steel, Jr.

Regarding your comment on the interaction with the ALGOL community, it is the case that efforts at cooperation *were* pursued. The authorization for the original ANSI effort explicitly called for this as a result of a compromise negotiated at a meeting held during a coffee break at an ANSI/X3 meeting in Phoenix. The workers on both sides ignored management.

David Zook

Why 31 character names, i.e., one more than COBOL's 30 characters?

BIOGRAPHY OF GEORGE RADIN

George Radin holds a B.A. in English Literature from Brooklyn College (1951), an M.A. in English Literature from Columbia (1952), and an M.S. in Math from N.Y.U. (1961). After managing the N.Y.U. College of Engineering Computer Center and Applications Programming at Columbia University Computing Center, he became an Instructor at IBM's Systems Research Institute.

In 1963 he joined the Advanced Computer Utilization Department, where he worked on advanced compiler technology and PL/I.

Since the PL/I work he has been: a member of the design groups for OS/360 and TSS; Manager of Program Product Planning and Advanced Technology; Manager of Advanced Systems Architecture and Design; and a Senior Manager at Thomas J. Watson Research Center. He is currently in charge of a research project, developing a new, fast minicomputer system.

In April 1980 he was appointed a Fellow of the IBM Corporation.

SNOBOL Session

Chairman: JAN Lee
Speaker: Ralph E. Griswold

PAPER: A HISTORY OF THE SNOBOL PROGRAMMING LANGUAGES

Ralph E. Griswold

Department of Computer Science
The University of Arizona

Development of the SNOBOL language began in 1962. It was followed by SNOBOL2, SNOBOL3, and SNOBOL4. Except for SNOBOL2 and SNOBOL3 (which were closely related), the others differ substantially and hence are more properly considered separate languages than versions of one language. In this paper historical emphasis is placed on the original language, SNOBOL, although important aspects of the subsequent languages are covered.

1. Background

1.1. Setting

The initiative for the development of a new string manipulation language that was to become SNOBOL arose in the Programming Research Studies Department at Bell Telephone Laboratories, Incorporated (BTL). This organization was originally situated at Whippany, New Jersey, but moved to the new Holmdel, New Jersey, Laboratory in mid-1962. The department was part of the Switching Engineering Laboratory, which was mainly responsible at that time for advanced planning and engineering for the Electronic Switching System (ESS) telephone offices. The department itself, although not part of the Research Division of BTL, was concerned with computer-related research and its members were relatively isolated from ESS concerns. Departmental work was in areas of automata theory (Lee, 1960, 1961b), graph analysis (Lee, 1961a; Griswold and Polonsky, 1962;

Ralph E. Griswold

Griswold, 1962), associative processors (Lee and Paull, 1963), and high-level programming languages for formula manipulation (Lee *et al.*, 1962).

To understand what follows, the environment within the department needs to be understood. The department was small by BTL standards (six persons) and had no internal supervisory structure. The department head, C. Y. (Chester) Lee was mainly concerned with his own research and other members of the department worked relatively independently, either individually or in small groups that formed naturally. In 1962 Ivan P. Polonsky and I were working with the SCL programming language that had been developed at BTL by Chester (Lee *et al.*, 1962) and were dividing our efforts between problem solving and the application of SCL to such problems as symbolic integration, factoring of multivariate polynomials, and the analysis of Markov chains. David J. Farber was also in the department, but he was more concerned with operating systems and software itself. At that time, he was also secretary of SHARE and was involved in many activities inside and outside BTL that were not directly related to the other research going on in that department.

Although SCL had a number of interesting features, it had notable deficiencies: poor performance, a severely limited data region, and an intricate, low-level syntax that required lengthy programs for realizing simple operations. As Ivan and I became increasingly frustrated with the limitations of SCL, Dave obtained COMIT (Yngve, 1958; MIT Press, 1962) for our use. Although COMIT was interesting, its difficult syntax and orientation toward natural-language processing made it unsuitable for formula manipulation and graph analysis. In the fall of 1962, the decision to attempt the design of a new programming language came spontaneously from Dave, Ivan, and myself. We simply felt that we could produce a language that was superior, for our purposes, to any one that existed at that time. Because of the relative independence of the members of the department and the absence of any formal channels of communication or approval, the early work that led to SNOBOL went on without the specific knowledge of Chester and, in fact, in an air of considerable secrecy. At the same time, Chester was working on an improved version of SCL, although we were not then aware of his work either.

These two independent movements to develop a new programming language surfaced with Chester's presentation of his new version of SCL in November 1962. While his proposal added a number of new facilities to SCL, it retained and expanded the features that had led to our divergent work. When we subsequently revealed our design (which was considerably more developed than Chester's) the conflict was evident: the department could not support the development of two languages. Without our help, Chester did not have the resources to implement his proposal. Since Chester was head of the department, we could not continue our work if Chester directed us not to. While Chester did not stop our work, there was considerable tension within the department in the ensuing months.

1.2. Initial Design

The group that was developing SNOBOL worked out its own internal relationships on the basis of the personalities and the qualifications of the persons involved. Dave was the acknowledged leader. He was the only member of the group with substantial software development experience and with contacts in the professional computing community. I had virtually no computing experience prior to coming to BTL and Ivan's background was largely in application areas rather than in software development.

The group operated autonomously and without outside direction. Dave provided an interface with other computing organizations within BTL, most notably the computer center and the research department at the Murray Hill Laboratory. His discussions with persons there—M. Douglas McIlroy, Robert Morris, and Victor A. Vyssotsky—undoubtedly had an indirect influence on the design and implementation of SNOBOL.

It should be noted that Dave viewed himself primarily as a language designer and implementor, while Ivan and I initially viewed ourselves primarily as eventual users. This view changed over a period of time as SNOBOL became more important to us than the problems it was intitially designed to solve. All members of the group regarded the effort as tentative, with its ultimate direction depending on the success of the initial efforts.

1.3. The Implementation

Consideration of how the implementation might be handled was present in the early language design stage. When the initial design was satisfactory to the group, actual implementation became the next goal. A trial implementation was undertaken on an IBM 7090 early in 1963. At that time the group felt that a running system was essential in order to determine whether or not the new language was worthwhile. We did not think that a large initial investment was justified, reasoning that if the language proved valuable, more design and another implementation would be required.

Dave felt that a true compiler for a language like SNOBOL was impossible and that an interpretive system would give us the flexibility to implement the kinds of language features we wanted. Source-language statements were translated into intermediate forms of flags and pointers suitable for efficient interpretation. This style of interpretation provided the model for future implementations. With its flexibility, it also provided a vehicle suitable for developing esoteric language features.

Dave sketched out the organization of an interpretive system and wrote the compiler and interpreter. The attitude toward the implementation is exemplified by the compiler, which Dave literally coded in macro FAP on the back of a business envelope one evening. (It has been said that the compiler *ran* as if it had been coded on the back of an envelope.) Doug McIlroy's string manipulation macros (McIlroy, 1962) were used extensively in the initial implementation and were to figure prominently in subsequent work. Ivan and I implemented the pattern-matching portion of the interpreter. This proved to be a challenge, since I had no prior assembly-language programming experience and Ivan's experience was limited. Laura White Noll assisted the group by implementing the symbol table and storage management routines, again relying on work done by Vic Vyssotsky and Doug McIlroy on scatter storage techniques (McIlroy, 1962, 1963; Morris, 1968).

The short period of time required to achieve the first usable implementation of SNOBOL—about three weeks—was a matter of pride within the group and was held as proof that the implementation of a programming language need not be time consuming and costly.

While the original implementation was not of the "toy" variety, it nonetheless required considerable incremental improvement and debugging, especially in the area of storage management. By the summer of 1963, however, the implementation was in extensive use within BTL, mainly in the Research Department at Murray Hill and the Electronic Switching Systems groups at Holmdel.

1.4. Reaction to SNOBOL

Dave, Ivan, and I were the first users of SNOBOL, although use spread rapidly through BTL. The earliest recorded applications were in the evaluation of algebraic expressions (Griswold, 1963c), a program to convert network descriptions into FORTRAN programs that performed statistical analyses of these networks (Faulhaber, 1963), a program to convert descriptions of ESS data into IPL-V programs that generated the corresponding assembly-language code to provide data regions for ESS programs (Griswold and Polonsky, 1963b), and a FORTRAN compiler (Farber, 1963a).

The initial reaction of users to SNOBOL was surprisingly enthusiastic. Programmers at BTL quickly learned the new language and began using it for a variety of problems. By late 1963 and early 1964, SNOBOL had been used within BTL for text generation (Manacher, 1963), graph analysis (Magnani, 1964), syntax analysis (Griswold, 1964a), and simulation of automata (Faulhaber, 1964). It was also being considered for application to several engineering problems of interest to the Bell System. There was no question that SNOBOL was a success. Chester acknowledged its value (Lee, 1963) and permitted work on SNOBOL to continue.

The first official announcement of SNOBOL outside BTL came in a talk by Dave at the University of Michigan in October 1963 (Farber, 1963b). Other talks followed and information spread by word of mouth. With distribution of the SNOBOL system, interest increased rapidly. Obviously a long pent-up need for such a programming language had been satisfied. Programmers began using SNOBOL for problems which they were formerly unwilling to undertake. Examples were programs to generate other programs (Faulhaber, 1963; Griswold and Polonsky, 1963b) and "quick-and-dirty" experimental compilers (Farber, 1963a).

1.5. The Problem of a Name

While SNOBOL is the only name for the language that most persons have ever heard, several other names were used tentatively and the final choice came with some difficulty. The language was initially called SCL7, reflecting its origins. At that time SCL was officially at version 5 (SCL5) and the name SCL7 reflected a feeling of advancement beyond the next potential version. Actually the new language was very much different from SCL. With Chester's separate language design and an increasing disaffection with SCL on our part, we sought a new name.

The first choice was the acronym SEXI (*S*tring *EX*pression *I*nterpreter). The first implementation of SNOBOL in fact printed this name on output listings (Griswold, 1963c). The name SEXI produced some problems, however. Dave recalls submitting a program deck with the job card comment SEXI FARBER as per BTL standards, to which the I/O clerk is said to have responded, "that's what *you* think." In the original draft report, the typed name SCL7 was changed by hand to SEXI except in the opening sentence (Griswold, 1963b). In Chester's critique of this draft (Lee, 1963), he commented:

> I feel the use of a name such as SEXI may be justified if the language is so poor that it needs something to spice it up. Here we have an extremely good language. The use of SEXI may be interpreted as a lack of confidence on our part.

The draft report itself acknowledged the problem of a name in its last paragraph (Griswold, 1963a):

A suitable name for such a string manipulation language is also badly needed . . . in addition to the two names referred to in this report [SCL7 and SEXI] . . . PENELOPE has been suggested, after the wife of Ulysses.

In fact the name PENELOPE was considered because of its graceful sound—the reference to Ulysses was an afterthought.

Despite a continued attachment to the name SEXI, we recognized that such a name was unlikely to gain approval from the authorities who controlled the release of information from BTL. Consequently the search for a new name began. This search was long and frustrating. We have since jokingly commented that it took longer to find a name than it did to design and implement the language (and that it was harder). The result was less satisfactory, as well, in most views.

We concentrated mainly on acronyms, working with words that described significant aspects of the language, such as "expression," "language," "manipulation," and "symbol." Hundreds of suggestions were made and rejected. I take personal credit and blame for the name SNOBOL. However, the name was quickly accepted by Dave and Ivan. As I recall, I came up with the name first and then put together the phrase from which it was supposedly derived—*S*tri*N*g *O*riented sym*BO*lic *L*anguage. This "pseudo-acronym" was intended to be a joke of sorts and a lampoon on the then current practice of selecting "cute" names for programming languages. Our humor was not appreciated and explanations of the origin of the name met with puzzled or pained expressions. With Steve Unger's comment, "that's *disgusting*," we suppressed the basis for the name SNOBOL until some years later when a publisher insisted on an explanation (Griswold, 1972a, p. ix).

The relatively lame humor exhibited in the choice of SNOBOL was not limited to the name of the language itself. Dave's error messages such as "ALL OUT OF SPACE, YELL FOR HELP" and "NO END STATEMENT, WHISPER FOR HELP" and the cryptic "RECOMPILE NOT ENABLED" quickly became wearisome to users.

Had we realized the extent to which SNOBOL would become popular, we probably would have selected a more dignified name. I recall that it was years before I could give a talk on SNOBOL without a sense of embarrassment about the name. SNOBOL has, of course, attracted many puns and bad jokes (e.g., the chance of a SNOBOL in hell). For some curious reason the lame humor of the name has been carried on by others. An example is Jim Gimpel's ICEBOL program for compressing SNOBOL programs (Griswold *et al.*, 1968b, pp. 197–202). Probably the worst pun is SPITBOL, *SP*eedy *I*mplemen*T*ation of SNO*BOL* (Dewar, 1971). Other examples are FASBOL (Santos, 1971), SNOFLAKE (Haight, 1970), ELFBOL (Gimpel and Hanson, 1973), SNOBAT (Silverston, 1976a), and most recently SLOBOL (Dalgleish, 1977).

A curious aspect of the choice of a name arose in the conflict with Chester between his language and ours and how the personnel would be affiliated. Implicitly acknowledging the success of the language, ultimately to be named SNOBOL, Chester offered to join our effort if we retained the name SCL but not if we picked another name. We decided to pick another name.

1.6. SNOBOL2 and SNOBOL3

A successor to SNOBOL was almost inevitable. Since there was no question of the demand for SNOBOL, issues in the original design and implementation had to be faced. The most notable design problem was the lack of any built-in function mechanism. As a result, even the simplest computations often required contorted, laborious, and inefficient programming techniques. In addition, the original implementation, while workable, was not sufficiently complete and not robust enough for wide use.

SNOBOL2 included a few minor changes to SNOBOL and a number of built-in functions for string and numeric computation. In addition, a facility for adding separately compiled assembly-language functions was included (Farber *et al.*, 1965b). The implementation was mostly redone from the ground up but again for the IBM 7090. This time more extensive use was made of the string manipulation macros (McIlroy, 1962) and their repertoire was extended (Farber *et al.*, 1965a).

SNOBOL2 was placed in use at BTL in April of 1964 (Farber *et al.*, 1964c). Although SNOBOL2 was used briefly at Project MAC under CTSS (Corbató *et al.*, 1963), it was never generally distributed outside BTL.

From the inception of SNOBOL2, it was clear to us that it had a serious deficiency: the lack of a mechanism for programmer-defined functions. This mechanism was designed, but not implemented because of the lack of personnel resources. With the summer assignment of Lee C. Varian (then a student at Princeton University) we had the necessary support, and the implementation of SNOBOL3 was undertaken. Glenn K. Manacher, on loan from the research division at Murray Hill, assisted in the design and implementation. SNOBOL3 was running in July of 1964 (Griswold, 1964b), and it officially replaced SNOBOL2 at BTL in October (Griswold, 1964c).

1.7. A Refractory Period

SNOBOL3 was greeted enthusiastically in the user community and its distribution to IBM 7090/94 installations was widespread. As a result, we became more and more involved in distribution, maintenance, and documentation.

As a result of increased interaction with the computing community after the release of SNOBOL3, we received many suggestions for changes and additions to the language. One of the evident deficiencies of SNOBOL3 was its lack of facilities for manipulating structures. Ivan and I began a series of investigations and experiments in this area using the external function mechanism of SNOBOL3 to add structure manipulation functions written in assembly language (Griswold and Polonsky, 1965; Griswold, 1965). While the results were interesting, they were inconclusive and did not provide clear direction for any substantial changes to SNOBOL3. Some related work continued, but language design and development were largely inactive. Unlike the progression from SNOBOL to SNOBOL2 and SNOBOL3, the progression to SNOBOL4 was not inevitable.

1.8. The Setting for SNOBOL4

This refractory period coincided with major changes in computing at BTL. In 1965 badly overloaded computing facilities and dissatisfaction with batch-mode operation, coupled with the imminence of the third-generation large-scale scientific computers, led to a corporate decision to revamp the computing facility and its mode of operation. The MULTICS project (Corbató and Vyssotsky, 1965) came into being, with large-scale interactive computing on GE 645s proposed as a replacement for the IBM 7094 batch operations then in use.

This major transition to new hardware of course implied major software development, including development of a replacement for SNOBOL3. The reimplementation of SNO-BOL3 was not an interesting or challenging project, but new ideas on language design coincided with this concern and led to the proposal for the development of SNOBOL4 on the new computer. We proposed to implement a SNOBOL-type language for the new computer, provided we could develop a new language as well. Our proposal was accepted, although no description of the new language was offered or requested.

In September 1965 a working group for production of GE 645 software was established within the local organization and James F. Poage was given the "technical responsibility for the implementation of SNOBOL IV [sic]" (Poage, 1965).

There was some reconsideration of an alternative for the name SNOBOL4. There were two main issues. On one hand, we expected SNOBOL4 to be substantially different from SNOBOL, SNOBOL2, and SNOBOL3. Hence there was an advantage to the selection of a completely new name to avoid the implication that SNOBOL4 was simply another version of SNOBOL3 with some minor changes. On the other hand, we felt the identification associated with the name SNOBOL would be valuable. We eventually made the decision to retain that identification.

1.9. Early SNOBOL4 Work

An early decision had to be made on the method to be used to implement SNOBOL4, since there was no GE 645 available for use. Most MULTICS-related GE 645 software development was done at Project MAC, originally using a 645 simulator running on a GE 635. EPL (Cambridge Information Systems Laboratory, 1968), an early version of PL/I, was used for most systems programming. Since our work on SNOBOL4 had low priority within the MULTICS project, and at Holmdel we were remote from the sites of major development work, we decided to do our original implementation of SNOBOL4 on our local IBM 7094, which had good, running software and to which we had access. We anticipated, of course, the need to transport our implementation to the new computer.

In retrospect, it is interesting to note that although SNOBOL4 was officially part of the MULTICS project, the affiliation was largely ignored by both sides. No schedules were established, no goals were projected, and no reports of documentation were ever requested or supplied.

Work on SNOBOL4 began in earnest in February 1966. The principals in the design and implementation of SNOBOL4 were Jim Poage, Ivan, and myself. Robert A. Yates served in a supporting role in the implementation of storage management routines and Al R. Breithaupt, on a temporary internship assignment, provided general programming support. By this time Dave Farber had other interests and responsibilities. He served primarily as an advisor on implementation and helped in providing support software. Although Jim Poage was the supervisor of the group developing SNOBOL4, I assumed de facto leadership of the technical aspects of the project.

Several important concerns affected the design of SNOBOL4. One was the need for a portable implementation that could be transferred to the GE 645 easily when the new computer became available. Another, more fundamental concern was our desire for more generality in the implementation. We expected SNOBOL4 to serve as a vehicle for language experimentation and to be sufficiently flexible that design and implementation could be concomitant—with new features tested experimentally in the context of a working system. From an implementation viewpoint, this led to the evolution of the machine-independent macro language SIL (Griswold, 1970, 1972a) that had origins in the use of McIlroy's string macros in the early implementation of SNOBOL.

Efficiency had been a minor concern in SNOBOL, SNOBOL2, and SNOBOL3, both to the designers and to the users, until a number of large applications raised questions about costs and memory limitations. During the initial design period of SNOBOL4, the prospects offered by third-generation hardware were the subject of much discussion. With the promise of cheaper, faster processors and virtual memory, software planners were envisioning an environment in which efficiency considerations could be ignored and memory could be treated as virtually unlimited. While we were skeptical, we nonetheless decided to design SNOBOL4 as if speed and space were not serious concerns. We recognized from the beginning that the resulting system would be inefficient and we anticipated the need for more efficient implementations if SNOBOL4 became popular.

The philosophy of generality, flexibility, and concomitant design and implementation had a greater effect on SNOBOL4 than on earlier languages. While SNOBOL, SNOBOL2, and SNOBOL3 were largely designed prior to implementation and completed as identifiable projects, SNOBOL4 development extended over a period of years and passed through many stages as new features were added and old ones discarded.

The implementation of SNOBOL4 was a metamorphic process. The first versions were obtained by gradual conversion of SNOBOL3, using external functions for features (such as pattern matching) that were substantially different from those of SNOBOL3. By April 1966 (Griswold, 1966b) a running version was used experimentally. The emphasis on flexibility and generality is evidenced by the fact that this version permitted source-language redefinition of internal executive procedures. Even the meaning of literals could be changed during program execution.

By August 1966 (Griswold, 1966d), a relatively complete preliminary version of SNOBOL4 was working on the IBM 7094 and language design and implementation were proceeding concomitantly as planned. In the meantime, the BTL decision to convert to GE 645s under MULTICS had been reconsidered and some of the laboratories had decided to change to other computers. Most notable was the Indian Hill Laboratory's change to an IBM 360/67 under TSS. In June 1966 (Martellotto, 1966) the Indian Hill Laboratory expressed interest in a "SNOBOL compiler" for the 360/67. The decision of our own Holmdel Laboratory in 1966 to go to a 360 under OS shifted our own implementation concerns.

Our first use of a 360 was at Princeton University, where Lee Varian arranged for us to obtain access to their computer facilities and supported our first attempt at transporting SNOBOL4 to a new computer. This work began in October 1966 and a 360 version of SNOBOL4 was running by the end of the year. In the spring of 1967, a 360/40 was installed at Holmdel. Although the first SNOBOL4 system sent outside BTL in June 1967 was for the IBM 7094 (Griswold, 1967), development work had been shifted entirely to the IBM 360 by this time.

1.10. Continuing SNOBOL4 Development

With the first release of SNOBOL4 outside BTL, work continued on new features. Beginning in mid 1967 considerable support was given as well to transported implementations in progress by other persons for the CDC 6000, GE 635, UNIVAC 1108, RCA Spectra 70, and CDC 3600.

Employees from other BTL organizations who were on temporary assignment to gain additional work experience augmented the personnel regularly assigned to the project. Paul D. Jensen and Bernard N. Dickman, who joined the project for the summer of 1967, designed and implemented tracing facilities (Dickman and Jensen, 1968). In the spring of 1968, Howard J. Strauss, also on temporary assignment, designed and implemented external functions (Strauss, 1968). James F. Gimpel was a contributor to continuing SNOBOL4 development, assisting in documentation, theoretical investigations of pattern matching (Gimpel, 1973a), and developing language extensions of his own (Gimpel, 1972). Michael D. Shapiro participated in the project intermittently from 1967, contributing ideas, testing the system, assisting with the documentation, and working on the CDC 6000 implementation (Shapiro, 1969).

The distribution of SNOBOL4 was substantially more widespread than that for SNOBOL3. By the end of 1967 (Griswold, 1968), some 58 IBM 360 systems had been distributed and documentation was being widely disseminated (Griswold *et al.*, 1967b). The decision to undertake extensive distribution was made by the implementors and I did most of the distribution myself, including copying magnetic tapes.

Despite the increased burden of distribution, correspondence, and maintenance, design and implementation continued. The first officially complete version was distributed in March 1968. Version 2, with substantial language changes, was distributed in December 1968 (Griswold *et al.*, 1968a), and Version 3, the last version released from BTL, was completed in November 1969 (Griswold *et al.*, 1971).

Subsequent work at BTL consisted of corrections and a substantial amount of documentation that was related to implementation and installation. In August 1971 I left BTL to join the faculty of the University of Arizona. At that time, active development of SNOBOL4 per se ceased, although Jim Gimpel at BTL continued his work on pattern matching (Gimpel, 1975), implementation techniques (Gimpel, 1974a,b), and the development of an efficient SNOBOL interpreter for the DEC-10 (Gimpel, 1973b). At the University of Arizona, work turned toward more research-oriented topics (Griswold, 1975c; Hallyburton, 1974; Druseikis and Griswold, 1973). Although some SNOBOL4 activity continues at various locations, it is now mostly concerned with implementations for new machines and with techniques for achieving greater efficiency.

1.11. Documentation

Until the first implementation of SNOBOL was working, little thought was given to documentation. The first attempt at documentation came in the form of a draft in March 1963 (Griswold, 1963a). The first complete document was an internal memorandum in May of that year (Farber *et al.*, 1963a), which was released in October for distribution outside BTL. A journal article based on this paper was submitted to the *Journal of the ACM* in October of 1963 and was published in January of 1964 (Farber *et al.*, 1964a). Rapid publication hastened the public awareness of SNOBOL. The manuscript had been distributed for review prior to submission and it was accepted the day after it was formally submitted (Farber *et al.*, 1963b; Hamming, 1963). The article appeared in print in less than three months.

The only documentation of SNOBOL2 was an internal draft memorandum (Farber *et al.*, 1964b). The lack of more formal documentation reflects the limited time that SNOBOL2 was in use.

Documentation for SNOBOL3 followed the pattern for SNOBOL—internal memoranda that were subsequently approved for release outside BTL as technical reports. A basic report describing the language (Farber *et al.*, 1964d) was followed by reports on the external function mechanism (Farber *et al.*, 1965b) and extensions to SNOBOL3 effected by use of the external function mechanism (Manacher, 1964; Manacher and Varian, 1964; Griswold and Varian, 1964; Griswold, 1965; Griswold and Polonsky, 1965). Official publication of a description of SNOBOL3 came in the form of a long article in the *Bell Systems Technical Journal* (Farber *et al.*, 1966). This journal was selected for the publication primarily because of its willingness to publish a paper of sufficient length to include a complete description of SNOBOL3. Prentice-Hall expressed interest in publishing a book on SNOBOL3, but after an investigation of the potential market, I discouraged this project. However, a SNOBOL3 primer was published by the MIT Press (Forte, 1967).

With SNOBOL4, documentation was taken much more seriously. Informal working papers on design and implementation were encouraged, but distribution was limited to those involved in the project. Several series of documents relating to the SNOBOL4 project were initiated for distribution outside BTL. These included installation notes and a series of technical reports (S4Ds) documenting the language and its implementation. The first S4Ds were concerned primarily with language descriptions (Griswold *et al.*, 1967b,c, 1968a). To date the S4D series has run to 56 documents, many of which have been revised repeatedly to reflect changes in SNOBOL4 (Griswold, 1978b).

By the time SNOBOL4 was available for general distribution, the language manual was finished (Griswold *et al.*, 1968a) and was being distributed by BTL. While distribution of earlier documentation had not been a significant problem, the demand for this manual was high. Before the publication of a book on SNOBOL4, over 2000 copies of the manual were distributed free of charge by BTL, and approval had been given for reprinting of over 1000 copies by organizations outside BTL.

In 1968 an adaptation of this manual was printed by Prentice-Hall (Griswold *et al.*, 1968b) and a revised, second edition (the "Green Book") was published in 1971 (Griswold *et al.*, 1971). This latter book remains the standard reference to the language. A primer more suitable for inexperienced programmers was published in 1973 (Griswold and Griswold, 1973), to be followed by other introductory books (Newsted, 1975; Maurer, 1976). Recently, more advanced books on the use of SNOBOL4 have appeared (Griswold, 1975a; Gimpel, 1976; Tharp, 1977). A book describing the implementation and especially its interaction with design appeared in 1972 (Griswold, 1972a).

Although there has never been an organized SNOBOL user's group, topical information has been published in the SNOBOL Bulletin of *SIGPLAN Notices* (Waite 1967–73) and the *SNOBOL4 Information Bulletin* which is issued aperiodically (Griswold, 1968–).

1.12. Support, Costs, and Schedules

Someone always wants to know how many man-years it took to develop a language and what the total cost was. Except in particularly highly structured and closely directed projects, such figures are difficult to determine at best and may be grossly misleading at worst. In addition, simple manpower estimates do not take into account the varying range of abilities of the persons involved.

For the SNOBOL languages, assignments of persons to the project were often informal or unofficial. Work was done spontaneously, motivation was generated within the group, and schedules were either nonexistent or generated internally to ensure adequate progress.

Since the development of SNOBOL spanned such a short period of time, fairly accurate manpower estimates are possible for it. Dave, Ivan, and I were involved for about nine months from the inception of the design to the completion of the first implementation. In addition, Laura White Noll provided about four months of programming support. Allowing for our other responsibilities, approximately one and one-half man-years were involved altogether.

SNOBOL2 was also produced in a relatively short time with a manpower expenditure of about two man-years. SNOBOL2 blended into SNOBOL3, but perhaps an additional two man-years were expended before the first public version appeared, although the time spent on subsequent maintenance was significant.

For SNOBOL4, accurate figures are impossible to determine. Part of the problem lies in the continuous evolution of design and development of SNOBOL4 over a period of years, making it difficult to know when one aspect ended and another began. Another confusing aspect was the responsibilities of the personnel involved. These duties became increasingly complex as the project continued. Jim Poage and I had major management responsibilities unrelated to SNOBOL4. As a rough estimate, perhaps six man-years were expended before the first running version of SNOBOL4 was available at BTL.

BTL always provided good physical support for SNOBOL. As far as costs are concerned, the major item was computer time. Although there were internal computer budgets, the accounting was never carried to the level of the persons involved in SNOBOL. Costs of SNOBOL development probably were never identified as such but instead were lumped with other projects. Certainly we used the computer resources at our disposal lavishly. In the absence of budget constraints, we felt that computer time was (in some sense) cheaper than our time, and we did not hesitate to make repeated batch runs to correct small errors if that speeded our work. While it was a luxury to have virtually unlimited computer access, budgets were only one constraint. We frequently were hampered by batch-mode operation and poor turnaround time, especially in the period between 1966 to 1968 when the second-generation computer facilities had become saturated and the transition to third-generation facilities introduced inevitable problems. Many entries in the SNOBOL4 log indicate continued frustration with computer facilities to the point that information about design and implementation is meager by comparison (Griswold, 1966–1969).

With the development of SNOBOL4 into a substantially larger project than any of the earlier languages had been, support of documentation, distribution, and maintenance by a small group became an increasing problem. The use of computer systems to support the work became essential. Emphasis was placed on document preparation systems, and we became leaders in introducing this technology to BTL. We first used TEXT90 and then TEXT360 (LeSeur, 1969) when the Holmdel Laboratory converted to third-generation hardware. The installation of ATS (IBM, 1969) provided the first interactive system for our use, and substantially reduced the effort of document preparation. We also developed a considerable amount of our own software (implemented in SNOBOL4, of course), including document formatting languages with interfaces to line printers and photocomposition equipment (Noll, 1971). As a result, the first Prentice-Hall book was delivered to the publisher as line-printer output in camera-ready form and the second edition was photocomposed. The use of camera-ready material significantly shortened the production period, and the use of a number of programs for tabulation and indexing produced unusually error-free copy for this kind of material.

Personnel support was another matter. While we generally favored a small, closely knit design and implementation group, there were many times when programming support and clerical help would have been welcome. What little help that was provided came in the form of temporary assignments: summer employees (as in the case of Lee Varian) or internal, rotational internships designed to broaden the background of employees by temporary assignments (Al Breithaupt and Howard Strauss were in this category).

SNOBOL4 produced our first serious manpower problem. Despite the enthusiasm with which SNOBOL4 was received and the accompanying publicity, no additional personnel support was available. Late in 1966, Jim Poage asked for additional personnel in programming support and clerical roles (Poage, 1966b). He listed 10 major areas in which work was needed and commented:

> It is unreasonable to expect that the people now working on SNOBOL4 (R. E. Griswold, I. P. Polonsky, and J. F. Poage) will be able to do all of the tasks listed, much less be willing to do them. Support for the SNOBOL4 effort is absolutely essential in the areas of debugging, the addition of routine features to all versions of the system, distribution of corrections to users, and conversion of SNOBOL4 to operate under MULTICS and TSS.

Nonetheless help was not forthcoming, and much of the burden of clerical work—even to making tape copies—fell to the developers themselves.

Certainly the attitude of BTL toward SNOBOL4 was reflected in its support of the project. Although SNOBOL4 was in considerable use within BTL and had received much favorable outside reaction, BTL's attention was directed toward the many important and pressing Bell System projects. SNOBOL4 could at best be considered peripheral. Because of its success, it was tolerated. The persons involved were allowed to work without significant hindrance. The lack of a formal project structure was mainly beneficial. Project members communicated informally but frequently. The notorious "11:15 lunch table" was the site of many exciting technical (and not-so-technical) discussions. The absence of a formal reporting structure, committee meetings, regular reports, and so on permitted the small, closely knit group to operate efficiently and effectively.

The local attitude toward research was exemplified by the "sand box" philosophy of our director, Bill Keister, who once told me that if you gave talented persons good facilities and left them alone, occasionally something good would happen (Keister, 1970). Clearly he placed SNOBOL in this category. There was no interference with our design nor were any features mandated by the needs of other projects at BTL.

1.13. The Release of SNOBOL

With the enthusiastic reception of SNOBOL within BTL, we were anxious to release it to outside users. Most software is developed with the goal of some sort of distribution to the computing community. In academic institutions, distribution of software is generally the concern and responsibility of the authors. Commercial ventures are predicated on distribution. SNOBOL, however, was developed within an industrial research organization and the original goal of the creators was to produce a tool for research going on there.

In 1963 there was little awareness within the computing community of the value of software. Most of the thorny issues regarding the protection of investments and proprietary rights had not been addressed. While BTL had mechanisms for reviewing and approving release of internal information outside the company, these procedures were designed for talks and papers. The specific question of the release of computer programs had not yet been addressed, nor was the management of the company then really aware of the significance of software.

Since we were anxious to release the SNOBOL system to installations outside BTL, this situation posed a problem. Clearly making an issue or test case of SNOBOL to get a corporate decision and policy would not speed SNOBOL's release. Dave Farber took the position that, in the absence of a policy that prevented release of a program, approval to give a talk or paper on the program constituted release of that program as well.

Using this basis, the first release of SNOBOL was obtained by release of the original SNOBOL paper (Farber *et al.*, 1963a) for "publication in SHARE Secretary's Distribution SSD" (Renne, 1963). The SNOBOL system subsequently was available to IBM 7090/94 users through SHARE.

Most of the interest in SNOBOL was in universities. With BTL's traditional identification with academic institutions, there was considerable management support for the distribution of SNOBOL outside BTL. However, as more and more of the work in BTL shifted from hardware to software there was increasing corporate concern with protection of the company's investment in software and its proprietary rights in this area. Early attempts to provide this protection centered on patents. Patentability became an issue for SNOBOL with the request for publication of an internal memorandum on the SNOBOL pattern-matching algorithm (Griswold and Polonsky, 1963a). Release of the paper was held up for nearly a year before BTL decided not to attempt to patent the algorithm (Renne, 1964).

Approval for release of SNOBOL3 outside BTL was granted in October 1964 with the comment (Keister, 1964):

> Since SNOBOL is a computer language which solves no particular problems directly and discloses no proprietary information, it is agreed that we could release information on recent modifications to this language. This can consist of user's manuals and program listings in appropriate form. We should use our judgement in individual cases as to whether the distribution of this information is to the benefit of the Laboratories and will contribute to advances in the programming art. The Patent Department should be kept informed of the institutions and individuals to whom we are releasing this information.

This process was followed and the Patent Department was notified periodically as copies of the SNOBOL3 system and its documentation were distributed.

Meanwhile the Patent Department continued to work on the patentability of computer programs, with SNOBOL3 as one of its specific test cases. We felt that it was in the best interests of BTL and the computing community for SNOBOL3 to be freely distributed. We therefore took a stand in opposition to the Patent Department. Many discussions followed and devolved into the intricacies of patent law. We were told that Euclid's algorithm could have been patented if it had not, unfortunately, been previously disclosed. Our sarcastic suggestion of a patent disclosure in the form of the initial state of core storage just prior to execution was considered to be reasonable (Kersey, 1967).

Our management supported our position on the value of the public release of SNOBOL3. Eventually the Patent Department capitulated with the statement (Hamlin, 1965):

> In view of the public disclosure of the SNOBOL program in 1963, this subject matter does not

appear to contain sufficient patentable novelty at this time to warrant the filing of an application for Letters Patent thereon.

Thus the first release of the original SNOBOL paper (Renne, 1963), which resulted in placing SNOBOL in the public domain, became the ultimate basis for public release of all subsequent material related to SNOBOL.

Release of SNOBOL4 outside BTL was of concern early in 1966 and release was obtained in May with the comment (Poage, 1966a):

> In the attached letter . . . dated October 20, 1964, principles were established for releasing information concerning SNOBOL outside of Bell Laboratories . . . . SNOBOL4, although different in syntax and implementation from SNOBOL, was not sufficiently new to consider for patent application. Therefore . . . the principles established in the attached letter should apply also to information concerning SNOBOL4. Further, since some economic benefit might be derived from the completed SNOBOL4 system, it was agreed that the final version should be submitted for copyright.

Once again the original release of SNOBOL provided the basis for releasing a new language. The phrase "final version" deserves note, since SNOBOL4 never reached a final version as such.

The issue was not completely settled until 1973 (Hirsch, 1973):

> SNOBOL, in its various forms, has been one of the most widely distributed of the Bell Laboratories–developed programs. Of the several versions of SNOBOL, the most current are designated as SNOBOL4 and SNOBOL4B. It is understood that the distribution of SNOBOL over the years has resulted in useful feedback and generally favorable reactions from those in the computing community at large.
>
> Because of the considerable administrative burden in reviewing individual requests for SNOBOL4 and SNOBOL4B, and because of the large number of copies already available to others, the Patent Division, with the concurrence of the Technical Relations Division, hereby grants a blanket approval for requests for these current versions of SNOBOL. Accordingly, any present or future requests for SNOBOL or its documentation need not be referred to the Patent or Technical Relations Divisions for approval. . . .
>
> The present grant of release approval is limited to the SNOBOL program (through versions 4 and 4B), and should not be considered applicable to other cases.

2. Rationale for the Content of the Language

2.1. Objectives

While the initial impetus for the development of SNOBOL was the need for a tool for formula manipulation, by the time the design of the language was under way, areas of interest had been extended to include graph processing and a number of text manipulation problems. Basically the objective was to provide a general-purpose language for manipulation of nonnumerical scientific data, such as formulas, that could be naturally represented by strings of characters. The interpretation of this objective was strongly influenced by the fact that we were oriented toward use of computers in research. An important criterion used in the design process was the "naïve user." We deliberately tried to produce a language that would be suitable for the person who was not primarily a programmer. We expected programs to be relatively small. In fact, the first implementation limited program size to 2000 "elements" (operators, operands, and so forth).

A main philosophical view emerged in the early design efforts: *ease of use*. To us, this implied several design criteria:

1. Conciseness: the language should have a small vocabulary and express high-level operations with a minimum of verbiage.
2. Simplicity: the language should be easy to learn and understand.
3. Problem orientation: the language facilities should be phrased in terms of the operations needed to solve problems, not the idiosyncrasies of computers.
4. Flexibility: users should be able to specify desired operations, even if these operations are difficult to implement. In particular, compile-time constraints should be minimized to allow maximum run-time freedom.

These objectives had several consequences, most of which can be characterized as a disregard for implementation problems and efficiency. This was a conscious decision and was justified by our contention that human resources were more precious than machine resources, especially in the research applications where SNOBOL was expected to be used. Our criterion for evaluating a proposed feature was more how it "felt" to us as programmers than how it conformed to conventional design criteria.

Specific consequences of this approach in SNOBOL were a single data type and the absence of declarations. In order to accommodate numerical computations in SNOBOL, arithmetic was performed (at least conceptually) on strings of digit characters that represented integers. This feature did not require declarations, and error checking was performed at run time. Declarations were viewed primarily as an aid to the implementation (Griswold, 1972a, p. 44), allowing compile-time decisions and the generation of efficient code. Since SNOBOL had only a single data type, the string, the most obvious declaration would have been for string length, either a fixed value or a maximum. However, the design criteria led us to support varying length strings with no specification by the user, placing all the burden of supporting this feature on the implementation. Similarly, SNOBOL contained no source-language storage management operations, again requiring the implementation to support allocation and garbage collection automatically.

From a language design viewpoint, such features amount to a design philosophy that the user of the language should not have to worry about how the computation is performed or what the actual implementation details are, but instead should be able to concentrate on the solution of problems. Without question, this philosophy was carried to the extreme in SNOBOL: deliberately and consciously so. It was the beginning of an attitude which I have sometimes described as "orthogonality to the mainstream."

2.2. Influence of Other Languages

One of the most fundamental problems we faced in the design of SNOBOL was determining the basic string manipulation operations and designing a notation for them. While algebraic languages had the well-established notation of mathematics as a natural basis for the elements of notation, no such independent notation existed for string manipulations. In developing the basic operations and notation, we were strongly influenced by earlier languages in this area.

Ivan and I were most familiar with SCL while Dave was more knowledgeable about COMIT. We had access to IPL-V, but we knew of other potentially relevant programming languages such as LISP only vicariously.

Since no information about SCL was ever released outside BTL, it is natural for observers to credit COMIT as the progenitor of SNOBOL. To us, however, SCL was a much more immediate influencing factor. The following quotation from the introductory section of the SCL manual (Lee *et al.*, 1962) characterizes its intent:

> The Symbolic Communication Language (SCL) is a language designed primarily for the processing of symbolic expressions. The basic unit which SCL deals with most conveniently is a line. A line may be an equation, an algebraic expression, a sentence, a set of pairs, etc. In mathematics, one often begins with a line, say an equation, and derives from it many other lines. Some of these derived lines are more important than others and are usually assigned a number. The general format in SCL is very much the same. The commands in SCL permit one to modify a line; the resulting line then appears next to the original line. If the new line is one which should be marked, a name can be assigned to that line. In this way it becomes particularly convenient to deal with mathematical expressions in SCL.

Since SCL had a strong influence on SNOBOL, it is appropriate to consider the factors that influenced SCL. Unfortunately, the only available source of information is the SCL manual. This manual references much of the prior literature on symbol manipulation languages, machine learning, and language translation. There is mention of IPL, LISP, COMIT, and macro processors, but no indication of how any of these might have influenced the design of SCL.

Aside from very different syntaxes, there is one clear difference between COMIT and SCL. While COMIT was oriented toward language translation with "constituent" units that typically were words, SCL was oriented toward algebraic manipulations on parenthesis-balanced strings of characters. While both SCL and COMIT had pattern matching and string transformation facilities, COMIT's facilities were constituent-based, while those of SCL demanded balanced parentheses. Both COMIT and SCL were organized around the concept of a workspace on which operations were performed. Other data was contained in "shelves" in COMIT and "data buffers" in SCL. Both SCL and COMIT were essentially single data type languages in which numerical computation was awkward. In COMIT, (integer) arithmetic was managed through operations on constituent subscripts. SCL, on the other hand, performed arithmetic only on rational numbers represented in prefix form as strings of character digits.

While it is difficult even for the designers of a language to recognize the influences of systems with which they are familiar, it was certainly the case that both SCL and COMIT were well known to us and we considered both to be inadequate for our needs. The resulting design of SNOBOL is certainly a synthesis of some features from both languages along with the introduction of new ideas. The extent of influence of SCL and COMIT is shown by that fact that SNOBOL contains their properties of basic string orientation, pattern matching and string transformation, and limited arithmetic facilities. SNOBOL departs by introducing the complete string (as opposed to a workspace of characters) as a data object that can be assigned to a variable. A more significant difference to users was that SNOBOL was considerably simpler than either COMIT or SCL, yet it provided more facilities for most text manipulation problems. Both SCL and COMIT were relatively slow and inefficient in their use of storage. Since we were confident that we easily could implement a language that made considerably more economical use of resources, efficiency and storage utilization were not serious concerns. Similarly, neither SCL nor COMIT permitted really large programs, so we did not think in these terms in the design of SNOBOL. Therefore SCL and COMIT had the indirect influence of causing us, for the most part, to disregard questions of efficiency and the possible consequences of large SNOBOL programs.

The influence of machine language is shown in the indirect referencing operator, which elevated the apparently low-level operation of indirect addressing to a high-level language and allowed the value of an identifier to be used as a variable. This operation proved to be extremely important, since it provided a method for representing associative relationships among strings and hence for representing structures in a pure string context. Since indirect referencing could be applied to any string constructed at run time, it implied the existence of an internal run-time symbol table.

2.3. Basic Decisions

The choice of syntax for SNOBOL was closely related to the selections of its control structures and was primarily motivated by the desire to make SNOBOL convenient for the "naïve user." In the choice of syntax, the influence of COMIT is evident. The statement format, in which an operation was specified, resembles that of COMIT. However, in SNOBOL the subject specifies the string on which the operation is performed, while in COMIT the string is implicit, namely the current workspace. The selection of the next statement to be executed, conditioned on the success or failure of the operation, is found both in COMIT and in SCL. In SCL, however, it resembles the multiple-exit operations of machine order structures of the time. The decision to rely on conditional gotos instead of introducing more sophisticated control structures was a deliberate one. We felt that providing a statement with a test-and-goto format would allow division of program logic into simple units and that inexperienced users would find a more technical, highly structured language difficult to learn and to use. The decision not to introduce reserved words or something similar was motivated by the same concern. The initial enthusiastic response to the simplicity of the language reinforced this decision for future development. Changing to a more "modern" syntax was not seriously considered, even for SNOBOL4.

At the time of the development of SNOBOL, its free-form syntax with the absence of fixed field positions and lack of limitations on the length of identifiers was somewhat of a novelty. Again, these choices were deliberate and were designed to make SNOBOL easy to use. Users of SNOBOL, accustomed to languages with more rigid syntaxes, greeted the new freedom enthusiastically.

The positional syntax of the statement with a subject followed by an operation was motivated by the feeling that the subject as a focus of attention was a useful construct and would aid users in organizing their approach to writing programs. The importance of this view is described by Galler and Perlis (1970, p. 78).

The most controversial aspect of the syntax of SNOBOL was its use of blanks. The decision not to have an explicit operator for concatenation, but instead just to use blanks to separate the strings to be concatenated, was motivated by a belief in the fundamental role of concatenation in a string-manipulation language. The model for this feature was simply the convention used in natural languages to separate words by blanks. Furthermore, an explicit operator for concatenation was thought to be overbearing, especially considering the frequency of the appearance of concatenation in SNOBOL programs.

Ralph E. Griswold

(The consequence of the ambiguous use of blanks, such as to separate subjects from the operations performed on them, is discussed in Section 3.3.1.)

One important early decision was to include backtracking in SNOBOL pattern matching. COMIT did not include backtracking, so that once a constituent matched, no alternative match was attempted, even if a subsequent constituent failed to match. Yngve justified this decision on the basis that someone had shown a pattern that would take 300 years of computer time to complete if backtracking were allowed (Yngve, 1964). We had observed that COMIT pattern matches sometimes failed when they should have succeeded, at least intuitively. We felt that it was conceptually important for a pattern to be a specification of the structural properties of a string and that all alternatives should be attempted to fit the pattern to these structural properties. The theoretical possibility of pattern matching taking arbitrarily long did not seem as important to us as the practical issues. In any event, we did not believe that this problem would arise in practice although steps were taken to minimize the problem (see Section 3.3.3). I know of only one instance where a pattern match actually took so long that it was mistaken for an endless loop within the system.

It is interesting that the issue of character sets was never given much consideration, despite SNOBOL's emphasis on string manipulation. The 48-character BCD character set was in general use when SNOBOL was designed, and it was accepted without much thought. Even with SNOBOL4, where various implementations were undertaken on computers with characters sets of different sizes, orderings, and graphics, no design consideration was given to the problem. Instead, it was considered to be an implementation problem specific to the target computer.

Machine independence and portability were given no consideration in the original design of SNOBOL, although use of string-manipulation macros (McIlroy, 1962) in the implementation laid the basis for later work. Our horizons were limited and our concerns were for providing a string manipulation language for the local computer, an IBM 7090. At that time, all BTL computer centers had 7090s as their main computers, and the possibility of implementations for other computers had not yet risen.

2.4. Progression to SNOBOL2 and SNOBOL3

Users quickly outgrew SNOBOL and the absence of certain facilities in SNOBOL made some programming tasks impractical or impossible. In one sense, SNOBOL was too simple. In another sense, the success of SNOBOL attracted users from areas in which the use of SNOBOL had not been anticipated.

An example of the deficiency of SNOBOL was the absence of any direct method for determining the length of a string. This computation had to be programmed using pattern matching. A naïve, although typical, method was to remove a character at a time until the string was exhausted, meanwhile incrementing a running count. Since the length of every string was readily accessible internally, this deficiency was doubly indefensible. There were no numerical comparison operations and these computations also had to be accomplished by pattern matching.

An obvious solution to these and a host of similar problems was the introduction of built-in functions to provide a repertoire of operations under a single syntactic cloak.

While the repertoire of built-in functions in SNOBOL2 handled the most commonly needed computations, special needs (such as interfacing operating system facilities) could not be accommodated by any fixed set of built-in functions. This motivated the introduction of an external function mechanism (Farber *et al.,* 1965b) whereby users could augment SNOBOL2 by functions coded in assembly language. This facility was used extensively (Manacher, 1964; Manacher and Varian, 1964; Griswold and Varian, 1964; Flannery, 1964; Griswold and Polonksy, 1965, Griswold, 1965, 1966a; Calise, 1966; Hall and McCabe, 1967; Wilson, 1967).

Like SNOBOL, SNOBOL2 lacked any mechanism for allowing the programmer to extend the operation repertoire at the source level. More serious, perhaps, was the fact that there was not even a mechanism for programming subroutines at the source level. While a subroutine linkage mechanism could be simulated using indirect referencing and computed gotos, this technique was awkward and was not obvious to the novice. By modern standards, most SNOBOL programs were extremely unstructured.

The introduction of a mechanism for defining functions distinguished SNOBOL3 from SNOBOL2. In this case, serious design problems arose. SNOBOL and SNOBOL2 had no block structure or mechanism for the declaration of the scope of identifiers, and all labels were global. We decided to retain this "simplicity" by adding a built-in function, DEFINE, which established the existence of programmer-defined functions at run time. The mechanism itself was simple. The bodies of defined functions were written as segments of a SNOBOL3 program. When a DEFINE was executed at run time, the entry point, function name, formal arguments, and local variables were bound. This mechanism avoided the need for declarations and provided considerable run-time flexibility, since the arguments of DEFINE, including even the name of the function, could be computed at run time. By saving and restoring the values associated with the formal parameters and local variables on call and return, respectively, a form of dynamic scoping was obtained and recursion worked properly.

In the design of the defined-function mechanism, the original SNOBOL design philosophy was clearly in conflict with contemporary concepts of program structure and the growing needs of users. The flexibility of run-time definition with the possibility of redefinition and computation of function attributes had some appeal for esoteric applications, but the lack of scope declarations and locality of labels virtually precluded well-structured programs and separately compilable modules. The mechanism chosen was partly the result of adherence to the orginal SNOBOL tradition and philosophy and partly the unwillingness to become involved in more substantive issues that an alternative approach would have forced. Another factor was limited personnel resources, which certainly inhibited radical departures from previous design. Even the chosen design for defined functions was set aside until Lee Varian became available on a summer assignment. Since Dave, Ivan, and I were doing essentially all of the implementation, distribution, documentation, and maintenance, other language features that would have required a substantial implementation effort were virtually unthinkable.

2.5. SNOBOL4

Despite the addition of the function mechanisms, SNOBOL3 retained most of the original SNOBOL design: a single string data type, static specification of patterns with a limited repertoire of pattern types, and indirect referencing as the only mechanism for representing structural relationships.

Work on structural manipulation functions (Griswold and Polonsky 1965 and Griswold

1965) had shown the usefulness of including facilities for processing data structures in a string-based language. Other inadequacies of SNOBOL3 were also apparent, notably the static, limited range of pattern specification and particularly the absence of a mechanism for specifying alternative matches.

The solutions to these problems were not so evident. While there were many suggestions, including a multitude of specific data structures and a variety of syntactic elaborations for pattern specifications, the unification needed for good language design was lacking. For my part, I resisted further embellishments to SNOBOL3. In addition, SNOBOL3 generally satisfied most of the users' needs and there was not the pressure to go to a new language that there had been in the transition from SNOBOL to SNOBOL2.

As mentioned in Section 1.8, the pressure eventually came from another source—the impending transition to third-generation hardware. The possibility of new computers compounded our earlier concerns with implementations of SNOBOL and SNOBOL3 done outside BTL. These independent implementations had proved difficult because of lack of previous consideration of machine independence and because the only implementation information was the assembly-language listings of the programs. We began to see the basis for a portable implementation in the extension of McIlroy's string manipulation macros to a complete set of machine-independent assembly-language operations.

During this period, the idea came that satisfied my reservations about the design of a new language—the concept of patterns as data objects that could be built, combined, and manipulated dynamically as opposed to the static pattern specification of SNOBOL3.

While SNOBOL introduced a new, simple string language and SNOBOL2 and SNOBOL3 fleshed out this design, SNOBOL4 departed radically from earlier work. Much of the simplicity of SNOBOL3 was abandoned for greater range and more powerful features. The semantic content of SNOBOL4 was substantially greater than that of SNOBOL3. While much of the early philosophy of flexibility was expanded, SNOBOL4 became a general-purpose language where SNOBOL3 had been a string manipulation language. The rationale for this change is found in the evolving sophistication of both the users and the designers. In a sense, it was an inevitable consequence of professional development and the interest in exploring new issues.

The issue of compatibility with previous languages was first seriously raised in the design of SNOBOL4. Except for a few minor syntactic changes, SNOBOL2 and SNOBOL3 were upward compatible with SNOBOL. There was concern that substantial changes in syntax for SNOBOL4 would make SNOBOL3 programs obsolete. We felt, however, that in order to realize the potential of new ideas, substantial changes were needed and that it would be best to make a clean break, regardless of the impact on SNOBOL3 programmers. The attempt to maintain upward compatibility in the progression from COMIT to COMIT II (Yngve, 1972) provided us with an example of the inhibiting effects of the alternative choice.

However, features of SNOBOL3, except those specifically marked for redesign, were not critically examined for modification or deletion. For example, indirect referencing was included in SNOBOL4 without much thought, despite the fact that its primary justification (representation of structural relationships) no longer applied with the introduction of arrays and defined data objects in SNOBOL4. Similarly, the lack of declarations persisted, even though the variety of data types that had been introduced would have made type declarations meaningful. Defined functions in the style of SNOBOL3 were also retained despite the otherwise radical departure of SNOBOL4 from SNOBOL3.

The computing environment at BTL until this time had been entirely batch oriented and we had not given any consideration to operation in an interactive environment, although there was beginning to be local use of outside time-sharing services. Since MULTICS was slated to replace the batch operation with a BTL-wide time-sharing facility, language features for interactive computing might have been given major consideration. I recall, however, that we gave relatively little attention to this issue. We were influenced by the opinion of local users of time sharing who placed more importance on run-time capabilities than on interactive compiling (Sinowitz, 1966).

The main attributes of SNOBOL4 that deserve mention are:

1. The multitude of data types.
2. Patterns as data objects with a large variety of pattern types.
3. Data structures, including arrays, tables, and defined (record-type) objects.
4. Run-time compilation.
5. Unevaluated expressions.

The need for more than one data type was a consequence of patterns as data objects. The inclusion of other data types followed naturally, but slowly. The gradual addition of data types characterizes the evolutionary development of the design of SNOBOL4. SNOBOL4 started with three data types: strings, integers, and patterns. In late 1966, arrays and defined data objects were added. Real numbers, code, and names were added in 1967, unevaluated expressions were added in mid-1968, and tables in mid-1969.

The introduction of data types such as integers and real numbers raised the issue of coercion, the automatic conversion of the data type to suit the context. We viewed coercion together with the absence of declarations as an important aspect of ease of use. Thus a string representing an integer could be read in and used in arithmetic contexts without specification on the part of the programmer. Mixed-mode arithmetic and other polymorphic operations followed naturally from this philosophy.

Patterns as data objects represented a major design change. Previously each type of pattern was represented by a different syntactic notation and each pattern had to be explicitly written in line at the place where it was used. The addition of new pattern types in this scheme would have required a proliferation of syntax. Furthermore, the requirement for statically specified, in-line patterns placed practical limitations on their complexity. With patterns as data objects, however, an unlimited number of pattern types was possible without additional syntax. Built-in patterns were included as the initial values of selected identifiers and a repertoire of pattern-valued functions was provided as a means of constructing more complex patterns. Thus patterns could be built incrementally, reducing the complexity needed at each step, and the same pattern could be used wherever needed without the user having to duplicate its construction.

Data structures were significant in providing a natural method of organizing data. In the spirit of SNOBOL, SNOBOL4 arrays were designed so that they were created at run time with dimensionality and size that could be computed. The decision to treat arrays as objects with a distinct data type allowed passing arrays as values and treating them like other program objects. Again in the spirit of SNOBOL, there were no type declarations for arrays and hence they were heterogeneous.

Defined, record-type data objects were added to provide a mechanism whereby the user could create data structures. This method was motivated by the opinion that no number of specific built-in data types such as lists, trees, and stacks, could satisfy all user needs. Thus the philosophy was to provide a means whereby the user could construct any kind of data structure and define operations on it.

Tables, which provided a kind of associative data structure, had been suggested a number of times, notably by Doug McIlroy and Mike Shapiro. It was Doug's persistence that resulted in their addition to SNOBOL4 in mid-1969, at a very late stage in the development of SNOBOL4 and at a time when there were very few remaining personnel resources for additional changes. Doug commented, as I recall, that tables seemed like a natural thing to have in a language such as SNOBOL4, since many of the applications of SNOBOL4 involved the need for operating on symbol tables at the source-language level. This one instance of outside influence, which proved to be very beneficial, stands out in my mind, since most other issues of language design were raised and decided within the project group.

The strong influence of a flexible, machine-independent implementation is shown in run-time compilation and unevaluated expressions. The interest in run-time compilation dates back to the influence of SCL, which not only had run-time compilation, but in fact routinely required its use. SNOBOL was designed with the idea of run-time compilation, in which labels were treated as variables that had their associated statements as values. The idea was that if a new value was assigned to a variable that occurred as a label, this new value would be considered as a string representing a statement and consequently compiled. While the treatment of labels as variables was supported, compilation of newly assigned values was not. As a result, if a label was accidentally used as a variable in a program, subsequent execution of the statement corresponding to that label produced the error message "RECOMPILE NOT ENABLED" (which soon became infamous).

SNOBOL2 and SNOBOL3 did not attempt run-time compilation, but the idea was not forgotten. In the design of SNOBOL4, the issue of run-time compilation was again raised, but a method of handling it still was not evident (the SNOBOL method was clearly unsatisfactory, since an accidental use of a label as a variable, possibly depending on data, could destroy a program). It was the implementation of SNOBOL4 that eventually suggested the design of run-time compilation.

To provide machine independence, portability, and flexibility, the implementation was designed around the generalization of McIlroy's string macros as a hypothetical assembly language for an abstract machine (Griswold, 1972a, 1976a). To achieve uniformity, all data were represented in terms of *descriptors,* the "word" in this abstract machine. Each SNOBOL4 data object was represented by a descriptor, either containing the datum or a pointer to it. An array, for example, consisted of a descriptor pointing to a block of descriptors, each of which represented an element of the array. Code compiled for a SNOBOL4 program also consisted of a block of descriptors. The idea for run-time compilation came as a result of the observation that a block of code could be treated as a source-language data object merely by having a descriptor point to it. It was a simple matter to add a function that would call the compiler at run time to convert a string representing a sequence of SNOBOL4 statements into a block of code, thus augmenting the original source-language program. In fact, it took just two days from the inception of the idea until run-time compilation was available in SNOBOL4.

An essential component for the practicality of this feature was the availability of the compiler during program execution. This was the consequence of environmental factors and the desire for a portable implementation. In the first place, the compiler was small (since SNOBOL4 has few compile-time operations and the interpretive implementation avoided the need for a bulky code generator or optimizer). As a result, there was not a great motivation to segment the implementation into a compilation component followed by an execution component. In the second place, the desire for a portable system discouraged an organization that required linkage between separate segments, overlays, and the like. Thus the compiler was just "there," which turned out not only to be handy, but also actually to make run-time compilation conceivable.

One concern from the initial SNOBOL design was dynamic components in patterns. The need for such a feature is typified by a specification such as locating two occurrences of the same character in a string. In SNOBOL this was handled in a rather ad hoc fashion by "back-referencing" identifiers that had values assigned earlier in a match. A more general problem, however, lies in recursive definitions such as those found in production grammars for languages.

The solution to these problems in SNOBOL4 first came in the form of "deferred evaluation," in which a variable could be flagged so that its value was not fetched until it was encountered during pattern matching. Thus a pattern could contain a deferred reference to itself, producing the effect of a recursive definition. While this scheme solved some of the problems related to the need for dynamic evaluation during pattern matching, it did not solve the general problem.

Again the implementation suggested a better mechanism. Since expressions were compiled into sequences of descriptors within code blocks, a descriptor pointing to the code for an expression could also be a source-language data object. As a result any expression could be left "unevaluated" by providing an operator that simply returned a pointer to the appropriate position in the code and then skipped over the code instead of executing it. Subsequent evaluation of the code could then be accomplished by temporarily changing the position for execution to the previously unevaluated code. When appearing in patterns, such unevaluated expressions were evaluated during pattern matching, which provided the same facility as deferred evaluation. Since any expression could be left unevaluated, however, there was the possibility for performing any arbitrary computation during pattern matching. With this feature, all the theoretical limitations of pattern matching were removed. Not only was there a natural isomorphism between production grammars and SNOBOL4 patterns (Griswold, 1975a, pp. 7–12, 233–234), but context sensitivity and Turing grammars could be represented within SNOBOL4 patterns.

Experimentation was one consequence of the evolutionary development of SNOBOL4 and especially the continuing design with the availability of a flexible implementation. It was easy to try out design ideas in practice and to modify or discard them on the basis of actual use. While there were certainly ideas that were tried and discarded, most experimental features were, in fact, retained in some form. This method of language development was largely responsible for the large semantic size of SNOBOL4 compared with the earlier SNOBOL languages

Most features suggested for SNOBOL4 were implemented. Among suggestions that were not implemented were some cosmetic improvements, such as a program cross-reference listing, which was implemented experimentally but was never incorporated into the official version, and structure dumps, which have since been incorporated, after a fashion, in SPITBOL (Dewar, 1971) and SITBOL (Gimpel, 1974c).

Ralph E. Griswold

2.6. Language Definition

Definition of the SNOBOL languages was always treated informally. The earliest documentation of SNOBOL included a BNF grammar describing the syntax, but the semantics were dealt with in an informal manner (Griswold, 1963a). The first published paper on SNOBOL treated the syntax informally as well (Farber *et al.*, 1964a). This informality continued with SNOBOL2 and SNOBOL3 (Farber *et al.*, 1966).

With SNOBOL4, more care was given to the definition of the syntax. Here the "LSD" notation originally used by IBM for describing the syntax for PL/I was applied (IBM, 1970, pp. 241–242). Since SNOBOL4 itself provides a notation for describing syntax, it is not surprising that SNOBOL4 has been used to describe its own syntax (Griswold, 1966; Griswold *et al.*, Polonsky, 1971, pp. 226–229). The idea of enriching BNF-style syntax description systems by adding constructions in the style of SNOBOL4 appears in Griswold (1972a, pp. 261–264).

Language semantics were always treated casually by the designers of SNOBOL. It has been a long-standing joke that the only real description of the formal semantics of SNOBOL4 is contained in the program listing of the SIL implementation (Griswold, 1976b). Despite the difficulties posed by SNOBOL4's dynamic characteristics, work has been done by others on more formal approaches to its semantics (Herriot, 1973a,b, 1974; Mickel, 1973; Tennent, 1973; Stewart, 1975).

2.7. Standardization

Until SNOBOL4, there was no serious consideration of standardization. In fact there was a conscious decision to discourage both standardization and control by user groups. However, dialects and variant implementations of SNOBOL3 done outside our group were posing significant problems for users and the question of standardization for SNOBOL4 was considered. As a matter of philosophy, we felt that SNOBOL was a living language and that change and experimentation were more beneficial than constraint and standardization. The machine-readable source was freely distributed to encourage experimentation. In fact, standardization would have been impractical in any event, since there was no mechanism to control or prevent the development of independent implementations or language variants.

However, the SIL implementation imposed de facto standardization on SNOBOL4 that exceeded most of the deliberate standardization attempts. SIL implementations of SNOBOL4 are more nearly compatible than those of most other generally available programming languages.

3. A Posteriori Evaluation

3.1. Meeting of Objectives

With the evolution of SNOBOL, SNOBOL2, SNOBOL3, and SNOBOL4, the original objective of developing a tool for string manipulation gradually broadened to include a wider range of non-numeric applications. The desire to provide a tool for our own research became more a desire to provide a tool for a large community of users and to make contributions to the design and implementation of programming languages.

In retrospect, the original objectives were greatly exceeded, but the areas of application for SNOBOL4 (the only one of the SNOBOL languages now in significant use) are substantially different from those originally anticipated. For example, during the development of SNOBOL, the designers gave no thought to potential uses for document formatting or for computing in the humanities, although these have become some of the most significant applications of SNOBOL4 (Griswold, 1977b). While SNOBOL has had some applications in formula manipulation (Bailey *et al.*, 1969; Rodgers, 1966; Roosen-Runge, 1967), the problem that provided the initial motivation for the development of the new language, it has never enjoyed significant popularity in this area. Similarly, use of SNOBOL as a compiler-writing tool was envisioned (Farber, 1963a), but the suitability of SNOBOL4 in this area is at best controversial (Dunn, 1973; Hanson, 1973; Gimpel, 1976, pp. 406, 411–432; Wetherell, 1978, p. 146). In fact SNOBOL4 is not now widely used for implementing production compilers.

For the areas in which SNOBOL4 has proved useful, the users generally like SNOBOL4 and feel that it meets its objectives (as they perceive them). SNOBOL4, like its predecessors, is the kind of language that has its adherents and ardent supporters (as well as its detractors). It is similar to APL in this respect, although the feelings about SNOBOL4 generally are not as strong as those about APL.

It is interesting to note that not all users greeted the increased capacity of SNOBOL2, SNOBOL3, and SNOBOL4 with enthusiasm. Some preferred the simplicity of the original SNOBOL, and SNOBOL4 was resisted by some experienced programmers despite the additional power it provided (Uhr, 1968; McIlroy, 1977).

The objectives of the designers of the SNOBOL languages have not always been well understood. In my opinion, the computing community as a whole has little accurate knowledge of SNOBOL and treats it more by hearsay than by actual knowledge. While there is a substantial amount of available material on the SNOBOL languages (Griswold, 1977b), effort is required to extract the real attributes of SNOBOL4. In general, one must use SNOBOL4 to understand it; it does not come naturally as yet another "algebraic" language might to a FORTRAN or PL/I user. Similarly, many persons are unaware of the substantial differences between SNOBOL and SNOBOL4. Here a decision to go to an entirely new name might have avoided the assumption that all the SNOBOL languages were similar.

User acceptance has been strongly influenced by the ready availability of the SNOBOL languages. From the earliest development, SNOBOL was distributed without charge or restriction of use to anyone interested in it. Its source code was provided without restriction, which facilitated its installation. For the most part, documentation and program material were distributed by BTL without charge. An interested person had only to supply a tape. Thus individuals and organizations with limited financial resources were able to get the programs. With SNOBOL4 the portable implementation was made freely available, and technical support was provided for implementation on a variety of machines. The exchange of program material for the portable implementation of SNOBOL4 in return for effort freely given by implementors on other machines was essential, especially in the absence of vendor support or a commercial base. It is my opinion that this free distribution and open attitude toward release of information was, in fact, *essential* to the acceptance and success of SNOBOL. If SNOBOL had been protected, if its distribution had been controlled, or if a charge had been made for the program material, it is likely that SNOBOL would have remained one of the many interesting, but noninfluential ideas of computer science. The use and influence of COMIT, for example, was probably substantially diminished by tight control over release of the source program. For an interesting debate of the issue of unrestricted distribution, see Galler (1968) and Mooers (1968).

3.2. Contributions of the Languages

SNOBOL is responsible, primarily, for introducing to high-level languages the idea of the string of characters as a single data object rather than as a workspace or an array of characters. This is a conceptual matter, and one of considerable importance, since the treatment of a varying length string as a single data object permits a global view of string processing that character aggregates inhibit.

One of the most formidable design problems faced by the architects of the SNOBOL languages, particularly at the beginning, was the implementation of storage management for a large number of varying length strings. However, the freedom that string data objects provide the programmer is enormous. Compare the 127 shelves of COMIT and the 64 possible string variables and two data buffers of SCL to SNOBOL, where strings were simply data objects in the sense that integers are data objects in FORTRAN.

SNOBOL's most obvious specific contribution is a viable high-level approach to string analysis through pattern matching. Where COMIT and SCL introduced pattern-matching features that were intriguing but of limited practical use, SNOBOL, and SNOBOL4 in particular, have made this tool generally well known and widely used.

More personally, I view the best points of SNOBOL to be the ease of use and its "comfortable feeling." It is somewhat like an old shoe. SNOBOL programmers characterize it as a hospitable, friendly language that allows much to be accomplished quickly and easily. Its "one-line" programs for problems such as character-code conversion and reformatting data cards are famous.

Some of the esoteric features in SNOBOL4 have proved valuable and have allowed comparatively easy treatment of otherwise intractable problems. Run-time compilation, for example, permits SNOBOL4 code to be imbedded in data, thus allowing easy run-time extension of programs such as document processors (Griswold, 1975a, pp. 189–191, 270; Anderson and Griswold, 1976; Conrow, 1977). Similarly, the capability to redefine any built-in SNOBOL4 operator allows extensions and experimental simulation of more advanced language features (Griswold, 1975a, pp. 26–30, 115, 256–257). This capability was used by John Doyle to simulate extensions to pattern matching in SNOBOL4 (Doyle, 1975).

As SNOBOL progressed to SNOBOL2, SNOBOL3, and then SNOBOL4, I applied one personal benchmark: could problems be solved by the new language that were not practical with the old one? In each case, the answer was yes. There are two aspects to this measure. In some cases, ease of programming made the solution feasible in terms of the effort or time required. As Kernighan and Plauger (1976, p. 84) remark, "many jobs will not get done at all unless they can be done quickly." In other cases, solutions to problems that were formerly intractable or unthinkable because of the degree of programming difficulty became reasonable and attractive. This latter situation applies particularly to researchers in areas such as the humanities, where sophisticated programming skills are less common.

3.2.1. Other Implementations

A measure of the importance of SNOBOL is given by the number of implementations carried on outside BTL. Many other persons and groups decided to implement various versions of SNOBOL. One of the earliest implementations was an "ALGOLized" version of SNOBOL for a Soviet computer (Kostalansky, 1967; Lavrov, 1968). Parallel to the development of SNOBOL2 and SNOBOL3, there were several implementations motivated both by the need for a SNOBOL language on machines other than the IBM 7090/94 and by an interest in experimentation with extensions and changes. The first implementations were completed for the RCA 601 (Simon and Walters, 1964), the PDP-6 (Guard, 1967), the Burroughs 5500, the CDC 3600, the SDS 930 (Lampson, 1966; Kain and Bailey, 1967), the IBM 360 (Madnick, 1966), and the IBM 1620 (Wilson, 1966). Many stories have been told about the 1620 implementation. It was a pure interpreter, constantly reprocessing the source program text. The call of a built-in function is said to have taken 40 seconds and programs were (naturally) frequently left to run overnight. Nonetheless, this implementation apparently was satisfactory and is remembered with some fondness by its users.

With SNOBOL4, there was even more implementation activity by other groups. This activity took two forms: implementations of the portable SIL system (which produced standard SNOBOL4 implementations) and independent implementations with various goals (which produced various dialects and language variants). The SIL system has attracted implementors for two reasons: the desire for SNOBOL4 on a specific computer for which it was not available, and the interest in the implementation of portable software in its own right.

As mentioned in Section 1.9, the first transporting of the SIL implementation of SNOBOL4 was done by Jim, Ivan, and myself, when we moved the IBM 7094 implementation to the IBM 360 in late 1966. In 1967 and 1968, SIL implementations were started for the CDC 6000 series (Gaines, 1968; Shapiro, 1969), the GE 635 (at the BTL Murray Hill Laboratory), the UNIVAC 1108 (Osterweil, 1970), the RCA Spectra 70, the CDC 3600, the Atlas 2 (Moody, 1972), the XDS Sigma 7 (Barker, 1973), the DEC-10 (Wade, 1970), and the Datacraft 6000 (Datacraft Corporation, 1972). All of these implementations were completed. In the process, much valuable feedback was obtained about the language and problems in the design and structure of the implementation. In all, SIL implementations have been undertaken for 40 different computers, and most have been brought to a working state. Recently even an implementation for the IMSAI 8080 has been started. In the case of some computers, several independent implementations have been done by individuals who wanted the experience of implementing portable software, even though another implementation was already available.

The relative inefficiency and large size of the SIL implementation of SNOBOL4 has challenged a number of groups to attempt more economical implementations. CAL SNOBOL approached the problem by severely subsetting SNOBOL4 to gain a dramatic performance improvement (Gaskins, 1970). SPITBOL produced the first efficient "compiler" system that implemented a reasonable approximation to the entire language, including runtime compilation (Dewar, 1971; Dewar *et al.*, 1975; Berndl, 1975). FASBOL combined subsetting with optional declarations to achieve very efficient implementations for the UNIVAC 1108 and the DEC-10 (Santos, 1971). SITBOL proved that an interpretive implementation could be a sufficiently efficient for production work (Gimpel, 1973b). SNO-

BAT combined some subsetting with new implementation techniques to produce a fast batch compiler (Silverston, 1976a,b, 1977). Most recently MACRO SPITBOL, a machine-independent and portable interpretive implementation has been developed (Dewar and McCann, 1977). This system performs better than some implementations tailored to specific machines. To date, MACRO SPITBOL has been implemented for the ICL 1900 (Dewar and McCann, 1974), the Burroughs B1700 (Morse, 1976), the DEC-10 (McCann *et al.*, 1976), the CDC 6000 series (Druseikis and Griswold, 1977), and the PDP-11, (Dewar, 1977).

In total there are some 50 implementations of SNOBOL4 currently available for different computers and operating systems (Griswold, 1978a).

3.2.2. Dialects and Extensions

These implementations resulted in numerous dialects of the language. In FASBOL, Santos added optional declarations to permit the generation of efficient code. SPITBOL added a number of built-in functions and error recovery facilities that have proved useful. SITBOL included most of the SPITBOL enhancements and added others (Gimpel, 1973c, 1974c). SITBOL is also notable for its integration with the DEC-10 operating system environment, which makes it particularly pleasant to use.

Changes to the SNOBOL4 language made in these implementations divide them into two categories. Those with substantial differences (CAL SNOBOL, FASBOL, and SNO-BAT) tend to be limited in their use because they cannot run many standard SNOBOL4 programs. On the other hand, SPITBOL, SITBOL, and MACRO SPITBOL are sufficiently compatible with the standard version of SNOBOL4 that they usually can be used to run existing programs with few if any modifications. It is interesting to note that the support of run-time compilation is an important issue here. A surprising number of "production" SNOBOL4 programs use this feature in an essential way (Griswold, 1975a, pp. 189–191, 222–224; 1975d; Anderson and Griswold, 1976; Gimpel, 1976, pp. 353–359; Conrow, 1977).

A number of significant extensions have been made to SNOBOL4. Notable are SNOBOL4B, a SIL-based extension that includes three-dimensional character "blocks" (Gimpel, 1972) and SNOBOL+, which adds pattern matching on trees (Ophir, 1974).

3.2.3. Influences on Hardware

Chai and DiGiuseppe (1965) considered issues of hardware design to support SNOBOL-like features. M. D. Shapiro (1972a,b) designed a SNOBOL machine using conventional hardware. A number of attempts have been made to microprogram SNOBOL4 or SIL (Syrett, 1971; Rosin, 1969; Rossman and Jones, 1974). So far, such attempts have had only limited success. While the B5500 and CDC STAR computers have introduced interesting string operations, the influence of SNOBOL on machine order structures is apparently tangential.

3.2.4. Use of SNOBOL4 as an Experimental Tool

As mentioned in Section 1.9, one of our motivations for developing SNOBOL4 was to have a vehicle for experimentation with programming language features. Once the project got under way, it became so overwhelming that there was little possibility for experimentation outside of the main thrust of the language. After the language reached a stable condition in 1970, some experimentation was undertaken at BTL with a SIL-based variant of

SNOBOL4 into which some speculative language features were incorporated (Griswold, 1971).

One experiment, while not speculative as a language feature, was interesting in its use of the run-time compilation facility. Users had long wanted a program cross-reference facility. Instead of implementing this directly in SIL, it was coded as a SNOBOL4 program that constructed cross-reference listings. A string corresponding to this program was then incorporated in the SIL data region. During program initialization, this string was compiled as a SNOBOL4 program segment to provide the desired facility. While the implementation of SNOBOL4 was not designed for bootstrapping, the source-language run-time compilation facility nevertheless supported this kind of process, which Jim Gimpel calls "spatial bootstrapping" (Gimpel, 1973d). Jim used a similar technique to provide a histogram facility for SITBOL (Gimpel, 1974c).

Concentrated experimental work started in 1971 at the University of Arizona to exploit SNOBOL4 as a research tool. Early work led to several additions to SNOBOL4 to extend its usefulness in this area (Griswold, 1975c). Subsequent applications led to new parameter transmission techniques (Druseikis and Griswold, 1973), high-level data structure processing facilities (Hallyburton, 1974), a linguistic interface to the SIL abstract machine (Griswold, 1975b) and novel performance measurement facilities (Ripley and Griswold, 1975).

3.3. Mistakes and Problems

3.3.1. Syntax and Control Structure

There are many things to criticize about any programming language and SNOBOL is no exception. The most controversial aspect of SNOBOL4 is its primitive syntax and lack of "modern" control structures. This is a debatable issue. SNOBOL has long been popular among nonprofessional and "novice" programmers who find the simple test-and-goto structure of SNOBOL to be much preferable to the nested control structures of languages that are more sophisticated in this respect. While the syntax and control structures of SNOBOL have been continually criticized by the more sophisticated component of the computing community, it may just be that this aspect of SNOBOL was primarily responsible for its initial acceptance and its practical usefulness.

At the present time, such a syntax and control structure would be "socially unacceptable" in the design of a new language. With the maturation of the programming community, the time for a SNOBOL-style syntax may be past; it certainly is not a necessity. Alternatives have been suggested (Griswold, 1974; Lindsay, 1975; Tamir, 1974) and SL5 provides an integration of the SNOBOL-style signaling mechanism with conventional control structures (Griswold and Hanson, 1977).

A less controversial problem is the defined function mechanism of SNOBOL4, which separates the defining statement from the procedure body, provides no static specification to delimit the procedure body, and does not provide scoping for labels. SNOBOL4 programmers "get around" these problems, but not happily (Abrahams, 1974). In retrospect, this aspect of SNOBOL4 seems to be an out-and-out mistake.

A few minor aspects of the syntax of SNOBOL have caused problems all out of proportion to their apparent significance. The use of blanks is the most notable of these problems. It is debatable whether the absence of a specific operator for concatenation was the

Ralph E. Griswold

best choice. While it is convenient to write strings to be concatenated with only separating blanks, many programmers find that the resulting requirement for blanks to surround infix operators is a compensating inconvenience. Many program errors result from the failure to provide mandatory blanks and the absence of a concatenation operator makes programs harder to read. The dual use of blanks to separate labels and gotos from the rest of statements and to separate the subject from the pattern compounds the problem. If I were to do it over again, I would, at least, provide explicit operators for concatenation and pattern matching, although others disagree on this point (McIlroy, 1977).

The fact that assignment and pattern matching are statements, not expressions, is a curious anomaly that can be traced to the earliest design considerations where the subject as a focus of attention was held to be of primary importance. The burden of these restrictions is not as great as it would be if SNOBOL had more sophisticated control structures. Most programmers are not aware of the effects of these limitations on their programming styles. Later dialects such as SITBOL and MACRO SPITBOL have corrected these mistakes.

As might be expected, several preprocessors have been written to convert more conventional control structures into standard SNOBOL4 (Croff, 1974; Beyer, 1976; Hanson, 1977b; Sommerville, 1977).

3.3.2. Structures and Indirect Referencing

SNOBOL, SNOBOL2, and SNOBOL3 were hampered by the single string data type, which made arithmetic awkward (and inefficient) and required programmers to simulate structures by encoding them as strings or producing awkward and "dangerous" pointer networks using indirect referencing. SNOBOL4 corrected these problems with a vengeance, introducing nine built-in data types and the ability to create the effect of others by using defined data objects.

Indirect referencing itself is hard to understand, error-prone, and frequently misused. While indirect referencing was valuable in SNOBOL, SNOBOL2, and SNOBOL3 in the absence of more direct ways to represent structural relationships, its continuance in SNOBOL4 was probably a mistake. With the exception of computed gotos, indirect referencing is unnecessary in SNOBOL4, since tables provide the same facility with the added capability to restrict the domain of applicable strings. By the time that tables were added, however, indirect referencing was ingrained in the language.

3.3.3. String Processing and Pattern Matching

A curiosity of SNOBOL4 is its relative lack of primitive string operations. Since pattern matching is so powerful, it is possible to do virtually anything using it. The results may be bizarre and inefficient, however. For example, SNOBOL4 does not have a primitive substring operation and pattern matching is necessary to perform even this simple operation. While SPITBOL and SITBOL rectified this defect, even these dialects lack primitives for "lexical" operations such as locating the position of a substring within a string. SL5 shows that there is no conceptual barrier to such primitives (Griswold et al., 1977).

While pattern matching is certainly the most powerful facility in SNOBOL4, it has many defects, some of which are rarely recognized. The most obvious problem lies in the heuristics used in pattern matching. These were originally introduced to avoid "futile" attempts to match (Griswold, 1972a, pp. 35–36, 126–131). The need for heuristics can be justified in theory by the observation that there are situations in which backtracking can cause pattern matching to take arbitrarily long before failing, while the failure can nonetheless be predicted, a priori, on the basis of such a simple consideration as the length of the subject. Until SNOBOL4, these heuristics were strictly an implementation matter, since they did not affect the results of program execution except possibly in the amount of time required. With the introduction of unevaluated expressions and other dynamic effects during pattern matching in SNOBOL4, heuristics became a linguistic matter. Failure to complete pattern matching because of the heuristics might cause some component with significant effects to be bypassed. This problem was "solved" by placing the heuristics under the control of a programmable switch. The heuristics remained a problem, however. They are complex and difficult to understand (even the implementors have to resort to implementation listings to resolve some of the more subtle effects). The usefulness of the heuristics is also questionable. Experiments with a representative set of programs has shown that most programs run properly with or without the heuristics and the saving in execution time is small or nonexistent. It is quite possible that the overhead of supporting the heuristics is greater than the savings that they produce. The concern over the possible consequences of backtracking appears to be unjustified in practice, and the heuristics probably should have been removed.

Less obvious problems with pattern matching lie in its overly large vocabulary, its idiosyncrasies, and its lack of generality. The strict left-to-right direction of pattern matching and the lack of a facility for moving or resetting the focus of attention within the subject without advancing to the right except as a result of successful pattern matching produces awkward and inefficient programming techniques. The absence of synthesis facilities at the level of the analysis facilities results in an asymmetry and requires string construction to be carried out at an entirely different level and frame of reference from analysis. Doyle (1975) proposed solutions to some of these problems.

In addition, although analysis produces a complete "parse" of the subject according to the pattern, the results are unavailable to the programmer except in terms of success or failure and in the identification of specifically matched substrings. Thus the structure of the parse is lost. The power of pattern matching in SNOBOL4 is therefore somewhat illusory. It is trivial to write a recognizer for any context-free grammar (Griswold 1975a, pp. 7–12, 233–234), but the corresponding parser is much more difficult and requires use of side effects and unobvious techniques (Gimpel, 1976, pp. 411–415).

Another deficiency in pattern matching is the lack of any way to write source-language procedures to perform pattern matching. While defined functions can be used to extend the repertoire of built-in functions, there is no corresponding mechanism for extending the repertoire of built-in pattern-matching procedures. An approach to solving these problems has been recently suggested (Griswold, 1975e, 1976c, e).

The fact that decomposition of strings through pattern matching operates by the side effects has always been a problem. By its nature, this mechanism is error prone and unstructured. On the other hand, string analysis, by analogy with grammatical characterizations of languages, leads naturally to deriving multiple values from a single analysis. A well-structured, uncomplicated solution to this problem remains elusive.

3.3.4. Input and Output

Input and output have always been problems in SNOBOL. Although the language constructs that perform input and output are particularly simple, there are two distinct problems: the formatting capabilities are weak, and there is no concept of files other than sequential ones. These deficiencies have restricted the use of SNOBOL4 in some cases and led to extensions in dialects such as SPITBOL.

The use of FORTRAN I/O as a specification for SNOBOL4 I/O had historical bases and was a mistake. It was chosen because FORTRAN was well known and so that implementors could use FORTRAN I/O packages instead of having to implement their own, thus enhancing portability. With advances in the state of the art, both of these concerns seem to have been misplaced. In retrospect it would have been a better choice to develop I/O specifically suitable for SNOBOL. Implementations that have departed from the FORTRAN standards have produced much more satisfactory results (Dewar, 1971; Gimpel, 1973c).

3.4. Changes and Additions

Many changes and additions to SNOBOL have been suggested, but not adopted. Most of these have been of the "junky" variety (such as a keyword &TEBAHPLA that would have contained an order-reversed copy of the alphabet). Many suggestions were made to meet specific or idiosyncratic needs. Our general attitude toward such suggestions was reserved, but they were accumulated with a mind toward abstracting the essence from apparently unrelated suggestions and producing unified improvements (Griswold, 1972b,c). For example, many suggestions were received for making specific improvements to pattern matching in SNOBOL3, but none of these was incorporated into the language. Nonetheless, a more general concept of patterns as data objects evolved. This concept subsumed all of the pattern-matching facilities of SNOBOL3, as well as the suggestions for changes, but it placed them in a conceptually simpler framework.

In summary, the general attitude was not to include specific language features, however useful they might appear, unless they fit naturally into the existing semantic framework or until a broader conceptual basis could be found. Phrased another way, the decision to include suggested features was more a matter of philosophy than pragmatism.

3.5. User Problems

Inefficiency is the problem most frequently ascribed to the SNOBOL languages, and interpretive implementations are frequently cited as the source of the problem. In fact, it is mainly language features that require run-time binding that lie at the root of most of the problems. Even "compiler" implementations such as SPITBOL (Dewar, 1971) have a significant interpretive component (Griswold, 1977a), and there are interpreters that rival the performance of such compilers (Gimpel, 1973b; Dewar and McCann, 1977).

Until SNOBOL4 there was, in fact, relatively little user concern about the efficiency of the SNOBOL languages. Despite the fact that third-generation hardware and subsequent developments have lowered the actual cost of computation considerably, increased awareness of costs and increased competition for resources resulted in more and more concern about efficiency. Thus SNOBOL4 is criticized for its inefficiency, even though it is actually substantially more efficient than SNOBOL3.

Nonetheless, the major problem that most users have had with SNOBOL4 *is* the resources that it requires. Depending on the user's environment, this may translate into cost, poor turnaround time, or the inability to run a program altogether due to storage limitations. This problem extends to the unavailability of SNOBOL4 implementations on computers with limited memories. Naïve users, in particular, tend to get into difficulty with programs that run satisfactorily on small amounts of sample data, but are totally impractical when applied to real data. Although the developers of SNOBOL4 actively discouraged its use for large problems, recommending it instead for simple, "one-shot" uses (Poage, 1977), even when the advice was received it was seldom taken. An inherent problem is often overlooked: string data simply take large amounts of space. Programs are written, for example, to keep a dictionary in core and tests are made with only a few words. The user fails to see the consequences of using the full dictionary. This problem is, of course, not specific to SNOBOL4, but it is more severe there because of the emphasis on nonnumeric data and the ease of expressing otherwise complex operations on such data.

As mentioned in Section 1.9, the SIL implementation of SNOBOL4 was not expected to be efficient. In practice, this implementation carried SNOBOL4 very close to the fine line between practicality and impracticality. In a sense, the implementation succeeded almost too well. It is efficient enough for use in some environments and for some problems. As a consequence SNOBOL4 has come into wide use. On the other hand, it is too inefficient to run production programs in most environments. If the implementation had proved too inefficient for general use, early modification to the implementation or to the language itself might have produced a significantly more efficient system. To some extent, these concerns are of more historical than current interest, since more efficient implementations, notably SPITBOL, SITBOL, and MACRO SPITBOL are coming into widespread use (Griswold, 1976d).

3.6. Implementation Problems

Because of the design philosophy, which sometimes has been expressed as "the implementor be damned," SNOBOL has presented both serious and interesting implementation problems. Briefly summarized, these are:

1. Storage management, including varying length strings, dynamic allocation, and implicit garbage collection.
2. Maintenance of a changing symbol table at run time.
3. Implicit processes, such as input, output, and tracing.
4. Pattern matching.
5. Run-time compilation.
6. Delayed bindings, including redefinition of functions and operators at run time.

In addition, some language features have a disproportionate effect on implementation. For example, the ability to redefine any built-in operator at run time forces implementation techniques that impose a substantial execution overhead. The unevaluated expression operator provides a particularly glaring example. Since this operator must leave its operand unevaluated and any operation can be made synonymous with it at run time, in the SIL implementation all operations are handled in prefix mode. By simply exempting this operator from redefinition, and treating it specially during compilation, SITBOL allows more efficient suffix evaluation to be used in place of prefix evaluation (Griswold, 1977a). This exemption is certainly a minor concession of design to implementation effi-

Ralph E. Griswold

ciency. Interestingly, however, prefix evaluation in SNOBOL4 preceded the introduction of unevaluated expressions and, in fact, it was the existence of prefix code that suggested unevaluated expressions.

Related issues and their treatment constitute a large and complex subject, which is discussed elsewhere in detail (Griswold, 1972a, 1977a).

3.7. Tradeoffs and Compromises

Very few of the traditional tradeoffs and compromises in language design were made for SNOBOL. By the nature of the design philosophy, few conscious linguistic concessions were made to implementation difficulties or efficiency. Most concessions, in fact, were made because of limited personnel resources and because of pressure (both from within and without the development group) to produce systems that could be used. Certainly several interesting areas for language extension went unexplored for lack of time and resources.

4. Implications for Current and Future Languages

4.1. Influences on Other Languages

The SNOBOL languages have had little apparent direct effect on the mainstream of programming language development. This lack of direct influence is probably a necessary consequence of the direction SNOBOL has taken, which is deliberately contrary to the mainstream. Most of the direct influence has been reflected in offshoots and dialects of existing languages.

String processing extensions to FORTRAN represent the most prevalent influence of the basic string operations and pattern matching (Jessup, 1966; Puckett and Farlow, 1966; Zweig, 1970; Gimpel, 1970; Shapiro, 1970; Baron and Golini, 1970; Hanson, 1974). Similar proposals have been made for PL/I (Rosin, 1967), ALGOL 60 (Storm, 1968), and ALGOL 68 (Dewar, 1975a).

The obvious relationship between SNOBOL and macro processing has resulted in the use of SNOBOL-style pattern matching in a number of macro processors (Waite, 1967, 1969; Kagan, 1972; Brown, 1974; Wilson, 1975).

Where there has been official acceptance of SNOBOL-like features in major languages, it has been grudging. PL/I is an example. The designs of SNOBOL4 and PL/I were contemporaneous, although the mechanics of the designs were very different. While SNOBOL, SNOBOL2, and SNOBOL3 had for several years supported true varying length strings, the designers of PL/I were reluctant to accept this concept presumably because of implementation considerations. I particularly recall Dave Farber and Doug McIlroy urging that string length be handled implicitly in PL/I but to no avail (although the EPL dialect of PL/I (Cambridge Information Systems Laboratory, 1968) did dynamically allocate varying strings). Similarly, Bob Rosin carried on an early campaign for simple string matching functions (Rosin, 1967), but only recently has something of this kind been added in the form of AFTER and BEFORE (American National Standards Institute, 1976, pp. 318, 322). COBOL also has expanded its earlier EXAMINE facility to a more powerful INSPECT statement, along with STRING and UNSTRING statements for decomposition and concatenation (American National Standards Institute, 1974, Ch. II, pp. 68–73, 86–88, 91–94).

The influence of SNOBOL features on dialects and divergent language developments has been more marked, if less influential. The SNOBOL concept of patterns has been most significant. Notable examples occur in PL/I (Pfeffer and Furtado, 1973) and LISP (Smith and Enea, 1973; Tesler *et al.*, 1973).

Incorporation of SNOBOL features or philosophy into other language contexts has led to more radical departures for the conventional programming languages. APLBOL, for example, provides an amalgamation of APL and SNOBOL (Leichter, 1976). ESP3 extends the concept of SNOBOL4 pattern matching to three-dimensional objects (Shapiro, 1976; Shapiro and Baron, 1977).

Although SNOBOL has never enjoyed general popularity in the AI community, it has had an indirect, although evident, influence on AI languages such as 1.pak and 2.pak (Mylopoulos *et al.*, 1973; Melli, 1974). The usefulness of a simple SNOBOL-like language for AI work is evident in EASEy (Uhr, 1974).

Even the mainstream of SNOBOL development is not entirely dead. Development of a better understanding of pattern matching (Druseikis and Doyle, 1974; Griswold, 1975e) has led to the development of SL5 (*SNOBOL Language 5*) in the spirit of SNOBOL but specifically designed for research rather than for general use (Griswold *et al.*, 1977; Griswold, 1976c,e).

An important influence of SNOBOL has been its "orthogonality" to the mainstream of programming language development. Where there has been a movement for strong typing, SNOBOL has offered a "typeless" alternative. Where concern over program structure and verification has led to the condemnation of a number of "harmful" features and encouraged a "police-state" school of programming, SNOBOL has provided ease of programming and freedom from constraints. This is not to say that the current concern with structured programming is misplaced, but rather that there are a variety of concerns that make different alternatives appropriate in different situations.

SNOBOL has shown that language features, once thought to be impractical because of implementation considerations, are in fact both practical and valuable. Specifically, SNOBOL has led to the development of implementation techniques to meet challenges of language features. In short, as a "maverick," SNOBOL has offered an alternative and has led many persons to think of possibilities that might not have been considered otherwise.

In the area of pattern matching, SNOBOL has directed attention toward backtrack control structures (most notably in AI languages) and to the implementation of such features (Druseikis and Doyle, 1974). The resulting interest in the use of coroutine mechanisms for implementing search and backtracking algorithms (Griswold, 1976f; Hanson, 1976b; Hanson and Griswold, 1978) may have substantial future impact on programming language design.

Of all the features of SNOBOL4, one of the most important in practice has proved to be the table data type, which provides at the source level a feature similar to the internal symbol tables of assemblers and compilers. By eliminating the need for the programmer to handle all the tedious and error-prone details of symbol tables at the source-language level, SNOBOL4 has provided a way in which symbol table techniques can be used freely and in which concise, simple programs can be written where the programming burden would otherwise be unsupportable (Griswold, 1975a, pp. 42–43, 194–197). Probably no other single feature of SNOBOL4 has made programming simpler or opened the door to more application areas. I consider tables to be a prime candidate for inclusion in new high-level languages.

4.2. Influence on Implementation Techniques

The problems inherent in the efficient implementation of SNOBOL-like languages have stimulated the development of new techniques and have had the indirect effect of liberating the design of programming languages from many of the constraints formerly attributable to problems of implementation and efficiency. For example, automatic storage management was considered to be a major implementation problem at the time SNOBOL was designed. Now, due at least in part to SNOBOL, the concern is no longer a major issue (Griswold, 1972a, Hanson, 1977a).

Efficient interpretive systems and particularly the handling of run-time bindings have been considerably developed as a result of SNOBOL4 implementations (Gimpel, 1973b; Dewar, 1975b; Dewar and McCann, 1977). A number of other interesting implementation techniques have been developed (Griswold, 1972a, 1977a; Tye, 1972; Gimpel, 1973b, 1974b; Druseikis and Doyle, 1974; Sears, 1974, Hanson, 1976a; Silverston, 1976b).

4.3. Influences on Theoretical Work

While SNOBOL by its very nature is beyond the realm of the verificationists, it has posed some interesting problems in the description of formal semantics (Herriot, 1973a,b, 1974; Mickel, 1973; Pagan, 1978; Tennent, 1973). Most theoretical work has concentrated on the description of patterns and pattern matching (Gimpel, 1973a, 1975; Goyer, 1973; Tennent, 1973; Stewart, 1975; Fleck, 1977), their implementation (Goyer, 1973; Druseikis and Doyle, 1974), and on the relationships between patterns and data structures (Fleck, 1971; Fleck and Liu, 1973).

4.4. Advice from the Experience of SNOBOL

Other language designers should look to the success and durability of a language that is as contrary as SNOBOL for possible future directions. In my opinion, programming language development has a long way to go before it achieves ''perfection''—if that is meaningful, possible, desirable, or even definable. There is too much of a tendency to get caught up with the fad of the moment, whether it is goto-less programming, FORTRAN preprocessors for structured programming, or data abstraction. Someone needs to look at alternatives, to consider unpopular views, and perhaps, particularly, to seek unconventional approaches. SNOBOL serves as an example of the success of such an endeavor.

4.5. The Long-Range Future of SNOBOL

The long-range future of SNOBOL depends on several issues. For example, SNOBOL, like FORTRAN, might prove indestructible simply because of the extent of its acceptance, regardless of the availability of better languages. I regard that as possible but unlikely. It is likely that a new language will be developed that both shares the philosophy of SNOBOL and is also better at doing the things SNOBOL was designed to do. After all, SNOBOL3 replaced SNOBOL and SNOBOL4 has virtually replaced SNOBOL3.

It is also possible that the current interest (or fad) for structured programming will eventually erode the basis of support of SNOBOL so that it will gradually fall into disuse. There is little evidence that this is happening at the present and I regard this future possibility as unlikely.

Here it is worthwhile to consider again the major reason for the success of SNOBOL— its availability. There have been many "good" programming languages that have been designed but not implemented. Others have been implemented but not made generally available. Furthermore there are generally available languages that are not maintained or supported. SNOBOL is in the small class of nonvendor-supported languages that are available on a wide variety of machines and that are well documented and consistently supported (Griswold, 1978a). It is my personal opinion that it was the general availability of SNOBOL processors and language documentation that were responsible, more than any other factor, for SNOBOL's initial success. With the transition to SNOBOL4, the wide range of readily available SIL implementations further extended SNOBOL's use. Efficient implementations of SNOBOL4, most notably SPITBOL, significantly enlarged its audience. The increasing availability of smaller computers now raises the question of the availability of SNOBOL processors to the growing ranks of programmers. The recent development of implementations of SNOBOL4 for the PDP-11 (Dewar, 1977; Dalgleish, 1977) and work on implementations for other mid-range machines may be an important determining factor in the durability of SNOBOL4.

ACKNOWLEDGMENTS

The material generously supplied to me by a number of persons over a period of years has proved immensely valuable in the preparation of the paper. The questions, comments, suggestions, and critical reviews of this paper by Dave Farber, Dave Hanson, Doug McIlroy, Jim Poage, Ivan Polonsky, Bob Rosin, Jean Sammet, Mike Shapiro, and Hank Tropp have been invaluable. I am, of course, solely responsible for errors of omission and commission. I am indebted most of all to my wife, Madge. She has helped with all aspects of the development of the paper: as a historian, editor, critic, organizer, and keyboarder. Most of all she has provided constant support and encouragement during the entire project.

REFERENCES

Abrahams, P. W. (1974). Improving the control structure of SNOBOL4. *SIGPLAN NOTICES* **9**(5): 10–12.

American National Standards Institute (1974). *American National Standard Programming Language COBOL*, ANSI X3.23-1974, New York.

American National Standards Institute (1976). *American National Standard Programming Language PL/I*, ANSI X3.53-1976, New York.

Anderson, R. O., and Griswold, R. E. (1976) February 18. *ACOLYTE; A Document Formatting Program.* Tucson, Arizona: University of Arizona, Department of Computer Science. SNOBOL4 Project Doc. S4PD11b.

Bailey, F. N., Brann, J., and Kain, R. Y. (1969) August 10. *Algebra I Users Reference Manual.* Minneapolis, Minnesota: University of Minnesota. Department of Electrical Engineering.

Barber, C. L. R. (1973) December 10. *SNOBOL4 Version 3.7.* El Segundo, California: XDS User's Group. Program Library Catalog Number 890823-11A00.

Baron, R. J., and Golini, J. (1970) September. *Strings: Some FORTRAN Callable String Processing Routines* (Unpublished technical report). Iowa City, Iowa: University of Iowa, Department of Computer Science.

Berndl, W. (1975) October. *An Analysis of the SPITBOL System.* Toronto, Ontario: Department of Computer Science, University of Toronto. Technical Report No. 85.

Beyer, T. (1976) April 30. *SNECS.* Letter to R. E. Griswold.

Brown, P. J. (1974) November. *Towards More General String Manipulation—SNOBOL4 Compared With ML/I* (Unpublished technical report). Canterbury, England: University of Kent at Canterbury.

Ralph E. Griswold

Calise, M. F. (1966) February 11. *Disk Functions for SNOBOL3.* (Unpublished internal memorandum). Holmdel, New Jersey: Bell Laboratories.

Cambridge Information Systems Laboratory (1968) April. *ELP Users' Reference Manual.* Cambridge, Massachusetts.

Chai, D., and DiGiuseppe, J. (1965) May. *A Study of System Design Considerations in Computers for Symbol Manipulation.* Ann Arbor, Michigan: University of Michigan, Department of Electrical Engineering. Report No. 05635-1-F.

Conrow, K. (1977). A FAMULUS post-processor. *SIGDOC Newsletter* **4**(3): 7–8.

Corbató, F. J., and Vyssotsky, V. A. (1965). Introduction and overview of the MULTICS system. In *AFIPS Conference Proceedings, Fall Joint Computer Conference,* pp. 185–196. Washington, D.C.: Spartan Books.

Corbató, F. J., *et al.* (1963). *The Compatible Time-Sharing System: A Programmer's Guide.* Cambridge, Massachusetts: MIT Press.

Croff, D. L. (1974) November. *SNOFLEX Handbook* (unpublished technical report). Eugene, Oregon: University of Oregon, Department of Computer Science.

Dalgleish, R. (1977) September 15. Letter to R. E. Griswold.

Datacraft Corporation (1972) July. *Series 6000 SNOBOL4 General Specification.* Fort Lauderdale, Florida.

Dewar, C. E. S. (1977). *RE: Release of SPITBOL-11* Chicago, Illinois: Dewar Information Systems Corporation.

Dewar, R. B. K. (1971) February 12. *SPITBOL Version 2.0* (SNOBOL4 Project Document S4D23). Chicago, Illinois: Illinois Institute of Technology.

Dewar, R. B. K. (1975a). *String Processing in ALGOL-68* (Unpublished technical report). Chicago, Illinois: Illinois Institute of Technology.

Dewar, R. B. K. (1975b). Indirect threaded code. *Communications of the ACM* **18**(6): 330–331.

Dewar, R. B. K., and McCann, A. P. (1974) December. *1900 SPITBOL.* Leeds, England: University of Leeds, Centre for Computer Studies. Technical Report No. 55.

Dewar, R. B. K., and McCann, A. P. (1977). Macro SPITBOL—a SNOBOL4 compiler. *Software—Practice and Experience* **7**: 95–113.

Dewar, R. B. K., Belcher, K., and Cole, J. (1975) March. *UNIVAC/SPITBOL;* Version 1.0. Chicago, Illinois: Illinois Institute of Technology, Department of Computer Science.

Dickman, B. N., and Jensen, P. D. (1968) January 9. *Tracing Facilities for SNOBOL4* (Unpublished Technical Memorandum 68-3344-1). Holmdel, New Jersey: Bell Laboratories.

Doyle, J. N. (1975) February 11. *A Generalized Facility for the Analysis and Synthesis of Strings, and a Procedure Based Model of an Implementation.* Tucson, Arizona: University of Arizona, Department of Computer Science. SNOBOL4 Project Document S4D48.

Druseikis, F. C., and Doyle, J. N. (1974). A procedural approach to pattern matching in SNOBOL4. In *Proceedings of the ACM Annual Conference,* pp. 311–317. New York: Association for Computing Machinery.

Druseikis, F. C., and Griswold, R. E. (1973) October 11. *An Extended Function Definition Facility for SNOBOL4.* Tucson, Arizona: University of Arizona, Department of Computer Science. SNOBOL4 Project Document S4D36.

Druseikis, F. C., and Griswold, R. E. (1977) August 24. *SPITBOL 6000 User's Manual* (Unpublished technical report). Tucson, Arizona: University of Arizona, Department of Computer Science.

Dunn, R. (1973). SNOBOL4 as a language for bootstrapping a compiler. *SIGPLAN Notices* **8**(5): 28–32.

Farber, D. J. (1963a) October 8. *FORTRAN Compiler for "Double Presision* (sic) *Project"* (Program listing). Holmdel, New Jersey: Bell Laboratories.

Farber, D. J. (1963b) October 18. SNOBOL, an improved COMIT-like language (oral presentation). Ann Arbor, Michigan: University of Michigan, Computer Center.

Farber, D. J., Griswold, R. E., and Polonsky, I. P. (1963a) May 16. *A Preliminary Report on the String Manipulation Language SNOBOL* (Unpublished Technical Memorandum 63-3344-2). Holmdel, New Jersey: Bell Laboratories.

Farber, D. J., Griswold, R. E., and Polonsky, I. P. (1963b) October 24. Letter to R. W. Hamming.

Farber, D. J., Griswold, R. E., and Polonsky, I. P. (1964a). SNOBOL, a string manipulation language. *Journal of the ACM* **11**(1): 21–30.

Farber, D. J., Griswold, R. E., and Polonsky, I. P. (1964b) April. *SNOBOL 2* (sic) (Unpublished internal memorandum). Holmdel, New Jersey: Bell Laboratories.

Farber, D. J., Griswold, R. E., and Polonsky, I. P. (1964c) April 28. Internal memorandum. Holmdel, New Jersey: Bell Laboratories.

Farber, D. J., Griswold, R. E., and Polonsky, I. P. (1964d) October 13. *SNOBOL3* (Unpublished Technical Memorandum 64-3344-1). Holmdel, New Jersey: Bell Laboratories.

Farber, D. J., Griswold, R. E., and Polonsky, I. P. (1965a) October 7. *SNOBOL3 Source* (Program listing). Holmdel, New Jersey: Bell Laboratories.

Farber, D. J., *et al.*, (1965b) May 13. *Programming Machine-Language Functions for SNOBOL3* (Unpublished Technical Memorandum 64-3343-2). Holmdel, New Jersey: Bell Laboratories.

Farber, D. J., Griswold, R. E., and Polonsky, I. P. (1966). SNOBOL3 programming language. *Bell System Technical Journal* **45**: 895–944.

Faulhaber, G. R. (1963) August 26. *SNAFU* (program listing). Holmdel, New Jersey: Bell Laboratories.

Faulhaber, G. R. (1964) February 17. *A Simulation Program for One- and Two-Dimensional Automata* (Unpublished Engineers Notes). Holmdel, New Jersey: Bell Laboratories.

Flannery, M. G. (1964) July 22. *Push and Pop* (Unpublished Engineers Notes). Holmdel, New Jersey: Bell Laboratories.

Fleck, A. C. (1971). Towards a theory of data structures. *Journal of Computer and System Sciences* **5**: 475–488.

Fleck, A. C. (1977) March. *Formal Models of String Patterns* (Unpublished technical report). Iowa City, Iowa: University of Iowa, Computer Science Department and University Computer Center.

Fleck, A. C., and Liu, L.-C. (1973) June. *On the Realization of Data Graphs*. Iowa City, Iowa: University of Iowa, Department of Mathematics. Technical Report No. 67.

Forte, A. (1967). *SNOBOL3 Primer; An Introduction to the Computer Programming Language*. Cambridge, Massachusetts: MIT Press.

Gaines, R. S. (1968) March 1. *Preliminary Report on the SNOBOL4 Programming Language, Revised to Conform to the CDC 6000 Implementation* (Unpublished technical report). Princeton, New Jersey: Institute for Defense Analyses.

Galler, B. A. (1968) March. Letter to the Editor. *Communications of the ACM* **11**(3): 148

Galler, B. A., and Perlis, A. J. (1970). *A View of Programming Languages*. Reading, Massachusetts: Addison-Wesley.

Gaskins. R., Jr. (1970) March. *CAL SNOBOL Reference Manual* (Unpublished technical report). Berkeley, California: University of California, Computer Center.

Gimpel, J. F. (1970) March 23. SNOBOLizing FORTRAN. Letter to R. Zweig.

Gimpel, J. F. (1972). Blocks—A new datatype for SNOBOL4. *Communications of the ACM* **15**(6): 438–447.

Gimpel, J. F. (1973a). A theory of discrete patterns and their implementation in SNOBOL4. *Communications of the ACM* **16**(2): 91–100.

Gimpel, J. F. (1973b) May 10. *A Design for SNOBOL4 for the PDP-10, Part I—The General*. Holmdel, New Jersey: Bell Laboratories. SNOBOL4 Project Document S4D29b.

Gimpel, J. F. (1972c) June 1. *SITBOL Version 3.0*. Holmdel, New Jersey: Bell Laboratories. SNOBOL4 Project Document S4D30b.

Gimpel, J. F. (1973d). Private communication to R. E. Griswold.

Gimpel, J. F. (1974a). The minimization of spatially-multiplexed character sets. *Communications of the ACM* **17**(6): 315–318.

Gimpel, J. F. (1974b) May 1. *A Hierarchical Approach to the Design of Linkage Conventions*. Holmdel, New Jersey: Bell Laboratories. SNOBOL4 Project Document S4D41.

Gimpel, J. F. (1974c). Some highlights of the SITBOL language extensions for SNOBOL4. *SIGPLAN Notices* **9**(10): 11–20.

Gimpel, J. F. (1975). Nonlinear pattern theory. *Acta Informatica* **4**: 213–229.

Gimpel, J. F. (1976). *Algorithms in SNOBOL4*. New York: Wiley.

Gimpel, J. F., and Hanson, D. R. (1973) October 5. *The Design of ELFBOL—A Full SNOBOL4 for the PDP-11*. Holmdel, New Jersey: Bell Laboratories. SNOBOL4 Project Document S4D43.

Goyer, P. (1973) August. *Le language SNOBOL4 et la conformité chaîne-modèle*. Ph. D. Thesis, Université de Montreal.

Griswold, R. E. (1962) September 18. *The Separation of Flow Graphs*. (Unpublished Technical Memorandum 62-3344-3). Holmdel, New Jersey: Bell Laboratories.

Griswold, R. E. (1963a) March. *SCL7* (Unpublished draft). Holmdel, New Jersey: Bell Laboratories.

Griswold, R. E. (1963b) April. *A Preliminary Report on a String Manipulation Language* (Unpublished draft). Holmdel, New Jersey: Bell Laboratories.

Griswold, R. E. (1963c) July 18. *Algebraic Evaluation* (Program listing). Holmdel, New Jersey: Bell Laboratories.

Ralph E. Griswold

Griswold, R. E. (1964a) January 24. *Syntax Analysis* (Program listing). Holmdel, New Jersey: Bell Laboratories.

Griswold, R. E. (1964b) August 4. *Determinant Computation Using 7/29/63 SNOBOL3* (Program listing). Holmdel, New Jersey: Bell Laboratories.

Griswold, R. E. (1964c) October 6. *SNOBOL2 is Obsolete* (Program listing). Holmdel, New Jersey: Bell Laboratories.

Griswold, R. E. (1965) June 1. *Linked-List Functions for SNOBOL3* (Unpublished Technical Memorandum 65-3343-6). Holmdel, New Jersey: Bell Laboratories.

Griswold, R. E. (1966–1969). Entries in *SNOBOL4 Project Log*. Holmdel, New Jersey: Bell Laboratories.

Griswold, R. E. (1966a) April 18. *Special Purpose SNOBOL3 Functions —* II (Unpublished Technical Memorandum 65-3343-1). Holmdel, New Jersey: Bell Laboratories.

Griswold, R. E. (1966b) April 24. Entry in *SNOBOL4 Project Log*. Holmdel, New Jersey: Bell Laboratories.

Griswold, R. E. (1966c) May 9. *Tentative SNOBOL4 Syntax Described in SNOBOL4* (Unpublished draft). Holmdel, New Jersey: Bell Laboratories.

Griswold, R. E. (1966d) July 28. Entry in *SNOBOL4 Project Log*. Holmdel, New Jersey: Bell Laboratories.

Griswold, R. E. (1967) June 28. Entry in *SNOBOL4 Distribution Log*. Holmdel, New Jersey: Bell Laboratories.

Griswold, R. E. (1968–). *SNOBOL4 Information Bulletins*. Holmdel, New Jersey: Bell Laboratories and Tucson, Arizona: University of Arizona, Department of Computer Science. (Published irregularly.)

Griswold, R. E. (1968) January 1. Entry in *SNOBOL4 Distribution Log*. Holmdel, New Jersey: Bell Laboratories.

Griswold, R. E. (1970) February 27. *A Guide to the Macro Implementation of SNOBOL4* (Unpublished Technical Memorandum 70-8242-5). Holmdel, New Jersey: Bell Laboratories.

Griswold, R. E. (1971). *MAIN 79* (Program listing). Holmdel, New Jersey: Bell Laboratories.

Griswold, R. E. (1972a). *The Macro Implementation of SNOBOL4: A Case Study of Machine-Independent Software Development*. San Francisco, California: Freeman.

Griswold, R. E. (1972b) November 9. *Suggestions for New Features in SNOBOL4* (Unpublished technical report). Tucson, Arizona: University of Arizona, Department of Computer Science.

Griswold, R. E. (1972c) November 13. *Suggestions for New Features in SNOBOL4; Round 2—The Embellisher's Delight* (Unpublished technical report). Tucson, Arizona: University of Arizona, Department of Computer Science.

Griswold, R. E. (1974). Suggested revisions and additions to the syntax and control mechanism of SNOBOL4. *SIGPLAN Notices* **9**(2): 7–23.

Griswold, R. E. (1975a). *String and List Processing in SNOBOL4: Techniques and Applications*. Englewood Cliffs, New Jersey: Prentice-Hall.

Griswold, R. E. (1975b). A portable diagnostic facility for SNOBOL4. *Software—Practice and Experience* **5**: 93–104.

Griswold, R. E. (1975c) February 5. *Additions to SNOBOL4 to Facilitate Programming Language Research*. Tucson, Arizona: University of Arizona, Department of Computer Science. SNOBOL4 Project Document S4D37c.

Griswold, R. E. (1975d) May 22. *GENLAB II; A Program for Synthesizing Text*. Tucson, Arizona: University of Arizona, Department of Computer Science. SNOBOL4 Project Document S4PD9a.

Griswold, R. E. (1975e). Extensible pattern matching in SNOBOL4. In *Proceedings of the ACM Annual Conference*, pp. 248–252. New York: Association for Computing Machinery.

Griswold, R. E. (1976a). The macro implementation of SNOBOL4. In *Software Portability*, pp. 180–191. Cambridge, England: Cambridge University Press.

Griswold, R. E. (1976b) June 9. *Source and Cross-Reference Listings for the SIL Implementation of SNOBOL4*. Tucson, Arizona: University of Arizona, Department of Computer Science. SNOBOL4 Project Document S4D26b.

Griswold, R. E. (1976c) June 17. *String Scanning in SL5*. Tucson, Arizona: University of Arizona, Department of Computer Science. SL5 Project Document S5LD5a.

Griswold, R. E. (1976d) July 28. *SNOBOL4 Information Bulletin S4B17*. Tucson, Arizona: University of Arizona, Department of Computer Science.

Griswold, R. E. (1976e). String analysis and synthesis in SL5. In *Proceedings of the ACM Annual Conference*, pp. 410–414. New York: Association for Computing Machinery.

Griswold, R. E. (1976f). The SL5 programming language and its use for goal-oriented programming. In *Proceedings of the Fifth Texas Conference on Computing Systems*, pp. 1–5. Austin, Texas: University of Texas.

Griswold, R. E. (1977a) February 4. *Highlights of Two Implementations of SNOBOL4*. Tucson, Arizona: University of Arizona, Department of Computer Science. SNOBOL4 Project Document S4D55.

Griswold, R. E. (1977b) December 9. *Bibliography of Documents Related to the SNOBOL Programming Languages* (Unpublished draft). Tucson, Arizona: University of Arizona, Department of Computer Science.

Griswold, R. E. (1978a) January 7. *Sources of Implementations of SNOBOL4*. Tucson, Arizona: University of Arizona, Department of Computer Science. SNOBOL4 Project Document S4N21f.

Griswold, R. E. (1978b) January 11. *Bibliography of Numbered SNOBOL4 Documents; May 1967 through January 1978*. Tucson, Arizona: University of Arizona, Department of Computer Science. SNOBOL4 Project Document S4D43b.

Griswold, R. E., and Griswold, M. T. (1973). *A SNOBOL4 Primer*. Englewood Cliffs, New Jersey: Prentice-Hall.

Griswold, R. E., and Hanson, D. R. (1977). An Overview of SL5. *SIGPLAN Notices* 12(4): 40–50.

Griswold, R. E., and Polonsky, I. P. (1962) September 5. *The Classification of the States of a Finite Markov Chain* (Unpublished Technical Memorandum 62-3344-3). Holmdel, New Jersey: Bell Laboratories.

Griswold, R. E., and Polonsky, I. P. (1963a) July 1. *String Pattern Matching in the Programming Language SNOBOL* (Unpublished Technical Memorandum 63-3344-3). Holmdel, New Jersey: Bell Laboratories.

Griswold, R. E., and Polonsky, I. P. (1963b) September 24. *IPL Data Compiler* (Program listing). Holmdel, New Jersey: Bell Laboratories.

Griswold, R. E., and Polonsky, I. P. (1965) February 1. *Tree Functions for SNOBOL3* (Unpublished Technical Memorandum 65-3343-1). Holmdel, New Jersey: Bell Laboratories.

Griswold, R. E., and Varian, L. C. (1964) November 24. *Special Purpose SNOBOL3 Functions* (Unpublished Technical Memorandum 64-3344-2). Holmdel, New Jersey: Bell Laboratories.

Griswold, R. E., Poage, J. F., and Polonsky, I. P. (1967a) May 1. *Preliminary Description of the SNOBOL4 Programming Language* (Unpublished Technical Memorandum 67-3344-2). Holmdel, New Jersey: Bell Laboratories.

Griswold, R. E., Poage, J. F., and Polonsky, I. P. (1967b) May 1. *Preliminary Description of the SNOBOL4 Programming Language*. Holmdel, New Jersey: Bell Laboratories. SNOBOL4 Project Document S4D1.

Griswold, R. E., Poage, J. F., and Polonsky, I. P. (1967c) October 20. *Preliminary Report on the SNOBOL4 Programming Language—II*. Holmdel, New Jersey: Bell Laboratories. SNOBOL4 Project Document S4D4.

Griswold, R. E., Poage, J. F., and Polonsky, I. P. (1968a) August 8. *The SNOBOL4 Programming Language*. Holmdel, New Jersey: Bell Laboratories. SNOBOL4 Project Document S4D9.

Griswold, R. E., Poage, J. F., and Polonsky, I. P. (1968b). *The SNOBOL4 Programming Language*. Englewood Cliffs, New Jersey: Prentice-Hall.

Griswold, R. E., Poage, J. F., and Polonsky, I. P. (1971). *The SNOBOL4 Programming Language,* Second Edition. Englewood Cliffs, New Jersey: Prentice-Hall.

Griswold, R. E., Hanson, D. R., and Korb, J. T. (1977) October 18. *An Overview of the SL5 Programming Language*. Tucson, Arizona: University of Arizona, Department of Computer Science. SL5 Project Document S5LD1d.

Guard, J. R. (1967) December 29. *SNOBOL*. Princeton, New Jersey: Applied Logic Corporation. Program Bulletin #67-006.

Haight, R. C. (1970) October 21. *The SNOFLAKE Programming Language* (Unpublished Technical Memorandum 70-9155-2). Piscataway, New Jersey: Bell Laboratories.

Hall, J. T., and McCabe, P. S. (1967) October 17. *SNOBOL3 Primitive Functions—Binary Routines Store on Disk* (Unpublished Technical Memorandum 67-5744-1). Indian Hill, Illinois: Bell Laboratories.

Hallyburton, J. C., Jr. (1974). *Advanced Data Structure Manipulation Techniques for the SNOBOL4 Programming Language*. Ph.D. Thesis, University of Arizona, Department of Computer Science.

Hamlin, K. B. (1965) February 16. Letter to W. Keister and M. E. Terry.

Hamming, R. W. (1963) October 25. Letter to D. J. Farber, R. E. Griswold, and I. P. Polonsky.

Hanson, D. R. (1973) June 8. Letter to the editor of *SIGPLAN Notices*.

Hanson, D. R. (1974). A simple technique for representing strings in FORTRAN IV. *Communications of the ACM* 17(11): 646–647.

Hanson, D. R. (1976a). Variable associations in SNOBOL4. *Software—Practice and Experience* 6: 245–254.

Hanson, D. R. (1976b). A procedure mechanism for backtrack programming. In *Proceedings of the ACM Annual Conference,* pp. 401–405. New York: Association for Computing Machinery.

Hanson, D. R. (1977a). Storage management for an implementation of SNOBOL4. *Software—Practice and Experience* **7**: 179–192.

Hanson, D. R. (1977b). RATSNO—an experiment in software adaptability. *Software—Practice and Experience* **7**: 623–630.

Hanson, D. R., and Griswold, R. E. (1978). The SL5 procedure mechanism. *Communications of the ACM*, **21**(5): 392–400.

Herriot, R. G. (1973a). Gloss: a semantic model of programming languages. *SIGPLAN Notices* **8**(9): 70–73.

Herriot, R. G. (1973b). Gloss: a high level machine. *SIGPLAN Notices* **8**(11): 81–90.

Herriot, R. G. (1974). A uniform view of control structures in programming languages. In *Proceedings of IFIP Congress, Stockholm, 74*, pp. 331–335.

Hirsch, A. E., Jr. (1973) May 15. Letter to G. L. Baldwin.

IBM Corporation (1969). *System/360 Administrative Terminal System—OS; Terminal Operations Manual*. White Plains, New York, Application Program H20-0589-1.

IBM Corporation (1970). *PL/I(F) Language Reference Manual*. White Plains, New York, File No. 5360-29.

Jessup, R. F. (1966) November 30. *SNIFF, A Set of Subroutines for String Operations in FORTRAN* (Unpublished Technical Memorandum 66-6322-9). Holmdel, New Jersey: Bell Laboratories.

Kagan, C. A. R. (1972). The multigap extension to string language processors. *SIGPLAN Notices* **3**(3): 115–146.

Kain, R. Y., and Bailey, F. N. (1967) September 12. *SNOBOL 67 Users Reference Manual* (Unpublished technical report). Minneapolis, Minnesota: University of Minnesota, Department of Electrical Engineering.

Keister, W. (1964) October 20. Letter to R. E. Griswold.

Keister, W. (1970). Private communication to R. E. Griswold.

Kernighan, B. W., and Plauger, P. J. (1976). *Software Tools*. Reading, Massachusetts: Addison-Wesley.

Kersey, G. (1967). Private communication to R. E. Griswold.

Kostalansky, E. (1967). The definition of the syntax and semantics of the language SNOBOL I (in Slovak). *Kybernetika* **3**.

Lampson, B. W. (1966) April 18. *930 SNOBOL System Reference Manual*. Berkeley, California: University of California. Document 30.50.70, Contract No. SD-185, ARPA.

Lavrov, S. S. (1968). *SNOBOL-A; A String Manipulation Language* (in Russian). Moscow: USSR Academy of Science Computer Center.

Lee, C. Y. (1960). Automata and finite automata. *Bell System Technical Journal* **39**: 1276–1296.

Lee, C. Y. (1961a). An algorithm for path connections and its applications. *IRE Transactions on Electronic Computers* **EC-10**: 346–365.

Lee, C. Y. (1961b). Categorizing automata by W-machine programs. *Journal of the ACM* **10**(8): 384–399.

Lee, C. Y. (1963) April 14. Handwritten comments on *A Preliminary Report on a String Manipulation Language*. (See Griswold 1963b.)

Lee, C. Y., and Paull, M. C. (1963). A content addressable distributed logic memory with applications to information retrieval. *Proceedings of the IEEE* **51**(6): 924–932.

Lee, C. Y., et al. (1962) September 1. *A Language for Symbolic Communication* (Unpublished Technical Memorandum 62-3344-4). Holmdel, New Jersey: Bell Laboratories.

Leichter, J. (1976). *APLBOL* (Unpublished technical report). Waltham, Massachusetts: Brandeis University, Mathematics Department.

LeSeur, W. J. (1969) April 10. *Text 360*. White Plains, New York: IBM Corporation. Document 360D-29.4.001.

Lindsay, J. H. (1975). *SNOBOLY; A Counterproposal to SNOBOLX* (Unpublished technical report). Kingston, Ontario: Queen's University, Department of Computing and Information Science.

Madnick, S. E. (1966) June. *SPL/I: A String Processing Language*. Cambridge, Massachusetts: IBM Corporation, Cambridge Scientific Center. Report 36.006.

Magnani, R. (1964) March 2. *A SNOBOL Program for Detecting Isomorphism Between Pairs of Weighted, Directed Graphs* (Unpublished Technical Memorandum 64-3341-1). Holmdel, New Jersey: Bell Laboratories.

Manacher, G. K. (1963) October 14. *Syntactic Functions* (Program listing). Holmdel, New Jersey: Bell Laboratories.

Manacher, G. K. (1964) July 1. *A Package of Subroutines for the SNOBOL Language* (Unpublished Technical Memorandum 64-1222-4). Holmdel, New Jersey: Bell Laboratories.

Manacher, G. K., and Varian, L. C. (1964) October 23. *A Dimension Statement and Random Number Facility for the SNOBOL Language* (Unpublished Technical Memorandum 64-1222-10). Holmdel, New Jersey: Bell Laboratories.

Martellotto, N. A. (1966) June 9. *SNOBOL Questionnaire* (Internal memorandum). Holmdel, New Jersey: Bell Laboratories.

Maurer, W. D. (1976). *A Programmer's Introduction to SNOBOL.* New York: Am. Elsevier.

McCann, A. P., Holden, S. C., and Dewar, R. B. K. (1976) December. *MACRO SPITBOL—DECsystem-10 Version.* Leeds, England: University of Leeds, Centre for Computer Studies. Technical Report No. 94.

McIlroy, M. D. (1962) August 7. *A String Manipulation System for FAP Programs* (Unpublished Technical Memorandum 62-1271-4). Holmdel, New Jersey: Bell Laboratories.

McIlroy, M. D. (1963). A variant method for file searching. *Communications of the ACM* **6**(3): 101.

McIlroy, M. D. (1977) December 5. Letter to R. E. Griswold.

Melli, L. F. (1974) December. *The 2.pak Language Primitives for AI Applications,* Masters Thesis, University of Toronto, Department of Computer Science.

Mickel, A. B. (1973) August. *Comparative Study of the Semantics of Selected Programming Languages.* Minneapolis, Minnesota: University of Minnesota, Computer, Information and Control Sciences. Technical Report TR 73-9.

MIT Press (1962). *An Introduction to COMIT Programming.* Cambridge, Massachusetts.

Moody, J. K. M. (1972) November 1. *SNOBOL4 on Titan* (Unpublished technical report). Cambridge, England: University of Cambridge, Computer Laboratory.

Mooers, C. N. (1968) March. Reply to letter to the Editor. *Communications of the ACM* **11**(3): 148–149.

Morris, R. (1968). Scatter storage techniques. *Communications of the ACM* **11**(1): 38–44.

Morse, P. L. (1976) January. *User Manual for B1700 SPITBOL; Version 1.0* (Unpublished technical report). Amherst, New York: State University of New York at Buffalo, Department of Computer Science.

Mylopoulos, J., Radler, N., Melli, L., and Roussopoulas, N. (1973). 1.pak: A SNOBOL-based programming language for artificial intelligence applications. In *Proceedings of the Third International Joint Conference on Artificial Intelligence,* pp. 691–696. Stanford, California: Stanford University.

Newsted. P. R. (1975). *SNOBOL; An Introduction to Programming.* Rochelle Park, New Jersey: Hayden Book Co.

Noll, L. W. (1971) April 15. *A Text Formatting Program for Phototypesetting Documents* (Unpublished technical report). Holmdel, New Jersey: Bell Laboratories.

Ophir, D. (1974). *SNOBOL +* (Unpublished technical report). Beer-Sheva, Israel: Atomic Energy Commission, Nuclear Research Centre-Negev.

Osterweil, L. (1970) August 12. *SNOBOL4 Version 3.4 on the UNIVAC 1108 under Exec 8* (Unpublished technical report). Silver Spring, Maryland: Language and Systems Development, Inc.

Pagan, F. G. (1978). Formal semantics of a SNOBOL4 subset. *Computer Languages* **5**(12): 46–49.

Pfeffer, A. S., and Furtado, A. L. (1973). Pattern matching for structured programming. In *Conference Record of the Seventh Asilomar Conference on Circuits, Systems, and Computers, Pacific Grove, California,* pp. 466–469.

Poage, J. F. (1965) September 29. *GE 645 Software Working Group* (Memorandum for File). Holmdel, New Jersey: Bell Laboratories.

Poage, J. F. (1966a) May 13. Letter to R. E. Griswold.

Poage, J. F. (1966b) November 3. Letter to C. Y. Lee.

Poage, J. F. (1977) December 1. Letter to R. E. Griswold.

Puckett, A. L., and Farlow, C. W. (1966) April 28. *Character and Bit String Manipulation Facilities for FORTRAN IV* (Unpublished Technical Memorandum 66-6322-5). Holmdel, New Jersey: Bell Laboratories.

Renne, H. S. (1963) October 1. Letter to F. J. Singer.

Renne, H. S. (1964) August 18. Letter to J. A. Baird.

Ripley, G. D., and Griswold, R. E. (1975). Tools for the measurement of SNOBOL4 Programs. *SIGPLAN Notices* **10**(50): 36–52.

Rodgers, E. A. (1966) August 5. *Symbolic Differentiator and HSUB Compiler Using SNOBOL* (Unpublished Technical Memorandum 66-3241-4). Murray Hill, New Jersey: Bell Laboratories.

Roosen-Runge, P. H. (1967) August. *A Table of Bell Polynomials.* Ann Arbor, Michigan: University of Michigan, Mental Health Research Institute. Communication 212.

Rosin, R. F. (1967). Strings in PL/I. *PL/I Bulletin* No. 4, pp. 6–12. Attachment to *SIGPLAN Notices* **2**(8).

Rosin, R. F. (1969). Contemporary concepts of microprogramming and emulation. *Computing Surveys* **1**(4): 197–212.

Rossman, G. E., and Jones, L. H. (1974). Functional memory-based dynamic microprocessors for higher level languages. *SIGPLAN Notices* **9**(8): 37–65.

Santos, P. J., Jr. (1971) December. *FASBOL, A SNOBOL4 Compiler*. Berkeley, California: University of California, Electronics Research Laboratory. Memorandum No. ERL-M134.

Sears, W. R. (1974) November 25. *The Design of SIXBOL, A Fast Implementation of SNOBOL4 for the CDC 6000 Series Computers*. Tucson, Arizona: University of Arizona, Department of Computer Science. SNOBOL4 Project Document S4D45.

Shapiro, L. G. (1976) March. *Inexact Pattern Matching in ESP³*. Manhattan, Kansas: Kansas State University, Department of Computer Science. Technical Report CS76-10.

Shapiro, L. G., and Baron, R. J. (1977). ESP³: a language for pattern description and a system for pattern recognition. *IEEE Transactions on Software Engineering* SE-3(2): 169–183.

Shapiro, M. D. (1969) March 1. *CDC 6000 SNOBOL4 (Version 2.0) User's Guide*. Lafayette, Indiana: Purdue University, Computer Science Center. Report R0 SNOBOL4-1.

Shapiro, M. D. (1970) December. *An Introduction to Character String Operations Using FORTRAN IV and the Purdue University String Handling Utility Package (PUSHUP)* (Unpublished technical report). Lafayette, Indiana: Purdue University.

Shapiro, M. D. (1972a) June. *A SNOBOL Machine: Functional Architectural Concepts of a String Processor*. Ph.D. Thesis, Purdue University.

Shapiro, M. D. (1972b) September. A SNOBOL machine: a higher-level languge processor in a conventional hardware framework. In *Innovative Architecture, Digest of Papers from COMPCON '72, Sixth Annual IEEE Computer Society International Conference*, pp. 41–44. San Francisco, California.

Silverston, S. M. (1976a) August. *SNOBAT 1.9*. Ames, Iowa: Iowa State University, Computation Center. Technical Report No. 17.

Silverston, S. M. (1976b) December. *Storage Structure and Management in the SNOBAT Implementation of SNOBOL4*. Ames, Iowa: Iowa State University, Department of Computer Science. Technical Report 76-14.

Silverston, S. M. (1977). Extensions to SNOBOL4 in the SNOBAT implementation. *SIGPLAN Notices* 12(9): 77–84.

Simon, A. H., and Walters, D. A. (1964) December 28. *RCA SNOBOL Programmers' Manual* (Unpublished technical report). Princeton, New Jersey: RCA Laboratories.

Sinowitz, N. R. (1966). Private communication to R. E. Griswold.

Smith, D. C., and Enea, H. J. (1973). *MLISP2*. Stanford, California: Stanford University, Artificial Intelligence Laboratory. Report AIM-195.

Smith, E. (1970) September. *Interactive SNOBOL4*. El Segundo, California: XDS Program Library Catalog No. 890637-11A00.

Sommerville, I. (1977). *S-SNOBOL—Structured SNOBOL4*. (Unpublished technical report). Edinburgh: Heriot-Watt University, Department of Computer Science.

Stewart, G. F. (1975). An algebraic model for string patterns. In *Conference Record of the Second ACM Symposium on Principles of Programming Languages, Palo Alto, California*, pp. 167–184.

Storm, E. F. (1968) CHAMP—character manipulation procedures. *Communications of the ACM* 11(8): 561–566.

Strauss, H. J. (1968) July 15. *External Functions for SNOBOL4* (Unpublished Technical Memorandum 68-3344-3). Holmdel, New Jersey: Bell Laboratories.

Syrett, T. (1971). *The SNOBOL Machine: The First Virtual Machine Language for the SLAC MLP-900* (Unpublished draft). Stanford, California: Stanford Linear Accelerator Center.

Tamir, M. (1974) August. *Control Mechanisms in SNOBOL* (Unpublished technical report). Jerusalem: Hebrew University of Jerusalem.

Tennent, R. D. (1973). Mathematical semantics of SNOBOL4. In *Conference Record of ACM Symposium on Principles of Programming Languages, Boston, Massachusetts*, pp. 95–107.

Tesler, L. G., Enea, H. J., and Smith, D. C. (1973). The LISP70 pattern matching system. In *Proceedings of the Third International Joint Conference on Artificial Intelligence*, pp. 671–676. Stanford, California: Stanford University.

Tharp, A. L. (1977). *Applications of SPITBOL*. Raleigh, North Carolina: North Carolina State College.

Tye, T. T. (1972). *CISBOL; Compiler Implementation of SNOBOL* (Unpublished technical report). Tucson, Arizona: University of Arizona, Department of Computer Science.

Uhr, L. (1968). Private communication to R. E. Griswold.

Uhr, L. (1974) December. *EASEy: An English-Like Programming Language for Artificial Intelligence and Complex Information Processing*. Madison, Wisconsin: University of Wisconsin, Computer Sciences Department. Technical Report 233.

Wade, L. (1970) October 17. *PDP-10 SNOBOL4 User's Guide*. Maynard, Massachusetts: Digital Equipment Corporation. DECUS Program Library No. 10-104.

Waite, W. M. (1967–1973). SNOBOL Bulletins in *SIGPLAN Notices*. (Appearing irregularly.)

Waite, W. M. (1967). A language-independent macro processor. *Communications of the ACM* **10**(7): 433–440.

Waite, W. M. (1969). *The Stage2 Macro Processor*. Boulder, Colorado: University of Colorado, Computer Center. Report No. 69-3.

Wetherell, C. (1978). *Etudes for Programmers*. Englewood Cliffs, New Jersey: Prentice-Hall.

Wilson, D. L. (1966) August. *SNOBOL3*. Milwaukee, Wisconsin: University of Wisconsin, Computer Center. Technical Report.

Wilson, F. C. (1975) April. *A Macro Programming Language*. College Station, Texas: Texas A&M University Graduate Center. NTIS Report AD-A009294.

Wilson, T. C. (1967) July 19. *No. 1 ESS—Special Purpose SNOBOL3 Functions* (Unpublished Engineers Notes). Indian Hill, Illinois: Bell Laboratories.

Yngve, V. H. (1958). A programming language for mechanical translation. *Mechanical Translation* **5**(1): 25–41.

Yngve, V. H. (1964). COMIT (oral presentation). Holmdel, New Jersey: Bell Laboratories.

Yngve, V. H. (1972). *Computer Programming with COMIT II*. Cambridge, Massachusetts: MIT Press.

Zweig, R. (1970) February 17. *FORTRAN Language Extensions for Character String Manipulation* (Unpublished Technical Memorandum 70-9155-1). Holmdel, New Jersey: Bell Laboratories.

TRANSCRIPT OF PRESENTATION

JAN LEE: Our first speaker is Ralph Griswold. Ralph received his Ph.D. from Stanford in 1962, which, within the period that we are discussing, makes him one of the new kids on the block. At the time of work on SNOBOL languages, begun in 1962, he was a member of the technical staff of Bell Labs in the Programming Research Studies Department at Holmdel, New Jersey. The members of this department were engaged in a variety of research projects related to the use of computers for high-level, nonnumerical computation. The work on SNOBOL was motivated by a need for a better tool to support these research activities. Since that time Ralph has moved to the University of Arizona where he is Professor of Computer Science and the head of the department.

RALPH E. GRISWOLD: The SNOBOL languages constitute a development over quite a period of time, an evolutionary development [Frame 1]. [Frame 2] is a time line. The solid lines represent periods of active language development; the circles represent specific re-

```
1.   The Setting
2.   Original Goals
3.   SNOBOL Characteristics
4.   Goals for SNOBOL2 and SNOBOL3
5.   SNOBOL3 Characteristics
6.   Goals for SNOBOL4
7.   SNOBOL4 Characteristics
8.   Contributions of the SNOBOL Languages
9.   The Future of SNOBOL
```

Frame 1. The SNOBOL languages.

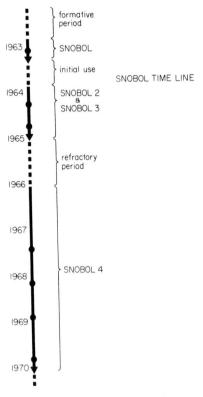

Frame 2. SNOBOL time line.

leases of the languages; and because of the period of time involved, some nearly 8 years, there is quite a bit of history that I'd like to cover [Frame 2†].

I propose to do that, essentially chronologically, concentrating more on philosophical, social, and political concerns than specific language features, although I'll try to give you a feeling for the course of the development of the languages during this time.

The talk will roughly follow these outlines. The setting that motivated the original development of SNOBOL; what the goals were; what the consequences were; the characteristics; successive languages—SNOBOL2 and SNOBOL3; and finally, SNOBOL4. I will summarize with my own views of what the major contributions of the SNOBOL languages are, and perhaps have a word to say about what I think the future of these languages or similar languages will be.

Before going on I'd like to comment that there have been a number of people involved in this work [Frame 3]. I am honored to give the talk. However, much of the work was done by other individuals, and I want to specifically give them credit for SNOBOL through SNOBOL3—Dave Farber, and Ivan Polonsky, in addition to myself, and SNOBOL4, Jim Poage and Ivan Polonsky. The comment "supported by a cast of thousands" is whimsical. I thought it a little silly to say "cast of two." It was always a relatively small effort in

† Frame 2 is referred back to several times in the talk.

```
SNOBOL - SNOBOL3
    Dave Farber
    Ralph Griswold
    Ivan Polonsky
SNOBOL4
    Ralph Griswold
    Jim Poage
    Ivan Polonsky
***** supported by a cast of thousands *****
```

Frame 3. SNOBOL principals.

terms of personnel. We felt uncomfortable if we got up to five, and perhaps for an hour or two we got up to six. But basically it was a small effort. Although over that substantial period of time, quite a few people were involved, and they all deserve credit. There were too many to list here, but I hope I've given adequate credit to them in the paper.

Now, the setting for this work was, as JAN indicated, in a research department at Bell Telephone Laboratories, where one of the main thrusts was high-level theorem proving with a kind of approach that a human being might take to it, which involved symbolic mathematics, manipulation of formulas, simplification of algebraic expressions, and so on.

At that time we were primarily using a language called SCL, which stands for Symbolic Communication Language. This language had been developed by Chester Lee, who was the head of the department and leader of the effort. And this language had the ability to manipulate strings of characters which were encoded in various ways; for example, as expressions and formulas. It had pattern-matching facilities, synthesis facilities, and a variety of other capabilities.

The difficulty of the language for us was that it was relatively slow, the amount of space available—this was on a 7090—was only 2000 characters, two different strings at one time. And the nature of the language was such that it required quite a bit of code to write a program. Yet we were trying to do high level operations and trying to do research.

We also had available to us IPL-V and COMIT, and we used those experimentally in this effort. We did not find them suitable for various reasons; COMIT, because it was designed primarily for linguistic processes, and it had a concept of constituents really intended to be words, which didn't help a great deal with algebraic expressions, and IPL-V, even with its list processing capabilities didn't give us really what we wanted.

Of all the languages in the conference, you might think what motivated their original development—why they were done. Some were done because of a specific desire to develop a tool for a community of users; others were done for related reasons; and some— and SNOBOL is a particular example of this case—were done because individuals needed a tool they didn't have, and in order to get that tool, set out to do development of their own.

Now, in that context, it's important to realize that we were trying to develop a tool for our own use; we had no expectation that it would develop into a language for general use. And we were not in the mainstream of computer science development. We were primarily influenced by what we had available—not what existed. As was mentioned in other talks in this conference, the communication of information at that time was not nearly as good as it is at the present time. We simply decided that we could produce a better tool for our own use and we set about to do that.

Ralph E. Griswold

Ivan Polonsky and I, who were doing this formula manipulation, were joined by Dave Farber, who had experience with language processors and what was going on with programming languages and computer science. We started out with what essentially was an amateur effort within this research group to develop a new tool. We did, however, set some goals, and these goals were influenced both by what we were doing and what we felt about what programming languages should be like for this kind of activity.

One of these was there would be research applications. We had already decided that the string of characters would be a good basis for representing a variety of nonnumerical scientific data such as formulas and graphs and so forth. We were looking for simplicity, ease of use, and suitability for what we then called "the naïve programmer"—that is a person who's not a professional programmer, but nonetheless had a good reason for using a computer as a tool in research. We rather deliberately took the position of disregarding questions of efficiency and difficulty of implementation. At this point we were primarily concerned with human resources and we took the position, which continued throughout the development of the languages, that human resources are far more precious than machine resources, and we should do what we could to make it easy to program.

We were able to disregard implementation problems because we were going to implement the language ourselves, and therefore we couldn't at least be accused of passing the buck. If we had troubles, that was our problem.

We certainly realized that what we were doing was experimental, and we started out with a quick implementation which was largely interpretive. Once the language was designed, this implementation was done in a great hurry. In fact it took about three weeks despite the fact that I had no experience with programming on the machine we were using —an IBM 7090. There's an anecdote about this. It's claimed that Dave Farber wrote the compiler portion of the system on the back of an envelope. That is literally true. And furthermore, it was a legal size envelope. He came in with it one morning. Unfortunately, to the best of our knowledge, the envelope doesn't survive unless it's somewhere in his personal effects. He hasn't found it. It's also been said that the resulting system ran like it was written on the back of an envelope! And I can personally verify that also!

Now, I'd like to look at this point—to give you an idea of what the original SNOBOL language looked like—since, although some of you may be familiar with SNOBOL4, you probably have not seen the original SNOBOL or, if you have, you may have forgotten it.

We are now up to the period in early 1963; we have an implementation. And a piece of a program that I resurrected looks like this [Frame 4]. I selected this program not because I understood exactly what it was doing, nor because it was elegant, but because it's the oldest existing listing to be found. The simple language statement structure—labels at the left; operations; line by line basis; optional GOTOs at the end, which may be conditional, indicated by F or S, or may be unconditional; with assignment operations, and where you see stars, these indicate patterns that match certain combinations of characters and symbols.

Now, one of the interesting things about this language which should tell you the level of development at this point is that it was extremely simple and quite crude. It had a single data type—the string. Even integers are represented as strings. It did have high-level pattern matching, but there were no declarations in the language for the reasons that I described earlier. We wanted it to be easy to use, and we felt that declarations were largely a concession to the implementation—an arguable point, I realize. However, we did have variable-length identifiers, and a free format, which in this time was somewhat unusual.

```
START     ,          = ","
          (          = "("
          )          = ")"
          AG         = ,
          N          = "0"
          SYS        .PRINT "GIVEN THE GRAPH"
I1        SYS        .READ   *A*  " "              /F(I3)
I2        A          *X* ( *Y* ) =                 /F(I1)
          $X         = , Y ,
          SYS        .PRINT X "  =" Y
          N          *N* = N + "1"
          AG         = AG X ,                      /(I2)
                        ⋮
```

Frame 4. Section of SNOBOL graph planarity program.

Also, we had automatic storage management. Strings were constructed, of arbitrary length, and that was taken care of automatically by the system. Yet, despite this sophistication, the syntax was so simple that anything that was not otherwise syntactically defined was an identifier. This statement actually uses comma as an identifier to assign its own literal value, and it is subsequently used down here in a concatenation statement. In fact, any string of characters whatsoever was a legal SNOBOL program and the compiler would compile anything at all. In fact, we accidentally gave it a COMIT program once, which it dutifully compiled. It didn't run very well, though.

Noticeably absent from this language were ordinary computational facilities. There were no functions, no mechanism of accessing any of the ordinary computational capabilities. The arithmetic was very primitive. Yet the language was simple, easy to learn, and useful things could be done with it very quickly.

The reaction to this language was unexpected, at least to me—and I'm again here speaking for myself. There was quite a bit of enthusiasm for this language within Bell Laboratories. By the time we had gotten it implemented, our colleagues were aware of it and we rather quickly found that there was both interest and use in the language. The early uses were formula manipulation from our own interests, graph analysis, some compiler construction and other language processors, and program generation. I think it's interesting to note that one of the first programs that was developed early in 1963 was a program that took a specification of the telephone network and produced as output a FORTRAN program which, when executed, did a network analysis. The FORTRAN program that was output was horrendous, and totally unreadable. It had been impractical for that person to generate this FORTRAN program by hand, so we had a feeling we had accomplished something when this individual was able to do something in a few weeks he was not able to do before with the tools that then existed.

Some knowledge of SNOBOL got outside of Bell Laboratories by word of mouth, and primarily to universities. University of Michigan was one of the early SNOBOL installations.

Going back to the chronology [Frame 2], following the period of initial use, it became clear that SNOBOL was sufficiently interesting, and there was a sufficient demand that it was necessary to go on to a more elaborate version of the language.

Ralph E. Griswold

The original SNOBOL implementation had been started by a group of individuals who were primarily interested in producing tools. They did it pretty much on their own as a closet activity, but it suddenly became very popular, and now we were in a position of deciding where to go. The public pressure, especially within Bell Laboratories, and our own need for more facilities, suggested that we go on, and instead of going back to our work in automatic theorem proving, we became more interested in the tools that we devised to do that work originally.

The necessity arose from the crudeness of the original language. For example, there was no function repertoire, no built-in function capability. In order to compute the length of the string, you had to literally decompose by pattern matching and increment a counter. And you could only compare numerical magnitudes by doing pattern matching. You might think what implications that has.

Well, we continued with this development. This led to SNOBOL2 and SNOBOL3. Not many individuals outside of Bell Laboratories realized that there really was a SNOBOL2. In fact, there was, and it was in existence for a good six months or so. The main difference between SNOBOL2 and SNOBOL3, which was its immediate successor, was a function repertoire. With SNOBOL2, built-in functions for doing various kinds of computations and numerical comparisons, and with SNOBOL3, a mechanism for defining recursive procedures.

This is an example of an early SNOBOL3 program [Frame 5]. It illustrates perhaps very little difference in syntax from SNOBOL. We did clean some things up so that parentheses could be used for grouping, as opposed to being identifiers; and you'll notice some function construction. But other than that, it was largely upward compatible. It retained the automatic storage regeneration, the single-string data type, and because of the lack of declarations, or conversely, the other way around, it had a dynamic component during execution where even procedure definitions were actually executed during the program execution. This is an example of some little piece of matrix manipulation; another example [Frame 6] taken from an existing listing shows that we were still doing a little formula ma-

```
              DEFINE ("MATRIX(X)","M.0",)
                            :
                            :
    M.0      D    =    "0"
             SYSPIT   *N*  " "                /F(FRETURN)
             I    =    "0"
    M.1      I    =    .NE(I,N) I + "1"        /F(RETURN)
             $("B" I)   =    "FALSE"
             SYSPOT   =    SYSPIT             /F(ERR)
             ROW    =    SYSPOT
             J    =    "1"
    M.2      ROW   *$("X" I "." J)/"6"*   =
    M.3      $("X" I "." J)    " "   =    /S(M.3)
             J    =    .NE(J,N) J + "1"        /S(M.2)F(M.1)
                            :
                            :
```

Frame 5. Section of SNOBOL 3 matrix manipulation program.

```
        DEFINE ("SIMPLIFY(EXP)","S1","U")
                          :
    S1    EXP     "("  *(U)*  "*0)"    = "0"   /S(S1)
          EXP     "(0*" *(U)*  ")"     = "0"   /S(S1)
          EXP     "("  *(U)*  "$1)"    = U     /S(S1)
          EXP     "("  *(U)*  "*1)"    = U     /S(S1)
          EXP     "(1*" *(U)*  ")"     = U     /S(S1)
          EXP     "(0+" *(U)*  ")"     = U     /S(S1)
          EXP     "("  *(U)*  "+0)"    = U     /S(S1)
          EXP     "("  *(U)*  "-0)"    = U     /S(S1)
          SIMPLIFY = EXP                       /(RETURN)
                          :
```

Frame 6. Section of SNOBOL3 formula manipulation program.

nipulation, if even only to test the program. This is a rather brief routine for doing an identity reduction, simplification of algebraic formulas. Again, it illustrates the general format of the language; string manipulation, pattern matching, modification, replacement, and conditional GOTOs. No additional control structures in SNOBOL3—no declarations—no new data types.

The reaction to SNOBOL3 was, in general, favorable. There were a few individuals, inside and outside of Bell Laboratories, who said we'd messed up SNOBOL1 by adding functions, and some of our programmers objected that functions were too hard to understand to use, and they preferred the simplicity of SNOBOL. I think that's probably a natural consequence of the fact that we attracted many nonprogrammers with SNOBOL because of the basic quite crude, simple, primitive nature of the language where you didn't have to learn a lot about conditionals, and control structures, and more mathematical concepts.

But for the most part, the reaction was positive. The implementation was more robust. It didn't compile anything anymore. I guess that's an advantage. And it was for the first time rather widely distributed outside Bell Laboratories and documented and published. There became a proliferation of implementations for other machines. This again was done for an IBM 7094, but there was enough interest in SNOBOL that students at various universities began implementing SNOBOL or versions and dialects of SNOBOL for their own machines.

Going back to the chronology [Frame 2], we've worked from a formative period when we were interested in problem solving, to developing a tool, to becoming interested in the tool, and then to what I call a refractory period in which we didn't respond to stimulus very much. This was still a closet effort to a large extent. There were few people involved in it. Bell Laboratories was of course aware of it. They supported it to the extent of allowing the individuals the time to work on it and the computer facilities and the physical support. But there was never an official project. It didn't have clerical support, and it didn't have programmer support. So the documentation, distribution of material, and dissemination of information was done by the same group that designed and implemented the language.

During this refractory period, however, we were contemplating the fact that SNOBOL3 had only a single data type—the string of characters, which meant that users tended to encode complex structures such as trees and graphs as strings, and we did some experimentation with list processing, tree processing, and various kinds of strings as experimental extensions to SNOBOL3.

Earlier, I alluded to the fact that the progression from SNOBOL to SNOBOL2 and 3 was virtually dictated by the acceptance of the language combined with its lack of facilities and lack of robustness of its implementation. SNOBOL4 is another matter. There was no force that dictated a transition from SNOBOL3 to SNOBOL4 in that fashion. In fact, the motivation came from within the group and because of outside influences of another nature. This was a period during which third-generation computing facilities were being developed and we were faced with a replacement of our IBM 7094s by GE 635s and 645s, or IBM 360s or similar machines, and we were our own largest user, which is not unusual. And we were facing the possibility of not having SNOBOL available for our own use on the new machines or having to emulate. This encouraged us to consider the possibility of implementing SNOBOL for the new machines. At the same time we had developed a greater interest in language design and language implementation, a greater interest in the concept of tool building than the tool itself, so our intellectual interests were more now in the computer science area.

We eventually decided to make a proposal to our management to implement SNOBOL for the new equipment that was coming in. To them this offered the opportunity of solving the problem with the users of SNOBOL; SNOBOL was now sufficiently widely used that there was a need for it. And the hooker that we attached to it is: "We'll be glad to do this provided you let us implement a new SNOBOL." Well, I don't know whether they realized what that meant or not, but they accepted the proposal without comment, on the spot, and again, left us alone to do what we wanted to do.

I have termed this attitude on the part of management "benign neglect." They provided a substantial amount of facilities, and largely left us to our own devices. There were never any schedules. There were never any reports. Versions of the language got done according to our own internal schedules. There were suggestions, input from our users, but none from management. So that you can see that this effort proceeded along much different lines than some of the other programming languages that have been described here. We did not have committees. We had our own internal discussions, but in a small group one can resolve those in various intellectual and physical fashions.

The project at this point became better organized. One of the things was that we were faced with new machines, possibly different machines at different Bell Laboratories locations, and weren't even sure what machine we would get at out own location. This encouraged us to give more consideration to the implementation, and in particular, develop a portable implementation. It is not a function of this conference to discuss implementation, but I will touch on that just enough to indicate that it's important to language development and that, in fact, this implementation was designed with the intent that it be easily implementable on a variety of machines. I'll come back to the significance of that later on.

We proceeded with the same philosophy, albeit developed and embellished by our own experience and the input that we had from users. We strove for more innovation. We were now more interested in producing new ideas and experimentation with programming language facilities than in the past. And we were willing to break with the concept of upward compatibility which had existed in going from SNOBOL to SNOBOL2 and SNOBOL3.

The result is, in some senses, quite similar, and in some senses, quite different. [Frame

```
        WC = "<";   SB = SPAN(" ")
        INT = SPAN("0123456789")
        REPL = WC SB "ALTER" SB (INT . I1 "," INT . I2  |
   +              INT. I1 I2)
        FOLL = WC SB "FOLLOW" SB INT . I1
        NEWC = WC ABORT | NULL

        CARD = ALTER                          :F(EOF)
        CARD   NEWC                           :S(NEW)
   ALT  CARD   REPL                           :S(REP)
        CARD   FOLL                           :F(ERR)
        N = N + 1
        OUT = CARD
                       :
                       :
```

Frame 7.   Section of SNOBOL4 editor.

7] is a section of a SNOBOL4 program for an editor. Although not immediately evident, one of the distinct differences between SNOBOL4 and previous versions of the language was a multitude of data types. As a matter of fact, we probably overdid it; having lived with strings for everything, we went to something like eight data types, plus the ability to define others. Among these data types were patterns which had previously been syntactic constructions. In the first few lines of this program you can see statements that construct patterns and assign them to identifiers, and then use these patterns subsequently in building larger and larger patterns. This capability did not exist in earlier languages, but it gives SNOBOL4 the capacity of building arbitrarily complex patterns in a piecewise fashion. For example, it's possible to write a pattern that completely describes the syntax of COBOL. It's not particularly useful, but it's possible to do that.

The other innovations, so far as SNOBOL is concerned, although not innovations with respect to other programming languages, were the introduction of arrays, record data types, and something that is somewhat innovative—a table data type which is illustrated in this program [Frame 8]. This incidentally perhaps expresses one of the advantages of SNOBOL4: it's an entirely self-contained program for counting the number of occurrences of words on input text. With a little bit of addition it can be made—the definition of the word can be made a little bit more sophisticated—it can be made into a concordance program, but I wanted it to fit on one slide. It is highly self-contained; no declarations. And I don't know whether it's bragging or not, but it ran the first time I tried it. That is not true of all my programs, I might add.

The table data type is illustrated here. Table is an associative structure much like a symbol table in an assembler or compiler so commonly used, but here it is represented in the high-level language at the source level, and the index to the table here is an arbitrary string of characters. There's no necessity for allocation statements, and there's no necessity to know in advance what strings may be indexed into the table. So this is an example of one of those facilities in SNOBOL4 that's substantially higher level than you would expect to find otherwise.

However, the syntax of the language is still primitive. Control structures still consist entirely of GOTOs and labels. There are no declarations. There are no scoping rules. De-

Ralph E. Griswold

```
          COUNT = TABLE()
          LETTERS = "ABCDEFGHIJKLMNOPQRSTUVWXYZ"
          GETWORD = BREAK(LFTTERS)  SPAN(LETTERS) . WORD
READ      LINE = INPUT                              :F(PRINT)
NEXTW     LINE   GETWORD =                          :F(READ)
          COUNT[WORD] = COUNT[WORD] + 1             :(NEXTW)
PRINT     COUNT = CONVERT(COUNT,"ARRAY")            :F(ERROR)
NEXTI     I = I + 1
          OUTPUT = COUNT[I,1] ":" COUNT[I,2]        :S(NEXTI)
FND
```

Frame 8.   SNOBOL4 word counter.

spite the multitude of data types, there are no declarations for types. All structures are heterogeneous, and any identifier can have any type of data at any time. So we have a combination of sophistication and high-level processing, with a rather primitive structure with respect to control both of program and of its allocation and storage.

However, SNOBOL4 classifies probably at this point as a general-purpose language as opposed to the earlier versions of SNOBOL which are primarily string processing languages. It's a general-purpose language with a heavy emphasis on string processing.

Well, the question is, what was the reaction to SNOBOL4? Again, primarily positive. The dissenting voices were more frequently heard, and there were a number of cases where individuals have felt that in going to many data types and going to more complex patterns and the ability to construct more complex patterns, that much of the virtue and simplicity of SNOBOL3 was lost. On the other hand, SNOBOL4 had the virtue of pragmatically permitting individuals to carry out work that they could not or would not be willing to carry out otherwise. So I think this is sort of typical of the history of programming language development; you gain something and you lose something.

The most significant aspect of SNOBOL4—and this has very little to do with programming language development—is its implementation, as I alluded to earlier. The implementation that was written at Bell Laboratories was written in machine-independent macrolanguage designed to be portable over the range of large-scale scientific computers. Very early, a number of individuals interested in SNOBOL languages undertook such experiments and, while SNOBOL4 was still under develoment at this time a number of specific periods in which individual versions of SNOBOL4 came out—there were simultaneously implementations on machines like the CDC 6600; the GE 635; the IBM 360; and so forth.

One of the facts of life about programming languages is their availability and support and implementation. We've had allusions earlier to the time you couldn't tell whether or not when you read a paper on programming language whether somebody was just talking about it or whether they'd implemented it, (and in the back of the room somebody said, "Nothing has changed!") And there have been many many important ideas in programming languages that have never reached the practical stage because they have either not been implemented, or their implementations have not been generally available. It's my personal view that it is the widespread and generally easy availability of the implementation of SNOBOL4 that's responsible for its extensive acceptance. It was distributed freely, without charge, from Bell Laboratories to anyone that wanted it. Support was provided for implementations on other machines, and there are today over some 50 implementations of this kind and there are thousands of installations of SNOBOL. So in some sense, it's one of the most widely available programming languages, if not among the top few that are most widely used. Because of the portable nature of the implementation, it also is one of the most widely standard implementations, de facto standardization imposed by portable implementation.

Now, there are a lot of ways you can look at the contributions of the SNOBOL languages. What I have to say is a personal opinion and I want to emphasize that again, because I think my colleagues might have other thoughts on the subject. There are some specifics relating to language features. It's hard to say that anything is totally original in a programming language because so many things come up in different contexts. But among widely used languages, SNOBOL certainly emphasized the string as a single data object rather than an aggregate of characters. From the very beginning, in the crudest implementation, it supported true varying length strings that were actual string data types, data objects, without the programmer having to think in terms of a structure imposed on the characters or to think of strings as an array or aggregate of characters. This permits a conceptualization of many problems that otherwise would be cluttered by the bookkeeping of indexing into aggregates.

Patterns as data objects are an important contribution of SNOBOL. Many languages had patterns, COMIT and SCL among the first. As I indicated earlier, SCL was more influential on our work than COMIT was. Patterns have been included in many other languages, but SNOBOL4 emphasized the concept of a pattern as a data object that could be constructed, manipulated and transmitted [and built] throughout program execution. This concept has occurred in a variety of suggestions and dialects for other languages, including—with apologies—ALGOL and PL/I. Quite commonly patterns now appear as constructs in artificial intelligence languages.

A single relatively simple feature of SNOBOL, the table data type, which was the original suggestion of Doug McIlroy, and was also a suggestion by Mike Shapiro, has turned out to be particularly useful. It represents essentially a hash structure at the source language level, with associative look-up, and it is easily documented. It's responsible for the use of SNOBOL in many areas where it otherwise would not have been used. I think it's one of the main candidates for inclusion in other high-level languages, and I'm sometimes puzzled by the fact that it isn't, because it is not something that is really difficult to implement as anyone who is familiar with compiler design knows.

I would personally like to think SNOBOL had some responsibility in opening the use of computers in areas that had previously been nontraditional: areas in the humanities— music theory, among the early uses. It's obvious that the application of quantitative methods in these areas has advantages and would come eventually, but because of SNOBOL's particular simplicity and orientation towards nonscientific and nontrained programmer individuals, it did attract early use in those areas, and I would like to think stimulated the development in those areas before it otherwise would have happened.

If I were to pick the most important contribution of SNOBOL to programming language development, I would say it's contrariness. A kinder way of putting it is the phrase that "its development has been orthogonal to the mainstream of programming language development." That was deliberate. We knew when we designed the original SNOBOL language what we were doing when we did not include declarations. We knew what

Ralph E. Griswold

we were doing when we kept the control structures simple. There were some times later when it's not too clear that we knew what we were doing, but we tried at most points in looking for new facilities for programming languages not to do what other people were doing better than they were doing it, but to try to find alternatives that might be useful and suitable in some circumstances and for some users. I think the fact that SNOBOL is as widely used as it is today, despite its relative primitiveness in terms of control structures, is evidence that there is a need for programming languages of different kinds for different uses and different users in particular.

Now, let me just close by commenting a little bit on the future of SNOBOL. This is a history conference and perhaps speculation isn't in order, but I think at the same time we might learn from history where we might be going and what we should do. We have a great deal of evidence that programming languages, however antique, develop durability by being used. The most marvelous example of course is FORTRAN, which is a monument to the insight of the original designers. Despite all of the complaints by computer scientists about problems that FORTRAN has, there is no evidence that FORTRAN is ever going to be displaced, and the same may in some sense apply to SNOBOL. Of course its audience is not nearly as large. Simply the fact that it exists, that it is in use, and that there are SNOBOL programs and SNOBOL programmers dictate that it will continue to a certain extent. This is both an economic and an inertial matter. There are many other programming languages with more attractive features, yet at the present time, there is no evidence that the use of SNOBOL4 is decreasing. In fact, it appears to be increasing.

However, there are some areas in which SNOBOL is certainly challenged, and these relate to its historical roots primarily. One is the concern with so-called structured programming. If there was ever a language that was ill-suited for structured programming, SNOBOL is it. It not only has GOTOs, it has side effects, it has all of the lovely things of assembly language, everything that goes with it. It's possible to write SNOBOL programs that are well structured, but the language certainly doesn't encourage it. Yet there are many people that like SNOBOL simply for that reason.

A serious question, and this is an economic question in the broad sense of economics, is the development of smaller, cheaper computers. With a change in our hardware technology, small computers are becoming more readily available to individuals, whether they be personal computers or small business machines, or educational machines. SNOBOL, by its nature, both as a language and what it does, is not well suited to small machines, if for no other reason than that string data occupies a great deal of space compared to numerical data, and SNOBOL is organized so that those strings are treated as data objects and must necessarily be represented that way.

It's somewhat encouraging to note that SNOBOL is sufficiently challenging that it has attracted a lot of effort on the part of clever implementers, and there are now production implementations of SNOBOL that rival processors such as PL/I for many purposes. And some of these are now becoming available on mid-range machines; for example, there is now a good solid SNOBOL4 for the PDP-11. This is an open area and we will see what happens here.

Another possibility is a successor to SNOBOL—something that does what SNOBOL does and does it better. This is a highly problematic area. If you recall the time line, you may have noticed that there is a substantial increase in the length of development in the versions of the language. Looked at linearly, it's about a ratio of 3 to 1. If in fact someone is working on SNOBOL5, I don't think you have to expect anything prior to 1984 at least.

Anyway, I think that the survival of SNOBOL is an open question. I think it will be interesting to see whether it is represented in a conference on fossil programming languages in 1980.

Thank you.

TRANSCRIPT OF QUESTION AND ANSWER SESSION

JAN LEE: There are a number of questions pertaining to the name of the language. If my memory serves me correctly, there are five columns in your paper which go into this in some detail, and I think the question by Raymond Bates of USC Information Science Institute probably summarizes most of them. He says that this footnote came from the PDP-10 SNOBOL User's Guide. Would you please comment on its accuracy. "Farber was once overheard to say that this name was largely contrived when the original *JACM* article was published. The name was apparently picked when one of the original implementers made a statement such as: "This program doesn't have a snowball's chance in hell of . . . .""

RALPH E. GRISWOLD: I'll be happy to respond to that. This is an area where the individuals' recollections differ, which is not surprising that far back. I will say this—that we struggled for a long time for a name. We spent more time trying to find a name than we did designing and implementing the language. And I'm not exaggerating. And I don't think that anyone should downplay the amount of effort it takes to derive names or the unfortunate consequences that they may have. You will recall that the original language was motivated as a tool for our internal use. We did not expect or anticipate that it might become a general-purpose language. We were looking for a name, and we felt that the acronyms that had been given for programming languages reflected a lack of maturity in the computer field. Everybody wanted to be cute. And we struggled for a long time to try to match that immaturity. There were a number of preliminary names—SCL7, indicating that it might be another generation of the SCL series of languages which I alluded to. There were a few other fanciful names. We were working with a string of words that might have something to do with the language. My recollection is that we manipulated them in various ways to see if we could come up with an acronym, and we found we couldn't although I observed that by taking a particular string of them and picking the letters out at appropriate points rather than at the beginning, I at least got a word. And my recollection is that I went into the office of Dave Farber and Ivan Polonsky and I said, "Well, I've really got a disgusting name." And for some reason they liked it, and I think at that time—my recollection is that Dave Farber said, "That sounds good because it doesn't have a snowball's chance in hell." That's my recollection.

LEE: Joel Gyllenskog of CSU, Sacramento, asks—or comments, first of all: "John McCarthy yesterday said that LISP was not an effort to implement a lambda calculus. What was the effect of Markov processes on the design of SNOBOL?"

GRISWOLD: None.

LEE: Does that mean you didn't know anything about them or . . .?

GRISWOLD: Essentially. At that time. We later discovered them.

Transcript of Question and Answer Session

LEE: During your talk you described the development of SNOBOL as being orthogonal to the mainstream of programming language development. I'm sure that that aroused this question from Richard Miller: "Do you think that your lack of knowledge of programming techniques resulted in the very different nature of the language?"

GRISWOLD: Partly. As I indicated earlier, the motivation came not from a group with a charter to develop a programming language, or from a computer science group per se, but from two individuals who were concerned with automatic theorem proving and formula manipulation, and another individual who was familiar with the area. We all contributed in one way or another. There was a certain amount of deliberateness, a certain amount of contrariness, but it was largely, I think, based on our experience with using other languages, rather than our intellectual thoughts about the way the languages should be developed. The answer to the question really depends on which individual you're talking about, and the resulting language was a mixture of several individuals' input.

LEE: What do you think would have been the effect on SNOBOL had it been promoted as actively as APL?

GRISWOLD: I think the effect would have been we wouldn't have had time to do it. I've indicated peripherally that SNOBOL was done by a small group of individuals largely out of their own initiative—we were *allowed* to do this work. We also had other responsibilities. But we did all the design, implementation, documentation, distribution including writing tapes, and publicity, if you like. And we had precious little time for proselytizing. I don't know what the effect would have been. Certainly in the early days of SNOBOL we did rather the contrary. The language sold itself, but I'm not kidding when I say that if we had undertaken that I think we probably would not have continued the development of the language.

LEE: Our next question comes from Ken Dickey of Humboldt State. He says, "You mention the free distribution as being a factor in SNOBOL's success. Outside the IBM structure, do you feel that there can be a successful language today without such a distribution?"

GRISWOLD: I assume that question means, "Can there be a successful language without free distribution outside of, say, some vendor structure?" Is that a good interpretation? I think it's very difficult. It's hard for me to convey how much effort it takes to distribute a language if you don't have an organization to support it. Now, of course, Bell Laboratories had organizational support in the sense of computer facilities, but there were many times in which I myself went in on Sundays and wrote distribution tapes, and all the things that go with it, and answered all the letters and documentation and so forth, personally. It takes a pretty fanatic person to do that over a period of time. I feel free saying that, standing here. I think it's becoming increasingly difficult, because of the economies of computing. But I don't think it's impossible. It does take a rather large amount of dedication and it does take continuity. The area that most programming languages fail in this, that are not vendor-supported, is in continuity. They come out of academic environments primarily, and then the individual moves to another organization, gets tired of all the trouble that goes with a language and stops supporting it, and the language dies. And this is one of the reasons why there is a hesitancy on the part of Federal funding agencies to support new programming languages in this context . . . and it's a very good reason.

LEE: Ralph, thank you very much.

FULL TEXT OF ALL QUESTIONS SUBMITTED

RAYMOND BATES

This footnote came from a PDP-10 SNOBOL User's Manual. Would you please comment on its accuracy? "Farber was once overheard to say that this name was largely contrived when the original *JACM* article was published. The name was apparently picked when one of the original implementers made a statement such as: 'This program doesn't have a snowball's chance in hell of succeeding.'"

KEN DICKEY

You mention "free" distribution as a factor in SNOBOL's success. Outside the IBM structure, do you feel that there can be a successful language today without such a distribution (i.e., nonproprietary such as PASCAL which would not be gaining wide use without such a distribution), or that the ready ability to freely design languages may make language distribution insignificant?

JOEL GYLLENSKOG

John McCarthey said that LISP was not an effort to implement the lambda calculus. What was the effect of Markov processes on the design of SNOBOL?

RICHARD MILLER

1. Do you think that your lack of knowledge of programming techniques affected the (very) different nature of the language (compared to FORTRAN or ALGOL)?
2. Could you comment on the evolution of the pattern concept?

BOB ROSIN

What do you think would have been the effect on SNOBOL had it been promoted as actively as was APL?

BRUCE WALKER

What does SNOBOL stand for?

PETER WEGNER

Both SNOBOL4 and APL achieve their attractiveness in part by their lack of declarations. Declarations force the programmer to plan ahead, and the attractiveness of SNOBOL and APL is due in part to the fact that programmers need not plan ahead as much in writing their programs. Should we encourage this attitude among programmers?

BIOGRAPHY OF RALPH E. GRISWOLD

Ralph E. Griswold was born in Modesto, California, on May 19, 1934. He received the B.S. degree in physics from Stanford University in 1956. Following service in the Navy, he returned to Stanford for his M.S. and Ph.D. degrees in 1960 and 1962, both in electrical engineering. His doctoral research was concerned with iterative switching networks.

Following the completion of his doctoral work he joined Bell Telephone Laboratories in New Jersey as a member of the technical staff. His initial assignment was in the Programming Research Studies Department, where he worked on developing programs for the manipulation of symbolic expressions.

This work led to the develoment of the SNOBOL programming language in collaboration with Ivan Polonsky and Dave Farber in 1963. Subsequent work led to SNOBOL2, SNOBOL3, and SNOBOL4.

In 1967 Dr. Griswold was made supervisor of the Computer Languages Research Group, and in 1969 he was appointed head of the Programming Research and Development Department with responsibility for a variety of activities ranging from programming language research to the operation of a time-sharing system for document preparation.

In 1971, Dr. Griswold left Bell Laboratories to head the computer science program at the University of Arizona. He has continued his work in programming languages there, with emphasis on the design of high-level facilities for the manipulation of nonnumeric data. His other interests include programming methodology, measurement of high-level programming languages, program portability, and computer-based phototypesetting systems.

APL Session

Chairman: JAN Lee
Speaker: Kenneth E. Iverson
Discussant: Frederick Brooks

PAPER: THE EVOLUTION OF APL

Adin D. Falkoff
Kenneth E. Iverson

IBM Corporation
Research Division

This paper is a discussion of the evolution of the APL language, and it treats implementations and applications only to the extent that they appear to have exercised a major influence on that evolution. Other sources of historical information are cited in References 1–3; in particular, *The Design of APL* [1] provides supplementary detail on the reasons behind many of the design decisions made in the development of the language. Readers requiring background on the current definition of the language should consult *APL Language* [4].

Although we have attempted to confirm our recollections by reference to written documents and to the memories of our colleagues, this remains a personal view which the reader should perhaps supplement by consulting the references provided. In particular, much information about individual contributions will be found in the Appendix to *The Design of APL* [1], and in the Acknowledgments in *A Programming Language* [10] and in *APL\360 User's Manual* [23]. Because Reference 23 may no longer be readily available, the acknowledgments from it are reprinted in Appendix A.

McDonnell's recent paper on the development of the notation for the circular functions [5] shows that the detailed evolution of any one facet of the language can be both interesting and illuminating. Too much detail in the present paper would, however, tend to obscure the main points, and we have therefore limited ourselves to one such example. We can only hope that other contributors will publish their views on the detailed developments of other facets of the language, and on the development of various applications of it.

The development of the language was first begun by Iverson as a tool for describing and

HISTORY OF PROGRAMMING LANGUAGES

analyzing various topics in data processing, for use in teaching classes, and in writing a book, *Automatic Data Processing* [6], undertaken together with Frederick P. Brooks, Jr., then a graduate student at Harvard. Because the work began as incidental to other work, it is difficult to pinpoint the beginning, but it was probably early 1956; the first explicit use of the language to provide communication between the designers and programmers of a complex system occurred during a leave from Harvard spent with the management consulting firm of McKinsey and Company in 1957. Even after others were drawn into the development of the language, this development remained largely incidental to the work in which it was used. For example, Falkoff was first attracted to it (shortly after Iverson joined IBM in 1960) by its use as a tool in his work in parallel search memories [7], and in 1964 we began to plan an implementation of the language to enhance its utility as a design tool, work which came to fruition when we were joined by Lawrence M. Breed in 1965.

The most important influences in the early phase appear to be Iverson's background in mathematics, his thesis work in the machine solutions of linear differential equations [8] for an economic input–output model proposed by Professor Wassily Leontief (who, with Professor Howard Aiken, served as thesis adviser), and Professor Aiken's interest in the newly developing field of commercial applications of computers. Falkoff brought to the work a background in engineering and technical development, with experience in a number of disciplines, which had left him convinced of the overriding importance of simplicity, particularly in a field as subject to complication as data processing.

Although the evolution has been continuous, it will be helpful to distinguish four phases according to the major use or preoccupation of the period: academic use (to 1960), machine description (1961–1963), implementation (1964–1968), and systems (after 1968).

1. Academic Use

The machine programming required in Iverson's thesis work was directed at the development of a set of subroutines designed to permit convenient experimentation with a variety of mathematical methods. This implementation experience led to an emphasis on implementable language constructs, and to an understanding of the role of the representation of data.

The mathematical background shows itself in a variety of ways, notably:

1. In the use of functions with explicit arguments and explicit results; even the relations $(< \leq = \geq > \neq)$ are treated as such functions.

2. In the use of logical functions and logical variables. For example, the compression function (denoted by /) uses as one argument a logical vector which is, in effect, the characteristic vector of the subset selected by compression.

3. In the use of concepts and terminology from tensor analysis, as in *inner product* and *outer product* and in the use of *rank* for the "dimensionality" of an array, and in the treatment of a scalar as an array of rank zero.

4. In the emphasis on generality. For example, the generalizations of summation (by $F/$), of inner product (by $F.G$), and of outer product (by $\circ.F$) extended the utility of these functions far beyond their original area of application.

5. In the emphasis on identities (already evident in [9]) which makes the language more useful for analytic purposes, and which leads to a uniform treatment of special cases as, for example, the definition of the reduction of an empty vector, first given in *A Programming Language* [10].

In 1954 Harvard University published an announcement [11] of a new graduate program in Automatic Data Processing organized by Professor Aiken. (The program was also reported in a conference on computer education [12]). Iverson was one of the new faculty appointed to prosecute the program; working under the guidance of Professor Aiken in the development of new courses provided a stimulus to his interest in developing notation, and the diversity of interests embraced by the program promoted a broad view of applications.

The state of the language at the end of the academic period is best represented by the presentation in *A Programming Language* [10], submitted for publication in early 1961. The evolution in the latter part of the period is best seen by comparing References 9 and 10. This comparison shows that *reduction* and *inner* and *outer product* were all introduced in that period, although not then recognized as a class later called *operators*. It also shows that specification was originally (in Reference 9) denoted by placing the specified name at the right, as in $P + Q \rightarrow Z$. The arguments (due in part to F. P. Brooks, Jr.) which led to the present form ($Z \leftarrow P + Q$) were that it better conformed to the mathematical form $Z = P + Q$, and that in reading a program, any backward reference to determine how a given variable was specified would be facilitated if the specified variables were aligned at the left margin. What this comparison does not show is the removal of a number of special comparison functions (such as the comparison of a vector with each row of a matrix) which were seen to be unnecessary when the power of the inner product began to be appreciated, as in the expression $M \wedge . = V$. This removal provides one example of the simplification of the language produced by generalizations.

2. Machine Description

The machine description phase was marked by the complete or partial description of a number of computer systems. The first use of the language to describe a complete computing system was begun in early 1962 when Falkoff discussed with Dr. W. C. Carter his work in the standardization of the instruction set for the machines that were to become the IBM System/360 family. Falkoff agreed to undertake a formal description of the machine language, largely as a vehicle for demonstrating how parallel processes could be rigorously represented. He was later joined in this work by Iverson when he returned from a short leave at Harvard, and still later by E. H. Sussenguth. This work was published as ''A Formal Description of System/360'' [13].

This phase was also marked by a consolidation and regularization of many aspects which had little to do with machine description. For example, the cumbersome definition of maximum and minimum (denoted in Reference 10 by $U\lceil V$ and $U\lfloor V$ and equivalent to what would now be written as $\lceil/U/V$ and $\lfloor/U/V$) was replaced, at the suggestion of Herbert Hellerman, by the present simple scalar functions. This simplification was deemed practical because of our increased understanding of the potential of reduction and inner and outer product.

The best picture of the evolution in this period is given by a comparison of *A Programming Language* [10] on the one hand, and ''A Formal Description of System/360'' [13] and ''Formalism in Programming Languages'' [14] on the other. Using explicit page references to Reference 10, we will now give some further examples of regularization during this period:

1. The elimination of embracing symbols (such as $|X|$ for absolute value, $\lfloor X \rfloor$ for floor, and $\lceil X \rceil$ for ceiling) and replacement by the leading symbol only, thus unifying the syntax for monadic functions.

2. The conscious use of a single function symbol to represent both a *monadic* and *dyadic* function (still referred to in Reference 10 as *unary* and *binary*).

3. The adoption of multicharacter names which, because of the failure (p. 11) to insist on no elision of the times sign, had been permitted (p. 10) only with a special indicator.

4. The rigorous adoption of a right-to-left order of execution which, although stated (p. 8) had been violated by the unconscious application of the familiar precedence rules of mathematics. Reasons for this choice are presented in *Elementary Functions* [15], in Berry's *APL\360 Primer* [16], and in *The Design of APL* [1].

5. The concomitant definition of reduction based on a right-to-left order of execution as opposed to the opposite convention defined on p. 16.

6. Elimination of the requirement for parentheses surrounding an expression involving a relation (p. 11). An example of the use without parentheses occurs near the bottom of p. 241 of Reference 13.

7. The elimination of implicit specification of a variable (that is, the specification of some function of it, as in the expression $\perp S \leftarrow 2$ on p. 81), and its replacement by an explicit inverse function ($\top$ in the cited example).

Perhaps the most important developments of this period were in the use of a collection of concurrent autonomous programs to describe a system, and the formalization of *shared variables* as the means of communication among the programs. Again, comparisons may be made between the system of programs of Reference 13, and the more informal use of concurrent programs introduced on p. 88 of Reference 10.

It is interesting to note that the need for a random function (denoted by the question mark) was first felt in describing the operation of the computer itself. The architects of the IBM System/360 wished to leave to the discretion of the designers of the individual machines of the 360 family the decision as to what was to be found in certain registers after the occurrence of certain errors, and this was done by stating that the result was to be random. Recognizing more general use for the function than the generation of random logical vectors, we subsequently defined the monadic question mark function as a scalar function whose argument specified the population from which the random elements were to be chosen.

3. Implementation

In 1964 a number of factors conspired to turn our attention seriously to the problem of implementation. One was the fact that the language was by now sufficiently well-defined to give us some confidence in its suitability for implementation. The second was the interest of Mr. John L. Lawrence, who, after managing the publication of our description of System/360, asked for our consultation in utilizing the language as a tool in his new responsibility (with Science Research Associates) for developing the use of computers in education. We quickly agreed with Mr. Lawrence on the necessity for a machine implementation in this work. The third was the interest of our then manager, Dr. Herbert Hellerman, who, after initiating some implementation work which did not see completion, himself undertook an implementation of an array-based language which he reported in the

Communications of the ACM [17]. Although this work was limited in certain important respects, it did prove useful as a teaching tool and tended to confirm the feasibility of implementation.

Our first step was to define a character set for APL. Influenced by Dr. Hellerman's interest in time-sharing systems, we decided to base the design on an 88-character set for the IBM 1050 terminal, which utilized the easily changed Selectric® typing element. The design of this character set exercised a surprising degree of influence on the development of the language.

As a practical matter it was clear that we would have to accept a linearization of the language (with no superscripts or subscripts) as well as a strict limit on the size of the primary character set. Although we expected these limitations to have a deleterious effect, and at first found unpleasant some of the linearity forced upon us, we now feel that the changes were beneficial, and that many led to important generalizations. For example:

1. On linearizing indexing we realized that the sub- and superscript form had inhibited the use of arrays of rank greater than 2, and had also inhibited the use of several levels of indexing; both inhibitions were relieved by the linear form $A[I; J; K]$.

2. The linearization of the inner and outer product notation (from $M \underset{\times}{+} N$ and $M \underset{\times}{\circ} N$ to $M + . \times N$ and $M \circ . \times N$) led eventually to the recognition of the operator (which was now represented by an explicit symbol, the period) as a separate and important component of the language.

3. Linearization led to a regularization of many functions of two arguments (such as $N \alpha J$ for $\alpha^j(n)$ and $A * B$ for a^b) and to the redefinition of certain functions of two or three arguments so as to eliminate one of the arguments. For example, $\iota^j(n)$ was replaced by ιN, with the simple expression $J + \iota N$ replacing the original definition. Moreover, the simple form ιN led to the recognition that $J \geq \iota N$ could replace $N \alpha J$ (for J a scalar) and that $J \circ . \geq \iota N$ could generalize $N \alpha J$ in a useful manner; as a result the functions α and ω were eventually withdrawn.

4. The limitation of the character set led to a more systematic exploitation of the notion of ambiguous valence, the representation of both a monadic and a dyadic function by the same symbol.

5. The limitation of the character set led to the replacement of the two functions for the number of rows and the number of columns of an array, by the single function (denoted by ρ) which gave the dimension vector of the array. This provided the necessary extension to arrays of arbitrary rank, and led to the simple expression $\rho \rho A$ for the rank of A. The resulting notion of the dimension vector also led to the definition of the dyadic reshape function $D \rho X$.

6. The limitation to 88 primary characters led to the important notion of composite characters formed by striking one of the basic characters over another. This scheme has provided a supply of easily read and easily written symbols which were needed as the language developed further. For example, the quad, overbar, and circle were included not for specific purposes but because they could be used to overstrike many characters. The overbar by itself also proved valuable for the representation of negative numbers, and the circle proved convenient in carrying out the idea, proposed by E. E. McDonnell, of representing the entire family of (monadic) circular functions by a single dyadic function.

7. The use of multiple fonts had to be reexamined, and this led to the realization that certain functions were defined not in terms of the value of the argument alone, but also in

terms of the form of the name of the argument. Such dependence on the forms of names was removed.

We did, however, include characters which could print above and below alphabetics to provide for possible font distinctions. The original typing element included both the present flat underscore, and a saw-tooth one (the *pralltriller* as shown, for example, in *Webster's Second*), and a hyphen. In practice, we found the two underscores somewhat difficult to distinguish, and the hyphen very difficult to distinguish from the minus, from which it differed only in length. We therefore made the rather costly change of two characters, substituting the present delta and del (inverted delta) for the pralltriller and the hyphen.

In the placement of the character set on the keyboard we were subject to a number of constraints imposed by the two forms of the IBM 2741 terminal (which differed in the encoding from keyboard-position to element-position), but were able to devise a grouping of symbols which most users find easy to learn. One pleasant surprise has been the discovery that numbers of people who do not use APL have adopted the type element for use in mathematical typing. The first publication of the character set appears to be in *Elementary Functions* [15].

Implementation led to a new class of questions, including the formal definition of functions, the localization and scope of names, and the use of tolerances in comparisons and in printing output. It also led to systems questions concerning the environment and its management, including the matter of libraries and certain parameters such as index origin, printing precision, and printing width.

Two early decisions set the tone of the implementation work: (1) The implementation was to be experimental, with primary emphasis on flexibility to permit experimentation with language concepts, and with questions of execution efficiency subordinated, and (2) the language was to be compromised as little as possible by machine considerations.

These considerations led Breed and P. S. Abrams (both of whom had been attracted to our work by Reference 13) to propose and build an *interpretive* implementation in the summer of 1965. This was a batch system with punched-card input, using a multicharacter encoding of the primitive function symbols. It ran on the IBM 7090 computer, and we were later able to experiment with it interactively, using the typeball previously designed, by placing the interpreter under an experimental time-sharing monitor (TSM) available on a machine in a nearby IBM facility.

TSM was available to us for only a very short time, and in early 1966 we began to consider an implementation on System/360, work that started in earnest in July and culminated in a running system in the fall. The fact that this interpretive and experimental implementation also proved to be remarkably practical and efficient is a tribute to the skill of the implementers, recognized in 1973 by the award to the principals (L. M. Breed, R. H. Lathwell, and R. D. Moore) of ACM's Grace Murray Hopper Award. The fact that many APL implementations continue to be largely interpretive may be attributed to the array character of the language which makes possible efficient interpretive execution.

We chose to treat the occurrence of a statement as an order to evaluate it, and rejected the notion of an explicit function to indicate evaluation. In order to avoid the introduction of "names" as a distinct object class, we also rejected the notion of "call by name." The constraints imposed by this decision were eventually removed in a simple and general way by the introduction of the *execute* function, which served to execute its character string argument as an APL expression. The evolution of these notions is discussed at length in the section on "Execute and Format" in *The Design of APL* [1].

In earlier discussions with a number of colleagues, the introduction of declarations into the language was urged upon us as a requisite for implementation. We resisted this on the general basis of simplicity, but also on the basis that information in declarations would be redundant, or perhaps conflicting, in a language in which arrays are primitive. The choice of an interpretive implementation made the exclusion of declarations feasible, and this, coupled with the determination to minimize the influence of machine considerations such as the internal representations of numbers on the design of the language, led to an early decision to exclude them.

In providing a mechanism by which a user could define a new function, we wished to provide six forms in all: functions with 0, 1, or 2 explicit arguments, and functions with 0 or 1 explicit results. This led to the adoption of a *header* for the function definition which was, in effect, a paradigm for the way in which a function was used. For example, a function F of two arguments having an explicit result would typically be used in an expression such as $Z \leftarrow A \ F \ B$, and this was the form used for the header.

The names for arguments and results in the header were of course made local to the function definition, but at the outset no thought was given to the localization of other names. Fortunately, the design of the interpreter made it relatively easy to localize the names by adding them to the header (separated by semicolons), and this was soon done. Names so localized were strictly local to the defined function, and their scope did not extend to any other functions used within it. It was not until the spring of 1968 when Breed returned from a talk by Professor Alan Perlis on what he called "dynamic localization" that the present scheme was adopted, in which name scopes extend to functions called within a function.

We recognized that the finite limits on the representation of numbers imposed by an implementation would raise problems which might require some compromise in the definition of the language, and we tried to keep these compromises to a minimum. For example, it was clear that we would have to provide both integer and floating point representations of numbers and, because we anticipated use of the system in logical design, we wished to provide an efficient (one bit per element) representation of logical arrays as well. However, at the cost of considerable effort and some loss of efficiency, both well worthwhile, the transitions between representations were made to be imperceptible to the user, except for secondary effects such as storage requirements.

Problems such as overflow (i.e., a result outside the range of the representations available) were treated as domain errors, the term *domain* being understood as the domain of the machine function provided, rather than as the domain of the abstract mathematical function on which it was based.

One difficulty we had not anticipated was the provision of sensible results for the comparison of quantities represented to a limited precision. For example, if X and Y were specified by $Y \leftarrow 2 \div 3$ and $X \leftarrow 3 \times Y$, then we wished to have the comparison $2 = X$ yield 1 (representing *true*) even though the representation of the quantity X would differ slightly from 2.

This was solved by introducing a comparison tolerance (christened *fuzz* by L. M. Breed, who knew of its use in the Bell Interpreter [18]) which was multiplied by the larger in magnitude of the arguments to give a tolerance to be applied in the comparison. This tolerance was at first fixed (at $1E^-13$) and was later made specifiable by the user. The matter has proven more difficult than we first expected, and discussion of it still continues [19, 20].

A related, but less serious, question was what to do with the rational root of a negative number, a question which arose because the exponent (as in the expression $^-8 * 2 \div 3$) would normally be presented as an approximation to a rational. Since we wished to make the mathematics behave "as you thought it did in high school" we wished to treat such cases properly at least for rationals with denominators of reasonable size. This was achieved by determining the result sign by a continued fraction expansion of the right argument (but only for negative left arguments) and worked for all denominators up to 80 and "most" above.

Most of the mathematical functions required were provided by programs taken from the work of the late Hirondo Kuki in the FORTRAN IV Subroutine Library. Certain functions (such as the inverse hyperbolics) were, however, not available and were developed, during the summers of 1967 and 1968, by K. M. Brown, then on the faculty of Cornell University.

The fundamental decision concerning the systems environment was the adoption of the concept of a workspace. As defined in "The APL\360 Terminal System" [21]:

> APL\360 is built around the idea of a workspace, analogous to a notebook, in which one keeps work in progress. The workspace holds both defined functions and variables (data), and it may be stored into and retrieved from a library holding many such workspaces. When retrieved from a library by an appropriate command from a terminal, a copy of the stored workspace becomes active at that terminal, and the functions defined in it, together with all the APL primitives, become available to the user.
>
> The three commands required for managing a library are "save," "load," and "drop," which respectively store a copy of an active workspace into a library, make a copy of a stored workspace active, and destroy the library copy of a workspace. Each user of the system has a private library into which only he can store. However, he may load a workspace from any of a number of common libraries, or if he is privy to the necessary information, from another user's private library. Functions or variables in different workspaces can be combined, either item by item or all at once, by a fourth command, called "copy." By means of three cataloging commands, a user may get the names of workspaces in his own or a common library, or get a listing of functions or variables in his active workspace.

The language used to control the system functions of loading and storing workspaces was not APL, but comprised a set of *system commands*. The first character of each system command is a right parenthesis, which cannot occur at the left of a valid APL expression, and therefore acts as an "escape character," freeing the syntax of what follows. System commands were used for other aspects such as sign-on and sign-off, messages to other users, and for the setting and sensing of various system parameters such as the index origin, the printing precision, the print width, and the *random link* used in generating the pseudo-random sequence for the random function.

When it first became necessary to name the implementation we chose the acronym formed from the book title *A Programming Language* [10] and, to allow a clear distinction between the language and any particular implementation of it, initiated the use of the machine name as part of the name of the implementation (as in APL\1130 and APL\360). Within the design group we had until that time simply referred to "the language."

A brief working manual of the APL\360 system was first published in November 1966 [22], and a full manual appeared in 1968 [23]. The initial implementation (in FORTRAN on an IBM 7090) was discussed by Abrams [24], and the time-shared implementation on System/360 was discussed by Breed and Lathwell [25].

4. Systems

Use of the APL system by others in IBM began long before it had been completed to the point described in *APL\360 User's Manual* [23]. We quickly learned the difficulties associated with changing the specifications of a system already in use, and the impact of changes on established users and programs. As a result we learned to appreciate the importance of the relatively long period of development of the language which preceded the implementation; early implementation of languages tends to stifle radical change, limiting further development to the addition of features and frills.

On the other hand, we also learned the advantages of a running model of the language in exposing anomalies and, in particular, the advantage of input from a large population of users concerned with a broad range of applications. This use quickly exposed the major deficiencies of the system.

Some of these deficiencies were rectified by the generalization of certain functions and the addition of others in a process of gradual evolution. Examples include the extension of the catenation function to apply to arrays other than vectors and to permit *lamination,* and the addition of a generalized matrix inverse function discussed by M. A. Jenkins [26].

Other deficiencies were of a systems nature, concerning the need to communicate between concurrent APL programs (as in our description of System/360), to communicate with the APL system itself within APL rather than by the ad hoc device of system commands, to communicate with alien systems and devices (as in the use of file devices), and the need to define functions within the language in terms of their representation by APL arrays. These matters required more fundamental innovations and led to what we have called the *system* phase.

The most pressing practical need for the application of APL systems to commercial data processing was the provision of file facilities. One of the first commercial systems to provide this was the File Subsystem reported by Sharp [27] in 1970, and defined in a SHARE presentation by L. M. Breed [28], and in a manual published by Scientific Time Sharing Corporation [29]. As its name implies, it was not an integral part of the language but was, like the system commands, a practical ad hoc solution to a pressing problem.

In 1970 R. H. Lathwell proposed what was to become the basis of a general solution to many systems problems of APL\360, a *shared variable processor* [30] which implemented the shared variable scheme of communication among processors. This work culminated in the APLSV System [31] which became generally available in 1973.

Falkoff's "Some Implications of Shared Variables" [32] presents the essential notion of the shared variable system as follows:

> A user of early APL systems essentially had what appeared to be an "APL machine" at his disposal, but one which lacked access to the rest of the world. In more recent systems, such as APLSV and others, this isolation is overcome and communication with other users and the host system is provided for by *shared variables.*
>
> Two classes of shared variables are available in these systems. First, there is a *general shared variable* facility with which a user may establish arbitrary, *temporary,* interfaces with other users or with auxiliary processors. Through the latter, communication may be had with other elements of the host system, such as its file subsystem, or with other systems altogether. Second, there is a

Adin D. Falkoff and Kenneth E. Iverson

set of *system variables* which define parts of the *permanent* interface between an APL program and the underlying processor. These are used for interrogating and controlling the computing environment, such as the origin for array indexing or the action to be taken upon the occurrence of certain exceptional conditions.

5. A Detailed Example

At the risk of placing undue emphasis on one facet of the language, we will now examine in detail the evolution of the treatment of numeric constants, in order to illustrate how substantial changes were commonly arrived at by a sequence of small steps.

Any numeric constant, including a constant vector, can be written as an expression involving APL primitive functions applied to decimal numbers as, for example, in $3.14 \times 10 * -5$ and -2.718 and $(3.14 \times 10 * -5),(-2.718), 5$. At the outset we permitted only nonnegative decimal constants of the form 2.718; all other values had to be expressed as compound statements.

Use of the monadic negation function in producing negative values in vectors was particularly cumbersome, as in $(-4),3,(-5),-7$. We soon realized that the adoption of a specific "negative" symbol would solve the problem, and familiarity with Beberman's work [33] led us to the adoption of his "high minus" which we had, rather fortuitously, included in our character set. The constant vector used above could now be written as $^-4,3,^-5,^-7$.

Solution of the problem of negative numbers emphasized the remaining awkwardness of factors of the form $10 * N$. At a meeting of the principals in Chicago, which included Donald Mitchell and Peter Calingaert of Science Research Associates, it was realized that the introduction of a scaled form of constant in the manner used in FORTRAN would not complicate the syntax, and this was soon adopted.

These refinements left one function in the writing of any vector constant, namely, catenation. The straightforward execution of an expression for a constant vector of N elements involved $N - 1$ catenations of scalars with vectors of increasing length, the handling of roughly $.5 \times N \times N + 1$ elements in all. To avoid gross inefficiencies in the input of a constant vector from the keyboard, catenation was therefore given special treatment in the original implementation.

This system had been in use for perhaps six months when it occurred to Falkoff that since commas were not required in the normal representation of a matrix, vector constants might do without them as well. This seemed outrageously simple, and we looked for flaws. Finding none we adopted and implemented the idea immediately, but it took some time to overcome the habit of writing expressions such as $(3,3)\rho X$ instead of $3\ 3\rho X$.

6. Conclusions

Nearly all programming languages are rooted in mathematical notation, employing such fundamental notions as functions, variables, and the decimal (or other radix) representation of numbers, and a view of programming languages as part of the longer-range development of mathematical notation can serve to illuminate their development.

Before the advent of the general-purpose computer, mathematical notation had, in a long and painful evolution well-described in Cajori's history of mathematical notations [34], embraced a number of important notions:

1. The notion of assigning an alphabetic name to a variable or unknown quantity (Cajori, Sections 339–341).

2. The notion of a *function* which applies to an *argument* or arguments to produce an explicit result which can itself serve as argument to another function, and the associated adoption of specific symbols (such as + and ×) to denote the more common functions (Cajori, Sections 200–233).

3. *Aggregation* or *grouping* symbols (such as the parentheses) which make possible the use of composite expressions with an unambiguous specification of the order in which the component functions are to be executed (Cajori, Sections 342–355).

4. Simple uniform representations for numeric quantities (Cajori, Sections 276–289).

5. The treatment of quantities without concern for the particular representation used.

6. The notion of treating vectors, matrices, and higher-dimensional arrays as entities, which had by this time become fairly widespread in mathematics, physics, and engineering.

With the first computer languages (machine languages) all of these notions were, for good practical reasons, dropped; variable names were represented by "register numbers," application of a function (as in $A+B$) was necessarily broken into a sequence of operations (such as "Load register 801 into the Addend register, Load register 802 into the Augend register, etc."), grouping of operations was therefore nonexistent, the various functions provided were represented by numbers rather than by familiar mathematical symbols, results depended sharply on the particular representation used in the machine, and the use of arrays, as such, disappeared.

Some of these limitations were soon removed in early "automatic programming" languages, and languages such as FORTRAN introduced a limited treatment of arrays, but many of the original limitations remain. For example, in FORTRAN and related languages the size of an array is not a language concept, the asterisk is used instead of any of the familiar mathematical symbols for multiplication, the power function is represented by two occurrences of this symbol rather than by a distinct symbol, and concern with representation still survives in declarations.

APL has, in its development, remained much closer to mathematical notation, retaining (or selecting one of) established symbols where possible, and employing mathematical terminology. Principles of simplicity and uniformity have, however, been given precedence, and these have led to certain departures from conventional mathematical notation as, for example, the adoption of a single form (analogous to 3+4) for the dyadic functions, a single form (analogous to −4) for monadic functions, and the adoption of a uniform rule for the application of all scalar functions to arrays. This relationship to mathematical notation has been discussed in *The Design of APL* [1] and in "Algebra as a Language" which occurs as Appendix A in *Algebra: An Algorithmic Treatment* [35].

The close ties with mathematical notation are evident in such things as the reduction operator (a generalization of sigma notation), the inner product (a generalization of matrix product), and the outer product (a generalization of the outer product used in tensor analysis). In other aspects the relation to mathematical notation is closer than might appear. For example, the order of execution of the conventional expression $F\,G\,H\,(X)$ can be expressed by saying that the right argument of each function is the value of the entire expression to its right; this rule, extended to dyadic as well as monadic functions, is the rule used in APL. Moreover, the term *operator* is used in the same sense as in "derivative operator'' or ''convolution operator'' in mathematics, and to avoid conflict it is not used as a synonym for *function*.

As a corollary we may remark that the other major programming languages, although known to the designers of APL, exerted little or no influence, because of their radical departures from the line of development of mathematical notation which APL continued. A concise view of the current use of the language, together with comments on matters such as writing style, may be found in Falkoff's review of the 1975 and 1976 International APL Congresses [36].

Although this is not the place to discuss the future, it should be remarked that the evolution of APL is far from finished. In particular, there remain large areas of mathematics, such as set theory and vector calculus, which can clearly be incorporated in APL through the introduction of further operators.

There are also a number of important features which are already in the abstract language, in the sense that their incorporation requires little or no new definition, but are as yet absent from most implementations. Examples include complex numbers, the possibility of defining functions of ambiguous valence (already incorporated in at least two systems [37, 38]), the use of user defined functions in conjunction with operators, and the use of selection functions other than indexing to the left of the assignment arrow.

We conclude with some general comments, taken from *The Design of APL* [1], on principles which guided, and circumstances which shaped, the evolution of APL:

> The actual operative principles guiding the design of any complex system must be few and broad. In the present instance we believe these principles to be simplicity and practicality. Simplicity enters in four guises: uniformity (rules are few and simple), generality (a small number of general functions provide as special cases a host of more specialized functions), familiarity (familiar symbols and usages are adopted whenever possible), and brevity (economy of expression is sought). Practicality is manifested in two respects: concern with actual application of the language, and concern with the practical limitations imposed by existing equipment.

> We believe that the design of APL was also affected in important respects by a number of procedures and circumstances. Firstly, from its inception APL has been developed by using it in a succession of areas. This emphasis on application clearly favors practicality and simplicity. The treatment of many different areas fostered generalization: for example, the general inner product was developed in attempting to obtain the advantages of ordinary matrix algebra in the treatment of symbolic logic.

> Secondly, the lack of any machine realization of the language during the first seven or eight years of its development allowed the designers the freedom to make radical changes, a freedom not normally enjoyed by designers who must observe the needs of a large working population dependent on the language for their daily computing needs. This circumstance was due more to the dearth of interest in the language than to foresight.

> Thirdly, at every stage the design of the language was controlled by a small group of not more than five people. In particular, the men who designed (and coded) the implementation were part of the language design group, and all members of the design group were involved in broad decisions affecting the implementation. On the other hand, many ideas were received and accepted from people outside the design group, particularly from active users of some implementation of APL.

> Finally, design decisions were made by Quaker consensus; controversial innovations were deferred until they could be revised or reevaluated so as to obtain unanimous agreement. Unanimity was not achieved without cost in time and effort, and many divergent paths were explored and assessed. For example, many different notations for the circular and hyperbolic functions were entertained over a period of more than a year before the present scheme was proposed, whereupon it was quickly adopted. As the language grows, more effort is needed to explore the ramifi-

cations of any major innovation. Moreover, greater care is needed in introducing new facilities, to avoid the possibility of later retraction that would inconvenience thousands of users.

Appendix. Acknowledgments†

The APL language was first defined by K. E. Iverson in *A Programming Language* (Wiley, 1962) and has since been developed in collaboration with A. D. Falkoff. The APL\360 Terminal System was designed with the additional collaboration of L. M. Breed, who with R. D. Moore (I. P. Sharp Associates, Toronto, Canada), also designed the S/360 implementation. The system was programmed for S/360 by Breed, Moore, and R. H. Lathwell, with continuing assistance from L. J. Woodrum (General Systems Architecture, IBM Corporation, Poughkeepsie, New York), and contributions by C. H. Brenner, H. A. Driscoll (Science Research Associates, Chicago, Illinois), and S. E. Krueger. The present implementation also benefitted from experience with an earlier version, designed and programmed for the IBM 7090 by Breed and P. S. Abrams (Computer Science Department, Stanford University, Stanford, California).

The development of the system has also profited from ideas contributed by many other users and colleagues, notably E. E. McDonnell, who suggested the notation for the signum and the circular functions.

In the preparation of the present manual, the authors are indebted to L. M. Breed for many discussions and suggestions; to R. H. Lathwell, E. E. McDonnell, and J. G. Arnold (Industry Development, IBM Corporation, White Plains, New York) for critical reading of successive drafts; and to Mrs. G. K. Sedlmayer and Miss Valerie Gilbert for superior clerical assistance.

A special acknowledgement is due to John L. Lawrence, who provided important support and encouragement during the early development of APL implementation, and who pioneered the application of APL in computer-related instruction.

For critical comments arising from their reading of this paper, we are indebted to a number of our colleagues who were there when it happened, particularly P. S. Abrams of Scientific Time Sharing Corporation, R. H. Lathwell and R. D. Moore of I. P. Sharp Associates, and L. M. Breed and E. E. McDonnell of IBM Corporation.

REFERENCES

1. Falkoff, A. D., and K. E. Iverson, The Design of APL. *IBM Journal of Research and Development,* **17**(4): 324–334 (1973) July.
2. The Story of APL, *Computing Report in Science and Engineering,* **6** (2): 14–18 (1970) April. IBM Corp.
3. Origin of APL, a videotape prepared by John Clark for the Fourth APL Conference, 1974, with the participation of P. S. Abrams, L. M. Breed, A. D. Falkoff, K. E. Iverson, and R. D. Moore. Available from Orange Coast Community College, Costa Mesa, California.
4. Falkoff, A. D., and K. E. Iverson, *APL Language,* Form No. GC26-3847, IBM Corp., White Plains, New York, 1975.
5. McDonnell, E. E., The Story of ○. *APL Quote-Quad.* **8**(2): 48–45 (1977) Dec. ACM, SIGPLAN Technical Committee on APL (STAPL).
6. Brooks, F. P., and K. E. Iverson, *Automatic Data Processing.* New York: Wiley, 1973.
7. Falkoff, A. D., Algorithms for Parallel Search Memories. *Journal of the ACM,* **9**: 488–511 (1962).
8. Iverson, K. E., *Machine Solutions of Linear Differential Equations: Applications to a Dynamic Economic Model, Ph.D. Thesis,* Harvard University, 1954.
9. Iverson, K. E. The Description of Finite Sequential Processes. *Proceedings of the Fourth London Symposium on Information Theory* (Colin Cherry, ed.), pp. 447–457. 1960.
10. Iverson, K. E., *A Programming Language.* New York: Wiley, 1962.
11. *Graduate Program in Automatic Data Processing* (brochure), Harvard University, 1954.
12. Iverson, K. E., Graduate Research and Instruction. *Proceedings of First Conference on Training Personnel*

† Reprinted from *APL\360 User's Manual* [23].

Kenneth E. Iverson

for the Computing Machine Field, Wayne State University, Detroit, Michigan (Arvid W. Jacobson, ed.), pp. 25–29. June 1954.

13. Falkoff, A. D., K. E. Iverson, and E. H. Sussenguth, A Formal Description of System/360. *IBM Systems Journal,* **4**(4): 198–262 (1964) Oct.
14. Iverson, K. E., Formalism in Programming Languages. *Communications of the ACM,* **7**(2): 80–88 (1964) Feb.
15. Iverson, K. E., *Elementary Functions,* Science Research Associates, Chicago, Illinois, 1966.
16. Berry, P. C., *APL\360 Primer* (GH20-0689), IBM Corp., White Plains, New York, 1969.
17. Hellerman, H., Experimental Personalized Array Translator System. *Communications of the ACM,* **7**(7): 433–438 (1964) July.
18. Wolontis, V. M., *A Complete Floating Point Decimal Interpretive System,* Tech. Newsl. No. 11, IBM Applied Science Division, 1956.
19. Lathwell, R. H., APL Comparison Tolerance. *APL 76 Conference Proceedings,* pp. 255–258. Association for Computing Machinery, 1976.
20. Breed, L. M., *Definitions for Fuzzy Floor and Ceiling,* Tech. Rep. No. TR03.024, IBM Corp., White Plains, New York, March 1977.
21. Falkoff, A. D., and K. E. Iverson, The APL\360 Terminal System. *Symposium on Interactive Systems for Experimental Applied Mathematics* (M. Klerer and J. Reinfelds, eds.), pp. 22–37. New York: Academic Press, 1968.
22. Falkoff, A. D., and K. E. Iverson, *APL\360,* IBM Corp., White Plains, New York, November 1966.
23. Falkoff, A. D., and K. E. Iverson, *APL\360 User's Manual,* IBM Corp., White Plains, New York, August 1968.
24. Abrams, P. S., *An Interpreter for Iverson Notation,* Tech. Rep. CS47, Computer Science Department, Stanford University, 1966.
25. Breed, L. M., and R. H. Lathwell, The Implementation of APL\360. *Symposium on Interactive Systems for Experimental and Applied Mathematics* (M. Klerer and J. Reinfelds, eds.), pp. 390–399. New York: Academic Press, 1968.
26. Jenkins, M. A., *The Solution of Linear Systems of Equations and Linear Least Squares Problems in APL,* IBM Tech. Rep. No. 320-2989, 1970.
27. Sharp, Ian P., The Future of APL to Benefit from a New File System. *Canadian Data Systems,* March 1970.
28. Breed, L. M., The APL PLUS File System. *Proceedings of SHARE XXXV,* p. 392. August 1970.
29. *APL PLUS File Subsystem Instruction Manual,* Scientific Time Sharing Corp., Washington, D.C., 1970.
30. Lathwell, R. H., System Formulation and APL Shared Variables. *IBM Journal of Research and Development,* **17**(4): 353–359 (1973) July.
31. Falkoff, A. D., and K. E. Iverson, *APLSV User's Manual,* IBM Corp., White Plains, New York, 1973.
32. Falkoff, A. D., Some Implications of Shared Variables. In *Formal Languages and Programming* (R. Aguilar, ed.), pp. 65–75. Amsterdam: North-Holland Publ., 1976. Reprinted in *APL 76 Conference Proceedings,* pp. 141–148. Association for Computing Machinery, 1976.
33. Beberman, M., and H. E. Vaughn, *High School Mathematics Course 1.* Indianapolis, Indiana: Heath, 1964.
34. Cajori, F., *A History of Mathematical Notations,* Vol. I, *Notations in Elementary Mathematics.* La Salle, Illinois: Open Court Publ., 1928.
35. Iverson, K. E., *Algebra: An Algorithmic Treatment.* Reading, Massachusetts: Addison Wesley, 1972.
36. Falkoff, A. D., APL75 and APL76: an overview of the Proceedings of the Pisa and Ottawa Congresses. *ACM Computing Reviews,* **18**(4): 139–141 (1977) Apr.
37. Weidmann, Clark, *APLUM Reference Manual,* University of Massachusetts, Amherst, Massachusetts, 1975.
38. *Sharp APL Tech. Note No.25,* I. P. Sharp Associates, Toronto, Canada, 1976.

TRANSCRIPT OF PRESENTATION

JAN LEE: For the devotees of the one-liners and APL, I'd now like to present Ken Iverson. Ken received his Bachelor's Degree from Queen's University of Kingston, Ontario, Canada, and his Master's and Ph.D. from Harvard University. In looking through his *vita,* it is very interesting to me to note his progress and to note that he's only had two jobs since he graduated. One at Harvard as Assistant Professor of Applied Mathematics, and then he joined IBM in 1960 and has progressed through the ranks since that time. In progressing through the ranks, he was appointed an IBM Fellow in 1971 for his work on APL, I believe. It's also interesting to note that three years later, having been awarded his Fellowship from IBM, he was then appointed the Manager of the APL Design Group. Ken Iverson.

KENNETH IVERSON: Thank you, JAN. They say never quarrel with a newspaper, because they will have the last word, and I suppose the same applies to chairmen. So I won't even comment on that introduction.

Once launched on a topic it's very easy to forget to mention the contributions of others, and although I have a very good memory, it is, in the words of one of my colleagues, very short, so I feel I must begin with acknowledgments, and I first want to mention Adin Falkoff, my co-author and colleague of nearly 20 years. In musing on the contributors to APL in the light of Radin's speculations last night about the relationship between the characteristics of artifacts and the characteristics of the designers, it struck me that we in the APL work tend to remember one another not for the fantastic ideas that we've contributed, but for the arrant nonsense that we have fought to keep out. Now, I think there's really a serious point here; namely, that design really should be concerned largely, not so much with collecting a lot of ideas, but with shaping them with a view of economy and balance. I think a good designer should make more use of Occam's razor than of the dustbag of a vacuum cleaner, and I thought this was important enough that it would be worthwhile looking for some striking examples of sort of overelaborate design. I was surprised that I didn't find it all that easy, except perhaps for the designers of programming languages and American automobiles, I think that designers seem to have this feeling, a gut feeling of a need for parsimony.

We tried to organize this discussion according to what seemed to be the major phases, and to label these phases with what would seem to be the major preoccupation of the period; and then to try to identify what were the main points of advance in that period, and also to try to identify what seemed to be the main influences at work at that time [Frame 1].

When I say "academic," this is simply a reflection of the fact that when I began to think about this, it was when I was teaching at Harvard, and my main concern was a need for clear expression, some sort of notation for use in classroom work and in writing. As a matter of fact, at the time I was engaged in trying to write a book together with Fred Brooks, and this was one of the motivations for the development of notation.

But it really was as a tool for communication and exposition that I was thinking of it. What seemed to me the major influence at that time was primarily my mathematical background. I was a renegade from mathematics. There are lots of renegades but many

MAJOR PHASES

ACADEMIC	1957–1960
MACHINE DESCRIPTION	1961–1963
IMPLEMENTATION	1964–1968
SYSTEMS	1968–

Frame 1

Kenneth E. Iverson

MATHEMATICAL INFLUENCE
FUNCTIONS WITH EXPLICIT ARGUMENTS
    AND RESULTS
USE OF LOGICAL FUNCTIONS
CONCEPTS FROM TENSOR ANALYSIS
EXPHASIS ON IDENTITIES
OPERATORS

Frame 2

of them didn't desert as early as I did. [Frame 2] lists the main aspects: the idea of functions with explicit arguments and explicit results, the use of logical functions.

Let me just mention one thing. You may have noticed that, for example, relations in APL are not treated separately as assertions, but simply as more logical functions. They are functions, they produce results which you can think of as true or false, but which in fact are represented by ordinary numbers, 1 and 0.

Also, in the treatment of arrays, let me mention—well, the number of concepts from tensor analysis, primarily the idea of simply thinking of the array as the one and only argument in the language and simply treating scalars, vectors, and matrices as special cases which had rank 0, 1, and 2.

The emphasis on identities—by this I mean that we tended to analyze any function to worry about end conditions. Like, what happens in the case of an empty vector and so on? And if you look at this, you'll see that many of the decisions have really come out as simply making identities hold over as wide a range as possible, and so avoid all kinds of special cases.

Finally, the idea of operators, and let me clarify the terminology. I was assured that everybody in the audience would have read the summary, and therefore this won't be necessary, but I will say something about it anyway. Commonly, "functions" are referred to indiscriminately as "functions," "procedures," "operators," and so on, and we tend to say that we call a function a function, and reserve the term "operator" for the way it is used in certain branches of mathematics when we speak about a derivative operator, a convolution operator, and so on. The basic notion is that it's something that applies to a function or functions, and produces a new function. You think of the "slash" in the reduction, for example. It's an operator that applies to any function to produce a new function. Similarly, the dot in the inner product and so on. And this too, I think, was probably because of the mathematical influence.

The next phase, then, was the machine description phase [Frame 3]. I joined IBM in

MACHINE DESCRIPTION PHASE
ORDER OF EXECUTION

SHARED VARIABLES

TYPOGRAPHY
    Linearization
    Single Symbols $|X$ for $|X|$
    Divalence $X * Y$ and $* Y$
    Vector Shape Function
    Compound Characters

Frame 3

1960 and shortly thereafter began to work with Adin Falkoff. We turned much more attention to the problem of describing machines themselves. Let me just mention a couple of the things that were sharpened up in this period. One, the order of execution which, if I have time, I will return to a little later, in a different context. And the other was the idea of shared variables. In describing machines one faces very directly the problem of concurrent processes. You have the CPU, you have the channel, so on. They are concurrent processes, and the only thing that makes them a system is the fact that they are able to communicate. And how do they communicate? We chose the idea that any communication has got to take place somehow through the sharing of some medium, some variable. And that is the general notion which has become, in fact, a rather important aspect of later APL.

Let me just give you an example of this machine description [Frame 4]. That is a 37-line description of the CPU of the 360, and although it obviously subordinates detail, by invoking certain other functions which themselves have definitions, it does exhibit I think in a very straightforward way, the essential detail of the CPU.

You would expect that the channel would be a separate process, but you might not expect that to really describe what happens in a control panel clearly, you've got to recognize that it's a concurrent process, and it may be in different states. And so it turned out that even the control panel seemed to lend itself very nicely to a clear description as a separate processor. There are certain variables that it shares with the CPU and possibly with other units.

The third phase was the one of implementation. I think it was about 1964 that we started thinking seriously of implementation, although this had always been in the back of our minds. We are sometimes asked "had we thought about implementation?" The answer is yes and no. We simply took it for granted that a language that's good for communication [of algorithms] between you and me is also good for communication with a machine, and I still feel the same way about that.

The first thing that we really started thinking seriously about was the question of typography. Earlier we had, in effect, a publication form. We didn't have to worry seriously about the particular symbols used. And once we faced the question of designing an actual implementation, we had to face that question. And I think pretty much following the advice of Herbert Hellerman who was also with IBM at the time, and his interest in time sharing systems, we decided to take the Selectric typing element and design ourselves an 88-character set, and constrain it to that.

Well, this had what to me were surprising implications for the language. It forced us to think seriously about linearizing things. We could no longer afford superscripts, subscripts, and so on, and somewhat to our surprise we found that this really generalized, and in many cases, simplified the language. The problems of addressing more than a two-dimensional arrray disappeared—you seem to soon run out of corners on a letter. But when you linearize things, you can go to any dimension.

We faced the problem of things like absolute value. We standardize that, and simply say all monadic functions appear to the left and they are represented by a single symbol.

The idea from mathematics where a function may have two valences—the minus sign, for example, can represent either subtraction or negation, and there's never any confusion because it's resolved by context. We simply exploited that, and that was one of the ways that we greatly conserved symbols. Thus, $X * Y$ for example, is X to the power Y and, $* Y$, as you might guess, is e to the power Y, in other words, the exponential.

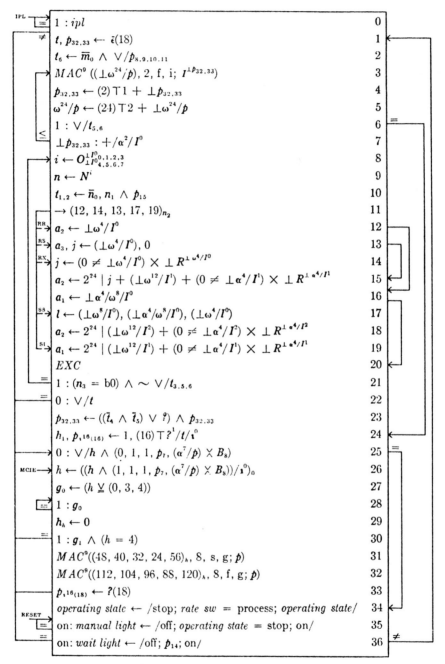

IPL		$1 : ipl$	0
	$\neq$	$t, p_{32.33} \leftarrow \bar{\epsilon}(18)$	1
		$t_6 \leftarrow \bar{m}_0 \wedge \vee/p_{8.9.10.11}$	2
		$MAC^9 ((\perp\omega^{24}/p), 2, f, i; I^{\perp p_{32.33}})$	3
		$p_{32.33} \leftarrow (2)\top 1 + \perp p_{32.33}$	4
		$\omega^{24}/p \leftarrow (24)\top 2 + \perp\omega^{24}/p$	5
		$1 : \vee/t_{5.6}$	6
	$\leq$	$\perp p_{32.33} : +/\alpha^2/I^0$	7
		$i \leftarrow O^{\perp I^0_{0.1.2.3}}_{\perp I^0_{4.5.6.7}}$	8
		$n \leftarrow N^i$	9
		$t_{1.2} \leftarrow \bar{n}_0, n_1 \wedge p_{15}$	10
		$\rightarrow (12, 14, 13, 17, 19)_{n_2}$	11
RR		$a_2 \leftarrow \perp\omega^4/I^0$	12
RS		$a_3, j \leftarrow (\perp\omega^4/I^0), 0$	13
RX		$j \leftarrow (0 \neq \perp\omega^4/I^0) \times \perp R^{\perp\omega^4/I^0}$	14
		$a_2 \leftarrow 2^{24} \mid j + (\perp\omega^{12}/I^1) + (0 \neq \perp\alpha^4/I^1) \times \perp R^{\perp\alpha^4/I^1}$	15
		$a_1 \leftarrow \perp\alpha^4/\omega^8/I^0$	16
S3		$l \leftarrow (\perp\omega^8/I^0), (\perp\alpha^4/\omega^8/I^0), (\perp\omega^4/I^0)$	17
		$a_2 \leftarrow 2^{24} \mid (\perp\omega^{12}/I^2) + (0 \neq \perp\alpha^4/I^2) \times \perp R^{\perp\alpha^4/I^2}$	18
S1		$a_1 \leftarrow 2^{24} \mid (\perp\omega^{12}/I^1) + (0 \neq \perp\alpha^4/I^1) \times \perp R^{\perp\alpha^4/I^1}$	19
		EXC	20
	$=$	$1 : (n_3 = b0) \wedge \sim \vee/t_{3.5.6}$	21
	$=$	$0 : \vee/t$	22
		$p_{32.33} \leftarrow ((\bar{t}_4 \wedge \bar{t}_5) \vee ?) \wedge p_{32.33}$	23
		$h_1, p_{,16(16)} \leftarrow 1, (16)\top ?^1/t/\imath^0$	24
		$0 : \vee/h \wedge (0, 1, 1, p_7, (\alpha^7/p) \times B_8)$	25
MCIE		$h \leftarrow ((h \wedge (1, 1, 1, p_7, (\alpha^7/p) \times B_8))/\imath^0)_0$	26
		$g_0 \leftarrow (h \veebar (0, 3, 4))$	27
	$=$	$1 : g_0$	28
		$h_h \leftarrow 0$	29
	$=$	$1 : g_1 \wedge (h = 4)$	30
		$MAC^9((48, 40, 32, 24, 56)_h, 8, s, g; p)$	31
		$MAC^9((112, 104, 96, 88, 120)_h, 8, f, g; p)$	32
		$p_{,16(18)} \leftarrow ?(18)$	33
RESET		$operating\ state \leftarrow /stop;\ rate\ sw = process;\ operating\ state/$	34
	$=$	on: $manual\ light \leftarrow /off;\ operating\ state = stop;\ on/$	35
	$=$	on: $wait\ light \leftarrow /off;\ p_{14};\ on/$	36

Frame 4. CPU, central processing unit *system program*.

IMPLEMENTATION
   EXPERIMENTAL
   MACHINE COMPROMISES
   INTERPRETER
   TSM
   FUNCTION DEFINITION
   NAME SCOPE
   FUZZ
   WORKSPACE
   Frame 5

Faced with only 88 characters you have to have some way of extending them, and I think the first thing that occurred to us was that when we adopted the exclamation mark for the factorial, we didn't really want to give it space on the keyboard, and recognized we could use a quote symbol and a period. That opened up the idea that is now very familiar, of forming compound characters. And this has given us a large enough number of easily writeable and easily readable characters.

Back to the question of the implementation [Frame 5]. In 1965 when we were joined by Larry Breed, who was very much interested in actually producing an implementation, we sort of arrived at two decisions. First of all that it should be experimental. We really were not necessarily aiming at something of practical application, but something that we could experiment with and refine our ideas about the language, and secondly that compromises with the machine, with the representation and so on, should be absolutely minimized. And with those two ideas in mind, Larry Breed and Phil [P. S.] Abrams proposed that we should do this, at the outset at least, as an interpreter. Somewhat surprisingly, I think that all APL implementations have essentially remained that way, and I think not because it's all that difficult to do compilation, but rather, because of its array nature, it is a language which allows reasonably efficient interpretation. And so there hasn't been quite the pressure to make a compiler. Also interpreters do have advantages, particularly for interactive use.

The first implementation was on a 7090. We actually had card input, so we had to have transliteration of symbols, AV for absolute value and all that kind of nonsense. But we did have a system running. We could run it and try it out with card input. Then, there became available to us a system called TSM, for Time Sharing Monitor, which allowed us to really use our typing element and a terminal, and so then we had essentially a terminal implementation very much like what you see today—of course, much more limited.

TSM unfortunately remained available to us for a relatively short period, and shortly thereafter, early in 1966 it must have been, we turned attention to an implementation on the 360. And in fact, I might mention that the first interpreter took $2\frac{1}{2}$ people $4\frac{1}{2}$ months, but not as complete as what you see today. The first implementation on the 360 took about the same length of time.

The implementation forced us to think seriously about certain aspects that we had so far been able to ignore: The question of a formal way of making function definitions. Once we faced the question of function definition, then there are questions of name scope. At the

SYSTEM PHASE
SHARED VARIABLE PROCESSOR
SYSTEM VARIABLES
SYSTEM FUNCTIONS
Frame 6

outset we had a very simple thing, that names were simply localized. I guess the closest thing would be to say that they were like "own" variables in a function. And then at one point, Larry Breed came back from a talk he attended given by Al Perlis in which Al was talking about what I think he called at the time "dynamic localization" or "dynamic local name scope" and we very quickly adopted that, and got what we have now. Names are localized to the function, but in effect can propagate downwards.

The machine representation of numbers raised questions about comparisons. For example, when I say Y is 2 divided by 3, and then try and compare 2 with Y times 3, do I want it to agree or not? Well, we wanted the mathematics to behave the way you thought it did in high school, more or less, and so we introduced this notion of what we then called "fuzz" but we now more respectably call a "comparison tolerance" and that, too, I think has become a very very important element of APL.

Finally, the idea of what we called the workspace. Most languages of the time, and perhaps still, tend to give you a library of functions. There are your tools. And your data is someplace else. So we thought it more convenient to work in terms of what we called eventually a "workspace," which was, if you like, a place where you have your tools and your materials. And this, too, has proved a very nice concept which has survived in all the later implementations.

I guess it was probably about 1968, when we got this system running and pretty well cleaned up, that we began to think more seriously about some very serious limitations of that system, effectively the absence of files or more generally, the absence of communication with the outside world, with outside resources. And what was chosen was the notion of shared variables [Frame 6]. In other words, to get our communication with the outside world in effect by allowing an APL user to offer to share a variable with some other processor. It might be a processor written in APL. It might be a file subsystem. It might be anything. And this in fact was an idea which, as I said, was implicit in some of our earlier work, but I think it was primarily Dick [R. H.] Lathwell who pressed this idea and saw it as a general solution to a lot of these problems, and that too has become, I think, a very important aspect in present APL systems. Certainly as a practical matter it's been very important.

And it also allowed us to systematize or rationalize some ideas in the language. We had, in the case of some functions like indexing, the idea of index origin. You could set the system to use 0-origin indexing or 1-origin indexing. And this essentially allowed us to rationalize that by recognizing that here was a variable that we really wanted to communicate to the APL system itself. This is what we call a system variable, a variable that is in effect shared with the interpreter itself, so that we now handle not only index origin but a host of other things like this, printing width, printing precision and so on; by simply treating them as variables that are shared with the system.

RELATION TO MATHEMATICAL NOTATION
VARIABLE NAMES
FUNCTIONS
GROUPING
REPRESENTATION
ARRAYS

Frame 7

System functions are related to that in the following way. There are certain variables to which you might like to have a programmer have access, such as, for example, some information from the symbol table—but even for APL programmers it would be dangerous to give them complete access to the symbol table and allow them to respecify it, for example. And so we gave a limited form of access to variables like that through what we called "system functions."

In talking about the development of all programming languages, not just APL, I think we tend to make a mistake in thinking of them as starting, ab initio, in the 1940s when machines first came along. And I think that that is a very serious mistake because, in fact, the essential notions are notions that were worked out in mathematics, and in related disciplines, over centuries [Frame 7]. I mean, just the idea of a formula, the idea of a procedure—although in mathematics we never had a really nice formal way of specifying this —it's clear that this is what we do. In fact, in a lecture, you sort of give the kernel of the thing and then you wave your arms and that replaces the looping and what-not. But the idea of algorithms and so on is very central to mathematics. And so I think it's a mistake to think of the development as starting from the computer. I think it's worthwhile trying to examine this in the following sense: if we look at mathematical notation, say, at the time of the development of the computer we had some very important notations. If you don't think they're important, I would recommend strongly that you take a look at some source like [Florian] Cajori's *History of Mathematical Notations*; it's just incredible the time and effort that went into introducing what we now just take as obvious. For example, the idea of a variable name: a very painful thing. At the outset you wrote calculations in terms of specific quantities. Then it was recognized that you really wanted to make some sort of a universal statement and so they actually wrote out things like "universalis" which, because we are all lazy, gradually got abbreviated, and I suppose by the time it reached u, somebody said, "Aha! We've got a lot of letters like that. And now we can talk about several universals," and so on.

But the serious thing is that this is a very important notion. The idea of identifying certain important functions like addition, multiplication, and assigning symbols to them. These symbols are not as old as you think. Take the times sign for example. It's only about 200 years old; it's too young to die. That's why we resist the things like the asterisk and so on, that happen to be on tabulating machines because of the need for check protection.

There were other things like grouping. It took a long time for what seems now the obviously beautiful way of showing grouping in an expression by parentheses. It was almost superseded by what is called the "vinculum"—where you drew a line over the top of the subexpression—linearization again. I think the main reason that the parentheses won out was because when you have what would now just be a series of parentheses you got lines going up higher and higher on the page, and that was awkward for printing.

The question of representation—certainly mathematics had long since reached the stage where you don't think about how the numbers are represented. When you think about multiplication, division, and so on, you don't think, "Ah—that's got to be carried out in roman numeral, or in arabic, or in base-2" or anything like that. You simply think of it as multiplication. Representation is subordinated.

And of course, the idea of arrays has been in mathematical notation and other applications for something like 150 years. They still haven't really been recognized, but they've been there.

Now, what happened when the first computer came along? For perfectly good practical reasons every one of these notions disappeared. You couldn't even say "A + B." You had to say, "Load A into accumulator; load B into so-and-so"—you couldn't even say that. You had to say, "Load register 800 into the so-and-so and so on." So all of these things disappeared, for perfectly practical reasons. The sad thing is that 30 years later we're still following that same aberration, and this is where I think it's interesting to look at APL [Frame 7]. But there are many more similarities than you might think; if you look in the paper, there are some of these things pointed out. One of these is the order of execution. Let me just take one second for that. People in programming seem to think that APL has a strange order of execution. The order of execution in APL is very simply this: every function takes as its right hand argument the value of an entire expression to the right of it. This came straight from expression in mathematics like *F* of *G* of *H* of *X*. And all we did in APL was to recognize that this was a really nice scheme, and let it extend to functions of two arguments as well. This has some very nice consequences. But it came from mathematics.

Now, let me say one last word of a more general character about the influences.

In our earlier paper on the design of APL [Reference 1 of Paper], Falkoff and I tried to figure out (in retrospect, obviously) what really were the main principles that had guided us. And we concluded that there were really just two: one was simplicity, and the other was practicality. Now, I expect that every one of the other participants in the APL work could cite some sort of important influence that led him to this kind of bias, but I would like to mention where I'm sure that mine came from. I'm sure it came from studying under Professor [Howard] Aiken [of Harvard]. This is a name that I think occurs much less prominently than it should in the history of computing. And Aiken was raised as an engineer. Although he had a very theoretical turn of mind, he always spoke of himself as an engineer. And an engineer he characterized as being a man who could build for one buck what any damn fool could do for ten. He also emphasized simplicity, and one of the most striking things that I think all of his graduate students remember was, when faced with the usual sort of enthusiastic presentation of something, he would say, "I'm a simple man. I don't understand that. Could you try to make it clear?" And this is a most effective way of dealing with graduate students. I know it had a decided impact on me.

Finally, he had some more general pieces of advice, which I found always useful. Let me just cite one of them. I don't know what the occasion was, but one of his graduate students was becoming a little paranoid that somebody might steal one of the fantastic ideas from his thesis, and so he was stamping every copy "Confidential." Aiken just shook his head and said, "Don't worry about people stealing your ideas. If they're any good, you'll have to ram them down their throats!"

TRANSCRIPT OF DISCUSSANT'S REMARKS

JAN LEE: Thank you, Ken. Our discussant for the APL paper is one of those gentlemen at whom all faculty members look with some awe. This is the student who made good! The one who was your assistant at one time, and then eventually you discover that he becomes the full professor! So I'd like to introduce Fred Brooks. Fred is the Professor and Chairman of the Computer Science Department at the University of North Carolina. He is probably best known as the father of System/360, having served as the Project Manager for its development and later as the Manager of the Operating System/360 Software Project. You can't blame him for that, though. Now, in the later years, Fred was responsible for what has become known as the one-language concept, which we alluded to in the PL/I session earlier on this morning, and he is going to comment on that and on APL.

FREDERICK BROOKS: In introduction, I'd like to say a word about the conference that I think should appropriately come from a part of the APL community—and that is, the thing I like best about this conference is its character set! I cannot recall a time since the 1976 Los Alamos machine history conference [International Research Conference on the History of Computing] when such a set of characters has been gathered under one roof.

I think one of the themes of the conference—very illuminating—is to study the processes by which languages are not only designed, but by which their adoption is accomplished. If you look back over the papers, you see a sharp dichotomy between what one can call the "committee" languages. The papers about those almost completely concern themselves with process; and the author languages, and the papers about those have almost completely concerned themselves with technical issues. I think there's a lesson there.

I myself have not ever been a major participant in the design of a high-level language, but I have been midwife at two: APL and PL/I. And I would like to remark that there is a class of programming languages which have not been discussed here at all, and that's appropriate. But these are the languages which are intended for direct interpretation by machine hardware. They're called "machine" languages, and Gerry Blaauw and I are working on an approach to computer architecture that treats that as a problem in programming language design where the utterances are costly.

Today I'd like to remark on two things that I can perhaps illuminate about the APL history. One is what Ken calls the "academic" period at Harvard; and the other is the third, the implementation period at IBM.

Ken accurately identifies the most important influence on his development of APL as being the mathematical background and orientation with which he set out to tackle the description of data processing problems. He set out to do it with ordinary mathematics. He discovered that on the one hand the notations had to be made consistent, and on the other hand, they had to be generalized. And I think it accurate to say that if one asks what other programming language ideas had an influence on APL, the answer is none. It is very much Ken's invention. For those of you who are in the academic community, I will give you a word of comfort and consolation. And that is that when Harvard decided that he was not to be reappointed, the excuse was that he had published nothing but one little book!!!

The other important thing to understand about the academic period, because it explains the answers to many commonly asked questions about APL, is that Ken conceived of APL as a language for thinking about computing and data processing. And this I think is, in the first place, helpful for explanation, and in the second place, a very great advantage. It means that the language was not constrained by the machines available in 1956, the keypunches, the typewriters, the tabulators, or the computers, or the machines available in the 1960s, or the machines available in the 1970s. And, as a consequence, I think the language goes more directly to the heart of the relevant concepts because at no point has the language been constrained by the equipment available. And for that reason I expect it to last for quite a while.

But some of the questions that are best answered by understanding this orientation as a thinking language are some, for example, that the management asked us: What is the motivation for the terrific compression of programs? It's a thinking language. And you don't want to spend a lot of time writing. Why was such an unusual character set adopted? It is a thinking language, and the principle was one character per operator. In that case, one per "function," if you will. In its original form, was the language expected to require such a large run-time system? The whole notion of run time was an alien notion in its original form. It was a thinking language. Why require an entirely new character set, instead of using built-in function names? Why not? It's a thinking language. And I think that that is a very important matter to arrive at.

With respect to the implementation period, IBM at the mid 1960s, as George Radin has very accurately, and I think very deeply characterized it, and indeed the whole community, was characterized by a spirit of unification. That was the spirit of the time, and it was one to which Bob Evans and I were professionally and emotionally committed very deeply in the 360 project. An outgrowth of the development of PL/I was an enunciation of an attempt to take on FORTRAN, ALGOL, and COBOL and replace them all with PL/I— what was known as the "one-language policy." These languages each had sufficiently strong community groups. The one-language policy had no noticeable effect on them. The only one that it had any effect on that I could see was unfortunately the implementation of APL that was underway at the time. So it's rather like one draws his sword and goes out to slay the foe, and in the process of drawing it back, clobbers the friend in the head!

For the remainder of my time I'd like to give a little bit of outside-the-APL-development-group view—hindsight—of what one might do differently, knowing what one knows about languages today, and what seemed to be the strengths that I think are very important and very instructive.

Control structures—it seems to me we know a lot more about control structures. Parameter passing, character strings; in George Radin's paper he documents my urging the APL approach of character vectors on PL/I and his rebuttal that correctly identifies character strings as a different kind of thing. And that rebuttal in there is instructive and dead right.

I think one would, today, make the decision to declare global variables rather than local variables as the thing to be explicitly declared. Ken and Adin might not agree with how I would do it differently. I think one of the things we recognize today that we did not, any of us, recognize then is the fact that APL incorporates a quite separate system language— the command language, and this is true of most programming language systems. We didn't recognize in OS/360 that JCL was a different language and a full language and had to be designed as such. And the incorporation of system variables and system functions in the on-going development of APL means that they have now recognized this and are building that concept into the system.

What's right, what's very right and still very instructive about APL? I think first of all, the conceptual integrity of the language which very much reflects the unification of mind of Ken and Adin in the working out of it; and the courtesy of the APL community which has refrained, by and large, from ad hoc additions to the language without at least going back to the intellectual source and trying to arrive at a consensus.

Next, I think the consistency of the language. I once long ago asked Ken, "Why are the human factors of APL so good?" And he said it does what you expect it to do. And that's a pretty good statement.

The generality: the symbols are new but the concepts are not. And the power: it works the way we think. I would say to a child, "Go to the basement and bring back all the good apples." That's the APL way of saying it. "Go to the basement—pick up an apple—examine it for goodness; if so, put in . . . ." The direct interaction, JOSS-like, the economy of keystrokes, the workspace concept where whole environments are called by name, and the fact that it is exciting to use because it improves and generalizes on mathematics.

Thank you.

TRANSCRIPT OF QUESTION AND ANSWER SESSION

JAN LEE: I have a question from Peter Wegner from Brown University. "Both SNOBOL4 and APL achieve their attractiveness in part by their lack of declarations; that is, declarations force the programmer to plan ahead, and the attractiveness of SNOBOL and APL is due to the fact that programmers need not plan ahead. Should we encourage this attitude amongst programmers?"

KENNETH IVERSON: Well, as I said at the outset, the ones that I wanted to duck, I'd ask Adin. You want to grab that one, Adin? The answer is no—he doesn't want to. But he's going to.

LEE: Basically, the question is that no declarations are required in either SNOBOL 4 or APL and that seems to be against the trend of software engineering.

ADIN FALKOFF: Right, and the second part of the question is—isn't that going to cause programmers to suffer some kind of mental debilitation.

LEE: I think that's a good paraphrasing.

FALKOFF: And I'm reminded of a conference on programming systems for mathematics that was held in 1966 or 1967, in which the question was, "Should we have interactive systems because that's going to cause a degeneration of the mathematical ability of the populace?" I think that the presence or absence of declarations has very little to do with the acceptability of the language. I think there are good technical reasons for not having them. By and large they tend to be redundant, and therefore incur many new rules, and thereby make life more complicated.

LEE: I have two questions—one from Bob Rosin at Bell Labs; one from Joseph De Kerf of Agfa Gevaert. Let me paraphrase them. There is an APL interpreter for most medium-scale and large-scale computers. But the manufacturers don't really promote the language. Why not?

IVERSON: I don't know! I haven't had the time to try and crawl inside their skulls and know why not. I think one reason is very simply that any industry, any organization, when they come to marketing, pushing things, feel very comforted with numbers, some sort of prediction of how many are they going to sell, and so on; and because our prediction processes seem to always simply predict more of what's happened in the past, it's very difficult for them to predict the possibilities of something that's at all radical. And I think that probably explains why it takes not only APL but a lot of new things time to take hold.

LEE: Let me close off with one from Aaron Finerman. He says, "Periodically we hear that APL is the wave of the future; that IBM will mount a major effort to spread the use of APL. Users of APL also tend to propagate the gospel. Do you believe the use of APL will grow, or that future use will be approximately at the present level?"

IVERSON: Adin Falkoff is presently the Manager of the APL Design Group, and so I really think I have to call on him to speak for IBM.

FALKOFF: And of course in the total spirit of this meeting, I must start with a disclaimer, and that is that I don't speak for IBM. I think that the growth of the use of APL will probably continue to expand, and I base that simply on a very direct extrapolation of what's happened so far. I see no evidence and no reason why it shouldn't. And I think that Ken really touched at the end of his talk on the fundamental reason for it, and that is that APL does represent, I believe, a return to the main trend line in the development of mathematics, and thereby represents the means for a rapprochement. if you like, between mathematics and programming.

LEE: Thank you, Adin, and thank you, Ken.

FULL TEXT OF ALL QUESTIONS SUBMITTED†

KENNETH BROOKS

(1) How did the distinction between APL operators and system commands come about?

(2) Was any thought ever given to including an IF–THEN construction in APL?

Answers: (1) APL system commands were introduced as an ad hoc "escape" from APL to handle peripheral matters which we did not see how to introduce cleanly into the language at the time. If you compare APL\360 with APLSV, you will see that many system commands have been superseded by the use of system variables and other devices which bring the required function within the language.

(2) APL operators provide "program structures" in the sense of applying functions to arrays or subsets thereof, and any extensions to include further types will be done by introducing further operators and not by introducing an anomalous syntax.

---

† Dr. Iverson has been kind enough to provide answers for many of the questions that were not asked at the session. References here refer to the bibliography on pp. 673–674. Ed.

NEIL G. CUADRA

(1) You have observed in the past that APL operators, unlike functions, are not treated in a uniform manner. How might a more uniform treatment be given to operators? In particular, would operators be applicable to user-defined functions, and could user-defined operators be permitted?

(2) The APL notation for function application introduces syntactic ambiguity in certain expressions. Were this fact and its effect on the implementation of APL realized at the time this notation was adopted?

Answer: (1) Formalization of the syntax of APL operators is discussed in Iverson, *Operators and Functions,* IBM Research Report No. 7091, and further discussions of APL operators appear in the Proceedings of the 1979 APL Conference sponsored by STAPL. In particular, operators should apply to user-defined functions, and user-defined operators should be permitted. The earlier observation that operators are not treated uniformly was not accurate.

(2) Since I am not aware of any such syntactic ambiguity and since the matter was not clarified during the session, this question is omitted.

JOSEPH DE KERF

There is an APL interpreter for most medium-scale and large computers. The manufacturers generally don't *really* promote this language, however. Why?

(Answered during session)

AARON FINERMAN

Periodically we hear that APL is the wave of the future—that IBM will mount a major effort to spread the use of APL. Users of APL also tend to propagate the gospel. Do you believe that the use of APL will grow or that its future use will be at approximately the present level?

(Answered by Falkoff during session.)

DAN FRIEDMAN

Why did you limit functions to just two arguments?

Answer: The limitation is to two formal arguments, which may themselves be arrays. This is the method used in mathematics, both in the use of vector arguments and in the use of expressions such as $f(a, b, c, d)$. If $a, b, c,$ and d are scalars, the latter can be written directly in APL, and if they are not, the matter can be handled by the enclose function discussed in Iverson's Research Report 7091 (already cited) and elsewhere.

BERNIE GALLER

Why the decision to avoid an operator precedence ordering?

Answer: In APL, different classes of functions are used together so freely that no precedence scheme can reduce the amount of parenthesization required. The ill-defined precedence in mathematics is limited to five functions and appears to have evolved to make convenient the writing of polynomials. The use of vectors in APL makes the use of polynomials convenient without precedence, as in $+ / C \times Y * \iota\rho\ C$. The eight- (or more) level schemes commonly used in programming languages are too cumbersome to even contemplate.

HELEN GIGLEY

Both APL and LISP provide functions to execute or evaluate character strings respectively as expressions. Was this feature an original design feature in APL? Why or why not? If not, why was it added?

Answer: The execute function was not present in the original APL\360 implementation and was added several years later. Arguments for its inclusion were presented at length in our *Design of APL* [Ref. 1 in Paper] from which I quote one brief section as follows:

> The concept of an execute function is a very powerful one. In a sense, it makes the language "self-conscious", and introduces endless possibilities for obscurity in programs. This might have been a reason for not allowing it, but we had long since realized that a general-purpose language cannot be made foolproof and remain effective.

JAMES P. HOBBS

Please comment on comments. At what point were they added to the language? The placement of comments requires a left to right scan to the comment symbol before the statement can be evaluated right to left. This seems inconsistent.

Answer: Comments were included in APL\360 (1968). The leading symbol of an entry must be examined in any case to detect system commands; and the order of execution is independent of the parsing algorithm.

J. B. HARVILL

How much, if any, influence did Aiken's algebra have in your work in APL?

Answer: He must be thinking of Aitken. [I.e., not Howard Aiken.]

TOM KURTZ

In designing BASIC, we briefly considered "fuzz," following the practice in Cornell's CORC, but dropped the idea because we didn't know how much fuzz to allow in a given situation. How does APL decide how much fuzz to use?

Answer: The comparison tolerance (fuzz) in APL is controllable by the user by assigning a value to the system variable $\Box CT$. The default value is $1E^-13$.

RICHARD MILLER

(1) Did you have any other applications in mind besides a notational one during the early design phase?
(2) How much parallelism did you intend to exploit in the problems run? With the machines used?

Answers: (1) Six of the seven chapters of Iverson's original book were devoted to various applications, including sorting, searching, trees, and logic. Moreover, as stated in our Design of APL [Ref. 1 in Paper]:

> . . . from its inception APL has been developed by using it in a succession of areas. This emphasis on application clearly favors practicality and simplicity. The treatment of many different areas fostered generalization; for example, the general inner product was developed in attempts to obtain the advantages of ordinary matrix algebra in the treatment of symbolic logic.

(2) As stated in our paper, "The language was to be compromised as little as possibly by machine considerations," and the possibilities of parallel execution (or lack thereof) in computers had no effect. However, the abundant possibilities for parallel execution of APL are there for exploitation by machine and software designers.

BOB ROSIN

What do you think would have been the effect on APL had it been promoted as little as was SNOBOL?

Answer: The answer to this question must either be so brief as to be useless, or so long as to be impractical.

JOE SCHWEBEL

In view of the fact that business programmers are reluctant to use even a "+" or "−" when they can use "ADD" or "SUBTRACT", did the designers expect APL to be usable as a business data processing language as is now proposed by some?

Answer: Expectation of its use in business data processing is clear from examples used as early as my 1962 book [10] and as recently as the current APL Language manual [4]. Not only is APL usable as a business data processing language "as is now proposed by some," but this has long been its major area of use.

DANIEL SOLOMON

If you had used a right arrow rather than a left arrow for the assignment operator then the direction of evaluation of an APL statement would be left to right.

Answer: This is a statement, not a question, and appears irrelevant.

HENRY TROPP

(1) Is the history of APL part of the history of mathematics, or vice versa?
(2) When I look at the architecture of the Harvard Mark I, its architecture closely resembles the way Howard Aiken solved mathematical problems. Can you briefly comment on the personal influence that Howard Aiken had on you as you approached the design of APL?

Answer: (1) Since chronology alone makes it impossible to consider the history of mathematics part of the history of APL, I assume that the question is put facetiously to challenge the claim that APL is closely related to mathematical notation. If this assumption is correct, I can only recommend a careful study of the relevant part of our paper

Biography

(Section 5) and of Reference 35 and other works which employ APL in the treatment of mathematical topics.

(2) I know the architecture of Mark I and I knew Professor Aiken, but I cannot presume to characterize "the way Howard Aiken solved mathematical problems," nor do I see how it could be related to the architecture of the Mark I. I have already commented on the general influence of Aiken on my work; however, he took no direct interest in APL.

PETER WEGNER

Both SNOBOL4 and APL achieve their attractiveness in part by their lack of declarations. Declarations force the programmer to plan ahead, and the attractiveness of SNO-BOL and APL is due in part to the fact that programmers need not plan ahead as usual in writing their programs. Should we encourage this attitude among programmers?

(Answered by Falkoff during session.)

BIOGRAPHY OF ADIN D. FALKOFF

Adin Falkoff holds the degrees of B.Ch.E. from the City College of New York (1941) and M.A. in Mathematics from Yale University (1963). He has worked for IBM since 1955, specializing in computer science and language design since 1960. He was a part-time staff member of the IBM Systems Research Institute from 1963 to 1967 and a Visiting Lecturer in Computer Science at Yale from 1968 to 1970. During the period 1970–1974, he managed the IBM Philadelphia Scientific Center and he is currently manager of the APL Design Group at the T. J. Watson Research Center.

BIOGRAPHY OF KENNETH E. IVERSON

Ken Iverson received the B.A. degree in Mathematics and Physics at Queen's University in Kingston, Ontario, in 1950. He holds an A.M. in Mathematics (1951) and a Ph.D. in Applied Mathematics (1954), both from Harvard. He was an Assistant Professor of Applied Math at Harvard from 1955 to 1960 and then joined IBM as a Research Staff Member. He was made an IBM Fellow in 1971.

He received the AFIPS Harry Goode Award in 1975 and was given ACM's Turing Award in 1979.

Appendixes

APPENDIX A. LANGUAGE SUMMARIES

These summaries are meant to give the flavor of each language and not to be a tutorial or overview. In most cases the language described here is the version that existed at the time covered by the formal paper and does not represent the 1978 version of the language. Except for APL, each of the summaries is the same as was published in the preprints. Each summary was prepared by a different person.

APL

APL is a general-purpose programming language with the following characteristics [reprinted from *APL Language* (Ref. 4 in APL Session Paper)]:

The primitive objects of the language are arrays (lists, tables, lists of tables, etc.). For example, $A + B$ is meaningful for any arrays A and B, the size of an array (ρA) is a primitive function, and arrays may be indexed by arrays as in $A[3\ 1\ 4\ 2]$.

The syntax is simple: there are only three statement types (name assignment, branch, or neither), there is no function precedence hierarchy, functions have either one, two, or no arguments, and primitive functions and defined functions (programs) are treated alike.

For example, $A \times B + C$ is computed by a right to left scan and would be equivalent to $A \times (B + C)$.

The semantic rules are few: the definitions of primitive functions are independent of the representations of data to which they apply, all scalar functions are extended to other arrays in the same way (that is, item-by-item), and primitive functions have no hidden effects (so-called side effects).

The sequence control is simple: one statement type embraces all types of branches (conditional, unconditional, computed, etc.), and the termination of the execution of any function always returns control to the point of use.

For example, $\rightarrow (A > 3)/LOOP$ is equivalent to the ALGOL statement **if** $A > 3$ **then goto** *LOOP*.

External communication is established by means of variables which are shared between APL and other systems or subsystems. These *shared variables* are treated both syntactically and semantically like other variables. A subclass of shared variables, *system variables* provides convenient communication between APL programs and their environment.

The utility of the primitive functions is vastly enhanced by operators which modify their behavior in a systematic manner. For example, *reduction* (denoted by /) modifies a function to apply over all elements of a list, as in $+/L$ for summation of the items of L. The remaining operators are *scan* (running totals, running maxima, etc.), the *axis* operator which, for example, allows reduction and scan to be applied over a specified axis (rows or columns) of a table, the *outer product,* which produces tables of values as in $RATE \circ . *YEARS$ for an interest table, and the *inner product,* a simple generalization of matrix product which is exceedingly useful in data processing and other nonmathematical applications.

The number of primitive functions is small enough that each is represented by a single easily read and easily written symbol, yet the set of primitives embraces operations from simple addition to grading (sorting) and formatting. The complete set can be classified as follows:

Arithmetic: + - × ÷ ⋆ ⊛ ○ | ⌊ ⌈ ! ⊞

Boolean and Relational: ∨ ∧ ⩾ ⩝ ~ < ≤ = ≥ > ≠

Selection and Structural: / \ ⌿ ⍀ [;] ↑ ↓ ρ , φ ⍉ ⊖

General: ∈ ι ? ⊥ ⊤ ⍋ ⍒ ⌽ ⍫

Symbol	Name/Function	Symbol	Name/Function
<	Less than	≤	Less than or equal
>	Greater than	≥	Greater than or equal
=	Equal	≠	Not equal
∨	Or	⩝	Nor
∧	And	⩘	Nand
−	Negation, Subtraction	+	Identity, Addition
÷	Reciprocal, Division	×	Signum, Multiplication
?	Monadic random, Dyadic random	ρ	Shape, Reshape
∈	Membership	~	Not
↑	Take	↓	Drop
ι	Index generator, Index of	○	Pi times, Circular
φ	Reversal, Rotation	⍉	Monadic transposition, Dyadic transposition
⊛	Natural logarithm, Logarithm	⋆	Exponential, Exponentiation
⌈	Ceiling, Maximum	⌊	Floor, Minimum
⍒	Grade down	⍋	Grade up
⊥	Base value	⊤	Representation
|	Absolute value, Residue		
/	Compression	\	Expansion
○.d	Outer product	d.D	Inner product
d/	Reduction	[ ]	Indexing
⊞	Matrix inverse, Matrix division	,	Ravel, Catenation/Lamination
!	Factorial, Combination	⌶	System Information

Each APL system is generally embedded in a specialized operating system which permits the user to define APL functions through the use of the ∇ operator, to manipulate workspaces and to specify the shared variables between programs in APL and external systems. Within this operating system the user may execute APL statements directly or defer execution by the placement of statements in function descriptions.

APT

APT is a programming language for describing how parts are to be produced by a numerically controlled machine tool. Within the language a programmer can define points, lines, planes, spheres, etc. and specify the movement of a cutting tool in terms of these shapes.

In the accompanying paper on the origins of the APT language, Figs. 7 and 9 give fairly self-explanatory examples of APT programs. This summary gives additional introductory information. [See pp. 325 and 328.]

Most statements in APT programs are used either to define geometric shapes or to specify the motion of a cutter. In describing shapes, the general APT principle is that any geometrically sensible form of description can be used. For example, a point can be described in terms of X, Y, and Z coordinates, or as the intersection of two lines, or as the point tangent to a circle and a line. A line can be described as passing through two points, as passing through a point and parallel or perpendicular to another line, as passing through a point and tangent to a circle, etc. A circle can be described in terms of a center and radius, as a center and tangent to a line, as tangent to two intersecting lines, etc. For example, the geometry of Fig. 1 (below) can be described as follows:

```
A = POINT/1, 5
B = POINT/2, 3
SIDE = LINE/A, B
JILL = CIRCLE/CTR AT, B, THRU, A
```

JILL is a circle passing through point A and centered at B.

When a geometric description is ambiguous, the ambiguity can be resolved by specifying the relative magnitude of X and Y coordinates. For example, the line through A and

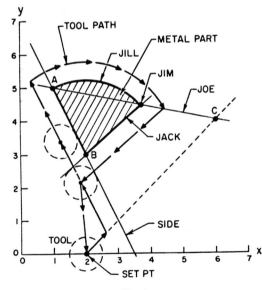

Fig. 1

C intersects the circle JILL at two points. To select the desired point, a programmer must write:

```
JIM = POINT/XLARGE, INT OF, JOE, WITH, JILL
```

Note that A is the point selected by XSMALL.

Motions of a cutter are controlled either by explicitly positioning the cutter (in terms of coordinates or increments from the present position) or by specifying continuous cutter motion along a curve. Motion of the cutter is constrained by a tangency condition to each of two surfaces, the so-called *part* surface and *drive* surface. Motions are terminated by specifying a tangency condition to a third surface, the *check* surface. When this required terminal tangency condition is met, the motion is complete. An initial motion statement positions the cutter within a specified tolerance from the drive and part surfaces and on the correct side of the part surface, e.g.,

```
FROM, POINT/2, 0
IN DIR, POINT/C
SIDE = LINE/A, B
GO TO/SIDE
TL LFT, GO LFT/SIDE
```

As the diagram shows, this command sequence states that the initial cutter position is at point 2,0; it is moved from this point in the direction of (the previously defined) point C. Motion continues until the cutter reaches (i.e., is tangent to) the line passing through points A or B. With the tool (i.e., cutter) on the left side of that line (TL LFT), the tool is moved to the left (with respect to the preceding motion toward point C) along the line called SIDE. GO LFT, GO RGT, GO FWD, etc., are commands used to indicate when the cutter is to follow a different curve as the part surface. For example, the next motion command is GO RGT, CIRCLE/CTR AT, B, THRU, A, meaning the cutter continues along SIDE until tangent to the specified circle and then it goes to the right along the specified circle.

The geometric definitions and motion commands in an APT program are transformed first into a broken line cutter path encoded as the cutter location tape (CLTAPE). The CLTAPE also includes commands for special functions such as turning coolant on and off. The CLTAPE is then transformed into codes for a specific controller-machine tool configuration. The mathematical computations yielding the coordinate sequences are performed by a part of the APT system called the ARELEM (arithmetic element) program; the transformation into machine tool codes is done by the APT *post-processor*. The use of different post-processors permits the APT language to be used for a wide variety of machine tools.

ALGOL 60

The term ALGOL is reported to have sprung from "ALGOrithmic Language." Many forget, however, that ALGOL is the second brightest star in the constellation Perseus and part of an eclipsing binary. ALGOL exhibits a variation in light, which is caused by the fact that once every 69-odd hours it is partially eclipsed by a dark body, its partner star, for about 10 hours. But note that ALGOL always manages to regain its brilliance. ALGOL and its eclipsing companion (could it be FORTRAN?) are miles and miles apart (about 6,000,000).

ALGOL 60 and FORTRAN are both algebraic languages designed primarily for writing programs to solve numerical problems. Both have simple variables and arrays, declarations, assignment statements, conditional and iterative statements, and procedures (subroutines).

ALGOL had the advantage of being developed several years after FORTRAN, and it exhibited several significant advances in programming language design. Of prime importance was its sense of simplicity, structure, and conciseness—its mathematical elegance if you will. The term "ALGOL-like" refers to these qualities as well as to the basic structure of the language. In attempting to popularize a new language many a designer has encroached upon the term "ALGOL-like", causing one eminent computer scientist to remark that "ALGOL was indeed an achievement; it was a significant advance over most of its successors."

Of course, ALGOL has its faults, and some aspects of it that were earlier praised are now considered to be clumsy, awkward and ill-defined. In many respects, by today's standards ALGOL is as inadequate as FORTRAN.

Listed below are some major features of ALGOL.

1. ALGOL 60 is described using a formal notation for syntax (Backus–Naur Form, or BNF). The defining document (only 16 pages in *Communications of the ACM*) is short, concise, and exceptionally clear. The document differentiates between the publication language and the hardware language for ALGOL.

2. The possible types of variables are *integer, real,* and *Boolean* (or logical). Each variable and array has to be declared.

3. The language has a nested statement structure; thus one can write:

> **if** f **then begin** $h := y$; $z := w$ **end**
> **else if** $h \neq z$ **then** $h := y$

4. The nested statement structure allows the introduction of *blocks,* which in turn allows the declaration of variables *local* to a program segment and brings on scope problems.

> $\vdots$
> $x := y$;
> **begin real** r;
>   use r in here only
> **end;**
> $\vdots$

5. Blocks introduce the possibility of *dynamic arrays* and systematic *dynamic storage allocation.* In the following, the size of array b depends on the value of *global variable* n:

> **begin array** $b[1:n]$;
>   use array b here only
> **end**

6. Procedures (subroutines) can be recursive. Parameters are call-by-value or call-by-name, a concept not thought well of these days. The following example illustrates *procedure definition, specification* of a *formal parameter* (n), *declaration* of a *local variable* (i), *assignment* to the procedure name (*factorial* := 1), recursive *function invocation* (*factorial* ($n - 1$)), and *nested statement structure:*

```
integer procedure factorial (n);
    value n; integer n;
    begin integer i;
        if n = 0 then factorial := 1
                    else begin i := factorial (n − 1);
                              factorial := n*i
                    end
    end
end
```

BASIC

Beginner's All-purpose Symbolic Instruction Code or BASIC was originally developed by T. E. Kurtz and J. G. Kemeny at Dartmouth College in 1963–1964. The original version consisted of 14 statement constructs. BASIC was one of several languages operating in a general-purpose time-sharing system also developed at Dartmouth. The simpler user commands, numbering about 8 or 10, have since become associated with the BASIC language.

A BASIC program is created via the NEW command, listed by the LIST command, edited by a DELETE command, executed by the RUN command, and saved by the SAVE command. Previously saved programs are retrieved from their file by entering OLD and the desired program name.

Every program statement begins with an integer line number and a statement keyword. Thus, assignment statements are exactly like the FORTRAN assignment, but are prefixed with an integer label and the keyword LET. For example,

```
1150 LET X = B*B − 4.0*A*C
```

computes $B^2 − 4AC$ and stores the result in X.

BASIC manages three data types: (1) numeric variables, (2) string variables, and (3) one- or two-dimensional array variables of either string or numeric type. All numeric computation is presumably performed in floating-point arithmetic, with truncation being performed during indexing. The subscript 0 is defined for array variables. If an array variable appears without a corresponding DIM statement, default subscript ranges of 0–10 in each dimension are provided.

Input–output is done in BASIC by the READ, INPUT, PRINT, and DATA statements, READ and DATA work together by assigning values from the DATA statements to the variable list in READ. INPUT and PRINT produce results at the user's terminal, interactively.

Control is performed by GOTO, IF THEN, ON GOTO, FOR NEXT, and GOSUB statements. The GOTO statement causes an unconditional branch to any statement in the program. The IF THEN statement causes a conditional branch (two-way), e.g., IF A = B THEN 350. The ON statement produces a branch to one of many statements depending on the value of a truncated integer index.

Subroutines are part of the same global environment as the main program and other routines. Thus, all data is accessible to all program "modules." A GOSUB 1000 causes subroutine invocation beginning with statement 1000 and continuing until a RETURN is reached. The subroutine has access to any variable used in any other segment of the program.

698

FORTRAN influenced "statement functions" provide single statement functions in BASIC. A function is "called" by an instance identical to array variable usage.

The following program segment illustrates the nature of BASIC programs. The program does nothing of importance, except illustrate most of BASIC's constructs.

```
 1  LET I = 0
 5  REMARK A$ IS A STRING, B IS AN ARRAY.
10  DIM A$(3), B(10)
15  PRINT "READY?"
20  INPUT A$
25  REMARK A$ = "YES" OR "NO".
30  IF A$ = "YES" THEN 50
35  LET I = I + 1
40  IF I < 3 THEN 15
45  GO TO 99
50  REMARK "YES"
55  INPUT N
60  ON N GO TO 70, 80
65  GO TO 55
70  PRINT "N=", N
75  READ B
80  PRINT "N=", N
85  REM SHORT FOR REMARK.
90  DATA 10,20,30,35,40,50,55,60,70,80
99  STOP
```

BASIC is unusual in that variable names are limited to a single letter followed by an optional digit if numeric, and further followed by a $ if of type string.

The looping construct

$$FOR \ I = 1 \ TO \ 10$$
$$\vdots$$
$$NEXT \ I$$

is bracketed with a NEXT statement following the loop body, but the loop counter is tested upon entry of the loop.

Subroutines are defined by an instance of a GOSUB, thus making modularity and scope a vague concept! Built-in functions resemble a pocket calculator's capability, and arithmetic uses the exponentiation caret as current versions of ASCII have eliminated the ↑.

Later versions of BASIC (various names, depending on the vendor) include string functions, matrix operations, and sequential and random file I/O.

COBOL 60

Notation

The syntax of COBOL 60 is defined through a metalanguage that uses:

lowercase letters for metalinguistic variable names;

uppercase letters for optional fixed words in the language, which are called "noise words";

underlined uppercase letters for required fixed words in the language;

brackets, [and], to enclose optional elements,

braces, { and }, to enclose elements from which a choice must be made; these are usually listed vertically;

ellipsis, ..., to show that the previous syntactic unit is to be repeated an arbitrary number of times.

The character set in COBOL 60 consists of 51 characters, comprising the 10 digits, the 26 uppercase letters and the special symbols:

$$+ \quad - \quad * \quad / \quad = \quad \$ \quad < \quad > \quad , \quad \cdot \quad ; \quad " \quad (\quad) \quad \text{blank}$$

Identifiers are composed of not more than 30 digits, letters, and hyphens. Certain keywords and connectives, which have been defined to improve the readability of the language, are reserved and may not be used as identifiers.

Programs

COBOL 60 programs are divided into four *divisions:*

IDENTIFICATION division: This begins each program and names the program and provides overall program documentation.

PROCEDURE division: This contains the algorithms specified as a sequence of executable units. These units are arranged hierarchically as *sections, paragraphs, sentences,* and imperative or conditional *statements.* An imperative statement consists of a *verb* followed by operands. The verbs of COBOL 60 are:

ACCEPT—obtain input from a low volume device.

ADD—add two or more quantities and store the sum.

ALTER—modify a predetermined sequence of operations.

CLOSE—terminate the processing of both input and output files.

COMPUTE—permit the use of formulas.

DEFINE—allow the introduction of new verbs.

DISPLAY—allow for visual display of low volume information.

DIVIDE—divide one number into another and store the result.

ENTER—allow more than one language in the same program.

EXAMINE—replace or count occurrences of a given character in data.

EXIT—mark the end point of a loop if needed.

GO TO—depart from the normal control sequence

INCLUDE—incorporate a library subroutine into the source program.

MOVE—transfer data, with editing, to one or more data fields.

MULTIPLY—multiply two quantities and store the result.

NOTE—mark a comment.

OPEN—initiate the processing of both input and output files.

PERFORM—depart from the normal control sequence to execute one or more statements a specified number of times and return.

READ—obtain the next logical record from an input file.

STOP—halt the computer either permanently or temporarily.

SUBTRACT—subtract one quantity from another and store the result.

USE—specify special I/O exception handling procedures.

WRITE—release a logical record for an output file.

The conditional statement is of the form

$$\text{IF} \dots \text{THEN} \dots \text{ELSE} \dots$$

Conditional statements can be nested to any depth.

DATA division: This contains descriptions of the data and files used by algorithms in the PROCEDURE division. The basic data structure is a *record* which is a multidimensional heterogeneous array. Records are also the basis for external files. The specifications in the DATA division consist of a sequence of *entries,* each of which consists of a *level-number, data name,* followed by a series of *clauses* that describe the data. The level-number specifies the hierarchical relationship between the data item described in the entry and the data described in other entries. Level-numbers start at 01 for records and higher level-numbers (less than 50) are used for subordinate items. There are also *special* level-numbers with specific meanings. The clauses are used to specify:

data type—alphabetic, numeric, or alphanumeric,
range of values,
location of editing symbols, e.g., dollar signs and commas,
location of radix point,
location of sign,
number of occurrences in a list or table
alignment in computer words
dominant usage—computational or display.

ENVIRONMENT division: contains information about the hardware on which the program is to be compiled and executed.

FORTRAN

The FORTRAN language was intended to be a vehicle for expressing scientific and mathematical computation, while allowing efficient object code to be produced. Since there was an emphasis on scientific computation in FORTRAN and FORTRAN II, little provision was made for heterogeneous data structures. Only arrays of up to three dimensions were possible, and they had to be declared explicitly†:

```
DIMENSION ALPHA(10,15), BETA(12)
```

Input and output statements allowed a little more flexibility, in that provision was made for controlling the format of information read from or written to the outside world (as opposed to reading and writing binary information on disk or tape):

```
      WRITE (5,200) MTH, BETA, Y
200   FORMAT (6H MONTH, I3, 8H; QUOTAS, 12F4.0, 10H; FORECAST, F6.2)
```

where MTH was assigned type integer because its first character was one of I, J, K, L, M,

---

† Examples are given here in FORTRAN II notation.

and N, and BETA was assumed to have been declared a vector as in the earlier example. The character string 6H MONTH specified that the word MONTH should print (i.e., be written on unit 5, as indicated in the WRITE statement), with an initial space character for carriage control. The format information could be changed at "run time" in later versions of FORTRAN, but not at first.

Actual computation was accomplished by using the assignment statement, which allowed expressions on the "right-hand side," but did not allow mixed types (such as integer and floating-point). The following was acceptable:

$$X1 = F(I+1,M1) * DAD - (C + 1.0)/Y$$

In this example, F was understood to be a function name, and F(I+1,M1) a function call, if F was not previously declared to be a two-dimensional array in a DIMENSION statement. As indicated, arguments in a function call could be expressions (with expressions called "by value" and variables called "by reference"). If F were an array name, the subscripts could only have the form $c_1 v \pm c_2$, where c_1 and c_2 were integer constants or missing, and v was a variable of integer type. If the variable (possibly subscripted) on the "left-hand side" of the assignment statement was not of the same type as the value of the "right-hand side" expression, the value was converted (at "run time") to the appropriate type before assignment.

Unconditional transfer of control was created by: (i) the "unconditional GO TO," as in

$$GO\ TO\ 31$$

where 31 is a statement label; (ii) the "computed GO TO," as in

$$GO\ TO\ (30,31,32,33),I1$$

where I1 took one of the values 1, 2, 3, or 4, to indicate the position in the list of the label of the next statement to be executed; and (iii) the related "assigned GO TO."

Conditional sequencing of control was accomplished by the IF statement:

$$IF\ (A+B-1.2)\ 7,6,9$$

which transferred control to the statement labeled 7, 6, or 9, respectively, depending on whether the expression A + B − 1.2 was negative, zero or positive.

Iteration was provided for the DO statement:

$$DO\ 17\ I = 1,N,2$$

which specified that the set of statements which followed, up to and including that labeled 17, was to be executed with I first assigned the value 1, and again with I successively incremented by 2, until I exceeded the value of N. (The statements in the "body" of the iteration would always be executed at least once, since the comparison of I with N occurred after their execution.)

Programmer influence on storage allocation occurred through the COMMON and EQUIVALENCE declarations, as in:

```
COMMON X,Y,Q
DIMENSION X(17,3),Q(20),R(5)
EQUIVALENCE (R(2),Q(6))
```

which would indicate that addresses were to be assigned in a region known as COMMON so that the array X would occupy the first 51 spaces, the variable Y would come next, and the vector Q would occupy the next 20 spaces. The vector R would also be assigned in COMMON, with the same address assigned to R(2) and Q(6). (Then R(1) and Q(5) would occupy the same space, and so on.)

In FORTRAN it was possible to call a number of "built-in" functions and functions defined by the user on a single line, but it was not possible, until FORTRAN II was available, to compile a separate subroutine or function (which differed from a subroutine in that it returned a value as a result). In FORTRAN II, a typical (a) subroutine and (b) function might be:

```
(a)  SUBROUTINE SWAP(I,J)      (b)      FUNCTION LESS(M,N)
       M = I                             LESS = N
       I = J                             IF (M-N) 1,2,2
       J = M                        1    LESS = M
       RETURN                       2    RETURN
       END                               END
```

where the name of the function LESS received the (integer) value to be returned. The facility for independent translation of subroutines and functions in FORTRAN II made it possible to provide subprogram libraries in the host operating system.

GPSS

The General Purpose Simulation System language has been developed over many years and implemented on several different manufacturers' machines. Of the two current versions, GPSS/360 models can operate with GPSS V, with some minor exemptions and modifications. GPSS V is more powerful and has more language statements and facilities.

The system to be simulated in GPSS is described as a block diagram in which the blocks represent the activities, and lines joining the blocks indicate the sequence in which the activities can be executed. Where there is a choice of activities, more than one line leaves a block and the condition for the choice is stated at the block.

The use of block diagrams to describe systems is, of course, very familiar. To base a programming language on this descriptive method, each block must be given a precise meaning. The approach taken in GPSS is to define a set of 48 specific block types, each of which represents a characteristic action of systems. Each block type is given a name that is descriptive of the block action. The entities that move through the system being simulated depend upon the nature of the system. For example, a communication system is concerned with the movement of messages, a road transportation system with motor vehicles, and a data processing system with records. In the simulation, these entities are called transactions. The sequence of events in real time is reflected in the movement of transactions from block to block in simulated time.

Transactions are created at one or more GENERATE blocks and are removed from the simulation at TERMINATE blocks. There can be many transactions simultaneously moving through the block diagram. Each transaction is always positioned at a block and most blocks can hold many transactions simultaneously. The transfer of a transaction from one block to another occurs instantaneously at a specific time or when some change of system condition occurs.

A GPSS block diagram can consist of many blocks. An identification number called a location is given to each block, and the movement of transactions is usually from one block to the block with the next highest location. The locations are assigned automatically by an assembly program within GPSS so that, when a problem is coded, the blocks are listed in sequential order. Blocks that need to be identified in the programming of a problem must be given a symbolic name.

Clock time is represented by an integral number, with the interval of real time corresponding to a unit of time chosen by the program user. The unit of time is not specifically stated but is implied by giving all times in terms of the same unit. One block type, ADVANCE, is concerned with representing the expenditure of time. The program computes an interval of time called an action time for each transaction as it enters an AD-VANCE block, and the transaction remains at the block for the interval of simulated time before attempting to proceed.

The action time may be a fixed interval, including zero, or a random variable and it can be made to depend upon conditions in the system in various ways. An action time is defined by giving a mean and modifier for the block.

Transactions have a priority level and they carry items of data called parameters. These can be signed integers of fullword, halfword, or byte size, or they can be signed floating point numbers.

The program maintains records of when each transaction in the system is due to move. It proceeds by completing all movements that are scheduled for execution at a particular instant of time and that can be logically performed. Where there is more than one transaction due to move, GPSS processes transactions in their priority order, and on a first-come, first-serve basis within the priority class.

Normally, a transaction spends time only at an ADVANCE block. Once the program has begun moving a transaction, therefore, it continues to move the transaction through the block diagram until one of several circumstances arises. The transaction may enter an ADVANCE block with a nonzero action time, in which case, the program will turn its attention to other transactions in the system and return after the action time has been expended. Secondly, the conditions in the system may be such that the action the transaction is attempting to execute by entering the block cannot be performed at the current time. The transaction is said to be blocked and it remains at the block it last entered. The program will automatically detect when the blocking condition has been removed and will start to move the transaction again at that time. A third possibility is that the transaction enters a TERMINATE block, in which case it is removed from the simulation. A fourth possibility is that a transaction is placed on a chain to be removed by a change in the simulation or another transaction.

When the program has moved one transaction as far as it can go, it turns its attention to any other transactions due to move at the same time instant. If all such movements are complete, the program advances the clock to the time of the next imminent event and repeats the process.

The TRANSFER and TEST blocks allow some location other than the next sequential location to be selected. This permits the path of the transaction to vary according to the criteria set in the block.

A simple illustration of GPSS provides some of the flavor of the language. A machine tool in a manufacturing shop is turning out parts at the rate of one every five minutes. As they are finished, the parts go to an inspector who takes 4 ± 3 minutes to examine each one and rejects about ten percent of the parts. Each part will be represented by one transaction, and the time unit selected is one minute. This problem coded in fixed format is presented below:

```
        GENERATE    5           CREATE PARTS
        ADVANCE     4,3         INSPECT
        TEST GE     RN1,100,REJ             REJECTS
        TERMINATE   1           ACCEPTED    PARTS
   REJ  TERMINATE   1           REJECTED    PARTS
        START       1000
```

A GENERATE block is used to represent the output of the machine by creating one transaction every five units of time. An ADVANCE block with a mean of 4 and modifer of 3 is used to represent inspection. This results in the equal probabilty of the values 1, 2, 3, 4, 5, 6, or 7. After inspection 90% of the parts go to the next block. Ten percent, those which draw a random number of less than 100 out of the range of 0 to 999 proceed to the REJ location. Since there is no further interest in following the history of the parts in this simulation, both locations reached from the TEST block are TERMINATE blocks.

The last line is for a control statement START, which indicates the end of the problem definition and contains the value of the terminating counter. In this case the START statement is set to stop the simulation after 1000 transactions have reached the two TERMINATE blocks.

When the simulation is completed, the program automatically prints an output report, in a prearranged format, unless it has been instructed otherwise. The first line gives the time at which the simulation stopped. This is followed by a listing of block counts. Two numbers are shown for each block. The first is a count of how many transactions were in the block at the time the simulation stopped. The second shows the total number of transactions that have entered the block during the simulation.

The results as indicated by the total block counts at the two TERMINATE blocks were 888 and 112, respectively. These results show that of the 1000 parts inspected, 88.8% were accepted and 11.2% were rejected. The simulation results differ from the expected results of 90% and 10%, but are within the expected values for 1000 trials.

Certain block types are constructed for the purpose of gathering statistics. A realistic modification of the example allows parts to accumulate on the inspectors work bench if the inspection does not finish quickly enough. It would be of interest to measure the size of the queue of work that occurs. GPSS will automatically measure the length of stay in QUEUE block and print the results showing the average stay duration, the maximum stay, and the number of transactions which passed through the QUEUE block without delay.

JOSS

JOSS is one of the earliest interactive, multiuser languages to become operational (the first demonstration was in 1963) and as such had a strong influence on many similar systems and languages which proliferated shortly thereafter. The system (hardware and software design and implementation) was developed by J. C. Shaw, T. O. Ellis, I. D. Nehama, A. Newell, and K. W. Uncapher at the RAND Corporation. The name is an acronym derived from: JOHNNIAC—the RAND-built Princeton-type computer named in honor of the mathematician John von Neumann; OPEN SHOP—designating operation by personnel other than those attached to the computing center; and SYSTEM—implying that JOSS is more than just a computer language.

At the time of initial system hardware specification, no acceptable typewriter-based terminals were commercially available, nor was the JOHNNIAC configured to accept multiuser input–output of this type. Therefore, special equipment was designed and built at RAND to meet these needs. The user terminal was based on the IBM model B typewriter, essentially equivalent to those used by RAND secretaries at that time. A special character set was specified to provide the symbols required by the JOSS language. Control and interface of up to eight remote consoles was provided by multiple-typewriter-control-system (MTCS) hardware. The development of these JOSS hardware components overlapped the development of the JOSS language.

The design of the JOSS language itself was purposely limited in scope: the goal was to attract the casual user in need of modest computational power. For this reason, JOSS was restricted to numeric calculations with no attempt to provide any of the many symbolic capabilities of the general purpose computer. At the same time, a conscious effort was made to avoid any stumbling blocks—however subtle—which might deter a potential user, and this constraint eventually became the limiting factor in language and system design. For example, JOSS provides *exact* input and output of both numbers and commands. (By this is meant that there is a one-to-one correspondence between internal and external representations, thus obviating the need to learn "computer arithmetic.") In order to make JOSS a primary rather than a secondary tool, special consideration was given to the ease of specification of report-quality output on standard $8\frac{1}{2}$" × 11" paper, ready for inclusion in formal RAND publications.

In operation, JOSS and the user take turns using the typewriter, and change of control is communicated to the user by visual, audible, and tactile feedback. A permanent record is supplied by the use of a two-color (black–green) typewriter ribbon. The user may enter a *direct command* on one line, followed by a carriage return; JOSS immediately carries out this command and returns control to the user. Alternately, the user may enter one or more *indirect commands:* each takes the form of a direct command preceded by a number which serves to indicate that the command is to be stored (but not carried out), to uniquely identify the stored command, and to specify a hierarchical organization of commands when a collection of these is to be carried out automatically.

Each JOSS command takes the form of an imperative English sentence (which may actually be verbalized). The command begins with a verb, and obeys the conventional rules of English for spacing, capitalization, punctuation, and spelling. Any command, direct or indirect, may be modified by appending a conditional clause; the command will be carried out (at the appropriate time) only if the expressed relationship holds. Several related commands are available to the user for controlling the sequence of execution and/or iteration of stored indirect commands.

All calculation is carried out (in decimal, to 10-digit pencil-and-paper accuracy) using explicit numeric values and/or variables designated by a single lower- or uppercase letter. Additionally, variables may be indexed to provide vector and array capability. Computational expressions are represented in the conventional way, and may be used freely. Indeed, wherever a numeric value may appear in a command, an arbitrarily complex expression denoting a numeric value may equally well appear, subject to the limitations of one line per command and one command per line.

For directing the production of formal output, the user may enter one or more *forms* composed of strings of characters to be output directly, and of field indicators for specifying the output of numeric results in fixed and/or scientific notation. Pagination control is also provided.

These are all of the essential features of the system; with this background, the accompanying summary provides a complete description of the initial 1963 implementation of JOSS.

DIRECT or INDIRECT

```
Set x=a.

Do step 1.1.
Do step 1.1 for x = a, b, c(d)e.
Do part 1.
Do part 1 for x = a(b)c(d)e, f, g.

Type a,b,c,__.
Type a,b in form 2.
Type "ABCDE".
Type step 1.1.
Type part 1.
Type form 2.
Type all steps.
Type all parts.
Type all forms.
Type all values.
Type all.
Type size.
Type time.
Type users.

Delete x,y.
Delete all values.

Line.

Page.
```

INDIRECT (Only):

```
1.1 To step 3.1.
1.1 To part 3.

1.1 Done.

1.1 Stop.

1.1 Demand x.
```

DIRECT (Only)

```
Cancel.

Delete step 1.1.
Delete part 1.
Delete form 2.
Delete all steps.
Delete all parts.
Delete all forms.
Delete all.

Go.

Form 2:
dist.= ...... accel.= __.____

x=a
```

RELATIONS

$= \neq \leq \geq < >$

OPERATIONS

$+ - \cdot / * ( ) [ ] | |$

CONDITIONS

if a<b<c and d=e or f≠g

FUNCTIONS

sqrt(a)	(square root)
log(a)	(natural logarithm)
exp(a)	
sin(a)	
cos(a)	
arg(a,b)	(argument of point [a,b])
ip(a)	(integer part)
fp(a)	(fraction part)
dp(a)	(digit part)
xp(a)	(exponent part)
sgn(a)	(sign)
max(a,b)	
min(a,b,c)	

Punctuation and Special Characters

. , ; : ' " _ # $?

____._____ indicates a field for a number in a form.

. . . . indicates scientific notation in a form.

is the strike-out symbol.

$ carries the value of the current line number.

* at the beginning or end kills an instruction line.

Brackets may be used above in place of parentheses.

Indexed letters (e.g., v(a), w[a,b]) may be used in place of x, y.

Arbitrary expressions (e.g., 3·[sin(2·p+3) −q]+r) may be used in place of a, b, c, ...

JOVIAL

JOVIAL (Jules' Own Version of the International Algebraic Language) was one of the first programming languages developed primarily to aid in programming large complex real time systems. Today it remains a major language for these applications and versions of JOVIAL have been implemented on dozens of different computers. The language and its compilers have been developed primarily by the Systems Development Corporation.

JOVIAL was based on ALGOL 58 but includes numerous features not in ALGOL (58 or 60) which make it particularly useful for programming large scale systems. The most important of these is the COMPOOL (COMmunications POOL), a central repository of data descriptions which permits programmers to reference data items without concerns as to how they are represented on some particular computer.

The structure of JOVIAL programs is very similar to those of ALGOL. JOVIAL provides a block structure for compound statements; its statement structure, loop structures, and procedure calls are very similar to those of ALGOL.

Basic data items include integer and real numbers, booleans, strings, and status items for example, RED, BLUE, GREEN may be the three possible values of some status items. If the variable *x* were such an item then the assignment

$$X = RED$$

and the equality relation

$$X\ EQ\ GREEN$$

are permitted.

There are the usual arithmetic, relational, and logical operators and it has a conditional statement which can have multiple arms. Thus one can write

```
IFEITH P $ I = 1 $
ORIF   Q $ I = 2 $
ORIF   R $ I = 3 $
END
```

to set I to 1, 2, or 3 or leave it unmodified according to the truth of the booleans P, Q, and R.

JOVIAL differs markedly from ALGOL (and most other languages) in the area of data definitions. At the lowest level, JOVIAL provides for *items* (basic data elements like numbers, strings, and so on). At the next level are *entries*—ordered collections of items (they would be called structure or records today). At the top level are *tables,* which are sequences of entries. JOVIAL has means for the user to control how tables are actually represented in some computer, permitting for example, the user to call for "serial" or "parallel" storage of tables to simplify indexing operations when more than one word of storage is required to accomodate all items in an entry. In serial tables all words containing an entry are contiguous;

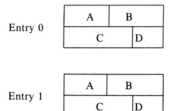

A parallel table with the same items is depicted

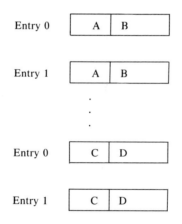

JOVIAL also permits machine language code inserts and provides some pseudo-operations which reference the COMPOOL to provide the shifting and masking operations required to extract items from an entry thus relieving programmers from being concerned with the detailed structure of tables and permitting this structure to change without programs being adversely affected. For example the code sequence

```
CLA ITEM  Move ITEM to accumulator
ETR ITEM  AND with a mask.
POS ITEM  Position least significant bit
          to be rightmost
```

will extract ITEM from the word containing it and position it in the accumulator.

A Micro-Manual for LISP

LISP data are symbolic expressions that can be either *atoms* or *lists*. *Atoms* are strings of letters and digits and other characters not otherwise used in LISP. A list consists of a left parenthesis followed by zero or more atoms or lists separated by spaces and ending with a right parenthesis. Examples:

A, ONION, (), (A), (A ONION A), (PLUS 3(TIMES X PI)1), (CAR (QUOTE(A B))).

The LISP programming language is defined by rules whereby certain LISP expressions have other LISP expressions as *values*. The function called *value* that we will use in giving these rules is not part of the LISP language but rather part of the informal mathematical language used to define LISP. Likewise, the italic letters *e* and *a* (sometimes with subscripts) denote LISP expressions, the letter *v* (usually subscripted) denotes an atom serving as a variable, and the letter *f* stands for a LISP expression serving as a function name.

1. *value* (QUOTE *e*) = *e*. Thus the value of (QUOTE A) is A.
2. *value* (CAR *e*), where *value e* is a nonempty *list,* is the first element of *value e*. Thus *value* (CAR (QUOTE(A B C))) = A.
3. *value* (CDR *e*), where *value e* is a nonempty list, is the list that remains when the first element of *value e* is deleted. Thus *value* (CDR (QUOTE(A B C))) = (B C).
4. *value* (CONS *e*1 *e*2), is the list that results from prefixing *value e*1 onto the list *value e*2. Thus *value* (CONS (QUOTE A)(QUOTE(B C))) = (A B C).
5. *value* (EQUAL *e*1 *e*2) is T if *value e*1 = *value e*2. Otherwise, it value is NIL. Thus *value*(EQUAL (CAR (QUOTE(A B))) (QUOTE A)) = T.
6. *value* (ATOM *e*) = T if *value e* is an atom; otherwise its value is NIL.
7. *value* (COND (p_1 e_1) . . . (p_n e_n)) = *value* e_i, where p_i is the first *p* whose value is not NIL. Thus

value (COND ((ATOM (QUOTE A)) (QUOTE B)) ((QUOTE T) (QUOTE C))) = B.

8. An atom *v*, regarded as an variable, may have a value.
9. *value* ((LAMBDA (v_1 . . . v_n)*e*)e_1 . . . e_n) is the same as *value e* but in an environment in which the variables $v_1, . . . , v_n$ take the values of the expressions $e_1, . . . , e_n$ in the original environment. Thus

value ((LAMBDA (X Y) (CONS (CAR X) Y)) (QUOTE (A B)) (CDR (QUOTE (C D))))
$$= (A D).$$

10. Here's the hard one. *value* ((LABEL *f* (LAMBDA (v_1 . . . v_n) *e*)) e_1 . . . e_n) is the same as *value* ((LAMBDA (v_1 . . . v_n) *e*) e_1 . . . e_n) with the additional rule that when (f a_1 . . . a_n) must be evaluated, *f* is replaced by (LABEL *f* (LAMBDA (v_1 . . . v_n)*e*)). Lists beginning with LABEL define functions recursively.

This is the core of LISP, and here are more examples:

value (CAR X) = (A B) if *value* X = ((A B) C), and *value* ((LABEL FF (LAMBDA (X) (COND ((ATOM X) X) ((QUOTE T) (FF (CAR X)))))) (QUOTE ((A B) C))) = A. Thus ((LABEL FF (LAMBDA (X) (COND ((ATOM X) X) ((QUOTE T) (FF (CAR X)))))), is the LISP name of a function *ff* such that *ff e* is the first atom in the written form of *e*. Note that the list *ff* is substituted for the atom FF twice.

Difficult mathematical type exercise: find a list *e* such that *value e* = *e*.

Abbreviations

The above LISP needs some abbreviations for practical use.

1. The variables T and NIL are permanently assigned the values T and NIL, and NIL is the name of the null list ().

2. So as not to describe a LISP function each time it is used we define it permanently by typing (DEFUN $f(v_1 \ldots v_n)e$). Thereafter $(f\, e_1 \ldots e_n)$ is evaluated by evaluating e with the variables $v_1, \ldots, v_n$ taking the values value $e_1, \ldots,$ value e_n respectively. Thus, after we define (DEFUN FF (X) (COND ((ATOM X) X) (T (FF (CAR X))))), typing (FF(QUOTE ((A B) C))), gets A from LISP.

3. We have the permanent function definitions

(DEFUN NULL (X) (EQUAL X NIL))   and
(DEFUN CADR (X) (CAR (CDR X))),

and similarly for arbitrary combinations of A and D.

4. (LIST $e_1 \ldots e_n$) is defined for each n to be

(CONS e_1 (CONS . . . (CONS e_n NIL))).

5. (AND $p\ q$) abbreviates (COND ($p\ q$) (T NIL)). ANDs with more terms are defined similarly, and the propositional connectives OR and NOT are used in abbreviating corresponding conditional expressions.

Here are more examples of LISP function definitions:

(DEFUN ALT (X) (COND ((OR (NULL X) (NULL (CDR X))) X)
                     (T (CONS (CAR X) (ALT (CDRR X))))))

defines a function that gives alternate elements of a list starting with the first element. Thus (ALT (QUOTE (A B C D E))) = (A C E).

(DEFUN SUBST (X Y Z) (COND ((ATOM Z) (COND ((EQUAL Z Y) X) (T Z)))
                          (T(CONS (SUBST X Y (CAR Z)) (SUBST X Y (CDR Z)))))),

where Y is an atom, gives the result of substituting X for Y in Z. Thus

(SUBST (QUOTE (PLUS X Y)) (QUOTE V) (QUOTE (TIMES X V)))
                                      = (TIMES X (PLUS X Y))

You may now program in LISP. Call LISP on a time-sharing computer, define some functions, type in a LISP expression, and LISP will output its value on your terminal.

The LISP Interpreter Written in LISP

The rules we have given for evaluating LISP expressions can themselves be expressed as a LISP function (EVAL $e\ a$), where e is an expression to be evaluated, and a is a list of variable-value pairs. a is used in the recursion and is often initially NIL. The long LISP expression that follows is just such an evaluator. It is presented as a single LABEL expressions with all auxiliary functions also defined by LABEL expressions internally, so that it references only the basic function of LISP and some of abbreviations like CADR and friends. It knows about all the functions that are used in its own definition so that it

```
(LABEL EVAL (LAMBDA (E A)
       (COND ((ATOM E)
              (COND ((EQ E NIL) NIL)
                    ((EQ E T) T)
                    (T (CDR ((LABEL
                             ASSOC
                             (LAMBDA (E A)
                                     (COND ((NULL A) NIL)
                                           ((EQ E (CAAR A)) (CAR A))
                                           (T (ASSOC E (CDR A))))))
                            E
                            A)))))
             ((ATOM (CAR E))
              (COND ((EQ (CAR E) (QUOTE QUOTE)) (CADR E))
                    ((EQ (CAR E) (QUOTE CAR))
                     (CAR (EVAL (CADR E) A)))
                    ((EQ (CAR E) (QUOTE CDR))
                     (CDR (EVAL (CADR E) A)))
                    ((EQ (CAR E) (QUOTE CADR))
                     (CADR (EVAL (CADR E) A)))
                    ((EQ (CAR E) (QUOTE CADDR))
                     (CADDR (EVAL (CADR E) A)))
                    ((EQ (CAR E) (QUOTE CAAR))
                     (CAAR (EVAL (CADR E) A)))
                    ((EQ (CAR E) (QUOTE CADAR))
                     (CADAR (EVAL (CADR E) A)))
                    ((EQ (CAR E) (QUOTE CADDAR))
                     (CADDAR (EVAL (CADR E) A)))
                    ((EQ (CAR E) (QUOTE ATOM))
                     (ATOM (EVAL (CADR E) A)))
                    ((EQ (CAR E) (QUOTE NULL))
                     (NULL (EVAL (CADR E) A)))
                    ((EQ (CAR E) (QUOTE CONS))
                     (CONS (EVAL (CADR E) A) (EVAL (CADDR E) A)))
                    ((EQ (CAR E) (QUOTE EQ))
                     (EQ (EVAL (CADR E) A) (EVAL (CADDR E) A)))
                    ((EQ (CAR E) (QUOTE COND))
                     ((LABEL EVCOND
                             (LAMBDA (U A) (COND ((EVAL (CAAR U) A)
                                                  (EVAL (CADAR U)
                                                        A))
                                                 (T (EVCOND (CDR U)
                                                            A)))))
                      (CDR E)
                      A))
                    (T (EVAL (CONS (CDR ((LABEL
                                         ASSOC
                                         (LAMBDA (E A)
                                                 (COND
                                                  ((NULL A) NIL)
                                                  ((EQ E (CAAR A))
                                                   (CAR A))
                                                  (T (ASSOC E
                                                            (CDR A))))))
                                        (CAR E)
                                        A))
                                   (CDR E))
                             A))))
             ((EQ (CAAR E) (QUOTE LAMBDA))
              (EVAL (CADDAR E)
                    ((LABEL FFAPPEND
                            (LAMBDA (U V)
                                    (COND ((NULL U) V)
                                          (T (CONS (CAR U)
                                                   (FFAPPEND (CDR U)
                                                             V))))))
                     ((LABEL
                       PAIRUP
                       (LAMBDA (U V)
                               (COND ((NULL U) NIL)
                                     (T (CONS (CONS (CAR U) (CAR V))
                                              (PAIRUP (CDR U)
                                                      (CDR V)))))))
                      (CADAR E)
                      ((LABEL
                        EVLIS
                        (LAMBDA (U A)
                                (COND ((NULL U) NIL)
                                      (T (CONS (EVAL (CAR U) A)
                                               (EVLIS (CDR U)
                                                      A))))))
                       (CDR E)
                       A))
                     A)))
             ((EQ (CAAR E) (QUOTE LABEL))
              (EVAL (CONS (CADDAR E) (CDR E))
                    (CONS (CONS (CADAR E) (CAR E)) A)))))
```

Fig. 2. LISP EVAL function.

can evaluate itself evaluating some other expression. It does not know about DEFUNs or any features of LISP not explained in this micro-manual such as functional arguments, property list functions, input-output, or sequential programs.

The function EVAL can serve as an interpreter for LISP, and LISP interpreters are actually made by hand-compiling EVAL into machine language or by cross-compiling it on a machine for which a LISP system already exists.

The definition would have been easier to follow had we defined auxiliary functions separately rather than include them using LABEL. However, we would then have needed property list functions in order to make the EVAL self-applicable. These auxiliary functions are EVLIS which evaluates lists of expressions, EVCOND which evaluates conditional expressions, ASSOC which finds the value associated with a variable in the environment, and PAIRUP which pairs up the corresponding elements of two lists.

EVAL is shown in Fig. 2 on page 712.

PL/I

PL/I was developed in two distinct stages. First the language NPL was conceived by a joint user–IBM committee. IBM alone then developed PL/I by clarifying and refining the rather incomplete specification of NPL. This overview describes the major features of PL/I, and George Radin's paper makes clear the distinctions between these two languages.

The characteristics of PL/I were strongly influenced by two factors: what was known (in 1964–65) about commercial, scientific, real-time, and system programming applications; and the features of FORTRAN, COBOL, and ALGOL which were useful in implementing those applications. The result is a language of great expressive power, which occasionally requires the programmer to manage great complexity.

PL/I supports a broad spectrum of scalar data types, which can be combined in arrays and structures. Each scalar constant or variable is specified within a broad range of numeric, string, label, file, and pointer data types. In addition, each numeric data element has a mode, base, scale, and precision. While the user can specify values for each of these attributes for every variable, the language provides a set of default values. PL/I also supports considerable generality in both the syntax and semantics of arithmetic expressions and provides for automatic conversion between data of widely different types. For example:

```
SALAD: PROCEDURE OPTIONS(MAIN);

        DECLARE APPLES FIXED,
        ORANGES          CHARACTER(40),
        MIXED_FRUIT      FLOAT;

        APPLES = 4.7;
        ORANGES = 6.31;
        MIXED_FRUIT = 2 * APPLES + 2 * ORANGES;

END SALAD;
```

Appendix A. Language Summaries

The form of PL/I programs generally follows ALGOL block and procedure structure, with the addition of multiple entry points and possibly separate compilation of procedures. Parameters, including labels and pointers, are passed by reference. Control constructs in PL/I reflect the influence of ALGOL. The following example illustrates many of these features in PL/I.

```
OUTER: PROCEDURE OPTIONS(MAIN);
        DECLARE X (10) FIXED;
                /* 10 ELEMENTS OF DEFAULT BASE AND PRECISION */

        SORT: PROCEDURE (A); /* EXCHANGE SORT */
              DECLARE A (*) FIXED,
                       /* THE SIZE OF A IS INHERITED
                          FROM THE ACTUAL PARAMETER */
                       (I, TEMP) FIXED,
                       FLAG BIT(1) INITIAL ( '1'B );

              DO WHILE (FLAG);
                      FLAG = '0'B;
                      DO I = 1 TO HBOUND(A, 1) -1;

                            IF (A(I) > A(I + 1) THEN DO;
                                    TEMP = A(I);
                                    A(I) = A(I + 1);
                                    A(I + 1) = TEMP;
                                    FLAG = '1'B;
                            END;

                      END;

              END;
        END SORT;

        GET LIST (X); /* READS 10 ITEMS INTO X */
        CALL SORT(X);
        PUT LIST (X);
END OUTER;
```

When corresponding formal and actual parameters are of differing types, PL/I converts the actual parameter and stores it in a local temporary on procedure entry. However, a similar conversion does not take place on exit. Therefore, in this example, if A and X differed in one or more attributes, the contents of X would not have been changed on exit from the procedure SORT.

PL/I also provides exception handling facilities (ON-conditions and ON-units) as well as programmer controlled storage allocations and deallocation. All of these may require changing the run-time context of a program at points other than block and procedure boundaries.

714

SIMULA

1. Motivation

SIMULA was conceived in the early 1960s by Ole-Johan Dahl and Kristen Nygaard of the Norwegian Computing Center [3]. The most prevalent version of the language today is SIMULA 67 [1].

SIMULA was designed for system description and system simulation. A system in this case is a collection of interdependent elements with a common goal [4]. A natural way to simulate a system is to describe the life cycle scenarios of its elements. This approach combines the local attributes of elements and the protocols for interelement communication into a single structure. Elements may exist for the duration of the simulation or be created and destroyed during its course.

2. Response

SIMULA permits the description of life cycle scenarios by means of the *class* concept. This, like the rest of SIMULA, is an extension of the basic concepts of ALGOL 60; in this case, procedures and blocks. SIMULA extends the ALGOL 60 block concept by freeing it from its inherently nested structure and allowing the generation and naming of coexisting block instances. These block instances are known as *objects* and are generated from templates called *class declarations*. The principal extensions which convert ALGOL 60 to SIMULA provide the ability to:

1. Declare a *class;*
2. Generate *objects* of a declared *class;*
3. Name the generated *objects;*
4. Form a hierarchical structure of *class declarations.*

3. Classes and Objects

The form of a class declaration in SIMULA parallels the form of a procedure declaration in ALGOL 60. The run-time consequences, however, are substantially different. In ALGOL 60, a reference to a declared procedure creates an instance of that procedure which only exists for the length of time that control is "inside" the procedure, i.e., executing statements from the procedure body. The ALGOL 60 procedure semantics are typically realized by the familiar mechanism of the run-time stack.

SIMULA, in contrast, permits objects to exist even though control is "outside" of them. Control is transferred to the first statement in the object upon object creation, as in ALGOL 60. Control passes out of the object either upon completion of the last statement or by means of the special statements *detach* and *resume*. Once control has left, the incarnations of the variables of the object persist, and may be accessed by a later execution of the same object or by other objects. This differs from the ALGOL 60 semantics, which define the incarnations of variables local to a block or procedure to be lost when control passes from that block or procedure.

The *detach* statement allows an object to be separated from the block in which it was created, and thereby survive the termination of the creating block. This contrasts with

ALGOL 60 where the created block or procedure instance is always "inside" its creator, and is terminated simultaneously with it. An object which executes a *detach* is said to be detached [1, 4]. The *resume* statement causes the resumption of execution of a named object at the point where that object last ceased execution (by means of a *detach* or *resume*). As a consequence objects have a control relationship like that of coroutines [2]: a single control point that moves from object to object at predetermined points, with no "nesting" or "return" structure imposed.

Objects are generated by means of the *new* statement which gives the *class* (template) name and the actual parameters to be associated with the instance. The name of a newly created object can be stored in a variable for subsequent reference.

4. Object–Object References

Each element of a simulation will have attributes whose values determine the state of the element. Since elements are specified in SIMULA by *class declarations,* their attributes are naturally represented by the variables which appear in the declarations. Objects which are created from these declarations. Objects which are created from these declarations may have occasion to reference the variables of other objects. SIMULA provides two notations to allow such reference. The first, the "dot" notation, is of the form $X \cdot Y$, and defines a reference to variable Y in the object whose name is X. (Recall that objects can be named upon creation.) The second notation is *inspect* X which allows direct access to the variables of some outside object X by use of the names given to them in the declaration of the class of which X is an instance.

5. Hierarchical Declarations

SIMULA permits the construction of complex objects from simple ones by a process of concatenation of declarations. Consider a *class* declaration C1, which consists of a formal parameter list, a specification part, a set of variable declarations, and a body of statements. This class declaration can be used as a basis for a subsequent class declaration C2, in a manner that causes the formal parameter list given for C2 to be concatenated with that of C1, the specification part of C2 to be concatenated with the specification part of C1, etc. C2 is therefore defined as an extension or increment over the existing C1, and is called a *subclass* of C1. Objects which are generated from subclass declarations are called *compound objects*. The process can continue indefinitely; C3 could be declared by concatenation on C1, etc.

6. Declaration Libraries

SIMULA allows class declarations to be collected in a library and included into a program by a simple reference in that program.

7. The Supplied Simulation System

The *class* concept of SIMULA is quite general and does not directly provide a useful simulation system. Most simulations using SIMULA are built on top of two supplied classes. The first, called SIMSET, provides a doubly linked circular list processing facility. The second, called SIMULATION is built using SIMSET, and provides support for the element life cycle scenarios of a given model. This supplied simulation system is quite compact, requiring less than twenty pages for its description [4] and can be very simply incorporated into a specific model.

8. The Process View of Simulation

The life cycle scenarios supported by the supplied class SIMULATION are called *processes,* and consequently SIMULA is said to support the *process view* of simulation. Processes proceed logically in parallel (by means of multiplexing over a single processor), and the objects which comprise them may be executed piecemeal (by the coroutine structure provided by *detach/resume*) or as single procedures. The model builder can combine piecemeal and single-procedure execution as he sees fit, and thereby achieve a natural representation of the system being simulated. The expressive power of SIMULA can be described also by considering the universal structure of simulations: a two-level hierarchy, consisting of a control program which manages the simulation clock and selects lower-level modules for execution. In SIMULA, these lower level modules can be processes, SIMSCRIPT event routines, GPSS block handlers, CSL activity modules, or the modules of continuous system simulations (see [4]). In this view SIMULA includes all of the aspects of the named systems and approaches as well as one distinctively its own.

9. Concluding Observations

The supplied simulation system is described completely in SIMULA, and therefore may be modified or enhanced as necessary to support the needs of a given model. Recent additions to SIMULA permit modification of the supplied system without loss of any of the compile and run time features the supplied system provides to uncover logical inconsistencies in the model. The supplied simulation system of SIMULA has been extended to form, for example, the database and operating system language OASIS [10] and the information system of SOL [5].

```
SIMULA begin integer uninfected;
   activity sick person;
   begin integer day;  Boolean symtoms;  set environment;
      uninfected := uninfected-1;  symptoms := false;
      hold(incubation);  symptoms := true;
      for day := 1 step 1 until length do
      begin if draw(probtreat[day], u1)
         then activate new treatment (current);
         infect(Poisson(contacts, u2), environment);
         hold(1) end
      end sick person;
      procedure infect(n, S);  value n;  integer n;  set S;
   begin integer i;
      for i := 1 step 1 until n do
      if draw(prinf×uninfected/population, u3) then
```

```
    begin include (new sick person, S);
        activate last (S) end
end infect;
activity treatment(patient);    element patient;
begin element X;
    extract patient when sick person do
    if symptoms then
    begin terminate(patient);
        for X : = first(environment) while exist(X) do
        activate new treatment(X) end
    else if draw(probmass, u4) then terminate (patient)
    end treatment;
    unifected := population;
    activate new sick person;   hold(simperiod)
end SIMULA
```

REFERENCES

1. Birtwistle, Graham, M., Ole-Johan Dahl, Bjorn Myhrhaug, and Kristen Nygaard, SIMULA *Begin*, student-litteratur, 1973.
2. Conway, Melvin E., Design of a Separable Transition-Diagram Compiler. *CACM*, **6**(7) (1963) July.
3. Dahl, Ole-Johan, and K. Nygaard, SIMULA—An Algol based Simulation Language. *CACM*, **9** (9): 671–681 (1966).
4. Franta, W. R., *The Process View of Simulation*. Amsterdam: Elsevier/North-Holland, 1977.
5. Sol, H. G., *SIMULA Software for the Development of Information Systems*, Technical Report, Department of Management Science and Business Economics, State University of Groningen, Groningen, the Netherlands.
6. Unger, Brian, and Donald Bibulock, James Gosling, and Doug Robinson, *OASIS Reference Manual*, TR No. 7711514, Dept. Computer Science, University of Calgary, February 1977.

SNOBOL

The SNOBOL programming languages introduced or popularized most of the concepts of character string processing. The original SNOBOL had just one data type: a string of characters. It could appear in a program as a literal delimited by quotation marks, or as a value assigned to a variable:

```
PET = "MY CALICO CAT"
```

Concatenation, a basic string operation, forms a new string from two or more strings placed end to end:

```
MYPET = "HERE IS" PET "."
```

concatenates the string "HERE IS", the value in the variable PET, and the string "." to form the string "HERE IS MY CALICO CAT." and assigns it to the variable MYPET.

Another fundamental operation is the pattern match. It examines the contents of a string as specified by a sequence of pattern elements. The elements may be strings (variables or literals) or special patterns delimited by asterisks. The original special patterns matched a fixed length string, an arbitrary string (between two other elements), or a string "balanced with respect to parentheses" (for algebraic expression processing).

A program is a sequence of statements. Each statement may contain up to three parts; all are optional. The first part of a statement is a label, allowing branching to that statement. The second part is the rule, specifying the action to be taken. The final part, the go to, controls flow to the next program statement. The sample SNOBOL program shown below demonstrates several of the language features. It reads lines of text, changes the vowels to asterisks, and prints the result.

```
[1] NEXTL  SYS .READ *LINE/"80"*      /F(END)
[2]        VOWEL = "A,E,I,O,U,"
[3] NEXTV  VOWEL *V* "," =            /F(LIST)
[4] VSTAR  LINE V = "*"               /S(VSTAR)F(NEXTV)
[5] LIST   SYS .PRINT "LINE=" LINE  /(NEXTL)
[6] END    NEXTL
```

The rule of a statement can specify assignment, pattern matching, or pattern matching with replacement. In an assignment rule (as shown in line 2 of the sample), an expression to the right of an equals sign is evaluated and assigned to the variable name on the left of the sign. The expression can be a variable or literal, a string concatenation expression, or a simple arithmetic expression. (Numeric literals are represented as strings of digit characters: "80".) In a pattern match the string to be examined is named, followed by the pattern definition (shown in line 1, combined with an input request). Execution of a match will either succeed or fail; this outcome is tested by the go to. The programmer may optionally specify a replacement for a matched substring in a match-and-replace rule by placing an equals sign after the pattern definition and specifying a replacement string expression to its right (line 4). The resulting string is expanded or contracted as required.

The go to of a statement can specify either an unconditional transfer to another statement after the statement is executed or can test the success or failure of the operation. The go to field is introduced by a slash character. For an unconditional go to (line 5), the destination label appears in parentheses as the remainder of the field. Conditional branching is indicated by preceding the open parenthesis by an S for success or an F for failure. Both may be specified, in either order (line 4). If no go to field appears or the condition which occurs was not specified, execution continues with the next statement.

As a detailed description of the actions in the sample, line 1 reads a card image from the system input file and assigns the 80 characters to the variable LINE. If there is no input data, the program branches to END to terminate execution. Line 2 assigns the string of vowels and commas to the variable VOWEL. Line 3, labeled NEXTV, pattern matches on the string VOWEL, assigns the letter to the variable V and replaces the letter and comma by a null (zero length) string. When VOWEL is null, the statement fails, branching to LIST (line 5). Line 4 matches and replaces the first occurrence of the vowel in V with an asterisk. If the match fails, the program goes to NEXTV to get the next vowel. Line 5 (LIST) prints the line, preceded by "LINE=", and branches to NEXTL in line 1 to read the next data line. The label END on line 6 indicates it is the last line of the program which begins execution at statement NEXTL.

SNOBOL2 and SNOBOL3 did not significantly change the basic concepts or structure. They did provide additional operations, such as numeric comparison functions: .LE(N,"10")

Appendix A. Language Summaries

SNOBOL4, the latest version, expanded the basic concepts to a more general data manipulation language. The general form of the language remained the same, but with major changes in the syntax rules for patterns. Patterns and pattern structures were expanded and became new assignable data types. Both integer and real numeric types and a full set of their operations were added. Data structuring was introduced, with predefined structure data types ARRAY and TABLE. An ARRAY is a collection of data items, which need not be of uniform data type, referenced by numeric subscripts. A TABLE is an associative array, with each element referenced with a unique associated value which is not necessarily an integer PET["DOG"] The programmer may define data structures as additional data types.

This example of a SNOBOL4 program performs the same functions as the previous SNOBOL program, but demonstrates use of the pattern data type:

```
[1]        VOWEL = ANY("AEIOU")
[2] NEXTL LINE = INPUT               :F(END)
[3] VSTAR LINE VOWEL = "*"           :S(VSTAR)
[4]        OUTPUT = "LINE=" LINE     :(NEXTL)
[5] END
```

Line 1 defines the pattern VOWEL to be any of the characters listed in the string. Line 2 reads the next input line and assigns it to the variable LINE, with a branch to END if data has been exhausted. Line 3 examines each character, replacing the first vowel by an asterisk. The program loops on this line until all have been replaced. Line 4 writes the line to the output file and goes back for more input. Line 5, with the label END, indicates the end of the program.

A single-statement SNOBOL4 program which produces the same result is:

```
[1] LOOP OUTPUT = "LINE=" REPLACE(INPUT,
    +        "AEIOU","*****")  :S(LOOP)
[2] END
```

The REPLACE function provides the desired action with only a single pass over the input line.

REFERENCES

1. Griswold, Ralph E. *The SNOBOL4 Programming Language,* 2nd edition. Englewood Cliffs, New Jersey: Prentice-Hall, 1971.
2. Griswold, Ralph E., and Griswold, Madge T. *A SNOBOL4 Primer.* Englewood Cliffs, New Jersey: Prentice-Hall, 1974.
3. Gimpel, James F. *Algorithms in SNOBOL4.* New York: Wiley, 1976.

ACKNOWLEDGMENTS

The following people prepared language summaries: Charles L. Baker (JOSS), Thomas Cheatham (JOVIAL), William R. Franta (SIMULA), Bernard A. Galler (FORTRAN), David Gries (ALGOL), Kenneth Iverson (APL), Ted G. Lewis (BASIC), John McCarthy (LISP), Julian Reitman (GPSS), Robert F. Rosin (PL/I), Douglas T. Ross (APT), Michael Shapiro (SNOBOL). The COBOL summary was anonymous.

APPENDIX B. CONFERENCE ORGANIZATION†

Major Elements

A number of steps were taken for this conference to enhance its quality (and hence its value) for both the people attending it and for the historical record that we were trying to create. First and foremost were those steps taken to obtain the highest quality papers possible. To do this, two knowledgeable people (one of whom was on the Program Committee) were designated as "language coordinators" and were assigned to work with each speaker in suggesting specific questions to be answered about the language, in reviewing drafts of the paper, in suggesting other reviewers, and generally in attempting to assist the speaker in preparing the paper and also the talk. The emphasis was on high technical quality papers and talks, not on papers full of reminiscences. In addition, an experienced historian, Henry Tropp, who is a specialist in the field of technological history guided the authors and the Program Committee on the significant historical elements which should be included in each paper. Since the authors for the papers to be presented were selected by the Program Committee rather than being volunteers in reply to a "call for papers," each was assisted by a set of guidelines which provided the rationale behind the conference and the items of major concern relevant to constructing a complete historical record.

Perhaps the most significant guidance received by the speakers was ten single spaced pages of questions which apply to all languages. These are listed below. While we did not expect each author to be able to answer all the questions, it is believed that most have been answered for most of the languages. In addition to these general questions, each speaker was given a list of questions directly related to his language, e.g., "Why were there exactly three subscripts in FORTRAN?" and "Why does COBOL have a COMPUTE verb for formulas and also ADD, SUBTRACT, MULTIPLY, and DIVIDE verbs to do arithmetic?" It should be emphasized that the purpose of the general questions was to (a) provide a framework within which the speaker could present his material and (b) specify those factors of the history which should be included in the paper.

Four steps were taken to enhance the value of the conference for those who could, as well as those who could not attend it. The first was to include in the preprints and in this book a very brief description of each language. We recognized that most people in the audience (and most readers) would be unfamiliar with all of the 13 languages, and to understand both the presentations and the written papers some basic introduction to each language was needed.

The second step involved the possibility of having a "discussant" to supplement the speaker. The Program Committee considered this at great length and established a philosophy of considering each language and speaker individually. Thus there was a discussant for some languages but not for others.

In considering the third step, it was felt from the very start of planning the conference that an essential objective was to preserve the actual results of the conference itself in ways that go beyond the issuing of a preliminary set of papers. Two actions were taken to achieve this step. First, the entire conference was audio and video taped. The resulting

---

† Revised from Conference Preprints.

tapes (or their equivalent) have now been made available to any person or group that wishes to acquire them. The tapes may be obtained from the ACM. [See Appendix F.]

Another action taken to preserve the results of this conference was to recognize that printed matter is frequently more useful than the tapes themselves. (After all, it will take about two and one half working days to listen to them!) Thus, from the beginning it was planned that a full-length book be prepared. Thus, its preparation was not an after thought, but rather was inherent in our plans from the very beginning.

Fourth, it was recognized that the languages had differing historical importance and potential interest to the audience. Hence, a different amount of time was allowed for each presentation, based on the Program Committee's consideration of these factors.

Part of the NSF grant received was allocated for student scholarships. Four graduate students were selected to have their expenses paid to the conference, but they also performed certain intellectual tasks under the supervision of our volunteer consulting historian. These students were selected in a competition, on the basis of applications received in response to a notification to computer science departments and other types of publicity. The students read all the material prior to the conference, and each was responsible for carefully monitoring several specific languages.

General Questions Asked of All Authors

The following set of questions was sent to all speakers, with a request that they answer as many of these in the paper as possible. However, the speakers were definitely not requested to provide a "question–answer" paper. The questions were provided as guidance, to indicate the type of material which we thought should be included in the papers, and to assist the author in determining what type of material to look for in preparing the paper. Clearly not all questions were answered by all authors.

Background

1. Basic Facts about Project Organization and People

(a) Under what organizational auspices was the language developed (e.g., name of company, department/division in the company, university)? Be as specific as possible about organizational subunits involved.

(b) Were there problems or conflicts within the organization in getting the project started? If so, please indicate what these were and how they were resolved.

(c) What was the source of funding (e.g., research grant, company R&D, company production funds, government contract)?

(d) Who were the people on the project and what was their relationship to the speaker (e.g., team members, subordinates)? To the largest extent possible, name all people involved, including part-timers, and when each person joined the project and what each worked on. Indicate the technical experience and background of each participant.

(e) Was the development done originally as a research project, as a development project, as a committee effort, as a one-person effort with some minor assistance, or . . . ?

(f) Was there a defined leader to the group? If so, what was his exact position and how did he get to be the leader? (e.g., appointed "from above," self-starter, volunteer, elected)?

(g) Was there a de facto leader different from the defined leader? If so, who defined him, i.e., was it some "higher authority" or the leader of the group, or . . . ?

(h) Were there consultants from outside the project that had a formal connection to it? If so, who where they, how and why were they chosen, and how much help were they? Were there informal consultants and if so, please answer the same questions.

(i) Did the participants in the project view *themselves* primarily as language designers, or implementers, or eventual users? If there were some of each working on the project, indicate the split as much as possible. How did this internal view of the people involved affect the initial planning and organization of the project?

(j) Did the language designers know (or believe) they would also have the responsibility for implementing the first version? Regardless of whether the answer is yes or no, how much was the technical language design affected by this?

2. Costs and Schedules

(a) Was there a budget providing a fixed upper limit on the costs? If so, how much money was to be allocated and in what ways? What external or internal factors led to the budget constraints? Was the money allocation formally divided between language design and actual implementation, and if so, indicate in what way?

(b) Was there a fixed deadline for completion and if so, what phases did it apply to?

(c) What is the best estimate of the amount of manpower involved (i.e., in man-years)? How much of that was for language design, for documentation, and for implementation?

(d) What is the best estimate of the costs until the first system was in the hands of the first users? If possible, show as much breakdown on this as possible.

(e) If there were cost and/or schedule constraints, how did that affect the language design and in what ways?

3. Basic Facts about Documentation

(a) In the planning stage, was there consideration of the need for documentation of the work as it progressed? If so, was it for internal communication among project members or for external monitoring of the project by others, or both?

(b) What types of documentation were decided upon?

(c) To the largest extent possible, cite both dates and documents for the following (including internal papers which may not have been released outside of the project) by title, date, and author. Recycle wherever possible and appropriate.†

(c1) Initial idea

(c2) First documentation of initial idea

(c3) Preliminary specifications

(c4) "Final" specifications (i.e., those which were intended to be implemented)

(c5) "Prototype" running (i.e., as thoroughly debugged as the state of the art permitted, but perhaps not all of the features were included)

---

† In items (c3), (c4), (c9), and (c10), indicate the level of formality of the specifications (e.g., English, formal notation) and what kind.

(c6) "Full" language compiler (or interpreter) was running

(c7) Usage on real problems was done by the developers

(c8) Usage on real problems was done by people other than the developers

(c9) Documentation by formal manuals

(c10) Paper(s) in professional journals or conference proceedings

(c11) Extension, modification and new versions

4. Languages/Systems Known at the Time

(a) What specific languages were known to you and/or other members of the development group at the time the work started? Which others did any of you learn about as the work progressed? How much did you know about these and in what ways (e.g., as users, from having read unpublished and/or published papers, informal conversations)? (Try to distinguish between what you as the writer knew and what the other members of the project knew.)

(b) Were these languages considered as formal inputs which you were definitely supposed to consider in your own language development, or did they merely provide background?

(c) How influenced were you by these languages? Put another way, how much did the prior language background of you and other members of the group influence the early language design? Regardless of whether the answer is "a lot" or "a little," why did these other languages have that level of influence? (This point may be more easily answered in Section 2 of *Rationale of Content of Language*.)

(d) Was there a *primary* source of inspiration for the language and if so, what was it? Was the language modeled after this (or any other predecessor or prototype)?

5. Intended Purposes and Users

(a) For what application area was the language designed, i.e., what types of problems was it supposed to be used for? Be as specific as possible in describing the application area; for example, was "business data processing" or "scientific applications" ever carefully defined? Was the apparent application area of some other language used as a model?

(b) For what types of users was the language intended (e.g., experienced programmers, mathematicians, business people, novice programmers)? Was there any conflict within the group on this? Were compromises made, and if so, were they for technical or nontechnical reasons?

(c) What equipment was the language intended to be implemented on? Wherever possible, cite specific machines by manufacturer and number, or alternatively, give the broad descriptions of the time period with examples (e.g., "COBOL was defined to be used on 'large' machines which at that time include UNIVAC I and II, IBM 705.") Was machine independence a significant design goal, albeit within this class of machines? (See also Question (1b) in *Rationale of Content of Language*.)

(d) What type of physical environment was envisioned for the use of this language (e.g., stand-alone system, to be used under control of an operating system, batch or interactive, particular input–output equipment)?

6. Source and Motivation

(a) What (or who) was the real origin of the idea to develop this language?

(b) What was the primary motivation in developing the language (e.g., research, task assigned by management)?

Rationale of Content of Language

These questions are intended to stimulate thought about various factors that affect almost any language design effort. Not all the questions are relevant for every language. They are intended to suggest areas that might be addressed in each paper.

1. Environment Factors

To what extent was the design of a language influenced by:

(a) Program size: Was it explicitly thought that programs written in the language would be large and/or written by more than one programmer? What features were explicitly included (or excluded) for this reason? If this factor wasn't considered, did it turn out to be a mistake?

(b) Program Libraries: Were program libraries envisioned as necessary or desirable, and if so, how much provision was made for them?

(c) Portability: How important was the goal of machine independence? What features reflect concern for portability? How well was this goal attained? See also question (1) on Standardization and question (5c) under *Background*.

(d) User Background and Training: What features catered to the expected background of intended users? In retrospect what features of the language proved to be difficult for programmers to use correctly? What features fell into disuse and why? How difficult did it prove to train users in the correct and effective use of the language, and was the difficulty a surprise? What changes in the language would have alleviated training problems? Were any proposed features rejected because it was felt users would not be able to use them correctly or appropriately?

(e) Object Code Efficiency: How did requirements for object code size and speed affect the language design? Were programs in the language expected to execute on large or small computers (i.e., was the size of object programs expected to pose a problem)? What design decisions were explicitly motivated by the concern (or lack of concern) for object code efficiency? Did these concerns turn out to be accurate and satisfied by the feature as designed? How was the design of features changed to make it easier to optimize object code?

(f) Object Computer Architecture: To what extent were features in the language dictated by the anticipated object computer, e.g., its work size, presence or lack of floating-point hardware, instruction set peculiarities, availability and use of index registers, etc.?

(g) Compilation Environment: To what extent, if any, did concerns about compilation efficiency affect the design? Were features rejected or included primarily to make it easier to implement compilers for the language or to ensure that the compilers would execute quickly? In retrospect, how correct or incorrect do you feel these decisions were?

(h) Programming Ease: To what extent was ease of coding an important consideration and what features in the language reflect the relative importance of this goal? Did maintainability considerations affect any design decisions? Which ones?

(i) Execution Environment: To what extent did the language design reflect its anticipated use in a batch as opposed to interactive program development (and use) environment? What features reflect these concerns?

(j) Character Set: How much attention was paid to the choice of a character set and what were the reasons for that decision? How much influence did the choice of the character set have on the syntax of the language?

(k) Parallel Implementation: Were there implementations being developed at the same time as the later part of the language development? If so, was the language design hampered or influenced by this in any way?

(l) Standardization: In addition to (or possibly separate from) the issue of portability, what considerations were given to possible standardization? What types of standardization were considered, and what groups were involved and when?

2. Functions to be Programmed

(a) How did the operations and data types in the language support the writing of particular kinds of algorithms in the language?

(b) What features might have been left out if a slightly different application area had been in mind?

(c) What features were considered essential to express properly the kinds of programs to be written in the language?

(d) What misconceptions about application requirements turned up that necessitated redesign of these application-specific language features before the language was actually released?

3. Language Design Principles

(a) What consideration, if any, was given to designing the language so programming errors could be detected at compile time? Was there consideration of problems of debugging? Were debugging facilities deliberately included in the language?

(b) To what extent was the goal of keeping the language simple considered important and what kind of simplicity was considered most important? What did *your* group mean by simplicity?

(c) What thought was given to make programs more understandable and how did these considerations influence the design? Was there conscious consideration of making programs in the language easy to read versus easy to write? If so, which did you choose and why?

(d) Did you consciously develop the data types first and then the operations, or did you use the opposite order, or did you try to develop both in parallel with appropriate iteration?

(e) To what extent did the design reflect a conscious philosophy of how languages should be designed (or how programs should be developed), and what was this philosophy?

4. Language Definition

(a) What techniques for defining languages were known to you? Did you use these or modify them, or did you develop new ones?

(b) To what extent—if any—was the language itself influenced by the technique used for the definition?

5. *Concepts about Other Languages*

(a) Were you consciously trying to introduce new concepts it so, what were they? Do you feel that you succeeded?

(b) If you were not trying to introduce new concepts, what was the justification for introducing this new language? (Such justification might involve technical, political, or economical factors.)

(c) To what extent did the design consciously borrow from previous language designs or attempt to correct perceived mistakes in other languages?

6. *Influence of Nontechnical Factors*

(a) How did time and cost constraints (as described in the *Background* section) influence the technical design?

(b) How did the size and structure of the design group affect the technical design?

(c) Provide any other information you have pertaining to ways in which the technical language design was influenced or affected by nontechnical factors.

A Posteriori Evaluation

1. *Meeting of Objectives*

(a) How well do you think the language met its original objectives?

(b) How well do you feel the *users* seem to think the language met its objectives?

(c) As best you can tell, how well do you think the computing community as a whole thinks the objectives were met?

(d) How much impact did portability (i.e., machine independence) have on user acceptance?

(e) Did the objectives change over time from the original statement of them? If so, when and in what ways? See also question (2d) under *Rationale of Content of Language* and answer here if appropriate.

2. *Contributions of Language*

(a) What is the biggest contribution (or several of them) made by this language? Was this one of the objectives? Was this contribution a technical or a nontechnical contribution, or both?

(b) What do you consider the best points of the language, even if they are not considered to be a contribution to the field (i.e., what are *you* proudest of about this language regardless of what anybody else thinks)?

(c) How many other people or groups decided to implement this language because of its inherent value?

(d) Did this language have any effect on the development of later hardware?

(e) Did this language spawn any "dialects"? Were they major or minor changes to the language definition? How significant did the dialects themselves become?

(f) In what way do you feel the computer field is better off (or worse) for having this language?

(g) What fundamental effects on the future of language design resulted from this language development (e.g., theoretical discoveries, new data types, new control structures)?

3. Mistakes or Desired Changes

(a) What mistakes do you think were made in the design of the language? Were any of these able to be corrected in a later version of the language? If you feel several mistakes were made, list as many as possible with some indication of the severity of each.

(b) Even if not considered mistakes, what changes would you make if you could do it all over again?

(c) What have been the biggest changes made to the language (albeit probably by other people) since its early development? Were these changes items considered originally and dropped in the initial development, or were they truly later thoughts?

(d) Have changes been *suggested* but not adopted? If so, be as explicit as possible about what changes were suggested and why they were not adopted.

4. Problems

(a) What were the biggest problems you had during the language design process? Did these affect the end result significantly?

(b) What are the biggest problems the users have had?

(c) What are the biggest problems the implementers have had? Were these deliberate, in the sense that a conscious decision was made to do something in the language design even if it made the implementation more difficult?

(d) What tradeoffs did you consciously make during the language design process? What tradeoffs did you unconsciously make which you realize only later were actually tradeoffs?

(e) What compromises did you have to make to meet other constraints such as time or budget, or user demands or political factors?

Implications for Current and Future Languages

1. Direct Influence

(a) What language developments of today and the foreseeable future are being directly influenced by your language? Regardless of whether your answer is "none" or "many, such as . . . ," please indicate the reasons.

(b) Is there anything in the experience of your language development which should influence current and future languages? If so, what is it? Put another way, in light of your experience, do you have advice for current and future language designers?

(c) Does your language have a long-range future? Regardless of whether your answer is yes or no, please indicate the reasons.

2. Indirect Influence

(a) Are there indirect influences which your language is now having or can be expected to have in the near future? What, and why?

APPENDIX C. LIST OF ATTENDEES†

Paul Abrahams
Courant Institute

Elizabeth S. Adams

James C. Ague
Cibar, Inc.

Daniel J. Alderson

Deanna M. Allen
Southern University

John R. Allen

Allen Ambler
Amdahl Corporation

Dan Anderson

Ruth Anderson
System Development Corporation

William Anderson

John. V. Andrisan
McAuto

Paul Armer

Alex J. Arthur
IBM Corporation

Bill Arthur
Sperry Univac

Karel Babcicky
Norwegian Computing Center

John Backus
IBM Corporation

Fred Bahr

Charles Baker
Ocean Data Systems

Dan Baker
Instructional TV Services
Long Beach State University

Deborah A. Baker

Lawrence M. Baker
U.S. Geological Survey

Avron Barr
Heuristic Programming Project
Stanford University

Raymond L. Bates
USC/Information Sciences Institute

F. L. Bauer
Munich Institute of Technology

Gloria M. Bauer

D. Beech
IBM Corporation

Peter Belmont
Intermetrics, Inc.

R. W. Bemer
Honeywell Information Systems

Donald J. Berchtold

Daniel M. Berry
University of California at Los Angeles

Paul Berry
I. P. Sharp Associates

Ulf Beyschlag

Mike Binkley
Hughes Aircraft Co.

Thomas P. Blinn

Joseph Blum

Carl R. Boehme
Carl R. Boehme & Assoc., Inc.

Erwin Book
SDC

Lorraine Borman
Vogelback Computing Center
Northwestern University

Spec Bowers
General Instrument Corporation

Allen H. Brady
University of Nevada

Donald R. Brandt
E G & G

Harvey Bratman
SDC

M. A. Brebner
Department of Computer Science
University of Calgary, Canada

Mary Ellen Brennan
Aerospace Corporation

Per Brinch-Hansen
Computer Science Department
University of Southern California

Frederick P. Brooks, Jr.
Computer Science Department
University of North Carolina

Kenneth P. Brooks
University of Virginia

Sheldon E. Brown
State of California Department of Corrections

James D. Buchan

Tim Budd
Yale University

James E. Burns

† Taken from registration forms. Affiliation given where it was provided on the forms.

729

Appendix C

Beverly A. Butcher

Walter M. Carlson
IBM Corporation

John Carnal

Curt Carr

Sergio Carvalho
University of Colorado

Jim Chase

Thomas Cheatham
Harvard University

Carl Cheney
Scientific Time Sharing Corporation

Billy Claybrook
Department of Computer Science
Virginia Polytechnic Institute

Janet Cook
Illinois State University

Donald L. Coss
Aerospace Division
Ball Corporation

Cary A. Coutant
University of Arizona

James L. Cox
IBM Corporation

Earl Crabb

Tim Croy

Floyd Crump
Scientific Time Sharing Corporation

Neil G. Cuadra

Ole-Johan Dahl
Institute of Informatics
Oslo University

David M. Dahm
Burroughs Corporation

Greg Davidson
Instructional TV Services
Long Beach State University

Ruth E. Davis

James C. Dehnert

Joseph De Kerf

William S. Derby
Lawrence Livermore Laboratory

Kenneth A. Dickey

Michael A. DiLoreta

Paul N. Dixon

Karen Denu Dodson

W. S. Dorsey

Melvin O. Duke
IBM Corporation

Richard Dunn

Cristopher Earnest
TRW

Harold Engelsohns

Bruce Englar

Adin Falkoff
IBM Corporation

John M. Favaro

Aaron Finerman

Roger M. Firestone
Sperry Univac

Steve Fitzgerald
Kimberly Clark

Joseph M. Fontana
University of Alabama

Robert Fraley
HP Laboratories

David A. Frangquist

Deborah G. Frangquist

Stephen D. Franklin
University of California at Irvine

Daniel P. Friedman
Computer Science Department
Indiana University

Robert M. Friedman
IBM Corporation

Raymond W. Frohnhoefer

Sandra Fuller
National Center for Atmospheric Research

Bernard Galler
University of Michigan

Bruce I. Galler

Susan Gerhart
USC Information Sciences Institute

Carol S. Giammo

Helen M. Gigley

John Gilmore

James F. Gimpel
Bell Laboratories

Karl Glaesser

John Goodenough
SofTech, Inc.

Geoffrey Gordon
IBM Corporation

Susan L. Graham
Computer Science Division
University of California

F. T. Grampp

Alan Grannell
Eagle Rock High School

Vin Grannell
Physics Department
Los Angeles City College

Fred Greene
Los Angeles City College

Madge T. Griswold

Ralph Griswold
University of Arizona

Richard E. Grove
Computer Center
University of Mississippi

Scott B. Guthery
Mathematica

John Guttag
Department of Computer Science
University of Southern California

Joel Gyllenskog
Department of Computer Science
California State University

Patrick E. Hagerty
Sperry Univac

John Halbur

Josn S. Hale
SUNY–Stony Brook
Computing Center

Scott L. Hanna
Hughes Aircraft Co.

Walter J. Hansen

Michael A. Harrison
University of California

J. B. Harvill
Texas Christian University

J. A. Hayes
Computer Center
California State University, Northridge

John F. Heafner
Virginia Polytechnic Institute & State University

John E. Heiser
Hughes Aircraft Co.

William R. Heller
Computer Science Department
Caltech

Robert Herriot
Computer Science Department
University of Washington

G. Steve Hirst

James P. Hobbs
Computing Facility
University of California

Frances Holberton
National Bureau of Standards

Grace M. Hopper
U.S. Navy

Greg Hopwood
Sperry Univac

Marsha Hopwood
The RAND Corp.

Gregory T. Horne

J. J. Horning
Xerox Corporation

Ellis Horowitz
Computer Science Department
University of Southern California

Forrest Howard
Commercial Union

Heather J. Hubbard
JPL

Charles E. Hughes
Computer Science Department
University of Tennessee

Cuthbert C. Hurd

Dr. Daniel Hyde
Department of Computer Science
Bucknell University

Richard Hyde
The Evergreen State College

Edgar T. Irons

Kenneth Iverson
IBM Research Center

Richard Johnson
Xerox Corporation

Jeremy Aldan Jones
Xerox PARC

William B. Jones
Math Department
California State University

Paul Jubinski
Shipboard Computer Facility
Hawaii Institute

Philip L. Karlton
Xerox Corporation

John Kattari

David G. Kay
Computer Science Department
UCLA

Thomas A. Keenan
National Science Foundation

William B. Kehl
UCLA

Dennis Kibler
University of California at Irvine

731

K. H. Kim
Department of Electrical Engineering
University of Southern California

Tom Knoche

Barbara A. Koalkin
Xerox Corporation

Susanne C. Kolb
Hewlett-Packard

John T. Korb

Bob Korsan
SRI International

Mary Kosinski

Martin G. Krebs
Northrop Ventura

Raveesh K. Kumra
Intel Corporation

Thomas Kurtz
Dartmouth College

Stephen Langdon

Dallas Lankford
Information Sciences Institute
USC

Thomas W. Lawhorn
Cibar, Inc.

Charles Ledbetter

J. A. N. Lee
Department of Computer Science
Virginia Polytechnic Institute

Ted Lewis

David E. Liddle
Xerox Corporation

Doris K. Lidtke
Computer Science Department
University of Oregon

Bob Linnenkohl
Interactive Systems Associates

Barbara Liskov
MIT Laboratory for Computer Science

Ralph L. London
Information Sciences Institute
USC

A. S. McAllister
IBM Corporation

Scott Mcauley
Scientific Time Sharing Corporation

John McCarthy
Artificial Intelligence Laboratory
Stanford University

Robert M. McClure

William M. McCormack
Syracuse University

Daniel D. McCracken

Beverly McFarland

Clay McFarland

John J. McGarvey

J. A. McHenry

Stephen McHenry
Pertec Computer Corporation

Donald B. McIntyre
Department of Geology
Pomona College

Bruce McLemore
Informatics

David MacNeil
Stanford University

John McNeley
Xerox Corporation

William P. McQuillan

Rex Malik

Keith B. Marcelius
Marcelius Associates

Michael Marcotty
General Motors Research Laboratories

Daniel S. Marcus

James Matheny
Computer Sciences Corporation

Terry Mellon
ICS Department
University of California at Irvine

Robert J. Mercer

Michael J. Merchant
E. G. & G., Inc.

Steven Meyer
Zilog, Inc.

Richard J. Miller
Department of Computer Science
University of Illinois

Terrence C. Miller
University of California

Roger Mills
TRW

Charles Minter
Department of Computer Science
Caltech

Shakib Hadi Misherghi

James G. Mitchell
Xerox PARC

Mark S. Moriconi
SRI International

Charles B. Morrill
IBM Corporation

R. Morgan Morrison

Harrison Morse
Functional Automation, Inc.

Stephen P. Morse
Intel Corp.

John Motil
Department of Computer Science
California State University

David Moulding
Xerox Corporation

Richard Nance
Department of Computer Science
Virginia Polytechnic Institute

Peter Naur

John Nestor
Intermetrics, Inc.

Erich J. Neuhold
IBM Thomas J. Watson Research Center

Dung T. Nguyen

Peter Nielsen
U.C.L.A.

Leo Nikora
Xerox Corporation

Roy Nutt
Computer Sciences Corporation

Kristen Nygaard
Norwegian Computing Center

David K. Oppenheim
Abacus Programming Corporation

Rex Page
Department of Computer Science
Colorado State University

Ted C. Park
Medical Data Consultants

T. H. Payne
University of California at Riverside

Billie J. Pease

Maria Heloisa Penedo

Alan Perlis
Yale University

R. H. Perrott
Institute for Advanced Computation

Norman Peterson
Bonneville Power Administration

Frank W. Pfeiffer
Northrop Research & Technology Center

Charles Pfleeger
Computer Science Department
University of Tennessee

Laurence G. Platt
Scientific Time Sharing Corporation

Barry Pollack
Department of Computer Science
University of British Columbia

Terrence Pratt
Department Applied Mathematics and Computer
    Science
University of Virginia

Andrezej Proskurowski
Department of Computer Science
University of Oregon

Arthur Pyster

George Radin
IBM Corporation

M. K. Randall
Sperry Univac

Peter Rathbun

Rorrie Ratkevich
Hughes Aircraft Company

Robert W. Rector
AFIPS

Matthias F. Reese

Juris Reinfelds
Department of Computing Science
University of Wollongong, Australia

Norman Richert

Ruth H. Richert

William Roch

Saul Rosen
Computing Center
Purdue University

Bruce Rosenblatt

Robert Rosin
Bell Laboratories

Douglas Ross
SofTech, Inc.

Lawrence A. Rowe
Computer Science Division, EECS Department
University of California at Berkley

Arlene Ruginis

David L. Russell
Computer Science Department
Univ. of Southern California

Paul Rutter
Bell Laboratories

George Ryckman
Computer Science Department
General Motors Research Laboratory

David J. Sager

Phillip Shaw

Sabina Saib
General Research Corporation

733

Appendix C

Daniel J. Salomon

Jean Sammet
IBM Corporation

James G. Sandman, Jr.
Xerox Corporation

Marilyn E. Sander

Edwin H. Satterthwaite, Jr.
Xerox Corporation

Jean Saylor
System Development Corporation

Jon J. Schild

C. T. Schlegel
Bell Laboratories

Charles J. Schmitt

Samuel A. Schmitt
IDA

Jules Schwartz
Computer Sciences Corporation

Joseph P. Schwebel
College of St. Thomas

Earl J. Schweppe
Computer Science Department
The University of Kansas

Michael Shapiro
NCR Corporation

Lynne C. Shaw
Sybron Corporation

Alan D. Sherer
Computer Sciences Corporation

Peter B. Sheridan
IBM Research

Steve Shipper

William Shirado
UCLA

John Sigle
Department of Computer Information Sciences
Trinity University

Paul L. Sinclair
Ryan–McFarland Corporation

Patrick G. Skelly

Stephen Slemmons
Ryan–McFarland Corporation

David Smallberg
UCLA

Robert A. Smith

David F. Speer
Illinois State University

Thomas B. Steel, Jr.
AT&T

Steven Stepanek

Nancy Stern
Hofstra University

Shelden Stewart
National Bureau of Standards

Jochanan Stier
Computing Center
State University of New York

Grace H. Sturgess
Burroughs Corporation

Howard E. Sturvis

Richard E. Sweet
Xerox Corporation

Daniel C. Swinehart
Xerox Corporation

Randy Tamura

Joseph J. Tardo
UCLA

David Taylor
Information Sciences Institute
USC

William P. Taylor

David H. Thompson
System Development Corporation

Luika A. Timmerman
Xerox PARC

Erwin Tomash
The Charles Babbage Institute

Henry Tropp
Department of Mathematics
Humboldt State University

Richard D. Tucker

Joey K. Tuttle

R. E. Utman

H. J. Vale

Bruce W. Van Atta
Computing Center
University of Rochester

Jerrold L. Wagener

Neal R. Wagner
Department of Mathematics
University of Texas at El Paso

Bruce W. Walker
Logicon

Jim Ward
The Evergreen State College

Alfred C. Weaver
University of Virginia

Bryan Webb
Pertec Computer Corporation

Peter Wegner
Brown University

J. H. Wegstein
National Bureau of Standards

Mark B. Wells
LASL

John Werth
Math Sciences Department
University of Nevada

Laurie H. Werth
EG&G

R. L. Wexelblat
Sperry Univac

John R. White
Computer Science Division EECS
University of Connecticut

Stanley J. Whitlock

John D. Wick
Xerox Corporation

David S. Wile
Information Sciences Institutes
USC

Belinda Wilkinson
Burroughs Corporation

Mark Will

John Thomas Williams

Norman F. Williamson

Shelburne D. Wilson, M.D.

David S. Wise

T. Wolfe

David A. Workman
Florida Technological University

Paul B. Yale
Pomona College

Bruce J. Zak

Joan R. Zak
Digital Equipment Corporation

Stephen N. Zilles
IBM Corporation

D. J. Zook

APPENDIX D. CONFERENCE PUBLICITY: ORIGINAL ANNOUNCEMENT, PRELIMINARY PROGRAM, AND FINAL PROGRAM

 **SIGPLAN**

HISTORY OF PROGRAMMING LANGUAGES CONFERENCE

LOS ANGELES, CALIFORNIA
JUNE 1-3, 1978

THEY CHANGED THE FACE OF COMPUTING

The conference is intended: (1) to initiate the preservation of a historical record for some major current languages and to give impetus to others to continue adding to this record, and (2) to provide information from one or two key contributors to the early technical development of the selected languages.

An opportunity to hear and to participate in discussions with a key technical contributor to the initial development of 13 of the most significant programming languages which: (1) were created and in use by 1967, (2) are in use in 1977, and (3) have had considerable influence on the field of computing.

The planned list of languages, speakers, and language coordinators is

LANGUAGE	SPEAKER(S)	LANGUAGE COORDINATORS
ALGOL(58, 60)	Alan Perlis, Peter Naur	David Gries, Tom Cheatham
APL	Ken Iverson	Phil Abrams, Jan Lee
APT	Douglas Ross	John Goodenough, Shizuo Hori
BASIC	Tom Kurtz	Henry Ledgard, Ted Lewis
COBOL	Jean Sammet	Michael Marcotty, Henry Ledgard
FORTRAN	John Backus	Bernard Galler, Jan Lee
GPSS	Geoff Gordon	Julian Reitman, John Goodenough
JOSS	Cliff Shaw	Charles Baker, Tom Cheatham
JOVIAL	Jules Schwartz	Tom Cheatham, Christopher Shaw
LISP	John McCarthy	Carl Hewitt, Barbara Liskov
PL/I	George Radin	Bob Rosin, Michael Marcotty
SIMULA	Ole Johan Dahl, Kristen Nygaard	Barbara Liskov, Richard Nance
SNOBOL	Ralph Griswold	Michael Shapiro, Bob Rosin

The language coordinators will work with each speaker by suggesting questions to be answered and by assisting the speaker in preparing the paper and then the talk.

The keynote speaker will be Captain Grace Murray Hopper.

Jean E. Sammet (IBM) is General Chairman and Program Chairman of the conference. Program Committee members are Tom Cheatham (Harvard U.), John Goodenough (SofTech), Henry Ledgard (U. Mass.), Jan Lee (VPI&SU), Barbara Liskov (MIT), Bob Rosin (Bell Labs), and Henry Tropp (Humboldt State U.).

Papers written by the invited authors will be distributed as preprints at the conference as an issue of SIGPLAN Notices. A final edited proceedings will be published after the conference.

Everyone interested in programming languages is invited to attend this meeting. Attendance will be open up to the capacity of the facilities on a first-come first-served basis. Advanced registration is strongly recommended. General information, including hotel and registration information, can be received by mailing the cutoff at the bottom of this announcement to the Publicity Chairman Billy G. Claybrook, Department of Computer Science, VPI&SU, Blacksburg, VA 24061. Advanced registration and hotel forms will be sent automatically to SIGPLAN members.

Please forward information, including Hotel and Registration information, for the History of Programming Languages Conference, June 1-3, 1978 to

Name_____

Affiliation_____

Street_____

City/State_____ Zip_____

This conference will consider and report on the technical factors which influenced the development of 13 languages which: (1) were created and in use by 1967, (2) remain in use in 1977, and (3) have had considerable influence on the field of computing. The criteria for choosing the languages included: usage, influence on language design, overall impact on the environment, novelty and uniqueness.

This is not a conference on the entire history of programming languages nor entirely a conference on history. It is not even a conference on the entire history of even the selected languages but will cover primarily their early developments. The emphasis is on the technical aspects of the language design and creation, and a number of significant steps have been taken in advance to assure the high technical quality of the meeting. As a result of this conference, it is expected that the field of computer science will have a better understanding of the processes of language design as related to the environment in which languages are developed and as related to the knowledge base available to the originators. The speakers were chosen with careful consideration of the technical role played by each of them during the early development of each language and also considering their availability and willingness to undertake the large task of writing a significant paper.

In order to achieve maximum technical quality, two knowledgeable language coordinators (one of whom is a member of the program committee) were assigned to work with each speaker in suggesting questions to be answered, in reviewing drafts of the paper, and generally attempting to assist the speaker in preparing the paper and also the talk. An experienced historian, who is a specialist in the field of technological history, has given guidance to the authors as to the significant historical elements which should be included in each paper.

The conference is expected to assemble a balance of language developers, users, and critics to consider the key issues. Attendees will hear what issues developers of key languages faced, including what events and environments motivated development of a particular language, the reasons for various features, internal controversies between developers and later between developers and those proposing subsequent modifications, and other factors influencing the evolution of what have proved to be significant languages.

The impact of the conference on future language evolution and development can be significant.

(acm) SIGPLAN

HISTORY OF PROGRAMMING LANGUAGES CONFERENCE

ALGOL APL
APT BASIC COBOL
FORTRAN GPSS
JOSS JOVIAL LISP
PL/I SIMULA
SNOBOL

THEY CHANGED THE FACE OF COMPUTING

LOS ANGELES, CALIFORNIA
JUNE 1-3, 1978

ACM
1133 Ave. of the Americas
New York NY 10036

The conference is intended: (1) to initiate the preservation of a historical record for some major current languages and to give impetus to others to continue adding to this record, and (2) to provide information from one or two key contributors to the early technical development of the selected languages.

PROGRAM

Wednesday, May 31st
7:00-10:00pm Informal Reception (Hyatt House Hotel)

Thursday, June 1st
9:15am-1:00pm
Keynote address - Grace Murray Hopper
FORTRAN - John Backus
2:30-5:30pm
ALGOL - Alan Perlis and Peter Naur
LISP - John McCarthy
8:00pm *
"Doing History" - Henry Tropp
Other informal sessions to be arranged

Friday, June 2nd
9:00am-12:30pm
COBOL - Jean Sammet
APT - Douglas Ross
2:00-5:30pm
JOVIAL - Jules Schwartz
GPSS - Geoffrey Gordon
SIMULA - Kristen Nygaard
JOSS - Cliff Shaw
BASIC - Tom Kurtz
7:00pm
Banquet with "Light Language Anecdotes"
Master of Ceremonies - Bernard Galler

Saturday, June 3rd
8:30am-12:30pm
PL/I - George Radin
SNOBOL - Ralph Griswold
APL - Ken Iverson
Closing

REGISTRATION HOURS
Wed. May 31.   7:00-10:00pm
Thu. June 1.   7:30am-5:30pm
Fri. June 2,   7:30am-5:30pm
Sat. June 3.   7:30am-9:30am

*INFORMAL EVENING SESSIONS
The evening of Thursday, June 1st, will be devoted to a set of informal sessions on topics of the attendees' choice. The one pre-arranged session will be lead by the Conference Historian, Henry Tropp who will discuss the problems of "doing the history" of contemporary technology with a special emphasis on programming languages.

REGISTRATION FEES

	Advance Registration (received by May 1)	Late Registration (after May 1)
ACM-SIGPLAN members	$50	$65
ACM members	55	70
SIGPLAN members	60	75
ACM Student members *	20	25
Non-members	65	80
Daily Attendance °	20/day	20/day

Registration Fees, except for those indicated by *, includes admittance to the technical sessions, the conference banquet and the preprinted proceedings. Tickets for the reception and extra tickets for the banquet may be purchased at the conference.
° Technical Meeting attendance only.

ORGANIZING COMMITTEES
General Chairman - Jean Sammet (IBM)
Consulting Historian - Henry Tropp (Humboldt State U.)
Administrative Chairman - J. A. N. Lee (VPI&SU)
Registrar - Rorrie Ratkevich (Hughes Aircraft)
Treasurer - Susan Gerhart (USC/ISI)
Local Arrangements - Erwin Book (SDC)
Publicity - Billy Claybrook (VPI&SU)
Exhibits - Walter Carlson (IBM)
Publications - Richard Wexelblat (Sperry-Univac)
Program Committee - Jean Sammet (IBM) Chairman,
Tom Cheatham (Harvard U.), John Goodenough (SofTech),
Henry Ledgard (UMass), Jan Lee (VPI&SU), Barbara
Liskov (MIT), Bob Rosin (Bell Labs) and Henry Tropp
(Humboldt State U.)
Language Coordinators - Phil Abrams, Charles Baker,
Tom Cheatham, Bernard Galler, John Goodenough,
David Gries, Carl Hewitt, Shizuo Hori, Henry Ledgard,
Jan Lee, Ted Lewis, Barbara Liskov, Michael Marcotty,
Richard Nance, Julian Reitman, Bob Rosin, Michael
Shapiro, Christopher Shaw.

EXHIBITS
A special display of memorabelia associated with these languages is planned. At the time of this printing, the form of this display has not been finalized.

CONFERENCE HOTEL
The conference sessions will be held at the Hyatt House Hotel at Los Angeles International Airport.
Accomodations for participants have been reserved at the Hyatt House at a special rate of $34 per room, deluxe, single or double, per night. A request form for individual reservations is attached to this advance program and should be returned directly to the hotel.

CONFERENCE REGISTRATION

Name _____

Address _____
_____
_____

ACM Member # _____ SIGPLAN Member (yes/no) _____

Student Member (yes/no) _____ Reg. Fee enclosed $ _____

Daily Attendance for Thursday ◯ Friday ◯ Saturday ◯ (mark all desired)

I expect to purchase tickets for the reception _____ and banquet _____ °
*Included in regular registration fee _____ (give numbers required)
Send this form with check made out to "History of Programming Languages"
to: Rorrie Ratkevich, Ground Systems Grp., Hughes Aircraft Corporation,
1901 West Malvern, Mail Drop 606-K126, Fullerton CA 92634

Send to:
HYATT HOUSE HOTEL at L.A. International Airport
6225 West Century Blvd. Los Angeles CA 90045
(213) 670-9000

Name _____

Address _____
_____
_____

Arrival date _____ time _____ m.° Occupancy: single/double

Departure date _____ Name of additional person
° Reservations must be received 15 days prior to the opening of the conference, and arrivals after 6:00pm must be guaranteed either by including a one night lodging fee of $34 or providing a credit card company number:

Credit Card Company (American Express, VISA/Bankamericard, Diners)
Card Number _____

(acm) **SIGPLAN**

HISTORY OF PROGRAMMING LANGUAGES CONFERENCE

FINAL PROGRAM

ALGOL APL
APT BASIC COBOL
FORTRAN GPSS
JOSS JOVIAL LISP
PL/I SIMULA
SNOBOL

THEY CHANGED THE FACE OF COMPUTING

LOS ANGELES, CALIFORNIA

JUNE 1-3, 1978

REGISTRATION HOURS
Wed. May 31   7:00pm-10:00pm
Thu. June 1   7:30am-5:30pm
Fri. June 2   7:30am-5:30pm
Sat. June 3   7:30am-9:30am

Daily and Student Registration fees do not include admission to either the Reception (Wednesday evening) nor the Banquet (Friday evening), nor a copy of the Preprints.

Tickets for the Reception (Wednesday evening) are included in each regular 3-day registration; additional tickets may be purchased in the registration area at $2 each.

Tickets for the Conference Banquet (Friday evening) are included in each regular 3-day registration; additional tickets will be available for purchase at the Registration desk at $15 each. Tickets must be purchased by 11:00am on Friday, June 2nd.

Additional copies of the Preprints of the Conference Papers may be purchased at the Registration desk at $18 each ($13.50 each for ACM or SIGPLAN members.)

MAILING SERVICE
Participants who desire to have Preprints of the Conference papers mailed to them instead of receiving them at the Conference may arrange this service at the Conference Office in the Plaza del Oro at an additional charge of $2 .

MESSAGES
A message board is available in the registration area for the posting of messages to participants. Messages received for participants by the Hotel will normally be directed to their room by the Hotel switchboard.

FINAL PROCEEDINGS
A statement of interest in receiving a copy of the final proceedings of the Conference is included in the Preprints. This form should be returned as soon as possible to enable the organizers to determine the number of copies to be printed.

NSF STUDENT SCHOLARSHIP HOLDERS
Included in a grant in aid of the conference provided by the National Science Foundation, four students were awarded scholarships to attend this conference. The students will assist the conference historian and the proceedings editor in preserving both the factual record of the events of the conference, as well as their impressions of the atmosphere and response of the participants.
The recipients of the scholarships are:

John M. Favaro, Univ. of California, Berkeley
Bruce I. Galler, Univ. of Michigan, Ann Arbor
Helen M. Gigley, Univ. of Massachusetts, Amherst
Richard J. Miller, Univ. of Illinois, Urbana

NATIONAL COMPUTER CONFERENCE
A panel discussion describing this conference will be presented on Tuesday, June 6th at the National Computer Conference (Anaheim Convention Center). The panelists will be Jean Sammet (Conference Chairman), Ralph Griswold (author of the SNOBOL paper), James Horning (attendee), JAN Lee (Administrative Chairman) and Henry Tropp (Conference Historian.)

REFUNDS
There will be no refunds of any portion of the registration fees.

RECEIPTS
Detailed receipts, itemizing each portion of the registration fee as required by some companies will be available from the conference office in exchange for the standard receipt issued by the Registrar.

CHECK OUT TIME
The Hyatt House Hotel requests that guests vacate their rooms by 2:00pm on the day of their departure. In special cases, extensions may be arranged by the guest at the front desk.

Wednesday May 31st
7:00-10:00pm Informal Reception in the International Ballroom

Thursday June 1st
9:15-11:00am Opening Session
    Session Chairman - Jean Sammet
    Keynote Speaker - Grace Murray Hopper
11:30am-1:00pm (Chairman: JAN Lee)
    FORTRAN - John Backus
    Discussant - George Ryckman
2:30-4:00pm (Chairman: Thomas Cheatham)
    ALGOL - Alan Perlis
          - Peter Naur
4:30-5:30pm (Chairman: Barbara Liskov)
    LISP - John McCarthy
    Discussant - Paul Abrahams
8:00pm Informal Session
    "Doing Contemporary History"
    Chairman and Speaker - Henry Tropp in the Bombay Room
6:00-8:00pm and 8:00-10:00pm
    Other informal sessions to be arranged in the Essex Rooms

INFORMAL THURSDAY EVENING SESSIONS

The evening of Thursday, June 1st will be devoted to a set of informal sessions of the attendee's choice. Sign-up sheets will be posted in the registration area and anyone is permitted to initiate a session by writing in the title of the topic to be discussed and by volunteering to be the session chairman. Interested attendees should also sign the sheets. The organizing commitee will then schedule sessions into the Essex rooms as space allows. This schedule will be announced during the last session on Thursday afternoon.

A pre-arranged session is to be held in the Bombay Room on the topic "Doing Contemporary History". This session will be led by the Conference Historian, Henry Tropp, who will discuss the problems and opportunities of preserving the history of contemporary technology with special emphasis on programming languages. There will be no sign-up sheet for this session. It is open to all interested attendees.

Friday June 2nd
9:00-10:30am (Chairman: Michael Marcotty)
    COBOL - Jean Sammet
    Discussant - Betty Holberton
11:00am-12:15pm (Chairman: John Goodenough)
    APT - Douglas Ross
    JOVIAL - Jules Schwartz
2:15-3:30pm (Chairman: Barbara Liskov)
    GPSS - Geoffrey Gordon
    SIMULA - Kristen Nygaard
    Discussant - Ole-Johan Dahl
4:00-5:15pm (Chairman: Thomas Cheatham)
    JOSS - Charles Baker
    BASIC - Thomas Kurtz

7:00pm Conference Banquet
    "The Way We (Really) Were"
    Master of Ceremonies: Bernard Galler in the International Ballroom

CONFERENCE BANQUET

The Conference Banquet will be held at 7:00pm on Friday, June 2nd in the International Ballroom. The Master of Ceremonies will be Bernard Galler, Associate Dean, University of Michigan. The meal will be followed by a special program entitled:
    "The Way We (Really) Were",
a program of light anecdotes prepared by the conference speakers.

An opportunity will be provided at the Banquet for attendees to sit at a table identified for a specific language, if they so desire. Sign-up sheets for specific language tables will be posted in the registration area on Thursday evening and throughout Friday.

SESSION FORMAT

Consideration of each language will be divided into three sections: an uninterrupted presentation of the paper, comments by a discussant (in those cases so identified) and questions from the audience. Priority will be given to written questions submitted on the forms which will be provided.

Saturday June 3rd
8:30-10:00am (Chairman: Robert Rosin)
    PL/I - George Radin
    Discussant - Bruce Rosenblatt
10:30am-12:15pm (Chairman: JAN Lee)
    SNOBOL - Ralph Griswold
    APL - Kenneth Iverson
    Discussant - Frederick Brooks
12:15-12:30pm (Chairman: Henry Tropp)
    Closing Remarks - Bernard Galler

Unless otherwise noted sessions will be held in the International Ballroom.

LANGUAGE SUMMARIES

The Preprints for the conference include a short language summary for each of the languages being discussed. Participants are urged to study these summaries prior to each session.
This will make it easier for the audience to understand the speakers since they will not have time to explain the basic concepts of the language features during the talk.

THE CONFERENCE RECORD

The entire conference, including the Keynote Address and the anecdotal program within the Banquet, will be audio-recorded for the purpose of preserving a historical record of the events of the conference and as a basis for the preparation of the final published proceedings.

Any discussion from the floor during the sessions will be conducted only through the use of the microphones provided. Each question or comment must be preceded by the identification of the speaker even though this may seem repetitious.
The informal evening sessions will be audio-recorded also.

ACM will hold the copyright to all the recorded material; thus recording of any part of the conference by individuals other than those explicitly authorized by the organizing committee of the conference is prohibited.
Copies of the audio-recordings will be made available for listening by interested persons or groups.

APPENDIX E. PHOTOGRAPHS FROM CONFERENCE

Here are some photos taken by Bob McClure and Dick Wexelblat at the conference. Some are individual and group photos of conference workers and attendees. Except for the pictures of the discussants, the photos were selected primarily for composition and interest. It was not possible to make a complete photographic record of the entire conference, nor was it possible to include all of the snapshots we would have liked to include.

Discussant Paul Abrahams.

Discussant Fred Brooks.

Discussant Betty Holberton.

Discussant Bruce Rosenblatt.

Discussant George Ryckman.

Algolists: (standing) J. McCarthy, F. L. Bauer, J. Wegstein; (seated) J. Backus, P. Naur, A. Perlis.

Dick Wexelblat, Dick Nance, Dan McCracken.

Erwin Book, Local Arrangements Chairman.

JAN Lee (making himself useful).

Robert Rosin.

F. L. Bauer.

Capt. Hopper (between talks).

Bernie Galler, JAN Lee, Henry Tropp.

Peter Naur at the lecturn.

The TV taping setup.

Part of the Program Committee: (standing) J. Goodenough, R. Rosin, H. Tropp: (seated) JAN Lee, J. Sammet, M. Marcotty. (Missing: T. Cheatham, H. Ledgard, B. Liskoff.)

APPENDIX F. CONFERENCE AUDIO AND VIDEO RECORDINGS

As mentioned in the Editor's Introduction, audio- and videocassettes are part of the permanent record of the conference. More information about the recordings is given below to help readers determine whether they want HOPL Cassette order blanks. (Order blanks may be obtained from Association for Computing Machinery, Order Department, P. O. Box 64145, Baltimore, Maryland 21264.)

Video recording was done by Educational TV Services of the University of California, Long Beach; postproduction facilities were provided by Bell Laboratories, Holmdel and the Learning Resources Center of Virginia Tech. With assistance from Jean Sammet, Henry Tropp, and Robert F. Rosin, the video programs were directed and produced by J. A. N. Lee.

There are 16 video programs (on 23 videocassettes) in U-Matic $\frac{3}{4}$-inch format, black and white, with audio track. They can also be obtained in VHS and Beta formats. The audiocassettes are in the conventional format and correspond exactly to the sound on the videocassettes. There is a separate "program" for each language, and, in addition, there is a program of conference excerpts which contains some material from each speaker. There is also a complete recording of the anecdotes told at the conference banquet, and they are quite amusing to hear. The conference excerpts are also available in a slide/audio format, with two audiocassettes synchronized with 174 35-mm slides.

The table on the next page provides the information on the number of cassettes in the program and the actual running time of each.

Please note that these tapes were produced under the guidance of ACM volunteers rather than professional producers and are of variable visual quality; the videocassettes are not commercial productions. A few videocassettes, as noted in the table, show only still photos; most other videocassettes have some still photos inserted to improve the visual quality. The audio portions and the individual audiocassettes have no problems.

Program	Speakers	Number of cassettes in program	Program running time (min)
Conference Excerpts	All speakers from technical program	2[a]	54 + 49
Conference Excerpts (slides & audio)	Two audiocassettes synchronized with 174 35-mm slides featuring all speakers from technical program		103
Banquet Anecdotes	Galler as M.C., many speakers	2	50 + 49
Opening Session	Conference Introduction—Sammet Keynote Address—Hopper	2[b]	59 + 38
ALGOL	Perlis and Naur	2[a]	60 + 30
APL	Iverson	1	48
APT	Ross	1	30
BASIC	Kurtz	1	39
COBOL	Sammet	2	60 + 28
FORTRAN	Backus	2[b]	58 + 32
GPSS	Gordon	1	33
JOSS	Baker	1	32
JOVIAL	Schwartz	1	40
LISP	McCarthy	1	56
PL/I	Radin	2	60 + 40
SIMULA	Nygaard and Dahl	1	46
SNOBOL	Griswold	1	47

[a] Due to problems in video recording, a significant portion of these videocassettes show only still photos. The audio has no problem.

[b] Due to problems in video recording, these videocassettes show only still photos. The audio has no problem.

Afterword

More than any other person, Jean Sammet is responsible for the success of the (dare I say: First?) History of Programming Languages Conference. Certainly she, with the very able assistance of JAN Lee, brought off what is probably the only conference I was ever at where virtually all attendees attended virtually every session. It is only fitting that she be allowed to have the last word and this I will achieve by reprinting verbatim her foreword to the conference preprints volume.

R. L. WEXELBLAT
PROCEEDINGS EDITOR

747

Afterword

General Chairman's Message

This is an unusual conference, and has had more difficulties in organizing it than most ACM SIGPLAN conferences; we hope it will be the start of a sequence of conferences sponsored by ACM and other organizations to provide information on various aspects of work done early in the life of the computing field. Detailed information on the objectives of this conference and how it was organized appear elsewhere in these proceedings.

A number of people have worked hard to make these proceedings, and the conference itself, a success. (In this case I define success as meaning (a) a significant contribution to the history of the computing field and (b) interesting material for those who wish to learn about—or be reminded of—the early technical development of these programming languages.) Only the readers and the conference attendees can judge whether or not we have succeeded. For some of the participants, their major work is finished when the conference ends; for others, the preparation of a book based on this conference, and the other aspects which involve making the audio tapes available to interested scholars will be a continuing task of major scope.

I want to express my deep personal thanks to the authors, who took time from current pursuits to rummage through many ancient files and resurrect both factual data and memories of these early events. Many of the language coordinators worked diligently to assist the authors in producing their papers.

Finally, I want to take this opportunity to particularly thank JAN Lee, who has so ably handled the administrative aspects of this conference in addition to serving on the Program Committee.

JEAN E. SAMMET
CONFERENCE GENERAL CHAIRMAN
AND
PROGRAM COMMITTEE CHAIRMAN

Index

Index

Index

Index

Index

Index

Note: The index primarily contains proper nouns—names of people, languages, and computers that were part of the history of programming languages. I have omitted names that appear only in figures or slide frames, but included all mentioned in the formal paper or the talk. People acknowledged for helping in the preparation of papers and talks are also omitted. People who asked questions at the conference are not listed in the index; however, everyone who answered a question is included. Ed.